## A BRIEF GUIDE TO ~~GETTING THE MO~~ST FROM THIS BOOK

### 1 Read the Book

| Feature | Description | Benefit | Page |
|---|---|---|---|
| Section-Opening Scenarios | Every section opens with a scenario presenting a unique application of algebra or trigonometry in your life outside the classroom. | Realizing that algebra and trigonometry are everywhere will help motivate your learning. | 2 |
| Detailed Worked-Out Examples | Examples are clearly written and provide step-by-step solutions. No steps are omitted, and each step is thoroughly explained to the right of the mathematics. | The blue annotations will help you understand the solutions by providing the reason why every algebraic and trigonometric step is true. | 592 |
| Applications Using Real-World Data | Interesting applications from nearly every discipline, supported by up-to-date real-world data, are included in every section. | Ever wondered how you'll use algebra and trigonometry? This feature will show you how algebra and trigonometry can solve real problems. | 187 |
| Study Tips | The book's study tip boxes offer suggestions for problem solving, point out common errors to avoid, and provide informal hints and suggestions. | By seeing common mistakes, you'll be able to avoid them. | 512 |
| Explanatory Voice Balloons | Voice balloons help to demystify algebra and trigonometry. They translate mathematical language into plain English, clarify problem-solving procedures, and present alternative ways of understanding. | Does math ever look foreign to you? This feature often translates math into everyday English. | 253 |
| Learning Objectives | Every section begins with a list of objectives. Each objective is restated in the margin where the objective is covered. | The objectives focus your reading by emphasizing what is most important and where to find it. | 550 |
| Technology | The screens displayed in the technology boxes show how graphing utilities verify and visualize algebraic and trigonometric results. | Even if you are not using a graphing utility in the course, this feature will help you understand different approaches to problem solving. | 307 |

### 2 Work the Problems

| Feature | Description | Benefit | Page |
|---|---|---|---|
| Check Point Examples | Each example is followed by a similar matched problem, called a Check Point, that offers you the opportunity to work a similar exercise. The answers to the Check Points are provided in the answer section. | You learn best by doing. You'll solidify your understanding of worked examples if you try a similar problem right away to be sure you understand what you've just read. | 651 |
| Extensive and Varied Exercise Sets | An abundant collection of exercises is included in an exercise set at the end of each section. Exercises are organized within categories. Your instructor will usually provide guidance on which exercises to work. The exercises in the first category, Practice Exercises, follow the same order as the section's worked examples. | The parallel order of the Practice Exercises lets you refer to the worked examples and use them as models for solving these problems. | 533–536 |
| | | NEW to This Edition The "make sense" exercises ask you to determine whether statements are sensible, and to explain why or why not. This enables you to test your conceptual understanding of the section's objectives. | 285 |

# A BRIEF GUIDE TO GETTING THE MOST FROM THIS BOOK

| Feature | Description | Benefit | Page |
|---|---|---|---|
| Practice Plus Problems | This category of exercises contains more challenging problems that often require you to combine several skills or concepts. | It is important to dig in and develop your problem-solving skills. Practice Plus Exercises provide you with ample opportunity to do so. | 336 |
| Preview Problems | NEW to This Edition Each exercise set concludes with three problems to help you prepare for the next section. | These exercises let you review previously covered material that you'll need to be successful for the forthcoming section. Some of these problems will get you thinking about concepts you'll soon encounter. | 576 |

## ③ Review for Quizzes and Tests

| Feature | Description | Benefit | Page |
|---|---|---|---|
| Mid-Chapter Check Points | At approximately the midway point in the chapter, an integrated set of review exercises allows you to review the skills and concepts you learned separately over several sections. | By combining exercises from the first half of the chapter, the Mid-Chapter Check Points give a comprehensive review before you move on to the material in the remainder of the chapter. | 685 |
| Chapter Review Grids | Each chapter contains a review chart that summarizes the definitions and concepts in every section of the chapter. Examples that illustrate these key concepts are also included in the chart. | Review this chart and you'll know the most important material in the chapter! | 577-579 |
| Chapter Review Exercises | A comprehensive collection of review exercises for each of the chapter's sections follows the grid. | Practice makes perfect. These exercises contain the most significant problems for each of the chapter's sections. | 580-583 |
| Chapter Tests | Each chapter contains a practice test with approximately 25 problems that cover the important concepts in the chapter. Take the practice test, check your answers, and then watch the Chapter Test Prep Video CD to see worked-out solutions for any exercises you miss. | You can use the chapter test to determine whether you have mastered the material covered in the chapter. | 583 |
| Chapter Test Prep Video CDs | These video CDs found at the back of your text contain worked-out solutions to every exercise in each chapter test. | The videos let you review any exercises you miss on the chapter test. | 583 |
| Cumulative Review Exercises | Beginning with Chapter 2, each chapter concludes with a comprehensive collection of mixed cumulative review exercises. These exercises combine problems from previous chapters and the present chapter, providing an ongoing cumulative review. | Ever forget what you've learned? These exercises ensure that you are not forgetting anything as you move forward. | 584 |

# Precalculus

# Precalculus

4e PART 2

# Robert Blitzer
Miami Dade College

PEARSON

**Library of Congress Cataloging-in-Publication Data**

Blitzer, Robert.
    Precalculus/Robert Blitzer. —4th ed.
        p.   cm.
    Includes index.
    ISBN 0-321-55984-3
    1.  Algebra—Textbooks.   I.  Title.
    QA154.3.B586   2010
    512—dc22                              2008048515

Editorial Director, Mathematics: Christine Hoag
Senior Acquisitions Editor: Adam Jaworski
Sponsoring Editor: Dawn Murrin
Editorial Assistant/Print Supplements Editor: Joseph Colella
Project Manager: Barbara Mack
Associate Managing Editor: Bayani Mendoza de Leon
Senior Managing Editor: Linda Mihatov Behrens
Senior Operations Supervisor: Diane Peirano
Marketing Manager: Katherine Greig
Art Director: Heather Scott
Interior Designer: Tamara Newnam
Cover Designer: Tamara Newnam
AV Project Manager: Thomas Benfatti
Senior Content Developer: Mary Durnwald
Project Manager, MathXL®: Eileen Moore
Associate Producer, Media: Christina Maestri
Cover Photo: John E. Kelly/FoodPix/Getty Images
Manager, Cover Visual Research and Permissions: Karen Sanatar
Manager, Rights and Permissions: Zina Arabia
Manager, Visual Research: Elaine Soares
Image Permission Coordinator: Debbie Hewitson
Photo Researcher: Sheila Norman
Art Studios: Scientific Illustrators/Laserwords
Compositor: Prepare, Inc.

Cover Art: John E. Kelly/Food Pix/Getty Images

Taken from:
*Precalculus*, Fourth Edition
By Robert Blitzer

This special edition published in cooperation with Pearson Learning Solutions.

Pearson Learning Solutions, 501 Boylston Street, Suite 900
Boston, MA 02116
A Pearson Education Company
www.pearsoned.com

Printed in the United States of America

 3 4 5 6 7 8 9 10 V0ZN 16 15 14


000200010271275876

CT

ISBN 10: 1-256-46786-3
ISBN 13: 978-1-256-46786-1

Preface    xi
Acknowledgments    xiv
To the Student    xv
About the Author    xvi

# CONTENTS

**P** Prerequisites: Fundamental Concepts of Algebra  1

P.1  Algebraic Expressions, Mathematical Models, and Real Numbers    2
P.2  Exponents and Scientific Notation    19
P.3  Radicals and Rational Exponents    30
P.4  Polynomials    46
P.5  Factoring Polynomials    56
*Mid-Chapter Check Point*    67
P.6  Rational Expressions    68
P.7  Equations    82
P.8  Modeling with Equations    101
P.9  Linear Inequalities and Absolute Value Inequalities    114
SUMMARY, REVIEW, AND TEST    129
REVIEW EXERCISES    129
CHAPTER P TEST    133

**7** Systems of Equations and Inequalities 727

7.1  Systems of Linear Equations in Two Variables    728
7.2  Systems of Linear Equations in Three Variables    748
7.3  Partial Fractions    756
7.4  Systems of Nonlinear Equations in Two Variables    767
*Mid-Chapter Check Point*    777
7.5  Systems of Inequalities    778
7.6  Linear Programming    790
SUMMARY, REVIEW, AND TEST    798
REVIEW EXERCISES    799
CHAPTER 7 TEST    802
CUMULATIVE REVIEW EXERCISES (CHAPTERS P–7)    803

**8** Matrices and Determinants 805

8.1 Matrix Solutions to Linear Systems   806

8.2 Inconsistent and Dependent Systems and Their Applications   818

8.3 Matrix Operations and Their Applications   827

*Mid-Chapter Check Point*   842

8.4 Multiplicative Inverses of Matrices and Matr Equations   842

8.5 Determinants and Cramer's Rule   856

SUMMARY, REVIEW, AND TEST   868

REVIEW EXERCISES   869

CHAPTER 8 TEST   871

CUMULATIVE REVIEW EXERCISES (CHAPTERS P–8)   872

**9** Conic Sections and Analytic Geometry 873

9.1 The Ellipse   874

9.2 The Hyperbola   886

9.3 The Parabola   900

*Mid-Chapter Check Point*   912

9.4 Rotation of Axes   913

9.5 Parametric Equations   925

9.6 Conic Sections in Polar Coordinates   935

SUMMARY, REVIEW, AND TEST   944

REVIEW EXERCISES   946

CHAPTER 9 TEST   948

CUMULATIVE REVIEW EXERCISES (CHAPTERS P–9)   949

**10** Sequences, Induction, and Probability 951

10.1 Sequences and Summation Notation    952
10.2 Arithmetic Sequences    963
10.3 Geometric Sequences and Series    972
*Mid-Chapter Check Point*    986
10.4 Mathematical Induction    987
10.5 The Binomial Theorem    996
10.6 Counting Principles, Permutations, and Combinations    1003
10.7 Probability    1015
SUMMARY, REVIEW, AND TEST    1029
REVIEW EXERCISES    1031
CHAPTER 10 TEST    1034
CUMULATIVE REVIEW EXERCISES (CHAPTERS P–10)    1035

**11** Introduction to Calculus 1037

11.1 Finding Limits Using Tables and Graphs    1038
11.2 Finding Limits Using Properties of Limits    1050
11.3 Limits and Continuity    1062
*Mid-Chapter Check Point*    1069
11.4 Introduction to Derivates    1070
SUMMARY, REVIEW, AND TEST    1083
REVIEW EXERCISES    1084
CHAPTER 11 TEST    1085
CUMULATIVE REVIEW EXERCISES (CHAPTERS P–11)    1086

Appendix A Where Did That Come From?
          Selected Proofs    A-1

Appendix B The Transition from
          Precalculus to Calculus    B-1

Answers to Selected Exercises    AA1
Subject Index    I-1
Photo Credits    P-1

# Preface

I've written **Precalculus, Fourth Edition**, to help diverse students, with different backgrounds and future goals, to succeed. The book has three fundamental goals:

1. To help students acquire a solid foundation in algebra and trigonometry, preparing them for other courses such as calculus, business calculus, and finite mathematics.
2. To show students how algebra and trigonometry can model and solve authentic real-world problems.
3. To enable students to develop problem-solving skills, while fostering critical thinking, within an interesting setting.

One major obstacle in the way of achieving these goals is the fact that very few students actually read their textbook. This has been a regular source of frustration for me and for my colleagues in the classroom. Anecdotal evidence gathered over years highlights two basic reasons that students do not take advantage of their textbook:

- "I'll never use this information."
- "I can't follow the explanations."

I've written every page of the Fourth Edition with the intent of eliminating these two objections. The ideas and tools I've used to do so are described for the student in "A Brief Guide to Getting the Most from This Book," which appears in the front of this book.

## How Does Precalculus Differ from Algebra and Trigonometry?

**Precalculus** is not simply a condensed version of my Algebra and Trigonometry book. Precalculus students are different from algebra and trigonometry students, and this text reflects those differences. Here are a few examples:

- **Algebra and Trigonometry** devotes an entire chapter to linear equations, rational equations, quadratic equations, radical equations, linear inequalities, and developing models involving these equations and inequalities. **Precalculus** reviews these topics in three sections of the prerequisites chapter (P.7: Equations; P.8 Modeling with Equations; P.9: Linear Inequalities and Absolute Value Inequalities). Functions, the core of any precalculus course, are then introduced in Chapter 1.
- **Precalculus** contains a section on constructing functions from verbal descriptions and formulas (1.10: Modeling with Functions) that is not included in **Algebra and Trigonometry**. Modeling skills are applied to situations that students are likely to see in calculus when solving applied problems involving maximum or minimum values.

- **Precalculus** develops trigonometry from the perspective of the unit circle (4.2: Trigonometric Functions: The Unit Circle). In **Algebra and Trigonometry**, trigonometry is developed using right triangles.
- **Precalculus** contains a chapter (Chapter 11: Introduction to Calculus) that takes the student into calculus with discussions of limits, continuity, and derivatives. This chapter is not included in **Algebra and Trigonometry**.
- Many of the liberal arts applications in **Algebra and Trigonometry** are replaced by more scientific or higher level applications in **Precalculus**. Some examples:
  - → Black Holes in Space (P.2: Exponents and Scientific Notation)
  - → Average Velocity (1.5: More on Slope)
  - → Newton's Law of Cooling (3.5: Exponential Growth and Decay; Modeling Data)
  - → Modeling Involving Mixtures and Uniform Motion (7.1: Systems of Linear Equations in Two Variables)

## What's New in the Fourth Edition?

- **New Applications and Real-World Data.** I'm on a constant search for real-world data that can be used to illustrate unique algebraic and trigonometric applications. I researched hundreds of books, magazines, newspapers, almanacs, and online sites to prepare the Fourth Edition. Among the 265 worked-out examples and application exercises based on new data sets, you'll find models that describe changing attitudes of college students over time.

- **"Make Sense?" Classroom Discussion Exercises.** Each exercise set contains four Critical Thinking exercises intended for classroom discussion in order to engage participation in the learning process. These items test conceptual understanding by asking students to determine whether statements are sensible, and to explain why or why not. Although sample answers are provided, students have skills and perspectives that frequently differ from those of math teachers, so answers and explanations may vary. The important part of this new feature is to let you ask students what they think about selected statements, determine whether they understand the concepts, and give them feedback to clarify any misunderstandings.

- **New Directions for the True/False Critical Thinking Exercises.** The Fourth Edition asks students to determine whether each statement in an itemized list is true or false. If the statement is false, students are then asked to make the necessary change or changes to produce a true statement.

- **Preview Exercises.** Each exercise set concludes with three problems to help students prepare for the next section. Some of these problems review previously covered material that students will need to be successful in the forthcoming section. Other problems are designed to get students thinking about concepts they will soon encounter.

- **More Detailed Directions When Comparing Mathematical Models with Actual Data.** The Fourth Edition asks students if values obtained from mathematical models understimate or over-estimate data displayed by graphs, and, if so, by how much.

- **Increased Study Tip Boxes.** The book's Study Tip boxes offer suggestions for problem solving, point out common errors to avoid, and provide informal hints and suggestions. These invaluable hints appear in greater abundance in the Fourth Edition.

- **New Chapter-Opening and Section-Opening Scenarios.** Every chapter and every section open with a scenario based on an application, the majority of which are unique to the Fourth Edition. These scenarios are revisited in the course of the chapter or section in one of the book's new examples, exercises, or discussions. The often-humorous tone of these openers is intended to help fearful and reluctant students overcome their negative perceptions about math.

- **867 New Examples and Exercises.** The Fourth Edition contains 24 detailed worked-out examples involving new data, 241 new application exercises, 324 "make sense" discussion exercises, 237 preview exercises, and 41 new exercises that appear in the various other categories of the exercise sets.

## What Content and Organizational Changes Have Been Made to the Fourth Edition?

- **Section P.1 (Algebraic Expressions, Mathematical Models, and Real Numbers)** contains a more detailed number line that illustrates both rational and irrational numbers. A new essay based on humorist Garth Sundem's *Geek Logik* sets the stage for the book's engaging collection of unique applications.

- **Section P.9 (Linear Inequalities and Absolute Value Inequalities)** presents a new example of an inequality that contains fractions.

- **Section 1.1 (Graphs and Graphing Utilities)** contains additional exercises that ask students to select the graph that best illustrates a given description or story.

- **Section 1.2 (Basics of Functions and Their Graphs)** adds to the discussion of identifying domain and range from a function's graph with a new example in which the range is not determined by looking at a graph's endpoints.

- **Section 1.3 (More on Functions and Their Graphs)** now opens with a discussion of intervals on which a function increases, decreases, or is constant. This serves as a fluid transition from the information on analyzing the graph of a function in the previous section, as well as an immediate connection to the section's introduction. With the revised order of objectives, the section closes with a discussion of the difference quotient. There is also a more detailed presentation on piecewise functions, including an example on graphing such a function.

- **Section 1.4 (Linear Functions and Slope)** contains a new modeling example on climate change that is connected to the chapter opener.

- **Section 2.3 (Polynomial Functions and Their Graphs)** follows the definition of a polynomial function with examples of functions that are polynomial functions and examples of functions that are not polynomial functions. There is a new example on the Leading Coefficient Test where a function's degree and leading coefficient are determined for an equation in factored form.

- **Section 3.5 (Exponential Growth and Decay; Modeling Data)** has a greater variety of exercises on half-life and exponential decay.

- **Section 10.3 (Geometric Sequences and Series)** has a more thoroughly developed example on determining the value of an annuity, supported by an essay on "Stashing Cash and Making Taxes Less Taxing." Finance problems have been expanded in the exercise set.

- **Appendix B (The Transition from Precalculus to Calculus)** has been added to indicate how various topics in the course are extended to more general situations in calculus.

I hope that my passion for teaching, as well as my respect for the diversity of students I have taught and learned from over the years, is apparent throughout this new edition. By connecting algebra to the whole spectrum of learning, it is my intent to show students that their world is profoundly mathematical, and indeed, $\pi$ is in the sky.

*Robert Blitzer*

## Supplements

| STUDENT RESOURCES | TEACHER RESOURCES |
|---|---|
| • *Student's Solutions Manual*<br>Fully worked solutions to odd-numbered exercises.<br>Available for purchase. ISBN: 0321575326<br><br>• *Videos on DVD*<br>A comprehensive set of DVDs, tied to the textbook, containing 10–13-minute lectures for each section of the textbook. Each lecture covers the key topics of the section including definitions and formulas when applicable. Videos also have optional English and Spanish subtitles.<br>Available for purchase. ISBN: 0321575342<br><br>• *Chapter Test Prep CD*<br>Students can watch teachers work through step-by-step solutions to all the Chapter Test exercises from the textbook. The Chapter Test Prep Videos CD is included with each new student text.<br>A replacement CD is available for purchase. ISBN: 0131362224 | Most of the teacher supplements and resources for this book are available electronically on the Instructor Resource Center. Upon adoption or to preview, please go to PearsonSchool.com/Advanced and click "Online Teacher Supplements." You will be required to complete a one-time registration subject to verification before being emailed access information to download materials.<br><br>The following supplements are available to qualified adopters:<br><br>**Instructor's Edition**<br>Provides answers to *all* exercises in the back of the text. ISBN: 0321575385<br><br>• *Instructor's Solutions Manual*<br>Fully worked solutions to all textbook exercises. ISBN: 0321575318<br><br>• *PowerPoint Lecture Slides*<br>Fully editable slides that follow the textbook. Project in class or post to a website in an online course. Included in these presentations are slides designed to work with Classroom Response Systems (Clickers). Available for download only.<br><br>• *Test Item File*<br>A test bank derived from TestGen®. Available for download only.<br><br>• *TestGen®*<br>Enables teachers to build, edit, print, and administer tests using a computerized bank of questions developed to cover all the objectives of the text. TestGen® is algorithmically based, allowing teachers to create multiple but equivalent versions of the same question or test with the click of a button. Teachers can also modify test bank questions or add new questions. Tests can be printed or administered online. The software and test bank are available for download. ISBN: 0137151578<br><br>• *Mini Lecture Notes*<br>These include additional examples and helpful teaching tips, by section. Available for download only. |

### MathXL® for School

MathXL® for School is a powerful online homework, tutorial, and assessment system that accompanies Pearson Education's textbooks in mathematics or statistics. With MathXL® for School, teachers can create, edit, and assign online homework and tests using algorithmically generated exercises correlated at the objective level to the textbook. They can also create and assign their own online exercises and import TestGen tests for added flexibility. All student work is tracked in MathXL® for School's online gradebook. Students can take chapter tests in MathXL® for School and receive personalized study plans based on their test results. The study plan diagnoses weaknesses and links students directly to tutorial exercises for the objectives they need to study and retest. Students can also access supplemental animations and video clips directly from selected exercises. MathXL® for School is available to qualified adopters. For more information, visit our website at www.MathXLforSchool.com, or contact your Pearson sales representative.

### MathXL® Tutorials on CD ISBN: 0321575369

This interactive tutorial CD-ROM provides algorithmically generated practice exercises that are correlated at the objective level to the exercises in the textbook. Every practice exercise is accompanied by an example and a guided solution designed to involve students in the solution process. Selected exercises may also include a video clip to help students visualize concepts. The software provides helpful feedback for incorrect answers and can generate printed summaries of students' progress.

### InterAct Math Tutorial Website: www.interactmath.com

Get practice and tutorial help online! This interactive tutorial website provides algorithmically generated practice exercises that correlate directly to the exercises in the textbook. Students can retry an exercise as many times as they like with new values each time for unlimited practice and mastery. Every exercise is accompanied by an interactive guided solution that provides helpful feedback for incorrect answers, and students can also view a worked-out sample problem that steps them through an exercise similar to the one they're working on.

# Acknowledgments

An enormous benefit of authoring a successful series is the broad-based feedback I receive from the students, dedicated users, and reviewers. Every change to this edition is the result of their thoughtful comments and suggestions. I would like to express my appreciation to all the reviewers, whose collective insights form the backbone of this revision. In particular, I would like to thank the following people for reviewing *College Algebra, Algebra and Trigonometry*, and *Precalculus*.

Barnhill, Kayoko Yates, *Clark College*
Beaver, Timothy, *Isothermal Community College*
Best, Lloyd, *Pacific Union College*
Burgin, Bill, *Gaston College*
Chang, Jimmy, *St. Petersburg College*
Colt, Diana, *University of Minnesota-Duluth*
Davidson, Wendy, *Georgia Perimeter College-Newton*
Densmore, Donna, *Bossier Parish Community College*
Enegren, Disa, *Rose State College*
Fisher, Nancy, *University of Alabama*
Gerken, Donna, *Miami Dade College*
Glickman, Cynthia, *Community College of Southern Nevada*
Goel, Sudhir Kumar, *Valdosta State University*
Gordon, Donald, *Manatee Community College*
Gross, David L., *University of Connecticut*
Haack, Joel K., *University of Northern Iowa*
Haefner, Jeremy, *University of Colorado*
Hague, Joyce, *University of Wisconsin at River Falls*
Hall, Mike, *University of Mississippi*
Hayes, Tom, *Montana State University*
Hay-Jahans, Christopher N., *University of South Dakota*
Hernandez, Celeste, *Richland College*
Howard, Heidi, *FCCJ South*
Ihlow, Winfield A., *SUNY College at Oswego*
Johnson, Nancy Raye, *Manatee Community College*
Leesburg, Mary, *Manatee Community College*
Lehmann, Christine Heinecke, *Purdue University North Central*
Levichev, Alexander, *Boston University*
Lin, Zongzhu, *Kansas State University*
Marlin, Benjamin, *Northwestern Oklahoma State University*
Massey, Marilyn, *Collin County Community College*
McCarthy-Germaine, Yvelyne, *University of New Orleans*
Mertens, Owen, *Missouri State University-Springfield*
Miller, James, *West Virginia University*

Nega, Martha, *Georgia Perimeter College-Decatur*
Pharo, Debra A., *Northwestern Michigan College*
Phoenix, Gloria, *North Carolina Agricultural and Technical State University*
Platt, David, *Front Range Community College*
Pohjanpelto, Juha, *Oregon State University*
Quinlan, Brooke, *Hillsborough Community College*
Rech, Janice, *University of Nebraska at Omaha*
Rouhani, Behnaz, *Georgia Perimeter College-Dunwoody*
Salmon, Judith, *Fitchburg State College*
Schultz, Cynthia, *Illinois Valley Community College*
Shelton, Pat, *North Carolina Agricultural and Technical State University*
Spillman, Caroline, *Georgia Perimeter College-Clarkston*
Stump, Chris, *Bethel College*
Sykes, Scott, *University of Western Georgia*
Trim, Pamela, *Southwest Tennessee Community College*
Turner, Chris, *Arkansas State University*
Van Lommel, Richard E., *California State University-Sacramento*
Van Peursem, Dan, *University of South Dakota*
Van Veldhuizen, Philip, *University of Nevada at Reno*
White, David, *The Victoria College*
Wienckowski, Tracy, *University of Buffalo*

Additional acknowledgments are extended to Dan Miller and Kelly Barber, for preparing the solutions manuals, Brad Davis, for preparing the answer section and serving as accuracy checker, the Preparè, Inc. formatting team, for the book's brilliant paging, Brian Morris at Scientific Illustrators, for superbly illustrating the book, Sheila Norman, photo researcher, for obtaining the book's new photographs, and Barbara Mack, whose talents as production editor kept every aspect of this complex project moving through its many stages.

I would like to thank my editor at Pearson, Adam Jaworski, and sponsoring editor, Dawn Murrin, who guided and coordinated the book from manuscript through production. Thanks to Heather Scott for the beautiful covers and interior design. Finally, thanks to Katherine Greig, for your innovative marketing efforts, and to the entire Pearson sales force, for your confidence and enthusiasm about the book.

Robert Blitzer

# To the Student

What unique insights can algebra and trigonometry offer me regarding

- whether or not I should apologize to a friend for a blunder I committed? (Chapter P, page 15)
- global warming and climate change? (Chapter 1, pages 187–188)
- becoming a safer driver? (Chapter 2, page 359 and pages 367–368)
- making my financial goals a reality? (Chapter 3, page 431, and Chapter 10, page 979)
- the cycles of my physical, intellectual, and emotional potentials? (Chapter 4, pages 459 and 534)
- maximizing athletic performance? (Chapter 5, pages 585 and 616)
- creating intricate computer images of chaotic behavior? (Chapter 6, pages 643, 686 and 695)
- symptoms of physical illness among students who are procrastinators? (Chapter 7, pages 728 and 745)
- the path on which humanity journeys through space? (Chapter 9, pages 873 and 881)

I've written this book so that you can learn about the power of algebra and trigonometry and how they relate directly to your life outside the classroom. A great deal of attention has been given to applying algebra and trigonometry to your life to make your learning experience both interesting and relevant.

Although the pages that follow are filled with unique applications, I understand that your primary goal in reading the book is to acquire a solid understanding of the required topics in your precalculus course. In order to achieve this goal, I've carefully explained each topic, using voice balloons to help you understand the objectives while avoiding dense paragraphs with an intimidating amount of information. Important definitions and procedures are set off in boxes, and worked-out examples that present solutions in a step-by-step manner appear in every section. Each example is followed by a similar matched problem, called a Check Point, for you to try so that you can actively participate in the learning process as you read the book. (Answers to all Check Points appear in the back of the book.) Study Tips offer hints and suggestions and often point out common errors to avoid.

As you begin your studies, I would like to offer some specific suggestions for using this book and for being successful in this course:

- **Attend all classes.** No book is intended to be a substitute for valuable insights and interactions that occur in the classroom. In addition to arriving on time and being prepared, you will find it useful to read the section before it is covered in class. This will give you a clear idea of the new material that will be discussed.

- **Read the book.** Read each section with pen (or pencil) in hand. Move through the worked-out examples with great care. These examples provide a model for doing exercises in the exercise sets. As you proceed through the reading, do not give up if you do not understand every single word. Things will become clearer as you read on and see how various procedures are applied to specific worked-out examples.

- **Work problems every day and check your answers.** The way to learn mathematics is by doing mathematics, which means working the Check Points and assigned exercises in the exercise sets. The more exercises you work, the better you will understand the material.

- **Review for quizzes and tests.** After completing a chapter, study the chapter review chart, work the exercises in the Chapter Review, and work the exercises in the Chapter Test. Answers to all these exercises are given in the back of the book.

The methods that I've used to help you read the book, work the problems, and review for tests are described in "A Brief Guide to Getting the Most from This Book," which appears in the front of this book. Spend a few minutes reviewing the guide to familiarize yourself with the book's features and their benefits.

- **Use the resources available with this book.** Additional resources to aid your study are described on page xiii. These resources include a Solutions Manual; a Chapter Test Prep Video CD; and MathXL® for School, an online homework, tutorial, and assessment system of the text.

I wrote this book in Point Reyes National Seashore, 40 miles north of San Francisco. The park consists of 75,000 acres with miles of pristine surf-washed beaches, forested ridges, and bays bordered by white cliffs. It was my hope to convey the beauty and excitement of mathematics using nature's unspoiled beauty as a source of inspiration and creativity. Enjoy the pages that follow as you empower yourself with the algebra and trigonometry needed to succeed in college, your career, and in your life.

Regards,
*Bob*
Robert Blitzer

# About the Author

*Bob and his horse Jerid*

**Bob Blitzer** is a native of Manhattan and received a Bachelor of Arts degree with dual majors in mathematics and psychology (minor: English literature) from the City College of New York. His unusual combination of academic interests led him toward a Master of Arts in mathematics from the University of Miami and a doctorate in behavioral sciences from Nova University. Bob's love for teaching mathematics was nourished for nearly 30 years at Miami Dade College, where he received numerous teaching awards, including Innovator of the Year from the League for Innovations in the Community College and an endowed chair based on excellence in the classroom. In addition to *Precalculus*, Bob has written textbooks covering introductory algebra, intermediate algebra, college algebra, algebra and trigonometry, and liberal arts mathematics, all published by Prentice Hall. When not secluded in his Northern California writer's cabin, Bob can be found hiking the beaches and trails of Point Reyes National Seashore, and tending to the chores required by his beloved entourage of horses, chickens, and irritable roosters.

# Precalculus

# Prerequisites:
## Fundamental Concepts of Algebra

# P

What can algebra possibly have to tell me about

- the skyrocketing cost of a college education?
- my workouts?
- apologizing to a friend for a blunder I committed?
- the meaning of the national debt that exceeds $9 trillion?
- time dilation on a futuristic high-speed journey to a nearby star?
- the widening imbalance between numbers of women and men on college campuses?

This chapter reviews fundamental concepts of algebra that are prerequisites for the study of precalculus. Throughout the chapter, you will see how the special language of algebra describes your world.

*Here's where you'll find these applications:*

- College costs: Section P.1, Example 2; Exercise Set P.1, Exercises 131–132
- Workouts: Exercise Set P.1, Exercises 129–130
- Apologizing: Essay on page 15
- The national debt: Section P.2, Example 6
- Time dilation: Essay on page 42
- College gender imbalance: Chapter P Test, Exercise 32.

1

# Algebraic Expressions, Mathematical Models, and Real Numbers

## Objectives

1 Evaluate algebraic expressions.

2 Use mathematical models.

3 Find the intersection of two sets.

4 Find the union of two sets.

5 Recognize subsets of the real numbers.

6 Use inequality symbols.

7 Evaluate absolute value.

8 Use absolute value to express distance.

9 Identify properties of the real numbers.

10 Simplify algebraic expressions.

How would your lifestyle change if a gallon of gas cost $9.15? Or if the price of a staple such as milk was $15? That's how much those products would cost if their prices had increased at the same rate college tuition has increased since 1980. (*Source*: Center for College Affordability and Productivity) In this section, you will learn how the special language of algebra describes your world, including the skyrocketing cost of a college education.

## Algebraic Expressions

Algebra uses letters, such as $x$ and $y$, to represent numbers. If a letter is used to represent various numbers, it is called a **variable**. For example, imagine that you are basking in the sun on the beach. We can let $x$ represent the number of minutes that you can stay in the sun without burning with no sunscreen. With a number 6 sunscreen, exposure time without burning is six times as long, or 6 times $x$. This can be written $6 \cdot x$, but it is usually expressed as $6x$. Placing a number and a letter next to one another indicates multiplication.

Notice that $6x$ combines the number 6 and the variable $x$ using the operation of multiplication. A combination of variables and numbers using the operations of addition, subtraction, multiplication, or division, as well as powers or roots, is called an **algebraic expression**. Here are some examples of algebraic expressions:

$$x + 6, \quad x - 6, \quad 6x, \quad \frac{x}{6}, \quad 3x + 5, \quad x^2 - 3, \quad \sqrt{x} + 7.$$

Many algebraic expressions involve *exponents*. For example, the algebraic expression

$$17x^2 + 261x + 3257$$

approximates the average cost of tuition and fees at public U.S. colleges for the school year ending $x$ years after 2000. The expression $x^2$ means $x \cdot x$, and is read "$x$ to the second power" or "$x$ squared." The exponent, 2, indicates that the base, $x$, appears as a factor two times.

### Exponential Notation

If $n$ is a counting number (1, 2, 3, and so on),

$$
\boxed{\text{Exponent or Power}}
$$

$$b^n = \underbrace{b \cdot b \cdot b \cdots \cdot b}_{b \text{ appears as a factor } n \text{ times.}}$$

$$\boxed{\text{Base}}$$

$b^n$ is read "the $n$th power of $b$" or "$b$ to the $n$th power." Thus, the $n$th power of $b$ is defined as the product of $n$ factors of $b$. The expression $b^n$ is called an **exponential expression**. Furthermore, $b^1 = b$.

For example,

$$8^2 = 8 \cdot 8 = 64, \quad 5^3 = 5 \cdot 5 \cdot 5 = 125, \quad \text{and} \quad 2^4 = 2 \cdot 2 \cdot 2 \cdot 2 = 16.$$

**①** Evaluate algebraic expressions.

## Evaluating Algebraic Expressions

**Evaluating an algebraic expression** means to find the value of the expression for a given value of the variable.

Many algebraic expressions involve more than one operation. Evaluating an algebraic expression without a calculator involves carefully applying the following order of operations agreement:

### The Order of Operations Agreement

1. Perform operations within the innermost parentheses and work outward. If the algebraic expression involves a fraction, treat the numerator and the denominator as if they were each enclosed in parentheses.
2. Evaluate all exponential expressions.
3. Perform multiplications and divisions as they occur, working from left to right.
4. Perform additions and subtractions as they occur, working from left to right.

**( EXAMPLE 1 )** **Evaluating an Algebraic Expression**

Evaluate $7 + 5(x - 4)^3$ for $x = 6$.

**Solution**

$$7 + 5(x - 4)^3 = 7 + 5(6 - 4)^3 \quad \text{Replace x with 6.}$$
$$= 7 + 5(2)^3 \quad \text{First work inside parentheses: } 6 - 4 = 2.$$
$$= 7 + 5(8) \quad \text{Evaluate the exponential expression:}$$
$$\quad 2^3 = 2 \cdot 2 \cdot 2 = 8.$$
$$= 7 + 40 \quad \text{Multiply: } 5(8) = 40.$$
$$= 47 \quad \text{Add.}$$

🖉 Check Point **1**   Evaluate $8 + 6(x - 3)^2$ for $x = 13$.

**②** Use mathematical models.

## Formulas and Mathematical Models

An **equation** is formed when an equal sign is placed between two algebraic expressions. One aim of algebra is to provide a compact, symbolic description of the world. These descriptions involve the use of *formulas*. A **formula** is an equation that uses variables to express a relationship between two or more quantities.

Here are two examples of formulas related to heart rate and exercise.

**Couch-Potato Exercise**

$$H = \frac{1}{5}(220 - a)$$

Heart rate, in beats per minute, | is | $\frac{1}{5}$ of | the difference between 220 and your age.

**Working It**

$$H = \frac{9}{10}(220 - a)$$

Heart rate, in beats per minute, | is | $\frac{9}{10}$ of | the difference between 220 and your age.

The process of finding formulas to describe real-world phenomena is called **mathematical modeling**. Such formulas, together with the meaning assigned to the variables, are called **mathematical models**. We often say that these formulas model, or describe, the relationships among the variables.

(**EXAMPLE 2**)   **Modeling the Cost of Attending a Public College**

The bar graph in **Figure P.1** shows the average cost of tuition and fees for public four-year colleges, adjusted for inflation. The formula

$$T = 17x^2 + 261x + 3257$$

models the average cost of tuition and fees, $T$, for public U.S. colleges for the school year ending $x$ years after 2000.

   **a.** Use the formula to find the average cost of tuition and fees at public U.S. colleges for the school year ending in 2007.

   **b.** By how much does the formula underestimate or overestimate the actual cost shown in **Figure P.1**?

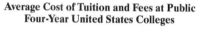

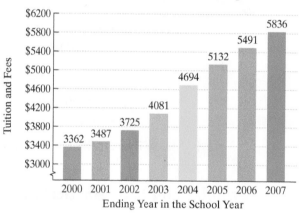

**Average Cost of Tuition and Fees at Public Four-Year United States Colleges**

Figure P.1
Source: The College Board

## Solution

   **a.** Because 2007 is 7 years after 2000, we substitute 7 for $x$ in the given formula. Then we use the order of operations to find $T$, the average cost of tuition and fees for the school year ending in 2007.

| | |
|---|---|
| $T = 17x^2 + 261x + 3257$ | This is the given mathematical model. |
| $T = 17(7)^2 + 261(7) + 3257$ | Replace each occurrence of x with 7. |
| $T = 17(49) + 261(7) + 3257$ | Evaluate the exponential expression $7^2 = 7 \cdot 7 = 49$. |
| $T = 833 + 1827 + 3257$ | Multiply from left to right: $17(49) = 833$ and $261(7) = 1827$. |
| $T = 5917$ | Add. |

The formula indicates that for the school year ending in 2007, the average cost of tuition and fees at public U.S. colleges was $5917.

   **b.** **Figure P.1** shows that the average cost of tuition and fees for the school year ending in 2007 was $5836.

The cost obtained from the formula, $5917, overestimates the actual data value by $5917 − $5836, or by $81.

⏣ Check Point **2** Assuming trends indicated by the data in **Figure P.1** continue, use the formula $T = 17x^2 + 261x + 3257$, described in Example 2, to project the average cost of tuition and fees at public U.S. colleges for the school year ending in 2010.

Sometimes a mathematical model gives an estimate that is not a good approximation or is extended to include values of the variable that do not make sense. In these cases, we say that **model breakdown** has occurred. For example, it is not likely that the formula in Example 2 would give a good estimate of tuition and fees in 2050 because it is too far in the future. Thus, model breakdown would occur.

## Sets

Before we describe the set of real numbers, let's be sure you are familiar with some basic ideas about sets. A **set** is a collection of objects whose contents can be clearly determined. The objects in a set are called the **elements** of the set. For example, the set of numbers used for counting can be represented by

$$\{1, 2, 3, 4, 5, \dots \}.$$

The braces, $\{\ \}$, indicate that we are representing a set. This form of representation, called the **roster method**, uses commas to separate the elements of the set. The symbol consisting of three dots after the 5, called an *ellipsis*, indicates that there is no final element and that the listing goes on forever.

A set can also be written in **set-builder notation**. In this notation, the elements of the set are described, but not listed. Here is an example:

$$\{x | x \text{ is a counting number less than 6}\}.$$

The set of all $x$    such that    $x$ is a counting number less than 6.

The same set written using the roster method is

$$\{1, 2, 3, 4, 5\}.$$

If $A$ and $B$ are sets, we can form a new set consisting of all elements that are in both $A$ and $B$. This set is called the *intersection* of the two sets.

 Find the intersection of two sets.

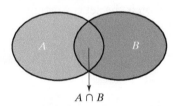

$A \cap B$

**Figure P.2** Picturing the intersection of two sets

### Definition of the Intersection of Sets

The **intersection** of sets $A$ and $B$, written $A \cap B$, is the set of elements common to both set $A$ **and** set $B$. This definition can be expressed in set-builder notation as follows:

$$A \cap B = \{x | x \text{ is an element of } A \text{ AND } x \text{ is an element of } B\}.$$

**Figure P.2** shows a useful way of picturing the intersection of sets $A$ and $B$. The figure indicates that $A \cap B$ contains those elements that belong to both $A$ and $B$ at the same time.

( EXAMPLE 3 )  **Finding the Intersection of Two Sets**

Find the intersection: $\{7, 8, 9, 10, 11\} \cap \{6, 8, 10, 12\}$.

**Solution**    The elements common to $\{7, 8, 9, 10, 11\}$ and $\{6, 8, 10, 12\}$ are 8 and 10. Thus,

$$\{7, 8, 9, 10, 11\} \cap \{6, 8, 10, 12\} = \{8, 10\}.$$

⏣ Check Point **3** Find the intersection: $\{3, 4, 5, 6, 7\} \cap \{3, 7, 8, 9\}$.

If a set has no elements, it is called the **empty set**, or the **null set**, and is represented by the symbol ∅ (the Greek letter phi). Here is an example that shows how the empty set can result when finding the intersection of two sets:

$$\{2, 4, 6\} \cap \{3, 5, 7\} = \emptyset.$$

These sets have no common elements.

Their intersection has no elements and is the empty set.

 Find the union of two sets.

Another set that we can form from sets $A$ and $B$ consists of elements that are in $A$ or $B$ or in both sets. This set is called the *union* of the two sets.

### Definition of the Union of Sets

The **union** of sets $A$ and $B$, written $A \cup B$, is the set of elements that are members of set $A$ **or** of set $B$ or of both sets. This definition can be expressed in set-builder notation as follows:

$$A \cup B = \{x \mid x \text{ is an element of } A \text{ OR } x \text{ is an element of } B\}.$$

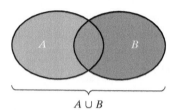

$A \cup B$

Figure P.3   Picturing the union of two sets

**Figure P.3** shows a useful way of picturing the union of sets $A$ and $B$. The figure indicates that $A \cup B$ is formed by joining the sets together.

We can find the union of set $A$ and set $B$ by listing the elements of set $A$. Then, we include any elements of set $B$ that have not already been listed. Enclose all elements that are listed with braces. This shows that the union of two sets is also a set.

( **EXAMPLE 4** )   **Finding the Union of Two Sets**

Find the union: $\{7, 8, 9, 10, 11\} \cup \{6, 8, 10, 12\}$.

**Solution**   To find $\{7, 8, 9, 10, 11\} \cup \{6, 8, 10, 12\}$, start by listing all the elements from the first set, namely 7, 8, 9, 10, and 11. Now list all the elements from the second set that are not in the first set, namely 6 and 12. The union is the set consisting of all these elements. Thus,

$$\{7, 8, 9, 10, 11\} \cup \{6, 8, 10, 12\} = \{6, 7, 8, 9, 10, 11, 12\}.$$   ●

⊘ Check Point 4   Find the union: $\{3, 4, 5, 6, 7\} \cup \{3, 7, 8, 9\}$.

 Recognize subsets of the real numbers.

## The Set of Real Numbers

The sets that make up the real numbers are summarized in **Table P.1**. We refer to these sets as **subsets** of the real numbers, meaning that all elements in each subset are also elements in the set of real numbers.

Notice the use of the symbol ≈ in the examples of irrational numbers. The symbol means "is approximately equal to." Thus,

$$\sqrt{2} \approx 1.414214.$$

We can verify that this is only an approximation by multiplying 1.414214 by itself. The product is very close to, but not exactly, 2:

$$1.414214 \times 1.414214 = 2.000001237796.$$

**Table P.1    Important Subsets of the Real Numbers**

| Name | Description | Examples |
|------|-------------|----------|
| Natural numbers $\mathbb{N}$ | $\{1, 2, 3, 4, 5, \dots\}$ <br> These are the numbers that we use for counting. | $2, 3, 5, 17$ |
| Whole numbers $\mathbb{W}$ | $\{0, 1, 2, 3, 4, 5, \dots\}$ <br> The set of whole numbers includes 0 and the natural numbers. | $0, 2, 3, 5, 17$ |
| Integers $\mathbb{Z}$ | $\{\dots, -5, -4, -3, -2, -1, 0, 1, 2, 3, 4, 5, \dots\}$ <br> The set of integers includes the negatives of the natural numbers and the whole numbers. | $-17, -5, -3, -2, 0, 2, 3, 5, 17$ |
| Rational numbers $\mathbb{Q}$ | $\left\{\frac{a}{b} \mid a \text{ and } b \text{ are integers and } b \neq 0\right\}$ <br> *This means that $b$ is not equal to zero.* <br><br> The set of rational numbers is the set of all numbers that can be expressed as a quotient of two integers, with the denominator not 0. Rational numbers can be expressed as terminating or repeating decimals. | $-17 = \frac{-17}{1}, -5 = \frac{-5}{1}, -3, -2,$ <br> $0, 2, 3, 5, 17,$ <br> $\frac{2}{5} = 0.4,$ <br> $\frac{-2}{3} = -0.6666\ldots = -0.\overline{6}$ |
| Irrational numbers $\mathbb{I}$ | The set of irrational numbers is the set of all numbers whose decimal representations are neither terminating nor repeating. Irrational numbers cannot be expressed as a quotient of integers. | $\sqrt{2} \approx 1.414214$ <br> $-\sqrt{3} \approx -1.73205$ <br> $\pi \approx 3.142$ <br> $-\frac{\pi}{2} \approx -1.571$ |

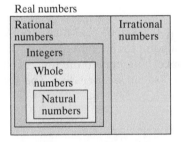

**Figure P.4** Every real number is either rational or irrational.

**Not all square roots are irrational.** For example, $\sqrt{25} = 5$ because $5^2 = 5 \cdot 5 = 25$. Thus, $\sqrt{25}$ is a natural number, a whole number, an integer, and a rational number $\left(\sqrt{25} = \frac{5}{1}\right)$.

The set of *real numbers* is formed by taking the union of the sets of rational numbers and irrational numbers. Thus, every real number is either rational or irrational, as shown in **Figure P.4**.

### Real Numbers

The set of **real numbers** is the set of numbers that are either rational or irrational:

$$\{x \mid x \text{ is rational or } x \text{ is irrational}\}.$$

The symbol $\mathbb{R}$ is used to represent the set of real numbers. Thus,

$$\mathbb{R} = \{x \mid x \text{ is rational}\} \cup \{x \mid x \text{ is irrational}\}.$$

**EXAMPLE 5    Recognizing Subsets of the Real Numbers**

Consider the following set of numbers:

$$\left\{-7, -\frac{3}{4}, 0, 0.\overline{6}, \sqrt{5}, \pi, 7.3, \sqrt{81}\right\}.$$

List the numbers in the set that are

**a.** natural numbers.     **b.** whole numbers.     **c.** integers.

**d.** rational numbers.    **e.** irrational numbers.    **f.** real numbers.

### Solution

**a.** Natural numbers: The natural numbers are the numbers used for counting. The only natural number in the set $\left\{-7, -\frac{3}{4}, 0, 0.\overline{6}, \sqrt{5}, \pi, 7.3, \sqrt{81}\right\}$ is $\sqrt{81}$ because $\sqrt{81} = 9$. (9 multiplied by itself, or $9^2$, is 81.)

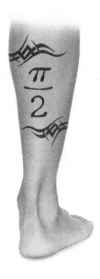

**b.** Whole numbers: The whole numbers consist of the natural numbers and 0. The elements of the set $\{-7, -\frac{3}{4}, 0, 0.\overline{6}, \sqrt{5}, \pi, 7.3, \sqrt{81}\}$ that are whole numbers are 0 and $\sqrt{81}$.

**c.** Integers: The integers consist of the natural numbers, 0, and the negatives of the natural numbers. The elements of the set $\{-7, -\frac{3}{4}, 0, 0.\overline{6}, \sqrt{5}, \pi, 7.3, \sqrt{81}\}$ that are integers are $\sqrt{81}$, 0, and $-7$.

**d.** Rational numbers: All numbers in the set $\{-7, -\frac{3}{4}, 0, 0.\overline{6}, \sqrt{5}, \pi, 7.3, \sqrt{81}\}$ that can be expressed as the quotient of integers are rational numbers. These include $-7\left(-7 = \frac{-7}{1}\right)$, $-\frac{3}{4}$, $0\left(0 = \frac{0}{1}\right)$, and $\sqrt{81}\left(\sqrt{81} = \frac{9}{1}\right)$. Furthermore, all numbers in the set that are terminating or repeating decimals are also rational numbers. These include $0.\overline{6}$ and 7.3.

**e.** Irrational numbers: The irrational numbers in the set $\{-7, -\frac{3}{4}, 0, 0.\overline{6}, \sqrt{5}, \pi, 7.3, \sqrt{81}\}$ are $\sqrt{5}\left(\sqrt{5} \approx 2.236\right)$ and $\pi(\pi \approx 3.14)$. Both $\sqrt{5}$ and $\pi$ are only approximately equal to 2.236 and 3.14, respectively. In decimal form, $\sqrt{5}$ and $\pi$ neither terminate nor have blocks of repeating digits.

**f.** Real numbers: All the numbers in the given set $\{-7, -\frac{3}{4}, 0, 0.\overline{6}, \sqrt{5}, \pi, 7.3, \sqrt{81}\}$ are real numbers.

⊘ Check Point **5**  Consider the following set of numbers:

$$\left\{-9, -1.3, 0, 0.\overline{3}, \frac{\pi}{2}, \sqrt{9}, \sqrt{10}\right\}.$$

List the numbers in the set that are

| | | |
|---|---|---|
| **a.** natural numbers. | **b.** whole numbers. | **c.** integers. |
| **d.** rational numbers. | **e.** irrational numbers. | **f.** real numbers. |

## The Real Number Line

The **real number line** is a graph used to represent the set of real numbers. An arbitrary point, called the **origin**, is labeled 0. Select a point to the right of 0 and label it 1. The distance from 0 to 1 is called the **unit distance**. Numbers to the right of the origin are **positive** and numbers to the left of the origin are **negative**. The real number line is shown in **Figure P.5**.

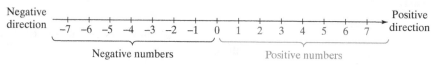

**Figure P.5**  The real number line

### Study Tip

Wondering how we located $\sqrt{2}$ as a precise point on the number line in **Figure P.6**? We used a right triangle with both legs of length 1. The remaining side measures $\sqrt{2}$.

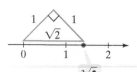

We'll have lots more to say about right triangles later in the chapter.

Real numbers are **graphed** on a number line by placing a dot at the correct location for each number. The integers are easiest to locate. In **Figure P.6**, we've graphed six rational numbers and three irrational numbers on a real number line.

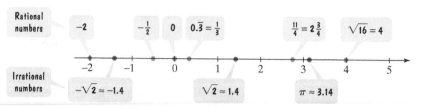

**Figure P.6**  Graphing numbers on a real number line

Every real number corresponds to a point on the number line and every point on the number line corresponds to a real number. We say that there is a **one-to-one correspondence** between all the real numbers and all points on a real number line.

**6** Use inequality symbols.

## Ordering the Real Numbers

On the real number line, the real numbers increase from left to right. The lesser of two real numbers is the one farther to the left on a number line. The greater of two real numbers is the one farther to the right on a number line.

Look at the number line in **Figure P.7**. The integers $-4$ and $-1$ are graphed.

Figure P.7

Observe that $-4$ is to the left of $-1$ on the number line. This means that $-4$ is less than $-1$.

$$-4 < -1$$

−4 is less than −1 because −4 is to the **left** of −1 on the number line.

In **Figure P.7**, we can also observe that $-1$ is to the right of $-4$ on the number line. This means that $-1$ is greater than $-4$.

$$-1 > -4$$

−1 is greater than −4 because −1 is to the **right** of −4 on the number line.

The symbols $<$ and $>$ are called **inequality symbols**. These symbols always point to the lesser of the two real numbers when the inequality statement is true.

−4 is less than −1.    $-4 < -1$   The symbol points to −4, the lesser number.

−1 is greater than −4.    $-1 > -4$   The symbol still points to −4, the lesser number.

The symbols $<$ and $>$ may be combined with an equal sign, as shown in the following table:

| | Symbols | Meaning | Examples | Explanation |
|---|---|---|---|---|
| This inequality is true if either the < part or the = part is true. | $a \leq b$ | $a$ is less than or equal to $b$. | $2 \leq 9$ $9 \leq 9$ | Because $2 < 9$ Because $9 = 9$ |
| This inequality is true if either the > part or the = part is true. | $b \geq a$ | $b$ is greater than or equal to $a$. | $9 \geq 2$ $2 \geq 2$ | Because $9 > 2$ Because $2 = 2$ |

**7** Evaluate absolute value.

## Absolute Value

The **absolute value** of a real number $a$, denoted by $|a|$, is the distance from 0 to $a$ on the number line. This distance is always taken to be nonnegative. For example, the real number line in **Figure P.8** shows that

$$|-3| = 3 \quad \text{and} \quad |5| = 5.$$

Figure P.8 Absolute value as the distance from 0

The absolute value of $-3$ is 3 because $-3$ is 3 units from 0 on the number line. The absolute value of 5 is 5 because 5 is 5 units from 0 on the number line. The absolute value of a positive real number or 0 is the number itself. The absolute value of a negative real number, such as $-3$, is the number without the negative sign.

We can define the absolute value of the real number $x$ without referring to a number line. The algebraic definition of the absolute value of $x$ is given as follows:

### Definition of Absolute Value

$$|x| = \begin{cases} x & \text{if } x \geq 0 \\ -x & \text{if } x < 0 \end{cases}$$

If $x$ is nonnegative (that is, $x \geq 0$), the absolute value of $x$ is the number itself. For example,

$$|5| = 5 \qquad |\pi| = \pi \qquad \left|\frac{1}{3}\right| = \frac{1}{3} \qquad |0| = 0. \quad \boxed{\text{Zero is the only number whose absolute value is 0.}}$$

If $x$ is a negative number (that is, $x < 0$), the absolute value of $x$ is the opposite of $x$. This makes the absolute value positive. For example,

$$|-3| = -(-3) = 3 \qquad |-\pi| = -(-\pi) = \pi \qquad \left|-\frac{1}{3}\right| = -\left(-\frac{1}{3}\right) = \frac{1}{3}.$$

$\boxed{\text{This middle step is usually omitted.}}$

( **EXAMPLE 6** ) **Evaluating Absolute Value**

Rewrite each expression without absolute value bars:

**a.** $\left|\sqrt{3} - 1\right|$     **b.** $|2 - \pi|$     **c.** $\dfrac{|x|}{x}$ if $x < 0$.

### Solution

**a.** Because $\sqrt{3} \approx 1.7$, the number inside the absolute value bars, $\sqrt{3} - 1$, is positive. The absolute value of a positive number is the number itself. Thus,

$$\left|\sqrt{3} - 1\right| = \sqrt{3} - 1.$$

**b.** Because $\pi \approx 3.14$, the number inside the absolute value bars, $2 - \pi$, is negative. The absolute value of $x$ when $x < 0$ is $-x$. Thus,

$$|2 - \pi| = -(2 - \pi) = \pi - 2.$$

**c.** If $x < 0$, then $|x| = -x$. Thus,

$$\frac{|x|}{x} = \frac{-x}{x} = -1.$$

⬤

○ Check Point **6** Rewrite each expression without absolute value bars:

**a.** $\left|1 - \sqrt{2}\right|$     **b.** $|\pi - 3|$     **c.** $\dfrac{|x|}{x}$ if $x > 0$.

Listed below are several basic properties of absolute value. Each of these properties can be derived from the definition of absolute value.

### Properties of Absolute Value

For all real numbers $a$ and $b$,

1. $|a| \geq 0$
2. $|-a| = |a|$
3. $a \leq |a|$
4. $|ab| = |a||b|$
5. $\left|\dfrac{a}{b}\right| = \dfrac{|a|}{|b|}, \quad b \neq 0$
6. $|a + b| \leq |a| + |b|$ (called the triangle inequality)

⑧ Use absolute value to express distance.

## Distance between Points on a Real Number Line

Absolute value is used to find the distance between two points on a real number line. If $a$ and $b$ are any real numbers, the **distance between $a$ and $b$** is the absolute value of their difference. For example, the distance between 4 and 10 is 6. Using absolute value, we find this distance in one of two ways:

$$|10 - 4| = |6| = 6 \quad \text{or} \quad |4 - 10| = |-6| = 6.$$

The distance between 4 and 10 on the real number line is 6.

Notice that we obtain the same distance regardless of the order in which we subtract.

### Distance between Two Points on the Real Number Line

If $a$ and $b$ are any two points on a real number line, then the distance between $a$ and $b$ is given by

$$|a - b| \quad \text{or} \quad |b - a|.$$

$\boxed{\text{EXAMPLE 7}}$  **Distance between Two Points on a Number Line**

Find the distance between $-5$ and 3 on the real number line.

**Solution**  Because the distance between $a$ and $b$ is given by $|a - b|$, the distance between $-5$ and 3 is

$$|-5 - 3| = |-8| = 8.$$

$a = -5 \quad b = 3$

**Figure P.9**  The distance between $-5$ and 3 is 8.

**Figure P.9** verifies that there are 8 units between $-5$ and 3 on the real number line. We obtain the same distance if we reverse the order of the subtraction:

$$|3 - (-5)| = |8| = 8.$$

⬤

⊘ Check Point **7**  Find the distance between $-4$ and 5 on the real number line.

⑨ Identify properties of the real numbers.

## Properties of Real Numbers and Algebraic Expressions

When you use your calculator to add two real numbers, you can enter them in any order. The fact that two real numbers can be added in any order is called the **commutative property of addition**. You probably use this property, as well as other properties of real numbers listed in **Table P.2**, without giving it much thought. The properties of the real numbers are especially useful when working with algebraic expressions. For each property listed in **Table P.2**, $a$, $b$, and $c$ represent real numbers, variables, or algebraic expressions.

**Table P.2    Properties of the Real Numbers**

| Name | Meaning | Examples |
|------|---------|----------|
| Commutative Property of Addition | Changing order when adding does not affect the sum. $a + b = b + a$ | • $13 + 7 = 7 + 13$ <br> • $13x + 7 = 7 + 13x$ |
| Commutative Property of Multiplication | Changing order when multiplying does not affect the product. $ab = ba$ | • $\sqrt{2} \cdot \sqrt{5} = \sqrt{5} \cdot \sqrt{2}$ <br> • $x \cdot 6 = 6x$ |
| Associative Property of Addition | Changing grouping when adding does not affect the sum. $(a + b) + c = a + (b + c)$ | • $3 + (8 + x) = (3 + 8) + x$ <br> $\qquad\qquad = 11 + x$ |
| Associative Property of Multiplication | Changing grouping when multiplying does not affect the product. $(ab)c = a(bc)$ | • $-2(3x) = (-2 \cdot 3)x = -6x$ |
| Distributive Property of Multiplication over Addition | Multiplication distributes over addition. $a \cdot (b + c) = a \cdot b + a \cdot c$ | • $7(4 + \sqrt{3}) = 7 \cdot 4 + 7 \cdot \sqrt{3}$ <br> $\qquad\qquad = 28 + 7\sqrt{3}$ <br> • $5(3x + 7) = 5 \cdot 3x + 5 \cdot 7$ <br> $\qquad\qquad = 15x + 35$ |
| Identity Property of Addition | Zero can be deleted from a sum. $a + 0 = a$ <br> $0 + a = a$ | • $\sqrt{3} + 0 = \sqrt{3}$ <br> • $0 + 6x = 6x$ |
| Identity Property of Multiplication | One can be deleted from a product. $a \cdot 1 = a$ <br> $1 \cdot a = a$ | • $1 \cdot \pi = \pi$ <br> • $13x \cdot 1 = 13x$ |
| Inverse Property of Addition | The sum of a real number and its additive inverse gives 0, the additive identity. $a + (-a) = 0$ <br> $(-a) + a = 0$ | • $\sqrt{5} + (-\sqrt{5}) = 0$ <br> • $-\pi + \pi = 0$ <br> • $6x + (-6x) = 0$ <br> • $(-4y) + 4y = 0$ |
| Inverse Property of Multiplication | The product of a nonzero real number and its multiplicative inverse gives 1, the multiplicative identity. $a \cdot \dfrac{1}{a} = 1, \quad a \neq 0$ <br> $\dfrac{1}{a} \cdot a = 1, \quad a \neq 0$ | • $7 \cdot \dfrac{1}{7} = 1$ <br> • $\left(\dfrac{1}{x - 3}\right)(x - 3) = 1, \quad x \neq 3$ |

## The Associative Property and the English Language

In the English language, phrases can take on different meanings depending on the way the words are associated with commas.

Here are three examples.

• Woman, without her man, is nothing.
  Woman, without her, man is nothing.

• What's the latest dope?
  What's the latest, dope?

• Population of Amsterdam broken down by age and sex
  Population of Amsterdam, broken down by age and sex

The properties of the real numbers in **Table P.2** apply to the operations of addition and multiplication. Subtraction and division are defined in terms of addition and multiplication.

## Definitions of Subtraction and Division

Let $a$ and $b$ represent real numbers.

**Subtraction:** $a - b = a + (-b)$
We call $-b$ the **additive inverse** or **opposite** of $b$.

**Division:** $a \div b = a \cdot \frac{1}{b}$, where $b \neq 0$
We call $\frac{1}{b}$ the **multiplicative inverse** or **reciprocal** of $b$. The quotient of $a$ and $b$, $a \div b$, can be written in the form $\frac{a}{b}$, where $a$ is the **numerator** and $b$ the **denominator** of the fraction.

Because subtraction is defined in terms of adding an inverse, the distributive property can be applied to subtraction:

$$a(b - c) = ab - ac$$
$$(b - c)a = ba - ca.$$

For example,

$$4(2x - 5) = 4 \cdot 2x - 4 \cdot 5 = 8x - 20.$$

⑩ Simplify algebraic expressions.

## Simplifying Algebraic Expressions

The **terms** of an algebraic expression are those parts that are separated by addition. For example, consider the algebraic expression

$$7x - 9y + z - 3,$$

which can be expressed as

$$7x + (-9y) + z + (-3).$$

This expression contains four terms, namely $7x$, $-9y$, $z$, and $-3$.

The numerical part of a term is called its **coefficient**. In the term $7x$, the 7 is the coefficient. If a term containing one or more variables is written without a coefficient, the coefficient is understood to be 1. Thus, $z$ means $1z$. If a term is a constant, its coefficient is that constant. Thus, the coefficient of the constant term $-3$ is $-3$.

$$7x + (-9y) + z + (-3)$$

| Coefficient is 7. | Coefficient is −9. | Coefficient is 1; $z$ means $1z$. | Coefficient is −3. |

The parts of each term that are multiplied are called the **factors** of the term. The factors of the term $7x$ are 7 and $x$.

**Like terms** are terms that have exactly the same variable factors. For example, $3x$ and $7x$ are like terms. The distributive property in the form

$$ba + ca = (b + c)a$$

enables us to add or subtract like terms. For example,

$$3x + 7x = (3 + 7)x = 10x$$
$$7y^2 - y^2 = 7y^2 - 1y^2 = (7 - 1)y^2 = 6y^2.$$

This process is called **combining like terms**.

An algebraic expression is **simplified** when parentheses have been removed and like terms have been combined.

**Study Tip**

To combine like terms mentally, add or subtract the coefficients of the terms. Use this result as the coefficient of the terms' variable factor(s).

**EXAMPLE 8** **Simplifying an Algebraic Expression**

Simplify: $6(2x^2 + 4x) + 10(4x^2 + 3x)$.

**Solution**

$$6(2x^2 + 4x) + 10(4x^2 + 3x)$$

$$= 6 \cdot 2x^2 + 6 \cdot 4x + 10 \cdot 4x^2 + 10 \cdot 3x \qquad \text{Use the distributive property to remove the parentheses.}$$

$$= 12x^2 + 24x + 40x^2 + 30x \qquad \text{Multiply.}$$

$$= (12x^2 + 40x^2) + (24x + 30x) \qquad \text{Group like terms.}$$

$$= 52x^2 + 54x \qquad \text{Combine like terms.}$$

> $52x^2$ and $54x$ are not like terms. They contain different variable factors, $x^2$ and $x$, and cannot be combined.

✓ Check Point **8** Simplify: $7(4x^2 + 3x) + 2(5x^2 + x)$.

## Properties of Negatives

The distributive property can be extended to cover more than two terms within parentheses. For example,

> This sign represents subtraction.

> This sign tells us that the number is negative.

$$-3(4x - 2y + 6) = -3 \cdot 4x - (-3) \cdot 2y - 3 \cdot 6$$

$$= -12x - (-6y) - 18$$

$$= -12x + 6y - 18.$$

The voice balloons illustrate that negative signs can appear side by side. They can represent the operation of subtraction or the fact that a real number is negative. Here is a list of properties of negatives and how they are applied to algebraic expressions:

### Properties of Negatives

Let $a$ and $b$ represent real numbers, variables, or algebraic expressions.

| **Property** | **Examples** |
|---|---|
| **1.** $(-1)a = -a$ | $(-1)4xy = -4xy$ |
| **2.** $-(-a) = a$ | $-(-6y) = 6y$ |
| **3.** $(-a)b = -ab$ | $(-7)4xy = -7 \cdot 4xy = -28xy$ |
| **4.** $a(-b) = -ab$ | $5x(-3y) = -5x \cdot 3y = -15xy$ |
| **5.** $-(a + b) = -a - b$ | $-(7x + 6y) = -7x - 6y$ |
| **6.** $-(a - b) = -a + b$ | $-(3x - 7y) = -3x + 7y$ |
| $\qquad\qquad = b - a$ | $\qquad\qquad = 7y - 3x$ |

It is not uncommon to see algebraic expressions with parentheses preceded by a negative sign or subtraction. Properties 5 and 6 in the box, $-(a + b) = -a - b$ and $-(a - b) = -a + b$, are related to this situation. An expression of the form $-(a + b)$ can be simplified as follows:

$$-(a + b) = -1(a + b) = (-1)a + (-1)b = -a + (-b) = -a - b.$$

Do you see a fast way to obtain the simplified expression on the right at the bottom of the previous page? **If a negative sign or a subtraction symbol appears outside parentheses, drop the parentheses and change the sign of every term within the parentheses.** For example,

$$-(3x^2 - 7x - 4) = -3x^2 + 7x + 4.$$

**EXAMPLE 9** **Simplifying an Algebraic Expression**

Simplify: $8x + 2[5 - (x - 3)]$.

**Solution**

$$8x + 2[5 - (x - 3)]$$

$= 8x + 2[5 - x + 3]$     Drop parentheses and change the sign of each term in parentheses: $-(x - 3) = -x + 3$.

$= 8x + 2[8 - x]$     Simplify inside brackets: $5 + 3 = 8$.

$= 8x + 16 - 2x$     Apply the distributive property:

$$2[8 - x] = 2 \cdot 8 - 2x = 16 - 2x.$$

$= (8x - 2x) + 16$     Group like terms.

$= (8 - 2)x + 16$     Apply the distributive property.

$= 6x + 16$     Simplify.

⊘ Check Point **9** Simplify: $6 + 4[7 - (x - 2)]$.

## Using Algebra to Solve Problems in Your Everyday Life

In *Geek Logik* (Workman Publishing, 2006), humorist Garth Sundem presents formulas covering dating, romance, career, finance, everyday decisions, and health. On the right is a sample of one of his formulas that "takes the guesswork out of life, providing easier living through algebra."

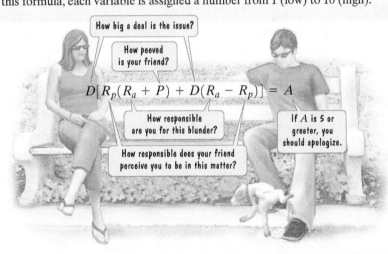

**Should You Apologize to Your Friend?**
In this formula, each variable is assigned a number from 1 (low) to 10 (high).

## Exercise Set P.1

### Practice Exercises

*In Exercises 1–16, evaluate each algebraic expression for the given value or values of the variable(s).*

**1.** $7 + 5x$, for $x = 10$

**2.** $8 + 6x$, for $x = 5$

**3.** $6x - y$, for $x = 3$ and $y = 8$

**4.** $8x - y$, for $x = 3$ and $y = 4$

**5.** $x^2 + 3x$, for $x = 8$

**6.** $x^2 + 5x$, for $x = 6$

**7.** $x^2 - 6x + 3$, for $x = 7$

**8.** $x^2 - 7x + 4$, for $x = 8$

**9.** $4 + 5(x - 7)^3$, for $x = 9$

**10.** $6 + 5(x - 6)^3$, for $x = 8$

**11.** $x^2 - 3(x - y)$, for $x = 8$ and $y = 2$

**12.** $x^2 - 4(x - y)$, for $x = 8$ and $y = 3$

**13.** $\dfrac{5(x + 2)}{2x - 14}$, for $x = 10$     **14.** $\dfrac{7(x - 3)}{2x - 16}$, for $x = 9$

**15.** $\dfrac{2x + 3y}{x + 1}$, for $x = -2$ and $y = 4$

**16.** $\dfrac{2x + y}{xy - 2x}$, for $x = -2$ and $y = 4$

The formula

$$C = \frac{5}{9}(F - 32)$$

expresses the relationship between Fahrenheit temperature, F, and Celsius temperature, C. In Exercises 17–18, use the formula to convert the given Fahrenheit temperature to its equivalent temperature on the Celsius scale.

**17.** 50°F     **18.** 86°F

A football was kicked vertically upward from a height of 4 feet with an initial speed of 60 feet per second. The formula

$$h = 4 + 60t - 16t^2$$

describes the ball's height above the ground, h, in feet, t seconds after it was kicked. Use this formula to solve Exercises 19–20.

**19.** What was the ball's height 2 seconds after it was kicked?

**20.** What was the ball's height 3 seconds after it was kicked?

In Exercises 21–28, find the intersection of the sets.

**21.** $\{1, 2, 3, 4\} \cap \{2, 4, 5\}$     **22.** $\{1, 3, 7\} \cap \{2, 3, 8\}$

**23.** $\{s, e, t\} \cap \{t, e, s\}$     **24.** $\{r, e, a, l\} \cap \{l, e, a, r\}$

**25.** $\{1, 3, 5, 7\} \cap \{2, 4, 6, 8, 10\}$

**26.** $\{0, 1, 3, 5\} \cap \{-5, -3, -1\}$

**27.** $\{a, b, c, d\} \cap \varnothing$     **28.** $\{w, y, z\} \cap \varnothing$

In Exercises 29–34, find the union of the sets.

**29.** $\{1, 2, 3, 4\} \cup \{2, 4, 5\}$     **30.** $\{1, 3, 7, 8\} \cup \{2, 3, 8\}$

**31.** $\{1, 3, 5, 7\} \cup \{2, 4, 6, 8, 10\}$     **32.** $\{0, 1, 3, 5\} \cup \{2, 4, 6\}$

**33.** $\{a, e, i, o, u\} \cup \varnothing$     **34.** $\{e, m, p, t, y\} \cup \varnothing$

In Exercises 35–38, list all numbers from the given set that are **a.** natural numbers, **b.** whole numbers, **c.** integers, **d.** rational numbers, **e.** irrational numbers, **f.** real numbers.

**35.** $\left\{-9, -\frac{4}{5}, 0, 0.25, \sqrt{3}, 9.2, \sqrt{100}\right\}$

**36.** $\left\{-7, -0.\overline{6}, 0, \sqrt{49}, \sqrt{50}\right\}$

**37.** $\left\{-11, -\frac{5}{6}, 0, 0.75, \sqrt{5}, \pi, \sqrt{64}\right\}$

**38.** $\left\{-5, -0.\overline{3}, 0, \sqrt{2}, \sqrt{4}\right\}$

**39.** Give an example of a whole number that is not a natural number.

**40.** Give an example of a rational number that is not an integer.

**41.** Give an example of a number that is an integer, a whole number, and a natural number.

**42.** Give an example of a number that is a rational number, an integer, and a real number.

Determine whether each statement in Exercises 43–50 is true or false.

**43.** $-13 \leq -2$     **44.** $-6 > 2$

**45.** $4 \geq -7$     **46.** $-13 < -5$

**47.** $-\pi \geq -\pi$     **48.** $-3 > -13$

**49.** $0 \geq -6$     **50.** $0 \geq -13$

In Exercises 51–60, rewrite each expression without absolute value bars.

**51.** $|300|$     **52.** $|-203|$

**53.** $|12 - \pi|$     **54.** $|7 - \pi|$

**55.** $|\sqrt{2} - 5|$     **56.** $|\sqrt{5} - 13|$

**57.** $\dfrac{-3}{|-3|}$     **58.** $\dfrac{-7}{|-7|}$

**59.** $\|-3| - |-7\|$     **60.** $\|-5| - |-13\|$

In Exercises 61–66, evaluate each algebraic expression for $x = 2$ and $y = -5$.

**61.** $|x + y|$     **62.** $|x - y|$

**63.** $|x| + |y|$     **64.** $|x| - |y|$

**65.** $\dfrac{y}{|y|}$     **66.** $\dfrac{|x|}{x} + \dfrac{|y|}{y}$

In Exercises 67–74, express the distance between the given numbers using absolute value. Then find the distance by evaluating the absolute value expression.

**67.** 2 and 17     **68.** 4 and 15

**69.** −2 and 5     **70.** −6 and 8

**71.** −19 and −4     **72.** −26 and −3

**73.** −3.6 and −1.4     **74.** −5.4 and −1.2

In Exercises 75–84, state the name of the property illustrated.

**75.** $6 + (-4) = (-4) + 6$

**76.** $11 \cdot (7 + 4) = 11 \cdot 7 + 11 \cdot 4$

**77.** $6 + (2 + 7) = (6 + 2) + 7$

**78.** $6 \cdot (2 \cdot 3) = 6 \cdot (3 \cdot 2)$

**79.** $(2 + 3) + (4 + 5) = (4 + 5) + (2 + 3)$

**80.** $7 \cdot (11 \cdot 8) = (11 \cdot 8) \cdot 7$

**81.** $2(-8 + 6) = -16 + 12$

**82.** $-8(3 + 11) = -24 + (-88)$

**83.** $\dfrac{1}{(x + 3)}(x + 3) = 1, x \neq -3$

**84.** $(x + 4) + [-(x + 4)] = 0$

In Exercises 85–96, simplify each algebraic expression.

**85.** $5(3x + 4) - 4$     **86.** $2(5x + 4) - 3$

**87.** $5(3x - 2) + 12x$     **88.** $2(5x - 1) + 14x$

**89.** $7(3y - 5) + 2(4y + 3)$     **90.** $4(2y - 6) + 3(5y + 10)$

**91.** $5(3y - 2) - (7y + 2)$     **92.** $4(5y - 3) - (6y + 3)$

**93.** $7 - 4[3 - (4y - 5)]$     **94.** $6 - 5[8 - (2y - 4)]$

**95.** $18x^2 + 4 - [6(x^2 - 2) + 5]$

**96.** $14x^2 + 5 - [7(x^2 - 2) + 4]$

In Exercises 97–102, write each algebraic expression without parentheses.

**97.** $-(-14x)$     **98.** $-(-17y)$

**99.** $-(2x - 3y - 6)$     **100.** $-(5x - 13y - 1)$

**101.** $\frac{1}{3}(3x) + [(4y) + (-4y)]$

**102.** $\frac{1}{2}(2y) + [(-7x) + 7x]$

## Practice Plus

*In Exercises 103–110, insert either* $<$, $>$, *or* $=$ *in the shaded area to make a true statement.*

**103.** $|-6|$ ▨ $|-3|$

**104.** $|-20|$ ▨ $|-50|$

**105.** $\left|\dfrac{3}{5}\right|$ ▨ $|-0.6|$

**106.** $\left|\dfrac{5}{2}\right|$ ▨ $|-2.5|$

**107.** $\dfrac{30}{40} - \dfrac{3}{4}$ ▨ $\dfrac{14}{15} \cdot \dfrac{15}{14}$

**108.** $\dfrac{17}{18} \cdot \dfrac{18}{17}$ ▨ $\dfrac{50}{60} - \dfrac{5}{6}$

**109.** $\dfrac{8}{13} \div \dfrac{8}{13}$ ▨ $|-1|$

**110.** $|-2|$ ▨ $\dfrac{4}{17} \div \dfrac{4}{17}$

*In Exercises 111–120, use the order of operations to simplify each expression.*

**111.** $8^2 - 16 \div 2^2 \cdot 4 - 3$

**112.** $10^2 - 100 \div 5^2 \cdot 2 - 3$

**113.** $\dfrac{5 \cdot 2 - 3^2}{[3^2 - (-2)]^2}$

**114.** $\dfrac{10 \div 2 + 3 \cdot 4}{(12 - 3 \cdot 2)^2}$

**115.** $8 - 3[-2(2 - 5) - 4(8 - 6)]$

**116.** $8 - 3[-2(5 - 7) - 5(4 - 2)]$

**117.** $\dfrac{2(-2) - 4(-3)}{5 - 8}$

**118.** $\dfrac{6(-4) - 5(-3)}{9 - 10}$

**119.** $\dfrac{(5 - 6)^2 - 2|3 - 7|}{89 - 3 \cdot 5^2}$

**120.** $\dfrac{12 \div 3 \cdot 5|2^2 + 3^2|}{7 + 3 - 6^2}$

*In Exercises 121–128, write each English phrase as an algebraic expression. Then simplify the expression. Let x represent the number.*

**121.** A number decreased by the sum of the number and four

**122.** A number decreased by the difference between eight and the number

**123.** Six times the product of negative five and a number

**124.** Ten times the product of negative four and a number

**125.** The difference between the product of five and a number and twice the number

**126.** The difference between the product of six and a number and negative two times the number

**127.** The difference between eight times a number and six more than three times the number

**128.** Eight decreased by three times the sum of a number and six

## Application Exercises

*The maximum heart rate, in beats per minute, that you should achieve during exercise is 220 minus your age:*

$$220 - a.$$

> This algebraic expression gives maximum
> heart rate in terms of age, $a$.

*The bar graph at the top of the next column shows the target heart rate ranges for four types of exercise goals. The lower and upper*

*limits of these ranges are fractions of the maximum heart rate, 220 − a. Exercises 129–130 are based on the information in the graph.*

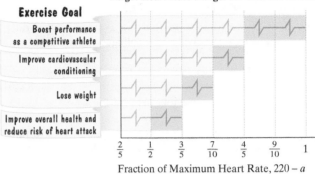

**Target Heart Rate Ranges for Exercise Goals**

Fraction of Maximum Heart Rate, 220 − a

**129.** If your exercise goal is to improve cardiovascular conditioning, the graph shows the following range for target heart rate, $H$, in beats per minute:

Lower limit of range  $H = \dfrac{7}{10}(220 - a)$

Upper limit of range  $H = \dfrac{4}{5}(220 - a)$.

  **a.** What is the lower limit of the heart range, in beats per minute, for a 20-year-old with this exercise goal?

  **b.** What is the upper limit of the heart range, in beats per minute, for a 20-year-old with this exercise goal?

**130.** If your exercise goal is to improve overall health, the graph shows the following range for target heart rate, $H$, in beats per minute:

Lower limit of range  $H = \dfrac{1}{2}(220 - a)$

Upper limit of range  $H = \dfrac{3}{5}(220 - a)$.

  **a.** What is the lower limit of the heart range, in beats per minute, for a 30-year-old with this exercise goal?

  **b.** What is the upper limit of the heart range, in beats per minute, for a 30-year-old with this exercise goal?

*The bar graph shows the average cost of tuition and fees at private four-year colleges in the United States.*

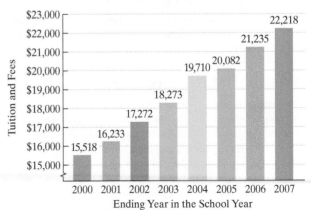

**Average Cost of Tuition and Fees at Private Four-Year United States Colleges**

Ending Year in the School Year

Source: The College Board

*The formula*

$$T = 15,395 + 988x - 2x^2$$

*models the average cost of tuition and fees, T, at private U.S. colleges for the school year ending x years after 2000. Use this information to solve Exercises 131–132.*

**131. a.** Use the formula to find the average cost of tuition and fees at private U.S. colleges for the school year ending in 2007.

   **b.** By how much does the formula underestimate or overestimate the actual cost shown by the graph at the bottom of the previous page for the school year ending in 2007?

   **c.** Use the formula to project the average cost of tuition and fees at private U.S. colleges for the school year ending in 2010.

**132. a.** Use the formula to find the average cost of tuition and fees at private U.S. colleges for the school year ending in 2006.

   **b.** By how much does the formula underestimate or overestimate the actual cost shown by the graph at the bottom of the previous page for the school year ending in 2006?

   **c.** Use the formula to project the average cost of tuition and fees at private U.S. colleges for the school year ending in 2012.

**133.** You had $10,000 to invest. You put *x* dollars in a safe, government-insured certificate of deposit paying 5% per year. You invested the remainder of the money in noninsured corporate bonds paying 12% per year. Your total interest earned at the end of the year is given by the algebraic expression

$$0.05x + 0.12(10,000 - x).$$

   **a.** Simplify the algebraic expression.

   **b.** Use each form of the algebraic expression to determine your total interest earned at the end of the year if you invested $6000 in the safe, government-insured certificate of deposit.

**134.** It takes you 50 minutes to get to campus. You spend *t* minutes walking to the bus stop and the rest of the time riding the bus. Your walking rate is 0.06 mile per minute and the bus travels at a rate of 0.5 mile per minute. The total distance walking and traveling by bus is given by the algebraic expression

$$0.06t + 0.5(50 - t).$$

   **a.** Simplify the algebraic expression.

   **b.** Use each form of the algebraic expression to determine the total distance that you travel if you spend 20 minutes walking to the bus stop.

## Writing in Mathematics

*Writing about mathematics will help you learn mathematics. For all writing exercises in this book, use complete sentences to respond to the question. Some writing exercises can be answered in a sentence; others require a paragraph or two. You can decide how much you need to write as long as your writing clearly and directly answers the question in the exercise. Standard references such as a dictionary and a thesaurus should be helpful.*

**135.** What is an algebraic expression? Give an example with your explanation.

**136.** If *n* is a natural number, what does $b^n$ mean? Give an example with your explanation.

**137.** What does it mean when we say that a formula models real-world phenomena?

**138.** What is the intersection of sets *A* and *B*?

**139.** What is the union of sets *A* and *B*?

**140.** How do the whole numbers differ from the natural numbers?

**141.** Can a real number be both rational and irrational? Explain your answer.

**142.** If you are given two real numbers, explain how to determine which is the lesser.

**143.** Think of a situation where you either apologized or did not apologize for a blunder you committed. Use the formula in the essay on page 15 to determine whether or not you should have apologized. How accurately does the formula model what you actually did?

**144.** Read *Geek Logik* by Garth Sundem (Workman Publishing, 2006). Would you recommend the book to college algebra students? Were you amused by the humor? Which formulas did you find most useful? Apply at least one of the formulas by plugging your life data into the equation, using the order of operations, and coming up with an answer to one of life's dilemmas.

## Critical Thinking Exercises

**Make Sense?** *In Exercises 145–148, determine whether each statement makes sense or does not make sense, and explain your reasoning.*

**145.** My mathematical model describes the data for tuition and fees at public four-year colleges for the past ten years extremely well, so it will serve as an accurate prediction for the cost of public colleges in 2050.

**146.** A model that describes the average cost of tuition and fees at private U.S. colleges for the school year ending *x* years after 2000 cannot be used to estimate the cost of private education for the school year ending in 2000.

**147.** The humor in this cartoon is based on the fact that the football will never be hiked.

**148.** Just as the commutative properties change groupings, the associative properties change order.

*In Exercises 149–156, determine whether each statement is true or false. If the statement is false, make the necessary change(s) to produce a true statement.*

**149.** Every rational number is an integer.

**150.** Some whole numbers are not integers.

**151.** Some rational numbers are not positive.

**152.** Irrational numbers cannot be negative.

**153.** The term $x$ has no coefficient.

**154.** $5 + 3(x - 4) = 8(x - 4) = 8x - 32$

**155.** $-x - x = -x + (-x) = 0$

**156.** $x - 0.02(x + 200) = 0.98x - 4$

*In Exercises 157–159, insert either $<$ or $>$ in the shaded area between the numbers to make the statement true.*

**157.** $\sqrt{2}$ ▢ $1.5$

**158.** $-\pi$ ▢ $-3.5$

**159.** $-\dfrac{3.14}{2}$ ▢ $-\dfrac{\pi}{2}$

## Preview Exercises

*Exercises 160–162 will help you prepare for the material covered in the next section.*

**160.** In parts (a) and (b), complete each statement.

    **a.** $b^4 \cdot b^3 = (b \cdot b \cdot b \cdot b)(b \cdot b \cdot b) = b^?$

    **b.** $b^5 \cdot b^5 = (b \cdot b \cdot b \cdot b \cdot b)(b \cdot b \cdot b \cdot b \cdot b) = b^?$

    **c.** Generalizing from parts (a) and (b), what should be done with the exponents when multiplying exponential expressions with the same base?

**161.** In parts (a) and (b), complete each statement.

    **a.** $\dfrac{b^7}{b^3} = \dfrac{\cancel{b} \cdot \cancel{b} \cdot \cancel{b} \cdot b \cdot b \cdot b \cdot b}{\cancel{b} \cdot \cancel{b} \cdot \cancel{b}} = b^?$

    **b.** $\dfrac{b^8}{b^2} = \dfrac{\cancel{b} \cdot \cancel{b} \cdot b \cdot b \cdot b \cdot b \cdot b \cdot b}{\cancel{b} \cdot \cancel{b}} = b^?$

    **c.** Generalizing from parts (a) and (b), what should be done with the exponents when dividing exponential expressions with the same base?

**162.** If 6.2 is multiplied by $10^3$, what does this multiplication do to the decimal point in 6.2?

---

## Section P.2  Exponents and Scientific Notation

### Objectives

1. Use properties of exponents.
2. Simplify exponential expressions.
3. Use scientific notation.

Listening to the radio on the way to campus, you hear politicians discussing the problem of the national debt, which exceeds \$9 trillion. They state that it's more than the gross domestic product of China, the world's second-richest nation, and four times greater than the combined net worth of America's 691 billionaires. They make it seem like the national debt is a real problem, but later you realize that you don't really know what a number like 9 trillion means. If the national debt were evenly divided among all citizens of the country, how much would every man, woman, and child have to pay? Is economic doomsday about to arrive?

In this section, you will learn to use exponents to provide a way of putting large and small numbers in perspective. Using this skill, we will explore the meaning of the national debt.

**1** Use properties of exponents.

## Properties of Exponents

The major properties of exponents are summarized in the box that follows and continues on the next page.

### Properties of Exponents

| Property | Examples |
|---|---|
| **The Negative-Exponent Rule** <br><br> If $b$ is any real number other than 0 and $n$ is a natural number, then $$b^{-n} = \frac{1}{b^n}.$$ | • $5^{-3} = \dfrac{1}{5^3} = \dfrac{1}{125}$ <br><br> • $\dfrac{1}{4^{-2}} = \dfrac{1}{\frac{1}{4^2}} = 4^2 = 16$ |

### Study Tip

When a negative integer appears as an exponent, switch the position of the base (from numerator to denominator or from denominator to numerator) and make the exponent positive.

**The Zero-Exponent Rule**

If $b$ is any real number other than 0,

$$b^0 = 1.$$

- $7^0 = 1$
- $(-5)^0 = 1$
- $-5^0 = -1$

Only 5 is raised to the zero power.

**The Product Rule**

If $b$ is a real number or algebraic expression, and $m$ and $n$ are integers,

$$b^m \cdot b^n = b^{m+n}.$$

- $2^2 \cdot 2^3 = 2^{2+3} = 2^5 = 32$
- $x^{-3} \cdot x^7 = x^{-3+7} = x^4$

When multiplying exponential expressions with the same base, add the exponents. Use this sum as the exponent of the common base.

**The Power Rule**

If $b$ is a real number or algebraic expression, and $m$ and $n$ are integers,

$$(b^m)^n = b^{mn}.$$

- $(2^2)^3 = 2^{2 \cdot 3} = 2^6 = 64$
- $(x^{-3})^4 = x^{-3 \cdot 4} = x^{-12} = \dfrac{1}{x^{12}}$

When an exponential expression is raised to a power, multiply the exponents. Place the product of the exponents on the base and remove the parentheses.

## Study Tip

$\dfrac{4^3}{4^5}$ and $\dfrac{4^5}{4^3}$ represent different numbers:

$$\frac{4^3}{4^5} = 4^{3-5} = 4^{-2} = \frac{1}{4^2} = \frac{1}{16}$$

$$\frac{4^5}{4^3} = 4^{5-3} = 4^2 = 16.$$

**The Quotient Rule**

If $b$ is a nonzero real number or algebraic expression, and $m$ and $n$ are integers,

$$\frac{b^m}{b^n} = b^{m-n}.$$

- $\dfrac{2^8}{2^4} = 2^{8-4} = 2^4 = 16$
- $\dfrac{x^3}{x^7} = x^{3-7} = x^{-4} = \dfrac{1}{x^4}$

When dividing exponential expressions with the same nonzero base, subtract the exponent in the denominator from the exponent in the numerator. Use this difference as the exponent of the common base.

**Products Raised to Powers**

If $a$ and $b$ are real numbers or algebraic expressions, and $n$ is an integer,

$$(ab)^n = a^n b^n.$$

- $(-2y)^4 = (-2)^4 y^4 = 16y^4$
- $(-2xy)^3 = (-2)^3 x^3 y^3 = -8x^3 y^3$

When a product is raised to a power, raise each factor to that power.

**Quotients Raised to Powers**

If $a$ and $b$ are real numbers, $b \neq 0$, or algebraic expressions, and $n$ is an integer,

$$\left(\frac{a}{b}\right)^n = \frac{a^n}{b^n}.$$

- $\left(\dfrac{2}{5}\right)^4 = \dfrac{2^4}{5^4} = \dfrac{16}{625}$
- $\left(-\dfrac{3}{x}\right)^3 = \dfrac{(-3)^3}{x^3} = -\dfrac{27}{x^3}$

When a quotient is raised to a power, raise the numerator to that power and divide by the denominator to that power.

② Simplify exponential
expressions.

## Simplifying Exponential Expressions

Properties of exponents are used to simplify exponential expressions. An exponential expression is **simplified** when

- No parentheses appear.
- No powers are raised to powers.
- Each base occurs only once.
- No negative or zero exponents appear.

### Simplifying Exponential Expressions

|  | **Example** |
|---|---|
| **1.** If necessary, remove parentheses by using $$(ab)^n = a^n b^n \quad \text{or} \quad \left(\frac{a}{b}\right)^n = \frac{a^n}{b^n}.$$ | $(xy)^3 = x^3 y^3$ |
| **2.** If necessary, simplify powers to powers by using $$(b^m)^n = b^{mn}.$$ | $(x^4)^3 = x^{4 \cdot 3} = x^{12}$ |
| **3.** If necessary, be sure that each base appears only once by using $$b^m \cdot b^n = b^{m+n} \quad \text{or} \quad \frac{b^m}{b^n} = b^{m-n}.$$ | $x^4 \cdot x^3 = x^{4+3} = x^7$ |
| **4.** If necessary, rewrite exponential expressions with zero powers as 1 ($b^0 = 1$). Furthermore, write the answer with positive exponents by using $$b^{-n} = \frac{1}{b^n} \quad \text{or} \quad \frac{1}{b^{-n}} = b^n.$$ | $\dfrac{x^5}{x^8} = x^{5-8} = x^{-3} = \dfrac{1}{x^3}$ |

The following example shows how to simplify exponential expressions. Throughout the example, assume that no variable in a denominator is equal to zero.

( EXAMPLE 1 ) **Simplifying Exponential Expressions**

Simplify:

**a.** $(-3x^4 y^5)^3$     **b.** $(-7xy^4)(-2x^5 y^6)$     **c.** $\dfrac{-35x^2 y^4}{5x^6 y^{-8}}$     **d.** $\left(\dfrac{4x^2}{y}\right)^{-3}.$

### Solution

**a.** $(-3x^4 y^5)^3 = (-3)^3 (x^4)^3 (y^5)^3$    Raise each factor inside the parentheses to the third power.

$= (-3)^3 x^{4 \cdot 3} y^{5 \cdot 3}$    Multiply the exponents when raising powers to powers.

$= -27 x^{12} y^{15}$    $(-3)^3 = (-3)(-3)(-3) = -27$

**b.** $(-7xy^4)(-2x^5 y^6) = (-7)(-2)xx^5 y^4 y^6$    Group factors with the same base.

$= 14x^{1+5} y^{4+6}$    When multiplying expressions with the same base, add the exponents.

$= 14x^6 y^{10}$    Simplify.

**c.** $\dfrac{-35x^2y^4}{5x^6y^{-8}} = \left(\dfrac{-35}{5}\right)\left(\dfrac{x^2}{x^6}\right)\left(\dfrac{y^4}{y^{-8}}\right)$   *Group factors with the same base.*

$= -7x^{2-6}y^{4-(-8)}$   *When dividing expressions with the same base, subtract the exponents.*

$= -7x^{-4}y^{12}$   *Simplify. Notice that $4 - (-8) = 4 + 8 = 12$.*

$= \dfrac{-7y^{12}}{x^4}$   *Write as a fraction and move the base with the negative exponent, $x^{-4}$, to the other side of the fraction bar and make the negative exponent positive.*

**d.** $\left(\dfrac{4x^2}{y}\right)^{-3} = \dfrac{(4x^2)^{-3}}{y^{-3}}$   *Raise the numerator and the denominator to the $-3$ power.*

$= \dfrac{4^{-3}(x^2)^{-3}}{y^{-3}}$   *Raise each factor in the numerator to the $-3$ power.*

$= \dfrac{4^{-3}x^{-6}}{y^{-3}}$   *Multiply the exponents when raising a power to a power: $(x^2)^{-3} = x^{2(-3)} = x^{-6}$.*

$= \dfrac{y^3}{4^3x^6}$   *Move each base with a negative exponent to the other side of the fraction bar and make each negative exponent positive.*

$= \dfrac{y^3}{64x^6}$   $4^3 = 4 \cdot 4 \cdot 4 = 64$

✓ Check Point **I** Simplify:

**a.** $(2x^3y^6)^4$     **b.** $(-6x^2y^5)(3xy^3)$     **c.** $\dfrac{100x^{12}y^2}{20x^{16}y^{-4}}$     **d.** $\left(\dfrac{5x}{y^4}\right)^{-2}.$

## Study Tip

Try to avoid the following common errors that can occur when simplifying exponential expressions.

| Correct | Incorrect | Description of Error |
|---|---|---|
| $b^3 \cdot b^4 = b^7$ | $b^3 \cdot b^4 = b^{12}$ | The exponents should be added, not multiplied. |
| $3^2 \cdot 3^4 = 3^6$ | $3^2 \cdot 3^4 = 9^6$ | The common base should be retained, not multiplied. |
| $\dfrac{5^{16}}{5^4} = 5^{12}$ | $\dfrac{5^{16}}{5^4} = 5^4$ | The exponents should be subtracted, not divided. |
| $(4a)^3 = 64a^3$ | $(4a)^3 = 4a^3$ | Both factors should be cubed. |
| $b^{-n} = \dfrac{1}{b^n}$ | $b^{-n} = -\dfrac{1}{b^n}$ | Only the exponent should change sign. |
| $(a + b)^{-1} = \dfrac{1}{a + b}$ | $(a + b)^{-1} = \dfrac{1}{a} + \dfrac{1}{b}$ | The exponent applies to the entire expression $a + b$. |

**③** Use scientific notation.

**Table P.3 Names of Large Numbers**

| | |
|---|---|
| $10^2$ | hundred |
| $10^3$ | thousand |
| $10^6$ | million |
| $10^9$ | billion |
| $10^{12}$ | trillion |
| $10^{15}$ | quadrillion |
| $10^{18}$ | quintillion |
| $10^{21}$ | sextillion |
| $10^{24}$ | septillion |
| $10^{27}$ | octillion |
| $10^{30}$ | nonillion |
| $10^{100}$ | googol |
| $10^{googol}$ | googolplex |

## Scientific Notation

As of December 2007, the national debt of the United States was about \$9.2 trillion. This is the amount of money the government has had to borrow over the years, mostly by selling bonds, because it has spent more than it has collected in taxes. A stack of \$1 bills equaling the national debt would rise to twice the distance from Earth to the moon. Because a trillion is $10^{12}$ (see **Table P.3**), the national debt can be expressed as

$$9.2 \times 10^{12}.$$

The number $9.2 \times 10^{12}$ is written in a form called *scientific notation*.

### Scientific Notation

A number is written in **scientific notation** when it is expressed in the form

$$a \times 10^n,$$

where the absolute value of $a$ is greater than or equal to 1 and less than 10 ($1 \le |a| < 10$), and $n$ is an integer.

It is customary to use the multiplication symbol, $\times$, rather than a dot, when writing a number in scientific notation.

## Converting from Scientific to Decimal Notation

Here are two examples of numbers in scientific notation:

$$6.4 \times 10^5 \quad \text{means} \quad 640{,}000.$$
$$2.17 \times 10^{-3} \quad \text{means} \quad 0.00217.$$

Do you see that the number with the positive exponent is relatively large and the number with the negative exponent is relatively small?

We can use $n$, the exponent on the 10 in $a \times 10^n$, to change a number in scientific notation to decimal notation. If $n$ is **positive**, move the decimal point in $a$ to the **right** $n$ places. If $n$ is **negative**, move the decimal point in $a$ to the **left** $|n|$ places.

**EXAMPLE 2** **Converting from Scientific to Decimal Notation**

Write each number in decimal notation:

**a.** $6.2 \times 10^7$ **b.** $-6.2 \times 10^7$ **c.** $2.019 \times 10^{-3}$ **d.** $-2.019 \times 10^{-3}$.

**Solution** In each case, we use the exponent on the 10 to determine how far to move the decimal point and in which direction. In parts (a) and (b), the exponent is positive, so we move the decimal point to the right. In parts (c) and (d), the exponent is negative, so we move the decimal point to the left.

**a.** $6.2 \times 10^7 = 62{,}000{,}000$

$n = 7$ | Move the decimal point 7 places to the right.

**b.** $-6.2 \times 10^7 = -62{,}000{,}000$

$n = 7$ | Move the decimal point 7 places to the right.

**c.** $2.019 \times 10^{-3} = 0.002019$

$n = -3$ | Move the decimal point $|-3|$ places, or 3 places, to the left.

**d.** $-2.019 \times 10^{-3} = -0.002019$

$n = -3$ | Move the decimal point $|-3|$ places, or 3 places, to the left.

✓ **Check Point 2** Write each number in decimal notation:

**a.** $-2.6 \times 10^9$ **b.** $3.017 \times 10^{-6}$.

## Converting from Decimal to Scientific Notation

To convert from decimal notation to scientific notation, we reverse the procedure of Example 2.

### Converting from Decimal to Scientific Notation

Write the number in the form $a \times 10^n$.

* Determine $a$, the numerical factor. Move the decimal point in the given number to obtain a number whose absolute value is between 1 and 10, including 1.
* Determine $n$, the exponent on $10^n$. The absolute value of $n$ is the number of places the decimal point was moved. The exponent $n$ is positive if the decimal point was moved to the left, negative if the decimal point was moved to the right, and 0 if the decimal point was not moved.

**EXAMPLE 3** Converting from Decimal Notation to Scientific Notation

Write each number in scientific notation:

**a.** 34,970,000,000,000
**b.** −34,970,000,000,000
**c.** 0.0000000000802
**d.** −0.0000000000802.

**Solution**

**a.** $34{,}970{,}000{,}000{,}000 = 3.497 \times 10^{13}$

> Move the decimal point to get a number whose absolute value is between 1 and 10.

> The decimal point was moved 13 places to the left, so $n = 13$.

**b.** $-34{,}970{,}000{,}000{,}000 = -3.497 \times 10^{13}$

**c.** $0.0000000000802 = 8.02 \times 10^{-11}$

> Move the decimal point to get a number whose absolute value is between 1 and 10.

> The decimal point was moved 11 places to the right, so $n = -11$.

**d.** $-0.0000000000802 = -8.02 \times 10^{-11}$

**Technology**

You can use your calculator's $\boxed{\text{EE}}$ (enter exponent) or $\boxed{\text{EXP}}$ key to convert from decimal to scientific notation. Here is how it's done for 0.0000000000802.

**Many Scientific Calculators**

Keystrokes

.0000000000802 $\boxed{\text{EE}}$ $\boxed{=}$

Display

$8.02 - 11$

**Many Graphing Calculators**

Use the mode setting for scientific notation.

Keystrokes

.0000000000802 $\boxed{\text{ENTER}}$

Display

$8.02\text{E} - 11$

**Study Tip**

If the absolute value of a number is greater than 10, it will have a positive exponent in scientific notation. If the absolute value of a number is less than 1, it will have a negative exponent in scientific notation.

✓ Check Point **3** Write each number in scientific notation:

**a.** 5,210,000,000
**b.** −0.00000006893.

**EXAMPLE 4** Expressing the U.S. Population in Scientific Notation

As of December 2007, the population of the United States was approximately 303 million. Express the population in scientific notation.

**Solution** Because a million is $10^6$, the 2007 population can be expressed as

$$303 \times 10^6.$$

> This factor is not between 1 and 10, so the number is not in scientific notation.

The voice balloon indicates that we need to convert 303 to scientific notation.

$$303 \times 10^6 = (3.03 \times 10^2) \times 10^6 = 3.03 \times 10^{2+6} = 3.03 \times 10^8$$

$$303 = 3.03 \times 10^2$$

In scientific notation, the population is $3.03 \times 10^8$.

⌀ Check Point **4** Express $410 \times 10^7$ in scientific notation.

## Computations with Scientific Notation

Properties of exponents are used to perform computations with numbers that are expressed in scientific notation.

( EXAMPLE 5 ) **Computations with Scientific Notation**

Perform the indicated computations, writing the answers in scientific notation:

**a.** $(6.1 \times 10^5)(4 \times 10^{-9})$      **b.** $\dfrac{1.8 \times 10^4}{3 \times 10^{-2}}$.

### Solution

**Technology**

$(6.1 \times 10^5)(4 \times 10^{-9})$
On a Calculator:

**Many Scientific Calculators**

6.1 [EE] 5 [×] 4 [EE] 9 [+/−] [=]

Display

2.44 − 03

**Many Graphing Calculators**

6.1 [EE] 5 [×] 4 [EE] [(−)] 9 [ENTER]

Display (in scientific notation mode)

2.44ᴇ − 3

**a.** $(6.1 \times 10^5)(4 \times 10^{-9})$

$= (6.1 \times 4) \times (10^5 \times 10^{-9})$    Regroup factors.

$= 24.4 \times 10^{5+(-9)}$    Add the exponents on 10 and multiply the other parts.

$= 24.4 \times 10^{-4}$    Simplify.

$= (2.44 \times 10^1) \times 10^{-4}$    Convert 24.4 to scientific notation: $24.4 = 2.44 \times 10^1$.

$= 2.44 \times 10^{-3}$    $10^1 \times 10^{-4} = 10^{1+(-4)} = 10^{-3}$

**b.** $\dfrac{1.8 \times 10^4}{3 \times 10^{-2}} = \left(\dfrac{1.8}{3}\right) \times \left(\dfrac{10^4}{10^{-2}}\right)$    Regroup factors.

$= 0.6 \times 10^{4-(-2)}$    Subtract the exponents on 10 and divide the other parts.

$= 0.6 \times 10^6$    Simplify: $4 - (-2) = 4 + 2 = 6$.

$= (6 \times 10^{-1}) \times 10^6$    Convert 0.6 to scientific notation: $0.6 = 6 \times 10^{-1}$.

$= 6 \times 10^5$    $10^{-1} \times 10^6 = 10^{-1+6} = 10^5$

⌀ Check Point **5** Perform the indicated computations, writing the answers in scientific notation:

**a.** $(7.1 \times 10^5)(5 \times 10^{-7})$      **b.** $\dfrac{1.2 \times 10^6}{3 \times 10^{-3}}$.

## Applications: Putting Numbers in Perspective

Due to tax cuts and spending increases, the United States began accumulating large deficits in the 1980s. To finance the deficit, the government had borrowed $9.2 trillion as of December 2007. The graph in **Figure P.10** shows the national debt increasing over time.

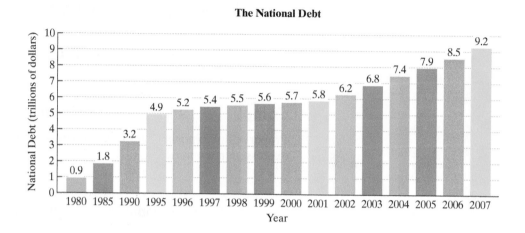

**The National Debt**

Figure P.10
*Source*: Office of Management and Budget

Example 6 shows how we can use scientific notation to comprehend the meaning of a number such as 9.2 trillion.

( **EXAMPLE 6** )  **The National Debt**

As of December 2007, the national debt was $9.2 trillion, or $9.2 \times 10^{12}$ dollars. At that time, the U.S. population was approximately 303,000,000 (303 million), or $3.03 \times 10^8$. If the national debt was evenly divided among every individual in the United States, how much would each citizen have to pay?

**Solution**  The amount each citizen must pay is the total debt, $9.2 \times 10^{12}$ dollars, divided by the number of citizens, $3.03 \times 10^8$.

$$\frac{9.2 \times 10^{12}}{3.03 \times 10^8} = \left(\frac{9.2}{3.03}\right) \times \left(\frac{10^{12}}{10^8}\right)$$
$$\approx 3.04 \times 10^{12-8}$$
$$= 3.04 \times 10^4$$
$$= 30,400$$

Every U.S. citizen would have to pay approximately $30,400 to the federal government to pay off the national debt.

⊘ Check Point **6** Pell Grants help low-income undergraduate students pay for college. In 2006, the federal cost of this program was $13 billion ($13 \times 10^9$) and there were 5.1 million ($5.1 \times 10^6$) grant recipients. How much, to the nearest hundred dollars, was the average grant?

## An Application: Black Holes in Space

The concept of a black hole, a region in space where matter appears to vanish, intrigues scientists and nonscientists alike. Scientists theorize that when massive stars run out of nuclear fuel, they begin to collapse under the force of their own gravity. As the star collapses, its density increases. In turn, the force of gravity increases so tremendously that even light cannot escape from the star. Consequently, it appears black.

A mathematical model, called the Schwarzchild formula, describes the critical value to which the radius of a massive body must be reduced for it to become a black hole. This model forms the basis of our next example.

**EXAMPLE 7** **An Application of Scientific Notation**

Use the Schwarzchild formula

$$R_s = \frac{2GM}{c^2}$$

where

$R_s$ = Radius of the star, in meters, that would cause it to become a black hole

$M$ = Mass of the star, in kilograms

$G$ = A constant, called the gravitational constant

$$= 6.7 \times 10^{-11} \frac{m^3}{kg \cdot s^2}$$

$c$ = Speed of light

$$= 3 \times 10^8 \text{ meters per second}$$

to determine to what length the radius of the sun must be reduced for it to become a black hole. The sun's mass is approximately $2 \times 10^{30}$ kilograms.

**Solution**

$$R_s = \frac{2GM}{c^2}$$

Use the given model.

$$= \frac{2 \times 6.7 \times 10^{-11} \times 2 \times 10^{30}}{(3 \times 10^8)^2}$$

Substitute the given values:
$G = 6.7 \times 10^{-11}$, $M = 2 \times 10^{30}$, and $c = 3 \times 10^8$.

$$= \frac{(2 \times 6.7 \times 2) \times (10^{-11} \times 10^{30})}{(3 \times 10^8)^2}$$

Rearrange factors in the numerator.

$$= \frac{26.8 \times 10^{-11+30}}{3^2 \times (10^8)^2}$$

Add exponents in the numerator. Raise each factor in the denominator to the power.

$$= \frac{26.8 \times 10^{19}}{9 \times 10^{16}}$$

Multiply powers to powers:
$(10^8)^2 = 10^{8 \cdot 2} = 10^{16}$.

$$= \frac{26.8}{9} \times 10^{19-16}$$

When dividing expressions with the same base, subtract the exponents.

$$\approx 2.978 \times 10^3$$

Simplify.

$$= 2978$$

Although the sun is not massive enough to become a black hole (its radius is approximately 700,000 kilometers), the Schwarzchild model theoretically indicates that if the sun's radius were reduced to approximately 2978 meters, that is, about $\frac{1}{235,000}$ its present size, it would become a black hole. ●

✓ Check Point **7** The speed of blood, $S$, in centimeters per second, located $r$ centimeters from the central axis of an artery is modeled by

$$S = (1.76 \times 10^5)[(1.44 \times 10^{-2}) - r^2].$$

Find the speed of blood at the central axis of this artery.

# Exercise Set P.2

## Practice Exercises

*Evaluate each exponential expression in Exercises 1–22.*

**1.** $5^2 \cdot 2$           **2.** $6^2 \cdot 2$

**3.** $(-2)^6$        **4.** $(-2)^4$

**5.** $-2^6$          **6.** $-2^4$

**7.** $(-3)^0$        **8.** $(-9)^0$

**9.** $-3^0$          **10.** $-9^0$

**11.** $4^{-3}$         **12.** $2^{-6}$

**13.** $2^2 \cdot 2^3$      **14.** $3^3 \cdot 3^2$

**15.** $(2^2)^3$       **16.** $(3^3)^2$

**17.** $\dfrac{2^8}{2^4}$         **18.** $\dfrac{3^8}{3^4}$

**19.** $3^{-3} \cdot 3$      **20.** $2^{-3} \cdot 2$

**21.** $\dfrac{2^3}{2^7}$         **22.** $\dfrac{3^4}{3^7}$

*Simplify each exponential expression in Exercises 23–64.*

**23.** $x^{-2}y$       **24.** $xy^{-3}$

**25.** $x^0 y^5$       **26.** $x^7 y^0$

**27.** $x^3 \cdot x^7$      **28.** $x^{11} \cdot x^5$

**29.** $x^{-5} \cdot x^{10}$    **30.** $x^{-6} \cdot x^{12}$

**31.** $(x^3)^7$       **32.** $(x^{11})^5$

**33.** $(x^{-5})^3$      **34.** $(x^{-6})^4$

**35.** $\dfrac{x^{14}}{x^7}$        **36.** $\dfrac{x^{30}}{x^{10}}$

**37.** $\dfrac{x^{14}}{x^{-7}}$       **38.** $\dfrac{x^{30}}{x^{-10}}$

**39.** $(8x^3)^2$      **40.** $(6x^4)^2$

**41.** $\left(-\dfrac{4}{x}\right)^3$    **42.** $\left(-\dfrac{6}{y}\right)^3$

**43.** $(-3x^2 y^5)^2$    **44.** $(-3x^4 y^6)^3$

**45.** $(3x^4)(2x^7)$    **46.** $(11x^5)(9x^{12})$

**47.** $(-9x^3 y)(-2x^6 y^4)$    **48.** $(-5x^4 y)(-6x^7 y^{11})$

**49.** $\dfrac{8x^{20}}{2x^4}$       **50.** $\dfrac{20x^{24}}{10x^6}$

**51.** $\dfrac{25a^{13}b^4}{-5a^2 b^3}$    **52.** $\dfrac{35a^{14}b^6}{-7a^7 b^3}$

**53.** $\dfrac{14b^7}{7b^{14}}$      **54.** $\dfrac{20b^{10}}{10b^{20}}$

**55.** $(4x^3)^{-2}$     **56.** $(10x^2)^{-3}$

**57.** $\dfrac{24x^3 y^5}{32x^7 y^{-9}}$    **58.** $\dfrac{10x^4 y^9}{30x^{12} y^{-3}}$

**59.** $\left(\dfrac{5x^3}{y}\right)^{-2}$    **60.** $\left(\dfrac{3x^4}{y}\right)^{-3}$

**61.** $\left(\dfrac{-15a^4 b^2}{5a^{10} b^{-3}}\right)^3$    **62.** $\left(\dfrac{-30a^{14} b^8}{10a^{17} b^{-2}}\right)^3$

**63.** $\left(\dfrac{3a^{-5} b^2}{12a^3 b^{-4}}\right)^0$    **64.** $\left(\dfrac{4a^{-5} b^3}{12a^3 b^{-5}}\right)^0$

*In Exercises 65–76, write each number in decimal notation without the use of exponents.*

**65.** $3.8 \times 10^2$       **66.** $9.2 \times 10^2$

**67.** $6 \times 10^{-4}$       **68.** $7 \times 10^{-5}$

**69.** $-7.16 \times 10^6$    **70.** $-8.17 \times 10^6$

**71.** $7.9 \times 10^{-1}$     **72.** $6.8 \times 10^{-1}$

**73.** $-4.15 \times 10^{-3}$   **74.** $-3.14 \times 10^{-3}$

**75.** $-6.00001 \times 10^{10}$   **76.** $-7.00001 \times 10^{10}$

*In Exercises 77–86, write each number in scientific notation.*

**77.** 32,000       **78.** 64,000

**79.** 638,000,000,000,000,000    **80.** 579,000,000,000,000,000

**81.** $-5716$       **82.** $-3829$

**83.** 0.0027       **84.** 0.0083

**85.** $-0.00000000504$    **86.** $-0.00000000405$

*In Exercises 87–106, perform the indicated computations. Write the answers in scientific notation. If necessary, round the decimal factor in your scientific notation answer to two decimal places.*

**87.** $(3 \times 10^4)(2.1 \times 10^3)$    **88.** $(2 \times 10^4)(4.1 \times 10^3)$

**89.** $(1.6 \times 10^{15})(4 \times 10^{-11})$    **90.** $(1.4 \times 10^{15})(3 \times 10^{-11})$

**91.** $(6.1 \times 10^{-8})(2 \times 10^{-4})$    **92.** $(5.1 \times 10^{-8})(3 \times 10^{-4})$

**93.** $(4.3 \times 10^8)(6.2 \times 10^4)$    **94.** $(8.2 \times 10^8)(4.6 \times 10^4)$

**95.** $\dfrac{8.4 \times 10^8}{4 \times 10^5}$    **96.** $\dfrac{6.9 \times 10^8}{3 \times 10^5}$

**97.** $\dfrac{3.6 \times 10^4}{9 \times 10^{-2}}$    **98.** $\dfrac{1.2 \times 10^4}{2 \times 10^{-2}}$

**99.** $\dfrac{4.8 \times 10^{-2}}{2.4 \times 10^6}$    **100.** $\dfrac{7.5 \times 10^{-2}}{2.5 \times 10^6}$

**101.** $\dfrac{2.4 \times 10^{-2}}{4.8 \times 10^{-6}}$    **102.** $\dfrac{1.5 \times 10^{-2}}{3 \times 10^{-6}}$

**103.** $\dfrac{480,000,000,000}{0.00012}$    **104.** $\dfrac{282,000,000,000}{0.00141}$

**105.** $\dfrac{0.00072 \times 0.003}{0.00024}$    **106.** $\dfrac{66,000 \times 0.001}{0.003 \times 0.002}$

## Practice Plus

*In Exercises 107–114, simplify each exponential expression. Assume that variables represent nonzero real numbers.*

**107.** $\dfrac{(x^{-2}y)^{-3}}{(x^2y^{-1})^3}$

**108.** $\dfrac{(xy^{-2})^{-2}}{(x^{-2}y)^{-3}}$

**109.** $(2x^{-3}yz^{-6})(2x)^{-5}$

**110.** $(3x^{-4}yz^{-7})(3x)^{-3}$

**111.** $\left(\dfrac{x^3y^4z^5}{x^{-3}y^{-4}z^{-5}}\right)^{-2}$

**112.** $\left(\dfrac{x^4y^5z^6}{x^{-4}y^{-5}z^{-6}}\right)^{-4}$

**113.** $\dfrac{(2^{-1}x^{-2}y^{-1})^{-2}(2x^{-4}y^3)^{-2}(16x^{-3}y^3)^0}{(2x^{-3}y^{-5})^2}$

**114.** $\dfrac{(2^{-1}x^{-3}y^{-1})^{-2}(2x^{-6}y^4)^{-2}(9x^3y^{-3})^0}{(2x^{-4}y^{-6})^2}$

## Application Exercises

*The bar graph shows the total amount Americans paid in federal taxes, in trillions of dollars, and the U.S. population, in millions, from 2003 through 2006. Exercises 115–116 are based on the numbers displayed by the graph.*

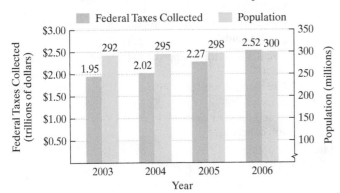

**Federal Taxes and the United States Population**

*Sources:* Internal Revenue Service and U.S. Census Bureau

**115. a.** In 2006, the United States government collected $2.52 trillion in taxes. Express this number in scientific notation.

   **b.** In 2006, the population of the United States was approximately 300 million. Express this number in scientific notation.

   **c.** Use your scientific notation answers from parts (a) and (b) to answer this question: If the total 2006 tax collections were evenly divided among all Americans, how much would each citizen pay? Express the answer in decimal notation.

**116. a.** In 2005, the United States government collected $2.27 trillion in taxes. Express this number in scientific notation.

   **b.** In 2005, the population of the United States was approximately 298 million. Express this number in scientific notation.

   **c.** Use your scientific notation answers from parts (a) and (b) to answer this question: If the total 2005 tax collections were evenly divided among all Americans, how much would each citizen pay? Express the answer in decimal notation, rounded to the nearest dollar.

*In the dramatic arts, ours is the era of the movies. As individuals and as a nation, we've grown up with them. Our images of love, war, family, country—even of things that terrify us—owe much to what we've seen on screen. The bar graph quantifies our love for movies by showing the number of tickets sold, in billions, and the average price per ticket for five selected years. Exercises 117–118 are based on the numbers displayed by the graph.*

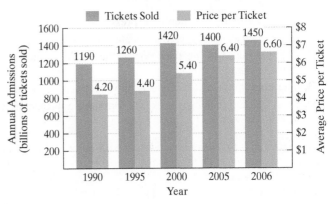

**United States Film Admissions and Admission Charges**

*Source:* National Association of Theater Owners

**117.** Use scientific notation to compute the amount of money that the motion picture industry made from box-office receipts in 2006. Express the answer in scientific notation.

**118.** Use scientific notation to compute the amount of money that the motion picture industry made from box office receipts in 2005. Express the answer in scientific notation.

**119.** The mass of one oxygen molecule is $5.3 \times 10^{-23}$ gram. Find the mass of 20,000 molecules of oxygen. Express the answer in scientific notation.

**120.** The mass of one hydrogen atom is $1.67 \times 10^{-24}$ gram. Find the mass of 80,000 hydrogen atoms. Express the answer in scientific notation.

**121.** In this exercise, use the fact that there are approximately $3.2 \times 10^7$ seconds in a year. According to the United States Department of Agriculture, Americans consume 127 chickens per second. How many chickens are eaten per year in the United States? Express the answer in scientific notation.

**122.** Convert 365 days (one year) to hours, to minutes, and, finally, to seconds, to determine how many seconds there are in a year. Express the answer in scientific notation.

## Writing in Mathematics

**123.** Describe what it means to raise a number to a power. In your description, include a discussion of the difference between $-5^2$ and $(-5)^2$.

**124.** Explain the product rule for exponents. Use $2^3 \cdot 2^5$ in your explanation.

**125.** Explain the power rule for exponents. Use $(3^2)^4$ in your explanation.

**126.** Explain the quotient rule for exponents. Use $\dfrac{5^8}{5^2}$ in your explanation.

**127.** Why is $(-3x^2)(2x^{-5})$ not simplified? What must be done to simplify the expression?

**128.** How do you know if a number is written in scientific notation?

**129.** Explain how to convert from scientific to decimal notation and give an example.

**130.** Explain how to convert from decimal to scientific notation and give an example.

## Critical Thinking Exercises

**Make Sense?** *In Exercises 131–134, determine whether each statement makes sense or does not make sense, and explain your reasoning.*

**131.** There are many exponential expressions that are equal to $36x^{12}$, such as $(6x^6)^2$, $(6x^3)(6x^9)$, $36(x^3)^9$, and $6^2(x^2)^6$.

**132.** If $5^{-2}$ is raised to the third power, the result is a number between 0 and 1.

**133.** The population of Colorado is approximately $4.6 \times 10^{12}$.

**134.** I just finished reading a book that contained approximately $1.04 \times 10^5$ words.

*In Exercises 135–142, determine whether each statement is true or false. If the statement is false, make the necessary change(s) to produce a true statement.*

**135.** $4^{-2} < 4^{-3}$

**136.** $5^{-2} > 2^{-5}$

**137.** $(-2)^4 = 2^{-4}$

**138.** $5^2 \cdot 5^{-2} > 2^5 \cdot 2^{-5}$

**139.** $534.7 = 5.347 \times 10^3$

**140.** $\dfrac{8 \times 10^{30}}{4 \times 10^{-5}} = 2 \times 10^{25}$

**141.** $(7 \times 10^5) + (2 \times 10^{-3}) = 9 \times 10^2$

**142.** $(4 \times 10^3) + (3 \times 10^2) = 4.3 \times 10^3$

**143.** The mad Dr. Frankenstein has gathered enough bits and pieces (so to speak) for $2^{-1} + 2^{-2}$ of his creature-to-be. Write a fraction that represents the amount of his creature that must still be obtained.

**144.** If $b^A = MN, b^C = M$, and $b^D = N$, what is the relationship among $A, C$, and $D$?

**145.** Our hearts beat approximately 70 times per minute. Express in scientific notation how many times the heart beats over a lifetime of 80 years. Round the decimal factor in your scientific notation answer to two decimal places.

## Group Exercise

**146. Putting Numbers into Perspective.** A large number can be put into perspective by comparing it with another number. For example, we put the $9.2 trillion national debt (Example 6) and the $2.52 trillion the government collected in taxes (Exercise 115) by comparing these numbers to the number of U.S. citizens.

For this project, each group member should consult an almanac, a newspaper, or the World Wide Web to find a number greater than one million. Explain to other members of the group the context in which the large number is used. Express the number in scientific notation. Then put the number into perspective by comparing it with another number.

## Preview Exercises

*Exercises 147–149 will help you prepare for the material covered in the next section.*

**147. a.** Find $\sqrt{16} \cdot \sqrt{4}$.
  **b.** Find $\sqrt{16 \cdot 4}$.
  **c.** Based on your answers to parts (a) and (b), what can you conclude?

**148. a.** Use a calculator to approximate $\sqrt{300}$ to two decimal places.
  **b.** Use a calculator to approximate $10\sqrt{3}$ to two decimal places.
  **c.** Based on your answers to parts (a) and (b), what can you conclude?

**149. a.** Simplify: $21x + 10x$.
  **b.** Simplify: $21\sqrt{2} + 10\sqrt{2}$.

---

**Section P.3**

## Radicals and Rational Exponents

### Objectives

1. Evaluate square roots.
2. Simplify expressions of the form $\sqrt{a^2}$.
3. Use the product rule to simplify square roots.
4. Use the quotient rule to simplify square roots.
5. Add and subtract square roots.
6. Rationalize denominators.
7. Evaluate and perform operations with higher roots.
8. Understand and use rational exponents.

This photograph shows mathematical models used by Albert Einstein at a lecture on relativity. Notice the radicals that appear in many of the formulas. Among these models, there is one describing how an astronaut in a moving spaceship ages more slowly than friends who remain on Earth. No description of your world can be complete without roots and radicals. In this section, in addition to reviewing the basics of radical expressions and the use of rational exponents to indicate radicals, you will see how radicals model time dilation for a futuristic high-speed trip to a nearby star.

**①** Evaluate square roots.

## Square Roots

From our earlier work with exponents, we are aware that the square of both 5 and −5 is 25:

$$5^2 = 25 \quad \text{and} \quad (-5)^2 = 25.$$

The reverse operation of squaring a number is finding the *square root* of the number. For example,

- One square root of 25 is 5 because $5^2 = 25$.
- Another square root of 25 is −5 because $(-5)^2 = 25$.

In general, **if $b^2 = a$, then $b$ is a square root of $a$.**

The symbol $\sqrt{\phantom{a}}$ is used to denote the *positive* or *principal square root* of a number. For example,

- $\sqrt{25} = 5$ because $5^2 = 25$ and 5 is positive.
- $\sqrt{100} = 10$ because $10^2 = 100$ and 10 is positive.

The symbol $\sqrt{\phantom{a}}$ that we use to denote the principal square root is called a **radical sign**. The number under the radical sign is called the **radicand**. Together we refer to the radical sign and its radicand as a **radical expression**.

Radical sign   $\sqrt{a}$   Radicand

Radical expression

### Definition of the Principal Square Root

If $a$ is a nonnegative real number, the nonnegative number $b$ such that $b^2 = a$, denoted by $b = \sqrt{a}$, is the **principal square root** of $a$.

The symbol $-\sqrt{\phantom{a}}$ is used to denote the negative square root of a number. For example,

- $-\sqrt{25} = -5$ because $(-5)^2 = 25$ and −5 is negative.
- $-\sqrt{100} = -10$ because $(-10)^2 = 100$ and −10 is negative.

(**EXAMPLE 1**)  **Evaluating Square Roots**

Evaluate:

**a.** $\sqrt{64}$    **b.** $-\sqrt{49}$    **c.** $\sqrt{\dfrac{1}{4}}$    **d.** $\sqrt{9 + 16}$    **e.** $\sqrt{9} + \sqrt{16}$.

**Solution**

**a.** $\sqrt{64} = 8$     The principal square root of 64 is 8. Check: $8^2 = 64$.

**b.** $-\sqrt{49} = -7$     The negative square root of 49 is −7. Check: $(-7)^2 = 49$.

**c.** $\sqrt{\dfrac{1}{4}} = \dfrac{1}{2}$     The principal square root of $\frac{1}{4}$ is $\frac{1}{2}$. Check: $\left(\frac{1}{2}\right)^2 = \frac{1}{4}$.

**d.** $\sqrt{9 + 16} = \sqrt{25}$     First simplify the expression under the radical sign.

$= 5$     Then take the principal square root of 25, which is 5.

**e.** $\sqrt{9} + \sqrt{16} = 3 + 4$     $\sqrt{9} = 3$ because $3^2 = 9$. $\sqrt{16} = 4$ because $4^2 = 16$.

$= 7$

**Study Tip**

In Example 1, parts (d) and (e), observe that $\sqrt{9 + 16}$ is not equal to $\sqrt{9} + \sqrt{16}$. In general,

$$\sqrt{a + b} \neq \sqrt{a} + \sqrt{b}$$

and

$$\sqrt{a - b} \neq \sqrt{a} - \sqrt{b}.$$

⊘ Check Point **1** Evaluate:

**a.** $\sqrt{81}$       **b.** $-\sqrt{9}$       **c.** $\sqrt{\dfrac{1}{25}}$

**d.** $\sqrt{36 + 64}$       **e.** $\sqrt{36} + \sqrt{64}$.

A number that is the square of a rational number is called a **perfect square**. All the radicands in Example 1 and Check Point 1 are perfect squares.

- 64 is a perfect square because $64 = 8^2$. Thus, $\sqrt{64} = 8$.
- $\dfrac{1}{4}$ is a perfect square because $\dfrac{1}{4} = \left(\dfrac{1}{2}\right)^2$. Thus, $\sqrt{\dfrac{1}{4}} = \dfrac{1}{2}$.

Let's see what happens to the radical expression $\sqrt{x}$ if $x$ is a negative number. Is the square root of a negative number a real number? For example, consider $\sqrt{-25}$. Is there a real number whose square is $-25$? No. Thus, $\sqrt{-25}$ is not a real number. In general, **a square root of a negative number is not a real number**.

If a number $a$ is nonnegative ($a \geq 0$), then $(\sqrt{a})^2 = a$. For example,

$$(\sqrt{2})^2 = 2, \quad (\sqrt{3})^2 = 3, \quad (\sqrt{4})^2 = 4, \quad \text{and} \quad (\sqrt{5})^2 = 5.$$

**②** Simplify expressions of the form $\sqrt{a^2}$.

## Simplifying Expressions of the Form $\sqrt{a^2}$

You may think that $\sqrt{a^2} = a$. However, this is not necessarily true. Consider the following examples:

$$\sqrt{4^2} = \sqrt{16} = 4$$
$$\sqrt{(-4)^2} = \sqrt{16} = 4.$$

> The result is not −4, but rather the absolute value of −4, or 4.

Here is a rule for simplifying expressions of the form $\sqrt{a^2}$:

### Simplifying $\sqrt{a^2}$

For any real number $a$,

$$\sqrt{a^2} = |a|.$$

In words, the principal square root of $a^2$ is the absolute value of $a$.

For example, $\sqrt{6^2} = |6| = 6$ and $\sqrt{(-6)^2} = |-6| = 6$.

**③** Use the product rule to simplify square roots.

## The Product Rule for Square Roots

A rule for multiplying square roots can be generalized by comparing $\sqrt{25} \cdot \sqrt{4}$ and $\sqrt{25 \cdot 4}$. Notice that

$$\sqrt{25} \cdot \sqrt{4} = 5 \cdot 2 = 10 \quad \text{and} \quad \sqrt{25 \cdot 4} = \sqrt{100} = 10.$$

Because we obtain 10 in both situations, the original radical expressions must be equal. That is,

$$\sqrt{25} \cdot \sqrt{4} = \sqrt{25 \cdot 4}.$$

This result is a special case of the **product rule for square roots** that can be generalized as follows:

### The Product Rule for Square Roots

If $a$ and $b$ represent nonnegative real numbers, then

$$\sqrt{ab} = \sqrt{a} \cdot \sqrt{b} \quad \text{and} \quad \sqrt{a} \cdot \sqrt{b} = \sqrt{ab}.$$

> The square root of a product is the product of the square roots.

> The product of two square roots is the square root of the product of the radicands.

A square root is **simplified** when its radicand has no factors other than 1 that are perfect squares. For example, $\sqrt{500}$ is not simplified because it can be expressed as $\sqrt{100 \cdot 5}$ and 100 is a perfect square. Example 2 shows how the product rule is used to remove from the square root any perfect squares that occur as factors.

> ### (EXAMPLE 2) Using the Product Rule to Simplify Square Roots
>
> Simplify:　**a.** $\sqrt{500}$　　**b.** $\sqrt{6x} \cdot \sqrt{3x}$.
>
> **Solution**
>
> **a.** $\sqrt{500} = \sqrt{100 \cdot 5}$　Factor 500; 100 is the greatest perfect square factor.
>
> $\phantom{\sqrt{500}} = \sqrt{100}\sqrt{5}$　Use the product rule: $\sqrt{ab} = \sqrt{a} \cdot \sqrt{b}$.
>
> $\phantom{\sqrt{500}} = 10\sqrt{5}$　Write $\sqrt{100}$ as 10. We read $10\sqrt{5}$ as "ten times the square root of 5."
>
> **b.** We can simplify $\sqrt{6x} \cdot \sqrt{3x}$ using the product rule only if $6x$ and $3x$ represent nonnegative real numbers. Thus, $x \geq 0$.
>
> $\sqrt{6x} \cdot \sqrt{3x} = \sqrt{6x \cdot 3x}$　Use the product rule: $\sqrt{a}\sqrt{b} = \sqrt{ab}$.
>
> $\phantom{\sqrt{6x} \cdot \sqrt{3x}} = \sqrt{18x^2}$　Multiply in the radicand.
>
> $\phantom{\sqrt{6x} \cdot \sqrt{3x}} = \sqrt{9x^2 \cdot 2}$　Factor 18; 9 is the greatest perfect square factor.
>
> $\phantom{\sqrt{6x} \cdot \sqrt{3x}} = \sqrt{9x^2}\sqrt{2}$　Use the product rule: $\sqrt{ab} = \sqrt{a} \cdot \sqrt{b}$.
>
> $\phantom{\sqrt{6x} \cdot \sqrt{3x}} = \sqrt{9}\sqrt{x^2}\sqrt{2}$　Use the product rule to write $\sqrt{9x^2}$ as the product of two square roots.
>
> $\phantom{\sqrt{6x} \cdot \sqrt{3x}} = 3x\sqrt{2}$　$\sqrt{x^2} = |x| = x$ because $x \geq 0$. ●

### Study Tip

When simplifying square roots, always look for the *greatest* perfect square factor possible. The following factorization will lead to further simplification:

$$\sqrt{500} = \sqrt{25 \cdot 20} = \sqrt{25}\sqrt{20} = 5\sqrt{20}.$$

25 is a perfect square factor of 500, but not the greatest perfect square factor.

Because 20 contains a perfect square factor, 4, the simplification is not complete.

$$5\sqrt{20} = 5\sqrt{4 \cdot 5} = 5\sqrt{4}\sqrt{5} = 5 \cdot 2\sqrt{5} = 10\sqrt{5}$$

Although the result checks with our simplification using $\sqrt{500} = \sqrt{100 \cdot 5}$, more work is required when the greatest perfect square factor is not used.

---

☑ Check Point **2** Simplify:

　　**a.** $\sqrt{75}$　　**b.** $\sqrt{5x} \cdot \sqrt{10x}$.

**④** Use the quotient rule to simplify square roots.

## The Quotient Rule for Square Roots

Another property for square roots involves division.

### The Quotient Rule for Square Roots

If $a$ and $b$ represent nonnegative real numbers and $b \neq 0$, then

$$\sqrt{\frac{a}{b}} = \frac{\sqrt{a}}{\sqrt{b}} \quad \text{and} \quad \frac{\sqrt{a}}{\sqrt{b}} = \sqrt{\frac{a}{b}}.$$

The square root of a quotient is the quotient of the square roots.

The quotient of two square roots is the square root of the quotient of the radicands.

**EXAMPLE 3** **Using the Quotient Rule to Simplify Square Roots**

Simplify: **a.** $\sqrt{\dfrac{100}{9}}$ **b.** $\dfrac{\sqrt{48x^3}}{\sqrt{6x}}$.

**Solution**

**a.** $\sqrt{\dfrac{100}{9}} = \dfrac{\sqrt{100}}{\sqrt{9}} = \dfrac{10}{3}$

**b.** We can simplify the quotient of $\sqrt{48x^3}$ and $\sqrt{6x}$ using the quotient rule only if $48x^3$ and $6x$ represent nonnegative real numbers and $6x \neq 0$. Thus, $x > 0$.

$$\frac{\sqrt{48x^3}}{\sqrt{6x}} = \sqrt{\frac{48x^3}{6x}} = \sqrt{8x^2} = \sqrt{4x^2}\sqrt{2} = \sqrt{4}\sqrt{x^2}\sqrt{2} = 2x\sqrt{2}$$

$\sqrt{x^2} = |x| = x$ because $x > 0$.

✓ Check Point **3** Simplify:

**a.** $\sqrt{\dfrac{25}{16}}$ **b.** $\dfrac{\sqrt{150x^3}}{\sqrt{2x}}$.

**⑤ Add and subtract square roots.**

## Adding and Subtracting Square Roots

Two or more square roots can be combined using the distributive property provided that they have the same radicand. Such radicals are called **like radicals**. For example,

$$7\sqrt{11} + 6\sqrt{11} = (7 + 6)\sqrt{11} = 13\sqrt{11}.$$

7 square roots of 11 plus 6 square roots of 11 result in 13 square roots of 11.

**EXAMPLE 4** **Adding and Subtracting Like Radicals**

Add or subtract as indicated:
**a.** $7\sqrt{2} + 5\sqrt{2}$ **b.** $\sqrt{5x} - 7\sqrt{5x}$.

**Solution**

**a.** $7\sqrt{2} + 5\sqrt{2} = (7 + 5)\sqrt{2}$     Apply the distributive property.

$= 12\sqrt{2}$     Simplify.

**b.** $\sqrt{5x} - 7\sqrt{5x} = 1\sqrt{5x} - 7\sqrt{5x}$     Write $\sqrt{5x}$ as $1\sqrt{5x}$.

$= (1 - 7)\sqrt{5x}$     Apply the distributive property.

$= -6\sqrt{5x}$     Simplify.

✓ Check Point **4** Add or subtract as indicated:

**a.** $8\sqrt{13} + 9\sqrt{13}$ **b.** $\sqrt{17x} - 20\sqrt{17x}$.

In some cases, radicals can be combined once they have been simplified. For example, to add $\sqrt{2}$ and $\sqrt{8}$, we can write $\sqrt{8}$ as $\sqrt{4 \cdot 2}$ because 4 is a perfect square factor of 8.

$$\sqrt{2} + \sqrt{8} = \sqrt{2} + \sqrt{4 \cdot 2} = 1\sqrt{2} + 2\sqrt{2} = (1 + 2)\sqrt{2} = 3\sqrt{2}$$

**EXAMPLE 5** **Combining Radicals That First Require Simplification**

Add or subtract as indicated:

    **a.** $7\sqrt{3} + \sqrt{12}$         **b.** $4\sqrt{50x} - 6\sqrt{32x}$.

**Solution**

    **a.** $7\sqrt{3} + \sqrt{12}$

$$= 7\sqrt{3} + \sqrt{4 \cdot 3} \quad \text{Split 12 into two factors such that one is a perfect square.}$$

$$= 7\sqrt{3} + 2\sqrt{3} \quad \sqrt{4 \cdot 3} = \sqrt{4}\sqrt{3} = 2\sqrt{3}$$

$$= (7 + 2)\sqrt{3} \quad \text{Apply the distributive property. You will find that this step is usually done mentally.}$$

$$= 9\sqrt{3} \quad \text{Simplify.}$$

    **b.** $4\sqrt{50x} - 6\sqrt{32x}$

$$= 4\sqrt{25 \cdot 2x} - 6\sqrt{16 \cdot 2x} \quad \text{25 is the greatest perfect square factor of 50x and 16 is the greatest perfect square factor of 32x.}$$

$$= 4 \cdot 5\sqrt{2x} - 6 \cdot 4\sqrt{2x} \quad \sqrt{25 \cdot 2x} = \sqrt{25}\sqrt{2x} = 5\sqrt{2x} \text{ and } \sqrt{16 \cdot 2x} = \sqrt{16}\sqrt{2x} = 4\sqrt{2x}.$$

$$= 20\sqrt{2x} - 24\sqrt{2x} \quad \text{Multiply: } 4 \cdot 5 = 20 \text{ and } 6 \cdot 4 = 24.$$

$$= (20 - 24)\sqrt{2x} \quad \text{Apply the distributive property.}$$

$$= -4\sqrt{2x} \quad \text{Simplify.}$$

✓ Check Point **5** Add or subtract as indicated:

    **a.** $5\sqrt{27} + \sqrt{12}$         **b.** $6\sqrt{18x} - 4\sqrt{8x}$.

**6** Rationalize denominators.

## Rationalizing Denominators

The calculator screen in **Figure P.11** shows approximate values for $\dfrac{1}{\sqrt{3}}$ and $\dfrac{\sqrt{3}}{3}$. The two approximations are the same. This is not a coincidence:

$$\frac{1}{\sqrt{3}} = \frac{1}{\sqrt{3}} \cdot \boxed{\frac{\sqrt{3}}{\sqrt{3}}} = \frac{\sqrt{3}}{\sqrt{9}} = \frac{\sqrt{3}}{3}.$$

Any number divided by itself is 1. Multiplication by 1 does not change the value of $\frac{1}{\sqrt{3}}$.

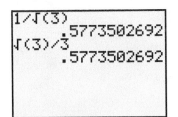

**Figure P.11** The calculator screen shows approximate values for $\dfrac{1}{\sqrt{3}}$ and $\dfrac{\sqrt{3}}{3}$.

This process involves rewriting a radical expression as an equivalent expression in which the denominator no longer contains any radicals. The process is called **rationalizing the denominator**. If the denominator consists of the square root of a natural number that is not a perfect square, **multiply the numerator and the denominator by the smallest number that produces the square root of a perfect square in the denominator.**

**EXAMPLE 6** **Rationalizing Denominators**

Rationalize the denominator:

    **a.** $\dfrac{15}{\sqrt{6}}$         **b.** $\dfrac{12}{\sqrt{8}}$.

**Study Tip**

Rationalizing a numerical denominator makes that denominator a rational number.

**Solution**

**a.** If we multiply the numerator and the denominator of $\dfrac{15}{\sqrt{6}}$ by $\sqrt{6}$, the denominator becomes $\sqrt{6} \cdot \sqrt{6} = \sqrt{36} = 6$. Therefore, we multiply by 1, choosing $\dfrac{\sqrt{6}}{\sqrt{6}}$ for 1.

$$\frac{15}{\sqrt{6}} = \frac{15}{\sqrt{6}} \cdot \frac{\sqrt{6}}{\sqrt{6}} = \frac{15\sqrt{6}}{\sqrt{36}} = \frac{15\sqrt{6}}{6} = \frac{5\sqrt{6}}{2}$$

Multiply by 1.      Simplify: $\frac{15}{6} = \frac{15 \div 3}{6 \div 3} = \frac{5}{2}$.

**b.** The *smallest* number that will produce the square root of a perfect square in the denominator of $\dfrac{12}{\sqrt{8}}$ is $\sqrt{2}$, because $\sqrt{8} \cdot \sqrt{2} = \sqrt{16} = 4$. We multiply by 1, choosing $\dfrac{\sqrt{2}}{\sqrt{2}}$ for 1.

$$\frac{12}{\sqrt{8}} = \frac{12}{\sqrt{8}} \cdot \frac{\sqrt{2}}{\sqrt{2}} = \frac{12\sqrt{2}}{\sqrt{16}} = \frac{12\sqrt{2}}{4} = 3\sqrt{2}$$

⦾

⊘ **Check Point 6** Rationalize the denominator:

     **a.** $\dfrac{5}{\sqrt{3}}$      **b.** $\dfrac{6}{\sqrt{12}}$.

Radical expressions that involve the sum and difference of the same two terms are called **conjugates**. Thus,

$$\sqrt{a} + \sqrt{b} \quad \text{and} \quad \sqrt{a} - \sqrt{b}$$

are conjugates. Conjugates are used to rationalize denominators because the product of such a pair contains no radicals:

Multiply each term of $\sqrt{a} - \sqrt{b}$ by each term of $\sqrt{a} + \sqrt{b}$.

$$(\sqrt{a} + \sqrt{b})(\sqrt{a} - \sqrt{b})$$
$$= \sqrt{a}(\sqrt{a} - \sqrt{b}) + \sqrt{b}(\sqrt{a} - \sqrt{b})$$

Distribute $\sqrt{a}$ over $\sqrt{a} - \sqrt{b}$.    Distribute $\sqrt{b}$ over $\sqrt{a} - \sqrt{b}$.

$$= \sqrt{a} \cdot \sqrt{a} - \sqrt{a} \cdot \sqrt{b} + \sqrt{b} \cdot \sqrt{a} - \sqrt{b} \cdot \sqrt{b}$$
$$= (\sqrt{a})^2 - \sqrt{ab} + \sqrt{ab} - (\sqrt{b})^2$$

$-\sqrt{ab} + \sqrt{ab} = 0$

$$= (\sqrt{a})^2 - (\sqrt{b})^2$$
$$= a - b.$$

**Multiplying Conjugates**

$$\left(\sqrt{a} + \sqrt{b}\right)\left(\sqrt{a} - \sqrt{b}\right) = (\sqrt{a})^2 - \left(\sqrt{b}\right)^2 = a - b$$

How can we rationalize a denominator if the denominator contains two terms with one or more square roots? **Multiply the numerator and the**

**denominator by the conjugate of the denominator.** Here are three examples of such expressions:

$$\bullet \; \frac{7}{5 + \sqrt{3}} \qquad \bullet \; \frac{8}{3\sqrt{2} - 4} \qquad \bullet \; \frac{h}{\sqrt{x + h} - \sqrt{x}}$$

| The conjugate of the denominator is $5 - \sqrt{3}$. | The conjugate of the denominator is $3\sqrt{2} + 4$. | The conjugate of the denominator is $\sqrt{x + h} + \sqrt{x}$. |

The product of the denominator and its conjugate is found using the formula

$$\left(\sqrt{a} + \sqrt{b}\right)\left(\sqrt{a} - \sqrt{b}\right) = \left(\sqrt{a}\right)^2 - \left(\sqrt{b}\right)^2 = a - b.$$

The simplified product will not contain a radical.

**EXAMPLE 7** **Rationalizing a Denominator Containing Two Terms**

Rationalize the denominator: $\dfrac{7}{5 + \sqrt{3}}$.

**Solution** The conjugate of the denominator is $5 - \sqrt{3}$. If we multiply the numerator and denominator by $5 - \sqrt{3}$, the simplified denominator will not contain a radical. Therefore, we multiply by 1, choosing $\dfrac{5 - \sqrt{3}}{5 - \sqrt{3}}$ for 1.

$$\frac{7}{5 + \sqrt{3}} = \frac{7}{5 + \sqrt{3}} \cdot \frac{5 - \sqrt{3}}{5 - \sqrt{3}} = \frac{7(5 - \sqrt{3})}{5^2 - (\sqrt{3})^2} = \frac{7(5 - \sqrt{3})}{25 - 3}$$

| Multiply by 1. | $(\sqrt{a} + \sqrt{b})(\sqrt{a} - \sqrt{b})$ $= (\sqrt{a})^2 - (\sqrt{b})^2$ |

$$= \frac{7(5 - \sqrt{3})}{22} \quad \text{or} \quad \frac{35 - 7\sqrt{3}}{22}$$

In either form of the answer, there is no radical in the denominator.

⬤

✍ Check Point **7** Rationalize the denominator: $\dfrac{8}{4 + \sqrt{5}}$.

**⑦** Evaluate and perform operations with higher roots.

## Other Kinds of Roots

We define the **principal $n$th root** of a real number $a$, symbolized by $\sqrt[n]{a}$, as follows:

### Definition of the Principal $n$th Root of a Real Number

$$\sqrt[n]{a} = b \text{ means that } b^n = a.$$

If $n$, the **index**, is even, then $a$ is nonnegative ($a \geq 0$) and $b$ is also nonnegative ($b \geq 0$). If $n$ is odd, $a$ and $b$ can be any real numbers.

For example,

$$\sqrt[3]{64} = 4 \text{ because } 4^3 = 64 \quad \text{and} \quad \sqrt[5]{-32} = -2 \text{ because } (-2)^5 = -32.$$

The same vocabulary that we learned for square roots applies to $n$th roots. The symbol $\sqrt[n]{\phantom{x}}$ is called a **radical** and the expression under the radical is called the **radicand**.

## Study Tip

Some higher even and odd roots occur so frequently that you might want to memorize them.

| Cube Roots | |
|---|---|
| $\sqrt[3]{1} = 1$ | $\sqrt[3]{125} = 5$ |
| $\sqrt[3]{8} = 2$ | $\sqrt[3]{216} = 6$ |
| $\sqrt[3]{27} = 3$ | $\sqrt[3]{1000} = 10$ |
| $\sqrt[3]{64} = 4$ | |

| Fourth Roots | Fifth Roots |
|---|---|
| $\sqrt[4]{1} = 1$ | $\sqrt[5]{1} = 1$ |
| $\sqrt[4]{16} = 2$ | $\sqrt[5]{32} = 2$ |
| $\sqrt[4]{81} = 3$ | $\sqrt[5]{243} = 3$ |
| $\sqrt[4]{256} = 4$ | |
| $\sqrt[4]{625} = 5$ | |

A number that is the $n$th power of a rational number is called a **perfect $n$th power**. For example, 8 is a perfect third power, or perfect cube, because $8 = 2^3$. Thus, $\sqrt[3]{8} = \sqrt[3]{2^3} = 2$. In general, one of the following rules can be used to find the $n$th root of a perfect $n$th power:

### Finding $n$th Roots of Perfect $n$th Powers

If $n$ is odd, $\sqrt[n]{a^n} = a$.
If $n$ is even, $\sqrt[n]{a^n} = |a|$.

For example,

$$\sqrt[3]{(-2)^3} = -2 \qquad \text{and} \qquad \sqrt[4]{(-2)^4} = |-2| = 2.$$

Absolute value is not needed with odd roots, but is necessary with even roots.

## The Product and Quotient Rules for Other Roots

The product and quotient rules apply to cube roots, fourth roots, and all higher roots.

### The Product and Quotient Rules for $n$th Roots

For all real numbers $a$ and $b$, where the indicated roots represent real numbers,

$$\sqrt[n]{ab} = \sqrt[n]{a} \cdot \sqrt[n]{b} \qquad \text{and} \qquad \sqrt[n]{a} \cdot \sqrt[n]{b} = \sqrt[n]{ab}$$

The $n$th root of a product is the product of the $n$th roots.

The product of two $n$th roots is the $n$th root of the product of the radicands.

$$\sqrt[n]{\frac{a}{b}} = \frac{\sqrt[n]{a}}{\sqrt[n]{b}}, b \neq 0 \qquad \text{and} \qquad \frac{\sqrt[n]{a}}{\sqrt[n]{b}} = \sqrt[n]{\frac{a}{b}}, b \neq 0.$$

The $n$th root of a quotient is the quotient of the $n$th roots.

The quotient of two $n$th roots is the $n$th root of the quotient of the radicands.

**EXAMPLE 8** Simplifying, Multiplying, and Dividing Higher Roots

Simplify: **a.** $\sqrt[3]{24}$   **b.** $\sqrt[4]{8} \cdot \sqrt[4]{4}$   **c.** $\sqrt[4]{\dfrac{81}{16}}$.

**Solution**

**a.** $\sqrt[3]{24} = \sqrt[3]{8 \cdot 3}$    Find the greatest perfect cube that is a factor of 24; $2^3 = 8$, so 8 is a perfect cube and is the greatest perfect cube factor of 24.

$\qquad = \sqrt[3]{8} \cdot \sqrt[3]{3}$   $\sqrt[n]{ab} = \sqrt[n]{a} \cdot \sqrt[n]{b}$

$\qquad = 2\sqrt[3]{3}$    $\sqrt[3]{8} = 2$

**b.** $\sqrt[4]{8} \cdot \sqrt[4]{4} = \sqrt[4]{8 \cdot 4}$    $\sqrt[n]{a} \cdot \sqrt[n]{b} = \sqrt[n]{ab}$

$\qquad = \sqrt[4]{32}$    Find the greatest perfect fourth power that is a factor of 32.

$\qquad = \sqrt[4]{16 \cdot 2}$    $2^4 = 16$, so 16 is a perfect fourth power and is the greatest perfect fourth power that is a factor of 32.

$\qquad = \sqrt[4]{16} \cdot \sqrt[4]{2}$    $\sqrt[n]{ab} = \sqrt[n]{a} \cdot \sqrt[n]{b}$

$\qquad = 2\sqrt[4]{2}$    $\sqrt[4]{16} = 2$

c. $\sqrt[4]{\dfrac{81}{16}} = \dfrac{\sqrt[4]{81}}{\sqrt[4]{16}}$     $\sqrt[n]{\dfrac{a}{b}} = \dfrac{\sqrt[n]{a}}{\sqrt[n]{b}}$

   $= \dfrac{3}{2}$     $\sqrt[4]{81} = 3$ because $3^4 = 81$ and $\sqrt[4]{16} = 2$ because $2^4 = 16$.

✓ Check Point **8**  Simplify:

a. $\sqrt[3]{40}$      b. $\sqrt[5]{8} \cdot \sqrt[5]{8}$      c. $\sqrt[3]{\dfrac{125}{27}}$.

We have seen that adding and subtracting square roots often involves simplifying terms. The same idea applies to adding and subtracting $n$th roots.

**EXAMPLE 9**  **Combining Cube Roots**

Subtract:  $5\sqrt[3]{16} - 11\sqrt[3]{2}$.

**Solution**

$$5\sqrt[3]{16} - 11\sqrt[3]{2}$$
$$= 5\sqrt[3]{8 \cdot 2} - 11\sqrt[3]{2}$$    Factor 16; 8 is the greatest perfect cube factor: $2^3 = 8$ and $\sqrt[3]{8} = 2$.

$$= 5 \cdot 2\sqrt[3]{2} - 11\sqrt[3]{2}$$    $\sqrt[3]{8 \cdot 2} = \sqrt[3]{8}\sqrt[3]{2} = 2\sqrt[3]{2}$
$$= 10\sqrt[3]{2} - 11\sqrt[3]{2}$$    Multiply: $5 \cdot 2 = 10$.
$$= (10 - 11)\sqrt[3]{2}$$    Apply the distributive property.
$$= -1\sqrt[3]{2} \text{ or } -\sqrt[3]{2}$$    Simplify.

✓ Check Point **9**  Subtract:  $3\sqrt[3]{81} - 4\sqrt[3]{3}$.

**⑧** Understand and use rational exponents.

## Rational Exponents

We define rational exponents so that their properties are the same as the properties for integer exponents. For example, we know that exponents are multiplied when an exponential expression is raised to a power. For this to be true,

$$\left(7^{\frac{1}{2}}\right)^2 = 7^{\frac{1}{2} \cdot 2} = 7^1 = 7.$$

We also know that

$$\left(\sqrt{7}\right)^2 = \sqrt{7} \cdot \sqrt{7} = \sqrt{49} = 7.$$

Can you see that the square of both $7^{\frac{1}{2}}$ and $\sqrt{7}$ is 7? It is reasonable to conclude that

$$7^{\frac{1}{2}} \quad \text{means} \quad \sqrt{7}.$$

We can generalize the fact that $7^{\frac{1}{2}}$ means $\sqrt{7}$ with the following definition:

The Definition of $a^{\frac{1}{n}}$

If $\sqrt[n]{a}$ represents a real number, where $n \geq 2$ is an integer, then

$$a^{\frac{1}{n}} = \sqrt[n]{a}.$$

The denominator of the rational exponent is the radical's index.

Furthermore,

$$a^{-\frac{1}{n}} = \dfrac{1}{a^{\frac{1}{n}}} = \dfrac{1}{\sqrt[n]{a}}, \quad a \neq 0.$$

---

**EXAMPLE 10** Using the Definition of $a^{\frac{1}{n}}$

Simplify:

**a.** $64^{\frac{1}{2}}$     **b.** $125^{\frac{1}{3}}$     **c.** $-16^{\frac{1}{4}}$     **d.** $(-27)^{\frac{1}{3}}$     **e.** $64^{-\frac{1}{3}}$.

**Solution**

**a.** $64^{\frac{1}{2}} = \sqrt{64} = 8$

**b.** $125^{\frac{1}{3}} = \sqrt[3]{125} = 5$

> The denominator is the index.

**c.** $-16^{\frac{1}{4}} = -\left(\sqrt[4]{16}\right) = -2$

> The base is 16 and the negative sign is not affected by the exponent.

**d.** $(-27)^{\frac{1}{3}} = \sqrt[3]{-27} = -3$

> Parentheses show that the base is −27 and that the negative sign is affected by the exponent.

**e.** $64^{-\frac{1}{3}} = \dfrac{1}{64^{\frac{1}{3}}} = \dfrac{1}{\sqrt[3]{64}} = \dfrac{1}{4}$

⊘ **Check Point 10** Simplify:

**a.** $25^{\frac{1}{2}}$     **b.** $8^{\frac{1}{3}}$     **c.** $-81^{\frac{1}{4}}$     **d.** $(-8)^{\frac{1}{3}}$     **e.** $27^{-\frac{1}{3}}$.

---

In Example 10 and Check Point 10, each rational exponent had a numerator of 1. If the numerator is some other integer, we still want to multiply exponents when raising a power to a power. For this reason,

$$a^{\frac{2}{3}} = \left(a^{\frac{1}{3}}\right)^2 \quad \text{and} \quad a^{\frac{2}{3}} = \left(a^2\right)^{\frac{1}{3}}.$$

> This means $\left(\sqrt[3]{a}\right)^2$.     This means $\sqrt[3]{a^2}$.

Thus,

$$a^{\frac{2}{3}} = \left(\sqrt[3]{a}\right)^2 = \sqrt[3]{a^2}.$$

Do you see that the denominator, 3, of the rational exponent is the same as the index of the radical? The numerator, 2, of the rational exponent serves as an exponent in each of the two radical forms. We generalize these ideas with the following definition:

---

### The Definition of $a^{\frac{m}{n}}$

If $\sqrt[n]{a}$ represents a real number and $\dfrac{m}{n}$ is a positive rational number, $n \geq 2$, then

$$a^{\frac{m}{n}} = \left(\sqrt[n]{a}\right)^m.$$

Also,

$$a^{\frac{m}{n}} = \sqrt[n]{a^m}.$$

Furthermore, if $a^{-\frac{m}{n}}$ is a nonzero real number, then

$$a^{-\frac{m}{n}} = \dfrac{1}{a^{\frac{m}{n}}}.$$

The first form of the definition of $a^{\frac{m}{n}}$, shown again below, involves taking the root first. This form is often preferable because smaller numbers are involved. Notice that the rational exponent consists of two parts, indicated by the following voice balloons:

The numerator is the exponent.

$$a^{\frac{m}{n}} = \left(\sqrt[n]{a}\right)^m.$$

The denominator is the radical's index.

**EXAMPLE 11** Using the Definition of $a^{\frac{m}{n}}$

Simplify:  **a.** $27^{\frac{2}{3}}$    **b.** $9^{\frac{3}{2}}$    **c.** $81^{-\frac{3}{4}}$.

**Solution**

**a.** $27^{\frac{2}{3}} = \left(\sqrt[3]{27}\right)^2 = 3^2 = 9$

**b.** $9^{\frac{3}{2}} = \left(\sqrt{9}\right)^3 = 3^3 = 27$

**c.** $81^{-\frac{3}{4}} = \dfrac{1}{81^{\frac{3}{4}}} = \dfrac{1}{\left(\sqrt[4]{81}\right)^3} = \dfrac{1}{3^3} = \dfrac{1}{27}$

## Technology

Here are the calculator keystroke sequences for $81^{-\frac{3}{4}}$:

**Many Scientific Calculators**

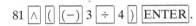

81 $\boxed{y^x}$ $\boxed{(}$ 3 $\boxed{+/-}$ $\boxed{\div}$ 4 $\boxed{)}$ $\boxed{=}$

**Many Graphing Calculators**

81 $\boxed{\wedge}$ $\boxed{(}$ $\boxed{(-)}$ 3 $\boxed{\div}$ 4 $\boxed{)}$ $\boxed{\text{ENTER}}$.

⊘ Check Point **11** Simplify:

**a.** $27^{\frac{4}{3}}$    **b.** $4^{\frac{3}{2}}$    **c.** $32^{-\frac{2}{5}}$.

---

Properties of exponents can be applied to expressions containing rational exponents.

**EXAMPLE 12** Simplifying Expressions with Rational Exponents

Simplify using properties of exponents:

**a.** $\left(5x^{\frac{1}{2}}\right)\left(7x^{\frac{3}{4}}\right)$    **b.** $\dfrac{32x^{\frac{5}{3}}}{16x^{\frac{3}{4}}}$.

**Solution**

**a.** $\left(5x^{\frac{1}{2}}\right)\left(7x^{\frac{3}{4}}\right) = 5 \cdot 7x^{\frac{1}{2}} \cdot x^{\frac{3}{4}}$   Group numerical factors and group variable factors with the same base.

$= 35x^{\frac{1}{2}+\frac{3}{4}}$   When multiplying expressions with the same base, add the exponents.

$= 35x^{\frac{5}{4}}$   $\frac{1}{2} + \frac{3}{4} = \frac{2}{4} + \frac{3}{4} = \frac{5}{4}$

**b.** $\dfrac{32x^{\frac{5}{3}}}{16x^{\frac{3}{4}}} = \left(\dfrac{32}{16}\right)\left(\dfrac{x^{\frac{5}{3}}}{x^{\frac{3}{4}}}\right)$   Group numerical factors and group variable factors with the same base.

$= 2x^{\frac{5}{3}-\frac{3}{4}}$   When dividing expressions with the same base, subtract the exponents.

$= 2x^{\frac{11}{12}}$   $\frac{5}{3} - \frac{3}{4} = \frac{20}{12} - \frac{9}{12} = \frac{11}{12}$

⊘ Check Point **12** Simplify using properties of exponents:

**a.** $\left(2x^{\frac{4}{3}}\right)\left(5x^{\frac{8}{3}}\right)$    **b.** $\dfrac{20x^4}{5x^{\frac{3}{2}}}$.

Rational exponents are sometimes useful for simplifying radicals by reducing the index.

**EXAMPLE 13** Reducing the Index of a Radical

Simplify: $\sqrt[9]{x^3}$.

**Solution**

$$\sqrt[9]{x^3} = x^{\frac{3}{9}} = x^{\frac{1}{3}} = \sqrt[3]{x}$$

✓ Check Point 13 Simplify: $\sqrt[6]{x^3}$.

# A Radical Idea: Time Is Relative

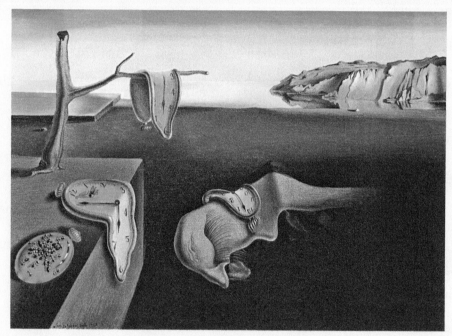

Salvador Dali "The Persistence of Memory" 1931, oil on canvas, $9\frac{1}{2} \times 13$ in. (24.1 × 33 cm). The Museum of Modern Art/Licensed by Scala-Art Resource, N.Y. © 1999 Demart Pro Arte, Geneva/Artists Rights Society (ARS), New York.

What does travel in space have to do with radicals? Imagine that in the future we will be able to travel at velocities approaching the speed of light (approximately 186,000 miles per second). According to Einstein's theory of special relativity, time would pass more quickly on Earth than it would in the moving spaceship. The special-relativity equation

$$R_a = R_f\sqrt{1 - \left(\frac{v}{c}\right)^2}$$

gives the aging rate of an astronaut, $R_a$, relative to the aging rate of a friend, $R_f$, on Earth. In this formula, $v$ is the astronaut's speed and $c$ is the speed of light. As the astronaut's speed approaches the speed of light, we can substitute $c$ for $v$.

$$R_a = R_f\sqrt{1 - \left(\frac{v}{c}\right)^2}$$  Einstein's equation gives the aging rate of an astronaut, $R_a$, relative to the aging rate of a friend, $R_f$, on Earth.

$$R_a = R_f\sqrt{1 - \left(\frac{c}{c}\right)^2}$$  The velocity, $v$, is approaching the speed of light, $c$, so let $v = c$.

$$= R_f\sqrt{1 - 1}$$  $\left(\frac{c}{c}\right)^2 = 1^2 = 1 \cdot 1 = 1$

$$= R_f\sqrt{0}$$  Simplify the radicand: $1 - 1 = 0$.

$$= R_f \cdot 0$$  $\sqrt{0} = 0$

$$= 0$$  Multiply: $R_f \cdot 0 = 0$.

Close to the speed of light, the astronaut's aging rate, $R_a$, relative to a friend, $R_f$, on Earth is nearly 0. What does this mean? As we age here on Earth, the space traveler would barely get older. The space traveler would return to an unknown futuristic world in which friends and loved ones would be long gone.

# Exercise Set P.3

## Practice Exercises

*Evaluate each expression in Exercises 1–12, or indicate that the root is not a real number.*

**1.** $\sqrt{36}$      **2.** $\sqrt{25}$

**3.** $-\sqrt{36}$      **4.** $-\sqrt{25}$

**5.** $\sqrt{-36}$      **6.** $\sqrt{-25}$

**7.** $\sqrt{25-16}$      **8.** $\sqrt{144+25}$

**9.** $\sqrt{25}-\sqrt{16}$      **10.** $\sqrt{144}+\sqrt{25}$

**11.** $\sqrt{(-13)^2}$      **12.** $\sqrt{(-17)^2}$

*Use the product rule to simplify the expressions in Exercises 13–22. In Exercises 17–22, assume that variables represent nonnegative real numbers.*

**13.** $\sqrt{50}$      **14.** $\sqrt{27}$

**15.** $\sqrt{45x^2}$      **16.** $\sqrt{125x^2}$

**17.** $\sqrt{2x}\cdot\sqrt{6x}$      **18.** $\sqrt{10x}\cdot\sqrt{8x}$

**19.** $\sqrt{x^3}$      **20.** $\sqrt{y^3}$

**21.** $\sqrt{2x^2}\cdot\sqrt{6x}$      **22.** $\sqrt{6x}\cdot\sqrt{3x^2}$

*Use the quotient rule to simplify the expressions in Exercises 23–32. Assume that $x > 0$.*

**23.** $\sqrt{\dfrac{1}{81}}$      **24.** $\sqrt{\dfrac{1}{49}}$

**25.** $\sqrt{\dfrac{49}{16}}$      **26.** $\sqrt{\dfrac{121}{9}}$

**27.** $\dfrac{\sqrt{48x^3}}{\sqrt{3x}}$      **28.** $\dfrac{\sqrt{72x^3}}{\sqrt{8x}}$

**29.** $\dfrac{\sqrt{150x^4}}{\sqrt{3x}}$      **30.** $\dfrac{\sqrt{24x^4}}{\sqrt{3x}}$

**31.** $\dfrac{\sqrt{200x^3}}{\sqrt{10x^{-1}}}$      **32.** $\dfrac{\sqrt{500x^3}}{\sqrt{10x^{-1}}}$

*In Exercises 33–44, add or subtract terms whenever possible.*

**33.** $7\sqrt{3}+6\sqrt{3}$      **34.** $8\sqrt{5}+11\sqrt{5}$

**35.** $6\sqrt{17x}-8\sqrt{17x}$      **36.** $4\sqrt{13x}-6\sqrt{13x}$

**37.** $\sqrt{8}+3\sqrt{2}$      **38.** $\sqrt{20}+6\sqrt{5}$

**39.** $\sqrt{50x}-\sqrt{8x}$      **40.** $\sqrt{63x}-\sqrt{28x}$

**41.** $3\sqrt{18}+5\sqrt{50}$      **42.** $4\sqrt{12}-2\sqrt{75}$

**43.** $3\sqrt{8}-\sqrt{32}+3\sqrt{72}-\sqrt{75}$

**44.** $3\sqrt{54}-2\sqrt{24}-\sqrt{96}+4\sqrt{63}$

*In Exercises 45–54, rationalize the denominator.*

**45.** $\dfrac{1}{\sqrt{7}}$      **46.** $\dfrac{2}{\sqrt{10}}$

**47.** $\dfrac{\sqrt{2}}{\sqrt{5}}$      **48.** $\dfrac{\sqrt{7}}{\sqrt{3}}$

**49.** $\dfrac{13}{3+\sqrt{11}}$      **50.** $\dfrac{3}{3+\sqrt{7}}$

**51.** $\dfrac{7}{\sqrt{5}-2}$      **52.** $\dfrac{5}{\sqrt{3}-1}$

**53.** $\dfrac{6}{\sqrt{5}+\sqrt{3}}$      **54.** $\dfrac{11}{\sqrt{7}-\sqrt{3}}$

*Evaluate each expression in Exercises 55–66, or indicate that the root is not a real number.*

**55.** $\sqrt[3]{125}$      **56.** $\sqrt[3]{8}$

**57.** $\sqrt[3]{-8}$      **58.** $\sqrt[3]{-125}$

**59.** $\sqrt[4]{-16}$      **60.** $\sqrt[4]{-81}$

**61.** $\sqrt[4]{(-3)^4}$      **62.** $\sqrt[4]{(-2)^4}$

**63.** $\sqrt[5]{(-3)^5}$      **64.** $\sqrt[5]{(-2)^5}$

**65.** $\sqrt[5]{-\dfrac{1}{32}}$      **66.** $\sqrt[6]{\dfrac{1}{64}}$

*Simplify the radical expressions in Exercises 67–74.*

**67.** $\sqrt[3]{32}$      **68.** $\sqrt[3]{150}$

**69.** $\sqrt[3]{x^4}$      **70.** $\sqrt[3]{x^5}$

**71.** $\sqrt[3]{9}\cdot\sqrt[3]{6}$      **72.** $\sqrt[3]{12}\cdot\sqrt[3]{4}$

**73.** $\dfrac{\sqrt[5]{64x^6}}{\sqrt[5]{2x}}$      **74.** $\dfrac{\sqrt[4]{162x^5}}{\sqrt[4]{2x}}$

*In Exercises 75–82, add or subtract terms whenever possible.*

**75.** $4\sqrt[5]{2}+3\sqrt[5]{2}$      **76.** $6\sqrt[5]{3}+2\sqrt[5]{3}$

**77.** $5\sqrt[3]{16}+\sqrt[3]{54}$      **78.** $3\sqrt[3]{24}+\sqrt[3]{81}$

**79.** $\sqrt[3]{54xy^3}-y\sqrt[3]{128x}$      **80.** $\sqrt[3]{24xy^3}-y\sqrt[3]{81x}$

**81.** $\sqrt{2}+\sqrt[3]{8}$      **82.** $\sqrt{3}+\sqrt[3]{15}$

*In Exercises 83–90, evaluate each expression without using a calculator.*

**83.** $36^{\frac{1}{2}}$      **84.** $121^{\frac{1}{2}}$

**85.** $8^{\frac{1}{3}}$      **86.** $27^{\frac{1}{3}}$

**87.** $125^{\frac{2}{3}}$      **88.** $8^{\frac{2}{3}}$

**89.** $32^{-\frac{4}{5}}$      **90.** $16^{-\frac{5}{2}}$

*In Exercises 91–100, simplify using properties of exponents.*

**91.** $\left(7x^{\frac{1}{3}}\right)\left(2x^{\frac{1}{4}}\right)$      **92.** $\left(3x^{\frac{2}{3}}\right)\left(4x^{\frac{3}{4}}\right)$

**93.** $\dfrac{20x^{\frac{1}{2}}}{5x^{\frac{1}{4}}}$      **94.** $\dfrac{72x^{\frac{3}{4}}}{9x^{\frac{1}{3}}}$

**95.** $\left(x^{\frac{2}{3}}\right)^3$      **96.** $\left(x^{\frac{4}{5}}\right)^5$

**97.** $(25x^4y^6)^{\frac{1}{2}}$

**98.** $(125x^9y^6)^{\frac{1}{3}}$

**99.** $\dfrac{\left(3y^{\frac{1}{4}}\right)^3}{y^{\frac{1}{12}}}$

**100.** $\dfrac{\left(2y^{\frac{1}{5}}\right)^4}{y^{\frac{3}{10}}}$

*In Exercises 101–108, simplify by reducing the index of the radical.*

**101.** $\sqrt[4]{5^2}$

**102.** $\sqrt[4]{7^2}$

**103.** $\sqrt[3]{x^6}$

**104.** $\sqrt[4]{x^{12}}$

**105.** $\sqrt[6]{x^4}$

**106.** $\sqrt[9]{x^6}$

**107.** $\sqrt[9]{x^6y^3}$

**108.** $\sqrt[12]{x^4y^8}$

## Practice Plus

*In Exercises 109–110, evaluate each expression.*

**109.** $\sqrt[3]{\sqrt[4]{16} + \sqrt{625}}$

**110.** $\sqrt[3]{\sqrt{\sqrt{169} + \sqrt{9}} + \sqrt{\sqrt[3]{1000} + \sqrt[3]{216}}}$

*In Exercises 111–114, simplify each expression. Assume that all variables represent positive numbers.*

**111.** $(49x^{-2}y^4)^{-\frac{1}{2}}\left(xy^{\frac{1}{2}}\right)$

**112.** $(8x^{-6}y^3)^{\frac{1}{3}}\left(x^{\frac{5}{6}}y^{-\frac{1}{3}}\right)^6$

**113.** $\left(\dfrac{x^{-\frac{5}{4}}y^{\frac{1}{3}}}{x^{-\frac{3}{4}}}\right)^{-6}$

**114.** $\left(\dfrac{x^{\frac{1}{2}}y^{-\frac{7}{4}}}{y^{-\frac{5}{4}}}\right)^{-4}$

## Application Exercises

**115.** The bar graph shows spam as a percentage of e-mail for four selected years. The data can be modeled by

$$y = 20.8\sqrt{x} + 21,$$

where $y$ is the percentage of e-mail that is spam and $x$ is the number of years after 1999.

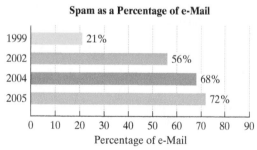

**Spam as a Percentage of e-Mail**

*Source*: IronPort

**a.** According to the model, what percentage of e-mail was spam in 2004? Use a calculator and round to the nearest tenth of a percent. Does this underestimate or overestimate the actual percentage given in the bar graph? By how much?

**b.** According to the model, what percentage of e-mail will be spam in 2011? Round to the nearest tenth of a percent.

**116.** America is getting older. The graph shows the projected elderly U.S. population for ages 65–84 and for ages 85 and older.

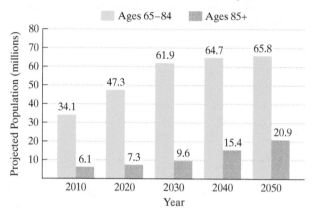

**Projected Elderly United States Population**

*Source:* U.S. Census Bureau

The formula $E = 5\sqrt{x} + 34.1$ models the projected number of elderly Americans ages 65–84, $E$, in millions, $x$ years after 2010.

**a.** Use the formula to find the projected increase in the number of Americans ages 65–84, in millions, from 2020 to 2050. Express this difference in simplified radical form.

**b.** Use a calculator and write your answer in part (a) to the nearest tenth. Does this rounded decimal overestimate or underestimate the difference in the projected data shown by the bar graph? By how much?

**117.** The early Greeks believed that the most pleasing of all rectangles were **golden rectangles**, whose ratio of width to height is

$$\frac{w}{h} = \frac{2}{\sqrt{5} - 1}.$$

The Parthenon at Athens fits into a golden rectangle once the triangular pediment is reconstructed.

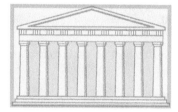

Rationalize the denominator of the golden ratio. Then use a calculator and find the ratio of width to height, correct to the nearest hundredth, in golden rectangles.

**118.** Use Einstein's special-relativity equation

$$R_a = R_f\sqrt{1 - \left(\frac{v}{c}\right)^2},$$

described in the essay on page 42, to solve this exercise. You are moving at 90% of the speed of light. Substitute $0.9c$ for $v$, your velocity, in the equation. What is your aging rate, correct to two decimal places, relative to a friend on Earth? If you are gone for 44 weeks, approximately how many weeks have passed for your friend?

*The perimeter, P, of a rectangle with length l and width w is given by the formula P = 2l + 2w. The area, A, is given by the formula A = lw. In Exercises 119–120, use these formulas to find the perimeter and area of each rectangle. Express answers in simplified radical form. Remember that perimeter is measured in linear units, such as feet or meters, and area is measured in square units, such as square feet, $ft^2$, or square meters, $m^2$.*

**119.**    $\sqrt{125}$ feet

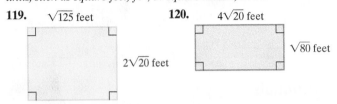

$2\sqrt{20}$ feet

**120.**    $4\sqrt{20}$ feet

$\sqrt{80}$ feet

## Writing in Mathematics

**121.** Explain how to simplify $\sqrt{10} \cdot \sqrt{5}$.

**122.** Explain how to add $\sqrt{3} + \sqrt{12}$.

**123.** Describe what it means to rationalize a denominator. Use both $\dfrac{1}{\sqrt{5}}$ and $\dfrac{1}{5 + \sqrt{5}}$ in your explanation.

**124.** What difference is there in simplifying $\sqrt[3]{(-5)^3}$ and $\sqrt[4]{(-5)^4}$?

**125.** What does $a^{\frac{m}{n}}$ mean?

**126.** Describe the kinds of numbers that have rational fifth roots.

**127.** Why must $a$ and $b$ represent nonnegative numbers when we write $\sqrt{a} \cdot \sqrt{b} = \sqrt{ab}$? Is it necessary to use this restriction in the case of $\sqrt[3]{a} \cdot \sqrt[3]{b} = \sqrt[3]{ab}$? Explain.

**128.** Read the essay on page 42. The future is now: You have the opportunity to explore the cosmos in a starship traveling near the speed of light. The experience will enable you to understand the mysteries of the universe in deeply personal ways, transporting you to unimagined levels of knowing and being. The down side: You return from your two-year journey to a futuristic world in which friends and loved ones are long gone. Do you explore space or stay here on Earth? What are the reasons for your choice?

## Critical Thinking Exercises

**Make Sense?**   *In Exercises 129–132, determine whether each statement makes sense or does not make sense, and explain your reasoning.*

**129.** The joke in this Peanuts cartoon would be more effective if Woodstock had rationalized the denominator correctly in the last frame.

PEANUTS © United Feature Syndicate, Inc.

**130.** Using my calculator, I determined that $6^7 = 279{,}936$, so 6 must be a seventh root of 279,936.

**131.** I simplified the terms of $2\sqrt{20} + 4\sqrt{75}$, and then I was able to add the like radicals.

**132.** When I use the definition for $a^{\frac{m}{n}}$, I usually prefer to first raise $a$ to the $m$ power because smaller numbers are involved.

*In Exercises 133–136, determine whether each statement is true or false. If the statement is false, make the necessary change(s) to produce a true statement.*

**133.** $7^{\frac{1}{2}} \cdot 7^{\frac{1}{2}} = 49$

**134.** $8^{-\frac{1}{3}} = -2$

**135.** The cube root of $-8$ is not a real number.

**136.** $\dfrac{\sqrt{20}}{8} = \dfrac{\sqrt{10}}{4}$

*In Exercises 137–138, fill in each box to make the statement true.*

**137.** $\left(5 + \sqrt{\phantom{x}}\right)\left(5 - \sqrt{\phantom{x}}\right) = 22$

**138.** $\sqrt{\phantom{x}x\phantom{x}} = 5x^7$

**139.** Find exact value of $\sqrt{13 + \sqrt{2} + \dfrac{7}{3 + \sqrt{2}}}$ without the use of a calculator.

**140.** Place the correct symbol, $>$ or $<$, in the shaded area between the given numbers. *Do not use a calculator.* Then check your result with a calculator.

**a.** $3^{\frac{1}{2}}$ ▨ $3^{\frac{1}{3}}$

**b.** $\sqrt{7} + \sqrt{18}$ ▨ $\sqrt{7 + 18}$

**141. a.** A mathematics professor recently purchased a birthday cake for her son with the inscription

$$\text{Happy } \left(2^{\frac{5}{2}} \cdot 2^{\frac{3}{4}} \div 2^{\frac{1}{4}}\right)\text{th Birthday.}$$

How old is the son?

**b.** The birthday boy, excited by the inscription on the cake, tried to wolf down the whole thing. Professor Mom, concerned about the possible metamorphosis of her son into a blimp, exclaimed, "Hold on! It is your birthday, so why not take $\dfrac{8^{-\frac{4}{3}} + 2^{-2}}{16^{-\frac{3}{4}} + 2^{-1}}$ of the cake? I'll eat half of what's left over." How much of the cake did the professor eat?

## Preview Exercises

*Exercises 142–144 will help you prepare for the material covered in the next section.*

**142.** Multiply:   $(2x^3y^2)(5x^4y^7)$.

**143.** Use the distributive property to multiply: $2x^4(8x^4 + 3x)$.

**144.** Simplify and express the answer in descending powers of $x$:

$$2x(x^2 + 4x + 5) + 3(x^2 + 4x + 5).$$

## Polynomials

### Objectives

① Understand the vocabulary of polynomials.

② Add and subtract polynomials.

③ Multiply polynomials.

④ Use FOIL in polynomial multiplication.

⑤ Use special products in polynomial multiplication.

⑥ Perform operations with polynomials in several variables.

Can that be Axl, your author's yellow lab, sharing a special moment with a baby chick? And if it is (it is), what possible relevance can this have to polynomials? An answer is promised before you reach the exercise set. For now, we open the section by defining and describing polynomials.

### How We Define Polynomials

More education results in a higher income. The mathematical models

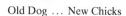

Old Dog ... New Chicks

$$M = -18x^3 + 923x^2 - 9603x + 48{,}446$$

$$\text{and} \quad W = 17x^3 - 450x^2 + 6392x - 14{,}764$$

describe the median, or middlemost, annual income for men, $M$, and women, $W$, who have completed $x$ years of education. We'll be working with these models and the data upon which they are based in the exercise set.

The algebraic expressions that appear on the right sides of the models are examples of *polynomials*. A **polynomial** is a single term or the sum of two or more terms containing variables with whole-number exponents. The polynomials above each contain four terms. Equations containing polynomials are used in such diverse areas as science, business, medicine, psychology, and sociology. In this section, we review basic ideas about polynomials and their operations.

① Understand the vocabulary of polynomials.

### How We Describe Polynomials

Consider the polynomial

$$7x^3 - 9x^2 + 13x - 6.$$

We can express this polynomial as

$$7x^3 + (-9x^2) + 13x + (-6).$$

The polynomial contains four terms. It is customary to write the terms in the order of descending powers of the variable. This is the **standard form** of a polynomial.

Some polynomials contain only one variable. Each term of such a polynomial in $x$ is of the form $ax^n$. If $a \neq 0$, the **degree** of $ax^n$ is $n$. For example, the degree of the term $7x^3$ is 3.

### Study Tip

We can express 0 in many ways, including $0x$, $0x^2$, and $0x^3$. It is impossible to assign a unique exponent to the variable. This is why 0 has no defined degree.

### The Degree of $ax^n$

If $a \neq 0$, the degree of $ax^n$ is $n$. The degree of a nonzero constant is 0. The constant 0 has no defined degree.

Here is an example of a polynomial and the degree of each of its four terms:

$$6x^4 - 3x^3 + 2x - 5.$$

| degree 4 | degree 3 | degree 1 | degree of nonzero constant: 0 |

Notice that the exponent on $x$ for the term $2x$, meaning $2x^1$, is understood to be 1. For this reason, the degree of $2x$ is 1. You can think of $-5$ as $-5x^0$; thus, its degree is 0.

A polynomial is simplified when it contains no grouping symbols and no like terms. A simplified polynomial that has exactly one term is called a **monomial**. A **binomial** is a simplified polynomial that has two terms. A **trinomial** is a simplified polynomial with three terms. Simplified polynomials with four or more terms have no special names.

The **degree of a polynomial** is the greatest degree of all the terms of the polynomial. For example, $4x^2 + 3x$ is a binomial of degree 2 because the degree of the first term is 2, and the degree of the other term is less than 2. Also, $7x^5 - 2x^2 + 4$ is a trinomial of degree 5 because the degree of the first term is 5, and the degrees of the other terms are less than 5.

Up to now, we have used $x$ to represent the variable in a polynomial. However, any letter can be used. For example,

- $7x^5 - 3x^3 + 8$     is a polynomial (in $x$) of degree 5. Because there are three terms, the polynomial is a trinomial.

- $6y^3 + 4y^2 - y + 3$     is a polynomial (in $y$) of degree 3. Because there are four terms, the polynomial has no special name.

- $z^7 + \sqrt{2}$     is a polynomial (in $z$) of degree 7. Because there are two terms, the polynomial is a binomial.

We can tie together the threads of our discussion with the formal definition of a polynomial in one variable. In this definition, the coefficients of the terms are represented by $a_n$ (read "$a$ sub $n$"), $a_{n-1}$ (read "$a$ sub $n$ minus 1"), $a_{n-2}$, and so on. The small letters to the lower right of each $a$ are called **subscripts** and are *not exponents*. Subscripts are used to distinguish one constant from another when a large and undetermined number of such constants are needed.

---

### Definition of a Polynomial in $x$

A **polynomial in $x$** is an algebraic expression of the form

$$a_n x^n + a_{n-1}x^{n-1} + a_{n-2}x^{n-2} + \cdots + a_1 x + a_0,$$

where $a_n, a_{n-1}, a_{n-2}, \ldots, a_1$, and $a_0$ are real numbers, $a_n \neq 0$, and $n$ is a non-negative integer. The polynomial is of **degree $n$**, $a_n$ is the **leading coefficient**, and $a_0$ is the **constant term**.

---

**2** Add and subtract polynomials.

## Adding and Subtracting Polynomials

Polynomials are added and subtracted by combining like terms. For example, we can combine the monomials $-9x^3$ and $13x^3$ using addition as follows:

$$-9x^3 + 13x^3 = (-9 + 13)x^3 = 4x^3.$$

| These like terms both contain $x$ to the third power. | Add coefficients and keep the same variable factor, $x^3$. |

**EXAMPLE 1** **Adding and Subtracting Polynomials**

Perform the indicated operations and simplify:

**a.** $(-9x^3 + 7x^2 - 5x + 3) + (13x^3 + 2x^2 - 8x - 6)$

**b.** $(7x^3 - 8x^2 + 9x - 6) - (2x^3 - 6x^2 - 3x + 9)$.

**Solution**

**a.** $(-9x^3 + 7x^2 - 5x + 3) + (13x^3 + 2x^2 - 8x - 6)$

$= (-9x^3 + 13x^3) + (7x^2 + 2x^2) + (-5x - 8x) + (3 - 6)$    Group like terms.

$= 4x^3 + 9x^2 + (-13x) + (-3)$    Combine like terms.

$= 4x^3 + 9x^2 - 13x - 3$    Simplify.

**b.** $(7x^3 - 8x^2 + 9x - 6) - (2x^3 - 6x^2 - 3x + 9)$

Change the sign of each coefficient.

$= (7x^3 - 8x^2 + 9x - 6) + (-2x^3 + 6x^2 + 3x - 9)$    Rewrite subtraction as addition of the additive inverse.

$= (7x^3 - 2x^3) + (-8x^2 + 6x^2) + (9x + 3x) + (-6 - 9)$    Group like terms.

$= 5x^3 + (-2x^2) + 12x + (-15)$    Combine like terms.

$= 5x^3 - 2x^2 + 12x - 15$    Simplify. ●

**⊘ Check Point 1** Perform the indicated operations and simplify:

**a.** $(-17x^3 + 4x^2 - 11x - 5) + (16x^3 - 3x^2 + 3x - 15)$

**b.** $(13x^3 - 9x^2 - 7x + 1) - (-7x^3 + 2x^2 - 5x + 9)$.

> **Study Tip**
>
> You can also arrange like terms in columns and combine vertically:
>
> $$\begin{array}{r} 7x^3 - 8x^2 + 9x - 6 \\ -2x^3 + 6x^2 + 3x - 9 \\ \hline 5x^3 - 2x^2 + 12x - 15 \end{array}$$
>
> The like terms can be combined by adding their coefficients and keeping the same variable factor.

**③ Multiply polynomials.**

> **Study Tip**
>
> Don't confuse adding and multiplying monomials.
>
> **Addition:**
> $$5x^4 + 6x^4 = 11x^4$$
>
> **Multiplication:**
> $$(5x^4)(6x^4) = (5 \cdot 6)(x^4 \cdot x^4)$$
> $$= 30x^{4+4}$$
> $$= 30x^8$$
>
> Only like terms can be added or subtracted, but unlike terms may be multiplied.
>
> **Addition:**
> $5x^4 + 3x^2$ cannot be simplified.
>
> **Multiplication:**
> $$(5x^4)(3x^2) = (5 \cdot 3)(x^4 \cdot x^2)$$
> $$= 15x^{4+2}$$
> $$= 15x^6$$

## Multiplying Polynomials

The product of two monomials is obtained by using properties of exponents. For example,

$$(-8x^6)(5x^3) = -8 \cdot 5x^{6+3} = -40x^9.$$

Multiply coefficients and add exponents.

Furthermore, we can use the distributive property to multiply a monomial and a polynomial that is not a monomial. For example,

$$3x^4(2x^3 - 7x + 3) = 3x^4 \cdot 2x^3 - 3x^4 \cdot 7x + 3x^4 \cdot 3 = 6x^7 - 21x^5 + 9x^4.$$

Monomial    Trinomial

How do we multiply two polynomials if neither is a monomial? For example, consider

$$(2x + 3)(x^2 + 4x + 5).$$

Binomial    Trinomial

One way to perform $(2x + 3)(x^2 + 4x + 5)$ is to distribute $2x$ throughout the trinomial

$$2x(x^2 + 4x + 5)$$

and 3 throughout the trinomial

$$3(x^2 + 4x + 5).$$

Then combine the like terms that result.

> **Multiplying Polynomials When Neither Is a Monomial**
> Multiply each term of one polynomial by each term of the other polynomial. Then combine like terms.

( **EXAMPLE 2** ) **Multiplying a Binomial and a Trinomial**

Multiply:   $(2x + 3)(x^2 + 4x + 5)$.

**Solution**

$$(2x + 3)(x^2 + 4x + 5)$$

$$= 2x(x^2 + 4x + 5) + 3(x^2 + 4x + 5) \qquad \text{Multiply the trinomial by each term of the binomial.}$$

$$= 2x \cdot x^2 + 2x \cdot 4x + 2x \cdot 5 + 3x^2 + 3 \cdot 4x + 3 \cdot 5 \qquad \text{Use the distributive property.}$$

$$= 2x^3 + 8x^2 + 10x + 3x^2 + 12x + 15 \qquad \text{Multiply monomials: Multiply coefficients and add exponents.}$$

$$= 2x^3 + 11x^2 + 22x + 15 \qquad \text{Combine like terms:}$$
$$8x^2 + 3x^2 = 11x^2 \text{ and}$$
$$10x + 12x = 22x.$$

Another method for performing the multiplication is to use a vertical format similar to that used for multiplying whole numbers.

$$
\begin{array}{r}
x^2 + 4x + 5 \\
2x + 3 \\
\hline
3x^2 + 12x + 15 \\
2x^3 + 8x^2 + 10x \\
\hline
2x^3 + 11x^2 + 22x + 15
\end{array}
$$

Write like terms in the same column.

Combine like terms.

$3(x^2 + 4x + 5)$

$2x(x^2 + 4x + 5)$

✓ Check Point **2** Multiply:   $(5x - 2)(3x^2 - 5x + 4)$.

**4** Use FOIL in polynomial multiplication.

## The Product of Two Binomials: FOIL

Frequently, we need to find the product of two binomials. One way to perform this multiplication is to distribute each term in the first binomial through the second binomial. For example, we can find the product of the binomials $3x + 2$ and $4x + 5$ as follows:

$$(3x + 2)(4x + 5) = 3x(4x + 5) + 2(4x + 5)$$
$$= 3x(4x) + 3x(5) + 2(4x) + 2(5)$$
$$= 12x^2 + 15x + 8x + 10.$$

Distribute $3x$ over $4x + 5$.   Distribute 2 over $4x + 5$.

> We'll combine these like terms later. For now, our interest is in how to obtain *each* of these four terms.

We can also find the product of $3x + 2$ and $4x + 5$ using a method called FOIL, which is based on our work shown at the bottom of the previous page. Any two binomials can be quickly multiplied by using the FOIL method, in which **F** represents the product of the **first** terms in each binomial, **O** represents the product of the **outside** terms, **I** represents the product of the **inside** terms, and **L** represents the product of the **last**, or second, terms in each binomial. For example, we can use the FOIL method to find the product of the binomials $3x + 2$ and $4x + 5$ as follows:

$$(3x + 2)(4x + 5) = 12x^2 + 15x + 8x + 10$$

| Product of First terms | Product of Outside terms | Product of Inside terms | Product of Last terms |

$$= 12x^2 + 23x + 10 \qquad \text{Combine like terms.}$$

In general, here's how to use the FOIL method to find the product of $ax + b$ and $cx + d$:

### Using the FOIL Method to Multiply Binomials

$$(ax + b)(cx + d) = ax \cdot cx + ax \cdot d + b \cdot cx + b \cdot d$$

| Product of First terms | Product of Outside terms | Product of Inside terms | Product of Last terms |

(EXAMPLE 3) **Using the FOIL Method**

Multiply: $(3x + 4)(5x - 3)$.

**Solution**

$$(3x + 4)(5x - 3) = 3x \cdot 5x + 3x(-3) + 4 \cdot 5x + 4(-3)$$
$$= 15x^2 - 9x + 20x - 12$$
$$= 15x^2 + 11x - 12 \qquad \text{Combine like terms.}$$

Check Point **3** Multiply: $(7x - 5)(4x - 3)$.

⑤ Use special products in polynomial multiplication.

## Special Products

There are several products that occur so frequently that it's convenient to memorize the form, or pattern, of these formulas.

## Special Products

Let $A$ and $B$ represent real numbers, variables, or algebraic expressions.

| **Special Product** | **Example** |
|---|---|

*Sum and Difference of Two Terms*

$$(A + B)(A - B) = A^2 - B^2$$

$$(2x + 3)(2x - 3) = (2x)^2 - 3^2$$
$$= 4x^2 - 9$$

*Squaring a Binomial*

$$(A + B)^2 = A^2 + 2AB + B^2$$

$$(y + 5)^2 = y^2 + 2 \cdot y \cdot 5 + 5^2$$
$$= y^2 + 10y + 25$$

$$(A - B)^2 = A^2 - 2AB + B^2$$

$$(3x - 4)^2$$
$$= (3x)^2 - 2 \cdot 3x \cdot 4 + 4^2$$
$$= 9x^2 - 24x + 16$$

*Cubing a Binomial*

$$(A + B)^3 = A^3 + 3A^2B + 3AB^2 + B^3$$

$$(x + 4)^3$$
$$= x^3 + 3x^2(4) + 3x(4)^2 + 4^3$$
$$= x^3 + 12x^2 + 48x + 64$$

$$(A - B)^3 = A^3 - 3A^2B + 3AB^2 - B^3$$

$$(x - 2)^3$$
$$= x^3 - 3x^2(2) + 3x(2)^2 - 2^3$$
$$= x^3 - 6x^2 + 12x - 8$$

**⑥** Perform operations with polynomials in several variables.

## Polynomials in Several Variables

A **polynomial in two variables**, $x$ and $y$, contains the sum of one or more monomials in the form $ax^ny^m$. The constant, $a$, is the **coefficient**. The exponents, $n$ and $m$, represent whole numbers. The **degree** of the monomial $ax^ny^m$ is $n + m$.

Here is an example of a polynomial in two variables:

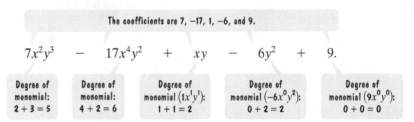

The **degree of a polynomial in two variables** is the highest degree of all its terms. For the preceding polynomial, the degree is 6.

Polynomials containing two or more variables can be added, subtracted, and multiplied just like polynomials that contain only one variable. For example, we can add the monomials $-7xy^2$ and $13xy^2$ as follows:

$$-7xy^2 + 13xy^2 = (-7 + 13)xy^2 = 6xy^2.$$

These like terms both contain the variable factors $x$ and $y^2$.

Add coefficients and keep the same variable factors, $xy^2$.

$\boxed{\text{EXAMPLE 4}}$  **Multiplying Polynomials in Two Variables**

Multiply:  **a.** $(x + 4y)(3x - 5y)$    **b.** $(5x + 3y)^2$.

**Solution**   We will perform the multiplication in part (a) using the FOIL method. We will multiply in part (b) using the formula for the square of a binomial sum, $(A + B)^2$.

**a.** $(x + 4y)(3x - 5y)$   Multiply these binomials using the FOIL method.

$$\overset{\text{F}}{\phantom{x}}\quad\overset{\text{O}}{\phantom{x}}\quad\overset{\text{I}}{\phantom{x}}\quad\overset{\text{L}}{\phantom{x}}$$

$$= (x)(3x) + (x)(-5y) + (4y)(3x) + (4y)(-5y)$$
$$= 3x^2 - 5xy + 12xy - 20y^2$$
$$= 3x^2 + 7xy - 20y^2 \quad \text{Combine like terms.}$$

$$(A + B)^2 \;=\; A^2 \;+\; 2 \cdot A \cdot B \;+\; B^2$$

**b.** $(5x + 3y)^2 = (5x)^2 + 2(5x)(3y) + (3y)^2$
$$= 25x^2 + 30xy + 9y^2$$

✓ Check Point **4**  Multiply:

   **a.** $(7x - 6y)(3x - y)$       **b.** $(2x + 4y)^2$.

Special products can sometimes be used to find the products of certain trinomials, as illustrated in Example 5.

$\boxed{\text{EXAMPLE 5}}$  **Using the Special Products**

Multiply:  **a.** $(7x + 5 + 4y)(7x + 5 - 4y)$       **b.** $(3x + y + 1)^2$.

**Solution**

   **a.** By grouping the first two terms within each of the parentheses, we can find the product using the form for the sum and difference of two terms.

$$(A \;+\; B) \;\cdot\; (A \;-\; B) \;=\; A^2 \;-\; B^2$$

$$[(7x + 5) + 4y] \cdot [(7x + 5) - 4y] = (7x + 5)^2 - (4y)^2$$
$$= (7x)^2 + 2 \cdot 7x \cdot 5 + 5^2 - (4y)^2$$
$$= 49x^2 + 70x + 25 - 16y^2$$

   **b.** We can group the terms of $(3x + y + 1)^2$ so that the formula for the square of a binomial can be applied.

$$(A \;+\; B)^2 \;=\; A^2 \;+\; 2 \;\cdot\; A \;\cdot\; B \;+\; B^2$$

$$[(3x + y) + 1]^2 = (3x + y)^2 + 2 \cdot (3x + y) \cdot 1 + 1^2$$
$$= 9x^2 + 6xy + y^2 + 6x + 2y + 1$$

✓ Check Point **5**  Multiply:

   **a.** $(3x + 2 + 5y)(3x + 2 - 5y)$    **b.** $(2x + y + 3)^2$.

## Labrador Retrievers and Polynomial Multiplication

The color of a Labrador retriever is determined by its pair of genes. A single gene is inherited at random from each parent. The black-fur gene, B, is dominant. The yellow-fur gene, Y, is recessive. This means that labs with at least one black-fur gene (BB or BY) have black coats. Only labs with two yellow-fur genes (YY) have yellow coats.

Axl, your author's yellow lab, inherited his genetic makeup from two black BY parents.

Second BY parent, a black lab with a recessive yellow-fur gene

First BY parent, a black lab with a recessive yellow-fur gene

|   | B  | Y  |
|---|----|----|
| B | BB | BY |
| Y | BY | YY |

The table shows the four possible combinations of color genes that BY parents can pass to their offspring.

Because YY is one of four possible outcomes, the probability that a yellow lab like Axl will be the offspring of these black parents is $\frac{1}{4}$.

The probabilities suggested by the table can be modeled by the expression $\left(\frac{1}{2}B + \frac{1}{2}Y\right)^2$.

$$\left(\frac{1}{2}B + \frac{1}{2}Y\right)^2 = \left(\frac{1}{2}B\right)^2 + 2\left(\frac{1}{2}B\right)\left(\frac{1}{2}Y\right) + \left(\frac{1}{2}Y\right)^2$$

$$= \frac{1}{4}BB + \frac{1}{2}BY + \frac{1}{4}YY$$

The probability of a black lab with two dominant black genes is $\frac{1}{4}$.

The probability of a black lab with a recessive yellow gene is $\frac{1}{2}$.

The probability of a yellow lab with two recessive yellow genes is $\frac{1}{4}$.

## Exercise Set P.4

### Practice Exercises

*In Exercises 1–4, is the algebraic expression a polynomial? If it is, write the polynomial in standard form.*

1. $2x + 3x^2 - 5$
2. $2x + 3x^{-1} - 5$
3. $\dfrac{2x + 3}{x}$
4. $x^2 - x^3 + x^4 - 5$

*In Exercises 5–8, find the degree of the polynomial.*

5. $3x^2 - 5x + 4$
6. $-4x^3 + 7x^2 - 11$
7. $x^2 - 4x^3 + 9x - 12x^4 + 63$
8. $x^2 - 8x^3 + 15x^4 + 91$

*In Exercises 9–14, perform the indicated operations. Write the resulting polynomial in standard form and indicate its degree.*

9. $(-6x^3 + 5x^2 - 8x + 9) + (17x^3 + 2x^2 - 4x - 13)$
10. $(-7x^3 + 6x^2 - 11x + 13) + (19x^3 - 11x^2 + 7x - 17)$
11. $(17x^3 - 5x^2 + 4x - 3) - (5x^3 - 9x^2 - 8x + 11)$
12. $(18x^4 - 2x^3 - 7x + 8) - (9x^4 - 6x^3 - 5x + 7)$
13. $(5x^2 - 7x - 8) + (2x^2 - 3x + 7) - (x^2 - 4x - 3)$
14. $(8x^2 + 7x - 5) - (3x^2 - 4x) - (-6x^3 - 5x^2 + 3)$

*In Exercises 15–82, find each product.*

15. $(x + 1)(x^2 - x + 1)$
16. $(x + 5)(x^2 - 5x + 25)$
17. $(2x - 3)(x^2 - 3x + 5)$
18. $(2x - 1)(x^2 - 4x + 3)$
19. $(x + 7)(x + 3)$
20. $(x + 8)(x + 5)$
21. $(x - 5)(x + 3)$
22. $(x - 1)(x + 2)$
23. $(3x + 5)(2x + 1)$
24. $(7x + 4)(3x + 1)$
25. $(2x - 3)(5x + 3)$
26. $(2x - 5)(7x + 2)$
27. $(5x^2 - 4)(3x^2 - 7)$
28. $(7x^2 - 2)(3x^2 - 5)$
29. $(8x^3 + 3)(x^2 - 5)$
30. $(7x^3 + 5)(x^2 - 2)$
31. $(x + 3)(x - 3)$
32. $(x + 5)(x - 5)$
33. $(3x + 2)(3x - 2)$
34. $(2x + 5)(2x - 5)$
35. $(5 - 7x)(5 + 7x)$
36. $(4 - 3x)(4 + 3x)$
37. $(4x^2 + 5x)(4x^2 - 5x)$
38. $(3x^2 + 4x)(3x^2 - 4x)$
39. $(1 - y^5)(1 + y^5)$
40. $(2 - y^5)(2 + y^5)$
41. $(x + 2)^2$
42. $(x + 5)^2$

**43.** $(2x + 3)^2$

**44.** $(3x + 2)^2$

**45.** $(x - 3)^2$

**46.** $(x - 4)^2$

**47.** $(4x^2 - 1)^2$

**48.** $(5x^2 - 3)^2$

**49.** $(7 - 2x)^2$

**50.** $(9 - 5x)^2$

**51.** $(x + 1)^3$

**52.** $(x + 2)^3$

**53.** $(2x + 3)^3$

**54.** $(3x + 4)^3$

**55.** $(x - 3)^3$

**56.** $(x - 1)^3$

**57.** $(3x - 4)^3$

**58.** $(2x - 3)^3$

**59.** $(x + 5y)(7x + 3y)$

**60.** $(x + 9y)(6x + 7y)$

**61.** $(x - 3y)(2x + 7y)$

**62.** $(3x - y)(2x + 5y)$

**63.** $(3xy - 1)(5xy + 2)$

**64.** $(7x^2y + 1)(2x^2y - 3)$

**65.** $(7x + 5y)^2$

**66.** $(9x + 7y)^2$

**67.** $(x^2y^2 - 3)^2$

**68.** $(x^2y^2 - 5)^2$

**69.** $(x - y)(x^2 + xy + y^2)$

**70.** $(x + y)(x^2 - xy + y^2)$

**71.** $(3x + 5y)(3x - 5y)$

**72.** $(7x + 3y)(7x - 3y)$

**73.** $(x + y + 3)(x + y - 3)$

**74.** $(x + y + 5)(x + y - 5)$

**75.** $(3x + 7 - 5y)(3x + 7 + 5y)$

**76.** $(5x + 7y - 2)(5x + 7y + 2)$

**77.** $[5y - (2x + 3)][5y + (2x + 3)]$

**78.** $[8y + (7 - 3x)][8y - (7 - 3x)]$

**79.** $(x + y + 1)^2$

**80.** $(x + y + 2)^2$

**81.** $(2x + y + 1)^2$

**82.** $(5x + 1 + 6y)^2$

## Practice Plus

*In Exercises 83–90, perform the indicated operation or operations.*

**83.** $(3x + 4y)^2 - (3x - 4y)^2$

**84.** $(5x + 2y)^2 - (5x - 2y)^2$

**85.** $(5x - 7)(3x - 2) - (4x - 5)(6x - 1)$

**86.** $(3x + 5)(2x - 9) - (7x - 2)(x - 1)$

**87.** $(2x + 5)(2x - 5)(4x^2 + 25)$

**88.** $(3x + 4)(3x - 4)(9x^2 + 16)$

**89.** $\dfrac{(2x - 7)^5}{(2x - 7)^3}$

**90.** $\dfrac{(5x - 3)^6}{(5x - 3)^4}$

## Application Exercises

*As you complete more years of education, you can count on a greater income. The bar graph shows the median, or middlemost, annual income for Americans, by level of education, in 2004.*

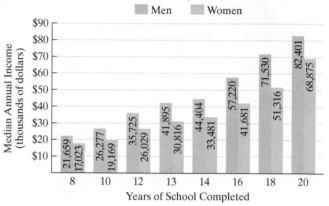

**Median Annual Income, by Level of Education, 2004**

*Source:* Bureau of the Census

*Here are polynomial models that describe the median annual income for men, M, and for women, W, who have completed x years of education:*

$$M = 177x^2 + 288x + 7075$$
$$W = 255x^2 - 2956x + 24{,}336$$

$$M = -18x^3 + 923x^2 - 9603x + 48{,}446$$
$$W = 17x^3 - 450x^2 + 6392x - 14{,}764.$$

*Exercises 91–92 are based on these models and the data displayed by the graph.*

**91. a.** Use the equation defined by a polynomial of degree 2 to find the median annual income for a man with 16 years of education. Does this underestimate or overestimate the median income shown by the bar graph? By how much?

**b.** Use the equations defined by polynomials of degree 3 to find a mathematical model for $M - W$.

**c.** According to the model in part (b), what is the difference in the median annual income between men and women with 14 years of education?

**d.** According to the data displayed by the graph, what is the actual difference in the median annual income between men and women with 14 years of education? Did the result of part (c) underestimate or overestimate this difference? By how much?

**92. a.** Use the equation defined by a polynomial of degree 2 to find the median annual income for a woman with 18 years of education. Does this underestimate or over-estimate the median income shown by the bar graph? By how much?

**b.** Use the equations defined by polynomials of degree 3 to find a mathematical model for $M - W$.

**c.** According to the model in part (b), what is the difference in the median annual income between men and women with 16 years of education?

**d.** According to the data displayed by the graph, what is the actual difference in the median annual income between men and women with 16 years of education? Did the result of part (c) underestimate or overestimate this difference? By how much?

*The volume, V, of a rectangular solid with length l, width w, and height h is given by the formula V = lwh. In Exercises 93–94, use this formula to write a polynomial in standard form that models, or represents, the volume of the open box.*

**93.**

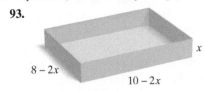

$8 - 2x$   $10 - 2x$   $x$

**94.**

$8 - 2x$   $5 - 2x$   $x$

*In Exercises 95–96, write a polynomial in standard form that models, or represents, the area of the shaded region.*

**95.**

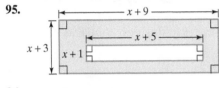

$x + 9$   $x + 5$   $x + 3$   $x + 1$

**96.**

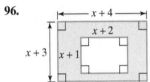

$x + 4$   $x + 2$   $x + 3$   $x + 1$

## Writing in Mathematics

**97.** What is a polynomial in $x$?

**98.** Explain how to subtract polynomials.

**99.** Explain how to multiply two binomials using the FOIL method. Give an example with your explanation.

**100.** Explain how to find the product of the sum and difference of two terms. Give an example with your explanation.

**101.** Explain how to square a binomial difference. Give an example with your explanation.

**102.** Explain how to find the degree of a polynomial in two variables.

## Critical Thinking Exercises

**Make Sense?** *In Exercises 103–106, determine whether each statement makes sense or does not make sense, and explain your reasoning.*

**103.** Knowing the difference between factors and terms is important: In $(3x^2y)^2$, I can distribute the exponent 2 on each factor, but in $(3x^2 + y)^2$, I cannot do the same thing on each term.

**104.** I used the FOIL method to find the product of $x + 5$ and $x^2 + 2x + 1$.

**105.** Many English words have prefixes with meanings similar to those used to describe polynomials, such as *monologue*, *binocular*, and *tricuspid*.

**106.** Special-product formulas have patterns that make their multiplications quicker than using the FOIL method.

**107.** Express the area of the plane figure shown as a polynomial in standard form.

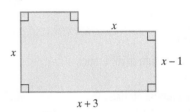

$x$   $x$   $x - 1$   $x + 3$

*In Exercises 108–109, represent the volume of each figure as a polynomial in standard form.*

**108.**

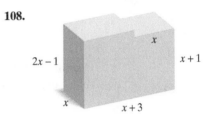

$2x - 1$   $x$   $x + 1$   $x$   $x + 3$

**109.**

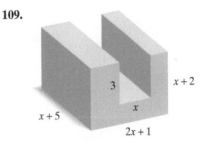

$3$   $x + 2$   $x + 5$   $x$   $2x + 1$

**110.** Simplify: $(y^n + 2)(y^n - 2) - (y^n - 3)^2$.

## Preview Exercises

*Exercises 111–113 will help you prepare for the material covered in the next section. In each exercise, replace the boxed question mark with an integer that results in the given product. Some trial and error may be necessary.*

**111.** $(x + 3)(x + \boxed{?}) = x^2 + 7x + 12$

**112.** $(x - \boxed{?})(x - 12) = x^2 - 14x + 24$

**113.** $(4x + 1)(2x - \boxed{?}) = 8x^2 - 10x - 3$

## Section P.5 Factoring Polynomials

### Objectives

1. Factor out the greatest common factor of a polynomial.
2. Factor by grouping.
3. Factor trinomials.
4. Factor the difference of squares.
5. Factor perfect square trinomials.
6. Factor the sum or difference of two cubes.
7. Use a general strategy for factoring polynomials.
8. Factor algebraic expressions containing fractional and negative exponents.

A two-year-old boy is asked, "Do you have a brother?" He answers, "Yes." "What is your brother's name?" "Tom." Asked if Tom has a brother, the two-year-old replies, "No." The child can go in the direction from self to brother, but he cannot reverse this direction and move from brother back to self.

As our intellects develop, we learn to reverse the direction of our thinking. Reversibility of thought is found throughout algebra. For example, we can multiply polynomials and show that

$$5x(2x + 3) = 10x^2 + 15x.$$

We can also reverse this process and express the resulting polynomial as

$$10x^2 + 15x = 5x(2x + 3).$$

**Factoring** a polynomial containing the sum of monomials means finding an equivalent expression that is a product.

**Factoring $10x^2 + 15x$**

Sum of monomials

Equivalent expression that is a product

$$10x^2 + 15x = 5x(2x + 3)$$

The factors of $10x^2 + 15x$ are $5x$ and $2x + 3$.

In this section, we will be **factoring over the set of integers**, meaning that the coefficients in the factors are integers. Polynomials that cannot be factored using integer coefficients are called **irreducible over the integers**, or **prime**.

The goal in factoring a polynomial is to use one or more factoring techniques until each of the polynomial's factors, except possibly for a monomial factor, is prime or irreducible. In this situation, the polynomial is said to be **factored completely**.

We will now discuss basic techniques for factoring polynomials.

① Factor out the greatest common factor of a polynomial.

### Common Factors

In any factoring problem, the first step is to look for the *greatest common factor*. The **greatest common factor**, abbreviated GCF, is an expression of the highest degree that divides each term of the polynomial. The distributive property in the reverse direction

$$ab + ac = a(b + c)$$

can be used to factor out the greatest common factor.

EXAMPLE 1 **Factoring Out the Greatest Common Factor**

**Study Tip**

The variable part of the greatest common factor always contains the *smallest* power of a variable or algebraic expression that appears in all terms of the polynomial.

Factor:    **a.** $18x^3 + 27x^2$          **b.** $x^2(x + 3) + 5(x + 3)$.

**Solution**

**a.** First, determine the greatest common factor.

> 9 is the greatest integer that divides 18 and 27.

$$18x^3 + 27x^2$$

> $x^2$ is the greatest expression that divides $x^3$ and $x^2$.

The GCF of the two terms of the polynomial is $9x^2$.

$$18x^3 + 27x^2$$
$$= 9x^2(2x) + 9x^2(3) \quad \text{Express each term as the product of the GCF and its other factor.}$$
$$= 9x^2(2x + 3) \quad \text{Factor out the GCF.}$$

**b.** In this situation, the greatest common factor is the common binomial factor $(x + 3)$. We factor out this common factor as follows:

$$x^2(x + 3) + 5(x + 3) = (x + 3)(x^2 + 5). \quad \text{Factor out the common binomial factor.}$$

⊘ Check Point **1**  Factor:

**a.** $10x^3 - 4x^2$          **b.** $2x(x - 7) + 3(x - 7)$.

**2**  Factor by grouping.

## Factoring by Grouping

Some polynomials have only a greatest common factor of 1. However, by a suitable grouping of the terms, it still may be possible to factor. This process, called **factoring by grouping**, is illustrated in Example 2.

EXAMPLE 2 **Factoring by Grouping**

Factor:   $x^3 + 4x^2 + 3x + 12$.

**Solution**   There is no factor other than 1 common to all terms. However, we can group terms that have a common factor:

$$\boxed{x^3 + 4x^2} \quad + \quad \boxed{3x + 12}.$$

> Common factor is $x^2$.    Common factor is 3.

We now factor the given polynomial as follows:

$$x^3 + 4x^2 + 3x + 12$$
$$= (x^3 + 4x^2) + (3x + 12) \quad \text{Group terms with common factors.}$$
$$= x^2(x + 4) + 3(x + 4) \quad \text{Factor out the greatest common factor from the grouped terms. The remaining two terms have } x + 4 \text{ as a common binomial factor.}$$
$$= (x + 4)(x^2 + 3). \quad \text{Factor out the GCF, } x + 4.$$

**Discovery**

In Example 2, group the terms as follows:

$$(x^3 + 3x) + (4x^2 + 12).$$

Factor out the greatest common factor from each group and complete the factoring process. Describe what happens. What can you conclude?

Thus,  $x^3 + 4x^2 + 3x + 12 = (x + 4)(x^2 + 3)$.  Check the factorization by multiplying the right side of the equation using the FOIL method. Because the factorization is correct, you should obtain the original polynomial.

⊘ Check Point **2**  Factor:   $x^3 + 5x^2 - 2x - 10$.

**③ Factor trinomials.**

# Factoring Trinomials

To factor a trinomial of the form $ax^2 + bx + c$, a little trial and error may be necessary.

## A Strategy for Factoring $ax^2 + bx + c$

Assume, for the moment, that there is no greatest common factor.

**1.** Find two **First** terms whose product is $ax^2$:

$$(\Box x + \quad)(\Box x + \quad) = ax^2 + bx + c.$$

**2.** Find two **Last** terms whose product is $c$:

$$(\Box x + \Box)(\Box x + \Box) = ax^2 + bx + c.$$

**3.** By trial and error, perform steps 1 and 2 until the sum of the **O**utside product and **I**nside product is $bx$:

$$(\Box x + \Box)(\Box x + \Box) = ax^2 + bx + c.$$

I

O

Sum of O + I

If no such combination exists, the polynomial is prime.

**Study Tip**

The *error* part of the factoring strategy plays an important role in the process. If you do not get the correct factorization the first time, this is not a bad thing. This error is often helpful in leading you to the correct factorization.

( **EXAMPLE 3** ) **Factoring a Trinomial Whose Leading Coefficient Is 1**

Factor: $x^2 + 6x + 8$.

**Solution**

**Step 1  Find two First terms whose product is $x^2$.**

$$x^2 + 6x + 8 = (x \quad)(x \quad)$$

**Step 2  Find two Last terms whose product is 8.**

| Factors of 8 | 8, 1 | 4, 2 | −8, −1 | −4, −2 |
|---|---|---|---|---|

**Step 3  Try various combinations of these factors.** The correct factorization of $x^2 + 6x + 8$ is the one in which the sum of the **O**utside and **I**nside products is equal to $6x$. Here is a list of the possible factorizations:

| Possible Factorizations of $x^2 + 6x + 8$ | Sum of Outside and Inside Products (Should Equal 6x) |
|---|---|
| $(x + 8)(x + 1)$ | $x + 8x = 9x$ |
| $(x + 4)(x + 2)$ | $2x + 4x = 6x$ |
| $(x - 8)(x - 1)$ | $-x - 8x = -9x$ |
| $(x - 4)(x - 2)$ | $-2x - 4x = -6x$ |

This is the required middle term.

Thus, $x^2 + 6x + 8 = (x + 4)(x + 2)$ or $(x + 2)(x + 4)$. ●

In factoring a trinomial of the form $x^2 + bx + c$, you can speed things up by listing the factors of $c$ and then finding their sums. We are interested in a sum of $b$. For example, in factoring $x^2 + 6x + 8$, we are interested in the factors of 8 whose sum is 6.

| Factors of 8 | 8, 1 | 4, 2 | −8, −1 | −4, −2 |
|---|---|---|---|---|
| Sum of Factors | 9 | 6 | −9 | −6 |

This is the desired sum.

Thus, $x^2 + 6x + 8 = (x + 4)(x + 2)$.

☑ Check Point **3**  Factor:  $x^2 + 13x + 40$.

( **EXAMPLE 4** )  **Factoring a Trinomial Whose Leading Coefficient Is 1**

Factor:  $x^2 + 3x - 18$.

**Solution**

**Step 1  Find two First terms whose product is $x^2$.**

$$x^2 + 3x - 18 = (x \quad )(x \quad )$$

To find the second term of each factor, we must find two integers whose product is $-18$ and whose sum is 3.

**Step 2  Find two Last terms whose product is $-18$.**

| Factors of $-18$ | 18, $-1$ | $-18, 1$ | 9, $-2$ | $-9, 2$ | 6, $-3$ | $-6, 3$ |
|---|---|---|---|---|---|---|

**Step 3  Try various combinations of these factors.**  We are looking for the pair of factors whose sum is 3.

| Factors of $-18$ | 18, $-1$ | $-18, 1$ | 9, $-2$ | $-9, 2$ | 6, $-3$ | $-6, 3$ |
|---|---|---|---|---|---|---|
| Sum of Factors | 17 | $-17$ | 7 | $-7$ | 3 | $-3$ |

This is the desired sum.

Thus,  $x^2 + 3x - 18 = (x + 6)(x - 3)$  or  $(x - 3)(x + 6)$.

☑ Check Point **4**  Factor:  $x^2 - 5x - 14$.

( **EXAMPLE 5** )  **Factoring a Trinomial Whose Leading Coefficient Is Not 1**

Factor:  $8x^2 - 10x - 3$.

**Solution**

**Step 1  Find two First terms whose product is $8x^2$.**

$$8x^2 - 10x - 3 \overset{?}{=} (8x \quad )(x \quad )$$
$$8x^2 - 10x - 3 \overset{?}{=} (4x \quad )(2x \quad )$$

**Step 2  Find two Last terms whose product is $-3$.**  The possible factorizations are $1(-3)$ and $-1(3)$.

**Step 3  Try various combinations of these factors.**  The correct factorization of $8x^2 - 10x - 3$ is the one in which the sum of the **O**utside and **I**nside products is equal to $-10x$. Here is a list of the possible factorizations:

| Possible Factorizations of $8x^2 - 10x - 3$ | Sum of Outside and Inside Products (Should Equal $-10x$) |
|---|---|
| $(8x + 1)(x - 3)$ | $-24x + x = -23x$ |
| $(8x - 3)(x + 1)$ | $8x - 3x = 5x$ |
| $(8x - 1)(x + 3)$ | $24x - x = 23x$ |
| $(8x + 3)(x - 1)$ | $-8x + 3x = -5x$ |
| $(4x + 1)(2x - 3)$ | $-12x + 2x = -10x$ |
| $(4x - 3)(2x + 1)$ | $4x - 6x = -2x$ |
| $(4x - 1)(2x + 3)$ | $12x - 2x = 10x$ |
| $(4x + 3)(2x - 1)$ | $-4x + 6x = 2x$ |

These four factorizations use $(8x \quad )(x \quad )$ with $1(-3)$ and $-1(3)$ as factorizations of $-3$.

These four factorizations use $(4x \quad )(2x \quad )$ with $1(-3)$ and $-1(3)$ as factorizations of $-3$.

This is the required middle term.

Thus,  $8x^2 - 10x - 3 = (4x + 1)(2x - 3)$  or  $(2x - 3)(4x + 1)$.

Use FOIL multiplication to check either of these factorizations.

**Study Tip**

Here are some suggestions for reducing the list of possible factorizations for $ax^2 + bx + c$:

1. If $b$ is relatively small, avoid the larger factors of $a$.
2. If $c$ is positive, the signs in both binomial factors must match the sign of $b$.
3. If the trinomial has no common factor, no binomial factor can have a common factor.
4. Reversing the signs in the binomial factors reverses the sign of $bx$, the middle term.

⊘ Check Point **5** Factor: $6x^2 + 19x - 7$.

(**EXAMPLE 6**) **Factoring a Trinomial in Two Variables**

Factor: $2x^2 - 7xy + 3y^2$.

**Solution**

**Step 1  Find two First terms whose product is $2x^2$.**

$$2x^2 - 7xy + 3y^2 = (2x \quad )(x \quad )$$

**Step 2  Find two Last terms whose product is $3y^2$.** The possible factorizations are $(y)(3y)$ and $(-y)(-3y)$.

**Step 3  Try various combinations of these factors.** The correct factorization of $2x^2 - 7xy + 3y^2$ is the one in which the sum of the **O**utside and **I**nside products is equal to $-7xy$. Here is a list of possible factorizations:

| Possible Factorizations of $2x^2 - 7xy + 3y^2$ | Sum of Outside and Inside Products (Should Equal $-7xy$) |
|---|---|
| $(2x + 3y)(x + y)$ | $2xy + 3xy = 5xy$ |
| $(2x + y)(x + 3y)$ | $6xy + xy = 7xy$ |
| $(2x - 3y)(x - y)$ | $-2xy - 3xy = -5xy$ |
| $(2x - y)(x - 3y)$ | $-6xy - xy = -7xy$ |

This is the required middle term.

Thus,

$$2x^2 - 7xy + 3y^2 = (2x - y)(x - 3y) \quad \text{or} \quad (x - 3y)(2x - y).$$

Use FOIL multiplication to check either of these factorizations. ●

⊘ Check Point **6** Factor: $3x^2 - 13xy + 4y^2$.

④ Factor the difference of squares.

## Factoring the Difference of Two Squares

A method for factoring the difference of two squares is obtained by reversing the special product for the sum and difference of two terms.

### The Difference of Two Squares

If $A$ and $B$ are real numbers, variables, or algebraic expressions, then

$$A^2 - B^2 = (A + B)(A - B).$$

In words: The difference of the squares of two terms factors as the product of a sum and a difference of those terms.

(**EXAMPLE 7**) **Factoring the Difference of Two Squares**

Factor:  **a.** $x^2 - 4$   **b.** $81x^2 - 49$.

**Solution**  We must express each term as the square of some monomial. Then we use the formula for factoring $A^2 - B^2$.

**a.**  $x^2 - 4 = x^2 - 2^2 = (x + 2)(x - 2)$

$$A^2 - B^2 = (A + B)(A - B)$$

**b.**  $81x^2 - 49 = (9x)^2 - 7^2 = (9x + 7)(9x - 7)$  ●

⊘ Check Point **7**  Factor:

**a.**  $x^2 - 81$     **b.**  $36x^2 - 25$.

We have seen that a polynomial is factored completely when it is written as the product of prime polynomials. To be sure that you have factored completely, check to see whether any factors with more than one term in the factored polynomial can be factored further. If so, continue factoring.

**( EXAMPLE 8 )  A Repeated Factorization**

Factor completely:  $x^4 - 81$.

**Solution**

$x^4 - 81 = (x^2)^2 - 9^2$    *Express as the difference of two squares.*

$= (x^2 + 9)(x^2 - 9)$    *The factors are the sum and the difference of the expressions being squared.*

$= (x^2 + 9)(x^2 - 3^2)$    *The factor $x^2 - 9$ is the difference of two squares and can be factored.*

$= (x^2 + 9)(x + 3)(x - 3)$    *The factors of $x^2 - 9$ are the sum and the difference of the expressions being squared.*  ●

### Study Tip

Factoring $x^4 - 81$ as

$$(x^2 + 9)(x^2 - 9)$$

is not a complete factorization. The second factor, $x^2 - 9$, is itself a difference of two squares and can be factored.

⊘ Check Point **8**  Factor completely:  $81x^4 - 16$.

**⑤** Factor perfect square trinomials.

## Factoring Perfect Square Trinomials

Our next factoring technique is obtained by reversing the special products for squaring binomials. The trinomials that are factored using this technique are called **perfect square trinomials**.

### Factoring Perfect Square Trinomials

Let $A$ and $B$ be real numbers, variables, or algebraic expressions.

**1.**  $A^2 + 2AB + B^2 = (A + B)^2$    **2.**  $A^2 - 2AB + B^2 = (A - B)^2$

Same sign                          Same sign

The two items in the box show that perfect square trinomials, $A^2 + 2AB + B^2$ and $A^2 - 2AB + B^2$, come in two forms: one in which the coefficient of the middle term is positive and one in which the coefficient of the middle term is negative. Here's how to recognize a perfect square trinomial:

**1.** The first and last terms are squares of monomials or integers.

**2.** The middle term is twice the product of the expressions being squared in the first and last terms.

**EXAMPLE 9** **Factoring Perfect Square Trinomials**

Factor: **a.** $x^2 + 6x + 9$ **b.** $25x^2 - 60x + 36$.

**Solution**

**a.** $x^2 + 6x + 9 = x^2 + 2 \cdot x \cdot 3 + 3^2 = (x + 3)^2$    The middle term has a positive sign.

$$\underbrace{A^2}_{} + \underbrace{2AB}_{} + \underbrace{B^2}_{} = \underbrace{(A + B)^2}_{}$$

**b.** We suspect that $25x^2 - 60x + 36$ is a perfect square trinomial because $25x^2 = (5x)^2$ and $36 = 6^2$. The middle term can be expressed as twice the product of $5x$ and 6.

$$25x^2 - 60x + 36 = (5x)^2 - 2 \cdot 5x \cdot 6 + 6^2 = (5x - 6)^2$$

$$\underbrace{A^2}_{} - \underbrace{2AB}_{} + \underbrace{B^2}_{} = \underbrace{(A - B)^2}_{}$$

⊘ **Check Point 9** Factor:

**a.** $x^2 + 14x + 49$ **b.** $16x^2 - 56x + 49$.

**⑥** Factor the sum or difference of two cubes.

## Factoring the Sum or Difference of Two Cubes

We can use the following formulas to factor the sum or the difference of two cubes:

**Study Tip**

**A Cube of SOAP**

When factoring sums or differences of cubes, observe the sign patterns shown by the voice balloons in the box. The word *SOAP* is a way to remember these patterns:

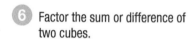

S O A P.

| Same signs | Opposite signs | Always Positive |

---

**Factoring the Sum or Difference of Two Cubes**

**1.** Factoring the Sum of Two Cubes

$$A^3 + B^3 = (A + B)(A^2 - AB + B^2)$$

| Same signs | Opposite signs | Always positive |

**2.** Factoring the Difference of Two Cubes

$$A^3 - B^3 = (A - B)(A^2 + AB + B^2)$$

| Same signs | Opposite signs | Always positive |

**EXAMPLE 10** **Factoring Sums and Differences of Two Cubes**

Factor: **a.** $x^3 + 8$ **b.** $64x^3 - 125$.

**Solution**

**a.** To factor $x^3 + 8$, we must express each term as the cube of some monomial. Then we use the formula for factoring $A^3 + B^3$.

$$x^3 + 8 = x^3 + 2^3 = (x + 2)(x^2 - x \cdot 2 + 2^2) = (x + 2)(x^2 - 2x + 4)$$

$$\underbrace{A^3}_{} + \underbrace{B^3}_{} = \underbrace{(A + B)}_{}\underbrace{(A^2 - AB + B^2)}_{}$$

**b.** To factor $64x^3 - 125$, we must express each term as the cube of some monomial. Then we use the formula for factoring $A^3 - B^3$.

$$64x^3 - 125 = (4x)^3 - 5^3 = (4x - 5)[(4x)^2 + (4x)(5) + 5^2]$$

$$A^3 - B^3 = (A - B)(A^2 + AB + B^2)$$

$$= (4x - 5)(16x^2 + 20x + 25)$$

⊘ Check Point **10** Factor:

**a.** $x^3 + 1$      **b.** $125x^3 - 8$.

**7** Use a general strategy for factoring polynomials.

## A Strategy for Factoring Polynomials

It is important to practice factoring a wide variety of polynomials so that you can quickly select the appropriate technique. The polynomial is factored completely when all its polynomial factors, except possibly for monomial factors, are prime. Because of the commutative property, the order of the factors does not matter.

> ### A Strategy for Factoring a Polynomial
>
> **1.** If there is a common factor, factor out the GCF.
> **2.** Determine the number of terms in the polynomial and try factoring as follows:
>
>     **a.** If there are two terms, can the binomial be factored by using one of the following special forms?
>
>        Difference of two squares: $A^2 - B^2 = (A + B)(A - B)$
>        Sum of two cubes:         $A^3 + B^3 = (A + B)(A^2 - AB + B^2)$
>        Difference of two cubes:  $A^3 - B^3 = (A - B)(A^2 + AB + B^2)$
>
>     **b.** If there are three terms, is the trinomial a perfect square trinomial? If so, factor by using one of the following special forms:
>
> $$A^2 + 2AB + B^2 = (A + B)^2$$
> $$A^2 - 2AB + B^2 = (A - B)^2.$$
>
>     If the trinomial is not a perfect square trinomial, try factoring by trial and error.
>
>     **c.** If there are four or more terms, try factoring by grouping.
> **3.** Check to see if any factors with more than one term in the factored polynomial can be factored further. If so, factor completely.

( **EXAMPLE 11** ) **Factoring a Polynomial**

Factor: $2x^3 + 8x^2 + 8x$.

**Solution**

**Step 1 If there is a common factor, factor out the GCF.** Because $2x$ is common to all terms, we factor it out.

$$2x^3 + 8x^2 + 8x = 2x(x^2 + 4x + 4) \quad \text{Factor out the GCF.}$$

**Step 2  Determine the number of terms and factor accordingly.** The factor $x^2 + 4x + 4$ has three terms and is a perfect square trinomial. We factor using $A^2 + 2AB + B^2 = (A + B)^2$.

$$2x^3 + 8x^2 + 8x = 2x(x^2 + 4x + 4)$$

$$= 2x(x^2 + 2 \cdot x \cdot 2 + 2^2)$$

$$\underbrace{\quad A^2 \quad + \quad \mathbf{2}AB \quad + \quad B^2 \quad}$$

$$= 2x(x + 2)^2 \qquad\qquad A^2 + 2AB + B^2 = (A + B)^2$$

**Step 3  Check to see if factors can be factored further.** In this problem, they cannot. Thus,

$$2x^3 + 8x^2 + 8x = 2x(x + 2)^2.$$

$\oslash$ Check Point **11**  Factor:  $3x^3 - 30x^2 + 75x.$

$\boxed{\text{EXAMPLE 12}}$  **Factoring a Polynomial**

Factor:  $x^2 - 25a^2 + 8x + 16.$

**Solution**

**Step 1  If there is a common factor, factor out the GCF.** Other than 1 or $-1$, there is no common factor.

**Step 2  Determine the number of terms and factor accordingly.** There are four terms. We try factoring by grouping. It can be shown that grouping into two groups of two terms does not result in a common binomial factor. Let's try grouping as a difference of squares.

$$x^2 - 25a^2 + 8x + 16$$

$$= (x^2 + 8x + 16) - 25a^2 \qquad \text{Rearrange terms and group as a perfect square trinomial minus } 25a^2 \text{ to obtain a difference of squares.}$$

$$= (x + 4)^2 - (5a)^2 \qquad \text{Factor the perfect square trinomial.}$$

$$= (x + 4 + 5a)(x + 4 - 5a) \qquad \text{Factor the difference of squares. The factors are the sum and difference of the expressions being squared.}$$

**Step 3  Check to see if factors can be factored further.** In this case, they cannot, so we have factored completely.

$\oslash$ Check Point **12**  Factor:  $x^2 - 36a^2 + 20x + 100.$

**8**  Factor algebraic expressions containing fractional and negative exponents.

## Factoring Algebraic Expressions Containing Fractional and Negative Exponents

Although expressions containing fractional and negative exponents are not polynomials, they can be simplified using factoring techniques.

$\boxed{\text{EXAMPLE 13}}$  **Factoring Involving Fractional and Negative Exponents**

Factor and simplify:  $x(x + 1)^{-\frac{3}{4}} + (x + 1)^{\frac{1}{4}}.$

**Solution** The greatest common factor of $x(x + 1)^{-\frac{3}{4}} + (x + 1)^{\frac{1}{4}}$ is $x + 1$ with the *smaller exponent* in the two terms. Thus, the greatest common factor is $(x + 1)^{-\frac{3}{4}}$.

$$x(x + 1)^{-\frac{3}{4}} + (x + 1)^{\frac{1}{4}}$$

$$= (x + 1)^{-\frac{3}{4}}x + (x + 1)^{-\frac{3}{4}}(x + 1) \qquad \text{Express each term as the product of the greatest common factor and its other factor.}$$

$$= (x + 1)^{-\frac{3}{4}}[x + (x + 1)] \qquad \text{Factor out the greatest common factor.}$$

$$= \frac{2x + 1}{(x + 1)^{\frac{3}{4}}} \qquad \qquad b^{-n} = \frac{1}{b^n}$$

✓ Check Point 13 Factor and simplify: $x(x - 1)^{-\frac{1}{2}} + (x - 1)^{\frac{1}{2}}$.

# Exercise Set P.5

## Practice Exercises

*In Exercises 1–10, factor out the greatest common factor.*

**1.** $18x + 27$

**2.** $16x - 24$

**3.** $3x^2 + 6x$

**4.** $4x^2 - 8x$

**5.** $9x^4 - 18x^3 + 27x^2$

**6.** $6x^4 - 18x^3 + 12x^2$

**7.** $x(x + 5) + 3(x + 5)$

**8.** $x(2x + 1) + 4(2x + 1)$

**9.** $x^2(x - 3) + 12(x - 3)$

**10.** $x^2(2x + 5) + 17(2x + 5)$

*In Exercises 11–16, factor by grouping.*

**11.** $x^3 - 2x^2 + 5x - 10$

**12.** $x^3 - 3x^2 + 4x - 12$

**13.** $x^3 - x^2 + 2x - 2$

**14.** $x^3 + 6x^2 - 2x - 12$

**15.** $3x^3 - 2x^2 - 6x + 4$

**16.** $x^3 - x^2 - 5x + 5$

*In Exercises 17–38, factor each trinomial, or state that the trinomial is prime.*

**17.** $x^2 + 5x + 6$

**18.** $x^2 + 8x + 15$

**19.** $x^2 - 2x - 15$

**20.** $x^2 - 4x - 5$

**21.** $x^2 - 8x + 15$

**22.** $x^2 - 14x + 45$

**23.** $3x^2 - x - 2$

**24.** $2x^2 + 5x - 3$

**25.** $3x^2 - 25x - 28$

**26.** $3x^2 - 2x - 5$

**27.** $6x^2 - 11x + 4$

**28.** $6x^2 - 17x + 12$

**29.** $4x^2 + 16x + 15$

**30.** $8x^2 + 33x + 4$

**31.** $9x^2 - 9x + 2$

**32.** $9x^2 + 5x - 4$

**33.** $20x^2 + 27x - 8$

**34.** $15x^2 - 19x + 6$

**35.** $2x^2 + 3xy + y^2$

**36.** $3x^2 + 4xy + y^2$

**37.** $6x^2 - 5xy - 6y^2$

**38.** $6x^2 - 7xy - 5y^2$

*In Exercises 39–48, factor the difference of two squares.*

**39.** $x^2 - 100$

**40.** $x^2 - 144$

**41.** $36x^2 - 49$

**42.** $64x^2 - 81$

**43.** $9x^2 - 25y^2$

**44.** $36x^2 - 49y^2$

**45.** $x^4 - 16$

**46.** $x^4 - 1$

**47.** $16x^4 - 81$

**48.** $81x^4 - 1$

*In Exercises 49–56, factor each perfect square trinomial.*

**49.** $x^2 + 2x + 1$

**50.** $x^2 + 4x + 4$

**51.** $x^2 - 14x + 49$

**52.** $x^2 - 10x + 25$

**53.** $4x^2 + 4x + 1$

**54.** $25x^2 + 10x + 1$

**55.** $9x^2 - 6x + 1$

**56.** $64x^2 - 16x + 1$

*In Exercises 57–64, factor using the formula for the sum or difference of two cubes.*

**57.** $x^3 + 27$

**58.** $x^3 + 64$

**59.** $x^3 - 64$

**60.** $x^3 - 27$

**61.** $8x^3 - 1$

**62.** $27x^3 - 1$

**63.** $64x^3 + 27$

**64.** $8x^3 + 125$

*In Exercises 65–92, factor completely, or state that the polynomial is prime.*

**65.** $3x^3 - 3x$

**66.** $5x^3 - 45x$

**67.** $4x^2 - 4x - 24$

**68.** $6x^2 - 18x - 60$

**69.** $2x^4 - 162$

**70.** $7x^4 - 7$

**71.** $x^3 + 2x^2 - 9x - 18$

**72.** $x^3 + 3x^2 - 25x - 75$

**73.** $2x^2 - 2x - 112$

**74.** $6x^2 - 6x - 12$

**75.** $x^3 - 4x$

**76.** $9x^3 - 9x$

**77.** $x^2 + 64$

**78.** $x^2 + 36$

**79.** $x^3 + 2x^2 - 4x - 8$

**80.** $x^3 + 2x^2 - x - 2$

**81.** $y^5 - 81y$

**82.** $y^5 - 16y$

**83.** $20y^4 - 45y^2$

**84.** $48y^4 - 3y^2$

**85.** $x^2 - 12x + 36 - 49y^2$

**86.** $x^2 - 10x + 25 - 36y^2$

**87.** $9b^2x - 16y - 16x + 9b^2y$

**88.** $16a^2x - 25y - 25x + 16a^2y$

**89.** $x^2y - 16y + 32 - 2x^2$

**90.** $12x^2y - 27y - 4x^2 + 9$

**91.** $2x^3 - 8a^2x + 24x^2 + 72x$

**92.** $2x^3 - 98a^2x + 28x^2 + 98x$

*In Exercises 93–102, factor and simplify each algebraic expression.*

**93.** $x^{\frac{3}{2}} - x^{\frac{1}{2}}$

**94.** $x^{\frac{3}{4}} - x^{\frac{1}{4}}$

**95.** $4x^{-\frac{2}{3}} + 8x^{\frac{1}{3}}$

**96.** $12x^{-\frac{3}{4}} + 6x^{\frac{1}{4}}$

**97.** $(x + 3)^{\frac{1}{2}} - (x + 3)^{\frac{3}{2}}$

**98.** $(x^2 + 4)^{\frac{3}{2}} + (x^2 + 4)^{\frac{7}{2}}$

**99.** $(x + 5)^{-\frac{1}{2}} - (x + 5)^{-\frac{3}{2}}$

**100.** $(x^2 + 3)^{-\frac{2}{3}} + (x^2 + 3)^{-\frac{5}{3}}$

**101.** $(4x - 1)^{\frac{1}{2}} - \frac{1}{3}(4x - 1)^{\frac{3}{2}}$

**102.** $-8(4x + 3)^{-2} + 10(5x + 1)(4x + 3)^{-1}$

## Practice Plus

*In Exercises 103–114, factor completely.*

**103.** $10x^2(x + 1) - 7x(x + 1) - 6(x + 1)$

**104.** $12x^2(x - 1) - 4x(x - 1) - 5(x - 1)$

**105.** $6x^4 + 35x^2 - 6$

**106.** $7x^4 + 34x^2 - 5$

**107.** $y^7 + y$

**108.** $(y + 1)^3 + 1$

**109.** $x^4 - 5x^2y^2 + 4y^4$

**110.** $x^4 - 10x^2y^2 + 9y^4$

**111.** $(x - y)^4 - 4(x - y)^2$

**112.** $(x + y)^4 - 100(x + y)^2$

**113.** $2x^2 - 7xy^2 + 3y^4$

**114.** $3x^2 + 5xy^2 + 2y^4$

## Application Exercises

**115.** Your computer store is having an incredible sale. The price on one model is reduced by 40%. Then the sale price is reduced by another 40%. If $x$ is the computer's original price, the sale price can be modeled by

$$(x - 0.4x) - 0.4(x - 0.4x).$$

**a.** Factor out $(x - 0.4x)$ from each term. Then simplify the resulting expression.

**b.** Use the simplified expression from part (a) to answer these questions. With a 40% reduction followed by a 40% reduction, is the computer selling at 20% of its original price? If not, at what percentage of the original price is it selling?

**116.** Your local electronics store is having an end-of-the-year sale. The price on a plasma television had been reduced by 30%. Now the sale price is reduced by another 30%. If $x$ is the television's original price, the sale price can be modeled by

$$(x - 0.3x) - 0.3(x - 0.3x).$$

**a.** Factor out $(x - 0.3x)$ from each term. Then simplify the resulting expression.

**b.** Use the simplified expression from part (a) to answer these questions. With a 30% reduction followed by a 30% reduction, is the television selling at 40% of its original price? If not, at what percentage of the original price is it selling?

*In Exercises 117–120,*

    **a.** Write an expression for the area of the shaded region.

    **b.** Write the expression in factored form.

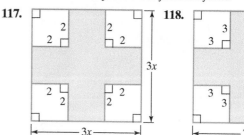

**117.**         **118.**

**119.**         **120.**

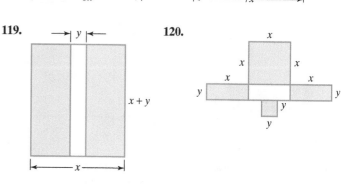

*In Exercises 121–122, find the formula for the volume of the region outside the smaller rectangular solid and inside the larger rectangular solid. Then express the volume in factored form.*

**121.**

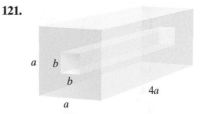

**122.**

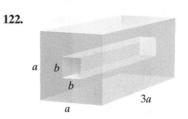

## Writing in Mathematics

**123.** Using an example, explain how to factor out the greatest common factor of a polynomial.

**124.** Suppose that a polynomial contains four terms. Explain how to use factoring by grouping to factor the polynomial.

**125.** Explain how to factor $3x^2 + 10x + 8$.

**126.** Explain how to factor the difference of two squares. Provide an example with your explanation.

**127.** What is a perfect square trinomial and how is it factored?

**128.** Explain how to factor $x^3 + 1$.

**129.** What does it mean to factor completely?

## Critical Thinking Exercises

**Make Sense?** *In Exercises 130–133, determine whether each statement makes sense or does not make sense, and explain your reasoning.*

**130.** Although $20x^3$ appears in both $20x^3 + 8x^2$ and $20x^3 + 10x$, I'll need to factor $20x^3$ in different ways to obtain each polynomial's factorization.

**131.** You grouped the polynomial's terms using different groupings than I did, yet we both obtained the same factorization.

**132.** I factored $4x^2 - 100$ completely and obtained $(2x + 10)(2x - 10)$.

**133.** First factoring out the greatest common factor makes it easier for me to determine how to factor the remaining factor, assuming that it is not prime.

*In Exercises 134–137, determine whether each statement is true or false. If the statement is false, make the necessary change(s) to produce a true statement.*

**134.** $x^4 - 16$ is factored completely as $(x^2 + 4)(x^2 - 4)$.

**135.** The trinomial $x^2 - 4x - 4$ is a prime polynomial.

**136.** $x^2 + 36 = (x + 6)^2$

**137.** $x^3 - 64 = (x + 4)(x^2 + 4x - 16)$

*In Exercises 138–141, factor completely.*

**138.** $x^{2n} + 6x^n + 8$         **139.** $-x^2 - 4x + 5$

**140.** $x^4 - y^4 - 2x^3y + 2xy^3$

**141.** $(x - 5)^{-\frac{1}{2}}(x + 5)^{-\frac{1}{2}} - (x + 5)^{\frac{1}{2}}(x - 5)^{-\frac{3}{2}}$

*In Exercises 142–143, find all integers b so that the trinomial can be factored.*

**142.** $x^2 + bx + 15$         **143.** $x^2 + 4x + b$

## Preview Exercises

*Exercises 144–146 will help you prepare for the material covered in the next section.*

**144.** Factor the numerator and the denominator. Then simplify by dividing out the common factor in the numerator and the denominator.

$$\frac{x^2 + 6x + 5}{x^2 - 25}$$

*In Exercises 145–146, perform the indicated operation. Where possible, reduce the answer to its lowest terms.*

**145.** $\dfrac{5}{4} \cdot \dfrac{8}{15}$         **146.** $\dfrac{1}{2} + \dfrac{2}{3}$

---

**Chapter** **P** **Mid-Chapter Check Point**

**What You Know:** We defined the real numbers $[\{x \mid x \text{ is rational}\} \cup \{x \mid x \text{ is irrational}\}]$ and graphed them as points on a number line. We reviewed the basic rules of algebra, using these properties to simplify algebraic expressions. We expanded our knowledge of exponents to include exponents other than natural numbers:

$$b^0 = 1; \quad b^{-n} = \frac{1}{b^n}; \quad \frac{1}{b^{-n}} = b^n; \quad b^{\frac{1}{n}} = \sqrt[n]{b};$$

$$b^{\frac{m}{n}} = \left(\sqrt[n]{b}\right)^m = \sqrt[n]{b^m}; \quad b^{-\frac{m}{n}} = \frac{1}{b^{\frac{m}{n}}}.$$

We used properties of exponents to simplify exponential expressions and properties of radicals to simplify radical expressions. Finally, we performed operations with polynomials. We used a number of fast methods for finding products of polynomials, including the FOIL method for multiplying binomials, a special-product formula for the product of the sum and difference of two terms $[(A + B)(A - B) = A^2 - B^2]$, and special-product formulas for squaring binomials $[(A + B)^2 = A^2 + 2AB + B^2; (A - B)^2 = A^2 - 2AB + B^2]$. We reversed the direction of these formulas and reviewed how to factor polynomials. We used a general strategy, summarized in the box on page 63, for factoring a wide variety of polynomials.

*In Exercises 1–27, simplify the given expression or perform the indicated operation (and simplify, if possible), whichever is appropriate.*

**1.** $(3x + 5)(4x - 7)$         **2.** $(3x + 5) - (4x - 7)$

**3.** $\sqrt{6} + 9\sqrt{6}$         **4.** $3\sqrt{12} - \sqrt{27}$

**5.** $7x + 3[9 - (2x - 6)]$         **6.** $(8x - 3)^2$

**7.** $\left(x^{\frac{1}{3}}y^{-\frac{1}{2}}\right)^6$         **8.** $\left(\dfrac{2}{7}\right)^0 - 32^{-\frac{2}{5}}$

**9.** $(2x - 5) - (x^2 - 3x + 1)$         **10.** $(2x - 5)(x^2 - 3x + 1)$

**11.** $x^3 + x^3 - x^3 \cdot x^3$         **12.** $(9a - 10b)(2a + b)$

**13.** $\{a, c, d, e\} \cup \{c, d, f, h\}$         **14.** $\{a, c, d, e\} \cap \{c, d, f, h\}$

**15.** $(3x^2y^3 - xy + 4y^2) - (-2x^2y^3 - 3xy + 5y^2)$

**16.** $\dfrac{24x^2y^{13}}{-2x^5y^{-2}}$         **17.** $\left(\dfrac{1}{3}x^{-5}y^4\right)(18x^{-2}y^{-1})$

**18.** $\sqrt[12]{x^4}$

**19.** $[4y - (3x + 2)][4y + (3x + 2)]$

**20.** $(x - 2y - 1)^2$

**21.** $\dfrac{24 \times 10^3}{2 \times 10^6}$ (Express the answer in scientific notation.)

**22.** $\dfrac{\sqrt[3]{32}}{\sqrt[3]{2}}$         **23.** $(x^3 + 2)(x^3 - 2)$

**24.** $(x^2 + 2)^2$

**25.** $\sqrt{50} \cdot \sqrt{6}$

**26.** $\dfrac{11}{7 - \sqrt{3}}$

**27.** $\dfrac{11}{\sqrt{3}}$

*In Exercises 28–34, factor completely, or state that the polynomial is prime.*

**28.** $7x^2 - 22x + 3$

**29.** $x^2 - 2x + 4$

**30.** $x^3 + 5x^2 + 3x + 15$

**31.** $3x^2 - 4xy - 7y^2$

**32.** $64y - y^4$

**33.** $50x^3 + 20x^2 + 2x$

**34.** $x^2 - 6x + 9 - 49y^2$

*In Exercises 35–36, factor and simplify each algebraic expression.*

**35.** $x^{-\frac{3}{2}} - 2x^{-\frac{1}{2}} + x^{\frac{1}{2}}$

**36.** $(x^2 + 1)^{\frac{1}{2}} - 10(x^2 + 1)^{-\frac{1}{2}}$

**37.** List all the rational numbers in this set:

$$\left\{ -11, -\frac{3}{7}, 0, 0.45, \sqrt{23}, \sqrt{25} \right\}.$$

*In Exercises 38–39, rewrite each expression without absolute value bars.*

**38.** $|2 - \sqrt{13}|$

**39.** $x^2|x|$ if $x < 0$

**40.** If the population of the United States is approximately $3.0 \times 10^8$ and each person spends about \$140 per year on ice cream, express the total annual spending on ice cream in scientific notation.

**41.** A human brain contains $3 \times 10^{10}$ neurons and a gorilla brain contains $7.5 \times 10^9$ neurons. How many times as many neurons are in the brain of a human as in the brain of a gorilla?

**42.** The number of TV channels is increasing. The bar graph shows the total channels available in the average U.S. household from 2000 through 2006.

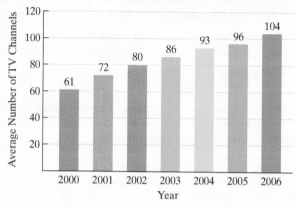

**Number of TV Channels in the Average United States Household**

*Source:* Nielsen Media Research

Here are two mathematical models for the data shown by the graph. In each formula, $N$ represents the number of TV channels in the average U.S. household $x$ years after 2000.

Model 1 — $N = 6.8x + 64$

Model 2 — $N = -0.5x^2 + 9.5x + 62$

**a.** Which model best describes the data for 2000?

**b.** Does the polynomial model of degree 2 underestimate or overestimate the number of channels for 2006? By how many channels?

**c.** According to the polynomial model of degree 1, how many channels will the average household have in 2010?

---

**Section P.6** **Rational Expressions**

**Objectives**

① Specify numbers that must be excluded from the domain of a rational expression.

② Simplify rational expressions.

③ Multiply rational expressions.

④ Divide rational expressions.

⑤ Add and subtract rational expressions.

⑥ Simplify complex rational expressions.

⑦ Simplify fractional expressions that occur in calculus.

⑧ Rationalize numerators.

How do we describe the costs of reducing environmental pollution? We often use algebraic expressions involving quotients of polynomials. For example, the algebraic expression

$$\frac{250x}{100 - x}$$

describes the cost, in millions of dollars, to remove $x$ percent of the pollutants that are discharged into a river. Removing a modest percentage of pollutants, say 40%, is far less costly than removing a substantially greater percentage, such as 95%. We see this by evaluating the algebraic expression for $x = 40$ and $x = 95$.

Evaluating $\dfrac{250x}{100 - x}$ for

| $x = 40$: | $x = 95$: |

Cost is $\dfrac{250(40)}{100 - 40} \approx 167.$  Cost is $\dfrac{250(95)}{100 - 95} = 4750.$

The cost increases from approximately \$167 million to a possibly prohibitive \$4750 million, or \$4.75 billion. Costs spiral upward as the percentage of removed pollutants increases.

Many algebraic expressions that describe costs of environmental projects are examples of *rational expressions*. First we will define rational expressions. Then we will review how to perform operations with such expressions.

## Rational Expressions

A **rational expression** is the quotient of two polynomials. Some examples are

$$\frac{x - 2}{4}, \quad \frac{4}{x - 2}, \quad \frac{x}{x^2 - 1}, \quad \text{and} \quad \frac{x^2 + 1}{x^2 + 2x - 3}.$$

The set of real numbers for which an algebraic expression is defined is the **domain** of the expression. Because rational expressions indicate division and division by zero is undefined, **we must exclude numbers from a rational expression's domain that make the denominator zero**.

(**EXAMPLE 1**)  **Excluding Numbers from the Domain**

Find all the numbers that must be excluded from the domain of each rational expression:

**a.** $\dfrac{4}{x - 2}$   **b.** $\dfrac{x}{x^2 - 1}.$

**Solution**   To determine the numbers that must be excluded from each domain, examine the denominators.

**a.** $\dfrac{4}{x - 2}$   **b.** $\dfrac{x}{x^2 - 1} = \dfrac{x}{(x + 1)(x - 1)}$

This denominator would equal zero if $x = 2$.  This factor would equal zero if $x = -1$.  This factor would equal zero if $x = 1$.

For the rational expression in part (a), we must exclude 2 from the domain. For the rational expression in part (b), we must exclude both $-1$ and 1 from the domain. These excluded numbers are often written to the right of a rational expression:

$$\frac{4}{x - 2}, x \neq 2 \qquad \frac{x}{x^2 - 1}, x \neq -1, x \neq 1$$

⏷ Check Point  **1**  Find all the numbers that must be excluded from the domain of each rational expression:

**a.** $\dfrac{7}{x + 5}$   **b.** $\dfrac{x}{x^2 - 36}.$

## Discovery

What happens if you try substituting 100 for $x$ in

$$\frac{250x}{100 - x}?$$

What does this tell you about the cost of cleaning up all of the river's pollutants?

**1** Specify numbers that must be excluded from the domain of a rational expression.

② Simplify rational expressions.

## Simplifying Rational Expressions

A rational expression is **simplified** if its numerator and denominator have no common factors other than 1 or −1. The following procedure can be used to simplify rational expressions:

### Simplifying Rational Expressions

1. Factor the numerator and the denominator completely.
2. Divide both the numerator and the denominator by any common factors.

**EXAMPLE 2** Simplifying Rational Expressions

Simplify:

$$\text{a. } \frac{x^3 + x^2}{x + 1} \qquad \text{b. } \frac{x^2 + 6x + 5}{x^2 - 25}.$$

### Solution

**a.** $\dfrac{x^3 + x^2}{x + 1} = \dfrac{x^2(x + 1)}{x + 1}$    Factor the numerator. Because the denominator is $x + 1$, $x \neq -1$.

$$= \frac{x^2 \overset{1}{\cancel{(x + 1)}}}{\underset{1}{\cancel{x + 1}}}$$    Divide out the common factor, $x + 1$.

$$= x^2, x \neq -1$$    Denominators of 1 need not be written because $\frac{a}{1} = a$.

**b.** $\dfrac{x^2 + 6x + 5}{x^2 - 25} = \dfrac{(x + 5)(x + 1)}{(x + 5)(x - 5)}$    Factor the numerator and denominator. Because the denominator is $(x + 5)(x - 5)$, $x \neq -5$ and $x \neq 5$.

$$= \frac{\overset{1}{\cancel{(x + 5)}}(x + 1)}{\underset{1}{\cancel{(x + 5)}}(x - 5)}$$    Divide out the common factor, $x + 5$.

$$= \frac{x + 1}{x - 5}, \quad x \neq -5, \quad x \neq 5$$

⊘ Check Point **2** Simplify:

$$\text{a. } \frac{x^3 + 3x^2}{x + 3} \qquad \text{b. } \frac{x^2 - 1}{x^2 + 2x + 1}.$$

③ Multiply rational expressions.

## Multiplying Rational Expressions

The product of two rational expressions is the product of their numerators divided by the product of their denominators. Here is a step-by-step procedure for multiplying rational expressions:

### Multiplying Rational Expressions

1. Factor all numerators and denominators completely.
2. Divide numerators and denominators by common factors.
3. Multiply the remaining factors in the numerators and multiply the remaining factors in the denominators.

**( EXAMPLE 3 )** **Multiplying Rational Expressions**

Multiply: $\dfrac{x-7}{x-1} \cdot \dfrac{x^2-1}{3x-21}$.

**Solution**

$\dfrac{x-7}{x-1} \cdot \dfrac{x^2-1}{3x-21}$

This is the given multiplication problem.

$= \dfrac{x-7}{x-1} \cdot \dfrac{(x+1)(x-1)}{3(x-7)}$

Factor as many numerators and denominators as possible. Because the denominators have factors of $x-1$ and $x-7$, $x \neq 1$ and $x \neq 7$.

$= \dfrac{\overset{1}{\cancel{x-7}}}{\underset{1}{\cancel{x-1}}} \cdot \dfrac{(x+1)\overset{1}{\cancel{(x-1)}}}{3\cancel{(x-7)}_{1}}$

Divide numerators and denominators by common factors.

$= \dfrac{x+1}{3}, x \neq 1, x \neq 7$

Multiply the remaining factors in the numerators and denominators.

> These excluded numbers from the domain must also be excluded from the simplified expression's domain.

**Check Point 3** Multiply:

$$\dfrac{x+3}{x^2-4} \cdot \dfrac{x^2-x-6}{x^2+6x+9}.$$

**④ Divide rational expressions.**

## Dividing Rational Expressions

The quotient of two rational expressions is the product of the first expression and the multiplicative inverse, or reciprocal, of the second expression. The reciprocal is found by interchanging the numerator and the denominator. Thus, **we find the quotient of two rational expressions by inverting the divisor and multiplying**.

**( EXAMPLE 4 )** **Dividing Rational Expressions**

Divide: $\dfrac{x^2-2x-8}{x^2-9} \div \dfrac{x-4}{x+3}$.

**Solution**

$\dfrac{x^2-2x-8}{x^2-9} \div \dfrac{x-4}{x+3}$

This is the given division problem.

$= \dfrac{x^2-2x-8}{x^2-9} \cdot \dfrac{x+3}{x-4}$

Invert the divisor and multiply.

$= \dfrac{(x-4)(x+2)}{(x+3)(x-3)} \cdot \dfrac{x+3}{x-4}$

Factor as many numerators and denominators as possible. For nonzero denominators, $x \neq -3, x \neq 3$, and $x \neq 4$.

$= \dfrac{\overset{1}{\cancel{(x-4)}}(x+2)}{(x+3)(x-3)} \cdot \dfrac{\overset{1}{\cancel{(x+3)}}}{\cancel{(x-4)}_{1}}$

Divide numerators and denominators by common factors.

$= \dfrac{x+2}{x-3}, x \neq -3, x \neq 3, x \neq 4$

Multiply the remaining factors in the numerators and in the denominators.

⟋ Check Point **4** Divide:

$$\frac{x^2 - 2x + 1}{x^3 + x} \div \frac{x^2 + x - 2}{3x^2 + 3}.$$

⑤ Add and subtract rational expressions.

## Adding and Subtracting Rational Expressions with the Same Denominator

We add or subtract rational expressions with the same denominator by (1) adding or subtracting the numerators, (2) placing this result over the common denominator, and (3) simplifying, if possible.

( EXAMPLE 5 ) **Subtracting Rational Expressions with the Same Denominator**

Subtract: $\dfrac{5x + 1}{x^2 - 9} - \dfrac{4x - 2}{x^2 - 9}.$

**Solution**

**Study Tip**

Example 5 shows that when a numerator is being subtracted, we must subtract every term in that expression.

Don't forget the parentheses.

$$\frac{5x + 1}{x^2 - 9} - \frac{4x - 2}{x^2 - 9} = \frac{5x + 1 - (4x - 2)}{x^2 - 9}$$

Subtract numerators and include parentheses to indicate that both terms are subtracted. Place this difference over the common denominator.

$$= \frac{5x + 1 - 4x + 2}{x^2 - 9}$$

Remove parentheses and then change the sign of each term in parentheses.

$$= \frac{x + 3}{x^2 - 9}$$

Combine like terms.

$$= \frac{\overset{1}{\cancel{x + 3}}}{\underset{1}{\cancel{(x + 3)}}(x - 3)}$$

Factor and simplify ($x \neq -3$ and $x \neq 3$).

$$= \frac{1}{x - 3}, x \neq -3, x \neq 3$$

⟋ Check Point **5** Subtract: $\dfrac{x}{x + 1} - \dfrac{3x + 2}{x + 1}.$

## Adding and Subtracting Rational Expressions with Different Denominators

Rational expressions that have no common factors in their denominators can be added or subtracted using one of the following properties:

$$\frac{a}{b} + \frac{c}{d} = \frac{ad + bc}{bd} \qquad \frac{a}{b} - \frac{c}{d} = \frac{ad - bc}{bd}, b \neq 0, d \neq 0.$$

The denominator, $bd$, is the product of the factors in the two denominators. Because we are considering rational expressions that have no common factors in their denominators, the product $bd$ gives the least common denominator.

**EXAMPLE 6** Subtracting Rational Expressions Having No Common Factors in Their Denominators

Subtract: $\dfrac{x+2}{2x-3} - \dfrac{4}{x+3}$.

**Solution** We need to find the least common denominator. This is the product of the distinct factors in each denominator, namely $(2x-3)(x+3)$. We can therefore use the subtraction property given previously as follows:

$$\frac{a}{b} - \frac{c}{d} = \frac{ad-bc}{bd}$$

$$\frac{x+2}{2x-3} - \frac{4}{x+3} = \frac{(x+2)(x+3) - (2x-3)4}{(2x-3)(x+3)}$$

*Observe that*
*$a = x + 2$, $b = 2x - 3$, $c = 4$,*
*and $d = x + 3$.*

$$= \frac{x^2 + 5x + 6 - (8x - 12)}{(2x-3)(x+3)}$$

*Multiply.*

$$= \frac{x^2 + 5x + 6 - 8x + 12}{(2x-3)(x+3)}$$

*Remove parentheses and then change the sign of each term in parentheses.*

$$= \frac{x^2 - 3x + 18}{(2x-3)(x+3)}, x \neq \frac{3}{2}, x \neq -3$$

*Combine like terms in the numerator.*

⊘ Check Point **6** Add: $\dfrac{3}{x+1} + \dfrac{5}{x-1}$.

---

The **least common denominator**, or LCD, of several rational expressions is a polynomial consisting of the product of all prime factors in the denominators, with each factor raised to the greatest power of its occurrence in any denominator. When adding and subtracting rational expressions that have different denominators with one or more common factors in the denominators, it is efficient to find the least common denominator first.

### Finding the Least Common Denominator

1. Factor each denominator completely.
2. List the factors of the first denominator.
3. Add to the list in step 2 any factors of the second denominator that do not appear in the list.
4. Form the product of the factors from the list in step 3. This product is the least common denominator.

**EXAMPLE 7** Finding the Least Common Denominator

Find the least common denominator of

$$\frac{7}{5x^2 + 15x} \quad \text{and} \quad \frac{9}{x^2 + 6x + 9}.$$

$$\frac{7}{5x^2 + 15x} \quad \text{and} \quad \frac{9}{x^2 + 6x + 9}$$

The given rational expressions (repeated)

**Solution**

**Step 1 Factor each denominator completely.**

$$5x^2 + 15x = 5x(x + 3)$$
$$x^2 + 6x + 9 = (x + 3)^2 \quad \text{or} \quad (x + 3)(x + 3)$$

| Factors are 5, *x*, and *x* + 3. | $\dfrac{7}{5x^2 + 15x}$ | $\dfrac{9}{x^2 + 6x + 9}$ | Factors are *x* + 3 and *x* + 3. |

**Step 2 List the factors of the first denominator.**

$$5, x, x + 3$$

**Step 3 Add any unlisted factors from the second denominator.** One factor of $x^2 + 6x + 9$ is already in our list. That factor is $x + 3$. However, the other factor of $x + 3$ is not listed in step 2. We add a second factor of $x + 3$ to the list. We have

$$5, x, x + 3, x + 3.$$

**Step 4 The least common denominator is the product of all factors in the final list.** Thus,

$$5x(x + 3)(x + 3) \quad \text{or} \quad 5x(x + 3)^2$$

is the least common denominator.

⊘ Check Point **7** Find the least common denominator of

$$\frac{3}{x^2 - 6x + 9} \quad \text{and} \quad \frac{7}{x^2 - 9}.$$

Finding the least common denominator for two (or more) rational expressions is the first step needed to add or subtract the expressions.

### Adding and Subtracting Rational Expressions That Have Different Denominators

1. Find the LCD of the rational expressions.
2. Rewrite each rational expression as an equivalent expression whose denominator is the LCD. To do so, multiply the numerator and the denominator of each rational expression by any factor(s) needed to convert the denominator into the LCD.
3. Add or subtract numerators, placing the resulting expression over the LCD.
4. If possible, simplify the resulting rational expression.

( EXAMPLE 8 ) **Adding Rational Expressions with Different Denominators**

Add: $\dfrac{x + 3}{x^2 + x - 2} + \dfrac{2}{x^2 - 1}.$

**Solution**

**Step 1 Find the least common denominator.** Start by factoring the denominators.

$$x^2 + x - 2 = (x + 2)(x - 1)$$
$$x^2 - 1 = (x + 1)(x - 1)$$

The factors of the first denominator are $x + 2$ and $x - 1$. The only factor from the second denominator that is not listed is $x + 1$. Thus, the least common denominator is

$$(x + 2)(x - 1)(x + 1).$$

**Step 2   Write equivalent expressions with the LCD as denominators.** We must rewrite each rational expression with a denominator of $(x + 2)(x - 1)(x + 1)$. We do so by multiplying both the numerator and the denominator of each rational expression by any factor(s) needed to convert the expression's denominator into the LCD.

$$\frac{x + 3}{(x + 2)(x - 1)} \cdot \frac{x + 1}{x + 1} = \frac{(x + 3)(x + 1)}{(x + 2)(x - 1)(x + 1)} \qquad \frac{2}{(x + 1)(x - 1)} \cdot \frac{x + 2}{x + 2} = \frac{2(x + 2)}{(x + 2)(x - 1)(x + 1)}$$

Multiply the numerator and denominator by
$x + 1$ to get $(x + 2)(x - 1)(x + 1)$, the LCD.

Multiply the numerator and denominator by
$x + 2$ to get $(x + 2)(x - 1)(x + 1)$, the LCD.

Because $\dfrac{x + 1}{x + 1} = 1$ and $\dfrac{x + 2}{x + 2} = 1$, we are not changing the value of either rational expression, only its appearance.

Now we are ready to perform the indicated addition.

$$\frac{x + 3}{x^2 + x - 2} + \frac{2}{x^2 - 1}$$

This is the given problem.

$$= \frac{x + 3}{(x + 2)(x - 1)} + \frac{2}{(x + 1)(x - 1)}$$

Factor the denominators.

The LCD is
$(x + 2)(x - 1)(x + 1)$.

$$= \frac{(x + 3)(x + 1)}{(x + 2)(x - 1)(x + 1)} + \frac{2(x + 2)}{(x + 2)(x - 1)(x + 1)}$$

Rewrite equivalent
expressions with the LCD.

**Step 3   Add numerators, putting this sum over the LCD.**

$$= \frac{(x + 3)(x + 1) + 2(x + 2)}{(x + 2)(x - 1)(x + 1)}$$

$$= \frac{x^2 + 4x + 3 + 2x + 4}{(x + 2)(x - 1)(x + 1)}$$

Perform the multiplications
in the numerator.

$$= \frac{x^2 + 6x + 7}{(x + 2)(x - 1)(x + 1)}, x \neq -2, x \neq 1, x \neq -1$$

Combine like terms in the
numerator: $4x + 2x = 6x$
and $3 + 4 = 7$.

**Step 4   If necessary, simplify.** Because the numerator is prime, no further simplification is possible.

⬭

☑ Check Point **8** Subtract:   $\dfrac{x}{x^2 - 10x + 25} - \dfrac{x - 4}{2x - 10}$.

**⑥** Simplify complex rational expressions.

## Complex Rational Expressions

**Complex rational expressions**, also called **complex fractions**, have numerators or denominators containing one or more rational expressions. Here are two examples of such expressions:

$$\frac{1 + \dfrac{1}{x}}{1 - \dfrac{1}{x}}$$

Separate rational
expressions occur
in the numerator
and the denominator.

$$\frac{\dfrac{1}{x + h} - \dfrac{1}{x}}{h}.$$

Separate rational
expressions occur
in the numerator.

One method for simplifying a complex rational expression is to combine its numerator into a single expression and combine its denominator into a single expression. Then perform the division by inverting the denominator and multiplying.

**EXAMPLE 9** **Simplifying a Complex Rational Expression**

Simplify: $\dfrac{1 + \dfrac{1}{x}}{1 - \dfrac{1}{x}}$.

**Solution**

**Step 1  Add to get a single rational expression in the numerator.**

$$1 + \frac{1}{x} = \frac{1}{1} + \frac{1}{x} = \frac{1 \cdot x}{1 \cdot x} + \frac{1}{x} = \frac{x}{x} + \frac{1}{x} = \frac{x + 1}{x}$$

> The LCD is 1 · x, or x.

**Step 2  Subtract to get a single rational expression in the denominator.**

$$1 - \frac{1}{x} = \frac{1}{1} - \frac{1}{x} = \frac{1 \cdot x}{1 \cdot x} - \frac{1}{x} = \frac{x}{x} - \frac{1}{x} = \frac{x - 1}{x}$$

> The LCD is 1 · x, or x.

**Step 3  Perform the division indicated by the main fraction bar: Invert and multiply. If possible, simplify.**

$$\frac{1 + \dfrac{1}{x}}{1 - \dfrac{1}{x}} = \frac{\dfrac{x + 1}{x}}{\dfrac{x - 1}{x}} = \frac{x + 1}{x} \cdot \frac{x}{x - 1} = \frac{x + 1}{\overset{1}{\cancel{x}}} \cdot \frac{\overset{1}{\cancel{x}}}{x - 1} = \frac{x + 1}{x - 1}$$

> Invert and multiply.

**Check Point 9** Simplify: $\dfrac{\dfrac{1}{x} - \dfrac{3}{2}}{\dfrac{1}{x} + \dfrac{3}{4}}$.

A second method for simplifying a complex rational expression is to find the least common denominator of all the rational expressions in its numerator and denominator. Then multiply each term in its numerator and denominator by this least common denominator. Because we are multiplying by a form of 1, we will obtain an equivalent expression that does not contain fractions in its numerator or denominator. Here we use this method to simplify the complex rational expression in Example 9.

$$\frac{1 + \dfrac{1}{x}}{1 - \dfrac{1}{x}} = \frac{\left(1 + \dfrac{1}{x}\right)}{\left(1 - \dfrac{1}{x}\right)} \cdot \frac{x}{x}$$

> The least common denominator of all the rational expressions is x. Multiply the numerator and denominator by x. Because $\frac{x}{x} = 1$, we are not changing the complex fraction $(x \neq 0)$.

$$= \frac{1 \cdot x + \dfrac{1}{x} \cdot x}{1 \cdot x - \dfrac{1}{x} \cdot x}$$

> Use the distributive property. Be sure to distribute x to every term.

$$= \frac{x + 1}{x - 1}, \ x \neq 0, \ x \neq 1$$

> Multiply. The complex rational expression is now simplified.

$\boxed{\text{EXAMPLE 10}}$ **Simplifying a Complex Rational Expression**

Simplify: $\dfrac{\dfrac{1}{x+h} - \dfrac{1}{x}}{h}$.

**Solution** We will use the method of multiplying each of the three terms, $\dfrac{1}{x+h}, \dfrac{1}{x}$, and $h$, by the least common denominator. The least common denominator is $x(x+h)$.

$\dfrac{\dfrac{1}{x+h} - \dfrac{1}{x}}{h}$

$= \dfrac{\left(\dfrac{1}{x+h} - \dfrac{1}{x}\right)x(x+h)}{hx(x+h)}$

Multiply the numerator and denominator by $x(x+h), h \neq 0, x \neq 0, x \neq -h$.

$= \dfrac{\dfrac{1}{x+h} \cdot x(x+h) - \dfrac{1}{x} \cdot x(x+h)}{hx(x+h)}$

Use the distributive property in the numerator.

$= \dfrac{x - (x+h)}{hx(x+h)}$

Simplify: $\dfrac{1}{x+h}x(x+h) = x$ and $\dfrac{1}{x} \cdot x(x+h) = x+h$.

$= \dfrac{x - x - h}{hx(x+h)}$

Subtract in the numerator. Remove parentheses and change the sign of each term in parentheses.

$= \dfrac{-\overset{1}{\cancel{h}}}{\underset{1}{\cancel{h}}x(x+h)}$

Simplify: $x - x - h = -h$.

$= -\dfrac{1}{x(x+h)}, h \neq 0, x \neq 0, x \neq -h$  Divide the numerator and denominator by $h$.

$\checkmark$ Check Point **10** Simplify: $\dfrac{\dfrac{1}{x+7} - \dfrac{1}{x}}{7}$.

**7** Simplify fractional expressions that occur in calculus.

## Fractional Expressions in Calculus

Fractional expressions containing radicals occur frequently in calculus. Because of the radicals, these expressions are not rational expressions. However, they can often be simplified using the procedure for simplifying complex rational expressions.

$\boxed{\text{EXAMPLE 11}}$ **Simplifying a Fractional Expression Containing Radicals**

Simplify: $\dfrac{\sqrt{9 - x^2} + \dfrac{x^2}{\sqrt{9 - x^2}}}{9 - x^2}$.

**Solution**

$$\frac{\sqrt{9-x^2}+\dfrac{x^2}{\sqrt{9-x^2}}}{9-x^2}$$

The least common denominator is $\sqrt{9-x^2}$.

$$=\frac{\sqrt{9-x^2}+\dfrac{x^2}{\sqrt{9-x^2}}}{9-x^2}\cdot\frac{\sqrt{9-x^2}}{\sqrt{9-x^2}}$$

Multiply the numerator and the denominator by $\sqrt{9-x^2}$.

$$=\frac{\sqrt{9-x^2}\sqrt{9-x^2}+\dfrac{x^2}{\sqrt{9-x^2}}\sqrt{9-x^2}}{(9-x^2)\sqrt{9-x^2}}$$

Use the distributive property in the numerator.

$$=\frac{(9-x^2)+x^2}{(9-x^2)^{\frac{3}{2}}}$$

In the denominator:
$$(9-x^2)^1(9-x^2)^{\frac{1}{2}}=(9-x^2)^{1+\frac{1}{2}}$$
$$=(9-x^2)^{\frac{3}{2}}.$$

$$=\frac{9}{\sqrt{(9-x^2)^3}}$$

Because the original expression was in radical form, write the denominator in radical form.  ●

○ Check Point **11** Simplify: $\dfrac{\sqrt{x}+\dfrac{1}{\sqrt{x}}}{x}$.

---

**8** Rationalize numerators.

Another fractional expression that you will encounter in calculus is

$$\frac{\sqrt{x+h}-\sqrt{x}}{h}.$$

Can you see that this expression is not defined if $h=0$? However, in calculus, you will ask the following question:

What happens to the expression as $h$ takes on values that get closer and closer to 0, such as $h=0.1$, $h=0.01$, $h=0.001$, $h=0.0001$, and so on?

The question is answered by first **rationalizing the numerator**. This process involves rewriting the fractional expression as an equivalent expression in which the numerator no longer contains any radicals. **To rationalize a numerator, multiply by 1 to eliminate the radicals in the *numerator*. Multiply the numerator and the denominator by the conjugate of the numerator.**

 **EXAMPLE 12** **Rationalizing a Numerator**

Rationalize the numerator:

$$\frac{\sqrt{x+h}-\sqrt{x}}{h}.$$

**Solution** The conjugate of the numerator is $\sqrt{x+h}+\sqrt{x}$. If we multiply the numerator and denominator by $\sqrt{x+h}+\sqrt{x}$, the simplified numerator will not contain a radical. Therefore, we multiply by 1, choosing $\dfrac{\sqrt{x+h}+\sqrt{x}}{\sqrt{x+h}+\sqrt{x}}$ for 1.

$$\frac{\sqrt{x+h}-\sqrt{x}}{h} = \frac{\sqrt{x+h}-\sqrt{x}}{h} \cdot \frac{\sqrt{x+h}+\sqrt{x}}{\sqrt{x+h}+\sqrt{x}}$$   Multiply by 1.

$$= \frac{\left(\sqrt{x+h}\right)^2 - \left(\sqrt{x}\right)^2}{h\left(\sqrt{x+h}+\sqrt{x}\right)}$$   $\left(\sqrt{a}-\sqrt{b}\right)\left(\sqrt{a}+\sqrt{b}\right) = \left(\sqrt{a}\right)^2 - \left(\sqrt{b}\right)^2$

$$= \frac{x+h-x}{h\left(\sqrt{x+h}+\sqrt{x}\right)}$$   $\left(\sqrt{x+h}\right)^2 = x+h$ and $\left(\sqrt{x}\right)^2 = x$.

$$= \frac{h}{h\left(\sqrt{x+h}+\sqrt{x}\right)}$$   Simplify: $x+h-x=h$.

$$= \frac{1}{\sqrt{x+h}+\sqrt{x}}, \quad h \neq 0$$   Divide both the numerator and denominator by $h$.

## Calculus Preview

In calculus, you will summarize the discussion on the right using the special notation

$$\lim_{h \to 0} \frac{\sqrt{x+h}-\sqrt{x}}{h} = \frac{1}{2\sqrt{x}}.$$

This is read "the limit of $\frac{\sqrt{x+h}-\sqrt{x}}{h}$ as $h$ approaches 0 equals $\frac{1}{2\sqrt{x}}$." Limits are discussed in Chapter 11, where we present an introduction to calculus.

What happens to $\dfrac{\sqrt{x+h}-\sqrt{x}}{h}$ as $h$ gets closer and closer to 0? In Example 12, we showed that

$$\frac{\sqrt{x+h}-\sqrt{x}}{h} = \frac{1}{\sqrt{x+h}+\sqrt{x}}.$$

As $h$ gets closer to 0, the expression on the right gets closer to $\dfrac{1}{\sqrt{x+0}+\sqrt{x}} = \dfrac{1}{\sqrt{x}+\sqrt{x}}$, or $\dfrac{1}{2\sqrt{x}}$. Thus, the fractional expression $\dfrac{\sqrt{x+h}-\sqrt{x}}{h}$ approaches $\dfrac{1}{2\sqrt{x}}$ as $h$ gets closer to 0.

✓ **Check Point 12** Rationalize the numerator: $\dfrac{\sqrt{x+3}-\sqrt{x}}{3}$.

## Exercise Set P.6

### Practice Exercises

*In Exercises 1–6, find all numbers that must be excluded from the domain of each rational expression.*

**1.** $\dfrac{7}{x-3}$   **2.** $\dfrac{13}{x+9}$   **3.** $\dfrac{x+5}{x^2-25}$

**4.** $\dfrac{x+7}{x^2-49}$   **5.** $\dfrac{x-1}{x^2+11x+10}$   **6.** $\dfrac{x-3}{x^2+4x-45}$

*In Exercises 7–14, simplify each rational expression. Find all numbers that must be excluded from the domain of the simplified rational expression.*

**7.** $\dfrac{3x-9}{x^2-6x+9}$   **8.** $\dfrac{4x-8}{x^2-4x+4}$

**9.** $\dfrac{x^2-12x+36}{4x-24}$   **10.** $\dfrac{x^2-8x+16}{3x-12}$

**11.** $\dfrac{y^2+7y-18}{y^2-3y+2}$   **12.** $\dfrac{y^2-4y-5}{y^2+5y+4}$

**13.** $\dfrac{x^2+12x+36}{x^2-36}$   **14.** $\dfrac{x^2-14x+49}{x^2-49}$

*In Exercises 15–32, multiply or divide as indicated.*

**15.** $\dfrac{x-2}{3x+9} \cdot \dfrac{2x+6}{2x-4}$   **16.** $\dfrac{6x+9}{3x-15} \cdot \dfrac{x-5}{4x+6}$

**17.** $\dfrac{x^2-9}{x^2} \cdot \dfrac{x^2-3x}{x^2+x-12}$   **18.** $\dfrac{x^2-4}{x^2-4x+4} \cdot \dfrac{2x-4}{x+2}$

**19.** $\dfrac{x^2-5x+6}{x^2-2x-3} \cdot \dfrac{x^2-1}{x^2-4}$   **20.** $\dfrac{x^2+5x+6}{x^2+x-6} \cdot \dfrac{x^2-9}{x^2-x-6}$

**21.** $\dfrac{x^3-8}{x^2-4} \cdot \dfrac{x+2}{3x}$   **22.** $\dfrac{x^2+6x+9}{x^3+27} \cdot \dfrac{1}{x+3}$

**23.** $\dfrac{x+1}{3} \div \dfrac{3x+3}{7}$   **24.** $\dfrac{x+5}{7} \div \dfrac{4x+20}{9}$

**25.** $\dfrac{x^2-4}{x} \div \dfrac{x+2}{x-2}$   **26.** $\dfrac{x^2-4}{x-2} \div \dfrac{x+2}{4x-8}$

**27.** $\dfrac{4x^2+10}{x-3} \div \dfrac{6x^2+15}{x^2-9}$   **28.** $\dfrac{x^2+x}{x^2-4} \div \dfrac{x^2-1}{x^2+5x+6}$

**29.** $\dfrac{x^2-25}{2x-2} \div \dfrac{x^2+10x+25}{x^2+4x-5}$

**30.** $\dfrac{x^2-4}{x^2+3x-10} \div \dfrac{x^2+5x+6}{x^2+8x+15}$

**31.** $\dfrac{x^2+x-12}{x^2+x-30} \cdot \dfrac{x^2+5x+6}{x^2-2x-3} \div \dfrac{x+3}{x^2+7x+6}$

**32.** $\dfrac{x^3-25x}{4x^2} \cdot \dfrac{2x^2-2}{x^2-6x+5} \div \dfrac{x^2+5x}{7x+7}$

*In Exercises 33–58, add or subtract as indicated.*

**33.** $\dfrac{4x+1}{6x+5} + \dfrac{8x+9}{6x+5}$

**34.** $\dfrac{3x+2}{3x+4} + \dfrac{3x+6}{3x+4}$

**35.** $\dfrac{x^2-2x}{x^2+3x} + \dfrac{x^2+x}{x^2+3x}$

**36.** $\dfrac{x^2-4x}{x^2-x-6} + \dfrac{4x-4}{x^2-x-6}$

**37.** $\dfrac{4x-10}{x-2} - \dfrac{x-4}{x-2}$

**38.** $\dfrac{2x+3}{3x-6} - \dfrac{3-x}{3x-6}$

**39.** $\dfrac{x^2+3x}{x^2+x-12} - \dfrac{x^2-12}{x^2+x-12}$

**40.** $\dfrac{x^2-4x}{x^2-x-6} - \dfrac{x-6}{x^2-x-6}$

**41.** $\dfrac{3}{x+4} + \dfrac{6}{x+5}$

**42.** $\dfrac{8}{x-2} + \dfrac{2}{x-3}$

**43.** $\dfrac{3}{x+1} - \dfrac{3}{x}$

**44.** $\dfrac{4}{x} - \dfrac{3}{x+3}$

**45.** $\dfrac{2x}{x+2} + \dfrac{x+2}{x-2}$

**46.** $\dfrac{3x}{x-3} - \dfrac{x+4}{x+2}$

**47.** $\dfrac{x+5}{x-5} + \dfrac{x-5}{x+5}$

**48.** $\dfrac{x+3}{x-3} + \dfrac{x-3}{x+3}$

**49.** $\dfrac{3}{2x+4} + \dfrac{2}{3x+6}$

**50.** $\dfrac{5}{2x+8} + \dfrac{7}{3x+12}$

**51.** $\dfrac{4}{x^2+6x+9} + \dfrac{4}{x+3}$

**52.** $\dfrac{3}{5x+2} + \dfrac{5x}{25x^2-4}$

**53.** $\dfrac{3x}{x^2+3x-10} - \dfrac{2x}{x^2+x-6}$

**54.** $\dfrac{x}{x^2-2x-24} - \dfrac{x}{x^2-7x+6}$

**55.** $\dfrac{x+3}{x^2-1} - \dfrac{x+2}{x-1}$

**56.** $\dfrac{x+5}{x^2-4} - \dfrac{x+1}{x-2}$

**57.** $\dfrac{4x^2+x-6}{x^2+3x+2} - \dfrac{3x}{x+1} + \dfrac{5}{x+2}$

**58.** $\dfrac{6x^2+17x-40}{x^2+x-20} + \dfrac{3}{x-4} - \dfrac{5x}{x+5}$

*In Exercises 59–72, simplify each complex rational expression.*

**59.** $\dfrac{\dfrac{x}{3}-1}{x-3}$

**60.** $\dfrac{\dfrac{x}{4}-1}{x-4}$

**61.** $\dfrac{1+\dfrac{1}{x}}{3-\dfrac{1}{x}}$

**62.** $\dfrac{8+\dfrac{1}{x}}{4-\dfrac{1}{x}}$

**63.** $\dfrac{\dfrac{1}{x}+\dfrac{1}{y}}{x+y}$

**64.** $\dfrac{1-\dfrac{1}{x}}{xy}$

**65.** $\dfrac{x-\dfrac{x}{x+3}}{x+2}$

**66.** $\dfrac{x-3}{x-\dfrac{3}{x-2}}$

**67.** $\dfrac{\dfrac{3}{x-2}-\dfrac{4}{x+2}}{\dfrac{7}{x^2-4}}$

**68.** $\dfrac{\dfrac{x}{x-2}+1}{\dfrac{3}{x^2-4}+1}$

**69.** $\dfrac{\dfrac{1}{x+1}}{\dfrac{1}{x^2-2x-3}+\dfrac{1}{x-3}}$

**70.** $\dfrac{\dfrac{6}{x^2+2x-15}-\dfrac{1}{x-3}}{\dfrac{1}{x+5}+1}$

**71.** $\dfrac{\dfrac{1}{(x+h)^2}-\dfrac{1}{x^2}}{h}$

**72.** $\dfrac{\dfrac{x+h}{x+h+1}-\dfrac{x}{x+1}}{h}$

*Exercises 73–78 contain fractional expressions that occur frequently in calculus. Simplify each expression.*

**73.** $\dfrac{\sqrt{x}-\dfrac{1}{3\sqrt{x}}}{\sqrt{x}}$

**74.** $\dfrac{\sqrt{x}-\dfrac{1}{4\sqrt{x}}}{\sqrt{x}}$

**75.** $\dfrac{\dfrac{x^2}{\sqrt{x^2+2}}-\sqrt{x^2+2}}{x^2}$

**76.** $\dfrac{\sqrt{5-x^2}+\dfrac{x^2}{\sqrt{5-x^2}}}{5-x^2}$

**77.** $\dfrac{\dfrac{1}{\sqrt{x+h}}-\dfrac{1}{\sqrt{x}}}{h}$

**78.** $\dfrac{\dfrac{1}{\sqrt{x+3}}-\dfrac{1}{\sqrt{x}}}{3}$

*In Exercises 79–82, rationalize the numerator.*

**79.** $\dfrac{\sqrt{x+5}-\sqrt{x}}{5}$

**80.** $\dfrac{\sqrt{x+7}-\sqrt{x}}{7}$

**81.** $\dfrac{\sqrt{x}+\sqrt{y}}{x^2-y^2}$

**82.** $\dfrac{\sqrt{x}-\sqrt{y}}{x^2-y^2}$

## Practice Plus

*In Exercises 83–90, perform the indicated operations. Simplify the result, if possible.*

**83.** $\left(\dfrac{2x+3}{x+1}\cdot\dfrac{x^2+4x-5}{2x^2+x-3}\right) - \dfrac{2}{x+2}$

**84.** $\dfrac{1}{x^2-2x-8} \div \left(\dfrac{1}{x-4}-\dfrac{1}{x+2}\right)$

**85.** $\left(2-\dfrac{6}{x+1}\right)\left(1+\dfrac{3}{x-2}\right)$

**86.** $\left(4-\dfrac{3}{x+2}\right)\left(1+\dfrac{5}{x-1}\right)$

**87.** $\dfrac{y^{-1}-(y+5)^{-1}}{5}$

**88.** $\dfrac{y^{-1}-(y+2)^{-1}}{2}$

**89.** $\left(\dfrac{1}{a^3-b^3}\cdot\dfrac{ac+ad-bc-bd}{1}\right) - \dfrac{c-d}{a^2+ab+b^2}$

**90.** $\dfrac{ab}{a^2+ab+b^2} + \left(\dfrac{ac-ad-bc+bd}{ac-ad+bc-bd} \div \dfrac{a^3-b^3}{a^3+b^3}\right)$

## Application Exercises

**91.** The rational expression

$$\dfrac{130x}{100-x}$$

describes the cost, in millions of dollars, to inoculate $x$ percent of the population against a particular strain of flu.

**a.** Evaluate the expression for $x = 40$, $x = 80$, and $x = 90$. Describe the meaning of each evaluation in terms of percentage inoculated and cost.

**b.** For what value of $x$ is the expression undefined?

**c.** What happens to the cost as $x$ approaches 100%? How can you interpret this observation?

**92.** The average rate on a round-trip commute having a one-way distance $d$ is given by the complex rational expression

$$\frac{2d}{\dfrac{d}{r_1} + \dfrac{d}{r_2}},$$

in which $r_1$ and $r_2$ are the average rates on the outgoing and return trips, respectively. Simplify the expression. Then find your average rate if you drive to campus averaging 40 miles per hour and return home on the same route averaging 30 miles per hour. Explain why the answer is not 35 miles per hour.

**93.** The bar graph shows the estimated number of calories per day needed to maintain energy balance for various gender and age groups for moderately active lifestyles. (Moderately active means a lifestyle that includes physical activity equivalent to walking 1.5 to 3 miles per day at 3 to 4 miles per hour, in addition to the light physical activity associated with typical day-to-day life.)

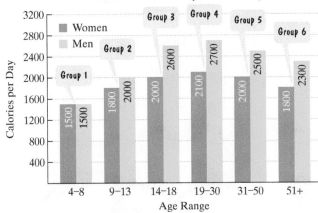

**Calories Needed to Maintain Energy Balance for Moderately Active Lifestyles**

*Source:* U.S.D.A.

**a.** The mathematical model

$$W = -66x^2 + 526x + 1030$$

describes the number of calories needed per day, $W$, by women in age group $x$ with moderately active lifestyles. According to the model, how many calories per day are needed by women between the ages of 19 and 30, inclusive, with this lifestyle? Does this underestimate or overestimate the number shown by the graph? By how much?

**b.** The mathematical model

$$M = -120x^2 + 998x + 590$$

describes the number of calories needed per day, $M$, by men in age group $x$ with moderately active lifestyles. According to the model, how many calories per day are needed by men between the ages of 19 and 30, inclusive, with this lifestyle? Does this underestimate or overestimate the number shown by the graph? By how much?

**c.** Write a simplified rational expression that describes the ratio of the number of calories needed per day by women in age group $x$ to the number of calories needed per day by men in age group $x$ for people with moderately active lifestyles.

**94.** If three resistors with resistances $R_1$, $R_2$, and $R_3$ are connected in parallel, their combined resistance is given by the expression

$$\frac{1}{\dfrac{1}{R_1} + \dfrac{1}{R_2} + \dfrac{1}{R_3}}.$$

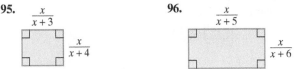

Simplify the complex rational expression. Then find the combined resistance when $R_1$ is 4 ohms, $R_2$ is 8 ohms, and $R_3$ is 12 ohms.

*In Exercises 95–96, express the perimeter of each rectangle as a single rational expression.*

**95.** $\dfrac{x}{x+3}$ ; $\dfrac{x}{x+4}$

**96.** $\dfrac{x}{x+5}$ ; $\dfrac{x}{x+6}$

## Writing in Mathematics

**97.** What is a rational expression?

**98.** Explain how to determine which numbers must be excluded from the domain of a rational expression.

**99.** Explain how to simplify a rational expression.

**100.** Explain how to multiply rational expressions.

**101.** Explain how to divide rational expressions.

**102.** Explain how to add or subtract rational expressions with the same denominators.

**103.** Explain how to add rational expressions having no common factors in their denominators. Use $\dfrac{3}{x+5} + \dfrac{7}{x+2}$ in your explanation.

**104.** Explain how to find the least common denominator for denominators of $x^2 - 100$ and $x^2 - 20x + 100$.

**105.** Describe two ways to simplify $\dfrac{\dfrac{3}{x} + \dfrac{2}{x^2}}{\dfrac{1}{x^2} + \dfrac{2}{x}}$.

*Explain the error in Exercises 106–108. Then rewrite the right side of the equation to correct the error that now exists.*

**106.** $\dfrac{1}{a} + \dfrac{1}{b} = \dfrac{1}{a+b}$

**107.** $\dfrac{1}{x} + 7 = \dfrac{1}{x+7}$

**108.** $\dfrac{a}{x} + \dfrac{a}{b} = \dfrac{a}{x+b}$

## Critical Thinking Exercises

**Make Sense?** *In Exercises 109–112, determine whether each statement makes sense or does not make sense, and explain your reasoning.*

**109.** I evaluated $\dfrac{3x-3}{4x(x-1)}$ for $x = 1$ and obtained 0.

**110.** The rational expressions

$$\frac{7}{14x} \quad \text{and} \quad \frac{7}{14+x}$$

can both be simplified by dividing each numerator and each denominator by 7.

**111.** When performing the division

$$\frac{7x}{x+3} \div \frac{(x+3)^2}{x-5},$$

I began by dividing the numerator and the denominator by the common factor, $x + 3$.

**112.** I subtracted $\frac{3x-5}{x-1}$ from $\frac{x-3}{x-1}$ and obtained a constant.

*In Exercises 113–116, determine whether each statement is true or false. If the statement is false, make the necessary change(s) to produce a true statement.*

**113.** $\frac{x^2 - 25}{x - 5} = x - 5$

**114.** The expression $\frac{-3y - 6}{y + 2}$ simplifies to the consecutive integer that follows $-4$.

**115.** $\frac{2x-1}{x-7} + \frac{3x-1}{x-7} - \frac{5x-2}{x-7} = 0$

**116.** $6 + \frac{1}{x} = \frac{7}{x}$

*In Exercises 117–119, perform the indicated operations.*

**117.** $\frac{1}{x^n - 1} - \frac{1}{x^n + 1} - \frac{1}{x^{2n} - 1}$

**118.** $\left(1 - \frac{1}{x}\right)\left(1 - \frac{1}{x+1}\right)\left(1 - \frac{1}{x+2}\right)\left(1 - \frac{1}{x+3}\right)$

**119.** $(x - y)^{-1} + (x - y)^{-2}$

**120.** In one short sentence, five words or less, explain what

$$\frac{\dfrac{1}{x} + \dfrac{1}{x^2} + \dfrac{1}{x^3}}{\dfrac{1}{x^4} + \dfrac{1}{x^5} + \dfrac{1}{x^6}}$$

does to each number $x$.

## Preview Exercises

*Exercises 121–123 will help you prepare for the material covered in the next section.*

**121.** If 6 is substituted for $x$ in the equation

$$2(x - 3) - 17 = 13 - 3(x + 2),$$

is the resulting statement true or false?

**122.** Multiply and simplify: $12\left(\dfrac{x+2}{4} - \dfrac{x-1}{3}\right)$.

**123.** Evaluate

$$\frac{-b - \sqrt{b^2 - 4ac}}{2a}$$

for $a = 2$, $b = 9$, and $c = -5$.

---

Section **P.7**

# Equations

## Objectives

1. Solve linear equations in one variable.
2. Solve linear equations containing fractions.
3. Solve rational equations with variables in the denominators.
4. Solve a formula for a variable.
5. Solve equations involving absolute value.
6. Solve quadratic equations by factoring.
7. Solve quadratic equations by the square root property.
8. Solve quadratic equations by completing the square.
9. Solve quadratic equations using the quadratic formula.
10. Use the discriminant to determine the number and type of solutions of quadratic equations.
11. Determine the most efficient method to use when solving a quadratic equation.
12. Solve radical equations.

**M**ath tattoos. Who knew? Do you recognize the significance of this tattoo? The algebraic expression gives the solutions of a *quadratic equation.*

In this section, we will review how to solve a variety of equations, including linear equations, quadratic equations, and radical equations.

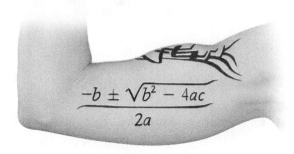

$$\frac{-b \pm \sqrt{b^2 - 4ac}}{2a}$$

## Solving Linear Equations in One Variable

We begin with a general definition of a linear equation in one variable.

### Definition of a Linear Equation

A **linear equation in one variable** $x$ is an equation that can be written in the form

$$ax + b = 0,$$

where $a$ and $b$ are real numbers, and $a \neq 0$.

An example of a linear equation in one variable is

$$4x + 12 = 0.$$

**Solving an equation** in $x$ involves determining all values of $x$ that result in a true statement when substituted into the equation. Such values are **solutions**, or **roots**, of the equation. For example, substitute $-3$ for $x$ in $4x + 12 = 0$. We obtain

$$4(-3) + 12 = 0, \quad \text{or} \quad -12 + 12 = 0.$$

This simplifies to the true statement $0 = 0$. Thus, $-3$ is a solution of the equation $4x + 12 = 0$. We also say that $-3$ **satisfies** the equation $4x + 12 = 0$, because when we substitute $-3$ for $x$, a true statement results. The set of all such solutions is called the equation's **solution set**. For example, the solution set of the equation $4x + 12 = 0$ is $\{-3\}$ because $-3$ is the equation's only solution.

Two or more equations that have the same solution set are called **equivalent equations**. For example, the equations

$$4x + 12 = 0 \quad \text{and} \quad 4x = -12 \quad \text{and} \quad x = -3$$

are equivalent equations because the solution set for each is $\{-3\}$. To solve a linear equation in $x$, we transform the equation into an equivalent equation one or more times. Our final equivalent equation should be of the form

$$x = \text{a number.}$$

The solution set of this equation is the set consisting of the number.

To generate equivalent equations, we will use the following principles:

## Generating Equivalent Equations

An equation can be transformed into an equivalent equation by one or more of the following operations:

**Example**

1. Simplify an expression by removing grouping symbols and combining like terms.

$$3(x - 6) = 6x - x$$
$$3x - 18 = 5x$$

2. Add (or subtract) the same real number or variable expression on *both* sides of the equation.

$$3x - 18 = 5x$$
$$3x - 18 - 3x = 5x - 3x \quad \boxed{\text{Subtract } 3x \text{ from both sides of the equation.}}$$
$$-18 = 2x$$

3. Multiply (or divide) by the same *nonzero* quantity on *both* sides of the equation.

$$-18 = 2x$$
$$\frac{-18}{2} = \frac{2x}{2} \quad \boxed{\text{Divide both sides of the equation by 2.}}$$
$$-9 = x$$

4. Interchange the two sides of the equation.

$$-9 = x$$
$$x = -9$$

If you look closely at the equations in the box, you will notice that we have solved the equation $3(x - 6) = 6x - x$. The final equation, $x = -9$, with $x$ isolated on the left side, shows that $\{-9\}$ is the solution set. The idea in solving a linear equation is to get the variable by itself on one side of the equal sign and a number by itself on the other side.

① Solve linear equations in one variable.

Here is a step-by-step procedure for solving a linear equation in one variable. Not all of these steps are necessary to solve every equation.

### Solving a Linear Equation

1. Simplify the algebraic expression on each side by removing grouping symbols and combining like terms.
2. Collect all the variable terms on one side and all the numbers, or constant terms, on the other side.
3. Isolate the variable and solve.
4. Check the proposed solution in the original equation.

**EXAMPLE 1** Solving a Linear Equation

Solve and check: $2(x - 3) - 17 = 13 - 3(x + 2)$.

**Solution**

**Step 1   Simplify the algebraic expression on each side.**

> Do not begin with $13 - 3$. Multiplication (the distributive property) is applied before subtraction.

$$2(x - 3) - 17 = 13 - 3(x + 2) \quad \text{This is the given equation.}$$
$$2x - 6 - 17 = 13 - 3x - 6 \quad \text{Use the distributive property.}$$
$$2x - 23 = -3x + 7 \quad \text{Combine like terms.}$$

**Step 2   Collect variable terms on one side and constant terms on the other side.** We will collect variable terms on the left by adding $3x$ to both sides. We will collect the numbers on the right by adding 23 to both sides.

$$2x - 23 + 3x = -3x + 7 + 3x \quad \text{Add } 3x \text{ to both sides.}$$
$$5x - 23 = 7 \quad \text{Simplify: } 2x + 3x = 5x.$$
$$5x - 23 + 23 = 7 + 23 \quad \text{Add 23 to both sides.}$$
$$5x = 30 \quad \text{Simplify.}$$

**Step 3   Isolate the variable and solve.** We isolate the variable, $x$, by dividing both sides of $5x = 30$ by 5.

$$\frac{5x}{5} = \frac{30}{5} \quad \text{Divide both sides by 5.}$$
$$x = 6 \quad \text{Simplify.}$$

**Step 4   Check the proposed solution in the original equation.** Substitute 6 for $x$ in the original equation.

**Discovery**

Solve the equation in Example 1 by collecting terms with the variable on the right and numerical terms on the left. What do you observe?

$$2(x - 3) - 17 = 13 - 3(x + 2) \quad \text{This is the original equation.}$$
$$2(6 - 3) - 17 \stackrel{?}{=} 13 - 3(6 + 2) \quad \text{Substitute 6 for x.}$$
$$2(3) - 17 \stackrel{?}{=} 13 - 3(8) \quad \text{Simplify inside parentheses.}$$
$$6 - 17 \stackrel{?}{=} 13 - 24 \quad \text{Multiply.}$$
$$-11 = -11 \quad \text{Subtract.}$$

The true statement $-11 = -11$ verifies that the solution set is $\{6\}$.

⊘ Check Point 1   Solve and check:  $4(2x + 1) = 29 + 3(2x - 5)$.

**② Solve linear equations containing fractions.**

## Linear Equations with Fractions

Equations are easier to solve when they do not contain fractions. How do we remove fractions from an equation? We begin by multiplying both sides of the equation by the least common denominator of any fractions in the equation. The least common denominator is the smallest number that all denominators will divide into. Multiplying every term on both sides of the equation by the least common denominator will eliminate the fractions in the equation. Example 2 shows how we "clear an equation of fractions."

**( EXAMPLE 2 ) Solving a Linear Equation Involving Fractions**

Solve and check: $\dfrac{x+2}{4} - \dfrac{x-1}{3} = 2.$

**Solution** The fractional terms have denominators of 4 and 3. The smallest number that is divisible by 4 and 3 is 12. We begin by multiplying both sides of the equation by 12, the least common denominator.

$$\dfrac{x+2}{4} - \dfrac{x-1}{3} = 2 \qquad \text{This is the given equation.}$$

$$12\left(\dfrac{x+2}{4} - \dfrac{x-1}{3}\right) = 12 \cdot 2 \qquad \text{Multiply both sides by 12.}$$

$$12\left(\dfrac{x+2}{4}\right) - 12\left(\dfrac{x-1}{3}\right) = 24 \qquad \begin{array}{l}\text{Use the distributive property and}\\\text{multiply each term on the left by 12.}\end{array}$$

$$\overset{3}{\cancel{12}}\left(\dfrac{x+2}{4}\right) - \overset{4}{\cancel{12}}\left(\dfrac{x-1}{3}\right) = 24 \qquad \begin{array}{l}\text{Divide out common factors in each}\\\text{multiplication on the left.}\end{array}$$

$$3(x+2) - 4(x-1) = 24 \qquad \text{The fractions are now cleared.}$$

$$3x + 6 - 4x + 4 = 24 \qquad \text{Use the distributive property.}$$

$$-x + 10 = 24 \qquad \begin{array}{l}\text{Combine like terms: } 3x - 4x = -x\\\text{and } 6 + 4 = 10.\end{array}$$

$$-x + 10 - 10 = 24 - 10 \qquad \text{Subtract 10 from both sides.}$$

$$-x = 14 \qquad \text{Simplify.}$$

> **We're not finished. A negative sign should not precede the variable.**

Isolate $x$ by multiplying or dividing both sides of this equation by $-1$.

$$\dfrac{-x}{-1} = \dfrac{14}{-1} \qquad \text{Divide both sides by } -1.$$

$$x = -14 \qquad \text{Simplify.}$$

Check the proposed solution. Substitute $-14$ for $x$ in the original equation. You should obtain $2 = 2$. This true statement verifies that the solution set is $\{-14\}$. ●

---

**✅ Check Point 2** Solve and check: $\dfrac{x-3}{4} = \dfrac{5}{14} - \dfrac{x+5}{7}.$

③ Solve rational equations with variables in the denominators.

## Rational Equations

A **rational equation** is an equation containing one or more rational expressions. In Example 2, we solved a rational equation with constants in the denominators. This rational equation was a linear equation. Now, let's consider a rational equation such as

$$\frac{3}{x+6} + \frac{1}{x-2} = \frac{4}{x^2+4x-12}.$$

Can you see how this rational equation differs from the rational equation that we solved earlier? The variable appears in the denominators. Although this rational equation is not a linear equation, the solution procedure still involves multiplying each side by the least common denominator. However, we must avoid any values of the variable that make a denominator zero.

( **EXAMPLE 3** ) **Solving a Rational Equation**

Solve: $\dfrac{3}{x+6} + \dfrac{1}{x-2} = \dfrac{4}{x^2+4x-12}.$

**Solution** To identify values of $x$ that make denominators zero, let's factor $x^2 + 4x - 12$, the denominator on the right. This factorization is also necessary in identifying the least common denominator.

$$\frac{3}{x+6} + \frac{1}{x-2} = \frac{4}{(x+6)(x-2)}$$

This denominator is zero if $x = -6$.   This denominator is zero if $x = 2$.   This denominator is zero if $x = -6$ or $x = 2$.

We see that $x$ cannot equal $-6$ or $2$. The least common denominator is $(x+6)(x-2)$.

$$\frac{3}{x+6} + \frac{1}{x-2} = \frac{4}{(x+6)(x-2)}, \quad x \neq -6, x \neq 2$$

This is the given equation with a denominator factored.

$$(x+6)(x-2)\left(\frac{3}{x+6} + \frac{1}{x-2}\right) = (x+6)(x-2) \cdot \frac{4}{(x+6)(x-2)}$$

Multiply both sides by $(x+6)(x-2)$, the LCD.

$$(x+6)(x-2)\cdot\frac{3}{x+6} + (x+6)(x-2)\cdot\frac{1}{x-2} = (x+6)(x-2)\cdot\frac{4}{(x+6)(x-2)}$$

Use the distributive property and divide out common factors.

$$3(x-2) + 1(x+6) = 4$$

Simplify. This equation is cleared of fractions.

$$3x - 6 + x + 6 = 4$$

Use the distributive property.

$$4x = 4$$

Combine like terms.

$$\frac{4x}{4} = \frac{4}{4}$$

Divide both sides by 4.

$$x = 1$$

Simplify. This is not part of the restriction that $x \neq -6$ and $x \neq 2$.

Check the proposed solution. Substitute 1 for $x$ in the original equation. You should obtain $-\frac{4}{7} = -\frac{4}{7}$. This true statement verifies that the solution set is $\{1\}$. ●

✓ Check Point **3** Solve: $\dfrac{6}{x+3} - \dfrac{5}{x-2} = \dfrac{-20}{x^2+x-6}.$

**EXAMPLE 4** Solving a Rational Equation

Solve: $\dfrac{1}{x+1} = \dfrac{2}{x^2-1} - \dfrac{1}{x-1}$.

**Solution** We begin by factoring $x^2 - 1$.

$$\underbrace{\frac{1}{x+1}}_{\substack{\text{This denominator}\\ \text{is zero if } x=-1.}} = \underbrace{\frac{2}{(x+1)(x-1)}}_{\substack{\text{This denominator}\\ \text{is zero if } x=-1 \text{ or } x=1.}} - \underbrace{\frac{1}{x-1}}_{\substack{\text{This denominator}\\ \text{is zero if } x=1.}}$$

We see that $x$ cannot equal $-1$ or $1$. The least common denominator is $(x+1)(x-1)$.

$$\frac{1}{x+1} = \frac{2}{(x+1)(x-1)} - \frac{1}{x-1}, \quad x \neq -1, x \neq 1 \qquad \text{This is the given equation with a denominator factored.}$$

$$(x+1)(x-1) \cdot \frac{1}{x+1} = (x+1)(x-1)\left(\frac{2}{(x+1)(x-1)} - \frac{1}{x-1}\right) \qquad \begin{array}{l}\text{Multiply both sides by}\\ (x+1)(x-1), \text{ the LCD.}\end{array}$$

$$\cancel{(x+1)}(x-1) \cdot \frac{1}{\cancel{x+1}} = \cancel{(x+1)}\,\cancel{(x-1)} \cdot \frac{2}{\cancel{(x+1)}\,\cancel{(x-1)}} - (x+1)\cancel{(x-1)} \cdot \frac{1}{\cancel{(x-1)}} \qquad \begin{array}{l}\text{Use the distributive property}\\ \text{and divide out common}\\ \text{factors.}\end{array}$$

$$1(x-1) = 2 - (x+1) \qquad \begin{array}{l}\text{Simplify. This equation is}\\ \text{cleared of fractions.}\end{array}$$

$$x - 1 = 2 - x - 1 \qquad \text{Simplify.}$$

$$x - 1 = -x + 1 \qquad \text{Combine numerical terms.}$$

$$x + x - 1 = -x + x + 1 \qquad \text{Add } x \text{ to both sides.}$$

$$2x - 1 = 1 \qquad \text{Simplify.}$$

$$2x - 1 + 1 = 1 + 1 \qquad \text{Add 1 to both sides.}$$

$$2x = 2 \qquad \text{Simplify.}$$

$$\frac{2x}{2} = \frac{2}{2} \qquad \text{Divide both sides by 2.}$$

$$x = 1 \qquad \text{Simplify.}$$

**Study Tip**

Reject any proposed solution that causes any denominator in an equation to equal 0.

The proposed solution, 1, is *not* a solution because of the restriction that $x \neq 1$. There is *no solution to this equation*. The solution set for this equation contains no elements. The solution set is $\varnothing$, the empty set. ●

○ Check Point **4** Solve: $\dfrac{1}{x+2} = \dfrac{4}{x^2-4} - \dfrac{1}{x-2}$.

**④** Solve a formula for a variable.

## Solving a Formula for One of Its Variables

**Solving a formula for a variable** means rewriting the formula so that the variable is isolated on one side of the equation. It does not mean obtaining a numerical value for that variable.

To solve a formula for one of its variables, treat that variable as if it were the only variable in the equation. Think of the other variables as if they were numbers.

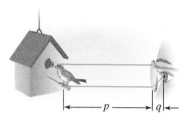

Figure P.12

### EXAMPLE 5 Solving a Formula for a Variable

If you wear glasses, did you know that each lens has a measurement called its focal length, $f$? When an object is in focus, its distance from the lens, $p$, and the distance from the lens to your retina, $q$, satisfy the formula

$$\frac{1}{p} + \frac{1}{q} = \frac{1}{f}.$$

(See **Figure P.12**.) Solve this formula for $p$.

**Solution** Our goal is to isolate the variable $p$. We begin by multiplying both sides by the least common denominator, $pqf$, to clear the equation of fractions.

| | |
|---|---|
| We need to isolate $p$. $\quad \dfrac{1}{p} + \dfrac{1}{q} = \dfrac{1}{f}$ | This is the given formula. |
| $pqf\left(\dfrac{1}{p} + \dfrac{1}{q}\right) = pqf\left(\dfrac{1}{f}\right)$ | Multiply both sides by $pqf$, the LCD. |
| $pqf\left(\dfrac{1}{p}\right) + pqf\left(\dfrac{1}{q}\right) = pqf\left(\dfrac{1}{f}\right)$ | Use the distributive property on the left side and divide out common factors. |
| $qf + pf = pq$ | Simplify. The formula is cleared of fractions. |

We need to isolate $p$.

**Study Tip**

You cannot solve $qf + pf = pq$ for $p$ by dividing both sides by $q$ and writing

$$\frac{qf + pf}{q} = p.$$

When a formula is solved for a specified variable, that variable must be isolated on one side. The variable $p$ occurs on both sides of

$$\frac{qf + pf}{q} = p.$$

To collect terms with $p$ on one side of the equation, subtract $pf$ from both sides. Then factor $p$ from the two resulting terms on the right to convert two occurrences of $p$ into one.

| | |
|---|---|
| $qf + pf = pq$ | This is the equation cleared of fractions. |
| $qf + pf - pf = pq - pf$ | Subtract $pf$ from both sides. |
| $qf = pq - pf$ | Simplify. |
| $qf = p(q - f)$ | Factor out $p$, the specified variable. |
| $\dfrac{qf}{q - f} = \dfrac{p(q - f)}{q - f}$ | Divide both sides by $q - f$ and solve for $p$. |
| $\dfrac{qf}{q - f} = p$ | Simplify. ● |

Check Point **5** Solve for $q$: $\dfrac{1}{p} + \dfrac{1}{q} = \dfrac{1}{f}$.

**⑤** Solve equations involving absolute value.

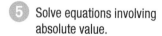

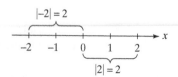

Figure P.13

## Equations Involving Absolute Value

We have seen that the absolute value of $x$, denoted $|x|$, describes the distance of $x$ from zero on a number line. Now consider an **absolute value equation**, such as

$$|x| = 2.$$

This means that we must determine real numbers whose distance from the origin on a number line is 2. **Figure P.13** shows that there are two numbers such that $|x| = 2$, namely, 2 and $-2$. We write $x = 2$ or $x = -2$. This observation can be generalized as follows:

Rewriting an Absolute Value Equation without Absolute Value Bars

If $c$ is a positive real number and $u$ represents any algebraic expression, then $|u| = c$ is equivalent to $u = c$ or $u = -c$.

(EXAMPLE 6) **Solving an Equation Involving Absolute Value**

Solve: $5|1 - 4x| - 15 = 0$.

**Solution**

$$5|1 - 4x| - 15 = 0 \qquad \text{This is the given equation.}$$

We need to isolate $|1 - 4x|$, the absolute value expression.

| | |
|---|---|
| $5|1 - 4x| = 15$ | Add 15 to both sides. |
| $|1 - 4x| = 3$ | Divide both sides by 5. |
| $1 - 4x = 3 \quad \text{or} \quad 1 - 4x = -3$ | Rewrite $|u| = c$ as $u = c$ or $u = -c$. |
| $-4x = 2 \qquad\qquad -4x = -4$ | Subtract 1 from both sides of each equation. |
| $x = -\frac{1}{2} \qquad\qquad x = 1$ | Divide both sides of each equation by $-4$. |

Take a moment to check $-\frac{1}{2}$ and 1, the proposed solutions, in the original equation, $5|1 - 4x| - 15 = 0$. In each case, you should obtain the true statement $0 = 0$. The solution set is $\left\{-\frac{1}{2}, 1\right\}$.

⊘ Check Point **6** Solve: $4|1 - 2x| - 20 = 0$.

The absolute value of a number is never negative. Thus, if $u$ is an algebraic expression and $c$ is a negative number, then $|u| = c$ has no solution. For example, the equation $|3x - 6| = -2$ has no solution because $|3x - 6|$ cannot be negative. The solution set is $\varnothing$, the empty set.

The absolute value of 0 is 0. Thus, if $u$ is an algebraic expression and $|u| = 0$, the solution is found by solving $u = 0$. For example, the solution of $|x - 2| = 0$ is obtained by solving $x - 2 = 0$. The solution is 2 and the solution set is $\{2\}$.

**⑥** Solve quadratic equations by factoring.

## Quadratic Equations and Factoring

Linear equations are first-degree polynomial equations of the form $ax + b = 0$. *Quadratic equations* are second-degree polynomial equations and contain an additional term involving the square of the variable.

Definition of a Quadratic Equation

A **quadratic equation** in $x$ is an equation that can be written in the **general form**

$$ax^2 + bx + c = 0,$$

where $a$, $b$, and $c$ are real numbers, with $a \neq 0$. A quadratic equation in $x$ is also called a **second-degree polynomial equation** in $x$.

Here are examples of quadratic equations in general form:

$$4x^2 - 2x = 0 \qquad\qquad 2x^2 + 7x - 4 = 0.$$

$a = 4 \quad b = -2 \quad c = 0$ $\qquad\qquad$ $a = 2 \quad b = 7 \quad c = -4$

Some quadratic equations, including the two shown above, can be solved by factoring and using the **zero-product principle**.

### The Zero-Product Principle

If the product of two algebraic expressions is zero, then at least one of the factors is equal to zero.

$$\text{If } AB = 0, \text{ then } A = 0 \text{ or } B = 0.$$

The zero-product principle can be applied only when a quadratic equation is in general form, with zero on one side of the equation.

### Solving a Quadratic Equation by Factoring

1. If necessary, rewrite the equation in the general form $ax^2 + bx + c = 0$, moving all terms to one side, thereby obtaining zero on the other side.
2. Factor completely.
3. Apply the zero-product principle, setting each factor containing a variable equal to zero.
4. Solve the equations in step 3.
5. Check the solutions in the original equation.

**EXAMPLE 7** **Solving Quadratic Equations by Factoring**

Solve by factoring:

a. $4x^2 - 2x = 0$  b. $2x^2 + 7x = 4$.

**Solution**

a.

| | |
|---|---|
| $4x^2 - 2x = 0$ | The given equation is in general form, with zero on one side. |
| $2x(2x - 1) = 0$ | Factor. |
| $2x = 0 \quad \text{or} \quad 2x - 1 = 0$ | Use the zero-product principle and set each factor equal to zero. |
| $x = 0 \qquad\qquad 2x = 1$ | Solve the resulting equations. |
| $\qquad\qquad\qquad x = \dfrac{1}{2}$ | |

Check the proposed solutions, $0$ and $\frac{1}{2}$, in the original equation.

| **Check 0:** | **Check $\frac{1}{2}$:** |
|---|---|
| $4x^2 - 2x = 0$ | $4x^2 - 2x = 0$ |
| $4 \cdot 0^2 - 2 \cdot 0 \overset{?}{=} 0$ | $4\left(\frac{1}{2}\right)^2 - 2\left(\frac{1}{2}\right) \overset{?}{=} 0$ |
| $0 - 0 \overset{?}{=} 0$ | $4\left(\frac{1}{4}\right) - 2\left(\frac{1}{2}\right) \overset{?}{=} 0$ |
| $0 = 0, \quad$ true | $1 - 1 \overset{?}{=} 0$ |
| | $0 = 0, \quad$ true |

The solution set is $\left\{0, \frac{1}{2}\right\}$.

b.

| | |
|---|---|
| $2x^2 + 7x = 4$ | This is the given equation. |
| $2x^2 + 7x - 4 = 4 - 4$ | Subtract 4 from both sides and write the quadratic equation in general form. |
| $2x^2 + 7x - 4 = 0$ | Simplify. |
| $(2x - 1)(x + 4) = 0$ | Factor. |
| $2x - 1 = 0 \quad \text{or} \quad x + 4 = 0$ | Use the zero-product principle and set each factor equal to zero. |
| $2x = 1 \qquad\qquad x = -4$ | Solve the resulting equations. |
| $x = \frac{1}{2}$ | |

Check the proposed solutions, $\frac{1}{2}$ and $-4$, in the original equation.

| Check $\frac{1}{2}$: | Check $-4$: |
|---|---|
| $2x^2 + 7x = 4$ | $2x^2 + 7x = 4$ |
| $2\left(\frac{1}{2}\right)^2 + 7\left(\frac{1}{2}\right) \stackrel{?}{=} 4$ | $2(-4)^2 + 7(-4) \stackrel{?}{=} 4$ |
| $\frac{1}{2} + \frac{7}{2} \stackrel{?}{=} 4$ | $32 + (-28) \stackrel{?}{=} 4$ |
| $4 = 4,$ true | $4 = 4,$ true |

The solution set is $\left\{-4, \frac{1}{2}\right\}$.

○ Check Point **7** Solve by factoring:

     **a.** $3x^2 - 9x = 0$      **b.** $2x^2 + x = 1$.

**7** Solve quadratic equations by the square root property.

## Quadratic Equations and the Square Root Property

Quadratic equations of the form $u^2 = d$, where $u$ is an algebraic expression and $d$ is a nonzero real number, can be solved by the *square root property*. First, isolate the squared expression $u^2$ on one side of the equation and the number $d$ on the other side. Then take the square root of both sides. Remember, there are two numbers whose square is $d$. One number is $\sqrt{d}$ and one is $-\sqrt{d}$.

     We can use factoring to verify that $u^2 = d$ has these two solutions.

| | |
|---|---|
| $u^2 = d$ | This is the given equation. |
| $u^2 - d = 0$ | Move all terms to one side and obtain zero on the other side. |
| $\left(u + \sqrt{d}\right)\left(u - \sqrt{d}\right) = 0$ | Factor. |
| $u + \sqrt{d} = 0$   or   $u - \sqrt{d} = 0$ | Set each factor equal to zero. |
| $u = -\sqrt{d}$        $u = \sqrt{d}$ | Solve the resulting equations. |

Because the solutions differ only in sign, we can write them in abbreviated notation as $u = \pm\sqrt{d}$. We read this as "$u$ equals positive or negative square root of $d$" or "$u$ equals plus or minus square root of $d$."

     Now that we have verified these solutions, we can solve $u^2 = d$ directly by taking square roots. This process is called the **square root property**.

---

### The Square Root Property

If $u$ is an algebraic expression and $d$ is a positive real number, then $u^2 = d$ has exactly two solutions:

$$\text{If } u^2 = d, \text{ then } u = \sqrt{d} \text{ or } u = -\sqrt{d}.$$

Equivalently,

$$\text{If } u^2 = d, \text{ then } u = \pm\sqrt{d}.$$

---

**EXAMPLE 8**   **Solving Quadratic Equations by the Square Root Property**

Solve by the square root property:

     **a.** $3x^2 - 15 = 0$      **b.** $(x - 2)^2 = 6$.

**Solution**   To apply the square root property, we need a squared expression by itself on one side of the equation.

$$3x^2 - 15 = 0 \qquad\qquad (x - 2)^2 = 6$$

We want $x^2$ by itself.

The squared expression is by itself.

a.     $3x^2 - 15 = 0$          This is the original equation.

$3x^2 = 15$          Add 15 to both sides.

$x^2 = 5$          Divide both sides by 3.

$x = \sqrt{5}$ or $x = -\sqrt{5}$          Apply the square root property.
          Equivalently, $x = \pm\sqrt{5}$.

By checking both proposed solutions in the original equation, we can confirm that the solution set is $\{-\sqrt{5}, \sqrt{5}\}$ or $\{\pm\sqrt{5}\}$.

b.   $(x - 2)^2 = 6$          This is the original equation.

$x - 2 = \pm\sqrt{6}$          Apply the square root property.

$x = 2 \pm \sqrt{6}$          Add 2 to both sides.

By checking both values in the original equation, we can confirm that the solution set is $\{2 + \sqrt{6}, 2 - \sqrt{6}\}$ or $\{2 \pm \sqrt{6}\}$.     ⬤

⊘ Check Point **8** Solve by the square root property:

a.  $3x^2 - 21 = 0$          b.  $(x + 5)^2 = 11$.

⑧ Solve quadratic equations by completing the square.

## Quadratic Equations and Completing the Square

How do we solve an equation in the form $ax^2 + bx + c = 0$ if the trinomial $ax^2 + bx + c$ cannot be factored? We cannot use the zero-product principle in such a case. However, we can convert the equation into an equivalent equation that can be solved using the square root property. This is accomplished by **completing the square**.

### Completing the Square

If $x^2 + bx$ is a binomial, then by adding $\left(\dfrac{b}{2}\right)^2$, which is the square of half the coefficient of $x$, a perfect square trinomial will result. That is,

$$x^2 + bx + \left(\frac{b}{2}\right)^2 = \left(x + \frac{b}{2}\right)^2.$$

We can solve any quadratic equation by completing the square. If the coefficient of the $x^2$-term is one, we add the square of half the coefficient of $x$ to both sides of the equation. **When you add a constant term to one side of the equation to complete the square, be certain to add the same constant to the other side of the equation.** These ideas are illustrated in Example 9.

( EXAMPLE 9 )  **Solving a Quadratic Equation by Completing the Square**

Solve by completing the square:   $x^2 - 6x + 4 = 0$.

**Solution**   We begin by subtracting 4 from both sides. This is done to isolate the binomial $x^2 - 6x$ so that we can complete the square.

$x^2 - 6x + 4 = 0$          This is the original equation.

$x^2 - 6x = -4$          Subtract 4 from both sides.

Next, we work with $x^2 - 6x = -4$ and complete the square. Find half the coefficient of the $x$-term and square it. The coefficient of the $x$-term is $-6$. Half of $-6$ is $-3$ and $(-3)^2 = 9$. Thus, we add 9 to both sides of the equation.

$$x^2 - 6x + 9 = -4 + 9 \qquad \text{Add 9 to both sides of } x^2 - 6x = -4$$
$$\text{to complete the square.}$$

$$(x - 3)^2 = 5 \qquad \text{Factor and simplify.}$$

$$x - 3 = \sqrt{5} \quad \text{or} \quad x - 3 = -\sqrt{5} \qquad \text{Apply the square root property.}$$

$$x = 3 + \sqrt{5} \qquad\qquad x = 3 - \sqrt{5} \qquad \text{Add 3 to both sides in each equation.}$$

The solutions are $3 \pm \sqrt{5}$ and the solution set is $\left\{3 + \sqrt{5}, 3 - \sqrt{5}\right\}$, or $\left\{3 \pm \sqrt{5}\right\}$.

**Check Point 9** Solve by completing the square: $x^2 + 4x - 1 = 0$.

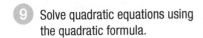

⑨ Solve quadratic equations using the quadratic formula.

## Quadratic Equations and the Quadratic Formula

We can use the method of completing the square to derive a formula that can be used to solve all quadratic equations. The derivation given here also shows a particular quadratic equation, $3x^2 - 2x - 4 = 0$, to specifically illustrate each of the steps.

Notice that if the coefficient of the $x^2$-term in a quadratic equation is not one, you must divide each side of the equation by this coefficient before completing the square.

### Deriving the Quadratic Formula

| General Form of a Quadratic Equation | Comment | A Specific Example |
|---|---|---|
| $ax^2 + bx + c = 0, a > 0$ | This is the given equation. | $3x^2 - 2x - 4 = 0$ |
| $x^2 + \dfrac{b}{a}x + \dfrac{c}{a} = 0$ | Divide both sides by $a$ so that the coefficient of $x^2$ is 1. | $x^2 - \dfrac{2}{3}x - \dfrac{4}{3} = 0$ |
| $x^2 + \dfrac{b}{a}x = -\dfrac{c}{a}$ | Isolate the binomial by adding $-\dfrac{c}{a}$ on both sides of the equation. | $x^2 - \dfrac{2}{3}x = \dfrac{4}{3}$ |
| $x^2 + \dfrac{b}{a}x + \left(\dfrac{b}{2a}\right)^2 = -\dfrac{c}{a} + \left(\dfrac{b}{2a}\right)^2$ $\underbrace{\qquad\qquad}_{(\text{half})^2}$ $x^2 + \dfrac{b}{a}x + \dfrac{b^2}{4a^2} = -\dfrac{c}{a} + \dfrac{b^2}{4a^2}$ | Complete the square. Add the square of half the coefficient of $x$ to both sides. | $x^2 - \dfrac{2}{3}x + \left(-\dfrac{1}{3}\right)^2 = \dfrac{4}{3} + \left(-\dfrac{1}{3}\right)^2$ $\underbrace{\qquad\qquad}_{(\text{half})^2}$ $x^2 - \dfrac{2}{3}x + \dfrac{1}{9} = \dfrac{4}{3} + \dfrac{1}{9}$ |
| $\left(x + \dfrac{b}{2a}\right)^2 = -\dfrac{c}{a}\cdot\dfrac{4a}{4a} + \dfrac{b^2}{4a^2}$ | Factor on the left side and obtain a common denominator on the right side. | $\left(x - \dfrac{1}{3}\right)^2 = \dfrac{4}{3}\cdot\dfrac{3}{3} + \dfrac{1}{9}$ |
| $\left(x + \dfrac{b}{2a}\right)^2 = \dfrac{-4ac + b^2}{4a^2}$ $\left(x + \dfrac{b}{2a}\right)^2 = \dfrac{b^2 - 4ac}{4a^2}$ | Add fractions on the right side. | $\left(x - \dfrac{1}{3}\right)^2 = \dfrac{12 + 1}{9}$ $\left(x - \dfrac{1}{3}\right)^2 = \dfrac{13}{9}$ |
| $x + \dfrac{b}{2a} = \pm\sqrt{\dfrac{b^2 - 4ac}{4a^2}}$ | Apply the square root property. | $x - \dfrac{1}{3} = \pm\sqrt{\dfrac{13}{9}}$ |
| $x + \dfrac{b}{2a} = \pm\dfrac{\sqrt{b^2 - 4ac}}{2a}$ | Take the square root of the quotient, simplifying the denominator. | $x - \dfrac{1}{3} = \pm\dfrac{\sqrt{13}}{3}$ |
| $x = \dfrac{-b}{2a} \pm \dfrac{\sqrt{b^2 - 4ac}}{2a}$ | Solve for $x$ by subtracting $\dfrac{b}{2a}$ from both sides. | $x = \dfrac{1}{3} \pm \dfrac{\sqrt{13}}{3}$ |
| $x = \dfrac{-b \pm \sqrt{b^2 - 4ac}}{2a}$ | Combine fractions on the right side. | $x = \dfrac{1 \pm \sqrt{13}}{3}$ |

The formula shown at the bottom of the left column is called the *quadratic formula*. A similar proof shows that the same formula can be used to solve quadratic equations if $a$, the coefficient of the $x^2$-term, is negative.

### The Quadratic Formula

The solutions of a quadratic equation in general form $ax^2 + bx + c = 0$, with $a \neq 0$, are given by the **quadratic formula**

$$x = \frac{-b \pm \sqrt{b^2 - 4ac}}{2a}.$$

> $x$ equals negative $b$ plus or minus the square root of $b^2 - 4ac$, all divided by $2a$.

To use the quadratic formula, write the quadratic equation in general form if necessary. Then determine the numerical values for $a$ (the coefficient of the $x^2$-term), $b$ (the coefficient of the $x$-term), and $c$ (the constant term). Substitute the values of $a$, $b$, and $c$ into the quadratic formula and evaluate the expression. The $\pm$ sign indicates that there are two solutions of the equation.

**EXAMPLE 10**  **Solving a Quadratic Equation Using the Quadratic Formula**

Solve using the quadratic formula:   $2x^2 - 6x + 1 = 0$.

**Solution**   The given equation is in general form. Begin by identifying the values for $a$, $b$, and $c$.

$$2x^2 - 6x + 1 = 0$$

$a = 2$    $b = -6$    $c = 1$

Substituting these values into the quadratic formula and simplifying gives the equation's solutions.

$$x = \frac{-b \pm \sqrt{b^2 - 4ac}}{2a}$$   Use the quadratic formula.

$$= \frac{-(-6) \pm \sqrt{(-6)^2 - 4(2)(1)}}{2 \cdot 2}$$   Substitute the values for $a$, $b$, and $c$: $a = 2$, $b = -6$, and $c = 1$.

$$= \frac{6 \pm \sqrt{36 - 8}}{4}$$   $-(-6) = 6$, $(-6)^2 = (-6)(-6) = 36$, and $4(2)(1) = 8$.

$$= \frac{6 \pm \sqrt{28}}{4}$$   Complete the subtraction under the radical.

$$= \frac{6 \pm 2\sqrt{7}}{4}$$   $\sqrt{28} = \sqrt{4 \cdot 7} = \sqrt{4}\sqrt{7} = 2\sqrt{7}$

$$= \frac{2(3 \pm \sqrt{7})}{4}$$   Factor out 2 from the numerator.

$$= \frac{3 \pm \sqrt{7}}{2}$$   Divide the numerator and denominator by 2.

**Study Tip**

Checking irrational solutions can be time-consuming. The solutions given by the quadratic formula are always correct, unless you have made a careless error. Checking for computational errors or errors in simplification is sufficient.

The solution set is $\left\{ \dfrac{3 + \sqrt{7}}{2}, \dfrac{3 - \sqrt{7}}{2} \right\}$ or $\left\{ \dfrac{3 \pm \sqrt{7}}{2} \right\}$.

**Check Point 10** Solve using the quadratic formula:

$$2x^2 + 2x - 1 = 0.$$

**10** Use the discriminant to determine the number and type of solutions of quadratic equations.

## Quadratic Equations and the Discriminant

The quantity $b^2 - 4ac$, which appears under the radical sign in the quadratic formula, is called the **discriminant**. **Table P.4** shows how the discriminant of the quadratic equation $ax^2 + bx + c = 0$ determines the number and type of solutions.

**Table P.4** The Discriminant and the Kinds of Solutions to $ax^2 + bx + c = 0$

| Discriminant $b^2 - 4ac$ | Kinds of Solutions to $ax^2 + bx + c = 0$ |
|---|---|
| $b^2 - 4ac > 0$ | **Two unequal real solutions:** If $a$, $b$, and $c$ are rational numbers and the discriminant is a perfect square, the solutions are rational. If the discriminant is not a perfect square, the solutions are irrational. |
| $b^2 - 4ac = 0$ | **One solution (a repeated solution) that is a real number:** If $a$, $b$, and $c$ are rational numbers, the repeated solution is also a rational number. |
| $b^2 - 4ac < 0$ | **No real solutions** |

**(EXAMPLE 11) Using the Discriminant**

Compute the discriminant of $4x^2 - 8x + 1 = 0$. What does the discriminant indicate about the number and type of solutions?

**Solution** Begin by identifying the values for $a$, $b$, and $c$.

$$2x^2 - 6x + 1 = 0$$

$$a = 2 \qquad b = -6 \qquad c = 1$$

Substitute and compute the discriminant:

$$b^2 - 4ac = (-8)^2 - 4 \cdot 4 \cdot 1 = 64 - 16 = 48.$$

The discriminant is 48. Because the discriminant is positive, the equation $4x^2 - 8x + 1 = 0$ has two unequal real solutions. ●

⬦ Check Point **11** Compute the discriminant of $3x^2 - 2x + 5 = 0$. What does the discriminant indicate about the number and type of solutions?

**11** Determine the most efficient method to use when solving a quadratic equation.

## Determining Which Method to Use

All quadratic equations can be solved by the quadratic formula. However, if an equation is in the form $u^2 = d$, such as $x^2 = 5$ or $(2x + 3)^2 = 8$, it is faster to use the square root property, taking the square root of both sides. If the equation is not in the form $u^2 = d$, write the quadratic equation in general form $(ax^2 + bx + c = 0)$. Try to solve the equation by factoring. If $ax^2 + bx + c$ cannot be factored, then solve the quadratic equation by the quadratic formula.

Because we used the method of completing the square to derive the quadratic formula, we no longer need it for solving quadratic equations. However, we will use completing the square later in the book to help graph circles and other kinds of equations.

**Table P.5** on the next page summarizes our observations about which technique to use when solving a quadratic equation.

**Table P.5    Determining the Most Efficient Technique to Use When Solving a Quadratic Equation**

| Description and Form of the Quadratic Equation | Most Efficient Solution Method | Example |
|---|---|---|
| $ax^2 + bx + c = 0$ and $ax^2 + bx + c$ can be factored easily. | Factor and use the zero-product principle. | $3x^2 + 5x - 2 = 0$ <br> $(3x - 1)(x + 2) = 0$ <br> $3x - 1 = 0 \quad$ or $\quad x + 2 = 0$ <br> $x = \dfrac{1}{3} \qquad\qquad x = -2$ |
| $ax^2 + bx = 0$ <br> The quadratic equation has no constant term. $(c = 0)$ | Factor and use the zero-product principle. | $6x^2 + 9x = 0$ <br> $3x(2x + 3) = 0$ <br> $3x = 0 \quad$ or $\quad 2x + 3 = 0$ <br> $x = 0 \qquad\qquad 2x = -3$ <br> $\qquad\qquad\qquad x = -\frac{3}{2}$ |
| $ax^2 + c = 0$ <br> The quadratic equation has no $x$-term. $(b = 0)$ | Solve for $x^2$ and apply the square root property. | $7x^2 - 4 = 0$ <br> $7x^2 = 4$ <br> $x^2 = \dfrac{4}{7}$ <br> $x = \pm\sqrt{\dfrac{4}{7}}$ <br> $= \pm\dfrac{2}{\sqrt{7}} = \pm\dfrac{2}{\sqrt{7}} \cdot \dfrac{\sqrt{7}}{\sqrt{7}} = \pm\dfrac{2\sqrt{7}}{7}$ |
| $u^2 = d$; $u$ is a first-degree polynomial. | Use the square root property. | $(x + 4)^2 = 5$ <br> $x + 4 = \pm\sqrt{5}$ <br> $x = -4 \pm \sqrt{5}$ |
| $ax^2 + bx + c = 0$ and $ax^2 + bx + c$ cannot be factored or the factoring is too difficult. | Use the quadratic formula: <br> $x = \dfrac{-b \pm \sqrt{b^2 - 4ac}}{2a}.$ | $x^2 - 2x - 6 = 0$ <br> $\boxed{a = 1} \quad \boxed{b = -2} \quad \boxed{c = -6}$ <br> $x = \dfrac{-(-2) \pm \sqrt{(-2)^2 - 4(1)(-6)}}{2(1)}$ <br> $= \dfrac{2 \pm \sqrt{4 + 24}}{2(1)}$ <br> $= \dfrac{2 \pm \sqrt{28}}{2} = \dfrac{2 \pm \sqrt{4}\sqrt{7}}{2}$ <br> $= \dfrac{2 \pm 2\sqrt{7}}{2} = \dfrac{2(1 \pm \sqrt{7})}{2}$ <br> $= 1 \pm \sqrt{7}$ |

🕛 Solve radical equations.

## Radical Equations

A **radical equation** is an equation in which the variable occurs in a square root, cube root, or any higher root. An example of a radical equation is

$$\sqrt{x} = 9.$$

We solve the equation by squaring both sides:

Squaring both sides eliminates the square root. $\qquad (\sqrt{x})^2 = 9^2$

$$x = 81.$$

The proposed solution, 81, can be checked in the original equation, $\sqrt{x} = 9$. Because $\sqrt{81} = 9$, the solution is 81 and the solution set is $\{81\}$.

In general, we solve radical equations with square roots by squaring both sides of the equation. We solve radical equations with $n$th roots by raising both sides of the equation to the $n$th power. Unfortunately, if $n$ is even, all the solutions of the equation raised to the even power may not be solutions of the original equation. Consider, for example, the equation

$$x = 4.$$

If we square both sides, we obtain

$$x^2 = 16.$$

Solving this equation using the square root property, we obtain

$$x = \pm\sqrt{16} = \pm 4.$$

The new equation $x^2 = 16$ has two solutions, $-4$ and $4$. By contrast, only $4$ is a solution of the original equation, $x = 4$. For this reason, **when raising both sides of an equation to an even power, always check proposed solutions in the original equation.**

Here is a general method for solving radical equations with $n$th roots:

### Solving Radical Equations Containing $n$th Roots

1. If necessary, arrange terms so that one radical is isolated on one side of the equation.
2. Raise both sides of the equation to the $n$th power to eliminate the isolated $n$th root.
3. Solve the resulting equation. If this equation still contains radicals, repeat steps 1 and 2.
4. Check all proposed solutions in the original equation.

Extra solutions may be introduced when you raise both sides of a radical equation to an even power. Such solutions, which are not solutions of the given equation, are called **extraneous solutions** or **extraneous roots**.

### EXAMPLE 12 Solving a Radical Equation

Solve: $\sqrt{2x - 1} + 2 = x$.

**Solution**

**Step 1  Isolate a radical on one side.** We isolate the radical, $\sqrt{2x - 1}$, by subtracting 2 from both sides.

| | |
|---|---|
| $\sqrt{2x - 1} + 2 = x$ | This is the given equation. |
| $\sqrt{2x - 1} = x - 2$ | Subtract 2 from both sides. |

**Step 2  Raise both sides to the $n$th power.** Because $n$, the index, is 2, we square both sides.

$$\left(\sqrt{2x - 1}\right)^2 = (x - 2)^2$$
$$2x - 1 = x^2 - 4x + 4 \qquad \text{Simplify. Use the formula } (A - B)^2 = A^2 - 2AB + B^2 \text{ on the right side.}$$

**Step 3  Solve the resulting equation.** Because of the $x^2$-term, the resulting equation is a quadratic equation. We can obtain 0 on the left side by subtracting $2x$ and adding 1 on both sides.

| | |
|---|---|
| $2x - 1 = x^2 - 4x + 4$ | The resulting equation is quadratic. |
| $0 = x^2 - 6x + 5$ | Write in general form, subtracting 2x and adding 1 on both sides. |
| $0 = (x - 1)(x - 5)$ | Factor. |
| $x - 1 = 0 \quad \text{or} \quad x - 5 = 0$ | Set each factor equal to 0. |
| $x = 1 \qquad\qquad x = 5$ | Solve the resulting equations. |

### Study Tip

Be sure to square *both sides* of an equation. Do *not* square each term.

**Correct:**

$$\left(\sqrt{2x - 1}\right)^2 = (x - 2)^2$$

**Incorrect!**

**Step 4  Check the proposed solutions in the original equation.**

| Check 1: | Check 5: |
|---|---|
| $\sqrt{2x-1}+2=x$ | $\sqrt{2x-1}+2=x$ |
| $\sqrt{2\cdot1-1}+2\overset{?}{=}1$ | $\sqrt{2\cdot5-1}+2\overset{?}{=}5$ |
| $\sqrt{1}+2\overset{?}{=}1$ | $\sqrt{9}+2\overset{?}{=}5$ |
| $1+2\overset{?}{=}1$ | $3+2\overset{?}{=}5$ |
| $3=1$,  false | $5=5$,  true |

Thus, 1 is an extraneous solution. The only solution is 5, and the solution set is $\{5\}$.

Check Point **12** Solve:  $\sqrt{x+3}+3=x$.

## Exercise Set P.7

### Practice Exercises

*In Exercises 1–16, solve each linear equation.*

**1.** $7x-5=72$       **2.** $6x-3=63$

**3.** $11x-(6x-5)=40$       **4.** $5x-(2x-10)=35$

**5.** $2x-7=6+x$       **6.** $3x+5=2x+13$

**7.** $7x+4=x+16$       **8.** $13x+14=12x-5$

**9.** $3(x-2)+7=2(x+5)$

**10.** $2(x-1)+3=x-3(x+1)$

**11.** $\dfrac{x+3}{6}=\dfrac{3}{8}+\dfrac{x-5}{4}$       **12.** $\dfrac{x+1}{4}=\dfrac{1}{6}+\dfrac{2-x}{3}$

**13.** $\dfrac{x}{4}=2+\dfrac{x-3}{3}$       **14.** $5+\dfrac{x-2}{3}=\dfrac{x+3}{8}$

**15.** $\dfrac{x+1}{3}=5-\dfrac{x+2}{7}$       **16.** $\dfrac{3x}{5}-\dfrac{x-3}{2}=\dfrac{x+2}{3}$

*Exercises 17–26 contain rational equations with variables in denominators. For each equation,* **a.** *Write the value or values of the variable that make a denominator zero. These are the restrictions on the variable.* **b.** *Keeping the restrictions in mind, solve the equation.*

**17.** $\dfrac{1}{x-1}+5=\dfrac{11}{x-1}$       **18.** $\dfrac{3}{x+4}-7=\dfrac{-4}{x+4}$

**19.** $\dfrac{8x}{x+1}=4-\dfrac{8}{x+1}$       **20.** $\dfrac{2}{x-2}=\dfrac{x}{x-2}-2$

**21.** $\dfrac{3}{2x-2}+\dfrac{1}{2}=\dfrac{2}{x-1}$

**22.** $\dfrac{3}{x+3}=\dfrac{5}{2x+6}+\dfrac{1}{x-2}$

**23.** $\dfrac{2}{x+1}-\dfrac{1}{x-1}=\dfrac{2x}{x^2-1}$

**24.** $\dfrac{4}{x+5}+\dfrac{2}{x-5}=\dfrac{32}{x^2-25}$

**25.** $\dfrac{1}{x-4}-\dfrac{5}{x+2}=\dfrac{6}{x^2-2x-8}$

**26.** $\dfrac{1}{x-3}-\dfrac{2}{x+1}=\dfrac{8}{x^2-2x-3}$

*In Exercises 27–42, solve each formula for the specified variable. Do you recognize the formula? If so, what does it describe?*

**27.** $I=Prt$ for $P$       **28.** $C=2\pi r$ for $r$

**29.** $T=D+pm$ for $p$       **30.** $P=C+MC$ for $M$

**31.** $A=\frac{1}{2}h(a+b)$ for $a$       **32.** $A=\frac{1}{2}h(a+b)$ for $b$

**33.** $S=P+Prt$ for $r$       **34.** $S=P+Prt$ for $t$

**35.** $B=\dfrac{F}{S-V}$ for $S$       **36.** $S=\dfrac{C}{1-r}$ for $r$

**37.** $IR+Ir=E$ for $I$       **38.** $A=2lw+2lh+2wh$ for $h$

**39.** $\dfrac{1}{p}+\dfrac{1}{q}=\dfrac{1}{f}$ for $f$       **40.** $\dfrac{1}{R}=\dfrac{1}{R_1}+\dfrac{1}{R_2}$ for $R_1$

**41.** $f=\dfrac{f_1f_2}{f_1+f_2}$ for $f_1$       **42.** $f=\dfrac{f_1f_2}{f_1+f_2}$ for $f_2$

*In Exercises 43–54, solve each absolute value equation or indicate the equation has no solution.*

**43.** $|x-2|=7$       **44.** $|x+1|=5$

**45.** $|2x-1|=5$       **46.** $|2x-3|=11$

**47.** $2|3x-2|=14$       **48.** $3|2x-1|=21$

**49.** $2\left|4-\dfrac{5}{2}x\right|+6=18$       **50.** $4\left|1-\dfrac{3}{4}x\right|+7=10$

**51.** $|x+1|+5=3$       **52.** $|x+1|+6=2$

**53.** $|2x-1|+3=3$       **54.** $|3x-2|+4=4$

*In Exercises 55–60, solve each quadratic equation by factoring.*

**55.** $x^2-3x-10=0$       **56.** $x^2-13x+36=0$

**57.** $x^2=8x-15$       **58.** $x^2=-11x-10$

**59.** $5x^2=20x$       **60.** $3x^2=12x$

In Exercises 61–66, solve each quadratic equation by the square root property.

**61.** $3x^2 = 27$

**62.** $5x^2 = 45$

**63.** $5x^2 + 1 = 51$

**64.** $3x^2 - 1 = 47$

**65.** $3(x - 4)^2 = 15$

**66.** $3(x + 4)^2 = 21$

In Exercises 67–74, solve each quadratic equation by completing the square.

**67.** $x^2 + 6x = 7$

**68.** $x^2 + 6x = -8$

**69.** $x^2 - 2x = 2$

**70.** $x^2 + 4x = 12$

**71.** $x^2 - 6x - 11 = 0$

**72.** $x^2 - 2x - 5 = 0$

**73.** $x^2 + 4x + 1 = 0$

**74.** $x^2 + 6x - 5 = 0$

In Exercises 75–82, solve each quadratic equation using the quadratic formula.

**75.** $x^2 + 8x + 15 = 0$

**76.** $x^2 + 8x + 12 = 0$

**77.** $x^2 + 5x + 3 = 0$

**78.** $x^2 + 5x + 2 = 0$

**79.** $3x^2 - 3x - 4 = 0$

**80.** $5x^2 + x - 2 = 0$

**81.** $4x^2 = 2x + 7$

**82.** $3x^2 = 6x - 1$

Compute the discriminant of each equation in Exercises 83–90. What does the discriminant indicate about the number and type of solutions?

**83.** $x^2 - 4x - 5 = 0$

**84.** $4x^2 - 2x + 3 = 0$

**85.** $2x^2 - 11x + 3 = 0$

**86.** $2x^2 + 11x - 6 = 0$

**87.** $x^2 = 2x - 1$

**88.** $3x^2 = 2x - 1$

**89.** $x^2 - 3x - 7 = 0$

**90.** $3x^2 + 4x - 2 = 0$

In Exercises 91–114, solve each quadratic equation by the method of your choice.

**91.** $2x^2 - x = 1$

**92.** $3x^2 - 4x = 4$

**93.** $5x^2 + 2 = 11x$

**94.** $5x^2 = 6 - 13x$

**95.** $3x^2 = 60$

**96.** $2x^2 = 250$

**97.** $x^2 - 2x = 1$

**98.** $2x^2 + 3x = 1$

**99.** $(2x + 3)(x + 4) = 1$

**100.** $(2x - 5)(x + 1) = 2$

**101.** $(3x - 4)^2 = 16$

**102.** $(2x + 7)^2 = 25$

**103.** $3x^2 - 12x + 12 = 0$

**104.** $9 - 6x + x^2 = 0$

**105.** $4x^2 - 16 = 0$

**106.** $3x^2 - 27 = 0$

**107.** $x^2 = 4x - 2$

**108.** $x^2 = 6x - 7$

**109.** $2x^2 - 7x = 0$

**110.** $2x^2 + 5x = 3$

**111.** $\dfrac{1}{x} + \dfrac{1}{x + 2} = \dfrac{1}{3}$

**112.** $\dfrac{1}{x} + \dfrac{1}{x + 3} = \dfrac{1}{4}$

**113.** $\dfrac{2x}{x - 3} + \dfrac{6}{x + 3} = -\dfrac{28}{x^2 - 9}$

**114.** $\dfrac{3}{x - 3} + \dfrac{5}{x - 4} = \dfrac{x^2 - 20}{x^2 - 7x + 12}$

In Exercises 115–124, solve each radical equation. Check all proposed solutions.

**115.** $\sqrt{3x + 18} = x$

**116.** $\sqrt{20 - 8x} = x$

**117.** $\sqrt{x + 3} = x - 3$

**118.** $\sqrt{x + 10} = x - 2$

**119.** $\sqrt{2x + 13} = x + 7$

**120.** $\sqrt{6x + 1} = x - 1$

**121.** $x - \sqrt{2x + 5} = 5$

**122.** $x - \sqrt{x + 11} = 1$

**123.** $\sqrt{2x + 19} - 8 = x$

**124.** $\sqrt{2x + 15} - 6 = x$

## Practice Plus

In Exercises 125–134, solve each equation.

**125.** $25 - [2 + 5x - 3(x + 2)] =$
$$-3(2x - 5) - [5(x - 1) - 3x + 3]$$

**126.** $45 - [4 - 2x - 4(x + 7)] =$
$$-4(1 + 3x) - [4 - 3(x + 2) - 2(2x - 5)]$$

**127.** $7 - 7x = (3x + 2)(x - 1)$

**128.** $10x - 1 = (2x + 1)^2$

**129.** $|x^2 + 2x - 36| = 12$

**130.** $|x^2 + 6x + 1| = 8$

**131.** $\dfrac{1}{x^2 - 3x + 2} = \dfrac{1}{x + 2} + \dfrac{5}{x^2 - 4}$

**132.** $\dfrac{x - 1}{x - 2} + \dfrac{x}{x - 3} = \dfrac{1}{x^2 - 5x + 6}$

**133.** $\sqrt{x + 8} - \sqrt{x - 4} = 2$

**134.** $\sqrt{x + 5} - \sqrt{x - 3} = 2$

In Exercises 135–136, list all numbers that must be excluded from the domain of each rational expression.

**135.** $\dfrac{3}{2x^2 + 4x - 9}$

**136.** $\dfrac{7}{2x^2 - 8x + 5}$

## Application Exercises

The latest guidelines, which apply to both men and women, give healthy weight ranges, rather than specific weights, for your height. The further you are above the upper limit of your range, the greater are the risks of developing weight-related health problems. The bar graph shows these ranges for various heights for people between the ages of 19 and 34, inclusive.

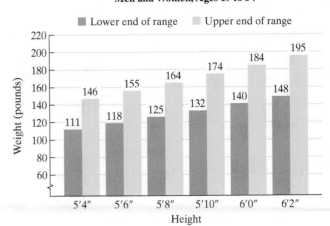

**Healthy Weight Ranges for Men and Women, Ages 19 to 34**

Source: U.S. Department of Health and Human Services

The mathematical model

$$\frac{W}{2} - 3H = 53$$

describes a weight, W, in pounds, that lies within the healthy weight range shown by the bar graph on the previous page for a person whose height is H inches over 5 feet. Use this information to solve Exercises 137–138.

**137.** Use the formula to find a healthy weight for a person whose height is 5′6″. (*Hint:* H = 6 because this person's height is 6 inches over 5 feet.) How many pounds is this healthy weight below the upper end of the range shown by the bar graph on the previous page?

**138.** Use the formula to find a healthy weight for a person whose height is 6′0″. (*Hint:* H = 12 because this person's height is 12 inches over 5 feet.) How many pounds is this healthy weight below the upper end of the range shown by the bar graph on the previous page?

**139.** A company wants to increase the 10% peroxide content of its product by adding pure peroxide (100% peroxide). If x liters of pure peroxide are added to 500 liters of its 10% solution, the concentration, C, of the new mixture is given by

$$C = \frac{x + 0.1(500)}{x + 500}.$$

How many liters of pure peroxide should be added to produce a new product that is 28% peroxide?

**140.** Suppose that x liters of pure acid are added to 200 liters of a 35% acid solution.

**a.** Write a formula that gives the concentration, C, of the new mixture. (*Hint:* See Exercise 139.)

**b.** How many liters of pure acid should be added to produce a new mixture that is 74% acid?

*A driver's age has something to do with his or her chance of getting into a fatal car crash. The bar graph shows the number of fatal vehicle crashes per 100 million miles driven for drivers of various age groups. For example, 25-year-old drivers are involved in 4.1 fatal crashes per 100 million miles driven. Thus, when a group of 25-year-old Americans have driven a total of 100 million miles, approximately 4 have been in accidents in which someone died.*

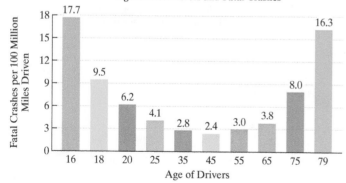

**Age of U.S. Drivers and Fatal Crashes**

*Source:* Insurance Institute for Highway Safety

*The number of fatal vehicle crashes per 100 million miles, y, for drivers of age x can be modeled by the formula*

$$y = 0.013x^2 - 1.19x + 28.24.$$

*Use the formula at the bottom of the previous column to solve Exercises 141–142.*

**141.** What age groups are expected to be involved in 3 fatal crashes per 100 million miles driven? How well does the formula model the trend in the actual data shown by the bar graph in the previous column?

**142.** What age groups are expected to be involved in 10 fatal crashes per 100 million miles driven? How well does the formula model the trend in the actual data shown by the bar graph in the previous column?

*By 2005, the amount of "clutter," including commercials and plugs for other shows, had increased to the point where an "hour-long" drama on cable TV was 45.4 minutes. The bar graph shows the average number of nonprogram minutes in an hour of prime-time cable television.*

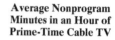

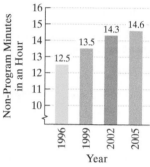

*Source:* Nielsen Monitor-Plus

*The data can be modeled by the formula*

$$M = 0.7\sqrt{x} + 12.5,$$

*where M is the average number of nonprogram minutes in an hour of prime-time cable x years after 1996. Use the formula to solve Exercises 143–144.*

**143.** Assuming the trend from 1996 through 2005 continues, use the model to project when there will be 15.1 cluttered minutes in every prime-time cable TV hour.

**144.** Assuming the trend from 1996 through 2005 continues, use the model to project when there will be 16 cluttered minutes in every prime-time cable TV hour.

## Writing in Mathematics

**145.** What is a linear equation in one variable? Give an example of this type of equation.

**146.** Explain how to determine the restrictions on the variable for the equation

$$\frac{3}{x + 5} + \frac{4}{x - 2} = \frac{7}{x^2 + 3x - 6}.$$

**147.** What does it mean to solve a formula for a variable?

**148.** Explain how to solve an equation involving absolute value.

**149.** Why does the procedure that you explained in Exercise 148 not apply to the equation $|x - 2| = -3$? What is the solution set for this equation?

**150.** What is a quadratic equation?

**151.** Explain how to solve $x^2 + 6x + 8 = 0$ using factoring and the zero-product principle.

**152.** Explain how to solve $x^2 + 6x + 8 = 0$ by completing the square.

**153.** Explain how to solve $x^2 + 6x + 8 = 0$ using the quadratic formula.

**154.** How is the quadratic formula derived?

**155.** What is the discriminant and what information does it provide about a quadratic equation?

**156.** If you are given a quadratic equation, how do you determine which method to use to solve it?

**157.** In solving $\sqrt{2x - 1} + 2 = x$, why is it a good idea to isolate the radical term? What if we don't do this and simply square each side? Describe what happens.

**158.** What is an extraneous solution to a radical equation?

## Critical Thinking Exercises

**Make Sense?** *In Exercises 159–162, determine whether each statement makes sense or does not make sense, and explain your reasoning.*

**159.** The model $P = -0.18n + 2.1$ describes the number of pay phones, $P$, in millions, $n$ years after 2000, so I have to solve a linear equation to determine the number of pay phones in 2006.

**160.** Although I can solve $3x + \frac{1}{5} = \frac{1}{4}$ by first subtracting $\frac{1}{5}$ from both sides, I find it easier to begin by multiplying both sides by 20, the least common denominator.

**161.** Because I want to solve $25x^2 - 169 = 0$ fairly quickly, I'll use the quadratic formula.

**162.** When checking a radical equation's proposed solution, I can substitute into the original equation or any equation that is part of the solution process.

*In Exercises 163–166, determine whether each statement is true or false. If the statement is false, make the necessary change(s) to produce a true statement.*

**163.** The equation $(2x - 3)^2 = 25$ is equivalent to $2x - 3 = 5$.

**164.** Every quadratic equation has two distinct numbers in its solution set.

**165.** The equations $3y - 1 = 11$ and $3y - 7 = 5$ are equivalent.

**166.** The equation $ax^2 + c = 0$, $a \neq 0$, cannot be solved by the quadratic formula.

**167.** Find $b$ such that $\frac{7x + 4}{b} + 13 = x$ will have a solution set given by $\{-6\}$.

**168.** Write a quadratic equation in general form whose solution set is $\{-3, 5\}$.

**169.** Solve for $C$: $V = C - \frac{C - S}{L}N$.

**170.** Solve for $t$: $s = -16t^2 + v_0 t$.

## Preview Exercises

*Exercises 171–173 will help you prepare for the material covered in the next section.*

**171.** Jane's salary exceeds Jim's by $150 per week. If $x$ represents Jim's weekly salary, write an algebraic expression that models Jane's weekly salary.

**172.** A long-distance telephone plan has a monthly fee of $20 with a charge of $0.05 per minute for all long-distance calls. Write an algebraic expression that models the plan's monthly cost for $x$ minutes of long-distance calls.

**173.** If the width of a rectangle is represented by $x$ and the length is represented by $x + 200$, write a simplified algebraic expression that models the rectangle's perimeter.

---

**Section P.8** **Modeling with Equations**

### Objective

① Use equations to solve problems.

**How Long It Takes to Earn $1000**

Howard Stern
Radio host
24 sec.

Dr. Phil McGraw
Television host
2 min. 24 sec.

Brad Pitt
Actor
4 min. 48 sec.

Kobe Bryant
Basketball player
5 min. 30 sec.

Chief executive
U.S. average
2 hr. 55 min.

Doctor, G.P.
U.S. average
13 hr. 5 min.

High school teacher
U.S. average
43 hours

Janitor
U.S. average
103 hours

*Source: Time*

In this section, you'll see examples and exercises focused on how much money Americans earn. These situations illustrate a step-by-step strategy for solving problems. As you become familiar with this strategy, you will learn to solve a wide variety of problems.

① Use equations to solve problems.

## Problem Solving with Equations

We have seen that a model is a mathematical representation of a real-world situation. In this section, we will be solving problems that are presented in English. This means that we must obtain models by translating from the ordinary language of English into the language of algebraic equations. To translate, however, we must understand the English prose and be familiar with the forms of algebraic language. Here are some general steps we will follow in solving word problems:

### Strategy for Solving Word Problems

**Step 1** Read the problem carefully. Attempt to state the problem in your own words and state what the problem is looking for. Let $x$ (or any variable) represent one of the unknown quantities in the problem.

**Step 2** If necessary, write expressions for any other unknown quantities in the problem in terms of $x$.

**Step 3** Write an equation in $x$ that models the verbal conditions of the problem.

**Step 4** Solve the equation and answer the problem's question.

**Step 5** Check the solution *in the original wording* of the problem, not in the equation obtained from the words.

( **EXAMPLE 1** ) **Celebrity Earnings**

*Forbes* magazine published a list of the highest paid TV celebrities between June 2006 and June 2007. The results are shown in **Figure P.14**.

**Highest Paid TV Celebrities between June 2006 and June 2007**

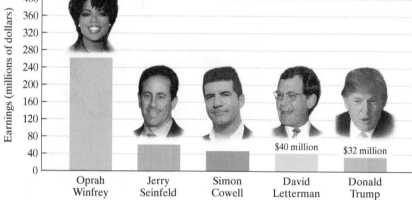

**Figure P.14**
*Source: Forbes*

The bar heights indicate that nobody came close to Oprah, who earned over four times more than any of the other TV stars. Although Seinfeld earned $15 million more than Cowell, Oprah's earnings exceeded Cowell's by $215 million. Combined, these three celebrities earned $365 million. How much did each of them earn?

### Solution

**Step 1 Let $x$ represent one of the unknown quantities.** We know something about Seinfeld's earnings and Oprah's earnings: Seinfeld earned $15 million more than Cowell, and Oprah's earnings exceeded Cowell's by $215 million. We will let

$x$ = Cowell's earnings (in millions of dollars).

**Step 2   Represent other unknown quantities in terms of *x*.** Because Seinfeld earned $15 million more than Cowell, let

$$x + 15 = \text{Seinfeld's earnings.}$$

Because Oprah's earnings exceeded Cowell's by $215 million, let

$$x + 215 = \text{Oprah's earnings.}$$

**Step 3   Write an equation in *x* that models the conditions.** Combined, the three celebrities earned $365 million.

| Oprah's earnings | plus | Seinfeld's earnings | plus | Cowell's earnings | equal | $365 million. |
|:---:|:---:|:---:|:---:|:---:|:---:|:---:|
| $(x + 215)$ | $+$ | $(x + 15)$ | $+$ | $x$ | $=$ | $365$ |

**Step 4   Solve the equation and answer the question.**

$$(x + 215) + (x + 15) + x = 365 \quad \text{This is the equation that models the problem's conditions.}$$

$$3x + 230 = 365 \quad \text{Remove parentheses, regroup, and combine like terms.}$$

$$3x = 135 \quad \text{Subtract 230 from both sides.}$$

$$x = 45 \quad \text{Divide both sides by 3.}$$

Thus,

$$\text{Cowell's earnings} = x = 45$$

$$\text{Seinfeld's earnings} = x + 15 = 45 + 15 = 60$$

$$\text{Oprah's earnings} = x + 215 = 45 + 215 = 260.$$

Between June 2006 and June 2007, Oprah earned $260 million, Seinfeld earned $60 million, and Cowell earned $45 million.

**Step 5   Check the proposed solution in the original wording of the problem.** The problem states that combined, the three celebrities earned $365 million. Using the earnings we determined in step 4, the sum is

$$\$45 \text{ million} + \$60 \text{ million} + \$260 \text{ million,}$$

or $365 million, which verifies the problem's conditions.

### Study Tip

Modeling with the word *exceeds* can be a bit tricky. It's helpful to identify the smaller quantity. Then add to this quantity to represent the larger quantity. For example, suppose that Tim's height exceeds Tom's height by *a* inches. Tom is the shorter person. If Tom's height is represented by *x*, then Tim's height is represented by $x + a$.

✓ Check Point **1**   According to the U.S. Department of Education (2007 data), there is a gap between teaching salaries for men and women at private colleges and universities. The average salary for men exceeds the average salary for women by $14,037. Combined, their average salaries are $130,015. Determine the average teaching salaries at private colleges for women and for men.

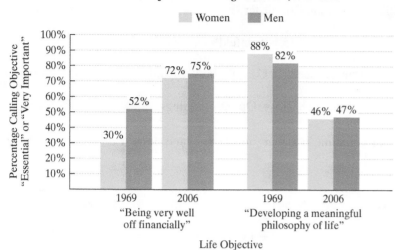

**Figure P.15**
*Source:* John Macionis, *Sociology*, Twelfth
Edition, Prentice Hall, 2008

**EXAMPLE 2** Modeling Attitudes of College Freshmen

Researchers have surveyed college freshmen every year since 1969. **Figure P.15** shows that attitudes about some life goals have changed dramatically. **Figure P.15** shows that the freshmen class of 2006 was more interested in making money than the freshmen of 1969 had been. In 1969, 52% of first-year college men considered "being very well off financially" essential or very important. For the period from 1969 through 2006, this percentage increased by approximately 0.6 each year. If this trend continues, by which year will all male freshmen consider "being very well off financially" essential or very important?

**Solution**

**Step 1  Let $x$ represent one of the unknown quantities.** We are interested in the year when all male freshmen, or 100% of the men, will consider this life objective essential or very important. Let

$x =$ the number of years after 1969 when all
male freshmen will consider "being very
well off financially" essential or very
important.

**Step 2  Represent other unknown quantities in terms of $x$.** There are no other unknown quantities to find, so we can skip this step.

**Step 3  Write an equation in $x$ that models the conditions.**

| The 1969 percentage | increased by | 0.6 each year for $x$ years | equals | 100% of the male freshmen. |
|:---:|:---:|:---:|:---:|:---:|
| 52 | + | 0.6$x$ | = | 100 |

**Step 4  Solve the equation and answer the question.**

$$52 + 0.6x = 100 \qquad \text{This is the equation that models the problem's conditions.}$$

$$52 - 52 + 0.6x = 100 - 52 \qquad \text{Subtract 52 from both sides.}$$

$$0.6x = 48 \qquad \text{Simplify.}$$

$$\frac{0.6x}{0.6} = \frac{48}{0.6} \qquad \text{Divide both sides by 0.6.}$$

$$x = 80 \qquad \text{Simplify.}$$

Using current trends, by 80 years after 1969, or in 2049, all male freshmen will consider "being very well off financially" essential or very important. (Do you agree with this projection that extends so far into the future? Are there unexpected events that might cause model breakdown to occur?)

**Step 5    Check the proposed solution in the original wording of the problem.** The problem states that all men (100%, represented by 100 using the model) will consider the objective essential or very important. Does this occur if we increase the 1969 percentage, 52%, by 0.6 each year for 80 years, our proposed solution?

$$52 + 0.6(80) = 52 + 48 = 100$$

This verifies that using trends shown in **Figure P.15**, all first-year college men will consider the objective essential or very important 80 years after 1969.

Check Point **2** **Figure P.15** shows that the freshmen class of 2006 was less interested in developing a philosophy of life than the freshmen of 1969 had been. In 1969, 88% of the women considered this objective essential or very important. Since then, this percentage has decreased by approximately 1.1 each year. If this trend continues, by which year will only 33% of female freshmen consider "developing a meaningful philosophy of life" essential or very important?

( **EXAMPLE 3** )  **A Price Reduction on a Digital Camera**

Your local computer store is having a terrific sale on digital cameras. After a 40% price reduction, you purchase a digital camera for $276. What was the camera's price before the reduction?

**Solution**

**Step 1    Let $x$ represent one of the unknown quantities.** We will let

$x =$ the original price of the digital camera prior to the reduction.

**Step 2    Represent other unknown quantities in terms of $x$.** There are no other unknown quantities to find, so we can skip this step.

**Step 3    Write an equation in $x$ that models the conditions.** The camera's original price minus the 40% reduction is the reduced price, $276.

| Original price | minus | the reduction (40% of the original price) | is | the reduced price, $276. |
|:---:|:---:|:---:|:---:|:---:|
| $x$ | $-$ | $0.4x$ | $=$ | $276$ |

**Study Tip**

Observe that the original price, $x$, reduced by 40% is $x - 0.4x$ and *not* $x - 0.4$.

**Step 4    Solve the equation and answer the question.**

$x - 0.4x = 276$   This is the equation that models the problem's conditions.

$0.6x = 276$   Combine like terms: $x - 0.4x = 1x - 0.4x = 0.6x$.

$\dfrac{0.6x}{0.6} = \dfrac{276}{0.6}$   Divide both sides by 0.6.

$x = 460$   Simplify: $0.6 \overline{)276.0}$ gives $460$.

The digital camera's price before the reduction was $460.

**Step 5    Check the proposed solution in the original wording of the problem.** The price before the reduction, $460, minus the 40% reduction should equal the reduced price given in the original wording, $276:

$$460 - 40\% \text{ of } 460 = 460 - 0.4(460) = 460 - 184 = 276.$$

This verifies that the digital camera's price before the reduction was $460.

Check Point **3**  After a 30% price reduction, you purchase a new computer for $840. What was the computer's price before the reduction?

Solving geometry problems usually requires a knowledge of basic geometric ideas and formulas. Formulas for area, perimeter, and volume are given in **Table P.6**.

### Table P.6 Common Formulas for Area, Perimeter, and Volume

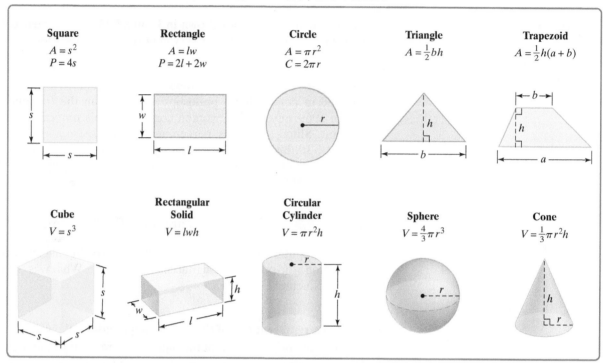

We will be using the formula for the perimeter of a rectangle, $P = 2l + 2w$, in our next example. The formula states that a rectangle's perimeter is the sum of twice its length and twice its width.

**EXAMPLE 4** **Finding the Dimensions of an American Football Field**

The length of an American football field is 200 feet more than the width. If the perimeter of the field is 1040 feet, what are its dimensions?

**Solution**

**Step 1 Let $x$ represent one of the unknown quantities.** We know something about the length; the length is 200 feet more than the width. We will let

$$x = \text{the width.}$$

**Step 2 Represent other unknown quantities in terms of $x$.** Because the length is 200 feet more than the width, we add 200 to the width to represent the length. Thus,

$$x + 200 = \text{the length.}$$

**Figure P.16** illustrates an American football field and its dimensions.

**Step 3 Write an equation in $x$ that models the conditions.** Because the perimeter of the field is 1040 feet,

**Figure P.16** An American football field

| Twice the length | plus | twice the width | is | the perimeter. |
|:---:|:---:|:---:|:---:|:---:|
| $2(x + 200)$ | $+$ | $2x$ | $=$ | $1040.$ |

**Step 4    Solve the equation and answer the question.**

$$2(x + 200) + 2x = 1040$$    This is the equation that models the problem's conditions.

$$2x + 400 + 2x = 1040$$    Apply the distributive property.

$$4x + 400 = 1040$$    Combine like terms: $2x + 2x = 4x$.

$$4x = 640$$    Subtract 400 from both sides.

$$x = 160$$    Divide both sides by 4.

Thus,

$$\text{width} = x = 160.$$
$$\text{length} = x + 200 = 160 + 200 = 360.$$

The dimensions of an American football field are 160 feet by 360 feet. (The 360-foot length is usually described as 120 yards.)

**Step 5    Check the proposed solution in the original wording of the problem.** The perimeter of the football field using the dimensions that we found is

$$2(360 \text{ feet}) + 2(160 \text{ feet}) = 720 \text{ feet} + 320 \text{ feet} = 1040 \text{ feet}.$$

Because the problem's wording tells us that the perimeter is 1040 feet, our dimensions are correct.

⊘ Check Point **4**   The length of a rectangular basketball court is 44 feet more than the width. If the perimeter of the basketball court is 288 feet, what are its dimensions?

We will use the formula for the area of a rectangle, $A = lw$, in our next example. The formula states that a rectangle's area is the product of its length and its width.

( **EXAMPLE 5** )   **Solving a Problem Involving Landscape Design**

A rectangular garden measures 80 feet by 60 feet. A large path of uniform width is to be added along both shorter sides and one longer side of the garden. The landscape designer doing the work wants to double the garden's area with the addition of this path. How wide should the path be?

**Solution**

**Step 1    Let $x$ represent one of the unknown quantities.** We will let

$$x = \text{the width of the path.}$$

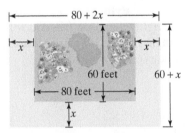

**Figure P.17**   The garden's area is to be doubled by adding the path.

The situation is illustrated in **Figure P.17**. The figure shows the original 80-by-60 foot rectangular garden and the path of width $x$ added along both shorter sides and one longer side.

**Step 2    Represent other unknown quantities in terms of $x$.** Because the path is added along both shorter sides and one longer side, **Figure P.17** shows that

$$80 + 2x = \text{the length of the new, expanded rectangle}$$

$$60 + x = \text{the width of the new, expanded rectangle.}$$

**Step 3    Write an equation in $x$ that models the conditions.** The area of the rectangle must be doubled by the addition of the path.

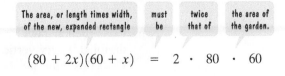

$$(80 + 2x)(60 + x) \;=\; 2 \cdot 80 \cdot 60$$

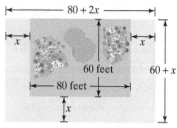

**Figure P.17** (repeated)

**Step 4** **Solve the equation and answer the question.**

$$(80 + 2x)(60 + x) = 2 \cdot 80 \cdot 60$$    This is the equation that models the problem's conditions.

$$4800 + 200x + 2x^2 = 9600$$    Multiply. Use FOIL on the left side.

$$2x^2 + 200x - 4800 = 0$$    Subtract 9600 from both sides and write the quadratic equation in general form.

$$2(x^2 + 100x - 2400) = 0$$    Factor out 2, the GCF.

$$2(x - 20)(x + 120) = 0$$    Factor the trinomial.

$$x - 20 = 0 \quad \text{or} \quad x + 120 = 0$$    Set each variable factor equal to 0.

$$x = 20 \qquad\qquad x = -120$$    Solve for x.

The path cannot have a negative width. Because $-120$ is geometrically impossible, we use $x = 20$. The width of the path should be 20 feet.

**Step 5** **Check the proposed solution in the original wording of the problem.** Has the landscape architect doubled the garden's area with the 20-foot-wide path? The area of the garden is 80 feet times 60 feet, or 4800 square feet. Because $80 + 2x$ and $60 + x$ represent the length and width of the expanded rectangle,

$$80 + 2x = 80 + 2 \cdot 20 = 120 \text{ feet is the expanded rectangle's length.}$$

$$60 + \phantom{2}x = 60 + 20 \phantom{20} = 80 \text{ feet is the expanded rectangle's width.}$$

The area of the expanded rectangle is 120 feet times 80 feet, or 9600 square feet. This is double the area of the garden, 4800 square feet, as specified by the problem's conditions. ●

**◯Check Point 5** A rectangular garden measures 16 feet by 12 feet. A path of uniform width is to be added so as to surround the entire garden. The landscape artist doing the work wants the garden and path to cover an area of 320 square feet. How wide should the path be?

The solution to our next problem relies on knowing the **Pythagorean Theorem**. The theorem relates the lengths of the three sides of a **right triangle**, a triangle with one angle measuring 90°. The side opposite the 90° angle is called the **hypotenuse**. The other sides are called **legs**. The legs form the two sides of the right angle.

### The Pythagorean Theorem

The sum of the squares of the lengths of the legs of a right triangle equals the square of the length of the hypotenuse.

    If the legs have lengths $a$ and $b$, and the hypotenuse has length $c$, then

$$a^2 + b^2 = c^2.$$

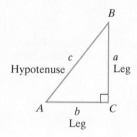

⬭**EXAMPLE 6** **Using the Pythagorean Theorem**

**a.** A wheelchair ramp with a length of 122 inches has a horizontal distance of 120 inches. What is the ramp's vertical distance?

**b.** Construction laws are very specific when it comes to access ramps for the disabled. Every vertical rise of 1 inch requires a horizontal run of 12 inches. Does this ramp satisfy the requirement?

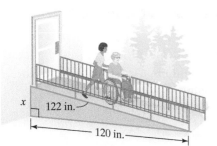

**Figure P.18**

## Solution

**a. Step 1   Let $x$ represent one of the unknown quantities.** We will let

$$x = \text{the ramp's vertical distance.}$$

The situation is illustrated in **Figure P.18**.

**Step 2   Represent other unknown quantities in terms of $x$.** There are no other unknown quantities, so we can skip this step.

**Step 3   Write an equation in $x$ that models the conditions. Figure P.18** shows the right triangle that is formed by the ramp, the wall, and the ground. We can find $x$, the ramp's vertical distance, using the Pythagorean Theorem.

| (leg)² | plus | (leg)² | equals | (hypotenuse)² |
|--------|------|--------|--------|---------------|
| $x^2$ | $+$ | $120^2$ | $=$ | $122^2$ |

**Step 4   Solve the equation and answer the question.** The quadratic equation $x^2 + 120^2 = 122^2$ can be solved most efficiently by the square root property.

$$x^2 + 120^2 = 122^2 \qquad \text{This is the equation resulting from the Pythagorean Theorem.}$$

$$x^2 + 14{,}400 = 14{,}884 \qquad \text{Square 120 and 122.}$$

$$x^2 = 484 \qquad \text{Isolate } x^2 \text{ by subtracting 14,400 from both sides.}$$

$$x = \sqrt{484} \quad \text{or} \quad x = -\sqrt{484} \qquad \text{Apply the square root property.}$$

$$x = 22 \qquad\qquad\quad x = -22 \qquad \text{Simplify.}$$

Because $x$ represents the ramp's vertical distance, this measurement must be positive. We reject $-22$. Thus, the ramp's vertical distance is 22 inches.

**Step 5   Check the proposed solution in the original wording of the problem.** The problem's wording implies that the ramp, the wall, and the ground form a right triangle. This can be checked using the **converse of the Pythagorean Theorem**: If a triangle has sides of lengths $a$, $b$, and $c$, where $c$ is the length of the longest side, and if $a^2 + b^2 = c^2$, then the triangle is a right triangle. Let's check that a vertical distance of 22 inches forms a right triangle with the ramp's length of 122 inches and its horizontal distance of 120 inches. Is $22^2 + 120^2 = 122^2$? Simplifying the arithmetic, we obtain the true statement $14{,}884 = 14{,}884$. Thus, a vertical distance of 22 inches forms a right triangle.

**b.** Every vertical rise of 1 inch requires a horizontal run of 12 inches. Because the ramp has a vertical distance of 22 inches, it requires a horizontal distance of $22(12)$ inches, or 264 inches. The horizontal distance is only 120 inches, so this ramp does not satisfy construction laws for access ramps for the disabled. ●

### Study Tip

The Pythagorean Theorem is an *if . . . then* statement: If a triangle is a right triangle, then $a^2 + b^2 = c^2$. The **converse** of *if p then q* is *if q then p*. Although the converse of a true statement may not be true, the converse of the Pythagorean Theorem is also a true statement: If $a^2 + b^2 = c^2$, then a triangle is a right triangle.

⊘ Check Point **6** A radio tower is supported by two wires that are each 130 yards long and attached to the ground 50 yards from the base of the tower. How tall is the tower?

### Study Tip

There is great value in reasoning through a word problem. This value comes from the problem-solving skills that are attained and is often more important than the specific problem or its solution.

In our final example, the conditions are modeled by a rational equation.

**EXAMPLE 7   Dividing the Cost of a Yacht**

A group of friends agrees to share the cost of a \$50,000 yacht equally. Before the purchase is made, one more person joins the group and enters the agreement. As a result, each person's share is reduced by \$2500. How many people were in the original group?

### Solution

**Step 1   Let $x$ represent one of the unknown quantities.** We will let

$$x = \text{the number of people in the original group.}$$

**Step 2   Represent other unknown quantities in terms of *x*.** Because one more person joined the original group, let

$$x + 1 = \text{the number of people in the final group.}$$

**Step 3   Write an equation in *x* that models the conditions.** As a result of one more person joining the original group, each person's share is reduced by $2500.

| Original cost per person | minus | $2500 | equals | the final cost per person. |
|:---:|:---:|:---:|:---:|:---:|
| $\dfrac{50{,}000}{x}$ | $-$ | $2500$ | $=$ | $\dfrac{50{,}000}{x + 1}$ |

This is the yacht's cost, $50,000, divided by the number of people, *x*.

This is the yacht's cost, $50,000, divided by the number of people, *x* + 1.

**Step 4   Solve the equation and answer the question.**

$$\frac{50{,}000}{x} - 2500 = \frac{50{,}000}{x + 1}$$

This is the equation that models the problem's conditions.

$$x(x + 1)\left(\frac{50{,}000}{x} - 2500\right) = x(x + 1) \cdot \frac{50{,}000}{x + 1}$$

Multiply both sides by $x(x + 1)$, the LCD.

$$\cancel{x}(x + 1) \cdot \frac{50{,}000}{\cancel{x}} - x(x + 1)2500 = x\cancel{(x + 1)} \cdot \frac{50{,}000}{\cancel{(x + 1)}}$$

Use the distributive property and divide out common factors.

$$50{,}000(x + 1) - 2500x(x + 1) = 50{,}000x$$

Simplify.

$$50{,}000x + 50{,}000 - 2500x^2 - 2500x = 50{,}000x$$

Use the distributive property.

$$-2500x^2 + 47{,}500x + 50{,}000 = 50{,}000x$$

Combine like terms: $50{,}000x - 2500x = 47{,}500x$.

$$-2500x^2 - 2500x + 50{,}000 = 0$$

Write the quadratic equation in general form, subtracting $50{,}000x$ from both sides.

$$-2500(x^2 + x - 20) = 0$$

Factor out $-2500$.

$$-2500(x + 5)(x - 4) = 0$$

Factor completely.

$$x + 5 = 0 \quad \text{or} \quad x - 4 = 0$$

Set each variable factor equal to zero.

$$x = -5 \qquad\qquad x = 4$$

Solve the resulting equations.

Because *x* represents the number of people in the original group, *x* cannot be negative. Thus, there were four people in the original group.

**Step 5   Check the proposed solution in the original wording of the problem.**

$$\text{original cost per person} \quad = \frac{\$50{,}000}{4} = \$12{,}500$$

$$\text{final cost per person} \quad = \frac{\$50{,}000}{5} = \$10{,}000$$

We see that each person's share is reduced by $12,500 − $10,000, or $2500, as specified by the problem's conditions.

Check Point **7** A group of people share equally in a $5,000,000 lottery. Before the money is divided, three more winning ticket holders are declared. As a result, each person's share is reduced by $375,000. How many people were in the original group of winners?

# Exercise Set P.8

## Practice and Application Exercises

**1.** The bar graph shows the time Americans spent using various media in 2007.

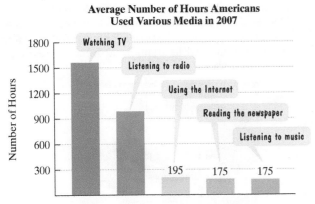

**Average Number of Hours Americans Used Various Media in 2007**

*Source:* Communication Industry Forecast and Report

Time spent watching TV exceeded time spent listening to the radio by 581 hours. The combined time devoted to these two media was 2529 hours. In 2007, how many hours did Americans spend listening to the radio and how many hours were spent watching TV?

**2.** Compared with Europeans, American employees use less vacation time.

**Average Vacation Time for Europeans and Americans**

*Source: The State of Working America 2006/2007*

The average time Italians spend on vacation exceeds the average American vacation time by 4 weeks. The combined average vacation time for Americans and Italians is 11.8 weeks. On average, how many weeks do Americans spend on vacation and how many weeks do Italians spend on vacation?

*Exercises 3–4 involve the average salaries represented by the bar graph.*

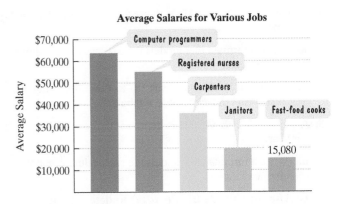

**Average Salaries for Various Jobs**

*Source:* 2007 data from salary.com

**3.** The average salary for computer programmers is $7740 less than twice the average salary for carpenters. Combined, their average salaries are $99,000. Determine the average salary for each of these jobs.

**4.** The average salary for registered nurses is $3500 less than three times the average salary for janitors. Combined, their average salaries are $74,060. Determine the average salary for each of these jobs.

*The bar graph indicates that American attitudes have become more tolerant over two decades on a variety of issues. Exercises 5–6 are based on the data displayed by the graph.*

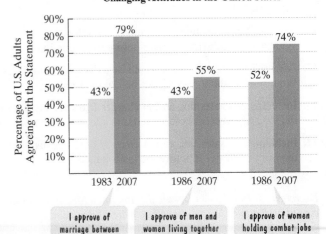

**Changing Attitudes in the United States**

*Source: USA Today*

*(Exercises 5–6 are illustrated by the bar graph at the bottom of the previous page.)*

**5.** In 1983, 43% of U.S. adults approved of marriage between blacks and whites. For the period from 1983 through 2007, the percentage approving of interracial marriage increased on average by 1.5 each year. If this trend continues, by which year will all American adults approve of interracial marriage?

**6.** In 1986, 43% of U.S. adults approved of men and women living together without being married. For the period from 1986 through 2007, the percentage approving of cohabitation increased on average by approximately 0.6 each year. If this trend continues, by which year will 61% of all American adults approve of cohabitation?

**7.** A new car worth $24,000 is depreciating in value by $3000 per year.

    **a.** Write a formula that models the car's value, $y$, in dollars, after $x$ years.

    **b.** Use the formula from part (a) to determine after how many years the car's value will be $9000.

**8.** A new car worth $45,000 is depreciating in value by $5000 per year.

    **a.** Write a formula that models the car's value, $y$, in dollars, after $x$ years.

    **b.** Use the formula from part (a) to determine after how many years the car's value will be $10,000.

**9.** In 2005, there were 13,300 students at college A, with a projected enrollment increase of 1000 students per year. In the same year, there were 26,800 students at college B, with a projected enrollment decline of 500 students per year. According to these projections, when will the colleges have the same enrollment? What will be the enrollment in each college at that time?

**10.** In 2000, the population of Greece was 10,600,000, with projections of a population decrease of 28,000 people per year. In the same year, the population of Belgium was 10,200,000, with projections of a population decrease of 12,000 people per year. (*Source*: United Nations) According to these projections, when will the two countries have the same population? What will be the population at that time?

**11.** After a 20% reduction, you purchase a television for $336. What was the television's price before the reduction?

**12.** After a 30% reduction, you purchase a dictionary for $30.80. What was the dictionary's price before the reduction?

**13.** Including 8% sales tax, an inn charges $162 per night. Find the inn's nightly cost before the tax is added.

**14.** Including 5% sales tax, an inn charges $252 per night. Find the inn's nightly cost before the tax is added.

*Exercises 15–16 involve markup, the amount added to the dealer's cost of an item to arrive at the selling price of that item.*

**15.** The selling price of a refrigerator is $584. If the markup is 25% of the dealer's cost, what is the dealer's cost of the refrigerator?

**16.** The selling price of a scientific calculator is $15. If the markup is 25% of the dealer's cost, what is the dealer's cost of the calculator?

**17.** A rectangular soccer field is twice as long as it is wide. If the perimeter of the soccer field is 300 yards, what are its dimensions?

**18.** A rectangular swimming pool is three times as long as it is wide. If the perimeter of the pool is 320 feet, what are its dimensions?

**19.** The length of the rectangular tennis court at Wimbledon is 6 feet longer than twice the width. If the court's perimeter is 228 feet, what are the court's dimensions?

**20.** The length of a rectangular pool is 6 meters less than twice the width. If the pool's perimeter is 126 meters, what are its dimensions?

**21.** The rectangular painting in the figure shown measures 12 inches by 16 inches and includes a frame of uniform width around the four edges. The perimeter of the rectangle formed by the painting and its frame is 72 inches. Determine the width of the frame.

**22.** The rectangular swimming pool in the figure shown measures 40 feet by 60 feet and includes a path of uniform width around the four edges. The perimeter of the rectangle formed by the pool and the surrounding path is 248 feet. Determine the width of the path.

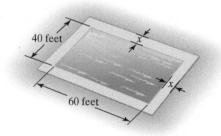

**23.** The length of a rectangular sign is 3 feet longer than the width. If the sign's area is 54 square feet, find its length and width.

**24.** A rectangular parking lot has a length that is 3 yards greater than the width. The area of the parking lot is 180 square yards. Find the length and the width.

**25.** Each side of a square is lengthened by 3 inches. The area of this new, larger square is 64 square inches. Find the length of a side of the original square.

**26.** Each side of a square is lengthened by 2 inches. The area of this new, larger square is 36 square inches. Find the length of a side of the original square.

**27.** A pool measuring 10 meters by 20 meters is surrounded by a path of uniform width. If the area of the pool and the path combined is 600 square meters, what is the width of the path?

**28.** A vacant rectangular lot is being turned into a community vegetable garden measuring 15 meters by 12 meters. A path of uniform width is to surround the garden. If the area of the lot is 378 square meters, find the width of the path surrounding the garden.

**29.** As part of a landscaping project, you put in a flower bed measuring 20 feet by 30 feet. To finish off the project, you are putting in a uniform border of pine bark around the outside of the rectangular garden. You have enough pine bark to cover 336 square feet. How wide should the border be?

**30.** As part of a landscaping project, you put in a flower bed measuring 10 feet by 12 feet. You plan to surround the bed with a uniform border of low-growing plants that require 1 square foot each when mature. If you have 168 of these plants, how wide a strip around the flower bed should you prepare for the border?

**31.** A 20-foot ladder is 15 feet from a house. How far up the house, to the nearest tenth of a foot, does the ladder reach?

**32.** The base of a 30-foot ladder is 10 feet from a building. If the ladder reaches the flat roof, how tall, to the nearest tenth of a foot, is the building?

**33.** A tree is supported by a wire anchored in the ground 5 feet from its base. The wire is 1 foot longer than the height that it reaches on the tree. Find the length of the wire.

**34.** A tree is supported by a wire anchored in the ground 15 feet from its base. The wire is 4 feet longer than the height that it reaches on the tree. Find the length of the wire.

**35.** A rectangular piece of land whose length its twice its width has a diagonal distance of 64 yards. How many yards, to the nearest tenth of a yard, does a person save by walking diagonally across the land instead of walking its length and its width?

**36.** A rectangular piece of land whose length is three times its width has a diagonal distance of 92 yards. How many yards, to the nearest tenth of a yard, does a person save by walking diagonally across the land instead of walking its length and its width?

**37.** A group of people share equally in a $20,000,000 lottery. Before the money is divided, two more winning ticket holders are declared. As a result, each person's share is reduced by $500,000. How many people were in the original group of winners?

**38.** A group of friends agrees to share the cost of a $480,000 vacation condominium equally. Before the purchase is made, four more people join the group and enter the agreement. As a result, each person's share is reduced by $32,000. How many people were in the original group?

*In Exercises 39–42, use the formula*

$$\text{Time traveled} = \frac{\text{Distance traveled}}{\text{Average velocity}}.$$

**39.** A car can travel 300 miles in the same amount of time it takes a bus to travel 180 miles. If the average velocity of the bus is 20 miles per hour slower than the average velocity of the car, find the average velocity for each.

**40.** A passenger train can travel 240 miles in the same amount of time it takes a freight train to travel 160 miles. If the average velocity of the freight train is 20 miles per hour slower than the average velocity of the passenger train, find the average velocity of each.

**41.** You ride your bike to campus a distance of 5 miles and return home on the same route. Going to campus, you ride mostly downhill and average 9 miles per hour faster than on your return trip home. If the round trip takes one hour and ten minutes—that is $\frac{7}{6}$ hours—what is your average velocity on the return trip?

**42.** An engine pulls a train 140 miles. Then a second engine, whose average velocity is 5 miles per hour faster than the first engine, takes over and pulls the train 200 miles. The total time required for both engines is 9 hours. Find the average velocity of each engine.

**43.** An automobile repair shop charged a customer $448, listing $63 for parts and the remainder for labor. If the cost of labor is $35 per hour, how many hours of labor did it take to repair the car?

**44.** A repair bill on a sailboat came to $1603, including $532 for parts and the remainder for labor. If the cost of labor is $63 per hour, how many hours of labor did it take to repair the sailboat?

**45.** An HMO pamphlet contains the following recommended weight for women: "Give yourself 100 pounds for the first 5 feet plus 5 pounds for every inch over 5 feet tall." Using this description, what height corresponds to a recommended weight of 135 pounds?

**46.** A job pays an annual salary of $33,150, which includes a holiday bonus of $750. If paychecks are issued twice a month, what is the gross amount for each paycheck?

**47.** You have 35 hits in 140 times at bat. Your batting average is $\frac{35}{140}$, or 0.25. How many consecutive hits must you get to increase your batting average to 0.30?

**48.** You have 30 hits in 120 times at bat. Your batting average is $\frac{30}{120}$, or 0.25. How many consecutive hits must you get to increase your batting average to 0.28?

## Writing in Mathematics

**49.** In your own words, describe a step-by-step approach for solving algebraic word problems.

**50.** Write an original word problem that can be solved using an equation. Then solve the problem.

**51.** In your own words, state the Pythagorean Theorem.

**52.** In the 1939 movie *The Wizard of Oz*, upon being presented with a Th.D. (Doctor of Thinkology), the Scarecrow proudly exclaims, "The sum of the square roots of any two sides of an isosceles triangle is equal to the square root of the remaining side." Did the Scarecrow get the Pythagorean Theorem right? In particular, describe four errors in the Scarecrow's statement.

## Critical Thinking Exercises

**Make Sense?** *In Exercises 53–56, determine whether each statement makes sense or does not make sense, and explain your reasoning.*

**53.** By modeling attitudes of college freshmen from 1969 through 2006, I can make precise predictions about the attitudes of the freshman class of 2020.

54. I find the hardest part in solving a word problem is writing the equation that models the verbal conditions.

55. After a 35% reduction, a computer's price is $780, so I determined the original price, $x$, by solving $x - 0.35 = 780$.

56. When I use the square root property to determine the length of a right triangle's side, I don't even bother to list the negative square root.

57. The perimeter of a plot of land in the shape of a right triangle is 12 miles. If one leg of the triangle exceeds the other leg by 1 mile, find the length of each boundary of the land.

58. The price of a dress is reduced by 40%. When the dress still does not sell, it is reduced by 40% of the reduced price. If the price of the dress after both reductions is $72, what was the original price?

59. In a film, the actor Charles Coburn plays an elderly "uncle" character criticized for marrying a woman when he is 3 times her age. He wittily replies, "Ah, but in 20 years time I shall only be twice her age." How old is the "uncle" and the woman?

60. Suppose that we agree to pay you 8¢ for every problem in this chapter that you solve correctly and fine you 5¢ for every problem done incorrectly. If at the end of 26 problems we do not owe each other any money, how many problems did you solve correctly?

61. It was wartime when the Ricardos found out Mrs. Ricardo was pregnant. Ricky Ricardo was drafted and made out a will, deciding that $14,000 in a savings account was to be divided between his wife and his child-to-be. Rather strangely, and certainly with gender bias, Ricky stipulated that if the child were a boy, he would get twice the amount of the mother's portion. If it were a girl, the mother would get twice the amount the girl was to receive. We'll never know what Ricky was thinking of, for (as fate would have it) he did not return from war. Mrs. Ricardo gave birth to twins—a boy and a girl. How was the money divided?

62. A thief steals a number of rare plants from a nursery. On the way out, the thief meets three security guards, one after another. To each security guard, the thief is forced to give one-half the plants that he still has, plus 2 more. Finally, the thief leaves the nursery with 1 lone palm. How many plants were originally stolen?

## Group Exercise

63. One of the best ways to learn how to *solve* a word problem in algebra is to *design* word problems of your own. Creating a word problem makes you very aware of precisely how much information is needed to solve the problem. You must also focus on the best way to present information to a reader and on how much information to give. As you write your problem, you gain skills that will help you solve problems created by others.

    The group should design five different word problems that can be solved using equations. All of the problems should be on different topics. For example, the group should not have more than one problem on the perimeter of a rectangle. The group should turn in both the problems and their algebraic solutions.

    (If you're not sure where to begin, consider the graph for Exercises 5–6 and the data that we did not use regarding attitudes about women in combat.)

## Preview Exercises

*Exercises 64–66 will help you prepare for the material covered in the next section.*

64. Is $-1$ a solution of $3 - 2x \leq 11$?

65. Solve: $-2x - 4 = x + 5$.

66. Solve: $\dfrac{x + 3}{4} = \dfrac{x - 2}{3} + \dfrac{1}{4}$.

---

## Section P.9 Linear Inequalities and Absolute Value Inequalities

### Objectives

1. Use interval notation.
2. Find intersections and unions of intervals.
3. Solve linear inequalities.
4. Solve compound inequalities.
5. Solve absolute value inequalities.

Rent-a-Heap, a car rental company, charges $125 per week plus $0.20 per mile to rent one of their cars. Suppose you are limited by how much money you can spend for the week: You can spend at most $335. If we let $x$ represent the number of miles you drive the heap in a week, we can write an inequality that models the given conditions:

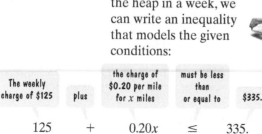

| The weekly charge of $125 | plus | the charge of $0.20 per mile for x miles | must be less than or equal to | $335. |
|---|---|---|---|---|
| 125 | + | 0.20x | ≤ | 335. |

Placing an inequality symbol between a polynomial of degree 1 and a constant results in a *linear inequality in one variable*. In this section, we will study how to solve linear inequalities such as $125 + 0.20x \leq 335$. **Solving an inequality** is the process of finding the set of numbers that make the inequality a true statement. These numbers are called the **solutions** of the inequality and we say that they **satisfy** the inequality. The set of all solutions is called the **solution set** of the inequality. Set-builder notation and a new notation, called *interval notation*, are used to represent these solution sets. We begin this section by looking at interval notation.

**1** Use interval notation.

## Interval Notation

Some sets of real numbers can be represented using **interval notation**. Suppose that $a$ and $b$ are two real numbers such that $a < b$.

| Interval Notation | Graph |
|---|---|
| The **open interval** $(a, b)$ represents the set of real numbers between, but not including, $a$ and $b$. $$(a, b) = \{x \mid a < x < b\}$$ $x$ is greater than $a$ $(a < x)$ and $x$ is less than $b$ $(x < b)$. | The parentheses in the graph and in interval notation indicate that $a$ and $b$, the endpoints, are excluded from the interval. |
| The **closed interval** $[a, b]$ represents the set of real numbers between, and including, $a$ and $b$. $$[a, b] = \{x \mid a \leq x \leq b\}$$ $x$ is greater than or equal to $a$ $(a \leq x)$ and $x$ is less than or equal to $b$ $(x \leq b)$. | The square brackets in the graph and in interval notation indicate that $a$ and $b$, the endpoints, are included in the interval. |
| The **infinite interval** $(a, \infty)$ represents the set of real numbers that are greater than $a$. $$(a, \infty) = \{x \mid x > a\}$$ The infinity symbol does not represent a real number. It indicates that the interval extends indefinitely to the right. | The parenthesis indicates that $a$ is excluded from the interval. |
| The **infinite interval** $(-\infty, b]$ represents the set of real numbers that are less than or equal to $b$. $$(-\infty, b] = \{x \mid x \leq b\}$$ The negative infinity symbol indicates that the interval extends indefinitely to the left. | The square bracket indicates that $b$ is included in the interval. |

## Parentheses and Brackets in Interval Notation

Parentheses indicate endpoints that are not included in an interval. Square brackets indicate endpoints that are included in an interval. Parentheses are always used with $\infty$ or $-\infty$.

**Table P.7** lists nine possible types of intervals used to describe subsets of real numbers.

**Table P.7   Intervals on the Real Number Line**

| Let $a$ and $b$ be real numbers such that $a < b$. | | |
|---|---|---|
| **Interval Notation** | **Set-Builder Notation** | **Graph** |
| $(a, b)$ | $\{x \mid a < x < b\}$ | ![graph: open a, open b]( ) $x$   $a$   $b$ |
| $[a, b]$ | $\{x \mid a \le x \le b\}$ | $x$   $a$   $b$ |
| $[a, b)$ | $\{x \mid a \le x < b\}$ | $x$   $a$   $b$ |
| $(a, b]$ | $\{x \mid a < x \le b\}$ | $x$   $a$   $b$ |
| $(a, \infty)$ | $\{x \mid x > a\}$ | $x$   $a$ |
| $[a, \infty)$ | $\{x \mid x \ge a\}$ | $x$   $a$ |
| $(-\infty, b)$ | $\{x \mid x < b\}$ | $x$   $b$ |
| $(-\infty, b]$ | $\{x \mid x \le b\}$ | $x$   $b$ |
| $(-\infty, \infty)$ | $\{x \mid x$ is a real number$\}$ or $\mathbb{R}$ (set of all real numbers) | $x$ |

**EXAMPLE 1**   **Using Interval Notation**

Express each interval in set-builder notation and graph:

    **a.** $(-1, 4]$       **b.** $[2.5, 4]$       **c.** $(-4, \infty)$.

**Solution**

    **a.** $(-1, 4] = \{x \mid -1 < x \le 4\}$

                 $-4$   $-3$   $-2$   $-1$   $0$   $1$   $2$   $3$   $4$

    **b.** $[2.5, 4] = \{x \mid 2.5 \le x \le 4\}$

                 $-4$   $-3$   $-2$   $-1$   $0$   $1$   $2$   $3$   $4$

    **c.** $(-4, \infty) = \{x \mid x > -4\}$

                 $-4$   $-3$   $-2$   $-1$   $0$   $1$   $2$   $3$   $4$

**Check Point 1**   Express each interval in set-builder notation and graph:

    **a.** $[-2, 5)$       **b.** $[1, 3.5]$       **c.** $(-\infty, -1)$.

**②** Find intersections and unions of intervals.

## Intersections and Unions of Intervals

In Section P.1, we learned how to find intersections and unions of sets. Recall that $A \cap B$ ($A$ intersection $B$) is the set of elements common to both set $A$ and set $B$. By contrast, $A \cup B$ ($A$ union $B$) is the set of elements in set $A$ or in set $B$ or in both sets.

Because intervals represent sets, it is possible to find their intersections and unions. Graphs are helpful in this process.

Finding Intersections and Unions of Two Intervals

1. Graph each interval on a number line.
2. **a.** To find the intersection, take the portion of the number line that the two graphs have in common.
   **b.** To find the union, take the portion of the number line representing the total collection of numbers in the two graphs.

**( EXAMPLE 2 )** **Finding Intersections and Unions of Intervals**

Use graphs to find each set:

**a.** $(1, 4) \cap [2, 8]$        **b.** $(1, 4) \cup [2, 8]$.

**Solution**

**a.** $(1, 4) \cap [2, 8]$, the intersection of the intervals $(1, 4)$ and $[2, 8]$, consists of the numbers that are in both intervals.

Graph of $(1, 4)$:     $\{x \mid 1 < x < 4\}$

Graph of $[2, 8]$:     $\{x \mid 2 \le x \le 8\}$

To find $(1, 4) \cap [2, 8]$, take the portion of the number line that the two graphs have in common.

Numbers in both
$(1, 4)$ and $[2, 8]$:     $\{x \mid 1 < x < 4$ and $2 \le x \le 8\}$

The numbers common to both intervals are those that are greater than or equal to 2 and less than 4: [2, 4).

Thus, $(1, 4) \cap [2, 8] = [2, 4)$.

**b.** $(1, 4) \cup [2, 8]$, the union of the intervals $(1, 4)$ and $[2, 8]$, consists of the numbers that are in either one interval or the other (or both).

Graph of $(1, 4)$:     $\{x \mid 1 < x < 4\}$

Graph of $[2, 8]$:     $\{x \mid 2 \le x \le 8\}$

To find $(1, 4) \cup [2, 8]$, take the portion of the number line representing the total collection of numbers in the two graphs.

Numbers in either
$(1, 4)$ or $[2, 8]$ or both:     $\{x \mid 1 < x < 4$ or $2 \le x \le 8\}$

The numbers in either one interval or the other (or both) are those that are greater than 1 and less than or equal to 8: (1, 8].

Thus, $(1, 4) \cup [2, 8] = (1, 8]$.

⊘ Check Point **2** Use graphs to find each set:

     **a.** $[1, 3] \cap (2, 6)$        **b.** $[1, 3] \cup (2, 6)$.

③ Solve linear inequalities.

## Solving Linear Inequalities in One Variable

We know that a linear equation in $x$ can be expressed as $ax + b = 0$. A **linear inequality in $x$** can be written in one of the following forms:

$$ax + b < 0, \, ax + b \leq 0, \, ax + b > 0, \, ax + b \geq 0.$$

In each form, $a \neq 0$.

Back to our question that opened this section: How many miles can you drive your Rent-a-Heap car if you can spend at most \$335? We answer the question by solving

$$0.20x + 125 \leq 335$$

for $x$. The solution procedure is nearly identical to that for solving

$$0.20x + 125 = 335.$$

Our goal is to get $x$ by itself on the left side. We do this by subtracting 125 from both sides to isolate $0.20x$:

$$0.20x + 125 \leq 335 \qquad \text{This is the given inequality.}$$
$$0.20x + 125 - 125 \leq 335 - 125 \qquad \text{Subtract 125 from both sides.}$$
$$0.02x \leq 210. \qquad \text{Simplify.}$$

Finally, we isolate $x$ from $0.20x$ by dividing both sides of the inequality by 0.20:

$$\frac{0.20x}{0.20} \leq \frac{210}{0.20} \qquad \text{Divide both sides by 0.20.}$$
$$x \leq 1050. \qquad \text{Simplify.}$$

### Study Tip

English phrases such as "at least" and "at most" can be modeled by inequalities.

| English Sentence | Inequality |
|---|---|
| $x$ is at least 5. | $x \geq 5$ |
| $x$ is at most 5. | $x \leq 5$ |
| $x$ is between 5 and 7. | $5 < x < 7$ |
| $x$ is no more than 5. | $x \leq 5$ |
| $x$ is no less than 5. | $x \geq 5$ |

With at most \$335 to spend, you can travel at most 1050 miles.

We started with the inequality $0.20x + 125 \leq 335$ and obtained the inequality $x \leq 1050$ in the final step. These inequalities have the same solution set, namely $\{x \mid x \leq 1050\}$. Inequalities such as these, with the same solution set, are said to be **equivalent**.

We isolated $x$ from $0.20x$ by dividing both sides of $0.20x \leq 210$ by 0.20, a positive number. Let's see what happens if we divide both sides of an inequality by a negative number. Consider the inequality $10 < 14$. Divide 10 and 14 by $-2$:

$$\frac{10}{-2} = -5 \quad \text{and} \quad \frac{14}{-2} = -7.$$

Because $-5$ lies to the right of $-7$ on the number line, $-5$ is greater than $-7$:

$$-5 > -7.$$

Notice that the direction of the inequality symbol is reversed:

$$10 < 14$$

Dividing by $-2$ changes the direction of the inequality symbol.

$$-5 > -7.$$

In general, **when we multiply or divide both sides of an inequality by a negative number, the direction of the inequality symbol is reversed**. When we reverse the direction of the inequality symbol, we say that we change the *sense* of the inequality.

We can isolate a variable in a linear inequality in the same way we isolate a variable in a linear equation. The properties on the next page are used to create equivalent inequalities.

## Properties of Inequalities

| Property | The Property in Words | Example |
|---|---|---|
| **The Addition Property of Inequality**<br>If $a < b$, then $a + c < b + c$.<br>If $a < b$, then $a - c < b - c$. | If the same quantity is added to or subtracted from both sides of an inequality, the resulting inequality is equivalent to the original one. | $2x + 3 < 7$<br>Subtract 3:<br>$2x + 3 - 3 < 7 - 3.$<br>Simplify:<br>$2x < 4.$ |
| **The Positive Multiplication Property of Inequality**<br>If $a < b$ and $c$ is positive, then $ac < bc$.<br>If $a < b$ and $c$ is positive, then $\dfrac{a}{c} < \dfrac{b}{c}$. | If we multiply or divide both sides of an inequality by the same positive quantity, the resulting inequality is equivalent to the original one. | $2x < 4$<br>Divide by 2:<br>$\dfrac{2x}{2} < \dfrac{4}{2}.$<br>Simplify:<br>$x < 2.$ |
| **The Negative Multiplication Property of Inequality**<br>If $a < b$ and $c$ is negative, then $ac > bc$.<br>If $a < b$ and $c$ is negative, $\dfrac{a}{c} > \dfrac{b}{c}$. | If we multiply or divide both sides of an inequality by the same negative quantity and reverse the direction of the inequality symbol, the resulting inequality is equivalent to the original one. | $-4x < 20$<br>Divide by $-4$ and change the sense of the inequality:<br>$\dfrac{-4x}{-4} > \dfrac{20}{-4}.$<br>Simplify:<br>$x > -5.$ |

### Discovery

As a partial check, select one number from the solution set of $3 - 2x \leq 11$. Substitute that number into the original inequality. Perform the resulting computations. You should obtain a true statement.

Is it possible to perform a partial check using a number that is not in the solution set? What should happen in this case? Try doing this.

**EXAMPLE 3** Solving a Linear Inequality

Solve and graph the solution set on a number line:

$$3 - 2x \leq 11.$$

**Solution**

| | |
|---|---|
| $3 - 2x \leq 11$ | This is the given inequality. |
| $3 - 2x - 3 \leq 11 - 3$ | Subtract 3 from both sides. |
| $-2x \leq 8$ | Simplify. |
| $\dfrac{-2x}{-2} \geq \dfrac{8}{-2}$ | Divide both sides by $-2$ and change the sense of the inequality. |
| $x \geq -4$ | Simplify. |

The solution set consists of all real numbers that are greater than or equal to $-4$, expressed as $\{x \mid x \geq -4\}$ in set-builder notation. The interval notation for this solution set is $[-4, \infty)$. The graph of the solution set is shown as follows:

**✓ Check Point 3** Solve and graph the solution set on a number line:

$$2 - 3x \leq 5.$$

**EXAMPLE 4** Solving a Linear Inequality

Solve and graph the solution set on a number line:

$$-2x - 4 > x + 5.$$

**Solution**

**Step 1  Simplify each side.** Because each side is already simplified, we can skip this step.

## Study Tip

You can solve

$$-2x - 4 > x + 5$$

by isolating $x$ on the right side. Add $2x$ to both sides.

$$-2x - 4 + 2x > x + 5 + 2x$$
$$-4 > 3x + 5$$

Now subtract 5 from both sides.

$$-4 - 5 > 3x + 5 - 5$$
$$-9 > 3x$$

Finally, divide both sides by 3.

$$\frac{-9}{3} > \frac{3x}{3}$$
$$-3 > x$$

This last inequality means the same thing as $x < -3$.

**Step 2   Collect variable terms on one side and constant terms on the other side.** We will collect the variable terms of $-2x - 4 > x + 5$ on the left and the constant terms on the right.

| | |
|---|---|
| $-2x - 4 > x + 5$ | This is the given inequality. |
| $-2x - 4 - x > x + 5 - x$ | Subtract x from both sides. |
| $-3x - 4 > 5$ | Simplify. |
| $-3x - 4 + 4 > 5 + 4$ | Add 4 to both sides. |
| $-3x > 9$ | Simplify. |

**Step 3   Isolate the variable and solve.** We isolate the variable, $x$, by dividing both sides by $-3$. Because we are dividing by a negative number, we must reverse the inequality symbol.

| | |
|---|---|
| $\dfrac{-3x}{-3} < \dfrac{9}{-3}$ | Divide both sides by $-3$ and change the sense of the inequality. |
| $x < -3$ | Simplify. |

**Step 4   Express the solution set in set-builder or interval notation and graph the set on a number line.** The solution set consists of all real numbers that are less than $-3$, expressed in set-builder notation as $\{x \mid x < -3\}$. The interval notation for this solution set is $(-\infty, -3)$. The graph of the solution set is shown as follows:

☑ Check Point **4** Solve and graph the solution set on a number line: $3x + 1 > 7x - 15$.

If an inequality contains fractions with constants in the denominators, begin by multiplying both sides by the least common denominator. This will clear the inequality of fractions.

( EXAMPLE 5 )  **Solving a Linear Inequality Containing Fractions**

Solve and graph the solution set on a number line:

$$\frac{x + 3}{4} \geq \frac{x - 2}{3} + \frac{1}{4}.$$

**Solution**   The denominators are 4, 3, and 4. The least common denominator is 12. We begin by multiplying both sides of the inequality by 12.

| | |
|---|---|
| $\dfrac{x + 3}{4} \geq \dfrac{x - 2}{3} + \dfrac{1}{4}$ | This is the given inequality. |
| $12\left(\dfrac{x + 3}{4}\right) \geq 12\left(\dfrac{x - 2}{3} + \dfrac{1}{4}\right)$ | Multiply both sides by 12. Multiplying by a positive number preserves the sense of the inequality. |
| $\dfrac{12}{1} \cdot \dfrac{x + 3}{4} \geq \dfrac{12}{1} \cdot \dfrac{x - 2}{3} + \dfrac{12}{1} \cdot \dfrac{1}{4}$ | Multiply each term by 12. Use the distributive property on the right side. |
| $\dfrac{\overset{3}{\cancel{12}}}{1} \cdot \dfrac{x + 3}{\underset{1}{\cancel{4}}} \geq \dfrac{\overset{4}{\cancel{12}}}{1} \cdot \dfrac{x - 2}{\underset{1}{\cancel{3}}} + \dfrac{\overset{3}{\cancel{12}}}{1} \cdot \dfrac{1}{\underset{1}{\cancel{4}}}$ | Divide out common factors in each multiplication. |
| $3(x + 3) \geq 4(x - 2) + 3$ | The fractions are now cleared. |

Now that the fractions have been cleared, we follow the four steps that we used in the previous example.

**Step 1   Simplify each side.**

$$3(x + 3) \geq 4(x - 2) + 3 \qquad \text{This is the inequality with the fractions cleared.}$$

$$3x + 9 \geq 4x - 8 + 3 \qquad \text{Use the distributive property.}$$

$$3x + 9 \geq 4x - 5 \qquad \text{Simplify.}$$

**Step 2   Collect variable terms on one side and constant terms on the other side.** We will collect variable terms on the left and constant terms on the right.

$$3x + 9 - 4x \geq 4x - 5 - 4x \qquad \text{Subtract 4x from both sides.}$$

$$-x + 9 \geq -5 \qquad \text{Simplify.}$$

$$-x + 9 - 9 \geq -5 - 9 \qquad \text{Subtract 9 from both sides.}$$

$$-x \geq -14 \qquad \text{Simplify.}$$

**Step 3   Isolate the variable and solve.** To isolate $x$, we must eliminate the negative sign in front of the $x$. Because $-x$ means $-1x$, we can do this by multiplying (or dividing) both sides of the inequality by $-1$. We are multiplying by a negative number. Thus, we must reverse the direction of the inequality symbol.

$$(-1)(-x) \leq (-1)(-14) \qquad \text{Multiply both sides by } -1 \text{ and change the sense of the in equality.}$$

$$x \leq 14 \qquad \text{Simplify.}$$

**Step 4   Express the solution set in set-builder or interval notation and graph the set on a number line.** The solution set consists of all real numbers that are less than or equal to 14, expressed in set-builder notation as $\{x | x \leq 14\}$. The interval notation for this solution set is $(-\infty, 14]$. The graph of the solution set is shown as follows:

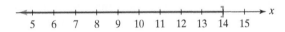

⊘ Check Point **5** Solve and graph the solution set on a number line:

$$\frac{x - 4}{2} \geq \frac{x - 2}{3} + \frac{5}{6}.$$

**④ Solve compound inequalities.**

## Solving Compound Inequalities

We now consider two inequalities such as

$$-3 < 2x + 1 \quad \text{and} \quad 2x + 1 \leq 3,$$

expressed as a **compound inequality**

$$-3 < 2x + 1 \leq 3.$$

The word *and* does not appear when the inequality is written in the shorter form, although intersection is implied. The shorter form enables us to solve both inequalities at once. By performing each operation on all three parts of the inequality, our goal is to **isolate $x$ in the middle.**

EXAMPLE 6   Solving a Compound Inequality

Solve and graph the solution set on a number line:

$$-3 < 2x + 1 \le 3.$$

**Solution**   We would like to isolate $x$ in the middle. We can do this by first subtracting 1 from all three parts of the compound inequality. Then we isolate $x$ from $2x$ by dividing all three parts of the inequality by 2.

| | |
|---|---|
| $-3 < 2x + 1 \le 3$ | This is the given inequality. |
| $-3 - 1 < 2x + 1 - 1 \le 3 - 1$ | Subtract 1 from all three parts. |
| $-4 < 2x \le 2$ | Simplify. |
| $\dfrac{-4}{2} < \dfrac{2x}{2} \le \dfrac{2}{2}$ | Divide each part by 2. |
| $-2 < x \le 1$ | Simplify. |

The solution set consists of all real numbers greater than $-2$ and less than or equal to 1, represented by $\{x \mid -2 < x \le 1\}$ in set-builder notation and $(-2, 1]$ in interval notation. The graph is shown as follows:

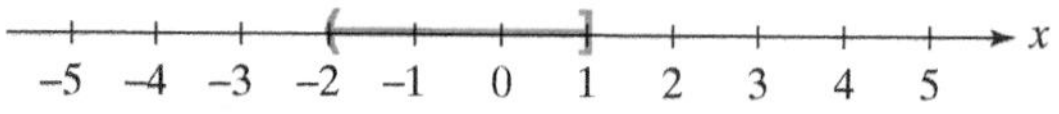

Check Point **6** Solve and graph the solution set on a number line: $1 \le 2x + 3 < 11.$

⑤ Solve absolute value inequalities.

## Solving Inequalities with Absolute Value

We know that $|x|$ describes the distance of $x$ from zero on a real number line. We can use this geometric interpretation to solve an inequality such as

$$|x| < 2.$$

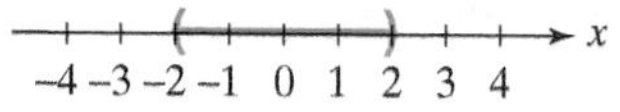

**Figure P.19**   $|x| < 2$, so $-2 < x < 2$.

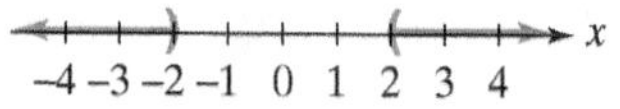

**Figure P.20**   $|x| > 2$, so $x < -2$ or $x > 2$.

This means that the distance of $x$ from 0 is *less than* 2, as shown in **Figure P.19**. The interval shows values of $x$ that lie less than 2 units from 0. Thus, $x$ can lie between $-2$ and 2. That is, $x$ is greater than $-2$ and less than 2. We write $(-2, 2)$ or $\{x \mid -2 < x < 2\}$.

   Some absolute value inequalities use the "greater than" symbol. For example, $|x| > 2$ means that the distance of $x$ from 0 is *greater than* 2, as shown in **Figure P.20**. Thus, $x$ can be less than $-2$ *or* greater than 2. We write $x < -2$ or $x > 2$. This can be expressed in interval notation as $(-\infty, -2) \cup (2, \infty)$.

   These observations suggest the following principles for solving inequalities with absolute value.

## Study Tip

In the $|u| < c$ case, we have one compound inequality to solve. In the $|u| > c$ case, we have two separate inequalities to solve.

### Solving an Absolute Value Inequality

If $u$ is an algebraic expression and $c$ is a positive number,

   **1.** The solutions of $|u| < c$ are the numbers that satisfy $-c < u < c$.

   **2.** The solutions of $|u| > c$ are the numbers that satisfy $u < -c$ or $u > c$.

These rules are valid if $<$ is replaced by $\le$ and $>$ is replaced by $\ge$.

**EXAMPLE 7** Solving an Absolute Value Inequality

Solve and graph the solution set on a number line: $|x - 4| < 3$.

**Solution** We rewrite the inequality without absolute value bars.

$$|u| < c \text{ means } -c < u < c.$$

$$|x - 4| < 3 \quad \text{means} \quad -3 < x - 4 < 3.$$

We solve the compound inequality by adding 4 to all three parts.

$$-3 < x - 4 < 3$$
$$-3 + 4 < x - 4 + 4 < 3 + 4$$
$$1 < x < 7$$

The solution set consists of all real numbers greater than 1 and less than 7, denoted by $\{x | 1 < x < 7\}$ or $(1, 7)$. The graph of the solution set is shown as follows:

○ **Check Point 7** Solve and graph the solution set on a number line: $|x - 2| < 5$.

**EXAMPLE 8** Solving an Absolute Value Inequality

Solve and graph the solution set on a number line: $-2|3x + 5| + 7 \geq -13$.

**Solution**

$$-2|3x + 5| + 7 \geq -13$$     This is the given inequality.

> We need to isolate $|3x + 5|$, the absolute value expression.

$$-2|3x + 5| + 7 - 7 \geq -13 - 7$$     Subtract 7 from both sides.

$$-2|3x + 5| \geq -20$$     Simplify.

$$\frac{-2|3x + 5|}{-2} \leq \frac{-20}{-2}$$     Divide both sides by $-2$ and change the sense of the inequality.

$$|3x + 5| \leq 10$$     Simplify.

$$-10 \leq 3x + 5 \leq 10$$     Rewrite without absolute value bars: $|u| \leq c$ means $-c \leq u \leq c$.

> Now we need to isolate $x$ in the middle.

$$-10 - 5 \leq 3x + 5 - 5 \leq 10 - 5$$     Subtract 5 from all three parts.

$$-15 \leq 3x \leq 5$$     Simplify.

$$\frac{-15}{3} \leq \frac{3x}{3} \leq \frac{5}{3}$$     Divide each part by 3.

$$-5 \leq x \leq \frac{5}{3}$$     Simplify.

The solution set is $\{x | -5 \le x \le \frac{5}{3}\}$ in set-builder notation and $[-5, \frac{5}{3}]$ in interval notation. The graph is shown as follows:

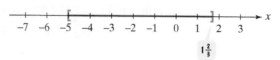

$1\frac{2}{3}$

⊘ Check Point **8** Solve and graph the solution set on a number line:
$-3|5x - 2| + 20 \ge -19$.

---

( **EXAMPLE 9** )   **Solving an Absolute Value Inequality**

Solve and graph the solution set on a number line:   $7 < |5 - 2x|$.

**Solution**   We begin by expressing the inequality with the absolute value expression on the left side:

$$|5 - 2x| > 7.$$

> $c < |u|$ means the same thing as $|u| > c$. In both cases, the inequality symbol points to $c$.

We rewrite this inequality without absolute value bars.

> $|u| \quad > \quad c \quad$ **means** $\quad u \quad < \quad -c \quad$ **or** $\quad u \quad > \quad c.$

$$|5 - 2x| > 7 \text{ means } 5 - 2x < -7 \text{ or } 5 - 2x > 7.$$

Because $|5 - 2x| > 7$ means $5 - 2x < -7$ or $5 - 2x > 7$, we solve $5 - 2x < -7$ and $5 - 2x > 7$ separately. Then we take the union of their solution sets.

| | | |
|---|---|---|
| $5 - 2x < -7$ **or** | $5 - 2x > 7$ | These are the inequalities without absolute value bars. |
| $5 - 5 - 2x < -7 - 5$ | $5 - 5 - 2x > 7 - 5$ | Subtract 5 from both sides. |
| $-2x < -12$ | $-2x > 2$ | Simplify. |
| $\dfrac{-2x}{-2} > \dfrac{-12}{-2}$ | $\dfrac{-2x}{-2} < \dfrac{2}{-2}$ | Divide both sides by $-2$ and change the sense of each inequality. |
| $x > 6$ | $x < -1$ | Simplify. |

The solution set consists of all numbers that are less than $-1$ or greater than 6. The solution set is $\{x | x < -1 \text{ or } x > 6\}$, or, in interval notation $(-\infty, -1) \cup (6, \infty)$. The graph of the solution set is shown as follows:

### Study Tip

The graph of the solution set for $|u| > c$ will be divided into two intervals whose union cannot be represented as a single interval. The graph of the solution set for $|u| < c$ will be a single interval. Avoid the common error of rewriting $|u| > c$ as $-c < u > c$.

⊘ Check Point **9** Solve and graph the solution set on a number line:
$18 < |6 - 3x|$.

## Applications

Our next example shows how to use an inequality to select the better deal between two pricing options. We use our strategy for solving word problems, modeling the verbal conditions of the problem with a linear inequality.

( **EXAMPLE 10** ) **Selecting the Better Deal**

Acme Car rental agency charges $4 a day plus $0.15 per mile, whereas Interstate rental agency charges $20 a day and $0.05 per mile. How many miles must be driven to make the daily cost of an Acme rental a better deal than an Interstate rental?

## Solution

**Step 1   Let *x* represent one of the unknown quantities.** We are looking for the number of miles that must be driven in a day to make Acme the better deal. Thus,

$$\text{let } x = \text{the number of miles driven in a day.}$$

**Step 2   Represent other unknown quantities in terms of *x*.** We are not asked to find another quantity, so we can skip this step.

**Step 3   Write an inequality in *x* that models the conditions.** Acme is a better deal than Interstate if the daily cost of Acme is less than the daily cost of Interstate.

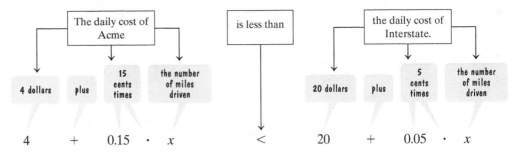

**Step 4   Solve the inequality and answer the question.**

$$4 + 0.15x < 20 + 0.05x$$     This is the inequality that models the verbal conditions.

$$4 + 0.15x - 0.05x < 20 + 0.05x - 0.05x$$     Subtract 0.05x from both sides.

$$4 + 0.1x < 20$$     Simplify.

$$4 + 0.1x - 4 < 20 - 4$$     Subtract 4 from both sides.

$$0.1x < 16$$     Simplify.

$$\frac{0.1x}{0.1} < \frac{16}{0.1}$$     Divide both sides by 0.1.

$$x < 160$$     Simplify.

Thus, driving fewer than 160 miles per day makes Acme the better deal.

**Step 5   Check the proposed solution in the original wording of the problem.** One way to do this is to take a mileage less than 160 miles per day to see if Acme is the better deal. Suppose that 150 miles are driven in a day.

$$\text{Cost for Acme} = 4 + 0.15(150) = 26.50$$

$$\text{Cost for Interstate} = 20 + 0.05(150) = 27.50$$

Acme has a lower daily cost, making Acme the better deal.

⊘ Check Point **10**  A car can be rented from Basic Rental for $260 per week with no extra charge for mileage. Continental charges $80 per week plus 25 cents for each mile driven to rent the same car. How many miles must be driven in a week to make the rental cost for Basic Rental a better deal than Continental's?

# Exercise Set P.9

## Practice Exercises

*In Exercises 1–14, express each interval in set-builder notation and graph the interval on a number line.*

**1.** $(1, 6]$      **2.** $(-2, 4]$

**3.** $[-5, 2)$      **4.** $[-4, 3)$

**5.** $[-3, 1]$      **6.** $[-2, 5]$

**7.** $(2, \infty)$      **8.** $(3, \infty)$

**9.** $[-3, \infty)$      **10.** $[-5, \infty)$

**11.** $(-\infty, 3)$      **12.** $(-\infty, 2)$

**13.** $(-\infty, 5.5)$      **14.** $(-\infty, 3.5]$

*In Exercises 15–26, use graphs to find each set.*

**15.** $(-3, 0) \cap [-1, 2]$      **16.** $(-4, 0) \cap [-2, 1]$

**17.** $(-3, 0) \cup [-1, 2]$      **18.** $(-4, 0) \cup [-2, 1]$

**19.** $(-\infty, 5) \cap [1, 8)$      **20.** $(-\infty, 6) \cap [2, 9)$

**21.** $(-\infty, 5) \cup [1, 8)$      **22.** $(-\infty, 6) \cup [2, 9)$

**23.** $[3, \infty) \cap (6, \infty)$      **24.** $[2, \infty) \cap (4, \infty)$

**25.** $[3, \infty) \cup (6, \infty)$      **26.** $[2, \infty) \cup (4, \infty)$

*In all exercises, other than ∅, use interval notation to express solution sets and graph each solution set on a number line.*

*In Exercises 27–48, solve each linear inequality.*

**27.** $5x + 11 < 26$      **28.** $2x + 5 < 17$

**29.** $3x - 7 \geq 13$      **30.** $8x - 2 \geq 14$

**31.** $-9x \geq 36$      **32.** $-5x \leq 30$

**33.** $8x - 11 \leq 3x - 13$      **34.** $18x + 45 \leq 12x - 8$

**35.** $4(x + 1) + 2 \geq 3x + 6$

**36.** $8x + 3 > 3(2x + 1) + x + 5$

**37.** $2x - 11 < -3(x + 2)$      **38.** $-4(x + 2) > 3x + 20$

**39.** $1 - (x + 3) \geq 4 - 2x$      **40.** $5(3 - x) \leq 3x - 1$

**41.** $\dfrac{x}{4} - \dfrac{3}{2} \leq \dfrac{x}{2} + 1$      **42.** $\dfrac{3x}{10} + 1 \geq \dfrac{1}{5} - \dfrac{x}{10}$

**43.** $1 - \dfrac{x}{2} > 4$      **44.** $7 - \dfrac{4}{5}x < \dfrac{3}{5}$

**45.** $\dfrac{x - 4}{6} \geq \dfrac{x - 2}{9} + \dfrac{5}{18}$      **46.** $\dfrac{4x - 3}{6} + 2 \geq \dfrac{2x - 1}{12}$

**47.** $3[3(x + 5) + 8x + 7] + 5[3(x - 6) - 2(3x - 5)]$
     $< 2(4x + 3)$

**48.** $5[3(2 - 3x) - 2(5 - x)] - 6[5(x - 2) - 2(4x - 3)]$
     $< 3x + 19$

*In Exercises 49–56, solve each compound inequality.*

**49.** $6 < x + 3 < 8$      **50.** $7 < x + 5 < 11$

**51.** $-3 \leq x - 2 < 1$      **52.** $-6 < x - 4 \leq 1$

**53.** $-11 < 2x - 1 \leq -5$      **54.** $3 \leq 4x - 3 < 19$

**55.** $-3 \leq \dfrac{2}{3}x - 5 < -1$      **56.** $-6 \leq \dfrac{1}{2}x - 4 < -3$

*In Exercises 57–92, solve each absolute value inequality.*

**57.** $|x| < 3$      **58.** $|x| < 5$

**59.** $|x - 1| \leq 2$      **60.** $|x + 3| \leq 4$

**61.** $|2x - 6| < 8$      **62.** $|3x + 5| < 17$

**63.** $|2(x - 1) + 4| \leq 8$      **64.** $|3(x - 1) + 2| \leq 20$

**65.** $\left|\dfrac{2x + 6}{3}\right| < 2$      **66.** $\left|\dfrac{3(x - 1)}{4}\right| < 6$

**67.** $|x| > 3$      **68.** $|x| > 5$

**69.** $|x - 1| \geq 2$      **70.** $|x + 3| \geq 4$

**71.** $|3x - 8| > 7$      **72.** $|5x - 2| > 13$

**73.** $\left|\dfrac{2x + 2}{4}\right| \geq 2$      **74.** $\left|\dfrac{3x - 3}{9}\right| \geq 1$

**75.** $\left|3 - \dfrac{2}{3}x\right| > 5$      **76.** $\left|3 - \dfrac{3}{4}x\right| > 9$

**77.** $3|x - 1| + 2 \geq 8$      **78.** $5|2x + 1| - 3 \geq 9$

**79.** $-2|x - 4| \geq -4$      **80.** $-3|x + 7| \geq -27$

**81.** $-4|1 - x| < -16$      **82.** $-2|5 - x| < -6$

**83.** $3 \leq |2x - 1|$      **84.** $9 \leq |4x + 7|$

**85.** $5 > |4 - x|$      **86.** $2 > |11 - x|$

**87.** $1 < |2 - 3x|$      **88.** $4 < |2 - x|$

**89.** $12 < \left|-2x + \dfrac{6}{7}\right| + \dfrac{3}{7}$      **90.** $1 < \left|x - \dfrac{11}{3}\right| + \dfrac{7}{3}$

**91.** $4 + \left|3 - \dfrac{x}{3}\right| \geq 9$      **92.** $\left|2 - \dfrac{x}{2}\right| - 1 \leq 1$

## Practice Plus

*In Exercises 93–96, use interval notation to represent all values of x satisfying the given conditions.*

**93.** $y = 1 - (x + 3) + 2x$    and    $y$ is at least 4.

**94.** $y = 2x - 11 + 3(x + 2)$    and    $y$ is at most 0.

**95.** $y = 7 - \left|\dfrac{x}{2} + 2\right|$    and    $y$ is at most 4.

**96.** $y = 8 - |5x + 3|$    and    $y$ is at least 6.

**97.** When 3 times a number is subtracted from 4, the absolute value of the difference is at least 5. Use interval notation to express the set of all numbers that satisfy this condition.

**98.** When 4 times a number is subtracted from 5, the absolute value of the difference is at most 13. Use interval notation to express the set of all numbers that satisfy this condition.

## Application Exercises

*The graphs show that the three components of love, namely passion, intimacy, and commitment, progress differently over time. Passion peaks early in a relationship and then declines. By contrast, intimacy and commitment build gradually. Use the graphs to solve Exercises 99–106.*

**The Course of Love Over Time**

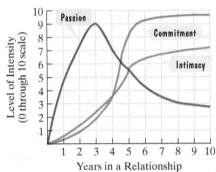

*Source*: R. J. Sternberg. A Triangular Theory of Love, *Psychological Review*, 93, 119–135.

**99.** Use interval notation to write an inequality that expresses for which years in a relationship intimacy is greater than commitment.

**100.** Use interval notation to write an inequality that expresses for which years in a relationship passion is greater than or equal to intimacy.

**101.** What is the relationship between passion and intimacy on for years [5, 7)?

**102.** What is the relationship between intimacy and commitment for years [4, 7)?

**103.** What is the relationship between passion and commitment for years (6, 8)?

**104.** What is the relationship between passion and commitment for years (7, 9)?

**105.** What is the maximum level of intensity for passion? After how many years in a relationship does this occur?

**106.** After approximately how many years do levels of intensity for commitment exceed the maximum level of intensity for passion?

**107.** The percentage, $P$, of U.S. voters who used electronic voting systems, such as optical scans, in national elections can be modeled by the formula

$$P = 3.1x + 25.8,$$

where $x$ is the number of years after 1994. In which years will more than 63% of U.S. voters use electronic systems?

**108.** The percentage, $P$, of U.S. voters who used punch cards or lever machines in national elections can be modeled by the formula

$$P = -2.5x + 63.1,$$

where $x$ is the number of years after 1994. In which years will fewer than 38.1% of U.S. voters use punch cards or lever machines?

**109.** A basic cellular phone plan costs $20 per month for 60 calling minutes. Additional time costs $0.40 per minute. The formula

$$C = 20 + 0.40(x - 60)$$

gives the monthly cost for this plan, $C$, for $x$ calling minutes, where $x > 60$. How many calling minutes are possible for a monthly cost of at least $28 and at most $40?

**110.** The formula for converting Fahrenheit temperature, $F$, to Celsius temperature, $C$, is

$$C = \frac{5}{9}(F - 32).$$

If Celsius temperature ranges from 15° to 35°, inclusive, what is the range for the Fahrenheit temperature? Use interval notation to express this range.

**111.** If a coin is tossed 100 times, we would expect approximately 50 of the outcomes to be heads. It can be demonstrated that a coin is unfair if $h$, the number of outcomes that result in heads, satisfies $\left|\dfrac{h - 50}{5}\right| \geq 1.645$. Describe the number of outcomes that determine an unfair coin that is tossed 100 times.

*In Exercises 112–123, use the strategy for solving word problems, modeling the verbal conditions of the problem with a linear inequality.*

**112.** A truck can be rented from Basic Rental for $50 per day plus $0.20 per mile. Continental charges $20 per day plus $0.50 per mile to rent the same truck. How many miles must be driven in a day to make the rental cost for Basic Rental a better deal than Continental's?

**113.** You are choosing between two long-distance telephone plans. Plan A has a monthly fee of $15 with a charge of $0.08 per minute for all long-distance calls. Plan B has a monthly fee of $3 with a charge of $0.12 per minute for all long-distance calls. How many minutes of long-distance calls in a month make plan A the better deal?

**114.** A city commission has proposed two tax bills. The first bill requires that a homeowner pay $1800 plus 3% of the assessed home value in taxes. The second bill requires taxes of $200 plus 8% of the assessed home value. What price range of home assessment would make the first bill a better deal?

**115.** A local bank charges $8 per month plus 5¢ per check. The credit union charges $2 per month plus 8¢ per check. How many checks should be written each month to make the credit union a better deal?

**116.** A company manufactures and sells blank audiocassette tapes. The weekly fixed cost is $10,000 and it costs $0.40 to produce each tape. The selling price is $2.00 per tape. How many tapes must be produced and sold each week for the company to generate a profit?

**117.** A company manufactures and sells personalized stationery. The weekly fixed cost is $3000 and it costs $3.00 to produce each package of stationery. The selling price is $5.50 per package. How many packages of stationery must be produced and sold each week for the company to generate a profit?

**118.** An elevator at a construction site has a maximum capacity of 2800 pounds. If the elevator operator weighs 265 pounds and each cement bag weighs 65 pounds, how many bags of cement can be safely lifted on the elevator in one trip?

**119.** An elevator at a construction site has a maximum capacity of 3000 pounds. If the elevator operator weighs 245 pounds and each cement bag weighs 95 pounds, how many bags of cement can be safely lifted on the elevator in one trip?

**120.** To earn an A in a course, you must have a final average of at least 90%. On the first four examinations, you have grades of 86%, 88%, 92%, and 84%. If the final examination counts as two grades, what must you get on the final to earn an A in the course?

**121.** On two examinations, you have grades of 86 and 88. There is an optional final examination, which counts as one grade. You decide to take the final in order to get a course grade of A, meaning a final average of at least 90.

   **a.** What must you get on the final to earn an A in the course?

   **b.** By taking the final, if you do poorly, you might risk the B that you have in the course based on the first two exam grades. If your final average is less than 80, you will lose your B in the course. Describe the grades on the final that will cause this to happen.

**122.** Parts for an automobile repair cost $175. The mechanic charges $34 per hour. If you receive an estimate for at least $226 and at most $294 for fixing the car, what is the time interval that the mechanic will be working on the job?

**123.** The toll to a bridge is $3.00. A three-month pass costs $7.50 and reduces the toll to $0.50. A six-month pass costs $30 and permits crossing the bridge for no additional fee. How many crossings per three-month period does it take for the three-month pass to be the best deal?

## Writing in Mathematics

**124.** When graphing the solutions of an inequality, what does a parenthesis signify? What does a bracket signify?

**125.** Describe ways in which solving a linear inequality is similar to solving a linear equation.

**126.** Describe ways in which solving a linear inequality is different than solving a linear equation.

**127.** What is a compound inequality and how is it solved?

**128.** Describe how to solve an absolute value inequality involving the symbol $<$. Give an example.

**129.** Describe how to solve an absolute value inequality involving the symbol $>$. Give an example.

**130.** Explain why $|x| < -4$ has no solution.

**131.** Describe the solution set of $|x| > -4$.

## Critical Thinking Exercises

**Make Sense?** *In Exercises 132–135, determine whether each statement makes sense or does not make sense, and explain your reasoning.*

**132.** I prefer interval notation over set-builder notation because it takes less space to write solution sets.

**133.** I can check inequalities by substituting 0 for the variable: When 0 belongs to the solution set, I should obtain a true statement, and when 0 does not belong to the solution set, I should obtain a false statement.

**134.** In an inequality such as $5x + 4 < 8x - 5$, I can avoid division by a negative number depending on which side I collect the variable terms and on which side I collect the constant terms.

**135.** I'll win the contest if I can complete the crossword puzzle in 20 minutes plus or minus 5 minutes, so my winning time, $x$, is modeled by $|x - 20| \leq 5$.

*In Exercises 136–139, determine whether each statement is true or false. If the statement is false, make the necessary change(s) to produce a true statement.*

**136.** $(-\infty, -1] \cap [-4, \infty) = [-4, -1]$

**137.** $(-\infty, 3) \cup (-\infty, -2) = (-\infty, -2)$

**138.** The inequality $3x > 6$ is equivalent to $2 > x$.

**139.** All irrational numbers satisfy $|x - 4| > 0$.

**140.** What's wrong with this argument? Suppose $x$ and $y$ represent two real numbers, where $x > y$.

| | |
|---|---|
| $2 > 1$ | This is a true statement. |
| $2(y - x) > 1(y - x)$ | Multiply both sides by $y - x$. |
| $2y - 2x > y - x$ | Use the distributive property. |
| $y - 2x > -x$ | Subtract $y$ from both sides. |
| $y > x$ | Add $2x$ to both sides. |

The final inequality, $y > x$, is impossible because we were initially given $x > y$.

**141.** Write an absolute value inequality for which the interval shown is the solution.

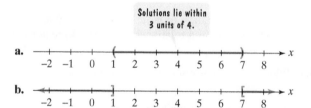

## Group Exercise

**142.** Each group member should research one situation that provides two different pricing options. These can involve areas such as public transportation options (with or without discount passes), cell phone plans, long-distance telephone plans, or anything of interest. Be sure to bring in all the details for each option. At a second group meeting, select the two pricing situations that are most interesting and relevant. Using each situation, write a word problem about selecting the better of the two options. The word problem should be one that can be solved using a linear inequality. The group should turn in the two problems and their solutions.

## Preview Exercises

*Exercises 143–145 will help you prepare for the material covered in the first section of the next chapter.*

**143.** If $y = 4 - x$, find the value of $y$ that corresponds to values of $x$ for each integer starting with $-3$ and ending with 3.

**144.** If $y = 4 - x^2$, find the value of $y$ that corresponds to values of $x$ for each integer starting with $-3$ and ending with 3.

**145.** If $y = |x + 1|$, find the value of $y$ that corresponds to values of $x$ for each integer starting with $-4$ and ending with 2.

# Chapter **P** Summary, Review, and Test

## Summary: Basic Formulas

### Definition of Absolute Value

$$|x| = \begin{cases} x & \text{if } x \geq 0 \\ -x & \text{if } x < 0 \end{cases}$$

### Distance between Points $a$ and $b$ on a Number Line

$|a - b|$  or  $|b - a|$

### Properties of Real Numbers

Commutative   $a + b = b + a$
$ab = ba$

Associative   $(a + b) + c = a + (b + c)$
$(ab)c = a(bc)$

Distributive   $a(b + c) = ab + ac$

Identity   $a + 0 = a$
$a \cdot 1 = a$

Inverse   $a + (-a) = 0$
$a \cdot \dfrac{1}{a} = 1, a \neq 0$

### Properties of Exponents

$b^{-n} = \dfrac{1}{b^n}, \quad b^0 = 1, \quad b^m \cdot b^n = b^{m+n},$

$(b^m)^n = b^{mn}, \quad \dfrac{b^m}{b^n} = b^{m-n}, \quad (ab)^n = a^n b^n, \quad \left(\dfrac{a}{b}\right)^n = \dfrac{a^n}{b^n}$

### Product and Quotient Rules for $n$th Roots

$$\sqrt[n]{ab} = \sqrt[n]{a} \cdot \sqrt[n]{b}, \qquad \sqrt[n]{\dfrac{a}{b}} = \dfrac{\sqrt[n]{a}}{\sqrt[n]{b}}$$

### Rational Exponents

$a^{\frac{1}{n}} = \sqrt[n]{a}, \quad a^{-\frac{1}{n}} = \dfrac{1}{a^{\frac{1}{n}}} = \dfrac{1}{\sqrt[n]{a}},$

$a^{\frac{m}{n}} = \left(\sqrt[n]{a}\right)^m = \sqrt[n]{a^m}, \quad a^{-\frac{m}{n}} = \dfrac{1}{a^{\frac{m}{n}}}$

### Special Products

$(A + B)(A - B) = A^2 - B^2$

$(A + B)^2 = A^2 + 2AB + B^2$

$(A - B)^2 = A^2 - 2AB + B^2$

$(A + B)^3 = A^3 + 3A^2B + 3AB^2 + B^3$

$(A - B)^3 = A^3 - 3A^2B + 3AB^2 - B^3$

### Factoring Formulas

$A^2 - B^2 = (A + B)(A - B)$

$A^2 + 2AB + B^2 = (A + B)^2$

$A^2 - 2AB + B^2 = (A - B)^2$

$A^3 + B^3 = (A + B)(A^2 - AB + B^2)$

$A^3 - B^3 = (A - B)(A^2 + AB + B^2)$

### Absolute Value Equations and Inequalities

1. If $c > 0$, then $|u| = c$ is equivalent to
   $u = c$ or $u = -c$.

2. If $c > 0$, then $|u| < c$ is equivalent to
   $-c < u < c$.

3. If $c > 0$, then $|u| > c$ is equivalent to
   $u < -c$ or $u > c$.

### The Quadratic Formula

All quadratic equations

$$ax^2 + bx + c = 0, \quad a \neq 0$$

can be solved by the quadratic formula

$$x = \dfrac{-b \pm \sqrt{b^2 - 4ac}}{2a}.$$

## Review Exercises

*You can use these review exercises, like the review exercises at the end of each chapter, to test your understanding of the chapter's topics. However, you can also use these exercises as a prerequisite test to check your mastery of the fundamental algebra skills needed in this book.*

### P.1

*In Exercises 1–2, evaluate each algebraic expression for the given value or values of the variable(s).*

1. $3 + 6(x - 2)^3$  for  $x = 4$
2. $x^2 - 5(x - y)$  for  $x = 6$  and  $y = 2$

3. You are riding along an expressway traveling $x$ miles per hour. The formula

$$S = 0.015x^2 + x + 10$$

models the recommended safe distance, $S$, in feet, between your car and other cars on the expressway. What is the recommended safe distance when your speed is 60 miles per hour?

*In Exercises 4–7, let $A = \{a, b, c\}, B = \{a, c, d, e\}$, and $C = \{a, d, f, g\}$. Find the indicated set.*

4. $A \cap B$
5. $A \cup B$
6. $A \cup C$
7. $C \cap A$

**8.** Consider the set:

$$\left\{-17, -\tfrac{9}{13}, 0, 0.75, \sqrt{2}, \pi, \sqrt{81}\right\}.$$

List all numbers from the set that are **a.** natural numbers, **b.** whole numbers, **c.** integers, **d.** rational numbers, **e.** irrational numbers, **f.** real numbers.

*In Exercises 9–11, rewrite each expression without absolute value bars.*

**9.** $|-103|$     **10.** $|\sqrt{2} - 1|$     **11.** $|3 - \sqrt{17}|$

**12.** Express the distance between the numbers $-17$ and $4$ using absolute value. Then evaluate the absolute value.

*In Exercises 13–18, state the name of the property illustrated.*

**13.** $3 + 17 = 17 + 3$     **14.** $(6 \cdot 3) \cdot 9 = 6 \cdot (3 \cdot 9)$
**15.** $\sqrt{3}(\sqrt{5} + \sqrt{3}) = \sqrt{15} + 3$
**16.** $(6 \cdot 9) \cdot 2 = 2 \cdot (6 \cdot 9)$
**17.** $\sqrt{3}(\sqrt{5} + \sqrt{3}) = (\sqrt{5} + \sqrt{3})\sqrt{3}$
**18.** $(3 \cdot 7) + (4 \cdot 7) = (4 \cdot 7) + (3 \cdot 7)$

*In Exercises 19–22, simplify each algebraic expression.*

**19.** $5(2x - 3) + 7x$
**20.** $\tfrac{1}{5}(5x) + [(3y) + (-3y)] - (-x)$
**21.** $3(4y - 5) - (7y + 2)$
**22.** $8 - 2[3 - (5x - 1)]$

**23.** The bar graph shows the percentage of U.S. adults who have been tested for HIV, by age.

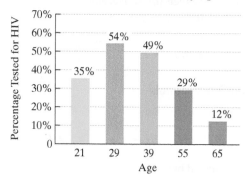

**Percentage of Adults in the United States Tested for HIV, by Age**

*Source:* National Center for Health Statistics

The data in the graph can be modeled by the formula

$$P = -0.05x^2 + 3.6x - 15,$$

where $P$ represents the percentage of U.S. adults tested for HIV at age $x$. According to the formula, what percentage of U.S. adults who are 21 years old have been tested for HIV? Does the model underestimate or overestimate the percent displayed by the bar graph? By how much?

## P.2

*Evaluate each exponential expression in Exercises 24–27.*

**24.** $(-3)^3(-2)^2$     **25.** $2^{-4} + 4^{-1}$

**26.** $5^{-3} \cdot 5$     **27.** $\dfrac{3^3}{3^6}$

*Simplify each exponential expression in Exercises 28–31.*

**28.** $(-2x^4y^3)^3$     **29.** $(-5x^3y^2)(-2x^{-11}y^{-2})$

**30.** $(2x^3)^{-4}$     **31.** $\dfrac{7x^5y^6}{28x^{15}y^{-2}}$

*In Exercises 32–33, write each number in decimal notation.*

**32.** $3.74 \times 10^4$     **33.** $7.45 \times 10^{-5}$

*In Exercises 34–35, write each number in scientific notation.*

**34.** $3,590,000$     **35.** $0.00725$

*In Exercises 36–37, perform the indicated operation and write the answer in decimal notation.*

**36.** $(3 \times 10^3)(1.3 \times 10^2)$     **37.** $\dfrac{6.9 \times 10^3}{3 \times 10^5}$

**38.** In this exercise, use $10^6$ for one million and $10^9$ for one billion to rewrite the number in each statement in scientific notation.

  **a.** According to the Tax Foundation, in 2005, individuals and companies in the United States spent approximately \$257 billion on tax preparation costs.

  **b.** According to the Internal Revenue Service, in 2005, approximately 175 million tax returns were filed.

**39.** Use your scientific notation answers from Exercise 38 to answer this question: If the total 2005 tax preparation costs were evenly divided among all tax returns, how much would it cost to prepare each return? Express the answer in decimal notation, rounded to the nearest dollar.

## P.3

*Use the product rule to simplify the expressions in Exercises 40–43. In Exercises 42–43, assume that variables represent nonnegative real numbers.*

**40.** $\sqrt{300}$     **41.** $\sqrt{12x^2}$
**42.** $\sqrt{10x} \cdot \sqrt{2x}$     **43.** $\sqrt{r^3}$

*Use the quotient rule to simplify the expressions in Exercises 44–45.*

**44.** $\sqrt{\dfrac{121}{4}}$     **45.** $\dfrac{\sqrt{96x^3}}{\sqrt{2x}}$ (Assume that $x > 0$.)

*In Exercises 46–48, add or subtract terms whenever possible.*

**46.** $7\sqrt{5} + 13\sqrt{5}$     **47.** $2\sqrt{50} + 3\sqrt{8}$
**48.** $4\sqrt{72} - 2\sqrt{48}$

*In Exercises 49–52, rationalize the denominator.*

**49.** $\dfrac{30}{\sqrt{5}}$     **50.** $\dfrac{\sqrt{2}}{\sqrt{3}}$

**51.** $\dfrac{5}{6 + \sqrt{3}}$     **52.** $\dfrac{14}{\sqrt{7} - \sqrt{5}}$

*Evaluate each expression in Exercises 53–56 or indicate that the root is not a real number.*

**53.** $\sqrt[3]{125}$     **54.** $\sqrt[5]{-32}$
**55.** $\sqrt[4]{-125}$     **56.** $\sqrt[4]{(-5)^4}$

*Simplify the radical expressions in Exercises 57–61.*

**57.** $\sqrt[3]{81}$     **58.** $\sqrt[3]{y^5}$
**59.** $\sqrt[3]{8} \cdot \sqrt[3]{10}$     **60.** $4\sqrt[3]{16} + 5\sqrt[3]{2}$
**61.** $\dfrac{\sqrt[4]{32x^5}}{\sqrt[4]{16x}}$ (Assume that $x > 0$.)

In Exercises 62–67, evaluate each expression.

**62.** $16^{\frac{1}{2}}$

**63.** $25^{-\frac{1}{2}}$

**64.** $125^{\frac{1}{3}}$

**65.** $27^{-\frac{1}{3}}$

**66.** $64^{\frac{2}{3}}$

**67.** $27^{-\frac{4}{3}}$

In Exercises 68–70, simplify using properties of exponents.

**68.** $\left(5x^{\frac{2}{3}}\right)\left(4x^{\frac{1}{4}}\right)$

**69.** $\dfrac{15x^{\frac{3}{4}}}{5x^{\frac{1}{2}}}$

**70.** $(125x^6)^{\frac{2}{3}}$

**71.** Simplify by reducing the index of the radical: $\sqrt[6]{y^3}$.

## P.4

In Exercises 72–73, perform the indicated operations. Write the resulting polynomial in standard form and indicate its degree.

**72.** $(-6x^3 + 7x^2 - 9x + 3) + (14x^3 + 3x^2 - 11x - 7)$

**73.** $(13x^4 - 8x^3 + 2x^2) - (5x^4 - 3x^3 + 2x^2 - 6)$

In Exercises 74–80, find each product.

**74.** $(3x - 2)(4x^2 + 3x - 5)$ **75.** $(3x - 5)(2x + 1)$

**76.** $(4x + 5)(4x - 5)$ **77.** $(2x + 5)^2$

**78.** $(3x - 4)^2$ **79.** $(2x + 1)^3$

**80.** $(5x - 2)^3$

In Exercises 81–87, find each product.

**81.** $(x + 7y)(3x - 5y)$ **82.** $(3x - 5y)^2$

**83.** $(3x^2 + 2y)^2$ **84.** $(7x + 4y)(7x - 4y)$

**85.** $(a - b)(a^2 + ab + b^2)$

**86.** $[5y - (2x + 1)][5y + (2x + 1)]$

**87.** $(x + 2y + 4)^2$

## P.5

In Exercises 88–104, factor completely, or state that the polynomial is prime.

**88.** $15x^3 + 3x^2$ **89.** $x^2 - 11x + 28$

**90.** $15x^2 - x - 2$ **91.** $64 - x^2$

**92.** $x^2 + 16$ **93.** $3x^4 - 9x^3 - 30x^2$

**94.** $20x^7 - 36x^3$ **95.** $x^3 - 3x^2 - 9x + 27$

**96.** $16x^2 - 40x + 25$ **97.** $x^4 - 16$

**98.** $y^3 - 8$ **99.** $x^3 + 64$

**100.** $3x^4 - 12x^2$ **101.** $27x^3 - 125$

**102.** $x^5 - x$ **103.** $x^3 + 5x^2 - 2x - 10$

**104.** $x^2 + 18x + 81 - y^2$

In Exercises 105–107, factor and simplify each algebraic expression.

**105.** $16x^{-\frac{3}{4}} + 32x^{\frac{1}{4}}$

**106.** $(x^2 - 4)(x^2 + 3)^{\frac{1}{2}} - (x^2 - 4)^2(x^2 + 3)^{\frac{3}{2}}$

**107.** $12x^{-\frac{1}{2}} + 6x^{-\frac{3}{2}}$

## P.6

In Exercises 108–110, simplify each rational expression. Also, list all numbers that must be excluded from the domain.

**108.** $\dfrac{x^3 + 2x^2}{x + 2}$

**109.** $\dfrac{x^2 + 3x - 18}{x^2 - 36}$

**110.** $\dfrac{x^2 + 2x}{x^2 + 4x + 4}$

In Exercises 111–113, multiply or divide as indicated.

**111.** $\dfrac{x^2 + 6x + 9}{x^2 - 4} \cdot \dfrac{x + 3}{x - 2}$ **112.** $\dfrac{6x + 2}{x^2 - 1} \div \dfrac{3x^2 + x}{x - 1}$

**113.** $\dfrac{x^2 - 5x - 24}{x^2 - x - 12} \div \dfrac{x^2 - 10x + 16}{x^2 + x - 6}$

In Exercises 114–117, add or subtract as indicated.

**114.** $\dfrac{2x - 7}{x^2 - 9} - \dfrac{x - 10}{x^2 - 9}$ **115.** $\dfrac{3x}{x + 2} + \dfrac{x}{x - 2}$

**116.** $\dfrac{x}{x^2 - 9} + \dfrac{x - 1}{x^2 - 5x + 6}$ **117.** $\dfrac{4x - 1}{2x^2 + 5x - 3} - \dfrac{x + 3}{6x^2 + x - 2}$

In Exercises 118–120, simplify each expression.

**118.** $\dfrac{\dfrac{1}{x} - \dfrac{1}{2}}{\dfrac{1}{3} - \dfrac{x}{6}}$

**119.** $\dfrac{3 + \dfrac{12}{x}}{1 - \dfrac{16}{x^2}}$

**120.** $\dfrac{3 - \dfrac{1}{x + 3}}{3 + \dfrac{1}{x + 3}}$

**121.** $\dfrac{\sqrt{25 - x^2} + \dfrac{x^2}{\sqrt{25 - x^2}}}{25 - x^2}$

## P.7

In Exercises 122–135, solve each equation.

**122.** $1 - 2(6 - x) = 3x + 2$

**123.** $2(x - 4) + 3(x + 5) = 2x - 2$

**124.** $2x - 4(5x + 1) = 3x + 17$

**125.** $\dfrac{1}{x - 1} - \dfrac{1}{x + 1} = \dfrac{2}{x^2 - 1}$

**126.** $\dfrac{4}{x + 2} + \dfrac{2}{x - 4} = \dfrac{30}{x^2 - 2x - 8}$

**127.** $-4|2x + 1| + 12 = 0$ **128.** $2x^2 - 11x + 5 = 0$

**129.** $(3x + 5)(x - 3) = 5$ **130.** $3x^2 - 7x + 1 = 0$

**131.** $x^2 - 9 = 0$ **132.** $(x - 3)^2 - 24 = 0$

**133.** $\dfrac{2x}{x^2 + 6x + 8} = \dfrac{x}{x + 4} - \dfrac{2}{x + 2}$

**134.** $\sqrt{8 - 2x} - x = 0$ **135.** $\sqrt{2x - 3} + x = 3$

In Exercises 136–137, solve each formula for the specified variable.

**136.** $vt + gt^2 = s$ for $g$ **137.** $T = \dfrac{A - P}{Pr}$ for $P$

In Exercises 138–139, without solving the given quadratic equation, determine the number and type of solutions.

**138.** $x^2 = 2x - 19$ **139.** $9x^2 - 30x + 25 = 0$

## P.8

*In Exercises 140–149, use the five-step strategy for solving word problems.*

**140.** The bar graph represents the millions of barrels of oil consumed each day by the countries with the greatest oil consumption.

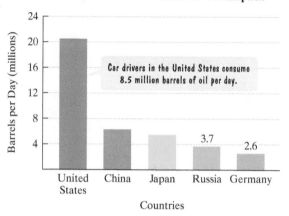

**Countries with the Greatest Oil Consumption**

Car drivers in the United States consume 8.5 million barrels of oil per day.

3.7    2.6

United States    China    Japan    Russia    Germany

Countries

*Source:* U.S. Energy Information Administration

Oil consumption in China exceeds Japan's by 0.8 million barrels per day, and oil consumption in the United States exceeds Japan's by 15 million barrels per day. Of the 82 million barrels of oil used by the world every day, the combined consumption for the United States, China, and Japan is 32.3 million barrels. Determine the daily oil consumption, in millions of barrels, for the United States, China, and Japan.

**141.** The line graph indicates that in 2000, 17.5% of people in the United States spoke a language other than English at home. For the period from 2000 through 2005, this percentage had been increasing by approximately 0.4 per year. If this trend continues, by which year will 25.1% of people in the United States speak a language other than English at home?

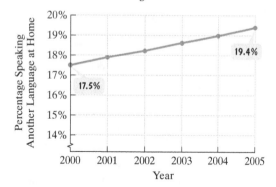

**Percentage of People in the United States Speaking a Language Other Than English at Home**

17.5%    19.4%

*Source:* U.S. Census Bureau

**142.** After a 20% price reduction, a cordless phone sold for $48. What was the phone's price before the reduction?

**143.** A salesperson earns $300 per week plus 5% commission of sales. How much must be sold to earn $800 in a week?

**144.** The length of a rectangular field is 6 yards less than triple the width. If the perimeter of the field is 340 yards, what are its dimensions?

**145.** In 2009, there were 14,100 students at college A, with a projected enrollment increase of 1500 students per year. In the same year, there were 41,700 students at college B, with a projected enrollment decline of 800 students per year. In which year will the colleges have the same enrollment? What will be the enrollment in each college at that time?

**146.** An architect is allowed 15 square yards of floor space to add a small bedroom to a house. Because of the room's design in relationship to the existing structure, the width of the rectangular floor must be 7 yards less than two times the length. Find the length and width of the rectangular floor that the architect is permitted.

**147.** A building casts a shadow that is double the length of its height. If the distance from the end of the shadow to the top of the building is 300 meters, how high is the building? Round to the nearest meter.

**148.** A painting measuring 10 inches by 16 inches is surrounded by a frame of uniform width. If the combined area of the painting and frame is 280 square inches, determine the width of the frame.

**149.** Club members equally share the cost of $1500 to charter a fishing boat. Shortly before the boat is to leave, four people decide not to go due to rough seas. As a result, the cost per person is increased by $100. How many people originally intended to go on the fishing trip?

## P.9

*In Exercises 150–152, express each interval in set-builder notation and graph the interval on a number line.*

**150.** $[-3, 5)$    **151.** $(-2, \infty)$    **152.** $(-\infty, 0]$

*In Exercises 153–156, use graphs to find each set.*

**153.** $(-2, 1] \cap [-1, 3)$    **154.** $(-2, 1] \cup [-1, 3)$

**155.** $[1, 3) \cap (0, 4)$    **156.** $[1, 3) \cup (0, 4)$

*In Exercises 157–166, solve each inequality. Use interval notation to express solution sets and graph each solution set on a number line.*

**157.** $-6x + 3 \leq 15$    **158.** $6x - 9 \geq -4x - 3$

**159.** $\dfrac{x}{3} - \dfrac{3}{4} - 1 > \dfrac{x}{2}$    **160.** $6x + 5 > -2(x - 3) - 25$

**161.** $3(2x - 1) - 2(x - 4) \geq 7 + 2(3 + 4x)$

**162.** $7 < 2x + 3 \leq 9$    **163.** $|2x + 3| \leq 15$

**164.** $\left| \dfrac{2x + 6}{3} \right| > 2$    **165.** $|2x + 5| - 7 \geq -6$

**166.** $-4|x + 2| + 5 \leq -7$

**167.** A car rental agency rents a certain car for $40 per day with unlimited mileage or $24 per day plus $0.20 per mile. How far can a customer drive this car per day for the $24 option to cost no more than the unlimited mileage option?

**168.** To receive a B in a course, you must have an average of at least 80% but less than 90% on five exams. Your grades on the first four exams were 95%, 79%, 91%, and 86%. What range of grades on the fifth exam will result in a B for the course?

CHAPTER
**Test Prep**
VIDEOS

**Chapter P  Test**

*In Exercises 1–18, simplify the given expression or perform the indicated operation (and simplify, if possible), whichever is appropriate.*

**1.** $5(2x^2 - 6x) - (4x^2 - 3x)$

**2.** $7 + 2[3(x + 1) - 2(3x - 1)]$

**3.** $\{1, 2, 5\} \cap \{5, a\}$

**4.** $\{1, 2, 5\} \cup \{5, a\}$

**5.** $\dfrac{30x^3y^4}{6x^9y^{-4}}$

**6.** $\sqrt{6r}\sqrt{3r}$ (Assume that $r \geq 0$.)

**7.** $4\sqrt{50} - 3\sqrt{18}$

**8.** $\dfrac{3}{5 + \sqrt{2}}$

**9.** $\sqrt[3]{16x^4}$

**10.** $\dfrac{x^2 + 2x - 3}{x^2 - 3x + 2}$

**11.** $\dfrac{5 \times 10^{-6}}{20 \times 10^{-8}}$ (Express the answer in scientific notation.)

**12.** $(2x - 5)(x^2 - 4x + 3)$

**13.** $(5x + 3y)^2$

**14.** $\dfrac{2x + 8}{x - 3} \div \dfrac{x^2 + 5x + 4}{x^2 - 9}$

**15.** $\dfrac{x}{x + 3} + \dfrac{5}{x - 3}$

**16.** $\dfrac{2x + 3}{x^2 - 7x + 12} - \dfrac{2}{x - 3}$

**17.** $\dfrac{1 - \dfrac{x}{x + 2}}{1 + \dfrac{1}{x}}$

**18.** $\dfrac{2x\sqrt{x^2 + 5} - \dfrac{2x^3}{\sqrt{x^2 + 5}}}{x^2 + 5}$

*In Exercises 19–24, factor completely, or state that the polynomial is prime.*

**19.** $x^2 - 9x + 18$

**20.** $x^3 + 2x^2 + 3x + 6$

**21.** $25x^2 - 9$

**22.** $36x^2 - 84x + 49$

**23.** $y^3 - 125$

**24.** $x^2 + 10x + 25 - 9y^2$

**25.** Factor and simplify:

$$x(x + 3)^{-\frac{3}{5}} + (x + 3)^{\frac{2}{5}}.$$

**26.** List all the rational numbers in this set:

$$\left\{-7, -\tfrac{4}{5}, 0, 0.25, \sqrt{3}, \sqrt{4}, \tfrac{22}{7}, \pi\right\}.$$

*In Exercises 27–28, state the name of the property illustrated.*

**27.** $3(2 + 5) = 3(5 + 2)$

**28.** $6(7 + 4) = 6 \cdot 7 + 6 \cdot 4$

**29.** Express in scientific notation: 0.00076.

**30.** Evaluate: $27^{-\frac{5}{3}}$.

**31.** In 2007, world population was approximately $6.6 \times 10^9$. By some projections, world population will double by 2040. Express the population at that time in scientific notation.

**32.** **Big (Lack of) Men on Campus** In 2007, 135 women received bachelor's degrees for every 100 men. According to the U.S. Department of Education, that gender imbalance will widen in the coming years, as shown by the bar graph.

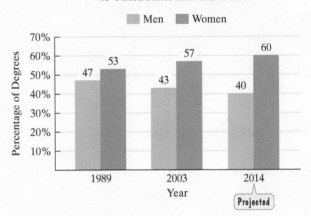

**Percentage of Bachelor's Degrees Awarded to United States Men and Women**

*Source:* U.S. Department of Education

The data for bachelor's degrees can be described by the following mathematical models:

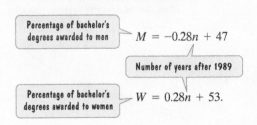

Percentage of bachelor's degrees awarded to men — $M = -0.28n + 47$

Number of years after 1989

Percentage of bachelor's degrees awarded to women — $W = 0.28n + 53$.

**a.** According to the first formula, what percentage of bachelor's degrees were awarded to men in 2003? Does this underestimate or overestimate the actual percent shown by the bar graph? By how much?

**b.** Use the given formulas to write a new formula with a rational expression that models the ratio of the percentage of bachelor's degrees received by men to the percentage received by women $n$ years after 1989. Name this new mathematical model $R$, for ratio.

**c.** Use the formula for $R$ to find the projected ratio of bachelor's degrees received by men to degrees received by women in 2014. According to the model, how many women will receive bachelor's degrees for every two men in 2014? How well does this describe the projections shown by the graph?

*In Exercises 33–47, solve each equation or inequality. Use interval notation to express solution sets of inequalities and graph these solution sets on a number line.*

**33.** $7(x - 2) = 4(x + 1) - 21$

**34.** $\dfrac{2x - 3}{4} = \dfrac{x - 4}{2} - \dfrac{x + 1}{4}$

**35.** $\dfrac{2}{x - 3} - \dfrac{4}{x + 3} = \dfrac{8}{x^2 - 9}$

**36.** $2x^2 - 3x - 2 = 0$

**37.** $(3x - 1)^2 = 75$

**38.** $x(x - 2) = 4$

**39.** $\sqrt{x - 3} + 5 = x$

**40.** $\sqrt{8 - 2x} - x = 0$

**41.** $\left|\dfrac{2}{3}x - 6\right| = 2$

**42.** $-3|4x - 7| + 15 = 0$

**43.** $\dfrac{2x}{x^2 + 6x + 8} + \dfrac{2}{x + 2} = \dfrac{x}{x + 4}$

**44.** $3(x + 4) \geq 5x - 12$

**45.** $\dfrac{x}{6} + \dfrac{1}{8} \leq \dfrac{x}{2} - \dfrac{3}{4}$

**46.** $-3 \leq \dfrac{2x + 5}{3} < 6$

**47.** $|3x + 2| \geq 3$

*In Exercises 48–50, solve each formula for the specified variable.*

**48.** $V = \dfrac{1}{3}lwh$ for $h$

**49.** $y - y_1 = m(x - x_1)$ for $x$

**50.** $R = \dfrac{as}{a + s}$ for $a$

*Without changes, the graphs show projections for the amount being paid in Social Security benefits and the amount going into the system. All data are expressed in billions of dollars.*

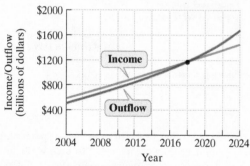

**Social Insecurity: Income and Outflow of the Social Security System**

*Source:* 2004 Social Security Trustees Report

*Exercises 51–53 are based on the data shown by the graphs.*

**51.** In 2004, the system's income was $575 billion, projected to increase at an average rate of $43 billion per year. In which year will the system's income be $1177 billion?

**52.** The data for the system's outflow can be modeled by the formula

$$B = 0.07x^2 + 47.4x + 500,$$

where $B$ represents the amount paid in benefits, in billions of dollars, $x$ years after 2004. According to this model, when will the amount paid in benefits be $1177 billion? Round to the nearest year.

**53.** How well do your answers to Exercises 51 and 52 model the data shown by the graphs?

**54.** For every one million U.S. residents, the number of movie theaters exceeds the number of drive-in theaters by 16 and the number of video rental stores exceeds the number of drive-in theaters by 64. Combined, there are 83 drive-in theaters, movie theaters, and video rental stores per one million U.S. residents. How many of each of these establishments are there per one million residents? (*Source:* U.S. Census Bureau)

**55.** The costs for two different kinds of heating systems for a small home are given in the following table. After how many years will total costs for solar heating and electric heating be the same? What will be the cost at that time?

| System | Cost to Install | Operating Cost/Year |
| --- | --- | --- |
| Solar | $29,700 | $150 |
| Electric | $5000 | $1100 |

**56.** The length of a rectangular carpet is 4 feet greater than twice its width. If the area is 48 square feet, find the carpet's length and width.

**57.** A vertical pole is to be supported by a wire that is 26 feet long and anchored 24 feet from the base of the pole. How far up the pole should the wire be attached?

**58.** After a 60% reduction, a jacket sold for $20. What was the jacket's price before the reduction?

**59.** A group of people would like to buy a vacation cabin for $600,000, sharing the cost equally. If they could find five more people to join them, each person's share would be reduced by $6000. How many people are in the group?

**60.** You are choosing between two telephone plans for local calls. Plan A charges $25 per month for unlimited calls. Plan B has a monthly fee of $13 with a charge of $0.06 per local call. How many local telephone calls in a month make plan A the better deal?

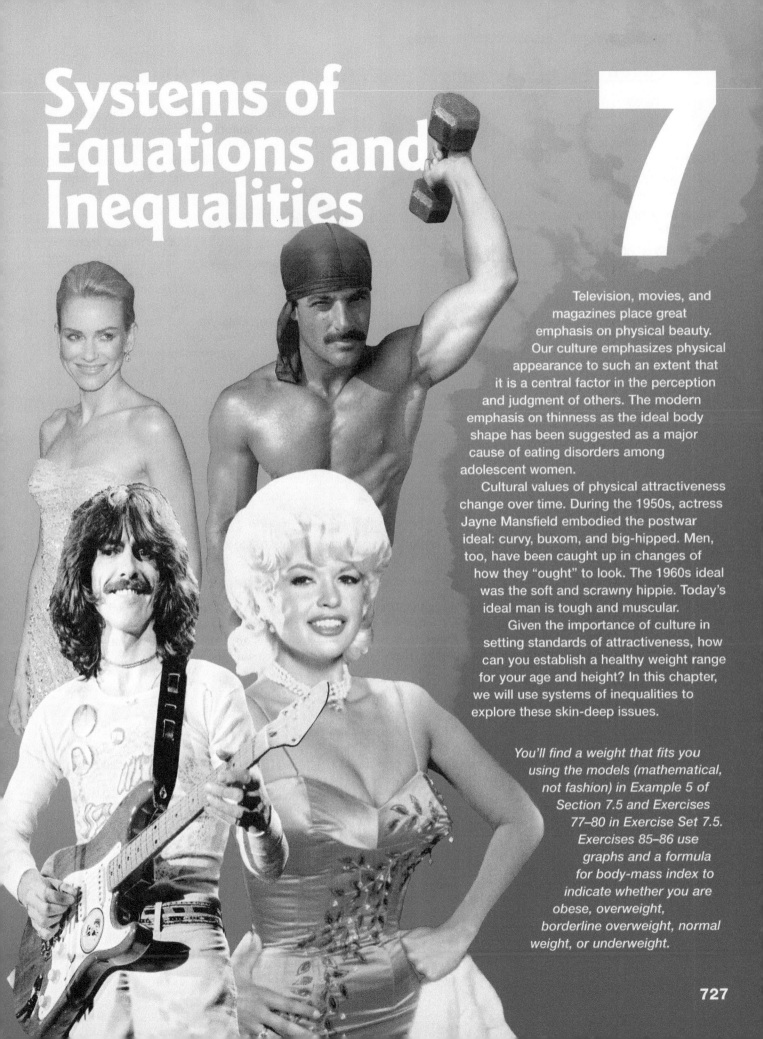

# Systems of Equations and Inequalities

# 7

Television, movies, and magazines place great emphasis on physical beauty. Our culture emphasizes physical appearance to such an extent that it is a central factor in the perception and judgment of others. The modern emphasis on thinness as the ideal body shape has been suggested as a major cause of eating disorders among adolescent women.

Cultural values of physical attractiveness change over time. During the 1950s, actress Jayne Mansfield embodied the postwar ideal: curvy, buxom, and big-hipped. Men, too, have been caught up in changes of how they "ought" to look. The 1960s ideal was the soft and scrawny hippie. Today's ideal man is tough and muscular.

Given the importance of culture in setting standards of attractiveness, how can you establish a healthy weight range for your age and height? In this chapter, we will use systems of inequalities to explore these skin-deep issues.

*You'll find a weight that fits you using the models (mathematical, not fashion) in Example 5 of Section 7.5 and Exercises 77–80 in Exercise Set 7.5. Exercises 85–86 use graphs and a formula for body-mass index to indicate whether you are obese, overweight, borderline overweight, normal weight, or underweight.*

727

## Section 7.1 Systems of Linear Equations in Two Variables

### Objectives

1. Decide whether an ordered pair is a solution of a linear system.
2. Solve linear systems by substitution.
3. Solve linear systems by addition.
4. Identify systems that do not have exactly one ordered-pair solution.
5. Solve problems using systems of linear equations.

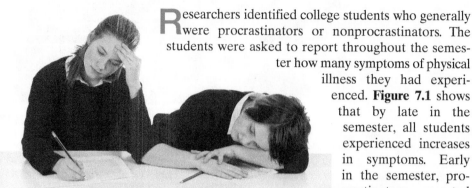

Researchers identified college students who generally were procrastinators or nonprocrastinators. The students were asked to report throughout the semester how many symptoms of physical illness they had experienced. **Figure 7.1** shows that by late in the semester, all students experienced increases in symptoms. Early in the semester, procrastinators reported fewer symptoms, but late in the semester, as work came due, they reported more symptoms than their nonprocrastinating peers.

The data in **Figure 7.1** can be analyzed using a pair of linear models in two variables. The figure shows that by week 6, both groups reported the same number of symptoms of illness, an average of approximately 3.5 symptoms per group. In this section, you will learn two algebraic methods, called *substitution* and *addition*, that will reinforce this graphic observation, verifying (6, 3.5) as the point of intersection.

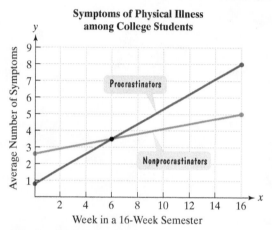

**Figure 7.1**
*Source:* Gerrig and Zimbardo, *Psychology and Life*, 18th Edition, Allyn and Bacon, 2008

1. Decide whether an ordered pair is a solution of a linear system.

### Systems of Linear Equations and Their Solutions

All equations in the form $Ax + By = C$ are straight lines when graphed. Two such equations are called a **system of linear equations** or a **linear system**. **A solution to a system of linear equations in two variables** is an ordered pair that satisfies both equations in the system. For example, (3, 4) satisfies the system

$$\begin{cases} x + y = 7 & \text{(3 + 4 is, indeed, 7.)} \\ x - y = -1. & \text{(3 - 4 is, indeed, -1.)} \end{cases}$$

Thus, (3, 4) satisfies both equations and is a solution of the system. The solution can be described by saying that $x = 3$ and $y = 4$. The solution can also be described using set notation. The solution set to the system is $\{(3, 4)\}$—that is, the set consisting of the ordered pair (3, 4).

A system of linear equations can have exactly one solution, no solution, or infinitely many solutions. We begin with systems that have exactly one solution.

**EXAMPLE 1** Determining Whether Ordered Pairs Are Solutions of a System

Consider the system:

$$\begin{cases} x + 2y = 2 \\ x - 2y = 6. \end{cases}$$

Determine if each ordered pair is a solution of the system:

**a.** $(4, -1)$     **b.** $(-4, 3)$.

## Solution

**a.** We begin by determining whether $(4, -1)$ is a solution. Because 4 is the $x$-coordinate and $-1$ is the $y$-coordinate of $(4, -1)$, we replace $x$ with 4 and $y$ with $-1$.

$$
\begin{array}{ll}
x + 2y = 2 & x - 2y = 6 \\
4 + 2(-1) \stackrel{?}{=} 2 & 4 - 2(-1) \stackrel{?}{=} 6 \\
4 + (-2) \stackrel{?}{=} 2 & 4 - (-2) \stackrel{?}{=} 6 \\
2 = 2, \quad \text{true} & 4 + 2 \stackrel{?}{=} 6 \\
& 6 = 6, \quad \text{true}
\end{array}
$$

The pair $(4, -1)$ satisfies both equations: It makes each equation true. Thus, the ordered pair is a solution of the system.

**b.** To determine whether $(-4, 3)$ is a solution, we replace $x$ with $-4$ and $y$ with 3.

$$
\begin{array}{ll}
x + 2y = 2 & x - 2y = 6 \\
-4 + 2 \cdot 3 \stackrel{?}{=} 2 & -4 - 2 \cdot 3 \stackrel{?}{=} 6 \\
-4 + 6 \stackrel{?}{=} 2 & -4 - 6 \stackrel{?}{=} 6 \\
2 = 2, \quad \text{true} & -10 = 6, \quad \text{false}
\end{array}
$$

The pair $(-4, 3)$ fails to satisfy *both* equations: It does not make both equations true. Thus, the ordered pair is not a solution of the system.

---

### Study Tip

When solving linear systems by graphing, neatly drawn graphs are essential for determining points of intersection.

- Use rectangular coordinate graph paper.
- Use a ruler or straightedge.
- Use a pencil with a sharp point.

---

The solution of a system of linear equations can sometimes be found by graphing both of the equations in the same rectangular coordinate system. For a system with one solution, the **coordinates of the point of intersection give the system's solution**. For example, the system in Example 1,

$$
\begin{cases}
x + 2y = 2 \\
x - 2y = 6,
\end{cases}
$$

is graphed in **Figure 7.2**. The solution of the system, $(4, -1)$, corresponds to the point of intersection of the lines.

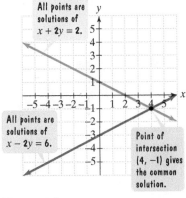

**Figure 7.2** Visualizing a system's solution

✓ Check Point **1** Consider the system:

$$
\begin{cases}
2x - 3y = -4 \\
2x + y = 4.
\end{cases}
$$

Determine if each ordered pair is a solution of the system:

**a.** $(1, 2)$    **b.** $(7, 6)$.

---

**2** Solve linear systems by substitution.

## Eliminating a Variable Using the Substitution Method

Finding the solution to a linear system by graphing equations may not be easy to do. For example, a solution of $\left(-\frac{2}{3}, \frac{157}{29}\right)$ would be difficult to "see" as an intersection point on a graph.

Let's consider a method that does not depend on finding a system's solution visually: the substitution method. This method involves converting the system to one equation in one variable by an appropriate substitution.

**Study Tip**

In step 1, you can choose which variable to isolate in which equation. If possible, solve for a variable whose coefficient is 1 or −1 to avoid working with fractions.

**Solving Linear Systems by Substitution**

1. Solve either of the equations for one variable in terms of the other. (If one of the equations is already in this form, you can skip this step.)
2. Substitute the expression found in step 1 into the *other* equation. This will result in an equation in one variable.
3. Solve the equation containing one variable.
4. Back-substitute the value found in step 3 into one of the original equations. Simplify and find the value of the remaining variable.
5. Check the proposed solution in both of the system's given equations.

**EXAMPLE 2**  **Solving a System by Substitution**

Solve by the substitution method:

$$\begin{cases} 5x - 4y = 9 \\ x - 2y = -3. \end{cases}$$

**Solution**

**Step 1   Solve either of the equations for one variable in terms of the other.** We begin by isolating one of the variables in either of the equations. By solving for $x$ in the second equation, which has a coefficient of 1, we can avoid fractions.

$$x - 2y = -3 \qquad \text{This is the second equation in the given system.}$$
$$x = 2y - 3 \qquad \text{Solve for x by adding 2y to both sides.}$$

**Step 2   Substitute the expression from step 1 into the other equation.** We substitute $2y - 3$ for $x$ in the first equation.

$$x = \boxed{2y - 3} \qquad\qquad 5\boxed{x} - 4y = 9$$

This gives us an equation in one variable, namely

$$5(2y - 3) - 4y = 9.$$

The variable $x$ has been eliminated.

**Step 3   Solve the resulting equation containing one variable.**

$$5(2y - 3) - 4y = 9 \qquad \text{This is the equation containing one variable.}$$
$$10y - 15 - 4y = 9 \qquad \text{Apply the distributive property.}$$
$$6y - 15 = 9 \qquad \text{Combine like terms.}$$
$$6y = 24 \qquad \text{Add 15 to both sides.}$$
$$y = 4 \qquad \text{Divide both sides by 6.}$$

**Study Tip**

The equation from step 1, in which one variable is expressed in terms of the other, is equivalent to one of the original equations. It is often easiest to back-substitute an obtained value into this equation to find the value of the other variable. After obtaining both values, get into the habit of checking the ordered-pair solution in *both* equations of the system.

**Step 4   Back-substitute the obtained value into one of the original equations.** Now that we have the $y$-coordinate of the solution, we back-substitute 4 for $y$ into one of the original equations to find $x$. Let's use both equations to show that we obtain the same value for $x$ in either case.

| **Using the first equation:** | **Using the second equation:** |
|---|---|
| $5x - 4y = 9$ | $x - 2y = -3$ |
| $5x - 4(4) = 9$ | $x - 2(4) = -3$ |
| $5x - 16 = 9$ | $x - 8 = -3$ |
| $5x = 25$ | $x = 5$ |
| $x = 5$ | |

With $x = 5$ and $y = 4$, the proposed solution is $(5, 4)$.

**Step 5   Check.** Take a moment to show that $(5, 4)$ satisfies both given equations. The solution set is $\{(5, 4)\}$.

## Technology

**Graphic Connections**

A graphing utility can be used to solve the system in Example 2. Solve each equation for $y$, graph the equations, and use the intersection feature. The utility displays the solution $(5, 4)$ as $x = 5$, $y = 4$.

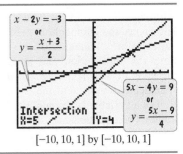

$[-10, 10, 1]$ by $[-10, 10, 1]$

☑ **Check Point 2** Solve by the substitution method:

$$\begin{cases} 3x + 2y = 4 \\ 2x + \phantom{2}y = 1. \end{cases}$$

③ Solve linear systems by addition.

## Eliminating a Variable Using the Addition Method

The substitution method is most useful if one of the given equations has an isolated variable. A second, and frequently the easiest, method for solving a linear system is the addition method. Like the substitution method, the addition method involves eliminating a variable and ultimately solving an equation containing only one variable. However, this time we eliminate a variable by adding the equations.

For example, consider the following system of linear equations:

$$\begin{cases} \phantom{-}3x - 4y = \phantom{-}11 \\ -3x + 2y = -7. \end{cases}$$

When we add these two equations, the $x$-terms are eliminated. This occurs because the coefficients of the $x$-terms, 3 and $-3$, are opposites (additive inverses) of each other:

$$\begin{cases} \phantom{-}3x - 4y = \phantom{-}11 \\ \underline{-3x + 2y = \phantom{-}{-7}} \end{cases}$$

$$-2y = 4 \quad \boxed{\text{The sum is an equation in one variable.}}$$

$$y = -2. \quad \textit{Divide both sides by } -2 \textit{ and solve for y.}$$

Now we can back-substitute $-2$ for $y$ into one of the original equations to find $x$. It does not matter which equation you use; you will obtain the same value for $x$ in either case. If we use either equation, we can show that $x = 1$ and the solution $(1, -2)$ satisfies both equations in the system.

When we use the addition method, we want to obtain two equations whose sum is an equation containing only one variable. The key step is to **obtain, for one of the variables, coefficients that differ only in sign**. To do this, we may need to multiply one or both equations by some nonzero number so that the coefficients of one of the variables, $x$ or $y$, become opposites. Then when the two equations are added, this variable is eliminated.

## Solving Linear Systems by Addition

1. If necessary, rewrite both equations in the form $Ax + By = C$.
2. If necessary, multiply either equation or both equations by appropriate nonzero numbers so that the sum of the $x$-coefficients or the sum of the $y$-coefficients is 0.
3. Add the equations in step 2. The sum is an equation in one variable.
4. Solve the equation in one variable.
5. Back-substitute the value obtained in step 4 into either of the given equations and solve for the other variable.
6. Check the solution in both of the original equations.

**EXAMPLE 3** Solving a System by the Addition Method

Solve by the addition method:

$$\begin{cases} 3x + 2y = 48 \\ 9x - 8y = -24. \end{cases}$$

**Solution**

**Step 1   Rewrite both equations in the form $Ax + By = C$.** Both equations are already in this form. Variable terms appear on the left and constants appear on the right.

**Step 2   If necessary, multiply either equation or both equations by appropriate numbers so that the sum of the $x$-coefficients or the sum of the $y$-coefficients is 0.** We can eliminate $x$ or $y$. Let's eliminate $x$. Consider the terms in $x$ in each equation, that is, $3x$ and $9x$. To eliminate $x$, we can multiply each term of the first equation by $-3$ and then add the equations.

$$\begin{cases} 3x + 2y = 48 \\ 9x - 8y = -24 \end{cases} \xrightarrow[\text{No change}]{\text{Multiply by } -3.} \begin{cases} -9x - 6y = -144 \\ \underline{9x - 8y = -24} \end{cases}$$

**Step 3   Add the equations.**   Add:   $-14y = -168$

**Step 4   Solve the equation in one variable.** We solve $-14y = -168$ by dividing both sides by $-14$.

$$\frac{-14y}{-14} = \frac{-168}{-14} \quad \text{Divide both sides by } -14.$$

$$y = 12 \quad \text{Simplify.}$$

**Step 5   Back-substitute and find the value for the other variable.** We can back-substitute 12 for $y$ into either one of the given equations. We'll use the first one.

$$3x + 2y = 48 \quad \text{This is the first equation in the given system.}$$

$$3x + 2(12) = 48 \quad \text{Substitute 12 for y.}$$

$$3x + 24 = 48 \quad \text{Multiply.}$$

$$3x = 24 \quad \text{Subtract 24 from both sides.}$$

$$x = 8 \quad \text{Divide both sides by 3.}$$

We found that $y = 12$ and $x = 8$. The proposed solution is $(8, 12)$.

**Step 6   Check.** Take a few minutes to show that $(8, 12)$ satisfies both of the original equations in the system. The solution set is $\{(8, 12)\}$.

⊘ Check Point **3** Solve by the addition method:

$$\begin{cases} 4x + 5y = 3 \\ 2x - 3y = 7. \end{cases}$$

Some linear systems have solutions that are not integers. If the value of one variable turns out to be a "messy" fraction, back-substitution might lead to cumbersome arithmetic. If this happens, you can return to the original system and use the addition method to find the value of the other variable.

( EXAMPLE 4 ) **Solving a System by the Addition Method**

Solve by the addition method:

$$\begin{cases} 2x = 7y - 17 \\ 5y = 17 - 3x. \end{cases}$$

**Solution**

**Step 1   Rewrite both equations in the form $Ax + By = C$.** We first arrange the system so that variable terms appear on the left and constants appear on the right. We obtain

$$\begin{cases} 2x - 7y = -17 & \text{Subtract 7y from both sides of the first equation.} \\ 3x + 5y = \phantom{-}17. & \text{Add 3x to both sides of the second equation.} \end{cases}$$

**Step 2   If necessary, multiply either equation or both equations by appropriate numbers so that the sum of the $x$-coefficients or the sum of the $y$-coefficients is 0.** We can eliminate $x$ or $y$. Let's eliminate $x$ by multiplying the first equation by 3 and the second equation by $-2$.

$$\begin{cases} 2x - 7y = -17 \\ 3x + 5y = \phantom{-}17 \end{cases} \xrightarrow[\text{Multiply by } -2.]{\text{Multiply by 3.}} \begin{cases} 6x - 21y = -51 \\ -6x - 10y = -34 \end{cases}$$

**Step 3   Add the equations.**     Add:     $-31y = -85$

**Step 4   Solve the equation in one variable.** We solve $-31y = -85$ by dividing both sides by $-31$.

$$\frac{-31y}{-31} = \frac{-85}{-31} \quad \text{Divide both sides by } -31.$$

$$y = \frac{85}{31} \quad \text{Simplify.}$$

**Step 5   Back-substitute and find the value for the other variable.** Back-substitution of $\frac{85}{31}$ for $y$ into either of the given equations results in cumbersome arithmetic. Instead, let's use the addition method on the given system in the form $Ax + By = C$ to find the value for $x$. Thus, we eliminate $y$ by multiplying the first equation by 5 and the second equation by 7.

$$\begin{cases} 2x - 7y = -17 \\ 3x + 5y = \phantom{-}17 \end{cases} \xrightarrow[\text{Multiply by 7.}]{\text{Multiply by 5.}} \begin{cases} 10x - 35y = -85 \\ 21x + 35y = \phantom{-}119 \end{cases}$$

Add:     $31x \phantom{- 35y} = \phantom{-}34$

$$x = \frac{34}{31} \quad \text{Divide both sides by 31.}$$

We found that $y = \dfrac{85}{31}$ and $x = \dfrac{34}{31}$. The proposed solution is $\left(\dfrac{34}{31}, \dfrac{85}{31}\right)$.

**Step 6   Check.** For this system, a calculator is helpful in showing that $\left(\frac{34}{31}, \frac{85}{31}\right)$ satisfies both of the original equations in the system. The solution set is $\left\{\left(\frac{34}{31}, \frac{85}{31}\right)\right\}$.

⊘ Check Point **4** Solve by the addition method:

$$\begin{cases} 2x = 9 + 3y \\ 4y = 8 - 3x. \end{cases}$$

**④** Identify systems that do not have exactly one ordered-pair solution.

## Linear Systems Having No Solution or Infinitely Many Solutions

We have seen that a system of linear equations in two variables represents a pair of lines. The lines either intersect at one point, are parallel, or are identical. Thus, there are three possibilities for the number of solutions to a system of two linear equations in two variables.

### The Number of Solutions to a System of Two Linear Equations

The number of solutions to a system of two linear equations in two variables is given by one of the following. (See **Figure 7.3**.)

| Number of Solutions | What This Means Graphically |
| --- | --- |
| Exactly one ordered-pair solution | The two lines intersect at one point. |
| No solution | The two lines are parallel. |
| Infinitely many solutions | The two lines are identical. |

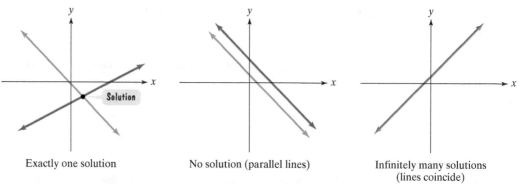

Exactly one solution     No solution (parallel lines)     Infinitely many solutions (lines coincide)

**Figure 7.3** Possible graphs for a system of two linear equations in two variables

A linear system with no solution is called an **inconsistent system**. If you attempt to solve such a system by substitution or addition, you will eliminate both variables. A false statement, such as $0 = 12$, will be the result.

( **EXAMPLE 5** ) **A System with No Solution**

Solve the system:

$$\begin{cases} 4x + 6y = 12 \\ 6x + 9y = 12. \end{cases}$$

**Solution**   Because no variable is isolated, we will use the addition method. To obtain coefficients of $x$ that differ only in sign, we multiply the first equation by 3 and multiply the second equation by $-2$.

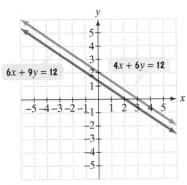

$$\begin{cases} 4x + 6y = 12 \\ 6x + 9y = 12 \end{cases}$$   $\xrightarrow{\text{Multiply by 3.}}$   $\begin{cases} 12x + 18y = \phantom{-}36 \\ -12x - 18y = -24 \end{cases}$

$\xrightarrow{\text{Multiply by } -2.}$

Add:   $\phantom{-12x - 18y = }0 = \phantom{-}12$

> There are no values of $x$ and $y$ for which $0 = 12$. No values of $x$ and $y$ satisfy $0x + 0y = 12$.

**Figure 7.4**   The graph of an inconsistent system

The false statement $0 = 12$ indicates that the system is inconsistent and has no solution. The solution set is the empty set, $\varnothing$.

The lines corresponding to the two equations in Example 5 are shown in **Figure 7.4**. The lines are parallel and have no point of intersection.

### Discovery

Show that the graphs of $4x + 6y = 12$ and $6x + 9y = 12$ must be parallel lines by solving each equation for $y$. What is the slope and $y$-intercept for each line? What does this mean? If a linear system is inconsistent, what must be true about the slopes and $y$-intercepts for the system's graphs?

✓ **Check Point 5**   Solve the system:

$$\begin{cases} 5x - 2y = 4 \\ -10x + 4y = 7. \end{cases}$$

A linear system that has at least one solution is called a **consistent system**. Lines that intersect and lines that coincide both represent consistent systems. If the lines coincide, then the consistent system has infinitely many solutions, represented by every point on either line.

The equations in a linear system with infinitely many solutions are called **dependent**. If you attempt to solve such a system by substitution or addition, you will eliminate both variables. However, a true statement, such as $10 = 10$, will be the result.

### EXAMPLE 6   A System with Infinitely Many Solutions

Solve the system:

$$\begin{cases} y = 3x - 2 \\ 15x - 5y = 10. \end{cases}$$

**Solution**   Because the variable $y$ is isolated in $y = 3x - 2$, the first equation, we can use the substitution method. We substitute the expression for $y$ into the second equation.

$y = \boxed{3x - 2}$      $15x - 5\boxed{y} = 10$   Substitute $3x - 2$ for $y$.

$15x - 5(3x - 2) = 10$   The substitution results in an equation in one variable.

$15x - 15x + 10 = 10$   Apply the distributive property.

> This statement is true for all values of $x$ and $y$.

$10 = 10$   Simplify.

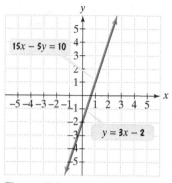

**Figure 7.5** The graph of a system with infinitely many solutions

In our final step, both variables have been eliminated and the resulting statement, $10 = 10$, is true. This true statement indicates that the system has infinitely many solutions. The solution set consists of all points $(x, y)$ lying on either of the coinciding lines, $y = 3x - 2$ or $15x - 5y = 10$, as shown in **Figure 7.5**.

We express the solution set for the system in one of two equivalent ways:

$$\{(x, y) \mid y = 3x - 2\} \quad \text{or} \quad \{(x, y) \mid 15x - 5y = 10\}.$$

The set of all ordered pairs $(x, y)$ such that $y = 3x - 2$

The set of all ordered pairs $(x, y)$ such that $15x - 5y = 10$

**Study Tip**

Although the system in Example 6 has infinitely many solutions, this does not mean that any ordered pair of numbers you can form will be a solution. The ordered pair $(x, y)$ must satisfy one of the system's equations, $y = 3x - 2$ or $15x - 5y = 10$, and there are infinitely many such ordered pairs. Because the graphs are coinciding lines, the ordered pairs that are solutions of one of the equations are also solutions of the other equation.

⊘ Check Point **6** Solve the system:

$$\begin{cases} x = 4y - 8 \\ 5x - 20y = -40. \end{cases}$$

**5** Solve problems using systems of linear equations.

## Applications

We begin with applications that involve two unknown quantities. We will let $x$ and $y$ represent these quantities. We then model the verbal conditions of the problem with a system of linear equations in $x$ and $y$.

### Strategy for Problem Solving Using Systems of Equations

**Step 1** Read the problem carefully. Attempt to state the problem in your own words and state what the problem is looking for. Use variables to represent unknown quantities.

**Step 2** Write a system of equations that models the problem's conditions.

**Step 3** Solve the system and answer the problem's question.

**Step 4** Check the proposed solution in the original wording of the problem.

Chemists and pharmacists often have to change the concentration of solutions and other mixtures. In these situations, the amount of a particular ingredient in the solution or mixture is expressed as a percentage of the total.

( **EXAMPLE 7** ) **Solving a Mixture Problem**

A chemist working on a flu vaccine needs to mix a 10% sodium-iodine solution with a 60% sodium-iodine solution to obtain 50 milliliters of a 30% sodium-iodine solution. How many milliliters of the 10% solution and of the 60% solution should be mixed?

**Solution**

**Step 1  Use variables to represent unknown quantities.**
Let $x$ = the number of milliliters of the 10% solution to be used in the mixture.
Let $y$ = the number of milliliters of the 60% solution to be used in the mixture.

**Step 2  Write a system of equations that models the problem's conditions.** The situation is illustrated in **Figure 7.6**.

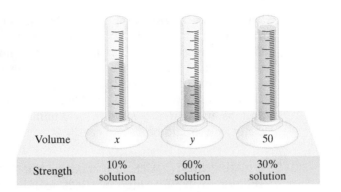

**Figure 7.6**

The chemist needs 50 milliliters of a 30% sodium-iodine solution. We form a table that shows the amount of sodium-iodine in each of the three solutions.

| Solution | Number of milliliters | × | Percent of Sodium-Iodine | = | Amount of Sodium-Iodine |
|---|---|---|---|---|---|
| 10% Solution | $x$ | | 10% = 0.1 | | $0.1x$ |
| 60% Solution | $y$ | | 60% = 0.6 | | $0.6y$ |
| 30% Mixture | 50 | | 30% = 0.3 | | $0.3(50) = 15$ |

The chemist needs to obtain a 50-milliliter mixture.

> The number of milliliters used of the 10% solution **plus** the number of milliliters used of the 60% solution **must equal** 50 milliliters.

$$x \quad + \quad y \quad = \quad 50$$

The 50-milliliter mixture must be 30% sodium-iodine. The amount of sodium-iodine must be 30% of 50, or $(0.3)(50) = 15$ milliliters.

> Amount of sodium-iodine in the 10% solution **plus** amount of sodium-iodine in the 60% solution **equals** amount of sodium-iodine in the mixture.

$$0.1x \quad + \quad 0.6y \quad = \quad 15$$

**Step 3 Solve the system and answer the problem's question.** The system

$$x + y = 50$$
$$0.1x + 0.6y = 15$$

can be solved by substitution or addition. Let's use substitution. Solving the first equation for $y$, we obtain $y = 50 - x$.

$$y = \boxed{50 - x} \qquad 0.1x + 0.6\boxed{y} = 15$$

We substitute $50 - x$ for $y$ in the second equation, $0.1x + 0.6y = 15$. This gives us an equation in one variable.

$$0.1x + 0.6(50 - x) = 15 \qquad \text{This equation contains one variable, } x.$$
$$0.1x + 30 - 0.6x = 15 \qquad \text{Apply the distributive property.}$$
$$-0.5x + 30 = 15 \qquad \text{Combine like terms.}$$
$$-0.5x = -15 \qquad \text{Subtract 30 from both sides.}$$
$$x = \frac{-15}{-0.5} = 30 \qquad \text{Divide both sides by } -0.5.$$

Back-substituting 30 for $x$ in either of the system's equations ($x + y = 50$ is easier to use) gives $y = 20$. Because $x$ represents the number of milliliters of the 10% solution and $y$ the number of milliliters of the 60% solution, the chemist should mix 30 milliliters of the 10% solution with 20 milliliters of the 60% solution.

**Step 4 Check the proposed solution in the original wording of the problem.** The problem states that the chemist needs 50 milliliters of a 30% sodium-iodine solution. The amount of sodium-iodine in this mixture is 0.3(50), or 15 milliliters. The amount of sodium-iodine in 30 milliliters of the 10% solution is 0.1(30), or 3 milliliters. The amount of sodium-iodine in 20 milliliters of the 60% solution is 0.6(20) = 12 milliliters. The amount of sodium-iodine in the two solutions used in the mixture is 3 milliliters + 12 milliliters, or 15 milliliters, exactly as it should be.

⬤

☑ Check Point 7 A chemist needs to mix an 18% acid solution with a 45% acid solution to obtain 12 liters of a 36% acid solution. How many liters of each of the acid solutions must be used?

We have seen that if an object moves at an average velocity $v$, the distance, $s$, covered in time $t$ is given by the formula

$$s = vt \quad \text{Distance equals velocity times time.}$$

Recall that objects that move in accordance with this formula are said to be in **uniform motion.** Wind and water current have the effect of increasing or decreasing a traveler's velocity.

( EXAMPLE 8 ) **Solving a Uniform Motion Problem**

When a small airplane flies with the wind, it can travel 450 miles in 3 hours. When the same airplane flies in the opposite direction against the wind, it takes 5 hours to fly the same distance. Find the average velocity of the plane in still air and the average velocity of the wind.

**Solution**

**Step 1 Use variables to represent unknown quantities.**
Let $x$ = the average velocity of the plane in still air.
Let $y$ = the average velocity of the wind.

**Step 2 Write a system of equations that models the problem's conditions.** As it travels with the wind, the plane's average velocity is increased. The net average velocity is its average velocity in still air, $x$, plus the average velocity of the wind, $y$, given by the expression $x + y$. As it travels against the wind, the plane's average velocity is decreased. The net average velocity is its average velocity in still air, $x$, minus the average velocity of the wind, $y$, given by the expression $x - y$. Here is a chart that summarizes the problem's information and includes the increased and decreased velocities:

| | Velocity $\times$ | Time $=$ | Distance |
|---|---|---|---|
| **Trip with the Wind** | $x + y$ | 3 | $3(x + y)$ |
| **Trip against the Wind** | $x - y$ | 5 | $5(x - y)$ |

The problem states that the distance in each direction is 450 miles. We use this information to write our system of equations.

The distance of the trip with the wind  is  450 miles.

$$3(x + y) \quad = \quad 450$$

The distance of the trip against the wind  is  450 miles.

$$5(x - y) \quad = \quad 450$$

**Step 3 Solve the system and answer the problem's question.** We can simplify the system by dividing both sides of the equations by 3 and 5, respectively.

$$\begin{cases} 3(x + y) = 450 \\ 5(x - y) = 450 \end{cases} \quad \xrightarrow[\text{Divide by 5.}]{\text{Divide by 3.}} \quad \begin{cases} x + y = 150 \\ x - y = \phantom{0}90 \end{cases}$$

Solve the system on the right by the addition method.

$$\begin{cases} x + y = 150 \\ \underline{x - y = \phantom{0}90} \end{cases}$$

Add:  $2x \phantom{- y} = 240$

$x = 120$   Divide both sides by 2.

Back-substituting 120 for $x$ in either of the system's equations gives $y = 30$. Because $x = 120$ and $y = 30$, the average velocity of the plane in still air is 120 miles per hour and the average velocity of the wind is 30 miles per hour.

**Step 4 Check the proposed solution in the original wording of the problem.** The problem states that the distance in each direction is 450 miles. The average velocity of the plane with the wind is $120 + 30 = 150$ miles per hour. In 3 hours, it travels $150 \cdot 3$, or 450 miles, which checks with the stated condition. Furthermore, the average velocity of the plane against the wind is $120 - 30 = 90$ miles per hour. In 5 hours, it travels $90 \cdot 5 = 450$ miles, which is the stated distance. ●

**Check Point 8** With the current, a motorboat can travel 84 miles in 2 hours. Against the current, the same trip takes 3 hours. Find the average velocity of the boat in still water and the average velocity of the current.

## Functions of Business: Break-Even Analysis

Suppose that a company produces and sells $x$ units of a product. Its *revenue* is the money generated by selling $x$ units of the product. Its *cost* is the cost of producing $x$ units of the product.

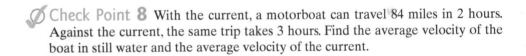

### Revenue and Cost Functions

A company produces and sells $x$ units of a product.

**Revenue Function**

$$R(x) = (\text{price per unit sold})x$$

**Cost Function**

$$C(x) = \text{fixed cost} + (\text{cost per unit produced})x$$

The point of intersection of the graphs of the revenue and cost functions is called the **break-even point**. The $x$-coordinate of the point reveals the number of units that a company must produce and sell so that money coming in, the revenue, is equal to money going out, the cost. The $y$-coordinate of the break-even point gives the amount of money coming in and going out. Example 9 illustrates the use of the substitution method in determining a company's break-even point.

(EXAMPLE 9) **Finding a Break-Even Point**

Technology is now promising to bring light, fast, and beautiful wheelchairs to millions of disabled people. A company is planning to manufacture these radically different wheelchairs. Fixed cost will be $500,000 and it will cost $400 to produce each wheelchair. Each wheelchair will be sold for $600.

**a.** Write the cost function, $C$, of producing $x$ wheelchairs.
**b.** Write the revenue function, $R$, from the sale of $x$ wheelchairs.
**c.** Determine the break-even point. Describe what this means.

**Solution**

**a.** The cost function is the sum of the fixed cost and variable cost.

| Fixed cost of $500,000 | plus | Variable cost: $400 for each chair produced |
|---|---|---|

$$C(x) = 500{,}000 + 400x$$

**b.** The revenue function is the money generated from the sale of $x$ wheelchairs.

| Revenue per chair, $600, times | the number of chairs sold |
|---|---|

$$R(x) = 600x$$

**c.** The break-even point occurs where the graphs of $C$ and $R$ intersect. Thus, we find this point by solving the system

$$\begin{cases} C(x) = 500{,}000 + 400x \\ R(x) = 600x \end{cases} \quad \text{or} \quad \begin{cases} y = 500{,}000 + 400x \\ y = 600x. \end{cases}$$

Using substitution, we can substitute $600x$ for $y$ in the first equation:

$$600x = 500{,}000 + 400x \qquad \text{Substitute } 600x \text{ for } y \text{ in } y = 500{,}000 + 400x.$$

$$200x = 500{,}000 \qquad \text{Subtract } 400x \text{ from both sides.}$$

$$x = 2500. \qquad \text{Divide both sides by } 200.$$

Back-substituting 2500 for $x$ in either of the system's equations (or functions), we obtain

$$R(2500) = 600(2500) = 1{,}500{,}000.$$

We used $R(x) = 600x$.

The break-even point is (2500, 1,500,000). This means that the company will break even if it produces and sells 2500 wheelchairs. At this level, the money coming in is equal to the money going out: $1,500,000. ●

**Figure 7.7** shows the graphs of the revenue and cost functions for the wheelchair business. Similar graphs and models apply no matter how small or large a business venture may be.

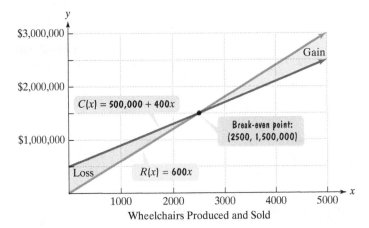

Figure 7.7
Wheelchairs Produced and Sold

The intersection point confirms that the company breaks even by producing and selling 2500 wheelchairs. Can you see what happens for $x < 2500$? The red cost graph lies above the blue revenue graph. The cost is greater than the revenue and the business is losing money. Thus, if they sell fewer than 2500 wheelchairs, the result is a *loss*. By contrast, look at what happens for $x > 2500$. The blue revenue graph lies above the red cost graph. The revenue is greater than the cost and the business is making money. Thus, if they sell more than 2500 wheelchairs, the result is a *gain*.

Ø Check Point **9** A company that manufactures running shoes has a fixed cost of $300,000. Additionally, it costs $30 to produce each pair of shoes. They are sold at $80 per pair.

   **a.** Write the cost function, $C$, of producing $x$ pairs of running shoes.

   **b.** Write the revenue function, $R$, from the sale of $x$ pairs of running shoes.

   **c.** Determine the break-even point. Describe what this means.

What does every entrepreneur, from a kid selling lemonade to Donald Trump, want to do? Generate profit, of course. The *profit* made is the money taken in, or the revenue, minus the money spent, or the cost. This relationship between revenue and cost allows us to define the *profit function, $P(x)$*.

### The Profit Function

The profit, $P(x)$, generated after producing and selling $x$ units of a product is given by the **profit function**

$$P(x) = R(x) - C(x),$$

where $R$ and $C$ are the revenue and cost functions, respectively.

The profit function for the wheelchair business in Example 9 is

$$\begin{aligned}
P(x) &= R(x) - C(x) \\
&= 600x - (500,000 + 400x) \\
&= 200x - 500,000.
\end{aligned}$$

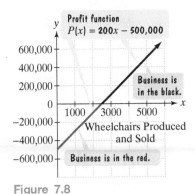

Figure 7.8

The graph of this profit function is shown in **Figure 7.8**. The red portion lies below the x-axis and shows a loss when fewer than 2500 wheelchairs are sold. The business is "in the red." The black portion lies above the x-axis and shows a gain when more than 2500 wheelchairs are sold. The wheelchair business is "in the black."

# Exercise Set 7.1

## Practice Exercises

In Exercises 1–4, determine whether the given ordered pair is a solution of the system.

**1.** $(2, 3)$
$$\begin{cases} x + 3y = 11 \\ x - 5y = -13 \end{cases}$$

**2.** $(-3, 5)$
$$\begin{cases} 9x + 7y = 8 \\ 8x - 9y = -69 \end{cases}$$

**3.** $(2, 5)$
$$\begin{cases} 2x + 3y = 17 \\ x + 4y = 16 \end{cases}$$

**4.** $(8, 5)$
$$\begin{cases} 5x - 4y = 20 \\ 3y = 2x + 1 \end{cases}$$

In Exercises 5–18, solve each system by the substitution method.

**5.** $\begin{cases} x + y = 4 \\ y = 3x \end{cases}$

**6.** $\begin{cases} x + y = 6 \\ y = 2x \end{cases}$

**7.** $\begin{cases} x + 3y = 8 \\ y = 2x - 9 \end{cases}$

**8.** $\begin{cases} 2x - 3y = -13 \\ y = 2x + 7 \end{cases}$

**9.** $\begin{cases} x = 4y - 2 \\ x = 6y + 8 \end{cases}$

**10.** $\begin{cases} x = 3y + 7 \\ x = 2y - 1 \end{cases}$

**11.** $\begin{cases} 5x + 2y = 0 \\ x - 3y = 0 \end{cases}$

**12.** $\begin{cases} 4x + 3y = 0 \\ 2x - y = 0 \end{cases}$

**13.** $\begin{cases} 2x + 5y = -4 \\ 3x - y = 11 \end{cases}$

**14.** $\begin{cases} 2x + 5y = 1 \\ -x + 6y = 8 \end{cases}$

**15.** $\begin{cases} 2x - 3y = 8 - 2x \\ 3x + 4y = x + 3y + 14 \end{cases}$

**16.** $\begin{cases} 3x - 4y = x - y + 4 \\ 2x + 6y = 5y - 4 \end{cases}$

**17.** $\begin{cases} y = \dfrac{1}{3}x + \dfrac{2}{3} \\ y = \dfrac{5}{7}x - 2 \end{cases}$

**18.** $\begin{cases} y = -\dfrac{1}{2}x + 2 \\ y = \dfrac{3}{4}x + 7 \end{cases}$

In Exercises 19–30, solve each system by the addition method.

**19.** $\begin{cases} x + y = 1 \\ x - y = 3 \end{cases}$

**20.** $\begin{cases} x + y = 6 \\ x - y = -2 \end{cases}$

**21.** $\begin{cases} 2x + 3y = 6 \\ 2x - 3y = 6 \end{cases}$

**22.** $\begin{cases} 3x + 2y = 14 \\ 3x - 2y = 10 \end{cases}$

**23.** $\begin{cases} x + 2y = 2 \\ -4x + 3y = 25 \end{cases}$

**24.** $\begin{cases} 2x - 7y = 2 \\ 3x + y = -20 \end{cases}$

**25.** $\begin{cases} 4x + 3y = 15 \\ 2x - 5y = 1 \end{cases}$

**26.** $\begin{cases} 3x - 7y = 13 \\ 6x + 5y = 7 \end{cases}$

**27.** $\begin{cases} 3x - 4y = 11 \\ 2x + 3y = -4 \end{cases}$

**28.** $\begin{cases} 2x + 3y = -16 \\ 5x - 10y = 30 \end{cases}$

**29.** $\begin{cases} 3x = 4y + 1 \\ 3y = 1 - 4x \end{cases}$

**30.** $\begin{cases} 5x = 6y + 40 \\ 2y = 8 - 3x \end{cases}$

In Exercises 31–42, solve by the method of your choice. Identify systems with no solution and systems with infinitely many solutions, using set notation to express their solution sets.

**31.** $\begin{cases} x = 9 - 2y \\ x + 2y = 13 \end{cases}$

**32.** $\begin{cases} 6x + 2y = 7 \\ y = 2 - 3x \end{cases}$

**33.** $\begin{cases} y = 3x - 5 \\ 21x - 35 = 7y \end{cases}$

**34.** $\begin{cases} 9x - 3y = 12 \\ y = 3x - 4 \end{cases}$

**35.** $\begin{cases} 3x - 2y = -5 \\ 4x + y = 8 \end{cases}$

**36.** $\begin{cases} 2x + 5y = -4 \\ 3x - y = 11 \end{cases}$

**37.** $\begin{cases} x + 3y = 2 \\ 3x + 9y = 6 \end{cases}$

**38.** $\begin{cases} 4x - 2y = 2 \\ 2x - y = 1 \end{cases}$

**39.** $\begin{cases} \dfrac{x}{4} - \dfrac{y}{4} = -1 \\ x + 4y = -9 \end{cases}$

**40.** $\begin{cases} \dfrac{x}{6} - \dfrac{y}{2} = \dfrac{1}{3} \\ x + 2y = -3 \end{cases}$

**41.** $\begin{cases} 2x = 3y + 4 \\ 4x = 3 - 5y \end{cases}$

**42.** $\begin{cases} 4x = 3y + 8 \\ 2x = -14 + 5y \end{cases}$

In Exercises 43–46, let x represent one number and let y represent the other number. Use the given conditions to write a system of equations. Solve the system and find the numbers.

**43.** The sum of two numbers is 7. If one number is subtracted from the other, their difference is −1. Find the numbers.

**44.** The sum of two numbers is 2. If one number is subtracted from the other, their difference is 8. Find the numbers.

**45.** Three times a first number decreased by a second number is 1. The first number increased by twice the second number is 12. Find the numbers.

**46.** The sum of three times a first number and twice a second number is 8. If the second number is subtracted from twice the first number, the result is 3. Find the numbers.

## Practice Plus

In Exercises 47–48, solve each system by the method of your choice.

**47.** $\begin{cases} \dfrac{x + 2}{2} - \dfrac{y + 4}{3} = 3 \\ \dfrac{x + y}{5} = \dfrac{x - y}{2} - \dfrac{5}{2} \end{cases}$

**48.** $\begin{cases} \dfrac{x - y}{3} = \dfrac{x + y}{2} - \dfrac{1}{2} \\ \dfrac{x + 2}{2} - 4 = \dfrac{y + 4}{3} \end{cases}$

In Exercises 49–50, solve each system for x and y, expressing either value in terms of a or b, if necessary. Assume that $a \neq 0$ and $b \neq 0$.

**49.** $\begin{cases} 5ax + 4y = 17 \\ ax + 7y = 22 \end{cases}$

**50.** $\begin{cases} 4ax + by = 3 \\ 6ax + 5by = 8 \end{cases}$

51. For the linear function $f(x) = mx + b$, $f(-2) = 11$ and $f(3) = -9$. Find $m$ and $b$.

52. For the linear function $f(x) = mx + b$, $f(-3) = 23$ and $f(2) = -7$. Find $m$ and $b$.

*Use the graphs of the linear functions to solve Exercises 53–54.*

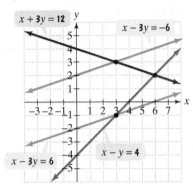

53. Write the linear system whose solution set is $\{(6, 2)\}$. Express each equation in the system in slope-intercept form.

54. Write the linear system whose solution set is $\varnothing$. Express each equation in the system in slope-intercept form.

## Application Exercises

55. A wine company needs to blend a California wine with a 5% alcohol content and a French wine with a 9% alcohol content to obtain 200 gallons of wine with a 7% alcohol content. How many gallons of each kind of wine must be used?

56. A jeweler needs to mix an alloy with a 16% gold content and an alloy with a 28% gold content to obtain 32 ounces of a new alloy with a 25% gold content. How many ounces of each of the original alloys must be used?

57. For thousands of years, gold has been considered one of Earth's most precious metals. One hundred percent pure gold is 24-karat gold, which is too soft to be made into jewelry. In the United States, most gold jewelry is 14-karat gold, approximately 58% gold. If 18-karat gold is 75% gold and 12-karat gold is 50% gold, how much of each should be used to make a 14-karat gold bracelet weighing 300 grams?

58. In the "Peanuts" cartoon shown, solve the problem that is sending Peppermint Patty into an agitated state. How much cream and how much milk, to the nearest thousandth of a gallon, must be mixed together to obtain 50 gallons of cream that contains 12.5% butterfat?

© 1978 United Media/United Feature Syndicate, Inc.

59. The manager of a candystand at a large multiplex cinema has a popular candy that sells for $1.60 per pound. The manager notices a different candy worth $2.10 per pound that is not selling well. The manager decides to form a mixture of both types of candy to help clear the inventory of the more expensive type. How many pounds of each kind of candy should be used to create a 75-pound mixture selling for $1.90 per pound?

60. A grocer needs to mix raisins at $2.00 per pound with granola at $3.25 per pound to obtain 10 pounds of a mixture that costs $2.50 per pound. How many pounds of raisins and how many pound of granola must be used?

61. When a small plane flies with the wind, it can travel 800 miles in 5 hours. When the plane flies in the opposite direction, against the wind, it takes 8 hours to fly the same distance. Find the average velocity of the plane in still air and the average velocity of the wind.

62. When a plane flies with the wind, it can travel 4200 miles in 6 hours. When the plane flies in the opposite direction, against the wind, it takes 7 hours to fly the same distance. Find the average velocity of the plane in still air and the average velocity of the wind.

63. A boat's crew rowed 16 kilometers downstream, with the current, in 2 hours. The return trip upstream, against the current, covered the same distance, but took 4 hours. Find the crew's average rowing velocity in still water and the average velocity of the current.

64. A motorboat traveled 36 miles downstream, with the current, in 1.5 hours. The return trip upstream, against the current, covered the same distance, but took 2 hours. Find the boat's average velocity in still water and the average velocity of the current.

65. With the current, you can canoe 24 miles in 4 hours. Against the same current, you can canoe only $\frac{3}{4}$ of this distance in 6 hours. Find your average velocity in still water and the average velocity of the current.

66. With the current, you can row 24 miles in 3 hours. Against the same current, you can row only $\frac{3}{4}$ of this distance in 4 hours. Find your average rowing velocity in still water and the average velocity of the current.

*The figure shows the graphs of the cost and revenue functions for a company that manufactures and sells small radios. Use the information in the figure to solve Exercises 67–72.*

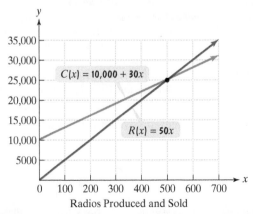

67. How many radios must be produced and sold for the company to break even?

68. More than how many radios must be produced and sold for the company to have a profit?

*(Exercises 69–72 are based on the graphs at the bottom of the previous page.)*

69. Use the formulas shown in the voice balloons to find $R(200) - C(200)$. Describe what this means for the company.

70. Use the formulas shown in the voice balloons to find $R(300) - C(300)$. Describe what this means for the company.

71. **a.** Use the formulas shown in the voice balloons to write the company's profit function, $P$, from producing and selling $x$ radios.

   **b.** Find the company's profit if 10,000 radios are produced and sold.

72. **a.** Use the formulas shown in the voice balloons to write the company's profit function, $P$, from producing and selling $x$ radios.

   **b.** Find the company's profit if 20,000 radios are produced and sold.

*Exercises 73–76 describe a number of business ventures. For each exercise,*

   **a.** *Write the cost function, C.*

   **b.** *Write the revenue function, R.*

   **c.** *Determine the break-even point. Describe what this means.*

73. A company that manufactures small canoes has a fixed cost of $18,000. It costs $20 to produce each canoe. The selling price is $80 per canoe. (In solving this exercise, let $x$ represent the number of canoes produced and sold.)

74. A company that manufactures bicycles has a fixed cost of $100,000. It costs $100 to produce each bicycle. The selling price is $300 per bike. (In solving this exercise, let $x$ represent the number of bicycles produced and sold.)

75. You invest in a new play. The cost includes an overhead of $30,000, plus production costs of $2500 per performance. A sold-out performance brings in $3125. (In solving this exercise, let $x$ represent the number of sold-out performances.)

76. You invested $30,000 and started a business writing greeting cards. Supplies cost 2¢ per card and you are selling each card for 50¢. (In solving this exercise, let $x$ represent the number of cards produced and sold.)

*An important application of systems of equations arises in connection with supply and demand. As the price of a product increases, the demand for that product decreases. However, at higher prices, suppliers are willing to produce greater quantities of the product. The price at which supply and demand are equal is called the* **equilibrium price**. *The quantity supplied and demanded at that price is called the* **equilibrium quantity**. *Exercises 77–78 involve supply and demand.*

77. The following models describe wages for low-skilled labor.

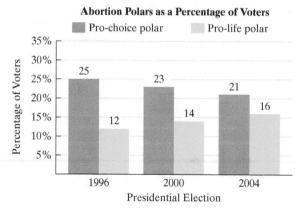

| **Demand Model** | **Supply Model** |
| --- | --- |
| $p = -0.325x + 5.8$ | $p = 0.375x + 3$ |

*Source:* O'Sullivan and Sheffrin, *Economics*, Prentice Hall, 2007

**a.** Solve the system and find the equilibrium number of workers, in millions, and the equilibrium hourly wage.

**b.** Use your answer from part (a) to complete this statement:

   If workers are paid _____ per hour, there will be ___ million available workers and ___ million workers will be hired.

**c.** In 2007, the federal minimum wage was set at $5.15 per hour. Substitute 5.15 for $p$ in the demand model, $p = -0.325x + 5.8$, and determine the millions of workers employers will hire at this price.

**d.** At a minimum wage of $5.15 per hour, use the supply model, $p = 0.375x + 3$, to determine the millions of available workers. Round to one decimal place.

**e.** At a minimum wage of $5.15 per hour, use your answers from parts (c) and (d) to determine how many more people are looking for work than employers are willing to hire.

78. The following models describe demand and supply for three-bedroom rental apartments.

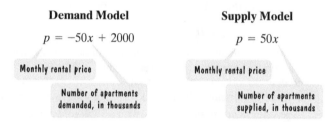

| **Demand Model** | **Supply Model** |
| --- | --- |
| $p = -50x + 2000$ | $p = 50x$ |

**a.** Solve the system and find the equilibrium quantity and the equilibrium price.

**b.** Use your answer from part (a) to complete this statement:

   When rents are _____ per month, consumers will demand _____ apartments and suppliers will offer _____ apartments for rent.

79. In each of the 1996, 2000, and 2004 presidential elections, 37% of voters believed abortion should be "always legal" or "always illegal." The bar graph shows the breakdown of these abortion "polars" as a percentage of voters in each election.

**Abortion Polars as a Percentage of Voters**

■ Pro-choice polar    ■ Pro-life polar

*(Bar graph: Percentage of Voters vs. Presidential Election)*

1996: Pro-choice polar 25, Pro-life polar 12
2000: Pro-choice polar 23, Pro-life polar 14
2004: Pro-choice polar 21, Pro-life polar 16

*Source: Newsweek*

The data in the bar graph on the previous page can be modeled by the following system of equations:

$$\begin{cases} x + 2y = 50 \\ -x + 2y = 24. \end{cases}$$

The percentage of pro-choice polars, $y$, $x$ years after 1996

The percentage of pro-life polars, $y$, $x$ years after 1996

In which year will the percentage of voters who are pro-choice polars be the same as the percentage of voters who are pro-life polars? For that year, what percent will be pro-choice and what percent will be pro-life?

80. The bar graph shows the percentage of Americans for and against the death penalty for a person convicted of murder.

**Are You in Favor of the Death Penalty for a Person Convicted of Murder?**

- For the death penalty
- Against the death penalty

*Source: Newsweek poll*

The data can be modeled by the following system of equations:

$$\begin{cases} 13x + 12y = 992 \\ -x + y = 16. \end{cases}$$

The percent, $y$, in favor of the death penalty $x$ years after 1988

The percent, $y$, against the death penalty $x$ years after 1988

In which year will the percentage of Americans in favor of the death penalty be the same as the percentage of Americans who oppose it? For that year, what percent will be for the death penalty and what percent will be against it?

81. We opened this section with a study showing that late in the semester, procrastinating students reported more symptoms of physical illness than their nonprocrastinating peers.

   a. At the beginning of the semester, procrastinators reported an average of 0.8 symptoms, increasing at a rate of 0.45 symptoms per week. Write a function that models the average number of symptoms after $x$ weeks.

   b. At the beginning of the semester, nonprocrastinators reported an average of 2.6 symptoms, increasing at a rate of 0.15 symptoms per week. Write a function that models the average number of symptoms after $x$ weeks.

   c. By which week in the semester did both groups report the same number of symptoms of physical illness? For that week, how many symptoms were reported by each group? How is this shown in **Figure 7.1** on page 728?

82. Although Social Security is a problem, some projections indicate that there's a much bigger time bomb ticking in the federal budget, and that's Medicare. In 2000, the cost of Social Security was 5.48% of the gross domestic product, increasing by 0.04% of the GDP per year. In 2000, the cost of Medicare was 1.84% of the gross domestic product, increasing by 0.17% of the GDP per year.

(*Source:* Congressional Budget Office)

   a. Write a function that models the cost of Social Security as a percentage of the GDP $x$ years after 2000.

   b. Write a function that models the cost of Medicare as a percentage of the GDP $x$ years after 2000.

   c. In which year will the cost of Medicare and Social Security be the same? For that year, what will be the cost of each program as a percentage of the GDP? Which program will have the greater cost after that year?

*The bar graph shows the percentage of Americans who used cigarettes, by ethnicity, in 1985 and 2005. For each of the groups shown, cigarette use has been linearly decreasing. Use this information to solve Exercises 83–84.*

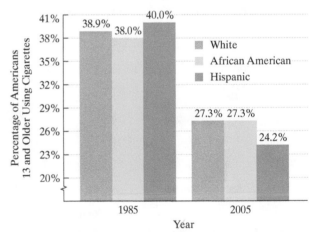

**Cigarette Use in the United States**

- White
- African American
- Hispanic

*Source:* Department of Health and Human Services

83. In this exercise, let $x$ represent the number of years after 1985 and let $y$ represent the percentage of Americans in one of the groups shown who used cigarettes.

   a. Use the data points $(0, 38)$ and $(20, 27.3)$ to find the slope-intercept equation of the line that models the percentage of African Americans who used cigarettes, $y$, $x$ years after 1985. Round the value of the slope $m$ to two decimal places.

   b. Use the data points $(0, 40)$ and $(20, 24.2)$ to find the slope-intercept equation of the line that models the percentage of Hispanics who used cigarettes, $y$, $x$ years after 1985.

   c. Use the models from parts (a) and (b) to find the year during which cigarette use was the same for African Americans and Hispanics. What percentage of each group used cigarettes during that year?

*(Exercise 84 is based on the bar graph in the second column on the previous page.)*

**84.** In this exercise, let $x$ represent the number of years after 1985 and let $y$ represent the percentage of Americans in one of the groups shown who used cigarettes.

  **a.** Use the data points $(0, 38.9)$ and $(20, 27.3)$ to find the slope-intercept equation of the line that models the percentage of whites who used cigarettes, $y$, $x$ years after 1985.

  **b.** Use the data points $(0, 40)$ and $(20, 24.2)$ to find the slope-intercept equation of the line that models the percentage of Hispanics who used cigarettes, $y$, $x$ years after 1985.

  **c.** Use the models from parts (a) and (b) to find the year, to the nearest whole year, during which cigarette use was the same for whites and Hispanics. What percentage of each group, to the nearest percent, used cigarettes during that year?

*Use a system of linear equations to solve Exercises 85–92.*

*Looking for Mr. Goodbar? It's probably not a good idea if you want to look like Mr. Universe or Julia Roberts. The graph shows the four candy bars with the highest fat content, representing grams of fat and calories in each bar. Exercises 85–88 are based on the graph.*

**Candy Bars with the Highest Fat Content**

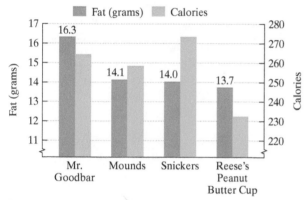

*Source:* Krantz and Sveum, *The World's Worsts*, HarperCollins, 2005

**85.** One Mr. Goodbar and two Mounds bars contain 780 calories. Two Mr. Goodbars and one Mounds bar contain 786 calories. Find the caloric content of each candy bar.

**86.** One Snickers bar and two Reese's Peanut Butter Cups contain 737 calories. Two Snickers bars and one Reese's Peanut Butter Cup contain 778 calories. Find the caloric content of each candy bar.

**87.** A collection of Halloween candy contains a total of five Mr. Goodbars and Mounds bars. Chew on this: The grams of fat in these candy bars exceed the daily maximum desirable fat intake of 70 grams by 7.1 grams. How many bars of each kind of candy are contained in the Halloween collection?

**88.** A collection of Halloween candy contains a total of 12 Snickers bars and Reese's Peanut Butter Cups. Chew on this: The grams of fat in these candy bars exceed twice the daily maximum desirable fat intake of 70 grams by 26.5 grams. How many bars of each kind of candy are contained in the Halloween collection?

**89.** A hotel has 200 rooms. Those with kitchen facilities rent for $100 per night and those without kitchen facilities rent for $80 per night. On a night when the hotel was completely occupied, revenues were $17,000. How many of each type of room does the hotel have?

**90.** A new restaurant is to contain two-seat tables and four-seat tables. Fire codes limit the restaurant's maximum occupancy to 56 customers. If the owners have hired enough servers to handle 17 tables of customers, how many of each kind of table should they purchase?

**91.** A rectangular lot whose perimeter is 360 feet is fenced along three sides. An expensive fencing along the lot's length costs $20 per foot and an inexpensive fencing along the two side widths costs only $8 per foot. The total cost of the fencing along the three sides comes to $3280. What are the lot's dimensions?

**92.** A rectangular lot whose perimeter is 320 feet is fenced along three sides. An expensive fencing along the lot's length costs $16 per foot and an inexpensive fencing along the two side widths costs only $5 per foot. The total cost of the fencing along the three sides comes to $2140. What are the lot's dimensions?

*In Exercises 93–94, an isosceles triangle containing two angles with equal measure is shown. The degree measure of each triangle's three interior angles and an exterior angle is represented with variables. Find the measure of the three interior angles.*

**93.**                    **94.**

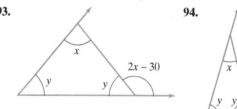

## Writing in Mathematics

**95.** What is a system of linear equations? Provide an example with your description.

**96.** What is the solution of a system of linear equations?

**97.** Explain how to solve a system of equations using the substitution method. Use $y = 3 - 3x$ and $3x + 4y = 6$ to illustrate your explanation.

**98.** Explain how to solve a system of equations using the addition method. Use $3x + 5y = -2$ and $2x + 3y = 0$ to illustrate your explanation.

**99.** When is it easier to use the addition method rather than the substitution method to solve a system of equations?

**100.** When using the addition or substitution method, how can you tell if a system of linear equations has infinitely many solutions? What is the relationship between the graphs of the two equations?

**101.** When using the addition or substitution method, how can you tell if a system of linear equations has no solution? What is the relationship between the graphs of the two equations?

**102.** Describe the break-even point for a business.

## Technology Exercise

**103.** Verify your solutions to any five exercises in Exercises 5–42 by using a graphing utility to graph the two equations in the system in the same viewing rectangle. Then use the intersection feature to display the solution.

## Critical Thinking Exercises

**Make Sense?** *In Exercises 104–107, determine whether each statement makes sense or does not make sense, and explain your reasoning.*

**104.** Each equation in a system of linear equations has infinitely many ordered-pair solutions.

**105.** Every linear system has infinitely many ordered-pair solutions.

**106.** I should mix 6 liters of a 50% acid solution with 4 liters of a 25% acid solution to obtain 10 liters of a 75% acid solution.

**107.** You told me that you flew against the wind from Miami to Seattle, 2800 miles, in 7 hours and, at the same time, your friend flew with the wind from Seattle to Miami in only 5.6 hours. You have not given me enough information to determine the average velocity of the wind.

**108.** Write a system of equations having $\{(-2, 7)\}$ as a solution set. (More than one system is possible.)

**109.** Solve the system for $x$ and $y$ in terms of $a_1, b_1, c_1, a_2, b_2,$ and $c_2$:

$$\begin{cases} a_1x + b_1y = c_1 \\ a_2x + b_2y = c_2. \end{cases}$$

**110.** Two identical twins can only be distinguished by the characteristic that one always tells the truth and the other always lies. One twin tells you of a lucky number pair: "When I multiply my first lucky number by 3 and my second lucky number by 6, the addition of the resulting numbers produces a sum of 12. When I add my first lucky number and twice my second lucky number, the sum is 5." Which twin is talking?

**111.** A marching band has 52 members, and there are 24 in the pom-pom squad. They wish to form several hexagons and squares like those diagrammed below. Can it be done with no people left over?

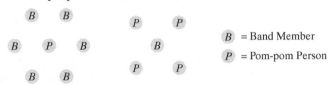

$B$ = Band Member

$P$ = Pom-pom Person

## Group Exercise

**112.** The group should write four different word problems that can be solved using a system of linear equations in two variables. All of the problems should be on different topics. The group should turn in the four problems and their algebraic solutions.

## Preview Exercises

*Exercises 113–115 will help you prepare for the material covered in the next section.*

**113.** If $x = 3, y = 2,$ and $z = -3,$ does the ordered triple $(x, y, z)$ satisfy the equation $2x - y + 4z = -8$?

**114.** Consider the following equations:

$$\begin{cases} 5x - 2y - 4z = 3 & \text{Equation 1} \\ 3x + 3y + 2z = -3. & \text{Equation 2} \end{cases}$$

Use these equations to eliminate $z$. Copy Equation 1 and multiply Equation 2 by 2. Then add the equations.

**115.** Write an equation involving $a, b,$ and $c$ based on the following description:

When the value of $x$ in $y = ax^2 + bx + c$ is 4, the value of $y$ is 1682.

Section 7.2

# Systems of Linear Equations in Three Variables

## Objectives

① Verify the solution of a system of linear equations in three variables.

② Solve systems of linear equations in three variables.

③ Solve problems using systems in three variables.

All animals sleep, but the length of time they sleep varies widely: Cattle sleep for only a few minutes at a time. We humans seem to need more sleep than other animals, up to eight hours a day. Without enough sleep, we have difficulty concentrating, make mistakes in routine tasks, lose energy, and feel bad-tempered. There is a relationship between hours of sleep and death rate per year per 100,000 people. How many hours of sleep will put you in the group with the minimum death rate? In this section, we will answer this question by solving a system of linear equations with more than two variables.

① Verify the solution of a system of linear equations in three variables.

## Systems of Linear Equations in Three Variables and Their Solutions

An equation such as $x + 2y - 3z = 9$ is called a *linear equation in three variables*. In general, any equation of the form

$$Ax + By + Cz = D,$$

where $A$, $B$, $C$, and $D$ are real numbers such that $A$, $B$, and $C$ are not all 0, is a **linear equation in three variables: $x$, $y$, and $z$**. The graph of this linear equation in three variables is a plane in three-dimensional space.

The process of solving a system of three linear equations in three variables is geometrically equivalent to finding the point of intersection (assuming that there is one) of three planes in space. (See **Figure 7.9**.) A **solution** of a system of linear equations in three variables is an ordered triple of real numbers that satisfies all equations of the system. The **solution set** of the system is the set of all its solutions.

Point of intersection

$P$

**Figure 7.9**

---

**EXAMPLE 1** Determining Whether an Ordered Triple Satisfies a System

Show that the ordered triple $(-1, 2, -2)$ is a solution of the system:

$$\begin{cases} x + 2y - 3z = 9 \\ 2x - y + 2z = -8 \\ -x + 3y - 4z = 15. \end{cases}$$

**Solution**  Because $-1$ is the $x$-coordinate, 2 is the $y$-coordinate, and $-2$ is the $z$-coordinate of $(-1, 2, -2)$, we replace $x$ with $-1$, $y$ with 2, and $z$ with $-2$ in each of the three equations.

$$x + 2y - 3z = 9$$
$$-1 + 2(2) - 3(-2) \stackrel{?}{=} 9$$
$$-1 + 4 + 6 \stackrel{?}{=} 9$$
$$9 = 9, \quad \text{true}$$

$$2x - y + 2z = -8$$
$$2(-1) - 2 + 2(-2) \stackrel{?}{=} -8$$
$$-2 - 2 - 4 \stackrel{?}{=} -8$$
$$-8 = -8, \quad \text{true}$$

$$-x + 3y - 4z = 15$$
$$-(-1) + 3(2) - 4(-2) \stackrel{?}{=} 15$$
$$1 + 6 + 8 \stackrel{?}{=} 15$$
$$15 = 15, \quad \text{true}$$

The ordered triple $(-1, 2, -2)$ satisfies the three equations: It makes each equation true. Thus, the ordered triple is a solution of the system.

Check Point I Show that the ordered triple $(-1, -4, 5)$ is a solution of the system:

$$\begin{cases} x - 2y + 3z = 22 \\ 2x - 3y - z = 5 \\ 3x + y - 5z = -32. \end{cases}$$

② Solve systems of linear equations in three variables.

## Solving Systems of Linear Equations in Three Variables by Eliminating Variables

The method for solving a system of linear equations in three variables is similar to that used on systems of linear equations in two variables. We use addition to eliminate any variable, reducing the system to two equations in two variables. Once we obtain a system of two equations in two variables, we use addition or substitution to eliminate a variable. The result is a single equation in one variable. We solve this equation to get the value of the remaining variable. Other variable values are found by back-substitution.

**Study Tip**

It does not matter which variable you eliminate, as long as you do it in two different pairs of equations.

### Solving Linear Systems in Three Variables by Eliminating Variables

1. Reduce the system to two equations in two variables. This is usually accomplished by taking two different pairs of equations and using the addition method to eliminate the same variable from both pairs.

2. Solve the resulting system of two equations in two variables using addition or substitution. The result is an equation in one variable that gives the value of that variable.

3. Back-substitute the value of the variable found in step 2 into either of the equations in two variables to find the value of the second variable.

4. Use the values of the two variables from steps 2 and 3 to find the value of the third variable by back-substituting into one of the original equations.

5. Check the proposed solution in each of the original equations.

**EXAMPLE 2** Solving a System in Three Variables

Solve the system:

$$\begin{cases} 5x - 2y - 4z = 3 & \text{Equation 1} \\ 3x + 3y + 2z = -3 & \text{Equation 2} \\ -2x + 5y + 3z = 3. & \text{Equation 3} \end{cases}$$

$$\begin{cases} 5x - 2y - 4z = 3 & \text{Equation 1} \\ 3x + 3y + 2z = -3 & \text{Equation 2} \\ -2x + 5y + 3z = 3 & \text{Equation 3} \end{cases}$$

The given system (repeated)

**Solution**  There are many ways to proceed. Because our initial goal is to reduce the system to two equations in two variables, **the central idea is to take two different pairs of equations and eliminate the same variable from both pairs.**

**Step 1  Reduce the system to two equations in two variables.** We choose any two equations and use the addition method to eliminate a variable. Let's eliminate $z$ using Equations 1 and 2. We do so by multiplying Equation 2 by 2. Then we add equations.

(Equation 1) $\begin{cases} 5x - 2y - 4z = 3 & \xrightarrow{\text{No change}} \\ 3x + 3y + 2z = -3 & \xrightarrow{\text{Multiply by 2.}} \end{cases}$ $\begin{cases} 5x - 2y - 4z = 3 \\ 6x + 6y + 4z = -6 \end{cases}$
(Equation 2)

Add:  $11x + 4y \qquad = -3$  Equation 4

Now we must eliminate the *same* variable using another pair of equations. We can eliminate $z$ from Equations 2 and 3. First, we multiply Equation 2 by $-3$. Next, we multiply Equation 3 by 2. Finally, we add equations.

(Equation 2) $\begin{cases} 3x + 3y + 2z = -3 & \xrightarrow{\text{Multiply by } -3.} \\ -2x + 5y + 3z = 3 & \xrightarrow{\text{Multiply by 2.}} \end{cases}$ $\begin{cases} -9x - 9y - 6z = 9 \\ -4x + 10y + 6z = 6 \end{cases}$
(Equation 3)

Add:  $-13x + y \qquad = 15$  Equation 5

Equations 4 and 5 give us a system of two equations in two variables:

$$\begin{cases} 11x + 4y = -3 & \text{Equation 4} \\ -13x + y = 15. & \text{Equation 5} \end{cases}$$

**Step 2  Solve the resulting system of two equations in two variables.** We will use the addition method to solve Equations 4 and 5 for $x$ and $y$. To do so, we multiply Equation 5 on both sides by $-4$ and add this to Equation 4.

(Equation 4) $\begin{cases} 11x + 4y = -3 & \xrightarrow{\text{No change}} \\ -13x + y = 15 & \xrightarrow{\text{Multiply by } -4.} \end{cases}$ $\begin{cases} 11x + 4y = -3 \\ 52x - 4y = -60 \end{cases}$
(Equation 5)

$63x \qquad = -63$

Add:  $x \qquad = -1$  Divide both sides by 63.

**Step 3  Use back-substitution in one of the equations in two variables to find the value of the second variable.** We back-substitute $-1$ for $x$ in either Equation 4 or 5 to find the value of $y$.

$$-13x + y = 15 \qquad \text{Equation 5}$$
$$-13(-1) + y = 15 \qquad \text{Substitute } -1 \text{ for } x.$$
$$13 + y = 15 \qquad \text{Multiply.}$$
$$y = 2 \qquad \text{Subtract 13 from both sides.}$$

**Step 4  Back-substitute the values found for two variables into one of the original equations to find the value of the third variable.** We can now use any one of the original equations and back-substitute the values of $x$ and $y$ to find the value for $z$. We will use Equation 2.

$$3x + 3y + 2z = -3 \qquad \text{Equation 2}$$
$$3(-1) + 3(2) + 2z = -3 \qquad \text{Substitute } -1 \text{ for } x \text{ and } 2 \text{ for } y.$$
$$3 + 2z = -3 \qquad \text{Multiply and then add:}$$
$$\qquad\qquad\qquad 3(-1) + 3(2) = -3 + 6 = 3.$$
$$2z = -6 \qquad \text{Subtract 3 from both sides.}$$
$$z = -3 \qquad \text{Divide both sides by 2.}$$

With $x = -1$, $y = 2$, and $z = -3$, the proposed solution is the ordered triple $(-1, 2, -3)$.

**Step 5 Check.** Check the proposed solution, $(-1, 2, -3)$, by substituting the values for $x$, $y$, and $z$ into each of the three original equations. These substitutions yield three true statements. Thus, the solution set is $\{(-1, 2, -3)\}$.

⬤

✓ Check Point **2** Solve the system:

$$\begin{cases} x + 4y - z = 20 \\ 3x + 2y + z = 8 \\ 2x - 3y + 2z = -16. \end{cases}$$

In some examples, one of the variables is already eliminated from a given equation. In this case, the missing variable should be eliminated from the other two equations, thereby making it possible to omit one of the elimination steps. We illustrate this idea in Example 3.

( **EXAMPLE 3** ) **Solving a System of Equations with a Missing Term**

Solve the system:

$$\begin{cases} x + \phantom{2y +} z = 8 & \text{Equation 1} \\ x + y + 2z = 17 & \text{Equation 2} \\ x + 2y + z = 16. & \text{Equation 3} \end{cases}$$

**Solution**

**Step 1 Reduce the system to two equations in two variables.** Because Equation 1 contains only $x$ and $z$, we could omit one of the elimination steps by eliminating $y$ using Equations 2 and 3. This will give us two equations in $x$ and $z$. To eliminate $y$ using Equations 2 and 3, we multiply Equation 2 by $-2$ and add Equation 3.

(Equation 2) $\begin{cases} x + y + 2z = 17 \end{cases}$ $\xrightarrow{\text{Multiply by } -2.}$ $\begin{cases} -2x - 2y - 4z = -34 \end{cases}$
(Equation 3) $\begin{cases} x + 2y + z = 16 \end{cases}$ $\xrightarrow{\text{No change}}$ $\begin{cases} \underline{x + 2y + z = \phantom{-}16} \end{cases}$

Add: $\phantom{xxx} -x \phantom{xxxxxx} - 3z = -18$ Equation 4

Equation 4 and the given Equation 1 provide us with a system of two equations in two variables:

$$\begin{cases} x + \phantom{3}z = 8 & \text{Equation 1} \\ -x - 3z = -18. & \text{Equation 4} \end{cases}$$

**Step 2 Solve the resulting system of two equations in two variables.** We will solve Equations 1 and 4 for $x$ and $z$.

$$\begin{cases} x + \phantom{3}z = \phantom{-}8 & \text{Equation 1} \\ \underline{-x - 3z = -18} & \text{Equation 4} \end{cases}$$

Add: $\phantom{xxxx} -2z = -10$

$\phantom{xxxxxxx} z = \phantom{-}5$ Divide both sides by $-2$.

**Step 3 Use back-substitution in one of the equations in two variables to find the value of the second variable.** To find $x$, we back-substitute $5$ for $z$ in either Equation 1 or 4. We will use Equation 1.

$x + z = 8$ Equation 1

$x + 5 = 8$ Substitute 5 for z.

$x = 3$ Subtract 5 from both sides.

$$\begin{cases} x + \phantom{y} + z = 8 & \text{Equation 1} \\ x + y + 2z = 17 & \text{Equation 2} \\ x + 2y + z = 16 & \text{Equation 3} \end{cases}$$

The given system (repeated)

**Step 4   Back-substitute the values found for two variables into one of the original equations to find the value of the third variable.** To find $y$, we back-substitute 3 for $x$ and 5 for $z$ into Equation 2 or 3. We cannot use Equation 1 because $y$ is missing in this equation. We will use Equation 2.

$$\begin{aligned} x + y + 2z &= 17 & &\text{Equation 2} \\ 3 + y + 2(5) &= 17 & &\text{Substitute 3 for x and 5 for z.} \\ y + 13 &= 17 & &\text{Multiply and add.} \\ y &= 4 & &\text{Subtract 13 from both sides.} \end{aligned}$$

We found that $z = 5$, $x = 3$, and $y = 4$. Thus, the proposed solution is the ordered triple $(3, 4, 5)$.

**Step 5   Check.** Substituting 3 for $x$, 4 for $y$, and 5 for $z$ into each of the three original equations yields three true statements. Consequently, the solution set is $\{(3, 4, 5)\}$.  ●

⊘ Check Point **3** Solve the system:

$$\begin{cases} 2y - z = 7 \\ x + 2y + z = 17 \\ 2x - 3y + 2z = -1. \end{cases}$$

A system of linear equations in three variables represents three planes. The three planes may not always intersect at one point. The planes may have no common point of intersection and represent an inconsistent system with no solution. By contrast, the planes may coincide or intersect along a line. In these cases, the planes have infinitely many points in common and represent systems with infinitely many solutions. Systems of linear equations in three variables that are inconsistent or that contain dependent equations will be discussed in Chapter 8.

③ Solve problems using systems in three variables.

## Applications

Systems of equations may allow us to find models for data without using a graphing utility. Three data points that do not lie on or near a line determine the graph of a quadratic function of the form $y = ax^2 + bx + c, a \neq 0$. Quadratic functions often model situations in which values of $y$ are decreasing and then increasing, suggesting the bowl-like shape of a parabola.

(EXAMPLE 4)  **Modeling Data Relating Sleep and Death Rate**

In a study relating sleep and death rate, the following data were obtained. Use the function $y = ax^2 + bx + c$ to model the data.

| $x$ (Average Number of Hours of Sleep) | $y$ (Death Rate per Year per 100,000 Males) |
|---|---|
| 4 | 1682 |
| 7 | 626 |
| 9 | 967 |

**Solution** We need to find values for $a, b,$ and $c$ in $y = ax^2 + bx + c$. We can do so by solving a system of three linear equations in $a, b,$ and $c$. We obtain the three equations by using the values of $x$ and $y$ from the data as follows:

$$y = ax^2 + bx + c \qquad \text{Use the quadratic function to model the data.}$$

When $x = 4, y = 1682$:    $\begin{cases} 1682 = a \cdot 4^2 + b \cdot 4 + c \\ 626 = a \cdot 7^2 + b \cdot 7 + c \quad \text{or} \\ 967 = a \cdot 9^2 + b \cdot 9 + c \end{cases}$  $\begin{cases} 16a + 4b + c = 1682 \\ 49a + 7b + c = 626 \\ 81a + 9b + c = 967. \end{cases}$

When $x = 7, y = 626$:

When $x = 9, y = 967$:

The easiest way to solve this system is to eliminate $c$ from two pairs of equations, obtaining two equations in $a$ and $b$. Solving this system gives $a = 104.5, b = -1501.5,$ and $c = 6016$. We now substitute the values for $a, b,$ and $c$ into $y = ax^2 + bx + c$. The function that models the given data is

$$y = 104.5x^2 - 1501.5x + 6016.$$

We can use the model that we obtained in Example 4 to find the death rate of males who average, say, 6 hours of sleep. First, write the model in function notation:

$$f(x) = 104.5x^2 - 1501.5x + 6016.$$

Substitute 6 for $x$:

$$f(6) = 104.5(6)^2 - 1501.5(6) + 6016 = 769.$$

According to the model, the death rate for males who average 6 hours of sleep is 769 deaths per 100,000 males.

⌀ Check Point **4** Find the quadratic function $y = ax^2 + bx + c$ whose graph passes through the points $(1, 4), (2, 1),$ and $(3, 4)$.

## Technology

The graph of

$$y = 104.5x^2 - 1501.5x + 6016$$

is displayed in a [3, 12, 1] by [500, 2000, 100] viewing rectangle. The minimum function feature shows that the lowest point on the graph, the vertex, is approximately (7.2, 622.5). Men who average 7.2 hours of sleep are in the group with the lowest death rate, approximately 622.5 deaths per 100,000 males.

# Exercise Set 7.2

## Practice Exercises

*In Exercises 1–4, determine if the given ordered triple is a solution of the system.*

**1.** $(2, -1, 3)$
$\begin{cases} x + y + z = 4 \\ x - 2y - z = 1 \\ 2x - y - 2z = -1 \end{cases}$

**2.** $(5, -3, -2)$
$\begin{cases} x + y + z = 0 \\ x + 2y - 3z = 5 \\ 3x + 4y + 2z = -1 \end{cases}$

**3.** $(4, 1, 2)$
$\begin{cases} x - 2y = 2 \\ 2x + 3y = 11 \\ y - 4z = -7 \end{cases}$

**4.** $(-1, 3, 2)$
$\begin{cases} x - 2z = -5 \\ y - 3z = -3 \\ 2x - z = -4 \end{cases}$

*Solve each system in Exercises 5–18.*

**5.** $\begin{cases} x + y + 2z = 11 \\ x + y + 3z = 14 \\ x + 2y - z = 5 \end{cases}$

**6.** $\begin{cases} 2x + y - 2z = -1 \\ 3x - 3y - z = 5 \\ x - 2y + 3z = 6 \end{cases}$

**7.** $\begin{cases} 4x - y + 2z = 11 \\ x + 2y - z = -1 \\ 2x + 2y - 3z = -1 \end{cases}$

**8.** $\begin{cases} x - y + 3z = 8 \\ 3x + y - 2z = -2 \\ 2x + 4y + z = 0 \end{cases}$

**9.** $\begin{cases} 3x + 2y - 3z = -2 \\ 2x - 5y + 2z = -2 \\ 4x - 3y + 4z = 10 \end{cases}$

**10.** $\begin{cases} 2x + 3y + 7z = 13 \\ 3x + 2y - 5z = -22 \\ 5x + 7y - 3z = -28 \end{cases}$

**11.** $\begin{cases} 2x - 4y + 3z = 17 \\ x + 2y - z = 0 \\ 4x - y - z = 6 \end{cases}$

**12.** $\begin{cases} x + z = 3 \\ x + 2y - z = 1 \\ 2x - y + z = 3 \end{cases}$

**13.** $\begin{cases} 2x + y = 2 \\ x + y - z = 4 \\ 3x + 2y + z = 0 \end{cases}$

**14.** $\begin{cases} x + 3y + 5z = 20 \\ y - 4z = -16 \\ 3x - 2y + 9z = 36 \end{cases}$

**15.** $\begin{cases} x + y = -4 \\ y - z = 1 \\ 2x + y + 3z = -21 \end{cases}$

**16.** $\begin{cases} x + y = 4 \\ x + z = 4 \\ y + z = 4 \end{cases}$

**17.** $\begin{cases} 3(2x + y) + 5z = -1 \\ 2(x - 3y + 4z) = -9 \\ 4(1 + x) = -3(z - 3y) \end{cases}$

**18.** $\begin{cases} 7z - 3 = 2(x - 3y) \\ 5y + 3z - 7 = 4x \\ 4 + 5z = 3(2x - y) \end{cases}$

*In Exercises 19–22, find the quadratic function $y = ax^2 + bx + c$ whose graph passes through the given points.*

**19.** $(-1, 6), (1, 4), (2, 9)$      **20.** $(-2, 7), (1, -2), (2, 3)$

**21.** $(-1, -4), (1, -2), (2, 5)$      **22.** $(1, 3), (3, -1), (4, 0)$

*In Exercises 23–24, let x represent the first number, y the second number, and z the third number. Use the given conditions to write a system of equations. Solve the system and find the numbers.*

**23.** The sum of three numbers is 16. The sum of twice the first number, 3 times the second number, and 4 times the third number is 46. The difference between 5 times the first number and the second number is 31. Find the three numbers.

**24.** The following is known about three numbers: Three times the first number plus the second number plus twice the third number is 5. If 3 times the second number is subtracted from the sum of the first number and 3 times the third number, the result is 2. If the third number is subtracted from 2 times the first number and 3 times the second number, the result is 1. Find the numbers.

## Practice Plus

*Solve each system in Exercises 25–26.*

**25.**
$$\begin{cases} \dfrac{x+2}{6} - \dfrac{y+4}{3} + \dfrac{z}{2} = 0 \\ \dfrac{x+1}{2} + \dfrac{y-1}{2} - \dfrac{z}{4} = \dfrac{9}{2} \\ \dfrac{x-5}{4} + \dfrac{y+1}{3} + \dfrac{z-2}{2} = \dfrac{19}{4} \end{cases}$$

**26.**
$$\begin{cases} \dfrac{x+3}{2} - \dfrac{y-1}{2} + \dfrac{z+2}{4} = \dfrac{3}{2} \\ \dfrac{x-5}{2} + \dfrac{y+1}{3} - \dfrac{z}{4} = -\dfrac{25}{6} \\ \dfrac{x-3}{4} - \dfrac{y+1}{2} + \dfrac{z-3}{2} = -\dfrac{5}{2} \end{cases}$$

*In Exercises 27–28, find the equation of the quadratic function $y = ax^2 + bx + c$ whose graph is shown. Select three points whose coordinates appear to be integers.*

**27.**
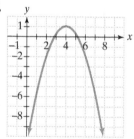

**28.**
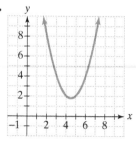

*In Exercises 29–30, solve each system for $(x, y, z)$ in terms of the nonzero constants a, b, and c.*

**29.**
$$\begin{cases} ax - by - 2cz = 21 \\ ax + by + cz = 0 \\ 2ax - by + cz = 14 \end{cases}$$

**30.**
$$\begin{cases} ax - by + 2cz = -4 \\ ax + 3by - cz = 1 \\ 2ax + by + 3cz = 2 \end{cases}$$

## Application Exercises

**31.** You throw a ball straight up from a rooftop. The ball misses the rooftop on its way down and eventually strikes the ground. A mathematical model can be used to describe the relationship for the ball's height above the ground, $y$, after $x$ seconds. Consider the following data:

| $x$, seconds after the ball is thrown | $y$, ball's height, in feet, above the ground |
|---|---|
| 1 | 224 |
| 3 | 176 |
| 4 | 104 |

   **a.** Find the quadratic function $y = ax^2 + bx + c$ whose graph passes through the given points.

   **b.** Use the function in part (a) to find the value for $y$ when $x = 5$. Describe what this means.

**32.** A mathematical model can be used to describe the relationship between the number of feet a car travels once the brakes are applied, $y$, and the number of seconds the car is in motion after the brakes are applied, $x$. A research firm collects the following data:

| $x$, seconds in motion after brakes are applied | $y$, feet car travels once the brakes are applied |
|---|---|
| 1 | 46 |
| 2 | 84 |
| 3 | 114 |

   **a.** Find the quadratic function $y = ax^2 + bx + c$ whose graph passes through the given points.

   **b.** Use the function in part (a) to find the value for $y$ when $x = 6$. Describe what this means.

*Use a system of linear equations in three variables to solve Exercises 33–39.*

*The bar graph compares the body composition of a 160-pound adult male and a 135-pound adult female. Exercises 33–34 are based on the data displayed by the graph.*

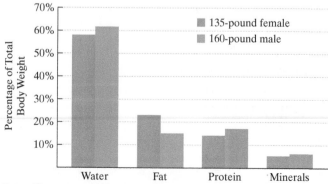

Source: Thompson et al., *The Science of Nutrition*, Benjamin Cummings, 2008

**33.** This exercise refers to the body composition of a 135-pound adult female, shown by the graph on the previous page. Ninety-five percent of her total body weight consists of water, fat, and protein. The difference between the percentage of body weight consisting of water and fat is 35%. The difference between the percentage of body weight consisting of fat and protein is 9%. Find the percentage of total body weight consisting of water, of fat, and of protein.

**34.** This exercise refers to the body composition of a 160-pound adult male, shown by the graph on the previous page. Ninety-four percent of his total body weight consists of water, fat, and protein. The difference between the percentage of body weight consisting of water and fat is 47%. The difference between the percentage of body weight consisting of protein and fat is 2%. Find the percentage of total body weight consisting of water, of fat, and of protein.

**35.** At a college production of *Streetcar Named Desire*, 400 tickets were sold. The ticket prices were $8, $10, and $12, and the total income from ticket sales was $3700. How many tickets of each type were sold if the combined number of $8 and $10 tickets sold was 7 times the number of $12 tickets sold?

**36.** A certain brand of razor blades comes in packages of 6, 12, and 24 blades, costing $2, $3, and $4 per package, respectively. A store sold 12 packages containing a total of 162 razor blades and took in $35. How many packages of each type were sold?

**37.** A person invested $6700 for one year, part at 8%, part at 10%, and the remainder at 12%. The total annual income from these investments was $716. The amount of money invested at 12% was $300 more than the amount invested at 8% and 10% combined. Find the amount invested at each rate.

**38.** A person invested $17,000 for one year, part at 10%, part at 12%, and the remainder at 15%. The total annual income from these investments was $2110. The amount of money invested at 12% was $1000 less than the amount invested at 10% and 15% combined. Find the amount invested at each rate.

**39.** In the following triangle, the degree measures of the three interior angles and two of the exterior angles are represented with variables. Find the measure of each interior angle.

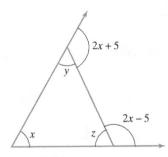

## Writing in Mathematics

**40.** What is a system of linear equations in three variables?

**41.** How do you determine whether a given ordered triple is a solution of a system in three variables?

**42.** Describe in general terms how to solve a system in three variables.

**43.** AIDS is taking a deadly toll on southern Africa. Describe how to use the techniques that you learned in this section to obtain a model for African life span using projections with AIDS, shown by the red graph in the figure. Let $x$ represent the number of years after 1985 and let $y$ represent African life span in that year.

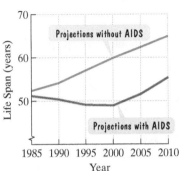

*Source:* United Nations

## Technology Exercises

**44.** Does your graphing utility have a feature that allows you to solve linear systems by entering coefficients and constant terms? If so, use this feature to verify the solutions to any five exercises that you worked by hand from Exercises 5–16.

**45.** Verify your results in Exercises 19–22 by using a graphing utility to graph the resulting parabola. Trace along the curve and convince yourself that the three points given in the exercise lie on the parabola.

## Critical Thinking Exercises

**Make Sense?** *In Exercises 46–49, determine whether each statement makes sense or does not make sense, and explain your reasoning.*

**46.** Solving a system in three variables, I found that $x = 3$ and $y = -1$. Because $z$ represents a third variable, $z$ cannot equal 3 or −1.

**47.** A system of linear equations in three variables, $x$, $y$, and $z$, cannot contain an equation in the form $y = mx + b$.

**48.** I'm solving a three-variable system in which one of the given equations has a missing term, so it will not be necessary to use any of the original equations twice when I reduce the system to two equations in two variables.

**49.** Because the percentage of the U.S. population that was foreign-born decreased from 1910 through 1970 and then increased after that, a quadratic function of the form $f(x) = ax^2 + bx + c$, rather than a linear function of the form $f(x) = mx + b$, should be used to model the data.

**50.** Describe how the system

$$\begin{cases} x + y - z - 2w = -8 \\ x - 2y + 3z + w = 18 \\ 2x + 2y + 2z - 2w = 10 \\ 2x + y - z + w = 3 \end{cases}$$

could be solved. Is it likely that in the near future a graphing utility will be available to provide a geometric solution (using intersecting graphs) to this system? Explain.

**51.** A modernistic painting consists of triangles, rectangles, and pentagons, all drawn so as to not overlap or share sides. Within each rectangle are drawn 2 red roses and each pentagon contains 5 carnations. How many triangles, rectangles, and pentagons appear in the painting if the painting contains a total of 40 geometric figures, 153 sides of geometric figures, and 72 flowers?

## Group Exercise

**52.** Group members should develop appropriate functions that model each of the projections shown in Exercise 43.

## Preview Exercises

*Exercises 53–55 will help you prepare for the material covered in the next section.*

**53.** Subtract: $\dfrac{3}{x-4} - \dfrac{2}{x+2}$.

**54.** Add: $\dfrac{5x-3}{x^2+1} + \dfrac{2x}{(x^2+1)^2}$.

**55.** Solve:

$$\begin{cases} A + B = 3 \\ 2A - 2B + C = 17 \\ 4A - 2C = 14. \end{cases}$$

---

## Section 7.3  Partial Fractions

### Objectives

1. Decompose $\dfrac{P}{Q}$, where $Q$ has only distinct linear factors.

2. Decompose $\dfrac{P}{Q}$, where $Q$ has repeated linear factors.

3. Decompose $\dfrac{P}{Q}$, where $Q$ has a nonrepeated prime quadratic factor.

4. Decompose $\dfrac{P}{Q}$, where $Q$ has a prime, repeated quadratic factor.

The rising and setting of the sun suggest the obvious: Things change over time. Calculus is the study of rates of change, allowing the motion of the rising sun to be measured by "freezing the frame" at one instant in time. If you are given a function, calculus reveals its rate of change at any "frozen" instant. In this section, you will learn an algebraic technique used in calculus to find a function if its rate of change is known. The technique involves expressing a given function in terms of simpler functions.

### The Idea behind Partial Fraction Decomposition

We know how to use common denominators to write a sum or difference of rational expressions as a single rational expression. For example,

$$\frac{3}{x-4} - \frac{2}{x+2} = \frac{3(x+2) - 2(x-4)}{(x-4)(x+2)}$$

$$= \frac{3x+6-2x+8}{(x-4)(x+2)} = \frac{x+14}{(x-4)(x+2)}.$$

For solving the kind of calculus problem described in the section opener, we must reverse this process:

$\dfrac{x+14}{(x-4)(x+2)}$ is expressed as the sum of two simpler fractions.

Partial fraction    Partial fraction

$$\frac{x+14}{(x-4)(x+2)} = \frac{3}{x-4} + \frac{-2}{x+2}.$$

This is the partial fraction decomposition of $\dfrac{x+14}{(x-4)(x+2)}$.

Each of the two fractions on the right is called a **partial fraction**. The sum of these fractions is called the **partial fraction decomposition** of the rational expression on the left-hand side.

Partial fraction decompositions can be written for rational expressions of the form $\dfrac{P(x)}{Q(x)}$, where $P$ and $Q$ have no common factors and the highest power in the numerator is less than the highest power in the denominator. In this section, we will show you how to write the partial fraction decompositions for each of the following rational expressions:

$$\frac{9x^2 - 9x + 6}{(2x - 1)(x + 2)(x - 2)}$$

> $P(x) = 9x^2 - 9x + 6$; highest power = 2
>
> $Q(x) = (2x - 1)(x + 2)(x - 2)$; multiplying factors, highest power = 3.

$$\frac{5x^3 - 3x^2 + 7x - 3}{(x^2 + 1)^2}.$$

> $P(x) = 5x^3 - 3x^2 + 7x - 3$; highest power = 3
>
> $Q(x) = (x^2 + 1)^2$; squaring the expression, highest power = 4.

The partial fraction decomposition of a rational expression depends on the factors of the denominator. We consider four cases involving different kinds of factors in the denominator:

1. The denominator is a product of distinct linear factors.
2. The denominator is a product of linear factors, some of which are repeated.
3. The denominator has prime quadratic factors, none of which is repeated.
4. The denominator has a repeated prime quadratic factor.

**1** Decompose $\dfrac{P}{Q}$, where $Q$ has only distinct linear factors.

## The Partial Fraction Decomposition of a Rational Expression with Distinct Linear Factors in the Denominator

If the denominator of a rational expression has a linear factor of the form $ax + b$, then the partial fraction decomposition will contain a term of the form

$$\frac{A}{ax + b}.$$

> Constant
>
> Linear factor

Each distinct linear factor in the denominator produces a partial fraction of the form *constant over linear factor*. For example,

$$\frac{9x^2 - 9x + 6}{(2x - 1)(x + 2)(x - 2)} = \frac{A}{2x - 1} + \frac{B}{x + 2} + \frac{C}{x - 2}.$$

> We write a constant over each linear factor in the denominator.

### The Partial Fraction Decomposition of $\dfrac{P(x)}{Q(x)}$: $Q(x)$ Has Distinct Linear Factors

The form of the partial fraction decomposition for a rational expression with distinct linear factors in the denominator is

$$\frac{P(x)}{(a_1x + b_1)(a_2x + b_2)(a_3x + b_3) \cdots (a_nx + b_n)}$$

$$= \frac{A_1}{a_1x + b_1} + \frac{A_2}{a_2x + b_2} + \frac{A_3}{a_3x + b_3} + \cdots + \frac{A_n}{a_nx + b_n}.$$

(**EXAMPLE 1**) **Partial Fraction Decomposition with Distinct Linear Factors**

Find the partial fraction decomposition of

$$\frac{x + 14}{(x - 4)(x + 2)}.$$

**Solution** We begin by setting up the partial fraction decomposition with the unknown constants. Write a constant over each of the two distinct linear factors in the denominator.

$$\frac{x + 14}{(x - 4)(x + 2)} = \frac{A}{x - 4} + \frac{B}{x + 2}$$

Our goal is to find $A$ and $B$. We do this by multiplying both sides of the equation by the least common denominator, $(x - 4)(x + 2)$.

$$(x - 4)(x + 2)\frac{x + 14}{(x - 4)(x + 2)} = (x - 4)(x + 2)\left(\frac{A}{x - 4} + \frac{B}{x + 2}\right)$$

We use the distributive property on the right side.

$$\cancel{(x - 4)}\,\cancel{(x + 2)}\frac{x + 14}{\cancel{(x - 4)}\,\cancel{(x + 2)}}$$

$$= \cancel{(x - 4)}(x + 2)\frac{A}{\cancel{(x - 4)}} + (x - 4)\cancel{(x + 2)}\frac{B}{\cancel{(x + 2)}}$$

Dividing out common factors in numerators and denominators, we obtain

$$x + 14 = A(x + 2) + B(x - 4).$$

To find values for $A$ and $B$ that make both sides equal, we'll express the sides in exactly the same form by writing the variable $x$-terms and then writing the constant terms. Apply the distributive property on the right side.

$x + 14 = Ax + 2A + Bx - 4B$     *Distribute A and B over the parentheses.*

$x + 14 = Ax + Bx + 2A - 4B$     *Rearrange terms.*

$1x + 14 = (A + B)x + (2A - 4B)$     *Rewrite to identify the coefficient of $x$ and the constant term.*

As shown by the arrows, if two polynomials are equal, coefficients of like powers of $x$ must be equal $(A + B = 1)$ and their constant terms must be equal $(2A - 4B = 14)$. Consequently, $A$ and $B$ satisfy the following two equations:

$$\begin{cases} A + B = 1 \\ 2A - 4B = 14. \end{cases}$$

We can use the addition method to solve this linear system in two variables. By multiplying the first equation by $-2$ and adding equations, we obtain $A = 3$ and $B = -2$. Thus,

$$\frac{x + 14}{(x - 4)(x + 2)} = \frac{A}{x - 4} + \frac{B}{x + 2} = \frac{3}{x - 4} + \frac{-2}{x + 2} \left( \text{or } \frac{3}{x - 4} - \frac{2}{x + 2} \right).$$

### Steps in Partial Fraction Decomposition

1. Set up the partial fraction decomposition with the unknown constants $A, B, C$, etc., in the numerators of the decomposition.
2. Multiply both sides of the resulting equation by the least common denominator.
3. Simplify the right side of the equation.
4. Write both sides in descending powers, equate coefficients of like powers of $x$, and equate constant terms.
5. Solve the resulting linear system for $A, B, C$, etc.
6. Substitute the values for $A, B, C$, etc., into the equation in step 1 and write the partial fraction decomposition.

### Study Tip

You will encounter some examples in which the denominator of the given rational expression is not already factored. If necessary, begin by factoring the denominator. Then apply the six steps needed to obtain the partial fraction decomposition.

✓ **Check Point** **1** Find the partial fraction decomposition of $\dfrac{5x - 1}{(x - 3)(x + 4)}$.

**2** Decompose $\dfrac{P}{Q}$, where $Q$ has repeated linear factors.

## The Partial Fraction Decomposition of a Rational Expression with Linear Factors in the Denominator, Some of Which Are Repeated

Suppose that $(ax + b)^n$ is a factor of the denominator. This means that the linear factor $ax + b$ is repeated $n$ times. When this occurs, the partial fraction decomposition will contain a sum of $n$ fractions for this factor of the denominator.

### The Partial Fraction Decomposition of $\dfrac{P(x)}{Q(x)}$: $Q(x)$ Has Repeated Linear Factors

The form of the partial fraction decomposition for a rational expression containing the linear factor $ax + b$ occurring $n$ times as its denominator is

$$\frac{P(x)}{(ax + b)^n} = \frac{A_1}{ax + b} + \frac{A_2}{(ax + b)^2} + \frac{A_3}{(ax + b)^3} + \cdots + \frac{A_n}{(ax + b)^n}.$$

> Include one fraction with a constant numerator for each power of $ax + b$.

**Partial Fraction Decomposition with Repeated Linear Factors**

Find the partial fraction decomposition of $\dfrac{x - 18}{x(x - 3)^2}$.

**Solution**

**Step 1 Set up the partial fraction decomposition with the unknown constants.** Because the linear factor $x - 3$ occurs twice, we must include one fraction with a constant numerator for each power of $x - 3$.

$$\frac{x - 18}{x(x - 3)^2} = \frac{A}{x} + \frac{B}{x - 3} + \frac{C}{(x - 3)^2}$$

**Step 2 Multiply both sides of the resulting equation by the least common denominator.** We clear fractions, multiplying both sides by $x(x - 3)^2$, the least common denominator.

$$x(x - 3)^2\left[\frac{x - 18}{x(x - 3)^2}\right] = x(x - 3)^2\left[\frac{A}{x} + \frac{B}{x - 3} + \frac{C}{(x - 3)^2}\right]$$

We use the distributive property on the right side.

$$\cancel{x}\,\cancel{(x-3)^2} \cdot \frac{x - 18}{\cancel{x}\,\cancel{(x-3)^2}} = \cancel{x}(x - 3)^2 \cdot \frac{A}{\cancel{x}} + x(x - 3)^2 \cdot \frac{B}{(x - 3)} + x\cancel{(x-3)^2} \cdot \frac{C}{\cancel{(x-3)^2}}$$

Dividing out common factors in numerators and denominators, we obtain

$$x - 18 = A(x - 3)^2 + Bx(x - 3) + Cx.$$

**Step 3 Simplify the right side of the equation.** Square $x - 3$. Then apply the distributive property.

$$x - 18 = A(x^2 - 6x + 9) + Bx(x - 3) + Cx \qquad \text{Square } x - 3 \text{ using}$$
$$(A - B)^2 = A^2 - 2AB + B^2.$$

$$x - 18 = Ax^2 - 6Ax + 9A + Bx^2 - 3Bx + Cx \qquad \text{Apply the distributive property.}$$

**Step 4 Write both sides in descending powers, equate coefficients of like powers of $x$, and equate constant terms.** The left side, $x - 18$, is in descending powers of $x$: $x - 18x^0$. We will write the right side in descending powers of $x$.

$$x - 18 = Ax^2 + Bx^2 - 6Ax - 3Bx + Cx + 9A \qquad \text{Rearrange terms on the right side.}$$

Express both sides in the same form.

$$0x^2 + 1x - 18 = (A + B)x^2 + (-6A - 3B + C)x + 9A \qquad \text{Rewrite to identify coefficients and the constant term.}$$

---

**Study Tip**

Avoid this common error:

$$\frac{x - 18}{x(x - 3)^2} = \frac{A}{x} + \frac{B}{x - 3} + \frac{C}{x - 3}$$

Listing $x - 3$ twice does not take into account $(x - 3)^2$.

Equating coefficients of like powers of $x$ and equating constant terms results in the following system of linear equations:

$$\begin{cases} A + B = 0 \\ -6A - 3B + C = 1 \\ 9A = -18. \end{cases}$$

**Step 5   Solve the resulting system for $A, B,$ and $C$.** Dividing both sides of the last equation by 9, we obtain $A = -2$. Substituting $-2$ for $A$ in the first equation, $A + B = 0$, gives $-2 + B = 0$, so $B = 2$. We find $C$ by substituting $-2$ for $A$ and 2 for $B$ in the middle equation, $-6A - 3B + C = 1$. We obtain $C = -5$.

**Step 6   Substitute the values of $A, B,$ and $C,$ and write the partial fraction decomposition.** With $A = -2, B = 2,$ and $C = -5$, the required partial fraction decomposition is

$$\frac{x - 18}{x(x - 3)^2} = \frac{A}{x} + \frac{B}{x - 3} + \frac{C}{(x - 3)^2} = -\frac{2}{x} + \frac{2}{x - 3} - \frac{5}{(x - 3)^2}.$$

⬤

◯ Check Point **2** Find the partial fraction decomposition of $\dfrac{x + 2}{x(x - 1)^2}$.

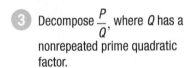 **3** Decompose $\dfrac{P}{Q}$, where $Q$ has a nonrepeated prime quadratic factor.

# The Partial Fraction Decomposition of a Rational Expression with Prime, Nonrepeated Quadratic Factors in the Denominator

Our final two cases of partial fraction decomposition involve prime quadratic factors of the form $ax^2 + bx + c$. Based on our work with the discriminant, we know that $ax^2 + bx + c$ is prime and cannot be factored over the integers if $b^2 - 4ac < 0$ or if $b^2 - 4ac$ is not a perfect square.

---

**The Partial Fraction Decomposition of $\dfrac{P(x)}{Q(x)}$: $Q(x)$ Has a Nonrepeated, Prime Quadratic Factor**

If $ax^2 + bx + c$ is a prime quadratic factor of $Q(x)$, the partial fraction decomposition will contain a term of the form

$$\frac{Ax + B}{ax^2 + bx + c}.$$

Linear numerator

Quadratic factor

---

The voice balloons in the box show that each distinct prime quadratic factor in the denominator produces a partial fraction of the form *linear numerator over quadratic factor*. For example,

$$\frac{3x^2 + 17x + 14}{(x - 2)(x^2 + 2x + 4)} = \frac{A}{x - 2} + \frac{Bx + C}{x^2 + 2x + 4}.$$

We write a constant over the linear factor in the denominator.

We write a linear numerator over the prime quadratic factor in the denominator.

Our next example illustrates how a linear system in three variables is used to determine values for $A$, $B$, and $C$.

$\boxed{\text{EXAMPLE 3}}$ **Partial Fraction Decomposition**

Find the partial fraction decomposition of

$$\frac{3x^2 + 17x + 14}{(x - 2)(x^2 + 2x + 4)}.$$

### Solution

**Step 1   Set up the partial fraction decomposition with the unknown constants.** We put a constant $(A)$ over the linear factor and a linear expression $(Bx + C)$ over the prime quadratic factor.

$$\frac{3x^2 + 17x + 14}{(x - 2)(x^2 + 2x + 4)} = \frac{A}{x - 2} + \frac{Bx + C}{x^2 + 2x + 4}$$

**Step 2   Multiply both sides of the resulting equation by the least common denominator.** We clear fractions, multiplying both sides by $(x - 2)(x^2 + 2x + 4)$, the least common denominator.

$$(x - 2)(x^2 + 2x + 4)\left[\frac{3x^2 + 17x + 14}{(x - 2)(x^2 + 2x + 4)}\right] = (x - 2)(x^2 + 2x + 4)\left[\frac{A}{x - 2} + \frac{Bx + C}{x^2 + 2x + 4}\right]$$

We use the distributive property on the right side.

$$(x - 2)(x^2 + 2x + 4) \cdot \frac{3x^2 + 17x + 14}{(x - 2)(x^2 + 2x + 4)}$$

$$= (x - 2)(x^2 + 2x + 4) \cdot \frac{A}{x - 2} + (x - 2)(x^2 + 2x + 4) \cdot \frac{Bx + C}{x^2 + 2x + 4}$$

Dividing out common factors in numerators and denominators, we obtain

$$3x^2 + 17x + 14 = A(x^2 + 2x + 4) + (Bx + C)(x - 2).$$

**Step 3   Simplify the right side of the equation.** We simplify on the right side by distributing $A$ over each term in parentheses and multiplying $(Bx + C)(x - 2)$ using the FOIL method.

$$3x^2 + 17x + 14 = Ax^2 + 2Ax + 4A + Bx^2 - 2Bx + Cx - 2C$$

**Step 4   Write both sides in descending powers, equate coefficients of like powers of $x$, and equate constant terms.** The left side, $3x^2 + 17x + 14$, is in descending powers of $x$. We write the right side in descending powers of $x$

$$3x^2 + 17x + 14 = Ax^2 + Bx^2 + 2Ax - 2Bx + Cx + 4A - 2C$$

and express both sides in the same form.

$$3x^2 + 17x + 14 = (A + B)x^2 + (2A - 2B + C)x + (4A - 2C)$$

Equating coefficients of like powers of $x$ and equating constant terms results in the following system of linear equations:

$$\begin{cases} A + B = 3 \\ 2A - 2B + C = 17 \\ 4A - 2C = 14. \end{cases}$$

**Step 5  Solve the resulting system for $A, B,$ and $C$.** Because the first equation involves $A$ and $B$, we can obtain another equation in $A$ and $B$ by eliminating $C$ from the second and third equations. Multiply the second equation by 2 and add equations. Solving in this manner, we obtain $A = 5, B = -2,$ and $C = 3$.

**Step 6  Substitute the values of $A, B,$ and $C$, and write the partial fraction decomposition.** With $A = 5, B = -2,$ and $C = 3$, the required partial fraction decomposition is

$$\frac{3x^2 + 17x + 14}{(x - 2)(x^2 + 2x + 4)} = \frac{A}{x - 2} + \frac{Bx + C}{x^2 + 2x + 4} = \frac{5}{x - 2} + \frac{-2x + 3}{x^2 + 2x + 4}.$$

### Technology

**Numeric Connections**

You can use the $\boxed{\text{TABLE}}$ feature of a graphing utility to check a partial fraction decomposition. To check the result of Example 3, enter the given rational function and its partial fraction decomposition:

$$y_1 = \frac{3x^2 + 17x + 14}{(x - 2)(x^2 + 2x + 4)}$$

$$y_2 = \frac{5}{x - 2} + \frac{-2x + 3}{x^2 + 2x + 4}.$$

| X | Y1 | Y2 |
|---|---|---|
| -3 | .28571 | .28571 |
| -2 | .5 | .5 |
| -1 | 0 | 0 |
| 0 | -1.75 | -1.75 |
| 1 | -4.857 | -4.857 |
| 2 | ERROR | ERROR |
| 3 | 4.8421 | 4.8421 |

X=-3

No matter how far up or down we scroll, $y_1 = y_2$, so the decomposition appears to be correct.

✓ **Check Point 3** Find the partial fraction decomposition of

$$\frac{8x^2 + 12x - 20}{(x + 3)(x^2 + x + 2)}.$$

④ Decompose $\dfrac{P}{Q}$, where $Q$ has a prime, repeated quadratic factor.

## The Partial Fraction Decomposition of a Rational Expression with a Prime, Repeated Quadratic Factor in the Denominator

Suppose that $(ax^2 + bx + c)^n$ is a factor of the denominator and that $ax^2 + bx + c$ cannot be factored further. This means that the quadratic factor $ax^2 + bx + c$ occurs $n$ times. When this occurs, the partial fraction decomposition will contain a linear numerator for each power of $ax^2 + bx + c$.

## The Partial Fraction Decomposition of $\frac{P(x)}{Q(x)}$: $Q(x)$ Has a Prime, Repeated Quadratic Factor

The form of the partial fraction decomposition for a rational expression containing the prime factor $ax^2 + bx + c$ occurring $n$ times as its denominator is

$$\frac{P(x)}{(ax^2 + bx + c)^n} = \frac{A_1x + B_1}{ax^2 + bx + c} + \frac{A_2x + B_2}{(ax^2 + bx + c)^2} + \frac{A_3x + B_3}{(ax^2 + bx + c)^3} + \cdots + \frac{A_nx + B_n}{(ax^2 + bx + c)^n}.$$

Include one fraction with a linear numerator for each power of $ax^2 + bx + c$.

**EXAMPLE 4** **Partial Fraction Decomposition with a Repeated Quadratic Factor**

### Study Tip

When the denominator of a rational expression contains a **power of a linear factor**, set up the partial fraction decomposition with **constant numerators** ($A, B, C$, etc.). When the denominator of a rational expression contains a **power of a prime quadratic factor**, set up the partial fraction decomposition with **linear numerators** ($Ax + B, Cx + D$, etc.).

Find the partial fraction decomposition of

$$\frac{5x^3 - 3x^2 + 7x - 3}{(x^2 + 1)^2}.$$

### Solution

**Step 1 Set up the partial fraction decomposition with the unknown constants.** Because the quadratic factor $x^2 + 1$ occurs twice, we must include one fraction with a linear numerator for each power of $x^2 + 1$.

$$\frac{5x^3 - 3x^2 + 7x - 3}{(x^2 + 1)^2} = \frac{Ax + B}{x^2 + 1} + \frac{Cx + D}{(x^2 + 1)^2}$$

**Step 2 Multiply both sides of the resulting equation by the least common denominator.** We clear fractions, multiplying both sides by $(x^2 + 1)^2$, the least common denominator.

$$(x^2 + 1)^2\left[\frac{5x^3 - 3x^2 + 7x - 3}{(x^2 + 1)^2}\right] = (x^2 + 1)^2\left[\frac{Ax + B}{x^2 + 1} + \frac{Cx + D}{(x^2 + 1)^2}\right]$$

Now we multiply and simplify.

$$5x^3 - 3x^2 + 7x - 3 = (x^2 + 1)(Ax + B) + Cx + D$$

**Step 3 Simplify the right side of the equation.** We multiply $(x^2 + 1)(Ax + B)$ using the FOIL method.

$$5x^3 - 3x^2 + 7x - 3 = Ax^3 + Bx^2 + Ax + B + Cx + D$$

**Step 4 Write both sides in descending powers, equate coefficients of like powers of $x$, and equate constant terms.**

$$5x^3 - 3x^2 + 7x - 3 = Ax^3 + Bx^2 + Ax + Cx + B + D$$

$$5x^3 - 3x^2 + 7x - 3 = Ax^3 + Bx^2 + (A + C)x + (B + D)$$

Equating coefficients of like powers of $x$ and equating constant terms results in the following system of linear equations:

$$\begin{cases} A = 5 \\ B = -3 \\ A + C = 7 \\ B + D = -3. \end{cases}$$

With $A = 5$, we immediately obtain $C = 2$.

With $B = -3$, we immediately obtain $D = 0$.

**Step 5 Solve the resulting system for A, B, C, and D.** Based on our observations in step 4, $A = 5, B = -3, C = 2$, and $D = 0$.

**Step 6 Substitute the values of A, B, C, and D, and write the partial fraction decomposition.**

$$\frac{5x^3 - 3x^2 + 7x - 3}{(x^2 + 1)^2} = \frac{Ax + B}{x^2 + 1} + \frac{Cx + D}{(x^2 + 1)^2} = \frac{5x - 3}{x^2 + 1} + \frac{2x}{(x^2 + 1)^2}$$

⊘ Check Point **4** Find the partial fraction decomposition of $\dfrac{2x^3 + x + 3}{(x^2 + 1)^2}$.

### Study Tip

When a rational expression contains a power of a factor in the denominator, be sure to set up the partial fraction decomposition to allow for every natural-number power of that factor less than or equal to the power. Example:

$$\frac{2x + 1}{(x - 5)^2 x^3}$$

$$= \frac{A}{x - 5} + \frac{B}{(x - 5)^2} + \frac{C}{x} + \frac{D}{x^2} + \frac{E}{x^3}$$

Although $(x - 5)^2$ and $x^2$ are quadratic, they are still expressed as powers of linear factors, $x - 5$ and $x$. Thus, the numerators are constant.

## Exercise Set 7.3

### Practice Exercises

*In Exercises 1–8, write the form of the partial fraction decomposition of the rational expression. It is not necessary to solve for the constants.*

**1.** $\dfrac{11x - 10}{(x - 2)(x + 1)}$

**2.** $\dfrac{5x + 7}{(x - 1)(x + 3)}$

**3.** $\dfrac{6x^2 - 14x - 27}{(x + 2)(x - 3)^2}$

**4.** $\dfrac{3x + 16}{(x + 1)(x - 2)^2}$

**5.** $\dfrac{5x^2 - 6x + 7}{(x - 1)(x^2 + 1)}$

**6.** $\dfrac{5x^2 - 9x + 19}{(x - 4)(x^2 + 5)}$

**7.** $\dfrac{x^3 + x^2}{(x^2 + 4)^2}$

**8.** $\dfrac{7x^2 - 9x + 3}{(x^2 + 7)^2}$

*In Exercises 9–42, write the partial fraction decomposition of each rational expression.*

**9.** $\dfrac{x}{(x - 3)(x - 2)}$

**10.** $\dfrac{1}{x(x - 1)}$

**11.** $\dfrac{3x + 50}{(x - 9)(x + 2)}$

**12.** $\dfrac{5x - 1}{(x - 2)(x + 1)}$

**13.** $\dfrac{7x - 4}{x^2 - x - 12}$

**14.** $\dfrac{9x + 21}{x^2 + 2x - 15}$

**15.** $\dfrac{4}{2x^2 - 5x - 3}$

**16.** $\dfrac{x}{x^2 + 2x - 3}$

**17.** $\dfrac{4x^2 + 13x - 9}{x(x - 1)(x + 3)}$

**18.** $\dfrac{4x^2 - 5x - 15}{x(x + 1)(x - 5)}$

**19.** $\dfrac{4x^2 - 7x - 3}{x^3 - x}$

**20.** $\dfrac{2x^2 - 18x - 12}{x^3 - 4x}$

**21.** $\dfrac{6x - 11}{(x - 1)^2}$

**22.** $\dfrac{x}{(x + 1)^2}$

**23.** $\dfrac{x^2 - 6x + 3}{(x - 2)^3}$

**24.** $\dfrac{2x^2 + 8x + 3}{(x + 1)^3}$

**25.** $\dfrac{x^2 + 2x + 7}{x(x - 1)^2}$

**26.** $\dfrac{3x^2 + 49}{x(x + 7)^2}$

**27.** $\dfrac{x^2}{(x - 1)^2(x + 1)}$

**28.** $\dfrac{x^2}{(x - 1)^2(x + 1)^2}$

**29.** $\dfrac{5x^2 - 6x + 7}{(x-1)(x^2+1)}$

**30.** $\dfrac{5x^2 - 9x + 19}{(x-4)(x^2+5)}$

**31.** $\dfrac{5x^2 + 6x + 3}{(x+1)(x^2+2x+2)}$

**32.** $\dfrac{9x+2}{(x-2)(x^2+2x+2)}$

**33.** $\dfrac{x+4}{x^2(x^2+4)}$

**34.** $\dfrac{10x^2 + 2x}{(x-1)^2(x^2+2)}$

**35.** $\dfrac{6x^2 - x + 1}{x^3 + x^2 + x + 1}$

**36.** $\dfrac{3x^2 - 2x + 8}{x^3 + 2x^2 + 4x + 8}$

**37.** $\dfrac{x^3 + x^2 + 2}{(x^2+2)^2}$

**38.** $\dfrac{x^2 + 2x + 3}{(x^2+4)^2}$

**39.** $\dfrac{x^3 - 4x^2 + 9x - 5}{(x^2 - 2x + 3)^2}$

**40.** $\dfrac{3x^3 - 6x^2 + 7x - 2}{(x^2 - 2x + 2)^2}$

**41.** $\dfrac{4x^2 + 3x + 14}{x^3 - 8}$

**42.** $\dfrac{3x - 5}{x^3 - 1}$

## Practice Plus

*In Exercises 43–46, perform each long division and write the partial fraction decomposition of the remainder term.*

**43.** $\dfrac{x^5 + 2}{x^2 - 1}$

**44.** $\dfrac{x^5}{x^2 - 4x + 4}$

**45.** $\dfrac{x^4 - x^2 + 2}{x^3 - x^2}$

**46.** $\dfrac{x^4 + 2x^3 - 4x^2 + x - 3}{x^2 - x - 2}$

*In Exercises 47–50, write the partial fraction decomposition of each rational expression.*

**47.** $\dfrac{1}{x^2 - c^2}$ $\quad (c \neq 0)$

**48.** $\dfrac{ax + b}{x^2 - c^2}$ $\quad (c \neq 0)$

**49.** $\dfrac{ax + b}{(x - c)^2}$ $\quad (c \neq 0)$

**50.** $\dfrac{1}{x^2 - ax - bx + ab}$ $\quad (a \neq b)$

## Application Exercises

**51.** Find the partial fraction decomposition for $\dfrac{1}{x(x+1)}$ and use the result to find the following sum:

$$\dfrac{1}{1 \cdot 2} + \dfrac{1}{2 \cdot 3} + \dfrac{1}{3 \cdot 4} + \cdots + \dfrac{1}{99 \cdot 100}.$$

**52.** Find the partial fraction decomposition for $\dfrac{2}{x(x+2)}$ and use the result to find the following sum:

$$\dfrac{2}{1 \cdot 3} + \dfrac{2}{3 \cdot 5} + \dfrac{2}{5 \cdot 7} + \cdots + \dfrac{2}{99 \cdot 101}.$$

## Writing in Mathematics

**53.** Explain what is meant by the partial fraction decomposition of a rational expression.

**54.** Explain how to find the partial fraction decomposition of a rational expression with distinct linear factors in the denominator.

**55.** Explain how to find the partial fraction decomposition of a rational expression with a repeated linear factor in the denominator.

**56.** Explain how to find the partial fraction decomposition of a rational expression with a prime quadratic factor in the denominator.

**57.** Explain how to find the partial fraction decomposition of a rational expression with a repeated, prime quadratic factor in the denominator.

**58.** How can you verify your result for the partial fraction decomposition for a given rational expression without using a graphing utility?

## Technology Exercise

**59.** Use the $\boxed{\text{TABLE}}$ feature of a graphing utility to verify any three of the decompositions that you obtained in Exercises 9–42.

## Critical Thinking Exercises

**Make Sense?** *In Exercises 60–63, determine whether each statement makes sense or does not make sense, and explain your reasoning.*

**60.** Partial fraction decomposition involves finding a single rational expression for a given sum or difference of rational expressions.

**61.** I apply partial fraction decompositions for rational expressions of the form $\dfrac{P(x)}{Q(x)}$, where $P$ and $Q$ have no common factors and the degree of $P$ is greater than the degree of $Q$.

**62.** Because $x + 5$ is linear and $x^2 - 3x + 2$ is quadratic, I set up the following partial fraction decomposition:

$$\dfrac{7x^2 + 9x + 3}{(x+5)(x^2 - 3x + 2)} = \dfrac{A}{x+5} + \dfrac{Bx + C}{x^2 - 3x + 2}.$$

**63.** Because $(x + 3)^2$ consists of two factors of $x + 3$, I set up the following partial fraction decomposition:

$$\dfrac{5x + 2}{(x+3)^2} = \dfrac{A}{x+3} + \dfrac{B}{x+3}.$$

**64.** Use an extension of the Study Tip on page 764 to describe how to set up the partial fraction decomposition of a rational expression that contains powers of a prime cubic factor in the denominator. Give an example of such a decomposition.

**65.** Find the partial fraction decomposition of

$$\dfrac{4x^2 + 5x - 9}{x^3 - 6x - 9}.$$

## Preview Exercises

*Exercises 66–68 will help you prepare for the material covered in the next section.*

**66.** Solve by the substitution method:

$$\begin{cases} 4x + 3y = 4 \\ y = 2x - 7. \end{cases}$$

**67.** Solve by the addition method:

$$\begin{cases} 2x + 4y = -4 \\ 3x + 5y = -3. \end{cases}$$

**68.** Graph $x - y = 3$ and $(x - 2)^2 + (y + 3)^2 = 4$ in the same rectangular coordinate system. What are the two intersection points? Show that each of these ordered pairs satisfies both equations.

---

**Section 7.4** **Systems of Nonlinear Equations in Two Variables**

### Objectives

① Recognize systems of nonlinear equations in two variables.

② Solve nonlinear systems by substitution.

③ Solve nonlinear systems by addition.

④ Solve problems using systems of nonlinear equations.

Scientists debate the probability that a "doomsday rock" will collide with Earth. It has been estimated that an asteroid, a tiny planet that revolves around the sun, crashes into Earth about once every 250,000 years, and that such a collision would have disastrous results. In 1908, a small fragment struck Siberia, leveling thousands of acres of trees. One theory about the extinction of dinosaurs 65 million years ago involves Earth's collision with a large asteroid and the resulting drastic changes in Earth's climate.

Understanding the path of Earth and the path of a comet is essential to detecting threatening space debris. Orbits about the sun are not described by linear equations in the form $Ax + By = C$. The ability to solve systems that contain nonlinear equations provides NASA scientists watching for troublesome asteroids with a way to locate possible collision points with Earth's orbit.

① Recognize systems of nonlinear equations in two variables.

### Systems of Nonlinear Equations and Their Solutions

A **system of** two **nonlinear equations** in two variables, also called a **nonlinear system**, contains at least one equation that cannot be expressed in the form $Ax + By = C$. Here are two examples:

$$\begin{cases} x^2 = 2y + 10 \\ 3x - y = 9 \end{cases}$$

Not in the form $Ax + By = C$. The term $x^2$ is not linear.

$$\begin{cases} y = x^2 + 3 \\ x^2 + y^2 = 9. \end{cases}$$

Neither equation is in the form $Ax + By = C$. The terms $x^2$ and $y^2$ are not linear.

A **solution** of a nonlinear system in two variables is an ordered pair of real numbers that satisfies both equations in the system. The **solution set** of the system is the set of all such ordered pairs. As with linear systems in two variables, the solution of a nonlinear system (if there is one) corresponds to the intersection point(s) of the graphs of the equations in the system. Unlike linear systems, the graphs can be circles, parabolas, or anything other than two lines. We will solve nonlinear systems using the substitution method and the addition method.

**②** Solve nonlinear systems by substitution.

## Eliminating a Variable Using the Substitution Method

The substitution method involves converting a nonlinear system into one equation in one variable by an appropriate substitution. The steps in the solution process are exactly the same as those used to solve a linear system by substitution. However, when you obtain an equation in one variable, this equation may not be linear. In our first example, this equation is quadratic.

**( EXAMPLE 1 )** Solving a Nonlinear System by the Substitution Method

Solve by the substitution method:

$$\begin{cases} x^2 = 2y + 10 & \text{(The graph is a parabola.)} \\ 3x - y = 9. & \text{(The graph is a line.)} \end{cases}$$

**Solution**

**Step 1 Solve one of the equations for one variable in terms of the other.** We begin by isolating one of the variables raised to the first power in either of the equations. By solving for $y$ in the second equation, which has a coefficient of $-1$, we can avoid fractions.

$$3x - y = 9 \qquad \text{This is the second equation in the given system.}$$
$$3x = y + 9 \qquad \text{Add } y \text{ to both sides.}$$
$$3x - 9 = y \qquad \text{Subtract 9 from both sides.}$$

**Step 2 Substitute the expression from step 1 into the other equation.** We substitute $3x - 9$ for $y$ in the first equation.

$$y = \boxed{3x - 9} \qquad x^2 = 2\boxed{y} + 10$$

This gives us an equation in one variable, namely

$$x^2 = 2(3x - 9) + 10.$$

The variable $y$ has been eliminated.

**Step 3 Solve the resulting equation containing one variable.**

$$x^2 = 2(3x - 9) + 10 \qquad \text{This is the equation containing one variable.}$$
$$x^2 = 6x - 18 + 10 \qquad \text{Use the distributive property.}$$
$$x^2 = 6x - 8 \qquad \text{Combine numerical terms on the right.}$$
$$x^2 - 6x + 8 = 0 \qquad \text{Move all terms to one side and set the quadratic equation equal to 0.}$$
$$(x - 4)(x - 2) = 0 \qquad \text{Factor.}$$
$$x - 4 = 0 \quad \text{or} \quad x - 2 = 0 \qquad \text{Set each factor equal to 0.}$$
$$x = 4 \qquad\qquad x = 2 \qquad \text{Solve for } x.$$

**Step 4 Back-substitute the obtained values into the equation from step 1.** Now that we have the $x$-coordinates of the solutions, we back-substitute 4 for $x$ and 2 for $x$ into the equation $y = 3x - 9$.

$$\text{If } x \text{ is 4,} \quad y = 3(4) - 9 = 3, \quad \text{so } (4, 3) \text{ is a solution.}$$
$$\text{If } x \text{ is 2,} \quad y = 3(2) - 9 = -3, \quad \text{so } (2, -3) \text{ is a solution.}$$

**Step 5   Check the proposed solutions in both of the system's given equations.** We begin by checking $(4, 3)$. Replace $x$ with $4$ and $y$ with $3$.

| | | |
|---|---|---|
| $x^2 = 2y + 10$ | $3x - y = 9$ | *These are the given equations.* |
| $4^2 \overset{?}{=} 2(3) + 10$ | $3(4) - 3 \overset{?}{=} 9$ | *Let x = 4 and y = 3.* |
| $16 \overset{?}{=} 6 + 10$ | $12 - 3 \overset{?}{=} 9$ | *Simplify.* |
| $16 = 16,$   true | $9 = 9,$   true | *True statements result.* |

The ordered pair $(4, 3)$ satisfies both equations. Thus, $(4, 3)$ is a solution of the system. Now let's check $(2, -3)$. Replace $x$ with $2$ and $y$ with $-3$ in both given equations.

| | | |
|---|---|---|
| $x^2 = 2y + 10$ | $3x - y = 9$ | *These are the given equations.* |
| $2^2 \overset{?}{=} 2(-3) + 10$ | $3(2) - (-3) \overset{?}{=} 9$ | *Let x = 2 and y = -3.* |
| $4 \overset{?}{=} -6 + 10$ | $6 + 3 \overset{?}{=} 9$ | *Simplify.* |
| $4 = 4,$   true | $9 = 9,$   true | *True statements result.* |

The ordered pair $(2, -3)$ also satisfies both equations and is a solution of the system. The solutions are $(4, 3)$ and $(2, -3)$, and the solution set is $\{(4, 3), (2, -3)\}$.

    **Figure 7.10** shows the graphs of the equations in the system and the solutions as intersection points.

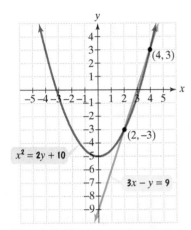

**Figure 7.10**   Points of intersection illustrate the nonlinear system's solutions.

✓ **Check Point 1** Solve by the substitution method:

$$\begin{cases} x^2 = y - 1 \\ 4x - y = -1. \end{cases}$$

---

( **EXAMPLE 2** ) **Solving a Nonlinear System by the Substitution Method**

Solve by the substitution method:

$$\begin{cases} x - y = 3 & \text{(The graph is a line.)} \\ (x - 2)^2 + (y + 3)^2 = 4. & \text{(The graph is a circle.)} \end{cases}$$

**Solution**   Graphically, we are finding the intersection of a line and a circle with center $(2, -3)$ and radius 2.

**Step 1   Solve one of the equations for one variable in terms of the other.** We will solve for $x$ in the linear equation—that is, the first equation. (We could also solve for $y$.)

| | |
|---|---|
| $x - y = 3$ | *This is the first equation in the given system.* |
| $x = y + 3$ | *Add y to both sides.* |

**Step 2   Substitute the expression from step 1 into the other equation.** We substitute $y + 3$ for $x$ in the second equation.

$$x = \boxed{y + 3} \qquad (\boxed{x} - 2)^2 + (y + 3)^2 = 4$$

This gives an equation in one variable, namely

$$(y + 3 - 2)^2 + (y + 3)^2 = 4.$$

The variable $x$ has been eliminated.

**Study Tip**

Recall that

$$(x - h)^2 + (y - k)^2 = r^2$$

describes a circle with center $(h, k)$ and radius $r$.

**Step 3 Solve the resulting equation containing one variable.**

$$(y + 3 - 2)^2 + (y + 3)^2 = 4 \qquad \text{This is the equation containing one variable.}$$

$$(y + 1)^2 + (y + 3)^2 = 4 \qquad \text{Combine numerical terms in the first parentheses.}$$

$$y^2 + 2y + 1 + y^2 + 6y + 9 = 4 \qquad \text{Use the formula } (A + B)^2 = A^2 + 2AB + B^2 \text{ to square } y + 1 \text{ and } y + 3.$$

$$2y^2 + 8y + 10 = 4 \qquad \text{Combine like terms on the left.}$$

$$2y^2 + 8y + 6 = 0 \qquad \text{Subtract 4 from both sides and set the quadratic equation equal to 0.}$$

$$2(y^2 + 4y + 3) = 0 \qquad \text{Factor out 2.}$$

$$2(y + 3)(y + 1) = 0 \qquad \text{Factor completely.}$$

$$y + 3 = 0 \quad \text{or} \quad y + 1 = 0 \qquad \text{Set each variable factor equal to 0.}$$

$$y = -3 \qquad\qquad y = -1 \qquad \text{Solve for y.}$$

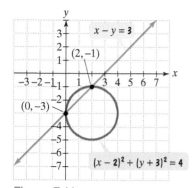

**Figure 7.11** Points of intersection illustrate the nonlinear system's solutions.

**Step 4 Back-substitute the obtained values into the equation from step 1.** Now that we have the $y$-coordinates of the solutions, we back-substitute $-3$ for $y$ and $-1$ for $y$ in the equation $x = y + 3$.

> If $y = -3$:   $x = -3 + 3 = 0$,   so $(0, -3)$ is a solution.
>
> If $y = -1$:   $x = -1 + 3 = 2$,   so $(2, -1)$ is a solution.

**Step 5 Check the proposed solutions in both of the system's given equations.** Take a moment to show that each ordered pair satisfies both given equations, $x - y = 3$ and $(x - 2)^2 + (y + 3)^2 = 4$. The solutions are $(0, -3)$ and $(2, -1)$, and the solution set of the given system is $\{(0, -3), (2, -1)\}$.

Figure 7.11 shows the graphs of the equations in the system and the solutions as intersection points.

⬤ Check Point **2** Solve by the substitution method:

$$\begin{cases} x + 2y = 0 \\ (x - 1)^2 + (y - 1)^2 = 5. \end{cases}$$

③ Solve nonlinear systems by addition.

## Eliminating a Variable Using the Addition Method

In solving linear systems with two variables, we learned that the addition method works well when each equation is in the form $Ax + By = C$. For nonlinear systems, the addition method can be used when each equation is in the form $Ax^2 + By^2 = C$. If necessary, we will multiply either equation or both equations by appropriate numbers so that the coefficients of $x^2$ or $y^2$ will have a sum of 0. We then add equations. The sum will be an equation in one variable.

( **EXAMPLE 3** ) **Solving a Nonlinear System by the Addition Method**

Solve the system:

$$\begin{cases} 4x^2 + y^2 = 13 & \text{Equation 1} \\ x^2 + y^2 = 10. & \text{Equation 2} \end{cases}$$

**Solution** We can use the same steps that we did when we solved linear systems by the addition method.

**Step 1  Write both equations in the form $Ax^2 + By^2 = C$.** Both equations are already in this form, so we can skip this step.

**Step 2  If necessary, multiply either equation or both equations by appropriate numbers so that the sum of the $x^2$-coefficients or the sum of the $y^2$-coefficients is 0.** We can eliminate $y^2$ by multiplying Equation 2 by $-1$.

$$\begin{cases} 4x^2 + y^2 = 13 \\ x^2 + y^2 = 10 \end{cases} \xrightarrow[\text{Multiply by }-1.]{\text{No change}} \begin{cases} 4x^2 + y^2 = 13 \\ -x^2 - y^2 = -10 \end{cases}$$

**Steps 3 and 4  Add equations and solve for the remaining variable.**

$$\begin{cases} 4x^2 + y^2 = 13 \\ -x^2 - y^2 = -10 \end{cases}$$

$$3x^2 \qquad = 3 \qquad \text{Add equations.}$$

$$x^2 = 1 \qquad \text{Divide both sides by 3.}$$

$$x = \pm 1 \qquad \text{Use the square root property:}$$
$$\text{If } x^2 = c, \text{ then } x = \pm\sqrt{c}.$$

**Step 5  Back-substitute and find the values for the other variable.** We must back-substitute each value of $x$ into either one of the original equations. Let's use $x^2 + y^2 = 10$, Equation 2. If $x = 1$,

$$1^2 + y^2 = 10 \qquad \text{Replace x with 1 in Equation 2.}$$

$$y^2 = 9 \qquad \text{Subtract 1 from both sides.}$$

$$y = \pm 3. \qquad \text{Apply the square root property.}$$

$(1, 3)$ and $(1, -3)$ are solutions. If $x = -1$,

$$(-1)^2 + y^2 = 10 \qquad \text{Replace x with }-1 \text{ in Equation 2.}$$

$$y^2 = 9 \qquad \text{The steps are the same as before.}$$

$$y = \pm 3.$$

$(-1, 3)$ and $(-1, -3)$ are solutions.

**Step 6  Check.** Take a moment to show that each of the four ordered pairs satisfies the given equations, $4x^2 + y^2 = 13$ and $x^2 + y^2 = 10$. The solution set of the given system is $\{(1, 3), (1, -3), (-1, 3), (-1, -3)\}$.

  **Figure 7.12** shows the graphs of the equations in the system and the solutions as intersection points.

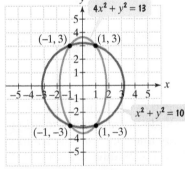

**Figure 7.12**  A system with four solutions

✓ Check Point **3**  Solve the system:

$$\begin{cases} 3x^2 + 2y^2 = 35 \\ 4x^2 + 3y^2 = 48. \end{cases}$$

  In solving nonlinear systems, we include only ordered pairs with real numbers in the solution set. We have seen that each of these ordered pairs corresponds to a point of intersection of the system's graphs.

**EXAMPLE 4** Solving a Nonlinear System by the Addition Method

Solve the system:

$$\begin{cases} y = x^2 + 3 & \text{Equation 1 (The graph is a parabola.)} \\ x^2 + y^2 = 9. & \text{Equation 2 (The graph is a circle.)} \end{cases}$$

**Solution** We could use substitution because Equation 1, $y = x^2 + 3$, has $y$ expressed in terms of $x$, but substituting $x^2 + 3$ for $y$ in $x^2 + y^2 = 9$ would result in a fourth-degree equation. However, we can rewrite Equation 1 by subtracting $x^2$ from both sides and adding the equations to eliminate the $x^2$-terms.

Notice how like terms are arranged in columns.

$$\begin{cases} -x^2 + y & = 3 & \text{Subtract } x^2 \text{ from both sides of Equation 1.} \\ \phantom{-}x^2 \phantom{+y} + y^2 & = 9 & \text{This is Equation 2.} \end{cases}$$
$$\overline{\phantom{-x^2}\ y + y^2 = 12} \quad \text{Add the equations.}$$

We now solve this quadratic equation.

$$y + y^2 = 12 \quad \text{This is the equation containing one variable.}$$

$$y^2 + y - 12 = 0 \quad \text{Subtract 12 from both sides and set the quadratic equation equal to 0.}$$

$$(y + 4)(y - 3) = 0 \quad \text{Factor.}$$

$$y + 4 = 0 \quad \text{or} \quad y - 3 = 0 \quad \text{Set each factor equal to 0.}$$

$$y = -4 \qquad\quad y = 3 \quad \text{Solve for } y.$$

To complete the solution, we must back-substitute each value of $y$ into either one of the original equations. We will use $y = x^2 + 3$, Equation 1. First, we substitute $-4$ for $y$.

$$-4 = x^2 + 3$$

$$-7 = x^2 \quad \text{Subtract 3 from both sides.}$$

Because the square of a real number cannot be negative, the equation $x^2 = -7$ does not have real-number solutions. We will not include the imaginary solutions, $x = \pm\sqrt{-7}$, or $i\sqrt{7}$ and $-i\sqrt{7}$, in the ordered pairs that make up the solution set. Thus, we move on to our other value for $y$, 3, and substitute this value into Equation 1.

$$y = x^2 + 3 \quad \text{This is Equation 1.}$$

$$3 = x^2 + 3 \quad \text{Back-substitute 3 for } y.$$

$$0 = x^2 \quad \text{Subtract 3 from both sides.}$$

$$0 = x \quad \text{Solve for } x.$$

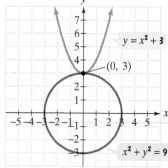

**Figure 7.13** A system with one real solution

We showed that if $y = 3$, then $x = 0$. Thus, $(0, 3)$ is the solution with a real ordered pair. Take a moment to show that $(0, 3)$ satisfies the given equations, $y = x^2 + 3$ and $x^2 + y^2 = 9$. The solution set of the system is $\{(0, 3)\}$. **Figure 7.13** shows the system's graphs and the solution as an intersection point.

✓ Check Point **4** Solve the system:

$$\begin{cases} y = x^2 + 5 \\ x^2 + y^2 = 25. \end{cases}$$

④ Solve problems using systems of nonlinear equations.

## Applications

Many geometric problems can be modeled and solved by the use of systems of nonlinear equations. We will use our step-by-step strategy for solving problems using mathematical models that are created from verbal conditions.

( EXAMPLE 5 ) **An Application of a Nonlinear System**

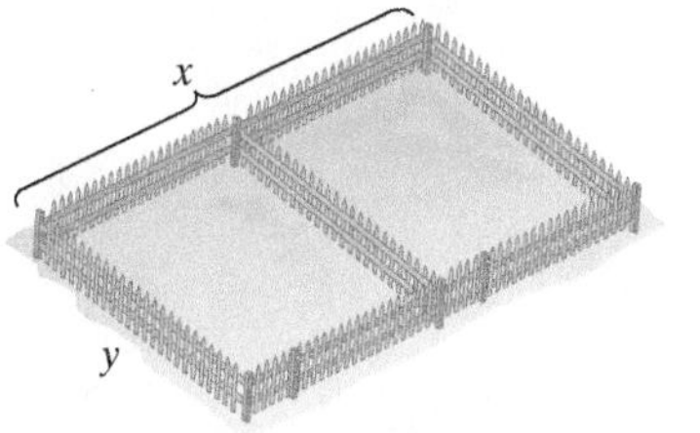

You have 36 yards of fencing to build the enclosure in **Figure 7.14**. Some of this fencing is to be used to build an internal divider. If you'd like to enclose 54 square yards, what are the dimensions of the enclosure?

Figure 7.14   Building an enclosure

## Solution

**Step 1   Use variables to represent unknown quantities.** Let $x$ = the enclosure's length and $y$ = the enclosure's width. These variables are shown in **Figure 7.14**.

**Step 2   Write a system of equations modeling the problem's conditions.** The first condition is that you have 36 yards of fencing.

| Fencing along both lengths | plus | fencing along both widths | plus | fencing for the internal divider | equals | 36 yards. |
|---|---|---|---|---|---|---|
| $2x$ | $+$ | $2y$ | $+$ | $y$ | $=$ | $36$ |

Adding like terms, we can express the equation that models the verbal conditions for the fencing as $2x + 3y = 36$.

The second condition is that you'd like to enclose 54 square yards. The rectangle's area, the product of its length and its width, must be 54 square yards.

| Length | times | width | is | 54 square yards. |
|---|---|---|---|---|
| $x$ | $\cdot$ | $y$ | $=$ | $54$ |

**Step 3   Solve the system and answer the problem's question.** We must solve the system

$$\begin{cases} 2x + 3y = 36 & \text{Equation 1} \\ xy = 54. & \text{Equation 2} \end{cases}$$

We will use substitution. Because Equation 1 has no coefficients of 1 or $-1$, we will work with Equation 2 and solve for $y$. Dividing both sides of $xy = 54$ by $x$, we obtain

$$y = \frac{54}{x}.$$

Now we substitute $\dfrac{54}{x}$ for $y$ in Equation 1 and solve for $x$.

$$2x + 3y = 36 \quad \text{This is Equation 1.}$$

$$2x + 3 \cdot \frac{54}{x} = 36 \quad \text{Substitute } \frac{54}{x} \text{ for } y.$$

$$2x + \frac{162}{x} = 36 \quad \text{Multiply.}$$

$$x\left(2x + \frac{162}{x}\right) = 36 \cdot x \qquad \text{Clear fractions by multiplying both sides by x.}$$

$$2x^2 + 162 = 36x \qquad \text{Use the distributive property on the left side.}$$

$$2x^2 - 36x + 162 = 0 \qquad \text{Subtract 36x from both sides and set the quadratic equation equal to 0.}$$

$$2(x^2 - 18x + 81) = 0 \qquad \text{Factor out 2.}$$

$$2(x - 9)^2 = 0 \qquad \text{Factor completely using } A^2 - 2AB + B^2 = (A - B)^2.$$

$$x - 9 = 0 \qquad \text{Set the repeated factor equal to zero.}$$

$$x = 9 \qquad \text{Solve for x.}$$

We back-substitute this value of $x$ into $y = \dfrac{54}{x}$.

$$\text{If } x = 9, \quad y = \frac{54}{9} = 6.$$

This means that the dimensions of the enclosure in **Figure 7.14** are 9 yards by 6 yards.

**Step 4   Check the proposed solution in the original wording of the problem.** Take a moment to check that a length of 9 yards and a width of 6 yards results in 36 yards of fencing and an area of 54 square yards. ●

Figure 7.14   (repeated)

⊘ Check Point **5**  Find the length and width of a rectangle whose perimeter is 20 feet and whose area is 21 square feet.

# Exercise Set 7.4

## Practice Exercises

*In Exercises 1–18, solve each system by the substitution method.*

**1.** $\begin{cases} x + y = 2 \\ y = x^2 - 4 \end{cases}$

**2.** $\begin{cases} x - y = -1 \\ y = x^2 + 1 \end{cases}$

**3.** $\begin{cases} x + y = 2 \\ y = x^2 - 4x + 4 \end{cases}$

**4.** $\begin{cases} 2x + y = -5 \\ y = x^2 + 6x + 7 \end{cases}$

**5.** $\begin{cases} y = x^2 - 4x - 10 \\ y = -x^2 - 2x + 14 \end{cases}$

**6.** $\begin{cases} y = x^2 + 4x + 5 \\ y = x^2 + 2x - 1 \end{cases}$

**7.** $\begin{cases} x^2 + y^2 = 25 \\ x - y = 1 \end{cases}$

**8.** $\begin{cases} x^2 + y^2 = 5 \\ 3x - y = 5 \end{cases}$

**9.** $\begin{cases} xy = 6 \\ 2x - y = 1 \end{cases}$

**10.** $\begin{cases} xy = -12 \\ x - 2y + 14 = 0 \end{cases}$

**11.** $\begin{cases} y^2 = x^2 - 9 \\ 2y = x - 3 \end{cases}$

**12.** $\begin{cases} x^2 + y = 4 \\ 2x + y = 1 \end{cases}$

**13.** $\begin{cases} xy = 3 \\ x^2 + y^2 = 10 \end{cases}$

**14.** $\begin{cases} xy = 4 \\ x^2 + y^2 = 8 \end{cases}$

**15.** $\begin{cases} x + y = 1 \\ x^2 + xy - y^2 = -5 \end{cases}$

**16.** $\begin{cases} x + y = -3 \\ x^2 + 2y^2 = 12y + 18 \end{cases}$

**17.** $\begin{cases} x + y = 1 \\ (x - 1)^2 + (y + 2)^2 = 10 \end{cases}$

**18.** $\begin{cases} 2x + y = 4 \\ (x + 1)^2 + (y - 2)^2 = 4 \end{cases}$

*In Exercises 19–28, solve each system by the addition method.*

**19.** $\begin{cases} x^2 + y^2 = 13 \\ x^2 - y^2 = 5 \end{cases}$

**20.** $\begin{cases} 4x^2 - y^2 = 4 \\ 4x^2 + y^2 = 4 \end{cases}$

**21.** $\begin{cases} x^2 - 4y^2 = -7 \\ 3x^2 + y^2 = 31 \end{cases}$

**22.** $\begin{cases} 3x^2 - 2y^2 = -5 \\ 2x^2 - y^2 = -2 \end{cases}$

**23.** $\begin{cases} 3x^2 + 4y^2 - 16 = 0 \\ 2x^2 - 3y^2 - 5 = 0 \end{cases}$

**24.** $\begin{cases} 16x^2 - 4y^2 - 72 = 0 \\ x^2 - y^2 - 3 = 0 \end{cases}$

**25.** $\begin{cases} x^2 + y^2 = 25 \\ (x - 8)^2 + y^2 = 41 \end{cases}$  **26.** $\begin{cases} x^2 + y^2 = 5 \\ x^2 + (y - 8)^2 = 41 \end{cases}$

**27.** $\begin{cases} y^2 - x = 4 \\ x^2 + y^2 = 4 \end{cases}$  **28.** $\begin{cases} x^2 - 2y = 8 \\ x^2 + y^2 = 16 \end{cases}$

*In Exercises 29–42, solve each system by the method of your choice.*

**29.** $\begin{cases} 3x^2 + 4y^2 = 16 \\ 2x^2 - 3y^2 = 5 \end{cases}$  **30.** $\begin{cases} x + y^2 = 4 \\ x^2 + y^2 = 16 \end{cases}$

**31.** $\begin{cases} 2x^2 + y^2 = 18 \\ xy = 4 \end{cases}$  **32.** $\begin{cases} x^2 + 4y^2 = 20 \\ xy = 4 \end{cases}$

**33.** $\begin{cases} x^2 + 4y^2 = 20 \\ x + 2y = 6 \end{cases}$  **34.** $\begin{cases} 3x^2 - 2y^2 = 1 \\ 4x - y = 3 \end{cases}$

**35.** $\begin{cases} x^3 + y = 0 \\ x^2 - y = 0 \end{cases}$  **36.** $\begin{cases} x^3 + y = 0 \\ 2x^2 - y = 0 \end{cases}$

**37.** $\begin{cases} x^2 + (y - 2)^2 = 4 \\ x^2 - 2y = 0 \end{cases}$  **38.** $\begin{cases} x^2 - y^2 - 4x + 6y - 4 = 0 \\ x^2 + y^2 - 4x - 6y + 12 = 0 \end{cases}$

**39.** $\begin{cases} y = (x + 3)^2 \\ x + 2y = -2 \end{cases}$  **40.** $\begin{cases} (x - 1)^2 + (y + 1)^2 = 5 \\ 2x - y = 3 \end{cases}$

**41.** $\begin{cases} x^2 + y^2 + 3y = 22 \\ 2x + y = -1 \end{cases}$  **42.** $\begin{cases} x - 3y = -5 \\ x^2 + y^2 - 25 = 0 \end{cases}$

*In Exercises 43–46, let x represent one number and let y represent the other number. Use the given conditions to write a system of nonlinear equations. Solve the system and find the numbers.*

**43.** The sum of two numbers is 10 and their product is 24. Find the numbers.

**44.** The sum of two numbers is 20 and their product is 96. Find the numbers.

**45.** The difference between the squares of two numbers is 3. Twice the square of the first number increased by the square of the second number is 9. Find the numbers.

**46.** The difference between the squares of two numbers is 5. Twice the square of the second number subtracted from three times the square of the first number is 19. Find the numbers.

## Practice Plus

*In Exercises 47–52, solve each system by the method of your choice.*

**47.** $\begin{cases} 2x^2 + xy = 6 \\ x^2 + 2xy = 0 \end{cases}$  **48.** $\begin{cases} 4x^2 + xy = 30 \\ x^2 + 3xy = -9 \end{cases}$

**49.** $\begin{cases} -4x + y = 12 \\ y = x^3 + 3x^2 \end{cases}$  **50.** $\begin{cases} -9x + y = 45 \\ y = x^3 + 5x^2 \end{cases}$

**51.** $\begin{cases} \dfrac{3}{x^2} + \dfrac{1}{y^2} = 7 \\ \dfrac{5}{x^2} - \dfrac{2}{y^2} = -3 \end{cases}$  **52.** $\begin{cases} \dfrac{2}{x^2} + \dfrac{1}{y^2} = 11 \\ \dfrac{4}{x^2} - \dfrac{2}{y^2} = -14 \end{cases}$

*In Exercises 53–54, make a rough sketch in a rectangular coordinate system of the graphs representing the equations in each system.*

**53.** The system, whose graphs are a line with positive slope and a parabola whose equation has a positive leading coefficient, has two solutions.

**54.** The system, whose graphs are a line with negative slope and a parabola whose equation has a negative leading coefficient, has one solution.

## Application Exercises

**55.** A planet's orbit follows a path described by $16x^2 + 4y^2 = 64$. A comet follows the parabolic path $y = x^2 - 4$. Where might the comet intersect the orbiting planet?

**56.** A system for tracking ships indicates that a ship lies on a path described by $2y^2 - x^2 = 1$. The process is repeated and the ship is found to lie on a path described by $2x^2 - y^2 = 1$. If it is known that the ship is located in the first quadrant of the coordinate system, determine its exact location.

**57.** Find the length and width of a rectangle whose perimeter is 36 feet and whose area is 77 square feet.

**58.** Find the length and width of a rectangle whose perimeter is 40 feet and whose area is 96 square feet.

*Use the formula for the area of a rectangle and the Pythagorean Theorem to solve Exercises 59–60.*

**59.** A small television has a picture with a diagonal measure of 10 inches and a viewing area of 48 square inches. Find the length and width of the screen.

**60.** The area of a rug is 108 square feet and the length of its diagonal is 15 feet. Find the length and width of the rug.

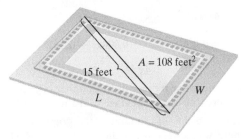

**61.** The figure shows a square floor plan with a smaller square area that will accommodate a combination fountain and pool. The floor with the fountain-pool area removed has an area of 21 square meters and a perimeter of 24 meters. Find the dimensions of the floor and the dimensions of the square that will accommodate the pool.

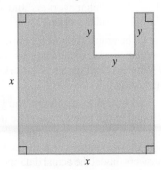

**62.** The area of the rectangular piece of cardboard shown below is 216 square inches. The cardboard is used to make an open box by cutting a 2-inch square from each corner and turning up the sides. If the box is to have a volume of 224 cubic inches, find the length and width of the cardboard that must be used.

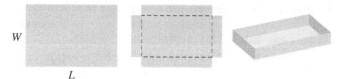

$W$

$L$

**63.** The bar graph shows that compared to a century ago, work in the United States now involves mostly white-collar service jobs.

**The Changing Pattern of Work in the United States, 1900–2005**

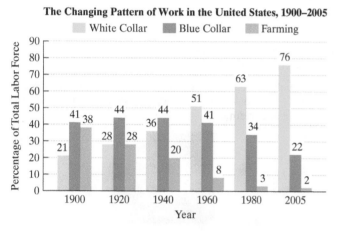

*Source:* U.S. Department of Labor

The data can be modeled by linear and quadratic functions.

White collar   $0.5x - y = -18$

Blue collar   $y = -0.004x^2 + 0.23x + 41$

Farming   $0.4x + y = 35$

In each function, $x$ represents the number of years after 1900 and $y$ represents the percentage of the total U.S. labor force.

**a.** Based on the information in the graph, it appears that there was a year when the percentage of white-collar workers in the labor force was the same as the percentage of blue-collar workers in the labor force. According to the graph, between which two decades did this occur?

**b.** Solve a nonlinear system to determine the year described in part (a). Round to the nearest year. What percentage of the labor force, to the nearest percent, consisted of white-collar workers and what percentage consisted of blue-collar workers?

**c.** According to the graph, for which year was the percentage of white-collar workers the same as the percentage of farmers? What percentage of U.S. workers were in each of these groups?

**d.** Solve a linear system to determine the year described in part (c). Round to the nearest year. Use the models to find the percentage of the labor force consisting of white-collar workers and the percentage consisting of farmers. How well do your answers model the actual data specified in part (c)?

## Writing in Mathematics

**64.** What is a system of nonlinear equations? Provide an example with your description.

**65.** Explain how to solve a nonlinear system using the substitution method. Use $x^2 + y^2 = 9$ and $2x - y = 3$ to illustrate your explanation.

**66.** Explain how to solve a nonlinear system using the addition method. Use $x^2 - y^2 = 5$ and $3x^2 - 2y^2 = 19$ to illustrate your explanation.

## Technology Exercises

**67.** Verify your solutions to any five exercises from Exercises 1–42 by using a graphing utility to graph the two equations in the system in the same viewing rectangle. Then use the intersection feature to verify the solutions.

**68.** Write a system of equations, one equation whose graph is a line and the other whose graph is a parabola, that has no ordered pairs that are real numbers in its solution set. Graph the equations using a graphing utility and verify that you are correct.

## Critical Thinking Exercises

**Make Sense?** *In Exercises 69–72, determine whether each statement makes sense or does not make sense, and explain your reasoning.*

**69.** I use the same steps to solve nonlinear systems as I did to solve linear systems, although I don't obtain linear equations when a variable is eliminated.

**70.** I graphed a nonlinear system that modeled the orbits of Earth and Mars, and the graphs indicated the system had a solution with a real ordered pair.

**71.** Without using any algebra, it's obvious that the nonlinear system consisting of $x^2 + y^2 = 4$ and $x^2 + y^2 = 25$ does not have real-number solutions.

**72.** I think that the nonlinear system consisting of $x^2 + y^2 = 36$ and $y = (x - 2)^2 - 3$ is easier to solve graphically than by using the substitution method or the addition method.

*In Exercises 73–76, determine whether each statement is true or false. If the statement is false, make the necessary change(s) to produce a true statement.*

**73.** A system of two equations in two variables whose graphs are a circle and a line can have four real ordered-pair solutions.

**74.** A system of two equations in two variables whose graphs are a parabola and a circle can have four real ordered-pair solutions.

**75.** A system of two equations in two variables whose graphs are two circles must have at least two real ordered-pair solutions.

**76.** A system of two equations in two variables whose graphs are a parabola and a circle cannot have only one real ordered-pair solution.

**77.** The points of intersection of the graphs of $xy = 20$ and $x^2 + y^2 = 41$ are joined to form a rectangle. Find the area of the rectangle.

**78.** Find $a$ and $b$ in this figure.

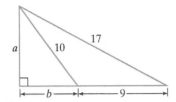

*Solve the systems in Exercises 79–80.*

**79.** $\begin{cases} \log_y x = 3 \\ \log_y(4x) = 5 \end{cases}$

**80.** $\begin{cases} \log x^2 = y + 3 \\ \log x = y - 1 \end{cases}$

## Preview Exercises

*Exercises 81–83 will help you prepare for the material covered in the next section. In each exercise, graph the linear function.*

**81.** $2x - 3y = 6$

**82.** $f(x) = -\frac{2}{3}x$

**83.** $f(x) = -2$

---

# Chapter 7 Mid-Chapter Check Point

**What You Know:** We learned to solve systems of equations. We solved linear and nonlinear systems in two variables by the substitution method and by the addition method. We solved linear systems in three variables by eliminating a variable, reducing the system to two equations in two variables. We saw that some linear systems, called inconsistent systems, have no solution, whereas other linear systems, called dependent systems, have infinitely many solutions. We applied systems to a variety of situations, including finding the break-even point for a business, finding a quadratic function from three points on its graph, and finding a rational function's partial fraction decomposition.

*In Exercises 1–12, solve each system by the method of your choice.*

**1.** $\begin{cases} x = 3y - 7 \\ 4x + 3y = 2 \end{cases}$

**2.** $\begin{cases} 3x + 4y = -5 \\ 2x - 3y = 8 \end{cases}$

**3.** $\begin{cases} \dfrac{2x}{3} + \dfrac{y}{5} = 6 \\ \dfrac{x}{6} - \dfrac{y}{2} = -4 \end{cases}$

**4.** $\begin{cases} y = 4x - 5 \\ 8x - 2y = 10 \end{cases}$

**5.** $\begin{cases} 2x + 5y = 3 \\ 3x - 2y = 1 \end{cases}$

**6.** $\begin{cases} \dfrac{x}{12} - y = \dfrac{1}{4} \\ 4x - 48y = 16 \end{cases}$

**7.** $\begin{cases} 2x - y + 2z = -8 \\ x + 2y - 3z = 9 \\ 3x - y - 4z = 3 \end{cases}$

**8.** $\begin{cases} x - 3z = -5 \\ 2x - y + 2z = 16 \\ 7x - 3y - 5z = 19 \end{cases}$

**9.** $\begin{cases} x^2 + y^2 = 9 \\ x + 2y - 3 = 0 \end{cases}$

**10.** $\begin{cases} 3x^2 + 2y^2 = 14 \\ 2x^2 - y^2 = 7 \end{cases}$

**11.** $\begin{cases} y = x^2 - 6 \\ x^2 + y^2 = 8 \end{cases}$

**12.** $\begin{cases} x - 2y = 4 \\ 2y^2 + xy = 8 \end{cases}$

*In Exercises 13–16, write the partial fraction decomposition of each rational expression.*

**13.** $\dfrac{x^2 - 6x + 3}{(x - 2)^3}$

**14.** $\dfrac{10x^2 + 9x - 7}{(x + 2)(x^2 - 1)}$

**15.** $\dfrac{x^2 + 4x - 23}{(x + 3)(x^2 + 4)}$

**16.** $\dfrac{x^3}{(x^2 + 4)^2}$

**17.** A company is planning to manufacture PDAs (personal digital assistants). The fixed cost will be \$400,000 and it will cost \$20 to produce each PDA. Each PDA will be sold for \$100.

  **a.** Write the cost function, $C$, of producing $x$ PDAs.

  **b.** Write the revenue function, $R$, from the sale of $x$ PDAs.

  **c.** Write the profit function, $P$, from producing and selling $x$ PDAs.

  **d.** Determine the break-even point. Describe what this means.

**18.** Roses sell for \$3 each and carnations for \$1.50 each. If a mixed bouquet of 20 flowers consisting of roses and carnations costs \$39, how many of each type of flower is in the bouquet?

**19.** At the north campus of a small liberal arts college, 10% of the students are women. At the south campus, 50% of the students are women. The campuses are merged into one east campus. If 40% of the 1200 students at the east campus are women, how many students did the north and south campuses have before the merger?

**20.** With the current, you can row 9 miles in 2 hours. Against the current, your return trip takes 6 hours. Find your average rowing velocity in still water and the average velocity of the current.

**21.** Find the measure of each angle whose degree measure is represented with a variable.

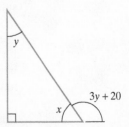

**22.** Find the quadratic function $y = ax^2 + bx + c$ whose graph passes through the points $(-1, 0)$, $(1, 4)$, and $(2, 3)$.

**23.** Find the length and width of a rectangle whose perimeter is 21 meters and whose area is 20 square meters.

## Section 7.5 Systems of Inequalities

### Objectives

1. Graph a linear inequality in two variables.
2. Graph a nonlinear inequality in two variables.
3. Use mathematical models involving linear inequalities.
4. Graph a system of inequalities.

We opened the chapter noting that the modern emphasis on thinness as the ideal body shape has been suggested as a major cause of eating disorders. In this section, as well as in the exercise set, we use systems of linear inequalities in two variables that will enable you to establish a healthy weight range for your height and age.

### Linear Inequalities in Two Variables and Their Solutions

We have seen that equations in the form $Ax + By = C$ are straight lines when graphed. If we change the symbol $=$ to $>$, $<$, $\geq$, or $\leq$, we obtain a **linear inequality in two variables**. Some examples of linear inequalities in two variables are $x + y > 2$, $3x - 5y \leq 15$, and $2x - y < 4$.

A **solution of an inequality in two variables**, $x$ and $y$, is an ordered pair of real numbers with the following property: When the $x$-coordinate is substituted for $x$ and the $y$-coordinate is substituted for $y$ in the inequality, we obtain a true statement. For example, $(3, 2)$ is a solution of the inequality $x + y > 1$. When 3 is substituted for $x$ and 2 is substituted for $y$, we obtain the true statement $3 + 2 > 1$, or $5 > 1$. Because there are infinitely many pairs of numbers that have a sum greater than 1, the inequality $x + y > 1$ has infinitely many solutions. Each ordered-pair solution is said to **satisfy** the inequality. Thus, $(3, 2)$ satisfies the inequality $x + y > 1$.

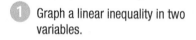

1 Graph a linear inequality in two variables.

### The Graph of a Linear Inequality in Two Variables

We know that the graph of an equation in two variables is the set of all points whose coordinates satisfy the equation. Similarly, the **graph of an inequality in two variables** is the set of all points whose coordinates satisfy the inequality.

Let's use **Figure 7.15** to get an idea of what the graph of a linear inequality in two variables looks like. Part of the figure shows the graph of the linear equation $x + y = 2$. The line divides the points in the rectangular coordinate system into three sets. First, there is the set of points along the line, satisfying $x + y = 2$. Next, there is the set of points in the green region above the line. Points in the green region satisfy the linear inequality $x + y > 2$. Finally, there is the set of points in the purple region below the line. Points in the purple region satisfy the linear inequality $x + y < 2$.

A **half-plane** is the set of all the points on one side of a line. In **Figure 7.15**, the green region is a half-plane. The purple region is also a half-plane. A half-plane is the graph of a linear inequality that involves $>$ or $<$. The graph of an inequality that involves $\geq$ or $\leq$ is a half-plane and a line. A solid line is used to show that a line is part of a graph. A dashed line is used to show that a line is not part of a graph.

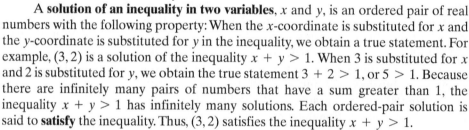

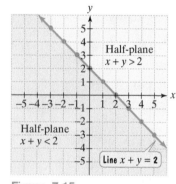

Figure 7.15

### Graphing a Linear Inequality in Two Variables

**1.** Replace the inequality symbol with an equal sign and graph the corresponding linear equation. Draw a solid line if the original inequality contains a $\leq$ or $\geq$ symbol. Draw a dashed line if the original inequality contains a $<$ or $>$ symbol.

**2.** Choose a test point from one of the half-planes. (Do not choose a point on the line.) Substitute the coordinates of the test point into the inequality.

**3.** If a true statement results, shade the half-plane containing this test point. If a false statement results, shade the half-plane not containing this test point.

( **EXAMPLE 1** ) **Graphing a Linear Inequality in Two Variables**

Graph:  $2x - 3y \geq 6$.

**Solution**

**Step 1  Replace the inequality symbol by = and graph the linear equation.** We need to graph $2x - 3y = 6$. We can use intercepts to graph this line.

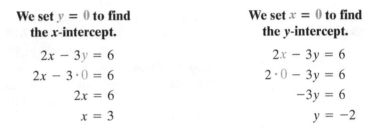

| We set $y = 0$ to find the $x$-intercept. | We set $x = 0$ to find the $y$-intercept. |
|---|---|
| $2x - 3y = 6$ | $2x - 3y = 6$ |
| $2x - 3 \cdot 0 = 6$ | $2 \cdot 0 - 3y = 6$ |
| $2x = 6$ | $-3y = 6$ |
| $x = 3$ | $y = -2$ |

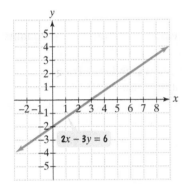

**Figure 7.16**  Preparing to graph $2x - 3y \geq 6$

The $x$-intercept is 3, so the line passes through $(3, 0)$. The $y$-intercept is $-2$, so the line passes through $(0, -2)$. Using the intercepts, the line is shown in **Figure 7.16** as a solid line. This is because the inequality $2x - 3y \geq 6$ contains a $\geq$ symbol, in which equality is included.

**Step 2  Choose a test point from one of the half-planes and not from the line. Substitute its coordinates into the inequality.** The line $2x - 3y = 6$ divides the plane into three parts—the line itself and two half-planes. The points in one half-plane satisfy $2x - 3y > 6$. The points in the other half-plane satisfy $2x - 3y < 6$. We need to find which half-plane belongs to the solution of $2x - 3y \geq 6$. To do so, we test a point from either half-plane. The origin, $(0, 0)$, is the easiest point to test.

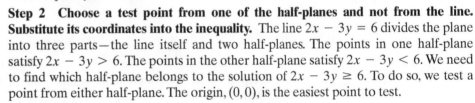

$$2x - 3y \geq 6 \qquad \text{This is the given inequality.}$$
$$2 \cdot 0 - 3 \cdot 0 \overset{?}{\geq} 6 \qquad \text{Test } (0, 0) \text{ by substituting 0 for x and 0 for y.}$$
$$0 - 0 \overset{?}{\geq} 6 \qquad \text{Multiply.}$$
$$0 \geq 6 \qquad \text{This statement is false.}$$

**Step 3  If a false statement results, shade the half-plane not containing the test point.** Because 0 is not greater than or equal to 6, the test point, $(0, 0)$, is not part of the solution set. Thus, the half-plane below the solid line $2x - 3y = 6$ is part of the solution set. The solution set is the line and the half-plane that does not contain the point $(0, 0)$, indicated by shading this half-plane. The graph is shown using green shading and a blue line in **Figure 7.17**.

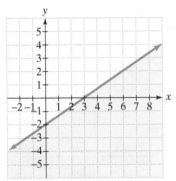

**Figure 7.17**  The graph of $2x - 3y \geq 6$

⊘ Check Point **1**  Graph:  $4x - 2y \geq 8$.

When graphing a linear inequality, choose a test point that lies in one of the half-planes and *not on the line dividing the half-planes*. The test point $(0, 0)$ is convenient because it is easy to calculate when 0 is substituted for each variable. However, if $(0, 0)$ lies on the dividing line and not in a half-plane, a different test point must be selected.

### ( EXAMPLE 2 ) Graphing a Linear Inequality in Two Variables

Graph: $y > -\dfrac{2}{3}x$.

#### Solution

**Step 1 Replace the inequality symbol by = and graph the linear equation.** Because we are interested in graphing $y > -\frac{2}{3}x$, we begin by graphing $y = -\frac{2}{3}x$. We can use the slope and the $y$-intercept to graph this linear function.

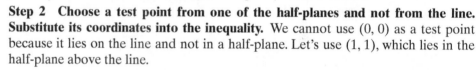

$$y = -\frac{2}{3}x + 0$$

Slope $= \dfrac{-2}{3} = \dfrac{\text{rise}}{\text{run}}$   $y$-intercept $= 0$

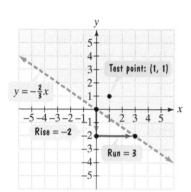

**Figure 7.18** The graph of $y > -\frac{2}{3}x$

The $y$-intercept is 0, so the line passes through $(0, 0)$. Using the $y$-intercept and the slope, the line is shown in **Figure 7.18** as a dashed line. This is because the inequality $y > -\frac{2}{3}x$ contains a $>$ symbol, in which equality is not included.

**Step 2 Choose a test point from one of the half-planes and not from the line. Substitute its coordinates into the inequality.** We cannot use $(0, 0)$ as a test point because it lies on the line and not in a half-plane. Let's use $(1, 1)$, which lies in the half-plane above the line.

$$y > -\frac{2}{3}x \qquad \text{This is the given inequality.}$$

$$1 \overset{?}{>} -\frac{2}{3} \cdot 1 \qquad \text{Test } (1, 1) \text{ by substituting 1 for x and 1 for y.}$$

$$1 > -\frac{2}{3} \qquad \text{This statement is true.}$$

**Step 3 If a true statement results, shade the half-plane containing the test point.** Because 1 is greater than $-\frac{2}{3}$, the test point $(1, 1)$ is part of the solution set. All the points on the same side of the line $y = -\frac{2}{3}x$ as the point $(1, 1)$ are members of the solution set. The solution set is the half-plane that contains the point $(1, 1)$, indicated by shading this half-plane. The graph is shown using green shading and a dashed blue line in **Figure 7.18**. ●

### Technology

Most graphing utilities can graph inequalities in two variables with the $\boxed{\text{SHADE}}$ feature. The procedure varies by model, so consult your manual. For most graphing utilities, you must first solve for $y$ if it is not already isolated. The figure shows the graph of $y > -\frac{2}{3}x$. Most displays do not distinguish between dashed and solid boundary lines.

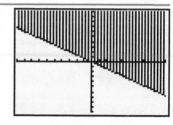

⊘Check Point **2** Graph: $y > -\dfrac{3}{4}x$.

## Graphing Linear Inequalities without Using Test Points

You can graph inequalities in the form $y > mx + b$ or $y < mx + b$ without using test points. The inequality symbol indicates which half-plane to shade.

- If $y > mx + b$, shade the half-plane above the line $y = mx + b$.
- If $y < mx + b$, shade the half-plane below the line $y = mx + b$.

Observe how this is illustrated in **Figure 7.18** in the margin on the previous page. The graph of $y > -\frac{2}{3}x$ is the half-plane above the line $y = -\frac{2}{3}x$.

It is also not necessary to use test points when graphing inequalities involving half-planes on one side of a vertical or a horizontal line.

| For the Vertical Line $x = a$: | For the Horizontal Line $y = b$: |
|---|---|
| • If $x > a$, shade the half-plane to the right of $x = a$. | • If $y > b$, shade the half-plane above $y = b$. |
| • If $x < a$, shade the half-plane to the left of $x = a$. | • If $y < b$, shade the half-plane below $y = b$. |

**Study Tip**

Continue using test points to graph inequalities in the form $Ax + By > C$ or $Ax + By < C$. The graph of $Ax + By > C$ can lie above or below the line given by $Ax + By = C$, depending on the value of $B$. The same comment applies to the graph of $Ax + By < C$.

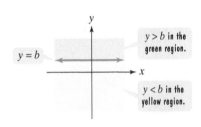

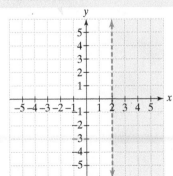

___EXAMPLE 3___ **Graphing Inequalities without Using Test Points**

Graph each inequality in a rectangular coordinate system:

    **a.** $y \le -3$         **b.** $x > 2$.

**Solution**

    **a.** $y \le -3$                                  **b.** $x > 2$

Graph $y = -3$, a horizontal line with $y$-intercept $-3$. The line is solid because equality is included in $y \le -3$. Because of the less than part of $\le$, shade the half-plane below the horizontal line.

Graph $x = 2$, a vertical line with $x$-intercept 2. The line is dashed because equality is not included in $x > 2$. Because of $>$, the greater than symbol, shade the half-plane to the right of the vertical line.

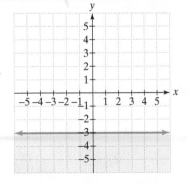

⊘ Check Point **3** Graph each inequality in a rectangular coordinate system:

**a.** $y > 1$          **b.** $x \leq -2$.

② Graph a nonlinear inequality in two variables.

## Graphing a Nonlinear Inequality in Two Variables

Example 4 illustrates that a nonlinear inequality in two variables is graphed in the same way that we graph a linear inequality.

( EXAMPLE 4 ) **Graphing a Nonlinear Inequality in Two Variables**

Graph: $x^2 + y^2 \leq 9$.

### Solution

**Step 1  Replace the inequality symbol with = and graph the nonlinear equation.** We need to graph $x^2 + y^2 = 9$. The graph is a circle of radius 3 with its center at the origin. The graph is shown in **Figure 7.19** as a solid circle because equality is included in the $\leq$ symbol.

**Step 2  Choose a test point from one of the regions and not from the circle. Substitute its coordinates into the inequality.** The circle divides the plane into three parts—the circle itself, the region inside the circle, and the region outside the circle. We need to determine whether the region inside or outside the circle is included in the solution. To do so, we will use the test point $(0, 0)$ from inside the circle.

$$x^2 + y^2 \leq 9 \qquad \text{This is the given inequality.}$$

$$0^2 + 0^2 \overset{?}{\leq} 9 \qquad \text{Test } (0, 0) \text{ by substituting } 0 \text{ for } x \text{ and } 0 \text{ for } y.$$

$$0 + 0 \overset{?}{\leq} 9 \qquad \text{Square } 0: 0^2 = 0.$$

$$0 \leq 9 \qquad \text{Add. This statement is true.}$$

**Step 3  If a true statement results, shade the region containing the test point.** The true statement tells us that all the points inside the circle satisfy $x^2 + y^2 \leq 9$. The graph is shown using green shading and a solid blue circle in **Figure 7.20**.

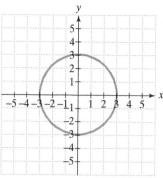

**Figure 7.19** Preparing to graph $x^2 + y^2 \leq 9$

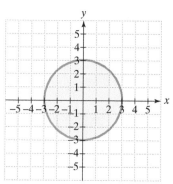

**Figure 7.20** The graph of $x^2 + y^2 \leq 9$

⊘ Check Point **4** Graph: $x^2 + y^2 \geq 16$.

③ Use mathematical models
involving linear inequalities.

## Modeling with Systems of Linear Inequalities

Just as two or more linear equations make up a system of linear equations, two or more linear inequalities make up a **system of linear inequalities**. A **solution of a system of linear inequalities** in two variables is an ordered pair that satisfies each inequality in the system.

(**EXAMPLE 5**) **Does Your Weight Fit You?**

The latest guidelines, which apply to both men and women, give healthy weight ranges, rather than specific weights, for your height. **Figure 7.21** shows the healthy weight region for various heights for people between the ages of 19 and 34, inclusive.

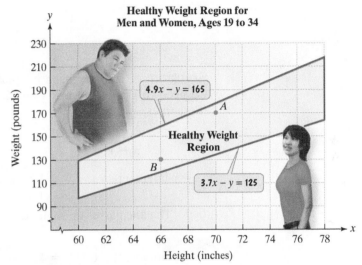

**Figure 7.21**
*Source:* U.S. Department of Health and Human Services

If $x$ represents height, in inches, and $y$ represents weight, in pounds, the healthy weight region in **Figure 7.21** can be modeled by the following system of linear inequalities:

$$\begin{cases} 4.9x - y \geq 165 \\ 3.7x - y \leq 125. \end{cases}$$

Show that point $A$ in **Figure 7.21** is a solution of the system of inequalities that describes healthy weight.

**Solution**   Point $A$ has coordinates $(70, 170)$. This means that if a person is 70 inches tall, or 5 feet 10 inches, and weighs 170 pounds, then that person's weight is within the healthy weight region. We can show that $(70, 170)$ satisfies the system of inequalities by substituting 70 for $x$ and 170 for $y$ in each inequality in the system.

| | |
|---|---|
| $4.9x - y \geq 165$ | $3.7x - y \leq 125$ |
| $4.9(70) - 170 \overset{?}{\geq} 165$ | $3.7(70) - 170 \overset{?}{\leq} 125$ |
| $343 - 170 \overset{?}{\geq} 165$ | $259 - 170 \overset{?}{\leq} 125$ |
| $173 \geq 165,$   true | $89 \leq 125,$   true |

The coordinates $(70, 170)$ make each inequality true. Thus, $(70, 170)$ satisfies the system for the healthy weight region and is a solution of the system. ●

⌀ Check Point 5   Show that point $B$ in **Figure 7.21** is a solution of the system of inequalities that describes healthy weight.

④ Graph a system of inequalities.

## Graphing Systems of Linear Inequalities

The **solution set of a system of linear inequalities in two variables** is the set of all ordered pairs that satisfy each inequality in the system. Thus, to graph a system of inequalities in two variables, begin by graphing each individual inequality in the same rectangular coordinate system. Then find the region, if there is one, that is common to every graph in the system. This region of intersection gives a picture of the system's solution set.

(EXAMPLE 6) **Graphing a System of Linear Inequalities**

Graph the solution set of the system:

$$\begin{cases} x - y < 1 \\ 2x + 3y \geq 12. \end{cases}$$

**Solution** Replacing each inequality symbol with an equal sign indicates that we need to graph $x - y = 1$ and $2x + 3y = 12$. We can use intercepts to graph these lines.

| $x - y = 1$ | | $2x + 3y = 12$ |
|---|---|---|
| $x$-intercept: $x - 0 = 1$ | Set $y = 0$ in each equation. | $x$-intercept: $2x + 3 \cdot 0 = 12$ |
| $x = 1$ | | $2x = 12$ |
| The line passes through $(1, 0)$. | | $x = 6$ |
| | | The line passes through $(6, 0)$. |
| $y$-intercept: $0 - y = 1$ | Set $x = 0$ in each equation. | $y$-intercept: $2 \cdot 0 + 3y = 12$ |
| $-y = 1$ | | $3y = 12$ |
| $y = -1$ | | $y = 4$ |
| The line passes through $(0, -1)$. | | The line passes through $(0, 4)$. |

Now we are ready to graph the solution set of the system of linear inequalities.

Graph $x - y < 1$. The blue line, $x - y = 1$, is dashed: Equality is not included in $x - y < 1$. Because $(0, 0)$ makes the inequality true $(0 - 0 < 1$, or $0 < 1$, is true), shade the half-plane containing $(0, 0)$ in yellow.

Add the graph of $2x + 3y \geq 12$. The red line, $2x + 3y = 12$, is solid: Equality is included in $2x + 3y \geq 12$. Because $(0, 0)$ makes the inequality false $(2 \cdot 0 + 3 \cdot 0 \geq 12$, or $0 \geq 12$, is false), shade the half-plane not containing $(0, 0)$ using green vertical shading.

The solution set of the system is graphed as the intersection (the overlap) of the two half-planes. This is the region in which the yellow shading and the green vertical shading overlap.

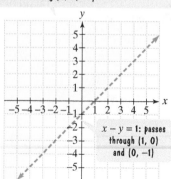

The graph of $x - y < 1$

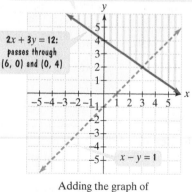

Adding the graph of $2x + 3y \geq 12$

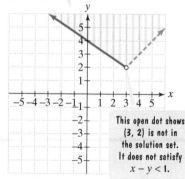

The graph of $x - y < 1$ and $2x + 3y \geq 12$

✓ Check Point **6** Graph the solution set of the system:

$$\begin{cases} x - 3y < 6 \\ 2x + 3y \geq -6. \end{cases}$$

( **EXAMPLE 7** )  **Graphing a System of Inequalities**

Graph the solution set of the system:

$$\begin{cases} y \geq x^2 - 4 \\ x - y \geq 2. \end{cases}$$

**Solution**  We begin by graphing $y \geq x^2 - 4$. Because equality is included in $\geq$, we graph $y = x^2 - 4$ as a solid parabola. Because $(0, 0)$ makes the inequality $y \geq x^2 - 4$ true (we obtain $0 \geq -4$), we shade the interior portion of the parabola containing $(0, 0)$, shown in yellow in **Figure 7.22**.

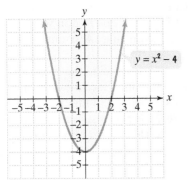

Figure 7.22  The graph of $y \geq x^2 - 4$

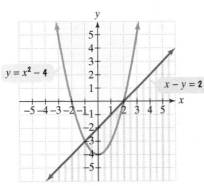

Figure 7.23  Adding the graph of $x - y \geq 2$

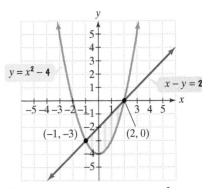

Figure 7.24  The graph of $y \geq x^2 - 4$ and $x - y \geq 2$

Now we graph $x - y \geq 2$ in the same rectangular coordinate system. First we graph the line $x - y = 2$ using its $x$-intercept, 2, and its $y$-intercept, $-2$. Because $(0, 0)$ makes the inequality $x - y \geq 2$ false (we obtain $0 \geq 2$), we shade the half-plane below the line. This is shown in **Figure 7.23** using green vertical shading.

The solution of the system is shown in **Figure 7.24** by the intersection (the overlap) of the solid yellow and green vertical shadings. The graph of the system's solution set consists of the region enclosed by the parabola and the line. To find the points of intersection of the parabola and the line, use the substitution method to solve the nonlinear system

$$\begin{cases} y = x^2 - 4 \\ x - y = 2. \end{cases}$$

Take a moment to show that the solutions are $(-1, -3)$ and $(2, 0)$, as shown in **Figure 7.24**.  ●

✓ Check Point **7** Graph the solution set of the system:

$$\begin{cases} y \geq x^2 - 4 \\ x + y \leq 2. \end{cases}$$

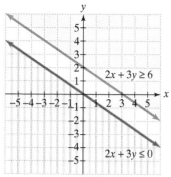

**Figure 7.25** A system of inequalities with no solution

A system of inequalities has no solution if there are no points in the rectangular coordinate system that simultaneously satisfy each inequality in the system. For example, the system

$$\begin{cases} 2x + 3y \geq 6 \\ 2x + 3y \leq 0, \end{cases}$$

whose separate graphs are shown in **Figure 7.25**, has no overlapping region. Thus, the system has no solution. The solution set is $\varnothing$, the empty set.

**EXAMPLE 8** Graphing a System of Inequalities

Graph the solution set of the system:

$$\begin{cases} x - y < 2 \\ -2 \leq x < 4 \\ \qquad y < 3. \end{cases}$$

**Solution** We begin by graphing $x - y < 2$, the first given inequality. The line $x - y = 2$ has an $x$-intercept of 2 and a $y$-intercept of $-2$. The test point $(0, 0)$ makes the inequality $x - y < 2$ true, and its graph is shown in **Figure 7.26**.

Now, let's consider the second given inequality, $-2 \leq x < 4$. Replacing the inequality symbols by $=$, we obtain $x = -2$ and $x = 4$, graphed as red vertical lines in **Figure 7.27**. The line of $x = 4$ is not included. Because $x$ is between $-2$ and 4, we shade the region between the vertical lines. We must intersect this region with the yellow region in **Figure 7.26**. The resulting region is shown in yellow and green vertical shading in **Figure 7.27**.

Finally, let's consider the third given inequality, $y < 3$. Replacing the inequality symbol by $=$, we obtain $y = 3$, which graphs as a horizontal line. Because of the less than symbol in $y < 3$, the graph consists of the half-plane below the line $y = 3$. We must intersect this half-plane with the region in **Figure 7.27**. The resulting region is shown in yellow and green vertical shading in **Figure 7.28**. This region represents the graph of the solution set of the given system.

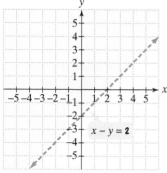

**Figure 7.26** The graph of $x - y < 2$

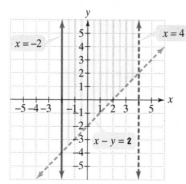

**Figure 7.27** The graph of $x - y < 2$ and $-2 \leq x < 4$

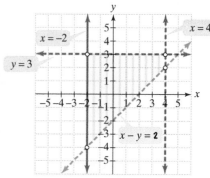

**Figure 7.28** The graph of $x - y < 2$ and $-2 \leq x < 4$ and $y < 3$

In **Figure 7.28** it may be difficult to tell where the graph of $x - y = 2$ intersects the vertical line $x = 4$. Using the substitution method, it can be determined that this intersection point is $(4, 2)$. Take a moment to verify that the four intersection points in **Figure 7.28** are, clockwise from upper left, $(-2, 3)$, $(4, 3)$, $(4, 2)$, and $(-2, -4)$. These points are shown as open dots because none satisfies all three of the system's inequalities.

⊘ Check Point **8** Graph the solution set of the system:

$$\begin{cases} x + y < 2 \\ -2 \leq x < 1 \\ \qquad y > -3. \end{cases}$$

# Exercise Set 7.5

## Practice Exercises

*In Exercises 1–26, graph each inequality.*

**1.** $x + 2y \le 8$

**2.** $3x - 6y \le 12$

**3.** $x - 2y > 10$

**4.** $2x - y > 4$

**5.** $y \le \frac{1}{3}x$

**6.** $y \le \frac{1}{4}x$

**7.** $y > 2x - 1$

**8.** $y > 3x + 2$

**9.** $x \le 1$

**10.** $x \le -3$

**11.** $y > 1$

**12.** $y > -3$

**13.** $x^2 + y^2 \le 1$

**14.** $x^2 + y^2 \le 4$

**15.** $x^2 + y^2 > 25$

**16.** $x^2 + y^2 > 36$

**17.** $(x - 2)^2 + (y + 1)^2 < 9$

**18.** $(x + 2)^2 + (y - 1)^2 < 16$

**19.** $y < x^2 - 1$

**20.** $y < x^2 - 9$

**21.** $y \ge x^2 - 9$

**22.** $y \ge x^2 - 1$

**23.** $y > 2^x$

**24.** $y \le 3^x$

**25.** $y \ge \log_2(x + 1)$

**26.** $y \ge \log_3(x - 1)$

*In Exercises 27–62, graph the solution set of each system of inequalities or indicate that the system has no solution.*

**27.** $\begin{cases} 3x + 6y \le 6 \\ 2x + y \le 8 \end{cases}$

**28.** $\begin{cases} x - y \ge 4 \\ x + y \le 6 \end{cases}$

**29.** $\begin{cases} 2x - 5y \le 10 \\ 3x - 2y > 6 \end{cases}$

**30.** $\begin{cases} 2x - y \le 4 \\ 3x + 2y > -6 \end{cases}$

**31.** $\begin{cases} y > 2x - 3 \\ y < -x + 6 \end{cases}$

**32.** $\begin{cases} y < -2x + 4 \\ y < x - 4 \end{cases}$

**33.** $\begin{cases} x + 2y \le 4 \\ y \ge x - 3 \end{cases}$

**34.** $\begin{cases} x + y \le 4 \\ y \ge 2x - 4 \end{cases}$

**35.** $\begin{cases} x \le 2 \\ y \ge -1 \end{cases}$

**36.** $\begin{cases} x \le 3 \\ y \le -1 \end{cases}$

**37.** $-2 \le x < 5$

**38.** $-2 < y \le 5$

**39.** $\begin{cases} x - y \le 1 \\ x \ge 2 \end{cases}$

**40.** $\begin{cases} 4x - 5y \ge -20 \\ x \ge -3 \end{cases}$

**41.** $\begin{cases} x + y > 4 \\ x + y < -1 \end{cases}$

**42.** $\begin{cases} x + y > 3 \\ x + y < -2 \end{cases}$

**43.** $\begin{cases} x + y > 4 \\ x + y > -1 \end{cases}$

**44.** $\begin{cases} x + y > 3 \\ x + y > -2 \end{cases}$

**45.** $\begin{cases} y \ge x^2 - 1 \\ x - y \ge -1 \end{cases}$

**46.** $\begin{cases} y \ge x^2 - 4 \\ x - y \ge 2 \end{cases}$

**47.** $\begin{cases} x^2 + y^2 \le 16 \\ x + y > 2 \end{cases}$

**48.** $\begin{cases} x^2 + y^2 \le 4 \\ x + y > 1 \end{cases}$

**49.** $\begin{cases} x^2 + y^2 > 1 \\ x^2 + y^2 < 16 \end{cases}$

**50.** $\begin{cases} x^2 + y^2 > 1 \\ x^2 + y^2 < 9 \end{cases}$

**51.** $\begin{cases} (x - 1)^2 + (y + 1)^2 < 25 \\ (x - 1)^2 + (y + 1)^2 \ge 16 \end{cases}$

**52.** $\begin{cases} (x + 1)^2 + (y - 1)^2 < 16 \\ (x + 1)^2 + (y - 1)^2 \ge 4 \end{cases}$

**53.** $\begin{cases} x^2 + y^2 \le 1 \\ y - x^2 > 0 \end{cases}$

**54.** $\begin{cases} x^2 + y^2 < 4 \\ y - x^2 \ge 0 \end{cases}$

**55.** $\begin{cases} x^2 + y^2 < 16 \\ y \ge 2^x \end{cases}$

**56.** $\begin{cases} x^2 + y^2 \le 16 \\ y < 2^x \end{cases}$

**57.** $\begin{cases} x - y \le 2 \\ x > -2 \\ y \le 3 \end{cases}$

**58.** $\begin{cases} 3x + y \le 6 \\ x > -2 \\ y \le 4 \end{cases}$

**59.** $\begin{cases} x \ge 0 \\ y \ge 0 \\ 2x + 5y < 10 \\ 3x + 4y \le 12 \end{cases}$

**60.** $\begin{cases} x \ge 0 \\ y \ge 0 \\ 2x + y < 4 \\ 2x - 3y \le 6 \end{cases}$

**61.** $\begin{cases} 3x + y \le 6 \\ 2x - y \le -1 \\ x > -2 \\ y < 4 \end{cases}$

**62.** $\begin{cases} 2x + y \le 6 \\ x + y > 2 \\ 1 \le x \le 2 \\ y < 3 \end{cases}$

## Practice Plus

*In Exercises 63–64, write each sentence as an inequality in two variables. Then graph the inequality.*

**63.** The $y$-variable is at least 4 more than the product of $-2$ and the $x$-variable.

**64.** The $y$-variable is at least 2 more than the product of $-3$ and the $x$-variable.

*In Exercises 65–68, write the given sentences as a system of inequalities in two variables. Then graph the system.*

**65.** The sum of the $x$-variable and the $y$-variable is at most 4. The $y$-variable added to the product of 3 and the $x$-variable does not exceed 6.

**66.** The sum of the $x$-variable and the $y$-variable is at most 3. The $y$-variable added to the product of 4 and the $x$-variable does not exceed 6.

**67.** The sum of the $x$-variable and the $y$-variable is no more than 2. The $y$-variable is no less than the difference between the square of the $x$-variable and 4.

**68.** The sum of the squares of the $x$-variable and the $y$-variable is no more than 25. The sum of twice the $y$-variable and the $x$-variable is no less than 5.

In Exercises 69–70, rewrite each inequality in the system without absolute value bars. Then graph the rewritten system in rectangular coordinates.

**69.** $\begin{cases} |x| \leq 2 \\ |y| \leq 3 \end{cases}$     **70.** $\begin{cases} |x| \leq 1 \\ |y| \leq 2 \end{cases}$

The graphs of solution sets of systems of inequalities involve finding the intersection of the solution sets of two or more inequalities. By contrast, in Exercises 71–72, you will be graphing the **union** of the solution sets of two inequalities.

**71.** Graph the union of $y > \frac{3}{2}x - 2$ and $y < 4$.

**72.** Graph the union of $x - y \geq -1$ and $5x - 2y \leq 10$.

Without graphing, in Exercises 73–76, determine if each system has no solution or infinitely many solutions.

**73.** $\begin{cases} 3x + y < 9 \\ 3x + y > 9 \end{cases}$

**74.** $\begin{cases} 6x - y \leq 24 \\ 6x - y > 24 \end{cases}$

**75.** $\begin{cases} (x + 4)^2 + (y - 3)^2 \leq 9 \\ (x + 4)^2 + (y - 3)^2 \geq 9 \end{cases}$

**76.** $\begin{cases} (x - 4)^2 + (y + 3)^2 \leq 24 \\ (x - 4)^2 + (y + 3)^2 \geq 24 \end{cases}$

## Application Exercises

The figure shows the healthy weight region for various heights for people ages 35 and older.

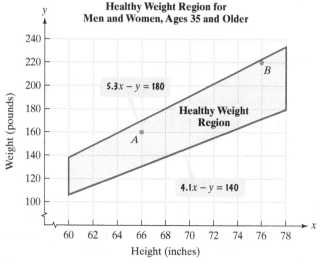

**Healthy Weight Region for Men and Women, Ages 35 and Older**

Source: U.S. Department of Health and Human Services

If x represents height, in inches, and y represents weight, in pounds, the healthy weight region can be modeled by the following system of linear inequalities:

$$\begin{cases} 5.3x - y \geq 180 \\ 4.1x - y \leq 140. \end{cases}$$

Use this information to solve Exercises 77–80.

**77.** Show that point $A$ is a solution of the system of inequalities that describes healthy weight for this age group.

**78.** Show that point $B$ is a solution of the system of inequalities that describes healthy weight for this age group.

**79.** Is a person in this age group who is 6 feet tall weighing 205 pounds within the healthy weight region?

**80.** Is a person in this age group who is 5 feet 8 inches tall weighing 135 pounds within the healthy weight region?

**81.** Many elevators have a capacity of 2000 pounds.

  **a.** If a child averages 50 pounds and an adult 150 pounds, write an inequality that describes when $x$ children and $y$ adults will cause the elevator to be overloaded.

  **b.** Graph the inequality. Because $x$ and $y$ must be positive, limit the graph to quadrant I only.

  **c.** Select an ordered pair satisfying the inequality. What are its coordinates and what do they represent in this situation?

**82.** A patient is not allowed to have more than 330 milligrams of cholesterol per day from a diet of eggs and meat. Each egg provides 165 milligrams of cholesterol. Each ounce of meat provides 110 milligrams.

  **a.** Write an inequality that describes the patient's dietary restrictions for $x$ eggs and $y$ ounces of meat.

  **b.** Graph the inequality. Because $x$ and $y$ must be positive, limit the graph to quadrant I only.

  **c.** Select an ordered pair satisfying the inequality. What are its coordinates and what do they represent in this situation?

**83.** On your next vacation, you will divide lodging between large resorts and small inns. Let $x$ represent the number of nights spent in large resorts. Let $y$ represent the number of nights spent in small inns.

  **a.** Write a system of inequalities that models the following conditions:

    You want to stay at least 5 nights. At least one night should be spent at a large resort. Large resorts average $200 per night and small inns average $100 per night. Your budget permits no more than $700 for lodging.

  **b.** Graph the solution set of the system of inequalities in part (a).

  **c.** Based on your graph in part (b), what is the greatest number of nights you could spend at a large resort and still stay within your budget?

**84.** A person with no more than $15,000 to invest plans to place the money in two investments. One investment is high risk, high yield; the other is low risk, low yield. At least $2000 is to be placed in the high-risk investment. Furthermore, the amount invested at low risk should be at least three times the amount invested at high risk. Find and graph a system of inequalities that describes all possibilities for placing the money in the high- and low-risk investments.

The graph of an inequality in two variables is a region in the rectangular coordinate system. Regions in coordinate systems have numerous applications. For example, the regions in the following two graphs indicate whether a person is obese, overweight, borderline overweight, normal weight, or underweight.

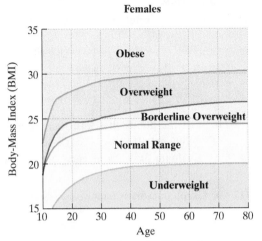

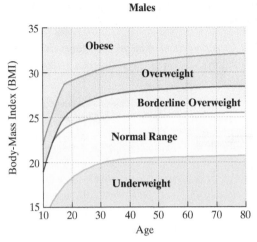

*Source:* Centers for Disease Control and Prevention

The horizontal axis shows a person's age. The vertical axis shows that person's body-mass index (BMI), computed using the following formula:

$$\text{BMI} = \frac{703W}{H^2}.$$

The variable W represents weight, in pounds. The variable H represents height, in inches. Use this information to solve Exercises 85–86.

**85.** A man is 20 years old, 72 inches (6 feet) tall, and weighs 200 pounds.

    **a.** Compute the man's BMI. Round to the nearest tenth.

    **b.** Use the man's age and his BMI to locate this information as a point in the coordinate system for males. Is this person obese, overweight, borderline overweight, normal weight, or underweight?

**86.** A woman is 25 years old, 66 inches (5 feet, 6 inches) tall, and weighs 105 pounds.

    **a.** Compute the woman's BMI. Round to the nearest tenth.

    **b.** Use the woman's age and her BMI to locate this information as a point in the coordinate system for females. Is this person obese, overweight, borderline overweight, normal weight, or underweight?

## Writing in Mathematics

**87.** What is a linear inequality in two variables? Provide an example with your description.

**88.** How do you determine if an ordered pair is a solution of an inequality in two variables, $x$ and $y$?

**89.** What is a half-plane?

**90.** What does a solid line mean in the graph of an inequality?

**91.** What does a dashed line mean in the graph of an inequality?

**92.** Compare the graphs of $3x - 2y > 6$ and $3x - 2y \leq 6$. Discuss similarities and differences between the graphs.

**93.** What is a system of linear inequalities?

**94.** What is a solution of a system of linear inequalities?

**95.** Explain how to graph the solution set of a system of inequalities.

**96.** What does it mean if a system of linear inequalities has no solution?

## Technology Exercises

Graphing utilities can be used to shade regions in the rectangular coordinate system, thereby graphing an inequality in two variables. Read the section of the user's manual for your graphing utility that describes how to shade a region. Then use your graphing utility to graph the inequalities in Exercises 97–102.

**97.** $y \leq 4x + 4$

**98.** $y \geq \frac{2}{3}x - 2$

**99.** $y \geq x^2 - 4$

**100.** $y \geq \frac{1}{2}x^2 - 2$

**101.** $2x + y \leq 6$

**102.** $3x - 2y \geq 6$

**103.** Does your graphing utility have any limitations in terms of graphing inequalities? If so, what are they?

**104.** Use a graphing utility with a ⌐SHADE⌐ feature to verify any five of the graphs that you drew by hand in Exercises 1–26.

**105.** Use a graphing utility with a ⌐SHADE⌐ feature to verify any five of the graphs that you drew by hand for the systems in Exercises 27–62.

## Critical Thinking Exercises

**Make Sense?** *In Exercises 106–109, determine whether each statement makes sense or does not make sense, and explain your reasoning.*

**106.** When graphing a linear inequality, I should always use $(0, 0)$ as a test point because it's easy to perform the calculations when 0 is substituted for each variable.

**107.** When graphing $3x - 4y < 12$, it's not necessary for me to graph the linear equation $3x - 4y = 12$ because the inequality contains a $<$ symbol, in which equality is not included.

**108.** The reason that systems of linear inequalities are appropriate for modeling healthy weight is because guidelines give healthy weight ranges, rather than specific weights, for various heights.

**109.** I graphed the solution set of $y \geq x + 2$ and $x \geq 1$ without using test points.

*In Exercises 110–113, write a system of inequalities for each graph.*

**110.**

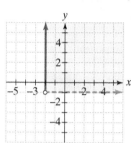

**111.**

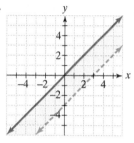

**112.**

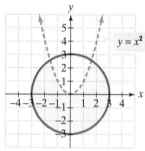

**113.**

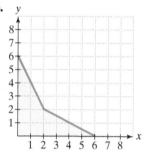

**114.** Write a system of inequalities whose solution set includes every point in the rectangular coordinate system.

**115.** Sketch the graph of the solution set for the following system of inequalities:

$$\begin{cases} y \geq nx + b \ (n < 0, b > 0) \\ y \leq mx + b \ (m > 0, b > 0). \end{cases}$$

## Preview Exercises

*Exercises 116–118 will help you prepare for the material covered in the next section.*

**116. a.** Graph the solution set of the system:

$$\begin{cases} x + y \geq 6 \\ x \leq 8 \\ y \geq 5. \end{cases}$$

**b.** List the points that form the corners of the graphed region in part (a).

**c.** Evaluate $3x + 2y$ at each of the points obtained in part (b).

**117. a.** Graph the solution set of the system:

$$\begin{cases} x \geq 0 \\ y \geq 0 \\ 3x - 2x \leq 6 \\ y \leq -x + 7. \end{cases}$$

**b.** List the points that form the corners of the graphed region in part (a).

**c.** Evaluate $2x + 5y$ at each of the points obtained in part (b).

**118.** Bottled water and medical supplies are to be shipped to survivors of an earthquake by plane. The bottled water weighs 20 pounds per container and medical kits weigh 10 pounds per kit. Each plane can carry no more than 80,000 pounds. If $x$ represents the number of bottles of water to be shipped per plane and $y$ represents the number of medical kits per plane, write an inequality that models each plane's 80,000-pound weight restriction.

---

## Section 7.6 Linear Programming

### Objectives

**1** Write an objective function describing a quantity that must be maximized or minimized.

**2** Use inequalities to describe limitations in a situation.

**3** Use linear programming to solve problems.

West Berlin children at Tempelhof airport watch fleets of U.S. airplanes bringing in supplies to circumvent the Soviet blockade. The airlift began June 28, 1948 and continued for 15 months.

The Berlin Airlift (1948 – 1949) was an operation by the United States and Great Britain in response to military action by the former Soviet Union: Soviet troops closed all roads and rail lines between West Germany and Berlin, cutting off supply routes to the city. The Allies used a mathematical technique developed during World

War II to maximize the amount of supplies transported. During the 15-month airlift, 278,228 flights provided basic necessities to blockaded Berlin, saving one of the world's great cities.

In this section, we will look at an important application of systems of linear inequalities. Such systems arise in **linear programming**, a method for solving problems in which a particular quantity that must be maximized or minimized is limited by other factors. Linear programming is one of the most widely used tools in management science. It helps businesses allocate resources to manufacture products in a way that will maximize profit. Linear programming accounts for more than 50% and perhaps as much as 90% of all computing time used for management decisions in business. The Allies used linear programming to save Berlin.

**①** Write an objective function describing a quantity that must be maximized or minimized.

## Objective Functions in Linear Programming

Many problems involve quantities that must be maximized or minimized. Businesses are interested in maximizing profit. An operation in which bottled water and medical kits are shipped to earthquake survivors needs to maximize the number of survivors helped by this shipment. An **objective function** is an algebraic expression in two or more variables describing a quantity that must be maximized or minimized.

( **EXAMPLE 1** ) **Writing an Objective Function**

Bottled water and medical supplies are to be shipped to survivors of an earthquake by plane. Each container of bottled water will serve 10 people and each medical kit will aid 6 people. If $x$ represents the number of bottles of water to be shipped and $y$ represents the number of medical kits, write the objective function that models the number of people that can be helped.

**Solution** Because each bottle of water serves 10 people and each medical kit aids 6 people, we have

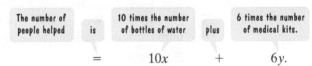

$$= \quad 10x \quad + \quad 6y.$$

Using $z$ to represent the number of people helped, the objective function is

$$z = 10x + 6y.$$

Unlike the functions that we have seen so far, the objective function is an equation in three variables. For a value of $x$ and a value of $y$, there is one and only one value of $z$. Thus, $z$ is a function of $x$ and $y$.

⬤

✓ Check Point **1** A company manufactures bookshelves and desks for computers. Let $x$ represent the number of bookshelves manufactured daily and $y$ the number of desks manufactured daily. The company's profits are $25 per bookshelf and $55 per desk. Write the objective function that models the company's total daily profit, $z$, from $x$ bookshelves and $y$ desks. (Check Points 2 through 4 are related to this situation, so keep track of your answers.)

**②** Use inequalities to describe limitations in a situation.

## Constraints in Linear Programming

Ideally, the number of earthquake survivors helped in Example 1 should increase without restriction so that every survivor receives water and medical kits. However, the planes that ship these supplies are subject to weight and volume restrictions. In linear programming problems, such restrictions are called **constraints**. Each

constraint is expressed as a linear inequality. The list of constraints forms a system of linear inequalities.

### EXAMPLE 2  Writing a Constraint

Each plane can carry no more than 80,000 pounds. The bottled water weighs 20 pounds per container and each medical kit weighs 10 pounds. Let $x$ represent the number of bottles of water to be shipped and $y$ the number of medical kits. Write an inequality that models this constraint.

**Solution**  Because each plane can carry no more than 80,000 pounds, we have

| The total weight of the water bottles | plus | the total weight of the medical kits | must be less than or equal to | 80,000 pounds. |
|---|---|---|---|---|

$$20x \quad + \quad 10y \quad \leq \quad 80{,}000.$$

Each bottle weighs 20 pounds.     Each kit weighs 10 pounds.

The plane's weight constraint is modeled by the inequality

$$20x + 10y \leq 80{,}000.$$

⊘ **Check Point 2** To maintain high quality, the company in Check Point 1 should not manufacture more than a total of 80 bookshelves and desks per day. Write an inequality that models this constraint.

In addition to a weight constraint on its cargo, each plane has a limited amount of space in which to carry supplies. Example 3 demonstrates how to express this constraint.

### EXAMPLE 3  Writing a Constraint

Each plane can carry a total volume of supplies that does not exceed 6000 cubic feet. Each water bottle is 1 cubic foot and each medical kit also has a volume of 1 cubic foot. With $x$ still representing the number of water bottles and $y$ the number of medical kits, write an inequality that models this second constraint.

**Solution**  Because each plane can carry a volume of supplies that does not exceed 6000 cubic feet, we have

| The total volume of the water | plus | the total volume of the medical kits | must be less than or equal to | 6000 cubic feet. |
|---|---|---|---|---|

$$1x \quad + \quad 1y \quad \leq \quad 6000.$$

Each bottle is 1 cubic foot.     Each kit is 1 cubic foot.

The plane's volume constraint is modeled by the inequality $x + y \leq 6000$.
In summary, here's what we have described so far in this aid-to-earthquake-victims situation:

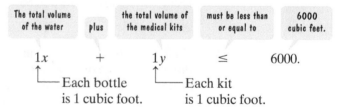

$$z = 10x + 6y \qquad \text{This is the objective function modeling the number of people helped with x bottles of water and y medical kits.}$$

$$\begin{cases} 20x + 10y \leq 80{,}000 \\ x + y \leq 6000. \end{cases} \qquad \text{These are the constraints based on each plane's weight and volume limitations.}$$

⊘ **Check Point 3** To meet customer demand, the company in Check Point 1 must manufacture between 30 and 80 bookshelves per day, inclusive. Furthermore, the company must manufacture at least 10 and no more than 30 desks per day. Write an inequality that models each of these sentences. Then summarize what you have described about this company by writing the objective function for its profits and the three constraints.

③ Use linear programming to solve problems.

## Solving Problems with Linear Programming

The problem in the earthquake situation described previously is to maximize the number of survivors who can be helped, subject to each plane's weight and volume constraints. The process of solving this problem is called *linear programming*, based on a theorem that was proven during World War II.

### Solving a Linear Programming Problem

Let $z = ax + by$ be an objective function that depends on $x$ and $y$. Furthermore, $z$ is subject to a number of constraints on $x$ and $y$. If a maximum or minimum value of $z$ exists, it can be determined as follows:

1. Graph the system of inequalities representing the constraints.
2. Find the value of the objective function at each corner, or **vertex**, of the graphed region. The maximum and minimum of the objective function occur at one or more of the corner points.

### EXAMPLE 4  Solving a Linear Programming Problem

Determine how many bottles of water and how many medical kits should be sent on each plane to maximize the number of earthquake victims who can be helped.

**Solution**  We must maximize $z = 10x + 6y$ subject to the following constraints:

$$\begin{cases} 20x + 10y \le 80{,}000 \\ x + y \le 6000. \end{cases}$$

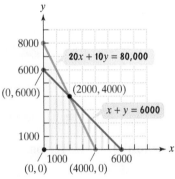

**Step 1  Graph the system of inequalities representing the constraints.** Because $x$ (the number of bottles of water per plane) and $y$ (the number of medical kits per plane) must be nonnegative, we need to graph the system of inequalities in quadrant I and its boundary only.

To graph the inequality $20x + 10y \le 80{,}000$, we graph the equation $20x + 10y = 80{,}000$ as a solid blue line (**Figure 7.29**). Setting $y = 0$, the $x$-intercept is 4000 and setting $x = 0$, the $y$-intercept is 8000. Using $(0, 0)$ as a test point, the inequality is satisfied, so we shade below the blue line, as shown in yellow in **Figure 7.29**.

Now we graph $x + y \le 6000$ by first graphing $x + y = 6000$ as a solid red line. Setting $y = 0$, the $x$-intercept is 6000. Setting $x = 0$, the $y$-intercept is 6000. Using $(0, 0)$ as a test point, the inequality is satisfied, so we shade below the red line, as shown using green vertical shading in **Figure 7.29**.

We use the addition method to find where the lines $20x + 10y = 80{,}000$ and $x + y = 6000$ intersect.

**Figure 7.29** The region in quadrant I representing the constraints $20x + 10y \le 80{,}000$ and $x + y \le 6000$

$$\begin{cases} 20x + 10y = 80{,}000 \\ x + y = 6000 \end{cases} \xrightarrow[\text{Multiply by } -10.}]{\text{No change}} \begin{cases} 20x + 10y = 80{,}000 \\ -10x - 10y = -60{,}000 \end{cases}$$

$$\text{Add:} \quad 10x = 20{,}000$$
$$x = 2000$$

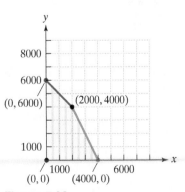

**Figure 7.30**

Back-substituting 2000 for $x$ in $x + y = 6000$, we find $y = 4000$, so the intersection point is $(2000, 4000)$.

The system of inequalities representing the constraints is shown by the region in which the yellow shading and the green vertical shading overlap in **Figure 7.29**. The graph of the system of inequalities is shown again in **Figure 7.30**. The red and blue line segments are included in the graph.

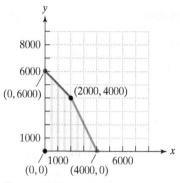

Figure 7.30 (repeated)

**Step 2 Find the value of the objective function at each corner of the graphed region. The maximum and minimum of the objective function occur at one or more of the corner points.** We must evaluate the objective function, $z = 10x + 6y$, at the four corners, or vertices, of the region in **Figure 7.30**.

| Corner $(x, y)$ | Objective Function $z = 10x + 6y$ |
|---|---|
| $(0, 0)$ | $z = 10(0) + 6(0) = 0$ |
| $(4000, 0)$ | $z = 10(4000) + 6(0) = 40,000$ |
| $(2000, 4000)$ | $z = 10(2000) + 6(4000) = 44,000$ ← maximum |
| $(0, 6000)$ | $z = 10(0) + 6(6000) = 36,000$ |

Thus, the maximum value of $z$ is 44,000 and this occurs when $x = 2000$ and $y = 4000$. In practical terms, this means that the maximum number of earthquake survivors who can be helped with each plane shipment is 44,000. This can be accomplished by sending 2000 water bottles and 4000 medical kits per plane. ⬤

✓ Check Point **4** For the company in Check Points 1–3, how many bookshelves and how many desks should be manufactured per day to obtain maximum profit? What is the maximum daily profit?

( EXAMPLE 5 ) **Solving a Linear Programming Problem**

Find the maximum value of the objective function

$$z = 2x + y$$

subject to the following constraints:

$$\begin{cases} x \geq 0, \, y \geq 0 \\ x + 2y \leq 5 \\ x - y \leq 2. \end{cases}$$

**Solution** We begin by graphing the region in quadrant I ($x \geq 0, \, y \geq 0$) formed by the constraints. The graph is shown in **Figure 7.31**.

Now we evaluate the objective function at the four vertices of this region.

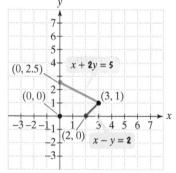

Figure 7.31 The graph of $x + 2y \leq 5$ and $x - y \leq 2$ in quadrant I

**Objective function:** $z = 2x + y$

At $(0, 0)$:  $z = 2 \cdot 0 + 0 = 0$

At $(2, 0)$:  $z = 2 \cdot 2 + 0 = 4$

At $(3, 1)$:  $z = 2 \cdot 3 + 1 = 7$   Maximum value of $z$

At $(0, 2.5)$:  $z = 2 \cdot 0 + 2.5 = 2.5$

Thus, the maximum value of $z$ is 7, and this occurs when $x = 3$ and $y = 1$. ⬤

We can see why the objective function in Example 5 has a maximum value that occurs at a vertex by solving the equation for $y$.

$z = 2x + y$    This is the objective function of Example 5.

$y = -2x + z$    Solve for $y$. Recall that the slope-intercept form of a line is $y = mx + b$.

Slope $= -2$    y-intercept $= z$

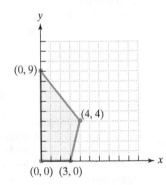

In this form, $z$ represents the $y$-intercept of the objective function. The equation describes infinitely many parallel lines, each with slope $-2$. The process in linear programming involves finding the maximum $z$-value for all lines that intersect the region determined by the constraints. Of all the lines whose slope is $-2$, we're looking for the one with the greatest $y$-intercept that intersects the given region. As we see in **Figure 7.32**, such a line will pass through one (or possibly more) of the vertices of the region.

**Figure 7.32** The line with slope $-2$ with the greatest $y$-intercept that intersects the shaded region passes through one of its vertices.

⌀ Check Point **5** Find the maximum value of the objective function $z = 3x + 5y$ subject to the constraints $x \geq 0$, $y \geq 0$, $x + y \geq 1$, $x + y \leq 6$.

# Exercise Set 7.6

## Practice Exercises

*In Exercises 1–4, find the value of the objective function at each corner of the graphed region. What is the maximum value of the objective function? What is the minimum value of the objective function?*

**1.** Objective Function
$z = 5x + 6y$

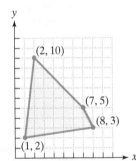

**2.** Objective Function
$z = 3x + 2y$

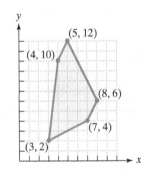

**3.** Objective Function
$z = 40x + 50y$

**4.** Objective Function
$z = 30x + 45y$

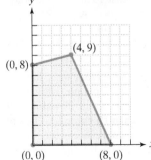

*In Exercises 5–14, an objective function and a system of linear inequalities representing the constraints are given.*

   **a.** *Graph the system of inequalities representing the constraints.*

   **b.** *Find the value of the objective function at each corner of the graphed region.*

   **c.** *Use the values in part (b) to determine the maximum value of the objective function and the values of x and y for which the maximum occurs.*

**5.** Objective Function         $z = 3x + 2y$
    Constraints
$$\begin{cases} x \geq 0, y \geq 0 \\ 2x + y \leq 8 \\ x + y \geq 4 \end{cases}$$

**6.** Objective Function         $z = 2x + 3y$
    Constraints
$$\begin{cases} x \geq 0, y \geq 0 \\ 2x + y \leq 8 \\ 2x + 3y \leq 12 \end{cases}$$

**7.** Objective Function         $z = 4x + y$
    Constraints
$$\begin{cases} x \geq 0, y \geq 0 \\ 2x + 3y \leq 12 \\ x + y \geq 3 \end{cases}$$

**8.** Objective Function         $z = x + 6y$
    Constraints
$$\begin{cases} x \geq 0, y \geq 0 \\ 2x + y \leq 10 \\ x - 2y \geq -10 \end{cases}$$

**9.** Objective Function         $z = 3x - 2y$
    Constraints
$$\begin{cases} 1 \leq x \leq 5 \\ y \geq 2 \\ x - y \geq -3 \end{cases}$$

**10.** Objective Function         $z = 5x - 2y$
    Constraints
$$\begin{cases} 0 \leq x \leq 5 \\ 0 \leq y \leq 3 \\ x + y \geq 2 \end{cases}$$

**11.** Objective Function         $z = 4x + 2y$
    Constraints
$$\begin{cases} x \geq 0, y \geq 0 \\ 2x + 3y \leq 12 \\ 3x + 2y \leq 12 \\ x + y \geq 2 \end{cases}$$

**12.** Objective Function

Constraints

$z = 2x + 4y$

$$\begin{cases} x \geq 0, \ y \geq 0 \\ x + 3y \geq 6 \\ x + y \geq 3 \\ x + y \leq 9 \end{cases}$$

**13.** Objective Function

Constraints

$z = 10x + 12y$

$$\begin{cases} x \geq 0, \ y \geq 0 \\ x + y \leq 7 \\ 2x + y \leq 10 \\ 2x + 3y \leq 18 \end{cases}$$

**14.** Objective Function

Constraints

$z = 5x + 6y$

$$\begin{cases} x \geq 0, \ y \geq 0 \\ 2x + y \geq 10 \\ x + 2y \geq 10 \\ x + y \leq 10 \end{cases}$$

## Application Exercises

**15.** A television manufacturer makes rear-projection and plasma televisions. The profit per unit is $125 for the rear-projection televisions and $200 for the plasma televisions.

**a.** Let $x$ = the number of rear-projection televisions manufactured in a month and let $y$ = the number of plasma televisions manufactured in a month. Write the objective function that models the total monthly profit.

**b.** The manufacturer is bound by the following constraints:

- Equipment in the factory allows for making at most 450 rear-projection televisions in one month.

- Equipment in the factory allows for making at most 200 plasma televisions in one month.

- The cost to the manufacturer per unit is $600 for the rear-projection televisions and $900 for the plasma televisions. Total monthly costs cannot exceed $360,000.

Write a system of three inequalities that models these constraints.

**c.** Graph the system of inequalities in part (b). Use only the first quadrant and its boundary, because $x$ and $y$ must both be nonnegative.

**d.** Evaluate the objective function for total monthly profit at each of the five vertices of the graphed region. [The vertices should occur at $(0, 0)$, $(0, 200)$, $(300, 200)$, $(450, 100)$, and $(450, 0)$.]

**e.** Complete the missing portions of this statement: The television manufacturer will make the greatest profit by manufacturing _____ rear-projection televisions each month and _____ plasma televisions each month. The maximum monthly profit is $ _____.

**16. a.** A student earns $10 per hour for tutoring and $7 per hour as a teacher's aid. Let $x$ = the number of hours each week spent tutoring and let $y$ = the number of hours each week spent as a teacher's aid. Write the objective function that models total weekly earnings.

**b.** The student is bound by the following constraints:

- To have enough time for studies, the student can work no more than 20 hours per week.

- The tutoring center requires that each tutor spend at least three hours per week tutoring.

- The tutoring center requires that each tutor spend no more than eight hours per week tutoring.

Write a system of three inequalities that models these constraints.

**c.** Graph the system of inequalities in part (b). Use only the first quadrant and its boundary, because $x$ and $y$ are non-negative.

**d.** Evaluate the objective function for total weekly earnings at each of the four vertices of the graphed region. [The vertices should occur at $(3, 0)$, $(8, 0)$, $(3, 17)$, and $(8, 12)$.]

**e.** Complete the missing portions of this statement: The student can earn the maximum amount per week by tutoring for _____ hours per week and working as a teacher's aid for _____ hours per week. The maximum amount that the student can earn each week is $ _____.

*Use the two steps for solving a linear programming problem, given in the box on page 793, to solve the problems in Exercises 17–23.*

**17.** A manufacturer produces two models of mountain bicycles. The times (in hours) required for assembling and painting each model are given in the following table:

|  | Model $A$ | Model $B$ |
|---|---|---|
| **Assembling** | 5 | 4 |
| **Painting** | 2 | 3 |

The maximum total weekly hours available in the assembly department and the paint department are 200 hours and 108 hours, respectively. The profits per unit are $25 for model $A$ and $15 for model $B$. How many of each type should be produced to maximize profit?

**18.** A large institution is preparing lunch menus containing foods A and B. The specifications for the two foods are given in the following table:

| Food | Units of Fat per Ounce | Units of Carbohydrates per Ounce | Units of Protein per Ounce |
|---|---|---|---|
| A | 1 | 2 | 1 |
| B | 1 | 1 | 1 |

Each lunch must provide at least 6 units of fat per serving, no more than 7 units of protein, and at least 10 units of carbohydrates. The institution can purchase food A for $0.12 per ounce and food B for $0.08 per ounce. How many ounces of each food should a serving contain to meet the dietary requirements at the least cost?

**19.** Food and clothing are shipped to survivors of a natural disaster. Each carton of food will feed 12 people, while each carton of clothing will help 5 people. Each 20-cubic-foot box of food weighs 50 pounds and each 10-cubic-foot box of clothing weighs 20 pounds. The commercial carriers transporting food and clothing are bound by the following constraints:

- The total weight per carrier cannot exceed 19,000 pounds.

- The total volume must be less than 8000 cubic feet.

How many cartons of food and clothing should be sent with each plane shipment to maximize the number of people who can be helped?

**20.** On June 24, 1948, the former Soviet Union blocked all land and water routes through East Germany to Berlin. A gigantic airlift was organized using American and British planes to bring food, clothing, and other supplies to the more than 2 million people in West Berlin. The cargo capacity was 30,000 cubic feet for an American plane and 20,000 cubic feet for a British plane. To break the Soviet blockade, the Western Allies had to maximize cargo capacity, but were subject to the following restrictions:

- No more than 44 planes could be used.

- The larger American planes required 16 personnel per flight, double that of the requirement for the British planes. The total number of personnel available could not exceed 512.

- The cost of an American flight was $9000 and the cost of a British flight was $5000. Total weekly costs could not exceed $300,000.

Find the number of American and British planes that were used to maximize cargo capacity.

**21.** A theater is presenting a program for students and their parents on drinking and driving. The proceeds will be donated to a local alcohol information center. Admission is $2.00 for parents and $1.00 for students. However, the situation has two constraints: The theater can hold no more than 150 people and every two parents must bring at least one student. How many parents and students should attend to raise the maximum amount of money?

**22.** You are about to take a test that contains computation problems worth 6 points each and word problems worth 10 points each. You can do a computation problem in 2 minutes and a word problem in 4 minutes. You have 40 minutes to take the test and may answer no more than 12 problems. Assuming you answer all the problems attempted correctly, how many of each type of problem must you answer to maximize your score? What is the maximum score?

**23.** In 1978, a ruling by the Civil Aeronautics Board allowed Federal Express to purchase larger aircraft. Federal Express's options included 20 Boeing 727s that United Airlines was retiring and/or the French-built Dassault Fanjet Falcon 20. To aid in their decision, executives at Federal Express analyzed the following data:

| | Boeing 727 | Falcon 20 |
|---|---|---|
| **Direct Operating Cost** | $1400 per hour | $500 per hour |
| **Payload** | 42,000 pounds | 6000 pounds |

Federal Express was faced with the following constraints:

- Hourly operating cost was limited to $35,000.

- Total payload had to be at least 672,000 pounds.

- Only twenty 727s were available.

Given the constraints, how many of each kind of aircraft should Federal Express have purchased to maximize the number of aircraft?

## Writing in Mathematics

**24.** What kinds of problems are solved using the linear programming method?

**25.** What is an objective function in a linear programming problem?

**26.** What is a constraint in a linear programming problem? How is a constraint represented?

**27.** In your own words, describe how to solve a linear programming problem.

**28.** Describe a situation in your life in which you would really like to maximize something, but you are limited by at least two constraints. Can linear programming be used in this situation? Explain your answer.

## Critical Thinking Exercises

**Make Sense?** *In Exercises 29–32, determine whether each statement makes sense or does not make sense, and explain your reasoning.*

**29.** In order to solve a linear programming problem, I use the graph representing the constraints and the graph of the objective function.

**30.** I use the coordinates of each vertex from my graph representing the constraints to find the values that maximize or minimize an objective function.

**31.** I need to be able to graph systems of linear inequalities in order to solve linear programming problems.

**32.** An important application of linear programming for businesses involves maximizing profit.

**33.** Suppose that you inherit $10,000. The will states how you must invest the money. Some (or all) of the money must be invested in stocks and bonds. The requirements are that at least $3000 be invested in bonds, with expected returns of $0.08 per dollar, and at least $2000 be invested in stocks, with expected returns of $0.12 per dollar. Because the stocks are medium risk, the final stipulation requires that the investment in bonds should never be less than the investment in stocks. How should the money be invested so as to maximize your expected returns?

**34.** Consider the objective function $z = Ax + By$ $(A > 0$ and $B > 0)$ subject to the following constraints: $2x + 3y \leq 9, x - y \leq 2, x \geq 0$, and $y \geq 0$. Prove that the objective function will have the same maximum value at the vertices $(3, 1)$ and $(0, 3)$ if $A = \frac{2}{3}B$.

## Group Exercises

**35.** Group members should choose a particular field of interest. Research how linear programming is used to solve problems in that field. If possible, investigate the solution of a specific practical problem. Present a report on your findings, including the contributions of George Dantzig, Narendra Karmarkar, and L. G. Khachion to linear programming.

**36.** Members of the group should interview a business executive who is in charge of deciding the product mix for a business. How are production policy decisions made? Are other methods used in conjunction with linear programming? What are these methods? What sort of academic background, particularly in mathematics, does this executive have? Present a group report addressing these questions, emphasizing the role of linear programming for the business.

## Preview Exercises

*Exercises 37–39 will help you prepare for the material covered in the first section of the next chapter.*

**37.** Solve the system:

$$\begin{cases} x + y + 2z = 19 \\ y + 2z = 13 \\ z = 5. \end{cases}$$

What makes it fairly easy to find the solution?

**38.** Solve the system:

$$\begin{cases} w - x + 2y - 2z = -1 \\ x - \frac{1}{3}y + z = \frac{8}{3} \\ y - z = 1 \\ z = 3. \end{cases}$$

Express the solution set in the form $\{(w, x, y, z)\}$. What makes it fairly easy to find the solution?

**39.** Consider the following array of numbers:

$$\begin{bmatrix} 1 & 2 & -1 \\ 4 & -3 & -15 \end{bmatrix}.$$

Rewrite the array as follows: Multiply each number in the top row by $-4$ and add this product to the corresponding number in the bottom row. Do not change the numbers in the top row.

# Chapter 7  Summary, Review, and Test

## Summary

| DEFINITIONS AND CONCEPTS | EXAMPLES |
|---|---|
| **7.1  Systems of Linear Equations in Two Variables** | |
| **a.** Two equations in the form $Ax + By = C$ are called a system of linear equations. A solution of the system is an ordered pair that satisfies both equations in the system. | Ex. 1, p. 728 |
| **b.** Systems of linear equations in two variables can be solved by eliminating a variable, using the substitution method (see the box on page 730) or the addition method (see the box on page 732). | Ex. 2, p. 730; Ex. 3, p. 732; Ex. 4, p. 733 |
| **c.** Some linear systems have no solution and are called inconsistent systems; others have infinitely many solutions. The equations in a linear system with infinitely many solutions are called dependent. For details, see the box on page 734. | Ex. 5, p. 734; Ex. 6, p. 735 |
| **d.** Functions of Business <br><br> *Revenue Function* <br><br> $$R(x) = (\text{price per unit sold})x$$ <br><br> *Cost Function* <br><br> $$C(x) = \text{fixed cost} + (\text{cost per unit produced})x$$ <br><br> *Profit Function* <br><br> $$P(x) = R(x) - C(x)$$ <br><br> The point of intersection of the graphs of $R$ and $C$ is the break-even point. The $x$-coordinate of the point reveals the number of units that a company must produce and sell so that the money coming in, the revenue, is equal to the money going out, the cost. The $y$-coordinate gives the amount of money coming in and going out. | Ex. 9, p. 740; Figure 7.8, p. 741 |
| **7.2  Systems of Linear Equations in Three Variables** | |
| **a.** Three equations in the form $Ax + By + Cz = D$ are called a system of linear equations in three variables. A solution of the system is an ordered triple that satisfies all three equations in the system. | Ex. 1, p. 748 |
| **b.** A system of linear equations in three variables can be solved by eliminating variables. Use the addition method to eliminate any variable, reducing the system to two equations in two variables. Use substitution or the addition method to solve the resulting system in two variables. Details are found in the box on page 749. | Ex. 2, p. 749; Ex. 3, p. 751 |
| **c.** Three points that do not lie on a line determine the graph of a quadratic function $y = ax^2 + bx + c$. Use the three given points to create a system of three equations. Solve the system to find $a$, $b$, and $c$. | Ex. 4, p. 752 |

| DEFINITIONS AND CONCEPTS | EXAMPLES |
|---|---|

### 7.3 Partial Fractions

a. Partial fraction decomposition is used on rational expressions in which the numerator and denominator have no common factors and the highest power in the numerator is less than the highest power in the denominator. The steps in partial fraction decomposition are given in the box on page 759.

| | |
|---|---|
| b. Include one partial fraction with a constant numerator for each distinct linear factor in the denominator. Include one partial fraction with a constant numerator for each power of a repeated linear factor in the denominator. | Ex. 1, p. 758; Ex. 2, p. 760 |
| c. Include one partial fraction with a linear numerator for each distinct prime quadratic factor in the denominator. Include one partial fraction with a linear numerator for each power of a prime, repeated quadratic factor in the denominator. | Ex. 3, p. 762; Ex. 4, p. 764 |

### 7.4 Systems of Nonlinear Equations in Two Variables

a. A system of two nonlinear equations in two variables contains at least one equation that cannot be expressed as $Ax + By = C$.

| | |
|---|---|
| b. Systems of nonlinear equations in two variables can be solved algebraically by eliminating all occurrences of one of the variables by the substitution or addition methods. | Ex. 1, p. 768; Ex. 2, p. 769; Ex. 3, p. 770; Ex. 4, p. 772 |

### 7.5 Systems of Inequalities

a. A linear inequality in two variables can be written in the form $Ax + By > C$, $Ax + By \geq C$, $Ax + By < C$, or $Ax + By \leq C$.

| | |
|---|---|
| b. The procedure for graphing a linear inequality in two variables is given in the box on page 779. A nonlinear inequality in two variables is graphed using the same procedure. | Ex. 1, p. 779; Ex. 2, p. 780; Ex. 3, p. 781; Ex. 4, p. 782 |
| c. To graph the solution set of a system of inequalities, graph each inequality in the system in the same rectangular coordinate system. Then find the region, if there is one, that is common to every graph in the system. | Ex. 6, p. 784; Ex. 7, p. 785; Ex. 8, p. 786 |

### 7.6 Linear Programming

| | |
|---|---|
| a. An objective function is an algebraic expression in three variables describing a quantity that must be maximized or minimized. | Ex. 1, p. 791 |
| b. Constraints are restrictions, expressed as linear inequalities. | Ex. 2, p. 792; Ex. 3, p. 792 |
| c. Steps for solving a linear programming problem are given in the box on page 793. | Ex. 4, p. 793; Ex. 5, p. 794 |

## Review Exercises

### 7.1

In Exercises 1–5, solve by the method of your choice. Identify systems with no solution and systems with infinitely many solutions, using set notation to express their solution sets.

**1.** $\begin{cases} y = 4x + 1 \\ 3x + 2y = 13 \end{cases}$

**2.** $\begin{cases} x + 4y = 14 \\ 2x - y = 1 \end{cases}$

**3.** $\begin{cases} 5x + 3y = 1 \\ 3x + 4y = -6 \end{cases}$

**4.** $\begin{cases} 2y - 6x = 7 \\ 3x - y = 9 \end{cases}$

**5.** $\begin{cases} 4x - 8y = 16 \\ 3x - 6y = 12 \end{cases}$

**6.** A company is planning to manufacture computer desks. The fixed cost will be $60,000 and it will cost $200 to produce each desk. Each desk will be sold for $450.

    **a.** Write the cost function, $C$, of producing $x$ desks.

    **b.** Write the revenue function, $R$, from the sale of $x$ desks.

    **c.** Determine the break-even point. Describe what this means.

**7.**

Gustav Klimt (1826–1918) "Mrs. Adele Bloch-Bauer, I", 1907. Oil on canvas, 138 × 138 cm. Private Collection. Photo: Erich Lessing/Art Resource, NY

Pablo Picasso (1881–1973) "Boy with a Pipe", 1905 (oil on canvas). Collection of Mr. and Mrs. John Hay Whitney, New York, USA. © DACS/The Bridgeman Art Library. © 2008 Estate of Pablo Picasso/Artists Rights Society (ARS), New York

Talk about paintings by numbers: In 2007, this glittering Klimt set the record for the most ever paid for a painting, a title that had been held by Picasso's *Boy with a Pipe*. Combined, the two paintings sold for $239 million. The difference between the selling price for Klimt's work and the selling price for Picasso's work was $31 million. Find the amount paid for each painting.

**8.** The graph shows that from 2000 through 2006, Americans unplugged land lines and switched to cellphones.

**Number of Cellphone and Land-Line Customers in the United States**

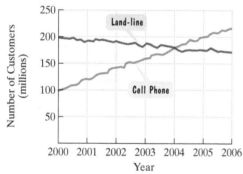

*Source:* Federal Communications Commission

**a.** Use the graphs to estimate the point of intersection. In what year was the number of cellphone and land-line customers the same? How many millions of customers were there for each?

**b.** In 2000, there were 98 million cellphone customers. For the period shown by the graph, this has increased at an average rate of 19.8 million customers per year. Write a function that models the number of cellphone customers, $y$, in millions, $x$ years after 2000.

**c.** The function $4.3x + y = 198$ models the number of land-line customers, $y$, in millions, $x$ years after 2000. Use this model and the model you obtained in part (b) to determine the year, rounded to the nearest year, when the number of cellphone and land-line customers was the same. According to the models, how many millions of customers, rounded to the nearest ten million, were there for each?

**d.** How well do the models in parts (b) and (c) describe the point of intersection of the graphs that you estimated in part (a)?

**9.** A travel agent offers two package vacation plans. The first plan costs $360 and includes 3 days at a hotel and a rental car for 2 days. The second plan costs $500 and includes 4 days at a hotel and a rental car for 3 days. The daily charge for the hotel is the same under each plan, as is the daily charge for the car. Find the cost per day for the hotel and for the car.

**10.** A chemist needs to mix a solution that is 34% silver nitrate with one that is 4% silver nitrate to obtain 100 milliliters of a mixture that is 7% silver nitrate. How many milliliters of each of the solutions must be used?

**11.** When a plane flies with the wind, it can travel 2160 miles in 3 hours. When the plane flies in the opposite direction, against the wind, it takes 4 hours to fly the same distance. Find the average velocity of the plane in still air and the average velocity of the wind.

## 7.2

*Solve each system in Exercises 12–13.*

**12.** $\begin{cases} 2x - y + z = 1 \\ 3x - 3y + 4z = 5 \\ 4x - 2y + 3z = 4 \end{cases}$

**13.** $\begin{cases} x + 2y - z = 5 \\ 2x - y + 3z = 0 \\ 2y + z = 1 \end{cases}$

**14.** Find the quadratic function $y = ax^2 + bx + c$ whose graph passes through the points $(1, 4), (3, 20)$, and $(-2, 25)$.

**15.** The bar graph shows the average debt in the United States, not including real estate mortgages, by age group. The difference between the average debt for the 30–39 age group and the 18–29 age group is $8100. The difference between the average debt for the 40–49 age group and the 30–39 age group is $3100. The combined average debt for these three age groups is $44,200. Find the average debt for each of these age groups.

**Average Debt by Age**

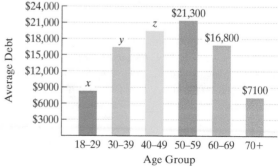

*Source:* Experian

## 7.3

*In Exercises 16–24, write the partial fraction decomposition of each rational expression.*

**16.** $\dfrac{x}{(x-3)(x+2)}$

**17.** $\dfrac{11x-2}{x^2-x-12}$

**18.** $\dfrac{4x^2-3x-4}{x(x+2)(x-1)}$

**19.** $\dfrac{2x+1}{(x-2)^2}$

**20.** $\dfrac{2x-6}{(x-1)(x-2)^2}$

**21.** $\dfrac{3x}{(x-2)(x^2+1)}$

**22.** $\dfrac{7x^2-7x+23}{(x-3)(x^2+4)}$

**23.** $\dfrac{x^3}{(x^2+4)^2}$

**24.** $\dfrac{4x^3+5x^2+7x-1}{(x^2+x+1)^2}$

## 7.4

*In Exercises 25–35, solve each system by the method of your choice.*

**25.** $\begin{cases} 5y = x^2 - 1 \\ x - y = 1 \end{cases}$

**26.** $\begin{cases} y = x^2 + 2x + 1 \\ x + y = 1 \end{cases}$

**27.** $\begin{cases} x^2 + y^2 = 2 \\ x + y = 0 \end{cases}$

**28.** $\begin{cases} 2x^2 + y^2 = 24 \\ x^2 + y^2 = 15 \end{cases}$

**29.** $\begin{cases} xy - 4 = 0 \\ y - x = 0 \end{cases}$

**30.** $\begin{cases} y^2 = 4x \\ x - 2y + 3 = 0 \end{cases}$

**31.** $\begin{cases} x^2 + y^2 = 10 \\ y = x + 2 \end{cases}$

**32.** $\begin{cases} xy = 1 \\ y = 2x + 1 \end{cases}$

**33.** $\begin{cases} x + y + 1 = 0 \\ x^2 + y^2 + 6y - x = -5 \end{cases}$

**34.** $\begin{cases} x^2 + y^2 = 13 \\ x^2 - y = 7 \end{cases}$

**35.** $\begin{cases} 2x^2 + 3y^2 = 21 \\ 3x^2 - 4y^2 = 23 \end{cases}$

**36.** The perimeter of a rectangle is 26 meters and its area is 40 square meters. Find its dimensions.

**37.** Find the coordinates of all points $(x, y)$ that lie on the line whose equation is $2x + y = 8$, so that the area of the rectangle shown in the figure is 6 square units.

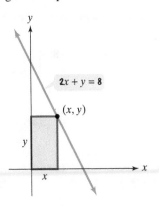

**38.** Two adjoining square fields with an area of 2900 square feet are to be enclosed with 240 feet of fencing. The situation is represented in the figure. Find the length of each side where a variable appears.

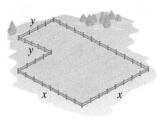

## 7.5

*In Exercises 39–45, graph each inequality.*

**39.** $3x - 4y > 12$

**40.** $y \le -\dfrac{1}{2}x + 2$

**41.** $x < -2$

**42.** $y \ge 3$

**43.** $x^2 + y^2 > 4$

**44.** $y \le x^2 - 1$

**45.** $y \le 2^x$

*In Exercises 46–55, graph the solution set of each system of inequalities or indicate that the system has no solution.*

**46.** $\begin{cases} 3x + 2y \ge 6 \\ 2x + y \ge 6 \end{cases}$

**47.** $\begin{cases} 2x - y \ge 4 \\ x + 2y < 2 \end{cases}$

**48.** $\begin{cases} y < x \\ y \le 2 \end{cases}$

**49.** $\begin{cases} x + y \le 6 \\ y \ge 2x - 3 \end{cases}$

**50.** $\begin{cases} 0 \le x \le 3 \\ y > 2 \end{cases}$

**51.** $\begin{cases} 2x + y < 4 \\ 2x + y > 6 \end{cases}$

**52.** $\begin{cases} x^2 + y^2 \le 16 \\ x + y < 2 \end{cases}$

**53.** $\begin{cases} x^2 + y^2 \le 9 \\ y < -3x + 1 \end{cases}$

**54.** $\begin{cases} y > x^2 \\ x + y < 6 \\ y < x + 6 \end{cases}$

**55.** $\begin{cases} y \ge 0 \\ 3x + 2y \ge 4 \\ x - y \le 3 \end{cases}$

## 7.6

**56.** Find the value of the objective function $z = 2x + 3y$ at each corner of the graphed region shown. What is the maximum value of the objective function? What is the minimum value of the objective function?

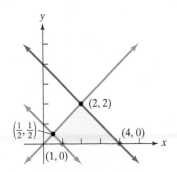

*In Exercises 57–59, graph the region determined by the constraints. Then find the maximum value of the given objective function, subject to the constraints.*

**57.** Objective Function $z = 2x + 3y$
Constraints
$$\begin{cases} x \geq 0, y \geq 0 \\ x + y \leq 8 \\ 3x + 2y \geq 6 \end{cases}$$

**58.** Objective Function $z = x + 4y$
Constraints
$$\begin{cases} 0 \leq x \leq 5, 0 \leq y \leq 7 \\ x + y \geq 3 \end{cases}$$

**59.** Objective Function $z = 5x + 6y$
Constraints
$$\begin{cases} x \geq 0, y \geq 0 \\ y \leq x \\ 2x + y \leq 12 \\ 2x + 3y \geq 6 \end{cases}$$

**60.** A paper manufacturing company converts wood pulp to writing paper and newsprint. The profit on a unit of writing paper is $500 and the profit on a unit of newsprint is $350.

  **a.** Let $x$ represent the number of units of writing paper produced daily. Let $y$ represent the number of units of newsprint produced daily. Write the objective function that models total daily profit.

  **b.** The manufacturer is bound by the following constraints:

  • Equipment in the factory allows for making at most 200 units of paper (writing paper and newsprint) in a day.

  • Regular customers require at least 10 units of writing paper and at least 80 units of newsprint daily.

  Write a system of inequalities that models these constraints.

  **c.** Graph the inequalities in part (b). Use only the first quadrant, because $x$ and $y$ must both be positive. (*Suggestion:* Let each unit along the $x$- and $y$-axes represent 20.)

  **d.** Evaluate the objective function at each of the three vertices of the graphed region.

  **e.** Complete the missing portions of this statement: The company will make the greatest profit by producing ＿＿＿ units of writing paper and ＿＿＿ units of newsprint each day. The maximum daily profit is $ ＿＿＿.

**61.** A manufacturer of lightweight tents makes two models whose specifications are given in the following table:

| | Cutting Time per Tent | Assembly Time per Tent |
|---|---|---|
| **Model A** | 0.9 hour | 0.8 hour |
| **Model B** | 1.8 hours | 1.2 hours |

On a monthly basis, the manufacturer has no more than 864 hours of labor available in the cutting department and at most 672 hours in the assembly division. The profits come to $25 per tent for model A and $40 per tent for model B. How many of each should be manufactured monthly to maximize the profit?

CHAPTER
**Test Prep**
VIDEOS
Chapter 7 Test

*In Exercises 1–5, solve the system.*

**1.** $\begin{cases} x = y + 4 \\ 3x + 7y = -18 \end{cases}$

**2.** $\begin{cases} 2x + 5y = -2 \\ 3x - 4y = 20 \end{cases}$

**3.** $\begin{cases} x + y + z = 6 \\ 3x + 4y - 7z = 1 \\ 2x - y + 3z = 5 \end{cases}$

**4.** $\begin{cases} x^2 + y^2 = 25 \\ x + y = 1 \end{cases}$

**5.** $\begin{cases} 2x^2 - 5y^2 = -2 \\ 3x^2 + 2y^2 = 35 \end{cases}$

**6.** Find the partial fraction decomposition for $\dfrac{x}{(x+1)(x^2+9)}$.

*In Exercises 7–10, graph the solution set of each inequality or system of inequalities.*

**7.** $x - 2y < 8$

**8.** $\begin{cases} x \geq 0, y \geq 0 \\ 3x + y \leq 9 \\ 2x + 3y \geq 6 \end{cases}$

**9.** $\begin{cases} x^2 + y^2 > 1 \\ x^2 + y^2 < 4 \end{cases}$

**10.** $\begin{cases} y \leq 1 - x^2 \\ x^2 + y^2 \leq 9 \end{cases}$

**11.** Find the maximum value of the objective function $z = 3x + 5y$ subject to the following constraints: $x \geq 0, y \geq 0, x + y \leq 6, x \geq 2$.

12. Health experts agree that cholesterol intake should be limited to 300 mg or less each day. Three ounces of shrimp and 2 ounces of scallops contain 156 mg of cholesterol. Five ounces of shrimp and 3 ounces of scallops contain 45 mg of cholesterol less than the suggested maximum daily intake. Determine the cholesterol content in an ounce of each item.

13. A company is planning to produce and sell a new line of computers. The fixed cost will be $360,000 and it will cost $850 to produce each computer. Each computer will be sold for $1150.

    **a.** Write the cost function, $C$, of producing $x$ computers.

    **b.** Write the revenue function, $R$, from the sale of $x$ computers.

    **c.** Determine the break-even point. Describe what this means.

14. A chemist needs to mix a 20% acid solution with a 50% acid solution to obtain 60 ounces of a 30% acid solution. How many ounces of each of the solutions must be used?

15. When a plane flies with the wind, it can travel 1600 kilometers in 2 hours. When the plane flies in the opposite direction, against the wind, it takes 3 hours to travel 1950 kilometers. Find the average velocity of the plane in still air and the average velocity of the wind.

16. Find the quadratic function whose graph passes through the points $(-1, -2)$, $(2, 1)$, and $(-2, 1)$.

17. The rectangular plot of land shown in the figure is to be fenced along three sides using 39 feet of fencing. No fencing is to be placed along the river's edge. The area of the plot is 180 square feet. What are its dimensions?

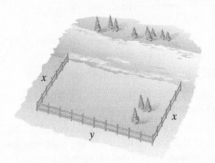

18. A manufacturer makes two types of jet skis, regular and deluxe. The profit on a regular jet ski is $200 and the profit on the deluxe model is $250. To meet customer demand, the company must manufacture at least 50 regular jet skis per week and at least 75 deluxe models. To maintain high quality, the total number of both models of jet skis manufactured by the company should not exceed 150 per week. How many jet skis of each type should be manufactured per week to obtain maximum profit? What is the maximum weekly profit?

## Cumulative Review Exercises (Chapters P–7)

*The figure shows the graph of $y = f(x)$ and its two vertical asymptotes. Use the graph to solve Exercises 1–10.*

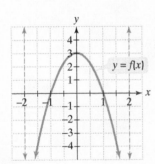

1. Find the domain and the range of $f$.

2. Find the zeros.

3. What is the relative maximum and where does it occur?

4. Find the interval(s) on which $f$ is decreasing.

5. Is $f(-0.7)$ positive or negative?

6. Find $(f \circ f)(-1)$.

7. Use arrow notation to complete this statement:

    $f(x) \rightarrow -\infty$ as _____ or as _____.

8. Does $f$ appear to be even, odd, or neither?

9. Graph $g(x) = f(x + 2) - 1$.

10. Graph $h(x) = \frac{1}{2}f\left(\frac{1}{2}x\right)$.

*In Exercises 11–21, solve each equation, inequality, or system of equations.*

11. $\sqrt{x^2 - 3x} = 2x - 6$

12. $4x^2 = 8x - 7$

13. $\left|\dfrac{x}{3} + 2\right| < 4$

14. $\dfrac{x + 5}{x - 1} > 2$

15. $2x^3 + x^2 - 13x + 6 = 0$

16. $6x - 3(5x + 2) = 4(1 - x)$

17. $\log(x + 3) + \log x = 1$

18. $3^{x+2} = 11$

19. $x^{\frac{1}{2}} - 2x^{\frac{1}{4}} - 15 = 0$

20. $\begin{cases} 3x - y = -2 \\ 2x^2 - y = 0 \end{cases}$

21. $\begin{cases} x + 2y + 3z = -2 \\ 3x + 3y + 10z = -2 \\ 2y - 5z = 6 \end{cases}$

*In Exercises 22–28, graph each equation, function, or inequality in a rectangular coordinate system. If two functions are indicated, graph both in the same system.*

22. $f(x) = (x + 2)^2 - 4$

23. $2x - 3y \le 6$

24. $y = 3^{x-2}$

25. $f(x) = \dfrac{x^2 - x - 6}{x + 1}$

26. $f(x) = 2x - 4$ and $f^{-1}$

27. $(x - 2)^2 + (y - 4)^2 > 9$

28. $f(x) = |x|$ and $g(x) = -|x - 2|$

*In Exercises 29–30, let $f(x) = 2x^2 - x - 1$ and $g(x) = 1 - x$.*

**29.** Find $(f \circ g)(x)$ and $(g \circ f)(x)$.

**30.** Find $\dfrac{f(x + h) - f(x)}{h}$ and simplify.

*In Exercises 31–32, write the linear function in slope-intercept form satisfying the given conditions.*

**31.** Graph of $f$ passes through $(2, 4)$ and $(4, -2)$.

**32.** Graph of $g$ passes through $(-1, 0)$ and is perpendicular to the line whose equation is $x + 3y - 6 = 0$.

**33.** You invested $4000 in two stocks paying 12% and 14% annual interest. At the end of the year, the total interest from these investments was $508. How much was invested at each rate?

**34.** The length of a rectangle is 1 meter more than twice the width. If the rectangle's area is 36 square meters, find its dimensions.

**35.** What interest rate is required for an investment of $6000 subject to continuous compounding to grow to $18,000 in 10 years?

*In Exercises 36–37, verify each identity.*

**36.** $\sec \theta - \cos \theta = \tan \theta \sin \theta$

**37.** $\tan x + \tan y = \dfrac{\sin (x + y)}{\cos x \cos y}$

*In Exercises 38–39, solve each equation.*

**38.** $\sin \theta = \tan \theta, \quad 0 \le \theta < 2\pi$

**39.** $2 + \cos 2\theta = 3 \cos \theta, \quad 0 \le \theta < 2\pi$

**40.** In oblique triangle $ABC$, $A = 12°$, $B = 75°$, and $a = 20$. Find $b$ to the nearest tenth.

# Matrices and Determinants

# 8

You are being drawn deeper into cyberspace, spending more time online each week. With constantly improving high-resolution images, cyberspace is reshaping your life by nourishing shared enthusiasms. The people who built your computer talk of bandwidth that will give you the visual experience, in high-definition 3-D format, of being in the same room with a person who is actually in another city. Rectangular arrays of numbers, called matrices, play a central role in representing computer images and in the forthcoming technology of tele-immersion.

*The use of rectangular arrays of numbers in the digital representation of images and the manipulation of images on a computer screen is discussed in Examples 8 and 9 in Section 8.3.*

**Section 8.1**

# Matrix Solutions to Linear Systems

## Objectives

1. Write the augmented matrix for a linear system.

2. Perform matrix row operations.

3. Use matrices and Gaussian elimination to solve systems.

4. Use matrices and Gauss-Jordan elimination to solve systems.

The data below show that we spend a lot of time sprucing up.

**Average Number of Minutes per Day Americans Spend on Grooming**

| | Ages 15–19 | Ages 20–24 | Ages 45–54 | Ages 65+ | Married | Single |
|---|---|---|---|---|---|---|
| Men | 37 | 37 | 34 | 28 | 31 | 34 |
| Women | 59 | 49 | 46 | 46 | 44 | 50 |

*Source:* Bureau of Labor Statistics' American Time-Use Survey

The 12 numbers inside the brackets are arranged in two rows and six columns. This rectangular array of 12 numbers, arranged in rows and columns and placed in brackets, is an example of a **matrix** (plural: **matrices**). The numbers inside the brackets are called **elements** of the matrix. Matrices are used to display information and to solve systems of linear equations. Because systems involving two equations in two variables can easily be solved by substitution or addition, we will focus on matrix solutions to systems of linear equations in three or more variables.

1 Write the augmented matrix for a linear system.

## Augmented Matrices

A matrix gives us a shortened way of writing a system of equations. The first step in solving a system of linear equations using matrices is to write the *augmented matrix*. An **augmented matrix** has a vertical bar separating the columns of the matrix into two groups. The coefficients of each variable are placed to the left of the vertical line and the constants are placed to the right. If any variable is missing, its coefficient is 0. Here are two examples:

| **System of Linear Equations** | **Augmented Matrix** |
|---|---|

$$\begin{cases} 3x + y + 2z = 31 \\ x + y + 2z = 19 \\ x + 3y + 2z = 25 \end{cases} \qquad \left[\begin{array}{ccc|c} 3 & 1 & 2 & 31 \\ 1 & 1 & 2 & 19 \\ 1 & 3 & 2 & 25 \end{array}\right]$$

$$\begin{cases} x + 2y - 5z = -19 \\ y + 3z = 9 \\ z = 4 \end{cases} \qquad \left[\begin{array}{ccc|c} 1 & 2 & -5 & -19 \\ 0 & 1 & 3 & 9 \\ 0 & 0 & 1 & 4 \end{array}\right].$$

Our goal in solving a system of linear equations in three variables using matrices is to produce a matrix with 1s down the diagonal from upper left to lower right on the left side of the vertical bar, called the **main diagonal**, and 0s below the 1s. In general, the matrix will be of the form

$$\begin{bmatrix} 1 & a & b & | & c \\ 0 & 1 & d & | & e \\ 0 & 0 & 1 & | & f \end{bmatrix},$$

where $a$ through $f$ represent real numbers. The third row of this matrix gives us the value of one variable. The other variables can then be found by back-substitution.

**2** Perform matrix row operations.

## Matrix Row Operations

A matrix with 1s down the main diagonal and 0s below the 1s is said to be in **row-echelon form**. How do we produce a matrix in this form? We use **row operations** on the augmented matrix. These row operations are just like what you did when solving a linear system by the addition method. The difference is that we no longer write the variables, usually represented by $x$, $y$, and $z$.

### Matrix Row Operations

The following row operations produce matrices that represent systems with the same solution set:

1. Two rows of a matrix may be interchanged. This is the same as interchanging two equations in a linear system.

2. The elements in any row may be multiplied by a nonzero number. This is the same as multiplying both sides of an equation by a nonzero number.

3. The elements in any row may be multiplied by a nonzero number, and these products may be added to the corresponding elements in any other row. This is the same as multiplying both sides of an equation by a nonzero number and then adding equations to eliminate a variable.

Two matrices are **row equivalent** if one can be obtained from the other by a sequence of row operations.

**Study Tip**

When performing the row operation

$$kR_i + R_j$$

you use row $i$ to find the products. However, **elements in row $i$ do not change. It is the elements in row $j$ that change:** Add $k$ times the elements in row $i$ to the corresponding elements in row $j$. Replace elements in row $j$ by these sums.

Each matrix row operation in the preceding box can be expressed symbolically as follows:

1. Interchange the elements in the $i$th and $j$th rows: $R_i \leftrightarrow R_j$.
2. Multiply each element in the $i$th row by $k$: $kR_i$.
3. Add $k$ times the elements in row $i$ to the corresponding elements in row $j$: $kR_i + R_j$.

**EXAMPLE 1** Performing Matrix Row Operations

Use the matrix

$$\begin{bmatrix} 3 & 18 & -12 & | & 21 \\ 1 & 2 & -3 & | & 5 \\ -2 & -3 & 4 & | & -6 \end{bmatrix}$$

and perform each indicated row operation:

**a.** $R_1 \leftrightarrow R_2$      **b.** $\frac{1}{3}R_1$      **c.** $2R_2 + R_3$.

$$\begin{bmatrix} 3 & 18 & -12 & | & 21 \\ 1 & 2 & -3 & | & 5 \\ -2 & -3 & 4 & | & -6 \end{bmatrix}$$

The given matrix (repeated)

### Solution

**a.** The notation $R_1 \leftrightarrow R_2$ means to interchange the elements in row 1 and row 2. This results in the row-equivalent matrix

$$\begin{bmatrix} 1 & 2 & -3 & | & 5 \\ 3 & 18 & -12 & | & 21 \\ -2 & -3 & 4 & | & -6 \end{bmatrix}.$$

This was row 2; now it's row 1.

This was row 1; now it's row 2.

**b.** The notation $\frac{1}{3}R_1$ means to multiply each element in row 1 by $\frac{1}{3}$. This results in the row-equivalent matrix

$$\begin{bmatrix} \frac{1}{3}(3) & \frac{1}{3}(18) & \frac{1}{3}(-12) & | & \frac{1}{3}(21) \\ 1 & 2 & -3 & | & 5 \\ -2 & -3 & 4 & | & -6 \end{bmatrix} = \begin{bmatrix} 1 & 6 & -4 & | & 7 \\ 1 & 2 & -3 & | & 5 \\ -2 & -3 & 4 & | & -6 \end{bmatrix}.$$

**c.** The notation $2R_2 + R_3$ means to add 2 times the elements in row 2 to the corresponding elements in row 3. Replace the elements in row 3 by these sums. First, we find 2 times the elements in row 2, namely, 1, 2, −3, and 5:

$$2(1) \text{ or } 2, \qquad 2(2) \text{ or } 4, \qquad 2(-3) \text{ or } -6, \qquad 2(5) \text{ or } 10.$$

Now we add these products to the corresponding elements in row 3. Although we use row 2 to find the products, row 2 does not change. It is the elements in row 3 that change, resulting in the row-equivalent matrix

Replace row 3 by the sum of itself and 2 times row 2.

$$\begin{bmatrix} 3 & 18 & -12 & | & 21 \\ 1 & 2 & -3 & | & 5 \\ -2+2=0 & -3+4=1 & 4+(-6)=-2 & | & -6+10=4 \end{bmatrix} = \begin{bmatrix} 3 & 18 & -12 & | & 21 \\ 1 & 2 & -3 & | & 5 \\ 0 & 1 & -2 & | & 4 \end{bmatrix}.$$

⬭ **Check Point** ❙ Use the matrix

$$\begin{bmatrix} 4 & 12 & -20 & | & 8 \\ 1 & 6 & -3 & | & 7 \\ -3 & -2 & 1 & | & -9 \end{bmatrix}$$

and perform each indicated row operation:

**a.** $R_1 \leftrightarrow R_2$     **b.** $\frac{1}{4}R_1$     **c.** $3R_2 + R_3$.

**3**   Use matrices and Gaussian elimination to solve systems.

## Solving Linear Systems Using Gaussian Elimination

The process that we use to solve linear systems using matrix row operations is called **Gaussian elimination**, after the German mathematician Carl Friedrich Gauss (1777–1855). Here are the steps used in Gaussian elimination:

### Solving Linear Systems of Three Equations with Three Variables Using Gaussian Elimination

**1.** Write the augmented matrix for the system.

**2.** Use matrix row operations to simplify the matrix to a row-equivalent matrix in row-echelon form, with 1s down the main diagonal from upper left to lower right, and 0s below the 1s in the first and second columns.

$$\begin{bmatrix} 1 & * & * & | & * \\ * & * & * & | & * \\ * & * & * & | & * \end{bmatrix} \rightarrow \begin{bmatrix} 1 & * & * & | & * \\ 0 & * & * & | & * \\ 0 & * & * & | & * \end{bmatrix} \rightarrow \begin{bmatrix} 1 & * & * & | & * \\ 0 & 1 & * & | & * \\ 0 & * & * & | & * \end{bmatrix} \rightarrow \begin{bmatrix} 1 & * & * & | & * \\ 0 & 1 & * & | & * \\ 0 & 0 & * & | & * \end{bmatrix} \rightarrow \begin{bmatrix} 1 & * & * & | & * \\ 0 & 1 & * & | & * \\ 0 & 0 & 1 & | & * \end{bmatrix}$$

Get 1 in the upper left-hand corner.

Use the 1 in the first column to get 0s below it.

Get 1 in the second row, second column position.

Use the 1 in the second column to get 0 below it.

Get 1 in the third row, third column position.

**3.** Write the system of linear equations corresponding to the matrix in step 2 and use back-substitution to find the system's solution.

( **EXAMPLE 2** ) **Gaussian Elimination with Back-Substitution**

Use matrices to solve the system:

$$\begin{cases} 3x + y + 2z = 31 \\ x + y + 2z = 19 \\ x + 3y + 2z = 25. \end{cases}$$

**Solution**

**Step 1  Write the augmented matrix for the system.**

**Linear System**  **Augmented Matrix**

$$\begin{cases} 3x + y + 2z = 31 \\ x + y + 2z = 19 \\ x + 3y + 2z = 25 \end{cases} \qquad \begin{bmatrix} 3 & 1 & 2 & | & 31 \\ 1 & 1 & 2 & | & 19 \\ 1 & 3 & 2 & | & 25 \end{bmatrix}$$

**Step 2  Use matrix row operations to simplify the matrix to row-echelon form, with 1s down the main diagonal from upper left to lower right, and 0s below the 1s in the first and second columns.** Our first step in achieving this goal is to get 1 in the top position of the first column.

We want 1 in this position. $\begin{bmatrix} 3 & 1 & 2 & | & 31 \\ 1 & 1 & 2 & | & 19 \\ 1 & 3 & 2 & | & 25 \end{bmatrix}$

To get 1 in this position, we interchange row 1 and row 2: $R_1 \leftrightarrow R_2$. (We could also interchange row 1 and row 3 to attain our goal.)

$\begin{bmatrix} 1 & 1 & 2 & | & 19 \\ 3 & 1 & 2 & | & 31 \\ 1 & 3 & 2 & | & 25 \end{bmatrix}$ This was row 2; now it's row 1.

This was row 1; now it's row 2.

Now we want to get 0s below the 1 in the first column.

We want 0 in these positions. $\begin{bmatrix} 1 & 1 & 2 & | & 19 \\ 3 & 1 & 2 & | & 31 \\ 1 & 3 & 2 & | & 25 \end{bmatrix}$

To get a 0 where there is now a 3, multiply the top row of numbers by $-3$ and add these products to the second row of numbers: $-3R_1 + R_2$. To get a 0 where there is now a 1, multiply the top row of numbers by $-1$ and add these products to the third row of numbers: $-1R_1 + R_3$. Although we are using row 1 to find the products, the numbers in row 1 do not change.

Replace row 2 by $-3R_1 + R_2$.

Replace row 3 by $-1R_1 + R_3$.

$$\begin{bmatrix} 1 & 1 & 2 & | & 19 \\ -3(1)+3 & -3(1)+1 & -3(2)+2 & | & -3(19)+31 \\ -1(1)+1 & -1(1)+3 & -1(2)+2 & | & -1(19)+25 \end{bmatrix} = \begin{bmatrix} 1 & 1 & 2 & | & 19 \\ 0 & -2 & -4 & | & -26 \\ 0 & 2 & 0 & | & 6 \end{bmatrix}$$

We want 1 in this position.

We move on to the second column. To get 1 in the desired position, we multiply $-2$ by its reciprocal, $-\frac{1}{2}$. Therefore, we multiply all the numbers in the second row by $-\frac{1}{2}$: $-\frac{1}{2}R_2$.

$$-\frac{1}{2}R_2 \quad \begin{bmatrix} 1 & 1 & 2 & | & 19 \\ -\frac{1}{2}(0) & -\frac{1}{2}(-2) & -\frac{1}{2}(-4) & | & -\frac{1}{2}(-26) \\ 0 & 2 & 0 & | & 6 \end{bmatrix} = \begin{bmatrix} 1 & 1 & 2 & | & 19 \\ 0 & 1 & 2 & | & 13 \\ 0 & 2 & 0 & | & 6 \end{bmatrix}.$$

We want 0 in this position.

$$\begin{bmatrix} 1 & 1 & 2 & | & 19 \\ 0 & 1 & 2 & | & 13 \\ 0 & 2 & 0 & | & 6 \end{bmatrix}$$

**We want 0 in this position.**

The matrix from the bottom
of the previous page (repeated)

So far, our matrix row operations have resulted in the matrix that we repeated in the margin. We are not yet done with the second column. The voice balloon shows that we want to get a 0 where there is now a 2. If we multiply the second row of numbers by $-2$ and add these products to the third row of numbers, we will get 0 in this position: $-2R_2 + R_3$. Although we are using the numbers in row 2 to find the products, the numbers in row 2 do not change.

**Replace row 3 by**
$-2R_2 + R_3.$

$$\begin{bmatrix} 1 & 1 & 2 & | & 19 \\ 0 & 1 & 2 & | & 13 \\ -2(0) + 0 & -2(1) + 2 & -2(2) + 0 & | & -2(13) + 6 \end{bmatrix} = \begin{bmatrix} 1 & 1 & 2 & | & 19 \\ 0 & 1 & 2 & | & 13 \\ 0 & 0 & -4 & | & -20 \end{bmatrix}$$

**We want 1 in this position.**

We move on to the third column. To get 1 in the desired position, we multiply $-4$ by its reciprocal, $-\frac{1}{4}$. Therefore, we multiply all the numbers in the third row by $-\frac{1}{4}$: $-\frac{1}{4}R_3$.

$-\frac{1}{4}R_3$
$$\begin{bmatrix} 1 & 1 & 2 & | & 19 \\ 0 & 1 & 2 & | & 13 \\ -\frac{1}{4}(0) & -\frac{1}{4}(0) & -\frac{1}{4}(-4) & | & -\frac{1}{4}(-20) \end{bmatrix} = \begin{bmatrix} 1 & 1 & 2 & | & 19 \\ 0 & 1 & 2 & | & 13 \\ 0 & 0 & 1 & | & 5 \end{bmatrix}$$

We now have the desired matrix in row-echelon form, with 1s down the main diagonal and 0s below the 1s in the first and second columns.

**Step 3   Write the system of linear equations corresponding to the matrix in step 2 and use back-substitution to find the system's solution.** The system represented by the matrix in step 2 is

$$\begin{bmatrix} 1 & 1 & 2 & | & 19 \\ 0 & 1 & 2 & | & 13 \\ 0 & 0 & 1 & | & 5 \end{bmatrix} \rightarrow \begin{cases} 1x + 1y + 2z = 19 \\ 0x + 1y + 2z = 13 \\ 0x + 0y + 1z = 5 \end{cases} \text{ or } \begin{cases} x + y + 2z = 19 & (1) \\ y + 2z = 13. & (2) \\ z = 5 & (3) \end{cases}$$

We immediately see from equation (3) that the value for $z$ is 5. To find $y$, we back-substitute 5 for $z$ in the second equation.

$$y + 2z = 13 \quad \text{Equation (2)}$$
$$y + 2(5) = 13 \quad \text{Substitute 5 for z.}$$
$$y + 10 = 13 \quad \text{Multiply.}$$
$$y = 3 \quad \text{Subtract 10 from both sides and solve for y.}$$

Finally, back-substitute 3 for $y$ and 5 for $z$ in the first equation.

$$x + y + 2z = 19 \quad \text{Equation (1)}$$
$$x + 3 + 2(5) = 19 \quad \text{Substitute 3 for y and 5 for z.}$$
$$x + 13 = 19 \quad \text{Multiply and add.}$$
$$x = 6 \quad \text{Subtract 13 from both sides and solve for x.}$$

## Technology

Most graphing utilities can convert an augmented matrix to row-echelon form, with 1s down the main diagonal and 0s below the 1s. However, row-echelon form is not unique. Your graphing utility might give a row-echelon form different from the one you obtained by hand. However, all row-echelon forms for a given system's augmented matrix produce the same solution to the system. Enter the augmented matrix and name it $A$. Then use the $\boxed{\text{REF}}$ (row-echelon form) command on matrix $A$.

With $z = 5$, $y = 3$, and $x = 6$, the solution set of the original system is $\{(6, 3, 5)\}$. Check to see that the solution satisfies all three equations in the given system.

⦿ Check Point **2** Use matrices to solve the system:

$$\begin{cases} 2x + y + 2z = 18 \\ x - y + 2z = 9 \\ x + 2y - z = 6. \end{cases}$$

Modern supercomputers are capable of solving systems with more than 600,000 variables. The augmented matrices for such systems are huge, but the solution using matrices is exactly like what we did in Example 2. Work with the augmented matrix, one column at a time. Get 1s down the main diagonal from upper left to lower right and 0s below the 1s. Let's see how this works for a linear system involving four equations in four variables.

( **EXAMPLE 3** ) **Gaussian Elimination with Back-Substitution**

Use matrices to solve the system:

$$\begin{cases} 2w + x + 3y - z = 6 \\ w - x + 2y - 2z = -1 \\ w - x - y + z = -4 \\ -w + 2x - 2y - z = -7. \end{cases}$$

**Solution**

**Step 1   Write the augmented matrix for the system.**

**Linear System**

$$\begin{cases} 2w + x + 3y - z = 6 \\ w - x + 2y - 2z = -1 \\ w - x - y + z = -4 \\ -w + 2x - 2y - z = -7 \end{cases}$$

**Augmented Matrix**

$$\left[\begin{array}{cccc|c} 2 & 1 & 3 & -1 & 6 \\ 1 & -1 & 2 & -2 & -1 \\ 1 & -1 & -1 & 1 & -4 \\ -1 & 2 & -2 & -1 & -7 \end{array}\right]$$

**Step 2   Use matrix row operations to simplify the matrix to row-echelon form, with 1s down the main diagonal from upper left to lower right, and 0s below the 1s in the first, second, and third columns.** Our first step in achieving this goal is to get 1 in the top position of the first column. To do this, we interchange row 1 and row 2: $R_1 \leftrightarrow R_2$.

We want 0s in these positions.

$$\left[\begin{array}{cccc|c} 1 & -1 & 2 & -2 & -1 \\ 2 & 1 & 3 & -1 & 6 \\ 1 & -1 & -1 & 1 & -4 \\ -1 & 2 & -2 & -1 & -7 \end{array}\right]$$

This was row 2; now it's row 1.

This was row 1; now it's row 2.

Now we use the 1 at the top of the first column to get 0s below it.

Use the previous matrix and:
Replace row 2 by $-2R_1 + R_2$.
Replace row 3 by $-1R_1 + R_3$.
Replace row 4 by $1R_1 + R_4$.

$$\left[\begin{array}{cccc|c} 1 & -1 & 2 & -2 & -1 \\ 0 & 3 & -1 & 3 & 8 \\ 0 & 0 & -3 & 3 & -3 \\ 0 & 1 & 0 & -3 & -8 \end{array}\right]$$

We want 1 in this position.

We move on to the second column. We can obtain 1 in the desired position by multiplying the numbers in the second row by $\frac{1}{3}$, the reciprocal of 3.

$$\left[\begin{array}{cccc|c} 1 & -1 & 2 & -2 & -1 \\ \frac{1}{3}(0) & \frac{1}{3}(3) & \frac{1}{3}(-1) & \frac{1}{3}(3) & \frac{1}{3}(8) \\ 0 & 0 & -3 & 3 & -3 \\ 0 & 1 & 0 & -3 & -8 \end{array}\right] = \left[\begin{array}{cccc|c} 1 & -1 & 2 & -2 & -1 \\ 0 & 1 & -\frac{1}{3} & 1 & \frac{8}{3} \\ 0 & 0 & -3 & 3 & -3 \\ 0 & 1 & 0 & -3 & -8 \end{array}\right] \quad \frac{1}{3}R_2$$

We want 0s in these positions.
The top position already has a 0.

$$\begin{bmatrix} 1 & -1 & 2 & -2 & | & -1 \\ 0 & 1 & -\frac{1}{3} & 1 & | & \frac{8}{3} \\ 0 & 0 & -3 & 3 & | & -3 \\ 0 & 1 & 0 & -3 & | & -8 \end{bmatrix}$$

We want 0s in these positions. The top position already has a 0.

The matrix from the bottom of the previous page (repeated)

So far, our matrix row operations have resulted in the matrix that we repeated in the margin. Now we use the 1 in the second row, second column position to get 0s below it.

Replace row 4 in the previous matrix by $-1R_2 + R_4$.

$$\begin{bmatrix} 1 & -1 & 2 & -2 & | & -1 \\ 0 & 1 & -\frac{1}{3} & 1 & | & \frac{8}{3} \\ 0 & 0 & -3 & 3 & | & -3 \\ 0 & 0 & \frac{1}{3} & -4 & | & -\frac{32}{3} \end{bmatrix}$$

We want 1 in this position.

We move on to the third column. We can obtain 1 in the desired position by multiplying the numbers in the third row by $-\frac{1}{3}$, the reciprocal of $-3$.

$$\begin{bmatrix} 1 & -1 & 2 & -2 & | & -1 \\ 0 & 1 & -\frac{1}{3} & 1 & | & \frac{8}{3} \\ -\frac{1}{3}(0) & -\frac{1}{3}(0) & -\frac{1}{3}(-3) & -\frac{1}{3}(3) & | & -\frac{1}{3}(-3) \\ 0 & 0 & \frac{1}{3} & -4 & | & -\frac{32}{3} \end{bmatrix} = \begin{bmatrix} 1 & -1 & 2 & -2 & | & -1 \\ 0 & 1 & -\frac{1}{3} & 1 & | & \frac{8}{3} \\ 0 & 0 & 1 & -1 & | & 1 \\ 0 & 0 & \frac{1}{3} & -4 & | & -\frac{32}{3} \end{bmatrix} \quad -\frac{1}{3}R_3$$

We want 0 in this position.

Now we use the 1 in the third column to get 0 below it.

Replace row 4 in the previous matrix by $-\frac{1}{3}R_3 + R_4$.

$$\begin{bmatrix} 1 & -1 & 2 & -2 & | & -1 \\ 0 & 1 & -\frac{1}{3} & 1 & | & \frac{8}{3} \\ 0 & 0 & 1 & -1 & | & 1 \\ 0 & 0 & 0 & -\frac{11}{3} & | & -11 \end{bmatrix}$$

We want 1 in this position.

We move on to the fourth column. Because we want 1s down the diagonal from upper left to lower right, we want 1 where there is now $-\frac{11}{3}$. We can obtain 1 in this position by multiplying the numbers in the fourth row by $-\frac{3}{11}$.

$$\begin{bmatrix} 1 & -1 & 2 & -2 & | & -1 \\ 0 & 1 & -\frac{1}{3} & 1 & | & \frac{8}{3} \\ 0 & 0 & 1 & -1 & | & 1 \\ -\frac{3}{11}(0) & -\frac{3}{11}(0) & -\frac{3}{11}(0) & -\frac{3}{11}(-\frac{11}{3}) & | & -\frac{3}{11}(-11) \end{bmatrix}$$

$$= \begin{bmatrix} 1 & -1 & 2 & -2 & | & -1 \\ 0 & 1 & -\frac{1}{3} & 1 & | & \frac{8}{3} \\ 0 & 0 & 1 & -1 & | & 1 \\ 0 & 0 & 0 & 1 & | & 3 \end{bmatrix} \quad -\frac{3}{11}R_4$$

We now have the desired matrix in row-echelon form, with 1s down the main diagonal and 0s below the 1s. An equivalent row-echelon matrix can be obtained using a graphing utility and the $\boxed{\text{REF}}$ command on the augmented matrix.

**Step 3  Write the system of linear equations corresponding to the matrix in step 2 and use back-substitution to find the system's solution.** The system represented by the matrix in step 2 is

$$\begin{bmatrix} 1 & -1 & 2 & -2 & | & -1 \\ 0 & 1 & -\frac{1}{3} & 1 & | & \frac{8}{3} \\ 0 & 0 & 1 & -1 & | & 1 \\ 0 & 0 & 0 & 1 & | & 3 \end{bmatrix} \rightarrow \begin{cases} 1w - 1x + 2y - 2z = -1 \\ 0w + 1x - \frac{1}{3}y + 1z = \frac{8}{3} \\ 0w + 0x + 1y - 1z = 1 \\ 0w + 0x + 0y + 1z = 3 \end{cases} \text{ or } \begin{cases} w - x + 2y - 2z = -1 \\ x - \frac{1}{3}y + z = \frac{8}{3} \\ y - z = 1 \\ z = 3. \end{cases}$$

We immediately see that the value for $z$ is 3. We can now use back-substitution to find the values for $y$, $x$, and $w$.

These are the
four equations
from the last column.

$$z = 3 \quad\Big|\quad y - z = 1 \quad\Big|\quad x - \frac{1}{3}y + z = \frac{8}{3} \quad\Big|\quad w - x + 2y - 2z = -1$$

$$y - 3 = 1 \quad\Big|\quad x - \frac{1}{3}(4) + 3 = \frac{8}{3} \quad\Big|\quad w - 1 + 2(4) - 2(3) = -1$$

$$y = 4 \qquad\qquad x + \frac{5}{3} = \frac{8}{3} \qquad\qquad w - 1 + 8 - 6 = -1$$

$$x = 1 \qquad\qquad\qquad w + 1 = -1$$

$$w = -2$$

Let's agree to write the solution for the system in the alphabetical order of the variables from left to right, namely $(w, x, y, z)$. Thus, the solution set is $\{(-2, 1, 4, 3)\}$. We can verify the solution by substituting the value for each variable into the original system of equations and obtaining four true statements.

⬤ Check Point 3 Use matrices to solve the system:

$$\begin{cases} w - 3x - 2y + z = -3 \\ 2w - 7x - y + 2z = 1 \\ 3w - 7x - 3y + 3z = -5 \\ 5w + x + 4y - 2z = 18. \end{cases}$$

④ Use matrices and Gauss-Jordan elimination to solve systems.

## Solving Linear Systems Using Gauss-Jordan Elimination

Using Gaussian elimination, we obtain a matrix in row-echelon form, with 1s down the main diagonal and 0s below the 1s. A second method, called **Gauss-Jordan elimination**, after Carl Friedrich Gauss and Wilhelm Jordan (1842–1899), continues the process until a matrix with 1s down the main diagonal and 0s in every position *above and below* each 1 is found. Such a matrix is said to be in **reduced row-echelon form**. For a system of three linear equations in three variables, $x$, $y$, and $z$, we must get the augmented matrix into the form

$$\begin{bmatrix} 1 & 0 & 0 & a \\ 0 & 1 & 0 & b \\ 0 & 0 & 1 & c \end{bmatrix}.$$

Based on this matrix, we conclude that $x = a$, $y = b$, and $z = c$.

### Solving Linear Systems Using Gauss-Jordan Elimination

1. Write the augmented matrix for the system.

2. Use matrix row operations to simplify the matrix to a row-equivalent matrix in reduced row-echelon form, with 1s down the main diagonal from upper left to lower right, and 0s above and below the 1s.

   a. Get 1 in the upper left-hand corner.

   b. Use the 1 in the first column to get 0s below it.

   c. Get 1 in the second row, second column.

   d. Use the 1 in the second column to make the remaining entries in the second column 0.

   e. Get 1 in the third row, third column.

   f. Use the 1 in the third column to make the remaining entries in the third column 0.

   g. Continue this procedure as far as possible.

3. Use the reduced row-echelon form of the matrix in step 2 to write the system's solution set. (Back-substitution is not necessary.)

## Technology

Most graphing utilities can convert a matrix to reduced row-echelon form. Enter the system's augmented matrix and name it $A$. Then use the RREF (reduced row-echelon form) command on matrix $A$.

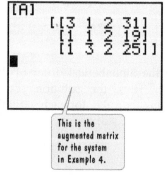

This is the augmented matrix for the system in Example 4.

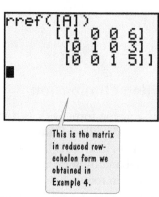

This is the matrix in reduced row-echelon form we obtained in Example 4.

**EXAMPLE 4** Using Gauss-Jordan Elimination

Use Gauss-Jordan elimination to solve the system:

$$\begin{cases} 3x + y + 2z = 31 \\ x + y + 2z = 19 \\ x + 3y + 2z = 25. \end{cases}$$

**Solution** In Example 2, we used Gaussian elimination to obtain the following matrix:

We want 0s in these positions.
$$\begin{bmatrix} 1 & 1 & 2 & | & 19 \\ 0 & 1 & 2 & | & 13 \\ 0 & 0 & 1 & | & 5 \end{bmatrix}.$$

To use Gauss-Jordan elimination, we need 0s both above and below the 1s in the main diagonal. We use the 1 in the second row, second column to get a 0 above it.

Replace row 1 in the previous matrix by $-1R_2 + R_1$.
$$\begin{bmatrix} 1 & 0 & 0 & | & 6 \\ 0 & 1 & 2 & | & 13 \\ 0 & 0 & 1 & | & 5 \end{bmatrix}$$
We want 0s in these positions.

We use the 1 in the third column to get 0s above it.

$$\begin{bmatrix} 1 & 0 & 0 & | & 6 \\ 0 & 1 & 0 & | & 3 \\ 0 & 0 & 1 & | & 5 \end{bmatrix}$$
Replace row 2 in the previous matrix by $-2R_3 + R_2$.

This last matrix corresponds to

$$x = 6, \quad y = 3, \quad z = 5.$$

As we found in Example 2, the solution set is $\{(6, 3, 5)\}$.

⊘ Check Point **4** Solve the system in Check Point 2 using Gauss-Jordan elimination. Begin by working with the matrix that you obtained in Check Point 2.

## Exercise Set 8.1

### Practice Exercises

*In Exercises 1–8, write the augmented matrix for each system of linear equations.*

**1.** $\begin{cases} 2x + y + 2z = 2 \\ 3x - 5y - z = 4 \\ x - 2y - 3z = -6 \end{cases}$

**2.** $\begin{cases} 3x - 2y + 5z = 31 \\ x + 3y - 3z = -12 \\ -2x - 5y + 3z = 11 \end{cases}$

**3.** $\begin{cases} x - y + z = 8 \\ y - 12z = -15 \\ z = 1 \end{cases}$

**4.** $\begin{cases} x - 2y + 3z = 9 \\ y + 3z = 5 \\ z = 2 \end{cases}$

**5.** $\begin{cases} 5x - 2y - 3z = 0 \\ x + y = 5 \\ 2x - 3z = 4 \end{cases}$

**6.** $\begin{cases} x - 2y + z = 10 \\ 3x + y = 5 \\ 7x + 2z = 2 \end{cases}$

**7.** $\begin{cases} 2w + 5x - 3y + z = 2 \\ 3x + y = 4 \\ w - x + 5y = 9 \\ 5w - 5x - 2y = 1 \end{cases}$

**8.** $\begin{cases} 4w + 7x - 8y + z = 3 \\ 5x + y = 5 \\ w - x - y = 17 \\ 2w - 2x + 11y = 4 \end{cases}$

*In Exercises 9–12, write the system of linear equations represented by the augmented matrix. Use x, y, and z, or, if necessary, w, x, y, and z, for the variables.*

**9.** $\begin{bmatrix} 5 & 0 & 3 & | & -11 \\ 0 & 1 & -4 & | & 12 \\ 7 & 2 & 0 & | & 3 \end{bmatrix}$

**10.** $\begin{bmatrix} 7 & 0 & 4 & | & -13 \\ 0 & 1 & -5 & | & 11 \\ 2 & 7 & 0 & | & 6 \end{bmatrix}$

**11.** $\begin{bmatrix} 1 & 1 & 4 & 1 & | & 3 \\ -1 & 1 & -1 & 0 & | & 7 \\ 2 & 0 & 0 & 5 & | & 11 \\ 0 & 0 & 12 & 4 & | & 5 \end{bmatrix}$

**12.** $\begin{bmatrix} 4 & 1 & 5 & 1 & | & 6 \\ 1 & -1 & 0 & -1 & | & 8 \\ 3 & 0 & 0 & 7 & | & 4 \\ 0 & 0 & 11 & 5 & | & 3 \end{bmatrix}$

*In Exercises 13–18, perform each matrix row operation and write the new matrix.*

**13.** $\begin{bmatrix} 2 & -6 & 4 & | & 10 \\ 1 & 5 & -5 & | & 0 \\ 3 & 0 & 4 & | & 7 \end{bmatrix}$ $\frac{1}{2}R_1$

**14.** $\begin{bmatrix} 3 & -12 & 6 & | & 9 \\ 1 & -4 & 4 & | & 0 \\ 2 & 0 & 7 & | & 4 \end{bmatrix} \quad \frac{1}{3}R_1$

**15.** $\begin{bmatrix} 1 & -3 & 2 & | & 0 \\ 3 & 1 & -1 & | & 7 \\ 2 & -2 & 1 & | & 3 \end{bmatrix} \quad -3R_1 + R_2$

**16.** $\begin{bmatrix} 1 & -1 & 5 & | & -6 \\ 3 & 3 & -1 & | & 10 \\ 1 & 3 & 2 & | & 5 \end{bmatrix} \quad -3R_1 + R_2$

**17.** $\begin{bmatrix} 1 & -1 & 1 & 1 & | & 3 \\ 0 & 1 & -2 & -1 & | & 0 \\ 2 & 0 & 3 & 4 & | & 11 \\ 5 & 1 & 2 & 4 & | & 6 \end{bmatrix} \quad \begin{matrix} \\ \\ -2R_1 + R_3 \\ -5R_1 + R_4 \end{matrix}$

**18.** $\begin{bmatrix} 1 & -5 & 2 & -2 & | & 4 \\ 0 & 1 & -3 & -1 & | & 0 \\ 3 & 0 & 2 & -1 & | & 6 \\ -4 & 1 & 4 & 2 & | & -3 \end{bmatrix} \quad \begin{matrix} \\ \\ -3R_1 + R_3 \\ 4R_1 + R_4 \end{matrix}$

*In Exercises 19–20, a few steps in the process of simplifying the given matrix to row-echelon form, with 1s down the diagonal from upper left to lower right, and 0s below the 1s, are shown. Fill in the missing numbers in the steps that are shown.*

**19.** $\begin{bmatrix} 1 & -1 & 1 & | & 8 \\ 2 & 3 & -1 & | & -2 \\ 3 & -2 & -9 & | & 9 \end{bmatrix} \rightarrow \begin{bmatrix} 1 & -1 & 1 & | & 8 \\ 0 & 5 & \square & | & \square \\ 0 & 1 & \square & | & \square \end{bmatrix}$

$\rightarrow \begin{bmatrix} 1 & -1 & 1 & | & 8 \\ 0 & 1 & \square & | & \square \\ 0 & 1 & \square & | & \square \end{bmatrix}$

**20.** $\begin{bmatrix} 1 & -2 & 3 & | & 4 \\ 2 & 1 & -4 & | & 3 \\ -3 & 4 & -1 & | & -2 \end{bmatrix} \rightarrow \begin{bmatrix} 1 & -2 & 3 & | & 4 \\ 0 & 5 & \square & | & \square \\ 0 & -2 & \square & | & \square \end{bmatrix}$

$\rightarrow \begin{bmatrix} 1 & -2 & 3 & | & 4 \\ 0 & 1 & \square & | & \square \\ 0 & -2 & \square & | & \square \end{bmatrix}$

*In Exercises 21–38, solve each system of equations using matrices. Use Gaussian elimination with back-substitution or Gauss-Jordan elimination.*

**21.** $\begin{cases} x + y - z = -2 \\ 2x - y + z = 5 \\ -x + 2y + 2z = 1 \end{cases}$

**22.** $\begin{cases} x - 2y - z = 2 \\ 2x - y + z = 4 \\ -x + y - 2z = -4 \end{cases}$

**23.** $\begin{cases} x + 3y = 0 \\ x + y + z = 1 \\ 3x - y - z = 11 \end{cases}$

**24.** $\begin{cases} 3y - z = -1 \\ x + 5y - z = -4 \\ -3x + 6y + 2z = 11 \end{cases}$

**25.** $\begin{cases} 2x - y - z = 4 \\ x + y - 5z = -4 \\ x - 2y = 4 \end{cases}$

**26.** $\begin{cases} x - 3z = -2 \\ 2x + 2y + z = 4 \\ 3x + y - 2z = 5 \end{cases}$

**27.** $\begin{cases} x + y + z = 4 \\ x - y - z = 0 \\ x - y + z = 2 \end{cases}$

**28.** $\begin{cases} 3x + y - z = 0 \\ x + y + 2z = 6 \\ 2x + 2y + 3z = 10 \end{cases}$

**29.** $\begin{cases} x + 2y = z - 1 \\ x = 4 + y - z \\ x + y - 3z = -2 \end{cases}$

**30.** $\begin{cases} 2x + y = z + 1 \\ 2x = 1 + 3y - z \\ x + y + z = 4 \end{cases}$

**31.** $\begin{cases} 3a - b - 4c = 3 \\ 2a - b + 2c = -8 \\ a + 2b - 3c = 9 \end{cases}$

**32.** $\begin{cases} 3a + b - c = 0 \\ 2a + 3b - 5c = 1 \\ a - 2b + 3c = -4 \end{cases}$

**33.** $\begin{cases} 2x + 2y + 7z = -1 \\ 2x + y + 2z = 2 \\ 4x + 6y + z = 15 \end{cases}$

**34.** $\begin{cases} 3x + 2y + 3z = 3 \\ 4x - 5y + 7z = 1 \\ 2x + 3y - 2z = 6 \end{cases}$

**35.** $\begin{cases} w + x + y + z = 4 \\ 2w + x - 2y - z = 0 \\ w - 2x - y - 2z = -2 \\ 3w + 2x + y + 3z = 4 \end{cases}$

**36.** $\begin{cases} w + x + y + z = 5 \\ w + 2x - y - 2z = -1 \\ w - 3x - 3y - z = -1 \\ 2w - x + 2y - z = -2 \end{cases}$

**37.** $\begin{cases} 3w - 4x + y + z = 9 \\ w + x - y - z = 0 \\ 2w + x + 4y - 2z = 3 \\ -w + 2x + y - 3z = 3 \end{cases}$

**38.** $\begin{cases} 2w + y - 3z = 8 \\ w - x + 4z = -10 \\ 3w + 5x - y - z = 20 \\ w + x - y - z = 6 \end{cases}$

## Practice Plus

**39.** Find the quadratic function $f(x) = ax^2 + bx + c$ for which $f(-2) = -4$, $f(1) = 2$, and $f(2) = 0$.

**40.** Find the quadratic function $f(x) = ax^2 + bx + c$ for which $f(-1) = 5$, $f(1) = 3$, and $f(2) = 5$.

**41.** Find the cubic function $f(x) = ax^3 + bx^2 + cx + d$ for which $f(-1) = 0$, $f(1) = 2$, $f(2) = 3$, and $f(3) = 12$.

**42.** Find the cubic function $f(x) = ax^3 + bx^2 + cx + d$ for which $f(-1) = 3$, $f(1) = 1$, $f(2) = 6$, and $f(3) = 7$.

**43.** Solve the system:

$$\begin{cases} 2\ln w + \ln x + 3\ln y - 2\ln z = -6 \\ 4\ln w + 3\ln x + \ln y - \ln z = -2 \\ \ln w + \ln x + \ln y + \ln z = -5 \\ \ln w + \ln x - \ln y - \ln z = 5. \end{cases}$$

(*Hint:* Let $A = \ln w$, $B = \ln x$, $C = \ln y$, and $D = \ln z$. Solve the system for $A, B, C,$ and $D$. Then use the logarithmic equations to find $w, x, y,$ and $z$.)

**44.** Solve the system:

$$\begin{cases} \ln w + \ln x + \ln y + \ln z = -1 \\ -\ln w + 4\ln x + \ln y - \ln z = 0 \\ \ln w - 2\ln x + \ln y - 2\ln z = 11 \\ -\ln w - 2\ln x + \ln y + 2\ln z = -3. \end{cases}$$

(*Hint:* Let $A = \ln w$, $B = \ln x$, $C = \ln y$, and $D = \ln z$. Solve the system for $A, B, C,$ and $D$. Then use the logarithmic equations to find $w, x, y,$ and $z$.)

## Application Exercises

**45.** A ball is thrown straight upward. A position function
$$s(t) = \tfrac{1}{2}at^2 + v_0t + s_0$$
can be used to describe the ball's height, $s(t)$, in feet, after $t$ seconds.

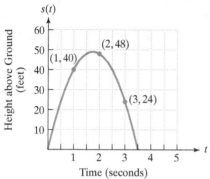

**a.** Use the points labeled in the graph to find the values of $a$, $v_0$, and $s_0$. Solve the system of linear equations involving $a$, $v_0$, and $s_0$ using matrices.

**b.** Find and interpret $s(3.5)$. Identify your solution as a point on the graph shown.

**c.** After how many seconds does the ball reach its maximum height? What is its maximum height?

**46.** A football is kicked straight upward. A position function
$$s(t) = \tfrac{1}{2}at^2 + v_0t + s_0$$
can be used to describe the ball's height, $s(t)$, in feet, after $t$ seconds.

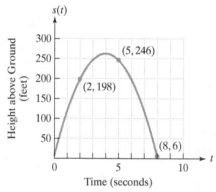

**a.** Use the points labeled in the graph to find the values of $a$, $v_0$, and $s_0$. Solve the system of linear equations involving $a$, $v_0$, and $s_0$ using matrices.

**b.** Find and interpret $s(7)$. Identify your solution as a point on the graph shown.

**c.** After how many seconds does the ball reach its maximum height? What is its maximum height?

*Write a system of linear equations in three or four variables to solve Exercises 47–50. Then use matrices to solve the system.*

**47.** Three foods have the following nutritional content per ounce.

|  | Calories | Protein (in grams) | Vitamin C (in milligrams) |
|---|---|---|---|
| **Food A** | 40 | 5 | 30 |
| **Food B** | 200 | 2 | 10 |
| **Food C** | 400 | 4 | 300 |

If a meal consisting of the three foods allows exactly 660 calories, 25 grams of protein, and 425 milligrams of vitamin C, how many ounces of each kind of food should be used?

**48.** A furniture company produces three types of desks: a children's model, an office model, and a deluxe model. Each desk is manufactured in three stages: cutting, construction, and finishing. The time requirements for each model and manufacturing stage are given in the following table.

|  | Children's model | Office model | Deluxe model |
|---|---|---|---|
| **Cutting** | 2 hr | 3 hr | 2 hr |
| **Construction** | 2 hr | 1 hr | 3 hr |
| **Finishing** | 1 hr | 1 hr | 2 hr |

Each week the company has available a maximum of 100 hours for cutting, 100 hours for construction, and 65 hours for finishing. If all available time must be used, how many of each type of desk should be produced each week?

**49.** Imagine the entire global population as a village of precisely 200 people. The bar graph shows some numeric observations based on this scenario.

**Earth's Population as a Village of 200 People**

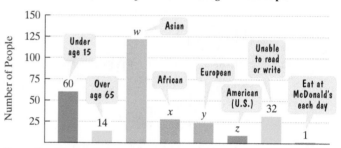

*Source:* Gary Rimmer, *Number Freaking*, The Disinformation Company Ltd., 2006

Combined, there are 183 Asians, Africans, Europeans, and Americans in the village. The number of Asians exceeds the number of Africans and Europeans by 70. The difference between the number of Europeans and Americans is 15. If the number of Africans is doubled, their population exceeds the number of Europeans and Americans by 23. Determine the number of Asians, Africans, Europeans, and Americans in the global village.

**50.** The bar graph shows the number of rooms, bathrooms, fireplaces, and elevators in the U.S. White House.

**The U.S. White House by the Numbers**

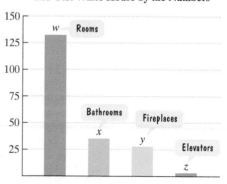

*Source:* The White House

Combined, there are 198 rooms, bathrooms, fireplaces, and elevators. The number of rooms exceeds the number of bathrooms and fireplaces by 69. The difference between the number of fireplaces and elevators is 25. If the number of bathrooms is doubled, it exceeds the number of fireplaces and elevators by 39. Determine the number of rooms, bathrooms, fireplaces, and elevators in the U.S. White House.

## Writing in Mathematics

**51.** What is a matrix?

**52.** Describe what is meant by the augmented matrix of a system of linear equations.

**53.** In your own words, describe each of the three matrix row operations. Give an example with each of the operations.

**54.** Describe how to use row operations and matrices to solve a system of linear equations.

**55.** What is the difference between Gaussian elimination and Gauss-Jordan elimination?

## Technology Exercises

**56.** Most graphing utilities can perform row operations on matrices. Consult the owner's manual for your graphing utility to learn proper keystrokes for performing these operations. Then duplicate the row operations of any three exercises that you solved from Exercises 13–18.

**57.** If your graphing utility has a ⃞ REF ⃞ (row-echelon form) command or a ⃞ RREF ⃞ (reduced row-echelon form) command, use this feature to verify your work with any five systems that you solved from Exercises 21–38.

**58.** Solve using a graphing utility's ⃞ REF ⃞ or ⃞ RREF ⃞ command:

$$\begin{cases} 2x_1 - 2x_2 + 3x_3 - x_4 = 12 \\ x_1 + 2x_2 - x_3 + 2x_4 - x_5 = -7 \\ x_1 + x_3 + x_4 - 5x_5 = 1 \\ -x_1 + x_2 - x_3 - 2x_4 - 3x_5 = 0 \\ x_1 - x_2 - x_4 + x_5 = 4. \end{cases}$$

## Critical Thinking Exercises

**Make Sense?**   *In Exercises 59–62, determine whether each statement makes sense or does not make sense, and explain your reasoning.*

**59.** Matrix row operations remind me of what I did when solving a linear system by the addition method, although I no longer write the variables.

**60.** When I use matrices to solve linear systems, the only arithmetic involves multiplication or a combination of multiplication and addition.

**61.** When I use matrices to solve linear systems, I spend most of my time using row operations to express the system's augmented matrix in row-echelon form.

**62.** Using row operations on an augmented matrix, I obtain a row in which 0s appear to the left of the vertical bar, but 6 appears on the right, so the system I'm working with has no solution.

*In Exercises 63–66, determine whether each statement is true or false. If the statement is false, make the necessary change(s) to produce a true statement.*

**63.** A matrix row operation such as $-\frac{4}{5}R_1 + R_2$ is not permitted because of the negative fraction.

**64.** The augmented matrix for the system

$$\begin{matrix} x - 3y = 5 \\ y - 2z = 7 \\ 2x + z = 4 \end{matrix} \quad \text{is} \quad \begin{bmatrix} 1 & -3 & | & 5 \\ 1 & -2 & | & 7 \\ 2 & 1 & | & 4 \end{bmatrix}.$$

**65.** In solving a linear system of three equations in three variables, we begin with the augmented matrix and use row operations to obtain a row-equivalent matrix with 0s down the diagonal from left to right and 1s below each 0.

**66.** The row operation $kR_i + R_j$ indicates that it is the elements in row $i$ that change.

**67.** The table shows the daily production level and profit for a business.

| $x$ (Number of Units Produced Daily) | 30 | 50 | 100 |
|---|---|---|---|
| $y$ (Daily Profit) | $5900 | $7500 | $4500 |

Use the quadratic function $y = ax^2 + bx + c$ to determine the number of units that should be produced each day for maximum profit. What is the maximum daily profit?

## Preview Exercises

*Exercises 68–70 will help you prepare for the material covered in the next section. In each exercise, refer to the following system:*

$$\begin{cases} 3x - 4y + 4z = 7 \\ x - y - 2z = 2 \\ 2x - 3y + 6z = 5. \end{cases}$$

**68.** Show that $(12z + 1, 10z - 1, z)$ satisfies the system for $z = 0$.

**69.** Show that $(12z + 1, 10z - 1, z)$ satisfies the system for $z = 1$.

**70. a.** Select a value for $z$ other than 0 or 1 and show that $(12z + 1, 10z - 1, z)$ satisfies the system.

**b.** Based on your work in Exercises 68–70(a), how does this system differ from those in Exercises 21–34?

# Inconsistent and Dependent Systems and Their Applications

## Objectives

① Apply Gaussian elimination to systems without unique solutions.

② Apply Gaussian elimination to systems with more variables than equations.

③ Solve problems involving systems without unique solutions.

Traffic jams getting you down? Powerful computers, able to solve systems with hundreds of thousands of variables in a single bound, may promise a gridlock-free future. The computer in your car could be linked to a central computer that manages traffic flow by controlling traffic lights, rerouting you away from raffic congestion, issuing weather reports, and selecting the best route to your destination. New technologies could eventually drive your car at a steady 75 miles per hour along automated highways as you comfortably nap. In this section, we look at the role of linear systems without unique solutions in a future free of traffic jams.

Linear systems can have one solution, no solution, or infinitely many solutions. We can use Gaussian elimination on systems with three or more variables to determine how many solutions such systems may have. In the case of systems with no solution or infinitely many solutions, it is impossible to rewrite the augmented matrix in the desired form with 1s down the main diagonal from upper left to lower right, and 0s below the 1s. Let's see what this means by looking at a system that has no solution.

① Apply Gaussian elimination to systems without unique solutions.

**EXAMPLE 1** A System with No Solution

Use Gaussian elimination to solve the system:

$$\begin{cases} x - y - 2z = 2 \\ 2x - 3y + 6z = 5 \\ 3x - 4y + 4z = 12. \end{cases}$$

**Solution**

**Step 1  Write the augmented matrix for the system.**

## Discovery

Use the addition method to solve Example 1. Describe what happens. Why does this mean that there is no solution?

**Linear System**

$$\begin{cases} x - y - 2z = 2 \\ 2x - 3y + 6z = 5 \\ 3x - 4y + 4z = 12 \end{cases}$$

**Augmented Matrix**

$$\begin{bmatrix} 1 & -1 & -2 & | & 2 \\ 2 & -3 & 6 & | & 5 \\ 3 & -4 & 4 & | & 12 \end{bmatrix}$$

**Step 2  Attempt to simplify the matrix to row-echelon form, with 1s down the main diagonal and 0s below the 1s.** Notice that the augmented matrix already has a 1 in the top position of the first column. Now we want 0s below the 1. To get the first 0, multiply row 1 by −2 and add these products to row 2. To get the second 0, multiply row 1 by $-3$ and add these products to row 3. Performing these operations, we obtain the following matrix:

We want 1 in this position.

$$\begin{bmatrix} 1 & -1 & -2 & 2 \\ 0 & -1 & 10 & 1 \\ 0 & -1 & 10 & 6 \end{bmatrix}.$$

Use the augmented matrix and:
Replace row 2 by $-2R_1 + R_2$.
Replace row 3 by $-3R_1 + R_3$.

Moving on to the second column, we obtain 1 in the desired position by multiplying row 2 by $-1$.

$$\begin{bmatrix} 1 & -1 & -2 & 2 \\ -1(0) & -1(-1) & -1(10) & -1(1) \\ 0 & -1 & 10 & 6 \end{bmatrix} = \begin{bmatrix} 1 & -1 & -2 & 2 \\ 0 & 1 & -10 & -1 \\ 0 & -1 & 10 & 6 \end{bmatrix} \quad -1R_2$$

We want 0 in this position.

Now we want a 0 below the 1 in column 2. To get the 0, multiply row 2 by 1 and add these products to row 3. (Equivalently, add row 2 to row 3.) We obtain the following matrix:

$$\begin{bmatrix} 1 & -1 & -2 & 2 \\ 0 & 1 & -10 & -1 \\ 0 & 0 & 0 & 5 \end{bmatrix}.$$

Replace row 3 in the previous matrix by $1R_2 + R_3$.

It is impossible to convert this last matrix to the desired form of 1s down the main diagonal. If we translate the last row back into equation form, we get

$$0x + 0y + 0z = 5,$$

There are no values of $x$, $y$, and $z$ for which $0 = 5$.

which is false. Regardless of which values we select for $x$, $y$, and $z$, the last equation can never be a true statement. Consequently, the system has no solution. The solution set is $\varnothing$, the empty set.

⬤

⊘ Check Point **1**  Use Gaussian elimination to solve the system:

$$\begin{cases} x - 2y - z = -5 \\ 2x - 3y - z = 0 \\ 3x - 4y - z = 1. \end{cases}$$

Recall that the graph of a system of three linear equations in three variables consists of three planes. When these planes intersect in a single point, the system has precisely one ordered-triple solution. When the planes have no point in common, the system has no solution, like the one in Example 1. **Figure 8.1** illustrates some of the geometric possibilities for these inconsistent systems.

Three planes are parallel with no common intersection point.

Two planes are parallel with no common intersection point.

Planes intersect two at a time. There is no intersection point common to all three planes.

**Figure 8.1**  Three planes may have no common point of intersection.

Now let's see what happens when we apply Gaussian elimination to a system with infinitely many solutions. Representing the solution set for these systems can be a bit tricky.

> **EXAMPLE 2** A System with an Infinite Number of Solutions

Use Gaussian elimination to solve the following system:

$$\begin{cases} 3x - 4y + 4z = 7 \\ x - y - 2z = 2 \\ 2x - 3y + 6z = 5. \end{cases}$$

**Solution** As always, we start with the augmented matrix.

$$\begin{bmatrix} 3 & -4 & 4 & | & 7 \\ 1 & -1 & -2 & | & 2 \\ 2 & -3 & 6 & | & 5 \end{bmatrix} \xrightarrow[\substack{\text{Interchange rows} \\ \text{1 and 2.}}]{R_1 \leftrightarrow R_2} \begin{bmatrix} 1 & -1 & -2 & | & 2 \\ 3 & -4 & 4 & | & 7 \\ 2 & -3 & 6 & | & 5 \end{bmatrix} \xrightarrow[\substack{\text{Replace row 3} \\ \text{by } -2R_1 + R_3.}]{\substack{\text{Replace row 2} \\ \text{by } -3R_1 + R_2.}}$$

$$\begin{bmatrix} 1 & -1 & -2 & | & 2 \\ 0 & -1 & 10 & | & 1 \\ 0 & -1 & 10 & | & 1 \end{bmatrix} \xrightarrow[\substack{\text{Multiply row} \\ \text{2 by } -1.}]{-1R_2} \begin{bmatrix} 1 & -1 & -2 & | & 2 \\ 0 & 1 & -10 & | & -1 \\ 0 & -1 & 10 & | & 1 \end{bmatrix} \xrightarrow[\substack{\text{Replace row 3} \\ \text{by } 1R_2 + R_3.}]{}$$

$$\begin{bmatrix} 1 & -1 & -2 & | & 2 \\ 0 & 1 & -10 & | & -1 \\ 0 & 0 & 0 & | & 0 \end{bmatrix}$$

If we translate row 3 of the matrix into equation form, we obtain

$$0x + 0y + 0z = 0$$

or

$$0 = 0.$$

This equation results in a true statement regardless of which values we select for $x, y,$ and $z$. Consequently, the equation $0x + 0y + 0z = 0$ is *dependent* on the other two equations in the system in the sense that it adds no new information about the variables. Thus, we can drop it from the system, which can now be expressed in the form

$$\begin{bmatrix} 1 & -1 & -2 & | & 2 \\ 0 & 1 & -10 & | & -1 \end{bmatrix}.$$  This is the last matrix from above with row 3 omitted.

The original system is equivalent to the system

$$\begin{cases} x - y - 2z = 2 \\ y - 10z = -1. \end{cases}$$  This is the system represented by the above matrix.

Although neither of these equations gives a value for $z$, we can use them to express $x$ and $y$ in terms of $z$. From the last equation, we obtain

$$y = 10z - 1.$$  Add 10z to both sides and isolate y.

Back-substituting for $y$ into the first equation obtained from the final matrix, we can find $x$ in terms of $z$.

$$x - y - 2z = 2$$  This is the first equation obtained from the final matrix.

$$x - (10z - 1) - 2z = 2$$  Because y = 10z − 1, substitute 10z − 1 for y.

$$x - 10z + 1 - 2z = 2$$  Apply the distributive property.

$$x - 12z + 1 = 2$$  Combine like terms.

$$x = 12z + 1$$  Solve for x in terms of z.

We have now found two equations expressing $x$ and $y$ in terms of $z$:

$$x = 12z + 1$$
$$y = 10z - 1.$$

Because no value is determined for $z$, we can find a solution of the system by letting $z$ equal any real number and then using these equations to obtain $x$ and $y$. For example, if $z = 1$, then

$$x = 12z + 1 = 12(1) + 1 = 13 \text{ and}$$
$$y = 10z - 1 = 10(1) - 1 = 9.$$

Consequently, (13, 9, 1) is a solution of the system. On the other hand, if we let $z = -1$, then

$$x = 12z + 1 = 12(-1) + 1 = -11 \text{ and}$$
$$y = 10z - 1 = 10(-1) - 1 = -11.$$

Thus, $(-11, -11, -1)$ is another solution of the system.

We see that for any arbitrary choice of $z$, every ordered triple of the form $(12z + 1, 10z - 1, z)$ is a solution of the system. The solution set of this system with dependent equations is

$$\{(12z + 1, 10z - 1, z)\}.$$

We have seen that when three planes have no point in common, the corresponding system has no solution. When the system has infinitely many solutions, like the one in Example 2, the three planes intersect in more than one point. **Figure 8.2** illustrates geometric possibilities for systems with dependent equations.

The planes intersect
along a common line.

The planes coincide.

**Figure 8.2** Three planes may intersect at infinitely many points.

Check Point **2** Use Gaussian elimination to solve the following system:

$$\begin{cases} x - 2y - z = 5 \\ 2x - 5y + 3z = 6 \\ x - 3y + 4z = 1. \end{cases}$$

**2** Apply Gaussian elimination to systems with more variables than equations.

## Nonsquare Systems

Up to this point, we have encountered only *square* systems in which the number of equations is equal to the number of variables. In a **nonsquare system**, the number of variables differs from the number of equations. In Example 3, we have two equations and three variables.

**EXAMPLE 3** **A System with Fewer Equations Than Variables**

Use Gaussian elimination to solve the system:

$$\begin{cases} 3x + 7y + 6z = 26 \\ x + 2y + z = 8. \end{cases}$$

**Solution** We begin with the augmented matrix.

$$\begin{bmatrix} 3 & 7 & 6 & | & 26 \\ 1 & 2 & 1 & | & 8 \end{bmatrix} \xrightarrow{R_1 \leftrightarrow R_2} \begin{bmatrix} 1 & 2 & 1 & | & 8 \\ 3 & 7 & 6 & | & 26 \end{bmatrix} \xrightarrow[\text{by } -3R_1 + R_2.]{\text{Replace row 2}} \begin{bmatrix} 1 & 2 & 1 & | & 8 \\ 0 & 1 & 3 & | & 2 \end{bmatrix}$$

Because the matrix $\begin{bmatrix} 1 & 2 & 1 & 8 \\ 0 & 1 & 3 & 2 \end{bmatrix}$ has 1s down the diagonal that begins with the upper-left entry and a 0 below the leading 1, we translate this matrix back into equation form.

$$\begin{cases} x + 2y + z = 8 & \text{Equation 1} \\ y + 3z = 2 & \text{Equation 2} \end{cases}$$

We can let $z$ equal any real number and use back-substitution to express $x$ and $y$ in terms of $z$.

**Equation 2**

$$y + 3z = 2$$
$$y = -3z + 2$$

**Equation 1**

$$x + 2y + z = 8$$
$$x + 2(-3z + 2) + z = 8$$
$$x - 6z + 4 + z = 8$$
$$x - 5z + 4 = 8$$
$$x = 5z + 4$$

For any arbitrary choice of $z$, every ordered triple of the form $(5z + 4, -3z + 2, z)$ is a solution of the system. We can express the system's solution set as

$$\{(5z + 4, -3z + 2, z)\}.$$

⬤ Check Point **3** Use Gaussian elimination to solve the system:

$$\begin{cases} x + 2y + 3z = 70 \\ x + y + z = 60. \end{cases}$$

**③** Solve problems involving systems without unique solutions.

## Applications

How will computers be programmed to control traffic flow and avoid congestion? They will be required to solve systems continually based on the following premise: If traffic is to keep moving, during any period of time the number of cars entering an intersection must equal the number of cars leaving that intersection. Let's see what this means by looking at the intersections of four one-way city streets.

( **EXAMPLE 4** ) **Traffic Control**

**Figure 8.3** shows the intersections of four one-way streets. As you study the figure, notice that 300 cars per hour want to enter intersection $I_1$ from the north on 27th Avenue. Also, 200 cars per hour want to head east from intersection $I_2$ on Palm Drive. The letters $w$, $x$, $y$, and $z$ stand for the number of cars passing between the intersections.

**a.** If the traffic is to keep moving, at each intersection the number of cars entering per hour must equal the number of cars leaving per hour. Use this idea to set up a linear system of equations involving $w$, $x$, $y$, and $z$.

**b.** Use Gaussian elimination to solve the system.

**c.** If construction on 27th Avenue limits $z$ to 50 cars per hour, how many cars per hour must pass between the other intersections to keep traffic flowing?

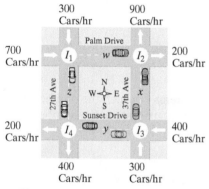

**Figure 8.3** The intersections of four one-way streets

**Solution**

**a.** Set up the system by considering one intersection at a time, referring to **Figure 8.3**.

For Intersection $I_1$: Because $300 + 700 = 1000$ cars enter $I_1$ and $w + z$ cars leave the intersection, then $w + z = 1000$.

For Intersection $I_2$: Because $w + x$ cars enter the intersection and $200 + 900 = 1100$ cars leave $I_2$, then $w + x = 1100$.

For Intersection $I_3$: **Figure 8.3** indicates that $300 + 400 = 700$ cars enter and $x + y$ leave, so $x + y = 700$.

For Intersection $I_4$: With $y + z$ cars entering and $200 + 400 = 600$ cars exiting, traffic will keep flowing if $y + z = 600$.

The system of equations that models this situation is given by

$$\begin{cases} w + z = 1000 \\ w + x = 1100 \\ x + y = 700 \\ y + z = 600. \end{cases}$$

**b.** To solve this system using Gaussian elimination, we begin with the augmented matrix.

**System of Linear Equations (showing missing variables with 0 coefficients)**

$$\begin{cases} 1w + 0x + 0y + 1z = 1000 \\ 1w + 1x + 0y + 0z = 1100 \\ 0w + 1x + 1y + 0z = 700 \\ 0w + 0x + 1y + 1z = 600 \end{cases}$$

**Augmented Matrix**

$$\begin{bmatrix} 1 & 0 & 0 & 1 & | & 1000 \\ 1 & 1 & 0 & 0 & | & 1100 \\ 0 & 1 & 1 & 0 & | & 700 \\ 0 & 0 & 1 & 1 & | & 600 \end{bmatrix}$$

We can now use row operations to obtain the following matrix:

$$\begin{bmatrix} 1 & 0 & 0 & 1 & | & 1000 \\ 0 & 1 & 0 & -1 & | & 100 \\ 0 & 0 & 1 & 1 & | & 600 \\ 0 & 0 & 0 & 0 & | & 0 \end{bmatrix}.$$

$w + z = 1000$

$x - z = 100$

$y + z = 600$

The last row of the matrix shows that the system in the voice balloons has dependent equations and infinitely many solutions. To write the solution set containing these infinitely many solutions, let $z$ equal any real number. Use the three equations in the voice balloons to express $w$, $x$, and $y$ in terms of $z$:

$$w = 1000 - z, \quad x = 100 + z, \quad \text{and} \quad y = 600 - z.$$

With $z$ arbitrary, the alphabetically ordered solution $(w, x, y, z)$ enables us to express the system's solution set as

$$\{(1000 - z, 100 + z, 600 - z, z)\}.$$

**c.** We are given that construction limits $z$ to 50 cars per hour. Because $z = 50$, we substitute 50 for $z$ in the system's ordered solution:

$$(1000 - z, 100 + z, 600 - z, z)$$  Use the system's solution.

$$= (1000 - 50, 100 + 50, 600 - 50, 50)$$  $z = 50$

$$= (950, 150, 550, 50).$$

Thus, $w = 950$, $x = 150$, and $y = 550$. (See **Figure 8.4**.) With construction on 27th Avenue, this means that to keep traffic flowing, 950 cars per hour must be routed between $I_1$ and $I_2$, 150 per hour between $I_3$ and $I_2$, and 550 per hour between $I_3$ and $I_4$. ●

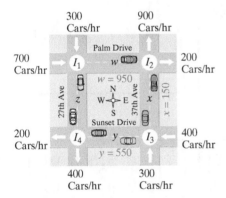

**Figure 8.4** With $z$ limited to 50 cars per hour, values for $w$, $x$, and $y$ are determined.

✔ Check Point **4** **Figure 8.5** shows a system of four one-way streets. The numbers in the figure denote the number of cars per minute that travel in the direction shown.

**a.** Use the requirement that the number of cars entering each of the intersections per minute must equal the number of cars leaving per minute to set up a system of equations in $w$, $x$, $y$, and $z$.

**b.** Use Gaussian elimination to solve the system.

**c.** If construction limits $z$ to 10 cars per minute, how many cars per minute must pass between the other intersections to keep traffic flowing?

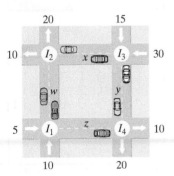

**Figure 8.5**

# Exercise Set 8.2

## Practice Exercises

*In Exercises 1–24, use Gaussian elimination to find the complete solution to each system of equations, or show that none exists.*

**1.** $\begin{cases} 5x + 12y + z = 10 \\ 2x + 5y + 2z = -1 \\ x + 2y - 3z = 5 \end{cases}$

**2.** $\begin{cases} 2x - 4y + z = 3 \\ x - 3y + z = 5 \\ 3x - 7y + 2z = 12 \end{cases}$

**3.** $\begin{cases} 5x + 8y - 6z = 14 \\ 3x + 4y - 2z = 8 \\ x + 2y - 2z = 3 \end{cases}$

**4.** $\begin{cases} 5x - 11y + 6z = 12 \\ -x + 3y - 2z = -4 \\ 3x - 5y + 2z = 4 \end{cases}$

**5.** $\begin{cases} 3x + 4y + 2z = 3 \\ 4x - 2y - 8z = -4 \\ x + y - z = 3 \end{cases}$

**6.** $\begin{cases} 2x - y - z = 0 \\ x + 2y + z = 3 \\ 3x + 4y + 2z = 8 \end{cases}$

**7.** $\begin{cases} 8x + 5y + 11z = 30 \\ -x - 4y + 2z = 3 \\ 2x - y + 5z = 12 \end{cases}$

**8.** $\begin{cases} x + y - 10z = -4 \\ x - 7z = -5 \\ 3x + 5y - 36z = -10 \end{cases}$

**9.** $\begin{cases} w - 2x - y - 3z = -9 \\ w + x - y = 0 \\ 3w + 4x + z = 6 \\ 2x - 2y + z = 3 \end{cases}$

**10.** $\begin{cases} 2w + x - 2y - z = 3 \\ w - 2x + y + z = 4 \\ -w - 8x + 7y + 5z = 13 \\ 3w + x - 2y + 2z = 6 \end{cases}$

**11.** $\begin{cases} 2w + x - y = 3 \\ w - 3x + 2y = -4 \\ 3w + x - 3y + z = 1 \\ w + 2x - 4y - z = -2 \end{cases}$

**12.** $\begin{cases} 2w - x + 3y + z = 0 \\ 3w + 2x + 4y - z = 0 \\ 5w - 2x - 2y - z = 0 \\ 2w + 3x - 7y - 5z = 0 \end{cases}$

**13.** $\begin{cases} w - 3x + y - 4z = 4 \\ -2w + x + 2y = -2 \\ 3w - 2x + y - 6z = 2 \\ -w + 3x + 2y - z = -6 \end{cases}$

**14.** $\begin{cases} 3w + 2x - y + 2z = -12 \\ 4w - x + y + 2z = 1 \\ w + x + y + z = -2 \\ -2w + 3x + 2y - 3z = 10 \end{cases}$

**15.** $\begin{cases} 2x + y - z = 2 \\ 3x + 3y - 2z = 3 \end{cases}$

**16.** $\begin{cases} 3x + 2y - z = 5 \\ x + 2y - z = 1 \end{cases}$

**17.** $\begin{cases} x + 2y + 3z = 5 \\ y - 5z = 0 \end{cases}$

**18.** $\begin{cases} 3x - y + 4z = 8 \\ y + 2z = 1 \end{cases}$

**19.** $\begin{cases} x + y - 2z = 2 \\ 3x - y - 6z = -7 \end{cases}$

**20.** $\begin{cases} -2x - 5y + 10z = 19 \\ x + 2y - 4z = 12 \end{cases}$

**21.** $\begin{cases} w + x - y + z = -2 \\ 2w - x + 2y - z = 7 \\ -w + 2x + y + 2z = -1 \end{cases}$

**22.** $\begin{cases} 2w - 3x + 4y + z = 7 \\ w - x + 3y - 5z = 10 \\ 3w + x - 2y - 2z = 6 \end{cases}$

**23.** $\begin{cases} w + 2x + 3y - z = 7 \\ 2x - 3y + z = 4 \\ w - 4x + y = 3 \end{cases}$

**24.** $\begin{cases} w - x + z = 0 \\ w - 4x + y + 2z = 0 \\ 3w - y + 2z = 0 \end{cases}$

## Practice Plus

*In Exercises 25–28, the first screen shows the augmented matrix, A, for a nonsquare linear system of three equations in four variables, w, x, y, and z. The second screen shows the reduced row-echelon form of matrix A. For each exercise,*

  **a.** Write the system represented by A.

  **b.** Use the reduced row-echelon form of A to find the system's complete solution.

**25.**

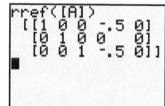

**26.**

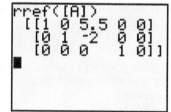

**27.**

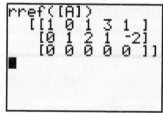

**28.**

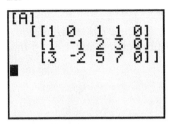 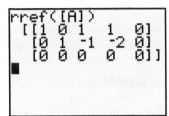

## Application Exercises

*The figure for Exercises 29–32 shows the intersections of three one-way streets. To keep traffic moving, the number of cars per minute entering an intersection must equal the number exiting that intersection. For intersection $I_1$, $x + 10$ cars enter and $y + 14$ cars exit per minute. Thus, $x + 10 = y + 14$.*

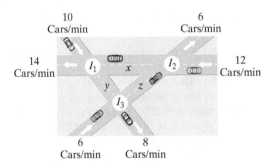

**29.** Write an equation for intersection $I_2$ that keeps traffic moving.

**30.** Write an equation for intersection $I_3$ that keeps traffic moving.

**31.** Use Gaussian elimination to solve the system formed by the equation given prior to Exercise 29 and the two equations that you obtained in Exercises 29–30.

**32.** Use your ordered solution obtained in Exercise 31 to solve this exercise. If construction limits $z$ to 4 cars per minute, how many cars per minute must pass between the other intersections to keep traffic flowing?

**33.** The figure shows the intersections of four one-way streets.

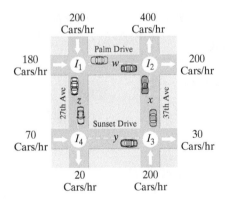

**a.** Set up a system of equations that keeps traffic moving.

**b.** Use Gaussian elimination to solve the system.

**c.** If construction limits $z$ to 50 cars per hour, how many cars per hour must pass between the other intersections to keep traffic moving?

**34.** The vitamin content per ounce for three foods is given in the following table.

| | Milligrams per Ounce | | |
| --- | --- | --- | --- |
| | Thiamin | Riboflavin | Niacin |
| **Food A** | 3 | 7 | 1 |
| **Food B** | 1 | 5 | 3 |
| **Food C** | 3 | 8 | 2 |

**a.** Use matrices to show that no combination of these foods can provide exactly 14 mg of thiamin, 32 mg of riboflavin, and 9 mg of niacin.

**b.** Use matrices to describe in practical terms what happens if the riboflavin requirement is increased by 5 mg and the other requirements stay the same.

**35.** Three foods have the following nutritional content per ounce.

| | Units per Ounce | | |
| --- | --- | --- | --- |
| | Vitamin A | Iron | Calcium |
| **Food 1** | 20 | 20 | 10 |
| **Food 2** | 30 | 10 | 10 |
| **Food 3** | 10 | 10 | 30 |

**a.** A diet must consist precisely of 220 units of vitamin A, 180 units of iron, and 340 units of calcium. However, the dietician runs out of Food 1. Use a matrix approach to show that under these conditions the dietary requirements cannot be met.

**b.** Now suppose that all three foods are available. Use matrices to give two possible ways to meet the iron and calcium requirements with the three foods.

**36.** A company that manufactures products $A$, $B$, and $C$ does both manufacturing and testing. The hours needed to manufacture and test each product are shown in the table.

| | Hours Needed Weekly to Manufacture | Hours Needed Weekly to Test |
| --- | --- | --- |
| **Product A** | 7 | 2 |
| **Product B** | 6 | 2 |
| **Product C** | 3 | 1 |

The company has exactly 67 hours per week available for manufacturing and 20 hours per week available for testing. Give two different combinations for the number of products that can be manufactured and tested weekly.

## Writing in Mathematics

**37.** Describe what happens when Gaussian elimination is used to solve an inconsistent system.

**38.** Describe what happens when Gaussian elimination is used to solve a system with dependent equations.

**39.** In solving a system of dependent equations in three variables, one student simply said that there are infinitely many solutions. A second student expressed the solution set as $\{(4z + 3, 5z - 1, z)\}$. Which is the better form of expressing the solution set and why?

## Technology Exercise

**40. a.** The figure shows the intersections of a number of one-way streets. The numbers given represent traffic flow at a peak period (from 4 P.M. to 5:30 P.M.). Use the figure to write a linear system of six equations in seven variables based on the idea that at each intersection the number of cars entering must equal the number of cars leaving.

**b.** Use a graphing utility with a | REF | or | RREF | command to find the complete solution to the system.

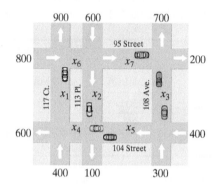

## Critical Thinking Exercises

**Make Sense?** *In Exercises 41–44, determine whether each statement makes sense or does not make sense, and explain your reasoning.*

**41.** I omitted row 3 from $\begin{bmatrix} 1 & -1 & -2 & | & 2 \\ 0 & 1 & -10 & | & -1 \\ 0 & 0 & 0 & | & 5 \end{bmatrix}$ and expressed

the system in the form $\begin{bmatrix} 1 & -1 & -2 & | & 2 \\ 0 & 1 & -10 & | & -1 \end{bmatrix}$.

**42.** I omitted row 3 from $\begin{bmatrix} 1 & -1 & -2 & | & 2 \\ 0 & 1 & -10 & | & -1 \\ 0 & 0 & 0 & | & 0 \end{bmatrix}$ and expressed

the system in the form $\begin{bmatrix} 1 & -1 & -2 & | & 2 \\ 0 & 1 & -10 & | & -1 \end{bmatrix}$.

**43.** I solved a nonsquare system in which the number of equations was the same as the number of variables.

**44.** Models for controlling traffic flow are based on an equal number of cars entering an intersection and leaving that intersection.

**45.** Consider the linear system

$$x + 3y + \quad z = \quad a^2$$
$$2x + 5y + 2az = \quad 0$$
$$x + \quad y + a^2z = -9.$$

For which values of $a$ will the system be inconsistent?

## Group Exercise

**46.** Before beginning this exercise, the group needs to read and solve Exercise 40.

**a.** A political group is planning a demonstration on 95th Street between 113th Place and 117th Court for 5 P.M. Wednesday. The problem becomes one of minimizing traffic flow on 95th Street (between 113th and 117th) without causing traffic tie-ups on other streets. One possible solution is to close off traffic on 95th Street between 113th and 117th (let $x_6 = 0$). What can group members conclude about $x_7$ under these conditions?

**b.** Working with a matrix allows us to simplify the problem caused by the political demonstration, but it did not actually solve the problem. There are an infinite number of solutions; each value of $x_7$ we choose gives us a new picture. We also assumed $x_6$ was equal to 0; changing that assumption would also lead to different solutions. With your group, design another solution to the traffic flow problem caused by the political demonstration.

## Preview Exercises

*Exercises 47–49 will help you prepare for the material covered in the next section. In each exercise, perform the indicated operation or operations.*

**47.** $-6 - (-5)$

**48.** $1(-4) + 2(5) + 3(-6)$

**49.** $\frac{1}{2}[8 - (-8)]$

## Section 8.3 Matrix Operations and Their Applications

### Objectives

1. Use matrix notation.
2. Understand what is meant by equal matrices.
3. Add and subtract matrices.
4. Perform scalar multiplication.
5. Solve matrix equations.
6. Multiply matrices.
7. Model applied situations with matrix operations.

Turn on your computer and read your e-mail or write a paper. When you need to do research, use the Internet to browse through art museums and photography exhibits. When you need a break, load a flight simulator program and fly through a photorealistic computer world. As different as these experiences may be, they all share one thing—you're looking at images based on matrices. Matrices have applications in numerous fields, including the new technology of digital photography in which pictures are represented by numbers rather than film. In this section, we turn our attention to matrix algebra and some of its applications.

1. Use matrix notation.

### Notations for Matrices

We have seen that an array of numbers, arranged in rows and columns and placed in brackets, is called a matrix. We can represent a matrix in two different ways.

- A capital letter, such as $A$, $B$, or $C$, can denote a matrix.
- A lowercase letter enclosed in brackets, such as that shown below, can denote a matrix.

$$A = [a_{ij}]$$ Matrix $A$ with elements $a_{ij}$

A general element in matrix $A$ is denoted by $a_{ij}$. This refers to the element in the $i$th row and $j$th column. For example, $a_{32}$ is the element of $A$ located in the third row, second column.

A matrix of **order $m \times n$** has $m$ rows and $n$ columns. If $m = n$, a matrix has the same number of rows as columns and is called a **square matrix.**

### EXAMPLE 1 Matrix Notation

Let

$$A = \begin{bmatrix} 3 & 2 & 0 \\ -4 & -5 & -\frac{1}{5} \end{bmatrix}.$$

**a.** What is the order of $A$?

**b.** If $A = [a_{ij}]$, identify $a_{23}$ and $a_{12}$.

### Solution

**a.** The matrix has 2 rows and 3 columns, so it is of order $2 \times 3$.

**b.** The element $a_{23}$ is in the second row and third column. Thus, $a_{23} = -\frac{1}{5}$. The element $a_{12}$ is in the first row and second column. Consequently, $a_{12} = 2$.

⊘ Check Point **|** Let

$$A = \begin{bmatrix} 5 & -2 \\ -3 & \pi \\ 1 & 6 \end{bmatrix}.$$

**a.** What is the order of $A$?     **b.** Identify $a_{12}$ and $a_{31}$.

---

**②** Understand what is meant by equal matrices.

## Equality of Matrices

Two matrices are **equal** if and only if they have the same order and corresponding elements are equal.

### Definition of Equality of Matrices

Two matrices $A$ and $B$ are **equal** if and only if they have the same order $m \times n$ and $a_{ij} = b_{ij}$ for $i = 1, 2, \ldots, m$ and $j = 1, 2, \ldots, n$.

For example, if $A = \begin{bmatrix} x & y+1 \\ z & 6 \end{bmatrix}$ and $B = \begin{bmatrix} 1 & 5 \\ 3 & 6 \end{bmatrix}$, then $A = B$ if and only if $x = 1$, $y + 1 = 5$ (so $y = 4$), and $z = 3$.

---

**③** Add and subtract matrices.

## Matrix Addition and Subtraction

**Table 8.1** shows that matrices of the same order can be added or subtracted by simply adding or subtracting corresponding elements.

### Table 8.1    Adding and Subtracting Matrices

Let $A = [a_{ij}]$ and $B = [b_{ij}]$ be matrices of order $m \times n$.

| Definition | The Definition in Words | Example |
|---|---|---|
| *Matrix Addition* <br><br> $A + B = [a_{ij} + b_{ij}]$ | Matrices of the same order are added by adding the elements in corresponding positions. | $\begin{bmatrix} 1 & -2 \\ 3 & 5 \end{bmatrix} + \begin{bmatrix} -1 & 6 \\ 0 & 4 \end{bmatrix}$ <br><br> $= \begin{bmatrix} 1+(-1) & -2+6 \\ 3+0 & 5+4 \end{bmatrix} = \begin{bmatrix} 0 & 4 \\ 3 & 9 \end{bmatrix}$ |
| *Matrix Subtraction* <br><br> $A - B = [a_{ij} - b_{ij}]$ | Matrices of the same order are subtracted by subtracting the elements in corresponding positions. | $\begin{bmatrix} 1 & -2 \\ 3 & 5 \end{bmatrix} - \begin{bmatrix} -1 & 6 \\ 0 & 4 \end{bmatrix}$ <br><br> $= \begin{bmatrix} 1-(-1) & -2-6 \\ 3-0 & 5-4 \end{bmatrix} = \begin{bmatrix} 2 & -8 \\ 3 & 1 \end{bmatrix}$ |

The sum or difference of two matrices of different orders is undefined. For example, consider the matrices

$$A = \begin{bmatrix} 0 & 3 \\ 4 & 3 \end{bmatrix} \quad \text{and} \quad B = \begin{bmatrix} 1 & 9 \\ 4 & 5 \\ 2 & 3 \end{bmatrix}.$$

The order of $A$ is $2 \times 2$; the order of $B$ is $3 \times 2$. These matrices are of different orders and cannot be added or subtracted.

**EXAMPLE 2** Adding and Subtracting Matrices

Perform the indicated matrix operations:

**a.** $\begin{bmatrix} 0 & 5 & 3 \\ -2 & 6 & -8 \end{bmatrix} + \begin{bmatrix} -2 & 3 & 5 \\ 7 & -9 & 6 \end{bmatrix}$

**b.** $\begin{bmatrix} -6 & 7 \\ 2 & -3 \end{bmatrix} - \begin{bmatrix} -5 & 6 \\ 0 & -4 \end{bmatrix}.$

**Solution**

**a.**

$$\begin{bmatrix} 0 & 5 & 3 \\ -2 & 6 & -8 \end{bmatrix} + \begin{bmatrix} -2 & 3 & 5 \\ 7 & -9 & 6 \end{bmatrix}$$

$$= \begin{bmatrix} 0 + (-2) & 5 + 3 & 3 + 5 \\ -2 + 7 & 6 + (-9) & -8 + 6 \end{bmatrix} \quad \text{Add the corresponding elements in the 2 × 3 matrices.}$$

$$= \begin{bmatrix} -2 & 8 & 8 \\ 5 & -3 & -2 \end{bmatrix} \quad \text{Simplify.}$$

**b.**

$$\begin{bmatrix} -6 & 7 \\ 2 & -3 \end{bmatrix} - \begin{bmatrix} -5 & 6 \\ 0 & -4 \end{bmatrix}$$

$$= \begin{bmatrix} -6 - (-5) & 7 - 6 \\ 2 - 0 & -3 - (-4) \end{bmatrix} \quad \text{Subtract the corresponding elements in the 2 × 2 matrices.}$$

$$= \begin{bmatrix} -1 & 1 \\ 2 & 1 \end{bmatrix} \quad \text{Simplify.}$$

**⊘ Check Point 2** Perform the indicated matrix operations:

**a.** $\begin{bmatrix} -4 & 3 \\ 7 & -6 \end{bmatrix} + \begin{bmatrix} 6 & -3 \\ 2 & -4 \end{bmatrix}$ **b.** $\begin{bmatrix} 5 & 4 \\ -3 & 7 \\ 0 & 1 \end{bmatrix} - \begin{bmatrix} -4 & 8 \\ 6 & 0 \\ -5 & 3 \end{bmatrix}.$

A matrix whose elements are all equal to 0 is called a **zero matrix**. If $A$ is an $m \times n$ matrix and 0 is the $m \times n$ zero matrix, then $A + 0 = A$. For example,

$$\begin{bmatrix} -5 & 2 \\ 3 & 6 \end{bmatrix} + \begin{bmatrix} 0 & 0 \\ 0 & 0 \end{bmatrix} = \begin{bmatrix} -5 & 2 \\ 3 & 6 \end{bmatrix}.$$

The $m \times n$ zero matrix is called the **additive identity** for $m \times n$ matrices.

For any matrix $A$, the **additive inverse** of $A$, written $-A$, is the matrix with the same order as $A$ such that every element of $-A$ is the opposite of the corresponding element of $A$. Because corresponding elements are added in matrix addition, $A + (-A)$ is a zero matrix. For example,

$$\begin{bmatrix} -5 & 2 \\ 3 & 6 \end{bmatrix} + \begin{bmatrix} 5 & -2 \\ -3 & -6 \end{bmatrix} = \begin{bmatrix} 0 & 0 \\ 0 & 0 \end{bmatrix}.$$

Properties of matrix addition are similar to properties for adding real numbers.

### Properties of Matrix Addition

If $A$, $B$, and $C$ are $m \times n$ matrices and 0 is the $m \times n$ zero matrix, then the following properties are true.

1. $A + B = B + A$ — Commutative property of addition
2. $(A + B) + C = A + (B + C)$ — Associative property of addition
3. $A + 0 = 0 + A = A$ — Additive identity property
4. $A + (-A) = (-A) + A = 0$ — Additive inverse property

④ Perform scalar multiplication.

## Scalar Multiplication

A matrix of order $1 \times 1$, such as [6], contains only one entry. To distinguish this matrix from the number 6, we refer to 6 as a **scalar**. In general, in our work with matrices, we will refer to real numbers as scalars.

To multiply a matrix $A$ by a scalar $c$, we multiply each entry in $A$ by $c$. For example,

$$\underset{\text{Scalar}}{4} \underset{\text{Matrix}}{\begin{bmatrix} 2 & 5 \\ -3 & 0 \end{bmatrix}} = \begin{bmatrix} 4(2) & 4(5) \\ 4(-3) & 4(0) \end{bmatrix} = \begin{bmatrix} 8 & 20 \\ -12 & 0 \end{bmatrix}.$$

### Definition of Scalar Multiplication

If $A = [a_{ij}]$ is a matrix of order $m \times n$ and $c$ is a scalar, then the matrix $cA$ is the $m \times n$ matrix given by

$$cA = [ca_{ij}].$$

This matrix is obtained by multiplying each element of $A$ by the real number $c$. We call $cA$ a **scalar multiple** of $A$.

**EXAMPLE 3** Scalar Multiplication

If $A = \begin{bmatrix} -1 & 4 \\ 3 & 0 \end{bmatrix}$ and $B = \begin{bmatrix} 2 & -3 \\ 5 & -6 \end{bmatrix}$, find the following matrices:

**a.** $-5B$      **b.** $2A + 3B$.

**Solution**

**a.** $-5B = -5 \begin{bmatrix} 2 & -3 \\ 5 & -6 \end{bmatrix} = \begin{bmatrix} -5(2) & -5(-3) \\ -5(5) & -5(-6) \end{bmatrix} = \begin{bmatrix} -10 & 15 \\ -25 & 30 \end{bmatrix}$

Multiply each element by −5.

### Technology

You can verify the algebraic solution in Example 3(b) by first entering the matrices [A] and [B] into your graphing utility. The screen below shows the required computation.

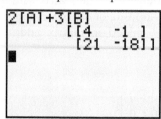

```
2[A]+3[B]
        [[4   -1 ]
         [21  -18]]
■
```

**b.** $2A + 3B = 2\begin{bmatrix} -1 & 4 \\ 3 & 0 \end{bmatrix} + 3\begin{bmatrix} 2 & -3 \\ 5 & -6 \end{bmatrix}$

$= \begin{bmatrix} 2(-1) & 2(4) \\ 2(3) & 2(0) \end{bmatrix} + \begin{bmatrix} 3(2) & 3(-3) \\ 3(5) & 3(-6) \end{bmatrix}$

Multiply each element in $A$ by 2.     Multiply each element in $B$ by 3.

$= \begin{bmatrix} -2 & 8 \\ 6 & 0 \end{bmatrix} + \begin{bmatrix} 6 & -9 \\ 15 & -18 \end{bmatrix} = \begin{bmatrix} -2 + 6 & 8 + (-9) \\ 6 + 15 & 0 + (-18) \end{bmatrix}$

Perform the addition of these 2 x 2 matrices by adding corresponding elements.

$= \begin{bmatrix} 4 & -1 \\ 21 & -18 \end{bmatrix}$

☑ Check Point **3** If $A = \begin{bmatrix} -4 & 1 \\ 3 & 0 \end{bmatrix}$ and $B = \begin{bmatrix} -1 & -2 \\ 8 & 5 \end{bmatrix}$, find the following matrices:

**a.** $-6B$      **b.** $3A + 2B$.

## Discovery

Verify each of the four properties listed in the box using

$$A = \begin{bmatrix} 2 & -4 \\ -5 & 3 \end{bmatrix},$$

$$B = \begin{bmatrix} 4 & 0 \\ 1 & -6 \end{bmatrix},$$

$c = 4$, and $d = 2$.

Properties of scalar multiplication are similar to properties for multiplying real numbers.

## Properties of Scalar Multiplication

If $A$ and $B$ are $m \times n$ matrices, and $c$ and $d$ are scalars, then the following properties are true.

**1.** $(cd)A = c(dA)$      Associative property of scalar multiplication

**2.** $1A = A$      Scalar identity property

**3.** $c(A + B) = cA + cB$      Distributive property

**4.** $(c + d)A = cA + dA$      Distributive property

**⑤** Solve matrix equations.

Have you noticed the many similarities between addition of real numbers and matrix addition, subtraction of real numbers and matrix subtraction, and multiplication of real numbers and scalar multiplication? Example 4 shows how these similarities can be used to solve matrix equations involving matrix addition, matrix subtraction, and scalar multiplication.

**EXAMPLE 4**    Solving a Matrix Equation

Solve for $X$ in the matrix equation

$$2X + A = B,$$

where $A = \begin{bmatrix} 1 & -5 \\ 0 & 2 \end{bmatrix}$ and $B = \begin{bmatrix} -6 & 5 \\ 9 & 1 \end{bmatrix}$.

**Solution**    We begin by solving the matrix equation for $X$.

$$2X + A = B$$      This is the given matrix equation.

$$2X = B - A$$      Subtract matrix A from both sides.

> We multiply both sides by $\frac{1}{2}$ rather than divide both sides by 2. This is in anticipation of performing scalar multiplication.

$$X = \frac{1}{2}(B - A)$$      Multiply both sides by $\frac{1}{2}$ and solve for matrix X.

Now we use the matrices $A$ and $B$ to find the matrix $X$.

$$X = \frac{1}{2}\left( \begin{bmatrix} -6 & 5 \\ 9 & 1 \end{bmatrix} - \begin{bmatrix} 1 & -5 \\ 0 & 2 \end{bmatrix} \right)$$      Substitute the matrices into $X = \frac{1}{2}(B - A)$.

$$= \frac{1}{2}\begin{bmatrix} -7 & 10 \\ 9 & -1 \end{bmatrix}$$      Subtract matrices by subtracting corresponding elements.

$$= \begin{bmatrix} -\dfrac{7}{2} & 5 \\ \dfrac{9}{2} & -\dfrac{1}{2} \end{bmatrix}$$      Perform the scalar multiplication by multiplying each element by $\frac{1}{2}$.

Take a few minutes to show that this matrix satisfies the given equation $2X + A = B$. Substitute the matrix for $X$ and the given matrices for $A$ and $B$ into the equation. The matrices on each side of the equal sign, $2X + A$ and $B$, should be equal. ⬤

⊘ Check Point **4** Solve for $X$ in the matrix equation $3X + A = B$, where

$$A = \begin{bmatrix} 2 & -8 \\ 0 & 4 \end{bmatrix} \quad \text{and} \quad B = \begin{bmatrix} -10 & 1 \\ -9 & 17 \end{bmatrix}.$$

⑥ Multiply matrices.

## Matrix Multiplication

We do not multiply two matrices by multiplying the corresponding entries of the matrices. Instead, we must think of matrix multiplication as *row-by-column multiplication*. To better understand how this works, let's begin with the definition of matrix multiplication for matrices of order $2 \times 2$.

### Definition of Matrix Multiplication: 2 × 2 Matrices

Row 1 of $A$ × Column 1 of $B$    Row 1 of $A$ × Column 2 of $B$

$$AB = \begin{bmatrix} a & b \\ c & d \end{bmatrix} \begin{bmatrix} e & f \\ g & h \end{bmatrix} = \begin{bmatrix} ae + bg & af + bh \\ ce + dg & cf + dh \end{bmatrix}$$

Row 2 of $A$ × Column 1 of $B$    Row 2 of $A$ × Column 2 of $B$

Notice that we obtain the element in the $i$th row and $j$th column in $AB$ by performing computations with elements in the $i$th row of $A$ and the $j$th column of $B$. For example, we obtain the element in the first row and first column of $AB$ by performing computations with elements in the first row of $A$ and the first column of $B$.

First row of $A$    First column of $B$

$$\begin{bmatrix} a & b \\ & \end{bmatrix} \begin{bmatrix} e \\ g \end{bmatrix} = \begin{bmatrix} ae + bg & \end{bmatrix}$$

1. Multiply each element in row 1 of $A$ by the corresponding element in column 1 of $B$.
2. Add these products.
3. Record the sum as the element in row 1, column 1 of the product matrix.

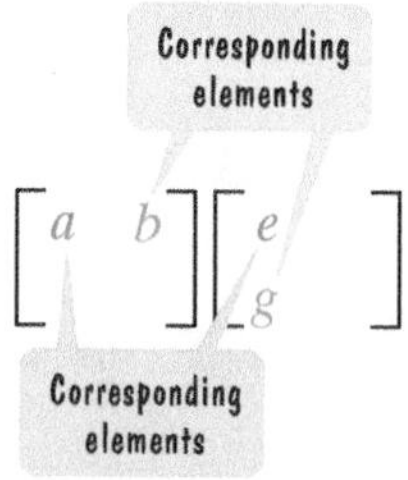

Corresponding elements

$$\begin{bmatrix} a & b \\ & \end{bmatrix} \begin{bmatrix} e \\ g \end{bmatrix}$$

Corresponding elements

**Figure 8.6** Finding corresponding elements when multiplying matrices

You may wonder how to find the corresponding elements in step 1 in the voice balloon. The element at the far left of row 1 corresponds to the element at the top of column 1. The second element from the left of row 1 corresponds to the second element from the top of column 1. This is illustrated in **Figure 8.6**.

(**EXAMPLE 5**) **Multiplying Matrices**

Find $AB$, given

$$A = \begin{bmatrix} 2 & 3 \\ 4 & 7 \end{bmatrix} \quad \text{and} \quad B = \begin{bmatrix} 0 & 1 \\ 5 & 6 \end{bmatrix}.$$

**Solution** We will perform a row-by-column computation.

$$AB = \begin{bmatrix} 2 & 3 \\ 4 & 7 \end{bmatrix} \begin{bmatrix} 0 & 1 \\ 5 & 6 \end{bmatrix}$$

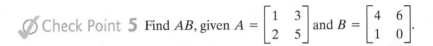

Row 1 of $A$ × Column 1 of $B$    Row 1 of $A$ × Column 2 of $B$

$$= \begin{bmatrix} 2(0) + 3(5) & 2(1) + 3(6) \\ 4(0) + 7(5) & 4(1) + 7(6) \end{bmatrix} = \begin{bmatrix} 15 & 20 \\ 35 & 46 \end{bmatrix}$$

Row 2 of $A$ × Column 1 of $B$    Row 2 of $A$ × Column 2 of $B$

✓ Check Point **5** Find $AB$, given $A = \begin{bmatrix} 1 & 3 \\ 2 & 5 \end{bmatrix}$ and $B = \begin{bmatrix} 4 & 6 \\ 1 & 0 \end{bmatrix}$.

We can generalize the process of Example 5 to multiply an $m \times n$ matrix and an $n \times p$ matrix. **For the product of two matrices to be defined, the number of columns of the first matrix must equal the number of rows of the second matrix.**

**First Matrix**      **Second Matrix**

$m \times n$            $n \times p$

The number of columns in the first matrix must be the same as the number of rows in the second matrix.

**Study Tip**

The following diagram illustrates the first sentence in the box defining matrix multiplication. The diagram is helpful in determining the order of the product $AB$.

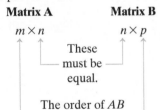

**Matrix A**          **Matrix B**

$m \times n$            $n \times p$

These must be equal.

The order of $AB$ is $m \times p$.

### Definition of Matrix Multiplication

The **product** of an $m \times n$ matrix, $A$, and an $n \times p$ matrix, $B$, is an $m \times p$ matrix, $AB$, whose elements are found as follows: The element in the $i$th row and $j$th column of $AB$ is found by multiplying each element in the $i$th row of $A$ by the corresponding element in the $j$th column of $B$ and adding the products.

To find a product $AB$, each row of $A$ must have the same number of elements as each column of $B$. We obtain $p_{ij}$, the element in the $i$th row and $j$th column in $AB$, by performing computations with elements in the $i$th row of $A$ and the $j$th column of $B$:

$i$th row of $A$    $j$th column of $B$    Element in the $i$th row and $j$th column of $AB$

$$\begin{bmatrix} * & \sqrt{} & \square \end{bmatrix} \begin{bmatrix} * \\ \sqrt{} \\ \square \end{bmatrix} = \begin{bmatrix} p_{ij} \end{bmatrix}.$$

When multiplying corresponding elements, keep in mind that the element at the far left of row $i$ corresponds to the element at the top of column $j$. The element second from the left in row $i$ corresponds to the element second from the top in column $j$. Likewise, the element third from the left in row $i$ corresponds to the element third from the top in column $j$, and so on.

**EXAMPLE 6** Multiplying Matrices

Matrices $A$ and $B$ are defined as follows:

$$A = \begin{bmatrix} 1 & 2 & 3 \end{bmatrix} \quad B = \begin{bmatrix} 4 \\ 5 \\ 6 \end{bmatrix}.$$

Find each product:    **a.** $AB$    **b.** $BA$.

**Solution**

**a.** Matrix $A$ is a $1 \times 3$ matrix and matrix $B$ is a $3 \times 1$ matrix. Thus, the product $AB$ is a $1 \times 1$ matrix.

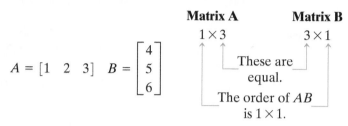

$$AB = \begin{bmatrix} 1 & 2 & 3 \end{bmatrix} \begin{bmatrix} 4 \\ 5 \\ 6 \end{bmatrix}$$   We will perform a row-by-column computation.

$$= [(1)(4) + (2)(5) + (3)(6)]$$   Multiply elements in row 1 of $A$ by corresponding elements in column 1 of $B$ and add the products.

$$= [4 + 10 + 18]$$   Perform the multiplications.

$$= [32]$$   Add.

**b.** Matrix $B$ is a $3 \times 1$ matrix and matrix $A$ is a $1 \times 3$ matrix. Thus, the product $BA$ is a $3 \times 3$ matrix.

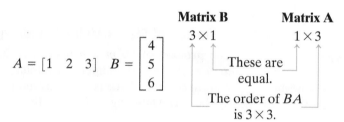

$$BA = \begin{bmatrix} 4 \\ 5 \\ 6 \end{bmatrix} \begin{bmatrix} 1 & 2 & 3 \end{bmatrix}$$   We perform a row-by-column computation.

**Technology**

The screens illustrate the solution of Example 6 using a graphing utility.

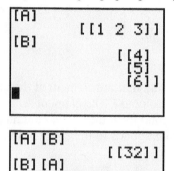

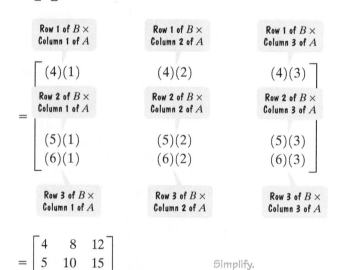

$$= \begin{bmatrix} 4 & 8 & 12 \\ 5 & 10 & 15 \\ 6 & 12 & 18 \end{bmatrix}$$   Simplify.

In Example 6, did you notice that $AB$ and $BA$ are different matrices? For most matrices $A$ and $B$, $AB \neq BA$. Because **matrix multiplication is not commutative**, be careful about the order in which matrices appear when performing this operation.

⊘ Check Point **6** If $A = \begin{bmatrix} 2 & 0 & 4 \end{bmatrix}$ and $B = \begin{bmatrix} 1 \\ 3 \\ 7 \end{bmatrix}$, find $AB$ and $BA$.

**Arthur Cayley**

The Granger Collection

Matrices were first studied intensively by the English mathematician Arthur Cayley (1821–1895). Before reaching the age of 25, he published 25 papers, setting a pattern of prolific creativity that lasted throughout his life. Cayley was a lawyer, painter, mountaineer, and Cambridge professor whose greatest invention was that of matrices and matrix theory. Cayley's matrix algebra, especially the noncommutativity of multiplication ($AB \neq BA$), opened up a new area of mathematics called abstract algebra.

( EXAMPLE 7 ) **Multiplying Matrices**

Where possible, find each product:

**a.** $\begin{bmatrix} 4 & 2 \\ 1 & 3 \end{bmatrix}\begin{bmatrix} 1 & 2 & 3 & 4 \\ 0 & 2 & -1 & 6 \end{bmatrix}$     **b.** $\begin{bmatrix} 1 & 2 & 3 & 4 \\ 0 & 2 & -1 & 6 \end{bmatrix}\begin{bmatrix} 4 & 2 \\ 1 & 3 \end{bmatrix}$.

**Solution**

**a.** The first matrix is a 2 × 2 matrix and the second is a 2 × 4 matrix. The product will be a 2 × 4 matrix.

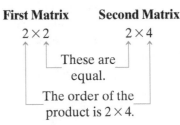

**First Matrix**     **Second Matrix**
$2 \times 2$         $2 \times 4$
These are equal.
The order of the product is $2 \times 4$.

$\begin{bmatrix} 4 & 2 \\ 1 & 3 \end{bmatrix}\begin{bmatrix} 1 & 2 & 3 & 4 \\ 0 & 2 & -1 & 6 \end{bmatrix}$   *We perform a row-by-column computation.*

Row 1 × Column 1   Row 1 × Column 2   Row 1 × Column 3   Row 1 × Column 4

$= \begin{bmatrix} 4(1) + 2(0) & 4(2) + 2(2) & 4(3) + 2(-1) & 4(4) + 2(6) \\ 1(1) + 3(0) & 1(2) + 3(2) & 1(3) + 3(-1) & 1(4) + 3(6) \end{bmatrix}$

Row 2 × Column 1   Row 2 × Column 2   Row 2 × Column 3   Row 2 × Column 4

$= \begin{bmatrix} 4 + 0 & 8 + 4 & 12 - 2 & 16 + 12 \\ 1 + 0 & 2 + 6 & 3 - 3 & 4 + 18 \end{bmatrix}$

$= \begin{bmatrix} 4 & 12 & 10 & 28 \\ 1 & 8 & 0 & 22 \end{bmatrix}$

**b.** $\begin{bmatrix} 1 & 2 & 3 & 4 \\ 0 & 2 & -1 & 6 \end{bmatrix}\begin{bmatrix} 4 & 2 \\ 1 & 3 \end{bmatrix}$   *First matrix     Second matrix*
*$2 \times 4$           $2 \times 2$*

*These numbers must be the same to multiply the matrices.*

The number of columns in the first matrix does not equal the number of rows in the second matrix. Thus, the product of these two matrices is undefined.   ●

⊘ Check Point **7** Where possible, find each product:

**a.** $\begin{bmatrix} 1 & 3 \\ 0 & 2 \end{bmatrix}\begin{bmatrix} 2 & 3 & -1 & 6 \\ 0 & 5 & 4 & 1 \end{bmatrix}$     **b.** $\begin{bmatrix} 2 & 3 & -1 & 6 \\ 0 & 5 & 4 & 1 \end{bmatrix}\begin{bmatrix} 1 & 3 \\ 0 & 2 \end{bmatrix}$.

Verify the properties listed in the box using

$$A = \begin{bmatrix} 3 & 2 \\ -1 & 4 \end{bmatrix},$$

$$B = \begin{bmatrix} 1 & 0 \\ 3 & 2 \end{bmatrix},$$

$$C = \begin{bmatrix} 1 & 2 \\ -1 & 1 \end{bmatrix},$$

and $c = 3$.

**7** Model applied situations with matrix operations.

Although matrix multiplication is not commutative, it does obey many of the properties of real numbers.

## Properties of Matrix Multiplication

If $A$, $B$, and $C$ are matrices and $c$ is a scalar, then the following properties are true. (Assume the order of each matrix is such that all operations in these properties are defined.)

**1.** $(AB)C = A(BC)$     Associative Property of Matrix Multiplication

**2.** $A(B + C) = AB + AC$     Distributive Properties of Matrix
$(A + B)C = AC + BC$     Multiplication

**3.** $c(AB) = (cA)B$     Associative Property of Scalar Multiplication

## Applications

All of the still images that you see on the Web have been created or manipulated on a computer in a digital format—made up of hundreds of thousands, or even millions, of tiny squares called **pixels**. Pixels are created by dividing an image into a grid. The computer can change the brightness of every square or pixel in this grid. A digital camera captures photos in this digital format. Also, you can scan pictures to convert them into digital format. Example 8 illustrates the role that matrices play in this new technology.

**EXAMPLE 8** **Matrices and Digital Photography**

The letter L in **Figure 8.7** is shown using 9 pixels in a 3 × 3 grid. The colors possible in the grid are shown in **Figure 8.8**. Each color is represented by a specific number: 0, 1, 2, or 3.

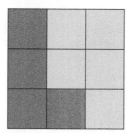

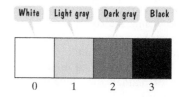

Figure 8.7   The letter L      Figure 8.8   Color levels

**a.** Find a matrix that represents a digital photograph of this letter L.

**b.** Increase the contrast of the letter L by changing the dark gray to black and the light gray to white. Use matrix addition to accomplish this.

### Solution

**a.** Look at the L and the background in **Figure 8.7**. Because the L is dark gray, color level 2, and the background is light gray, color level 1, a digital photograph of **Figure 8.7** can be represented by the matrix

$$\begin{bmatrix} 2 & 1 & 1 \\ 2 & 1 & 1 \\ 2 & 2 & 1 \end{bmatrix}.$$

**b.** We can make the L black, color level 3, by increasing each 2 in the above matrix to 3. We can make the background white, color level 0, by decreasing each 1 in the above matrix to 0. This is accomplished using the following matrix addition:

$$\begin{bmatrix} 2 & 1 & 1 \\ 2 & 1 & 1 \\ 2 & 2 & 1 \end{bmatrix} + \begin{bmatrix} 1 & -1 & -1 \\ 1 & -1 & -1 \\ 1 & 1 & -1 \end{bmatrix} = \begin{bmatrix} 3 & 0 & 0 \\ 3 & 0 & 0 \\ 3 & 3 & 0 \end{bmatrix}.$$

The picture corresponding to the matrix sum to the right of the equal sign is shown in **Figure 8.9**.

Figure 8.9   Changing contrast: the letter L

⊘ Check Point **8** Change the contrast of the letter L in **Figure 8.7** on the previous page by making the L light gray and the background black. Use matrix addition to accomplish this.

## Images of space

Photographs sent back from space use matrices with thousands of pixels. Each pixel is assigned a number from 0 to 63 representing its color–0 for pure white and 63 for pure black. In the image of Saturn shown here, matrix operations provide false colors that emphasize the banding of the planet's upper atmosphere.

We have seen how functions can be transformed using translations, reflections, stretching, and shrinking. In a similar way, matrix operations are used to transform and manipulate computer graphics.

**EXAMPLE 9**  **Transformations of an Image**

The quadrilateral in **Figure 8.10** can be represented by the matrix

Coordinates of vertices

$$A = \begin{bmatrix} -2 & -1 & 3 & 1 \\ -3 & 2 & 4 & -2 \end{bmatrix}.$$

*x*-coordinates
*y*-coordinates

Each column in the matrix gives the coordinates of a vertex, or corner, of the quadrilateral. Use matrix operations to perfom the following transformations:

**a.** Move the quadrilateral 4 units to the right and 1 unit down.

**b.** Shrink the quadrilateral to half its perimeter.

**c.** Let $B = \begin{bmatrix} -1 & 0 \\ 0 & 1 \end{bmatrix}$. Find $BA$. What effect does this have on the quadrilateral in **Figure 8.10**?

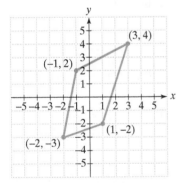

Figure 8.10

## Solution

**a.** We translate the quadrilateral 4 units right and 1 unit down by adding 4 to each *x*-coordinate and subtracting 1 from each *y*-coordinate. This is accomplished using the following matrix addition:

$$\begin{bmatrix} -2 & -1 & 3 & 1 \\ -3 & 2 & 4 & -2 \end{bmatrix} + \begin{bmatrix} 4 & 4 & 4 & 4 \\ -1 & -1 & -1 & -1 \end{bmatrix} = \begin{bmatrix} 2 & 3 & 7 & 5 \\ -4 & 1 & 3 & -3 \end{bmatrix}.$$

This matrix represents the original quadrilateral.

Shift 4 units to the right and 1 unit down.

This matrix represents the translated quadrilateral.

Each column in the matrix on the right gives the coordinates of a vertex of the translated quadrilateral. The original quadrilateral and the translated image are shown in **Figure 8.11**.

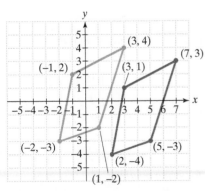

Figure 8.11  Shifting the quadrilateral 4 units right and 1 unit down

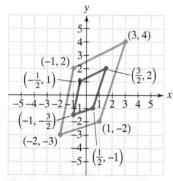

**Figure 8.12** Shrinking the quadrilateral to half the original perimeter

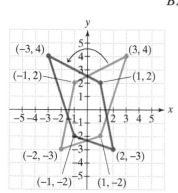

**Figure 8.13**

**b.** We shrink the quadrilateral in **Figure 8.10**, shown in blue in **Figure 8.12**, to half its perimeter by multiplying each $x$-coordinate and each $y$-coordinate by $\frac{1}{2}$. This is accomplished using the following scalar multiplication:

$$\frac{1}{2}\begin{bmatrix} -2 & -1 & 3 & 1 \\ -3 & 2 & 4 & -2 \end{bmatrix} = \begin{bmatrix} -1 & -\frac{1}{2} & \frac{3}{2} & \frac{1}{2} \\ -\frac{3}{2} & 1 & 2 & -1 \end{bmatrix}.$$

This matrix represents the original quadrilateral.

This matrix represents the quadrilateral with half the original perimeter.

Each column in the matrix on the right gives the coordinates of a vertex of the reduced quadrilateral. The original quadrilateral and the reduced image are shown in **Figure 8.12**.

**c.** We begin by finding $BA$. Keep in mind that $A$ represents the original quadrilateral, shown in blue in **Figure 8.13**.

$$BA = \begin{bmatrix} -1 & 0 \\ 0 & 1 \end{bmatrix}\begin{bmatrix} -2 & -1 & 3 & 1 \\ -3 & 2 & 4 & -2 \end{bmatrix}$$

$$= \begin{bmatrix} (-1)(-2) + 0(-3) & (-1)(-1) + 0(2) & (-1)(3) + 0(4) & (-1)(1) + 0(-2) \\ 0(-2) + 1(-3) & 0(-1) + 1(2) & 0(3) + 1(4) & 0(1) + 1(-2) \end{bmatrix}$$

$$= \begin{bmatrix} 2 & 1 & -3 & -1 \\ -3 & 2 & 4 & -2 \end{bmatrix}$$

Each column in the matrix multiplication gives the coordinates of a vertex of the transformed image. The original quadrilateral and this transformed image are shown in **Figure 8.13**. Notice that each $x$-coordinate on the original blue image is replaced with its opposite on the transformed red image.

We can conclude that multiplication by $\begin{bmatrix} -1 & 0 \\ 0 & 1 \end{bmatrix}$ reflected the blue quadrilateral about the $y$-axis. ●

**⊘ Check Point 9** Consider the triangle represented by the matrix

$$A = \begin{bmatrix} 0 & 3 & 4 \\ 0 & 5 & 2 \end{bmatrix}.$$

Use matrix operations to perform the following transformations:

**a.** Move the triangle 3 units to the left and 1 unit down.

**b.** Enlarge the triangle to twice its original perimeter.

Illustrate your results in parts (a) and (b) by showing the original triangle and the transformed image in a rectangular coordinate system.

**c.** Let $B = \begin{bmatrix} 1 & 0 \\ 0 & -1 \end{bmatrix}$. Find $BA$. What effect does this have on the original triangle?

## Exercise Set 8.3

### Practice Exercises

*In Exercises 1–4,*

**a.** *Give the order of each matrix.*

**b.** *If $A = [a_{ij}]$, identify $a_{32}$ and $a_{23}$, or explain why identification is not possible.*

**1.** $\begin{bmatrix} 4 & -7 & 5 \\ -6 & 8 & -1 \end{bmatrix}$

**2.** $\begin{bmatrix} -6 & 4 & -1 \\ -9 & 0 & \frac{1}{2} \end{bmatrix}$

**3.** $\begin{bmatrix} 1 & -5 & \pi & e \\ 0 & 7 & -6 & -\pi \\ -2 & \frac{1}{2} & 11 & -\frac{1}{5} \end{bmatrix}$

**4.** $\begin{bmatrix} -4 & 1 & 3 & -5 \\ 2 & -1 & \pi & 0 \\ 1 & 0 & -e & \frac{1}{5} \end{bmatrix}$

*In Exercises 5–8, find values for the variables so that the matrices in each exercise are equal.*

**5.** $\begin{bmatrix} x \\ 4 \end{bmatrix} = \begin{bmatrix} 6 \\ y \end{bmatrix}$

**6.** $\begin{bmatrix} x \\ 7 \end{bmatrix} = \begin{bmatrix} 11 \\ y \end{bmatrix}$

**7.** $\begin{bmatrix} x & 2y \\ z & 9 \end{bmatrix} = \begin{bmatrix} 4 & 12 \\ 3 & 9 \end{bmatrix}$

**8.** $\begin{bmatrix} x & y+3 \\ 2z & 8 \end{bmatrix} = \begin{bmatrix} 12 & 5 \\ 6 & 8 \end{bmatrix}$

*In Exercises 9–16, find the following matrices:*

**a.** $A + B$  **b.** $A - B$

**c.** $-4A$  **d.** $3A + 2B$.

**9.** $A = \begin{bmatrix} 4 & 1 \\ 3 & 2 \end{bmatrix}$, $B = \begin{bmatrix} 5 & 9 \\ 0 & 7 \end{bmatrix}$

**10.** $A = \begin{bmatrix} -2 & 3 \\ 0 & 1 \end{bmatrix}$, $B = \begin{bmatrix} 8 & 1 \\ 5 & 4 \end{bmatrix}$

**11.** $A = \begin{bmatrix} 1 & 3 \\ 3 & 4 \\ 5 & 6 \end{bmatrix}$, $B = \begin{bmatrix} 2 & -1 \\ 3 & -2 \\ 0 & 1 \end{bmatrix}$

**12.** $A = \begin{bmatrix} 3 & 1 & 1 \\ -1 & 2 & 5 \end{bmatrix}$, $B = \begin{bmatrix} 2 & -3 & 6 \\ -3 & 1 & -4 \end{bmatrix}$

**13.** $A = \begin{bmatrix} 2 \\ -4 \\ 1 \end{bmatrix}$, $B = \begin{bmatrix} -5 \\ 3 \\ -1 \end{bmatrix}$

**14.** $A = \begin{bmatrix} 6 & 2 & -3 \end{bmatrix}$, $B = \begin{bmatrix} 4 & -2 & 3 \end{bmatrix}$

**15.** $A = \begin{bmatrix} 2 & -10 & -2 \\ 14 & 12 & 10 \\ 4 & -2 & 2 \end{bmatrix}$, $B = \begin{bmatrix} 6 & 10 & -2 \\ 0 & -12 & -4 \\ -5 & 2 & -2 \end{bmatrix}$

**16.** $A = \begin{bmatrix} 6 & -3 & 5 \\ 6 & 0 & -2 \\ -4 & 2 & -1 \end{bmatrix}$, $B = \begin{bmatrix} -3 & 5 & 1 \\ -1 & 2 & -6 \\ 2 & 0 & 4 \end{bmatrix}$

*In Exercises 17–26, let*

$$A = \begin{bmatrix} -3 & -7 \\ 2 & -9 \\ 5 & 0 \end{bmatrix} \text{ and } B = \begin{bmatrix} -5 & -1 \\ 0 & 0 \\ 3 & -4 \end{bmatrix}.$$

*Solve each matrix equation for $X$.*

**17.** $X - A = B$      **18.** $X - B = A$

**19.** $2X + A = B$      **20.** $3X + A = B$

**21.** $3X + 2A = B$      **22.** $2X + 5A = B$

**23.** $B - X = 4A$      **24.** $A - X = 4B$

**25.** $4A + 3B = -2X$      **26.** $4B + 3A = -2X$

*In Exercises 27–36, find (if possible) the following matrices:*

    **a.** $AB$     **b.** $BA$.

**27.** $A = \begin{bmatrix} 1 & 3 \\ 5 & 3 \end{bmatrix}$, $B = \begin{bmatrix} 3 & -2 \\ -1 & 6 \end{bmatrix}$

**28.** $A = \begin{bmatrix} 3 & -2 \\ 1 & 5 \end{bmatrix}$, $B = \begin{bmatrix} 0 & 0 \\ 5 & -6 \end{bmatrix}$

**29.** $A = \begin{bmatrix} 1 & 2 & 3 & 4 \end{bmatrix}$, $B = \begin{bmatrix} 1 \\ 2 \\ 3 \\ 4 \end{bmatrix}$

**30.** $A = \begin{bmatrix} -1 \\ -2 \\ -3 \end{bmatrix}$, $B = \begin{bmatrix} 1 & 2 & 3 \end{bmatrix}$

**31.** $A = \begin{bmatrix} 1 & -1 & 4 \\ 4 & -1 & 3 \\ 2 & 0 & -2 \end{bmatrix}$, $B = \begin{bmatrix} 1 & 1 & 0 \\ 1 & 2 & 4 \\ 1 & -1 & 3 \end{bmatrix}$

**32.** $A = \begin{bmatrix} 1 & -1 & 1 \\ 5 & 0 & -2 \\ 3 & -2 & 2 \end{bmatrix}$, $B = \begin{bmatrix} 1 & 1 & 0 \\ 1 & -4 & 5 \\ 3 & -1 & 2 \end{bmatrix}$

**33.** $A = \begin{bmatrix} 4 & 2 \\ 6 & 1 \\ 3 & 5 \end{bmatrix}$, $B = \begin{bmatrix} 2 & 3 & 4 \\ -1 & -2 & 0 \end{bmatrix}$

**34.** $A = \begin{bmatrix} 2 & 4 \\ 3 & 1 \\ 4 & 2 \end{bmatrix}$, $B = \begin{bmatrix} 3 & 2 & 0 \\ -1 & -3 & 5 \end{bmatrix}$

**35.** $A = \begin{bmatrix} 2 & -3 & 1 & -1 \\ 1 & 1 & -2 & 1 \end{bmatrix}$, $B = \begin{bmatrix} 1 & 2 \\ -1 & 1 \\ 5 & 4 \\ 10 & 5 \end{bmatrix}$

**36.** $A = \begin{bmatrix} 2 & -1 & 3 & 2 \\ 1 & 0 & -2 & 1 \end{bmatrix}$, $B = \begin{bmatrix} -1 & 2 \\ 1 & 1 \\ 3 & -4 \\ 6 & 5 \end{bmatrix}$

*In Exercises 37–44, perform the indicated matrix operations given that $A$, $B$, and $C$ are defined as follows. If an operation is not defined, state the reason.*

$$A = \begin{bmatrix} 4 & 0 \\ -3 & 5 \\ 0 & 1 \end{bmatrix} \quad B = \begin{bmatrix} 5 & 1 \\ -2 & -2 \end{bmatrix} \quad C = \begin{bmatrix} 1 & -1 \\ -1 & 1 \end{bmatrix}$$

**37.** $4B - 3C$      **38.** $5C - 2B$

**39.** $BC + CB$      **40.** $A(B + C)$

**41.** $A - C$      **42.** $B - A$

**43.** $A(BC)$      **44.** $A(CB)$

## Practice Plus

*In Exercises 45–50, let*

$$A = \begin{bmatrix} 1 & 0 \\ 0 & 1 \end{bmatrix}, \quad B = \begin{bmatrix} 1 & 0 \\ 0 & -1 \end{bmatrix}, \quad C = \begin{bmatrix} -1 & 0 \\ 0 & 1 \end{bmatrix},$$

$$D = \begin{bmatrix} -1 & 0 \\ 0 & -1 \end{bmatrix}.$$

**45.** Find the product of the sum of $A$ and $B$ and the difference between $C$ and $D$.

**46.** Find the product of the difference between $A$ and $B$ and the sum of $C$ and $D$.

**47.** Use any three of the matrices to verify a distributive property.

**48.** Use any three of the matrices to verify an associative property.

*In Exercises 49–50, suppose that the vertices of a computer graphic are points, $(x, y)$, represented by the matrix*

$$Z = \begin{bmatrix} x \\ y \end{bmatrix}.$$

**49.** Find $BZ$ and explain why this reflects the graphic about the $x$-axis.

**50.** Find $CZ$ and explain why this reflects the graphic about the $y$-axis.

## Application Exercises

*The + sign in the figure is shown using 9 pixels in a 3 × 3 grid. The color levels are given to the right of the figure. Each color is represented by a specific number: 0, 1, 2, or 3. Use this information to solve Exercises 51–52.*

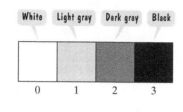

**51. a.** Find a matrix that represents a digital photograph of the + sign.

**b.** Adjust the contrast by changing the black to dark gray and the light gray to white. Use matrix addition to accomplish this.

**c.** Adjust the contrast by changing the black to light gray and the light gray to dark gray. Use matrix addition to accomplish this.

**52. a.** Find a matrix that represents a digital photograph of the + sign.

**b.** Adjust the contrast by changing the black to dark gray and the light gray to black. Use matrix addition to accomplish this.

**c.** Adjust the contrast by leaving the black alone and changing the light gray to white. Use matrix addition to accomplish this.

*The figure shows the letter L in a rectangular coordinate system.*

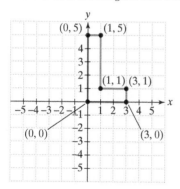

*The figure can be represented by the matrix*

$$B = \begin{bmatrix} 0 & 3 & 3 & 1 & 1 & 0 \\ 0 & 0 & 1 & 1 & 5 & 5 \end{bmatrix}.$$

*Each column in the matrix describes a point on the letter. The order of the columns shows the direction in which a pencil must move to draw the letter. The L is completed by connecting the last point in the matrix, (0, 5), to the starting point, (0, 0). Use these ideas to solve Exercises 53–60.*

**53.** Use matrix operations to move the L 2 units to the left and 3 units down. Then graph the letter and its transformation in a rectangular coordinate system.

**54.** Use matrix operations to move the L 2 units to the right and 3 units down. Then graph the letter and its transformation in a rectangular coordinate system.

**55.** Reduce the L to half its perimeter and move the reduced image 1 unit up. Then graph the letter and its transformation.

**56.** Reduce the L to half its perimeter and move the reduced image 2 units up. Then graph the letter and its transformation.

**57. a.** If $A = \begin{bmatrix} 1 & 0 \\ 0 & -1 \end{bmatrix}$, find $AB$.

**b.** Graph the object represented by matrix $AB$. What effect does the matrix multiplication have on the letter L represented by matrix $B$?

**58. a.** If $A = \begin{bmatrix} -1 & 0 \\ 0 & 1 \end{bmatrix}$, find $AB$.

**b.** Graph the object represented by matrix $AB$. What effect does the matrix multiplication have on the letter L represented by matrix $B$?

**59. a.** If $A = \begin{bmatrix} 0 & -1 \\ 1 & 0 \end{bmatrix}$, find $AB$.

**b.** Graph the object represented by matrix $AB$. What effect does the matrix multiplication have on the letter L represented by matrix $B$?

**60. a.** If $A = \begin{bmatrix} 2 & 0 \\ 0 & 1 \end{bmatrix}$, find $AB$.

**b.** Graph the object represented by matrix $AB$. What effect does the matrix multiplication have on the letter L represented by matrix $B$?

**61.** Completing the transition to adulthood is measured by one or more of the following: leaving home, finishing school, getting married, having a child, or being financially independent. The bar graph shows the percentage of Americans, ages 20 and 30, who had completed the transition to adulthood in 1960 and in 2000.

**Percentage Having Completed the Transition to Adulthood**

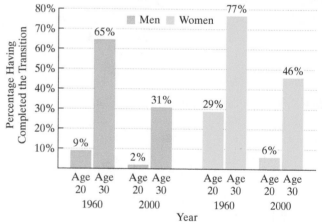

*Source:* James M. Henslin, *Sociology*, Eighth Edition, Allyn and Bacon, 2007

**a.** Use a 2 × 2 matrix to represent the data for 2000. Entries in the matrix should be percents that are organized as follows:

$$\begin{array}{c} \\ \text{Age 20} \\ \text{Age 30} \end{array} \begin{array}{cc} \text{Men} & \text{Women} \\ \left[ \begin{array}{cc} & \\ & \end{array} \right]. \end{array}$$

Call this matrix $A$.

**b.** Use a 2 × 2 matrix to represent the data for 1960. Call this matrix $B$.

**c.** Find $B - A$. What does this matrix represent?

**62.** The table gives an estimate of basic caloric needs for different age groups and activity levels.

| Age Range | Sedentary | | Moderately Active | | Active | |
|---|---|---|---|---|---|---|
| | Men | Women | Men | Women | Men | Women |
| 19 − 30 | 2400 | 2000 | 2700 | 2100 | 3000 | 2400 |
| 31 − 50 | 2200 | 1800 | 2500 | 2000 | 2900 | 2200 |
| 51 + | 2000 | 1600 | 2300 | 1800 | 2600 | 2100 |

*Source: USA Today*

a. Use a $3 \times 3$ matrix to represent the daily caloric needs, by age and activity level, for men. Call this matrix $M$.

b. Use a $3 \times 3$ matrix to represent the daily caloric needs, by age and activity level, for women. Call this matrix $W$.

c. Find $M - W$. What does this matrix represent?

**63.** The final grade in a particular course is determined by grades on the midterm and final. The grades for five students and the two grading systems are modeled by the following matrices. Call the first matrix $A$ and the second $B$.

$$
\begin{array}{c}
\text{Midterm} \quad \text{Final} \\
\begin{array}{c}
\text{Student 1} \\ \text{Student 2} \\ \text{Student 3} \\ \text{Student 4} \\ \text{Student 5}
\end{array}
\begin{bmatrix}
76 & 92 \\
74 & 84 \\
94 & 86 \\
84 & 62 \\
58 & 80
\end{bmatrix}
\end{array}
\qquad
\begin{array}{c}
\quad\;\; \text{System} \;\; \text{System} \\
\quad\;\; 1 \qquad\;\; 2 \\
\begin{array}{c}
\text{Midterm} \\ \text{Final}
\end{array}
\begin{bmatrix}
0.5 & 0.3 \\
0.5 & 0.7
\end{bmatrix}
\end{array}
$$

a. Describe the grading system that is represented by matrix $B$.

b. Compute the matrix $AB$ and assign each of the five students a final course grade first using system 1 and then using system 2. ($89.5 - 100 = A, 79.5 - 89.4 = B, 69.5 - 79.4 = C, 59.5 - 69.4 = D,$ below $59.5 = F$)

**64.** In a certain county, the proportion of voters in each age group registered as Republicans, Democrats, or Independents is given by the following matrix, which we'll call $A$.

$$
\begin{array}{c}
\qquad\qquad\qquad \text{Age} \\
\;\; \textbf{18–30} \qquad\quad \textbf{31–50} \qquad \textbf{Over 50} \\
\begin{array}{c}
\textbf{Republicans} \\ \textbf{Democrats} \\ \textbf{Independents}
\end{array}
\begin{bmatrix}
0.40 & 0.30 & 0.70 \\
0.30 & 0.60 & 0.25 \\
0.30 & 0.10 & 0.05
\end{bmatrix}
\end{array}
$$

The distribution, by age and gender, of this county's voting population is given by the following matrix, which we'll call $B$.

$$
\begin{array}{c}
\qquad\qquad \textbf{Male} \quad\;\; \textbf{Female} \\
\begin{array}{c}
\textbf{18–30} \\ \textbf{Age} \quad \textbf{31–50} \\ \textbf{Over 50}
\end{array}
\begin{bmatrix}
6000 & 8000 \\
12{,}000 & 14{,}000 \\
14{,}000 & 16{,}000
\end{bmatrix}
\end{array}
$$

a. Calculate the product $AB$.

b. How many female Democrats are there?

c. How many male Republicans are there?

## Writing in Mathematics

**65.** What is meant by the order of a matrix? Give an example with your explanation.

**66.** What does $a_{ij}$ mean?

**67.** What are equal matrices?

**68.** How are matrices added?

**69.** Describe how to subtract matrices.

**70.** Describe matrices that cannot be added or subtracted.

**71.** Describe how to perform scalar multiplication. Provide an example with your description.

**72.** Describe how to multiply matrices.

**73.** Describe when the multiplication of two matrices is not defined.

**74.** If two matrices can be multiplied, describe how to determine the order of the product.

**75.** Low-resolution digital photographs use 262,144 pixels in a $512 \times 512$ grid. If you enlarge a low-resolution digital photograph enough, describe what will happen.

## Technology Exercise

**76.** Use the matrix feature of a graphing utility to verify each of your answers to Exercises 37–44.

## Critical Thinking Exercises

**Make Sense?** *In Exercises 77–80, determine whether each statement makes sense or does not make sense, and explain your reasoning.*

**77.** I added matrices of the same order by adding corresponding elements.

**78.** I multiplied an $m \times n$ matrix and an $n \times p$ matrix by multiplying corresponding elements.

**79.** I'm working with two matrices that can be added but not multiplied.

**80.** I'm working with two matrices that can be multiplied but not added.

**81.** Find two matrices $A$ and $B$ such that $AB = BA$.

**82.** Consider a square matrix such that each element that is not on the diagonal from upper left to lower right is zero. Experiment with such matrices (call each matrix $A$) by finding $AA$. Then write a sentence or two describing a method for multiplying this kind of matrix by itself.

**83.** If $AB = -BA$, then $A$ and $B$ are said to be anticommutative.

Are $A = \begin{bmatrix} 0 & -1 \\ 1 & 0 \end{bmatrix}$ and $B = \begin{bmatrix} 1 & 0 \\ 0 & -1 \end{bmatrix}$ anticommutative?

## Group Exercise

**84.** The interesting and useful applications of matrix theory are nearly unlimited. Applications of matrices range from representing digital photographs to predicting long-range trends in the stock market. Members of the group should research an application of matrices that they find intriguing. The group should then present a seminar to the class about this application.

## Preview Exercises

*Exercises 85–87 will help you prepare for the material covered in the next section.*

**85.** Multiply:

$$\begin{bmatrix} a_{11} & a_{12} \\ a_{21} & a_{22} \end{bmatrix} \begin{bmatrix} 1 & 0 \\ 0 & 1 \end{bmatrix}.$$

After performing the multiplication, describe what happens to the elements in the first matrix.

**86.** Use Gauss-Jordan elimination to solve the system:

$$\begin{cases} -x - y - z = 1 \\ 4x + 5y \quad = 0 \\ \quad y - 3z = 0. \end{cases}$$

**87.** Multiply and write the linear system represented by the following matrix multiplication:

$$\begin{bmatrix} a_1 & b_1 & c_1 \\ a_2 & b_2 & c_2 \\ a_3 & b_3 & c_3 \end{bmatrix} \begin{bmatrix} x \\ y \\ z \end{bmatrix} = \begin{bmatrix} d_1 \\ d_2 \\ d_3 \end{bmatrix}.$$

---

## Chapter 8 Mid-Chapter Check Point

**What You Know:** We learned to use matrices to solve systems of linear equations. Gaussian elimination required simplifying the augmented matrix to one with 1s down the main diagonal and 0s below the 1s. Gauss-Jordan elimination simplified the augmented matrix to one with 1s down the main diagonal and 0s above and below each 1. Such a matrix, in reduced row-echelon form, did not require back-substitution to solve the system. We applied Gaussian elimination to systems with no solution, as well as to represent the solution set for systems with infinitely many solutions, including nonsquare systems. We learned how to perform operations with matrices, including matrix addition, matrix subtraction, scalar multiplication, and matrix multiplication.

*In Exercises 1–5, use matrices to find the complete solution to each system of equations, or show that none exists.*

**1.** $\begin{cases} x + 2y - 3z = -7 \\ 3x - y + 2z = 8 \\ 2x - y + z = 5 \end{cases}$

**2.** $\begin{cases} 2x + 4y + 5z = 2 \\ x + y + 2z = 1 \\ 3x + 5y + 7z = 4 \end{cases}$

**3.** $\begin{cases} x - 2y + 2z = -2 \\ 2x + 3y - z = 1 \end{cases}$

**4.** $\begin{cases} w + x + y + z = 6 \\ w - x + 3y + z = -14 \\ w + 2x - 3z = 12 \\ 2w + 3x + 6y + z = 1 \end{cases}$

**5.** $\begin{cases} 2x - 2y + 2z = 5 \\ x - y + z = 2 \\ 2x + y - z = 1 \end{cases}$

*In Exercises 6–10, perform the indicated matrix operations or solve the matrix equation for X given that A, B, and C are defined as follows. If an operation is not defined, state the reason.*

$$A = \begin{bmatrix} 0 & 2 \\ -1 & 3 \\ 1 & 0 \end{bmatrix} \quad B = \begin{bmatrix} 4 & 1 \\ -6 & -2 \end{bmatrix} \quad C = \begin{bmatrix} -1 & 0 \\ 0 & 1 \end{bmatrix}$$

**6.** $2C - \frac{1}{2}B$

**7.** $A(B + C)$

**8.** $A(BC)$

**9.** $A + C$

**10.** $2X - 3C = B$

---

## Section 8.4  Multiplicative Inverses of Matrices and Matrix Equations

### Objectives

1. Find the multiplicative inverse of a square matrix.
2. Use inverses to solve matrix equations.
3. Encode and decode messages.

This 1941 RCA radiogram shows an encoded message from the Japanese government.

In 1939, Britain's secret service hired top chess players, mathematicians, and other masters of logic to break the code used by the Nazis in communications between headquarters and troops. The project, which employed over 10,000 people, broke the code less than a year later, providing the Allies with information about Nazi troop movements throughout World War II.

Messages must often be sent in such a way that the real meaning is hidden from everyone but the sender and the recipient. In this section, we will look at the role that matrices and their inverses play in this process.

## The Multiplicative Identity Matrix

For the real numbers, we know that 1 is the multiplicative identity because $a \cdot 1 = 1 \cdot a = a$. Is there a similar property for matrix multiplication? That is, is there a matrix $I$ such that $AI = A$ and $IA = A$? The answer is yes. A square matrix with 1s down the main diagonal from upper left to lower right and 0s elsewhere does not change the elements in a matrix in products with that matrix. In the case of $2 \times 2$ matrices,

$$\begin{bmatrix} a_{11} & a_{12} \\ a_{21} & a_{22} \end{bmatrix} \begin{bmatrix} 1 & 0 \\ 0 & 1 \end{bmatrix} = \begin{bmatrix} a_{11} & a_{12} \\ a_{21} & a_{22} \end{bmatrix}$$

The elements in the matrix do not change.

and $\begin{bmatrix} 1 & 0 \\ 0 & 1 \end{bmatrix} \begin{bmatrix} a_{11} & a_{12} \\ a_{21} & a_{22} \end{bmatrix} = \begin{bmatrix} a_{11} & a_{12} \\ a_{21} & a_{22} \end{bmatrix}$.

The elements in the matrix do not change.

The $n \times n$ square matrix with 1s down the main diagonal from upper left to lower right and 0s elsewhere is called the **multiplicative identity matrix of order** $n$. This matrix is designated by $I_n$. For example,

$$I_2 = \begin{bmatrix} 1 & 0 \\ 0 & 1 \end{bmatrix}, \quad I_3 = \begin{bmatrix} 1 & 0 & 0 \\ 0 & 1 & 0 \\ 0 & 0 & 1 \end{bmatrix},$$

and so on.

**① Find the multiplicative inverse of a square matrix.**

## The Multiplicative Inverse of a Matrix

The multiplicative identity matrix, $I_n$, will help us to define a new concept: the multiplicative inverse of a matrix. To do so, let's consider a similar concept, the multiplicative inverse of a nonzero number, $a$. Recall that the multiplicative inverse of $a$ is $\frac{1}{a}$. The multiplicative inverse has the following property:

$$a \cdot \frac{1}{a} = 1 \quad \text{and} \quad \frac{1}{a} \cdot a = 1.$$

We can define the multiplicative inverse of a square matrix in a similar manner.

### Definition of the Multiplicative Inverse of a Square Matrix

Let $A$ be an $n \times n$ matrix. If there exists an $n \times n$ matrix $A^{-1}$ (read: "$A$ inverse") such that

$$AA^{-1} = I_n \quad \text{and} \quad A^{-1}A = I_n,$$

then $A^{-1}$ is the **multiplicative inverse** of $A$.

We have seen that matrix multiplication is not commutative. Thus, to show that a matrix $B$ is the multiplicative inverse of the matrix $A$, find both $AB$ and $BA$. If $B$ is the multiplicative inverse of $A$, both products ($AB$ and $BA$) will be the multiplicative identity matrix, $I_n$.

**EXAMPLE 1** The Multiplicative Inverse of a Matrix

Show that $B$ is the multiplicative inverse of $A$, where

$$A = \begin{bmatrix} -1 & 3 \\ 2 & -5 \end{bmatrix} \quad \text{and} \quad B = \begin{bmatrix} 5 & 3 \\ 2 & 1 \end{bmatrix}.$$

**Solution** To show that $B$ is the multiplicative inverse of $A$, we must find the products $AB$ and $BA$. If $B$ is the multiplicative inverse of $A$, then $AB$ will be the multiplicative identity matrix and $BA$ will be the multiplicative identity matrix. Because $A$ and $B$ are $2 \times 2$ matrices, $n = 2$. Thus, we denote the multiplicative identity matrix as $I_2$; it is also a $2 \times 2$ matrix. We must show that

- $AB = I_2 = \begin{bmatrix} 1 & 0 \\ 0 & 1 \end{bmatrix}$ and

- $BA = I_2 = \begin{bmatrix} 1 & 0 \\ 0 & 1 \end{bmatrix}.$

Let's first show $AB = I_2$.

$$AB = \begin{bmatrix} -1 & 3 \\ 2 & -5 \end{bmatrix} \begin{bmatrix} 5 & 3 \\ 2 & 1 \end{bmatrix}$$

$$= \begin{bmatrix} -1(5) + 3(2) & -1(3) + 3(1) \\ 2(5) + (-5)(2) & 2(3) + (-5)(1) \end{bmatrix} = \begin{bmatrix} 1 & 0 \\ 0 & 1 \end{bmatrix}$$

Let's now show $BA = I_2$.

$$BA = \begin{bmatrix} 5 & 3 \\ 2 & 1 \end{bmatrix} \begin{bmatrix} -1 & 3 \\ 2 & -5 \end{bmatrix}$$

$$= \begin{bmatrix} 5(-1) + 3(2) & 5(3) + 3(-5) \\ 2(-1) + 1(2) & 2(3) + 1(-5) \end{bmatrix} = \begin{bmatrix} 1 & 0 \\ 0 & 1 \end{bmatrix}$$

Both products give the multiplicative identity matrix. Thus, $B$ is the multiplicative inverse of $A$ and we can designate $B$ as $A^{-1} = \begin{bmatrix} 5 & 3 \\ 2 & 1 \end{bmatrix}.$

⊘ Check Point | Show that $B$ is the multiplicative inverse of $A$, where

$$A = \begin{bmatrix} 2 & 1 \\ 1 & 1 \end{bmatrix} \quad \text{and} \quad B = \begin{bmatrix} 1 & -1 \\ -1 & 2 \end{bmatrix}.$$

One method for finding the multiplicative inverse of a matrix $A$ is to begin by denoting the elements in $A^{-1}$ with variables. Using the equation $AA^{-1} = I_n$, we can find a value for each element in the multiplicative inverse that is represented by a variable. Example 2 shows how this is done.

( EXAMPLE 2 ) **Finding the Multiplicative Inverse of a Matrix**

Find the multiplicative inverse of

$$A = \begin{bmatrix} 2 & 1 \\ 5 & 3 \end{bmatrix}.$$

**Solution** Let us denote the multiplicative inverse by

$$A^{-1} = \begin{bmatrix} w & x \\ y & z \end{bmatrix}.$$

Because $A$ is a $2 \times 2$ matrix, we use the equation $AA^{-1} = I_2$ to find values for $w$, $x$, $y$, and $z$.

$$\overset{A}{\begin{bmatrix} 2 & 1 \\ 5 & 3 \end{bmatrix}} \overset{A^{-1}}{\begin{bmatrix} w & x \\ y & z \end{bmatrix}} = \overset{I_2}{\begin{bmatrix} 1 & 0 \\ 0 & 1 \end{bmatrix}}$$

$$\begin{bmatrix} 2w + y & 2x + z \\ 5w + 3y & 5x + 3z \end{bmatrix} = \begin{bmatrix} 1 & 0 \\ 0 & 1 \end{bmatrix}$$

Use row-by-column matrix multiplication on the left side of $\begin{bmatrix} 2 & 1 \\ 5 & 3 \end{bmatrix} \begin{bmatrix} w & x \\ y & z \end{bmatrix} = \begin{bmatrix} 1 & 0 \\ 0 & 1 \end{bmatrix}.$

We now equate corresponding elements to obtain the following two systems of linear equations:

$$\begin{cases} 2w + y = 1 \\ 5w + 3y = 0 \end{cases} \quad \text{and} \quad \begin{cases} 2x + z = 0 \\ 5x + 3z = 1. \end{cases}$$

Each of these systems can be solved using the addition method.

## Technology

You can use a graphing utility to find the inverse of the matrix in Example 2. Enter the matrix and name it $A$. The screens show $A$ and $A^{-1}$. Verify that this is correct by showing that

$$AA^{-1} = I_2 \quad \text{and} \quad A^{-1}A = I_2.$$

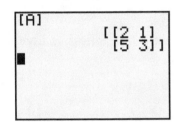

$$\begin{cases} 2w + y = 1 \\ 5w + 3y = 0 \end{cases} \xrightarrow[\text{No change}]{\text{Multiply by } -3.} \begin{array}{r} -6w - 3y = -3 \\ 5w + 3y = 0 \\ \hline \end{array}$$

Add: $\quad -w \quad\quad = -3$

$w = 3$

Use back-substitution. $\quad y = -5$

$$\begin{cases} 2x + z = 0 \\ 5x + 3z = 1 \end{cases} \xrightarrow[\text{No change}]{\text{Multiply by } -3.} \begin{array}{r} -6x - 3z = 0 \\ 5x + 3z = 1 \\ \hline \end{array}$$

Add: $\quad -x \quad\quad = 1$

$x = -1$

Use back-substitution. $\quad z = 2$

Using these values, we have

$$A^{-1} = \begin{bmatrix} w & x \\ y & z \end{bmatrix} = \begin{bmatrix} 3 & -1 \\ -5 & 2 \end{bmatrix}.$$

⊘ **Check Point 2** Find the multiplicative inverse of $A = \begin{bmatrix} 5 & 7 \\ 2 & 3 \end{bmatrix}$.

Only square matrices of order $n \times n$ have multiplicative inverses, but not every square matrix possesses a multiplicative inverse. For example, suppose that you apply the procedure of Example 2 to $A = \begin{bmatrix} -6 & 4 \\ -3 & 2 \end{bmatrix}$:

This is $A$.   This represents $A^{-1}$.   This is the multiplicative identity matrix.

$$\begin{bmatrix} -6 & 4 \\ -3 & 2 \end{bmatrix} \begin{bmatrix} w & x \\ y & z \end{bmatrix} = \begin{bmatrix} 1 & 0 \\ 0 & 1 \end{bmatrix}.$$

Multiplying matrices on the left and equating corresponding elements results in inconsistent systems with no solutions. There are no values for $w$, $x$, $y$, and $z$. This shows that matrix $A$ does not have a multiplicative inverse.

A nonsquare matrix, one with a different number of rows than columns, cannot have a multiplicative inverse. If $A$ is an $m \times n$ matrix and $B$ is an $n \times m$ matrix ($n \neq m$), then the products $AB$ and $BA$ are of different orders. This means that they could not be equal to each other, so that $AB$ and $BA$ could not both equal the multiplicative identity matrix.

If a square matrix has a multiplicative inverse, that inverse is unique. This means that the square matrix has no more than one inverse. If a square matrix has a multiplicative inverse, it is said to be **invertible** or **nonsingular**. If a square matrix has no multiplicative inverse, it is called **singular**.

## A Quick Method for Finding the Multiplicative Inverse of a 2 × 2 Matrix

The same method used in Example 2 can be used to develop the general form of the multiplicative inverse of a 2 × 2 matrix. The following rule enables us to calculate the multiplicative inverse, if there is one:

**Study Tip**

To find the matrix that appears as the second factor for the inverse of

$$A = \begin{bmatrix} a & b \\ c & d \end{bmatrix}:$$

- Reverse $a$ and $d$, the numbers in the diagonal from upper left to lower right.
- Negate $b$ and $c$, the numbers in the other diagonal.

**Multiplicative Inverse of a 2 × 2 Matrix**

If $A = \begin{bmatrix} a & b \\ c & d \end{bmatrix}$, then $A^{-1} = \dfrac{1}{ad - bc}\begin{bmatrix} d & -b \\ -c & a \end{bmatrix}$.

The matrix $A$ is invertible if and only if $ad - bc \neq 0$. If $ad - bc = 0$, then $A$ does not have a multiplicative inverse.

(EXAMPLE 3) **Using the Quick Method to Find a Multiplicative Inverse**

Find the multiplicative inverse of

$$A = \begin{bmatrix} -1 & -2 \\ 3 & 4 \end{bmatrix}.$$

**Solution**

**Study Tip**

When using the formula to find the multiplicative inverse, start by computing $ad - bc$. If the computed value is 0, there is no need to continue. The given matrix is singular—that is, it does not have a multiplicative inverse.

$$A = \begin{bmatrix} \overset{a}{-1} & \overset{b}{-2} \\ \underset{c}{3} & \underset{d}{4} \end{bmatrix}$$

This is the given matrix. We've designated the elements a, b, c, and d.

$$A^{-1} = \frac{1}{ad - bc}\begin{bmatrix} d & -b \\ -c & a \end{bmatrix}$$

This is the formula for the inverse of $\begin{bmatrix} a & b \\ c & d \end{bmatrix}$.

$$= \frac{1}{(-1)(4) - (-2)(3)}\begin{bmatrix} 4 & -(-2) \\ -3 & -1 \end{bmatrix}$$

Apply the formula with $a = -1$, $b = -2$, $c = 3$, and $d = 4$.

$$= \frac{1}{2}\begin{bmatrix} 4 & 2 \\ -3 & -1 \end{bmatrix}$$

Simplify.

$$= \begin{bmatrix} 2 & 1 \\ -\frac{3}{2} & -\frac{1}{2} \end{bmatrix}$$

Perform the scalar multiplication by multiplying each element in the matrix by $\frac{1}{2}$.

The inverse of $A = \begin{bmatrix} -1 & -2 \\ 3 & 4 \end{bmatrix}$ is $A^{-1} = \begin{bmatrix} 2 & 1 \\ -\frac{3}{2} & -\frac{1}{2} \end{bmatrix}$.

We can verify this result by showing that $AA^{-1} = I_2$ and $A^{-1}A = I_2$.　⬤

⊘ Check Point **3** Find the multiplicative inverse of

$$A = \begin{bmatrix} 3 & -2 \\ -1 & 1 \end{bmatrix}.$$

## Finding Multiplicative Inverses of $n \times n$ Matrices with $n$ Greater Than 2

To find the multiplicative inverse of a $3 \times 3$ invertible matrix, we begin by denoting the elements in the multiplicative inverse with variables. Here is an example:

$$\begin{bmatrix} -1 & -1 & -1 \\ 4 & 5 & 0 \\ 0 & 1 & -3 \end{bmatrix} \begin{bmatrix} x_1 & x_2 & x_3 \\ y_1 & y_2 & y_3 \\ z_1 & z_2 & z_3 \end{bmatrix} = \begin{bmatrix} 1 & 0 & 0 \\ 0 & 1 & 0 \\ 0 & 0 & 1 \end{bmatrix}.$$

This is matrix $A$ whose inverse we wish to find.  |  This represents $A^{-1}$.  |  This is the multiplicative identity matrix, $I_3$.

We multiply the matrices on the left, using the row-by-column definition of matrix multiplication.

$$\begin{bmatrix} -x_1 - y_1 - z_1 & -x_2 - y_2 - z_2 & -x_3 - y_3 - z_3 \\ 4x_1 + 5y_1 + 0z_1 & 4x_2 + 5y_2 + 0z_2 & 4x_3 + 5y_3 + 0z_3 \\ 0x_1 + 1y_1 - 3z_1 & 0x_2 + 1y_2 - 3z_2 & 0x_3 + 1y_3 - 3z_3 \end{bmatrix} = \begin{bmatrix} 1 & 0 & 0 \\ 0 & 1 & 0 \\ 0 & 0 & 1 \end{bmatrix}$$

We now equate corresponding entries to obtain the following three systems of linear equations:

$$\begin{cases} -x_1 - y_1 - z_1 = 1 \\ 4x_1 + 5y_1 + 0z_1 = 0 \\ 0x_1 + y_1 - 3z_1 = 0 \end{cases} \qquad \begin{cases} -x_2 - y_2 - z_2 = 0 \\ 4x_2 + 5y_2 + 0z_2 = 1 \\ 0x_2 + y_2 - 3z_2 = 0 \end{cases} \qquad \begin{cases} -x_3 - y_3 - z_3 = 0 \\ 4x_3 + 5y_3 + 0z_3 = 0 \\ 0x_3 + y_3 - 3z_3 = 1. \end{cases}$$

Notice that the variables on the left of the equal signs have the same coefficients in each system. We can use Gauss-Jordan elimination to solve all three systems at once. Form an augmented matrix that contains the coefficients of the three systems to the left of the vertical line and the constants for the systems to the right.

$$\left[ \begin{array}{ccc|ccc} -1 & -1 & -1 & 1 & 0 & 0 \\ 4 & 5 & 0 & 0 & 1 & 0 \\ 0 & 1 & -3 & 0 & 0 & 1 \end{array} \right]$$

Coefficients of the three systems  |  Constants on the right in each of the three systems

To solve all three systems using Gauss-Jordan elimination, we must obtain $\begin{bmatrix} 1 & 0 & 0 \\ 0 & 1 & 0 \\ 0 & 0 & 1 \end{bmatrix}$ to the left of the vertical line. Use matrix row operations, working one column at a time. Obtain 1 in the required position. Then obtain 0s in the other two positions. Using these operations, we obtain the matrix

$$\left[ \begin{array}{ccc|ccc} 1 & 0 & 0 & 15 & 4 & -5 \\ 0 & 1 & 0 & -12 & -3 & 4 \\ 0 & 0 & 1 & -4 & -1 & 1 \end{array} \right].$$

This augmented matrix provides the solutions to the three systems of equations. They are given by

$$\left[ \begin{array}{ccc|c} 1 & 0 & 0 & 15 \\ 0 & 1 & 0 & -12 \\ 0 & 0 & 1 & -4 \end{array} \right] \qquad \begin{array}{l} x_1 = 15 \\ y_1 = -12 \\ z_1 = -4 \end{array}$$

and $\left[ \begin{array}{ccc|c} 1 & 0 & 0 & 4 \\ 0 & 1 & 0 & -3 \\ 0 & 0 & 1 & -1 \end{array} \right]$ $\begin{array}{l} x_2 = 4 \\ y_2 = -3 \\ z_2 = -1 \end{array}$ and $\left[ \begin{array}{ccc|c} 1 & 0 & 0 & -5 \\ 0 & 1 & 0 & 4 \\ 0 & 0 & 1 & 1 \end{array} \right]$ $\begin{array}{l} x_3 = -5 \\ y_3 = 4 \\ z_3 = 1. \end{array}$

Using the nine values from the previous page, the inverse matrix is

$$\begin{bmatrix} x_1 & x_2 & x_3 \\ y_1 & y_2 & y_3 \\ z_1 & z_2 & z_3 \end{bmatrix} = \begin{bmatrix} 15 & 4 & -5 \\ -12 & -3 & 4 \\ -4 & -1 & 1 \end{bmatrix}.$$

Take a second look at the matrix obtained at the point where Gauss-Jordan elimination was completed. This matrix is shown, again, below. Notice that the $3 \times 3$ matrix to the right of the vertical bar is the multiplicative inverse of $A$. Also notice that the multiplicative identity matrix, $I_3$ is the matrix that appears to the left of the vertical bar.

$$\left[\begin{array}{ccc|ccc} 1 & 0 & 0 & 15 & 4 & -5 \\ 0 & 1 & 0 & -12 & -3 & 4 \\ 0 & 0 & 1 & -4 & -1 & 1 \end{array}\right].$$

This is the multiplicative identity, $I_3$.    This is the multiplicative inverse of $A$.

The observations in the voice balloons and the procedures followed above give us a general method for finding the multiplicative inverse of an invertible matrix.

## Study Tip

Because we have a quick method for finding the multiplicative inverse of a $2 \times 2$ matrix, the procedure on the right is recommended for matrices of order $3 \times 3$ or greater when a graphing utility is not being used.

## Procedure for Finding the Multiplicative Inverse of an Invertible Matrix

To find $A^{-1}$ for any $n \times n$ matrix $A$ for which $A^{-1}$ exists,

1. Form the augmented matrix $[A|I_n]$, where $I_n$ is the multiplicative identity matrix of the same order as the given matrix $A$.

2. Perform row operations on $[A|I_n]$ to obtain a matrix of the form $[I_n|B]$. This is equivalent to using Gauss-Jordan elimination to change $A$ into the identity matrix.

3. Matrix $B$ is $A^{-1}$.

4. Verify the result by showing that $AA^{-1} = I_n$ and $A^{-1}A = I_n$.

---

( **EXAMPLE 4** )  **Finding the Multiplicative Inverse of a 3 × 3 Matrix**

Find the multiplicative inverse of

$$A = \begin{bmatrix} 1 & -1 & 1 \\ 0 & -2 & 1 \\ -2 & -3 & 0 \end{bmatrix}.$$

### Solution

**Step 1   Form the augmented matrix $[A|I_3]$.**

$$\left[\begin{array}{ccc|ccc} 1 & -1 & 1 & 1 & 0 & 0 \\ 0 & -2 & 1 & 0 & 1 & 0 \\ -2 & -3 & 0 & 0 & 0 & 1 \end{array}\right]$$

This is matrix $A$.    This is $I_3$, the multiplicative identity matrix, with 1s down the main diagonal and 0s elsewhere.

**Step 2   Perform row operations on $[A|I_3]$ to obtain a matrix of the form $[I_3|B]$.** To the left of the vertical dividing line, we want 1s down the diagonal from upper left to lower right and 0s elsewhere.

$$\begin{bmatrix} 1 & -1 & 1 & | & 1 & 0 & 0 \\ 0 & -2 & 1 & | & 0 & 1 & 0 \\ -2 & -3 & 0 & | & 0 & 0 & 1 \end{bmatrix}$$
Replace row 3
by $2R_1 + R_3$.
$\longrightarrow$
$$\begin{bmatrix} 1 & -1 & 1 & | & 1 & 0 & 0 \\ 0 & -2 & 1 & | & 0 & 1 & 0 \\ 0 & -5 & 2 & | & 2 & 0 & 1 \end{bmatrix}$$
$\xrightarrow{-\frac{1}{2}R_2}$

$$\begin{bmatrix} 1 & -1 & 1 & | & 1 & 0 & 0 \\ 0 & 1 & -\frac{1}{2} & | & 0 & -\frac{1}{2} & 0 \\ 0 & -5 & 2 & | & 2 & 0 & 1 \end{bmatrix}$$
Replace row 1 by $1R_2 + R_1$.
Replace row 3 by $5R_2 + R_3$.
$\longrightarrow$
$$\begin{bmatrix} 1 & 0 & \frac{1}{2} & | & 1 & -\frac{1}{2} & 0 \\ 0 & 1 & -\frac{1}{2} & | & 0 & -\frac{1}{2} & 0 \\ 0 & 0 & -\frac{1}{2} & | & 2 & -\frac{5}{2} & 1 \end{bmatrix}$$
$\xrightarrow{-2R_3}$

$$\begin{bmatrix} 1 & 0 & \frac{1}{2} & | & 1 & -\frac{1}{2} & 0 \\ 0 & 1 & -\frac{1}{2} & | & 0 & -\frac{1}{2} & 0 \\ 0 & 0 & 1 & | & -4 & 5 & -2 \end{bmatrix}$$
Replace row 1 by $-\frac{1}{2}R_3 + R_1$.
Replace row 2 by $\frac{1}{2}R_3 + R_2$.
$\longrightarrow$
$$\begin{bmatrix} 1 & 0 & 0 & | & 3 & -3 & 1 \\ 0 & 1 & 0 & | & -2 & 2 & -1 \\ 0 & 0 & 1 & | & -4 & 5 & -2 \end{bmatrix}$$

This is the multiplicative identity, $I_3$.

This is the multiplicative inverse of $A$.

## Technology

We can use a graphing utility to verify the inverse matrix we found in Example 4. Enter the elements in matrix $A$ and press $\boxed{x^{-1}}$ to display $A^{-1}$.

```
[A]
      [[1  -1  1]
       [0  -2  1]
       [-2 -3  0]]
[A]-1
      [[3  -3  1 ]
       [-2  2  -1]
       [-4  5  -2]]
```

## Technology

The matrix

$$A = \begin{bmatrix} 4 & 6 \\ 2 & 3 \end{bmatrix} = \begin{bmatrix} a & b \\ c & d \end{bmatrix}$$

has no multiplicative inverse because

$$\begin{aligned} ad - bc &= 4 \cdot 3 - 6 \cdot 2 \\ &= 12 - 12 = 0. \end{aligned}$$

When we try to find the inverse with a graphing utility, an ERROR message occurs, indicating the matrix is singular.

```
[A]
      [[4  6]
       [2  3]]
[A]-1
■
```

```
ERR:SINGULAR MAT
1■Quit
2:Goto
```

**Step 3  Matrix $B$ is $A^{-1}$.** The last matrix shown is in the form $[I_3|B]$. The multiplicative identity matrix is on the left of the vertical bar. Matrix $B$, the multiplicative inverse of $A$, is on the right. Thus, the multiplicative inverse of $A$ is

$$A^{-1} = \begin{bmatrix} 3 & -3 & 1 \\ -2 & 2 & -1 \\ -4 & 5 & -2 \end{bmatrix}.$$

**Step 4  Verify the result by showing that $AA^{-1} = I_3$ and $A^{-1}A = I_3$.** Try confirming the result by multiplying $A$ and $A^{-1}$ to obtain $I_3$. Do you obtain $I_3$ if you reverse the order of the multiplication?

We have seen that not all square matrices have multiplicative inverses. If the row operations in step 2 result in all zeros in a row or column to the left of the vertical line, the given matrix does not have a multiplicative inverse.

⊘ Check Point **4** Find the multiplicative inverse of

$$A = \begin{bmatrix} 1 & 0 & 2 \\ -1 & 2 & 3 \\ 1 & -1 & 0 \end{bmatrix}.$$

## Summary: Finding Multiplicative Inverses for Invertible Matrices

Use a graphing utility with matrix capabilities, or

**a.** If the matrix is 2 × 2: The inverse of $A = \begin{bmatrix} a & b \\ c & d \end{bmatrix}$ is

$$A^{-1} = \frac{1}{ad - bc}\begin{bmatrix} d & -b \\ -c & a \end{bmatrix}.$$

**b.** If the matrix $A$ is $n \times n$ where $n > 2$: Use the procedure on page 848. Form $[A|I_n]$ and use row transformations to obtain $[I_n|B]$. Then $A^{-1} = B$.

## Solving Systems of Equations Using Multiplicative Inverses of Matrices

Matrix multiplication can be used to represent a system of linear equations.

**Linear System**

$$\begin{cases} a_1x + b_1y + c_1z = d_1 \\ a_2x + b_2y + c_2z = d_2 \\ a_3x + b_3y + c_3z = d_3 \end{cases}$$

**Matrix Form of the System**

$$\begin{bmatrix} a_1 & b_1 & c_1 \\ a_2 & b_2 & c_2 \\ a_3 & b_3 & c_3 \end{bmatrix} \begin{bmatrix} x \\ y \\ z \end{bmatrix} = \begin{bmatrix} d_1 \\ d_2 \\ d_3 \end{bmatrix}$$

The matrix contains the system's coefficients. | The matrix contains the system's variables. | The matrix contains the system's constants.

You can work with the matrix form of the system and obtain the form of the linear system on the left. To do so, perform the matrix multiplication on the left side of the matrix equation. Then equate the corresponding elements.

The matrix equation

$$\begin{bmatrix} a_1 & b_1 & c_1 \\ a_2 & b_2 & c_2 \\ a_3 & b_3 & c_3 \end{bmatrix} \begin{bmatrix} x \\ y \\ z \end{bmatrix} = \begin{bmatrix} d_1 \\ d_2 \\ d_3 \end{bmatrix}$$

$$\downarrow \qquad \quad \downarrow \quad \downarrow \quad \downarrow$$
$$A \qquad \quad X \; = \; B$$

is abbreviated as $AX = B$, where $A$ is the **coefficient matrix** of the system, and $X$ and $B$ are matrices containing one column, called **column matrices**. The matrix $B$ is called the **constant matrix**.

Here is a specific example of a linear system and its matrix form:

**Linear System**

$$\begin{cases} x - y + z = 2 \\ \phantom{x} -2y + z = 2 \\ -2x - 3y \phantom{+ z} = \tfrac{1}{2} \end{cases}$$

**Matrix Form**

Coefficients

$$\begin{bmatrix} 1 & -1 & 1 \\ 0 & -2 & 1 \\ -2 & -3 & 0 \end{bmatrix} \begin{bmatrix} x \\ y \\ z \end{bmatrix} = \begin{bmatrix} 2 \\ 2 \\ \tfrac{1}{2} \end{bmatrix}$$ Constants

$A$, the coefficent matrix | $X$ = | $B$, the constant matrix

The matrix equation $AX = B$ can be solved using $A^{-1}$ if it exists.

$AX = B$     This is the matrix equation.

$A^{-1}AX = A^{-1}B$     Multiply both sides by $A^{-1}$. Because matrix multiplication is not commutative, put $A^{-1}$ in the same left position on both sides.

$I_nX = A^{-1}B$     The multiplicative inverse property tells us that $A^{-1}A = I_n$.

$X = A^{-1}B$     Because $I_n$ is the multiplicative identity, $I_nX = X$.

We see that if $AX = B$, then $X = A^{-1}B$.

② Use inverses to solve matrix equations.

### Solving a System Using $A^{-1}$

If $AX = B$ has a unique solution, then $X = A^{-1}B$. To solve a linear system of equations, multiply $A^{-1}$ and $B$ to find $X$.

( EXAMPLE 5 ) **Using the Inverse of a Matrix to Solve a System**

Solve the system by using $A^{-1}$, the inverse of the coefficient matrix:

$$\begin{cases} x - y + z = 2 \\ -2y + z = 2 \\ -2x - 3y = \frac{1}{2}. \end{cases}$$

## Technology

We can use a graphing utility to solve a linear system with a unique solution by entering the elements in $A$, the coefficient matrix, and $B$, the column matrix. Then find the product of $A^{-1}$ and $B$. The screen below verifies our solution in Example 5.

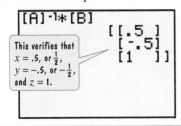

**Solution**   The linear system can be written as

$$\underset{A}{\begin{bmatrix} 1 & -1 & 1 \\ 0 & -2 & 1 \\ -2 & -3 & 0 \end{bmatrix}} \underset{X}{\begin{bmatrix} x \\ y \\ z \end{bmatrix}} = \underset{B}{\begin{bmatrix} 2 \\ 2 \\ \frac{1}{2} \end{bmatrix}}.$$

The solution is given by $X = A^{-1}B$. Consequently, we must find $A^{-1}$. We found the inverse of matrix $A$ in Example 4. Using this result,

$$X = A^{-1}B = \begin{bmatrix} 3 & -3 & 1 \\ -2 & 2 & -1 \\ -4 & 5 & -2 \end{bmatrix} \begin{bmatrix} 2 \\ 2 \\ \frac{1}{2} \end{bmatrix} = \begin{bmatrix} 3 \cdot 2 + (-3) \cdot 2 + 1 \cdot \frac{1}{2} \\ -2 \cdot 2 + 2 \cdot 2 + (-1) \cdot \frac{1}{2} \\ -4 \cdot 2 + 5 \cdot 2 + (-2) \cdot \frac{1}{2} \end{bmatrix} = \begin{bmatrix} \frac{1}{2} \\ -\frac{1}{2} \\ 1 \end{bmatrix}.$$

Thus, $x = \frac{1}{2}$, $y = -\frac{1}{2}$, and $z = 1$. The solution set is $\left\{\left(\frac{1}{2}, -\frac{1}{2}, 1\right)\right\}$.   ●

◯ Check Point **5**   Solve the system by using $A^{-1}$, the inverse of the coefficient matrix that you found in Check Point 4:

$$\begin{cases} x + 2z = 6 \\ -x + 2y + 3z = -5 \\ x - y = 6. \end{cases}$$

**③** Encode and decode messages.

## Applications of Matrix Inverses to Coding

A **cryptogram** is a message written so that no one other than the intended recipient can understand it. To encode a message, we begin by assigning a number to each letter in the alphabet: $A = 1, B = 2, C = 3, \ldots, Z = 26$, and a space $= 0$. For example, the numerical equivalent of the word MATH is 13, 1, 20, 8. The numerical equivalent of the message is then converted into a matrix. Finally, an invertible matrix can be used to convert the message into code. The multiplicative inverse of this matrix can be used to decode the message.

### Encoding a Word or Message

1. Express the word or message numerically.
2. List the numbers in step 1 by columns and form a square matrix. If you do not have enough numbers to form a square matrix, put zeros in any remaining spaces in the last column.
3. Select any square invertible matrix, called the **coding matrix**, the same size as the matrix in step 2. Multiply the coding matrix by the square matrix that expresses the message numerically. The resulting matrix is the **coded matrix**.
4. Use the numbers, by columns, from the coded matrix in step 3 to write the encoded message.

**EXAMPLE 6** Encoding a Word

Use matrices to encode the word MATH.

**Solution**

**Step 1 Express the word numerically.** As shown previously, the numerical equivalent of MATH is 13, 1, 20, 8.

**Step 2 List the numbers in step 1 by columns and form a square matrix.** The $2 \times 2$ matrix for the numerical equivalent of MATH, 13, 1, 20, 8, is

$$\begin{bmatrix} 13 & 20 \\ 1 & 8 \end{bmatrix}.$$

**Step 3 Multiply the matrix in step 2 by a square invertible matrix.** We will use $\begin{bmatrix} -2 & -3 \\ 3 & 4 \end{bmatrix}$ as the coding matrix.

$$\underbrace{\begin{bmatrix} -2 & -3 \\ 3 & 4 \end{bmatrix}}_{\substack{\text{Coding} \\ \text{matrix}}} \underbrace{\begin{bmatrix} 13 & 20 \\ 1 & 8 \end{bmatrix}}_{\substack{\text{Numerical} \\ \text{representation of} \\ \text{MATH}}} = \begin{bmatrix} -2(13) - 3(1) & -2(20) - 3(8) \\ 3(13) + 4(1) & 3(20) + 4(8) \end{bmatrix}$$

$$= \underbrace{\begin{bmatrix} -29 & -64 \\ 43 & 92 \end{bmatrix}}_{\substack{\text{Coded} \\ \text{matrix}}}$$

**Step 4 Use the numbers, by columns, from the coded matrix in step 3 to write the encoded message.** The encoded message is $-29, \ 43, -64, \ 92$. ●

⊘ Check Point 6 Use the coding matrix in Example 6, $\begin{bmatrix} -2 & -3 \\ 3 & 4 \end{bmatrix}$, to encode the word BASE.

The inverse of a coding matrix can be used to decode a word or message that was encoded.

### Decoding a Word or Message That Was Encoded

1. Find the multiplicative inverse of the coding matrix.
2. Multiply the multiplicative inverse of the coding matrix and the coded matrix.
3. Express the numbers, by columns, from the matrix in step 2 as letters.

**EXAMPLE 7** Decoding a Word

Decode $-29, 43, -64, 92$ from Example 6.

**Solution**

**Step 1 Find the inverse of the coding matrix.** The coding matrix in Example 6 was $\begin{bmatrix} -2 & -3 \\ 3 & 4 \end{bmatrix}$. We use the formula for the multiplicative inverse of a $2 \times 2$ matrix to find the multiplicative inverse of this matrix. It is $\begin{bmatrix} 4 & 3 \\ -3 & -2 \end{bmatrix}$.

**Step 2  Multiply the multiplicative inverse of the coding matrix and the coded matrix.**

$$\underbrace{\begin{bmatrix} 4 & 3 \\ -3 & -2 \end{bmatrix}}_{\substack{\text{Multiplicative inverse} \\ \text{of the coding matrix}}} \underbrace{\begin{bmatrix} -29 & -64 \\ 43 & 92 \end{bmatrix}}_{\substack{\text{Coded} \\ \text{matrix}}} = \begin{bmatrix} 4(-29) + 3(43) & 4(-64) + 3(92) \\ -3(-29) - 2(43) & -3(-64) - 2(92) \end{bmatrix}$$

$$= \begin{bmatrix} 13 & 20 \\ 1 & 8 \end{bmatrix}$$

**Step 3  Express the numbers, by columns, from the matrix in step 2 as letters.** The numbers are 13, 1, 20, and 8. Using letters, the decoded message is MATH.

✓ Check Point **7** Decode the word that you encoded in Check Point 6.

Decoding is simple for an authorized receiver who knows the coding matrix. Because any invertible matrix can be used for the coding matrix, decoding a cryptogram for an unauthorized receiver who does not know this matrix is extremely difficult.

# Exercise Set 8.4

## Practice Exercises

*In Exercises 1–12, find the products AB and BA to determine whether B is the multiplicative inverse of A.*

**1.** $A = \begin{bmatrix} 4 & -3 \\ -5 & 4 \end{bmatrix}$, $B = \begin{bmatrix} 4 & 3 \\ 5 & 4 \end{bmatrix}$

**2.** $A = \begin{bmatrix} -2 & -1 \\ -1 & 1 \end{bmatrix}$, $B = \begin{bmatrix} 1 & 1 \\ 1 & 2 \end{bmatrix}$

**3.** $A = \begin{bmatrix} -4 & 0 \\ 1 & 3 \end{bmatrix}$, $B = \begin{bmatrix} -2 & 4 \\ 0 & 1 \end{bmatrix}$

**4.** $A = \begin{bmatrix} -2 & 4 \\ 1 & -2 \end{bmatrix}$, $B = \begin{bmatrix} 1 & 2 \\ -1 & -2 \end{bmatrix}$

**5.** $A = \begin{bmatrix} -2 & 1 \\ \frac{3}{2} & -\frac{1}{2} \end{bmatrix}$, $B = \begin{bmatrix} 1 & 2 \\ 3 & 4 \end{bmatrix}$

**6.** $A = \begin{bmatrix} 4 & 5 \\ 2 & 3 \end{bmatrix}$, $B = \begin{bmatrix} \frac{3}{2} & -\frac{5}{2} \\ -1 & 2 \end{bmatrix}$

**7.** $A = \begin{bmatrix} 0 & 1 & 0 \\ 0 & 0 & 1 \\ 1 & 0 & 0 \end{bmatrix}$, $B = \begin{bmatrix} 0 & 0 & 1 \\ 1 & 0 & 0 \\ 0 & 1 & 0 \end{bmatrix}$

**8.** $A = \begin{bmatrix} -2 & 1 & -1 \\ -5 & 2 & -1 \\ 3 & -1 & 1 \end{bmatrix}$, $B = \begin{bmatrix} 1 & 0 & 1 \\ 2 & 1 & 3 \\ -1 & 1 & 1 \end{bmatrix}$

**9.** $A = \begin{bmatrix} 1 & 2 & 3 \\ 1 & 3 & 4 \\ 1 & 4 & 3 \end{bmatrix}$, $B = \begin{bmatrix} \frac{7}{2} & -3 & \frac{1}{2} \\ -\frac{1}{2} & 0 & \frac{1}{2} \\ -\frac{1}{2} & 1 & -\frac{1}{2} \end{bmatrix}$

**10.** $A = \begin{bmatrix} 0 & 2 & 0 \\ 3 & 3 & 2 \\ 2 & 5 & 1 \end{bmatrix}$, $B = \begin{bmatrix} -3.5 & -1 & 2 \\ 0.5 & 0 & 0 \\ 4.5 & 2 & -3 \end{bmatrix}$

**11.** $A = \begin{bmatrix} 0 & 0 & -2 & 1 \\ -1 & 0 & 1 & 1 \\ 0 & 1 & -1 & 0 \\ 1 & 0 & 0 & -1 \end{bmatrix}$, $B = \begin{bmatrix} 1 & 2 & 0 & 3 \\ 0 & 1 & 1 & 1 \\ 0 & 1 & 0 & 1 \\ 1 & 2 & 0 & 2 \end{bmatrix}$

**12.** $A = \begin{bmatrix} 1 & -2 & 1 & 0 \\ 0 & 1 & -2 & 1 \\ 0 & 0 & 1 & -2 \\ 0 & 0 & 0 & 1 \end{bmatrix}$, $B = \begin{bmatrix} 1 & 2 & 3 & 4 \\ 0 & 1 & 2 & 3 \\ 0 & 0 & 1 & 2 \\ 0 & 0 & 0 & 1 \end{bmatrix}$

*In Exercises 13–18, use the fact that if $A = \begin{bmatrix} a & b \\ c & d \end{bmatrix}$, then $A^{-1} = \dfrac{1}{ad - bc}\begin{bmatrix} d & -b \\ -c & a \end{bmatrix}$ to find the inverse of each matrix, if possible. Check that $AA^{-1} = I_2$ and $A^{-1}A = I_2$.*

**13.** $A = \begin{bmatrix} 2 & 3 \\ -1 & 2 \end{bmatrix}$

**14.** $A = \begin{bmatrix} 0 & 3 \\ 4 & -2 \end{bmatrix}$

**15.** $A = \begin{bmatrix} 3 & -1 \\ -4 & 2 \end{bmatrix}$

**16.** $A = \begin{bmatrix} 2 & -6 \\ 1 & -2 \end{bmatrix}$

**17.** $A = \begin{bmatrix} 10 & -2 \\ -5 & 1 \end{bmatrix}$

**18.** $A = \begin{bmatrix} 6 & -3 \\ -2 & 1 \end{bmatrix}$

*In Exercises 19–28, find $A^{-1}$ by forming $[A|I]$ and then using row operations to obtain $[I|B]$, where $A^{-1} = [B]$. Check that $AA^{-1} = I$ and $A^{-1}A = I$.*

**19.** $A = \begin{bmatrix} 2 & 0 & 0 \\ 0 & 4 & 0 \\ 0 & 0 & 6 \end{bmatrix}$

**20.** $A = \begin{bmatrix} 3 & 0 & 0 \\ 0 & 6 & 0 \\ 0 & 0 & 9 \end{bmatrix}$

**21.** $A = \begin{bmatrix} 1 & 2 & -1 \\ -2 & 0 & 1 \\ 1 & -1 & 0 \end{bmatrix}$

**22.** $A = \begin{bmatrix} 1 & -1 & 1 \\ 0 & 2 & -1 \\ 2 & 3 & 0 \end{bmatrix}$

**23.** $A = \begin{bmatrix} 2 & 2 & -1 \\ 0 & 3 & -1 \\ -1 & -2 & 1 \end{bmatrix}$

**24.** $A = \begin{bmatrix} 2 & 4 & -4 \\ 1 & 3 & -4 \\ 2 & 4 & -3 \end{bmatrix}$

**25.** $A = \begin{bmatrix} 5 & 0 & 2 \\ 2 & 2 & 1 \\ -3 & 1 & -1 \end{bmatrix}$

**26.** $A = \begin{bmatrix} 3 & 2 & 6 \\ 1 & 1 & 2 \\ 2 & 2 & 5 \end{bmatrix}$

**27.** $A = \begin{bmatrix} 1 & 0 & 0 & 0 \\ 0 & -1 & 0 & 0 \\ 0 & 0 & 3 & 0 \\ 1 & 0 & 0 & 1 \end{bmatrix}$

**28.** $A = \begin{bmatrix} 2 & 0 & 0 & 1 \\ 0 & 1 & 0 & 0 \\ 0 & 0 & -1 & 0 \\ 0 & 0 & 0 & 2 \end{bmatrix}$

*In Exercises 29–32, write each linear system as a matrix equation in the form $AX = B$, where $A$ is the coefficient matrix and $B$ is the constant matrix.*

**29.** $\begin{cases} 6x + 5y = 13 \\ 5x + 4y = 10 \end{cases}$
  **30.** $\begin{cases} 7x + 5y = 23 \\ 3x + 2y = 10 \end{cases}$

**31.** $\begin{cases} x + 3y + 4z = -3 \\ x + 2y + 3z = -2 \\ x + 4y + 3z = -6 \end{cases}$
  **32.** $\begin{cases} x + 4y - z = 3 \\ x + 3y - 2z = 5 \\ 2x + 7y - 5z = 12 \end{cases}$

*In Exercises 33–36, write each matrix equation as a system of linear equations without matrices.*

**33.** $\begin{bmatrix} 4 & -7 \\ 2 & -3 \end{bmatrix} \begin{bmatrix} x \\ y \end{bmatrix} = \begin{bmatrix} -3 \\ 1 \end{bmatrix}$

**34.** $\begin{bmatrix} 3 & 0 \\ -3 & 1 \end{bmatrix} \begin{bmatrix} x \\ y \end{bmatrix} = \begin{bmatrix} 6 \\ -7 \end{bmatrix}$

**35.** $\begin{bmatrix} 2 & 0 & -1 \\ 0 & 3 & 0 \\ 1 & 1 & 0 \end{bmatrix} \begin{bmatrix} x \\ y \\ z \end{bmatrix} = \begin{bmatrix} 6 \\ 9 \\ 5 \end{bmatrix}$

**36.** $\begin{bmatrix} -1 & 0 & 1 \\ 0 & -1 & 0 \\ 0 & 1 & 1 \end{bmatrix} \begin{bmatrix} x \\ y \\ z \end{bmatrix} = \begin{bmatrix} -4 \\ 2 \\ 4 \end{bmatrix}$

*In Exercises 37–42,*

**a.** *Write each linear system as a matrix equation in the form $AX = B$.*

**b.** *Solve the system using the inverse that is given for the coefficient matrix.*

**37.** $\begin{cases} 2x + 6y + 6z = 8 \\ 2x + 7y + 6z = 10 \\ 2x + 7y + 7z = 9 \end{cases}$

The inverse of $\begin{bmatrix} 2 & 6 & 6 \\ 2 & 7 & 6 \\ 2 & 7 & 7 \end{bmatrix}$ is $\begin{bmatrix} \frac{7}{2} & 0 & -3 \\ -1 & 1 & 0 \\ 0 & -1 & 1 \end{bmatrix}$.

**38.** $\begin{cases} x + 2y + 5z = 2 \\ 2x + 3y + 8z = 3 \\ -x + y + 2z = 3 \end{cases}$

The inverse of $\begin{bmatrix} 1 & 2 & 5 \\ 2 & 3 & 8 \\ -1 & 1 & 2 \end{bmatrix}$ is $\begin{bmatrix} 2 & -1 & -1 \\ 12 & -7 & -2 \\ -5 & 3 & 1 \end{bmatrix}$.

**39.** $\begin{cases} x - y + z = 8 \\ 2y - z = -7 \\ 2x + 3y = 1 \end{cases}$

The inverse of $\begin{bmatrix} 1 & -1 & 1 \\ 0 & 2 & -1 \\ 2 & 3 & 0 \end{bmatrix}$ is $\begin{bmatrix} 3 & 3 & -1 \\ -2 & -2 & 1 \\ -4 & -5 & 2 \end{bmatrix}$.

**40.** $\begin{cases} x - 6y + 3z = 11 \\ 2x - 7y + 3z = 14 \\ 4x - 12y + 5z = 25 \end{cases}$

The inverse of $\begin{bmatrix} 1 & -6 & 3 \\ 2 & -7 & 3 \\ 4 & -12 & 5 \end{bmatrix}$ is $\begin{bmatrix} 1 & -6 & 3 \\ 2 & -7 & 3 \\ 4 & -12 & 5 \end{bmatrix}$.

**41.** $\begin{cases} w - x + 2y = -3 \\ x - y + z = 4 \\ -w + x - y + 2z = 2 \\ -x + y - 2z = -4 \end{cases}$

The inverse of $\begin{bmatrix} 1 & -1 & 2 & 0 \\ 0 & 1 & -1 & 1 \\ -1 & 1 & -1 & 2 \\ 0 & -1 & 1 & -2 \end{bmatrix}$ is $\begin{bmatrix} 0 & 0 & -1 & -1 \\ 1 & 4 & 1 & 3 \\ 1 & 2 & 1 & 2 \\ 0 & -1 & 0 & -1 \end{bmatrix}$.

**42.** $\begin{cases} 2w + y + z = 6 \\ 3w + z = 9 \\ -w + x - 2y + z = 4 \\ 4w - x + y = 6 \end{cases}$

The inverse of $\begin{bmatrix} 2 & 0 & 1 & 1 \\ 3 & 0 & 0 & 1 \\ -1 & 1 & -2 & 1 \\ 4 & -1 & 1 & 0 \end{bmatrix}$ is $\begin{bmatrix} -1 & 2 & -1 & -1 \\ -4 & 9 & -5 & -6 \\ 0 & 1 & -1 & -1 \\ 3 & -5 & 3 & 3 \end{bmatrix}$.

## Practice Plus

*In Exercises 43–44, find $A^{-1}$ and check.*

**43.** $A = \begin{bmatrix} e^x & e^{3x} \\ -e^{3x} & e^{5x} \end{bmatrix}$
  **44.** $A = \begin{bmatrix} e^{2x} & -e^x \\ e^{3x} & e^{2x} \end{bmatrix}$

*In Exercises 45–46, if $I$ is the multiplicative identity matrix of order 2, find $(I - A)^{-1}$ for the given matrix $A$.*

**45.** $\begin{bmatrix} 8 & -5 \\ -3 & 2 \end{bmatrix}$
  **46.** $\begin{bmatrix} 7 & -5 \\ -4 & 3 \end{bmatrix}$

*In Exercises 47–48, find $(AB)^{-1}$, $A^{-1}B^{-1}$, and $B^{-1}A^{-1}$. What do you observe?*

**47.** $A = \begin{bmatrix} 2 & 1 \\ 3 & 1 \end{bmatrix}$  $B = \begin{bmatrix} 4 & 7 \\ 1 & 2 \end{bmatrix}$

**48.** $A = \begin{bmatrix} 2 & -9 \\ 1 & -4 \end{bmatrix}$  $B = \begin{bmatrix} 9 & 5 \\ 7 & 4 \end{bmatrix}$

**49.** Prove the following statement:

If $A = \begin{bmatrix} a & 0 & 0 \\ 0 & b & 0 \\ 0 & 0 & c \end{bmatrix}$, $a \neq 0, b \neq 0, c \neq 0$,

then $A^{-1} = \begin{bmatrix} \frac{1}{a} & 0 & 0 \\ 0 & \frac{1}{b} & 0 \\ 0 & 0 & \frac{1}{c} \end{bmatrix}$.

**50.** Prove the following statement:

If $A = \begin{bmatrix} a & b \\ c & d \end{bmatrix}$ and $ad - bc \neq 0$,

then $A^{-1} = \dfrac{1}{ad - bc} \begin{bmatrix} d & -b \\ -c & a \end{bmatrix}$.

(*Hint:* Use the method of Example 2 on page 844.)

## Application Exercises

*In Exercises 51–52, use the coding matrix*

$$A = \begin{bmatrix} 4 & -1 \\ -3 & 1 \end{bmatrix} \text{ and its inverse } A^{-1} = \begin{bmatrix} 1 & 1 \\ 3 & 4 \end{bmatrix}$$

*to encode and then decode the given message.*

**51.** HELP
  **52.** LOVE

*In Exercises 53–54, use the coding matrix*

$$A = \begin{bmatrix} 1 & -1 & 0 \\ 3 & 0 & 2 \\ -1 & 0 & -1 \end{bmatrix} \text{ and its inverse}$$

$$A^{-1} = \begin{bmatrix} 0 & 1 & 2 \\ -1 & 1 & 2 \\ 0 & -1 & -3 \end{bmatrix} \text{ to write a cryptogram for each}$$

*message. Check your result by decoding the cryptogram.*

**53.** S  E  N  D  _  C  A  S  H
19  5  14  4  0  3  1  19  8

Use $\begin{bmatrix} 19 & 4 & 1 \\ 5 & 0 & 19 \\ 14 & 3 & 8 \end{bmatrix}$.

**54.** S  T  A  Y  _  W  E  L  L
19  20  1  25  0  23  5  12  12

Use $\begin{bmatrix} 19 & 25 & 5 \\ 20 & 0 & 12 \\ 1 & 23 & 12 \end{bmatrix}$.

## Writing in Mathematics

**55.** What is the multiplicative identity matrix?

**56.** If you are given two matrices, $A$ and $B$, explain how to determine if $B$ is the multiplicative inverse of $A$.

**57.** Explain why a matrix that does not have the same number of rows and columns cannot have a multiplicative inverse.

**58.** Explain how to find the multiplicative inverse for a $2 \times 2$ invertible matrix.

**59.** Explain how to find the multiplicative inverse for a $3 \times 3$ invertible matrix.

**60.** Explain how to write a linear system of three equations in three variables as a matrix equation.

**61.** Explain how to solve the matrix equation $AX = B$.

**62.** What is a cryptogram?

**63.** It's January 1, and you've written down your major goal for the year. You do not want those closest to you to see what you've written in case you do not accomplish your objective. Consequently, you decide to use a coding matrix to encode your goal. Explain how this can be accomplished.

**64.** A year has passed since Exercise 63. (Time flies when you're solving exercises in algebra books.) It's been a terrific year and so many wonderful things have happened that you can't remember your goal from a year ago. You consult your personal journal and you find the encoded message and the coding matrix. How can you use these to find your original goal?

## Technology Exercises

*In Exercises 65–70, use a graphing utility to find the multiplicative inverse of each matrix. Check that the displayed inverse is correct.*

**65.** $\begin{bmatrix} 3 & -1 \\ -2 & 1 \end{bmatrix}$    **66.** $\begin{bmatrix} -4 & 1 \\ 6 & -2 \end{bmatrix}$

**67.** $\begin{bmatrix} -2 & 1 & -1 \\ -5 & 2 & -1 \\ 3 & -1 & 1 \end{bmatrix}$    **68.** $\begin{bmatrix} 1 & 1 & -1 \\ -3 & 2 & -1 \\ 3 & -3 & 2 \end{bmatrix}$

**69.** $\begin{bmatrix} 7 & -3 & 0 & 2 \\ -2 & 1 & 0 & -1 \\ 4 & 0 & 1 & -2 \\ -1 & 1 & 0 & -1 \end{bmatrix}$    **70.** $\begin{bmatrix} 1 & 2 & 0 & 0 \\ 0 & 0 & 1 & 0 \\ 1 & 3 & 0 & 1 \\ 4 & 0 & 0 & 2 \end{bmatrix}$

*In Exercises 71–76, write each system in the form $AX = B$. Then solve the system by entering $A$ and $B$ into your graphing utility and computing $A^{-1}B$.*

**71.** $\begin{cases} x - y + z = -6 \\ 4x + 2y + z = 9 \\ 4x - 2y + z = -3 \end{cases}$    **72.** $\begin{cases} y + 2z = 0 \\ -x + y = 1 \\ 2x - y + z = -1 \end{cases}$

**73.** $\begin{cases} 3x - 2y + z = -2 \\ 4x - 5y + 3z = -9 \\ 2x - y + 5z = -5 \end{cases}$    **74.** $\begin{cases} x - y = 1 \\ 6x + y + 20z = 14 \\ y + 3z = 1 \end{cases}$

**75.** $\begin{cases} v - 3x + z = -3 \\ w + y = -1 \\ x + z = 7 \\ v + w - x + 4y = -8 \\ v + w + x + y + z = 8 \end{cases}$

**76.** $\begin{cases} w + x + y + z = 4 \\ w + 3x - 2y + 2z = 7 \\ 2w + 2x + y + z = 3 \\ w - x + 2y + 3z = 5 \end{cases}$

*In Exercises 77–78, use a coding matrix $A$ of your choice. Use a graphing utility to find the multiplicative inverse of your coding matrix. Write a cryptogram for each message. Check your result by decoding the cryptogram. Use your graphing utility to perform all necessary matrix multiplications.*

**77.** A  R  R  I  V  E  D  _  S  A  F  E  L  Y
1  18  18  9  22  5  4  0  19  1  6  5  12  25

**78.** A  R  T  _  E  N  R  I  C  H  E  S
1  18  20  0  5  14  18  9  3  8  5  19

## Critical Thinking Exercises

**Make Sense?** *In Exercises 79–82, determine whether each statement makes sense or does not make sense, and explain your reasoning.*

**79.** I found the multiplicative inverse of a $2 \times 3$ matrix.

**80.** I used Gauss-Jordan elimination to find the multiplicative inverse of a $3 \times 3$ matrix.

**81.** I used matrix multiplication to represent a system of linear equations.

**82.** I made an encoding error by selecting the wrong square invertible matrix.

*In Exercises 83–88, determine whether each statement is true or false. If the statement is false, make the necessary change(s) to produce a true statement.*

**83.** All square $2 \times 2$ matrices have inverses because there is a formula for finding these inverses.

**84.** Two $2 \times 2$ invertible matrices can have a matrix sum that is not invertible.

**85.** To solve the matrix equation $AX = B$ for $X$, multiply $A$ and the inverse of $B$.

**86.** $(AB)^{-1} = A^{-1}B^{-1}$, assuming $A$, $B$, and $AB$ are invertible.

**87.** $(A + B)^{-1} = A^{-1} + B^{-1}$, assuming $A$, $B$, and $A + B$ are invertible.

**88.** $\begin{bmatrix} 1 & -3 \\ -1 & 3 \end{bmatrix}$ is an invertible matrix.

**89.** Give an example of a $2 \times 2$ matrix that is its own inverse.

**90.** If $A = \begin{bmatrix} 3 & 5 \\ 2 & 4 \end{bmatrix}$, find $(A^{-1})^{-1}$.

**91.** Find values of $a$ for which the following matrix is not invertible:
$$\begin{bmatrix} 1 & a+1 \\ a-2 & 4 \end{bmatrix}.$$

## Group Exercise

**92.** Each person in the group should work with one partner. Send a coded word or message to each other by giving your partner the coded matrix and the coding matrix that you selected. Once messages are sent, each person should decode the message received.

## Preview Exercises

*Exercises 93–95 will help you prepare for the material covered in the next section. Simplify the expression in each exercise.*

**93.** $2(-5) - (-3)(4)$

**94.** $\dfrac{2(-5) - 1(-4)}{5(-5) - 6(-4)}$

**95.** $2(-30 - (-3)) - 3(6 - 9) + (-1)(1 - 15)$

---

Section **8.5** **Determinants and Cramer's Rule**

### Objectives

1. Evaluate a second-order determinant.

2. Solve a system of linear equations in two variables using Cramer's rule.

3. Evaluate a third-order determinant.

4. Solve a system of linear equations in three variables using Cramer's rule.

5. Use determinants to identify inconsistent systems and systems with dependent equations.

6. Evaluate higher-order determinants.

A portion of Charles Babbage's unrealized Difference Engine

As cyberspace absorbs more and more of our work, play, shopping, and socializing, where will it all end? Which activities will still be offline in 2025?

Our technologically transformed lives can be traced back to the English inventor Charles Babbage (1792–1871). Babbage knew of a method for solving linear systems called *Cramer's rule*, in honor of the Swiss geometer Gabriel Cramer (1704–1752). Cramer's rule was simple, but involved numerous multiplications for large systems. Babbage designed a machine, called the "difference engine," that consisted of toothed wheels on shafts for performing these multiplications. Despite the fact that only one-seventh of the functions ever worked, Babbage's invention demonstrated how complex calculations could be handled mechanically. In 1944, scientists at IBM used the lessons of the difference engine to create the world's first computer.

Those who invented computers hoped to relegate the drudgery of repeated computation to a machine. In this section, we look at a method for solving linear systems that played a critical role in this process. The method uses real numbers, called *determinants*, that are associated with arrays of numbers. As with matrix methods, solutions are obtained by writing down the coefficients and constants of a linear system and performing operations with them.

1. Evaluate a second-order determinant.

### The Determinant of a 2 × 2 Matrix

Associated with every square matrix is a real number, called its **determinant**. The determinant for a 2 × 2 square matrix is defined as follows:

**Definition of the Determinant of a 2 × 2 Matrix**

The determinant of the matrix $\begin{bmatrix} a_1 & b_1 \\ a_2 & b_2 \end{bmatrix}$ is denoted by $\begin{vmatrix} a_1 & b_1 \\ a_2 & b_2 \end{vmatrix}$ and is defined by

$$\begin{vmatrix} a_1 & b_1 \\ a_2 & b_2 \end{vmatrix} = a_1b_2 - a_2b_1.$$

We also say that the **value** of the **second-order determinant** $\begin{vmatrix} a_1 & b_1 \\ a_2 & b_2 \end{vmatrix}$ is $a_1b_2 - a_2b_1$.

Example 1 illustrates that the determinant of a matrix may be positive or negative. A determinant can also have 0 as its value.

**( EXAMPLE 1 )  Evaluating the Determinant of a 2 × 2 Matrix**

Evaluate the determinant of each of the following matrices:

**a.** $\begin{bmatrix} 5 & 6 \\ 7 & 3 \end{bmatrix}$      **b.** $\begin{bmatrix} 2 & 4 \\ -3 & -5 \end{bmatrix}$.

**Solution**  We multiply and subtract as indicated.

**a.** $\begin{vmatrix} 5 & 6 \\ 7 & 3 \end{vmatrix} = 5 \cdot 3 - 7 \cdot 6 = 15 - 42 = -27$    *The value of the second-order determinant is −27.*

**b.** $\begin{vmatrix} 2 & 4 \\ -3 & -5 \end{vmatrix} = 2(-5) - (-3)(4) = -10 + 12 = 2$    *The value of the second-order determinant is 2.* ●

⊘ **Check Point 1**  Evaluate the determinant of each of the following matrices:

**a.** $\begin{bmatrix} 10 & 9 \\ 6 & 5 \end{bmatrix}$      **b.** $\begin{bmatrix} 4 & 3 \\ -5 & -8 \end{bmatrix}$.

**②** Solve a system of linear equations in two variables using Cramer's rule.

## Solving Systems of Linear Equations in Two Variables Using Determinants

Determinants can be used to solve a linear system in two variables. In general, such a system appears as

$$\begin{cases} a_1x + b_1y = c_1 \\ a_2x + b_2y = c_2. \end{cases}$$

Let's first solve this system for $x$ using the addition method. We can solve for $x$ by eliminating $y$ from the equations. Multiply the first equation by $b_2$ and the second equation by $-b_1$. Then add the two equations:

$$\begin{cases} a_1x + b_1y = c_1 \\ a_2x + b_2y = c_2 \end{cases} \xrightarrow[\text{Multiply by } -b_1.]{\text{Multiply by } b_2.} \begin{cases} a_1b_2x + b_1b_2y = \phantom{-}c_1b_2 \\ -a_2b_1x - b_1b_2y = -c_2b_1 \end{cases}$$

Add:    $(a_1b_2 - a_2b_1)x = c_1b_2 - c_2b_1$

$$x = \frac{c_1b_2 - c_2b_1}{a_1b_2 - a_2b_1}.$$

Because

$$\begin{vmatrix} c_1 & b_1 \\ c_2 & b_2 \end{vmatrix} = c_1b_2 - c_2b_1 \quad \text{and} \quad \begin{vmatrix} a_1 & b_1 \\ a_2 & b_2 \end{vmatrix} = a_1b_2 - a_2b_1,$$

we can express our answer for $x$ as the quotient of two determinants:

$$x = \frac{c_1 b_2 - c_2 b_1}{a_1 b_2 - a_2 b_1} = \frac{\begin{vmatrix} c_1 & b_1 \\ c_2 & b_2 \end{vmatrix}}{\begin{vmatrix} a_1 & b_1 \\ a_2 & b_2 \end{vmatrix}}.$$

Similarly, we could use the addition method to solve our system for $y$, again expressing $y$ as the quotient of two determinants. This method of using determinants to solve the linear system, called **Cramer's rule**, is summarized in the box.

### Solving a Linear System in Two Variables Using Determinants Cramer's Rule

If

$$\begin{cases} a_1 x + b_1 y = c_1 \\ a_2 x + b_2 y = c_2, \end{cases}$$

then

$$x = \frac{\begin{vmatrix} c_1 & b_1 \\ c_2 & b_2 \end{vmatrix}}{\begin{vmatrix} a_1 & b_1 \\ a_2 & b_2 \end{vmatrix}} \quad \text{and} \quad y = \frac{\begin{vmatrix} a_1 & c_1 \\ a_2 & c_2 \end{vmatrix}}{\begin{vmatrix} a_1 & b_1 \\ a_2 & b_2 \end{vmatrix}},$$

where

$$\begin{vmatrix} a_1 & b_1 \\ a_2 & b_2 \end{vmatrix} \neq 0.$$

Here are some helpful tips when solving

$$\begin{cases} a_1 x + b_1 y = c_1 \\ a_2 x + b_2 y = c_2 \end{cases}$$

using determinants:

1. Three different determinants are used to find $x$ and $y$. The determinants in the denominators for $x$ and $y$ are identical. The determinants in the numerators for $x$ and $y$ differ. In abbreviated notation, we write

   $$x = \frac{D_x}{D} \quad \text{and} \quad y = \frac{D_y}{D}, \text{ where } D \neq 0.$$

2. The elements of $D$, the determinant in the denominator, are the coefficients of the variables in the system.

   $$D = \begin{vmatrix} a_1 & b_1 \\ a_2 & b_2 \end{vmatrix}$$

3. $D_x$, the determinant in the numerator of $x$, is obtained by replacing the $x$-coefficients, in $D$, $a_1$ and $a_2$, with the constants on the right sides of the equations, $c_1$ and $c_2$.

   $$D = \begin{vmatrix} a_1 & b_1 \\ a_2 & b_2 \end{vmatrix} \quad \text{and} \quad D_x = \begin{vmatrix} c_1 & b_1 \\ c_2 & b_2 \end{vmatrix} \quad \begin{array}{l} \text{Replace the column with } a_1 \text{ and } a_2 \text{ with} \\ \text{the constants } c_1 \text{ and } c_2 \text{ to get } D_x. \end{array}$$

4. $D_y$, the determinant in the numerator for $y$, is obtained by replacing the $y$-coefficients, in $D$, $b_1$ and $b_2$, with the constants on the right sides of the equations, $c_1$ and $c_2$.

   $$D = \begin{vmatrix} a_1 & b_1 \\ a_2 & b_2 \end{vmatrix} \quad \text{and} \quad D_y = \begin{vmatrix} a_1 & c_1 \\ a_2 & c_2 \end{vmatrix} \quad \begin{array}{l} \text{Replace the column with } b_1 \text{ and } b_2 \text{ with} \\ \text{the constants } c_1 \text{ and } c_2 \text{ to get } D_y. \end{array}$$

(**EXAMPLE 2**) **Using Cramer's Rule to Solve a Linear System**

Use Cramer's rule to solve the system:

$$\begin{cases} 5x - 4y = 2 \\ 6x - 5y = 1. \end{cases}$$

**Solution**   Because

$$x = \frac{D_x}{D} \quad \text{and} \quad y = \frac{D_y}{D},$$

we will set up and evaluate the three determinants $D$, $D_x$, and $D_y$.

1. $D$, the determinant in both denominators, consists of the $x$- and $y$-coefficients.

$$D = \begin{vmatrix} 5 & -4 \\ 6 & -5 \end{vmatrix} = (5)(-5) - (6)(-4) = -25 + 24 = -1$$

Because this determinant is not zero, we continue to use Cramer's rule to solve the system.

2. $D_x$, the determinant in the numerator for $x$, is obtained by replacing the $x$-coefficients in $D$, 5 and 6, by the constants on the right sides of the equations, 2 and 1.

$$D_x = \begin{vmatrix} 2 & -4 \\ 1 & -5 \end{vmatrix} = (2)(-5) - (1)(-4) = -10 + 4 = -6$$

3. $D_y$, the determinant in the numerator for $y$, is obtained by replacing the $y$-coefficients in $D$, $-4$ and $-5$, by the constants on the right sides of the equations, 2 and 1.

$$D_y = \begin{vmatrix} 5 & 2 \\ 6 & 1 \end{vmatrix} = (5)(1) - (6)(2) = 5 - 12 = -7$$

4. Thus,

$$x = \frac{D_x}{D} = \frac{-6}{-1} = 6 \quad \text{and} \quad y = \frac{D_y}{D} = \frac{-7}{-1} = 7.$$

As always, the solution $(6, 7)$ can be checked by substituting these values into the original equations. The solution set is $\{(6, 7)\}$.   ●

⊘ Check Point **2**   Use Cramer's rule to solve the system:

$$\begin{cases} 5x + 4y = 12 \\ 3x - 6y = 24. \end{cases}$$

③ Evaluate a third-order determinant.

## The Determinant of a 3 × 3 Matrix

Associated with every square matrix is a real number called its determinant. The determinant for a 3 × 3 matrix is defined as follows:

### Definition of a Third-Order Determinant

$$\begin{vmatrix} a_1 & b_1 & c_1 \\ a_2 & b_2 & c_2 \\ a_3 & b_3 & c_3 \end{vmatrix} = a_1 b_2 c_3 + b_1 c_2 a_3 + c_1 a_2 b_3 - a_3 b_2 c_1 - b_3 c_2 a_1 - c_3 a_2 b_1$$

The six terms and the three factors in each term in this complicated evaluation formula, $a_1b_2c_3 + b_1c_2a_3 + c_1a_2b_3 - a_3b_2c_1 - b_3c_2a_1 - c_3a_2b_1$, can be rearranged, and then we can apply the distributive property. We obtain

$$a_1b_2c_3 - a_1b_3c_2 - a_2b_1c_3 + a_2b_3c_1 + a_3b_1c_2 - a_3b_2c_1$$

$$= a_1(b_2c_3 - b_3c_2) - a_2(b_1c_3 - b_3c_1) + a_3(b_1c_2 - b_2c_1)$$

$$= a_1 \begin{vmatrix} b_2 & c_2 \\ b_3 & c_3 \end{vmatrix} - a_2 \begin{vmatrix} b_1 & c_1 \\ b_3 & c_3 \end{vmatrix} + a_3 \begin{vmatrix} b_1 & c_1 \\ b_2 & c_2 \end{vmatrix}.$$

You can evaluate each of the second-order determinants and obtain the three expressions in parentheses in the second step.

In summary, we now have arranged the definition of a third-order determinant as follows:

### Definition of the Determinant of a 3 × 3 Matrix

A third-order determinant is defined by

$$\begin{vmatrix} a_1 & b_1 & c_1 \\ a_2 & b_2 & c_2 \\ a_3 & b_3 & c_3 \end{vmatrix} = a_1 \begin{vmatrix} b_2 & c_2 \\ b_3 & c_3 \end{vmatrix} - a_2 \begin{vmatrix} b_1 & c_1 \\ b_3 & c_3 \end{vmatrix} + a_3 \begin{vmatrix} b_1 & c_1 \\ b_2 & c_2 \end{vmatrix}.$$

> Subtract.    Add.

> Each $a$ on the right comes from the first column.

Here are some tips that may be helpful when evaluating the determinant of a 3 × 3 matrix:

### Evaluating the Determinant of a 3 × 3 Matrix

1. Each of the three terms in the definition contains two factors—a numerical factor and a second-order determinant.
2. The numerical factor in each term is an element from the first column of the third-order determinant.
3. The minus sign precedes the second term.
4. The second-order determinant that appears in each term is obtained by crossing out the row and the column containing the numerical factor.

$$a_1 \begin{vmatrix} b_2 & c_2 \\ b_3 & c_3 \end{vmatrix} - a_2 \begin{vmatrix} b_1 & c_1 \\ b_3 & c_3 \end{vmatrix} + a_3 \begin{vmatrix} b_1 & c_1 \\ b_2 & c_2 \end{vmatrix}$$

$$\begin{vmatrix} a_1 & b_1 & c_1 \\ a_2 & b_2 & c_2 \\ a_3 & b_3 & c_3 \end{vmatrix} \quad \begin{vmatrix} a_1 & b_1 & c_1 \\ a_2 & b_2 & c_2 \\ a_3 & b_3 & c_3 \end{vmatrix} \quad \begin{vmatrix} a_1 & b_1 & c_1 \\ a_2 & b_2 & c_2 \\ a_3 & b_3 & c_3 \end{vmatrix}$$

The **minor** of an element is the determinant that remains after deleting the row and column of that element. For this reason, we call this method **expansion by minors.**

(**EXAMPLE 3**) **Evaluating the Determinant of a 3 × 3 Matrix**

Evaluate the determinant of the following matrix:

$$\begin{bmatrix} 4 & 1 & 0 \\ -9 & 3 & 4 \\ -3 & 8 & 1 \end{bmatrix}.$$

**Solution** We know that each of the three terms in the determinant contains a numerical factor and a second-order determinant. The numerical factors are from the first column of the given matrix. They are highlighted in the following matrix:

$$\begin{bmatrix} 4 & 1 & 0 \\ -9 & 3 & 4 \\ -3 & 8 & 1 \end{bmatrix}.$$

We find the minor for each numerical factor by deleting the row and column of that element:

$$\begin{bmatrix} 4 & 1 & 0 \\ -9 & 3 & 4 \\ -3 & 8 & 1 \end{bmatrix} \quad \begin{bmatrix} 4 & 1 & 0 \\ -9 & 3 & 4 \\ -3 & 8 & 1 \end{bmatrix} \quad \begin{bmatrix} 4 & 1 & 0 \\ -9 & 3 & 4 \\ -3 & 8 & 1 \end{bmatrix}$$

The minor for
4 is $\begin{vmatrix} 3 & 4 \\ 8 & 1 \end{vmatrix}$.

The minor for
$-9$ is $\begin{vmatrix} 1 & 0 \\ 8 & 1 \end{vmatrix}$.

The minor for
$-3$ is $\begin{vmatrix} 1 & 0 \\ 3 & 4 \end{vmatrix}$.

Now we have three numerical factors, 4, $-9$, and $-3$, and three second-order determinants. We multiply each numerical factor by its second-order determinant to find the three terms of the third-order determinant:

$$4\begin{vmatrix} 3 & 4 \\ 8 & 1 \end{vmatrix}, \quad -9\begin{vmatrix} 1 & 0 \\ 8 & 1 \end{vmatrix}, \quad -3\begin{vmatrix} 1 & 0 \\ 3 & 4 \end{vmatrix}.$$

Based on the preceding definition, we subtract the second term from the first term and add the third term:

Don't forget to supply the minus sign.

$$\begin{vmatrix} 4 & 1 & 0 \\ -9 & 3 & 4 \\ -3 & 8 & 1 \end{vmatrix} = 4\begin{vmatrix} 3 & 4 \\ 8 & 1 \end{vmatrix} - (-9)\begin{vmatrix} 1 & 0 \\ 8 & 1 \end{vmatrix} - 3\begin{vmatrix} 1 & 0 \\ 3 & 4 \end{vmatrix} \quad \text{Begin by evaluating the three second-order determinants.}$$

$= 4(3 \cdot 1 - 8 \cdot 4) + 9(1 \cdot 1 - 8 \cdot 0) - 3(1 \cdot 4 - 3 \cdot 0)$

$= 4(3 - 32) + 9(1 - 0) - 3(4 - 0)$     Multiply within parentheses.

$= 4(-29) + 9(1) - 3(4)$     Subtract within parentheses.

$= -116 + 9 - 12$     Multiply.

$= -119$     Add and subtract as indicated. ●

### Technology

A graphing utility can be used to evaluate the determinant of a matrix. Enter the matrix and call it $A$. Then use the determinant command. The screen below verifies our result in Example 3.

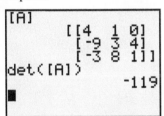

○ Check Point **3** Evaluate the determinant of the following matrix:

$$\begin{bmatrix} 2 & 1 & 7 \\ -5 & 6 & 0 \\ -4 & 3 & 1 \end{bmatrix}.$$

The six terms in the definition of a third-order determinant can be rearranged and factored in a variety of ways. Thus, it is possible to expand a determinant by minors about any row or any column. *Minus signs must be supplied preceding any element appearing in a position where the sum of its row and its column is an odd number.* For example, expanding about the elements in column 2 gives us

$$\begin{vmatrix} a_1 & b_1 & c_1 \\ a_2 & b_2 & c_2 \\ a_3 & b_3 & c_3 \end{vmatrix} = -b_1\begin{vmatrix} a_2 & c_2 \\ a_3 & c_3 \end{vmatrix} + b_2\begin{vmatrix} a_1 & c_1 \\ a_3 & c_3 \end{vmatrix} - b_3\begin{vmatrix} a_1 & c_1 \\ a_2 & c_2 \end{vmatrix}.$$

Minus sign is supplied because $b_1$ appears in row 1 and column 2; $1 + 2 = 3$, an odd number.

Minus sign is supplied because $b_3$ appears in row 3 and column 2; $3 + 2 = 5$, an odd number.

**Study Tip**

Keep in mind that you can expand a determinant by minors about any row or column. Use alternating plus and minus signs to precede the numerical factors of the minors according to the following sign array:

$$\begin{vmatrix} + & - & + \\ - & + & - \\ + & - & + \end{vmatrix}.$$

Expanding by minors about column 3, we obtain

$$\begin{vmatrix} a_1 & b_1 & c_1 \\ a_2 & b_2 & c_2 \\ a_3 & b_3 & c_3 \end{vmatrix} = c_1 \begin{vmatrix} a_2 & b_2 \\ a_3 & b_3 \end{vmatrix} - c_2 \begin{vmatrix} a_1 & b_1 \\ a_3 & b_3 \end{vmatrix} + c_3 \begin{vmatrix} a_1 & b_1 \\ a_2 & b_2 \end{vmatrix}.$$

> Minus sign must be supplied because $c_2$ appears in row 2 and column 3; $2 + 3 = 5$, an odd number.

When evaluating a $3 \times 3$ determinant using expansion by minors, you can expand about any row or column. To simplify the arithmetic, if a row or column contains one or more 0s, expand about that row or column.

( **EXAMPLE 4** ) **Evaluating a Third-Order Determinant**

Evaluate:

$$\begin{vmatrix} 9 & 5 & 0 \\ -2 & -3 & 0 \\ 1 & 4 & 2 \end{vmatrix}.$$

**Solution** Note that the last column has two 0s. We will expand the determinant about the elements in that column.

$$\begin{vmatrix} 9 & 5 & 0 \\ -2 & -3 & 0 \\ 1 & 4 & 2 \end{vmatrix} = 0 \begin{vmatrix} -2 & -3 \\ 1 & 4 \end{vmatrix} - 0 \begin{vmatrix} 9 & 5 \\ 1 & 4 \end{vmatrix} + 2 \begin{vmatrix} 9 & 5 \\ -2 & -3 \end{vmatrix}$$

$$= 0 - 0 + 2[9(-3) - (-2)5]$$

*Evaluate the second-order determinant whose numerical factor is not 0.*

$$= 2(-27 + 10)$$
$$= 2(-17)$$
$$= -34$$

⊘ Check Point **4** Evaluate:

$$\begin{vmatrix} 6 & 4 & 0 \\ -3 & -5 & 3 \\ 1 & 2 & 0 \end{vmatrix}.$$

**④** Solve a system of linear equations in three variables using Cramer's rule.

## Solving Systems of Linear Equations in Three Variables Using Determinants

Cramer's rule can be applied to solving systems of linear equations in three variables. The determinants in the numerator and denominator of all variables are third-order determinants.

**Solving Three Equations in Three Variables Using Determinants Cramer's Rule**

If

$$\begin{cases} a_1x + b_1y + c_1z = d_1 \\ a_2x + b_2y + c_2z = d_2 \\ a_3x + b_3y + c_3z = d_3 \end{cases}$$

then

$$x = \frac{D_x}{D}, y = \frac{D_y}{D}, \text{ and } z = \frac{D_z}{D}, \text{ where } D \neq 0.$$

These four third-order determinants are given by

$$D = \begin{vmatrix} a_1 & b_1 & c_1 \\ a_2 & b_2 & c_2 \\ a_3 & b_3 & c_3 \end{vmatrix}$$ These are the coefficients of the variables x, y, and z.

$$D_x = \begin{vmatrix} d_1 & b_1 & c_1 \\ d_2 & b_2 & c_2 \\ d_3 & b_3 & c_3 \end{vmatrix}$$ Replace x-coefficients in D with the constants on the right of the three equations.

$$D_y = \begin{vmatrix} a_1 & d_1 & c_1 \\ a_2 & d_2 & c_2 \\ a_3 & d_3 & c_3 \end{vmatrix}$$ Replace y-coefficients in D with the constants on the right of the three equations.

$$D_z = \begin{vmatrix} a_1 & b_1 & d_1 \\ a_2 & b_2 & d_2 \\ a_3 & b_3 & d_3 \end{vmatrix}$$ Replace z-coefficients in D with the constants on the right of the three equations.

( EXAMPLE 5 ) **Using Cramer's Rule to Solve a Linear System in Three Variables**

Use Cramer's rule to solve:

$$\begin{cases} x + 2y - z = -4 \\ x + 4y - 2z = -6 \\ 2x + 3y + z = 3. \end{cases}$$

**Solution** Because

$$x = \frac{D_x}{D}, \quad y = \frac{D_y}{D}, \quad \text{and} \quad z = \frac{D_z}{D},$$

we need to set up and evaluate four determinants.

**Step 1 Set up the determinants.**

1. $D$, the determinant in all three denominators, consists of the $x$-, $y$-, and $z$-coefficients.

$$D = \begin{vmatrix} 1 & 2 & -1 \\ 1 & 4 & -2 \\ 2 & 3 & 1 \end{vmatrix}$$

2. $D_x$, the determinant in the numerator for $x$, is obtained by replacing the $x$-coefficients in $D$, 1, 1, and 2, with the constants on the right sides of the equations, $-4$, $-6$, and 3.

$$D_x = \begin{vmatrix} -4 & 2 & -1 \\ -6 & 4 & -2 \\ 3 & 3 & 1 \end{vmatrix}$$

3. $D_y$, the determinant in the numerator for $y$, is obtained by replacing the $y$-coefficients in $D$, 2, 4, and 3, with the constants on the right sides of the equations, $-4$, $-6$, and 3.

$$D_y = \begin{vmatrix} 1 & -4 & -1 \\ 1 & -6 & -2 \\ 2 & 3 & 1 \end{vmatrix}$$

4. $D_z$, the determinant in the numerator for $z$, is obtained by replacing the $z$-coefficients in $D$, $-1$, $-2$, and 1, with the constants on the right sides of the equations, $-4$, $-6$, and 3.

$$D_z = \begin{vmatrix} 1 & 2 & -4 \\ 1 & 4 & -6 \\ 2 & 3 & 3 \end{vmatrix}$$

**Step 2 Evaluate the four determinants.**

$$D = \begin{vmatrix} 1 & 2 & -1 \\ 1 & 4 & -2 \\ 2 & 3 & 1 \end{vmatrix} = 1 \begin{vmatrix} 4 & -2 \\ 3 & 1 \end{vmatrix} - 1 \begin{vmatrix} 2 & -1 \\ 3 & 1 \end{vmatrix} + 2 \begin{vmatrix} 2 & -1 \\ 4 & -2 \end{vmatrix}$$

$$= 1(4 + 6) - 1(2 + 3) + 2(-4 + 4)$$
$$= 1(10) - 1(5) + 2(0) = 5$$

### Study Tip

To find $D_x$, $D_y$, and $D_z$, you'll need to apply the evaluation process for a $3 \times 3$ determinant three times. The values of $D_x$, $D_y$, and $D_z$ cannot be obtained from the numbers that occur in the computation of $D$.

Using the same technique to evaluate each determinant, we obtain

$$D_x = -10, \quad D_y = 5, \quad \text{and} \quad D_z = 20.$$

**Step 3 Substitute these four values and solve the system.**

$$x = \frac{D_x}{D} = \frac{-10}{5} = -2$$

$$y = \frac{D_y}{D} = \frac{5}{5} = 1$$

$$z = \frac{D_z}{D} = \frac{20}{5} = 4$$

The solution $(-2, 1, 4)$ can be checked by substitution into the original three equations. The solution set is $\{(-2, 1, 4)\}$.

🖊 Check Point **5** Use Cramer's rule to solve the system:

$$\begin{cases} 3x - 2y + z = 16 \\ 2x + 3y - z = -9 \\ x + 4y + 3z = 2. \end{cases}$$

**5** Use determinants to identify inconsistent systems and systems with dependent equations.

## Cramer's Rule with Inconsistent and Dependent Systems

If $D$, the determinant in the denominator, is 0, the variables described by the quotient of determinants are not real numbers. However, when $D = 0$, this indicates that the system is either inconsistent or contains dependent equations. This gives rise to the following two situations:

### Determinants: Inconsistent and Dependent Systems

1. If $D = 0$ and at least one of the determinants in the numerator is not 0, then the system is inconsistent. The solution set is $\varnothing$.
2. If $D = 0$ and all the determinants in the numerators are 0, then the equations in the system are dependent. The system has infinitely many solutions.

### Discovery

Write a system of two equations that is inconsistent. Now use determinants and the result boxed above to verify that this is truly an inconsistent system. Repeat the same process for a system with two dependent equations.

Although we have focused on applying determinants to solve linear systems, they have other applications, some of which we consider in the exercise set that follows Example 6.

⑥ Evaluate higher-order
determinants.

## The Determinant of Any $n \times n$ Matrix

The determinant of a matrix with $n$ rows and $n$ columns is said to be an ***nth*-order determinant**. The value of an $n$th-order determinant $(n > 2)$ can be found in terms of determinants of order $n - 1$. For example, we found the value of a third-order determinant in terms of determinants of order 2.

We can generalize this idea for fourth-order determinants and higher. We have seen that the **minor** of the element $a_{ij}$ is the determinant obtained by deleting the $i$th row and the $j$th column in the given array of numbers. The **cofactor** of the element $a_{ij}$ is $(-1)^{i+j}$ times the minor of $a_{ij}$. If the sum of the row and column $(i + j)$ is even, the cofactor is the same as the minor. If the sum of the row and column $(i + j)$ is odd, the cofactor is the opposite of the minor.

Let's see what this means in the case of a fourth-order determinant.

(**EXAMPLE 6**) **Evaluating the Determinant of a 4 × 4 Matrix**

Evaluate the determinant of the following matrix:

$$A = \begin{bmatrix} 1 & -2 & 3 & 0 \\ -1 & 1 & 0 & 2 \\ 0 & 2 & 0 & -3 \\ 2 & 3 & -4 & 1 \end{bmatrix}.$$

**Solution**

$$|A| = \begin{vmatrix} 1 & -2 & 3 & 0 \\ -1 & 1 & 0 & 2 \\ 0 & 2 & 0 & -3 \\ 2 & 3 & -4 & 1 \end{vmatrix}$$

*With two 0s in the third column, we will expand along the third column.*

$$= (-1)^{1+3}(3)\begin{vmatrix} -1 & 1 & 2 \\ 0 & 2 & -3 \\ 2 & 3 & 1 \end{vmatrix} + (-1)^{4+3}(-4)\begin{vmatrix} 1 & -2 & 0 \\ -1 & 1 & 2 \\ 0 & 2 & -3 \end{vmatrix}.$$

**3 is in row 1, column 3.**

**−4 is in row 4, column 3.**

$$= 3\begin{vmatrix} -1 & 1 & 2 \\ 0 & 2 & -3 \\ 2 & 3 & 1 \end{vmatrix} + 4\begin{vmatrix} 1 & -2 & 0 \\ -1 & 1 & 2 \\ 0 & 2 & -3 \end{vmatrix}$$

*The determinant that follows 3 is obtained by crossing out the row and the column (row 1, column 3) in the original determinant. The minor for −4 is obtained in a similar manner.*

Evaluate the two third-order determinants to get

$$|A| = 3(-25) + 4(-1) = -79.$$

⬤

✓ Check Point **6** Evaluate the determinant of the following matrix:

$$A = \begin{bmatrix} 0 & 4 & 0 & -3 \\ -1 & 1 & 5 & 2 \\ 1 & -2 & 0 & 6 \\ 3 & 0 & 0 & 1 \end{bmatrix}.$$

If a linear system has $n$ equations, Cramer's rule requires you to compute $n + 1$ determinants of $n$th order. The excessive number of calculations required to perform Cramer's rule for systems with four or more equations makes it an inefficient method for solving large systems.

## Exercise Set 8.5

### Practice Exercises

*Evaluate each determinant in Exercises 1–10.*

**1.** $\begin{vmatrix} 5 & 7 \\ 2 & 3 \end{vmatrix}$

**2.** $\begin{vmatrix} 4 & 8 \\ 5 & 6 \end{vmatrix}$

**3.** $\begin{vmatrix} -4 & 1 \\ 5 & 6 \end{vmatrix}$

**4.** $\begin{vmatrix} 7 & 9 \\ -2 & -5 \end{vmatrix}$

**5.** $\begin{vmatrix} -7 & 14 \\ 2 & -4 \end{vmatrix}$

**6.** $\begin{vmatrix} 1 & -3 \\ -8 & 2 \end{vmatrix}$

**7.** $\begin{vmatrix} -5 & -1 \\ -2 & -7 \end{vmatrix}$

**8.** $\begin{vmatrix} \frac{1}{5} & \frac{1}{6} \\ -6 & 5 \end{vmatrix}$

**9.** $\begin{vmatrix} \frac{1}{2} & \frac{1}{2} \\ \frac{1}{8} & -\frac{3}{4} \end{vmatrix}$

**10.** $\begin{vmatrix} \frac{2}{3} & \frac{1}{3} \\ -\frac{1}{2} & \frac{3}{4} \end{vmatrix}$

*For Exercises 11–26, use Cramer's rule to solve each system or to determine that the system is inconsistent or contains dependent equations.*

**11.** $\begin{cases} x + y = 7 \\ x - y = 3 \end{cases}$

**12.** $\begin{cases} 2x + y = 3 \\ x - y = 3 \end{cases}$

**13.** $\begin{cases} 12x + 3y = 15 \\ 2x - 3y = 13 \end{cases}$

**14.** $\begin{cases} x - 2y = 5 \\ 5x - y = -2 \end{cases}$

**15.** $\begin{cases} 4x - 5y = 17 \\ 2x + 3y = 3 \end{cases}$

**16.** $\begin{cases} 3x + 2y = 2 \\ 2x + 2y = 3 \end{cases}$

**17.** $\begin{cases} x + 2y = 3 \\ 5x + 10y = 15 \end{cases}$

**18.** $\begin{cases} 2x - 9y = 5 \\ 3x - 3y = 11 \end{cases}$

**19.** $\begin{cases} 3x - 4y = 4 \\ 2x + 2y = 12 \end{cases}$

**20.** $\begin{cases} 3x = 7y + 1 \\ 2x = 3y - 1 \end{cases}$

**21.** $\begin{cases} 2x = 3y + 2 \\ 5x = 51 - 4y \end{cases}$

**22.** $\begin{cases} y = -4x + 2 \\ 2x = 3y + 8 \end{cases}$

**23.** $\begin{cases} 3x = 2 - 3y \\ 2y = 3 - 2x \end{cases}$

**24.** $\begin{cases} x + 2y - 3 = 0 \\ 12 = 8y + 4x \end{cases}$

**25.** $\begin{cases} 4y = 16 - 3x \\ 6x = 32 - 8y \end{cases}$

**26.** $\begin{cases} 2x = 7 + 3y \\ 4x - 6y = 3 \end{cases}$

*Evaluate each determinant in Exercises 27–32.*

**27.** $\begin{vmatrix} 3 & 0 & 0 \\ 2 & 1 & -5 \\ 2 & 5 & -1 \end{vmatrix}$

**28.** $\begin{vmatrix} 4 & 0 & 0 \\ 3 & -1 & 4 \\ 2 & -3 & 5 \end{vmatrix}$

**29.** $\begin{vmatrix} 3 & 1 & 0 \\ -3 & 4 & 0 \\ -1 & 3 & -5 \end{vmatrix}$

**30.** $\begin{vmatrix} 2 & -4 & 2 \\ -1 & 0 & 5 \\ 3 & 0 & 4 \end{vmatrix}$

**31.** $\begin{vmatrix} 1 & 1 & 1 \\ 2 & 2 & 2 \\ -3 & 4 & -5 \end{vmatrix}$

**32.** $\begin{vmatrix} 1 & 2 & 3 \\ 2 & 2 & -3 \\ 3 & 2 & 1 \end{vmatrix}$

*In Exercises 33–40, use Cramer's rule to solve each system.*

**33.** $\begin{cases} x + y + z = 0 \\ 2x - y + z = -1 \\ -x + 3y - z = -8 \end{cases}$

**34.** $\begin{cases} x - y + 2z = 3 \\ 2x + 3y + z = 9 \\ -x - y + 3z = 11 \end{cases}$

**35.** $\begin{cases} 4x - 5y - 6z = -1 \\ x - 2y - 5z = -12 \\ 2x - y = 7 \end{cases}$

**36.** $\begin{cases} x - 3y + z = -2 \\ x + 2y = 8 \\ 2x - y = 1 \end{cases}$

**37.** $\begin{cases} x + y + z = 4 \\ x - 2y + z = 7 \\ x + 3y + 2z = 4 \end{cases}$

**38.** $\begin{cases} 2x + 2y + 3z = 10 \\ 4x - y + z = -5 \\ 5x - 2y + 6z = 1 \end{cases}$

**39.** $\begin{cases} x + 2z = 4 \\ 2y - z = 5 \\ 2x + 3y = 13 \end{cases}$

**40.** $\begin{cases} 3x + 2z = 4 \\ 5x - y = -4 \\ 4y + 3z = 22 \end{cases}$

*Evaluate each determinant in Exercises 41–44.*

**41.** $\begin{vmatrix} 4 & 2 & 8 & -7 \\ -2 & 0 & 4 & 1 \\ 5 & 0 & 0 & 5 \\ 4 & 0 & 0 & -1 \end{vmatrix}$

**42.** $\begin{vmatrix} 3 & -1 & 1 & 2 \\ -2 & 0 & 0 & 0 \\ 2 & -1 & -2 & 3 \\ 1 & 4 & 2 & 3 \end{vmatrix}$

**43.** $\begin{vmatrix} -2 & -3 & 3 & 5 \\ 1 & -4 & 0 & 0 \\ 1 & 2 & 2 & -3 \\ 2 & 0 & 1 & 1 \end{vmatrix}$

**44.** $\begin{vmatrix} 1 & -3 & 2 & 0 \\ -3 & -1 & 0 & -2 \\ 2 & 1 & 3 & 1 \\ 2 & 0 & -2 & 0 \end{vmatrix}$

### Practice Plus

*In Exercises 45–46, evaluate each determinant.*

**45.** $\begin{vmatrix} \begin{vmatrix} 3 & 1 \\ -2 & 3 \end{vmatrix} & \begin{vmatrix} 7 & 0 \\ 1 & 5 \end{vmatrix} \\ \begin{vmatrix} 3 & 0 \\ 0 & 7 \end{vmatrix} & \begin{vmatrix} 9 & -6 \\ 3 & 5 \end{vmatrix} \end{vmatrix}$

**46.** $\begin{vmatrix} \begin{vmatrix} 5 & 0 \\ 4 & -3 \end{vmatrix} & \begin{vmatrix} -1 & 0 \\ 0 & -1 \end{vmatrix} \\ \begin{vmatrix} 7 & -5 \\ 4 & 6 \end{vmatrix} & \begin{vmatrix} 4 & 1 \\ -3 & 5 \end{vmatrix} \end{vmatrix}$

*In Exercises 47–48, write the system of linear equations for which Cramer's rule yields the given determinants.*

**47.** $D = \begin{vmatrix} 2 & -4 \\ 3 & 5 \end{vmatrix}, \quad D_x = \begin{vmatrix} 8 & -4 \\ -10 & 5 \end{vmatrix}$

**48.** $D = \begin{vmatrix} 2 & -3 \\ 5 & 6 \end{vmatrix}, \quad D_x = \begin{vmatrix} 8 & -3 \\ 11 & 6 \end{vmatrix}$

*In Exercises 49–52, solve each equation for x.*

**49.** $\begin{vmatrix} -2 & x \\ 4 & 6 \end{vmatrix} = 32$

**50.** $\begin{vmatrix} x + 3 & -6 \\ x - 2 & -4 \end{vmatrix} = 28$

**51.** $\begin{vmatrix} 1 & x & -2 \\ 3 & 1 & 1 \\ 0 & -2 & 2 \end{vmatrix} = -8$

**52.** $\begin{vmatrix} 2 & x & 1 \\ -3 & 1 & 0 \\ 2 & 1 & 4 \end{vmatrix} = 39$

### Application Exercises

*Determinants are used to find the area of a triangle whose vertices are given by three points in a rectangular coordinate system. The area of a triangle with vertices $(x_1, y_1)$, $(x_2, y_2)$, and $(x_3, y_3)$ is*

$$\text{Area} = \pm\frac{1}{2}\begin{vmatrix} x_1 & y_1 & 1 \\ x_2 & y_2 & 1 \\ x_3 & y_3 & 1 \end{vmatrix},$$

*where the ± symbol indicates that the appropriate sign should be chosen to yield a positive area. Use this information to work Exercises 53–54.*

**53.** Use determinants to find the area of the triangle whose vertices are $(3, -5), (2, 6),$ and $(-3, 5).$

**54.** Use determinants to find the area of the triangle whose vertices are $(1, 1), (-2, -3),$ and $(11, -3).$

*Determinants are used to show that three points lie on the same line (are collinear). If*

$$\begin{vmatrix} x_1 & y_1 & 1 \\ x_2 & y_2 & 1 \\ x_3 & y_3 & 1 \end{vmatrix} = 0,$$

*then the points* $(x_1, y_1), (x_2, y_2),$ *and* $(x_3, y_3)$ *are collinear. If the determinant does not equal 0, then the points are not collinear. Use this information to work Exercises 55–56.*

**55.** Are the points $(3, -1), (0, -3),$ and $(12, 5)$ collinear?

**56.** Are the points $(-4, -6), (1, 0),$ and $(11, 12)$ collinear?

*Determinants are used to write an equation of a line passing through two points. An equation of the line passing through the distinct points* $(x_1, y_1)$ *and* $(x_2, y_2)$ *is given by*

$$\begin{vmatrix} x & y & 1 \\ x_1 & y_1 & 1 \\ x_2 & y_2 & 1 \end{vmatrix} = 0.$$

*Use this information to work Exercises 57–58.*

**57.** Use the determinant to write an equation of the line passing through $(3, -5)$ and $(-2, 6)$. Then expand the determinant, expressing the line's equation in slope-intercept form.

**58.** Use the determinant to write an equation of the line passing through $(-1, 3)$ and $(2, 4)$. Then expand the determinant, expressing the line's equation in slope-intercept form.

## Writing in Mathematics

**59.** Explain how to evaluate a second-order determinant.

**60.** Describe the determinants $D_x$ and $D_y$ in terms of the coefficients and constants in a system of two equations in two variables.

**61.** Explain how to evaluate a third-order determinant.

**62.** When expanding a determinant by minors, when is it necessary to supply minus signs?

**63.** Without going into too much detail, describe how to solve a linear system in three variables using Cramer's rule.

**64.** In applying Cramer's rule, what does it mean if $D = 0$?

**65.** The process of solving a linear system in three variables using Cramer's rule can involve tedious computation. Is there a way of speeding up this process, perhaps using Cramer's rule to find the value for only one of the variables? Describe how this process might work, presenting a specific example with your description. Remember that your goal is still to find the value for each variable in the system.

**66.** If you could use only one method to solve linear systems in three variables, which method would you select? Explain why this is so.

## Technology Exercises

**67.** Use the feature of your graphing utility that evaluates the determinant of a square matrix to verify any five of the determinants that you evaluated by hand in Exercises 1–10, 27–32, or 41–44.

*In Exercises 68–69, use a graphing utility to evaluate the determinant for the given matrix.*

**68.** $\begin{bmatrix} 3 & -2 & -1 & 4 \\ -5 & 1 & 2 & 7 \\ 2 & 4 & 5 & 0 \\ -1 & 3 & -6 & 5 \end{bmatrix}$

**69.** $\begin{bmatrix} 8 & 2 & 6 & -1 & 0 \\ 2 & 0 & -3 & 4 & 7 \\ 2 & 1 & -3 & 6 & -5 \\ -1 & 2 & 1 & 5 & -1 \\ 4 & 5 & -2 & 3 & -8 \end{bmatrix}$

**70.** What is the fastest method for solving a linear system with your graphing utility?

## Critical Thinking Exercises

**Make Sense?** *In Exercises 71–74, determine whether each statement makes sense or does not make sense, and explain your reasoning.*

**71.** I'm solving a linear system using a determinant that contains two rows and three columns.

**72.** I can speed up the tedious computations required by Cramer's rule by using the value of $D$ to determine the value of $D_x$.

**73.** When using Cramer's rule to solve a linear system, the number of determinants that I set up and evaluate is the same as the number of variables in the system.

**74.** Using Cramer's rule to solve a linear system, I found the value of $D$ to be zero, so the system is inconsistent.

**75. a.** Evaluate: $\begin{vmatrix} a & a \\ 0 & a \end{vmatrix}.$

**b.** Evaluate: $\begin{vmatrix} a & a & a \\ 0 & a & a \\ 0 & 0 & a \end{vmatrix}.$

**c.** Evaluate: $\begin{vmatrix} a & a & a & a \\ 0 & a & a & a \\ 0 & 0 & a & a \\ 0 & 0 & 0 & a \end{vmatrix}.$

**d.** Describe the pattern in the given determinants.

**e.** Describe the pattern in the evaluations.

**76.** Evaluate: $\begin{vmatrix} 2 & 0 & 0 & 0 & 0 \\ 0 & 3 & 0 & 0 & 0 \\ 0 & 0 & 2 & 0 & 0 \\ 0 & 0 & 0 & 1 & 0 \\ 0 & 0 & 0 & 0 & 4 \end{vmatrix}.$

**77.** What happens to the value of a second-order determinant if the two columns are interchanged?

**78.** Consider the system

$$a_1 x + b_1 y = c_1$$
$$a_2 x + b_2 y = c_2.$$

Use Cramer's rule to prove that if the first equation of the system is replaced by the sum of the two equations, the resulting system has the same solution as the original system.

**79.** Show that the equation of a line through $(x_1, y_1)$ and $(x_2, y_2)$ is given by the determinant equation in Exercises 57–58.

## Group Exercise

**80.** We have seen that determinants can be used to solve linear equations, give areas of triangles in rectangular coordinates, and determine equations of lines. Not impressed with these applications? Members of the group should research an application of determinants that they find intriguing. The group should then present a seminar to the class about this application.

## Preview Exercises

*Exercises 81–83 will help you prepare for the material covered in the first section of the next chapter.*

**81.** Consider the equation $\dfrac{x^2}{9} + \dfrac{y^2}{4} = 1$.

  **a.** Set $y = 0$ and find the $x$-intercepts.

  **b.** Set $x = 0$ and find the $y$-intercepts.

**82.** Divide both sides of $25x^2 + 16y^2 = 400$ by 400 and simplify.

**83.** Complete the square and write the circle's equation in standard form:

$$x^2 + y^2 - 2x + 4y = 4.$$

Then give the center and radius of the circle and graph the equation.

# Chapter 8 Summary, Review, and Test

## Summary

| DEFINITIONS AND CONCEPTS | EXAMPLES |
|---|---|
| **8.1 Matrix Solutions to Linear Systems** | |
| **a.** Matrix row operations are described in the box on page 807. | Ex. 1, p. 807 |
| **b.** To solve a linear system using Gaussian elimination, begin with the system's augmented matrix. Use matrix row operations to get 1s down the main diagonal from upper left to lower right, and 0s below the 1s. Such a matrix is in row-echelon form. Details are in the box on page 808. | Ex. 2, p. 809; Ex. 3, p. 811 |
| **c.** To solve a linear system using Gauss-Jordan elimination, use the procedure of Gaussian elimination, but obtain 0s above and below the 1s in the main diagonal from upper left to lower right. Such a matrix is in reduced row-echelon form. Details are in the box on page 813. | Ex. 4, p. 814 |
| **8.2 Inconsistent and Dependent Systems and Their Applications** | |
| **a.** If Gaussian elimination results in a matrix with a row containing all 0s to the left of the vertical line and a nonzero number to the right, the system has no solution (is inconsistent). | Ex. 1, p. 818 |
| **b.** In a square system, if Gaussian elimination results in a matrix with a row with all 0s, but not a row like the one in part (a), the system has an infinite number of solutions (contains dependent equations). | Ex. 2, p. 820 |
| **c.** In nonsquare systems, the number of variables differs from the number of equations. | Ex. 3, p. 821 |
| **8.3 Matrix Operations and Their Applications** | |
| **a.** A matrix of order $m \times n$ has $m$ rows and $n$ columns. Two matrices are equal if and only if they have the same order and corresponding elements are equal. | Ex. 1, p. 827 |
| **b.** Matrix Addition and Subtraction: Matrices of the same order are added or subtracted by adding or subtracting corresponding elements. Properties of matrix addition are given in the box on page 830. | Ex. 2, p. 829 |
| **c.** Scalar Multiplication: If $A$ is a matrix and $c$ is a scalar, then $cA$ is the matrix formed by multiplying each element in $A$ by $c$. Properties of scalar multiplication are given in the box on page 831. | Ex. 3, p. 830; Ex. 4, p. 831 |
| **d.** Matrix Multiplication: The product of an $m \times n$ matrix $A$ and an $n \times p$ matrix $B$ is an $m \times p$ matrix $AB$. The element in the $i$th row and $j$th column of $AB$ is found by multiplying each element in the $i$th row of $A$ by the corresponding element in the $j$th column of $B$ and adding the products. Matrix multiplication is not commutative: $AB \neq BA$. Properties of matrix multiplication are given in the box on page 836. | Ex. 5, p. 832; Ex. 6, p. 833; Ex. 7, p. 835 |
| **8.4 Multiplicative Inverses of Matrices and Matrix Equations** | |
| **a.** The multiplicative identity matrix $I_n$ is an $n \times n$ matrix with 1s down the main diagonal from upper left to lower right and 0s elsewhere. | |
| **b.** Let $A$ be an $n \times n$ square matrix. If there is a square matrix $A^{-1}$ such that $AA^{-1} = I_n$ and $A^{-1}A = I_n$, then $A^{-1}$ is the multiplicative inverse of $A$. | Ex. 1, p. 843 |
| **c.** If a square matrix has a multiplicative inverse, it is invertible or nonsingular. Methods for finding multiplicative inverses for invertible matrices, including a formula for $2 \times 2$ matrices, are given in the box on page 849. | Ex. 2, p. 844; Ex. 3, p. 846; Ex. 4, p. 848 |

| DEFINITIONS AND CONCEPTS | EXAMPLES |
|---|---|

**d.** Linear systems can be represented by matrix equations of the form $AX = B$ in which $A$ is the coefficient matrix and $B$ is the constant matrix. If $AX = B$ has a unique solution, then $X = A^{-1}B$.

Ex. 5, p. 851

**8.5  Determinants and Cramer's Rule**

**a.** Value of a second-order determinant:

$$\begin{vmatrix} a_1 & b_1 \\ a_2 & b_2 \end{vmatrix} = a_1 b_2 - a_2 b_1$$

Ex. 1, p. 857

**b.** Cramer's rule for solving systems of linear equations in two variables uses three second-order determinants and is stated in the box on page 858.

Ex. 2, p. 859

**c.** To evaluate an $n$th-order determinant, where $n > 2$,
  **1.** Select a row or column about which to expand.
  **2.** Multiply each element $a_{ij}$ in the row or column by $(-1)^{i+j}$ times the determinant obtained by deleting the $i$th row and the $j$th column in the given array of numbers.
  **3.** The value of the determinant is the sum of the products found in step 2.

Ex. 3, p. 860;
Ex. 4, p. 862;
Ex. 6, p. 865

**d.** Cramer's rule for solving systems of linear equations in three variables uses four third-order determinants and is stated in the box on pages 862–863.

Ex. 5, p. 863

**e.** Cramer's rule with inconsistent and dependent systems is summarized by the two situations in the box on page 864.

## Review Exercises

### 8.1

*In Exercises 1–2, perform each matrix row operation and write the new matrix.*

**1.** $\begin{bmatrix} 1 & 2 & 2 & | & 2 \\ 0 & 1 & -1 & | & 2 \\ 0 & 5 & 4 & | & 1 \end{bmatrix}$   $-5R_2 + R_3$

**2.** $\begin{bmatrix} 2 & -2 & 1 & | & -1 \\ 1 & 2 & -1 & | & 2 \\ 6 & 4 & 3 & | & 5 \end{bmatrix}$   $\frac{1}{2}R_1$

*In Exercises 3–5, solve each system of equations using matrices. Use Gaussian elimination with back-substitution or Gauss-Jordan elimination.*

**3.** $\begin{cases} x + 2y + 3z = -5 \\ 2x + y + z = 1 \\ x + y - z = 8 \end{cases}$

**4.** $\begin{cases} x - 2y + z = 0 \\ y - 3z = -1 \\ 2y + 5z = -2 \end{cases}$

**5.** $\begin{cases} 3x_1 + 5x_2 - 8x_3 + 5x_4 = -8 \\ x_1 + 2x_2 - 3x_3 + x_4 = -7 \\ 2x_1 + 3x_2 - 7x_3 + 3x_4 = -11 \\ 4x_1 + 8x_2 - 10x_3 + 7x_4 = -10 \end{cases}$

**6.** The table shows the pollutants in the air in a city on a typical summer day.

| $x$ (Hours after 6 A.M.) | $y$ (Amount of Pollutants in the Air, in parts per million) |
|---|---|
| 2 | 98 |
| 4 | 138 |
| 10 | 162 |

**a.** Use the function $y = ax^2 + bx + c$ to model the data. Use either Gaussian elimination with back-substitution or Gauss-Jordan elimination to find the values for $a$, $b$, and $c$.

**b.** Use the function to find the time of day at which the city's air pollution level is at a maximum. What is the maximum level?

**7.** Sociologists Joseph Kahl and Dennis Gilbert developed a six-tier model to portray the class structure of the United States. The bar graph represents the percentage of Americans who are members of each of the six social classes.

**The United States Social Class Ladder**

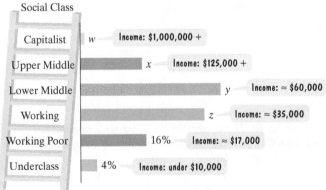

Percentage of the Population

*Source*: James Henslin, *Sociology*, Eighth Edition, Allyn and Bacon, 2007

Combined, members of the capitalist class, the upper-middle class, the lower-middle class, and the working class make up 80% of the U.S. population. The percentage of the population belonging to the lower-middle class exceeds the percentage belonging to capitalist and upper-middle classes by 18%. The difference between the percentage belonging to the lower-middle class and the working class is 4%. If the percentage belonging to the upper-middle class is tripled, it exceeds the percentage belonging to the capitalist and lower-middle classes by 10%. Determine the percentage of the U.S. population who are members of the capitalist class, the upper-middle class, the lower-middle class, and the working class.

## 8.2

*In Exercises 8–11, use Gaussian elimination to find the complete solution to each system, or show that none exists.*

**8.** $\begin{cases} 2x - 3y + z = 1 \\ x - 2y + 3z = 2 \\ 3x - 4y - z = 1 \end{cases}$

**9.** $\begin{cases} x - 3y + z = 1 \\ -2x + y + 3z = -7 \\ x - 4y + 2z = 0 \end{cases}$

**10.** $\begin{cases} x_1 + 4x_2 + 3x_3 - 6x_4 = 5 \\ x_1 + 3x_2 + x_3 - 4x_4 = 3 \\ 2x_1 + 8x_2 + 7x_3 - 5x_4 = 11 \\ 2x_1 + 5x_2 - 6x_4 = 4 \end{cases}$

**11.** $\begin{cases} 2x + 3y - 5z = 15 \\ x + 2y - z = 4 \end{cases}$

**12.** The figure shows the intersections of three one-way streets. The numbers given represent traffic flow, in cars per hour, at a peak period (from 4 P.M. to 6 P.M.).

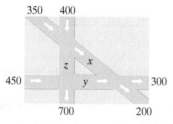

**a.** Use the idea that the number of cars entering each intersection per hour must equal the number of cars leaving per hour to set up a system of linear equations involving $x$, $y$, and $z$.

**b.** Use Gaussian elimination to solve the system.

**c.** If construction limits the value of $z$ to 400, how many cars per hour must pass between the other intersections to keep traffic flowing?

## 8.3

**13.** Find values for $x$, $y$, and $z$ so that the following matrices are equal:

$$\begin{bmatrix} 2x & y+7 \\ z & 4 \end{bmatrix} = \begin{bmatrix} -10 & 13 \\ 6 & 4 \end{bmatrix}.$$

*In Exercises 14–27, perform the indicated matrix operations given that A, B, C, and D are defined as follows. If an operation is not defined, state the reason.*

$$A = \begin{bmatrix} 2 & -1 & 2 \\ 5 & 3 & -1 \end{bmatrix} \quad B = \begin{bmatrix} 0 & -2 \\ 3 & 2 \\ 1 & -5 \end{bmatrix}$$

$$C = \begin{bmatrix} 1 & 2 & 3 \\ -1 & 1 & 2 \\ -1 & 2 & 1 \end{bmatrix} \quad D = \begin{bmatrix} -2 & 3 & 1 \\ 3 & -2 & 4 \end{bmatrix}$$

**14.** $A + D$

**15.** $2B$

**16.** $D - A$

**17.** $B + C$

**18.** $3A + 2D$

**19.** $-2A + 4D$

**20.** $-5(A + D)$

**21.** $AB$

**22.** $BA$

**23.** $BD$

**24.** $DB$

**25.** $AB - BA$

**26.** $(A - D)C$

**27.** $B(AC)$

**28.** Solve for $X$ in the matrix equation

$$3X + A = B,$$

where $A = \begin{bmatrix} 4 & 6 \\ -5 & 0 \end{bmatrix}$ and $B = \begin{bmatrix} -2 & -12 \\ 4 & 1 \end{bmatrix}.$

*In Exercises 29–30, use nine pixels in a 3 × 3 grid and the color levels shown.*

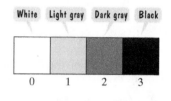

**29.** Write a 3 × 3 matrix that represents a digital photograph of the letter T in dark gray on a light gray background.

**30.** Find a matrix $B$ so that $A + B$ increases the contrast of the letter T by changing the dark gray to black and the light gray to white.

*The figure shows a right triangle in a rectangular coordinate system.*

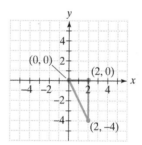

*The figure can be represented by the matrix*

$$B = \begin{bmatrix} 0 & 2 & 2 \\ 0 & 0 & -4 \end{bmatrix}.$$

*Use the triangle and the matrix that represents it to solve Exercises 31–36.*

**31.** Use matrix operations to move the triangle 2 units to the left and 1 unit up. Then graph the triangle and its transformation in a rectangular coordinate system.

**32.** Use matrix operations to reduce the triangle to half its perimeter and move the reduced image 2 units down. Then graph the triangle and its transformation in a rectangular coordinate system.

*In Exercises 33–36, find AB and graph the resulting image. What effect does the multiplication have on the triangle represented by matrix B?*

**33.** $A = \begin{bmatrix} 1 & 0 \\ 0 & -1 \end{bmatrix}$

**34.** $A = \begin{bmatrix} -1 & 0 \\ 0 & 1 \end{bmatrix}$

**35.** $A = \begin{bmatrix} 0 & -1 \\ 1 & 0 \end{bmatrix}$

**36.** $A = \begin{bmatrix} 2 & 0 \\ 0 & 1 \end{bmatrix}$

## 8.4

In Exercises 37–38, find the products $AB$ and $BA$ to determine whether $B$ is the multiplicative inverse of $A$.

**37.** $A = \begin{bmatrix} 2 & 7 \\ 1 & 4 \end{bmatrix}$, $B = \begin{bmatrix} 4 & -7 \\ -1 & 3 \end{bmatrix}$

**38.** $A = \begin{bmatrix} 1 & 0 & 0 \\ 0 & 2 & -7 \\ 0 & -1 & 4 \end{bmatrix}$, $B = \begin{bmatrix} 1 & 0 & 0 \\ 0 & 4 & 7 \\ 0 & 1 & 2 \end{bmatrix}$

In Exercises 39–42, find $A^{-1}$. Check that $AA^{-1} = I$ and $A^{-1}A = I$.

**39.** $A = \begin{bmatrix} 1 & -1 \\ -2 & 3 \end{bmatrix}$

**40.** $A = \begin{bmatrix} 0 & 1 \\ 5 & 3 \end{bmatrix}$

**41.** $A = \begin{bmatrix} 1 & 0 & -2 \\ 2 & 1 & 0 \\ 1 & 0 & -3 \end{bmatrix}$

**42.** $A = \begin{bmatrix} 1 & 3 & -2 \\ 4 & 13 & -7 \\ 5 & 16 & -8 \end{bmatrix}$

In Exercises 43–44,

**a.** Write each linear system as a matrix equation in the form $AX = B$.

**b.** Solve the system using the inverse that is given for the coefficient matrix.

**43.** $\begin{cases} x + y + 2z = 7 \\ \quad\; y + 3z = -2 \\ 3x \quad\; - 2z = 0 \end{cases}$ The inverse of $\begin{bmatrix} 1 & 1 & 2 \\ 0 & 1 & 3 \\ 3 & 0 & -2 \end{bmatrix}$ is $\begin{bmatrix} -2 & 2 & 1 \\ 9 & -8 & -3 \\ -3 & 3 & 1 \end{bmatrix}$.

**44.** $\begin{cases} x - y + 2z = 12 \\ \quad\; y - z = -5 \\ x \quad\quad + 2z = 10 \end{cases}$ The inverse of $\begin{bmatrix} 1 & -1 & 2 \\ 0 & 1 & -1 \\ 1 & 0 & 2 \end{bmatrix}$ is $\begin{bmatrix} 2 & 2 & -1 \\ -1 & 0 & 1 \\ -1 & -1 & 1 \end{bmatrix}$.

**45.** Use the coding matrix $A = \begin{bmatrix} 3 & 2 \\ 4 & 3 \end{bmatrix}$ and its inverse $A^{-1} = \begin{bmatrix} 3 & -2 \\ -4 & 3 \end{bmatrix}$ to encode and then decode the word RULE.

## 8.5

In Exercises 46–51, evaluate each determinant.

**46.** $\begin{vmatrix} 3 & 2 \\ -1 & 5 \end{vmatrix}$

**47.** $\begin{vmatrix} -2 & -3 \\ -4 & -8 \end{vmatrix}$

**48.** $\begin{vmatrix} 2 & 4 & -3 \\ 1 & -1 & 5 \\ -2 & 4 & 0 \end{vmatrix}$

**49.** $\begin{vmatrix} 4 & 7 & 0 \\ -5 & 6 & 0 \\ 3 & 2 & -4 \end{vmatrix}$

**50.** $\begin{vmatrix} 1 & 1 & 0 & 2 \\ 0 & 3 & 2 & 1 \\ 0 & -2 & 4 & 0 \\ 0 & 3 & 0 & 1 \end{vmatrix}$

**51.** $\begin{vmatrix} 2 & 2 & 2 & 2 \\ 0 & 2 & 2 & 2 \\ 0 & 0 & 2 & 2 \\ 0 & 0 & 0 & 2 \end{vmatrix}$

In Exercises 52–55, use Cramer's rule to solve each system.

**52.** $\begin{cases} x - 2y = 8 \\ 3x + 2y = -1 \end{cases}$

**53.** $\begin{cases} 7x + 2y = 0 \\ 2x + y = -3 \end{cases}$

**54.** $\begin{cases} x + 2y + 2z = 5 \\ 2x + 4y + 7z = 19 \\ -2x - 5y - 2z = 8 \end{cases}$

**55.** $\begin{cases} 2x + y \quad\quad = -4 \\ \quad\; y - 2z = 0 \\ 3x \quad\quad - 2z = -11 \end{cases}$

**56.** Use the quadratic function $y = ax^2 + bx + c$ to model the following data:

| $x$ (Age of a Driver) | $y$ (Average Number of Automobile Accidents per Day in the United States) |
| --- | --- |
| 20 | 400 |
| 40 | 150 |
| 60 | 400 |

Use Cramer's rule to determine values for $a$, $b$, and $c$. Then use the model to write a statement about the average number of automobile accidents in which 30-year-olds and 50-year-olds are involved daily.

---

**CHAPTER**
**Test Prep**
**VIDEOS**

**Chapter 8   Test**

In Exercises 1–2, solve each system of equations using matrices.

**1.** $\begin{cases} x + 2y - z = -3 \\ 2x - 4y + z = -7 \\ -2x + 2y - 3z = 4 \end{cases}$

**2.** $\begin{cases} x - 2y + z = 2 \\ 2x - y - z = 1 \end{cases}$

In Exercises 3–6, let

$$A = \begin{bmatrix} 3 & 1 \\ 1 & 0 \\ 2 & 1 \end{bmatrix}, \quad B = \begin{bmatrix} 1 & -1 \\ 2 & 1 \end{bmatrix}, \quad \text{and} \quad C = \begin{bmatrix} 1 & 2 \\ -1 & 3 \end{bmatrix}.$$

Carry out the indicated operations.

**3.** $2B + 3C$

**4.** $AB$

**5.** $C^{-1}$

**6.** $BC - 3B$

7. If $A = \begin{bmatrix} 1 & 2 & 2 \\ 2 & 3 & 3 \\ 1 & -1 & -2 \end{bmatrix}$ and $B = \begin{bmatrix} -3 & 2 & 0 \\ 7 & -4 & 1 \\ -5 & 3 & -1 \end{bmatrix}$, show that $B$ is the inverse of $A$.

8. Consider the system

$$3x + 5y = 9$$

$$2x - 3y = -13.$$

 a. Express the system in the form $AX = B$, where $A$, $X$, and $B$ are appropriate matrices.

 b. Find $A^{-1}$, the inverse of the coefficient matrix.

 c. Use $A^{-1}$ to solve the given system.

9. Evaluate: $\begin{vmatrix} 4 & -1 & 3 \\ 0 & 5 & -1 \\ 5 & 2 & 4 \end{vmatrix}$.

10. Solve for $x$ only using Cramer's rule:

$$\begin{cases} 3x + y - 2z = -3 \\ 2x + 7y + 3z = 9 \\ 4x - 3y - z = 7. \end{cases}$$

# Cumulative Review Exercises (Chapters P–8)

*Solve each equation or inequality in Exercises 1–6.*

1. $2x^2 = 4 - x$

2. $5x + 8 \le 7(1 + x)$

3. $x^3 + x^2 - 4x - 4 \ge 0$

4. $3x^3 + 8x^2 - 15x + 4 = 0$

5. $e^{2x} - 14e^x + 45 = 0$

6. $\log_3 x + \log_3(x + 2) = 1$

7. Use matrices to solve this system:

$$\begin{cases} x - y + z = 17 \\ 2x + 3y + z = 8 \\ -4x + y + 5z = -2. \end{cases}$$

8. Solve for $y$ using Cramer's rule:

$$\begin{cases} x - 2y + z = 7 \\ 2x + y - z = 0 \\ 3x + 2y - 2z = -2. \end{cases}$$

9. If $f(x) = \sqrt{4x - 7}$, find $f^{-1}(x)$.

10. Graph: $f(x) = \dfrac{x}{x^2 - 16}$.

11. Use the graph of $f(x) = 4x^4 - 4x^3 - 25x^2 + x + 6$ shown in the figure to factor the polynomial completely.

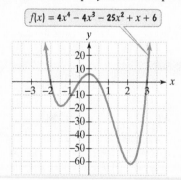

$f(x) = 4x^4 - 4x^3 - 25x^2 + x + 6$

12. Graph $y = \log_2 x$ and $y = \log_2(x + 1)$ in the same rectangular coordinate system.

13. Use the exponential decay model $A = A_0 e^{kt}$ to solve this problem. A radioactive substance has a half-life of 40 days. There are initially 900 grams of the substance.

 a. Find the decay model for this substance. Round $k$ to the nearest thousandth.

 b. How much of the substance will remain after 10 days? Round to the nearest hundredth of a gram.

14. Multiply the matrices: $\begin{bmatrix} 1 & -1 & 0 \\ 2 & 1 & 3 \end{bmatrix} \begin{bmatrix} 4 & -1 \\ 2 & 0 \\ 1 & 1 \end{bmatrix}$.

15. Find the partial fraction decomposition of

$$\frac{3x^2 + 17x - 38}{(x - 3)(x - 2)(x + 2)}.$$

*In Exercises 16–19, graph each equation, function, or inequality in a rectangular coordinate system.*

16. $y = -\frac{2}{3}x - 1$

17. $3x - 5y < 15$

18. $f(x) = x^2 - 2x - 3$

19. $(x - 1)^2 + (y + 1)^2 = 9$

20. Use synthetic division to divide $x^3 - 6x + 4$ by $x - 2$.

21. Graph: $y = 2 \sin 2\pi x$, $0 \le x \le 2$.

22. Find the exact value of $\cos\left[\tan^{-1}\left(-\frac{4}{3}\right)\right]$.

23. Verify the identity: $\dfrac{\cos 2x}{\cos x - \sin x} = \cos x + \sin x$.

24. Solve on the interval $[0, 2\pi)$: $\cos^2 x + \sin x + 1 = 0$.

25. If $\mathbf{v} = -6\mathbf{i} + 5\mathbf{j}$ and $\mathbf{w} = -7\mathbf{i} + 3\mathbf{j}$, find $4\mathbf{w} - 5\mathbf{v}$.

# Conic Sections and Analytic Geometry

# 9

From ripples in water to the path on which humanity journeys through space, certain curves occur naturally throughout the universe. Over two thousand years ago, the ancient Greeks studied these curves, called *conic sections*, without regard to their immediate usefulness simply because studying them elicited ideas that were exciting, challenging, and interesting. The ancient Greeks could not have imagined the applications of these curves in the twenty-first century. They enable the Hubble Space Telescope, a large satellite about the size of a school bus orbiting 375 miles above Earth, to gather distant rays of light and focus them into spectacular images of our evolving universe. They provide doctors with a procedure for dissolving kidney stones painlessly without invasive surgery. In this chapter, we use the rectangular coordinate system to study the conic sections and the mathematics behind their surprising applications.

Here's where you'll find applications that move beyond planet Earth:

- Planetary orbits: Section 9.1, page 881; Exercise Set 9.1, Exercise 78.
- Halley's Comet: Essay on page 882.
- Hubble Space Telescope: Section 9.3, pages 900 and 908.

*For a kidney stone here on Earth, see Section 9.1, page 882.*

## Section 9.1  The Ellipse

### Objectives

1 Graph ellipses centered at the origin.
2 Write equations of ellipses in standard form.
3 Graph ellipses not centered at the origin.
4 Solve applied problems involving ellipses.

You took on a summer job driving a truck, delivering books that were ordered online. You're an avid reader, so just being around books sounded appealing. However, now you're feeling a bit shaky driving the truck for the first time. It's 10 feet wide and 9 feet high; compared to your compact car, it feels like you're behind the wheel of a tank. Up ahead you see a sign at the semielliptical entrance to a tunnel: Caution! Tunnel is 10 Feet High at Center Peak. Then you see another sign: Caution! Tunnel Is 40 Feet Wide. Will your truck clear the opening of the tunnel's archway?

Mathematics is present in the movements of planets, bridge and tunnel construction, navigational systems used to keep track of a ship's location, manufacture of lenses for telescopes, and even in a procedure for disintegrating kidney stones. The mathematics behind these applications involves conic sections. Conic sections are curves that result from the intersection of a right circular cone and a plane. **Figure 9.1** illustrates the four conic sections: the circle, the ellipse, the parabola, and the hyperbola.

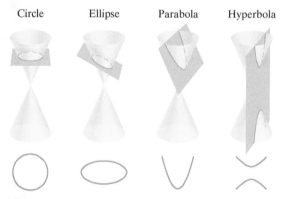

Figure 9.1 Obtaining the conic sections by intersecting a plane and a cone

In this section, we study the symmetric oval-shaped curve known as the ellipse. We will use a geometric definition for an ellipse to derive its equation. With this equation, we will determine if your delivery truck will clear the tunnel's entrance.

### Definition of an Ellipse

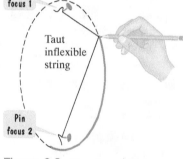

Figure 9.2 Drawing an ellipse

**Figure 9.2** illustrates how to draw an ellipse. Place pins at two fixed points, each of which is called a *focus* (plural: *foci*). If the ends of a fixed length of string are fastened to the pins and we draw the string taut with a pencil, the path traced by the pencil will be an ellipse. Notice that the sum of the distances of the pencil point from the foci remains constant because the length of the string is fixed. This procedure for drawing an ellipse illustrates its geometric definition.

#### Definition of an Ellipse

An **ellipse** is the set of all points, $P$, in a plane the sum of whose distances from two fixed points, $F_1$ and $F_2$, is constant (see **Figure 9.3**). These two fixed points are called the **foci** (plural of **focus**). The midpoint of the segment connecting the foci is the **center** of the ellipse.

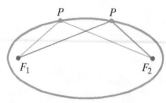

Figure 9.3

**Figure 9.4** illustrates that an ellipse can be elongated in any direction. In this section, we will limit our discussion to ellipses that are elongated horizontally or vertically. The line through the foci intersects the ellipse at two points, called the **vertices** (singular: **vertex**). The line segment that joins the vertices is the **major axis**. Notice that the midpoint of the major axis is the center of the ellipse. The line segment whose endpoints are on the ellipse and that is perpendicular to the major axis at the center is called the **minor axis** of the ellipse.

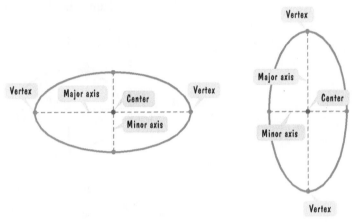

Figure 9.4   Horizontal and vertical elongations of an ellipse

## Standard Form of the Equation of an Ellipse

The rectangular coordinate system gives us a unique way of describing an ellipse. It enables us to translate an ellipse's geometric definition into an algebraic equation.

We start with **Figure 9.5** to obtain an ellipse's equation. We've placed an ellipse that is elongated horizontally into a rectangular coordinate system. The foci are on the $x$-axis at $(-c, 0)$ and $(c, 0)$, as in **Figure 9.5**. In this way, the center of the ellipse is at the origin. We let $(x, y)$ represent the coordinates of any point on the ellipse.

What does the definition of an ellipse tell us about the point $(x, y)$ in **Figure 9.5**? For any point $(x, y)$ on the ellipse, the sum of the distances to the two foci, $d_1 + d_2$, must be constant. As we shall see, it is convenient to denote this constant by $2a$. Thus, the point $(x, y)$ is on the ellipse if and only if

$$d_1 + d_2 = 2a.$$

$$\sqrt{(x + c)^2 + y^2} + \sqrt{(x - c)^2 + y^2} = 2a \quad \text{Use the distance formula.}$$

After eliminating radicals and simplifying, we obtain

$$(a^2 - c^2)x^2 + a^2 y^2 = a^2(a^2 - c^2).$$

Look at the triangle in **Figure 9.5**. Notice that the distance from $F_1$ to $F_2$ is $2c$. Because the length of any side of a triangle is less than the sum of the lengths of the other two sides, $2c < d_1 + d_2$. Equivalently, $2c < 2a$ and $c < a$. Consequently, $a^2 - c^2 > 0$. For convenience, let $b^2 = a^2 - c^2$. Substituting $b^2$ for $a^2 - c^2$ in the preceding equation, we obtain

$$b^2 x^2 + a^2 y^2 = a^2 b^2$$

$$\frac{b^2 x^2}{a^2 b^2} + \frac{a^2 y^2}{a^2 b^2} = \frac{a^2 b^2}{a^2 b^2} \quad \text{Divide both sides by } a^2 b^2.$$

$$\frac{x^2}{a^2} + \frac{y^2}{b^2} = 1. \quad \text{Simplify.}$$

This last equation is the **standard form of the equation of an ellipse centered at the origin**. There are two such equations, one for a horizontal major axis and one for a vertical major axis.

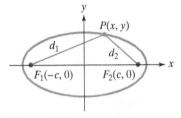

Figure 9.5

**Study Tip**

The algebraic details behind eliminating the radicals and obtaining the equation shown can be found in Appendix A. There you will find a step-by-step derivation of the ellipse's equation.

## Standard Forms of the Equations of an Ellipse

The **standard form of the equation of an ellipse** with center at the origin, and major and minor axes of lengths $2a$ and $2b$ (where $a$ and $b$ are positive, and $a^2 > b^2$) is

$$\frac{x^2}{a^2} + \frac{y^2}{b^2} = 1 \quad \text{or} \quad \frac{x^2}{b^2} + \frac{y^2}{a^2} = 1.$$

**Figure 9.6** illustrates that the vertices are on the major axis, $a$ units from the center. The foci are on the major axis, $c$ units from the center. For both equations, $b^2 = a^2 - c^2$. Equivalently, $c^2 = a^2 - b^2$.

**Study Tip**

The form $c^2 = a^2 - b^2$ is the one you should remember. When finding the foci, this form is easy to manipulate.

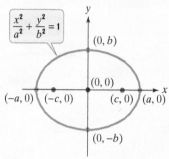

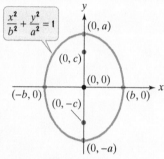

**Figure 9.6(a)**  Major axis is horizontal with length $2a$.

**Figure 9.6(b)**  Major axis is vertical with length $2a$.

The intercepts shown in **Figure 9.6(a)** can be obtained algebraically. Let's do this for

$$\frac{x^2}{a^2} + \frac{y^2}{b^2} = 1.$$

**$x$-intercepts: Set $y = 0$.**

$$\frac{x^2}{a^2} = 1$$

$$x^2 = a^2$$

$$x = \pm a$$

$x$-intercepts are $-a$ and $a$. The graph passes through $(-a, 0)$ and $(a, 0)$, which are the vertices.

**$y$-intercepts: Set $x = 0$.**

$$\frac{y^2}{b^2} = 1$$

$$y^2 = b^2$$

$$y = \pm b$$

$y$-intercepts are $-b$ and $b$. The graph passes through $(0, -b)$ and $(0, b)$.

## Using the Standard Form of the Equation of an Ellipse

We can use the standard form of an ellipse's equation to graph the ellipse. Although the definition of the ellipse is given in terms of its foci, the foci are not part of the graph. A complete graph of an ellipse can be obtained without graphing the foci.

**1** Graph ellipses centered at the origin.

**EXAMPLE 1** **Graphing an Ellipse Centered at the Origin**

Graph and locate the foci: $\dfrac{x^2}{9} + \dfrac{y^2}{4} = 1.$

**Solution**  The given equation is the standard form of an ellipse's equation with $a^2 = 9$ and $b^2 = 4$.

$$\frac{x^2}{9} + \frac{y^2}{4} = 1$$

$a^2 = 9$. This is the larger of the two denominators.

$b^2 = 4$. This is the smaller of the two denominators.

## Technology

We graph $\frac{x^2}{9} + \frac{y^2}{4} = 1$ with a graphing utility by solving for $y$.

$$\frac{y^2}{4} = 1 - \frac{x^2}{9}$$

$$y^2 = 4\left(1 - \frac{x^2}{9}\right)$$

$$y = \pm 2\sqrt{1 - \frac{x^2}{9}}$$

Notice that the square root property requires us to define two functions. Enter

$$y_1 = 2\ \boxed{\sqrt{\ }}\ (1\ \boxed{-}\ x\ \boxed{\wedge}\ 2\ \boxed{\div}\ 9)$$

and

$$y_2 = -y_1.$$

To see the true shape of the ellipse, use the

$$\boxed{\text{ZOOM SQUARE}}$$

feature so that one unit on the $y$-axis is the same length as one unit on the $x$-axis.

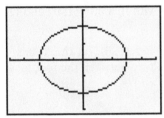

$[-5, 5, 1]$ by $[-3, 3, 1]$

Because the denominator of the $x^2$-term is greater than the denominator of the $y^2$-term, the major axis is horizontal. Based on the standard form of the equation, we know the vertices are $(-a, 0)$ and $(a, 0)$. Because $a^2 = 9$, $a = 3$. Thus, the vertices are $(-3, 0)$ and $(3, 0)$, shown in **Figure 9.7**.

Now let us find the endpoints of the vertical minor axis. According to the standard form of the equation, these endpoints are $(0, -b)$ and $(0, b)$. Because $b^2 = 4$, $b = 2$. Thus, the endpoints of the minor axis are $(0, -2)$ and $(0, 2)$. They are shown in **Figure 9.7**.

Finally, we find the foci, which are located at $(-c, 0)$ and $(c, 0)$. We can use the formula $c^2 = a^2 - b^2$ to do so. We know that $a^2 = 9$ and $b^2 = 4$. Thus,

$$c^2 = a^2 - b^2 = 9 - 4 = 5.$$

Because $c^2 = 5$, $c = \sqrt{5}$. The foci, $(-c, 0)$ and $(c, 0)$, are located at $\left(-\sqrt{5}, 0\right)$ and $\left(\sqrt{5}, 0\right)$. They are shown in **Figure 9.7**.

You can sketch the ellipse in **Figure 9.7** by locating endpoints on the major and minor axes.

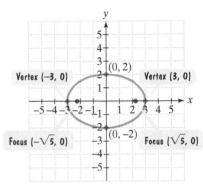

Figure 9.7   The graph of $\dfrac{x^2}{9} + \dfrac{y^2}{4} = 1$

$$\frac{x^2}{3^2} + \frac{y^2}{2^2} = 1$$

Endpoints of the major axis are 3 units to the right and left of the center.

Endpoints of the minor axis are 2 units up and down from the center.

**Check Point 1**   Graph and locate the foci: $\dfrac{x^2}{36} + \dfrac{y^2}{9} = 1$.

**EXAMPLE 2**   Graphing an Ellipse Centered at the Origin

Graph and locate the foci:   $25x^2 + 16y^2 = 400$.

**Solution**   We begin by expressing the equation in standard form. Because we want 1 on the right side, we divide both sides by 400.

$$\frac{25x^2}{400} + \frac{16y^2}{400} = \frac{400}{400}$$

$$\frac{x^2}{16} + \frac{y^2}{25} = 1$$

$b^2 = 16$. This is the smaller of the two denominators.

$a^2 = 25$. This is the larger of the two denominators.

The equation is the standard form of an ellipse's equation with $a^2 = 25$ and $b^2 = 16$. Because the denominator of the $y^2$-term is greater than the denominator of the $x^2$-term, the major axis is vertical. Based on the standard form of the equation, we know the vertices are $(0, -a)$ and $(0, a)$. Because $a^2 = 25$, $a = 5$. Thus, the vertices are $(0, -5)$ and $(0, 5)$, shown in **Figure 9.8**.

Now let us find the endpoints of the horizontal minor axis. According to the standard form of the equation, these endpoints are $(-b, 0)$ and $(b, 0)$. Because

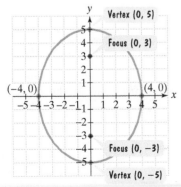

Figure 9.8   The graph of

$25x^2 + 16y^2 = 400$, or $\dfrac{x^2}{16} + \dfrac{y^2}{25} = 1$

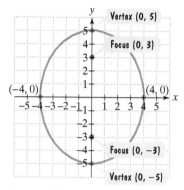

**Figure 9.8** (repeated) The graph of $\dfrac{x^2}{16} + \dfrac{y^2}{25} = 1$

$b^2 = 16$, $b = 4$. Thus, the endpoints of the minor axis are $(-4, 0)$ and $(4, 0)$. They are shown in **Figure 9.8**.

Finally, we find the foci, which are located at $(0, -c)$ and $(0, c)$. We can use the formula $c^2 = a^2 - b^2$ to do so. We know that $a^2 = 25$ and $b^2 = 16$. Thus,

$$c^2 = a^2 - b^2 = 25 - 16 = 9.$$

Because $c^2 = 9$, $c = 3$. The foci, $(0, -c)$ and $(0, c)$, are located at $(0, -3)$ and $(0, 3)$. They are shown in **Figure 9.8**.

You can sketch the ellipse in **Figure 9.8** by locating endpoints on the major and minor axes.

$$\frac{x^2}{4^2} + \frac{y^2}{5^2} = 1$$

| Endpoints of the minor axis are 4 units to the right and left of the center. | Endpoints of the major axis are 5 units up and down from the center. |

✓ **Check Point 2** Graph and locate the foci: $16x^2 + 9y^2 = 144$.

In Examples 1 and 2, we used the equation of an ellipse to find its foci and vertices. In the next example, we reverse this procedure.

**② Write equations of ellipses in standard form.**

---

**EXAMPLE 3** **Finding the Equation of an Ellipse from Its Foci and Vertices**

Find the standard form of the equation of an ellipse with foci at $(-1, 0)$ and $(1, 0)$ and vertices $(-2, 0)$ and $(2, 0)$.

**Solution** Because the foci are located at $(-1, 0)$ and $(1, 0)$, on the $x$-axis, the major axis is horizontal. The center of the ellipse is midway between the foci, located at $(0, 0)$. Thus, the form of the equation is

$$\frac{x^2}{a^2} + \frac{y^2}{b^2} = 1.$$

We need to determine the values for $a^2$ and $b^2$. The distance from the center, $(0, 0)$, to either vertex, $(-2, 0)$ or $(2, 0)$, is 2. Thus, $a = 2$.

$$\frac{x^2}{2^2} + \frac{y^2}{b^2} = 1 \qquad \text{or} \qquad \frac{x^2}{4} + \frac{y^2}{b^2} = 1$$

We must still find $b^2$. The distance from the center, $(0, 0)$, to either focus, $(-1, 0)$ or $(1, 0)$, is 1, so $c = 1$. Using $c^2 = a^2 - b^2$, we have

$$1^2 = 2^2 - b^2$$

and

$$b^2 = 2^2 - 1^2 = 4 - 1 = 3.$$

Substituting 3 for $b^2$ in $\dfrac{x^2}{4} + \dfrac{y^2}{b^2} = 1$ gives us the standard form of the ellipse's equation. The equation is

$$\frac{x^2}{4} + \frac{y^2}{3} = 1.$$

✓ **Check Point 3** Find the standard form of the equation of an ellipse with foci at $(-2, 0)$ and $(2, 0)$ and vertices $(-3, 0)$ and $(3, 0)$.

③ Graph ellipses not centered at the origin.

## Translations of Ellipses

Horizontal and vertical translations can be used to graph ellipses that are not centered at the origin. **Figure 9.9** illustrates that the graphs of

$$\frac{(x - h)^2}{a^2} + \frac{(y - k)^2}{b^2} = 1 \quad \text{and} \quad \frac{x^2}{a^2} + \frac{y^2}{b^2} = 1$$

have the same size and shape. However, the graph of the first equation is centered at $(h, k)$ rather than at the origin.

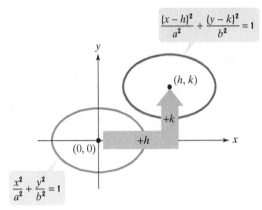

**Figure 9.9** Translating an ellipse's graph

**Table 9.1** gives the standard forms of equations of ellipses centered at $(h, k)$ and shows their graphs.

**Table 9.1 Standard Forms of Equations of Ellipses Centered at (h, k)**

| Equation | Center | Major Axis | Vertices | Graph |
|---|---|---|---|---|
| $\dfrac{(x - h)^2}{a^2} + \dfrac{(y - k)^2}{b^2} = 1$ <br><br> Endpoints of major axis are *a* units right and *a* units left of center. $a^2 > b^2$ <br><br> Foci are *c* units right and *c* units left of center, where $c^2 = a^2 - b^2$. | $(h, k)$ | Parallel to the *x*-axis, horizontal | $(h - a, k)$ <br> $(h + a, k)$ | Vertex $(h + a, k)$ <br> Focus $(h - c, k)$ <br> Major axis — $(h, k)$ <br> Vertex $(h - a, k)$ <br> Focus $(h + c, k)$ |
| $\dfrac{(x - h)^2}{b^2} + \dfrac{(y - k)^2}{a^2} = 1$ <br><br> $a^2 > b^2$   Endpoints of the major axis are *a* units above and *a* units below the center. <br><br> Foci are *c* units above and *c* units below the center, where $c^2 = a^2 - b^2$. | $(h, k)$ | Parallel to the *y*-axis, vertical | $(h, k - a)$ <br> $(h, k + a)$ | Vertex $(h, k + a)$ <br> Focus $(h, k + c)$ <br> $(h, k)$ <br> Vertex $(h, k - a)$ <br> Focus $(h, k - c)$ <br> Major axis |

**EXAMPLE 4** **Graphing an Ellipse Centered at $(h, k)$**

Graph: $\dfrac{(x-1)^2}{4} + \dfrac{(y+2)^2}{9} = 1$. Where are the foci located?

**Solution**   To graph the ellipse, we need to know its center, $(h, k)$. In the standard forms of equations centered at $(h, k)$, $h$ is the number subtracted from $x$ and $k$ is the number subtracted from $y$.

> This is $(x - h)^2$, with $h = 1$.   This is $(y - k)^2$, with $k = -2$.

$$\dfrac{(x-1)^2}{4} + \dfrac{(y-(-2))^2}{9} = 1$$

We see that $h = 1$ and $k = -2$. Thus, the center of the ellipse, $(h, k)$, is $(1, -2)$. We can graph the ellipse by locating endpoints on the major and minor axes. To do this, we must identify $a^2$ and $b^2$.

$$\dfrac{(x-1)^2}{4} + \dfrac{(y+2)^2}{9} = 1$$

> $b^2 = 4$. This is the smaller of the two denominators.   $a^2 = 9$. This is the larger of the two denominators.

The larger number is under the expression involving $y$. This means that the major axis is vertical and parallel to the $y$-axis.

We can sketch the ellipse by locating endpoints on the major and minor axes.

$$\dfrac{(x-1)^2}{2^2} + \dfrac{(y+2)^2}{3^2} = 1$$

> Endpoints of the minor axis are 2 units to the right and left of the center.   Endpoints of the major axis (the vertices) are 3 units up and down from the center.

We categorize the observations in the voice balloons as follows:

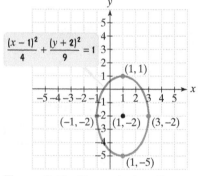

$\dfrac{(x-1)^2}{4} + \dfrac{(y+2)^2}{9} = 1$

$(1, 1)$

$(-1, -2)$  $(1, -2)$  $(3, -2)$

$(1, -5)$

**Figure 9.10**   The graph of an ellipse centered at $(1, -2)$

| For a Vertical Major Axis with Center $(1, -2)$ | |
|---|---|
| **Vertices** | **Endpoints of Minor Axis** |
| $(1, -2 + 3) = (1, 1)$ | $(1 + 2, -2) = (3, -2)$ |
| $(1, -2 - 3) = (1, -5)$ | $(1 - 2, -2) = (-1, -2)$ |

> 3 units above and below center      2 units right and left of center

Using the center and these four points, we can sketch the ellipse shown in **Figure 9.10**. With $c^2 = a^2 - b^2$, we have $c^2 = 9 - 4 = 5$. So the foci are located $\sqrt{5}$ units above and below the center, at $\left(1, -2 + \sqrt{5}\right)$ and $\left(1, -2 - \sqrt{5}\right)$. ●

⊘ **Check Point 4** Graph: $\dfrac{(x+1)^2}{9} + \dfrac{(y-2)^2}{4} = 1$. Where are the foci located?

In some cases, it is necessary to convert the equation of an ellipse to standard form by completing the square on $x$ and $y$. For example, suppose that we wish to graph the ellipse whose equation is

$$9x^2 + 4y^2 - 18x + 16y - 11 = 0.$$

Because we plan to complete the square on both $x$ and $y$, we need to rearrange terms so that

- $x$-terms are arranged in descending order.
- $y$-terms are arranged in descending order.
- the constant term appears on the right.

$$9x^2 + 4y^2 - 18x + 16y - 11 = 0$$ This is the given equation.

$$(9x^2 - 18x) + (4y^2 + 16y) = 11$$ Group terms and add 11 to both sides.

$$9(x^2 - 2x + \square) + 4(y^2 + 4y + \square) = 11$$ To complete the square, coefficients of $x^2$ and $y^2$ must be 1. Factor out 9 and 4, respectively.

> We added 9 · 1, or 9, to the left side.

> We also added 4 · 4, or 16, to the left side.

$$9(x^2 - 2x + 1) + 4(y^2 + 4y + 4) = 11 + 9 + 16$$ Complete each square by adding the square of half the coefficient of x and y, respectively.

> 9 and 16, added on the left side, must also be added on the right side.

$$9(x - 1)^2 + 4(y + 2)^2 = 36$$ Factor.

$$\frac{9(x - 1)^2}{36} + \frac{4(y + 2)^2}{36} = \frac{36}{36}$$ Divide both sides by 36.

$$\frac{(x - 1)^2}{4} + \frac{(y + 2)^2}{9} = 1$$ Simplify.

The equation is now in standard form. This is precisely the form of the equation that we graphed in Example 4.

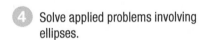
**4** Solve applied problems involving ellipses.

## Applications

Ellipses have many applications. German scientist Johannes Kepler (1571–1630) showed that the planets in our solar system move in elliptical orbits, with the sun at a focus. Earth satellites also travel in elliptical orbits, with Earth at a focus.

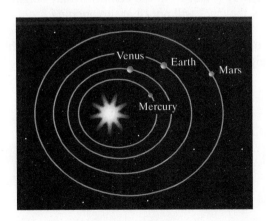

Planets move in elliptical orbits.

Whispering in an elliptical dome

One intriguing aspect of the ellipse is that a ray of light or a sound wave emanating from one focus will be reflected from the ellipse to exactly the other focus. A whispering gallery is an elliptical room with an elliptical, dome-shaped ceiling. People standing at the foci can whisper and hear each other quite clearly, while persons in other locations in the room cannot hear them. Statuary Hall in the U.S. Capitol Building is elliptical. President John Quincy Adams, while a member of the House of Representatives, was aware of this acoustical phenomenon. He situated his desk at a focal point of the elliptical ceiling, easily eavesdropping on the private conversations of other House members located near the other focus.

The elliptical reflection principle is used in a procedure for disintegrating kidney stones. The patient is placed within a device that is elliptical in shape. The patient is placed so the kidney is centered at one focus, while ultrasound waves from the other focus hit the walls and are reflected to the kidney stone. The convergence of the ultrasound waves at the kidney stone causes vibrations that shatter it into fragments. The small pieces can then be passed painlessly through the patient's system. The patient recovers in days, as opposed to up to six weeks if surgery is used instead.

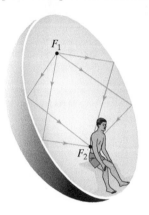

Disintegrating kidney stones

Ellipses are often used for supporting arches of bridges and in tunnel construction. This application forms the basis of our next example.

**EXAMPLE 5** **An Application Involving an Ellipse**

A semielliptical archway over a one-way road has a height of 10 feet and a width of 40 feet (see **Figure 9.11**). Your truck has a width of 10 feet and a height of 9 feet. Will your truck clear the opening of the archway?

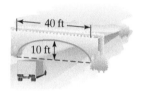

Figure 9.11
A semielliptical archway

**Solution** Because your truck's width is 10 feet, to determine the clearance, we must find the height of the archway 5 feet from the center. If that height is 9 feet or less, the truck will not clear the opening.

In **Figure 9.12**, we've constructed a coordinate system with the $x$-axis on the ground and the origin at the center of the archway. Also shown is the truck, whose height is 9 feet.

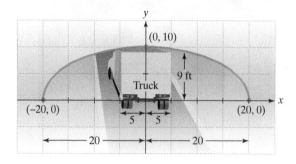

Figure 9.12

Using the equation $\frac{x^2}{a^2} + \frac{y^2}{b^2} = 1$, we can express the equation of the blue archway in **Figure 9.12** as $\frac{x^2}{20^2} + \frac{y^2}{10^2} = 1$, or $\frac{x^2}{400} + \frac{y^2}{100} = 1$.

As shown in **Figure 9.12**, the edge of the 10-foot-wide truck corresponds to $x = 5$. We find the height of the archway 5 feet from the center by substituting 5 for $x$ and solving for $y$.

## Halley's Comet

Halley's Comet has an elliptical orbit with the sun at one focus. The comet returns every 76.3 years. The first recorded sighting was in 239 B.C. It was last seen in 1986. At that time, spacecraft went close to the comet, measuring its nucleus to be 7 miles long and 4 miles wide. By 2024, Halley's Comet will have reached the farthest point in its elliptical orbit before returning to be next visible from Earth in 2062.

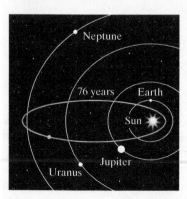

The elliptical orbit of Halley's Comet

$$\frac{5^2}{400} + \frac{y^2}{100} = 1 \qquad \text{Substitute 5 for } x \text{ in } \frac{x^2}{400} + \frac{y^2}{100} = 1.$$

$$\frac{25}{400} + \frac{y^2}{100} = 1 \qquad \text{Square 5.}$$

$$400\left(\frac{25}{400} + \frac{y^2}{100}\right) = 400(1) \qquad \text{Clear fractions by multiplying both sides by 400.}$$

$$25 + 4y^2 = 400 \qquad \text{Use the distributive property and simplify.}$$

$$4y^2 = 375 \qquad \text{Subtract 25 from both sides.}$$

$$y^2 = \frac{375}{4} \qquad \text{Divide both sides by 4.}$$

$$y = \sqrt{\frac{375}{4}} \qquad \text{Take only the positive square root. The archway is above the x-axis, so y is nonnegative.}$$

$$\approx 9.68 \qquad \text{Use a calculator.}$$

Thus, the height of the archway 5 feet from the center is approximately 9.68 feet. Because your truck's height is 9 feet, there is enough room for the truck to clear the archway.

Check Point **5** Will a truck that is 12 feet wide and has a height of 9 feet clear the opening of the archway described in Example 5?

# Exercise Set 9.1

## Practice Exercises

*In Exercises 1–18, graph each ellipse and locate the foci.*

**1.** $\frac{x^2}{16} + \frac{y^2}{4} = 1$    **2.** $\frac{x^2}{25} + \frac{y^2}{16} = 1$

**3.** $\frac{x^2}{9} + \frac{y^2}{36} = 1$    **4.** $\frac{x^2}{16} + \frac{y^2}{49} = 1$

**5.** $\frac{x^2}{25} + \frac{y^2}{64} = 1$    **6.** $\frac{x^2}{49} + \frac{y^2}{36} = 1$

**7.** $\frac{x^2}{49} + \frac{y^2}{81} = 1$    **8.** $\frac{x^2}{64} + \frac{y^2}{100} = 1$

**9.** $\frac{x^2}{\frac{9}{4}} + \frac{y^2}{\frac{25}{4}} = 1$    **10.** $\frac{x^2}{\frac{81}{4}} + \frac{y^2}{\frac{25}{16}} = 1$

**11.** $x^2 = 1 - 4y^2$    **12.** $y^2 = 1 - 4x^2$

**13.** $25x^2 + 4y^2 = 100$    **14.** $9x^2 + 4y^2 = 36$

**15.** $4x^2 + 16y^2 = 64$    **16.** $4x^2 + 25y^2 = 100$

**17.** $7x^2 = 35 - 5y^2$    **18.** $6x^2 = 30 - 5y^2$

*In Exercises 19–24, find the standard form of the equation of each ellipse and give the location of its foci.*

**19.**
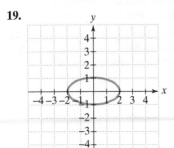

**20.**
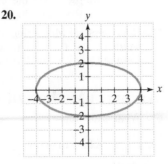

**21.**
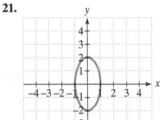

**22.**
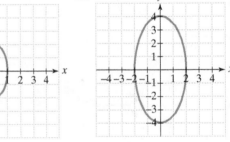

**23.**
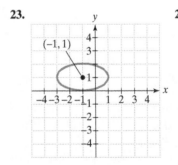

**24.**
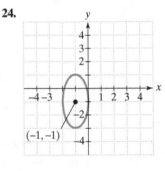

*In Exercises 25–36, find the standard form of the equation of each ellipse satisfying the given conditions.*

**25.** Foci: $(-5, 0), (5, 0)$; vertices: $(-8, 0), (8, 0)$

**26.** Foci: $(-2, 0), (2, 0)$; vertices: $(-6, 0), (6, 0)$

**27.** Foci: $(0, -4), (0, 4)$; vertices: $(0, -7), (0, 7)$

**28.** Foci: $(0, -3), (0, 3)$; vertices: $(0, -4), (0, 4)$

**29.** Foci: $(-2, 0), (2, 0)$; $y$-intercepts: $-3$ and $3$

**30.** Foci: $(0, -2), (0, 2)$; $x$-intercepts: $-2$ and $2$

**31.** Major axis horizontal with length 8; length of minor axis = 4; center: $(0, 0)$

**32.** Major axis horizontal with length 12; length of minor axis = 6; center: $(0, 0)$

**33.** Major axis vertical with length 10; length of minor axis = 4; center: $(-2, 3)$

**34.** Major axis vertical with length 20; length of minor axis = 10; center: $(2, -3)$

**35.** Endpoints of major axis: $(7, 9)$ and $(7, 3)$
Endpoints of minor axis: $(5, 6)$ and $(9, 6)$

**36.** Endpoints of major axis: $(2, 2)$ and $(8, 2)$
Endpoints of minor axis: $(5, 3)$ and $(5, 1)$

*In Exercises 37–50, graph each ellipse and give the location of its foci.*

**37.** $\dfrac{(x - 2)^2}{9} + \dfrac{(y - 1)^2}{4} = 1$

**38.** $\dfrac{(x - 1)^2}{16} + \dfrac{(y + 2)^2}{9} = 1$

**39.** $(x + 3)^2 + 4(y - 2)^2 = 16$

**40.** $(x - 3)^2 + 9(y + 2)^2 = 18$

**41.** $\dfrac{(x - 4)^2}{9} + \dfrac{(y + 2)^2}{25} = 1$

**42.** $\dfrac{(x - 3)^2}{9} + \dfrac{(y + 1)^2}{16} = 1$

**43.** $\dfrac{x^2}{25} + \dfrac{(y - 2)^2}{36} = 1$

**44.** $\dfrac{(x - 4)^2}{4} + \dfrac{y^2}{25} = 1$

**45.** $\dfrac{(x + 3)^2}{9} + (y - 2)^2 = 1$

**46.** $\dfrac{(x + 2)^2}{16} + (y - 3)^2 = 1$

**47.** $\dfrac{(x - 1)^2}{2} + \dfrac{(y + 3)^2}{5} = 1$

**48.** $\dfrac{(x + 1)^2}{2} + \dfrac{(y - 3)^2}{5} = 1$

**49.** $9(x - 1)^2 + 4(y + 3)^2 = 36$

**50.** $36(x + 4)^2 + (y + 3)^2 = 36$

*In Exercises 51–56, convert each equation to standard form by completing the square on x and y. Then graph the ellipse and give the location of its foci.*

**51.** $9x^2 + 25y^2 - 36x + 50y - 164 = 0$

**52.** $4x^2 + 9y^2 - 32x + 36y + 64 = 0$

**53.** $9x^2 + 16y^2 - 18x + 64y - 71 = 0$

**54.** $x^2 + 4y^2 + 10x - 8y + 13 = 0$

**55.** $4x^2 + y^2 + 16x - 6y - 39 = 0$

**56.** $4x^2 + 25y^2 - 24x + 100y + 36 = 0$

## Practice Plus

*In Exercises 57–62, find the solution set for each system by graphing both of the system's equations in the same rectangular coordinate system and finding points of intersection. Check all solutions in both equations.*

**57.** $\begin{cases} x^2 + y^2 = 1 \\ x^2 + 9y^2 = 9 \end{cases}$

**58.** $\begin{cases} x^2 + y^2 = 25 \\ 25x^2 + y^2 = 25 \end{cases}$

**59.** $\begin{cases} \dfrac{x^2}{25} + \dfrac{y^2}{9} = 1 \\ y = 3 \end{cases}$

**60.** $\begin{cases} \dfrac{x^2}{4} + \dfrac{y^2}{36} = 1 \\ x = -2 \end{cases}$

**61.** $\begin{cases} 4x^2 + y^2 = 4 \\ 2x - y = 2 \end{cases}$

**62.** $\begin{cases} 4x^2 + y^2 = 4 \\ x + y = 3 \end{cases}$

*In Exercises 63–64, graph each semiellipse.*

**63.** $y = -\sqrt{16 - 4x^2}$

**64.** $y = -\sqrt{4 - 4x^2}$

## Application Exercises

**65.** Will a truck that is 8 feet wide carrying a load that reaches 7 feet above the ground clear the semielliptical arch on the one-way road that passes under the bridge shown in the figure?

**66.** A semielliptic archway has a height of 20 feet and a width of 50 feet, as shown in the figure. Can a truck 14 feet high and 10 feet wide drive under the archway without going into the other lane?

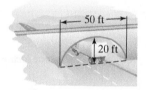

**67.** The elliptical ceiling in Statuary Hall in the U.S. Capitol Building is 96 feet long and 23 feet tall.

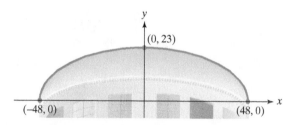

**a.** Using the rectangular coordinate system in the figure shown, write the standard form of the equation of the elliptical ceiling.

**b.** John Quincy Adams discovered that he could overhear the conversations of opposing party leaders near the left side of the chamber if he situated his desk at the focus at the right side of the chamber. How far from the center of the ellipse along the major axis did Adams situate his desk? (Round to the nearest foot.)

**68.** If an elliptical whispering room has a height of 30 feet and a width of 100 feet, where should two people stand if they would like to whisper back and forth and be heard?

## Writing in Mathematics

**69.** What is an ellipse?

**70.** Describe how to graph $\dfrac{x^2}{25} + \dfrac{y^2}{16} = 1$.

**71.** Describe how to locate the foci for $\frac{x^2}{25} + \frac{y^2}{16} = 1$.

**72.** Describe one similarity and one difference between the graphs of $\frac{x^2}{25} + \frac{y^2}{16} = 1$ and $\frac{x^2}{16} + \frac{y^2}{25} = 1$.

**73.** Describe one similarity and one difference between the graphs of $\frac{x^2}{25} + \frac{y^2}{16} = 1$ and $\frac{(x-1)^2}{25} + \frac{(y-1)^2}{16} = 1$.

**74.** An elliptipool is an elliptical pool table with only one pocket. A pool shark places a ball on the table, hits it in what appears to be a random direction, and yet it bounces off the edge, falling directly into the pocket. Explain why this happens.

## Technology Exercises

**75.** Use a graphing utility to graph any five of the ellipses that you graphed by hand in Exercises 1–18.

**76.** Use a graphing utility to graph any three of the ellipses that you graphed by hand in Exercises 37–50. First solve the given equation for $y$ by using the square root property. Enter each of the two resulting equations to produce each half of the ellipse.

**77.** Use a graphing utility to graph any one of the ellipses that you graphed by hand in Exercises 51–56. Write the equation as a quadratic equation in $y$ and use the quadratic formula to solve for $y$. Enter each of the two resulting equations to produce each half of the ellipse.

**78.** Write an equation for the path of each of the following elliptical orbits. Then use a graphing utility to graph the two ellipses in the same viewing rectangle. Can you see why early astronomers had difficulty detecting that these orbits are ellipses rather than circles?

- Earth's orbit: Length of major axis: 186 million miles

    Length of minor axis: 185.8 million miles

- Mars's orbit: Length of major axis: 283.5 million miles

    Length of minor axis: 278.5 million miles

## Critical Thinking Exercises

**Make Sense?** *In Exercises 79–82, determine whether each statement makes sense or does not make sense, and explain your reasoning.*

**79.** I graphed an ellipse with a horizontal major axis and foci on the $y$-axis.

**80.** I graphed an ellipse that was symmetric about its major axis but not symmetric about its minor axis.

**81.** You told me that an ellipse centered at the origin has vertices at $(-5, 0)$ and $(5, 0)$, so I was able to graph the ellipse.

**82.** In a whispering gallery at our science museum, I stood at one focus, my friend stood at the other focus, and we had a clear conversation, very little of which was heard by the 25 museum visitors standing between us.

**83.** Find the standard form of the equation of an ellipse with vertices at $(0, -6)$ and $(0, 6)$, passing through $(2, -4)$.

**84.** An Earth satellite has an elliptical orbit described by

$$\frac{x^2}{(5000)^2} + \frac{y^2}{(4750)^2} = 1.$$

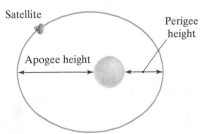

(All units are in miles.) The coordinates of the center of Earth are $(16, 0)$.

**a.** The perigee of the satellite's orbit is the point that is nearest Earth's center. If the radius of Earth is approximately 4000 miles, find the distance of the perigee above Earth's surface.

**b.** The apogee of the satellite's orbit is the point that is the greatest distance from Earth's center. Find the distance of the apogee above Earth's surface.

**85.** The equation of the red ellipse in the figure shown is

$$\frac{x^2}{25} + \frac{y^2}{9} = 1.$$

Write the equation for each circle shown in the figure.

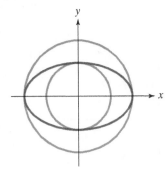

**86.** What happens to the shape of the graph of $\frac{x^2}{a^2} + \frac{y^2}{b^2} = 1$ as $\frac{c}{a} \to 0$, where $c^2 = a^2 - b^2$?

## Preview Exercises

*Exercises 87–89 will help you prepare for the material covered in the next section.*

**87.** Divide both sides of $4x^2 - 9y^2 = 36$ by 36 and simplify. How does the simplified equation differ from that of an ellipse?

**88.** Consider the equation $\frac{x^2}{16} - \frac{y^2}{9} = 1$.

**a.** Find the $x$-intercepts.

**b.** Explain why there are no $y$-intercepts.

**89.** Consider the equation $\frac{y^2}{9} - \frac{x^2}{16} = 1$.

**a.** Find the $y$-intercepts.

**b.** Explain why there are no $x$-intercepts.

## Section 9.2  The Hyperbola

### Objectives

1. Locate a hyperbola's vertices and foci.

2. Write equations of hyperbolas in standard form.

3. Graph hyperbolas centered at the origin.

4. Graph hyperbolas not centered at the origin.

5. Solve applied problems involving hyperbolas.

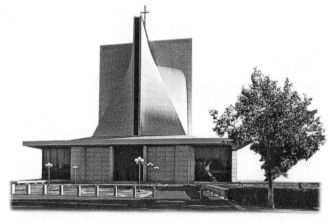

St. Mary's Cathedral

Conic sections are often used to create unusual architectural designs. The top of St. Mary's Cathedral in San Francisco is a 2135-cubic-foot dome with walls rising 200 feet above the floor and supported by four massive concrete pylons that extend 94 feet into the ground. Cross sections of the roof are parabolas and hyperbolas. In this section, we study the curve with two parts known as the hyperbola.

## Definition of a Hyperbola

**Figure 9.13** shows a cylindrical lampshade casting two shadows on a wall. These shadows indicate the distinguishing feature of hyperbolas: Their graphs contain two disjoint parts, called **branches**. Although each branch might look like a parabola, its shape is actually quite different.

The definition of a hyperbola is similar to that of an ellipse. For an ellipse, the *sum* of the distances to the foci is a constant. By contrast, for a hyperbola the *difference* of the distances to the foci is a constant.

**Figure 9.13** Casting hyperbolic shadows

### Definition of a Hyperbola

A **hyperbola** is the set of points in a plane the difference of whose distances from two fixed points, called foci, is constant.

**Figure 9.14** illustrates the two branches of a hyperbola. The line through the foci intersects the hyperbola at two points, called the **vertices**. The line segment that joins the vertices is the **transverse axis**. The midpoint of the transverse axis is the **center** of the hyperbola. Notice that the center lies midway between the vertices, as well as midway between the foci.

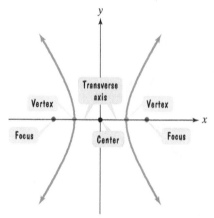

**Figure 9.14** The two branches of a hyperbola

## Standard Form of the Equation of a Hyperbola

The rectangular coordinate system enables us to translate a hyperbola's geometric definition into an algebraic equation. **Figure 9.15** is our starting point for obtaining an equation. We place the foci, $F_1$ and $F_2$, on the $x$-axis at the points $(-c, 0)$ and $(c, 0)$. Note that the center of this hyperbola is at the origin. We let $(x, y)$ represent the coordinates of any point, $P$, on the hyperbola.

What does the definition of a hyperbola tell us about the point $(x, y)$ in **Figure 9.15**? For any point $(x, y)$ on the hyperbola, the absolute value of the difference of the distances from the two foci, $|d_2 - d_1|$, must be constant. We denote this constant by $2a$, just as we did for the ellipse. Thus, the point $(x, y)$ is on the hyperbola if and only if

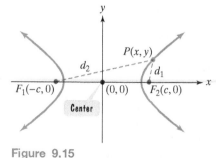

**Figure 9.15**

$$|d_2 - d_1| = 2a.$$

$$\left|\sqrt{(x + c)^2 + (y - 0)^2} - \sqrt{(x - c)^2 + (y - 0)^2}\right| = 2a \quad \text{Use the distance formula.}$$

After eliminating radicals and simplifying, we obtain

$$(c^2 - a^2)x^2 - a^2y^2 = a^2(c^2 - a^2).$$

For convenience, let $b^2 = c^2 - a^2$. Substituting $b^2$ for $c^2 - a^2$ in the preceding equation, we obtain

$$b^2x^2 - a^2y^2 = a^2b^2.$$

$$\frac{b^2x^2}{a^2b^2} - \frac{a^2y^2}{a^2b^2} = \frac{a^2b^2}{a^2b^2} \quad \text{Divide both sides by } a^2b^2.$$

$$\frac{x^2}{a^2} - \frac{y^2}{b^2} = 1 \quad \text{Simplify.}$$

This last equation is called the **standard form of the equation of a hyperbola centered at the origin**. There are two such equations. The first is for a hyperbola in which the transverse axis lies on the $x$-axis. The second is for a hyperbola in which the transverse axis lies on the $y$-axis.

## Standard Forms of the Equations of a Hyperbola

The **standard form of the equation of a hyperbola** with center at the origin is

$$\frac{x^2}{a^2} - \frac{y^2}{b^2} = 1 \quad \text{or} \quad \frac{y^2}{a^2} - \frac{x^2}{b^2} = 1.$$

**Figure 9.16(a)** illustrates that for the equation on the left, the transverse axis lies on the $x$-axis. **Figure 9.16(b)** illustrates that for the equation on the right, the transverse axis lies on the $y$-axis. The vertices are $a$ units from the center and the foci are $c$ units from the center. For both equations, $b^2 = c^2 - a^2$. Equivalently, $c^2 = a^2 + b^2$.

### Study Tip

The form $c^2 = a^2 + b^2$ is the one you should remember. When finding the foci, this form is easy to manipulate.

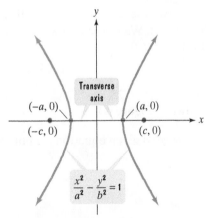

**Figure 9.16(a)** Transverse axis lies on the $x$-axis.

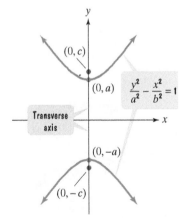

**Figure 9.16(b)** Transverse axis lies on the $y$-axis.

### Study Tip

When the $x^2$-term is preceded by a plus sign, the transverse axis is horizontal. When the $y^2$-term is preceded by a plus sign, the transverse axis is vertical.

① Locate a hyperbola's vertices and foci.

## Study Tip

Notice the sign difference between the following equations:
Finding an ellipse's foci:

$$c^2 = a^2 - b^2$$

Finding a hyperbola's foci:

$$c^2 = a^2 + b^2.$$

## Using the Standard Form of the Equation of a Hyperbola

We can use the standard form of the equation of a hyperbola to find its vertices and locate its foci. Because the vertices are $a$ units from the center, begin by identifying $a^2$ in the equation. In the standard form of a hyperbola's equation, **$a^2$ is the number under the variable whose term is preceded by a plus sign** (+). If the $x^2$-term is preceded by a plus sign, the transverse axis lies along the $x$-axis. Thus, the vertices are $a$ units to the left and right of the origin. If the $y^2$-term is preceded by a plus sign, the transverse axis lies along the $y$-axis. Thus, the vertices are $a$ units above and below the origin.

We know that the foci are $c$ units from the center. The substitution that is used to derive the hyperbola's equation, $c^2 = a^2 + b^2$, is needed to locate the foci when $a^2$ and $b^2$ are known.

**EXAMPLE 1** Finding Vertices and Foci from a Hyperbola's Equation

Find the vertices and locate the foci for each of the following hyperbolas with the given equation:

**a.** $\dfrac{x^2}{16} - \dfrac{y^2}{9} = 1$ **b.** $\dfrac{y^2}{9} - \dfrac{x^2}{16} = 1.$

**Solution** Both equations are in standard form. We begin by identifying $a^2$ and $b^2$ in each equation.

**a.** The first equation is in the form $\dfrac{x^2}{a^2} - \dfrac{y^2}{b^2} = 1.$

$$\frac{x^2}{16} - \frac{y^2}{9} = 1$$

$a^2 = 16$. This is the denominator of the term preceded by a plus sign. $b^2 = 9$. This is the denominator of the term preceded by a minus sign.

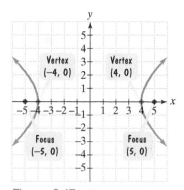

**Figure 9.17** The graph of $\dfrac{x^2}{16} - \dfrac{y^2}{9} = 1$

Because the $x^2$-term is preceded by a plus sign, the transverse axis lies along the $x$-axis. Thus, the vertices are $a$ units to the *left* and *right* of the origin. Based on the standard form of the equation, we know the vertices are $(-a, 0)$ and $(a, 0)$. Because $a^2 = 16$, $a = 4$. Thus, the vertices are $(-4, 0)$ and $(4, 0)$, shown in **Figure 9.17**.

We use $c^2 = a^2 + b^2$ to find the foci, which are located at $(-c, 0)$ and $(c, 0)$. We know that $a^2 = 16$ and $b^2 = 9$; we need to find $c^2$ in order to find $c$.

$$c^2 = a^2 + b^2 = 16 + 9 = 25$$

Because $c^2 = 25$, $c = 5$. The foci are located at $(-5, 0)$ and $(5, 0)$. They are shown in **Figure 9.17**.

**b.** The second given equation is in the form $\dfrac{y^2}{a^2} - \dfrac{x^2}{b^2} = 1.$

$$\frac{y^2}{9} - \frac{x^2}{16} = 1$$

$a^2 = 9$. This is the denominator of the term preceded by a plus sign. $b^2 = 16$. This is the denominator of the term preceded by a minus sign.

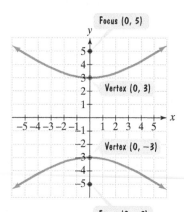

**Figure 9.18** The graph of $\dfrac{y^2}{9} - \dfrac{x^2}{16} = 1$

Because the $y^2$-term is preceded by a plus sign, the transverse axis lies along the $y$-axis. Thus, the vertices are $a$ units *above* and *below* the origin. Based on the standard form of the equation, we know the vertices are $(0, -a)$ and $(0, a)$. Because $a^2 = 9$, $a = 3$. Thus, the vertices are $(0, -3)$ and $(0, 3)$, shown in **Figure 9.18**.

We use $c^2 = a^2 + b^2$ to find the foci, which are located at $(0, -c)$ and $(0, c)$.

$$c^2 = a^2 + b^2 = 9 + 16 = 25$$

Because $c^2 = 25$, $c = 5$. The foci are located at $(0, -5)$ and $(0, 5)$. They are shown in **Figure 9.18**.

⊘Check Point 1 Find the vertices and locate the foci for each of the following hyperbolas with the given equation:

a. $\dfrac{x^2}{25} - \dfrac{y^2}{16} = 1$      b. $\dfrac{y^2}{25} - \dfrac{x^2}{16} = 1$.

In Example 1, we used equations of hyperbolas to find their foci and vertices. In the next example, we reverse this procedure.

**2** Write equations of hyperbolas in standard form.

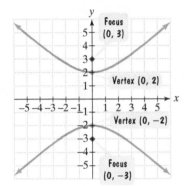
Figure 9.19

**EXAMPLE 2** **Finding the Equation of a Hyperbola from Its Foci and Vertices**

Find the standard form of the equation of a hyperbola with foci at $(0, -3)$ and $(0, 3)$ and vertices $(0, -2)$ and $(0, 2)$, shown in **Figure 9.19**.

**Solution** Because the foci are located at $(0, -3)$ and $(0, 3)$, on the $y$-axis, the transverse axis lies on the $y$-axis. The center of the hyperbola is midway between the foci, located at $(0, 0)$. Thus, the form of the equation is

$$\frac{y^2}{a^2} - \frac{x^2}{b^2} = 1.$$

We need to determine the values for $a^2$ and $b^2$. The distance from the center, $(0, 0)$, to either vertex, $(0, -2)$ or $(0, 2)$, is 2, so $a = 2$.

$$\frac{y^2}{2^2} - \frac{x^2}{b^2} = 1 \quad \text{or} \quad \frac{y^2}{4} - \frac{x^2}{b^2} = 1$$

We must still find $b^2$. The distance from the center, $(0, 0)$, to either focus, $(0, -3)$ or $(0, 3)$, is 3. Thus, $c = 3$. Using $c^2 = a^2 + b^2$, we have

$$3^2 = 2^2 + b^2$$

and

$$b^2 = 3^2 - 2^2 = 9 - 4 = 5.$$

Substituting 5 for $b^2$ in $\dfrac{y^2}{4} - \dfrac{x^2}{b^2} = 1$ gives us the standard form of the hyperbola's equation. The equation is

$$\frac{y^2}{4} - \frac{x^2}{5} = 1.$$

⊘Check Point 2 Find the standard form of the equation of a hyperbola with foci at $(0, -5)$ and $(0, 5)$ and vertices $(0, -3)$ and $(0, 3)$.

## The Asymptotes of a Hyperbola

As $x$ and $y$ get larger, the two branches of the graph of a hyperbola approach a pair of intersecting straight lines, called **asymptotes**. The asymptotes pass through the center of the hyperbola and are helpful in graphing hyperbolas.

**Figure 9.20** shows the asymptotes for the graphs of hyperbolas centered at the origin. The asymptotes pass through the corners of a rectangle. Note that the dimensions of this rectangle are $2a$ by $2b$. The line segment of length $2b$ is the **conjugate axis** of the hyperbola and is perpendicular to the transverse axis through the center of the hyperbola.

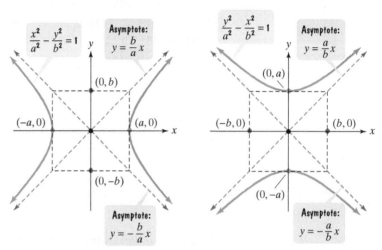

**Figure 9.20**    Asymptotes of a hyperbola

## The Asymptotes of a Hyperbola Centered at the Origin

The hyperbola $\dfrac{x^2}{a^2} - \dfrac{y^2}{b^2} = 1$ has a horizontal transverse axis and two asymptotes

$$y = \frac{b}{a}x \qquad \text{and} \qquad y = -\frac{b}{a}x.$$

The hyperbola $\dfrac{y^2}{a^2} - \dfrac{x^2}{b^2} = 1$ has a vertical transverse axis and two asymptotes

$$y = \frac{a}{b}x \qquad \text{and} \qquad y = -\frac{a}{b}x.$$

Why are $y = \pm\dfrac{b}{a}x$ the asymptotes for a hyperbola whose transverse axis is horizontal? The proof can be found in Appendix A.

③ Graph hyperbolas centered at the origin.

## Graphing Hyperbolas Centered at the Origin

Hyperbolas are graphed using vertices and asymptotes.

### Graphing Hyperbolas

1. Locate the vertices.
2. Use dashed lines to draw the rectangle centered at the origin with sides parallel to the axes, crossing one axis at $\pm a$ and the other at $\pm b$.
3. Use dashed lines to draw the diagonals of this rectangle and extend them to obtain the asymptotes.
4. Draw the two branches of the hyperbola by starting at each vertex and approaching the asymptotes.

**EXAMPLE 3** Graphing a Hyperbola

Graph and locate the foci: $\dfrac{x^2}{25} - \dfrac{y^2}{16} = 1$. What are the equations of the asymptotes?

**Solution**

**Step 1   Locate the vertices.** The given equation is in the form $\dfrac{x^2}{a^2} - \dfrac{y^2}{b^2} = 1$, with $a^2 = 25$ and $b^2 = 16$.

$$\underset{a^2\,=\,25}{\qquad}\dfrac{x^2}{25} - \dfrac{y^2}{16} = 1\underset{\qquad b^2\,=\,16}{}$$

Based on the standard form of the equation with the transverse axis on the $x$-axis, we know that the vertices are $(-a, 0)$ and $(a, 0)$. Because $a^2 = 25$, $a = 5$. Thus, the vertices are $(-5, 0)$ and $(5, 0)$, shown in **Figure 9.21**.

**Step 2   Draw a rectangle.** Because $a^2 = 25$ and $b^2 = 16$, $a = 5$ and $b = 4$. We construct a rectangle to find the asymptotes, using $-5$ and $5$ on the $x$-axis (the vertices are located here) and $-4$ and $4$ on the $y$-axis. The rectangle passes through these four points, shown using dashed lines in **Figure 9.21**.

**Step 3   Draw extended diagonals for the rectangle to obtain the asymptotes.** We draw dashed lines through the opposite corners of the rectangle, shown in **Figure 9.21**, to obtain the graph of the asymptotes. Based on the standard form of the hyperbola's equation, the equations for these asymptotes are

$$y = \pm\dfrac{b}{a}x \qquad \text{or} \qquad y = \pm\dfrac{4}{5}x.$$

**Technology**

Graph $\dfrac{x^2}{25} - \dfrac{y^2}{16} = 1$ by solving for $y$:

$$y_1 = \dfrac{\sqrt{16x^2 - 400}}{5}$$

$$y_2 = -\dfrac{\sqrt{16x^2 - 400}}{5} = -y_1.$$

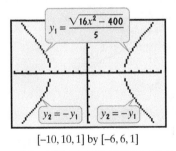

$[-10, 10, 1]$ by $[-6, 6, 1]$

**Figure 9.21**  Preparing to graph $\dfrac{x^2}{25} - \dfrac{y^2}{16} = 1$

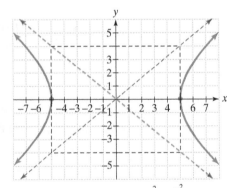

**Figure 9.22**  The graph of $\dfrac{x^2}{25} - \dfrac{y^2}{16} = 1$

**Step 4   Draw the two branches of the hyperbola by starting at each vertex and approaching the asymptotes.** The hyperbola is shown in **Figure 9.22**.

We now consider the foci, located at $(-c, 0)$ and $(c, 0)$. We find $c$ using $c^2 = a^2 + b^2$.

$$c^2 = 25 + 16 = 41$$

Because $c^2 = 41$, $c = \sqrt{41}$. The foci are located at $\left(-\sqrt{41}, 0\right)$ and $\left(\sqrt{41}, 0\right)$, approximately $(-6.4, 0)$ and $(6.4, 0)$.

✓ Check Point **3**  Graph and locate the foci: $\dfrac{x^2}{36} - \dfrac{y^2}{9} = 1$. What are the equations of the asymptotes?

**EXAMPLE 4** Graphing a Hyperbola

Graph and locate the foci: $9y^2 - 4x^2 = 36$. What are the equations of the asymptotes?

**Solution** We begin by writing the equation in standard form. The right side should be 1, so we divide both sides by 36.

$$\frac{9y^2}{36} - \frac{4x^2}{36} = \frac{36}{36}$$

$$\frac{y^2}{4} - \frac{x^2}{9} = 1 \qquad \text{Simplify. The right side is now 1.}$$

Now we are ready to use our four-step procedure for graphing hyperbolas.

**Step 1 Locate the vertices.** The equation that we obtained is in the form $\frac{y^2}{a^2} - \frac{x^2}{b^2} = 1$, with $a^2 = 4$ and $b^2 = 9$.

$$\underset{a^2 = 4}{\frac{y^2}{4}} - \underset{b^2 = 9}{\frac{x^2}{9}} = 1$$

Based on the standard form of the equation with the transverse axis on the $y$-axis, we know that the vertices are $(0, -a)$ and $(0, a)$. Because $a^2 = 4$, $a = 2$. Thus, the vertices are $(0, -2)$ and $(0, 2)$, shown in **Figure 9.23**.

**Step 2 Draw a rectangle.** Because $a^2 = 4$ and $b^2 = 9$, $a = 2$ and $b = 3$. We construct a rectangle to find the asymptotes, using $-2$ and $2$ on the $y$-axis (the vertices are located here) and $-3$ and $3$ on the $x$-axis. The rectangle passes through these four points, shown using dashed lines in **Figure 9.23**.

**Step 3 Draw extended diagonals of the rectangle to obtain the asymptotes.** We draw dashed lines through the opposite corners of the rectangle, shown in **Figure 9.23**, to obtain the graph of the asymptotes. Based on the standard form of the hyperbola's equation, the equations of these asymptotes are

$$y = \pm \frac{a}{b}x \qquad \text{or} \qquad y = \pm \frac{2}{3}x.$$

**Step 4 Draw the two branches of the hyperbola by starting at each vertex and approaching the asymptotes.** The hyperbola is shown in **Figure 9.24**.

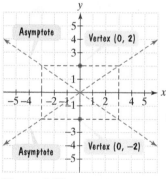

Figure 9.23 Preparing to graph $\frac{y^2}{4} - \frac{x^2}{9} = 1$

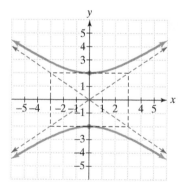

Figure 9.24 The graph of $\frac{y^2}{4} - \frac{x^2}{9} = 1$

We now consider the foci, located at $(0, -c)$ and $(0, c)$. We find $c$ using $c^2 = a^2 + b^2$.

$$c^2 = 4 + 9 = 13$$

Because $c^2 = 13, c = \sqrt{13}$. The foci are located at $\left(0, -\sqrt{13}\right)$ and $\left(0, \sqrt{13}\right)$, approximately $(0, -3.6)$ and $(0, 3.6)$.

⊘ Check Point **4** Graph and locate the foci: $y^2 - 4x^2 = 4$. What are the equations of the asymptotes?

**4** Graph hyperbolas not centered at the origin.

## Translations of Hyperbolas

The graph of a hyperbola can be centered at $(h, k)$, rather than at the origin. Horizontal and vertical translations are accomplished by replacing $x$ with $x - h$ and $y$ with $y - k$ in the standard form of the hyperbola's equation.

**Table 9.2** gives the standard forms of equations of hyperbolas centered at $(h, k)$ and shows their graphs.

**Table 9.2   Standard Forms of Equations of Hyperbolas Centered at $(h, k)$**

| Equation | Center | Transverse Axis | Vertices | Graph |
|---|---|---|---|---|
| $\dfrac{(x - h)^2}{a^2} - \dfrac{(y - k)^2}{b^2} = 1$<br><br>Vertices are $a$ units right and $a$ units left of center.<br><br>Foci are $c$ units right and $c$ units left of center, where $c^2 = a^2 + b^2$. | $(h, k)$ | Parallel to the $x$-axis; horizontal | $(h - a, k)$<br>$(h + a, k)$ | |
| $\dfrac{(y - k)^2}{a^2} - \dfrac{(x - h)^2}{b^2} = 1$<br><br>Vertices are $a$ units above and $a$ units below the center.<br><br>Foci are $c$ units above and $c$ units below the center, where $c^2 = a^2 + b^2$. | $(h, k)$ | Parallel to the $y$-axis; vertical | $(h, k - a)$<br>$(h, k + a)$ | |

**EXAMPLE 5** Graphing a Hyperbola Centered at $(h, k)$

Graph: $\dfrac{(x - 2)^2}{16} - \dfrac{(y - 3)^2}{9} = 1$. Where are the foci located? What are the equations of the asymptotes?

**Solution** In order to graph the hyperbola, we need to know its center, $(h, k)$. In the standard forms of equations centered at $(h, k)$, $h$ is the number subtracted from $x$ and $k$ is the number subtracted from $y$.

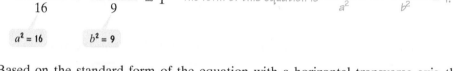

This is $(x - h)^2$, with $h = 2$.

$$\frac{(x - 2)^2}{16} - \frac{(y - 3)^2}{9} = 1$$

This is $(y - k)^2$, with $k = 3$.

We see that $h = 2$ and $k = 3$. Thus, the center of the hyperbola, $(h, k)$, is $(2, 3)$. We can graph the hyperbola by using vertices, asymptotes, and our four-step graphing procedure.

**Step 1   Locate the vertices.** To do this, we must identify $a^2$.

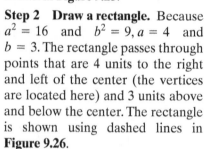

$$\frac{(x - 2)^2}{16} - \frac{(y - 3)^2}{9} = 1 \qquad \text{The form of this equation is } \frac{(x - h)^2}{a^2} - \frac{(y - k)^2}{b^2} = 1.$$

$a^2 = 16 \qquad b^2 = 9$

Based on the standard form of the equation with a horizontal transverse axis, the vertices are $a$ units to the left and right of the center. Because $a^2 = 16$, $a = 4$. This means that the vertices are 4 units to the left and right of the center, $(2, 3)$. Four units to the left of $(2, 3)$ puts one vertex at $(2 - 4, 3)$, or $(-2, 3)$. Four units to the right of $(2, 3)$ puts the other vertex at $(2 + 4, 3)$, or $(6, 3)$. The vertices are shown in **Figure 9.25**.

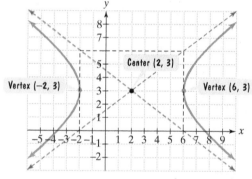

Figure 9.25 Locating a hyperbola's center and vertices

**Step 2   Draw a rectangle.** Because $a^2 = 16$ and $b^2 = 9$, $a = 4$ and $b = 3$. The rectangle passes through points that are 4 units to the right and left of the center (the vertices are located here) and 3 units above and below the center. The rectangle is shown using dashed lines in **Figure 9.26**.

**Figure 9.26** The graph of $\dfrac{(x - 2)^2}{16} - \dfrac{(y - 3)^2}{9} = 1$

**Step 3   Draw extended diagonals of the rectangle to obtain the asymptotes.** We draw dashed lines through the opposite corners of the rectangle, shown in **Figure 9.26**, to obtain the graph of the asymptotes. The equations of the asymptotes of the unshifted hyperbola $\dfrac{x^2}{16} - \dfrac{y^2}{9} = 1$ are $y = \pm \dfrac{b}{a}x$, or $y = \pm \dfrac{3}{4}x$. Thus, the asymptotes for the hyperbola that is shifted two units to the right and three units up, namely

$$\frac{(x - 2)^2}{16} - \frac{(y - 3)^2}{9} = 1$$

have equations that can be expressed as

$$y - 3 = \pm \frac{3}{4}(x - 2).$$

**Step 4   Draw the two branches of the hyperbola by starting at each vertex and approaching the asymptotes.** The hyperbola is shown in **Figure 9.26**.

We now consider the foci, located $c$ units to the right and left of the center. We find $c$ using $c^2 = a^2 + b^2$.

$$c^2 = 16 + 9 = 25$$

Because $c^2 = 25$, $c = 5$. This means that the foci are 5 units to the left and right of the center, $(2, 3)$. Five units to the left of $(2, 3)$ puts one focus at $(2 - 5, 3)$, or $(-3, 3)$. Five units to the right of $(2, 3)$ puts the other focus at $(2 + 5, 3)$, or $(7, 3)$. ●

**Study Tip**

You can also use the point-slope form of a line's equation

$$y - y_1 = m(x - x_1)$$

to find the equations of the asymptotes. The center of the hyperbola, $(h, k)$, is a point on each asymptote, so $x_1 = h$ and $y_1 = k$. The slopes, $m$, are $\pm \dfrac{b}{a}$ for a horizontal transverse axis and $\pm \dfrac{a}{b}$ for a vertical transverse axis.

✅ Check Point 5 Graph: $\dfrac{(x-3)^2}{4} - \dfrac{(y-1)^2}{1} = 1$. Where are the foci located? What are the equations of the asymptotes?

In our next example, it is necessary to convert the equation of a hyperbola to standard form by completing the square on $x$ and $y$.

( EXAMPLE 6 ) **Graphing a Hyperbola Centered at $(h, k)$**

Graph: $4x^2 - 24x - 25y^2 + 250y - 489 = 0$. Where are the foci located? What are the equations of the asymptotes?

**Solution**  We begin by completing the square on $x$ and $y$.

$$4x^2 - 24x - 25y^2 + 250y - 489 = 0$$

This is the given equation.

$$(4x^2 - 24x) + (-25y^2 + 250y) = 489$$

Group terms and add 489 to both sides.

$$4(x^2 - 6x + \square) - 25(y^2 - 10y + \square) = 489$$

Factor out 4 and −25, respectively, so coefficients of $x^2$ and $y^2$ are 1.

$$4(x^2 - 6x + 9) - 25(y^2 - 10y + 25) = 489 + 36 + (-625)$$

Complete each square by adding the square of half the coefficient of $x$ and $y$, respectively.

We added 4 · 9, or 36, to the left side.

We added −25 · 25, or −625, to the left side.

Add 36 + (−625) to the right side.

$$4(x-3)^2 - 25(y-5)^2 = -100$$

Factor.

$$\dfrac{4(x-3)^2}{-100} - \dfrac{25(y-5)^2}{-100} = \dfrac{-100}{-100}$$

Divide both sides by −100.

$$\dfrac{(x-3)^2}{-25} + \dfrac{(y-5)^2}{4} = 1$$

Simplify.

This is $(y-k)^2$, with $k = 5$.

This is $(x-h)^2$, with $h = 3$.

$$\dfrac{(y-5)^2}{4} - \dfrac{(x-3)^2}{25} = 1$$

Write the equation in standard form, $\dfrac{(y-k)^2}{a^2} - \dfrac{(x-h)^2}{b^2} = 1$.

**Study Tip**

The hyperbola's center is $(3, 5)$ because the last equation shows that 3 is subtracted from $x$ and 5 is subtracted from $y$. Many students tend to read the equation from left to right and get the center backward. The hyperbola's center is *not* $(5, 3)$.

We see that $h = 3$ and $k = 5$. Thus, the center of the hyperbola, $(h, k)$, is $(3, 5)$. Because the $x^2$-term is being subtracted, the transverse axis is vertical and the hyperbola opens upward and downward.

We use our four-step procedure to obtain the graph of

$$\dfrac{(y-5)^2}{4} - \dfrac{(x-3)^2}{25} = 1.$$

$a^2 = 4$     $b^2 = 25$

**Step 1   Locate the vertices.** Based on the standard form of the equation with a vertical transverse axis, the vertices are $a$ units above and below the center. Because $a^2 = 4$, $a = 2$. This means that the vertices are 2 units above and below the center, $(3, 5)$. This puts the vertices at $(3, 7)$ and $(3, 3)$, shown in **Figure 9.27**.

**Step 2   Draw a rectangle.** Because $a^2 = 4$ and $b^2 = 25$, $a = 2$ and $b = 5$. The rectangle passes through points that are 2 units above and below the center (the vertices are located here) and 5 units to the right and left of the center. The rectangle is shown using dashed lines in **Figure 9.27**.

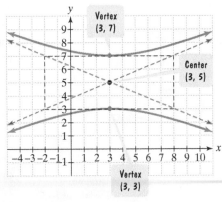

Figure 9.27  The graph of $\dfrac{(y-5)^2}{4} - \dfrac{(x-3)^2}{25} = 1$

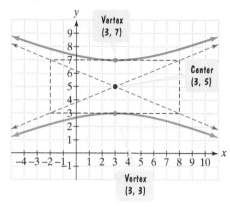

**Figure 9.27** (repeated) The graph of
$\dfrac{(y-5)^2}{4} - \dfrac{(x-3)^2}{25} = 1$

**Step 3  Draw extended diagonals of the rectangle to obtain the asymptotes.** We draw dashed lines through the opposite corners of the rectangle, shown in **Figure 9.27**, to obtain the graph of the asymptotes. The equations of the asymptotes of the unshifted hyperbola $\dfrac{y^2}{4} - \dfrac{x^2}{25} = 1$ are $y = \pm\dfrac{a}{b}x$, or $y = \pm\dfrac{2}{5}x$. Thus, the asymptotes for the hyperbola that is shifted three units to the right and five units up, namely

$$\frac{(y-5)^2}{4} - \frac{(x-3)^2}{25} = 1$$

have equations that can be expressed as

$$y - 5 = \pm\frac{2}{5}(x - 3).$$

**Step 4  Draw the two branches of the hyperbola by starting at each vertex and approaching the asymptotes.** The hyperbola is shown in **Figure 9.27**.

We now consider the foci, located $c$ units above and below the center, $(3, 5)$. We find $c$ using $c^2 = a^2 + b^2$.

$$c^2 = 4 + 25 = 29$$

Because $c^2 = 29$, $c = \sqrt{29}$. The foci are located at $\left(3, 5 + \sqrt{29}\right)$ and $\left(3, 5 - \sqrt{29}\right)$.

⊘ Check Point **6** Graph: $4x^2 - 24x - 9y^2 - 90y - 153 = 0$. Where are the foci located? What are the equations of the asymptotes?

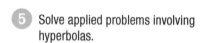

**⑤ Solve applied problems involving hyperbolas.**

## Applications

Hyperbolas have many applications. When a jet flies at a speed greater than the speed of sound, the shock wave that is created is heard as a sonic boom. The wave has the shape of a cone. The shape formed as the cone hits the ground is one branch of a hyperbola.

Halley's Comet, a permanent part of our solar system, travels around the sun in an elliptical orbit. Other comets pass through the solar system only once, following a hyperbolic path with the sun as a focus.

Hyperbolas are of practical importance in fields ranging from architecture to navigation. Cooling towers used in the design for nuclear power plants have cross sections that are both ellipses and hyperbolas. Three-dimensional solids whose cross sections are hyperbolas are used in some rather unique architectural creations, including the TWA building at Kennedy Airport in New York City and the St. Louis Science Center Planetarium.

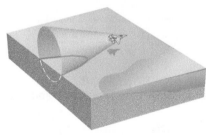

The hyperbolic shape of a sonic boom

(EXAMPLE 7) **An Application Involving Hyperbolas**

An explosion is recorded by two microphones that are 2 miles apart. Microphone $M_1$ received the sound 4 seconds before microphone $M_2$. Assuming sound travels at 1100 feet per second, determine the possible locations of the explosion relative to the location of the microphones.

**Solution**  We begin by putting the microphones in a coordinate system. Because 1 mile = 5280 feet, we place $M_1$ 5280 feet on a horizontal axis to the right of the origin and $M_2$ 5280 feet on a horizontal axis to the left of the origin. **Figure 9.28** illustrates that the two microphones are 2 miles apart.

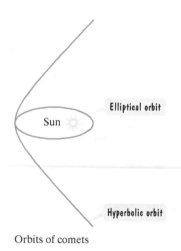

Orbits of comets

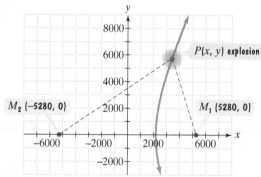

**Figure 9.28**  Locating an explosion on the branch of a hyperbola

We know that $M_2$ received the sound 4 seconds after $M_1$. Because sound travels at 1100 feet per second, the difference between the distance from $P$ to $M_1$ and the distance from $P$ to $M_2$ is 4400 feet. The set of all points $P$ (or locations of the explosion) satisfying these conditions fits the definition of a hyperbola, with microphones $M_1$ and $M_2$ at the foci.

$$\frac{x^2}{a^2} - \frac{y^2}{b^2} = 1 \qquad \textit{Use the standard form of the hyperbola's equation. } P(x, y), \textit{ the}$$
$$\textit{explosion point, lies on this hyperbola. We must find } a^2 \textit{ and } b^2.$$

The difference between the distances, represented by $2a$ in the derivation of the hyperbola's equation, is 4400 feet. Thus, $2a = 4400$ and $a = 2200$.

$$\frac{x^2}{(2200)^2} - \frac{y^2}{b^2} = 1 \qquad \textit{Substitute 2200 for a.}$$

$$\frac{x^2}{4,840,000} - \frac{y^2}{b^2} = 1 \qquad \textit{Square 2200.}$$

We must still find $b^2$. We know that $a = 2200$. The distance from the center, $(0, 0)$, to either focus, $(-5280, 0)$ or $(5280, 0)$, is 5280. Thus, $c = 5280$. Using $c^2 = a^2 + b^2$, we have

$$5280^2 = 2200^2 + b^2$$

and

$$b^2 = 5280^2 - 2200^2 = 23{,}038{,}400.$$

The equation of the hyperbola with a microphone at each focus is

$$\frac{x^2}{4,840,000} - \frac{y^2}{23,038,400} = 1. \qquad \textit{Substitute 23,038,400 for } b^2.$$

We can conclude that the explosion occurred somewhere on the right branch (the branch closer to $M_1$) of the hyperbola given by this equation. ●

In Example 7, we determined that the explosion occurred somewhere along one branch of a hyperbola, but not exactly where on the hyperbola. If, however, we had received the sound from another pair of microphones, we could locate the sound along a branch of another hyperbola. The exact location of the explosion would be the point where the two hyperbolas intersect.

⊘ Check Point **7** Rework Example 7 assuming microphone $M_1$ receives the sound 3 seconds before microphone $M_2$.

# Exercise Set 9.2

## Practice Exercises

In Exercises 1–4, find the vertices and locate the foci of each hyperbola with the given equation. Then match each equation to one of the graphs that are shown and labeled (a)–(d).

**1.** $\dfrac{x^2}{4} - \dfrac{y^2}{1} = 1$

**2.** $\dfrac{x^2}{1} - \dfrac{y^2}{4} = 1$

**3.** $\dfrac{y^2}{4} - \dfrac{x^2}{1} = 1$

**4.** $\dfrac{y^2}{1} - \dfrac{x^2}{4} = 1$

**a.**

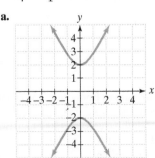

**b.**

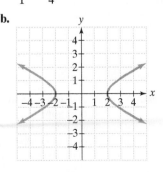

**c.**

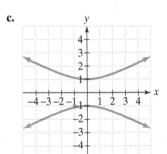

**d.**

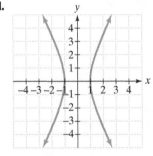

In Exercises 5–12, find the standard form of the equation of each hyperbola satisfying the given conditions.

**5.** Foci: $(0, -3)$, $(0, 3)$; vertices: $(0, -1)$, $(0, 1)$

**6.** Foci: $(0, -6)$, $(0, 6)$; vertices: $(0, -2)$, $(0, 2)$

**7.** Foci: $(-4, 0)$, $(4, 0)$; vertices: $(-3, 0)$, $(3, 0)$

**8.** Foci: $(-7, 0)$, $(7, 0)$; vertices: $(-5, 0)$, $(5, 0)$

**9.** Endpoints of transverse axis: $(0, -6)$, $(0, 6)$; asymptote: $y = 2x$

**10.** Endpoints of transverse axis: $(-4, 0)$, $(4, 0)$; asymptote: $y = 2x$

**11.** Center: $(4, -2)$; Focus: $(7, -2)$; vertex: $(6, -2)$

**12.** Center: $(-2, 1)$; Focus: $(-2, 6)$; vertex: $(-2, 4)$

*In Exercises 13–26, use vertices and asymptotes to graph each hyperbola. Locate the foci and find the equations of the asymptotes.*

**13.** $\dfrac{x^2}{9} - \dfrac{y^2}{25} = 1$      **14.** $\dfrac{x^2}{16} - \dfrac{y^2}{25} = 1$

**15.** $\dfrac{x^2}{100} - \dfrac{y^2}{64} = 1$      **16.** $\dfrac{x^2}{144} - \dfrac{y^2}{81} = 1$

**17.** $\dfrac{y^2}{16} - \dfrac{x^2}{36} = 1$      **18.** $\dfrac{y^2}{25} - \dfrac{x^2}{64} = 1$

**19.** $4y^2 - x^2 = 1$      **20.** $9y^2 - x^2 = 1$

**21.** $9x^2 - 4y^2 = 36$      **22.** $4x^2 - 25y^2 = 100$

**23.** $9y^2 - 25x^2 = 225$      **24.** $16y^2 - 9x^2 = 144$

**25.** $y = \pm\sqrt{x^2 - 2}$      **26.** $y = \pm\sqrt{x^2 - 3}$

*In Exercises 27–32, find the standard form of the equation of each hyperbola.*

**27.**
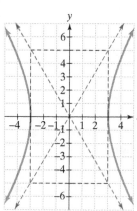

**28.**
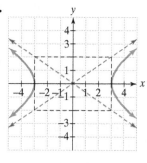

**29.**
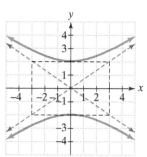

**30.**
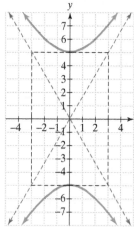

**31.**
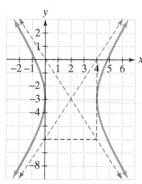

**32.**
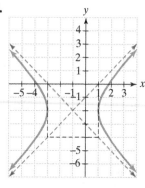

*In Exercises 33–42, use the center, vertices, and asymptotes to graph each hyperbola. Locate the foci and find the equations of the asymptotes.*

**33.** $\dfrac{(x + 4)^2}{9} - \dfrac{(y + 3)^2}{16} = 1$    **34.** $\dfrac{(x + 2)^2}{9} - \dfrac{(y - 1)^2}{25} = 1$

**35.** $\dfrac{(x + 3)^2}{25} - \dfrac{y^2}{16} = 1$    **36.** $\dfrac{(x + 2)^2}{9} - \dfrac{y^2}{25} = 1$

**37.** $\dfrac{(y + 2)^2}{4} - \dfrac{(x - 1)^2}{16} = 1$

**38.** $\dfrac{(y - 2)^2}{36} - \dfrac{(x + 1)^2}{49} = 1$

**39.** $(x - 3)^2 - 4(y + 3)^2 = 4$

**40.** $(x + 3)^2 - 9(y - 4)^2 = 9$

**41.** $(x - 1)^2 - (y - 2)^2 = 3$

**42.** $(y - 2)^2 - (x + 3)^2 = 5$

*In Exercises 43–50, convert each equation to standard form by completing the square on x and y. Then graph the hyperbola. Locate the foci and find the equations of the asymptotes.*

**43.** $x^2 - y^2 - 2x - 4y - 4 = 0$

**44.** $4x^2 - y^2 + 32x + 6y + 39 = 0$

**45.** $16x^2 - y^2 + 64x - 2y + 67 = 0$

**46.** $9y^2 - 4x^2 - 18y + 24x - 63 = 0$

**47.** $4x^2 - 9y^2 - 16x + 54y - 101 = 0$

**48.** $4x^2 - 9y^2 + 8x - 18y - 6 = 0$

**49.** $4x^2 - 25y^2 - 32x + 164 = 0$

**50.** $9x^2 - 16y^2 - 36x - 64y + 116 = 0$

## Practice Plus

*In Exercises 51–56, graph each relation. Use the relation's graph to determine its domain and range.*

**51.** $\dfrac{x^2}{9} - \dfrac{y^2}{16} = 1$      **52.** $\dfrac{x^2}{25} - \dfrac{y^2}{4} = 1$

**53.** $\dfrac{x^2}{9} + \dfrac{y^2}{16} = 1$      **54.** $\dfrac{x^2}{25} + \dfrac{y^2}{4} = 1$

**55.** $\dfrac{y^2}{16} - \dfrac{x^2}{9} = 1$      **56.** $\dfrac{y^2}{4} - \dfrac{x^2}{25} = 1$

*In Exercises 57–60, find the solution set for each system by graphing both of the system's equations in the same rectangular coordinate system and finding points of intersection. Check all solutions in both equations.*

**57.** $\begin{cases} x^2 - y^2 = 4 \\ x^2 + y^2 = 4 \end{cases}$    **58.** $\begin{cases} x^2 - y^2 = 9 \\ x^2 + y^2 = 9 \end{cases}$

**59.** $\begin{cases} 9x^2 + y^2 = 9 \\ y^2 - 9x^2 = 9 \end{cases}$    **60.** $\begin{cases} 4x^2 + y^2 = 4 \\ y^2 - 4x^2 = 4 \end{cases}$

## Application Exercises

**61.** An explosion is recorded by two microphones that are 1 mile apart. Microphone $M_1$ received the sound 2 seconds before microphone $M_2$. Assuming sound travels at 1100 feet per second, determine the possible locations of the explosion relative to the location of the microphones.

**62.** Radio towers $A$ and $B$, 200 kilometers apart, are situated along the coast, with $A$ located due west of $B$. Simultaneous radio signals are sent from each tower to a ship, with the signal from $B$ received 500 microseconds before the signal from $A$.

**a.** Assuming that the radio signals travel 300 meters per microsecond, determine the equation of the hyperbola on which the ship is located.

**b.** If the ship lies due north of tower $B$, how far out at sea is it?

**63.** An architect designs two houses that are shaped and positioned like a part of the branches of the hyperbola whose equation is $625y^2 - 400x^2 = 250{,}000$, where $x$ and $y$ are in yards. How far apart are the houses at their closest point?

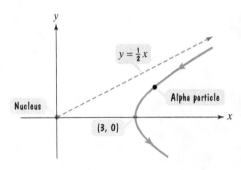

**64.** Scattering experiments, in which moving particles are deflected by various forces, led to the concept of the nucleus of an atom. In 1911, the physicist Ernest Rutherford (1871–1937) discovered that when alpha particles are directed toward the nuclei of gold atoms, they are eventually deflected along hyperbolic paths, illustrated in the figure. If a particle gets as close as 3 units to the nucleus along a hyperbolic path with an asymptote given by $y = \frac{1}{2}x$, what is the equation of its path?

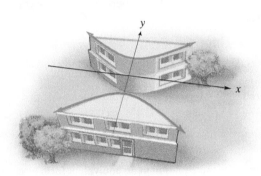

*Moiré patterns, such as those shown in Exercises 65–66, can appear when two repetitive patterns overlap to produce a third, sometimes unintended, pattern.*

**a.** *In each exercise, use the name of a conic section to describe the moiré pattern.*

**b.** *Select one of the following equations that can possibly describe a conic section within the moiré pattern:*

$$x^2 + y^2 = 1; \quad x^2 - y^2 = 1; \quad x^2 + 4y^2 = 4.$$

**65.**    **66.**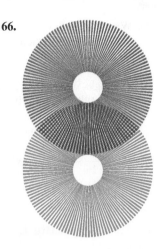

## Writing in Mathematics

**67.** What is a hyperbola?

**68.** Describe how to graph $\dfrac{x^2}{9} - \dfrac{y^2}{1} = 1$.

**69.** Describe how to locate the foci of the graph of $\dfrac{x^2}{9} - \dfrac{y^2}{1} = 1$.

**70.** Describe one similarity and one difference between the graphs of $\dfrac{x^2}{9} - \dfrac{y^2}{1} = 1$ and $\dfrac{y^2}{9} - \dfrac{x^2}{1} = 1$.

**71.** Describe one similarity and one difference between the graphs of $\dfrac{x^2}{9} - \dfrac{y^2}{1} = 1$ and $\dfrac{(x - 3)^2}{9} - \dfrac{(y + 3)^2}{1} = 1$.

**72.** How can you distinguish an ellipse from a hyperbola by looking at their equations?

**73.** In 1992, a NASA team began a project called Spaceguard Survey, calling for an international watch for comets that might collide with Earth. Why is it more difficult to detect a possible "doomsday comet" with a hyperbolic orbit than one with an elliptical orbit?

## Technology Exercises

**74.** Use a graphing utility to graph any five of the hyperbolas that you graphed by hand in Exercises 13–26.

**75.** Use a graphing utility to graph any three of the hyperbolas that you graphed by hand in Exercises 33–42. First solve the given equation for $y$ by using the square root property. Enter each of the two resulting equations to produce each branch of the hyperbola.

**76.** Use a graphing utility to graph any one of the hyperbolas that you graphed by hand in Exercises 43–50. Write the equation as a quadratic equation in $y$ and use the quadratic formula to solve for $y$. Enter each of the two resulting equations to produce each branch of the hyperbola.

**77.** Use a graphing utility to graph $\dfrac{x^2}{4} - \dfrac{y^2}{9} = 0$. Is the graph a hyperbola? In general, what is the graph of $\dfrac{x^2}{a^2} - \dfrac{y^2}{b^2} = 0$?

**78.** Graph $\dfrac{x^2}{a^2} - \dfrac{y^2}{b^2} = 1$ and $\dfrac{x^2}{a^2} - \dfrac{y^2}{b^2} = -1$ in the same viewing rectangle for values of $a^2$ and $b^2$ of your choice. Describe the relationship between the two graphs.

**79.** Write $4x^2 - 6xy + 2y^2 - 3x + 10y - 6 = 0$ as a quadratic equation in $y$ and then use the quadratic formula to express $y$ in terms of $x$. Graph the resulting two equations using a graphing utility in a $[-50, 70, 10]$ by $[-30, 50, 10]$ viewing rectangle. What effect does the $xy$-term have on the graph of the resulting hyperbola? What problems would you encounter if you attempted to write the given equation in standard form by completing the square?

**80.** Graph $\dfrac{x^2}{16} - \dfrac{y^2}{9} = 1$ and $\dfrac{x|x|}{16} - \dfrac{y|y|}{9} = 1$ in the same viewing rectangle. Explain why the graphs are not the same.

## Critical Thinking Exercises

**Make Sense?** *In Exercises 81–84, determine whether each statement makes sense or does not make sense, and explain your reasoning.*

**81.** I changed the addition in an ellipse's equation to subtraction and this changed its elongation from horizontal to vertical.

**82.** I noticed that the definition of a hyperbola closely resembles that of an ellipse in that it depends on the distances between a set of points in a plane to two fixed points, the foci.

**83.** I graphed a hyperbola centered at the origin that had $y$-intercepts, but no $x$-intercepts.

**84.** I graphed a hyperbola centered at the origin that was symmetric with respect to the $x$-axis and also symmetric with respect to the $y$-axis.

*In Exercises 85–88, determine whether each statement is true or false. If the statement is false, make the necessary change(s) to produce a true statement.*

**85.** If one branch of a hyperbola is removed from a graph, then the branch that remains must define $y$ as a function of $x$.

**86.** All points on the asymptotes of a hyperbola also satisfy the hyperbola's equation.

**87.** The graph of $\dfrac{x^2}{9} - \dfrac{y^2}{4} = 1$ does not intersect the line $y = -\dfrac{2}{3}x$.

**88.** Two different hyperbolas can never share the same asymptotes.

**89.** What happens to the shape of the graph of $\dfrac{x^2}{a^2} - \dfrac{y^2}{b^2} = 1$ as $\dfrac{c}{a} \to \infty$, where $c^2 = a^2 + b^2$?

**90.** Find the standard form of the equation of the hyperbola with vertices $(5, -6)$ and $(5, 6)$, passing through $(0, 9)$.

**91.** Find the equation of a hyperbola whose asymptotes are perpendicular.

## Preview Exercises

*Exercises 92–94 will help you prepare for the material covered in the next section.*

*In Exercises 92–93, graph each parabola with the given equation.*

**92.** $y = x^2 + 4x - 5$                **93.** $y = -3(x - 1)^2 + 2$

**94.** Isolate the terms involving $y$ on the left side of the equation:
$$y^2 + 2y + 12x - 23 = 0.$$
Then write the equation in an equivalent form by completing the square on the left side.

---

## Section 9.3  The Parabola

### Objectives

1. Graph parabolas with vertices at the origin.
2. Write equations of parabolas in standard form.
3. Graph parabolas with vertices not at the origin.
4. Solve applied problems involving parabolas.

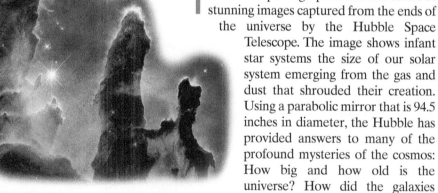

At first glance, this image looks like columns of smoke rising from a fire into a starry sky. Those are, indeed, stars in the background, but you are not looking at ordinary smoke columns. These stand almost 6 trillion miles high and are 7000 light-years from Earth—more than 400 million times as far away as the sun.

This NASA photograph is one of a series of stunning images captured from the ends of the universe by the Hubble Space Telescope. The image shows infant star systems the size of our solar system emerging from the gas and dust that shrouded their creation. Using a parabolic mirror that is 94.5 inches in diameter, the Hubble has provided answers to many of the profound mysteries of the cosmos: How big and how old is the universe? How did the galaxies come to exist? Do other Earth-like planets orbit other sun-like stars? In this section, we study parabolas and their applications, including parabolic shapes that gather distant rays of light and focus them into spectacular images.

### Definition of a Parabola

In Chapter 2, we studied parabolas, viewing them as graphs of quadratic functions in the form

$$y = a(x - h)^2 + k \quad \text{or} \quad y = ax^2 + bx + c.$$

## Study Tip

Here is a summary of what you should already know about graphing parabolas.

**Graphing $y = a(x - h)^2 + k$ and $y = ax^2 + bx + c$**

1. If $a > 0$, the graph opens upward. If $a < 0$, the graph opens downward.
2. The vertex of $y = a(x - h)^2 + k$ is $(h, k)$.

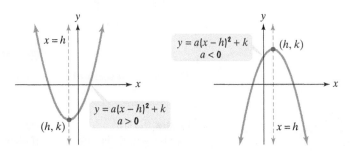

3. The $x$-coordinate of the vertex of $y = ax^2 + bx + c$ is $x = -\dfrac{b}{2a}$.

Parabolas can be given a geometric definition that enables us to include graphs that open to the left or to the right, as well as those that open obliquely. The definitions of ellipses and hyperbolas involved two fixed points, the foci. By contrast, the definition of a parabola is based on one point and a line.

### Definition of a Parabola

A **parabola** is the set of all points in a plane that are equidistant from a fixed line, the **directrix**, and a fixed point, the **focus**, that is not on the line (see **Figure 9.29**).

In **Figure 9.29**, find the line passing through the focus and perpendicular to the directrix. This is the **axis of symmetry** of the parabola. The point of intersection of the parabola with its axis of symmetry is called the **vertex**. Notice that the vertex is midway between the focus and the directrix.

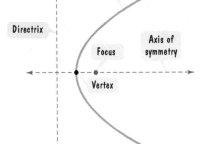

Figure 9.29

### Standard Form of the Equation of a Parabola

The rectangular coordinate system enables us to translate a parabola's geometric definition into an algebraic equation. **Figure 9.30** is our starting point for obtaining an equation. We place the focus on the $x$-axis at the point $(p, 0)$. The directrix has an equation given by $x = -p$. The vertex, located midway between the focus and the directrix, is at the origin.

What does the definition of a parabola tell us about the point $(x, y)$ in **Figure 9.30**? For any point $(x, y)$ on the parabola, the distance $d_1$ to the directrix is equal to the distance $d_2$ to the focus. Thus, the point $(x, y)$ is on the parabola if and only if

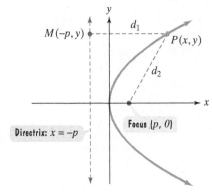

Figure 9.30

$$d_1 = d_2.$$

$$\sqrt{(x + p)^2 + (y - y)^2} = \sqrt{(x - p)^2 + (y - 0)^2} \quad \text{Use the distance formula.}$$

$$(x + p)^2 = (x - p)^2 + y^2 \quad \text{Square both sides of the equation.}$$

$$x^2 + 2px + p^2 = x^2 - 2px + p^2 + y^2 \quad \text{Square } x + p \text{ and } x - p.$$
$$2px = -2px + y^2 \quad \begin{array}{l}\text{Subtract } x^2 + p^2 \text{ from both} \\ \text{sides of the equation.}\end{array}$$
$$y^2 = 4px \quad \text{Solve for } y^2.$$

This last equation is called the **standard form of the equation of a parabola with its vertex at the origin**. There are two such equations, one for a focus on the $x$-axis and one for a focus on the $y$-axis.

### Standard Forms of the Equations of a Parabola

The **standard form of the equation of a parabola** with vertex at the origin is

$$y^2 = 4px \qquad \text{or} \qquad x^2 = 4py.$$

**Figure 9.31(a)** illustrates that for the equation on the left, the focus is on the $x$-axis, which is the axis of symmetry. **Figure 9.31(b)** illustrates that for the equation on the right, the focus is on the $y$-axis, which is the axis of symmetry.

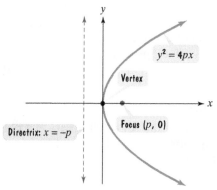

Figure 9.31(a)   Parabola with the $x$-axis as the axis of symmetry. If $p > 0$, the graph opens to the right. If $p < 0$, the graph opens to the left.

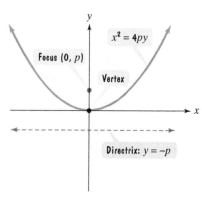

Figure 9.31(b)   Parabola with the $y$-axis as the axis of symmetry. If $p > 0$, the graph opens upward. If $p < 0$, the graph opens downward.

**1** Graph parabolas with vertices at the origin.

## Using the Standard Form of the Equation of a Parabola

We can use the standard form of the equation of a parabola to find its focus and directrix. Observing the graph's symmetry from its equation is helpful in locating the focus.

$$y^2 = 4px \qquad\qquad x^2 = 4py$$

The equation does not change if $y$ is replaced with $-y$. There is $x$-axis symmetry and the focus is on the $x$-axis at $(p, 0)$.

The equation does not change if $x$ is replaced with $-x$. There is $y$-axis symmetry and the focus is on the $y$-axis at $(0, p)$.

Although the definition of a parabola is given in terms of its focus and its directrix, the focus and directrix are not part of the graph. The vertex, located at the origin, is a point on the graph of $y^2 = 4px$ and $x^2 = 4py$. Example 1 illustrates how you can find two additional points on the parabola.

**EXAMPLE 1**  **Finding the Focus and Directrix of a Parabola**

Find the focus and directrix of the parabola given by $y^2 = 12x$. Then graph the parabola.

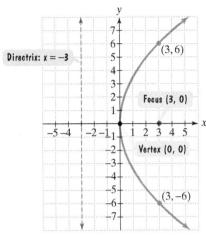

Figure 9.32  The graph of $y^2 = 12x$

## Technology

We graph $y^2 = 12x$ with a graphing utility by first solving for $y$. The screen shows the graphs of $y = \sqrt{12x}$ and $y = -\sqrt{12x}$. The graph fails the vertical line test. Because $y^2 = 12x$ is not a function, you were not familiar with this form of the parabola's equation in Chapter 2.

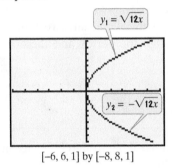

$y_1 = \sqrt{12x}$

$y_2 = -\sqrt{12x}$

[–6, 6, 1] by [–8, 8, 1]

**Solution**  The given equation, $y^2 = 12x$, is in the standard form $y^2 = 4px$, so $4p = 12$.

No change if $y$ is replaced with $-y$. The parabola has $x$-axis symmetry.

$y^2 = 12x$

This is $4p$.

We can find both the focus and the directrix by finding $p$.

$$4p = 12$$
$$p = 3 \quad \text{Divide both sides by 4.}$$

Because $p$ is positive, the parabola, with its $x$-axis symmetry, opens to the right. The focus is 3 units to the right of the vertex, $(0, 0)$.

$$\text{Focus:} \quad (p, 0) = (3, 0)$$
$$\text{Directrix:} \quad x = -p; x = -3$$

The focus, $(3, 0)$, and directrix, $x = -3$, are shown in **Figure 9.32**.

To graph the parabola, we will use two points on the graph that lie directly above and below the focus. Because the focus is at $(3, 0)$, substitute 3 for $x$ in the parabola's equation, $y^2 = 12x$.

$$y^2 = 12 \cdot 3 \quad \text{Replace } x \text{ with 3 in } y^2 = 12x.$$
$$y^2 = 36 \quad \text{Simplify.}$$
$$y = \pm\sqrt{36} = \pm 6 \quad \text{Apply the square root property.}$$

The points on the parabola above and below the focus are $(3, 6)$ and $(3, -6)$. The graph is sketched in **Figure 9.32**.

○ Check Point **1**  Find the focus and directrix of the parabola given by $y^2 = 8x$. Then graph the parabola.

In general, the points on a parabola $y^2 = 4px$ that lie above and below the focus, $(p, 0)$, are each at a distance $|2p|$ from the focus. This is because if $x = p$, then $y^2 = 4px = 4p^2$, so $y = \pm 2p$. The line segment joining these two points is called the *latus rectum*; its length is $|4p|$.

### The Latus Rectum and Graphing Parabolas

The **latus rectum** of a parabola is a line segment that passes through its focus, is parallel to its directrix, and has its endpoints on the parabola. **Figure 9.33** shows that the length of the latus rectum for the graphs of $y^2 = 4px$ and $x^2 = 4py$ is $|4p|$.

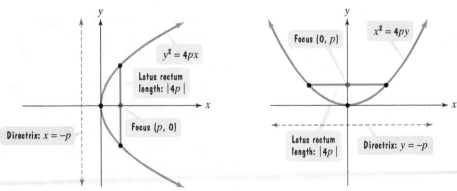

Figure 9.33  Endpoints of the latus rectum are helpful in determining a parabola's "width," or how it opens.

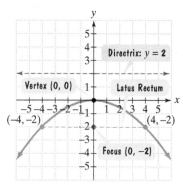

**Figure 9.34** The graph of $x^2 = -8y$

## Technology

Graph $x^2 = -8y$ by first solving for $y$: $y = -\dfrac{x^2}{8}$. The graph passes the vertical line test. Because $x^2 = -8y$ is a function, you were familiar with the parabola's alternate algebraic form, $y = -\dfrac{1}{8}x^2$, in Chapter 2. The form is $y = ax^2 + bx + c$, with $a = -\dfrac{1}{8}$, $b = 0$, and $c = 0$.

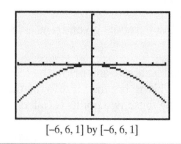

$[-6, 6, 1]$ by $[-6, 6, 1]$

**②** Write equations of parabolas in standard form.

**EXAMPLE 2** **Finding the Focus and Directrix of a Parabola**

Find the focus and directrix of the parabola given by $x^2 = -8y$. Then graph the parabola.

**Solution** The given equation, $x^2 = -8y$, is in the standard form $x^2 = 4py$, so $4p = -8$.

> No change if $x$ is replaced with $-x$. The parabola has $y$-axis symmetry.

$$x^2 = -8y$$

This is $4p$.

We can find both the focus and the directrix by finding $p$.

$$4p = -8$$
$$p = -2 \quad \text{Divide both sides by 4.}$$

Because $p$ is negative, the parabola, with its $y$-axis symmetry, opens downward. The focus is 2 units below the vertex, $(0, 0)$.

Focus:  $(0, p) = (0, -2)$
Directrix:  $y = -p; y = 2$

The focus and directrix are shown in **Figure 9.34**.

To graph the parabola, we will use the vertex, $(0, 0)$, and the two endpoints of the latus rectum. The length of the latus rectum is

$$|4p| = |4(-2)| = |-8| = 8.$$

Because the graph has $y$-axis symmetry, the latus rectum extends 4 units to the left and 4 units to the right of the focus, $(0, -2)$. The endpoints of the latus rectum are $(-4, -2)$ and $(4, -2)$. Passing a smooth curve through the vertex and these two points, we sketch the parabola, shown in **Figure 9.34**.

⊘ Check Point **2** Find the focus and directrix of the parabola given by $x^2 = -12y$. Then graph the parabola.

In Examples 1 and 2, we used the equation of a parabola to find its focus and directrix. In the next example, we reverse this procedure.

**EXAMPLE 3** **Finding the Equation of a Parabola from Its Focus and Directrix**

Find the standard form of the equation of a parabola with focus $(5, 0)$ and directrix $x = -5$, shown in **Figure 9.35**.

**Solution** The focus is $(5, 0)$. Thus, the focus is on the $x$-axis. We use the standard form of the equation in which there is $x$-axis symmetry, namely $y^2 = 4px$.

We need to determine the value of $p$. **Figure 9.35** shows that the focus is 5 units to the right of the vertex, $(0, 0)$. Thus, $p$ is positive and $p = 5$. We substitute 5 for $p$ in $y^2 = 4px$ to obtain the standard form of the equation of the parabola. The equation is

$$y^2 = 4 \cdot 5x \quad \text{or} \quad y^2 = 20x.$$

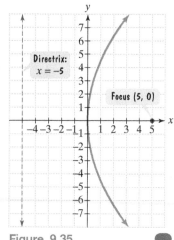

Figure 9.35

⊘ Check Point **3** Find the standard form of the equation of a parabola with focus $(8, 0)$ and directrix $x = -8$.

**3** Graph parabolas with vertices not at the origin.

## Translations of Parabolas

The graph of a parabola can have its vertex at $(h, k)$, rather than at the origin. Horizontal and vertical translations are accomplished by replacing $x$ with $x - h$ and $y$ with $y - k$ in the standard form of the parabola's equation.

**Table 9.3** gives the standard forms of equations of parabolas with vertex at $(h, k)$. **Figure 9.36** shows their graphs.

**Table 9.3** Standard Forms of Equations of Parabolas with Vertex at $(h, k)$

| Equation | Vertex | Axis of Symmetry | Focus | Directrix | Description |
|---|---|---|---|---|---|
| $(y - k)^2 = 4p(x - h)$ | $(h, k)$ | Horizontal | $(h + p, k)$ | $x = h - p$ | If $p > 0$, opens to the right. If $p < 0$, opens to the left. |
| $(x - h)^2 = 4p(y - k)$ | $(h, k)$ | Vertical | $(h, k + p)$ | $y = k - p$ | If $p > 0$, opens upward. If $p < 0$, opens downward. |

**Study Tip**

If $y$ is the squared term, there is horizontal symmetry and the parabola's equation is not a function. If $x$ is the squared term, there is vertical symmetry and the parabola's equation is a function. Continue to think of $p$ as the directed distance from the vertex, $(h, k)$, to the focus.

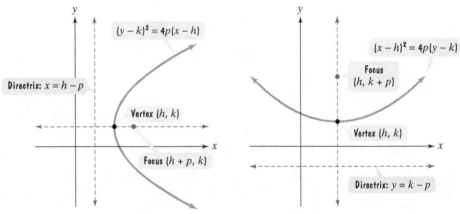

**Figure 9.36** Graphs of parabolas with vertex at $(h, k)$ and $p > 0$

The two parabolas shown in **Figure 9.36** illustrate standard forms of equations for $p > 0$. If $p < 0$, a parabola with a horizontal axis of symmetry will open to the left and the focus will lie to the left of the directrix. If $p < 0$, a parabola with a vertical axis of symmetry will open downward and the focus will lie below the directrix.

**EXAMPLE 4** **Graphing a Parabola with Vertex at $(h, k)$**

Find the vertex, focus, and directrix of the parabola given by

$$(x - 3)^2 = 8(y + 1).$$

Then graph the parabola.

**Solution** In order to find the focus and directrix, we need to know the vertex. In the standard forms of equations with vertex at $(h, k)$, $h$ is the number subtracted from $x$ and $k$ is the number subtracted from $y$.

$$(x - 3)^2 = 8(y - (-1))$$

This is $(x - h)^2$, with $h = 3$.     This is $y - k$, with $k = -1$.

We see that $h = 3$ and $k = -1$. Thus, the vertex of the parabola is $(h, k) = (3, -1)$.

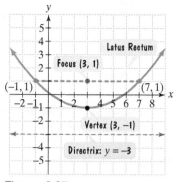

**Figure 9.37** The graph of $(x - 3)^2 = 8(y + 1)$

## Technology

Graph $(x - 3)^2 = 8(y + 1)$ by first solving for $y$:

$$\tfrac{1}{8}(x - 3)^2 = y + 1$$

$$y = \tfrac{1}{8}(x - 3)^2 - 1.$$

The graph passes the vertical line test. Because $(x - 3)^2 = 8(y + 1)$ is a function, you were familiar with the parabola's alternate algebraic form, $y = \tfrac{1}{8}(x - 3)^2 - 1$, in Chapter 2. The form is $y = a(x - h)^2 + k$ with $a = \tfrac{1}{8}$, $h = 3$, and $k = -1$.

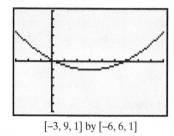

[-3, 9, 1] by [-6, 6, 1]

Now that we have the vertex, $(3, -1)$, we can find both the focus and directrix by finding $p$.

$$(x - 3)^2 = 8(y + 1)$$

The equation is in the standard form $(x - h)^2 = 4p(y - k)$. Because $x$ is the squared term, there is vertical symmetry and the parabola's equation is a function.

This is 4p.

Because $4p = 8$, $p = 2$. Based on the standard form of the equation, the axis of symmetry is vertical. With a positive value for $p$ and a vertical axis of symmetry, the parabola opens upward. Because $p = 2$, the focus is located 2 units above the vertex, $(3, -1)$. Likewise, the directrix is located 2 units below the vertex.

Focus:     $(h, k + p) = (3, -1 + 2) = (3, 1)$

The vertex, $(h, k)$, is $(3, -1)$.      The focus is 2 units above the vertex, $(3, -1)$.

Directrix:     $y = k - p$
$$y = -1 - 2 = -3$$

The directrix is 2 units below the vertex, $(3, -1)$.

Thus, the focus is $(3, 1)$ and the directrix is $y = -3$. They are shown in **Figure 9.37**. To graph the parabola, we will use the vertex, $(3, -1)$, and the two endpoints of the latus rectum. The length of the latus rectum is

$$|4p| = |4 \cdot 2| = |8| = 8.$$

Because the graph has vertical symmetry, the latus rectum extends 4 units to the left and 4 units to the right of the focus, $(3, 1)$. The endpoints of the latus rectum are $(3 - 4, 1)$, or $(-1, 1)$, and $(3 + 4, 1)$, or $(7, 1)$. Passing a smooth curve through the vertex and these two points, we sketch the parabola, shown in **Figure 9.37**. ●

✔ Check Point **4** Find the vertex, focus, and directrix of the parabola given by $(x - 2)^2 = 4(y + 1)$. Then graph the parabola.

In some cases, we need to convert the equation of a parabola to standard form by completing the square on $x$ or $y$, whichever variable is squared. Let's see how this is done.

**EXAMPLE 5** **Graphing a Parabola with Vertex at $(h, k)$**

Find the vertex, focus, and directrix of the parabola given by
$$y^2 + 2y + 12x - 23 = 0.$$
Then graph the parabola.

**Solution** We convert the given equation to standard form by completing the square on the variable $y$. We isolate the terms involving $y$ on the left side.

$$y^2 + 2y + 12x - 23 = 0 \qquad \text{This is the given equation.}$$
$$y^2 + 2y = -12x + 23 \qquad \text{Isolate the terms involving } y.$$
$$y^2 + 2y + 1 = -12x + 23 + 1 \qquad \text{Complete the square by adding the square of half the coefficient of } y.$$
$$(y + 1)^2 = -12x + 24 \qquad \text{Factor.}$$

To express the equation $(y + 1)^2 = -12x + 24$ in the standard form $(y - k)^2 = 4p(x - h)$, we factor out $-12$ on the right. The standard form of the parabola's equation is

$$(y + 1)^2 = -12(x - 2).$$

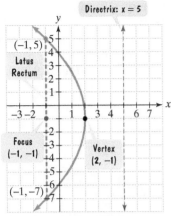

**Figure 9.38** The graph of $y^2 + 2y + 12x - 23 = 0$, or $(y + 1)^2 = -12(x - 2)$

## Technology

Graph $y^2 + 2y + 12x - 23 = 0$ by solving the equation for $y$.

$$y^2 + 2y + (12x - 23) = 0$$

$$a = 1 \quad b = 2 \quad c = 12x - 23$$

Use the quadratic formula to solve for $y$ and enter the resulting equations.

$$y_1 = \frac{-2 + \sqrt{4 - 4(12x - 23)}}{2}$$

$$y_2 = \frac{-2 - \sqrt{4 - 4(12x - 23)}}{2}$$

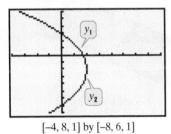

[−4, 8, 1] by [−8, 6, 1]

**4** Solve applied problems involving parabolas.

We use $(y + 1)^2 = -12(x - 2)$ to identify the vertex, $(h, k)$, and the value for $p$ needed to locate the focus and the directrix.

$$[y - (-1)]^2 = -12(x - 2)$$

*The equation is in the standard form $(y - k)^2 = 4p(x - h)$. Because $y$ is the squared term, there is horizontal symmetry and the parabola's equation is not a function.*

This is $(y - k)^2$, with $k = -1$.

This is $4p$.

This is $x - h$, with $h = 2$.

We see that $h = 2$ and $k = -1$. Thus, the vertex of the parabola is $(h, k) = (2, -1)$. Because $4p = -12$, $p = -3$. Based on the standard form of the equation, the axis of symmetry is horizontal. With a negative value for $p$ and a horizontal axis of symmetry, the parabola opens to the left. Because $p = -3$, the focus is located 3 units to the left of the vertex, $(2, -1)$. Likewise, the directrix is located 3 units to the right of the vertex.

Focus: $$(h + p, k) = (2 + (-3), -1) = (-1, -1)$$

The vertex, $(h, k)$, is $(2, -1)$.

The focus is 3 units to the left of the vertex, $(2, -1)$.

Directrix: $$x = h - p$$
$$x = 2 - (-3) = 5$$

The directrix is 3 units to the right of the vertex, $(2, -1)$.

Thus, the focus is $(-1, -1)$ and the directrix is $x = 5$. They are shown in **Figure 9.38**.

To graph the parabola, we will use the vertex, $(2, -1)$, and the two endpoints of the latus rectum. The length of the latus rectum is

$$|4p| = |4(-3)| = |-12| = 12.$$

Because the graph has horizontal symmetry, the latus rectum extends 6 units above and 6 units below the focus, $(-1, -1)$. The endpoints of the latus rectum are $(-1, -1 + 6)$, or $(-1, 5)$, and $(-1, -1 - 6)$, or $(-1, -7)$. Passing a smooth curve through the vertex and these two points, we sketch the parabola shown in **Figure 9.38**.

**Check Point 5** Find the vertex, focus, and directrix of the parabola given by $y^2 + 2y + 4x - 7 = 0$. Then graph the parabola.

## Applications

Parabolas have many applications. Cables hung between structures to form suspension bridges form parabolas. Arches constructed of steel and concrete, whose main purpose is strength, are usually parabolic in shape.

Suspension bridge

Arch bridge

We have seen that comets in our solar system travel in orbits that are ellipses and hyperbolas. Some comets follow parabolic paths. Only comets with elliptical orbits, such as Halley's Comet, return to our part of the galaxy.

If a parabola is rotated about its axis of symmetry, a parabolic surface is formed. **Figure 9.39(a)** shows how a parabolic surface can be used to reflect light. Light originates at the focus. Note how the light is reflected by the parabolic surface, so that the outgoing light is parallel to the axis of symmetry. The reflective properties of parabolic surfaces are used in the design of searchlights [see **Figure 9.39(b)**], automobile headlights, and parabolic microphones.

## The Hubble Space Telescope

The Hubble Space Telescope

For decades, astronomers hoped to create an observatory above the atmosphere that would provide an unobscured view of the universe. This vision was realized with the 1990 launching of the Hubble Space Telescope. The telescope initially had blurred vision due to problems with its parabolic mirror. The mirror had been ground two millionths of a meter smaller than design specifications. In 1993, astronauts from the Space Shuttle *Endeavor* equipped the telescope with optics to correct the blurred vision. "A small change for a mirror, a giant leap for astronomy," Christopher J. Burrows of the Space Telescope Science Institute said when clear images from the ends of the universe were presented to the public after the repair mission.

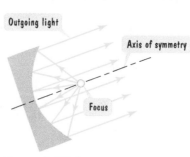

**Figure 9.39(a)** Parabolic surface reflecting light

**Figure 9.39(b)** Light from the focus is reflected parallel to the axis of symmetry.

**Figure 9.40(a)** shows how a parabolic surface can be used to reflect *incoming* light. Note that light rays strike the surface and are reflected *to the focus*. This principle is used in the design of reflecting telescopes, radar, and television satellite dishes. Reflecting telescopes magnify the light from distant stars by reflecting the light from these bodies to the focus of a parabolic mirror [see **Figure 9.40(b)**].

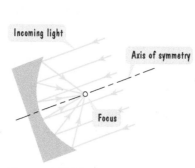

**Figure 9.40(a)** Parabolic surface reflecting incoming light

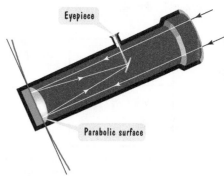

**Figure 9.40(b)** Incoming light rays are reflected to the focus.

---

( EXAMPLE 6 ) **Using the Reflection Property of Parabolas**

An engineer is designing a flashlight using a parabolic reflecting mirror and a light source, shown in **Figure 9.41**. The casting has a diameter of 4 inches and a depth of 2 inches. What is the equation of the parabola used to shape the mirror? At what point should the light source be placed relative to the mirror's vertex?

**Solution** We position the parabola with its vertex at the origin and opening upward (**Figure 9.42**). Thus, the focus is on the *y*-axis, located at $(0, p)$. We use the

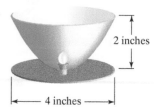

**Figure 9.41** Designing a flashlight

**Figure 9.42**

standard form of the equation in which there is $y$-axis symmetry, namely $x^2 = 4py$. We need to find $p$. Because $(2, 2)$ lies on the parabola, we let $x = 2$ and $y = 2$ in $x^2 = 4py$.

$$2^2 = 4p \cdot 2 \quad \text{Substitute 2 for x and 2 for y in } x^2 = 4py.$$

$$4 = 8p \quad \text{Simplify.}$$

$$p = \tfrac{1}{2} \quad \text{Divide both sides of the equation by 8 and reduce the resulting fraction.}$$

We substitute $\tfrac{1}{2}$ for $p$ in $x^2 = 4py$ to obtain the standard form of the equation of the parabola. The equation of the parabola used to shape the mirror is

$$x^2 = 4 \cdot \tfrac{1}{2} y \quad \text{or} \quad x^2 = 2y.$$

The light source should be placed at the focus, $(0, p)$. Because $p = \tfrac{1}{2}$, the light should be placed at $\left(0, \tfrac{1}{2}\right)$, or $\tfrac{1}{2}$ inch above the vertex.

⊘ Check Point **6** In Example 6, suppose that the casting has a diameter of 6 inches and a depth of 4 inches. What is the equation of the parabola used to shape the mirror? At what point should the light source be placed relative to the mirror's vertex?

## Degenerate Conic Sections

We opened the chapter by noting that conic sections are curves that result from the intersection of a cone and a plane. However, these intersections might not result in a conic section. Three degenerate cases occur when the cutting plane passes through the vertex. These **degenerate conic sections** are a point, a line, and a pair of intersecting lines, illustrated in **Figure 9.43**.

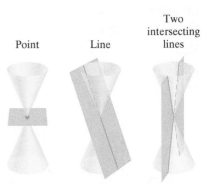

Point     Line     Two intersecting lines

Figure 9.43   Degenerate conics

# Exercise Set 9.3

## Practice Exercises

*In Exercises 1–4, find the focus and directrix of each parabola with the given equation. Then match each equation to one of the graphs that are shown and labeled (a)–(d).*

**1.** $y^2 = 4x$

**2.** $x^2 = 4y$

**3.** $x^2 = -4y$

**4.** $y^2 = -4x$

**a.**

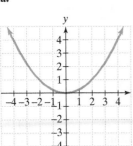

**b.**

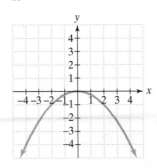

**c.**

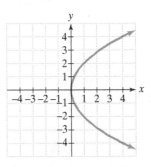

**d.**

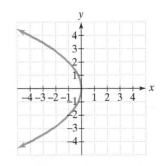

*In Exercises 5–16, find the focus and directrix of the parabola with the given equation. Then graph the parabola.*

**5.** $y^2 = 16x$

**6.** $y^2 = 4x$

**7.** $y^2 = -8x$

**8.** $y^2 = -12x$

**9.** $x^2 = 12y$

**10.** $x^2 = 8y$

**11.** $x^2 = -16y$

**12.** $x^2 = -20y$

**13.** $y^2 - 6x = 0$

**14.** $x^2 - 6y = 0$

**15.** $8x^2 + 4y = 0$

**16.** $8y^2 + 4x = 0$

*In Exercises 17–30, find the standard form of the equation of each parabola satisfying the given conditions.*

**17.** Focus: $(7, 0)$; Directrix: $x = -7$

**18.** Focus: $(9, 0)$; Directrix: $x = -9$

**19.** Focus: $(-5, 0)$; Directrix: $x = 5$

**20.** Focus: $(-10, 0)$; Directrix: $x = 10$

**21.** Focus: $(0, 15)$; Directrix: $y = -15$

**22.** Focus: $(0, 20)$; Directrix: $y = -20$

**23.** Focus: $(0, -25)$; Directrix: $y = 25$

**24.** Focus: $(0, -15)$; Directrix: $y = 15$

**25.** Vertex: $(2, -3)$; Focus: $(2, -5)$

**26.** Vertex: $(5, -2)$; Focus: $(7, -2)$

**27.** Focus: $(3, 2)$; Directrix: $x = -1$

**28.** Focus: $(2, 4)$; Directrix: $x = -4$

**29.** Focus: $(-3, 4)$; Directrix: $y = 2$

**30.** Focus: $(7, -1)$; Directrix: $y = -9$

*In Exercises 31–34, find the vertex, focus, and directrix of each parabola with the given equation. Then match each equation to one of the graphs that are shown and labeled (a)–(d).*

**31.** $(y - 1)^2 = 4(x - 1)$

**32.** $(x + 1)^2 = 4(y + 1)$

**33.** $(x + 1)^2 = -4(y + 1)$

**34.** $(y - 1)^2 = -4(x - 1)$

**a.**

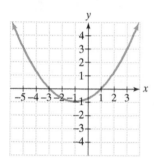

**b.**

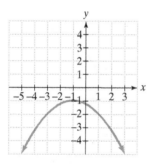

**c.**

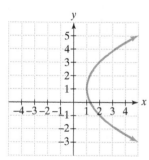

**d.**

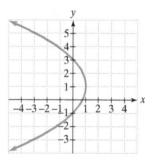

*In Exercises 35–42, find the vertex, focus, and directrix of each parabola with the given equation. Then graph the parabola.*

**35.** $(x - 2)^2 = 8(y - 1)$  **36.** $(x + 2)^2 = 4(y + 1)$

**37.** $(x + 1)^2 = -8(y + 1)$  **38.** $(x + 2)^2 = -8(y + 2)$

**39.** $(y + 3)^2 = 12(x + 1)$  **40.** $(y + 4)^2 = 12(x + 2)$

**41.** $(y + 1)^2 = -8x$  **42.** $(y - 1)^2 = -8x$

*In Exercises 43–48, convert each equation to standard form by completing the square on x or y. Then find the vertex, focus, and directrix of the parabola. Finally, graph the parabola.*

**43.** $x^2 - 2x - 4y + 9 = 0$  **44.** $x^2 + 6x + 8y + 1 = 0$

**45.** $y^2 - 2y + 12x - 35 = 0$  **46.** $y^2 - 2y - 8x + 1 = 0$

**47.** $x^2 + 6x - 4y + 1 = 0$  **48.** $x^2 + 8x - 4y + 8 = 0$

## Practice Plus

*In Exercises 49–54, use the vertex and the direction in which the parabola opens to determine the relation's domain and range. Is the relation a function?*

**49.** $y^2 + 6y - x + 5 = 0$  **50.** $y^2 - 2y - x - 5 = 0$

**51.** $y = -x^2 + 4x - 3$  **52.** $y = -x^2 - 4x + 4$

**53.** $x = -4(y - 1)^2 + 3$  **54.** $x = -3(y - 1)^2 - 2$

*In Exercises 55–60, find the solution set for each system by graphing both of the system's equations in the same rectangular coordinate system and finding points of intersection. Check all solutions in both equations.*

**55.** $\begin{cases} (y - 2)^2 = x + 4 \\ \qquad y = -\dfrac{1}{2}x \end{cases}$  **56.** $\begin{cases} (y - 3)^2 = x - 2 \\ \quad x + y = 5 \end{cases}$

**57.** $\begin{cases} x = y^2 - 3 \\ x = y^2 - 3y \end{cases}$  **58.** $\begin{cases} x = y^2 - 5 \\ x^2 + y^2 = 25 \end{cases}$

**59.** $\begin{cases} x = (y + 2)^2 - 1 \\ (x - 2)^2 + (y + 2)^2 = 1 \end{cases}$  **60.** $\begin{cases} x = 2y^2 + 4y + 5 \\ (x + 1)^2 + (y - 2)^2 = 1 \end{cases}$

## Application Exercises

**61.** The reflector of a flashlight is in the shape of a parabolic surface. The casting has a diameter of 4 inches and a depth of 1 inch. How far from the vertex should the light bulb be placed?

**62.** The reflector of a flashlight is in the shape of a parabolic surface. The casting has a diameter of 8 inches and a depth of 1 inch. How far from the vertex should the light bulb be placed?

**63.** A satellite dish, like the one shown below, is in the shape of a parabolic surface. Signals coming from a satellite strike the surface of the dish and are reflected to the focus, where the receiver is located. The satellite dish shown has a diameter of 12 feet and a depth of 2 feet. How far from the base of the dish should the receiver be placed?

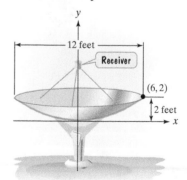

**64.** In Exercise 63, if the diameter of the dish is halved and the depth stays the same, how far from the base of the smaller dish should the receiver be placed?

**65.** The towers of the Golden Gate Bridge connecting San Francisco to Marin County are 1280 meters apart and rise 160 meters above the road. The cable between the towers has the shape of a parabola and the cable just touches the sides of the road midway between the towers. What is the height of the cable 200 meters from a tower? Round to the nearest meter.

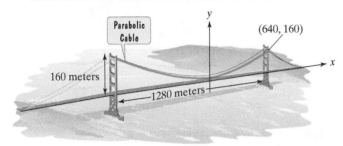

**66.** The towers of a suspension bridge are 800 feet apart and rise 160 feet above the road. The cable between the towers has the shape of a parabola and the cable just touches the sides of the road midway between the towers. What is the height of the cable 100 feet from a tower?

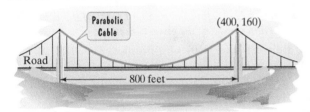

**67.** The parabolic arch shown in the figure is 50 feet above the water at the center and 200 feet wide at the base. Will a boat that is 30 feet tall clear the arch 30 feet from the center?

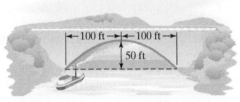

**68.** A satellite dish in the shape of a parabolic surface has a diameter of 20 feet. If the receiver is to be placed 6 feet from the base, how deep should the dish be?

## Writing in Mathematics

**69.** What is a parabola?

**70.** Explain how to use $y^2 = 8x$ to find the parabola's focus and directrix.

**71.** If you are given the standard form of the equation of a parabola with vertex at the origin, explain how to determine if the parabola opens to the right, left, upward, or downward.

**72.** Describe one similarity and one difference between the graphs of $y^2 = 4x$ and $(y - 1)^2 = 4(x - 1)$.

**73.** How can you distinguish parabolas from other conic sections by looking at their equations?

**74.** Look at the satellite dish shown in Exercise 63. Why must the receiver for a shallow dish be farther from the base of the dish than for a deeper dish of the same diameter?

## Technology Exercises

**75.** Use a graphing utility to graph any five of the parabolas that you graphed by hand in Exercises 5–16.

**76.** Use a graphing utility to graph any three of the parabolas that you graphed by hand in Exercises 35–42. First solve the given equation for $y$, possibly using the square root property. Enter each of the two resulting equations to produce the complete graph.

*Use a graphing utility to graph the parabolas in Exercises 77–78. Write the given equation as a quadratic equation in $y$ and use the quadratic formula to solve for $y$. Enter each of the equations to produce the complete graph.*

**77.** $y^2 + 2y - 6x + 13 = 0$     **78.** $y^2 + 10y - x + 25 = 0$

*In Exercises 79–80, write each equation as a quadratic equation in $y$ and then use the quadratic formula to express $y$ in terms of $x$. Graph the resulting two equations using a graphing utility. What effect does the $xy$-term have on the graph of the resulting parabola?*

**79.** $16x^2 - 24xy + 9y^2 - 60x - 80y + 100 = 0$

**80.** $x^2 + 2\sqrt{3}xy + 3y^2 + 8\sqrt{3}x - 8y + 32 = 0$

## Critical Thinking Exercises

**Make Sense?** *In Exercises 81–84, determine whether each statement makes sense or does not make sense, and explain your reasoning.*

**81.** I graphed a parabola that opened to the right and contained a maximum point.

**82.** Knowing that a parabola opening to the right has a vertex at $(-1, 1)$ gives me enough information to determine its graph.

**83.** I noticed that depending on the values for $A$ and $B$, assuming that they are both not zero, the graph of $Ax^2 + By^2 = C$ can represent any of the conic sections other than a parabola.

**84.** I'm using a telescope in which light from distant stars is reflected to the focus of a parabolic mirror.

*In Exercises 85–88, determine whether each statement is true or false. If the statement is false, make the necessary change(s) to produce a true statement.*

**85.** The parabola whose equation is $x = 2y - y^2 + 5$ opens to the right.

**86.** If the parabola whose equation is $x = ay^2 + by + c$ has its vertex at $(3, 2)$ and $a > 0$, then it has no $y$-intercepts.

**87.** Some parabolas that open to the right have equations that define $y$ as a function of $x$.

**88.** The graph of $x = a(y - k) + h$ is a parabola with vertex at $(h, k)$.

**89.** Find the focus and directrix of a parabola whose equation is of the form $Ax^2 + Ey = 0$, $A \neq 0$, $E \neq 0$.

**90.** Write the standard form of the equation of a parabola whose points are equidistant from $y = 4$ and $(-1, 0)$.

## Group Exercise

**91.** Consult the research department of your library or the Internet to find an example of architecture that incorporates one or more conic sections in its design. Share this example with other group members. Explain precisely how conic sections are used. Do conic sections enhance the appeal of the architecture? In what ways?

## Preview Exercises

*Exercises 92–94 will help you prepare for the material covered in the next section.*

**92.** Simplify and write the equation in standard form in terms of $x'$ and $y'$:

$$\left[ \frac{\sqrt{2}}{2}(x' - y') \right]\left[ \frac{\sqrt{2}}{2}(x' + y') \right] = 1.$$

**93. a.** Make a sketch showing that $\cot 2\theta = -\dfrac{7}{24}$ for $90° < 2\theta < 180°$.

**b.** Use your sketch from part (a) to determine the value of $\cos 2\theta$.

**c.** Use the value of $\cos 2\theta$ from part (b) and the identities

$$\sin \theta = \sqrt{\frac{1 - \cos 2\theta}{2}} \quad \text{and} \quad \cos \theta = \sqrt{\frac{1 + \cos 2\theta}{2}}$$

to determine the values of $\sin \theta$ and $\cos \theta$.

**d.** In part (c), why did we not write $\pm$ before the radical in each formula?

**94.** The equation $3x^2 - 2\sqrt{3}xy + y^2 + 2x + 2\sqrt{3}y = 0$ is in the form $Ax^2 + Bxy + Cy^2 + Dx + Ey + F = 0$. Use the equation to determine the value of $B^2 - 4AC$.

---

## Chapter 9 Mid-Chapter Check Point

**What You Know:** We learned that the four conic sections are the circle, the ellipse, the hyperbola, and the parabola. Prior to this chapter, we graphed circles with center $(h, k)$ and radius $r$:

$$(x - h)^2 + (y - k)^2 = r^2.$$

In this chapter, you learned to graph ellipses centered at the origin and ellipses centered at $(h, k)$:

$$\frac{(x - h)^2}{a^2} + \frac{(y - k)^2}{b^2} = 1 \quad \text{or}$$

$$\frac{(x - h)^2}{b^2} + \frac{(y - k)^2}{a^2} = 1, a^2 > b^2.$$

We saw that the larger denominator $(a^2)$ determines whether the major axis is horizontal or vertical. We used vertices and asymptotes to graph hyperbolas centered at the origin and hyperbolas centered at $(h, k)$:

$$\frac{(x - h)^2}{a^2} - \frac{(y - k)^2}{b^2} = 1 \quad \text{or} \quad \frac{(y - k)^2}{a^2} - \frac{(x - h)^2}{b^2} = 1.$$

We used $c^2 = a^2 - b^2$ to locate the foci of an ellipse. We used $c^2 = a^2 + b^2$ to locate the foci of a hyperbola. Finally, we used the vertex and the latus rectum to graph parabolas with vertices at the origin and parabolas with vertices at $(h, k)$:

$$(y - k)^2 = 4p(x - h) \quad \text{or} \quad (x - h)^2 = 4p(y - k).$$

*In Exercises 1–5, graph each ellipse. Give the location of the foci.*

**1.** $\dfrac{x^2}{25} + \dfrac{y^2}{4} = 1$      **2.** $9x^2 + 4y^2 = 36$

**3.** $\dfrac{(x - 2)^2}{16} + \dfrac{(y + 1)^2}{25} = 1$      **4.** $\dfrac{(x + 2)^2}{25} + \dfrac{(y - 1)^2}{16} = 1$

**5.** $x^2 + 9y^2 - 4x + 54y + 49 = 0$

*In Exercises 6–11, graph each hyperbola. Give the location of the foci and the equations of the asymptotes.*

**6.** $\dfrac{x^2}{9} - y^2 = 1$      **7.** $\dfrac{y^2}{9} - x^2 = 1$

**8.** $y^2 - 4x^2 = 16$      **9.** $4x^2 - 49y^2 = 196$

**10.** $\dfrac{(x - 2)^2}{9} - \dfrac{(y + 2)^2}{16} = 1$

**11.** $4x^2 - y^2 + 8x + 6y + 11 = 0$

*In Exercises 12–13, graph each parabola. Give the location of the focus and the directrix.*

**12.** $(x - 2)^2 = -12(y + 1)$      **13.** $y^2 - 2x - 2y - 5 = 0$

*In Exercises 14–21, graph each equation.*

**14.** $x^2 + y^2 = 4$      **15.** $x + y = 4$

**16.** $x^2 - y^2 = 4$      **17.** $x^2 + 4y^2 = 4$

**18.** $(x + 1)^2 + (y - 1)^2 = 4$      **19.** $x^2 + 4(y - 1)^2 = 4$

**20.** $(x - 1)^2 - (y - 1)^2 = 4$      **21.** $(y + 1)^2 = 4(x - 1)$

*In Exercises 22–27, find the standard form of the equation of the conic section satisfying the given conditions.*

**22.** Ellipse; Foci: $(-4, 0)$, $(4, 0)$; Vertices: $(-5, 0)$, $(5, 0)$

**23.** Ellipse; Endpoints of major axis: $(-8, 2)$, $(10, 2)$; Foci: $(-4, 2)$, $(6, 2)$

**24.** Hyperbola; Foci: $(0, -3)$, $(0, 3)$; Vertices: $(0, -2)$, $(0, 2)$

**25.** Hyperbola; Foci: $(-4, 5)$, $(2, 5)$; Vertices: $(-3, 5)$, $(1, 5)$

**26.** Parabola; Focus: $(4, 5)$; Directrix: $y = -1$

**27.** Parabola; Focus: $(-2, 6)$; Directrix: $x = 8$

**28.** A semielliptical archway over a one-way road has a height of 10 feet and a width of 30 feet. A truck has a width of 10 feet and a height of 9.5 feet. Will this truck clear the opening of the archway?

**29.** A lithotriper is used to disentegrate kidney stones. The patient is placed within an elliptical device with the kidney centered at one focus, while ultrasound waves from the other focus hit the walls and are reflected to the kidney stone, shattering the stone. Suppose that the length of the major axis of the ellipse is 40 centimeters and the length of the minor axis is 20 centimeters. How far from the kidney stone should the electrode that sends the ultrasound waves be placed in order to shatter the stone?

**30.** An explosion is recorded by two forest rangers, one at a primary station and the other at an outpost 6 kilometers away. The ranger at the primary station hears the explosion 6 seconds before the ranger at the outpost.

**a.** Assuming sound travels at 0.35 kilometer per second, write an equation in standard form that gives all the possible locations of the explosion. Use a coordinate system with the two ranger stations on the x-axis and the midpoint between the stations at the origin.

**b.** Graph the equation that gives the possible locations of the explosion. Show the locations of the ranger stations in your drawing.

**31.** A domed ceiling is a parabolic surface. Ten meters down from the top of the dome, the ceiling is 15 meters wide. For the best lighting on the floor, a light source should be placed at the focus of the parabolic surface. How far from the top of the dome, to the nearest tenth of a meter, should the light source be placed?

Section 9.4

# Rotation of Axes

## Objectives

1. Identify conics without completing the square.
2. Use rotation of axes formulas.
3. Write equations of rotated conics in standard form.
4. Identify conics without rotating axes.

Richard E. Prince "The Cone of Apollonius" (detail), fiberglass, steel, paint, graphite, 51 × 18 × 14 in. Collection: Vancouver Art Gallery, Vancouver, Canada. Photo courtesy of Equinox Gallery, Vancouver, Canada.

To recognize a conic section, you often need to pay close attention to its graph. Graphs powerfully enhance our understanding of algebra and trigonometry. However, it is not possible for people who are blind—or sometimes, visually impaired—to see a graph. Creating informative materials for the blind and visually impaired is a challenge for instructors and mathematicians. Many people who are visually impaired "see" a graph by touching a three-dimensional representation of that graph, perhaps while it is described verbally.

Is it possible to identify conic sections in nonvisual ways? The answer is yes, and the methods for doing so are related to the coefficients in their equations. As we present these methods, think about how you learn them. How would your approach to studying mathematics change if we removed all graphs and replaced them with verbal descriptions?

1. Identify conics without completing the square.

## Identifying Conic Sections without Completing the Square

Conic sections can be represented both geometrically (as intersecting planes and cones) and algebraically. The equations of the conic sections we have considered in the first three sections of this chapter can be expressed in the form

$$Ax^2 + Cy^2 + Dx + Ey + F = 0,$$

in which $A$ and $C$ are not both zero. You can use $A$ and $C$, the coefficients of $x^2$ and $y^2$, respectively, to identify a conic section without completing the square.

---

### Identifying a Conic Section without Completing the Square

A nondegenerate conic section of the form

$$Ax^2 + Cy^2 + Dx + Ey + F = 0,$$

in which $A$ and $C$ are not both zero, is

- a circle if $A = C$,
- a parabola if $AC = 0$,
- an ellipse if $A \neq C$ and $AC > 0$, and
- a hyperbola if $AC < 0$.

---

**EXAMPLE 1** Identifying a Conic Section without Completing the Square

Identify the graph of each of the following nondegenerate conic sections:

**a.** $4x^2 - 25y^2 - 24x + 250y - 489 = 0$

**b.** $x^2 + y^2 + 6x - 2y + 6 = 0$

**c.** $y^2 + 12x + 2y - 23 = 0$

**d.** $9x^2 + 25y^2 - 54x + 50y - 119 = 0.$

**Solution** We use $A$, the coefficient of $x^2$, and $C$, the coefficient of $y^2$, to identify each conic section.

**a.** $4x^2 - 25y^2 - 24x + 250y - 489 = 0$

$A = 4$    $C = -25$

$AC = 4(-25) = -100 < 0$

Because $AC < 0$, the graph of the equation is a hyperbola.

**b.** $x^2 + y^2 + 6x - 2y + 6 = 0$

$A = 1$    $C = 1$

Because $A = C$, the graph of the equation is a circle.

**c.** We can write $y^2 + 12x + 2y - 23 = 0$ as

$$0x^2 + y^2 + 12x + 2y - 23 = 0.$$

$A = 0$    $C = 1$

$AC = 0(1) = 0$

Because $AC = 0$, the graph of the equation is a parabola.

**d.** $9x^2 + 25y^2 - 54x + 50y - 119 = 0$

$A = 9$    $C = 25$

$AC = 9(25) = 225 > 0.$

Because $AC > 0$ and $A \neq C$, the graph of the equation is an ellipse. ●

⊘ **Check Point 1** Identify the graph of each of the following nondegenerate conic sections:

**a.** $3x^2 + 2y^2 + 12x - 4y + 2 = 0$
**b.** $x^2 + y^2 - 6x + y + 3 = 0$
**c.** $y^2 - 12x - 4y + 52 = 0$
**d.** $9x^2 - 16y^2 - 90x + 64y + 17 = 0.$

**②** Use rotation of axes formulas.

## Rotation of Axes

**Figure 9.44** shows the graph of

$$7x^2 - 6\sqrt{3}xy + 13y^2 - 16 = 0.$$

The graph looks like an ellipse, although its major axis neither lies along the $x$-axis or $y$-axis nor is parallel to the $x$-axis or $y$-axis. Do you notice anything unusual about the equation? It contains an $xy$-term. However, look at what happens if we rotate the $x$- and $y$-axes through an angle of $30°$. In the rotated $x'y'$-system, the major axis of the ellipse lies along the $x'$-axis. We can write the equation of the ellipse in this rotated $x'y'$-system as

$$\frac{x'^2}{4} + \frac{y'^2}{1} = 1.$$

Observe that there is no $x'y'$-term in the equation.

Except for degenerate cases, the **general second-degree equation**

$$Ax^2 + Bxy + Cy^2 + Dx + Ey + F = 0$$

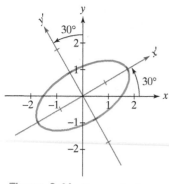

**Figure 9.44** The graph of $7x^2 - 6\sqrt{3}xy + 13y^2 - 16 = 0$, a rotated ellipse

represents one of the conic sections. However, due to the $xy$-term in the equation, these conic sections are rotated in such a way that their axes are no longer parallel to the $x$- and $y$-axes. To reduce these equations to forms of the conic sections with which you are already familiar, we use a procedure called **rotation of axes**.

Suppose that the $x$- and $y$-axes are rotated through a positive angle $\theta$, resulting in a new $x'y'$ coordinate system. This system is shown in **Figure 9.45(a)**. The origin in the $x'y'$-system is the same as the origin in the $xy$-system. Point $P$ in **Figure 9.45(b)** has coordinates $(x, y)$ relative to the $xy$-system and coordinates $(x', y')$ relative to the $x'y'$-system. Our goal is to obtain formulas relating the old and new coordinates. Thus, we need to express $x$ and $y$ in terms of $x'$, $y'$, and $\theta$.

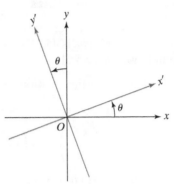

(a) Rotating the $x$- and $y$-axes through a positive angle $\theta$

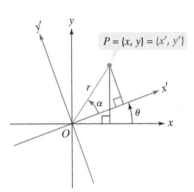

(b) Describing point $P$ relative to the $xy$-system and the rotated $x'y'$-system

Figure 9.45   Rotating axes

Look at **Figure 9.45(b)**. Notice that

$r =$ the distance from the origin $O$ to point $P$.

$\alpha =$ the angle from the positive $x'$-axis to the ray from $O$ through $P$.

Using the definitions of sine and cosine, we obtain

$$\cos \alpha = \frac{x'}{r} : x' = r \cos \alpha$$

> This is from the right triangle with a leg along the $x'$-axis.

$$\sin \alpha = \frac{y'}{r} : y' = r \sin \alpha$$

$$\cos (\theta + \alpha) = \frac{x}{r} : x = r \cos (\theta + \alpha)$$

> This is from the taller right triangle with a leg along the $x$-axis.

$$\sin (\theta + \alpha) = \frac{y}{r} : y = r \sin (\theta + \alpha).$$

Thus,

$$x = r \cos(\theta + \alpha)$$

> This is the third of the preceding equations.

$$= r(\cos \theta \cos \alpha - \sin \theta \sin \alpha)$$

> Use the formula for the cosine of the sum of two angles.

$$= (r \cos \alpha) \cos \theta - (r \sin \alpha) \sin \theta$$

> Apply the distributive property and rearrange factors.

$$= x' \cos \theta - y' \sin \theta.$$

> Use the first and second of the preceding equations: $x' = r \cos \alpha$ and $y' = r \sin \alpha$.

Similarly,

$$y = r \sin(\theta + \alpha) = r(\sin \theta \cos \alpha + \cos \theta \sin \alpha) = x' \sin \theta + y' \cos \theta.$$

### Rotation of Axes Formulas

Suppose an $xy$-coordinate system and an $x'y'$-coordinate system have the same origin and $\theta$ is the angle from the positive $x$-axis to the positive $x'$-axis. If the coordinates of point $P$ are $(x, y)$ in the $xy$-system and $(x', y')$ in the rotated $x'y'$-system, then

$$x = x' \cos \theta - y' \sin \theta$$

$$y = x' \sin \theta + y' \cos \theta.$$

$(\text{EXAMPLE 2})$ **Rotating Axes**

Write the equation $xy = 1$ in terms of a rotated $x'y'$-system if the angle of rotation from the $x$-axis to the $x'$-axis is $45°$. Express the equation in standard form. Use the rotated system to graph $xy = 1$.

**Solution**  With $\theta = 45°$, the rotation formulas for $x$ and $y$ are

$$x = x' \cos \theta - y' \sin \theta = x' \cos 45° - y' \sin 45°$$

$$= x'\left(\frac{\sqrt{2}}{2}\right) - y'\left(\frac{\sqrt{2}}{2}\right) = \frac{\sqrt{2}}{2}(x' - y')$$

$$y = x' \sin \theta + y' \cos \theta = x' \sin 45° + y' \cos 45°$$

$$= x'\left(\frac{\sqrt{2}}{2}\right) + y'\left(\frac{\sqrt{2}}{2}\right) = \frac{\sqrt{2}}{2}(x' + y').$$

Now substitute these expressions for $x$ and $y$ in the given equation, $xy = 1$.

$$xy = 1 \quad \text{This is the given equation.}$$

$$\left[\frac{\sqrt{2}}{2}(x' - y')\right]\left[\frac{\sqrt{2}}{2}(x' + y')\right] = 1 \quad \text{Substitute the expressions for } x \text{ and } y \text{ from the rotation formulas.}$$

$$\frac{2}{4}(x' - y')(x' + y') = 1 \quad \text{Multiply: } \frac{\sqrt{2}}{2} \cdot \frac{\sqrt{2}}{2} = \frac{2}{4}.$$

$$\frac{1}{2}(x'^2 - y'^2) = 1 \quad \text{Reduce } \frac{2}{4} \text{ and multiply the binomials.}$$

$$\frac{x'^2}{2} - \frac{y'^2}{2} = 1 \quad \text{Write the equation in standard form:}$$
$$\frac{x^2}{a^2} - \frac{y^2}{b^2} = 1.$$

$\boxed{a^2 = 2}$  $\boxed{b^2 = 2}$

This equation expresses $xy = 1$ in terms of the rotated $x'y'$-system. Can you see that this is the standard form of the equation of a hyperbola? The hyperbola's center is at $(0, 0)$, with the transverse axis on the $x'$-axis. The vertices are $(-a, 0)$ and $(a, 0)$. Because $a^2 = 2$, the vertices are $\left(-\sqrt{2}, 0\right)$ and $\left(\sqrt{2}, 0\right)$, located on the $x'$-axis. Based on the standard form of the hyperbola's equation, the equations for the asymptotes are

$$y' = \pm\frac{b}{a}x' \quad \text{or} \quad y' = \pm\frac{\sqrt{2}}{\sqrt{2}}x'.$$

The equations of the asymptotes can be simplified to $y' = x'$ and $y' = -x'$, which correspond to the original $x$- and $y$-axes. The graph of the hyperbola is shown in **Figure 9.46**. ●

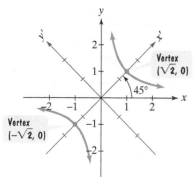

**Figure 9.46**  The graph of $xy = 1$ or $\dfrac{x'^2}{2} - \dfrac{y'^2}{2} = 1$

Vertex $(\sqrt{2}, 0)$

Vertex $(-\sqrt{2}, 0)$

⊘ Check Point **2**  Write the equation $xy = 2$ in terms of a rotated $x'y'$-system if the angle of rotation from the $x$-axis to the $x'$-axis is $45°$. Express the equation in standard form. Use the rotated system to graph $xy = 2$.

**③ Write equations of rotated conics in standard form.**

## Using Rotations to Transform Equations with xy-Terms to Standard Equations of Conic Sections

We have noted that the appearance of the term $Bxy$ $(B \neq 0)$ in the general second-degree equation indicates that the graph of the conic section has been rotated. A rotation of axes through an appropriate angle can transform the equation to one of the standard forms of the conic sections in $x'$ and $y'$ in which no $x'y'$-term appears.

### Amount of Rotation Formula

The general second-degree equation

$$Ax^2 + Bxy + Cy^2 + Dx + Ey + F = 0, B \neq 0$$

can be rewritten as an equation in $x'$ and $y'$ without an $x'y'$-term by rotating the axes through angle $\theta$, where

$$\cot 2\theta = \frac{A - C}{B}.$$

Before we learn to apply this formula, let's see how it can be derived. We begin with the general second-degree equation

$$Ax^2 + Bxy + Cy^2 + Dx + Ey + F = 0, B \neq 0.$$

Then we rotate the axes through an angle $\theta$. In terms of the rotated $x'y'$-system, the general second-degree equation can be written as

$$A(x' \cos \theta - y' \sin \theta)^2 + B(x' \cos \theta - y' \sin \theta)(x' \sin \theta + y' \cos \theta)$$
$$+ C(x' \sin \theta + y' \cos \theta)^2 + D(x' \cos \theta - y' \sin \theta)$$
$$+ E(x' \sin \theta + y' \cos \theta) + F = 0.$$

After a lot of simplifying that involves expanding and collecting like terms, you will obtain the following equation:

> We want a rotation that results in no $x'y'$-term.

$$(A \cos^2 \theta + B \sin \theta \cos \theta + C \sin^2 \theta)x'^2 + [B(\cos^2 \theta - \sin^2 \theta) + 2(C - A)(\sin \theta \cos \theta)]x'y'$$
$$+ (A \sin^2 \theta - B \sin \theta \cos \theta + C \cos^2 \theta)y'^2$$
$$+ (D \cos \theta + E \sin \theta)x'$$
$$+ (-D \sin \theta + E \cos \theta)y' + F = 0.$$

If this looks somewhat ghastly, take a deep breath and focus only on the $x'y'$-term. We want to choose $\theta$ so that the coefficient of this term is zero. This will give the required rotation that results in no $x'y'$-term.

$$B(\cos^2 \theta - \sin^2 \theta) + 2(C - A) \sin \theta \cos \theta = 0 \qquad \text{Set the coefficient of the } x'y'\text{-term equal to 0.}$$

$$B \cos 2\theta + (C - A) \sin 2\theta = 0 \qquad \text{Use the double-angle formulas:}$$
$$\cos 2\theta = \cos^2 \theta - \sin^2 \theta \text{ and}$$
$$\sin 2\theta = 2 \sin \theta \cos \theta.$$

$$B \cos 2\theta = -(C - A) \sin 2\theta \qquad \text{Subtract } (C - A) \sin 2\theta \text{ from both sides.}$$

$$B \cos 2\theta = (A - C) \sin 2\theta \qquad \text{Simplify.}$$

$$\frac{B \cos 2\theta}{B \sin 2\theta} = \frac{(A - C) \sin 2\theta}{B \sin 2\theta} \qquad \text{Divide both sides by } B \sin 2\theta.$$

$$\frac{\cos 2\theta}{\sin 2\theta} = \frac{A - C}{B} \qquad \text{Simplify.}$$

$$\cot 2\theta = \frac{A - C}{B} \qquad \text{Apply a quotient identity:}$$
$$\cot 2\theta = \frac{\cos 2\theta}{\sin 2\theta}.$$

If $\cot 2\theta$ is positive, we will select $\theta$ so that $0° < \theta < 45°$. If $\cot 2\theta$ is negative, we will select $\theta$ so that $45° < \theta < 90°$. Thus $\theta$, the angle of rotation, is always an acute angle.

Here is a step-by-step procedure for writing the equation of a rotated conic section in standard form:

### Writing the Equation of a Rotated Conic in Standard Form

**1.** Use the given equation

$$Ax^2 + Bxy + Cy^2 + Dx + Ey + F = 0, B \neq 0$$

to find cot $2\theta$.

$$\cot 2\theta = \frac{A - C}{B}$$

**2.** Use the expression for cot $2\theta$ to determine $\theta$, the angle of rotation.

**3.** Substitute $\theta$ in the rotation formulas

$$x = x' \cos \theta - y' \sin \theta \quad \text{and} \quad y = x' \sin \theta + y' \cos \theta$$

and simplify.

**4.** Substitute the expressions for $x$ and $y$ from the rotation formulas in the given equation and simplify. The resulting equation should have no $x'y'$-term.

**5.** Write the equation involving $x'$ and $y'$ in standard form.

Using the equation in step 5, you can graph the conic section in the rotated $x'y'$-system.

( **EXAMPLE 3** ) **Writing the Equation of a Rotated Conic Section in Standard Form**

Rewrite the equation

$$7x^2 - 6\sqrt{3}xy + 13y^2 - 16 = 0$$

in a rotated $x'y'$-system without an $x'y'$-term. Express the equation in the standard form of a conic section. Graph the conic section in the rotated system.

**Solution**

**Step 1  Use the given equation to find cot $2\theta$.** We need to identify the constants $A$, $B$, and $C$ in the given equation.

$$7x^2 - 6\sqrt{3}\,xy + 13y^2 - 16 = 0$$

| $A$ is the coefficient of the $x^2$-term: $A = 7$. | $B$ is the coefficient of the $xy$-term: $B = -6\sqrt{3}$. | $C$ is the coefficient of the $y^2$-term: $C = 13$. |

The appropriate angle $\theta$ through which to rotate the axes satisfies the equation

$$\cot 2\theta = \frac{A - C}{B} = \frac{7 - 13}{-6\sqrt{3}} = \frac{-6}{-6\sqrt{3}} = \frac{1}{\sqrt{3}} \text{ or } \frac{\sqrt{3}}{3}.$$

**Step 2  Use the expression for cot $2\theta$ to determine the angle of rotation.** We have $\cot 2\theta = \dfrac{\sqrt{3}}{3}$. Based on our knowledge of exact values for trigonometric functions, we conclude that $2\theta = 60°$. Thus, $\theta = 30°$.

**Step 3** **Substitute $\theta$ in the rotation formulas $x = x' \cos \theta - y' \sin \theta$ and $y = x' \sin \theta + y' \cos \theta$ and simplify.** Substituting $30°$ for $\theta$,

$$x = x' \cos 30° - y' \sin 30° = x'\left(\frac{\sqrt{3}}{2}\right) - y'\left(\frac{1}{2}\right) = \frac{\sqrt{3}x' - y'}{2}$$

$$y = x' \sin 30° + y' \cos 30° = x'\left(\frac{1}{2}\right) + y'\left(\frac{\sqrt{3}}{2}\right) = \frac{x' + \sqrt{3}y'}{2}.$$

**Step 4** **Substitute the expressions for $x$ and $y$ from the rotation formulas in the given equation and simplify.**

$$7x^2 - 6\sqrt{3}xy + 13y^2 - 16 = 0 \qquad \text{This is the given equation.}$$

$$7\left(\frac{\sqrt{3}x' - y'}{2}\right)^2 - 6\sqrt{3}\left(\frac{\sqrt{3}x' - y'}{2}\right)\left(\frac{x' + \sqrt{3}y'}{2}\right)$$

$$+ 13\left(\frac{x' + \sqrt{3}y'}{2}\right)^2 - 16 = 0 \qquad \begin{array}{l}\text{Substitute the expressions for } x \\ \text{and } y \text{ from the rotation formulas.}\end{array}$$

$$7\left(\frac{3x'^2 - 2\sqrt{3}x'y' + y'^2}{4}\right) - 6\sqrt{3}\left(\frac{\sqrt{3}x'^2 + 3x'y' - x'y' - \sqrt{3}y'^2}{4}\right)$$

$$+ 13\left(\frac{x'^2 + 2\sqrt{3}x'y' + 3y'^2}{4}\right) - 16 = 0 \qquad \text{Square and multiply.}$$

$$7\left(3x'^2 - 2\sqrt{3}x'y' + y'^2\right) - 6\sqrt{3}\left(\sqrt{3}x'^2 + 2x'y' - \sqrt{3}y'^2\right)$$

$$+ 13(x'^2 + 2\sqrt{3}x'y' + 3y'^2) - 64 = 0 \qquad \text{Multiply both sides by 4.}$$

$$21x'^2 - 14\sqrt{3}x'y' + 7y'^2 - 18x'^2 - 12\sqrt{3}x'y' + 18y'^2$$

$$+ 13x'^2 + 26\sqrt{3}x'y' + 39y'^2 - 64 = 0 \qquad \text{Distribute throughout parentheses.}$$

$$21x'^2 - 18x'^2 + 13x'^2 - 14\sqrt{3}x'y' - 12\sqrt{3}x'y' + 26\sqrt{3}x'y'$$

$$+ 7y'^2 + 18y'^2 + 39y'^2 - 64 = 0 \qquad \text{Rearrange terms.}$$

$$16x'^2 + 64y'^2 - 64 = 0 \qquad \text{Combine like terms.}$$

Do you see how we "lost" the $x'y'$-term in the last equation?

$$-14\sqrt{3}x'y' - 12\sqrt{3}x'y' + 26\sqrt{3}x'y' = -26\sqrt{3}x'y' + 26\sqrt{3}x'y' = 0x'y' = 0$$

**Step 5** **Write the equation involving $x'$ and $y'$ in standard form.** We can express $16x'^2 + 64y'^2 - 64 = 0$, an equation of an ellipse, in the standard form $\frac{x^2}{a^2} + \frac{y^2}{b^2} = 1$.

$$16x'^2 + 64y'^2 - 64 = 0 \qquad \begin{array}{l}\text{This equation describes the ellipse relative to a} \\ \text{system rotated through 30°.}\end{array}$$

$$16x'^2 + 64y'^2 = 64 \qquad \text{Add 64 to both sides.}$$

$$\frac{16x'^2}{64} + \frac{64y'^2}{64} = \frac{64}{64} \qquad \text{Divide both sides by 64.}$$

$$\frac{x'^2}{4} + \frac{y'^2}{1} = 1 \qquad \text{Simplify.}$$

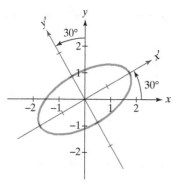

**Figure 9.44** (repeated) The graph of $7x^2 - 6\sqrt{3}xy + 13y^2 - 16 = 0$ or $\dfrac{x'^2}{4} - \dfrac{y'^2}{1} = 1$, a rotated ellipse

The equation $\dfrac{x'^2}{4} + \dfrac{y'^2}{1} = 1$ is the standard form of the equation of an ellipse. The major axis is on the $x'$-axis and the vertices are $(-2, 0)$ and $(2, 0)$. The minor axis is on the $y'$-axis with endpoints $(0, -1)$ and $(0, 1)$. The graph of the ellipse is shown in **Figure 9.44**. Does this graph look familiar? It should—you saw it earlier in this section on page 914.

**Check Point 3** Rewrite the equation

$$2x^2 + \sqrt{3}xy + y^2 - 2 = 0$$

in a rotated $x'y'$-system without an $x'y'$-term. Express the equation in the standard form of a conic section. Graph the conic section in the rotated system.

## Technology

In order to graph a general second-degree equation in the form

$$Ax^2 + Bxy + Cy^2 + Dx + Ey + F = 0$$

using a graphing utility, it is necessary to solve for $y$. Rewrite the equation as a quadratic equation in $y$.

$$Cy^2 + (Bx + E)y + (Ax^2 + Dx + F) = 0$$

By applying the quadratic formula, the graph of this equation can be obtained by entering

$$y_1 = \frac{-(Bx + E) + \sqrt{(Bx + E)^2 - 4C(Ax^2 + Dx + F)}}{2C}$$

and

$$y_2 = \frac{-(Bx + E) - \sqrt{(Bx + E)^2 - 4C(Ax^2 + Dx + F)}}{2C}.$$

The graph of

$$7x^2 - 6\sqrt{3}xy + 13y^2 - 16 = 0$$

is shown on the right in a $[-2, 2, 1]$ by $[-2, 2, 1]$ viewing rectangle. The graph was obtained by entering the equations for $y_1$ and $y_2$ shown above with

$$A = 7, B = -6\sqrt{3}, C = 13, D = 0, E = 0,$$

and $F = -16$.

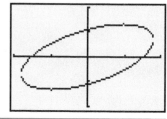

In Example 3 and Check Point 3, we found $\theta$, the angle of rotation, directly because we recognized $\dfrac{\sqrt{3}}{3}$ as the value of cot $60°$. What do we do if cot $2\theta$ is not the cotangent of one of the familiar angles? We use cot $2\theta$ to find sin $\theta$ and cos $\theta$ as follows:

- Use a sketch of cot $2\theta$ to find cos $2\theta$.
- Find sin $\theta$ and cos $\theta$ using the identities

$$\sin \theta = \sqrt{\frac{1 - \cos 2\theta}{2}} \qquad \text{and} \qquad \cos \theta = \sqrt{\frac{1 + \cos 2\theta}{2}}.$$

> **Because $\theta$ is an acute angle, the positive square roots are appropriate.**

The resulting values for sin $\theta$ and cos $\theta$ are used to write the rotation formulas that give an equation with no $x'y'$-term.

(EXAMPLE 4) **Graphing the Equation of a Rotated Conic**

Graph relative to a rotated $x'y'$-system in which the equation has no $x'y'$-term:

$$16x^2 - 24xy + 9y^2 + 110x - 20y + 100 = 0.$$

**Solution**

**Step 1   Use the given equation to find cot $2\theta$.** With $A = 16$, $B = -24$, and $C = 9$, we have

$$\cot 2\theta = \frac{A - C}{B} = \frac{16 - 9}{-24} = -\frac{7}{24}.$$

**Step 2   Use the expression for cot $2\theta$ to determine sin $\theta$ and cos $\theta$.** A rough sketch showing cot $2\theta$ is given in **Figure 9.47**. Because $\theta$ is always acute and cot $2\theta$ is negative, $2\theta$ is in quadrant II. The third side of the triangle is found using $r = \sqrt{x^2 + y^2}$. Thus, $r = \sqrt{(-7)^2 + 24^2} = \sqrt{625} = 25$. By the definition of the cosine function,

$$\cos 2\theta = \frac{x}{r} = \frac{-7}{25} = -\frac{7}{25}.$$

Now we use identities to find values for sin $\theta$ and cos $\theta$.

$$\sin \theta = \sqrt{\frac{1 - \cos 2\theta}{2}} = \sqrt{\frac{1 - \left(-\dfrac{7}{25}\right)}{2}}$$

$$= \sqrt{\frac{\dfrac{25}{25} + \dfrac{7}{25}}{2}} = \sqrt{\frac{\dfrac{32}{25}}{2}} = \sqrt{\frac{32}{50}} = \sqrt{\frac{16}{25}} = \frac{4}{5}$$

$$\cos \theta = \sqrt{\frac{1 + \cos 2\theta}{2}} = \sqrt{\frac{1 + \left(-\dfrac{7}{25}\right)}{2}}$$

$$= \sqrt{\frac{\dfrac{25}{25} - \dfrac{7}{25}}{2}} = \sqrt{\frac{\dfrac{18}{25}}{2}} = \sqrt{\frac{18}{50}} = \sqrt{\frac{9}{25}} = \frac{3}{5}$$

**Step 3   Substitute sin $\theta$ and cos $\theta$ in the rotation formulas**

$$x = x' \cos \theta - y' \sin \theta \quad \text{and} \quad y = x' \sin \theta + y' \cos \theta$$

**and simplify.** Substituting $\frac{4}{5}$ for sin $\theta$ and $\frac{3}{5}$ for cos $\theta$,

$$x = x'\left(\frac{3}{5}\right) - y'\left(\frac{4}{5}\right) = \frac{3x' - 4y'}{5}$$

$$y = x'\left(\frac{4}{5}\right) + y'\left(\frac{3}{5}\right) = \frac{4x' + 3y'}{5}.$$

**Step 4   Substitute the expressions for $x$ and $y$ from the rotation formulas in the given equation and simplify.**

$$16x^2 - 24xy + 9y^2 + 110x - 20y + 100 = 0 \qquad \text{This is the given equation.}$$

$$16\left(\frac{3x' - 4y'}{5}\right)^2 - 24\left(\frac{3x' - 4y'}{5}\right)\left(\frac{4x' + 3y'}{5}\right) + 9\left(\frac{4x' + 3y'}{5}\right)^2 \qquad \text{Substitute the expressions for } x \text{ and } y \text{ from the rotation formulas.}$$

$$+ 110\left(\frac{3x' - 4y'}{5}\right) - 20\left(\frac{4x' + 3y'}{5}\right) + 100 = 0$$

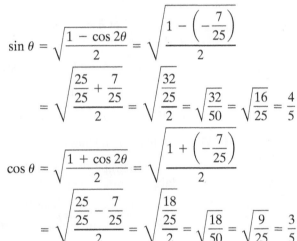

$$\sqrt{(-7)^2 + 24^2} = 25$$

24

$2\theta$

$-7$

**Figure 9.47** Using cot $2\theta$ to find cos $2\theta$

Work with the last equation at the bottom of the previous page. Take a few minutes to expand, multiply both sides of the equation by 25, and combine like terms. You should obtain

$$y'^2 + 2x' - 4y' + 4 = 0,$$

an equation that has no $x'y'$-term.

**Step 5   Write the equation involving $x'$ and $y'$ in standard form.** With only one variable that is squared, we have the equation of a parabola. We need to write the equation in the standard form $(y - k)^2 = 4p(x - h)$.

$$y'^2 + 2x' - 4y' + 4 = 0 \qquad \text{This is the equation without an x'y'-term.}$$

$$y'^2 - 4y' = -2x' - 4 \qquad \text{Isolate the terms involving y'.}$$

$$y'^2 - 4y' + 4 = -2x' - 4 + 4 \qquad \text{Complete the square by adding the square of half the coefficient of y'.}$$

$$(y' - 2)^2 = -2x' \qquad \text{Factor.}$$

The standard form of the parabola's equation in the rotated $x'y'$-system is

$$(y' - 2)^2 = -2x'.$$

This is $(y' - k)^2$, with $k = 2$.    This is $4p$.    This is $x' - h$, with $h = 0$.

We see that $h = 0$ and $k = 2$. Thus, the vertex of the parabola in the $x'y'$-system is $(h, k) = (0, 2)$.

We can use the $x'y'$-system to graph the parabola. Using a calculator to solve $\sin \theta = \frac{4}{5}$, we find that $\theta = \sin^{-1}\frac{4}{5} \approx 53°$. Rotate the axes through approximately 53°. With $4p = -2$ and $p = -\frac{1}{2}$, the parabola's focus is $\frac{1}{2}$ unit to the left of the vertex, $(0, 2)$. Thus, the focus in the $x'y'$-system is $\left(-\frac{1}{2}, 2\right)$.

To graph the parabola, we use the vertex, $(0, 2)$, and the two endpoints of the latus rectum.

$$\text{length of latus rectum} = |4p| = |-2| = 2$$

The latus rectum extends 1 unit above and 1 unit below the focus, $\left(-\frac{1}{2}, 2\right)$. Thus, the endpoints of the latus rectum in the $x'y'$-system are $\left(-\frac{1}{2}, 3\right)$ and $\left(-\frac{1}{2}, 1\right)$. Using the rotated system, pass a smooth curve through the vertex and the two endpoints of the latus rectum. The graph of the parabola is shown in **Figure 9.48**.   ●

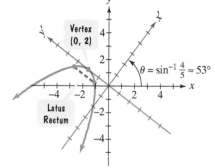

**Figure 9.48**   The graph of $(y' - 2)^2 = -2x'$ in a rotated $x'y'$-system

Ø Check Point **4**  Graph relative to a rotated $x'y'$-system in which the equation has no $x'y'$-term:

$$4x^2 - 4xy + y^2 - 8\sqrt{5}x - 16\sqrt{5}y = 0.$$

**④**  Identify conics without rotating axes.

## Identifying Conic Sections without Rotating Axes

We now know that the general second-degree equation

$$Ax^2 + Bxy + Cy^2 + Dx + Ey + F = 0, B \neq 0$$

can be rewritten as

$$A'x'^2 + C'y'^2 + D'x' + E'y' + F' = 0$$

in a rotated $x'y'$-system. A relationship between the coefficients of the two equations is given by

$$B^2 - 4AC = -4A'C'.$$

We also know that $A'$ and $C'$ can be used to identify the graph of the rotated equation. Thus, $B^2 - 4AC$ can also be used to identify the graph of the general second-degree equation.

## Identifying a Conic Section without a Rotation of Axes

A nondegenerate conic section of the form

$$Ax^2 + Bxy + Cy^2 + Dx + Ey + F = 0$$

is

- a parabola if $B^2 - 4AC = 0$,
- an ellipse or a circle if $B^2 - 4AC < 0$, and
- a hyperbola if $B^2 - 4AC > 0$.

### Technology

**Graphic Connections**

The graph of

$$11x^2 + 10\sqrt{3}xy + y^2 - 4 = 0$$

is shown in a $\left[-1, 1, \frac{1}{4}\right]$ by $\left[-1, 1, \frac{1}{4}\right]$ viewing rectangle. The graph verifies that the equation represents a rotated hyperbola.

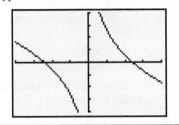

**EXAMPLE 5** **Identifying a Conic Section without Rotating Axes**

Identify the graph of

$$11x^2 + 10\sqrt{3}xy + y^2 - 4 = 0.$$

**Solution**   We use $A$, $B$, and $C$ to identify the conic section.

$$11x^2 + 10\sqrt{3}xy + y^2 - 4 = 0$$

$$A = 11 \qquad B = 10\sqrt{3} \qquad C = 1$$

$$B^2 - 4AC = \left(10\sqrt{3}\right)^2 - 4(11)(1) = 100 \cdot 3 - 44 = 256 > 0$$

Because $B^2 - 4AC > 0$, the graph of the equation is a hyperbola.

⦿ Check Point **5**   Identify the graph of $3x^2 - 2\sqrt{3}xy + y^2 + 2x + 2\sqrt{3}y = 0$.

## Exercise Set 9.4

### Practice Exercises

*In Exercises 1–8, identify each equation without completing the square.*

**1.** $y^2 - 4x + 2y + 21 = 0$

**2.** $y^2 - 4x - 4y = 0$

**3.** $4x^2 - 9y^2 - 8x - 36y - 68 = 0$

**4.** $9x^2 + 25y^2 - 54x - 200y + 256 = 0$

**5.** $4x^2 + 4y^2 + 12x + 4y + 1 = 0$

**6.** $9x^2 + 4y^2 - 36x + 8y + 31 = 0$

**7.** $100x^2 - 7y^2 + 90y - 368 = 0$

**8.** $y^2 + 8x + 6y + 25 = 0$

*In Exercises 9–14, write each equation in terms of a rotated x'y'-system using θ, the angle of rotation. Write the equation involving x' and y' in standard form.*

**9.** $xy = -1; \theta = 45°$

**10.** $xy = -4; \theta = 45°$

**11.** $x^2 - 4xy + y^2 - 3 = 0; \theta = 45°$

**12.** $13x^2 - 10xy + 13y^2 - 72 = 0; \theta = 45°$

**13.** $23x^2 + 26\sqrt{3}xy - 3y^2 - 144 = 0; \theta = 30°$

**14.** $13x^2 - 6\sqrt{3}xy + 7y^2 - 16 = 0; \theta = 60°$

*In Exercises 15–26, write the appropriate rotation formulas so that in a rotated system the equation has no x'y'-term.*

**15.** $x^2 + xy + y^2 - 10 = 0$

**16.** $x^2 + 4xy + y^2 - 3 = 0$

**17.** $3x^2 - 10xy + 3y^2 - 32 = 0$

**18.** $5x^2 - 8xy + 5y^2 - 9 = 0$

**19.** $11x^2 + 10\sqrt{3}xy + y^2 - 4 = 0$

**20.** $7x^2 - 6\sqrt{3}xy + 13y^2 - 16 = 0$

**21.** $10x^2 + 24xy + 17y^2 - 9 = 0$

**22.** $32x^2 - 48xy + 18y^2 - 15x - 20y = 0$

**23.** $x^2 + 4xy - 2y^2 - 1 = 0$

**24.** $3xy - 4y^2 + 18 = 0$

**25.** $34x^2 - 24xy + 41y^2 - 25 = 0$

**26.** $6x^2 - 6xy + 14y^2 - 45 = 0$

In Exercises 27–38,

   **a.** *Rewrite the equation in a rotated $x'y'$-system without an $x'y'$-term. Use the appropriate rotation formulas from Exercises 15–26.*

   **b.** *Express the equation involving $x'$ and $y'$ in the standard form of a conic section.*

   **c.** *Use the rotated system to graph the equation.*

**27.** $x^2 + xy + y^2 - 10 = 0$

**28.** $x^2 + 4xy + y^2 - 3 = 0$

**29.** $3x^2 - 10xy + 3y^2 - 32 = 0$

**30.** $5x^2 - 8xy + 5y^2 - 9 = 0$

**31.** $11x^2 + 10\sqrt{3}xy + y^2 - 4 = 0$

**32.** $7x^2 - 6\sqrt{3}xy + 13y^2 - 16 = 0$

**33.** $10x^2 + 24xy + 17y^2 - 9 = 0$

**34.** $32x^2 - 48xy + 18y^2 - 15x - 20y = 0$

**35.** $x^2 + 4xy - 2y^2 - 1 = 0$

**36.** $3xy - 4y^2 + 18 = 0$

**37.** $34x^2 - 24xy + 41y^2 - 25 = 0$

**38.** $6x^2 - 6xy + 14y^2 - 45 = 0$

In Exercises 39–44, identify each equation without applying a rotation of axes.

**39.** $5x^2 - 2xy + 5y^2 - 12 = 0$

**40.** $10x^2 + 24xy + 17y^2 - 9 = 0$

**41.** $24x^2 + 16\sqrt{3}xy + 8y^2 - x + \sqrt{3}y - 8 = 0$

**42.** $3x^2 - 2\sqrt{3}xy + y^2 + 2x + 2\sqrt{3}y = 0$

**43.** $23x^2 + 26\sqrt{3}xy - 3y^2 - 144 = 0$

**44.** $4xy + 3y^2 + 4x + 6y - 1 = 0$

## Practice Plus

In Exercises 45–48,

   • *If the graph of the equation is an ellipse, find the coordinates of the vertices on the minor axis.*

   • *If the graph of the equation is a hyperbola, find the equations of the asymptotes.*

   • *If the graph of the equation is a parabola, find the coordinates of the vertex.*

*Express answers relative to an $x'y'$-system in which the given equation has no $x'y'$-term. Assume that the $x'y'$-system has the same origin as the $xy$-system.*

**45.** $5x^2 - 6xy + 5y^2 - 8 = 0$

**46.** $2x^2 - 4xy + 5y^2 - 36 = 0$

**47.** $x^2 - 4xy + 4y^2 + 5\sqrt{5}y - 10 = 0$

**48.** $x^2 + 4xy - 2y^2 - 6 = 0$

## Writing in Mathematics

**49.** Explain how to identify the graph of
$$Ax^2 + Cy^2 + Dx + Ey + F = 0.$$

**50.** If there is a 60° angle from the positive $x$-axis to the positive $x'$-axis, explain how to obtain the rotation formulas for $x$ and $y$.

**51.** How do you obtain the angle of rotation so that a general second-degree equation has no $x'y'$-term in a rotated $x'y'$-system?

**52.** What is the most time-consuming part in using a graphing utility to graph a general second-degree equation with an $xy$-term?

**53.** Explain how to identify the graph of
$$Ax^2 + Bxy + Cy^2 + Dx + Ey + F = 0.$$

## Technology Exercises

In Exercises 54–60, use a graphing utility to graph each equation.

**54.** $x^2 + 4xy + y^2 - 3 = 0$

**55.** $7x^2 + 8xy + y^2 - 1 = 0$

**56.** $3x^2 + 4xy + 6y^2 - 7 = 0$

**57.** $3x^2 - 6xy + 3y^2 + 10x - 8y - 2 = 0$

**58.** $9x^2 + 24xy + 16y^2 + 90x - 130y = 0$

**59.** $x^2 + 4xy + 4y^2 + 10\sqrt{5}x - 9 = 0$

**60.** $7x^2 + 6xy + 2.5y^2 - 14x + 4y + 9 = 0$

## Critical Thinking Exercises

**Make Sense?** *In Exercises 61–64, determine whether each statement makes sense or does not make sense, and explain your reasoning.*

**61.** I graphed $2x^2 - 3y^2 + 6y + 4 = 0$ by using the procedure for writing the equation of a rotated conic in standard form.

**62.** In order to graph an ellipse whose equation contained an $xy$-term, I used a rotated coordinate system that placed the ellipse's center at the origin.

**63.** Although the algebra of rotations can get ugly, the main idea is that rotation through an appropriate angle will transform a general second-degree equation into an equation in $x'$ and $y'$ without an $x'y'$-term.

**64.** I can verify that $2xy - 9 = 0$ is the equation of a hyperbola by rotating the axes through 45° or by showing that $B^2 - 4AC > 0$.

**65.** Explain the relationship between the graph of $3x^2 - 2xy + 3y^2 + 2 = 0$ and the sound made by one hand clapping. Begin by following the directions for Exercises 27–38. (You will first need to write rotation formulas that eliminate the $x'y'$-term.)

**66.** What happens to the equation $x^2 + y^2 = r^2$ in a rotated $x'y'$-system?

In Exercises 67–68, let
$$Ax^2 + Bxy + Cy^2 + Dx + Ey + F = 0$$

be an equation of a conic section in an $xy$-coordinate system. Let $A'x'^2 + B'x'y' + C'y'^2 + D'x' + E'y' + F' = 0$ be the equation of the conic section in the rotated $x'y'$-coordinate system. Use the coefficients $A'$, $B'$, and $C'$, shown in the equation with the voice balloon pointing to $B'$ on page 917, to prove the following relationships.

**67.** $A' + C' = A + C$

**68.** $B'^2 - 4A'C' = B^2 - 4AC$

## Group Exercise

**69.** Many public and private organizations and schools provide educational materials and information for the blind and visually impaired. Using your library, resources on the World Wide Web, or local organizations, investigate how your group or college could make a contribution to enhance the study of mathematics for the blind and visually impaired. In relation to conic sections, group members should discuss how to create graphs in tactile, or touchable, form that show blind students the visual structure of the conics, including asymptotes, intercepts, end behavior, and rotations.

## Preview Exercises

*Exercises 70–72 will help you prepare for the material covered in the next section. In each exercise, graph the equation in a rectangular coordinate system.*

**70.** $y^2 = 4(x + 1)$

**71.** $y = \dfrac{1}{2}x^2 + 1, \quad x \geq 0$

**72.** $\dfrac{x^2}{25} + \dfrac{y^2}{4} = 1$

---

**Section 9.5**

## Parametric Equations

### Objectives

1. Use point plotting to graph plane curves described by parametric equations.
2. Eliminate the parameter.
3. Find parametric equations for functions.
4. Understand the advantages of parametric representations.

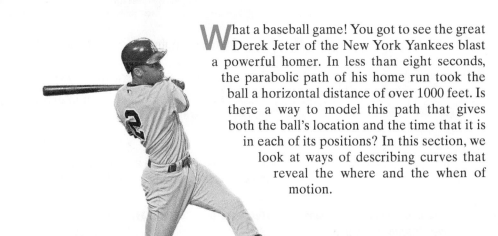

What a baseball game! You got to see the great Derek Jeter of the New York Yankees blast a powerful homer. In less than eight seconds, the parabolic path of his home run took the ball a horizontal distance of over 1000 feet. Is there a way to model this path that gives both the ball's location and the time that it is in each of its positions? In this section, we look at ways of describing curves that reveal the where and the when of motion.

### Plane Curves and Parametric Equations

You throw a ball from a height of 6 feet, with an initial velocity of 90 feet per second and at an angle of 40° with the horizontal. After $t$ seconds, the location of the ball can be described by

$$x = (90 \cos 40°)t \quad \text{and} \quad y = 6 + (90 \sin 40°)t - 16t^2.$$

> This is the ball's horizontal distance, in feet.

> This is the ball's vertical height, in feet.

Because we can use these equations to calculate the location of the ball at any time $t$, we can describe the path of the ball. For example, to determine the location when $t = 1$ second, substitute 1 for $t$ in each equation:

$$x = (90 \cos 40°)t = (90 \cos 40°)(1) \approx 68.9 \text{ feet}$$

$$y = 6 + (90 \sin 40°)t - 16t^2 = 6 + (90 \sin 40°)(1) - 16(1)^2 \approx 47.9 \text{ feet}.$$

This tells us that after one second, the ball has traveled a horizontal distance of approximately 68.9 feet, and the height of the ball is approximately 47.9 feet. **Figure 9.49** on the next page displays this information and the results for calculations corresponding to $t = 2$ seconds and $t = 3$ seconds.

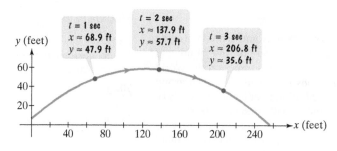

Figure 9.49   The location of a thrown ball after 1, 2, and 3 seconds

The voice balloons in **Figure 9.49** tell where the ball is located and when the ball is at a given point $(x, y)$ on its path. The variable $t$, called a **parameter**, gives the various times for the ball's location. The equations that describe where the ball is located express both $x$ and $y$ as functions of $t$ and are called **parametric equations**.

$$x = (90 \cos 40°)t \qquad y = 6 + (90 \sin 40°)t - 16t^2$$

This is the parametric equation for $x$.

This is the parametric equation for $y$.

The collection of points $(x, y)$ in **Figure 9.49** is called a **plane curve**.

### Plane Curves and Parametric Equations

Suppose that $t$ is a number in an interval $I$. A **plane curve** is the set of ordered pairs $(x, y)$, where

$$x = f(t), \quad y = g(t) \quad \text{for } t \text{ in interval } I.$$

The variable $t$ is called a **parameter**, and the equations $x = f(t)$ and $y = g(t)$ are called **parametric equations** for the curve.

**①** Use point plotting to graph plane curves described by parametric equations.

## Graphing Plane Curves

Graphing a plane curve represented by parametric equations involves plotting points in the rectangular coordinate system and connecting them with a smooth curve.

### Graphing a Plane Curve Described by Parametric Equations

1. Select some values of $t$ on the given interval.
2. For each value of $t$, use the given parametric equations to compute $x$ and $y$.
3. Plot the points $(x, y)$ in the order of increasing $t$ and connect them with a smooth curve.

Take a second look at **Figure 9.49**. Do you notice arrows along the curve? These arrows show the direction, or **orientation**, along the curve as $t$ increases. After graphing a plane curve described by parametric equations, use arrows between the points to show the orientation of the curve corresponding to increasing values of $t$.

**( EXAMPLE 1 )** **Graphing a Curve Defined by Parametric Equations**

Graph the plane curve defined by the parametric equations:

$$x = t^2 - 1, \qquad y = 2t, \qquad -2 \le t \le 2.$$

### Solution

**Step 1   Select some values of $t$ on the given interval.** We will select integral values of $t$ on the interval $-2 \le t \le 2$. Let $t = -2, -1, 0, 1,$ and $2$.

**Step 2    For each value of *t*, use the given parametric equations to compute *x* and *y*.** We organize our work in a table. The first column lists the choices for the parameter *t*. The next two columns show the corresponding values for *x* and *y*. The last column lists the ordered pair $(x, y)$.

| $t$ | $x = t^2 - 1$ | $y = 2t$ | $(x, y)$ |
|---|---|---|---|
| $-2$ | $(-2)^2 - 1 = 4 - 1 = 3$ | $2(-2) = -4$ | $(3, -4)$ |
| $-1$ | $(-1)^2 - 1 = 1 - 1 = 0$ | $2(-1) = -2$ | $(0, -2)$ |
| $0$ | $0^2 - 1 = -1$ | $2(0) = 0$ | $(-1, 0)$ |
| $1$ | $1^2 - 1 = 0$ | $2(1) = 2$ | $(0, 2)$ |
| $2$ | $2^2 - 1 = 4 - 1 = 3$ | $2(2) = 4$ | $(3, 4)$ |

**Step 3    Plot the points $(x, y)$ in the order of increasing *t* and connect them with a smooth curve.** The plane curve defined by the parametric equations on the given interval is shown in **Figure 9.50**. The arrows show the direction, or orientation, along the curve as *t* varies from $-2$ to 2.

**Figure 9.50**   The plane curve defined by $x = t^2 - 1$, $y = 2t$, $-2 \le t \le 2$

(Graph annotations: $t = 2, (3, 4)$; $t = 1, (0, 2)$; $t = 0, (-1, 0)$; $t = -1, (0, -2)$; $t = -2, (3, -4)$)

✓ Check Point  **|**  Graph the plane curve defined by the parametric equations:

$$x = t^2 + 1, \qquad y = 3t, \qquad -2 \le t \le 2.$$

## ② Eliminate the parameter.

## Eliminating the Parameter

The graph in **Figure 9.50** shows the plane curve for $x = t^2 - 1$, $y = 2t$, $-2 \le t \le 2$. Even if we examine the parametric equations carefully, we may not be able to tell that the corresponding plane curve is a portion of a parabola. By **eliminating the parameter**, we can write one equation in *x* and *y* that is equivalent to the two parametric equations. The voice balloons illustrate this process.

Begin with the parametric equations.

$$x = t^2 - 1$$
$$y = 2t$$

Solve for *t* in one of the equations.

Using $y = 2t$,
$$t = \frac{y}{2}.$$

Substitute the expression for *t* in the other parametric equation.

Using $t = \frac{y}{2}$ and $x = t^2 - 1$,
$$x = \left(\frac{y}{2}\right)^2 - 1.$$

The rectangular equation (the equation in *x* and *y*), $x = \dfrac{y^2}{4} - 1$, can be written as $y^2 = 4(x + 1)$. This is the standard form of the equation of a parabola with vertex at $(-1, 0)$ and axis of symmetry along the *x*-axis. Because the parameter *t* is restricted to the interval $[-2, 2]$, the plane curve in the technology box on the left shows only a part of the parabola.

Our discussion illustrates a second method for graphing a plane curve described by parametric equations. Eliminate the parameter *t* and graph the resulting rectangular equation in *x* and *y*. However, **you may need to change the domain of the rectangular equation to be consistent with the domain for the parametric equation in *x*.** This situation is illustrated in Example 2.

## Technology

A graphing utility can be used to obtain a plane curve represented by parametric equations. Set the mode to parametric and enter the equations. You must enter the minimum and maximum values for *t*, and an increment setting for *t* (*t*step). The setting *t*step determines the number of points the graphing utility will plot.

Shown below is the plane curve for

$$x = t^2 - 1$$
$$y = 2t$$

in a $[-5, 5, 1]$ by $[-5, 5, 1]$ viewing rectangle with *t*min $= -2$, *t*max $= 2$, and *t*step $= 0.01$.

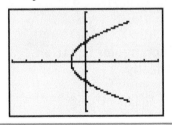

**EXAMPLE 2**   **Finding and Graphing the Rectangular Equation of a Curve Defined Parametrically**

Sketch the plane curve represented by the parametric equations

$$x = \sqrt{t} \quad \text{and} \quad y = \tfrac{1}{2}t + 1$$

by eliminating the parameter.

**Solution** We eliminate the parameter $t$ and then graph the resulting rectangular equation.

| Begin with the parametric equations. | Solve for $t$ in one of the equations. | Substitute the expression for $t$ in the other parametric equation. |
|---|---|---|

$x = \sqrt{t}$

$y = \dfrac{1}{2}t + 1$

Using $x = \sqrt{t}$ and squaring both sides, $t = x^2$.

Using $t = x^2$ and $y = \dfrac{1}{2}t + 1$,

$y = \dfrac{1}{2}x^2 + 1$.

Because $t$ is not limited to a closed interval, you might be tempted to graph the entire bowl-shaped parabola whose equation is $y = \frac{1}{2}x^2 + 1$. However, take a second look at the parametric equation for $x$:

$$x = \sqrt{t}.$$

This equation is defined only when $t \geq 0$. Thus, $x$ is nonnegative. The plane curve is the parabola given by $y = \frac{1}{2}x^2 + 1$ with the domain restricted to $x \geq 0$. The plane curve is shown in **Figure 9.51**.

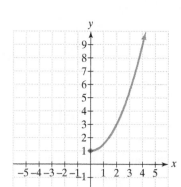

**Figure 9.51** The plane curve for $x = \sqrt{t}$ and $y = \frac{1}{2}t + 1$, or $y = \frac{1}{2}x^2 + 1, x \geq 0$

⌀ Check Point **2** Sketch the plane curve represented by the parametric equations

$$x = \sqrt{t} \quad \text{and} \quad y = 2t - 1$$

by eliminating the parameter.

Eliminating the parameter is not always a simple matter. In some cases, it may not be possible. When this occurs, you can use point plotting to obtain a plane curve.

Trigonometric identities can be helpful in eliminating the parameter. For example, consider the plane curve defined by the parametric equations

$$x = \sin t, \quad y = \cos t, \quad 0 \leq t < 2\pi.$$

We use the trigonometric identity $\sin^2 t + \cos^2 t = 1$ to eliminate the parameter. Square each side of each parametric equation and then add.

$$x^2 = \sin^2 t$$
$$\dfrac{y^2 = \cos^2 t}{x^2 + y^2 = \sin^2 t + \cos^2 t}$$

This is the sum of the two equations above the horizontal lines.

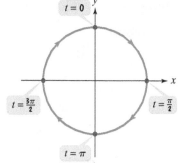

**Figure 9.52** The plane curve defined by $x = \sin t, y = \cos t,$ $0 \leq t < 2\pi$

Using a Pythagorean identity, we write this equation as $x^2 + y^2 = 1$. The plane curve is a circle with center $(0, 0)$ and radius 1. It is shown in **Figure 9.52**.

⟮ **EXAMPLE 3** ⟯ **Finding and Graphing the Rectangular Equation of a Curve Defined Parametrically**

Sketch the plane curve represented by the parametric equations

$$x = 5\cos t, \quad y = 2\sin t, \quad 0 \leq t \leq \pi$$

by eliminating the parameter.

**Solution** We eliminate the parameter using the identity $\cos^2 t + \sin^2 t = 1$. To apply the identity, divide the parametric equation for $x$ by 5 and the parametric equation for $y$ by 2.

$$\dfrac{x}{5} = \cos t \quad \text{and} \quad \dfrac{y}{2} = \sin t$$

Square and add these two equations.

$$\frac{x^2}{25} = \cos^2 t$$

$$\frac{y^2}{4} = \sin^2 t$$

$$\overline{\frac{x^2}{25} + \frac{y^2}{4} = \cos^2 t + \sin^2 t}$$

> This is the sum of the two equations above the horizontal lines.

Using a Pythagorean identity, we write this equation as

$$\frac{x^2}{25} + \frac{y^2}{4} = 1.$$

This rectangular equation is the standard form of the equation for an ellipse centered at $(0, 0)$.

$$\frac{x^2}{25} + \frac{y^2}{4} = 1$$

> $a^2 = 25$: Endpoints of major axis are 5 units left and right of center.

> $b^2 = 4$: Endpoints of minor axis are 2 units above and below center.

The ellipse is shown in **Figure 9.53(a)**. However, this is not the plane curve. Because $t$ is restricted to the interval $[0, \pi]$, the plane curve is only a portion of the ellipse. Use the starting and ending values for $t$, 0 and $\pi$, respectively, and a value of $t$ in the interval $(0, \pi)$ to find which portion to include.

> Begin at $t = 0$.

> Increase to $t = \frac{\pi}{2}$.

> End at $t = \pi$.

$x = 5 \cos t = 5 \cos 0 = 5 \cdot 1 = 5$

$y = 2 \sin t = 2 \sin 0 = 2 \cdot 0 = 0$

$x = 5 \cos t = 5 \cos \frac{\pi}{2} = 5 \cdot 0 = 0$

$y = 2 \sin t = 2 \sin \frac{\pi}{2} = 2 \cdot 1 = 2$

$x = 5 \cos t = 5 \cos \pi = 5(-1) = -5$

$y = 2 \sin t = 2 \sin \pi = 2(0) = 0$

Points on the plane curve include $(5, 0)$, which is the starting point, $(0, 2)$, and $(-5, 0)$, which is the ending point. The plane curve is the top half of the ellipse, shown in **Figure 9.53(b)**.

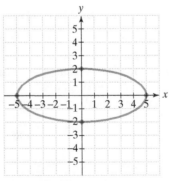

Figure 9.53(a)   The graph of $\frac{x^2}{25} + \frac{y^2}{4} = 1$

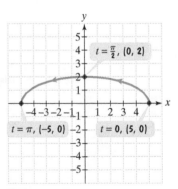

Figure 9.53(b)   The plane curve for $x = 5 \cos t$, $y = 2 \sin t$, $0 \le t \le \pi$

✓ Check Point **3** Sketch the plane curve represented by the parametric equations

$$x = 6 \cos t,\ y = 4 \sin t,\ \pi \le t \le 2\pi$$

by eliminating the parameter.

③ Find parametric equations for functions.

## Finding Parametric Equations

Infinitely many pairs of parametric equations can represent the same plane curve. If the plane curve is defined by the function $y = f(x)$, here is a procedure for finding a set of parametric equations:

### Parametric Equations for the Function $y = f(x)$

One set of parametric equations for the plane curve defined by $y = f(x)$ is

$$x = t \quad \text{and} \quad y = f(t),$$

in which $t$ is in the domain of $f$.

( **EXAMPLE 4** ) **Finding Parametric Equations**

Find a set of parametric equations for the parabola whose equation is $y = 9 - x^2$.

**Solution**  Let $x = t$. Parametric equations for $y = f(x)$ are $x = t$ and $y = f(t)$. Thus, parametric equations for $y = 9 - x^2$ are

$$x = t \quad \text{and} \quad y = 9 - t^2.$$

◯ Check Point 4 Find a set of parametric equations for the parabola whose equation is $y = x^2 - 25$.

You can write other sets of parametric equations for $y = 9 - x^2$ by starting with a different parametric equation for $x$. Here are three more sets of parametric equations for

$$y = 9 - x^2:$$

- If $x = t^3$, $y = 9 - (t^3)^2 = 9 - t^6$.

  Parametric equations are $x = t^3$ and $y = 9 - t^6$.

- If $x = t + 1$, $y = 9 - (t + 1)^2 = 9 - (t^2 + 2t + 1) = 8 - t^2 - 2t$.

  Parametric equations are $x = t + 1$ and $y = 8 - t^2 - 2t$.

- If $x = \dfrac{t}{2}$, $y = 9 - \left(\dfrac{t}{2}\right)^2 = 9 - \dfrac{t^2}{4}$.

  Parametric equations are $x = \dfrac{t}{2}$ and $y = 9 - \dfrac{t^2}{4}$.

Can you start with any choice for the parametric equation for $x$? The answer is no. **The substitution for $x$ must be a function that allows $x$ to take on all the values in the domain of the given rectangular equation.** For example, the domain of the function $y = 9 - x^2$ is the set of all real numbers. If you incorrectly let $x = t^2$, these values of $x$ exclude negative numbers that are included in $y = 9 - x^2$. The parametric equations

$$x = t^2 \quad \text{and} \quad y = 9 - (t^2)^2 = 9 - t^4$$

do not represent $y = 9 - x^2$ because only points for which $x \geq 0$ are obtained.

④ Understand the advantages of parametric representations.

## Advantages of Parametric Equations over Rectangular Equations

We opened this section with parametric equations that described the horizontal distance and the vertical height of your thrown baseball after $t$ seconds. Parametric equations are frequently used to represent the path of a moving object. If $t$

## Technology

The ellipse shown was obtained using the parametric mode and the radian mode of a graphing utility.

$$x(t) = 2 + 3 \cos t$$

$$y(t) = 3 + 2 \sin t$$

We used a $[-2, 6, 1]$ by $[-1, 6, 1]$ viewing rectangle with $t\text{min} = 0$, $t\text{max} = 6.2$, and $t\text{step} = 0.1$.

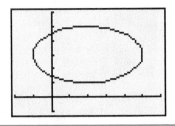

represents time, parametric equations give the location of a moving object and tell when the object is located at each of its positions. Rectangular equations tell where the moving object is located but do not reveal when the object is in a particular position.

When using technology to obtain graphs, parametric equations that represent relations that are not functions are often easier to use than their corresponding rectangular equations. It is far easier to enter the equation of an ellipse given by the parametric equations

$$x = 2 + 3 \cos t \quad \text{and} \quad y = 3 + 2 \sin t$$

than to use the rectangular equivalent

$$\frac{(x - 2)^2}{9} + \frac{(y - 3)^2}{4} = 1.$$

The rectangular equation must first be solved for $y$ and then entered as two separate equations before a graphing utility reveals the ellipse.

## The Parametrization of DNA

DNA, the molecule of biological inheritance, is hip. At least that's what a new breed of marketers would like you to believe. For $2500, you can spit into a test tube and a Web-based company will tell you your risks for heart attack and other conditions.

It's been more than 55 years since James Watson and Francis Crick defined the structure, or shape, of DNA. A knowledge of how a molecule is structured does not always lead to an understanding of how it works, but it did in the case of DNA. The structure, which Watson and Crick announced in *Nature* in 1953, immediately suggested how the molecule could be reproduced and how it could contain biological information.

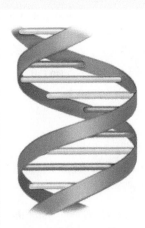

The DNA molecule, structured like a spiraled ladder, consists of two parallel helices (singular: helix) that are intertwined.

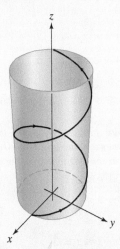

Each helix can be described by a curve in three dimensions represented by parametric equations in $x$, $y$, and $z$:
$x = a \cos t$, $y = a \sin t$, $z = bt$,
where $a$ and $b$ are positive constants.

The structure of the DNA molecule reveals the vital role that trigonometric functions play in the genetic information and instruction codes necessary for the maintenance and continuation of life.

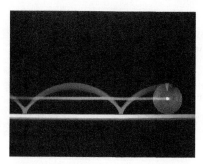

Linear functions and cycloids are used to describe rolling motion. The light at the rolling circle's center shows that it moves linearly. By contrast, the light at the circle's edge has rotational motion and traces out a cycloid.

A curve that is used in physics for much of the theory of light is called a **cycloid**. The path of a fixed point on the circumference of a circle as it rolls along a line is a cycloid. A point on the rim of a bicycle wheel traces out a cycloid curve, shown in **Figure 9.54**. If the radius of the circle is $a$, the parametric equations of the cycloid are

$$x = a(t - \sin t) \quad \text{and} \quad y = a(1 - \cos t).$$

It is an extremely complicated task to represent the cycloid in rectangular form.

Cycloids are used to solve problems that involve the "shortest time." For example, **Figure 9.55** shows a bead sliding down a wire. For the bead to travel along the wire in the shortest possible time, the shape of the wire should be that of an inverted cycloid.

**Figure 9.54** The curve traced by a fixed point on the circumference of a circle rolling along a straight line is a cycloid.

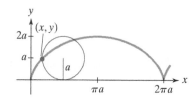

Figure 9.55

# Exercise Set 9.5

## Practice Exercises

*In Exercises 1–8, parametric equations and a value for the parameter t are given. Find the coordinates of the point on the plane curve described by the parametric equations corresponding to the given value of t.*

**1.** $x = 3 - 5t, y = 4 + 2t; t = 1$

**2.** $x = 7 - 4t, y = 5 + 6t; t = 1$

**3.** $x = t^2 + 1, y = 5 - t^3; t = 2$

**4.** $x = t^2 + 3, y = 6 - t^3; t = 2$

**5.** $x = 4 + 2\cos t, y = 3 + 5\sin t; t = \dfrac{\pi}{2}$

**6.** $x = 2 + 3\cos t, y = 4 + 2\sin t; t = \pi$

**7.** $x = (60\cos 30°)t, y = 5 + (60\sin 30°)t - 16t^2; t = 2$

**8.** $x = (80\cos 45°)t, y = 6 + (80\sin 45°)t - 16t^2; t = 2$

*In Exercises 9–20, use point plotting to graph the plane curve described by the given parametric equations. Use arrows to show the orientation of the curve corresponding to increasing values of t.*

**9.** $x = t + 2, y = t^2; -2 \le t \le 2$

**10.** $x = t - 1, y = t^2; -2 \le t \le 2$

**11.** $x = t - 2, y = 2t + 1; -2 \le t \le 3$

**12.** $x = t - 3, y = 2t + 2; -2 \le t \le 3$

**13.** $x = t + 1, y = \sqrt{t}; t \ge 0$

**14.** $x = \sqrt{t}, y = t - 1; t \ge 0$

**15.** $x = \cos t, y = \sin t; 0 \le t < 2\pi$

**16.** $x = -\sin t, y = -\cos t; 0 \le t < 2\pi$

**17.** $x = t^2, y = t^3; -\infty < t < \infty$

**18.** $x = t^2 + 1, y = t^3 - 1; -\infty < t < \infty$

**19.** $x = 2t, y = |t - 1|; -\infty < t < \infty$

**20.** $x = |t + 1|, y = t - 2; -\infty < t < \infty$

*In Exercises 21–40, eliminate the parameter t. Then use the rectangular equation to sketch the plane curve represented by the given parametric equations. Use arrows to show the orientation of the curve corresponding to increasing values of t. (If an interval for t is not specified, assume that $-\infty < t < \infty$.)*

**21.** $x = t, y = 2t$

**22.** $x = t, y = -2t$

**23.** $x = 2t - 4, y = 4t^2$

**24.** $x = t - 2, y = t^2$

**25.** $x = \sqrt{t}, y = t - 1$

**26.** $x = \sqrt{t}, y = t + 1$

**27.** $x = 2\sin t, y = 2\cos t; 0 \le t < 2\pi$

**28.** $x = 3\sin t, y = 3\cos t; 0 \le t < 2\pi$

**29.** $x = 1 + 3\cos t, y = 2 + 3\sin t; 0 \le t < 2\pi$

**30.** $x = -1 + 2\cos t, y = 1 + 2\sin t; 0 \le t < 2\pi$

**31.** $x = 2\cos t, y = 3\sin t; 0 \le t < 2\pi$

**32.** $x = 3\cos t, y = 5\sin t; 0 \le t < 2\pi$

**33.** $x = 1 + 3\cos t, y = -1 + 2\sin t; 0 \le t \le \pi$

**34.** $x = 2 + 4\cos t, y = -1 + 3\sin t; 0 \le t \le \pi$

**35.** $x = \sec t, y = \tan t$

**36.** $x = 5\sec t, y = 3\tan t$

**37.** $x = t^2 + 2, y = t^2 - 2$

**38.** $x = \sqrt{t} + 2, y = \sqrt{t} - 2$

**39.** $x = 2^t, y = 2^{-t}; t \ge 0$

**40.** $x = e^t, y = e^{-t}; t \ge 0$

*In Exercises 41–43, eliminate the parameter. Write the resulting equation in standard form.*

**41.** A circle: $x = h + r\cos t, y = k + r\sin t$

**42.** An ellipse: $x = h + a\cos t, y = k + b\sin t$

**43.** A hyperbola: $x = h + a\sec t, y = k + b\tan t$

**44.** The following are parametric equations of the line through $(x_1, y_1)$ and $(x_2, y_2)$:

$$x = x_1 + t(x_2 - x_1) \quad \text{and} \quad y = y_1 + t(y_2 - y_1).$$

Eliminate the parameter and write the resulting equation in point-slope form.

*In Exercises 45–52, use your answers from Exercises 41–44 and the parametric equations given in Exercises 41–44 to find a set of parametric equations for the conic section or the line.*

**45.** Circle: Center: $(3, 5)$; Radius: 6

**46.** Circle: Center: $(4, 6)$; Radius: 9

**47.** Ellipse: Center: $(-2, 3)$; Vertices: 5 units to the left and right of the center; Endpoints of Minor Axis: 2 units above and below the center

**48.** Ellipse: Center: $(4, -1)$; Vertices: 5 units above and below the center; Endpoints of Minor Axis: 3 units to the left and right of the center

**49.** Hyperbola: Vertices: $(4, 0)$ and $(-4, 0)$; Foci: $(6, 0)$ and $(-6, 0)$

**50.** Hyperbola: Vertices: $(0, 4)$ and $(0, -4)$; Foci: $(0, 5)$ and $(0, -5)$

**51.** Line: Passes through $(-2, 4)$ and $(1, 7)$

**52.** Line: Passes through $(3, -1)$ and $(9, 12)$

*In Exercises 53–56, find two different sets of parametric equations for each rectangular equation.*

**53.** $y = 4x - 3$       **54.** $y = 2x - 5$

**55.** $y = x^2 + 4$       **56.** $y = x^2 - 3$

*In Exercises 57–58, the parametric equations of four plane curves are given. Graph each plane curve and determine how they differ from each other.*

**57.** **a.** $x = t$ and $y = t^2 - 4$

     **b.** $x = t^2$ and $y = t^4 - 4$

     **c.** $x = \cos t$ and $y = \cos^2 t - 4$

     **d.** $x = e^t$ and $y = e^{2t} - 4$

**58.** **a.** $x = t, y = \sqrt{4 - t^2}; -2 \le t \le 2$

     **b.** $x = \sqrt{4 - t^2}, y = t; -2 \le t \le 2$

     **c.** $x = 2 \sin t, y = 2 \cos t; 0 \le t < 2\pi$

     **d.** $x = 2 \cos t, y = 2 \sin t; 0 \le t < 2\pi$

## Practice Plus

*In Exercises 59–62, sketch the plane curve represented by the given parametric equations. Then use interval notation to give each relation's domain and range.*

**59.** $x = 4 \cos t + 2, y = 4 \cos t - 1$

**60.** $x = 2 \sin t - 3, y = 2 \sin t + 1$

**61.** $x = t^2 + t + 1, y = 2t$

**62.** $x = t^2 - t + 6, y = 3t$

*In Exercises 63–68, sketch the function represented by the given parametric equations. Then use the graph to determine each of the following:*

     **a.** *intervals, if any, on which the function is increasing and intervals, if any, on which the function is decreasing.*

     **b.** *the number, if any, at which the function has a maximum and this maximum value, or the number, if any, at which the function has a minimum and this minimum value.*

**63.** $x = 2^t, y = t$       **64.** $x = e^t, y = t$

**65.** $x = \dfrac{t}{2}, y = 2t^2 - 8t + 3$    **66.** $x = \dfrac{t}{2}, y = -2t^2 + 8t - 1$

**67.** $x = 2(t - \sin t), y = 2(1 - \cos t); 0 \le t \le 2\pi$

**68.** $x = 3(t - \sin t), y = 3(1 - \cos t); 0 \le t \le 2\pi$

## Application Exercises

*The path of a projectile that is launched h feet above the ground with an initial velocity of $v_0$ feet per second and at an angle $\theta$ with the horizontal is given by the parametric equations*

$$x = (v_0 \cos \theta)t \quad \text{and} \quad y = h + (v_0 \sin \theta)t - 16t^2,$$

*where t is the time, in seconds, after the projectile was launched. The parametric equation for x gives the projectile's horizontal distance, in feet. The parametric equation for y gives the projectile's height, in feet. Use these parametric equations to solve Exercises 69–70.*

**69.** The figure shows the path for a baseball hit by Derek Jeter. The ball was hit with an initial velocity of 180 feet per second at an angle of 40° to the horizontal. The ball was hit at a height 3 feet off the ground.

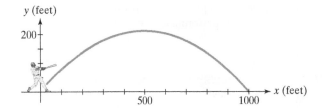

     **a.** Find the parametric equations that describe the position of the ball as a function of time.

     **b.** Describe the ball's position after 1, 2, and 3 seconds. Round to the nearest tenth of a foot. Locate your solutions on the plane curve.

     **c.** How long, to the nearest tenth of a second, is the ball in flight? What is the total horizontal distance that it travels before it lands? Is your answer consistent with the figure shown?

     **d.** You meet Derek Jeter and he asks you to tell him something interesting about the path of the baseball that he hit. Use the graph to respond to his request. Then verify your observation algebraically.

**70.** The figure shows the path for a baseball that was hit with an initial velocity of 150 feet per second at an angle of 35° to the horizontal. The ball was hit at a height of 3 feet off the ground.

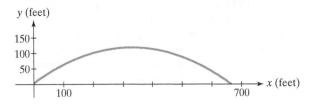

     **a.** Find the parametric equations that describe the position of the ball as a function of time.

     **b.** Describe the ball's position after 1, 2, and 3 seconds. Round to the nearest tenth of a foot. Locate your solutions on the plane curve.

**c.** How long is the ball in flight? (Round to the nearest tenth of a second.) What is the total horizontal distance that it travels, to the nearest tenth of a foot, before it lands? Is your answer consistent with the figure shown at the bottom of the previous page?

**d.** Use the graph on the previous page to describe something about the path of the baseball that might be of interest to the player who hit the ball. Then verify your observation algebraically.

## Writing in Mathematics

**71.** What are plane curves and parametric equations?

**72.** How is point plotting used to graph a plane curve described by parametric equations? Give an example with your description.

**73.** What is the significance of arrows along a plane curve?

**74.** What does it mean to eliminate the parameter? What useful information can be obtained by doing this?

**75.** Explain how the rectangular equation $y = 5x$ can have infinitely many sets of parametric equations.

**76.** Discuss how the parametric equations for the path of a projectile (see Exercises 69–70) and the ability to obtain plane curves with a graphing utility can be used by a baseball coach to analyze performances of team players.

## Technology Exercises

**77.** Use a graphing utility in a parametric mode to verify any five of your hand-drawn graphs in Exercises 9–40.

*In Exercises 78–82, use a graphing utility to obtain the plane curve represented by the given parametric equations.*

**78.** Cycloid: $x = 3(t - \sin t)$, $y = 3(1 - \cos t)$;
$[0, 60, 5] \times [0, 8, 1]$, $0 \leq t < 6\pi$

**79.** Cycloid: $x = 2(t - \sin t)$, $y = 2(1 - \cos t)$;
$[0, 60, 5] \times [0, 8, 1]$, $0 \leq t < 6\pi$

**80.** Witch of Agnesi: $x = 2 \cot t$, $y = 2 \sin^2 t$;
$[-6, 6, 1] \times [-4, 4, 1]$, $0 \leq t < 2\pi$

**81.** Hypocycloid: $x = 4 \cos^3 t$, $y = 4 \sin^3 t$;
$[-5, 5, 1] \times [-5, 5, 1]$, $0 \leq t < 2\pi$

**82.** Lissajous Curve: $x = 2 \cos t$, $y = \sin 2t$;
$[-3, 3, 1] \times [-2, 2, 1]$, $0 \leq t < 2\pi$

*Use the equations for the path of a projectile given prior to Exercises 69–70 to solve Exercises 83–85.*

*In Exercises 83–84, use a graphing utility to obtain the path of a projectile launched from the ground ($h = 0$) at the specified values of $\theta$ and $v_0$. In each exercise, use the graph to determine the maximum height and the time at which the projectile reaches its maximum height. Also use the graph to determine the range of the projectile and the time it hits the ground. Round all answers to the nearest tenth.*

**83.** $\theta = 55°$, $v_0 = 200$ feet per second

**84.** $\theta = 35°$, $v_0 = 300$ feet per second

**85.** A baseball player throws a ball with an initial velocity of 140 feet per second at an angle of 22° to the horizontal. The ball leaves the player's hand at a height of 5 feet.

**a.** Write the parametric equations that describe the ball's position as a function of time.

**b.** Use a graphing utility to obtain the path of the baseball.

**c.** Find the ball's maximum height and the time at which it reaches this height. Round all answers to the nearest tenth.

**d.** How long is the ball in the air?

**e.** How far does the ball travel?

## Critical Thinking Exercises

**Make Sense?** *In Exercises 86–89, determine whether each statement makes sense or does not make sense, and explain your reasoning.*

**86.** Parametric equations allow me to use functions to describe curves that are not graphs of functions.

**87.** Parametric equations let me think of a curve as a path traced out by a moving point.

**88.** I represented $y = x^2 - 9$ with the parametric equations $x = t^2$ and $y = t^4 - 9$.

**89.** I found alternate pairs of parametric equations for the same rectangular equation.

**90.** Eliminate the parameter: $x = \cos^3 t$ and $y = \sin^3 t$.

**91.** The plane curve described by the parametric equations $x = 3 \cos t$ and $y = 3 \sin t$, $0 \leq t < 2\pi$, has a counterclockwise orientation. Alter one or both parametric equations so that you obtain the same plane curve with the opposite orientation.

**92.** The figure shows a circle of radius $a$ rolling along a horizontal line. Point $P$ traces out a cycloid. Angle $t$, in radians, is the angle through which the circle has rolled. $C$ is the center of the circle.

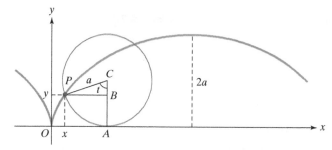

Use the suggestions in parts (a) and (b) to prove that the parametric equations of the cycloid are $x = a(t - \sin t)$ and $y = a(1 - \cos t)$.

**a.** Derive the parametric equation for $x$ using the figure and
$$x = OA - xA.$$

**b.** Derive the parametric equation for $y$ using the figure and
$$y = AC - BC.$$

## Preview Exercises

*Exercises 93–95 will help you prepare for the material covered in the next section.*

**93.** Rewrite $r = \dfrac{4}{2 + \cos \theta}$ by dividing the numerator and the denominator by 2.

**94.** Complete the table of coordinates at the top of the next page. Where necessary, round to two decimal places. Then plot the resulting points, $(r, \theta)$, using a polar coordinate system.

| $\theta$ | 0 | $\dfrac{\pi}{2}$ | $\dfrac{2\pi}{3}$ | $\dfrac{3\pi}{4}$ | $\dfrac{5\pi}{6}$ | $\pi$ |
|---|---|---|---|---|---|---|
| $r = \dfrac{4}{2 + \cos\theta}$ | | | | | | |

**95. a.** Showing all steps, rewrite $r = \dfrac{1}{3 - 3\cos\theta}$ as $9r^2 = (1 + 3r\cos\theta)^2$.

**b.** Express $9r^2 = (1 + 3r\cos\theta)^2$ in rectangular coordinates. Which conic section is represented by the rectangular equation?

Section 9.6

# Conic Sections in Polar Coordinates

## Objectives

**1** Define conics in terms of a focus and a directrix.

**2** Graph the polar equations of conics.

John Glenn made the first U.S.-manned flight around Earth on *Friendship 7*.

On the morning of February 20, 1962, millions of Americans collectively held their breath as the world's newest pioneer swept across the threshold of one of our last frontiers. Roughly one hundred miles above Earth, astronaut John Glenn sat comfortably in the weightless environment of a $9\frac{1}{2}$-by-6-foot space capsule that offered the leg room of a Volkswagen "Beetle" and the aesthetics of a garbage can. Glenn became the first American to orbit Earth in a three-orbit mission that lasted slightly under 5 hours.

In this section's exercise set, you will see how John Glenn's historic orbit can be described using conic sections in polar coordinates. To obtain this model, we begin with a definition that permits a unified approach to the conic sections.

**1** Define conics in terms of a focus and a directrix.

## The Focus-Directrix Definitions of the Conic Sections

The definition of a parabola is given in terms of a fixed point, the focus, and a fixed line, the directrix. By contrast, the definitions of an ellipse and a hyperbola are given in terms of two fixed points, the foci. It is possible to define each of these conic sections in terms of a point and a line. **Figure 9.56** shows a conic section in the polar coordinate system. The fixed point, the focus, is at the pole. The fixed line, the directrix, is perpendicular to the polar axis.

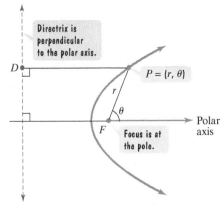

Figure 9.56   A conic in the polar coordinate system

### Focus-Directrix Definitions of the Conic Sections

Let $F$ be a fixed point, the focus, and let $D$ be a fixed line, the directrix, in a plane (**Figure 9.56**). A **conic section**, or **conic**, is the set of all points $P$ in the plane such that

$$\frac{PF}{PD} = e,$$

where $e$ is a fixed positive number, called the **eccentricity**.

If $e = 1$, the conic is a parabola.

If $e < 1$, the conic is an ellipse.

If $e > 1$, the conic is a hyperbola.

**Figure 9.57** illustrates the eccentricity for each type of conic. Notice that if $e = 1$, the definition of the parabola is the same as the focus-directrix definition with which you are familiar.

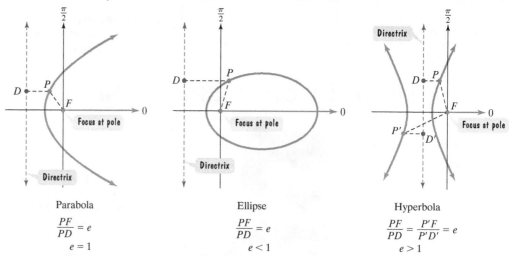

Parabola

$$\frac{PF}{PD} = e$$

$$e = 1$$

Ellipse

$$\frac{PF}{PD} = e$$

$$e < 1$$

Hyperbola

$$\frac{PF}{PD} = \frac{P'F}{P'D'} = e$$

$$e > 1$$

**Figure 9.57** The eccentricity for each conic

② Graph the polar equations of conics.

## Polar Equations of Conics

By locating a focus at the pole, all conics can be represented by similar equations in the polar coordinate system. In each of these equations,

- $(r, \theta)$ is a point on the graph of the conic.
- $e$ is the eccentricity. (Remember that $e > 0$.)
- $p$ is the distance between the focus (located at the pole) and the directrix.

## Standard Forms of the Polar Equations of Conics

Let the pole be a focus of a conic section of eccentricity $e$ with the directrix $p$ units from the focus. The equation of the conic is given by one of the four equations listed.

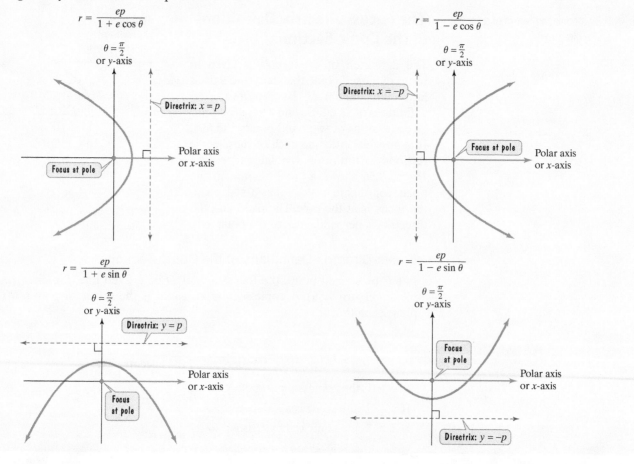

The graphs in the box illustrate two kinds of symmetry—symmetry with respect to the polar axis and symmetry with respect to the $y$-axis. If the equation contains $\cos \theta$, the polar axis is an axis of symmetry. If the equation contains $\sin \theta$, the line $\theta = \frac{\pi}{2}$, or the $y$-axis, is an axis of symmetry. Take a moment to verify these observations.

We will derive one of the equations displayed in the previous box. The other three equations are obtained in a similar manner. In **Figure 9.58**, let $P = (r, \theta)$ be any point on a conic section.

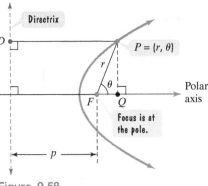

**Figure 9.58**

$$\frac{PF}{PD} = e \qquad \text{By definition, the ratio of the distance between } P \text{ and the focus to the distance between } P \text{ and the directrix equals the positive constant } e.$$

$$\frac{r}{PD} = e \qquad \text{Figure 9.58 shows that the distance from } P \text{ to the focus, located at the pole, is } r\text{: } PF = r.$$

$$\frac{r}{p + FQ} = e \qquad \text{Figure 9.58 shows that the distance from } P \text{ to the directrix is } p + FQ\text{: } PD = p + FQ.$$

$$\frac{r}{p + r \cos \theta} = e \qquad \text{Using the triangle in the figure, } \cos \theta = \frac{FQ}{r} \text{ and } FQ = r \cos \theta.$$

By solving this equation for $r$, we will obtain the desired equation. Clear fractions by multiplying both sides by the least common denominator.

$$r = e(p + r \cos \theta) \qquad \text{Multiply both sides by } p + r \cos \theta.$$

$$r = ep + er \cos \theta \qquad \text{Apply the distributive property.}$$

$$r - er \cos \theta = ep \qquad \text{Subtract } er \cos \theta \text{ from both sides to collect terms involving } r \text{ on the same side.}$$

$$r(1 - e \cos \theta) = ep \qquad \text{Factor out } r \text{ from the two terms on the left.}$$

$$r = \frac{ep}{1 - e \cos \theta} \qquad \text{Divide both sides by } 1 - e \cos \theta \text{ and solve for } r.$$

In summary, the standard forms of the polar equations of conics are

$$r = \frac{ep}{1 \pm e \cos \theta} \quad \text{and} \quad r = \frac{ep}{1 \pm e \sin \theta}.$$

In all forms, the constant term in the denominator is 1.

### Graphing the Polar Equation of a Conic

1. If necessary, write the equation in one of the standard forms.
2. Use the standard form to determine values for $e$ and $p$. Use the value of $e$ to identify the conic.
3. Use the appropriate figure for the standard form of the equation shown in the box on page 936 to help guide the graphing process.

**EXAMPLE 1** Graphing the Polar Equation of a Conic

Graph the polar equation:

$$r = \frac{4}{2 + \cos \theta}.$$

## Solution

**Step 1  Write the equation in one of the standard forms.** The equation is not in standard form because the constant term in the denominator is not 1.

$$r = \frac{4}{2 + \cos \theta}$$

To obtain 1 in this position, divide the numerator and denominator by 2.

The equation in standard form is

$$r = \frac{2}{1 + \frac{1}{2} \cos \theta}.$$

$ep = 2$

$e = \frac{1}{2}$

This equation is in the form $r = \dfrac{ep}{1 + e \cos \theta}$.

**Step 2  Use the standard form to find e and p, and identify the conic.** The voice balloons show that

$$e = \tfrac{1}{2} \quad \text{and} \quad ep = \tfrac{1}{2}p = 2.$$

Thus, $e = \tfrac{1}{2}$ and $p = 4$. Because $e = \tfrac{1}{2} < 1$, the conic is an ellipse.

**Step 3  Use the figure for the equation's standard form to guide the graphing process.** The figure for the conic's standard form is shown in **Figure 9.59(a)**. We have symmetry with respect to the polar axis. One focus is at the pole and the corresponding directrix is $x = 4$, located four units to the right of the pole.

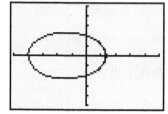
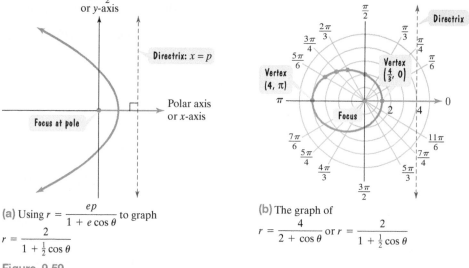

(a) Using $r = \dfrac{ep}{1 + e \cos \theta}$ to graph
$r = \dfrac{2}{1 + \frac{1}{2} \cos \theta}$

(b) The graph of
$r = \dfrac{4}{2 + \cos \theta}$ or $r = \dfrac{2}{1 + \frac{1}{2} \cos \theta}$

**Figure 9.59**

**Figure 9.59(a)** indicates that the major axis is on the polar axis. Thus, we find the vertices by selecting 0 and $\pi$ for $\theta$. The corresponding values for $r$ are $\tfrac{4}{3}$ and 4, respectively. **Figure 9.59(b)** shows the vertices, $\left(\tfrac{4}{3}, 0\right)$ and $(4, \pi)$.

You can sketch the upper half of the ellipse by plotting some points from $\theta = 0$ to $\theta = \pi$.

$$r = \frac{4}{2 + \cos \theta}$$

| $\theta$ | $\dfrac{\pi}{2}$ | $\dfrac{2\pi}{3}$ | $\dfrac{3\pi}{4}$ | $\dfrac{5\pi}{6}$ |
|---|---|---|---|---|
| $r$ | 2 | 2.7 | 3.1 | 3.5 |

Using symmetry with respect to the polar axis, you can sketch the lower half. The graph of the given equation is shown in **Figure 9.59(b)**.

⊘ Check Point **I** Use the three steps shown in the box on page 937 to graph the polar equation:

$$r = \frac{4}{2 - \cos \theta}.$$

(EXAMPLE 2) **Graphing the Polar Equation of a Conic**

Graph the polar equation:

$$r = \frac{12}{3 + 3 \sin \theta}.$$

**Solution**

**Step 1  Write the equation in one of the standard forms.** The equation is not in standard form because the constant term in the denominator is not 1. Divide the numerator and denominator by 3 to write the standard form.

$$r = \frac{4}{1 + 1 \sin \theta}$$

ep = 4

e = 1

This equation is in the form $r = \dfrac{ep}{1 + e \sin \theta}$.

**Step 2  Use the standard form to find $e$ and $p$, and identify the conic.** The voice balloons show that

$$e = 1 \quad \text{and} \quad ep = 1p = 4.$$

Thus, $e = 1$ and $p = 4$. Because $e = 1$, the conic is a parabola.

**Step 3  Use the figure for the equation's standard form to guide the graphing process. Figure 9.60(a)** indicates that we have symmetry with respect to $\theta = \dfrac{\pi}{2}$. The focus is at the pole and, with $p = 4$, the directrix is $y = 4$, located four units above the pole.

**Figure 9.60(a)** indicates that the vertex is on the line of $\theta = \dfrac{\pi}{2}$, or the $y$-axis. Thus, we find the vertex by selecting $\dfrac{\pi}{2}$ for $\theta$. The corresponding value for $r$ is 2. **Figure 9.60(b)** shows the vertex, $\left(2, \dfrac{\pi}{2}\right)$.

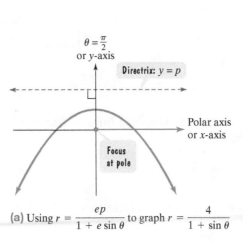

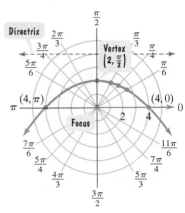

(a) Using $r = \dfrac{ep}{1 + e \sin \theta}$ to graph $r = \dfrac{4}{1 + \sin \theta}$

(b) The graph of $r = \dfrac{12}{3 + 3 \sin \theta}$ or $r = \dfrac{4}{1 + \sin \theta}$

**Figure 9.60**

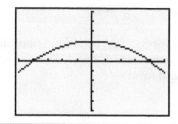
To find where the parabola crosses the polar axis, select $\theta = 0$ and $\theta = \pi$. The corresponding values for $r$ are 4 and 4, respectively. **Figure 9.60(b)** shows the points $(4, 0)$ and $(4, \pi)$ on the polar axis.

You can sketch the right half of the parabola by plotting some points from $\theta = 0$ to $\theta = \frac{\pi}{2}$.

$$r = \frac{12}{3 + 3 \sin \theta}$$

| $\theta$ | $\dfrac{\pi}{6}$ | $\dfrac{\pi}{4}$ | $\dfrac{\pi}{3}$ |
|---|---|---|---|
| $r$ | 2.7 | 2.3 | 2.1 |

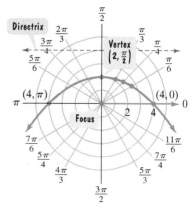

Figure 9.60(b) (repeated) The graph of $r = \dfrac{12}{3 + 3 \sin \theta}$ or $r = \dfrac{4}{1 + \sin \theta}$

Using symmetry with respect to $\theta = \dfrac{\pi}{2}$, you can sketch the left half. The graph of the given equation is shown in **Figure 9.60(b)**.

⏺ Check Point **2**  Use the three steps shown in the box on page 937 to graph the polar equation:

$$r = \frac{8}{4 + 4 \sin \theta}.$$

( EXAMPLE 3 )  **Graphing the Polar Equation of a Conic**

Graph the polar equation:

$$r = \frac{9}{3 - 6 \cos \theta}.$$

**Solution**

**Step 1  Write the equation in one of the standard forms.** We can obtain a constant term of 1 in the denominator by dividing each term by 3.

$$\underbrace{r = \frac{3}{1 - 2 \cos \theta}}_{}$$

$ep = 3$ · · · $e = 2$

This equation is in the form $r = \dfrac{ep}{1 - e \cos \theta}$.

**Step 2  Use the standard form to find $e$ and $p$, and identify the conic.** The voice balloons show that

$$e = 2 \quad \text{and} \quad ep = 2p = 3.$$

Thus, $e = 2$ and $p = \frac{3}{2}$. Because $e = 2 > 1$, the conic is a hyperbola.

**Step 3    Use the figure for the equation's standard form to guide the graphing process. Figure 9.61(a)** indicates that we have symmetry with respect to the polar axis. One focus is at the pole and, with $p = \frac{3}{2}$, the corresponding directrix is $x = -\frac{3}{2}$, located 1.5 units to the left of the pole.

**Figure 9.61(a)** indicates that the transverse axis is horizontal and the vertices lie on the polar axis. Thus, we find the vertices by selecting $0$ and $\pi$ for $\theta$. **Figure 9.61(b)** shows the vertices, $(-3, 0)$ and $(1, \pi)$.

To find where the hyperbola crosses the line $\theta = \frac{\pi}{2}$, select $\frac{\pi}{2}$ and $\frac{3\pi}{2}$ for $\theta$. **Figure 9.61(b)** shows the points $\left(3, \frac{\pi}{2}\right)$ and $\left(3, \frac{3\pi}{2}\right)$ on the graph.

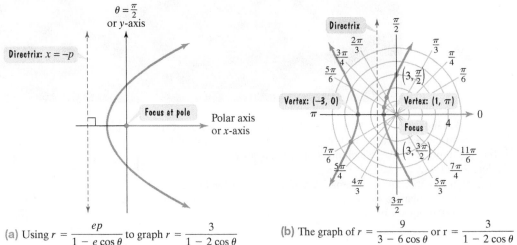

Figure 9.61    (a) Using $r = \dfrac{ep}{1 - e\cos\theta}$ to graph $r = \dfrac{3}{1 - 2\cos\theta}$    (b) The graph of $r = \dfrac{9}{3 - 6\cos\theta}$ or r $= \dfrac{3}{1 - 2\cos\theta}$

We sketch the hyperbola by plotting some points from $\theta = 0$ to $\theta = \pi$.

$$r = \frac{3}{1 - 2\cos\theta}$$

| $\theta$ | $\dfrac{\pi}{6}$ | $\dfrac{2\pi}{3}$ | $\dfrac{5\pi}{6}$ |
|---|---|---|---|
| $r$ | $-4.1$ | $1.5$ | $1.1$ |

**Figure 9.61(b)** shows the points $\left(\dfrac{\pi}{6}, -4.1\right)$, $\left(\dfrac{2\pi}{3}, 1.5\right)$, and $\left(\dfrac{5\pi}{6}, 1.1\right)$ on the graph. Observe that $\left(\dfrac{\pi}{6}, -4.1\right)$ is on the lower half of the hyperbola. Using symmetry with respect to the polar axis, we sketch the entire lower half. The graph of the given equation is shown in **Figure 9.61(b)**. ●

⊘ Check Point **3**    Use the three steps shown in the box on page 937 to graph the polar equation:

$$r = \frac{9}{3 - 9\cos\theta}.$$

# Modeling Planetary Motion

Polish astronomer Nicolaus Copernicus (1473–1543) was correct in stating that planets in our solar system revolve around the sun and not Earth. However, he incorrectly believed that celestial orbits move in perfect circles, calling his system "the ballet of the planets."

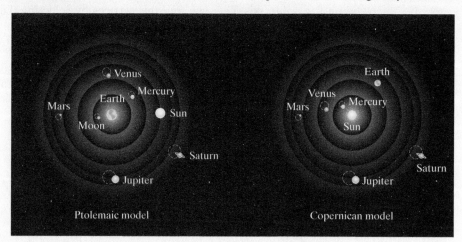

Ptolemaic model    Copernican model

Table **9.4** indicates that the planets in our solar system have orbits with eccentricities that are much closer to 0 than to 1. Most of these orbits are almost circular, which made it difficult for early astronomers to detect that they are actually ellipses.

German scientist and mathematician Johannes Kepler (1571–1630) discovered that planets move in elliptical orbits with the sun at one focus. The polar equation for these orbits is

$$r = \frac{(1 - e^2)a}{1 - e \cos \theta},$$

where the length of the orbit's major axis is $2a$. Describing planetary orbits, Kepler wrote, "The heavenly motions are nothing but a continuous song for several voices, to be perceived by the intellect, not by the ear."

**Table 9.4   Eccentricities of Planetary Orbits**

| Mercury | 0.2056 | Jupiter | 0.0484 |
|---------|--------|---------|--------|
| Venus | 0.0068 | Saturn | 0.0543 |
| Earth | 0.0167 | Uranus | 0.0460 |
| Mars | 0.0934 | Neptune | 0.0082 |

# Exercise Set 9.6

## Practice Exercises

*In Exercises 1–8,*

   **a.** *Identify the conic section that each polar equation represents.*

   **b.** *Describe the location of a directrix from the focus located at the pole.*

**1.** $r = \dfrac{3}{1 + \sin \theta}$        **2.** $r = \dfrac{3}{1 + \cos \theta}$

**3.** $r = \dfrac{6}{3 - 2 \cos \theta}$      **4.** $r = \dfrac{6}{3 + 2 \cos \theta}$

**5.** $r = \dfrac{8}{2 + 2 \sin \theta}$      **6.** $r = \dfrac{8}{2 - 2 \sin \theta}$

**7.** $r = \dfrac{12}{2 - 4 \cos \theta}$     **8.** $r = \dfrac{12}{2 + 4 \cos \theta}$

*In Exercises 9–20, use the three steps shown in the box on page 937 to graph each polar equation.*

**9.** $r = \dfrac{1}{1 + \sin \theta}$       **10.** $r = \dfrac{1}{1 + \cos \theta}$

**11.** $r = \dfrac{2}{1 - \cos \theta}$      **12.** $r = \dfrac{2}{1 - \sin \theta}$

**13.** $r = \dfrac{12}{5 + 3 \cos \theta}$     **14.** $r = \dfrac{12}{5 - 3 \cos \theta}$

**15.** $r = \dfrac{6}{2 - 2 \sin \theta}$     **16.** $r = \dfrac{6}{2 + 2 \sin \theta}$

**17.** $r = \dfrac{8}{2 - 4 \cos \theta}$     **18.** $r = \dfrac{8}{2 + 4 \cos \theta}$

**19.** $r = \dfrac{12}{3 - 6 \cos \theta}$     **20.** $r = \dfrac{12}{3 - 3 \cos \theta}$

## Practice Plus

*In Exercises 21–28, describe a viewing rectangle, or window, such as $[-30, 30, 3]$ by $[-8, 4, 1]$, that shows a complete graph of each polar equation and minimizes unused portions of the screen.*

**21.** $r = \dfrac{15}{3 - 2 \cos \theta}$     **22.** $r = \dfrac{16}{5 - 3 \cos \theta}$

**23.** $r = \dfrac{8}{1 - \cos \theta}$

**24.** $r = \dfrac{8}{1 + \cos \theta}$

**25.** $r = \dfrac{4}{1 + 3 \cos \theta}$

**26.** $r = \dfrac{16}{3 + 5 \cos \theta}$

**27.** $r = \dfrac{4}{5 + 5 \sin \theta}$

**28.** $r = \dfrac{2}{3 + 3 \sin \theta}$

## Application Exercises

*Halley's Comet has an elliptical orbit with the sun at one focus. Its orbit, shown in the figure below, is given approximately by*

$$r = \frac{1.069}{1 + 0.967 \sin \theta}.$$

*In the formula, r is measured in astronomical units. (One astronomical unit is the average distance from Earth to the sun, approximately 93 million miles.) Use the given formula and the figure to solve Exercises 29–30. Round to the nearest hundredth of an astronomical unit and the nearest million miles.*

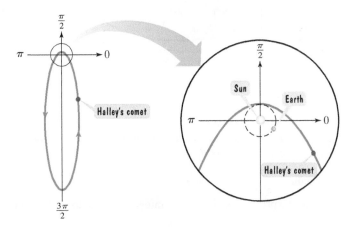

**29.** Find the distance from Halley's Comet to the sun at its shortest distance from the sun.

**30.** Find the distance from Halley's Comet to the sun at its greatest distance from the sun.

*On February 20, 1962, John Glenn made the first U.S.-manned flight around the Earth for three orbits on Friendship 7. With Earth at one focus, the orbit of Friendship 7 is given approximately by*

$$r = \frac{4090.76}{1 - 0.0076 \cos \theta},$$

*where r is measured in miles from Earth's center. Use the formula and the figure shown to solve Exercises 31–32.*

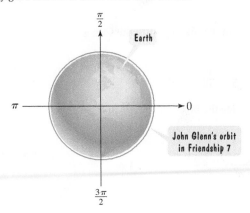

**31.** How far from Earth's center was John Glenn at his greatest distance from the planet? Round to the nearest mile. If the radius of Earth is 3960 miles, how far was he from Earth's surface at this point on the flight?

**32.** How far from Earth's center was John Glenn at his closest distance from the planet? Round to the nearest mile. If the radius of Earth is 3960 miles, how far was he from Earth's surface at this point on the flight?

## Writing in Mathematics

**33.** How are the conics described in terms of a fixed point and a fixed line?

**34.** If all conics are defined in terms of a fixed point and a fixed line, how can you tell one kind of conic from another?

**35.** If you are given the standard form of the polar equation of a conic, how do you determine its eccentricity?

**36.** If you are given the standard form of the polar equation of a conic, how do you determine the location of a directrix from the focus at the pole?

**37.** Describe a strategy for graphing $r = \dfrac{1}{1 + \sin \theta}$.

**38.** You meet John Glenn and he asks you to tell him something of interest about the elliptical orbit of his first space voyage in 1962. Describe how to use the polar equation for orbits in the essay on page 942, the equation for his 1962 journey in Exercises 31–32, and a graphing utility to provide him with an interesting visual analysis.

## Technology Exercises

*Use the polar mode of a graphing utility with angle measure in radians to solve Exercises 39–42. Unless otherwise indicated, use $\theta$min = 0, $\theta$max = $2\pi$, and $\theta$ step = $\dfrac{\pi}{48}$. If you are not satisfied with the quality of the graph, experiment with smaller values for $\theta$ step.*

**39.** Use a graphing utility to verify any five of your hand-drawn graphs in Exercises 9–20.

*In Exercises 40–42, identify the conic that each polar equation represents. Then use a graphing utility to graph the equation.*

**40.** $r = \dfrac{16}{4 - 3 \cos \theta}$

**41.** $r = \dfrac{12}{4 + 5 \sin \theta}$

**42.** $r = \dfrac{18}{6 - 6 \cos \theta}$

*In Exercises 43–44, use a graphing utility to graph the equation. Then answer the given question.*

**43.** $r = \dfrac{4}{1 - \sin\left(\theta - \dfrac{\pi}{4}\right)}$; How does the graph differ from the graph of $r = \dfrac{4}{1 - \sin \theta}$?

**44.** $r = \dfrac{3}{2 + 6 \cos\left(\theta + \dfrac{\pi}{3}\right)}$; How does the graph differ from the graph of $r = \dfrac{3}{2 + 6 \cos \theta}$?

**45.** Use the polar equation for planetary orbits,

$$r = \frac{(1 - e^2)a}{1 - e \cos \theta},$$

to find the polar equation of the orbit for Mercury and Earth.

Mercury: $e = 0.2056$ and $a = 36.0 \times 10^6$ miles

Earth: $e = 0.0167$ and $a = 92.96 \times 10^6$ miles

Use a graphing utility to graph both orbits in the same viewing rectangle. What do you see about the orbits from their graphs that is not obvious from their equations?

## Critical Thinking Exercises

**Make Sense?** *In Exercises 46–49, determine whether each statement makes sense or does not make sense, and explain your reasoning.*

**46.** Eccentricity and polar coordinates enable me to see that ellipses, hyperbolas, and parabolas are a unified group of interrelated curves.

**47.** I graphed a conic in the form $r = \dfrac{ep}{1 - e \cos \theta}$ that was symmetric with respect to the $y$-axis.

**48.** Given the focus is at the pole, I can write the polar equation of a conic section if I know its eccentricity and the rectangular equation of the directrix.

**49.** As long as I know how to graph in polar coordinates, a knowledge of conic sections is not necessary to graph the equations in Exercises 9–20.

**50.** Identify the conic and graph the equation:

$$r = \frac{4 \sec \theta}{2 \sec \theta - 1}.$$

*In Exercises 51–52, write a polar equation of the conic that is named and described.*

**51.** Ellipse: a focus at the pole; vertex: $(4, 0)$; $e = \frac{1}{2}$

**52.** Hyperbola: a focus at the pole; directrix: $x = -1$; $e = \frac{3}{2}$

**53.** Identify the conic and write its equation in rectangular coordinates: $r = \dfrac{1}{2 - 2 \cos \theta}$.

**54.** Prove that the polar equation of a planet's elliptical orbit is

$$r = \frac{(1 - e^2)a}{1 - e \cos \theta},$$

where $e$ is the eccentricity and $2a$ is the length of the major axis.

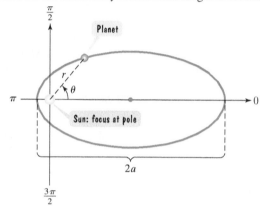

## Preview Exercises

*Exercises 55–57 will help you prepare for the material covered in the first section of the next chapter.*

**55.** Evaluate $\dfrac{(-1)^n}{3^n - 1}$ for $n = 1, 2, 3,$ and $4$.

**56.** Find the product of all positive integers from $n$ down through 1 for $n = 5$.

**57.** Evaluate $i^2 + 1$ for all consecutive integers from 1 to 6, inclusive. Then find the sum of the six evaluations.

# Chapter 9 Summary, Review, and Test

## Summary

| **DEFINITIONS AND CONCEPTS** | **EXAMPLES** |
|---|---|

### 9.1 The Ellipse

**a.** An ellipse is the set of all points in a plane the sum of whose distances from two fixed points, the foci, is constant.

| | |
|---|---|
| **b.** Standard forms of the equations of an ellipse with center at the origin are $\dfrac{x^2}{a^2} + \dfrac{y^2}{b^2} = 1$ [foci: $(-c, 0), (c, 0)$] and $\dfrac{x^2}{b^2} + \dfrac{y^2}{a^2} = 1$ [foci: $(0, -c), (0, c)$], where $c^2 = a^2 - b^2$ and $a^2 > b^2$. See the box on page 876 and Figure 9.6. | Ex. 1, p. 876; Ex. 2, p. 877; Ex. 3, p. 878 |
| **c.** Standard forms of the equations of an ellipse centered at $(h, k)$ are $\dfrac{(x - h)^2}{a^2} + \dfrac{(y - k)^2}{b^2} = 1$ and $\dfrac{(x - h)^2}{b^2} + \dfrac{(y - k)^2}{a^2} = 1, a^2 > b^2$. See Table 9.1 on page 879. | Ex. 4, p. 880 |

**DEFINITIONS AND CONCEPTS**                                                                    **EXAMPLES**

## 9.2   The Hyperbola

**a.** A hyperbola is the set of all points in a plane the difference of whose distances from two fixed points, the foci, is constant.

**b.** Standard forms of the equations of a hyperbola with center at the origin are $\dfrac{x^2}{a^2} - \dfrac{y^2}{b^2} = 1$ [foci: $(-c, 0)$, $(c, 0)$] and $\dfrac{y^2}{a^2} - \dfrac{x^2}{b^2} = 1$ [foci: $(0, -c)$, $(0, c)$], where $c^2 = a^2 + b^2$. See the box on page 887 and Figure 9.16.

Ex. 1, p. 888;
Ex. 2, p. 889

**c.** Asymptotes for $\dfrac{x^2}{a^2} - \dfrac{y^2}{b^2} = 1$ are $y = \pm\dfrac{b}{a}x$. Asymptotes for $\dfrac{y^2}{a^2} - \dfrac{x^2}{b^2} = 1$ are $y = \pm\dfrac{a}{b}x$.

**d.** A procedure for graphing hyperbolas is given in the lower box on page 890.

Ex. 3, p. 891;
Ex. 4, p. 892

**e.** Standard forms of the equations of a hyperbola centered at $(h, k)$ are $\dfrac{(x - h)^2}{a^2} - \dfrac{(y - k)^2}{b^2} = 1$ and $\dfrac{(y - k)^2}{a^2} - \dfrac{(x - h)^2}{b^2} = 1$. See Table 9.2 on page 893.

Ex. 5, p. 893;
Ex. 6, p. 895

## 9.3   The Parabola

**a.** A parabola is the set of all points in a plane that are equidistant from a fixed line, the directrix, and a fixed point, the focus.

**b.** Standard forms of the equations of parabolas with vertex at the origin are $y^2 = 4px$ [focus: $(p, 0)$] and $x^2 = 4py$ [focus: $(0, p)$]. See the box and Figure 9.31 on page 902.

Ex. 1, p. 902;
Ex. 3, p. 904

**c.** A parabola's latus rectum is a line segment that passes through its focus, is parallel to its directrix, and has its endpoints on the parabola. The length of the latus rectum for $y^2 = 4px$ and $x^2 = 4py$ is $|4p|$. A parabola can be graphed using the vertex and endpoints of the latus rectum.

Ex. 2, p. 904

**d.** Standard forms of the equations of a parabola with vertex at $(h, k)$ are $(y - k)^2 = 4p(x - h)$ and $(x - h)^2 = 4p(y - k)$. See Table 9.3 on page 905 and Figure 9.36.

Ex. 4, p. 905;
Ex. 5, p. 906

## 9.4   Rotation of Axes

**a.** A nondegenerate conic section with equation of the form $Ax^2 + Cy^2 + Dx + Ey + F = 0$ in which $A$ and $C$ are not both zero is **1.** a circle if $A = C$; **2.** a parabola if $AC = 0$; **3.** an ellipse if $A \neq C$ and $AC > 0$; **4.** a hyperbola if $AC < 0$.

Ex. 1, p. 913

**b.** Rotation of Axes Formulas
$\theta$ is the angle from the positive $x$-axis to the positive $x'$-axis.
$$x = x' \cos\theta - y' \sin\theta \quad \text{and} \quad y = x' \sin\theta + y' \cos\theta$$

Ex. 2, p. 916

**c.** Amount of Rotation Formula
The general second-degree equation
$$Ax^2 + Bxy + Cy^2 + Dx + Ey + F = 0$$
can be rewritten in $x'$ and $y'$ without an $x'y'$-term by rotating the axes through angle $\theta$, where
$$\cot 2\theta = \frac{A - C}{B} \text{ and } \theta \text{ is an acute angle.}$$

**d.** If $2\theta$ in $\cot 2\theta$ is one of the familiar angles such as $30°, 45°$, or $60°$, write the equation of a rotated conic in standard form using the five-step procedure in the box on page 918.

Ex. 3, p. 918

**e.** If $\cot 2\theta$ is not the cotangent of one of the more familiar angles, use a sketch of $\cot 2\theta$ to find $\cos 2\theta$. Then use
$$\sin\theta = \sqrt{\frac{1 - \cos 2\theta}{2}} \quad \text{and} \quad \cos\theta = \sqrt{\frac{1 + \cos 2\theta}{2}}$$
to find values for $\sin\theta$ and $\cos\theta$ in the rotation formulas.

Ex. 4, p. 921

**f.** A nondegenerate conic section of the form
$$Ax^2 + Bxy + Cy^2 + Dx + Ey + F = 0$$
is **1.** a parabola if $B^2 - 4AC = 0$; **2.** an ellipse or a circle if $B^2 - 4AC < 0$; **3.** a hyperbola if $B^2 - 4AC > 0$.

Ex. 5, p. 923

| DEFINITIONS AND CONCEPTS | EXAMPLES |
|---|---|

### 9.5 Parametric Equations

**a.** The relationship between the parametric equations $x = f(t)$ and $y = g(t)$ and plane curves is described in the first box on page 926.

**b.** Point plotting can be used to graph a plane curve described by parametric equations. See the second box on page 926.

Ex. 1, p. 926

**c.** Plane curves can be sketched by eliminating the parameter $t$ and graphing the resulting rectangular equation. It is sometimes necessary to change the domain of the rectangular equation to be consistent with the domain for the parametric equation in $x$.

Ex. 2, p. 927;
Ex. 3, p. 928

**d.** Infinitely many pairs of parametric equations can represent the same plane curve. One pair for $y = f(x)$ is $x = t$ and $y = f(t)$, in which $t$ is in the domain of $f$.

Ex. 4, p. 930

### 9.6 Conic Sections in Polar Coordinates

**a.** The focus-directrix definitions of the conic sections are given in the box on page 935. For all points on a conic, the ratio of the distance from a fixed point (focus) and the distance from a fixed line (directrix) is constant and is called its eccentricity. If $e = 1$, the conic is a parabola. If $e < 1$, the conic is an ellipse. If $e > 1$, the conic is a hyperbola.

**b.** Standard forms of the polar equations of conics are

$$r = \frac{ep}{1 \pm e \cos \theta} \quad \text{and} \quad r = \frac{ep}{1 \pm e \sin \theta},$$

in which $(r, \theta)$ is a point on the conic's graph, $e$ is the eccentricity, and $p$ is the distance between the focus (located at the pole) and the directrix. Details are shown in the box on page 936.

Ex. 1, p. 937;
Ex. 2, p. 939;
Ex. 3, p. 940

**c.** A procedure for graphing the polar equation of a conic is given in the box on page 937.

## Review Exercises

### 9.1

*In Exercises 1–8, graph each ellipse and locate the foci.*

**1.** $\dfrac{x^2}{36} + \dfrac{y^2}{25} = 1$

**2.** $\dfrac{y^2}{25} + \dfrac{x^2}{16} = 1$

**3.** $4x^2 + y^2 = 16$

**4.** $4x^2 + 9y^2 = 36$

**5.** $\dfrac{(x-1)^2}{16} + \dfrac{(y+2)^2}{9} = 1$

**6.** $\dfrac{(x+1)^2}{9} + \dfrac{(y-2)^2}{16} = 1$

**7.** $4x^2 + 9y^2 + 24x - 36y + 36 = 0$

**8.** $9x^2 + 4y^2 - 18x + 8y - 23 = 0$

*In Exercises 9–11, find the standard form of the equation of each ellipse satisfying the given conditions.*

**9.** Foci: $(-4, 0)$, $(4, 0)$; Vertices: $(-5, 0)$, $(5, 0)$

**10.** Foci: $(0, -3)$, $(0, 3)$; Vertices: $(0, -6)$, $(0, 6)$

**11.** Major axis horizontal with length 12; length of minor axis = 4; center: $(-3, 5)$.

**12.** A semielliptical arch supports a bridge that spans a river 20 yards wide. The center of the arch is 6 yards above the river's center. Write an equation for the ellipse so that the $x$-axis coincides with the water level and the $y$-axis passes through the center of the arch.

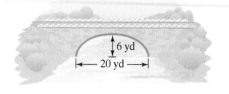

**13.** A semielliptic archway has a height of 15 feet at the center and a width of 50 feet, as shown in the figure. The 50-foot width consists of a two-lane road. Can a truck that is 12 feet high and 14 feet wide drive under the archway without going into the other lane?

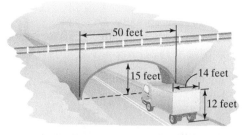

**14.** An elliptical pool table has a ball placed at each focus. If one ball is hit toward the side of the table, explain what will occur.

### 9.2

*In Exercises 15–22, graph each hyperbola. Locate the foci and find the equations of the asymptotes.*

**15.** $\dfrac{x^2}{16} - y^2 = 1$

**16.** $\dfrac{y^2}{16} - x^2 = 1$

**17.** $9x^2 - 16y^2 = 144$

**18.** $4y^2 - x^2 = 16$

**19.** $\dfrac{(x-2)^2}{25} - \dfrac{(y+3)^2}{16} = 1$

**20.** $\dfrac{(y+2)^2}{25} - \dfrac{(x-3)^2}{16} = 1$

**21.** $y^2 - 4y - 4x^2 + 8x - 4 = 0$

**22.** $x^2 - y^2 - 2x - 2y - 1 = 0$

In Exercises 23–24, find the standard form of the equation of each hyperbola satisfying the given conditions.

**23.** Foci: $(0, -4), (0, 4)$; Vertices: $(0, -2), (0, 2)$

**24.** Foci: $(-8, 0), (8, 0)$; Vertices: $(-3, 0), (3, 0)$

**25.** Explain why it is not possible for a hyperbola to have foci at $(0, -2)$ and $(0, 2)$ and vertices at $(0, -3)$ and $(0, 3)$.

**26.** Radio tower $M_2$ is located 200 miles due west of radio tower $M_1$. The situation is illustrated in the figure shown, where a coordinate system has been superimposed. Simultaneous radio signals are sent from each tower to a ship, with the signal from $M_2$ received 500 microseconds before the signal from $M_1$. Assuming that radio signals travel at 0.186 mile per microsecond, determine the equation of the hyperbola on which the ship is located.

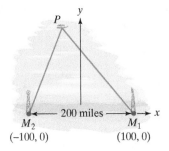

**9.3**

In Exercises 27–33, find the vertex, focus, and directrix of each parabola with the given equation. Then graph the parabola.

**27.** $y^2 = 8x$

**28.** $x^2 + 16y = 0$

**29.** $(y - 2)^2 = -16x$

**30.** $(x - 4)^2 = 4(y + 1)$

**31.** $x^2 + 4y = 4$

**32.** $y^2 - 4x - 10y + 21 = 0$

**33.** $x^2 - 4x - 2y = 0$

In Exercises 34–35, find the standard form of the equation of each parabola satisfying the given conditions.

**34.** Focus: $(12, 0)$; Directrix: $x = -12$

**35.** Focus: $(0, -11)$; Directrix: $y = 11$

**36.** An engineer is designing headlight units for automobiles. The unit has a parabolic surface with a diameter of 12 inches and a depth of 3 inches. The situation is illustrated in the figure, where a coordinate system has been superimposed. What is the equation of the parabola in this system? Where should the light source be placed? Describe this placement relative to the vertex.

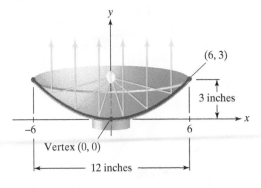

**37.** The George Washington Bridge spans the Hudson River from New York to New Jersey. Its two towers are 3500 feet apart and rise 316 feet above the road. As shown in the figure, the cable between the towers has the shape of a parabola and the cable just touches the sides of the road midway between the towers. What is the height of the cable 1000 feet from a tower?

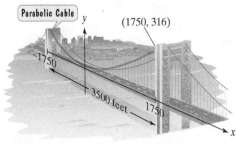

**38.** The giant satellite dish in the figure shown is in the shape of a parabolic surface. Signals strike the surface and are reflected to the focus, where the receiver is located. The diameter of the dish is 300 feet and its depth is 44 feet. How far, to the nearest foot, from the base of the dish should the receiver be placed?

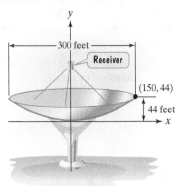

**9.4**

In Exercises 39–46, identify the conic represented by each equation without completing the square or using a rotation of axes.

**39.** $y^2 + 4x + 2y - 15 = 0$

**40.** $x^2 + 16y^2 - 160y + 384 = 0$

**41.** $16x^2 + 64x + 9y^2 - 54y + 1 = 0$

**42.** $4x^2 - 9y^2 - 8x + 12y - 144 = 0$

**43.** $5x^2 + 2\sqrt{3}xy + 3y^2 - 18 = 0$

**44.** $5x^2 - 8xy + 7y^2 - 9\sqrt{5}x - 9 = 0$

**45.** $x^2 + 6xy + 9y^2 - 2y = 0$

**46.** $x^2 - 2xy + 3y^2 + 2x + 4y - 1 = 0$

In Exercises 47–51,

**a.** Rewrite the equation in a rotated $x'y'$-system without an $x'y'$-term.

**b.** Express the equation involving $x'$ and $y'$ in the standard form of a conic section.

**c.** Use the rotated system to graph the equation.

**47.** $xy - 4 = 0$

**48.** $x^2 + xy + y^2 - 1 = 0$

**49.** $4x^2 + 10xy + 4y^2 - 9 = 0$

**50.** $6x^2 - 6xy + 14y^2 - 45 = 0$

**51.** $x^2 + 2\sqrt{3}xy + 3y^2 - 12\sqrt{3}x + 12y = 0$

## 9.5

*In Exercises 52–57, eliminate the parameter and graph the plane curve represented by the parametric equations. Use arrows to show the orientation of each plane curve.*

**52.** $x = 2t - 1$, $y = 1 - t$; $-\infty < t < \infty$

**53.** $x = t^2$, $y = t - 1$; $-1 \le t \le 3$.

**54.** $x = 4t^2$, $y = t + 1$; $-\infty < t < \infty$

**55.** $x = 4 \sin t$, $y = 3 \cos t$; $0 \le t < \pi$

**56.** $x = 3 + 2 \cos t$, $y = 1 + 2 \sin t$; $0 \le t < 2\pi$

**57.** $x = 3 \sec t$, $y = 3 \tan t$; $0 \le t \le \dfrac{\pi}{4}$

**58.** Find two different sets of parametric equations for $y = x^2 + 6$.

**59.** The path of a projectile that is launched $h$ feet above the ground with an initial velocity of $v_0$ feet per second and at an angle $\theta$ with the horizontal is given by the parametric equations

$$x = (v_0 \cos \theta)t \quad \text{and} \quad y = h + (v_0 \sin \theta)t - 16t^2,$$

where $t$ is the time, in seconds, after the projectile was launched. A football player throws a football with an initial velocity of 100 feet per second at an angle of 40° to the horizontal. The ball leaves the player's hand at a height of 6 feet.

  **a.** Find the parametric equations that describe the position of the ball as a function of time.

  **b.** Describe the ball's position after 1, 2, and 3 seconds. Round to the nearest tenth of a foot.

  **c.** How long, to the nearest tenth of a second, is the ball in flight? What is the total horizontal distance that it travels before it lands?

  **d.** Graph the parametric equations in part (a) using a graphing utility. Use the graph to determine when the ball is at its maximum height. What is its maximum height? Round answers to the nearest tenth.

## 9.6

*In Exercises 60–65,*

  **a.** *If necessary, write the equation in one of the standard forms for a conic in polar coordinates.*

  **b.** *Determine values for e and p. Use the value of e to identify the conic section.*

  **c.** *Graph the given polar equation.*

**60.** $r = \dfrac{4}{1 - \sin \theta}$        **61.** $r = \dfrac{6}{1 + \cos \theta}$

**62.** $r = \dfrac{6}{2 + \sin \theta}$        **63.** $r = \dfrac{2}{3 - 2 \cos \theta}$

**64.** $r = \dfrac{6}{3 + 6 \sin \theta}$        **65.** $r = \dfrac{8}{4 + 16 \cos \theta}$

---

### CHAPTER
## Test Prep VIDEOS — Chapter 9 Test

*In Exercises 1–5, graph the conic section with the given equation. For ellipses, find the foci. For hyperbolas, find the foci and give the equations of the asymptotes. For parabolas, find the vertex, focus, and directrix.*

**1.** $9x^2 - 4y^2 = 36$

**2.** $x^2 = -8y$

**3.** $\dfrac{(x + 2)^2}{25} + \dfrac{(y - 5)^2}{9} = 1$

**4.** $4x^2 - y^2 + 8x + 2y + 7 = 0$

**5.** $(x + 5)^2 = 8(y - 1)$

*In Exercises 6–8, find the standard form of the equation of the conic section satisfying the given conditions.*

**6.** Ellipse; Foci: $(-7, 0)$, $(7, 0)$; Vertices: $(-10, 0)$, $(10, 0)$

**7.** Hyperbola; Foci: $(0, -10)$, $(0, 10)$; Vertices: $(0, -7)$, $(0, 7)$

**8.** Parabola; Focus: $(50, 0)$; Directrix: $x = -50$

**9.** A sound whispered at one focus of a whispering gallery can be heard at the other focus. The figure at the top of the next column shows a whispering gallery whose cross section is a semielliptical arch with a height of 24 feet and a width of 80 feet. How far from the room's center should two people stand so that they can whisper back and forth and be heard?

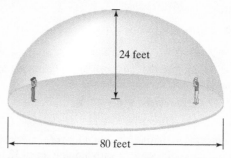

**10.** An engineer is designing headlight units for cars. The unit shown in the figure below has a parabolic surface with a diameter of 6 inches and a depth of 3 inches.

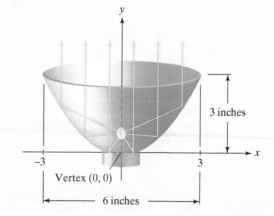

a. Using the coordinate system that has been positioned on the unit, find the parabola's equation.

b. If the light source is located at the focus, describe its placement relative to the vertex.

*In Exercises 11–12, identify each equation without completing the square or using a rotation of axes.*

**11.** $x^2 + 9y^2 + 10x - 18y + 25 = 0$

**12.** $x^2 + y^2 + xy + 3x - y - 3 = 0$

**13.** For the equation

$$7x^2 - 6\sqrt{3}xy + 13y^2 - 16 = 0,$$

determine what angle of rotation would eliminate the $x'y'$-term in a rotated $x'y'$-system.

*In Exercises 14–15, eliminate the parameter and graph the plane curve represented by the parametric equations. Use arrows to show the orientation of each plane curve.*

**14.** $x = t^2, y = t - 1; -\infty < t < \infty$

**15.** $x = 1 + 3 \sin t, y = 2 \cos t; 0 \le t < 2\pi$

*In Exercises 16–17, identify the conic section and graph the polar equation.*

**16.** $r = \dfrac{2}{1 - \cos \theta}$

**17.** $r = \dfrac{4}{2 + \sin \theta}$

## Cumulative Review Exercises (Chapters P–9)

*Solve each equation or inequality in Exercises 1–7.*

**1.** $2(x - 3) + 5x = 8(x - 1)$

**2.** $-3(2x - 4) > 2(6x - 12)$

**3.** $x - 5 = \sqrt{x + 7}$

**4.** $(x - 2)^2 = 20$

**5.** $|2x - 1| \ge 7$

**6.** $3x^3 + 4x^2 - 7x + 2 = 0$

**7.** $\log_2(x + 1) + \log_2(x - 1) = 3$

*Solve each system in Exercises 8–10.*

**8.** $\begin{cases} 3x + 4y = 2 \\ 2x + 5y = -1 \end{cases}$

**9.** $\begin{cases} 2x^2 - y^2 = -8 \\ x - y = 6 \end{cases}$

**10.** (Use matrices.)

$$\begin{cases} x - y + z = 17 \\ -4x + y + 5z = -2 \\ 2x + 3y + z = 8 \end{cases}$$

*In Exercises 11–13, graph each equation, function, or system in a rectangular coordinate system.*

**11.** $f(x) = (x - 1)^2 - 4$

**12.** $\dfrac{x^2}{9} + \dfrac{y^2}{4} = 1$

**13.** $\begin{cases} 5x + y \le 10 \\ y \ge \dfrac{1}{4}x + 2 \end{cases}$

**14. a.** List all possible rational roots of

$$32x^3 - 52x^2 + 17x + 3 = 0.$$

**b.** The graph of $f(x) = 32x^3 - 52x^2 + 17x + 3$ is shown in a $[-1, 3, 1]$ by $[-2, 6, 1]$ viewing rectangle. Use the graph of $f$ and synthetic division to solve the equation in part (a).

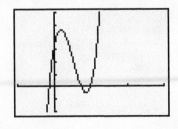

**15.** The figure shows the graph of $y = f(x)$ and its two vertical asymptotes.

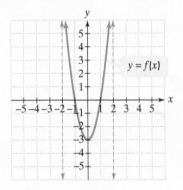

**a.** Find the domain and the range of $f$.

**b.** What is the relative minimum and where does it occur?

**c.** Find the interval on which $f$ is increasing.

**d.** Find $f(-1) - f(0)$.

**e.** Find $(f \circ f)(1)$.

**f.** Use arrow notation to complete this statement:

$$f(x) \to \infty \text{ as } \underline{\quad} \text{ or as } \underline{\quad}.$$

**g.** Graph $g(x) = f(x - 2) + 1$.

**h.** Graph $h(x) = -f(2x)$.

**16.** If $f(x) = x^2 - 4$ and $g(x) = x + 2$, find $(g \circ f)(x)$.

**17.** Expand using logarithmic properties. Where possible, evaluate logarithmic expressions.

$$\log_5 \left( \frac{x^3 \sqrt{y}}{125} \right)$$

**18.** Write the slope-intercept form of the equation of the line passing through $(1, -4)$ and $(-5, 8)$.

**19.** Rent-a-Truck charges a daily rental rate for a truck of $39 plus $0.16 a mile. A competing agency, Ace Truck Rentals, charges $25 a day plus $0.24 a mile for the same truck. How many miles must be driven in a day to make the daily cost of both agencies the same? What will be the cost?

**20.** The local cable television company offers two deals. Basic cable service with one movie channel costs $35 per month. Basic service with two movie channels cost $45 per month. Find the charge for the basic cable service and the charge for each movie channel.

**21.** Verify the identity: $\dfrac{\csc \theta - \sin \theta}{\sin \theta} = \cot^2 \theta$.

**22.** Graph one complete cycle of $y = 2 \cos(2x + \pi)$.

**23.** If $\mathbf{v} = 3\mathbf{i} - 6\mathbf{j}$ and $\mathbf{w} = \mathbf{i} + \mathbf{j}$, find $(\mathbf{v} \cdot \mathbf{w})\mathbf{w}$.

**24.** Solve for $\theta$: $\sin 2\theta = \sin \theta, 0 \leq \theta < 2\pi$.

**25.** In oblique triangle $ABC$, $A = 64°$, $B = 72°$, and $a = 13.6$. Solve the triangle. Round lengths to the nearest tenth.

# Sequences, Induction, and Probability

Something incredible has happened. Your college roommate, a gifted athlete, has been given a six-year contract with a professional baseball team. He will be playing against the likes of Alex Rodriguez and Manny Ramirez. Management offers him three options. One is a beginning salary of $1,700,000 with annual increases of $70,000 per year starting in the second year. A second option is $1,700,000 the first year with an annual increase of 2% per year beginning in the second year. The third option involves less money the first year—$1,500,000—but there is an annual increase of 9% yearly after that. Which option offers the most money over the six-year contract?

*A similar problem appears as Exercise 67 in Exercise Set 10.3, and this problem appears as the Group Exercise on page 986.*

**Sequences and Summation Notation**

## Sequences

Many creations in nature involve intricate mathematical designs, including a variety of spirals. For example, the arrangement of the individual florets in the head of a sunflower forms spirals. In some species, there are 21 spirals in the clockwise direction and 34 in the counterclockwise direction. The precise numbers depend on the species of sunflower: 21 and 34, or 34 and 55, or 55 and 89, or even 89 and 144.

This observation becomes even more interesting when we consider a sequence of numbers investigated by Leonardo of Pisa, also known as Fibonacci, an Italian mathematician of the thirteenth century. The **Fibonacci sequence** of numbers is an infinite sequence that begins as follows:

$$1, 1, 2, 3, 5, 8, 13, 21, 34, 55, 89, 144, 233, \ldots.$$

The first two terms are 1. Every term thereafter is the sum of the two preceding terms. For example, the third term, 2, is the sum of the first and second terms: $1 + 1 = 2$. The fourth term, 3, is the sum of the second and third terms: $1 + 2 = 3$, and so on. Did you know that the number of spirals in a daisy or a sunflower, 21 and 34, are two Fibonacci numbers? The number of spirals in a pine cone, 8 and 13, and a pineapple, 8 and 13, are also Fibonacci numbers.

We can think of the Fibonacci sequence as a function. The terms of the sequence

$$1, 1, 2, 3, 5, 8, 13, 21, 34, 55, 89, 144, 233, \ldots$$

are the range values for a function $f$ whose domain is the set of positive integers.

| Domain: | 1, | 2, | 3, | 4, | 5, | 6, | 7, | ... |
|---|---|---|---|---|---|---|---|---|
| | ↓ | ↓ | ↓ | ↓ | ↓ | ↓ | ↓ | |
| Range: | 1, | 1, | 2, | 3, | 5, | 8, | 13, | ... |

Thus, $f(1) = 1, f(2) = 1, f(3) = 2, f(4) = 3, f(5) = 5, f(6) = 8, f(7) = 13$, and so on.

The letter $a$ with a subscript is used to represent function values of a sequence, rather than the usual function notation. The subscripts make up the domain of the sequence and they identify the location of a term. Thus, $a_1$ represents the first term of the sequence, $a_2$ represents the second term, $a_3$ the third term, and so on. This notation is shown for the first six terms of the Fibonacci sequence:

$$1, \quad 1, \quad 2, \quad 3, \quad 5, \quad 8.$$

$a_1 = 1 \quad a_2 = 1 \quad a_3 = 2 \quad a_4 = 3 \quad a_5 = 5 \quad a_6 = 8$

The notation $a_n$ represents the $n$th term, or **general term**, of a sequence. The entire sequence is represented by $\{a_n\}$.

### Definition of a Sequence

An **infinite sequence** $\{a_n\}$ is a function whose domain is the set of positive integers. The function values, or **terms**, of the sequence are represented by

$$a_1, a_2, a_3, a_4, \ldots, a_n, \ldots.$$

Sequences whose domains consist only of the first $n$ positive integers are called **finite sequences**.

① Find particular terms of a sequence from the general term.

(EXAMPLE 1) **Writing Terms of a Sequence from the General Term**

Write the first four terms of the sequence whose $n$th term, or general term, is given:

**a.** $a_n = 3n + 4$  **b.** $a_n = \dfrac{(-1)^n}{3^n - 1}$.

**Solution**

**a.** We need to find the first four terms of the sequence whose general term is $a_n = 3n + 4$. To do so, we replace $n$ in the formula with $1, 2, 3,$ and $4$.

$a_1$, 1st term   $3 \cdot 1 + 4 = 3 + 4 = 7$   $a_2$, 2nd term   $3 \cdot 2 + 4 = 6 + 4 = 10$

$a_3$, 3rd term   $3 \cdot 3 + 4 = 9 + 4 = 13$   $a_4$, 4th term   $3 \cdot 4 + 4 = 12 + 4 = 16$

The first four terms are $7, 10, 13,$ and $16$. The sequence defined by $a_n = 3n + 4$ can be written as

$$7, 10, 13, 16, \ldots, 3n + 4, \ldots.$$

**b.** We need to find the first four terms of the sequence whose general term is $a_n = \dfrac{(-1)^n}{3^n - 1}$. To do so, we replace each occurrence of $n$ in the formula with $1, 2, 3,$ and $4$.

$a_1$, 1st term   $\dfrac{(-1)^1}{3^1 - 1} = \dfrac{-1}{3 - 1} = -\dfrac{1}{2}$   $a_2$, 2nd term   $\dfrac{(-1)^2}{3^2 - 1} = \dfrac{1}{9 - 1} = \dfrac{1}{8}$

$a_3$, 3rd term   $\dfrac{(-1)^3}{3^3 - 1} = \dfrac{-1}{27 - 1} = -\dfrac{1}{26}$   $a_4$, 4th term   $\dfrac{(-1)^4}{3^4 - 1} = \dfrac{1}{81 - 1} = \dfrac{1}{80}$

The first four terms are $-\frac{1}{2}, \frac{1}{8}, -\frac{1}{26},$ and $\frac{1}{80}$. The sequence defined by $\dfrac{(-1)^n}{3^n - 1}$ can be written as

$$-\frac{1}{2}, \frac{1}{8}, -\frac{1}{26}, \frac{1}{80}, \ldots, \frac{(-1)^n}{3^n - 1}, \ldots.$$

**Study Tip**

The factor $(-1)^n$ in the general term of a sequence causes the signs of the terms to alternate between positive and negative, depending on whether $n$ is even or odd.

⊘ Check Point **1** Write the first four terms of the sequence whose $n$th term, or general term, is given:

**a.** $a_n = 2n + 5$  **b.** $a_n = \dfrac{(-1)^n}{2^n + 1}$.

Although sequences are usually named with the letter $a$, any lowercase letter can be used. For example, the first four terms of the sequence $\{b_n\} = \left\{\left(\frac{1}{2}\right)^n\right\}$ are $b_1 = \frac{1}{2}, b_2 = \frac{1}{4}, b_3 = \frac{1}{8},$ and $b_4 = \frac{1}{16}$.

Because a sequence is a function whose domain is the set of positive integers, the **graph of a sequence** is a set of discrete points. For example, consider the sequence whose general term is $a_n = \frac{1}{n}$. How does the graph of this sequence differ

## Technology

Graphing utilities can write the terms of a sequence and graph them. For example, to find the first six terms of $\{a_n\} = \left\{\frac{1}{n}\right\}$, enter

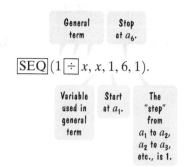

$$\boxed{\text{SEQ}}\,(1 \boxed{\div} x, x, 1, 6, 1).$$

| Variable used in general term | Start at $a_1$. | The "step" from $a_1$ to $a_2$, $a_2$ to $a_3$, etc., is 1. |

The first few terms of the sequence are shown in the viewing rectangle. By pressing the right arrow key to scroll right, you can see the remaining terms.

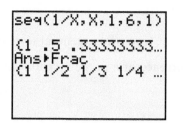

from the graph of the function $f(x) = \frac{1}{x}$? The graph of $f(x) = \frac{1}{x}$ is shown in **Figure 10.1(a)** for positive values of $x$. To obtain the graph of the sequence $\{a_n\} = \left\{\frac{1}{n}\right\}$, remove all the points from the graph of $f$ except those whose $x$-coordinates are positive integers. Thus, we remove all points except $(1, 1), \left(2, \frac{1}{2}\right), \left(3, \frac{1}{3}\right), \left(4, \frac{1}{4}\right)$, and so on. The remaining points are the graph of the sequence $\{a_n\} = \left\{\frac{1}{n}\right\}$, shown in **Figure 10.1(b)**. Notice that the horizontal axis is labeled $n$ and the vertical axis is labeled $a_n$.

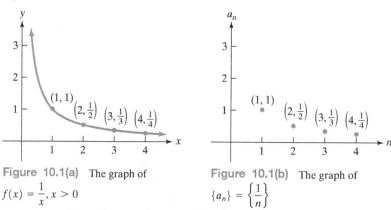

**Figure 10.1(a)** The graph of $f(x) = \dfrac{1}{x}, x > 0$

**Figure 10.1(b)** The graph of $\{a_n\} = \left\{\dfrac{1}{n}\right\}$

Comparing a continuous graph to the graph of a sequence

## Recursion Formulas

In Example 1, the formulas used for the $n$th term of a sequence expressed the term as a function of $n$, the number of the term. Sequences can also be defined using **recursion formulas**. A recursion formula defines the $n$th term of a sequence as a function of the previous term. Our next example illustrates that if the first term of a sequence is known, then the recursion formula can be used to determine the remaining terms.

② Use recursion formulas.

( EXAMPLE 2 ) **Using a Recursion Formula**

Find the first four terms of the sequence in which $a_1 = 5$ and $a_n = 3a_{n-1} + 2$ for $n \geq 2$.

**Solution**   Let's be sure we understand what is given.

$$a_1 = 5 \quad \text{and} \quad a_n = 3a_{n-1} + 2$$

| The first term is 5. | Each term after the first | is | 3 times the previous term | plus 2. |

Now let's write the first four terms of this sequence.

$$a_1 = 5 \qquad \text{This is the given first term.}$$

$$a_2 = 3a_1 + 2 \qquad \text{Use } a_n = 3a_{n-1} + 2, \text{ with } n = 2.$$
$$\text{Thus, } a_2 = 3a_{2-1} + 2 = 3a_1 + 2.$$

$$\quad\; = 3(5) + 2 = 17 \qquad \text{Substitute 5 for } a_1.$$

$$a_3 = 3a_2 + 2 \qquad \text{Again use } a_n = 3a_{n-1} + 2, \text{ with } n = 3.$$

$$\quad\; = 3(17) + 2 = 53 \qquad \text{Substitute 17 for } a_2.$$

$$a_4 = 3a_3 + 2 \qquad \text{Notice that } a_4 \text{ is defined in terms of } a_3.$$
$$\text{We used } a_n = 3a_{n-1} + 2, \text{ with } n = 4.$$

$$\quad\; = 3(53) + 2 = 161 \qquad \text{Use the value of } a_3, \text{ the third term, obtained above.}$$

The first four terms are 5, 17, 53, and 161.

⊘ Check Point **2** Find the first four terms of the sequence in which $a_1 = 3$ and $a_n = 2a_{n-1} + 5$ for $n \geq 2$.

**3** Use factorial notation.

## Factorial Notation

Products of consecutive positive integers occur quite often in sequences. These products can be expressed in a special notation, called **factorial notation**.

### Factorials from 0 through 20

| | |
|---|---|
| 0! | 1 |
| 1! | 1 |
| 2! | 2 |
| 3! | 6 |
| 4! | 24 |
| 5! | 120 |
| 6! | 720 |
| 7! | 5040 |
| 8! | 40,320 |
| 9! | 362,880 |
| 10! | 3,628,800 |
| 11! | 39,916,800 |
| 12! | 479,001,600 |
| 13! | 6,227,020,800 |
| 14! | 87,178,291,200 |
| 15! | 1,307,674,368,000 |
| 16! | 20,922,789,888,000 |
| 17! | 355,687,428,096,000 |
| 18! | 6,402,373,705,728,000 |
| 19! | 121,645,100,408,832,000 |
| 20! | 2,432,902,008,176,640,000 |

As $n$ increases, $n!$ grows very rapidly. Factorial growth is more explosive than exponential growth discussed in Chapter 3.

### Factorial Notation

If $n$ is a positive integer, the notation $n!$ (read "$n$ factorial") is the product of all positive integers from $n$ down through 1.

$$n! = n(n-1)(n-2) \cdots (3)(2)(1)$$

0! (zero factorial), by definition, is 1.

$$0! = 1$$

The values of $n!$ for the first six positive integers are

$$1! = 1$$
$$2! = 2 \cdot 1 = 2$$
$$3! = 3 \cdot 2 \cdot 1 = 6$$
$$4! = 4 \cdot 3 \cdot 2 \cdot 1 = 24$$
$$5! = 5 \cdot 4 \cdot 3 \cdot 2 \cdot 1 = 120$$
$$6! = 6 \cdot 5 \cdot 4 \cdot 3 \cdot 2 \cdot 1 = 720.$$

Factorials affect only the number or variable that they follow unless grouping symbols appear. For example,

$$2 \cdot 3! = 2(3 \cdot 2 \cdot 1) = 2 \cdot 6 = 12$$

whereas

$$(2 \cdot 3)! = 6! = 6 \cdot 5 \cdot 4 \cdot 3 \cdot 2 \cdot 1 = 720.$$

In this sense, factorials are similar to exponents.

### EXAMPLE 3  Finding Terms of a Sequence Involving Factorials

Write the first four terms of the sequence whose $n$th term is

$$a_n = \frac{2^n}{(n-1)!}.$$

**Solution**  We need to find the first four terms of the sequence. To do so, we replace each $n$ in $\dfrac{2^n}{(n-1)!}$ with $1, 2, 3,$ and $4$.

$a_1$, 1st term $\quad \dfrac{2^1}{(1-1)!} = \dfrac{2}{0!} = \dfrac{2}{1} = 2$

$a_2$, 2nd term $\quad \dfrac{2^2}{(2-1)!} = \dfrac{4}{1!} = \dfrac{4}{1} = 4$

$a_3$, 3rd term $\quad \dfrac{2^3}{(3-1)!} = \dfrac{8}{2!} = \dfrac{8}{\cdot 2 \cdot 1} = 4$

$a_4$, 4th term $\quad \dfrac{2^4}{(4-1)!} = \dfrac{16}{3!} = \dfrac{16}{3 \cdot 2 \cdot 1} = \dfrac{16}{6} = \dfrac{8}{3}$

The first four terms are $2, 4, 4,$ and $\frac{8}{3}$.

### Technology

Most calculators have factorial keys. To find 5!, most calculators use one of the following:

**Many Scientific Calculators**

$$5 \boxed{x!}$$

**Many Graphing Calculators**

$$5 \boxed{!} \ \boxed{\text{ENTER}}.$$

Because $n!$ becomes quite large as $n$ increases, your calculator will display these larger values in scientific notation.

⊘ Check Point **3** Write the first four terms of the sequence whose $n$th term is

$$a_n = \frac{20}{(n+1)!}.$$

When evaluating fractions with factorials in the numerator and the denominator, try to reduce the fraction before performing the multiplications. For example, consider $\frac{26!}{21!}$. Rather than write out 26! as the product of all integers from 26 down to 1, we can express 26! as

$$26! = 26 \cdot 25 \cdot 24 \cdot 23 \cdot 22 \cdot 21!.$$

In this way, we can divide both the numerator and the denominator by the common factor, 21!.

$$\frac{26!}{21!} = \frac{26 \cdot 25 \cdot 24 \cdot 23 \cdot 22 \cdot \cancel{21!}}{\cancel{21!}} = 26 \cdot 25 \cdot 24 \cdot 23 \cdot 22 = 7,893,600$$

**EXAMPLE 4** **Evaluating Fractions with Factorials**

Evaluate each factorial expression:

**a.** $\dfrac{10!}{2!8!}$ **b.** $\dfrac{(n+1)!}{n!}.$

**Solution**

**a.** $\dfrac{10!}{2!8!} = \dfrac{10 \cdot 9 \cdot \cancel{8!}}{2 \cdot 1 \cdot \cancel{8!}} = \dfrac{90}{2} = 45$

**b.** $\dfrac{(n+1)!}{n!} = \dfrac{(n+1) \cdot \cancel{n!}}{\cancel{n!}} = n + 1$

⊘ Check Point **4** Evaluate each factorial expression:

**a.** $\dfrac{14!}{2!12!}$ **b.** $\dfrac{n!}{(n-1)!}.$

**④ Use summation notation.**

## Summation Notation

It is sometimes useful to find the sum of the first $n$ terms of a sequence. For example, consider the cost of raising a child born in the United States in 2006 to a middle-income ($43,200–$72,600 per year) family, shown in **Table 10.1**.

**Table 10.1    The Cost of Raising a Child Born in the U.S. in 2006 to a Middle-Income Family**

| Year | 2006 | 2007 | 2008 | 2009 | 2010 | 2011 | 2012 | 2013 | 2014 |
|---|---|---|---|---|---|---|---|---|---|
| **Average Cost** | $10,600 | $10,930 | $11,270 | $11,960 | $12,330 | $12,710 | $12,950 | $13,350 | $13,760 |
| | Child is under 1. | Child is 1. | Child is 2. | Child is 3. | Child is 4. | Child is 5. | Child is 6. | Child is 7. | Child is 8. |

| Year | 2015 | 2016 | 2017 | 2018 | 2019 | 2020 | 2021 | 2022 | 2023 |
|---|---|---|---|---|---|---|---|---|---|
| **Average Cost** | $13,970 | $14,400 | $14,840 | $16,360 | $16,860 | $17,390 | $18,430 | $19,000 | $19,590 |
| | Child is 9. | Child is 10. | Child is 11. | Child is 12. | Child is 13. | Child is 14. | Child is 15. | Child is 16. | Child is 17. |

*Source:* U.S. Department of Agriculture

We can let $a_n$ represent the cost of raising a child in year $n$, where $n = 1$ corresponds to 2006, $n = 2$ to 2007, $n = 3$ to 2008, and so on. The terms of the finite sequence in **Table 10.1** are given as follows:

10,600,   10,930,   11,270,   11,960,   12,330,   12,710,   12,950,   13,350,   13,760,
$a_1$       $a_2$       $a_3$       $a_4$       $a_5$       $a_6$       $a_7$       $a_8$       $a_9$

13,970,   14,400,   14,840,   16,360,   16,860,   17,390,   18,430,   19,000,   19,590.
$a_{10}$     $a_{11}$     $a_{12}$     $a_{13}$     $a_{14}$     $a_{15}$     $a_{16}$     $a_{17}$     $a_{18}$

Why might we want to add the terms of this sequence? We do this to find the total cost of raising a child born in 2006 from birth through age 17. Thus,

$$a_1 + a_2 + a_3 + a_4 + a_5 + a_6 + a_7 + a_8 + a_9 + a_{10} + a_{11} + a_{12} + a_{13} + a_{14} + a_{15} + a_{16} + a_{17} + a_{18}$$
$$= 10{,}600 + 10{,}930 + 11{,}270 + 11{,}960 + 12{,}330 + 12{,}710 + 12{,}950 + 13{,}350 + 13{,}760$$
$$+ 13{,}970 + 14{,}400 + 14{,}840 + 16{,}360 + 16{,}860 + 17{,}390 + 18{,}430 + 19{,}000 + 19{,}590$$
$$= 260{,}700.$$

We see that the total cost of raising a child born in 2006 from birth through age 17 is $260,700.

There is a compact notation for expressing the sum of the first $n$ terms of a sequence. For example, rather than write

$$a_1 + a_2 + a_3 + a_4 + a_5 + a_6 + a_7 + a_8 + a_9 + a_{10} + a_{11} + a_{12} + a_{13} + a_{14} + a_{15} + a_{16} + a_{17} + a_{18},$$

we can use *summation notation* to express the sum as

$$\sum_{i=1}^{18} a_i.$$

We read this expression as "the sum as $i$ goes from 1 to 18 of $a_i$." The letter $i$ is called the *index of summation* and is not related to the use of $i$ to represent $\sqrt{-1}$.

You can think of the symbol $\Sigma$ (the uppercase Greek letter sigma) as an instruction to add up the terms of a sequence.

## Summation Notation

The sum of the first $n$ terms of a sequence is represented by the **summation notation**

$$\sum_{i=1}^{n} a_i = a_1 + a_2 + a_3 + a_4 + \cdots + a_n,$$

where $i$ is the **index of summation**, $n$ is the **upper limit of summation**, and 1 is the **lower limit of summation**.

Any letter can be used for the index of summation. The letters $i$, $j$, and $k$ are used commonly. Furthermore, the lower limit of summation can be an integer other than 1.

When we write out a sum that is given in summation notation, we are **expanding the summation notation**. Example 5 shows how to do this.

( **EXAMPLE 5** ) **Using Summation Notation**

Expand and evaluate the sum:

**a.** $\sum_{i=1}^{6} (i^2 + 1)$     **b.** $\sum_{k=4}^{7} [(-2)^k - 5]$     **c.** $\sum_{i=1}^{5} 3.$

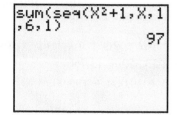

**Solution**

**a.** To find $\sum\limits_{i=1}^{6}(i^2 + 1)$, we must replace $i$ in the expression $i^2 + 1$ with all consecutive integers from $1$ to $6$, inclusive. Then we add.

$$\sum_{i=1}^{6}(i^2 + 1) = (1^2 + 1) + (2^2 + 1) + (3^2 + 1) + (4^2 + 1)$$
$$+ (5^2 + 1) + (6^2 + 1)$$
$$= 2 + 5 + 10 + 17 + 26 + 37$$
$$= 97$$

**b.** The index of summation in $\sum\limits_{k=4}^{7}[(-2)^k - 5]$ is $k$. First we evaluate $(-2)^k - 5$ for all consecutive integers from $4$ through $7$, inclusive. Then we add.

$$\sum_{k=4}^{7}[(-2)^k - 5] = [(-2)^4 - 5] + [(-2)^5 - 5]$$
$$+ [(-2)^6 - 5] + [(-2)^7 - 5]$$
$$= (16 - 5) + (-32 - 5) + (64 - 5) + (-128 - 5)$$
$$= 11 + (-37) + 59 + (-133)$$
$$= -100$$

**c.** To find $\sum\limits_{i=1}^{5} 3$, we observe that every term of the sum is 3. The notation $i = 1$ through 5 indicates that we must add the first five terms of a sequence in which every term is 3.

$$\sum_{i=1}^{5} 3 = 3 + 3 + 3 + 3 + 3 = 15$$

⬤

✓ Check Point **5** Expand and evaluate the sum:

**a.** $\sum\limits_{i=1}^{6} 2i^2$    **b.** $\sum\limits_{k=3}^{5} (2^k - 3)$    **c.** $\sum\limits_{i=1}^{5} 4$.

Although the domain of a sequence is the set of positive integers, any integers can be used for the limits of summation. For a given sum, we can vary the upper and lower limits of summation, as well as the letter used for the index of summation. By doing so, we can produce different-looking summation notations for the same sum. For example, the sum of the squares of the first four positive integers, $1^2 + 2^2 + 3^2 + 4^2$, can be expressed in a number of equivalent ways:

$$\sum_{i=1}^{4} i^2 = 1^2 + 2^2 + 3^2 + 4^2 = 30$$

$$\sum_{i=0}^{3} (i + 1)^2 = (0 + 1)^2 + (1 + 1)^2 + (2 + 1)^2 + (3 + 1)^2$$
$$= 1^2 + 2^2 + 3^2 + 4^2 = 30$$

$$\sum_{k=2}^{5} (k - 1)^2 = (2 - 1)^2 + (3 - 1)^2 + (4 - 1)^2 + (5 - 1)^2$$
$$= 1^2 + 2^2 + 3^2 + 4^2 = 30.$$

EXAMPLE 6  **Writing Sums in Summation Notation**

Express each sum using summation notation:

**a.** $1^3 + 2^3 + 3^3 + \cdots + 7^3$    **b.** $1 + \dfrac{1}{3} + \dfrac{1}{9} + \dfrac{1}{27} + \cdots + \dfrac{1}{3^{n-1}}$.

**Solution**  In each case, we will use 1 as the lower limit of summation and $i$ for the index of summation.

**a.** The sum $1^3 + 2^3 + 3^3 + \cdots + 7^3$ has seven terms, each of the form $i^3$, starting at $i = 1$ and ending at $i = 7$. Thus,

$$1^3 + 2^3 + 3^3 + \cdots + 7^3 = \sum_{i=1}^{7} i^3.$$

**b.** The sum

$$1 + \frac{1}{3} + \frac{1}{9} + \frac{1}{27} + \cdots + \frac{1}{3^{n-1}}$$

has $n$ terms, each of the form $\dfrac{1}{3^{i-1}}$, starting at $i = 1$ and ending at $i = n$. Thus,

$$1 + \frac{1}{3} + \frac{1}{9} + \frac{1}{27} + \cdots + \frac{1}{3^{n-1}} = \sum_{i=1}^{n} \frac{1}{3^{i-1}}.$$

⊘ Check Point **6**  Express each sum using summation notation:

**a.** $1^2 + 2^2 + 3^2 + \cdots + 9^2$    **b.** $1 + \dfrac{1}{2} + \dfrac{1}{4} + \dfrac{1}{8} + \cdots + \dfrac{1}{2^{n-1}}$.

**Table 10.2** contains some important properties of sums expressed in summation notation.

**Table 10.2   Properties of Sums**

| Property | Example |
|---|---|
| **1.** $\displaystyle\sum_{i=1}^{n} ca_i = c \sum_{i=1}^{n} a_i$, $c$ any real number | $\displaystyle\sum_{i=1}^{4} 3i^2 = 3 \cdot 1^2 + 3 \cdot 2^2 + 3 \cdot 3^2 + 3 \cdot 4^2$ <br> $3 \displaystyle\sum_{i=1}^{4} i^2 = 3(1^2 + 2^2 + 3^2 + 4^2) = 3 \cdot 1^2 + 3 \cdot 2^2 + 3 \cdot 3^2 + 3 \cdot 4^2$ <br> Conclusion: $\displaystyle\sum_{i=1}^{4} 3i^2 = 3 \sum_{i=1}^{4} i^2$ |
| **2.** $\displaystyle\sum_{i=1}^{n} (a_i + b_i) = \sum_{i=1}^{n} a_i + \sum_{i=1}^{n} b_i$ | $\displaystyle\sum_{i=1}^{4} (i + i^2) = (1 + 1^2) + (2 + 2^2) + (3 + 3^2) + (4 + 4^2)$ <br> $\displaystyle\sum_{i=1}^{4} i + \sum_{i=1}^{4} i^2 = (1 + 2 + 3 + 4) + (1^2 + 2^2 + 3^2 + 4^2)$ <br> $= (1 + 1^2) + (2 + 2^2) + (3 + 3^2) + (4 + 4^2)$ <br> Conclusion: $\displaystyle\sum_{i=1}^{4} (i + i^2) = \sum_{i=1}^{4} i + \sum_{i=1}^{4} i^2$ |
| **3.** $\displaystyle\sum_{i=1}^{n} (a_i - b_i) = \sum_{i=1}^{n} a_i - \sum_{i=1}^{n} b_i$ | $\displaystyle\sum_{i=3}^{5} (i^2 - i^3) = (3^2 - 3^3) + (4^2 - 4^3) + (5^2 - 5^3)$ <br> $\displaystyle\sum_{i=3}^{5} i^2 - \sum_{i=3}^{5} i^3 = (3^2 + 4^2 + 5^2) - (3^3 + 4^3 + 5^3)$ <br> $= (3^2 - 3^3) + (4^2 - 4^3) + (5^2 - 5^3)$ <br> Conclusion: $\displaystyle\sum_{i=3}^{5} (i^2 - i^3) = \sum_{i=3}^{5} i^2 - \sum_{i=3}^{5} i^3$ |

# Exercise Set 10.1

## Practice Exercises

*In Exercises 1–12, write the first four terms of each sequence whose general term is given.*

**1.** $a_n = 3n + 2$

**2.** $a_n = 4n - 1$

**3.** $a_n = 3^n$

**4.** $a_n = \left(\dfrac{1}{3}\right)^n$

**5.** $a_n = (-3)^n$

**6.** $a_n = \left(-\dfrac{1}{3}\right)^n$

**7.** $a_n = (-1)^n(n + 3)$

**8.** $a_n = (-1)^{n+1}(n + 4)$

**9.** $a_n = \dfrac{2n}{n + 4}$

**10.** $a_n = \dfrac{3n}{n + 5}$

**11.** $a_n = \dfrac{(-1)^{n+1}}{2^n - 1}$

**12.** $a_n = \dfrac{(-1)^{n+1}}{2^n + 1}$

*The sequences in Exercises 13–18 are defined using recursion formulas. Write the first four terms of each sequence.*

**13.** $a_1 = 7$ and $a_n = a_{n-1} + 5$ for $n \geq 2$

**14.** $a_1 = 12$ and $a_n = a_{n-1} + 4$ for $n \geq 2$

**15.** $a_1 = 3$ and $a_n = 4a_{n-1}$ for $n \geq 2$

**16.** $a_1 = 2$ and $a_n = 5a_{n-1}$ for $n \geq 2$

**17.** $a_1 = 4$ and $a_n = 2a_{n-1} + 3$ for $n \geq 2$

**18.** $a_1 = 5$ and $a_n = 3a_{n-1} - 1$ for $n \geq 2$

*In Exercises 19–22, the general term of a sequence is given and involves a factorial. Write the first four terms of each sequence.*

**19.** $a_n = \dfrac{n^2}{n!}$

**20.** $a_n = \dfrac{(n + 1)!}{n^2}$

**21.** $a_n = 2(n + 1)!$

**22.** $a_n = -2(n - 1)!$

*In Exercises 23–28, evaluate each factorial expression.*

**23.** $\dfrac{17!}{15!}$

**24.** $\dfrac{18!}{16!}$

**25.** $\dfrac{16!}{2!14!}$

**26.** $\dfrac{20!}{2!18!}$

**27.** $\dfrac{(n + 2)!}{n!}$

**28.** $\dfrac{(2n + 1)!}{(2n)!}$

*In Exercises 29–42, find each indicated sum.*

**29.** $\displaystyle\sum_{i=1}^{6} 5i$

**30.** $\displaystyle\sum_{i=1}^{6} 7i$

**31.** $\displaystyle\sum_{i=1}^{4} 2i^2$

**32.** $\displaystyle\sum_{i=1}^{5} i^3$

**33.** $\displaystyle\sum_{k=1}^{5} k(k + 4)$

**34.** $\displaystyle\sum_{k=1}^{4} (k - 3)(k + 2)$

**35.** $\displaystyle\sum_{i=1}^{4} \left(-\dfrac{1}{2}\right)^i$

**36.** $\displaystyle\sum_{i=2}^{4} \left(-\dfrac{1}{3}\right)^i$

**37.** $\displaystyle\sum_{i=5}^{9} 11$

**38.** $\displaystyle\sum_{i=3}^{7} 12$

**39.** $\displaystyle\sum_{i=0}^{4} \dfrac{(-1)^i}{i!}$

**40.** $\displaystyle\sum_{i=0}^{4} \dfrac{(-1)^{i+1}}{(i + 1)!}$

**41.** $\displaystyle\sum_{i=1}^{5} \dfrac{i!}{(i - 1)!}$

**42.** $\displaystyle\sum_{i=1}^{5} \dfrac{(i + 2)!}{i!}$

*In Exercises 43–54, express each sum using summation notation. Use 1 as the lower limit of summation and i for the index of summation.*

**43.** $1^2 + 2^2 + 3^2 + \cdots + 15^2$

**44.** $1^4 + 2^4 + 3^4 + \cdots + 12^4$

**45.** $2 + 2^2 + 2^3 + \cdots + 2^{11}$

**46.** $5 + 5^2 + 5^3 + \cdots + 5^{12}$

**47.** $1 + 2 + 3 + \cdots + 30$

**48.** $1 + 2 + 3 + \cdots + 40$

**49.** $\dfrac{1}{2} + \dfrac{2}{3} + \dfrac{3}{4} + \cdots + \dfrac{14}{14 + 1}$

**50.** $\dfrac{1}{3} + \dfrac{2}{4} + \dfrac{3}{5} + \cdots + \dfrac{16}{16 + 2}$

**51.** $4 + \dfrac{4^2}{2} + \dfrac{4^3}{3} + \cdots + \dfrac{4^n}{n}$

**52.** $\dfrac{1}{9} + \dfrac{2}{9^2} + \dfrac{3}{9^3} + \cdots + \dfrac{n}{9^n}$

**53.** $1 + 3 + 5 + \cdots + (2n - 1)$

**54.** $a + ar + ar^2 + \cdots + ar^{n-1}$

*In Exercises 55–60, express each sum using summation notation. Use a lower limit of summation of your choice and k for the index of summation.*

**55.** $5 + 7 + 9 + 11 + \cdots + 31$

**56.** $6 + 8 + 10 + 12 + \cdots + 32$

**57.** $a + ar + ar^2 + \cdots + ar^{12}$

**58.** $a + ar + ar^2 + \cdots + ar^{14}$

**59.** $a + (a + d) + (a + 2d) + \cdots + (a + nd)$

**60.** $(a + d) + (a + d^2) + \cdots + (a + d^n)$

## Practice Plus

*In Exercises 61–68, use the graphs of $\{a_n\}$ and $\{b_n\}$ to find each indicated sum.*

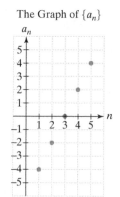

The Graph of $\{a_n\}$

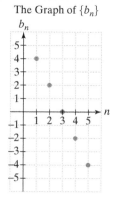

The Graph of $\{b_n\}$

**61.** $\displaystyle\sum_{i=1}^{5} (a_i^2 + 1)$

**62.** $\displaystyle\sum_{i=1}^{5} (b_i^2 - 1)$

**63.** $\displaystyle\sum_{i=1}^{5} (2a_i + b_i)$

**64.** $\displaystyle\sum_{i=1}^{5} (a_i + 3b_i)$

**65.** $\sum_{i=4}^{5}\left(\dfrac{a_i}{b_i}\right)^2$  **66.** $\sum_{i=4}^{5}\left(\dfrac{a_i}{b_i}\right)^3$

**67.** $\sum_{i=1}^{5} a_i^2 + \sum_{i=1}^{5} b_i^2$  **68.** $\sum_{i=1}^{5} a_i^2 - \sum_{i=3}^{5} b_i^2$

## Application Exercises

**69.** Advertisers don't have to fear that they'll face a sea of "sold out" signs as they rush to the Internet. The growing number of popular sites filled with user-created content, including MySpace.com and YouTube.com, provide plenty of inventory for advertisers who can't find space on top portals such as Yahoo. The bar graph shows U.S. online ad spending, in billions of dollars, from 2000 through 2006.

**United States Online Ad Spending**

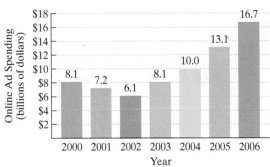

*Source:* eMarketer

Let $a_n$ represent online ad spending, in billions of dollars, $n$ years after 1999.

**a.** Use the numbers given in the graph to find and interpret $\dfrac{1}{7}\sum_{i=1}^{7} a_i$.

**b.** The finite sequence whose general term is
$$a_n = 0.5n^2 - 1.5n + 8,$$
where $n = 1, 2, 3, \ldots, 7$, models online ad spending, $a_n$, in billions of dollars, $n$ years after 1999. Use the model to find $\dfrac{1}{7}\sum_{i=1}^{7} a_i$. Does this underestimate or overestimate the actual sum in part (a)? By how much?

**70.** More and more television commercial time is devoted to drug companies as hucksters for the benefits and risks of their wares. The bar graph shows the amount that drug companies spent on consumer drug ads, in billions of dollars, from 2002 through 2006.

**Spending for Consumer Drug Ads**

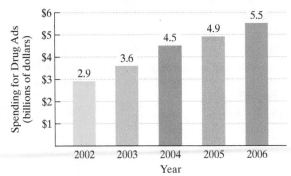

*Source:* Nielsen Monitor-Plus

Let $a_n$ represent spending for consumer drug ads, in billions of dollars, $n$ years after 2001.

**a.** Use the numbers given in the graph to find and interpret $\dfrac{1}{5}\sum_{i=1}^{5} a_i$.

**b.** The finite sequence whose general term is
$$a_n = 0.65n + 2.3,$$
where $n = 1, 2, 3, 4, 5$, models spending for consumer drug ads, in billions of dollars, $n$ years after 2001. Use the model to find $\dfrac{1}{5}\sum_{i=1}^{5} a_i$. Does this seem reasonable in terms of the actual sum in part (a), or has model breakdown occurred?

**71.** A deposit of $6000 is made in an account that earns 6% interest compounded quarterly. The balance in the account after $n$ quarters is given by the sequence
$$a_n = 6000\left(1 + \dfrac{0.06}{4}\right)^n, \quad n = 1, 2, 3, \ldots.$$
Find the balance in the account after five years. Round to the nearest cent.

**72.** A deposit of $10,000 is made in an account that earns 8% interest compounded quarterly. The balance in the account after $n$ quarters is given by the sequence
$$a_n = 10{,}000\left(1 + \dfrac{0.08}{4}\right)^n, \quad n = 1, 2, 3, \ldots.$$
Find the balance in the account after six years. Round to the nearest cent.

## Writing in Mathematics

**73.** What is a sequence? Give an example with your description.

**74.** Explain how to write terms of a sequence if the formula for the general term is given.

**75.** What does the graph of a sequence look like? How is it obtained?

**76.** What is a recursion formula?

**77.** Explain how to find $n!$ if $n$ is a positive integer.

**78.** Explain the best way to evaluate $\dfrac{900!}{899!}$ without a calculator.

**79.** What is the meaning of the symbol $\Sigma$? Give an example with your description.

**80.** You buy a new car for $24,000. At the end of $n$ years, the value of your car is given by the sequence
$$a_n = 24{,}000\left(\dfrac{3}{4}\right)^n, \quad n = 1, 2, 3, \ldots.$$
Find $a_5$ and write a sentence explaining what this value represents. Describe the $n$th term of the sequence in terms of the value of your car at the end of each year.

## Technology Exercises

*In Exercises 81–85, use a calculator's factorial key to evaluate each expression.*

**81.** $\dfrac{200!}{198!}$  **82.** $\left(\dfrac{300}{20}\right)!$  **83.** $\dfrac{20!}{300}$

**84.** $\dfrac{20!}{(20-3)!}$

**85.** $\dfrac{54!}{(54-3)!3!}$

**86.** Use the $\boxed{\text{SEQ}}$ (sequence) capability of a graphing utility to verify the terms of the sequences you obtained for any five sequences from Exercises 1–12 or 19–22.

**87.** Use the $\boxed{\text{SUM}}$ $\boxed{\text{SEQ}}$ (sum of the sequence) capability of a graphing utility to verify any five of the sums you obtained in Exercises 29–42.

**88.** As $n$ increases, the terms of the sequence

$$a_n = \left(1 + \frac{1}{n}\right)^n$$

get closer and closer to the number $e$ (where $e \approx 2.7183$). Use a calculator to find $a_{10}, a_{100}, a_{1000}, a_{10,000},$ and $a_{100,000}$, comparing these terms to your calculator's decimal approximation for $e$.

*Many graphing utilities have a sequence-graphing mode that plots the terms of a sequence as points on a rectangular coordinate system. Consult your manual; if your graphing utility has this capability, use it to graph each of the sequences in Exercises 89–92. What appears to be happening to the terms of each sequence as n gets larger?*

**89.** $a_n = \dfrac{n}{n+1}$  $n:[0, 10, 1]$ by $a_n:[0, 1, 0.1]$

**90.** $a_n = \dfrac{100}{n}$  $n:[0, 1000, 100]$ by $a_n:[0, 1, 0.1]$

**91.** $a_n = \dfrac{2n^2 + 5n - 7}{n^3}$  $n:[0, 10, 1]$ by $a_n:[0, 2, 0.2]$

**92.** $a_n = \dfrac{3n^4 + n - 1}{5n^4 + 2n^2 + 1}$  $n:[0, 10, 1]$ by $a_n:[0, 1, 0.1]$

## Critical Thinking Exercises

**Make Sense?**  *In Exercises 93–96, determine whether each statement makes sense or does not make sense, and explain your reasoning.*

**93.** Now that I've studied sequences, I realize that the joke in this cartoon is based on the fact that you can't have a negative number of sheep.

WHEN MATHEMATICIANS CAN'T SLEEP

**94.** By writing $a_1, a_2, a_3, a_4, \ldots, a_n, \ldots,$ I can see that the range of a sequence is the set of positive integers.

**95.** It makes a difference whether or not I use parentheses around the expression following the summation symbol, because the value of $\displaystyle\sum_{i=1}^{8} (i + 7)$ is 92, but the value of $\displaystyle\sum_{i=1}^{8} i + 7$ is 43.

**96.** Without writing out the terms, I can see that $(-1)^{2n}$ in $a_n = \dfrac{(-1)^{2n}}{3n}$ causes the terms to alternate in sign.

*In Exercises 97–100, determine whether each statement is true or false. If the statement is false, make the necessary change(s) to produce a true statement.*

**97.** $\dfrac{n!}{(n-1)!} = \dfrac{1}{n-1}$

**98.** The Fibonacci sequence 1, 1, 2, 3, 5, 8, 13, 21, 34, 55, 89, 144, … can be defined recursively using $a_0 = 1, a_1 = 1$; $a_n = a_{n-2} + a_{n-1}$, where $n \geq 2$.

**99.** $\displaystyle\sum_{i=1}^{2} (-1)^i 2^i = 0$

**100.** $\displaystyle\sum_{i=1}^{2} a_i b_i = \sum_{i=1}^{2} a_i \sum_{i=1}^{2} b_i$

**101.** Write the first five terms of the sequence whose first term is 9 and whose general term is

$$a_n = \begin{cases} \dfrac{a_{n-1}}{2} & \text{if } a_{n-1} \text{ is even} \\ 3a_{n-1} + 5 & \text{if } a_{n-1} \text{ is odd} \end{cases}$$

for $n \geq 2$.

## Group Exercise

**102.** Enough curiosities involving the Fibonacci sequence exist to warrant a flourishing Fibonacci Association, which publishes a quarterly journal. Do some research on the Fibonacci sequence by consulting the Internet or the research department of your library, and find one property that interests you. After doing this research, get together with your group to share these intriguing properties.

## Preview Exercises

*Exercises 103–105 will help you prepare for the material covered in the next section.*

**103.** Consider the sequence 8, 3, −2, −7, −12, …. Find $a_2 - a_1$, $a_3 - a_2, a_4 - a_3,$ and $a_5 - a_4$. What do you observe?

**104.** Consider the sequence whose $n$th term is $a_n = 4n - 3$. Find $a_2 - a_1, a_3 - a_2, a_4 - a_3,$ and $a_5 - a_4$. What do you observe?

**105.** Use the formula $a_n = 4 + (n - 1)(-7)$ to find the eighth term of the sequence 4, −3, −10, ….

## Section 10.2 Arithmetic Sequences

### Objectives

1. Find the common difference for an arithmetic sequence.
2. Write terms of an arithmetic sequence.
3. Use the formula for the general term of an arithmetic sequence.
4. Use the formula for the sum of the first $n$ terms of an arithmetic sequence.

Your grandmother and her financial counselor are looking at options in case an adult residential facility is needed in the future. The good news is that your grandmother's total assets are $500,000. The bad news is that adult residential community costs average $64,130 annually, increasing by $1800 each year. In this section, we will see how sequences can be used to model your grandmother's situation and help her to identify realistic options.

① Find the common difference for an arithmetic sequence.

### Arithmetic Sequences

The bar graph in **Figure 10.2** shows annual salaries, rounded to the nearest thousand dollars, of U.S. senators from 2000 to 2005. The graph illustrates that each year salaries increased by $4 thousand. The sequence of annual salaries

$$142, 146, 150, 154, 158, 162, \ldots$$

shows that each term after the first, 142, differs from the preceding term by a constant amount, namely 4. This sequence is an example of an *arithmetic sequence*.

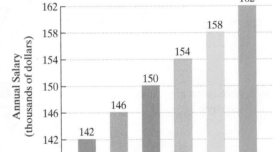

**Annual Salaries of U.S. Senators**

Figure 10.2 *Source:* U.S. Senate

### Definition of an Arithmetic Sequence

An **arithmetic sequence** is a sequence in which each term after the first differs from the preceding term by a constant amount. The difference between consecutive terms is called the **common difference** of the sequence.

The common difference, $d$, is found by subtracting any term from the term that directly follows it. In the following examples, the common difference is found by subtracting the first term from the second term, $a_2 - a_1$.

| Arithmetic Sequence | Common Difference |
|---|---|
| $142, 146, 150, 154, 158, \ldots$ | $d = 146 - 142 = 4$ |
| $-5, -2, 1, 4, 7, \ldots$ | $d = -2 - (-5) = -2 + 5 = 3$ |
| $8, 3, -2, -7, -12, \ldots$ | $d = 3 - 8 = -5$ |

**Figure 10.3** shows the graphs of the last two arithmetic sequences in our list. The common difference for the increasing sequence in **Figure 10.3(a)** is 3. The common difference for the decreasing sequence in **Figure 10.3(b)** is −5.

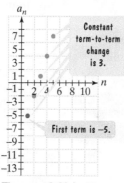

**Figure 10.3(a)** The graph of $\{a_n\} = -5, -2, 1, 4, 7, \dots$

**Figure 10.3(b)** The graph of $\{b_n\} = 8, 3, -2, -7, -12, \dots$

The graph of each arithmetic sequence in **Figure 10.3** forms a set of discrete points lying on a straight line. This illustrates that **an arithmetic sequence is a linear function whose domain is the set of positive integers**.

If the first term of an arithmetic sequence is $a_1$, each term after the first is obtained by adding $d$, the common difference, to the previous term. This can be expressed recursively as follows:

$$a_n = a_{n-1} + d.$$

Add $d$ to the term in any position to get the next term.

To use this recursion formula, we must be given the first term.

**②** Write terms of an arithmetic sequence.

**EXAMPLE 1** **Writing the Terms of an Arithmetic Sequence**

Write the first six terms of the arithmetic sequence in which $a_1 = 6$ and $a_n = a_{n-1} - 2$.

**Solution** The recursion formula $a_1 = 6$ and $a_n = a_{n-1} - 2$ indicates that each term after the first, 6, is obtained by adding −2 to the previous term.

| | |
|---|---|
| $a_1 = 6$ | This is given. |
| $a_2 = a_1 - 2 = 6 - 2 \quad = 4$ | Use $a_n = a_{n-1} - 2$ with $n = 2$. |
| $a_3 = a_2 - 2 = 4 - 2 \quad = 2$ | Use $a_n = a_{n-1} - 2$ with $n = 3$. |
| $a_4 = a_3 - 2 = 2 - 2 \quad = 0$ | Use $a_n = a_{n-1} - 2$ with $n = 4$. |
| $a_5 = a_4 - 2 = 0 - 2 \quad = -2$ | Use $a_n = a_{n-1} - 2$ with $n = 5$. |
| $a_6 = a_5 - 2 = -2 - 2 = -4$ | Use $a_n = a_{n-1} - 2$ with $n = 6$. |

The first six terms are

$$6, 4, 2, 0, -2, \text{ and } -4.$$

**Check Point 1** Write the first six terms of the arithmetic sequence in which $a_1 = 100$ and $a_n = a_{n-1} - 30$.

**③** Use the formula for the general term of an arithmetic sequence.

## The General Term of an Arithmetic Sequence

Consider an arithmetic sequence whose first term is $a_1$ and whose common difference is $d$. We are looking for a formula for the general term, $a_n$. Let's begin by writing the first six terms. The first term is $a_1$. The second term is $a_1 + d$. The third term is

$a_1 + d + d$, or $a_1 + 2d$. Thus, we start with $a_1$ and add $d$ to each successive term. The first six terms are

$$a_1, \quad a_1 + d, \quad a_1 + 2d, \quad a_1 + 3d, \quad a_1 + 4d, \quad a_1 + 5d.$$

| $a_1$, first term | $a_2$, second term | $a_3$, third term | $a_4$, fourth term | $a_5$, fifth term | $a_6$, sixth term |

Compare the coefficient of $d$ and the subscript of $a$ denoting the term number. Can you see that the coefficient of $d$ is 1 less than the subscript of $a$ denoting the term number?

$a_3$: third term $= a_1 + 2d$          $a_4$: fourth term $= a_1 + 3d$

One less than 3, or 2, is the coefficient of $d$.

One less than 4, or 3, is the coefficient of $d$.

Thus, the formula for the $n$th term is

$$a_n\text{: }n\text{th term} = a_1 + (n - 1)d.$$

One less than $n$, or $n - 1$, is the coefficient of $d$.

### General Term of an Arithmetic Sequence

The $n$th term (the general term) of an arithmetic sequence with first term $a_1$ and common difference $d$ is

$$a_n = a_1 + (n - 1)d.$$

**( EXAMPLE 2 ) Using the Formula for the General Term of an Arithmetic Sequence**

Find the eighth term of the arithmetic sequence whose first term is 4 and whose common difference is $-7$.

**Solution**   To find the eighth term, $a_8$, we replace $n$ in the formula with 8, $a_1$ with 4, and $d$ with $-7$.

$$a_n = a_1 + (n - 1)d$$
$$a_8 = 4 + (8 - 1)(-7) = 4 + 7(-7) = 4 + (-49) = -45$$

The eighth term is $-45$. We can check this result by writing the first eight terms of the sequence:

$$4, -3, -10, -17, -24, -31, -38, -45.$$

⬤

⊘ Check Point **2**  Find the ninth term of the arithmetic sequence whose first term is 6 and whose common difference is $-5$.

**( EXAMPLE 3 ) Using an Arithmetic Sequence to Model Teachers' Earnings**

According to the National Education Association, teachers in the United States earned an average of $44,600 in 2002. This amount has increased by approximately $1130 per year.

**a.** Write a formula for the $n$th term of the arithmetic sequence that describes teachers' average earnings $n$ years after 2001.

**b.** How much will U.S. teachers earn, on average, by the year 2012?

**Solution**

a. With a yearly increase of $1130, we can express teachers' earnings by the following arithmetic sequence:

$$44{,}600, \quad 44{,}600 + 1130 = 45{,}730, \quad 45{,}730 + 1130 = 46{,}860, \ldots .$$

| $a_1$: earnings in 2002, 1 year after 2001 | $a_2$: earnings in 2003, 2 years after 2001 | $a_3$: earnings in 2004, 3 years after 2001 |

In the sequence 44,600, 45,730, 46,860, …, $a_1$, the first term, represents the amount teachers earned in 2002. Each subsequent year this amount increases by $1130, so $d = 1130$. We use the formula for the general term of an arithmetic sequence to write the $n$th term of the sequence that describes teachers' earnings $n$ years after 2001.

$a_n = a_1 + (n - 1)d$     This is the formula for the general term of an arithmetic sequence.

$a_n = 44{,}600 + (n - 1)1130$     $a_1 = 44{,}600$ and $d = 1130$.

$a_n = 44{,}600 + 1130n - 1130$     Distribute 1130 to each term in parentheses.

$a_n = 1130n + 43{,}470$     Simplify.

Thus, teachers' earnings $n$ years after 2001 can be described by $a_n = 1130n + 43{,}470$.

b. Now we need to project teachers' earnings in 2012. The year 2012 is 11 years after 2001. Thus, $n = 11$. We substitute 11 for $n$ in $a_n = 1130n + 43{,}470$.

$$a_{11} = 1130 \cdot 11 + 43{,}470 = 55{,}900$$

The 11th term of the sequence is 55,900. Thus, U.S. teachers are projected to earn an average of $55,900 by the year 2012.   ●

⊘ Check Point **3** Thanks to drive-thrus and curbside delivery, Americans are eating more meals behind the wheel. In 2004, we averaged 32 à la car meals, increasing by approximately 0.7 meal per year. (*Source: Newsweek*)

a. Write a formula for the $n$th term of the arithmetic sequence that models the average number of car meals $n$ years after 2003.

b. How many car meals will Americans average by the year 2014?

④ Use the formula for the sum of the first $n$ terms of an arithmetic sequence.

## The Sum of the First n Terms of an Arithmetic Sequence

The sum of the first $n$ terms of an arithmetic sequence, denoted by $S_n$, and called the **$n$th partial sum**, can be found without having to add up all the terms. Let

$$S_n = a_1 + a_2 + a_3 + \cdots + a_n$$

be the sum of the first $n$ terms of an arithmetic sequence. Because $d$ is the common difference between terms, $S_n$ can be written forward and backward as follows:

| Forward: Start with the first term, $a_1$. Keep adding $d$. | |
| --- | --- |

$S_n = a_1 \qquad\qquad + (a_1 + d) + (a_1 + 2d) + \cdots + a_n$

$S_n = a_n \qquad\qquad + (a_n - d) + (a_n - 2d) + \cdots + a_1$

Backward: Start with the last term, $a_n$. Keep subtracting $d$.

$2S_n = (a_1 + a_n) + (a_1 + a_n) + (a_1 + a_n) + \cdots + (a_1 + a_n).$    Add the two equations.

Because there are $n$ sums of $(a_1 + a_n)$ on the right side, we can express this side as $n(a_1 + a_n)$. Thus, the last equation can be written as follows:

$$2S_n = n(a_1 + a_n)$$

$$S_n = \frac{n}{2}(a_1 + a_n). \quad \text{Solve for } S_n, \text{ dividing both sides by 2.}$$

We have proved the following result:

### The Sum of the First $n$ Terms of an Arithmetic Sequence

The sum, $S_n$, of the first $n$ terms of an arithmetic sequence is given by

$$S_n = \frac{n}{2}(a_1 + a_n),$$

in which $a_1$ is the first term and $a_n$ is the $n$th term.

To find the sum of the terms of an arithmetic sequence using $S_n = \frac{n}{2}(a_1 + a_n)$, we need to know the first term, $a_1$, the last term, $a_n$, and the number of terms, $n$. The following examples illustrate how to use this formula.

( EXAMPLE 4 ) **Finding the Sum of $n$ Terms of an Arithmetic Sequence**

Find the sum of the first 100 terms of the arithmetic sequence: $1, 3, 5, 7, \ldots$.

**Solution** By finding the sum of the first 100 terms of $1, 3, 5, 7, \ldots$, we are finding the sum of the first 100 odd numbers. To find the sum of the first 100 terms, $S_{100}$, we replace $n$ in the formula with 100.

$$S_n = \frac{n}{2}(a_1 + a_n)$$

$$S_{100} = \frac{100}{2}(a_1 + a_{100})$$

> The first term, $a_1$, is 1.

> We must find $a_{100}$, the 100th term.

We use the formula for the general term of a sequence to find $a_{100}$. The common difference, $d$, of $1, 3, 5, 7, \ldots$, is 2.

$$a_n = a_1 + (n - 1)d \qquad \text{This is the formula for the } n\text{th term of an arithmetic sequence. Use it to find the 100th term.}$$

$$a_{100} = 1 + (100 - 1) \cdot 2 \qquad \text{Substitute 100 for } n, 2 \text{ for } d, \text{ and } 1 \text{ (the first term) for } a_1.$$

$$= 1 + 99 \cdot 2 \qquad \text{Perform the subtraction in parentheses.}$$

$$= 1 + 198 = 199 \qquad \text{Multiply } (99 \cdot 2 = 198) \text{ and then add.}$$

Now we are ready to find the sum of the 100 terms $1, 3, 5, 7, \ldots, 199$.

$$S_n = \frac{n}{2}(a_1 + a_n) \qquad \text{Use the formula for the sum of the first } n \text{ terms of an arithmetic sequence. Let } n = 100, a_1 = 1, \text{ and } a_{100} = 199.$$

$$S_{100} = \frac{100}{2}(1 + 199) = 50(200) = 10{,}000$$

The sum of the first 100 odd numbers is 10,000. Equivalently, the 100th partial sum of the sequence $1, 3, 5, 7, \ldots$ is 10,000.

⊘ Check Point **4** Find the sum of the first 15 terms of the arithmetic sequence: $3, 6, 9, 12, \ldots$.

**Technology**

To find

$$\sum_{i=1}^{25} (5i - 9)$$

on a graphing utility, enter

SUM SEQ $(5x - 9, x, 1, 25, 1)$.

Then press ENTER.

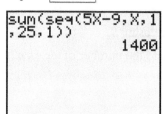

(EXAMPLE 5) **Using $S_n$ to Evaluate a Summation**

Find the following sum: $\sum_{i=1}^{25} (5i - 9)$.

**Solution**

$$\sum_{i=1}^{25} (5i - 9) = (5 \cdot 1 - 9) + (5 \cdot 2 - 9) + (5 \cdot 3 - 9) + \cdots + (5 \cdot 25 - 9)$$

$$= -4 \qquad + 1 \qquad + 6 \qquad + \cdots + 116$$

By evaluating the first three terms and the last term, we see that $a_1 = -4$; $d$, the common difference, is $1 - (-4)$, or 5; and $a_{25}$, the last term, is 116.

$$S_n = \frac{n}{2}(a_1 + a_n) \qquad \text{Use the formula for the sum of the first } n \text{ terms of an arithmetic sequence. Let } n = 25, a_1 = -4, \text{ and } a_{25} = 116.$$

$$S_{25} = \frac{25}{2}(-4 + 116) = \frac{25}{2}(112) = 1400$$

Thus,

$$\sum_{i=1}^{25} (5i - 9) = 1400. \qquad \bullet$$

⊘ Check Point **5** Find the following sum: $\sum_{i=1}^{30} (6i - 11)$.

(EXAMPLE 6) **Modeling Total Residential Community Costs over a Six-Year Period**

Your grandmother has assets of $500,000. One option that she is considering involves an adult residential community for a six-year period beginning in 2009. The model

$$a_n = 1800n + 64{,}130$$

describes yearly adult residential community costs $n$ years after 2008. Does your grandmother have enough to pay for the facility?

**Solution**  We must find the sum of an arithmetic sequence whose general term is $a_n = 1800n + 64{,}130$. The first term of the sequence corresponds to the facility's costs in the year 2009. The last term corresponds to costs in the year 2014. Because the model describes costs $n$ years after 2008, $n = 1$ describes the year 2009 and $n = 6$ describes the year 2014.

$$a_n = 1800n + 64{,}130 \qquad \text{This is the given formula for the general term of the sequence.}$$

$$a_1 = 1800 \cdot 1 + 64{,}130 = 65{,}930 \qquad \text{Find } a_1 \text{ by replacing } n \text{ with 1.}$$

$$a_6 = 1800 \cdot 6 + 64{,}130 = 74{,}930 \qquad \text{Find } a_6 \text{ by replacing } n \text{ with 6.}$$

The first year the facility will cost $65,930. By year six, the facility will cost $74,930. Now we must find the sum of the costs for all six years. We focus on the sum of the first six terms of the arithmetic sequence

$$65{,}930, \ 67{,}730, \ \ldots \ , \ 74{,}930.$$

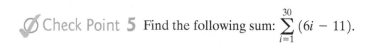

We find this sum using the formula for the sum of the first $n$ terms of an arithmetic sequence. We are adding 6 terms: $n = 6$. The first term is 65,930: $a_1 = 65{,}930$. The last term—that is, the sixth term—is 74,930: $a_6 = 74{,}930$.

$$S_n = \frac{n}{2}(a_1 + a_n)$$

$$S_6 = \frac{6}{2}(65{,}930 + 74{,}930) = 3(140{,}860) = 422{,}580$$

Total adult residential community costs for your grandmother are predicted to be $422,580. Because your grandmother's assets are $500,000, she has enough to pay for the facility for the six-year period. ●

⊘ Check Point **6** In Example 6, how much would it cost for the adult residential community for a ten-year period beginning in 2009?

## Exercise Set 10.2

### Practice Exercises

*In Exercises 1–14, write the first six terms of each arithmetic sequence.*

**1.** $a_1 = 200, d = 20$

**2.** $a_1 = 300, d = 50$

**3.** $a_1 = -7, d = 4$

**4.** $a_1 = -8, d = 5$

**5.** $a_1 = 300, d = -90$

**6.** $a_1 = 200, d = -60$

**7.** $a_1 = \frac{5}{2}, d = -\frac{1}{2}$

**8.** $a_1 = \frac{3}{4}, d = -\frac{1}{4}$

**9.** $a_n = a_{n-1} + 6, a_1 = -9$

**10.** $a_n = a_{n-1} + 4, a_1 = -7$

**11.** $a_n = a_{n-1} - 10, a_1 = 30$

**12.** $a_n = a_{n-1} - 20, a_1 = 50$

**13.** $a_n = a_{n-1} - 0.4, a_1 = 1.6$

**14.** $a_n = a_{n-1} - 0.3, a_1 = -1.7$

*In Exercises 15–22, find the indicated term of the arithmetic sequence with first term, $a_1$, and common difference, $d$.*

**15.** Find $a_6$ when $a_1 = 13, d = 4$.

**16.** Find $a_{16}$ when $a_1 = 9, d = 2$.

**17.** Find $a_{50}$ when $a_1 = 7, d = 5$.

**18.** Find $a_{60}$ when $a_1 = 8, d = 6$.

**19.** Find $a_{200}$ when $a_1 = -40, d = 5$.

**20.** Find $a_{150}$ when $a_1 = -60, d = 5$.

**21.** Find $a_{60}$ when $a_1 = 35, d = -3$.

**22.** Find $a_{70}$ when $a_1 = -32, d = 4$.

*In Exercises 23–34, write a formula for the general term (the nth term) of each arithmetic sequence. Do not use a recursion formula. Then use the formula for $a_n$ to find $a_{20}$, the 20th term of the sequence.*

**23.** $1, 5, 9, 13, \ldots$

**24.** $2, 7, 12, 17, \ldots$

**25.** $7, 3, -1, -5, \ldots$

**26.** $6, 1, -4, -9, \ldots$

**27.** $a_1 = 9, d = 2$

**28.** $a_1 = 6, d = 3$

**29.** $a_1 = -20, d = -4$

**30.** $a_1 = -70, d = -5$

**31.** $a_n = a_{n-1} + 3, a_1 = 4$

**32.** $a_n = a_{n-1} + 5, a_1 = 6$

**33.** $a_n = a_{n-1} - 10, a_1 = 30$

**34.** $a_n = a_{n-1} - 12, a_1 = 24$

**35.** Find the sum of the first 20 terms of the arithmetic sequence: $4, 10, 16, 22, \ldots$.

**36.** Find the sum of the first 25 terms of the arithmetic sequence: $7, 19, 31, 43, \ldots$.

**37.** Find the sum of the first 50 terms of the arithmetic sequence: $-10, -6, -2, 2, \ldots$.

**38.** Find the sum of the first 50 terms of the arithmetic sequence: $-15, -9, -3, 3, \ldots$.

**39.** Find $1 + 2 + 3 + 4 + \cdots + 100$, the sum of the first 100 natural numbers.

**40.** Find $2 + 4 + 6 + 8 + \cdots + 200$, the sum of the first 100 positive even integers.

**41.** Find the sum of the first 60 positive even integers.

**42.** Find the sum of the first 80 positive even integers.

**43.** Find the sum of the even integers between 21 and 45.

**44.** Find the sum of the odd integers between 30 and 54.

*For Exercises 45–50, write out the first three terms and the last term. Then use the formula for the sum of the first n terms of an arithmetic sequence to find the indicated sum.*

**45.** $\displaystyle\sum_{i=1}^{17} (5i + 3)$

**46.** $\displaystyle\sum_{i=1}^{20} (6i - 4)$

**47.** $\displaystyle\sum_{i=1}^{30} (-3i + 5)$

**48.** $\displaystyle\sum_{i=1}^{40} (-2i + 6)$

**49.** $\displaystyle\sum_{i=1}^{100} 4i$

**50.** $\displaystyle\sum_{i=1}^{50} (-4i)$

## Practice Plus

*Use the graphs of the arithmetic sequences {$a_n$} and {$b_n$} to solve Exercises 51–58.*

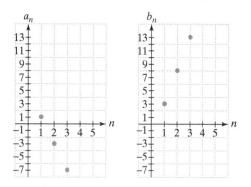

**51.** Find $a_{14} + b_{12}$.   **52.** Find $a_{16} + b_{18}$.

**53.** If {$a_n$} is a finite sequence whose last term is −83, how many terms does {$a_n$} contain?

**54.** If {$b_n$} is a finite sequence whose last term is 93, how many terms does {$b_n$} contain?

**55.** Find the difference between the sum of the first 14 terms of {$b_n$} and the sum of the first 14 terms of {$a_n$}.

**56.** Find the difference between the sum of the first 15 terms of {$b_n$} and the sum of the first 15 terms of {$a_n$}.

**57.** Write a linear function $f(x) = mx + b$, whose domain is the set of positive integers, that represents {$a_n$}.

**58.** Write a linear function $g(x) = mx + b$, whose domain is the set of positive integers, that represents {$b_n$}.

*Use a system of two equations in two variables, $a_1$ and $d$, to solve Exercises 59–60.*

**59.** Write a formula for the general term (the $n$th term) of the arithmetic sequence whose second term, $a_2$, is 4 and whose sixth term, $a_6$, is 16.

**60.** Write a formula for the general term (the $n$th term) of the arithmetic sequence whose third term, $a_3$, is 7 and whose eighth term, $a_8$, is 17.

## Application Exercises

*The bar graphs show changes that have taken place in the United States over time. Exercises 61–62 involve developing arithmetic sequences that model the data.*

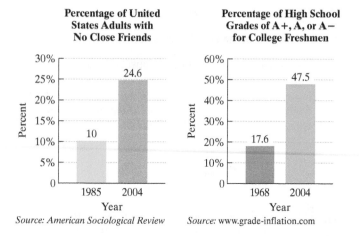

*Source: American Sociological Review*   *Source: www.grade-inflation.com*

**61.** In 1985, 10% of Americans had no close friends. On average, this has increased by approximately 0.77% per year.

   **a.** Write a formula for the $n$th term of the arithmetic sequence that models the percentage of Americans with no close friends $n$ years after 1984.

   **b.** If trends shown by the model in part (a) continue, what percentage of Americans will have no close friends in 2011? Round to one decimal place.

**62.** In 1968, 17.6% of high school grades for college freshmen consisted of A's (A+, A, or A−). On average, this has increased by approximately 0.83% per year.

   **a.** Write a formula for the $n$th term of the arithmetic sequence that models the percentage of high school grades of A for college freshmen $n$ years after 1967.

   **b.** If trends shown by the model in part (a) continue, what percentage of high school grades for college freshmen will consist of A's in 2018?

**63.** Company A pays $24,000 yearly with raises of $1600 per year. Company B pays $28,000 yearly with raises of $1000 per year. Which company will pay more in year 10? How much more?

**64.** Company A pays $23,000 yearly with raises of $1200 per year. Company B pays $26,000 yearly with raises of $800 per year. Which company will pay more in year 10? How much more?

*In Exercises 65–67, we revisit the data from Chapter P showing the average cost of tuition and fees at public and private four-year U.S. colleges.*

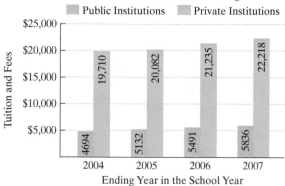

*Source:* The College Board

**65. a.** Use the numbers shown in the bar graph to find the total cost of tuition and fees at public colleges for a four-year period from the school year ending in 2004 through the school year ending in 2007.

   **b.** The model

$$a_n = 379n + 4342$$

describes the cost of tuition and fees at public colleges in academic year $n$, where $n = 1$ corresponds to the school year ending in 2004, $n = 2$ to the school year ending in 2005, and so on. Use this model and the formula for $S_n$ to find the total cost of tuition and fees at public colleges for a four-year period from the school year ending in 2004 through the school year ending in 2007. Does the model underestimate or overestimate the actual sum you obtained in part (a)? By how much?

**66. a.** Use the numbers shown in the bar graph to find the total cost of tuition and fees at private colleges for a four-year period from the school year ending in 2004 through the school year ending in 2007.

**b.** The model

$$a_n = 868n + 18{,}642$$

describes the cost of tuition and fees at private colleges in academic year $n$, where $n = 1$ corresponds to the school year ending in 2004, $n = 2$ to the school year ending in 2005, and so on. Use this model and the formula for $S_n$ to find the total cost of tuition and fees at private colleges for a four-year period from the school year ending in 2004 through the school year ending in 2007. Does the model underestimate or overestimate the actual sum that you obtained in part (a)? By how much?

**67.** Use one of the models in Exercises 65–66 and the formula for $S_n$ to find the total cost of tuition and fees for your undergraduate education. How well does the model describe your anticipated costs?

**68.** A company offers a starting yearly salary of $33,000 with raises of $2500 per year. Find the total salary over a ten-year period.

**69.** You are considering two job offers. Company A will start you at $19,000 a year and guarantee a raise of $2600 per year. Company B will start you at a higher salary, $27,000 a year, but will only guarantee a raise of $1200 per year. Find the total salary that each company will pay over a ten-year period. Which company pays the greater total amount?

**70.** A theater has 30 seats in the first row, 32 seats in the second row, increasing by 2 seats per row for a total of 26 rows. How many seats are there in the theater?

**71.** A section in a stadium has 20 seats in the first row, 23 seats in the second row, increasing by 3 seats each row for a total of 38 rows. How many seats are in this section of the stadium?

## Writing in Mathematics

**72.** What is an arithmetic sequence? Give an example with your explanation.

**73.** What is the common difference in an arithmetic sequence?

**74.** Explain how to find the general term of an arithmetic sequence.

**75.** Explain how to find the sum of the first $n$ terms of an arithmetic sequence without having to add up all the terms.

## Technology Exercises

**76.** Use the $\boxed{\text{SEQ}}$ (sequence) capability of a graphing utility and the formula you obtained for $a_n$ to verify the value you found for $a_{20}$ in any five exercises from Exercises 23–34.

**77.** Use the capability of a graphing utility to calculate the sum of a sequence to verify any five of your answers to Exercises 45–50.

## Critical Thinking Exercises

**Make Sense?** *In Exercises 78–81, determine whether each statement makes sense or does not make sense, and explain your reasoning.*

**78.** Rather than performing the addition, I used the formula $S_n = \frac{n}{2}(a_1 + a_n)$ to find the sum of the first thirty terms of the sequence $2, 4, 8, 16, 32, \ldots$.

**79.** I was able to find the sum of the first fifty terms of an arithmetic sequence even though I did not identify every term.

**80.** The sequence for the number of seats per row in our movie theater as the rows move toward the back is arithmetic with $d = 1$ so people don't block the view of those in the row behind them.

**81.** Beginning at 6:45 A.M., a bus stops on my block every 23 minutes, so I used the formula for the $n$th term of an arithmetic sequence to describe the stopping time for the $n$th bus of the day.

**82.** In the sequence $21{,}700, 23{,}172, 24{,}644, 26{,}116, \ldots$, which term is $314{,}628$?

**83.** A *degree-day* is a unit used to measure the fuel requirements of buildings. By definition, each degree that the average daily temperature is below $65°F$ is 1 degree-day. For example, a temperature of $42°F$ constitutes 23 degree-days. If the average temperature on January 1 was $42°F$ and fell $2°F$ for each subsequent day up to and including January 10, how many degree-days are included from January 1 to January 10?

**84.** Show that the sum of the first $n$ positive odd integers,

$$1 + 3 + 5 + \cdots + (2n - 1),$$

is $n^2$.

## Preview Exercises

*Exercises 85–87 will help you prepare for the material covered in the next section.*

**85.** Consider the sequence $1, -2, 4, -8, 16, \ldots$. Find $\dfrac{a_2}{a_1}, \dfrac{a_3}{a_2}, \dfrac{a_4}{a_3}$, and $\dfrac{a_5}{a_4}$. What do you observe?

**86.** Consider the sequence whose $n$th term is $a_n = 3 \cdot 5^n$. Find $\dfrac{a_2}{a_1}, \dfrac{a_3}{a_2}, \dfrac{a_4}{a_3}$, and $\dfrac{a_5}{a_4}$. What do you observe?

**87.** Use the formula $a_n = a_1 3^{n-1}$ to find the 7th term of the sequence $11, 33, 99, 297, \ldots$.

## Section 10.3 Geometric Sequences and Series

### Objectives

1 Find the common ratio of a geometric sequence.

2 Write terms of a geometric sequence.

3 Use the formula for the general term of a geometric sequence.

4 Use the formula for the sum of the first $n$ terms of a geometric sequence.

5 Find the value of an annuity.

6 Use the formula for the sum of an infinite geometric series.

Here we are at the closing moments of a job interview. You're shaking hands with the manager. You managed to answer all the tough questions without losing your poise, and now you've been offered a job. As a matter of fact, your qualifications are so terrific that you've been offered two jobs—one just the day before, with a rival company in the same field! One company offers $30,000 the first year, with increases of 6% per year for four years after that. The other offers $32,000 the first year, with annual increases of 3% per year after that. Over a five-year period, which is the better offer?

If salary raises amount to a certain percent each year, the yearly salaries over time form a geometric sequence. In this section, we investigate geometric sequences and their properties. After studying the section, you will be in a position to decide which job offer to accept: You will know which company will pay you more over five years.

1 Find the common ratio of a geometric sequence.

### Geometric Sequences

**Figure 10.4** shows a sequence in which the number of squares is increasing. From left to right, the number of squares is 1, 5, 25, 125, and 625. In this sequence, each term after the first, 1, is obtained by multiplying the preceding term by a constant amount, namely 5. This sequence of increasing numbers of squares is an example of a *geometric sequence*.

Figure 10.4  A geometric sequence of squares

### Definition of a Geometric Sequence

A **geometric sequence** is a sequence in which each term after the first is obtained by multiplying the preceding term by a fixed nonzero constant. The amount by which we multiply each time is called the **common ratio** of the sequence.

The common ratio, $r$, is found by dividing any term after the first term by the term that directly precedes it. In the following examples, the common ratio is found by dividing the second term by the first term, $\dfrac{a_2}{a_1}$.

| Geometric sequence | Common ratio |
|---|---|
| $1, 5, 25, 125, 625, \ldots$ | $r = \dfrac{5}{1} = 5$ |
| $4, 8, 16, 32, 64, \ldots$ | $r = \dfrac{8}{4} = 2$ |
| $6, -12, 24, -48, 96, \ldots$ | $r = \dfrac{-12}{6} = -2$ |
| $9, -3, 1, -\dfrac{1}{3}, \dfrac{1}{9}, \ldots$ | $r = \dfrac{-3}{9} = -\dfrac{1}{3}$ |

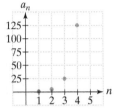

**Figure 10.5** The graph of $\{a_n\} = 1, 5, 25, 125, \ldots$

**Figure 10.5** shows a partial graph of the first geometric sequence in our list. The graph forms a set of discrete points lying on the exponential function $f(x) = 5^{x-1}$. This illustrates that **a geometric sequence with a positive common ratio other than 1 is an exponential function whose domain is the set of positive integers.**

How do we write out the terms of a geometric sequence when the first term and the common ratio are known? We multiply the first term by the common ratio to get the second term, multiply the second term by the common ratio to get the third term, and so on.

② Write terms of a geometric sequence.

**EXAMPLE 1**  **Writing the Terms of a Geometric Sequence**

Write the first six terms of the geometric sequence with first term 6 and common ratio $\frac{1}{3}$.

**Solution**  The first term is 6. The second term is $6 \cdot \frac{1}{3}$, or 2. The third term is $2 \cdot \frac{1}{3}$, or $\frac{2}{3}$. The fourth term is $\frac{2}{3} \cdot \frac{1}{3}$, or $\frac{2}{9}$, and so on. The first six terms are

$$6, 2, \frac{2}{3}, \frac{2}{9}, \frac{2}{27}, \text{ and } \frac{2}{81}.$$

⊘ Check Point **1**  Write the first six terms of the geometric sequence with first term 12 and common ratio $\frac{1}{2}$.

③ Use the formula for the general term of a geometric sequence.

## The General Term of a Geometric Sequence

Consider a geometric sequence whose first term is $a_1$ and whose common ratio is $r$. We are looking for a formula for the general term, $a_n$. Let's begin by writing the first six terms. The first term is $a_1$. The second term is $a_1 r$. The third term is $a_1 r \cdot r$, or $a_1 r^2$. The fourth term is $a_1 r^2 \cdot r$, or $a_1 r^3$, and so on. Starting with $a_1$ and multiplying each successive term by $r$, the first six terms are

$$a_1, \qquad a_1 r, \qquad a_1 r^2, \qquad a_1 r^3, \qquad a_1 r^4, \qquad a_1 r^5.$$

$a_1$, first term    $a_2$, second term    $a_3$, third term    $a_4$, fourth term    $a_5$, fifth term    $a_6$, sixth term

Can you see that the exponent on $r$ is 1 less than the subscript of $a$ denoting the term number?

$a_3$: third term $= a_1 r^2$    $a_4$: fourth term $= a_1 r^3$

One less than 3, or 2, is the exponent on $r$.    One less than 4, or 3, is the exponent on $r$.

Thus, the formula for the $n$th term is

$$a_n = a_1 r^{n-1}.$$

One less than $n$, or $n - 1$, is the exponent on $r$.

### General Term of a Geometric Sequence

The $n$th term (the general term) of a geometric sequence with first term $a_1$ and common ratio $r$ is

$$a_n = a_1 r^{n-1}.$$

**Study Tip**

Be careful with the order of operations when evaluating

$$a_1 r^{n-1}.$$

First find $r^{n-1}$. Then multiply the result by $a_1$.

**EXAMPLE 2** **Using the Formula for the General Term of a Geometric Sequence**

Find the eighth term of the geometric sequence whose first term is $-4$ and whose common ratio is $-2$.

**Solution** To find the eighth term, $a_8$, we replace $n$ in the formula with 8, $a_1$ with $-4$, and $r$ with $-2$.

$$a_n = a_1 r^{n-1}$$
$$a_8 = -4(-2)^{8-1} = -4(-2)^7 = -4(-128) = 512$$

The eighth term is 512. We can check this result by writing the first eight terms of the sequence:

$$-4, 8, -16, 32, -64, 128, -256, 512.$$

⊘ **Check Point 2** Find the seventh term of the geometric sequence whose first term is 5 and whose common ratio is $-3$.

In Chapter 3, we studied exponential functions of the form $f(x) = b^x$ and used an exponential function to model the growth of the U.S. population from 1970 through 2007 (Example 1 on page 437). In our next example, we revisit the country's population growth over a shorter period of time, 2000 through 2006. Because a geometric sequence is an exponential function whose domain is the set of positive integers, geometric and exponential growth mean the same thing.

**EXAMPLE 3** **Geometric Population Growth**

The table shows the population of the United States in 2000, with estimates given by the Census Bureau for 2001 through 2006.

| Year | 2000 | 2001 | 2002 | 2003 | 2004 | 2005 | 2006 |
|---|---|---|---|---|---|---|---|
| **Population (millions)** | 281.4 | 284.5 | 287.6 | 290.8 | 294.0 | 297.2 | 300.5 |

**a.** Show that the population is increasing geometrically.

**b.** Write the general term for the geometric sequence modeling the population of the United States, in millions, $n$ years after 1999.

**c.** Project the U.S. population, in millions, for the year 2009.

**Solution**

**a.** First, we use the sequence of population growth, 281.4, 284.5, 287.6, 290.8, and so on, to divide the population for each year by the population in the preceding year.

### Geometric Population Growth

Economist Thomas Malthus (1766–1834) predicted that population would increase as a geometric sequence and food production would increase as an arithmetic sequence. He concluded that eventually population would exceed food production. If two sequences, one geometric and one arithmetic, are increasing, the geometric sequence will eventually overtake the arithmetic sequence, regardless of any head start that the arithmetic sequence might initially have.

$$\frac{284.5}{281.4} \approx 1.011, \quad \frac{287.6}{284.5} \approx 1.011, \quad \frac{290.8}{287.6} \approx 1.011$$

Continuing in this manner, we will keep getting approximately 1.011. This means that the population is increasing geometrically with $r \approx 1.011$. The population of the United States in any year shown in the sequence is approximately 1.011 times the population the year before.

**b.** The sequence of the U.S. population growth is

$$281.4, 284.5, 287.6, 290.8, 294.0, 297.2, 300.5, \ldots.$$

Because the population is increasing geometrically, we can find the general term of this sequence using

$$a_n = a_1 r^{n-1}.$$

In this sequence, $a_1 = 281.4$ and [from part (a)] $r \approx 1.011$. We substitute these values into the formula for the general term. This gives the general term for the geometric sequence modeling the U.S. population, in millions, $n$ years after 1999.

$$a_n = 281.4(1.011)^{n-1}$$

**c.** We can use the formula for the general term, $a_n$, in part (b) to project the U.S. population for the year 2009. The year 2009 is 10 years after 1999 — that is, $2009 - 1999 = 10$. Thus, $n = 10$. We substitute $10$ for $n$ in $a_n = 281.4(1.011)^{n-1}$.

$$a_{10} = 281.4(1.011)^{10-1} = 281.4(1.011)^9 \approx 310.5$$

The model projects that the United States will have a population of approximately 310.5 million in the year 2009.

☑ Check Point **3** Write the general term for the geometric sequence

$$3, 6, 12, 24, 48, \ldots.$$

Then use the formula for the general term to find the eighth term.

**④ Use the formula for the sum of the first $n$ terms of a geometric sequence.**

## The Sum of the First n Terms of a Geometric Sequence

The sum of the first $n$ terms of a geometric sequence, denoted by $S_n$ and called the **nth partial sum**, can be found without having to add up all the terms. Recall that the first $n$ terms of a geometric sequence are

$$a_1, a_1 r, a_1 r^2, \ldots, a_1 r^{n-2}, a_1 r^{n-1}.$$

We proceed as follows:

$$S_n = a_1 + a_1 r + a_1 r^2 + \cdots + a_1 r^{n-2} + a_1 r^{n-1} \qquad S_n \text{ is the sum of the first } n \text{ terms of the sequence.}$$

$$r S_n = a_1 r + a_1 r^2 + a_1 r^3 + \cdots + a_1 r^{n-1} + a_1 r^n \qquad \text{Multiply both sides of the equation by } r.$$

$$S_n - r S_n = a_1 - a_1 r^n \qquad \text{Subtract the second equation from the first equation.}$$

$$S_n(1 - r) = a_1(1 - r^n) \qquad \text{Factor out } S_n \text{ on the left and } a_1 \text{ on the right.}$$

$$S_n = \frac{a_1(1 - r^n)}{1 - r}. \qquad \text{Solve for } S_n \text{ by dividing both sides by } 1 - r \text{ (assuming that } r \neq 1).$$

**Study Tip**

If the common ratio is 1, the geometric sequence is

$$a_1, a_1, a_1, a_1, \ldots.$$

The sum of the first $n$ terms of this sequence is $na_1$:

$$S_n = \underbrace{a_1 + a_1 + a_1 + \cdots + a_1}_{\text{There are } n \text{ terms.}}$$

$$= na_1.$$

We have proved the following result:

**The Sum of the First $n$ Terms of a Geometric Sequence**

The sum, $S_n$, of the first $n$ terms of a geometric sequence is given by

$$S_n = \frac{a_1(1 - r^n)}{1 - r},$$

in which $a_1$ is the first term and $r$ is the common ratio ($r \neq 1$).

To find the sum of the terms of a geometric sequence, we need to know the first term, $a_1$, the common ratio, $r$, and the number of terms, $n$. The following examples illustrate how to use this formula.

**EXAMPLE 4** Finding the Sum of the First $n$ Terms of a Geometric Sequence

Find the sum of the first 18 terms of the geometric sequence: $2, -8, 32, -128, \ldots.$

**Solution** To find the sum of the first 18 terms, $S_{18}$, we replace $n$ in the formula with 18.

$$S_n = \frac{a_1(1 - r^n)}{1 - r}$$

$$S_{18} = \frac{a_1(1 - r^{18})}{1 - r}$$

The first term, $a_1$, is 2.    We must find $r$, the common ratio.

We can find the common ratio by dividing the second term of $2, -8, 32, -128, \ldots$ by the first term.

$$r = \frac{a_2}{a_1} = \frac{-8}{2} = -4$$

Now we are ready to find the sum of the first 18 terms of $2, -8, 32, -128, \ldots.$

$$S_n = \frac{a_1(1 - r^n)}{1 - r}$$    Use the formula for the sum of the first $n$ terms of a geometric sequence.

$$S_{18} = \frac{2[1 - (-4)^{18}]}{1 - (-4)}$$    $a_1$ (the first term) $= 2$, $r = -4$, and $n = 18$ because we want the sum of the first 18 terms.

$$= -27{,}487{,}790{,}694$$    Use a calculator.

The sum of the first 18 terms is $-27{,}487{,}790{,}694$. Equivalently, this number is the 18th partial sum of the sequence $2, -8, 32, -128, \ldots.$

✓ Check Point **4**  Find the sum of the first nine terms of the geometric sequence: $2, -6, 18, -54, \ldots.$

**EXAMPLE 5** Using $S_n$ to Evaluate a Summation

Find the following sum: $\displaystyle\sum_{i=1}^{10} 6 \cdot 2^i.$

**Solution** Let's write out a few terms in the sum.

$$\sum_{i=1}^{10} 6 \cdot 2^i = 6 \cdot 2 + 6 \cdot 2^2 + 6 \cdot 2^3 + \cdots + 6 \cdot 2^{10}$$

## Technology

To find

$$\sum_{i=1}^{10} 6 \cdot 2^i$$

on a graphing utility, enter

[SUM] [SEQ] $(6 \times 2^x, x, 1, 10, 1)$.

Then press [ENTER].

```
sum(seq(6*2^X,X,
1,10,1))
            12276
```

Do you see that each term after the first is obtained by multiplying the preceding term by 2? To find the sum of the 10 terms ($n = 10$), we need to know the first term, $a_1$, and the common ratio, $r$. The first term is $6 \cdot 2$ or 12: $a_1 = 12$. The common ratio is 2.

$$S_n = \frac{a_1(1 - r^n)}{1 - r} \qquad \text{Use the formula for the sum of the first } n \text{ terms of a geometric sequence.}$$

$$S_{10} = \frac{12(1 - 2^{10})}{1 - 2} \qquad a_1 \text{ (the first term)} = 12, r = 2, \text{ and } n = 10 \\ \text{because we are adding ten terms.}$$

$$= 12{,}276 \qquad \text{Use a calculator.}$$

Thus,

$$\sum_{i=1}^{10} 6 \cdot 2^i = 12{,}276.$$

⊘ Check Point **5** Find the following sum: $\sum_{i=1}^{8} 2 \cdot 3^i$.

Some of the exercises in the previous exercise set involved situations in which salaries increased by a fixed amount each year. A more realistic situation is one in which salary raises increase by a certain percent each year. Example 6 shows how such a situation can be modeled using a geometric sequence.

### EXAMPLE 6  Computing a Lifetime Salary

A union contract specifies that each worker will receive a 5% pay increase each year for the next 30 years. One worker is paid $20,000 the first year. What is this person's total lifetime salary over a 30-year period?

**Solution**    The salary for the first year is $20,000. With a 5% raise, the second-year salary is computed as follows:

Salary for year 2 $= 20{,}000 + 20{,}000(0.05) = 20{,}000(1 + 0.05) = 20{,}000(1.05)$.

Each year, the salary is 1.05 times what it was in the previous year. Thus, the salary for year 3 is 1.05 times $20,000(1.05)$, or $20{,}000(1.05)^2$. The salaries for the first five years are given in the table.

**Yearly Salaries**

| Year 1 | Year 2 | Year 3 | Year 4 | Year 5 | ... |
|--------|--------|--------|--------|--------|-----|
| 20,000 | 20,000(1.05) | $20{,}000(1.05)^2$ | $20{,}000(1.05)^3$ | $20{,}000(1.05)^4$ | ... |

The numbers in the bottom row form a geometric sequence with $a_1 = 20{,}000$ and $r = 1.05$. To find the total salary over 30 years, we use the formula for the sum of the first $n$ terms of a geometric sequence, with $n = 30$.

$$S_n = \frac{a_1(1 - r^n)}{1 - r}$$

$$S_{30} = \frac{20{,}000[1 - (1.05)^{30}]}{1 - 1.05}$$

Total salary over 30 years

$$= \frac{20{,}000[1 - (1.05)^{30}]}{-0.05}$$

$$\approx 1{,}328{,}777 \qquad \text{Use a calculator.}$$

The total salary over the 30-year period is approximately $1,328,777.

⊘ Check Point **6** A job pays a salary of $30,000 the first year. During the next 29 years, the salary increases by 6% each year. What is the total lifetime salary over the 30-year period?

**⑤** Find the value of an annuity.

## Annuities

The compound interest formula

$$A = P(1 + r)^t$$

gives the future value, $A$, after $t$ years, when a fixed amount of money, $P$, the principal, is deposited in an account that pays an annual interest rate $r$ (in decimal form) compounded once a year. However, money is often invested in small amounts at periodic intervals. For example, to save for retirement, you might decide to place $1000 into an Individual Retirement Account (IRA) at the end of each year until you retire. An **annuity** is a sequence of equal payments made at equal time periods. An IRA is an example of an annuity.

Suppose $P$ dollars is deposited into an account at the end of each year. The account pays an annual interest rate, $r$, compounded annually. At the end of the first year, the account contains $P$ dollars. At the end of the second year, $P$ dollars is deposited again. At the time of this deposit, the first deposit has received interest earned during the second year. The **value of the annuity** is the sum of all deposits made plus all interest paid. Thus, the value of the annuity after two years is

$$P + P(1 + r).$$

| Deposit of $P$ dollars at end of second year | First-year deposit of $P$ dollars with interest earned for a year |
|---|---|

The value of the annuity after three years is

$$P \quad + \quad P(1 + r) \quad + \quad P(1 + r)^2.$$

| Deposit of $P$ dollars at end of third year | Second-year deposit of $P$ dollars with interest earned for a year | First-year deposit of $P$ dollars with interest earned over two years |
|---|---|---|

The value of the annuity after $t$ years is

$$P + P(1 + r) + P(1 + r)^2 + P(1 + r)^3 + \cdots + P(1 + r)^{t-1}.$$

| Deposit of $P$ dollars at end of year $t$ | First-year deposit of $P$ dollars with interest earned over $t - 1$ years |
|---|---|

This is the sum of the terms of a geometric sequence with first term $P$ and common ratio $1 + r$. We use the formula

$$S_n = \frac{a_1(1 - r^n)}{1 - r}$$

to find the sum of the terms:

$$S_t = \frac{P[1 - (1 + r)^t]}{1 - (1 + r)} = \frac{P[1 - (1 + r)^t]}{-r} = \frac{P[(1 + r)^t - 1]}{r}.$$

This formula gives the value of an annuity after $t$ years if interest is compounded once a year. We can adjust the formula to find the value of an annuity if equal payments are made at the end of each of $n$ yearly compounding periods.

### Value of an Annuity: Interest Compounded *n* Times per Year

If *P* is the deposit made at the end of each compounding period for an annuity at *r* percent annual interest compounded *n* times per year, the value, *A*, of the annuity after *t* years is

$$A = \frac{P\left[\left(1 + \dfrac{r}{n}\right)^{nt} - 1\right]}{\dfrac{r}{n}}.$$

## Stashing Cash and Making Taxes Less Taxing

As you prepare for your future career, retirement probably seems very far away. Making regular deposits into an IRA may not be fun, but there is a special incentive from Uncle Sam that makes it far more appealing. Traditional IRAs are **tax-deferred savings plans**. This means that you do not pay taxes on deposits and interest until you begin withdrawals, typically at retirement. Before then, yearly deposits count as adjustments to gross income and are not part of your taxable income. Not only do you get a tax break now, but you ultimately earn more. This is because you do not pay taxes on interest from year to year, allowing earnings to accumulate until you start withdrawals. With a tax code that encourages long-term savings, opening an IRA early in your career is a smart way to gain more control over how you will spend a large part of your life.

**EXAMPLE 7** **Determining the Value of an Annuity**

At age 25, to save for retirement, you decide to deposit $200 at the end of each month into an IRA that pays 7.5% compounded monthly.

**a.** How much will you have from the IRA when you retire at age 65?
**b.** Find the interest.

### Solution

**a.** Because you are 25, the amount that you will have from the IRA when you retire at 65 is its value after 40 years.

$$A = \frac{P\left[\left(1 + \dfrac{r}{n}\right)^{nt} - 1\right]}{\dfrac{r}{n}}$$

  Use the formula for the value of an annuity.

$$A = \frac{200\left[\left(1 + \dfrac{0.075}{12}\right)^{12\cdot40} - 1\right]}{\dfrac{0.075}{12}}$$

  The annuity involves month-end deposits of $200: *P* = 200. The interest rate is 7.5%: *r* = 0.075. The interest is compounded monthly: *n* = 12. The number of years is 40: *t* = 40.

$$= \frac{200\left[(1 + 0.00625)^{480} - 1\right]}{0.00625}$$

  Using parentheses keys, this can be performed in a single step on a graphing calculator.

$$= \frac{200\left[(1.00625)^{480} - 1\right]}{0.00625}$$

$$\approx \frac{200(19.8989 - 1)}{0.00625}$$

  Use a calculator to find $(1.00625)^{480}$:

  1.00625 $\boxed{y^x}$ 480 $\boxed{=}$ .

$$\approx 604{,}765$$

After 40 years, you will have approximately $604,765 when retiring at age 65.

**b.** Interest = Value of the IRA − Total deposits
$$\approx \$604{,}765 - \$200 \cdot 12 \cdot 40$$

$200 per month × 12 months per year × 40 years

$$= \$604{,}765 - \$96{,}000 = \$508{,}765$$

The interest is approximately $508,765, more than five times the amount of your contributions to the IRA.

⦰ Check Point **7** At age 30, to save for retirement, you decide to deposit $100 at the end of each month into an IRA that pays 9.5% compounded monthly.

    **a.** How much will you have from the IRA when you retire at age 65?

    **b.** Find the interest.

⑥ Use the formula for the sum of an infinite geometric series.

## Geometric Series

An infinite sum of the form

$$a_1 + a_1 r + a_1 r^2 + a_1 r^3 + \cdots + a_1 r^{n-1} + \cdots$$

with first term $a_1$ and common ratio $r$ is called an **infinite geometric series**. How can we determine which infinite geometric series have sums and which do not? We look at what happens to $r^n$ as $n$ gets larger in the formula for the sum of the first $n$ terms of this series, namely

$$S_n = \frac{a_1(1 - r^n)}{1 - r}.$$

If $r$ is any number between $-1$ and $1$, that is, $-1 < r < 1$, the term $r^n$ approaches 0 as $n$ gets larger. For example, consider what happens to $r^n$ for $r = \frac{1}{2}$:

$$\left(\frac{1}{2}\right)^1 = \frac{1}{2} \quad \left(\frac{1}{2}\right)^2 = \frac{1}{4} \quad \left(\frac{1}{2}\right)^3 = \frac{1}{8} \quad \left(\frac{1}{2}\right)^4 = \frac{1}{16} \quad \left(\frac{1}{2}\right)^5 = \frac{1}{32} \quad \left(\frac{1}{2}\right)^6 = \frac{1}{64}.$$

These numbers are approaching 0 as $n$ gets larger.

Take another look at the formula for the sum of the first $n$ terms of a geometric sequence.

$$S_n = \frac{a_1(1 - r^n)}{1 - r}$$

If $-1 < r < 1$, $r^n$ approaches 0 as $n$ gets larger.

Let us replace $r^n$ with 0 in the formula for $S_n$. This change gives us a formula for the sum of an infinite geometric series with a common ratio between $-1$ and 1.

### The Sum of an Infinite Geometric Series

If $-1 < r < 1$ (equivalently, $|r| < 1$), then the sum of the infinite geometric series

$$a_1 + a_1 r + a_1 r^2 + a_1 r^3 + \cdots,$$

in which $a_1$ is the first term and $r$ is the common ratio, is given by

$$S = \frac{a_1}{1 - r}.$$

If $|r| \geq 1$, the infinite series does not have a sum.

To use the formula for the sum of an infinite geometric series, we need to know the first term and the common ratio. For example, consider

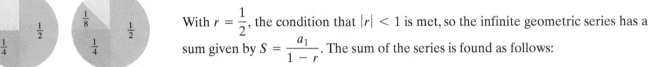

$$\text{First term, } a_1, \text{ is } \tfrac{1}{2}. \qquad \frac{1}{2} + \frac{1}{4} + \frac{1}{8} + \frac{1}{16} + \frac{1}{32} + \cdots.$$

$$\text{Common ratio, } r, \text{ is } \frac{a_2}{a_1}.$$

$$r = \tfrac{1}{4} \div \tfrac{1}{2} = \tfrac{1}{4} \cdot 2 = \tfrac{1}{2}$$

With $r = \dfrac{1}{2}$, the condition that $|r| < 1$ is met, so the infinite geometric series has a sum given by $S = \dfrac{a_1}{1-r}$. The sum of the series is found as follows:

$$\frac{1}{2} + \frac{1}{4} + \frac{1}{8} + \frac{1}{16} + \frac{1}{32} + \cdots = \frac{a_1}{1-r} = \frac{\dfrac{1}{2}}{1 - \dfrac{1}{2}} = \frac{\dfrac{1}{2}}{\dfrac{1}{2}} = 1.$$

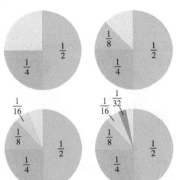

**Figure 10.6** The sum $\frac{1}{2} + \frac{1}{4} + \frac{1}{8} + \frac{1}{16} + \frac{1}{32} + \cdots$ is approaching 1.

Thus, the sum of the infinite geometric series is 1. Notice how this is illustrated in **Figure 10.6**. As more terms are included, the sum is approaching the area of one complete circle.

**EXAMPLE 8** **Finding the Sum of an Infinite Geometric Series**

Find the sum of the infinite geometric series: $\quad \frac{3}{8} - \frac{3}{16} + \frac{3}{32} - \frac{3}{64} + \cdots$.

**Solution**  Before finding the sum, we must find the common ratio.

$$r = \frac{a_2}{a_1} = \frac{-\dfrac{3}{16}}{\dfrac{3}{8}} = -\frac{3}{16} \cdot \frac{8}{3} = -\frac{1}{2}$$

Because $r = -\frac{1}{2}$, the condition that $|r| < 1$ is met. Thus, the infinite geometric series has a sum.

$$S = \frac{a_1}{1-r}$$

*This is the formula for the sum of an infinite geometric series. Let $a_1 = \dfrac{3}{8}$ and $r = -\dfrac{1}{2}$.*

$$= \frac{\dfrac{3}{8}}{1 - \left(-\dfrac{1}{2}\right)} = \frac{\dfrac{3}{8}}{\dfrac{3}{2}} = \frac{3}{8} \cdot \frac{2}{3} = \frac{1}{4}$$

Thus, the sum of $\frac{3}{8} - \frac{3}{16} + \frac{3}{32} - \frac{3}{64} + \cdots$ is $\frac{1}{4}$. Put in an informal way, as we continue to add more and more terms, the sum is approximately $\frac{1}{4}$.

⊘ Check Point **8**  Find the sum of the infinite geometric series:
$3 + 2 + \frac{4}{3} + \frac{8}{9} + \cdots$.

We can use the formula for the sum of an infinite geometric series to express a repeating decimal as a fraction in lowest terms.

**EXAMPLE 9** Writing a Repeating Decimal as a Fraction

Express $0.\overline{7}$ as a fraction in lowest terms.

**Solution**

$$0.\overline{7} = 0.7777\ldots = \frac{7}{10} + \frac{7}{100} + \frac{7}{1000} + \frac{7}{10,000} + \cdots$$

Observe that $0.\overline{7}$ is an infinite geometric series with first term $\frac{7}{10}$ and common ratio $\frac{1}{10}$. Because $r = \frac{1}{10}$, the condition that $|r| < 1$ is met. Thus, we can use our formula to find the sum. Therefore,

$$0.\overline{7} = \frac{a_1}{1 - r} = \frac{\frac{7}{10}}{1 - \frac{1}{10}} = \frac{\frac{7}{10}}{\frac{9}{10}} = \frac{7}{10} \cdot \frac{10}{9} = \frac{7}{9}.$$

An equivalent fraction for $0.\overline{7}$ is $\frac{7}{9}$.

⬭

🖋 Check Point **9** Express $0.\overline{9}$ as a fraction in lowest terms.

Infinite geometric series have many applications, as illustrated in Example 10.

**EXAMPLE 10** Tax Rebates and the Multiplier Effect

$1400

70% is spent.

$980

70% is spent.

$686

A tax rebate that returns a certain amount of money to taxpayers can have a total effect on the economy that is many times this amount. In economics, this phenomenon is called the **multiplier effect**. Suppose, for example, that the government reduces taxes so that each consumer has $2000 more income. The government assumes that each person will spend 70% of this (= $1400). The individuals and businesses receiving this $1400 in turn spend 70% of it (= $980), creating extra income for other people to spend, and so on. Determine the total amount spent on consumer goods from the initial $2000 tax rebate.

**Solution**   The total amount spent is given by the infinite geometric series

$$1400 + 980 + 686 + \cdots.$$

70% of 1400   70% of 980

The first term is 1400: $a_1 = 1400$. The common ratio is 70%, or 0.7: $r = 0.7$. Because $r = 0.7$, the condition that $|r| < 1$ is met. Thus, we can use our formula to find the sum. Therefore,

$$1400 + 980 + 686 + \cdots = \frac{a_1}{1 - r} = \frac{1400}{1 - 0.7} \approx 4667.$$

This means that the total amount spent on consumer goods from the initial $2000 rebate is approximately $4667.

⬭

🖋 Check Point **10** Rework Example 10 and determine the total amount spent on consumer goods with a $1000 tax rebate and 80% spending down the line.

# Exercise Set 10.3

## Practice Exercises

*In Exercises 1–8, write the first five terms of each geometric sequence.*

**1.** $a_1 = 5$, $r = 3$

**2.** $a_1 = 4$, $r = 3$

**3.** $a_1 = 20$, $r = \frac{1}{2}$

**4.** $a_1 = 24$, $r = \frac{1}{3}$

**5.** $a_n = -4a_{n-1}$, $a_1 = 10$

**6.** $a_n = -3a_{n-1}$, $a_1 = 10$

**7.** $a_n = -5a_{n-1}$, $a_1 = -6$

**8.** $a_n = -6a_{n-1}$, $a_1 = -2$

*In Exercises 9–16, use the formula for the general term (the nth term) of a geometric sequence to find the indicated term of each sequence with the given first term, $a_1$, and common ratio, r.*

**9.** Find $a_8$ when $a_1 = 6$, $r = 2$.

**10.** Find $a_8$ when $a_1 = 5$, $r = 3$.

**11.** Find $a_{12}$ when $a_1 = 5$, $r = -2$.

**12.** Find $a_{12}$ when $a_1 = 4$, $r = -2$.

**13.** Find $a_{40}$ when $a_1 = 1000$, $r = -\frac{1}{2}$.

**14.** Find $a_{30}$ when $a_1 = 8000$, $r = -\frac{1}{2}$.

**15.** Find $a_8$ when $a_1 = 1{,}000{,}000$, $r = 0.1$.

**16.** Find $a_8$ when $a_1 = 40{,}000$, $r = 0.1$.

*In Exercises 17–24, write a formula for the general term (the nth term) of each geometric sequence. Then use the formula for $a_n$ to find $a_7$, the seventh term of the sequence.*

**17.** $3, 12, 48, 192, \ldots$

**18.** $3, 15, 75, 375, \ldots$

**19.** $18, 6, 2, \frac{2}{3}, \ldots$

**20.** $12, 6, 3, \frac{3}{2}, \ldots$

**21.** $1.5, -3, 6, -12, \ldots$

**22.** $5, -1, \frac{1}{5}, -\frac{1}{25}, \ldots$

**23.** $0.0004, -0.004, 0.04, -0.4, \ldots$

**24.** $0.0007, -0.007, 0.07, -0.7, \ldots$

*Use the formula for the sum of the first n terms of a geometric sequence to solve Exercises 25–30.*

**25.** Find the sum of the first 12 terms of the geometric sequence: $2, 6, 18, 54, \ldots$.

**26.** Find the sum of the first 12 terms of the geometric sequence: $3, 6, 12, 24, \ldots$.

**27.** Find the sum of the first 11 terms of the geometric sequence: $3, -6, 12, -24, \ldots$.

**28.** Find the sum of the first 11 terms of the geometric sequence: $4, -12, 36, -108, \ldots$.

**29.** Find the sum of the first 14 terms of the geometric sequence: $-\frac{3}{2}, 3, -6, 12, \ldots$.

**30.** Find the sum of the first 14 terms of the geometric sequence: $-\frac{1}{24}, \frac{1}{12}, -\frac{1}{6}, \frac{1}{3}, \ldots$.

*In Exercises 31–36, find the indicated sum. Use the formula for the sum of the first n terms of a geometric sequence.*

**31.** $\sum_{i=1}^{8} 3^i$

**32.** $\sum_{i=1}^{6} 4^i$

**33.** $\sum_{i=1}^{10} 5 \cdot 2^i$

**34.** $\sum_{i=1}^{7} 4(-3)^i$

**35.** $\sum_{i=1}^{6} \left(\frac{1}{2}\right)^{i+1}$

**36.** $\sum_{i=1}^{6} \left(\frac{1}{3}\right)^{i+1}$

*In Exercises 37–44, find the sum of each infinite geometric series.*

**37.** $1 + \frac{1}{3} + \frac{1}{9} + \frac{1}{27} + \cdots$

**38.** $1 + \frac{1}{4} + \frac{1}{16} + \frac{1}{64} + \cdots$

**39.** $3 + \frac{3}{4} + \frac{3}{4^2} + \frac{3}{4^3} + \cdots$

**40.** $5 + \frac{5}{6} + \frac{5}{6^2} + \frac{5}{6^3} + \cdots$

**41.** $1 - \frac{1}{2} + \frac{1}{4} - \frac{1}{8} + \cdots$

**42.** $3 - 1 + \frac{1}{3} - \frac{1}{9} + \cdots$

**43.** $\sum_{i=1}^{\infty} 8(-0.3)^{i-1}$

**44.** $\sum_{i=1}^{\infty} 12(-0.7)^{i-1}$

*In Exercises 45–50, express each repeating decimal as a fraction in lowest terms.*

**45.** $0.\overline{5} = \frac{5}{10} + \frac{5}{100} + \frac{5}{1000} + \frac{5}{10{,}000} + \cdots$

**46.** $0.\overline{1} = \frac{1}{10} + \frac{1}{100} + \frac{1}{1000} + \frac{1}{10{,}000} + \cdots$

**47.** $0.\overline{47} = \frac{47}{100} + \frac{47}{10{,}000} + \frac{47}{1{,}000{,}000} + \cdots$

**48.** $0.\overline{83} = \frac{83}{100} + \frac{83}{10{,}000} + \frac{83}{1{,}000{,}000} + \cdots$

**49.** $0.\overline{257}$

**50.** $0.\overline{529}$

*In Exercises 51–56, the general term of a sequence is given. Determine whether the sequence is arithmetic, geometric, or neither. If the sequence is arithmetic, find the common difference; if it is geometric, find the common ratio.*

**51.** $a_n = n + 5$

**52.** $a_n = n - 3$

**53.** $a_n = 2^n$

**54.** $a_n = \left(\frac{1}{2}\right)^n$

**55.** $a_n = n^2 + 5$

**56.** $a_n = n^2 - 3$

## Practice Plus

*In Exercises 57–62, let*

$$\{a_n\} = -5, 10, -20, 40, \ldots,$$

$$\{b_n\} = 10, -5, -20, -35, \ldots,$$

*and*

$$\{c_n\} = -2, 1, -\frac{1}{2}, \frac{1}{4}, \ldots.$$

**57.** Find $a_{10} + b_{10}$.

**58.** Find $a_{11} + b_{11}$.

**59.** Find the difference between the sum of the first 10 terms of $\{a_n\}$ and the sum of the first 10 terms of $\{b_n\}$.

**60.** Find the difference between the sum of the first 11 terms of $\{a_n\}$ and the sum of the first 11 terms of $\{b_n\}$.

**61.** Find the product of the sum of the first 6 terms of $\{a_n\}$ and the sum of the infinite series containing all the terms of $\{c_n\}$.

**62.** Find the product of the sum of the first 9 terms of $\{a_n\}$ and the sum of the infinite series containing all the terms of $\{c_n\}$.

*In Exercises 63–64, find $a_2$ and $a_3$ for each geometric sequence.*

**63.** $8, a_2, a_3, 27$

**64.** $2, a_2, a_3, -54$

## Application Exercises

*Use the formula for the general term (the nth term) of a geometric sequence to solve Exercises 65–68.*

*In Exercises 65–66, suppose you save $1 the first day of a month, $2 the second day, $4 the third day, and so on. That is, each day you save twice as much as you did the day before.*

**65.** What will you put aside for savings on the fifteenth day of the month?

**66.** What will you put aside for savings on the thirtieth day of the month?

**67.** A professional baseball player signs a contract with a beginning salary of $3,000,000 for the first year and an annual increase of 4% per year beginning in the second year. That is, beginning in year 2, the athlete's salary will be 1.04 times what it was in the previous year. What is the athlete's salary for year 7 of the contract? Round to the nearest dollar.

**68.** You are offered a job that pays $30,000 for the first year with an annual increase of 5% per year beginning in the second year. That is, beginning in year 2, your salary will be 1.05 times what it was in the previous year. What can you expect to earn in your sixth year on the job?

*In Exercises 69–70, you will develop geometric sequences that model the population growth for California and Texas, the two most-populated U.S. states.*

**69.** The table shows population estimates for California from 2003 through 2006 from the U.S. Census Bureau.

| Year | 2003 | 2004 | 2005 | 2006 |
|---|---|---|---|---|
| **Population in millions** | 35.48 | 35.89 | 36.13 | 36.46 |

  **a.** Divide the population for each year by the population in the preceding year. Round to two decimal places and show that California has a population increase that is approximately geometric.

  **b.** Write the general term of the geometric sequence modeling California's population, in millions, $n$ years after 2002.

  **c.** Use your model from part (b) to project California's population, in millions, for the year 2010. Round to two decimal places.

**70.** The table shows population estimates for Texas from 2003 through 2006 from the U.S. Census Bureau.

| Year | 2003 | 2004 | 2005 | 2006 |
|---|---|---|---|---|
| **Population in millions** | 22.12 | 22.49 | 22.86 | 23.41 |

  **a.** Divide the population for each year by the population in the preceding year. Round to two decimal places and show that Texas has a population increase that is approximately geometric.

  **b.** Write the general term of the geometric sequence modeling Texas's population, in millions, $n$ years after 2002.

  **c.** Use your model from part (b) to project Texas's population, in millions, for the year 2010. Round to two decimal places.

*Use the formula for the sum of the first n terms of a geometric sequence to solve Exercises 71–76.*

*In Exercises 71–72, you save $1 the first day of a month, $2 the second day, $4 the third day, continuing to double your savings each day.*

**71.** What will your total savings be for the first 15 days?

**72.** What will your total savings be for the first 30 days?

**73.** A job pays a salary of $24,000 the first year. During the next 19 years, the salary increases by 5% each year. What is the total lifetime salary over the 20-year period? Round to the nearest dollar.

**74.** You are investigating two employment opportunities. Company A offers $30,000 the first year. During the next four years, the salary is guaranteed to increase by 6% per year. Company B offers $32,000 the first year, with guaranteed annual increases of 3% per year after that. Which company offers the better total salary for a five-year contract? By how much? Round to the nearest dollar.

**75.** A pendulum swings through an arc of 20 inches. On each successive swing, the length of the arc is 90% of the previous length.

$$20, \quad 0.9(20), \quad 0.9^2(20), \quad 0.9^3(20), \ldots$$

| 1st swing | 2nd swing | 3rd swing | 4th swing |

After 10 swings, what is the total length of the distance the pendulum has swung?

**76.** A pendulum swings through an arc of 16 inches. On each successive swing, the length of the arc is 96% of the previous length.

$$16, \quad 0.96(16), \quad (0.96)^2(16), \quad (0.96)^3(16), \ldots$$

| 1st swing | 2nd swing | 3rd swing | 4th swing |

After 10 swings, what is the total length of the distance the pendulum has swung?

*Use the formula for the value of an annuity to solve Exercises 77–84. Round answers to the nearest dollar.*

**77.** To save money for a sabbatical to earn a master's degree, you deposit $2000 at the end of each year in an annuity that pays 7.5% compounded annually.

  **a.** How much will you have saved at the end of five years?

  **b.** Find the interest.

**78.** To save money for a sabbatical to earn a master's degree, you deposit $2500 at the end of each year in an annuity that pays 6.25% compounded annually.

  **a.** How much will you have saved at the end of five years?

  **b.** Find the interest.

**79.** At age 25, to save for retirement, you decide to deposit $50 at the end of each month in an IRA that pays 5.5% compounded monthly.

  **a.** How much will you have from the IRA when you retire at age 65?

  **b.** Find the interest.

**80.** At age 25, to save for retirement, you decide to deposit $75 at the end of each month in an IRA that pays 6.5% compounded monthly.

   **a.** How much will you have from the IRA when you retire at age 65?

   **b.** Find the interest.

**81.** To offer scholarship funds to children of employees, a company invests $10,000 at the end of every three months in an annuity that pays 10.5% compounded quarterly.

   **a.** How much will the company have in scholarship funds at the end of ten years?

   **b.** Find the interest.

**82.** To offer scholarship funds to children of employees, a company invests $15,000 at the end of every three months in an annuity that pays 9% compounded quarterly.

   **a.** How much will the company have in scholarship funds at the end of ten years?

   **b.** Find the interest.

**83.** Here are two ways of investing $30,000 for 20 years.

| Lump-Sum Deposit | Rate | Time |
|---|---|---|
| $30,000 | 5% compounded annually | 20 years |

| Periodic Deposits | Rate | Time |
|---|---|---|
| $1500 at the end of each year | 5% compounded annually | 20 years |

After 20 years, how much more will you have from the lump-sum investment than from the annuity?

**84.** Here are two ways of investing $40,000 for 25 years.

| Lump-Sum Deposit | Rate | Time |
|---|---|---|
| $40,000 | 6.5% compounded annually | 25 years |

| Periodic Deposits | Rate | Time |
|---|---|---|
| $1600 at the end of each year | 6.5% compounded annually | 25 years |

After 25 years, how much more will you have from the lump-sum investment than from the annuity?

*Use the formula for the sum of an infinite geometric series to solve Exercises 85–87.*

**85.** A new factory in a small town has an annual payroll of $6 million. It is expected that 60% of this money will be spent in the town by factory personnel. The people in the town who receive this money are expected to spend 60% of what they receive in the town, and so on. What is the total of all this spending, called the *total economic impact* of the factory, on the town each year?

**86.** How much additional spending will be generated by a $10 billion tax rebate if 60% of all income is spent?

**87.** If the shading process shown in the figure is continued indefinitely, what fractional part of the largest square will eventually be shaded?

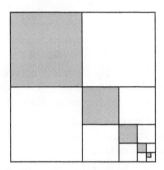

## Writing in Mathematics

**88.** What is a geometric sequence? Give an example with your explanation.

**89.** What is the common ratio in a geometric sequence?

**90.** Explain how to find the general term of a geometric sequence.

**91.** Explain how to find the sum of the first $n$ terms of a geometric sequence without having to add up all the terms.

**92.** What is an annuity?

**93.** What is the difference between a geometric sequence and an infinite geometric series?

**94.** How do you determine if an infinite geometric series has a sum? Explain how to find the sum of such an infinite geometric series.

**95.** Would you rather have $10,000,000 and a brand new BMW, or 1¢ today, 2¢ tomorrow, 4¢ on day 3, 8¢ on day 4, 16¢ on day 5, and so on, for 30 days? Explain.

**96.** For the first 30 days of a flu outbreak, the number of students on your campus who become ill is increasing. Which is worse: The number of students with the flu is increasing arithmetically or is increasing geometrically? Explain your answer.

## Technology Exercises

**97.** Use the ⟨SEQ⟩ (sequence) capability of a graphing utility and the formula you obtained for $a_n$ to verify the value you found for $a_7$ in any three exercises from Exercises 17–24.

**98.** Use the capability of a graphing utility to calculate the sum of a sequence to verify any three of your answers to Exercises 31–36.

*In Exercises 99–100, use a graphing utility to graph the function. Determine the horizontal asymptote for the graph of f and discuss its relationship to the sum of the given series.*

**99. Function**     **Series**

$$f(x) = \frac{2\left[1 - \left(\frac{1}{3}\right)^x\right]}{1 - \frac{1}{3}} \qquad 2 + 2\left(\frac{1}{3}\right) + 2\left(\frac{1}{3}\right)^2 + 2\left(\frac{1}{3}\right)^3 + \cdots$$

**100. Function**                **Series**

$$f(x) = \frac{4[1 - (0.6)^x]}{1 - 0.6} \qquad 4 + 4(0.6) + 4(0.6)^2 + 4(0.6)^3 + \cdots$$

## Critical Thinking Exercises

**Make Sense?** *In Exercises 101–104, determine whether each statement makes sense or does not make sense, and explain your reasoning.*

**101.** There's no end to the number of geometric sequences that I can generate whose first term is 5 if I pick nonzero numbers $r$ and multiply 5 by each value of $r$ repeatedly.

**102.** I've noticed that the big difference between arithmetic and geometric sequences is that arithmetic sequences are based on addition and geometric sequences are based on multiplication.

**103.** I modeled California's population growth with a geometric sequence, so my model is an exponential function whose domain is the set of natural numbers.

**104.** I used a formula to find the sum of the infinite geometric series $3 + 1 + \frac{1}{3} + \frac{1}{9} + \cdots$ and then checked my answer by actually adding all the terms.

*In Exercises 105–108, determine whether each statement is true or false. If the statement is false, make the necessary change(s) to produce a true statement.*

**105.** The sequence $2, 6, 24, 120, \ldots$ is an example of a geometric sequence.

**106.** The sum of the geometric series $\frac{1}{2} + \frac{1}{4} + \frac{1}{8} + \cdots + \frac{1}{512}$ can only be estimated without knowing precisely what terms occur between $\frac{1}{8}$ and $\frac{1}{512}$.

**107.** $10 - 5 + \dfrac{5}{2} - \dfrac{5}{4} + \cdots = \dfrac{10}{1 - \dfrac{1}{2}}$

**108.** If the $n$th term of a geometric sequence is $a_n = 3(0.5)^{n-1}$, the common ratio is $\frac{1}{2}$.

**109.** In a pest-eradication program, sterilized male flies are released into the general population each day. Ninety percent of those flies will survive a given day. How many flies should be released each day if the long-range goal of the program is to keep 20,000 sterilized flies in the population?

**110.** You are now 25 years old and would like to retire at age 55 with a retirement fund of $1,000,000. How much should you deposit at the end of each month for the next 30 years in an IRA paying 10% annual interest compounded monthly to achieve your goal? Round to the nearest dollar.

## Group Exercise

**111.** Group members serve as a financial team analyzing the three options given to the professional baseball player described in the chapter opener on page 951. As a group, determine which option provides the most amount of money over the six-year contract and which provides the least. Describe one advantage and one disadvantage to each option.

## Preview Exercises

*Exercises 112–114 will help you prepare for the material covered in the next section.*

*In Exercises 112–113, show that*

$$1 + 2 + 3 + \cdots + n = \frac{n(n + 1)}{2}$$

*is true for the given value of n.*

**112.** $n = 3$: Show that $1 + 2 + 3 = \dfrac{3(3 + 1)}{2}$.

**113.** $n = 5$: Show that $1 + 2 + 3 + 4 + 5 = \dfrac{5(5 + 1)}{2}$.

**114.** Simplify: $\dfrac{k(k + 1)(2k + 1)}{6} + (k + 1)^2$.

## Chapter 10 Mid-Chapter Check Point

**What You Know:** We learned that a sequence is a function whose domain is the set of positive integers. In an arithmetic sequence, each term after the first differs from the preceding term by a constant, the common difference, $d$. In a geometric sequence, each term after the first is obtained by multiplying the preceding term by a nonzero constant, the common ratio, $r$. We found the general term of arithmetic sequences $[a_n = a_1 + (n - 1)d]$ and geometric sequences $[a_n = a_1 r^{n-1}]$ and used these formulas to find particular terms. We determined the sum of the first $n$ terms of arithmetic sequences $\left[S_n = \dfrac{n}{2}(a_1 + a_n)\right]$ and geometric sequences $\left[S_n = \dfrac{a_1(1 - r^n)}{1 - r}\right]$. Finally, we determined the sum of an infinite geometric series,

$$a_1 + a_1 r + a_1 r^2 + a_1 r^3 + \cdots, \text{ if } -1 < r < 1 \left(S = \frac{a_1}{1 - r}\right).$$

*In Exercises 1–4, write the first five terms of each sequence. Assume that d represents the common difference of an arithmetic sequence and r represents the common ratio of a geometric sequence.*

**1.** $a_n = (-1)^{n+1} \dfrac{n}{(n - 1)!}$      **2.** $a_1 = 5, d = -3$

**3.** $a_1 = 5, r = -3$      **4.** $a_1 = 3, a_n = -a_{n-1} + 4$

*In Exercises 5–7, write a formula for the general term (the nth term) of each sequence. Then use the formula to find the indicated term.*

**5.** $2, 6, 10, 14, \ldots; a_{20}$      **6.** $3, 6, 12, 24, \ldots; a_{10}$

**7.** $\dfrac{3}{2}, 1, \dfrac{1}{2}, 0, \ldots; a_{30}$

**8.** Find the sum of the first ten terms of the sequence:

$$5, 10, 20, 40, \ldots.$$

**9.** Find the sum of the first 50 terms of the sequence:

$$-2, 0, 2, 4, \ldots.$$

**10.** Find the sum of the first ten terms of the sequence:

$$-20, 40, -80, 160, \ldots.$$

**11.** Find the sum of the first 100 terms of the sequence:

$$4, -2, -8, -14, \ldots.$$

*In Exercises 12–15, find each indicated sum.*

**12.** $\displaystyle\sum_{i=1}^{4} (i + 4)(i - 1)$    **13.** $\displaystyle\sum_{i=1}^{50} (3i - 2)$

**14.** $\displaystyle\sum_{i=1}^{6} \left(\frac{3}{2}\right)^{i}$    **15.** $\displaystyle\sum_{i=1}^{\infty} \left(-\frac{2}{5}\right)^{i-1}$

**16.** Express $0.\overline{45}$ as a fraction in lowest terms.

**17.** Express the sum using summation notation. Use $i$ for the index of summation.

$$\frac{1}{3} + \frac{2}{4} + \frac{3}{5} + \cdots + \frac{18}{20}$$

**18.** A skydiver falls 16 feet during the first second of a dive, 48 feet during the second second, 80 feet during the third second, 112 feet during the fourth second, and so on. Find the distance that the skydiver falls during the 15th second and the total distance the skydiver falls in 15 seconds.

**19.** If the average value of a house increases 10% per year, how much will a house costing $120,000 be worth in 10 years? Round to the nearest dollar.

---

**Section** **10.4** **Mathematical Induction**

### Objectives

❶ Understand the principle of mathematical induction.

❷ Prove statements using mathematical induction.

After ten years of work, Princeton University's Andrew Wiles proved Fermat's Last Theorem.

**P**ierre de Fermat (1601–1665) was a lawyer who enjoyed studying mathematics. In a margin of one of his books, he claimed that no positive integers satisfy

$$x^n + y^n = z^n$$

if $n$ is an integer greater than or equal to 3.

If $n = 2$, we can find positive integers satisfying $x^n + y^n = z^n$, or $x^2 + y^2 = z^2$:

$$3^2 + 4^2 = 5^2.$$

However, Fermat claimed that no positive integers satisfy

$$x^3 + y^3 = z^3, \quad x^4 + y^4 = z^4, \quad x^5 + y^5 = z^5,$$

and so on. Fermat claimed to have a proof of his conjecture, but added, "The margin of my book is too narrow to write it down." Some believe that he never had a proof and intended to frustrate his colleagues.

In 1994, 40-year-old Princeton math professor Andrew Wiles proved Fermat's Last Theorem using a principle called *mathematical induction*. In this section, you will learn how to use this powerful method to prove statements about the positive integers.

❶ Understand the principle of mathematical induction.

### The Principle of Mathematical Induction

How do we prove statements using mathematical induction? Let's consider an example. We will prove a statement that appears to give a correct formula for the sum of the first $n$ positive integers:

$$S_n: 1 + 2 + 3 + \cdots + n = \frac{n(n + 1)}{2}.$$

We can verify $S_n$: $1 + 2 + 3 + \cdots + n = \dfrac{n(n + 1)}{2}$ for, say, the first four positive integers. If $n = 1$, the statement $S_1$ is

| Take the first term on the left. | $1 \overset{?}{=} \dfrac{1(1 + 1)}{2}$ | Substitute 1 for $n$ on the right. |

$$1 \overset{?}{=} \dfrac{1 \cdot 2}{2}$$

$1 = 1$ ✓.  This true statement shows that $S_1$ is true.

If $n = 2$, the statement $S_2$ is

| Add the first two terms on the left. | $1 + 2 \overset{?}{=} \dfrac{2(2 + 1)}{2}$ | Substitute 2 for $n$ on the right. |

$$3 \overset{?}{=} \dfrac{2 \cdot 3}{2}$$

$3 = 3$ ✓.  This true statement shows that $S_2$ is true.

If $n = 3$, the statement $S_3$ is

| Add the first three terms on the left. | $1 + 2 + 3 \overset{?}{=} \dfrac{3(3 + 1)}{2}$ | Substitute 3 for $n$ on the right. |

$$6 \overset{?}{=} \dfrac{3 \cdot 4}{2}$$

$6 = 6$ ✓.  This true statement shows that $S_3$ is true.

Finally, if $n = 4$, the statement $S_4$ is

| Add the first four terms on the left. | $1 + 2 + 3 + 4 \overset{?}{=} \dfrac{4(4 + 1)}{2}$ | Substitute 4 for $n$ on the right. |

$$10 \overset{?}{=} \dfrac{4 \cdot 5}{2}$$

$10 = 10$ ✓.  This true statement shows that $S_4$ is true.

This approach does *not* prove that the given statement $S_n$ is true for every positive integer $n$. The fact that the formula produces true statements for $n = 1, 2, 3,$ and 4 does not guarantee that it is valid for all positive integers $n$. Thus, we need to be able to verify the truth of $S_n$ without verifying the statement for each and every one of the positive integers.

A legitimate proof of the given statement $S_n$ involves a technique called **mathematical induction**.

### The Principle of Mathematical Induction

Let $S_n$ be a statement involving the positive integer $n$. If

1. $S_1$ is true, and

2. the truth of the statement $S_k$ implies the truth of the statement $S_{k+1}$, for every positive integer $k$,

then the statement $S_n$ is true for all positive integers $n$.

**Figure 10.7** Falling dominoes illustrate the principle of mathematical induction.

The principle of mathematical induction can be illustrated using an unending line of dominoes, as shown in **Figure 10.7**. If the first domino is pushed over, it knocks down the next, which knocks down the next, and so on, in a chain reaction. To topple all the dominoes in the infinite sequence, two conditions must be satisfied:

1. The first domino must be knocked down.

2. If the domino in position $k$ is knocked down, then the domino in position $k + 1$ must be knocked down.

If the second condition is not satisfied, it does not follow that all the dominoes will topple. For example, suppose the dominoes are spaced far enough apart so that a falling domino does not push over the next domino in the line.

The domino analogy provides the two steps that are required in a proof by mathematical induction.

### The Steps in a Proof by Mathematical Induction

Let $S_n$ be a statement involving the positive integer $n$. To prove that $S_n$ is true for all positive integers $n$ requires two steps.

**Step 1** Show that $S_1$ is true.

**Step 2** Show that if $S_k$ is assumed to be true, then $S_{k+1}$ is also true, for every positive integer $k$.

Notice that to prove $S_n$, we work only with the statements $S_1$, $S_k$, and $S_{k+1}$. Our first example provides practice in writing these statements.

**EXAMPLE 1** Writing $S_1$, $S_k$, and $S_{k+1}$

For the given statement $S_n$, write the three statements $S_1$, $S_k$, and $S_{k+1}$.

**a.** $S_n: 1 + 2 + 3 + \cdots + n = \dfrac{n(n + 1)}{2}$

**b.** $S_n: 1^2 + 2^2 + 3^2 + \cdots + n^2 = \dfrac{n(n + 1)(2n + 1)}{6}$

### Solution

**a.** We begin with

$$S_n: 1 + 2 + 3 + \cdots + n = \frac{n(n + 1)}{2}.$$

Write $S_1$ by taking the first term on the left and replacing $n$ with 1 on the right.

$$S_1: 1 = \frac{1(1 + 1)}{2}$$

$S_n: 1 + 2 + 3 + \cdots + n = \dfrac{n(n+1)}{2}$

The statement for part (a) (repeated)

Write $S_k$ by taking the sum of the first $k$ terms on the left and replacing $n$ with $k$ on the right.

$$S_k: 1 + 2 + 3 + \cdots + k = \frac{k(k+1)}{2}$$

Write $S_{k+1}$ by taking the sum of the first $k+1$ terms on the left and replacing $n$ with $k+1$ on the right.

$$S_{k+1}: 1 + 2 + 3 + \cdots + (k+1) = \frac{(k+1)[(k+1)+1]}{2}$$

$$S_{k+1}: 1 + 2 + 3 + \cdots + (k+1) = \frac{(k+1)(k+2)}{2} \qquad \text{Simplify on the right.}$$

**b.** We begin with

$$S_n: 1^2 + 2^2 + 3^2 + \cdots + n^2 = \frac{n(n+1)(2n+1)}{6}.$$

Write $S_1$ by taking the first term on the left and replacing $n$ with 1 on the right.

$$S_1: 1^2 = \frac{1(1+1)(2 \cdot 1 + 1)}{6}$$

Using $S_n: 1^2 + 2^2 + 3^2 + \cdots + n^2 = \dfrac{n(n+1)(2n+1)}{6}$, we write $S_k$ by taking the sum of the first $k$ terms on the left and replacing $n$ with $k$ on the right.

$$S_k: 1^2 + 2^2 + 3^2 + \cdots + k^2 = \frac{k(k+1)(2k+1)}{6}$$

Write $S_{k+1}$ by taking the sum of the first $k+1$ terms on the left and replacing $n$ with $k+1$ on the right.

$$S_{k+1}: 1^2 + 2^2 + 3^2 + \cdots + (k+1)^2 = \frac{(k+1)[(k+1)+1][2(k+1)+1]}{6}$$

$$S_{k+1}: 1^2 + 2^2 + 3^2 + \cdots + (k+1)^2 = \frac{(k+1)(k+2)(2k+3)}{6} \qquad \text{Simplify on the right.} \quad \bullet$$

🖊 Check Point **1** For the given statement $S_n$, write the three statements $S_1$, $S_k$, and $S_{k+1}$.

**a.** $2 + 4 + 6 + \cdots + 2n = n(n+1)$

**b.** $1^3 + 2^3 + 3^3 + \cdots + n^3 = \dfrac{n^2(n+1)^2}{4}$

Always simplify $S_{k+1}$ before trying to use mathematical induction to prove that $S_n$ is true. For example, consider

$$S_n: 1^2 + 3^2 + 5^2 + \cdots + (2n-1)^2 = \frac{n(2n-1)(2n+1)}{3}.$$

Begin by writing $S_{k+1}$ as follows:

$$S_{k+1}: 1^2 + 3^2 + 5^2 + \cdots + [2(k+1)-1]^2$$

$$= \frac{(k+1)[2(k+1)-1][2(k+1)+1]}{3}.$$

The sum of the first $k+1$ terms

Replace $n$ with $k+1$ on the right side of $S_n$.

Now simplify both sides of the equation.

$$S_{k+1}: 1^2 + 3^2 + 5^2 + \cdots + (2k + 2 - 1)^2 = \frac{(k + 1)(2k + 2 - 1)(2k + 2 + 1)}{3}$$

$$S_{k+1}: 1^2 + 3^2 + 5^2 + \cdots + (2k + 1)^2 = \frac{(k + 1)(2k + 1)(2k + 3)}{3}$$

② Prove statements using mathematical induction.

## Proving Statements about Positive Integers Using Mathematical Induction

Now that we know how to find $S_1$, $S_k$, and $S_{k+1}$, let's see how we can use these statements to carry out the two steps in a proof by mathematical induction. In Examples 2 and 3, we will use the statements $S_1$, $S_k$, and $S_{k+1}$ to prove each of the statements $S_n$ that we worked with in Example 1.

(EXAMPLE 2) **Proving a Formula by Mathematical Induction**

Use mathematical induction to prove that

$$1 + 2 + 3 + \cdots + n = \frac{n(n + 1)}{2}$$

for all positive integers $n$.

**Solution**

**Step 1   Show that $S_1$ is true.** Statement $S_1$ is

$$1 = \frac{1(1 + 1)}{2}.$$

Simplifying on the right, we obtain $1 = 1$. This true statement shows that $S_1$ is true.

**Step 2   Show that if $S_k$ is true, then $S_{k+1}$ is true.** Using $S_k$ and $S_{k+1}$ from Example 1(a), show that the truth of $S_k$,

$$1 + 2 + 3 + \cdots + k = \frac{k(k + 1)}{2},$$

implies the truth of $S_{k+1}$,

$$1 + 2 + 3 + \cdots + (k + 1) = \frac{(k + 1)(k + 2)}{2}.$$

We will work with $S_k$. Because we assume that $S_k$ is true, we add the next consecutive integer after $k$—namely, $k + 1$—to both sides.

$$1 + 2 + 3 + \cdots + k = \frac{k(k + 1)}{2}$$

This is $S_k$, which we assume is true.

$$1 + 2 + 3 + \cdots + k + (k + 1) = \frac{k(k + 1)}{2} + (k + 1)$$

> We do not have to write this $k$ because $k$ is understood to be the integer that precedes $k + 1$.

Add $k + 1$ to both sides of the equation.

$$1 + 2 + 3 + \cdots + (k + 1) = \frac{k(k + 1)}{2} + \frac{2(k + 1)}{2}$$

Write the right side with a common denominator of 2.

$$1 + 2 + 3 + \cdots + (k + 1) = \frac{(k + 1)}{2}(k + 2)$$

Factor out the common factor $\frac{k + 1}{2}$ on the right.

$$1 + 2 + 3 + \cdots + (k + 1) = \frac{(k + 1)(k + 2)}{2}$$

This final result is the statement $S_{k+1}$.

We have shown that if we assume that $S_k$ is true and we add $k + 1$ to both sides of $S_k$, then $S_{k+1}$ is also true. By the principle of mathematical induction, the statement $S_n$, namely,

$$1 + 2 + 3 + \cdots + n = \frac{n(n + 1)}{2},$$

is true for every positive integer $n$.

✓ Check Point **2** Use mathematical induction to prove that

$$2 + 4 + 6 + \cdots + 2n = n(n + 1)$$

for all positive integers $n$.

(EXAMPLE 3) **Proving a Formula by Mathematical Induction**

Use mathematical induction to prove that

$$1^2 + 2^2 + 3^2 + \cdots + n^2 = \frac{n(n + 1)(2n + 1)}{6}$$

for all positive integers $n$.

**Solution**

**Step 1 Show that $S_1$ is true.** Statement $S_1$ is

$$1^2 = \frac{1(1 + 1)(2 \cdot 1 + 1)}{6}.$$

Simplifying, we obtain $1 = \dfrac{1 \cdot 2 \cdot 3}{6}$. Further simplification on the right gives the statement $1 = 1$. This true statement shows that $S_1$ is true.

**Step 2 Show that if $S_k$ is true, then $S_{k+1}$ is true.** Using $S_k$ and $S_{k+1}$ from Example 1(b), show that the truth of

$$S_k: 1^2 + 2^2 + 3^2 + \cdots + k^2 = \frac{k(k + 1)(2k + 1)}{6}$$

implies the truth of

$$S_{k+1}: 1^2 + 2^2 + 3^2 + \cdots + (k + 1)^2 = \frac{(k + 1)(k + 2)(2k + 3)}{6}.$$

We will work with $S_k$. Because we assume that $S_k$ is true, we add the square of the next consecutive integer after $k$, namely, $(k + 1)^2$, to both sides of the equation.

$$1^2 + 2^2 + 3^2 + \cdots + k^2 = \frac{k(k + 1)(2k + 1)}{6}$$
This is $S_k$, assumed to be true. We must work with this and show $S_{k+1}$ is true.

$$1^2 + 2^2 + 3^2 + \cdots + k^2 + (k + 1)^2 = \frac{k(k + 1)(2k + 1)}{6} + (k + 1)^2$$
Add $(k + 1)^2$ to both sides.

$$1^2 + 2^2 + 3^2 + \cdots + (k + 1)^2 = \frac{k(k + 1)(2k + 1)}{6} + \frac{6(k + 1)^2}{6}$$
It is not necessary to write $k^2$ on the left. Express the right side with the least common denominator, 6.

$$= \frac{(k + 1)}{6}[k(2k + 1) + 6(k + 1)]$$
Factor out the common factor $\dfrac{k + 1}{6}$.

$$= \frac{(k + 1)}{6}(2k^2 + 7k + 6)$$
Multiply and combine like terms.

$$= \frac{(k + 1)}{6}(k + 2)(2k + 3) \quad \text{Factor } 2k^2 + 7k + 6.$$

$$= \frac{(k + 1)(k + 2)(2k + 3)}{6} \quad \text{This final statement is } S_{k+1}.$$

We have shown that if we assume that $S_k$ is true, and we add $(k + 1)^2$ to both sides of $S_k$, then $S_{k+1}$ is also true. By the principle of mathematical induction, the statement $S_n$, namely,

$$1^2 + 2^2 + 3^2 + \cdots + n^2 = \frac{n(n + 1)(2n + 1)}{6},$$

is true for every positive integer $n$.

⬤

◯ Check Point **3** Use mathematical induction to prove that

$$1^3 + 2^3 + 3^3 + \cdots + n^3 = \frac{n^2(n + 1)^2}{4}$$

for all positive integers $n$.

Example 4 illustrates how mathematical induction can be used to prove statements about positive integers that do not involve sums.

( **EXAMPLE 4** ) **Using the Principle of Mathematical Induction**

Prove that 2 is a factor of $n^2 + 5n$ for all positive integers $n$.

**Solution**

**Step 1  Show that $S_1$ is true.** Statement $S_1$ reads

2 is a factor of $1^2 + 5 \cdot 1$.

Simplifying the arithmetic, the statement reads

2 is a factor of 6.

This statement is true: that is, $6 = 2 \cdot 3$. This shows that $S_1$ is true.

**Step 2  Show that if $S_k$ is true, then $S_{k+1}$ is true.** Let's write $S_k$ and $S_{k+1}$:

$S_k$:     2 is a factor of $k^2 + 5k$.

$S_{k+1}$:   2 is a factor of $(k + 1)^2 + 5(k + 1)$.

We can rewrite statement $S_{k+1}$ by simplifying the algebraic expression in the statement as follows:

$$(k + 1)^2 + 5(k + 1) = k^2 + 2k + 1 + 5k + 5 = k^2 + 7k + 6.$$

Use the formula $(A + B)^2 = A^2 + 2AB + B^2.$

Statement $S_{k+1}$ now reads

2 is a factor of $k^2 + 7k + 6$.

We need to use statement $S_k$ — that is, 2 is a factor of $k^2 + 5k$ — to prove statement $S_{k+1}$. We do this as follows:

$$k^2 + 7k + 6 = (k^2 + 5k) + (2k + 6) = (k^2 + 5k) + 2(k + 3).$$

We assume that 2 is a factor of $k^2 + 5k$ because we assume $S_k$ is true.

Factoring the last two terms shows that 2 is a factor of $2k + 6$.

$$k^2 + 7k + 6 = (k^2 + 5k) + (2k + 6) = (k^2 + 5k) + 2(k + 3)$$

We assume that 2 is
a factor of $k^2 + 5k$ because
we assume $S_k$ is true.

Factoring the last two
terms shows that 2 is
a factor of $2k + 6$.

We've repeated the equation from the bottom of the previous page. The voice balloons show that 2 is a factor of $k^2 + 5k$ and of $2(k + 3)$. Thus, if $S_k$ is true, 2 is a factor of the sum $(k^2 + 5k) + 2(k + 3)$, or of $k^2 + 7k + 6$. This is precisely statement $S_{k+1}$. We have shown that if we assume that $S_k$ is true, then $S_{k+1}$ is also true. By the principle of mathematical induction, the statement $S_n$, namely 2 is a factor of $n^2 + 5n$, is true for every positive integer $n$. ●

⬜ Check Point **4** Prove that 2 is a factor of $n^2 + n$ for all positive integers $n$.

## Exercise Set 10.4

### Practice Exercises

*In Exercises 1–4, a statement $S_n$ about the positive integers is given. Write statements $S_1, S_2,$ and $S_3$, and show that each of these statements is true.*

**1.** $S_n: 1 + 3 + 5 + \cdots + (2n - 1) = n^2$

**2.** $S_n: 3 + 4 + 5 + \cdots + (n + 2) = \dfrac{n(n + 5)}{2}$

**3.** $S_n:$ 2 is a factor of $n^2 - n$.

**4.** $S_n:$ 3 is a factor of $n^3 - n$.

*In Exercises 5–10, a statement $S_n$ about the positive integers is given. Write statements $S_k$ and $S_{k+1}$, simplifying statement $S_{k+1}$ completely.*

**5.** $S_n: 4 + 8 + 12 + \cdots + 4n = 2n(n + 1)$

**6.** $S_n: 3 + 4 + 5 + \cdots + (n + 2) = \dfrac{n(n + 5)}{2}$

**7.** $S_n: 3 + 7 + 11 + \cdots + (4n - 1) = n(2n + 1)$

**8.** $S_n: 2 + 7 + 12 + \cdots + (5n - 3) = \dfrac{n(5n - 1)}{2}$

**9.** $S_n:$ 2 is a factor of $n^2 - n + 2$.

**10.** $S_n:$ 2 is a factor of $n^2 - n$.

*In Exercises 11–24, use mathematical induction to prove that each statement is true for every positive integer $n$.*

**11.** $4 + 8 + 12 + \cdots + 4n = 2n(n + 1)$

**12.** $3 + 4 + 5 + \cdots + (n + 2) = \dfrac{n(n + 5)}{2}$

**13.** $1 + 3 + 5 + \cdots + (2n - 1) = n^2$

**14.** $3 + 6 + 9 + \cdots + 3n = \dfrac{3n(n + 1)}{2}$

**15.** $3 + 7 + 11 + \cdots + (4n - 1) = n(2n + 1)$

**16.** $2 + 7 + 12 + \cdots + (5n - 3) = \dfrac{n(5n - 1)}{2}$

**17.** $1 + 2 + 2^2 + \cdots + 2^{n-1} = 2^n - 1$

**18.** $1 + 3 + 3^2 + \cdots + 3^{n-1} = \dfrac{3^n - 1}{2}$

**19.** $2 + 4 + 8 + \cdots + 2^n = 2^{n+1} - 2$

**20.** $\dfrac{1}{2} + \dfrac{1}{4} + \dfrac{1}{8} + \cdots + \dfrac{1}{2^n} = 1 - \dfrac{1}{2^n}$

**21.** $1 \cdot 2 + 2 \cdot 3 + 3 \cdot 4 + \cdots + n(n + 1) = \dfrac{n(n + 1)(n + 2)}{3}$

**22.** $1 \cdot 3 + 2 \cdot 4 + 3 \cdot 5 + \cdots + n(n + 2) = \dfrac{n(n + 1)(2n + 7)}{6}$

**23.** $\dfrac{1}{1 \cdot 2} + \dfrac{1}{2 \cdot 3} + \dfrac{1}{3 \cdot 4} + \cdots + \dfrac{1}{n(n + 1)} = \dfrac{n}{n + 1}$

**24.** $\dfrac{1}{2 \cdot 3} + \dfrac{1}{3 \cdot 4} + \dfrac{1}{4 \cdot 5} + \cdots + \dfrac{1}{(n + 1)(n + 2)} = \dfrac{n}{2n + 4}$

### Practice Plus

*In Exercises 25–34, use mathematical induction to prove that each statement is true for every positive integer $n$.*

**25.** 2 is a factor of $n^2 - n$.

**26.** 2 is a factor of $n^2 + 3n$.

**27.** 6 is a factor of $n(n + 1)(n + 2)$.

**28.** 3 is a factor of $n(n + 1)(n - 1)$.

**29.** $\displaystyle\sum_{i=1}^{n} 5 \cdot 6^i = 6(6^n - 1)$

**30.** $\displaystyle\sum_{i=1}^{n} 7 \cdot 8^i = 8(8^n - 1)$

**31.** $n + 2 > n$

**32.** If $0 < x < 1$, then $0 < x^n < 1$.

**33.** $(ab)^n = a^n b^n$

**34.** $\left(\dfrac{a}{b}\right)^n = \dfrac{a^n}{b^n}$

## Writing in Mathematics

**35.** Explain how to use mathematical induction to prove that a statement is true for every positive integer $n$.

**36.** Consider the statement $S_n$ given by

$$n^2 - n + 41 \text{ is prime.}$$

Although $S_1, S_2, \ldots, S_{40}$ are true, $S_{41}$ is false. Verify that $S_{41}$ is false. Then describe how this is illustrated by the dominoes in the figure. What does this tell you about a pattern, or formula, that seems to work for several values of $n$?

## Critical Thinking Exercises

**Make Sense?** *In Exercises 37–40, determine whether each statement makes sense or does not make sense, and explain your reasoning.*

**37.** I use mathematical induction to prove that statements are true for all real numbers $n$.

**38.** I begin proofs by mathematical induction by writing $S_k$ and $S_{k+1}$, both of which I assume to be true.

**39.** When a line of falling dominoes is used to illustrate the principle of mathematical induction, it is not necessary for all the dominoes to topple.

**40.** This triangular arrangement of 36 circles illustrates that

$$1 + 2 + 3 + \cdots + n = \frac{n(n + 1)}{2}$$

is true for $n = 8$.

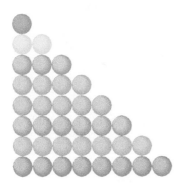

*Some statements are false for the first few positive integers, but true for some positive integer m on. In these instances, you can prove $S_n$ for $n \geq m$ by showing that $S_m$ is true and that $S_k$ implies $S_{k+1}$ when $k > m$. Use this extended principle of mathematical induction to prove that each statement in Exercises 41–42 is true.*

**41.** Prove that $n^2 > 2n + 1$ for $n \geq 3$. Show that the formula is true for $n = 3$ and then use step 2 of mathematical induction.

**42.** Prove that $2^n > n^2$ for $n \geq 5$. Show that the formula is true for $n = 5$ and then use step 2 of mathematical induction.

*In Exercises 43–44, find $S_1$ through $S_5$ and then use the pattern to make a conjecture about $S_n$. Prove the conjectured formula for $S_n$ by mathematical induction.*

**43.** $S_n: \dfrac{1}{4} + \dfrac{1}{12} + \dfrac{1}{24} + \cdots + \dfrac{1}{2n(n + 1)} = ?$

**44.** $S_n: \left(1 - \dfrac{1}{2}\right)\left(1 - \dfrac{1}{3}\right)\left(1 - \dfrac{1}{4}\right) \cdots \left(1 - \dfrac{1}{n + 1}\right) = ?$

## Group Exercise

**45.** Fermat's most notorious theorem, described in the section opener on page 987, baffled the greatest minds for more than three centuries. In 1994, after ten years of work, Princeton University's Andrew Wiles proved Fermat's Last Theorem. *People* magazine put him on its list of "the 25 most intriguing people of the year," the Gap asked him to model jeans, and Barbara Walters chased him for an interview. "Who's Barbara Walters?" asked the bookish Wiles, who had somehow gone through life without a television.

Using the 1993 PBS documentary "Solving Fermat: Andrew Wiles" or information about Andrew Wiles on the Internet, research and present a group seminar on what Wiles did to prove Fermat's Last Theorem, problems along the way, and the role of mathematical induction in the proof.

## Preview Exercises

*Exercises 46–48 will help you prepare for the material covered in the next section. Each exercise involves observing a pattern in the expanded form of the binomial expression $(a + b)^n$.*

$$(a + b)^1 = a + b$$
$$(a + b)^2 = a^2 + 2ab + b^2$$
$$(a + b)^3 = a^3 + 3a^2b + 3ab^2 + b^3$$
$$(a + b)^4 = a^4 + 4a^3b + 6a^2b^2 + 4ab^3 + b^4$$
$$(a + b)^5 = a^5 + 5a^4b + 10a^3b^2 + 10a^2b^3 + 5ab^4 + b^5$$

**46.** Describe the pattern for the exponents on $a$.

**47.** Describe the pattern for the exponents on $b$.

**48.** Describe the pattern for the sum of the exponents on the variables in each term.

## Section 10.5 The Binomial Theorem

### Objectives

① Evaluate a binomial coefficient.

② Expand a binomial raised to a power.

③ Find a particular term in a binomial expansion.

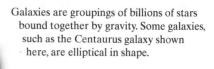

Galaxies are groupings of billions of stars bound together by gravity. Some galaxies, such as the Centaurus galaxy shown here, are elliptical in shape.

**I**s mathematics discovered or invented? For example, planets revolve in elliptical orbits. Does that mean that the ellipse is out there, waiting for the mind to discover it? Or do people create the definition of an ellipse just as they compose a song? And is it possible for the same mathematics to be discovered/invented by independent researchers separated by time, place, and culture? This is precisely what occurred when mathematicians attempted to find efficient methods for raising binomials to higher and higher powers, such as

$$(x + 2)^3, (x + 2)^4, (x + 2)^5, (x + 2)^6,$$

and so on. In this section, we study higher powers of binomials and a method first discovered/invented by great minds in Eastern and Western cultures working independently.

① Evaluate a binomial coefficient.

## Binomial Coefficients

Before turning to powers of binomials, we introduce a special notation that uses factorials.

### Definition of a Binomial Coefficient $\binom{n}{r}$

For nonnegative integers $n$ and $r$, with $n \geq r$, the expression $\binom{n}{r}$ (read "$n$ above $r$") is called a **binomial coefficient** and is defined by

$$\binom{n}{r} = \frac{n!}{r!(n - r)!}.$$

The symbol $_nC_r$ is often used in place of $\binom{n}{r}$ to denote binomial coefficients.

### Technology

Graphing utilities can compute binomial coefficients. For example, to find $\binom{6}{2}$, many utilities require the sequence

6 $_nC_r$ 2 ENTER.

The graphing utility will display 15. Consult your manual and verify the other evaluations in Example 1.

( EXAMPLE 1 )  **Evaluating Binomial Coefficients**

Evaluate:     **a.** $\binom{6}{2}$     **b.** $\binom{3}{0}$     **c.** $\binom{9}{3}$     **d.** $\binom{4}{4}$.

**Solution**   In each case, we apply the definition of the binomial coefficient.

**a.** $\binom{6}{2} = \frac{6!}{2!(6 - 2)!} = \frac{6!}{2!4!} = \frac{6 \cdot 5 \cdot 4!}{2 \cdot 1 \cdot 4!} = 15$

**b.** $\dbinom{3}{0} = \dfrac{3!}{0!(3-0)!} = \dfrac{3!}{0!3!} = \dfrac{1}{1} = 1$

Remember that 0! = 1.

**c.** $\dbinom{9}{3} = \dfrac{9!}{3!(9-3)!} = \dfrac{9!}{3!6!} = \dfrac{9 \cdot 8 \cdot 7 \cdot \cancel{6!}}{3 \cdot 2 \cdot 1 \cdot \cancel{6!}} = 84$

**d.** $\dbinom{4}{4} = \dfrac{4!}{4!(4-4)!} = \dfrac{\cancel{4!}}{\cancel{4!}0!} = \dfrac{1}{1} = 1$

⊘ Check Point **|** Evaluate:

**a.** $\dbinom{6}{3}$ **b.** $\dbinom{6}{0}$ **c.** $\dbinom{8}{2}$ **d.** $\dbinom{3}{3}$.

**②** Expand a binomial raised to a power.

## The Binomial Theorem

When we write out the *binomial expression* $(a + b)^n$, where $n$ is a positive integer, a number of patterns begin to appear.

$$(a + b)^1 = a + b$$
$$(a + b)^2 = a^2 + 2ab + b^2$$
$$(a + b)^3 = a^3 + 3a^2b + 3ab^2 + b^3$$
$$(a + b)^4 = a^4 + 4a^3b + 6a^2b^2 + 4ab^3 + b^4$$
$$(a + b)^5 = a^5 + 5a^4b + 10a^3b^2 + 10a^2b^3 + 5ab^4 + b^5$$

Each expanded form of the binomial expression is a polynomial. Observe the following patterns:

1. The first term in the expansion of $(a + b)^n$ is $a^n$. The exponents on $a$ decrease by 1 in each successive term.
2. The exponents on $b$ in the expansion of $(a + b)^n$ increase by 1 in each successive term. In the first term, the exponent on $b$ is 0. (Because $b^0 = 1$, $b$ is not shown in the first term.) The last term is $b^n$.
3. The sum of the exponents on the variables in any term in the expansion of $(a + b)^n$ is equal to $n$.
4. The number of terms in the polynomial expansion is one greater than the power of the binomial, $n$. There are $n + 1$ terms in the expanded form of $(a + b)^n$.

Using these observations, the variable parts of the expansion of $(a + b)^6$ are

$$a^6, \quad a^5b, \quad a^4b^2, \quad a^3b^3, \quad a^2b^4, \quad ab^5, \quad b^6.$$

The first term is $a^6$, with the exponents on $a$ decreasing by 1 in each successive term. The exponents on $b$ increase from 0 to 6, with the last term being $b^6$. The sum of the exponents in each term is equal to 6.

We can generalize from these observations to obtain the variable parts of the expansion of $(a + b)^n$. They are

$$a^n, \quad a^{n-1}b, \quad a^{n-2}b^2, \quad a^{n-3}b^3, \ldots, \quad ab^{n-1}, \quad b^n.$$

Exponents on $a$ are decreasing by 1.
Exponents on $b$ are increasing by 1.

Sum of exponents:
$n - 1 + 1 = n$

Sum of exponents:
$n - 3 + 3 = n$

Sum of exponents:
$1 + n - 1 = n$

If we use binomial coefficients and the pattern for the variable part of each term, a formula called the **Binomial Theorem** can be used to expand any positive integral power of a binomial.

### A Formula for Expanding Binomials: The Binomial Theorem

For any positive integer $n$,

$$(a + b)^n = \binom{n}{0}a^n + \binom{n}{1}a^{n-1}b + \binom{n}{2}a^{n-2}b^2 + \binom{n}{3}a^{n-3}b^3 + \cdots + \binom{n}{n}b^n$$

$$= \sum_{r=0}^{n} \binom{n}{r}a^{n-r}b^r.$$

**EXAMPLE 2** Using the Binomial Theorem

Expand: $(x + 2)^4$.

**Solution** We use the Binomial Theorem

$$(a + b)^n = \binom{n}{0}a^n + \binom{n}{1}a^{n-1}b + \binom{n}{2}a^{n-2}b^2 + \binom{n}{3}a^{n-3}b^3 + \cdots + \binom{n}{n}b^n$$

to expand $(x + 2)^4$. In $(x + 2)^4$, $a = x$, $b = 2$, and $n = 4$. In the expansion, powers of $x$ are in descending order, starting with $x^4$. Powers of 2 are in ascending order, starting with $2^0$. (Because $2^0 = 1$, a 2 is not shown in the first term.) The sum of the exponents on $x$ and 2 in each term is equal to 4, the exponent in the expression $(x + 2)^4$.

$$(x + 2)^4 = \binom{4}{0}x^4 + \binom{4}{1}x^3 \cdot 2 + \binom{4}{2}x^2 \cdot 2^2 + \binom{4}{3}x \cdot 2^3 + \binom{4}{4}2^4$$

These binomial coefficients are evaluated using $\binom{n}{r} = \frac{n!}{r!(n-r)!}$.

$$= \frac{4!}{0!4!}x^4 + \frac{4!}{1!3!}x^3 \cdot 2 + \frac{4!}{2!2!}x^2 \cdot 4 + \frac{4!}{3!1!}x \cdot 8 + \frac{4!}{4!0!} \cdot 16$$

$\frac{4!}{2!2!} = \frac{4 \cdot 3 \cdot 2!}{2! \cdot 2 \cdot 1} = \frac{12}{2} = 6$

Take a few minutes to verify the other factorial evaluations.

$$= 1 \cdot x^4 + 4x^3 \cdot 2 + 6x^2 \cdot 4 + 4x \cdot 8 + 1 \cdot 16$$

$$= x^4 + 8x^3 + 24x^2 + 32x + 16$$

⬤

### Technology

You can use a graphing utility's table feature to find the five binomial coefficients in Example 2.

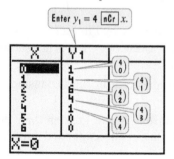

Enter $y_1 = 4$ nCr $x$.

⌀ Check Point **2** Expand: $(x + 1)^4$.

**EXAMPLE 3** Using the Binomial Theorem

Expand: $(2x - y)^5$.

**Solution** Because the Binomial Theorem involves the addition of two terms raised to a power, we rewrite $(2x - y)^5$ as $[2x + (-y)]^5$. We use the Binomial Theorem

$$(a + b)^n = \binom{n}{0}a^n + \binom{n}{1}a^{n-1}b + \binom{n}{2}a^{n-2}b^2 + \binom{n}{3}a^{n-3}b^3 + \cdots + \binom{n}{n}b^n$$

to expand $[2x + (-y)]^5$. In $[2x + (-y)]^5, a = 2x, b = -y,$ and $n = 5$. In the expansion, powers of $2x$ are in descending order, starting with $(2x)^5$. Powers of $-y$ are in ascending order, starting with $(-y)^0$. [Because $(-y)^0 = 1$, a $-y$ is not shown in the first term.] The sum of the exponents on $2x$ and $-y$ in each term is equal to 5, the exponent in the expression $(2x - y)^5$.

$$(2x - y)^5 = [2x + (-y)]^5$$

$$= \binom{5}{0}(2x)^5 + \binom{5}{1}(2x)^4(-y) + \binom{5}{2}(2x)^3(-y)^2 + \binom{5}{3}(2x)^2(-y)^3 + \binom{5}{4}(2x)(-y)^4 + \binom{5}{5}(-y)^5$$

Evaluate binomial coefficients using $\binom{n}{r} = \frac{n!}{r!(n-r)!}$.

$$= \frac{5!}{0!5!}(2x)^5 + \frac{5!}{1!4!}(2x)^4(-y) + \frac{5!}{2!3!}(2x)^3(-y)^2 + \frac{5!}{3!2!}(2x)^2(-y)^3 + \frac{5!}{4!1!}(2x)(-y)^4 + \frac{5!}{5!0!}(-y)^5$$

$$\frac{5!}{2!3!} = \frac{5 \cdot 4 \cdot 3!}{2 \cdot 1 \cdot 3!} = 10$$

Take a few minutes to verify the other factorial evaluations.

$$= 1(2x)^5 + 5(2x)^4(-y) + 10(2x)^3(-y)^2 + 10(2x)^2(-y)^3 + 5(2x)(-y)^4 + 1(-y)^5$$

Raise both factors in these parentheses to the indicated powers.

$$= 1(32x^5) + 5(16x^4)(-y) + 10(8x^3)(-y)^2 + 10(4x^2)(-y)^3 + 5(2x)(-y)^4 + 1(-y)^5$$

Now raise $-y$ to the indicated powers.

$$= 1(32x^5) + 5(16x^4)(-y) + 10(8x^3)y^2 + 10(4x^2)(-y^3) + 5(2x)y^4 + 1(-y^5)$$

Multiplying factors in each of the six terms gives us the desired expansion:

$$(2x - y)^5 = 32x^5 - 80x^4y + 80x^3y^2 - 40x^2y^3 + 10xy^4 - y^5.$$

$\checkmark$ **Check Point 3** Expand: $(x - 2y)^5$.

**③** Find a particular term in a binomial expansion.

## Finding a Particular Term in a Binomial Expansion

By observing the terms in the formula for expanding binomials, we can find a formula for finding a particular term without writing the entire expansion.

| 1st term | 2nd term | 3rd term |
|---|---|---|
| $\binom{n}{0}a^nb^0$ | $\binom{n}{1}a^{n-1}b^1$ | $\binom{n}{2}a^{n-2}b^2$ |

The exponent on $b$ is 1 less than the term number.

Based on the observation in the bottom voice balloon, the $(r + 1)$st term of the expansion of $(a + b)^n$ is the term that contains $b^r$.

### Finding a Particular Term in a Binomial Expansion

The $(r + 1)$st term of the expansion of $(a + b)^n$ is

$$\binom{n}{r}a^{n-r}b^r.$$

$\boxed{\text{EXAMPLE 4}}$  **Finding a Single Term of a Binomial Expansion**

Find the fourth term in the expansion of $(3x + 2y)^7$.

**Solution**   The fourth term in the expansion of $(3x + 2y)^7$ contains $(2y)^3$. To find the fourth term, first note that $4 = 3 + 1$. Equivalently, the fourth term of $(3x + 2y)^7$ is the $(3 + 1)$st term. Thus, $r = 3, a = 3x, b = 2y,$ and $n = 7$. The fourth term is

$$\binom{7}{3}(3x)^{7-3}(2y)^3 = \binom{7}{3}(3x)^4(2y)^3 = \frac{7!}{3!(7-3)!}(3x)^4(2y)^3.$$

Use the formula for the $(r + 1)$st term of $(a + b)^n$: $\binom{n}{r}a^{n-r}b^r$.

We use $\binom{n}{r} = \frac{n!}{r!(n-r)!}$ to evaluate $\binom{7}{3}$.

Now we need to evaluate the factorial expression and raise $3x$ and $2y$ to the indicated powers. We obtain

$$\frac{7!}{3!4!}(81x^4)(8y^3) = \frac{7 \cdot 6 \cdot 5 \cdot 4!}{3 \cdot 2 \cdot 1 \cdot 4!}(81x^4)(8y^3) = 35(81x^4)(8y^3) = 22{,}680x^4y^3.$$

The fourth term of $(3x + 2y)^7$ is $22{,}680x^4y^3$.

$\oslash$ Check Point **4**  Find the fifth term in the expansion of $(2x + y)^9$.

## The Universality of Mathematics

Pascal's triangle is an array of numbers showing coefficients of the terms in the expansions of $(a + b)^n$. Although credited to French mathematician Blaise Pascal (1623–1662), the triangular array of numbers appeared in a Chinese document printed in 1303. The Binomial Theorem was known in Eastern cultures prior to its discovery in Europe. The same mathematics is often discovered/invented by independent researchers separated by time, place, and culture.

| Binomial Expansions | Pascal's Triangle Coefficients in the Expansions | Chinese Document: 1303 |
|---|---|---|
| $(a + b)^0 = 1$ | 1 | |
| $(a + b)^1 = a + b$ | 1  1 | |
| $(a + b)^2 = a^2 + 2ab + b^2$ | 1  2  1 | |
| $(a + b)^3 = a^3 + 3a^2b + 3ab^2 + b^3$ | 1  3  3  1 | |
| $(a + b)^4 = a^4 + 4a^3b + 6a^2b^2 + 4ab^3 + b^4$ | 1  4  6  4  1 | |
| $(a + b)^5 = a^5 + 5a^4b + 10a^3b^2 + 10a^2b^3 + 5ab^4 + b^5$ | 1  5  10  10  5  1 | |
|  | 1  6  15  20  15  6  1 | |
|  | 1  7  21  35  35  21  7  1 | |
|  | 1  8  28  56  70  56  28  8  1 | |

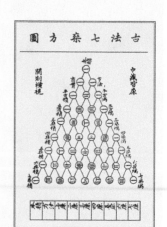

# Exercise Set 10.5

## Practice Exercises

*In Exercises 1–8, evaluate the given binomial coefficient.*

**1.** $\binom{8}{3}$     **2.** $\binom{7}{2}$     **3.** $\binom{12}{1}$

**4.** $\binom{11}{1}$     **5.** $\binom{6}{6}$     **6.** $\binom{15}{2}$

**7.** $\binom{100}{2}$     **8.** $\binom{100}{98}$

*In Exercises 9–30, use the Binomial Theorem to expand each binomial and express the result in simplified form.*

**9.** $(x + 2)^3$     **10.** $(x + 4)^3$

**11.** $(3x + y)^3$     **12.** $(x + 3y)^3$

**13.** $(5x - 1)^3$     **14.** $(4x - 1)^3$

**15.** $(2x + 1)^4$     **16.** $(3x + 1)^4$

**17.** $(x^2 + 2y)^4$     **18.** $(x^2 + y)^4$

**19.** $(y - 3)^4$     **20.** $(y - 4)^4$

**21.** $(2x^3 - 1)^4$     **22.** $(2x^5 - 1)^4$

**23.** $(c + 2)^5$     **24.** $(c + 3)^5$

**25.** $(x - 1)^5$     **26.** $(x - 2)^5$

**27.** $(3x - y)^5$     **28.** $(x - 3y)^5$

**29.** $(2a + b)^6$     **30.** $(a + 2b)^6$

*In Exercises 31–38, write the first three terms in each binomial expansion, expressing the result in simplified form.*

**31.** $(x + 2)^8$     **32.** $(x + 3)^8$

**33.** $(x - 2y)^{10}$     **34.** $(x - 2y)^9$

**35.** $(x^2 + 1)^{16}$     **36.** $(x^2 + 1)^{17}$

**37.** $(y^3 - 1)^{20}$     **38.** $(y^3 - 1)^{21}$

*In Exercises 39–48, find the term indicated in each expansion.*

**39.** $(2x + y)^6$; third term     **40.** $(x + 2y)^6$; third term

**41.** $(x - 1)^9$; fifth term     **42.** $(x - 1)^{10}$; fifth term

**43.** $(x^2 + y^3)^8$; sixth term     **44.** $(x^3 + y^2)^8$; sixth term

**45.** $\left(x - \frac{1}{2}\right)^9$; fourth term     **46.** $\left(x + \frac{1}{2}\right)^8$; fourth term

**47.** $(x^2 + y)^{22}$; the term containing $y^{14}$

**48.** $(x + 2y)^{10}$; the term containing $y^6$

## Practice Plus

*In Exercises 49–52, use the Binomial Theorem to expand each expression and write the result in simplified form.*

**49.** $(x^3 + x^{-2})^4$     **50.** $(x^2 + x^{-3})^4$

**51.** $\left(x^{\frac{1}{3}} - x^{-\frac{1}{3}}\right)^3$     **52.** $\left(x^{\frac{2}{3}} - \frac{1}{\sqrt[3]{x}}\right)^3$

*In Exercises 53–54, find $\dfrac{f(x + h) - f(x)}{h}$ and simplify.*

**53.** $f(x) = x^4 + 7$     **54.** $f(x) = x^5 + 8$

**55.** Find the middle term in the expansion of $\left(\dfrac{3}{x} + \dfrac{x}{3}\right)^{10}$.

**56.** Find the middle term in the expansion of $\left(\dfrac{1}{x} - x^2\right)^{12}$.

## Application Exercises

*The graph shows that U.S. smokers have a greater probability of suffering from some ailments than the general adult population. Exercises 57–58 are based on some of the probabilities, expressed as decimals, shown to the right of the bars. In each exercise, use a calculator to determine the probability, correct to four decimal places.*

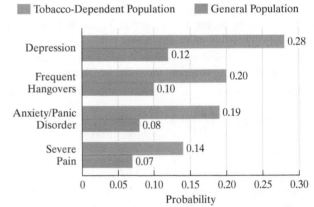

Probability That United States Adults Suffer from Various Ailments

*Source: MARS 2005 OTC/DTC*

*If the probability an event will occur is p and the probability it will not occur is q, then each term in the expansion of $(p + q)^n$ represents a probability.*

**57.** The probability that a smoker suffers from depression is 0.28. If five smokers are randomly selected, the probability that three of them will suffer from depression is the third term of the binomial expansion of

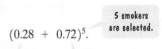

$(0.28 + 0.72)^5$.

What is this probability?

**58.** The probability that a person in the general population suffers from depression is 0.12. If five people from the general population are randomly selected, the probability that three of them will suffer from depression is the third term of the binomial expansion of

$$(0.12 + 0.88)^5.$$

5 people from the general population are selected.

Probability a person in the general population suffers from depression

Probability a person in the general population does not suffer from depression

What is this probability?

## Writing in Mathematics

**59.** Explain how to evaluate $\binom{n}{r}$. Provide an example with your explanation.

**60.** Describe the pattern on the exponents on $a$ in the expansion of $(a + b)^n$.

**61.** Describe the pattern on the exponents on $b$ in the expansion of $(a + b)^n$.

**62.** What is true about the sum of the exponents on $a$ and $b$ in any term in the expansion of $(a + b)^n$?

**63.** How do you determine how many terms there are in a binomial expansion?

**64.** Explain how to use the Binomial Theorem to expand a binomial. Provide an example with your explanation.

**65.** Explain how to find a particular term in a binomial expansion without having to write out the entire expansion.

**66.** Describe how you would use mathematical induction to prove

$$(a + b)^n = \binom{n}{0}a^n + \binom{n}{1}a^{n-1}b + \binom{n}{2}a^{n-2}b^2$$

$$+ \cdots + \binom{n}{n-1}ab^{n-1} + \binom{n}{n}b^n.$$

What happens when $n = 1$? Write the statement that we assume to be true. Write the statement that we must prove. What must be done to the left side of the assumed statement to make it look like the left side of the statement that must be proved? (More detail on the actual proof is found in Exercise 85.)

## Technology Exercises

**67.** Use the $\boxed{{}_nC_r}$ key on a graphing utility to verify your answers in Exercises 1–8.

In Exercises 68–69, graph each of the functions in the same viewing rectangle. Describe how the graphs illustrate the Binomial Theorem.

**68.** $f_1(x) = (x + 2)^3$          $f_2(x) = x^3$

$f_3(x) = x^3 + 6x^2$          $f_4(x) = x^3 + 6x^2 + 12x$

$f_5(x) = x^3 + 6x^2 + 12x + 8$

Use a $[-10, 10, 1]$ by $[-30, 30, 10]$ viewing rectangle.

**69.** $f_1(x) = (x + 1)^4$          $f_2(x) = x^4$

$f_3(x) = x^4 + 4x^3$          $f_4(x) = x^4 + 4x^3 + 6x^2$

$f_5(x) = x^4 + 4x^3 + 6x^2 + 4x$

$f_6(x) = x^4 + 4x^3 + 6x^2 + 4x + 1$

Use a $[-5, 5, 1]$ by $[-30, 30, 10]$ viewing rectangle.

In Exercises 70–72, use the Binomial Theorem to find a polynomial expansion for each function. Then use a graphing utility and an approach similar to the one in Exercises 68 and 69 to verify the expansion.

**70.** $f_1(x) = (x - 1)^3$          **71.** $f_1(x) = (x - 2)^4$

**72.** $f_1(x) = (x + 2)^6$

## Critical Thinking Exercises

**Make Sense?** In Exercises 73–76, determine whether each statement makes sense or does not make sense, and explain your reasoning.

**73.** In order to expand $(x^3 - y^4)^5$, I find it helpful to rewrite the expression inside the parentheses as $x^3 + (-y^4)$.

**74.** Without writing the expansion of $(x - 1)^6$, I can see that the terms have alternating positive and negative signs.

**75.** I use binomial coefficients to expand $(a + b)^n$, where $\binom{n}{1}$ is the coefficient of the first term, $\binom{n}{2}$ is the coefficient of the second term, and so on.

**76.** One of the terms in my binomial expansion is $\binom{7}{5}x^2y^4$.

In Exercises 77–80, determine whether each statement is true or false. If the statement is false, make the necessary change(s) to produce a true statement.

**77.** The binomial expansion for $(a + b)^n$ contains $n$ terms.

**78.** The Binomial Theorem can be written in condensed form as

$$(a + b)^n = \sum_{r=0}^{n} \binom{n}{r}a^{n-r}b^r.$$

**79.** The sum of the binomial coefficients in $(a + b)^n$ cannot be $2^n$.

**80.** There are no values of $a$ and $b$ such that

$$(a + b)^4 = a^4 + b^4.$$

**81.** Use the Binomial Theorem to expand and then simplify the result: $(x^2 + x + 1)^3$.

Hint: Write $x^2 + x + 1$ as $x^2 + (x + 1)$.

**82.** Find the term in the expansion of $(x^2 + y^2)^5$ containing $x^4$ as a factor.

**83.** Prove that

$$\binom{n}{r} = \binom{n}{n - r}.$$

**84.** Show that

$$\binom{n}{r} + \binom{n}{r + 1} = \binom{n + 1}{r + 1}.$$

Hints:

$$(n - r)! = (n - r)(n - r - 1)!$$

$$(r + 1)! = (r + 1)r!$$

**85.** Follow the outline below and use mathematical induction to prove the Binomial Theorem:

$$(a + b)^n = \binom{n}{0}a^n + \binom{n}{1}a^{n-1}b + \binom{n}{2}a^{n-2}b^2$$

$$+ \cdots + \binom{n}{n-1}ab^{n-1} + \binom{n}{n}b^n.$$

**a.** Verify the formula for $n = 1$.

**b.** Replace $n$ with $k$ and write the statement that is assumed true. Replace $n$ with $k + 1$ and write the statement that must be proved.

**c.** Multiply both sides of the statement assumed to be true by $a + b$. Add exponents on the left. On the right, distribute $a$ and $b$, respectively.

**d.** Collect like terms on the right. At this point, you should have

$$(a + b)^{k+1} = \binom{k}{0}a^{k+1} + \left[\binom{k}{0} + \binom{k}{1}\right]a^k b$$

$$+ \left[\binom{k}{1} + \binom{k}{2}\right]a^{k-1}b^2 + \left[\binom{k}{2} + \binom{k}{3}\right]a^{k-2}b^3$$

$$+ \cdots + \left[\binom{k}{k-1} + \binom{k}{k}\right]ab^k + \binom{k}{k}b^{k+1}.$$

**e.** Use the result of Exercise 84 to add the binomial sums in brackets. For example, because $\binom{n}{r} + \binom{n}{r+1}$

$= \binom{n+1}{r+1}$, then $\binom{k}{0} + \binom{k}{1} = \binom{k+1}{1}$ and

$\binom{k}{1} + \binom{k}{2} = \binom{k+1}{2}$.

**f.** Because $\binom{k}{0} = \binom{k+1}{0}$ (why?) and $\binom{k}{k} = \binom{k+1}{k+1}$

(why?), substitute these results and the results from part (e) into the equation in part (d). This should give the statement that we were required to prove in the second step of the mathematical induction process.

## Preview Exercises

*Exercises 86–88 will help you prepare for the material covered in the next section.*

**86.** Evaluate $\dfrac{n!}{(n-r)!}$ for $n = 20$ and $r = 3$.

**87.** Evaluate $\dfrac{n!}{(n-r)!\,r!}$ for $n = 8$ and $r = 3$.

**88.** You can choose from two pairs of jeans (one blue, one black) and three T-shirts (one beige, one yellow, and one blue), as shown in the diagram.

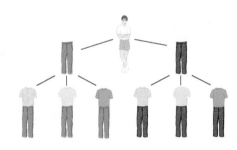

True or false: The diagram shows that you can form $2 \times 3$, or 6, different outfits.

---

## (Section) 10.6 Counting Principles, Permutations, and Combinations

### Objectives

1. Use the Fundamental Counting Principle.
2. Use the permutations formula.
3. Distinguish between permutation problems and combination problems.
4. Use the combinations formula.

Have you ever imagined what your life would be like if you won the lottery? What changes would you make? Before you fantasize about becoming a person of leisure with a staff of obedient elves, think about this: The probability of winning top prize in the lottery is about the same as the probability of being struck by lightning. There are millions of possible number combinations in lottery games and only one way of winning the grand prize. Determining the probability of winning involves calculating the chance of getting the winning combination from all possible outcomes. In this section, we begin preparing for the surprising world of probability by looking at methods for counting possible outcomes.

① Use the Fundamental Counting Principle.

## The Fundamental Counting Principle

It's early morning, you're groggy, and you have to select something to wear for your 8 A.M. class. (What *were* you thinking of when you signed up for a class at that hour?!) Fortunately, your "lecture wardrobe" is rather limited—just two pairs of jeans to choose from (one blue, one black), three T-shirts to choose from (one beige, one yellow, and one blue), and two pairs of sneakers to select from (one black pair, one red pair). Your possible outfits are shown in **Figure 10.8**.

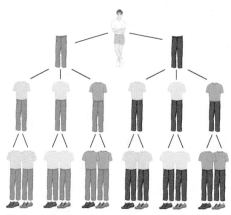

Figure 10.8 Selecting a wardrobe

The **tree diagram**, so named because of its branches, shows that you can form 12 outfits from your two pairs of jeans, three T-shirts, and two pairs of sneakers. Notice that the number of outfits can be obtained by multiplying the number of choices for jeans, 2, the number of choices for the T-shirts, 3, and the number of choices for the sneakers, 2:

$$2 \cdot 3 \cdot 2 = 12.$$

We can generalize this idea to any two or more groups of items—not just jeans, T-shirts, and sneakers—with the **Fundamental Counting Principle**:

### The Fundamental Counting Principle

The number of ways in which a series of successive things can occur is found by multiplying the number of ways in which each thing can occur.

For example, if you own 30 pairs of jeans, 20 T-shirts, and 12 pairs of sneakers, you have

$$30 \cdot 20 \cdot 12 = 7200$$

choices for your wardrobe!

( EXAMPLE 1 ) **Options in Planning a Course Schedule**

Next semester you are planning to take three courses—math, English, and humanities. Based on time blocks and highly recommended professors, there are 8 sections of math, 5 of English, and 4 of humanities that you find suitable. Assuming no scheduling conflicts, how many different three-course schedules are possible?

**Solution** This situation involves making choices with three groups of items.

| Math | English | Humanities |
| --- | --- | --- |
| 8 choices | 5 choices | 4 choices |

We use the Fundamental Counting Principle to find the number of three-course schedules. Multiply the number of choices for each of the three groups:

$$8 \cdot 5 \cdot 4 = 160.$$

Thus, there are 160 different three-course schedules.

⊘ Check Point **1** A pizza can be ordered with three choices of size (small, medium, or large), four choices of crust (thin, thick, crispy, or regular), and six choices of toppings (ground beef, sausage, pepperoni, bacon, mushrooms, or onions). How many different one-topping pizzas can be ordered?

**( EXAMPLE 2 )** **A Multiple-Choice Test**

You are taking a multiple-choice test that has ten questions. Each of the questions has four answer choices, with one correct answer per question. If you select one of these four choices for each question and leave nothing blank, in how many ways can you answer the questions?

**Solution** This situation involves making choices with ten questions.

| Question 1 | Question 2 | Question 3 | ⋯ | Question 9 | Question 10 |
| 4 choices | 4 choices | 4 choices | | 4 choices | 4 choices |

We use the Fundamental Counting Principle to determine the number of ways that you can answer the questions on the test. Multiply the number of choices, 4, for each of the ten questions.

$$4 \cdot 4 \cdot 4 \cdot 4 \cdot 4 \cdot 4 \cdot 4 \cdot 4 \cdot 4 \cdot 4 = 4^{10} = 1{,}048{,}576$$

Thus, you can answer the questions in 1,048,576 different ways.

Are you surprised that there are over one million ways of answering a ten-question multiple-choice test? Of course, there is only one way to answer the test and receive a perfect score. The probability of guessing your way into a perfect score involves calculating the chance of getting a perfect score, just one way from all 1,048,576 possible outcomes. In short, prepare for the test and do not rely on guessing!

⊘ Check Point **2** You are taking a multiple-choice test that has six questions. Each of the questions has three answer choices, with one correct answer per question. If you select one of these three choices for each question and leave nothing blank, in how many ways can you answer the questions?

**( EXAMPLE 3 )** **Telephone Numbers in the United States**

Telephone numbers in the United States begin with three-digit area codes followed by seven-digit local telephone numbers. Area codes and local telephone numbers cannot begin with 0 or 1. How many different telephone numbers are possible?

**Solution** This situation involves making choices with ten groups of items.

Area Code          Local Telephone Number
□ □ □              □ □ □   □ □ □ □

You cannot use 0 or 1 in these groups. There are only 8 choices: 2, 3, 4, 5, 6, 7, 8, or 9.

You can use 0, 1, 2, 3, 4, 5, 6, 7, 8, or 9 in these groups. There are 10 choices per group.

The number of possible ways of playing the first four moves on each side in a game of chess is 318,979,564,000.

**Running Out of Telephone Numbers**

By the year 2020, portable telephones used for business and pleasure will all be videophones. At that time, U.S. population is expected to be 323 million. Faxes, beepers, cell phones, computer phone lines, and business lines may result in certain areas running out of phone numbers. Solution: Add more digits!

With or without extra digits, we expect that the 2020 videophone greeting will still be "hello," a word created by Thomas Edison in 1877. Phone inventor Alexander Graham Bell preferred "ahoy," but "hello" won out, appearing in the *Oxford English Dictionary* in 1883.

*(Source: New York Times)*

Here are the numbers of choices for each of the ten groups of items:

**Area Code**
8  10  10

**Local Telephone Number**
8  10  10     10  10  10  10.

We use the Fundamental Counting Principle to determine the number of different telephone numbers that are possible. The total number of telephone numbers possible is

$$8 \cdot 10 \cdot 10 \cdot 8 \cdot 10 \cdot 10 \cdot 10 \cdot 10 \cdot 10 \cdot 10 = 6{,}400{,}000{,}000.$$

There are six billion four hundred million different telephone numbers that are possible.

⊘ Check Point **3** License plates in a particular state display two letters followed by three numbers, such as AT-887 or BB-013. How many different license plates can be manufactured?

**② Use the permutations formula.**

## Permutations

You are the coach of a little league baseball team. There are 13 players on the team (and lots of parents hovering in the background, dreaming of stardom for their little "Manny Ramirez"). You need to choose a batting order having 9 players. The order makes a difference, because, for instance, if bases are loaded and "Little Manny" is fourth or fifth at bat, his possible home run will drive in three additional runs. How many batting orders can you form?

You can choose any of 13 players for the first person at bat. Then you will have 12 players from which to choose the second batter, then 11 from which to choose the third batter, and so on. The situation can be shown as follows:

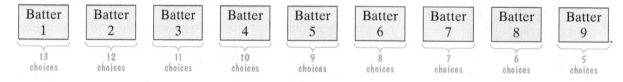

| Batter 1 | Batter 2 | Batter 3 | Batter 4 | Batter 5 | Batter 6 | Batter 7 | Batter 8 | Batter 9 |
|---|---|---|---|---|---|---|---|---|
| 13 choices | 12 choices | 11 choices | 10 choices | 9 choices | 8 choices | 7 choices | 6 choices | 5 choices |

We use the Fundamental Counting Principle to find the number of batting orders. The total number of batting orders is

$$13 \cdot 12 \cdot 11 \cdot 10 \cdot 9 \cdot 8 \cdot 7 \cdot 6 \cdot 5 = 259{,}459{,}200.$$

Nearly 260 million batting orders are possible for your 13-player little league team. Each batting order is called a *permutation* of 13 players taken 9 at a time. The number of permutations of 13 players taken 9 at a time is 259,459,200.

A **permutation** is an ordered arrangement of items that occurs when

• No item is used more than once. (Each of the 9 players in the batting order bats exactly once.)

• The order of arrangement makes a difference.

We can obtain a formula for finding the number of permutations of 13 players taken 9 at a time by rewriting our computation:

$$13 \cdot 12 \cdot 11 \cdot 10 \cdot 9 \cdot 8 \cdot 7 \cdot 6 \cdot 5$$
$$= \frac{13 \cdot 12 \cdot 11 \cdot 10 \cdot 9 \cdot 8 \cdot 7 \cdot 6 \cdot 5 \cdot \boxed{4 \cdot 3 \cdot 2 \cdot 1}}{\boxed{4 \cdot 3 \cdot 2 \cdot 1}} = \frac{13!}{4!} = \frac{13!}{(13 - 9)!}.$$

Thus, the number of permutations of 13 things taken 9 at a time is $\frac{13!}{(13 - 9)!}$. The special notation $_{13}P_9$ is used to replace the phrase "the number of permutations of 13 things taken 9 at a time." Using this new notation, we can write

$$_{13}P_9 = \frac{13!}{(13-9)!}.$$

The numerator of this expression is the number of items, 13 team members, expressed as a factorial: 13!. The denominator is also a factorial. It is the factorial of the difference between the number of items, 13, and the number of items in each permutation, 9 batters: $(13-9)!$.

The notation $_nP_r$ means the **number of permutations of n things taken r at a time**. We can generalize from the situation in which 9 batters were taken from 13 players. By generalizing, we obtain the following formula for the number of permutations if $r$ items are taken from $n$ items.

### Study Tip

Because all permutation problems are also fundamental counting problems, they can be solved using the formula for $_nP_r$ or using the Fundamental Counting Principle.

---

### Permutations of n Things Taken r at a Time

The number of possible permutations if $r$ items are taken from $n$ items is

$$_nP_r = \frac{n!}{(n-r)!}.$$

---

### Technology

Graphing utilities have a menu item for calculating permutations, usually labeled $\boxed{_nP_r}$. For example, to find $_{20}P_3$, the keystrokes are

$$20 \boxed{_nP_r} \; 3 \; \boxed{\text{ENTER}}.$$

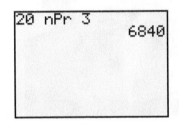

If you are using a scientific calculator, check your manual for the location of the menu item for calculating permutations and the required keystrokes.

### EXAMPLE 4  Using the Formula for Permutations

You and 19 of your friends have decided to form an Internet marketing consulting firm. The group needs to choose three officers—a CEO, an operating manager, and a treasurer. In how many ways can those offices be filled?

**Solution**  Your group is choosing $r = 3$ officers from a group of $n = 20$ people (you and 19 friends). The order in which the officers are chosen matters because the CEO, the operating manager, and the treasurer each have different responsibilities. Thus, we are looking for the number of permutations of 20 things taken 3 at a time. We use the formula

$$_nP_r = \frac{n!}{(n-r)!}$$

with $n = 20$ and $r = 3$.

$$_{20}P_3 = \frac{20!}{(20-3)!} = \frac{20!}{17!} = \frac{20 \cdot 19 \cdot 18 \cdot 17!}{17!} = \frac{20 \cdot 19 \cdot 18 \cdot \cancel{17!}}{\cancel{17!}} = 20 \cdot 19 \cdot 18 = 6840$$

Thus, there are 6840 different ways of filling the three offices.  ●

✍ **Check Point 4**  A corporation has seven members on its board of directors. In how many different ways can it elect a president, vice-president, secretary, and treasurer?

### How to Pass the Time for $2\frac{1}{2}$ Million Years

If you were to arrange 15 different books on a shelf and it took you one minute for each permutation, the entire task would take 2,487,965 years.

*Source:* Isaac Asimov's *Book of Facts.*

### EXAMPLE 5  Using the Formula for Permutations

You need to arrange seven of your favorite books along a small shelf. How many different ways can you arrange the books, assuming that the order of the books makes a difference to you?

**Solution**  Because you are using all seven of your books in every possible arrangement, you are arranging $r = 7$ books from a group of $n = 7$ books. Thus, we are looking for the number of permutations of 7 things taken 7 at a time. We use the formula

$$_nP_r = \frac{n!}{(n-r)!}$$

with $n = 7$ and $r = 7$.

$$_7P_7 = \frac{7!}{(7-7)!} = \frac{7!}{0!} = \frac{7!}{1} = 5040$$

Thus, you can arrange the books in 5040 ways. There are 5040 different possible permutations.

⬤

✓ **Check Point 5** In how many ways can six books be lined up along a shelf?

⟨3⟩ Distinguish between permutation problems and combination problems.

## Combinations

Discussing the tragic death of actor Heath Ledger at age 28, *USA Today* (Jan. 30, 2008) cited five people who had achieved cult-figure status after death. Made iconic by death: Marilyn Monroe (actress, 1927–1962), James Dean (actor, 1931–1955), Jim Morrison (musician and lead singer of The Doors, 1943–1971), Janis Joplin (blues/rock singer, 1943–1970), and Jimi Hendrix (guitar virtuoso, 1943–1970).

Imagine that you ask your friends the following question: "Of these five people, which three would you select to be included in a documentary featuring the best of their work?" You are not asking your friends to rank their three favorite artists in any kind of order—they should merely select the three to be included in the documentary.

One friend answers, "Jim Morrison, Janis Joplin, and Jimi Hendrix." Another responds, "Jimi Hendrix, Janis Joplin, and Jim Morrison." These two people have the same artists in their group of selections, even if they are named in a different order. We are interested *in which artists are named, not the order in which they are named*, for the documentary. Because the items are taken without regard to order, this is not a permutation problem. No ranking of any sort is involved.

Later on, you ask your roommate which three artists she would select for the documentary. She names Marilyn Monroe, James Dean, and Jimi Hendrix. Her selection is different from those of your two other friends because different entertainers are cited.

Mathematicians describe the group of artists given by your roommate as a *combination*. A **combination** of items occurs when

- The items are selected from the same group (the five stars who were made iconic by death).

- No item is used more than once. (You may view Jimi Hendrix as a guitar god, but your three selections cannot be Jimi Hendrix, Jimi Hendrix, and Jimi Hendrix.)

- The order of the items makes no difference. (Morrison, Joplin, Hendrix is the same group in the documentary as Hendrix, Joplin, Morrison.)

Do you see the difference between a permutation and a combination? A permutation is an ordered arrangement of a given group of items. A combination is a group of items taken without regard to their order. **Permutation** problems involve situations in which **order matters**. **Combination** problems involve situations in which the **order of the items makes no difference**.

**( EXAMPLE 6 )** **Distinguishing between Permutations and Combinations**

For each of the following problems, determine whether the problem is one involving permutations or combinations. (It is not necessary to solve the problem.)

a. Six students are running for student government president, vice-president, and treasurer. The student with the greatest number of votes becomes the president, the second highest vote-getter becomes vice-president, and the student who gets the third largest number of votes will be treasurer. How many different outcomes are possible for these three positions?

b. Six people are on the board of supervisors for your neighborhood park. A three-person committee is needed to study the possibility of expanding the park. How many different committees could be formed from the six people?

c. Baskin-Robbins offers 31 different flavors of ice cream. One of their items is a bowl consisting of three scoops of ice cream, each a different flavor. How many such bowls are possible?

**Solution**

a. Students are choosing three student government officers from six candidates. The order in which the officers are chosen makes a difference because each of the offices (president, vice-president, treasurer) is different. Order matters. This is a problem involving permutations.

b. A three-person committee is to be formed from the six-person board of supervisors. The order in which the three people are selected does not matter because they are not filling different roles on the committee. Because order makes no difference, this is a problem involving combinations.

c. A three-scoop bowl of three different flavors is to be formed from Baskin-Robbins's 31 flavors. The order in which the three scoops of ice cream are put into the bowl is irrelevant. A bowl with chocolate, vanilla, and strawberry is exactly the same as a bowl with vanilla, strawberry, and chocolate. Different orderings do not change things, and so this is a problem involving combinations.

Check Point 6 For each of the following problems, explain if the problem is one involving permutations or combinations. (It is not necessary to solve the problem.)

a. How many ways can you select 6 free DVDs from a list of 200 DVDs?

b. In a race in which there are 50 runners and no ties, in how many ways can the first three finishers come in?

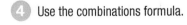
④ Use the combinations formula.

**A Formula for Combinations**

We have seen that the notation $_nP_r$ means the number of permutations of $n$ things taken $r$ at a time. Similarly, the notation $_nC_r$ **means the number of combinations of $n$ things taken $r$ at a time.**

We can develop a formula for $_nC_r$ by comparing permutations and combinations. Consider the letters A, B, C, and D. The number of permutations of these four letters taken three at a time is

$$_4P_3 = \frac{4!}{(4-3)!} = \frac{4!}{1!} = \frac{4 \cdot 3 \cdot 2 \cdot 1}{1} = 24.$$

Here are the 24 permutations:

| | | | |
|---|---|---|---|
| ABC, | ABD, | ACD, | BCD, |
| ACB, | ADB, | ADC, | BDC, |
| BAC, | BAD, | CAD, | CBD, |
| BCA, | BDA, | CDA, | CDB, |
| CAB, | DAB, | DAC, | DBC, |
| CBA, | DBA, | DCA, | DCB. |

This column contains only one combination, ABC.

This column contains only one combination, ABD.

This column contains only one combination, ACD.

This column contains only one combination, BCD.

Because the order of items makes no difference in determining combinations, each column of six permutations represents one combination. There is a total of four combinations:

$$ABC, \quad ABD, \quad ACD, \quad BCD.$$

Thus, $_4C_3 = 4$: The number of combinations of 4 things taken 3 at a time is 4. With 24 permutations and only four combinations, there are 6, or 3!, times as many permutations as there are combinations.

In general, there are $r!$ times as many permutations of $n$ things taken $r$ at a time as there are combinations of $n$ things taken $r$ at a time. Thus, we find the number of combinations of $n$ things taken $r$ at a time by dividing the number of permutations of $n$ things taken $r$ at a time by $r!$.

$$_nC_r = \frac{_nP_r}{r!} = \frac{\dfrac{n!}{(n-r)!}}{r!} = \frac{n!}{(n-r)!r!}$$

**Study Tip**

The number of combinations if $r$ items are taken from $n$ items cannot be found using the Fundamental Counting Principle and requires the use of the formula shown on the right.

### Combinations of $n$ Things Taken $r$ at a Time

The number of possible combinations if $r$ items are taken from $n$ items is

$$_nC_r = \frac{n!}{(n-r)!r!}.$$

Notice that the formula for $_nC_r$ is the same as the formula for the binomial coefficient $\binom{n}{r}$.

**EXAMPLE 7** Using the Formula for Combinations

A three-person committee is needed to study ways of improving public transportation. How many committees could be formed from the eight people on the board of supervisors?

**Solution** The order in which the three people are selected does not matter. This is a problem of selecting $r = 3$ people from a group of $n = 8$ people. We are

Graphing utilities have a menu item for calculating combinations, usually labeled $_nC_r$. For example, to find $_8C_3$, the keystrokes on most graphing utilities are

8 $\boxed{_nC_r}$ 3 $\boxed{\text{ENTER}}$.

If you are using a scientific calculator, check your manual to see whether there is a menu item for calculating combinations.

If you use your calculator's factorial key to find $\frac{8!}{5!3!}$, be sure to enclose the factorials in the denominator with parentheses

8 $\boxed{!}$ $\boxed{\div}$ $\boxed{(}$ 5 $\boxed{!}$ $\boxed{\times}$ 3 $\boxed{!}$ $\boxed{)}$

pressing $\boxed{=}$ or $\boxed{\text{ENTER}}$ to obtain the answer.

looking for the number of combinations of eight things taken three at a time. We use the formula

$$_nC_r = \frac{n!}{(n-r)!r!}$$

with $n = 8$ and $r = 3$.

$$_8C_3 = \frac{8!}{(8-3)!3!} = \frac{8!}{5!3!} = \frac{8 \cdot 7 \cdot 6 \cdot 5!}{5! \cdot 3 \cdot 2 \cdot 1} = \frac{8 \cdot 7 \cdot 6 \cdot 5!}{5! \cdot 3 \cdot 2 \cdot 1} = 56$$

Thus, 56 committees of three people each can be formed from the eight people on the board of supervisors.

**⊘ Check Point 7** From a group of 10 physicians, in how many ways can four people be selected to attend a conference on acupuncture?

**EXAMPLE 8** Using the Formula for Combinations

In poker, a person is dealt 5 cards from a standard 52-card deck. The order in which you are dealt the 5 cards does not matter. How many different 5-card poker hands are possible?

**Solution**  Because the order in which the 5 cards are dealt does not matter, this is a problem involving combinations. We are looking for the number of combinations of $n = 52$ cards dealt $r = 5$ at a time. We use the formula

$$_nC_r = \frac{n!}{(n-r)!r!}$$

with $n = 52$ and $r = 5$.

$$_{52}C_5 = \frac{52!}{(52-5)!5!} = \frac{52!}{47!5!} = \frac{52 \cdot 51 \cdot 50 \cdot 49 \cdot 48 \cdot 47!}{47! \cdot 5 \cdot 4 \cdot 3 \cdot 2 \cdot 1} = 2{,}598{,}960$$

Thus, there are 2,598,960 different 5-card poker hands possible. It surprises many people that more than 2.5 million 5-card hands can be dealt from a mere 52 cards.

If you are a card player, it does not get any better than to be dealt the 5-card poker hand shown in **Figure 10.9**. This hand is called a *royal flush*. It consists of an ace, king, queen, jack, and 10, all of the same suit: all hearts, all diamonds, all clubs, or all spades. The probability of being dealt a royal flush involves calculating the number of ways of being dealt such a hand: just 4 of all 2,598,960 possible hands. In the next section, we move from counting possibilities to computing probabilities.

**Figure 10.9**  A royal flush

**⊘ Check Point 8** How many different 4-card hands can be dealt from a deck that has 16 different cards?

## Exercise Set 10.6

### Practice Exercises

*In Exercises 1–8, use the formula for $_nP_r$ to evaluate each expression.*

**1.** $_9P_4$
**2.** $_7P_3$
**3.** $_8P_5$
**4.** $_{10}P_4$
**5.** $_6P_6$
**6.** $_9P_9$
**7.** $_8P_0$
**8.** $_6P_0$

*In Exercises 9–16, use the formula for $_nC_r$ to evaluate each expression.*

**9.** $_9C_5$
**10.** $_{10}C_6$
**11.** $_{11}C_4$
**12.** $_{12}C_5$
**13.** $_7C_7$
**14.** $_4C_4$
**15.** $_5C_0$
**16.** $_6C_0$

*In Exercises 17–20, does the problem involve permutations or combinations? Explain your answer. (It is not necessary to solve the problem.)*

17. A medical researcher needs 6 people to test the effectiveness of an experimental drug. If 13 people have volunteered for the test, in how many ways can 6 people be selected?

18. Fifty people purchase raffle tickets. Three winning tickets are selected at random. If first prize is $1000, second prize is $500, and third prize is $100, in how many different ways can the prizes be awarded?

19. How many different four-letter passwords can be formed from the letters A, B, C, D, E, F, and G if no repetition of letters is allowed?

20. Fifty people purchase raffle tickets. Three winning tickets are selected at random. If each prize is $500, in how many different ways can the prizes be awarded?

## Practice Plus

*In Exercises 21–28, evaluate each expression.*

21. $\dfrac{_7P_3}{3!} - {_7C_3}$

22. $\dfrac{_{20}P_2}{2!} - {_{20}C_2}$

23. $1 - \dfrac{_3P_2}{_4P_3}$

24. $1 - \dfrac{_5P_3}{_{10}P_4}$

25. $\dfrac{_7C_3}{_5C_4} - \dfrac{98!}{96!}$

26. $\dfrac{_{10}C_3}{_6C_4} - \dfrac{46!}{44!}$

27. $\dfrac{_4C_2 \cdot {_6C_1}}{_{18}C_3}$

28. $\dfrac{_5C_1 \cdot {_7C_2}}{_{12}C_3}$

## Application Exercises

*Use the Fundamental Counting Principle to solve Exercises 29–40.*

29. The model of the car you are thinking of buying is available in nine different colors and three different styles (hatchback, sedan, or station wagon). In how many ways can you order the car?

30. A popular brand of pen is available in three colors (red, green, or blue) and four writing tips (bold, medium, fine, or micro). How many different choices of pens do you have with this brand?

31. An ice cream store sells two drinks (sodas or milk shakes), in four sizes (small, medium, large, or jumbo), and five flavors (vanilla, strawberry, chocolate, coffee, or pistachio). In how many ways can a customer order a drink?

32. A restaurant offers the following lunch menu.

| Main Course | Vegetables | Beverages | Desserts |
|---|---|---|---|
| Ham | Potatoes | Coffee | Cake |
| Chicken | Peas | Tea | Pie |
| Fish | Green beans | Milk | Ice cream |
| Beef | | Soda | |

If one item is selected from each of the four groups, in how many ways can a meal be ordered? Describe two such orders.

33. You are taking a multiple-choice test that has five questions. Each of the questions has three answer choices, with one correct answer per question. If you select one of these three choices for each question and leave nothing blank, in how many ways can you answer the questions?

34. You are taking a multiple-choice test that has eight questions. Each of the questions has three answer choices, with one correct answer per question. If you select one of these three choices for each question and leave nothing blank, in how many ways can you answer the questions?

35. In the original plan for area codes in 1945, the first digit could be any number from 2 through 9, the second digit was either 0 or 1, and the third digit could be any number except 0. With this plan, how many different area codes were possible?

36. How many different four-letter radio station call letters can be formed if the first letter must be W or K?

37. Six performers are to present their comedy acts on a weekend evening at a comedy club. One of the performers insists on being the last stand-up comic of the evening. If this performer's request is granted, how many different ways are there to schedule the appearances?

38. Five singers are to perform at a night club. One of the singers insists on being the last performer of the evening. If this singer's request is granted, how many different ways are there to schedule the appearances?

39. In the *Cambridge Encyclopedia of Language* (Cambridge University Press, 1987), author David Crystal presents five sentences that make a reasonable paragraph regardless of their order. The sentences are as follows:

   * Mark had told him about the foxes.
   * John looked out the window.
   * Could it be a fox?
   * However, nobody had seen one for months.
   * He thought he saw a shape in the bushes.

   How many different five-sentence paragraphs can be formed if the paragraph begins with "He thought he saw a shape in the bushes" and ends with "John looked out of the window"?

40. A television programmer is arranging the order that five movies will be seen between the hours of 6 P.M. and 4 A.M. Two of the movies have a G rating and they are to be shown in the first two time blocks. One of the movies is rated NC-17 and it is to be shown in the last of the time blocks, from 2 A.M. until 4 A.M. Given these restrictions, in how many ways can the five movies be arranged during the indicated time blocks?

*Use the formula for $_nP_r$ to solve Exercises 41–48.*

41. A club with ten members is to choose three officers—president, vice-president, and secretary-treasurer. If each office is to be held by one person and no person can hold more than one office, in how many ways can those offices be filled?

42. A corporation has ten members on its board of directors. In how many different ways can it elect a president, vice-president, secretary, and treasurer?

43. For a segment of a radio show, a disc jockey can play 7 songs. If there are 13 songs to select from, in how many ways can the program for this segment be arranged?

44. Suppose you are asked to list, in order of preference, the three best movies you have seen this year. If you saw 20 movies during the year, in how many ways can the three best be chosen and ranked?

45. In a race in which six automobiles are entered and there are no ties, in how many ways can the first three finishers come in?

46. In a production of *West Side Story*, eight actors are considered for the male roles of Tony, Riff, and Bernardo. In how many ways can the director cast the male roles?

47. Nine bands have volunteered to perform at a benefit concert, but there is only enough time for five of the bands to play. How many lineups are possible?

48. How many arrangements can be made using four of the letters of the word COMBINE if no letter is to be used more than once?

*Use the formula for $_nC_r$ to solve Exercises 49–56.*

49. An election ballot asks voters to select three city commissioners from a group of six candidates. In how many ways can this be done?

50. A four-person committee is to be elected from an organization's membership of 11 people. How many different committees are possible?

51. Of 12 possible books, you plan to take 4 with you on vacation. How many different collections of 4 books can you take?

52. There are 14 standbys who hope to get seats on a flight, but only 6 seats are available on the plane. How many different ways can the 6 people be selected?

53. You volunteer to help drive children at a charity event to the zoo, but you can fit only 8 of the 17 children present in your van. How many different groups of 8 children can you drive?

54. Of the 100 people in the U.S. Senate, 18 serve on the Foreign Relations Committee. How many ways are there to select Senate members for this committee (assuming party affiliation is not a factor in selection)?

55. To win at LOTTO in the state of Florida, one must correctly select 6 numbers from a collection of 53 numbers (1 through 53). The order in which the selection is made does not matter. How many different selections are possible?

56. To win in the New York State lottery, one must correctly select 6 numbers from 59 numbers. The order in which the selection is made does not matter. How many different selections are possible?

*In Exercises 57–66, solve by the method of your choice.*

57. In a race in which six automobiles are entered and there are no ties, in how many ways can the first four finishers come in?

58. A book club offers a choice of 8 books from a list of 40. In how many ways can a member make a selection?

59. A medical researcher needs 6 people to test the effectiveness of an experimental drug. If 13 people have volunteered for the test, in how many ways can 6 people be selected?

60. Fifty people purchase raffle tickets. Three winning tickets are selected at random. If first prize is $1000, second prize is $500, and third prize is $100, in how many different ways can the prizes be awarded?

61. From a club of 20 people, in how many ways can a group of three members be selected to attend a conference?

62. Fifty people purchase raffle tickets. Three winning tickets are selected at random. If each prize is $500, in how many different ways can the prizes be awarded?

63. How many different four-letter passwords can be formed from the letters A, B, C, D, E, F, and G if no repetition of letters is allowed?

64. Nine comedy acts will perform over two evenings. Five of the acts will perform on the first evening and the order in which the acts perform is important. How many ways can the schedule for the first evening be made?

65. Using 15 flavors of ice cream, how many cones with three different flavors can you create if it is important to you which flavor goes on the top, middle, and bottom?

66. Baskin-Robbins offers 31 different flavors of ice cream. One of their items is a bowl consisting of three scoops of ice cream, each a different flavor. How many such bowls are possible?

*Exercises 67–72 are based on the following jokes about books:*

- *"Outside of a dog, a book is man's best friend. Inside of a dog, it's too dark to read."—Groucho Marx*

- *"I recently bought a book of free verse. For $12."—George Carlin*

- *"If a word in the dictionary was misspelled, how would we know?"—Steven Wright*

- *"Encyclopedia is a Latin term. It means 'to paraphrase a term paper.'"—Greg Ray*

- *"A bookstore is one of the only pieces of evidence we have that people are still thinking."—Jerry Seinfeld*

- *"I honestly believe there is absolutely nothing like going to bed with a good book. Or a friend who's read one."—Phyllis Diller*

67. In how many ways can these six jokes be ranked from best to worst?

68. If Phyllis Diller's joke about books is excluded, in how many ways can the remaining five jokes be ranked from best to worst?

69. In how many ways can people select their three favorite jokes from these comments about books?

70. In how many ways can people select their two favorite jokes from these comments about books?

71. If the order in which these jokes are told makes a difference in terms of how they are received, how many ways can they be delivered if George Carlin's joke is delivered first and Jerry Seinfeld's joke is told last?

72. If the order in which these jokes are told makes a difference in terms of how they are received, how many ways can they be delivered if a joke by a man is told first?

## Writing in Mathematics

73. Explain the Fundamental Counting Principle.

74. Write an original problem that can be solved using the Fundamental Counting Principle. Then solve the problem.

75. What is a permutation?

76. Describe what $_nP_r$ represents.

77. Write a word problem that can be solved by evaluating $_7P_3$.

78. What is a combination?

79. Explain how to distinguish between permutation and combination problems.

80. Write a word problem that can be solved by evaluating $_7C_3$.

## Technology Exercises

**81.** Use a graphing utility with an $\boxed{_nP_r}$ menu item to verify your answers in Exercises 1–8.

**82.** Use a graphing utility with an $\boxed{_nC_r}$ menu item to verify your answers in Exercises 9–16.

## Critical Thinking Exercises

**Make Sense?** *In Exercises 83–86, determine whether each statement makes sense or does not make sense, and explain your reasoning.*

**83.** I used the Fundamental Counting Principle to determine the number of five-digit ZIP codes that are available to the U.S. Postal Service.

**84.** I used the permutations formula to determine the number of ways the manager of a baseball team can form a 9-player batting order from a team of 25 players.

**85.** I used the combinations formula to determine how many different four-note sound sequences can be created from the notes C, D, E, F, G, A, and B.

**86.** I used the permutations formula to determine the number of ways people can select their 9 favorite baseball players from a team of 25 players.

*In Exercises 87–90, determine whether each statement is true or false. If the statement is false, make the necessary change(s) to produce a true statement.*

**87.** The number of ways to choose four questions out of ten questions on an essay test is $_{10}P_4$.

**88.** If $r > 1$, $_nP_r$ is less than $_nC_r$.

**89.** $_7P_3 = 3!\,_7C_3$

**90.** The number of ways to pick a winner and first runner-up in a talent contest with 20 contestants is $_{20}C_2$.

**91.** Five men and five women line up at a checkout counter in a store. In how many ways can they line up if the first person in line is a woman and the people in line alternate woman, man, woman, man, and so on?

**92.** How many four-digit odd numbers less than 6000 can be formed using the digits 2, 4, 6, 7, 8, and 9?

**93.** A mathematics exam consists of 10 multiple-choice questions and 5 open-ended problems in which all work must be shown. If an examinee must answer 8 of the multiple-choice questions and 3 of the open-ended problems, in how many ways can the questions and problems be chosen?

## Group Exercise

**94.** The group should select real-world situations where the Fundamental Counting Principle can be applied. These could involve the number of possible student ID numbers on your campus, the number of possible phone numbers in your community, the number of meal options at a local restaurant, the number of ways a person in the group can select outfits for class, the number of ways a condominium can be purchased in a nearby community, and so on. Once situations have been selected, group members should determine in how many ways each part of the task can be done. Group members will need to obtain menus, find out about telephone-digit requirements in the community, count shirts, pants, shoes in closets, visit condominium sales offices, and so on. Once the group reassembles, apply the Fundamental Counting Principle to determine the number of available options in each situation. Because these numbers may be quite large, use a calculator.

## Preview Exercises

*Exercises 95–97 will help you prepare for the material covered in the next section.*

*The figure shows that when a die is rolled, there are six equally likely outcomes: 1, 2, 3, 4, 5, or 6. Use this information to solve each exercise.*

**95.** What fraction of the outcomes are less than 5?

**96.** What fraction of the outcomes are not less than 5?

**97.** What fraction of the outcomes are even or greater than 3?

## Section 10.7 Probability

### Objectives

1. Compute empirical probability.
2. Compute theoretical probability.
3. Find the probability that an event will not occur.
4. Find the probability of one event or a second event occurring.
5. Find the probability of one event and a second event occurring.

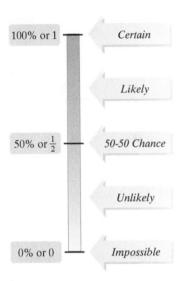

Possible Values for Probabilities

- 100% or 1 — Certain
- Likely
- 50% or $\frac{1}{2}$ — 50-50 Chance
- Unlikely
- 0% or 0 — Impossible

**Table 10.3 The Hours of Sleep Americans Get on a Typical Night**

| Hours of Sleep | Number of Americans, in millions |
|---|---|
| 4 or less | 12 |
| 5 | 27 |
| 6 | 75 |
| 7 | 90 |
| 8 | 81 |
| 9 | 9 |
| 10 or more | 6 |
| | Total: 300 |

*Source:* Discovery Health Media

How many hours of sleep do you typically get each night? **Table 10.3** indicates that 75 million out of 300 million Americans are getting six hours of sleep on a typical night. The *probability* of an American getting six hours of sleep on a typical night is $\frac{75}{300}$. This fraction can be reduced to $\frac{1}{4}$, or expressed as 0.25, or 25%. Thus, 25% of Americans get six hours of sleep each night.

We find a probability by dividing one number by another. Probabilities are assigned to an *event*, such as getting six hours of sleep on a typical night. Events that are certain to occur are assigned probabilities of 1, or 100%. For example, the probability that a given individual will eventually die is 1. Although Woody Allen whined, "I don't want to achieve immortality through my work. I want to achieve it through not dying," death (and taxes) are always certain. By contrast, if an event cannot occur, its probability is 0. Regrettably, the probability that Elvis will return and serenade us with one final reprise of "Don't Be Cruel" (and we hope we're not) is 0.

Probabilities of events are expressed as numbers ranging from 0 to 1, or 0% to 100%. The closer the probability of a given event is to 1, the more likely it is that the event will occur. The closer the probability of a given event is to 0, the less likely it is that the event will occur.

1 Compute empirical probability.

### Empirical Probability

Empirical probability applies to situations in which we observe how frequently an event occurs. We use the following formula to compute the empirical probability of an event:

#### Computing Empirical Probability

The **empirical probability** of event $E$, denoted by $P(E)$, is

$$P(E) = \frac{\text{observed number of times } E \text{ occurs}}{\text{total number of observed occurrences}}.$$

**EXAMPLE 1** Empirical Probabilities with Real-World Data

When women turn 40, their gynecologists typically remind them that it is time to undergo mammography screening for breast cancer. The data in **Table 10.4** on the next page are based on 100,000 U.S. women, ages 40 to 50, who participated in mammography screening.

Table 10.4   Mammography Screening on 100,000
U.S. Women, Ages 40 to 50

|  | Breast Cancer | No Breast Cancer |
|---|---|---|
| **Positive Mammogram** | 720 | 6944 |
| **Negative Mammogram** | 80 | 92,256 |

720 + 6944 = 7664 women have positive mammograms.

80 + 92,256 = 92,336 women have negative mammograms.

720 + 80 = 800 women have breast cancer.

6944 + 92,256 = 99,200 women do not have breast cancer.

*Source:* Gerd Gigerenzer, *Calculated Risks*, Simon and Schuster, 2002

**a.** Use **Table 10.4** to find the probability that a woman aged 40 to 50 has breast cancer.

**b.** Among women without breast cancer, find the probability of a positive mammogram.

**c.** Among women with positive mammograms, find the probability of not having breast cancer.

**Solution**

**a.** We begin with the probability that a woman aged 40 to 50 has breast cancer. The probability of having breast cancer is the number of women with breast cancer divided by the total number of women.

$$P(\text{breast cancer}) = \frac{\text{number of women with breast cancer}}{\text{total number of women}}$$

$$= \frac{800}{100,000} = \frac{1}{125} = 0.008$$

The empirical probability that a woman aged 40 to 50 has breast cancer is $\frac{1}{125}$, or 0.008.

**b.** Now, we find the probability of a positive mammogram among women without breast cancer. Thus, we restrict the data to women without breast cancer:

|  | No Breast Cancer |
|---|---|
| **Positive Mammogram** | 6944 |
| **Negative Mammogram** | 92,256 |

Within the restricted data, the probability of a positive mammogram is the number of women with positive mammograms divided by the total number of women.

$$P(\text{positive mammogram}) = \frac{\text{number of women with positive mammograms}}{\text{total number of women in the restricted data}}$$

$$= \frac{6944}{6944 + 92,256} = \frac{6944}{99,200} = 0.07$$

This is the total number of women without breast cancer.

Among women without breast cancer, the empirical probability of a positive mammogram is $\frac{6944}{99,200}$, or 0.07.

**c.** Now, we find the probability of not having breast cancer among women with positive mammograms. Thus, we restrict the data to women with positive mammograms:

| | Breast Cancer | No Breast Cancer |
|---|---|---|
| **Positive Mammogram** | 720 | 6944 |

Within the restricted data, the probability of not having breast cancer is the number of women with no breast cancer divided by the total number of women.

$$P(\text{no breast cancer}) = \frac{\text{number of women with no breast cancer}}{\text{total number of women in the restricted data}}$$

$$= \frac{6944}{720 + 6944} = \frac{6944}{7664} \approx 0.906$$

> This is the total number of women with positive mammograms.

Among women with positive mammograms, the probability of not having breast cancer is $\frac{6944}{7664}$, or approximately 0.906.

⊘ Check Point ❙ Use the data in **Table 10.4** to solve this exercise. Express probabilities as fractions and as decimals rounded to three decimal places.

   **a.** Find the probability that a woman aged 40 to 50 has a positive mammogram.

   **b.** Among women with breast cancer, find the probability of a positive mammogram.

   **c.** Among women with positive mammograms, find the probability of having breast cancer.

**② Compute theoretical probability.**

## Theoretical Probability

You toss a coin. Although it is equally likely to land either heads up, denoted by $H$, or tails up, denoted by $T$, the actual outcome is uncertain. Any occurrence for which the outcome is uncertain is called an **experiment**. Thus, tossing a coin is an example of an experiment. The set of all possible outcomes of an experiment is the **sample space** of the experiment, denoted by $S$. The sample space for the coin-tossing experiment is

$$S = \{H, T\}.$$

> Lands heads up    Lands tails up

We can define an event more formally using these concepts. An **event**, denoted by $E$, is any subcollection, or subset, of a sample space. For example, the subset $E = \{T\}$ is the event of landing tails up when a coin is tossed.

    Theoretical probability applies to situations like this, in which the sample space only contains equally likely outcomes, all of which are known. To calculate the theoretical probability of an event, we divide the number of outcomes resulting in the event by the number of outcomes in the sample space.

### Computing Theoretical Probability

If an event $E$ has $n(E)$ equally likely outcomes and its sample space $S$ has $n(S)$ equally likely outcomes, the **theoretical probability** of event $E$, denoted by $P(E)$, is

$$P(E) = \frac{\text{number of outcomes in event } E}{\text{number of outcomes in samples space } S} = \frac{n(E)}{n(S)}.$$

The sum of the theoretical probabilities of all possible outcomes in the sample space is 1.

How can we use this formula to compute the probability of a coin landing tails up? We use the following sets:

$$E = \{T\} \qquad S = \{H, T\}.$$

> This is the event of landing tails up.

> This is the sample space with all equally likely outcomes.

The probability of a coin landing tails up is

$$P(E) = \frac{\text{number of outcomes that result in tails up}}{\text{total number of possible outcomes}} = \frac{n(E)}{n(S)} = \frac{1}{2}.$$

Theoretical probability applies to many games of chance, including rolling dice, lotteries, card games, and roulette. The next example deals with the experiment of rolling a die. **Figure 10.10** illustrates that when a die is rolled, there are six equally likely outcomes. The sample space can be shown as

$$S = \{1, 2, 3, 4, 5, 6\}.$$

**Figure 10.10** Outcomes when a die is rolled

**EXAMPLE 2** **Computing Theoretical Probability**

A die is rolled. Find the probability of getting a number less than 5.

**Solution** The sample space of equally likely outcomes is $S = \{1, 2, 3, 4, 5, 6\}$. There are six outcomes in the sample space, so $n(S) = 6$.

We are interested in the probability of getting a number less than 5. The event of getting a number less than 5 can be represented by

$$E = \{1, 2, 3, 4\}.$$

There are four outcomes in this event, so $n(E) = 4$.

The probability of rolling a number less than 5 is

$$P(E) = \frac{n(E)}{n(S)} = \frac{4}{6} = \frac{2}{3}.$$

⊘ Check Point **2** A die is rolled. Find the probability of getting a number greater than 4.

**EXAMPLE 3** **Computing Theoretical Probability**

Two ordinary six-sided dice are rolled. What is the probability of getting a sum of 8?

**Solution** Each die has six equally likely outcomes. By the Fundamental Counting Principle, there are $6 \cdot 6$, or 36, equally likely outcomes in the sample space. That is, $n(S) = 36$. The 36 outcomes are shown below as ordered pairs. The five ways of rolling a sum of 8 appear in the green highlighted diagonal.

| | | Second Die | | | | |
|---|---|---|---|---|---|---|
| | ⚀ | ⚁ | ⚂ | ⚃ | ⚄ | ⚅ |
| ⚀ | (1,1) | (1,2) | (1,3) | (1,4) | (1,5) | (1,6) |
| ⚁ | (2,1) | (2,2) | (2,3) | (2,4) | (2,5) | (2,6) |
| ⚂ | (3,1) | (3,2) | (3,3) | (3,4) | (3,5) | (3,6) |
| ⚃ | (4,1) | (4,2) | (4,3) | (4,4) | (4,5) | (4,6) |
| ⚄ | (5,1) | (5,2) | (5,3) | (5,4) | (5,5) | (5,6) |
| ⚅ | (6,1) | (6,2) | (6,3) | (6,4) | (6,5) | (6,6) |

(First Die on left side)

$$S = \{(1, 1), (1, 2), (1, 3), (1, 4), \\ (1, 5), (1, 6), (2, 1), (2, 2), \\ (2, 3), (2, 4), (2, 5), (2, 6), \\ (3, 1), (3, 2), (3, 3), (3, 4), \\ (3, 5), (3, 6), (4, 1), (4, 2), \\ (4, 3), (4, 4), (4, 5), (4, 6), \\ (5, 1), (5, 2), (5, 3), (5, 4), \\ (5, 5), (5, 6), (6, 1), (6, 2), \\ (6, 3), (6, 4), (6, 5), (6, 6)\}$$

The phrase "getting a sum of 8" describes the event

$$E = \{(6, 2), (5, 3), (4, 4), (3, 5), (2, 6)\}.$$

This event has 5 outcomes, so $n(E) = 5$. Thus, the probability of getting a sum of 8 is

$$P(E) = \frac{n(E)}{n(S)} = \frac{5}{36}.$$

⚫

⊘ Check Point **3** What is the probability of getting a sum of 5 when two six-sided dice are rolled?

## Computing Theoretical Probability without Listing an Event and the Sample Space

In some situations, we can compute theoretical probability without having to write out each event and each sample space. For example, suppose you are dealt one card from a standard 52-card deck, illustrated in **Figure 10.11**. The deck has four suits: Hearts and diamonds are red, and clubs and spades are black. Each suit has 13 different face values — A(ace), 2, 3, 4, 5, 6, 7, 8, 9, 10, J(jack), Q(queen), and K(king). Jacks, queens, and kings are called **picture cards** or **face cards**.

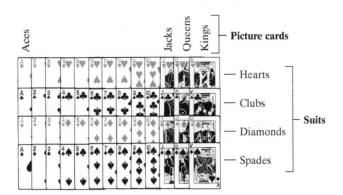

**Figure 10.11** A standard 52-card bridge deck

( EXAMPLE 4 ) **Probability and a Deck of 52 Cards**

You are dealt one card from a standard 52-card deck. Find the probability of being dealt a heart.

**Solution**   Let $E$ be the event of being dealt a heart. Because there are 13 hearts in the deck, the event of being dealt a heart can occur in 13 ways. The number of outcomes in event $E$ is 13: $n(E) = 13$. With 52 cards in the deck, the total number of possible ways of being dealt a single card is 52. The number of outcomes in the sample space is 52: $n(S) = 52$. The probability of being dealt a heart is

$$P(E) = \frac{n(E)}{n(S)} = \frac{13}{52} = \frac{1}{4}.$$

⚫

⊘ Check Point **4** If you are dealt one card from a standard 52-card deck, find the probability of being dealt a king.

If your state has a lottery drawing each week, the probability that someone will win the top prize is relatively high. If there is no winner this week, it is virtually certain that eventually someone will be graced with millions of dollars. So, why are you so unlucky compared to this undisclosed someone? In Example 5, we provide an answer to this question, using the counting principles discussed in Section 10.6.

State lotteries keep 50 cents on the dollar, resulting in $10 billion a year for public funding.
© Damon Higgins/*The Palm Beach Post*

### Comparing the Probability of Dying to the Probability of Winning Florida's LOTTO

As a healthy nonsmoking 30-year-old, your probability of dying this year is approximately 0.001. Divide this probability by the probability of winning LOTTO with one ticket:

$$\frac{0.001}{0.0000000436} \approx 22,936.$$

A healthy 30-year-old is nearly 23,000 times more likely to die this year than to win Florida's lottery.

③ Find the probability that an event will not occur.

---

**EXAMPLE 5** **Probability and Combinations: Winning the Lottery**

Florida's lottery game, LOTTO, is set up so that each player chooses six different numbers from 1 to 53. If the six numbers chosen match the six numbers drawn randomly, the player wins (or shares) the top cash prize. (As of this writing, the top cash prize has ranged from $7 million to $106.5 million.) With one LOTTO ticket, what is the probability of winning this prize?

**Solution**  Because the order of the six numbers does not matter, this is a situation involving combinations. Let $E$ be the event of winning the lottery with one ticket. With one LOTTO ticket, there is only one way of winning. Thus, $n(E) = 1$.

The sample space is the set of all possible six-number combinations. We can use the combinations formula

$$_nC_r = \frac{n!}{(n-r)!r!}$$

to find the total number of possible combinations. We are selecting $r = 6$ numbers from a collection of $n = 53$ numbers.

$$_{53}C_6 = \frac{53!}{(53-6)!6!} = \frac{53!}{47!6!} = \frac{53\cdot52\cdot51\cdot50\cdot49\cdot48\cdot\cancel{47!}}{\cancel{47!}\cdot6\cdot5\cdot4\cdot3\cdot2\cdot1} = 22,957,480$$

There are nearly 23 million number combinations possible in LOTTO. If a person buys one LOTTO ticket, the probability of winning is

$$P(E) = \frac{n(E)}{n(S)} = \frac{1}{22,957,480} \approx 0.0000000436.$$

The probability of winning the top prize with one LOTTO ticket is $\frac{1}{22,957,480}$, or about 1 in 23 million.

Suppose that a person buys 5000 different tickets in Florida's LOTTO. Because that person has selected 5000 different combinations of the six numbers, the probability of winning is

$$\frac{5000}{22,957,480} \approx 0.000218.$$

The chances of winning top prize are about 218 in a million. At $1 per LOTTO ticket, it is highly probable that our LOTTO player will be $5000 poorer. Knowing a little probability helps a lotto.

⊘ Check Point **5** People lose interest when they do not win at games of chance, including Florida's LOTTO. With drawings twice weekly instead of once, the game described in Example 5 was brought in to bring back lost players and increase ticket sales. The original LOTTO was set up so that each player chose six different numbers from 1 to 49, rather than from 1 to 53, with a lottery drawing only once a week. With one LOTTO ticket, what was the probability of winning the top cash prize in Florida's original LOTTO? Express the answer as a fraction and as a decimal correct to ten places.

## Probability of an Event Not Occurring

If we know $P(E)$, the probability of an event $E$, we can determine the probability that the event will not occur, denoted by $P(\text{not } E)$. Because the sum of the probabilities of all possible outcomes in any situation is 1,

$$P(E) + P(\text{not } E) = 1.$$

We now solve this equation for $P(\text{not } E)$, the probability that event $E$ will not occur, by subtracting $P(E)$ from both sides. The resulting formula is given in the box on the next page.

### The Probability of an Event Not Occurring

The probability that an event $E$ will not occur is equal to 1 minus the probability that it will occur.

$$P(\text{not } E) = 1 - P(E)$$

(EXAMPLE 6) **The Probability of an Event Not Occurring**

The circle graph in **Figure 10.12** shows the distribution, by age group, of the 191 million car drivers in the United States, with all numbers rounded to the nearest million. If one driver is randomly selected from this population, find the probability that the person is not in the 20–29 age group. Express the probability as a simplified fraction.

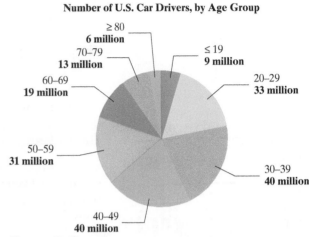

**Number of U.S. Car Drivers, by Age Group**

≥ 80
**6 million**

70–79
**13 million**

60–69
**19 million**

50–59
**31 million**

40–49
**40 million**

30–39
**40 million**

20–29
**33 million**

≤ 19
**9 million**

Figure 10.12   *Source:* U.S. Census Bureau

**Solution**   We use the probability that the selected person *is* in the 20–29 age group to find the probability that the selected person is not in this age group.

$P(\text{not in 20–29 age group})$

$= 1 - P(\text{in 20–29 age group})$

> The graph shows 33 million drivers in the 20–29 age group.

$$= 1 - \frac{33}{191}$$

> This number, 191 million drivers, was given, but can be obtained by adding the numbers in the eight sectors.

$$= \frac{191}{191} - \frac{33}{191} = \frac{158}{191}$$

The probability that a randomly selected driver is not in the 20–29 age group is $\frac{158}{191}$.

✓ Check Point **6**  If one driver is randomly selected from the population represented in **Figure 10.12**, find the probability, expressed as a simplified fraction, that the person is not in the 50–59 age group.

④ Find the probability of one event or a second event occurring.

## *Or* Probabilities with Mutually Exclusive Events

Suppose that you randomly select one card from a deck of 52 cards. Let $A$ be the event of selecting a king and let $B$ be the event of selecting a queen. Only one card is selected, so it is impossible to get both a king and a queen. The events of selecting a king and a queen cannot occur simultaneously. They are called *mutually exclusive events*. If it is impossible for any two events, $A$ and $B$, to occur simultaneously, they are said to be **mutually exclusive**. If $A$ and $B$ are mutually exclusive events, the probability that either $A$ or $B$ will occur is determined by adding their individual probabilities.

### *Or* Probabilities with Mutually Exclusive Events

If $A$ and $B$ are mutually exclusive events, then

$$P(A \text{ or } B) = P(A) + P(B).$$

Using set notation, $P(A \cup B) = P(A) + P(B)$.

(EXAMPLE 7) **The Probability of Either of Two Mutually Exclusive Events Occurring**

If one card is randomly selected from a deck of cards, what is the probability of selecting a king or a queen?

**Solution** We find the probability that either of these mutually exclusive events will occur by adding their individual probabilities.

$$P(\text{king or queen}) = P(\text{king}) + P(\text{queen}) = \frac{4}{52} + \frac{4}{52} = \frac{8}{52} = \frac{2}{13}$$

The probability of selecting a king or a queen is $\frac{2}{13}$.

⊘ Check Point **7** If you roll a single, six-sided die, what is the probability of getting either a 4 or a 5?

## Or Probabilities with Events That Are Not Mutually Exclusive

Consider the deck of 52 cards shown in **Figure 10.13**. Suppose that these cards are shuffled and you randomly select one card from the deck. What is the probability of selecting a diamond or a picture card (jack, queen, king)? Begin by adding their individual probabilities.

$$P(\text{diamond}) + P(\text{picture card}) = \frac{13}{52} + \frac{12}{52}$$

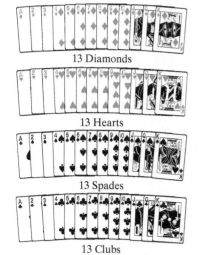

Figure 10.13  A deck of 52 cards

| There are 13 diamonds in the deck of 52 cards. | There are 12 picture cards in the deck of 52 cards. |

However, this sum is not the probability of selecting a diamond or a picture card. The problem is that there are three cards that are *simultaneously* diamonds and picture cards, shown in **Figure 10.14**. The events of selecting a diamond and selecting a picture card are not mutually exclusive. It is possible to select a card that is both a diamond and a picture card.

Figure 10.14  Three diamonds are picture cards.

The situation is illustrated in the diagram in **Figure 10.15**. Why can't we find the probability of selecting a diamond or a picture card by adding their individual probabilities? The diagram shows that three of the cards, the three diamonds that are picture cards, get counted twice when we add the individual probabilities. First the three cards get counted as diamonds and then they get counted as picture cards. In order to avoid the error of counting the three cards twice, we need to subtract the probability of getting a diamond and a picture card, $\frac{3}{52}$, as follows:

$P(\text{diamond or picture card})$

$$= P(\text{diamond}) + P(\text{picture card}) - P(\text{diamond and picture card})$$

$$= \frac{13}{52} + \frac{12}{52} - \frac{3}{52} = \frac{13 + 12 - 3}{52} = \frac{22}{52} = \frac{11}{26}.$$

Thus, the probability of selecting a diamond or a picture card is $\frac{11}{26}$.

In general, if $A$ and $B$ are events that are not mutually exclusive, the probability that $A$ or $B$ will occur is determined by adding their individual probabilities and then subtracting the probability that $A$ and $B$ occur simultaneously.

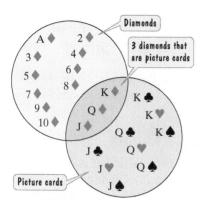

Figure 10.15

## Or Probabilities with Events That Are Not Mutually Exclusive

If $A$ and $B$ are not mutually exclusive events, then

$$P(A \text{ or } B) = P(A) + P(B) - P(A \text{ and } B).$$

Using set notation,

$$P(A \cup B) = P(A) + P(B) - P(A \cap B).$$

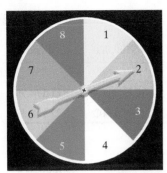

Figure 10.16 It is equally probable that the pointer will land on any one of the eight regions.

**EXAMPLE 8** An *Or* Probability with Events That Are Not Mutually Exclusive

**Figure 10.16** illustrates a spinner. It is equally probable that the pointer will land on any one of the eight regions, numbered 1 through 8. If the pointer lands on a borderline, spin again. Find the probability that the pointer will stop on an even number or a number greater than 5.

**Solution** It is possible for the pointer to land on a number that is both even and greater than 5. Two of the numbers, 6 and 8, are even and greater than 5. These events are not mutually exclusive. The probability of landing on a number that is even or greater than 5 is calculated as follows:

$$P\left(\begin{array}{c}\text{even or}\\\text{greater than 5}\end{array}\right) = P(\text{even}) + P(\text{greater than 5}) - P\left(\begin{array}{c}\text{even and}\\\text{greater than 5}\end{array}\right)$$

$$= \frac{4}{8} + \frac{3}{8} - \frac{2}{8}$$

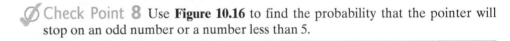

Four of the eight numbers, 2, 4, 6, and 8, are even.   Three of the eight numbers, 6, 7, and 8, are greater than 5.   Two of the eight numbers, 6 and 8, are even and greater than 5.

$$= \frac{4 + 3 - 2}{8} = \frac{5}{8}.$$

The probability that the pointer will stop on an even number or a number greater than 5 is $\frac{5}{8}$.

⊘ Check Point **8** Use **Figure 10.16** to find the probability that the pointer will stop on an odd number or a number less than 5.

**EXAMPLE 9** An *Or* Probability with Real-World Data

Each year the Internal Revenue Service audits a sample of tax forms to verify their accuracy. **Table 10.5** shows the number of tax returns filed and audited in 2006 by taxable income.

Table 10.5  Tax Returns Filed and Audited, by Taxable Income, 2006

|  | < $25,000 | $25,000–$49,999 | $50,000–$99,999 | ≥ $100,000 | Total |
|---|---|---|---|---|---|
| Audit | 461,729 | 191,150 | 163,711 | 166,839 | 983,429 |
| No audit | 51,509,900 | 30,637,782 | 26,300,262 | 12,726,963 | 121,174,907 |
| Total | 51,971,629 | 30,828,932 | 26,463,973 | 12,893,802 | 122,158,336 |

*Source:* Internal Revenue Service

If one person is randomly selected from the population represented in **Table 10.5**, find the probability that

**a.** the taxpayer had a taxable income less than $25,000 or was audited.

**b.** the taxpayer had a taxable income less than $25,000 or at least $100,000.

Express probabilities as decimals rounded to the nearest hundredth.

Table 10.5 (repeated)

|  | < $25,000 | $25,000–$49,999 | $50,000–$99,999 | ≥ $100,000 | Total |
|---|---|---|---|---|---|
| Audit | 461,729 | 191,150 | 163,711 | 166,839 | 983,429 |
| No audit | 51,509,900 | 30,637,782 | 26,300,262 | 12,726,963 | 121,174,907 |
| Total | 51,971,629 | 30,828,932 | 26,463,973 | 12,893,802 | 122,158,336 |

*Source:* Internal Revenue Service

### Solution

**a.** It is possible to select a taxpayer who both earned less than $25,000 and was audited. Thus, these events are not mutually exclusive.

$P$(less than $25,000 or audited)

$= P$(less than $25,000) $+ P$(audited) $- P$(less than $25,000 and audited)

$$= \frac{51,971,629}{122,158,336} + \frac{983,429}{122,158,336} - \frac{461,729}{122,158,336}$$

> Of the 122,158,336 taxpayers, 51,971,629 had taxable incomes less than $25,000.

> Of the 122,158,336 taxpayers, 983,429 were audited.

> Of the 122,158,336 taxpayers, 461,729 earned less than $25,000 and were audited.

$$= \frac{52,493,329}{122,158,336} \approx 0.43$$

The probability that a taxpayer had a taxable income less than $25,000 or was audited is approximately 0.43.

**b.** A taxable income of *at least* $100,000 means $100,000 or more. Thus, it is not possible to select a taxpayer with both a taxable income of less than $25,000 and at least $100,000. These events are mutually exclusive.

$P$(less than $25,000 or at least $100,000)

$= P$(less than $25,000) $+ P$(at least $100,000)

> Of the 122,158,336 taxpayers, 51,971,629 had taxable incomes less than $25,000.

> Of the 122,158,336 taxpayers, 12,893,802 had taxable incomes of $100,000 or more.

$$= \frac{51,971,629}{122,158,336} + \frac{12,893,802}{122,158,336}$$

$$= \frac{64,865,431}{122,158,336} \approx 0.53$$

The probability that a taxpayer had a taxable income less than $25,000 or at least $100,000 is approximately 0.53.

⏺ Check Point **9** If one person is randomly selected from the population represented in **Table 10.5**, find the probability, expressed as a decimal rounded to the nearest hundredth, that

**a.** the taxpayer had a taxable income of at least $100,000 or was not audited.

**b.** the taxpayer had a taxable income less than $25,000 or between $50,000 and $99,999, inclusive.

⑤ Find the probability of one event and a second event occurring.

## *And* Probabilities with Independent Events

Suppose that you toss a fair coin two times in succession. The outcome of the first toss, heads or tails, does not affect what happens when you toss the coin a second time. For example, the occurrence of tails on the first toss does not make tails more likely or less likely to occur on the second toss. The repeated toss of a coin produces *independent events* because the outcome of one toss does not influence the outcome of others. Two events are **independent events** if the occurrence of either of them has no effect on the probability of the other.

If two events are independent, we can calculate the probability of the first occurring and the second occurring by multiplying their probabilities.

### *And* Probabilities with Independent Events

If $A$ and $B$ are independent events, then

$$P(A \text{ and } B) = P(A) \cdot P(B).$$

Figure 10.17 A U.S. roulette wheel

---

**EXAMPLE 10** **Independent Events on a Roulette Wheel**

**Figure 10.17** shows a U.S. roulette wheel that has 38 numbered slots (1 through 36, 0, and 00). Of the 38 compartments, 18 are black, 18 are red, and two are green. A play has the dealer spin the wheel and a small ball in opposite directions. As the ball slows to a stop, it can land with equal probability on any one of the 38 numbered slots. Find the probability of red occurring on two consecutive plays.

**Solution**   The wheel has 38 equally likely outcomes and 18 are red. Thus, the probability of red occurring on a play is $\frac{18}{38}$, or $\frac{9}{19}$. The result that occurs on each play is independent of all previous results. Thus,

$$P(\text{red and red}) = P(\text{red}) \cdot P(\text{red}) = \frac{9}{19} \cdot \frac{9}{19} = \frac{81}{361} \approx 0.224.$$

The probability of red occurring on two consecutive plays is $\frac{81}{361}$.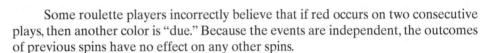

Some roulette players incorrectly believe that if red occurs on two consecutive plays, then another color is "due." Because the events are independent, the outcomes of previous spins have no effect on any other spins.

⊘ **Check Point 10** Find the probability of green occurring on two consecutive plays on a roulette wheel.

---

The *and* rule for independent events can be extended to cover three or more events. Thus, if $A$, $B$, and $C$ are independent events, then

$$P(A \text{ and } B \text{ and } C) = P(A) \cdot P(B) \cdot P(C).$$

**EXAMPLE 11** **Independent Events in a Family**

The picture in the margin shows a family that has had nine girls in a row. Find the probability of this occurrence.

**Solution**   If two or more events are independent, we can find the probability of them all occurring by multiplying their probabilities. The probability of a baby girl is $\frac{1}{2}$, so the probability of nine girls in a row is $\frac{1}{2}$ used as a factor nine times.

$$P(\text{nine girls in a row}) = \frac{1}{2} \cdot \frac{1}{2} \cdot \frac{1}{2} \cdot \frac{1}{2} \cdot \frac{1}{2} \cdot \frac{1}{2} \cdot \frac{1}{2} \cdot \frac{1}{2} \cdot \frac{1}{2}$$

$$= \left(\frac{1}{2}\right)^9 = \frac{1}{512}$$

The probability of a run of nine girls in a row is $\frac{1}{512}$. (If another child is born into the family, this event is independent of the other nine, and the probability of a girl is still $\frac{1}{2}$.)

⊘ **Check Point 11** Find the probability of a family having four boys in a row.

# Exercise Set 10.7

## Practice and Application Exercises

*The table shows the distribution, by marital status and gender, of the 212.5 million Americans ages 18 or older. Use the data in the table to solve Exercises 1–10.*

### Marital Status of the United States Population, Ages 18 or Older, in Millions

|  | Never Married | Married | Widowed | Divorced | Total |
|---|---|---|---|---|---|
| **Male** | 28.6 | 62.1 | 2.7 | 9.0 | 102.4 |
| **Female** | 23.3 | 62.8 | 11.3 | 12.7 | 110.1 |
| **Total** | 51.9 | 124.9 | 14.0 | 21.7 | 212.5 |

Total male:
28.6 + 62.1 + 2.7 + 9.0 = 102.4

Total female:
23.3 + 62.8 + 11.3 + 12.7 = 110.1

Total never married:
28.6 + 23.3 = 51.9

Total widowed:
2.7 + 11.3 = 14.0

Total adult population:
102.4 + 110.1 = 212.5

Total married:
62.1 + 62.8 = 124.9

Total divorced:
9.0 + 12.7 = 21.7

*Source:* U.S. Census Bureau

*If one person is randomly selected from the population described in the table, find the probability, to the nearest hundredth, that the person*

1. is divorced.
2. has never been married.
3. is female.
4. is male.
5. is a widowed male.
6. is a widowed female.
7. Among those who are divorced, find the probability of selecting a woman.
8. Among those who are divorced, find the probability of selecting a man.
9. Among adult men, find the probability of selecting a married person.
10. Among adult women, find the probability of selecting a married person.

*In Exercises 11–16, a die is rolled. Find the probability of getting*

11. a 4.
12. a 5.
13. an odd number.
14. a number greater than 3.
15. a number greater than 4.
16. a number greater than 7.

*In Exercises 17–20, you are dealt one card from a standard 52-card deck. Find the probability of being dealt*

17. a queen.
18. a diamond.
19. a picture card.
20. a card greater than 3 and less than 7.

*In Exercises 21–22, a fair coin is tossed two times in succession. The sample space of equally likely outcomes is $\{HH, HT, TH, TT\}$. Find the probability of getting*

21. two heads.
22. the same outcome on each toss.

*In Exercises 23–24, you select a family with three children. If M represents a male child and F a female child, the sample space of equally likely outcomes is $\{MMM, MMF, MFM, MFF, FMM, FMF, FFM, FFF\}$. Find the probability of selecting a family with*

23. at least one male child.
24. at least two female children.

*In Exercises 25–26, a single die is rolled twice. The 36 equally likely outcomes are shown as follows:*

|  | Second Roll | | | | | |
|---|---|---|---|---|---|---|
| First Roll | (1, 1) | (1, 2) | (1, 3) | (1, 4) | (1, 5) | (1, 6) |
|  | (2, 1) | (2, 2) | (2, 3) | (2, 4) | (2, 5) | (2, 6) |
|  | (3, 1) | (3, 2) | (3, 3) | (3, 4) | (3, 5) | (3, 6) |
|  | (4, 1) | (4, 2) | (4, 3) | (4, 4) | (4, 5) | (4, 6) |
|  | (5, 1) | (5, 2) | (5, 3) | (5, 4) | (5, 5) | (5, 6) |
|  | (6, 1) | (6, 2) | (6, 3) | (6, 4) | (6, 5) | (6, 6) |

*Find the probability of getting*

25. two numbers whose sum is 4.
26. two numbers whose sum is 6.
27. To play the California lottery, a person has to select 6 out of 51 numbers, paying $1 for each six-number selection. If you pick six numbers that are the same as the ones drawn by the lottery, you win mountains of money. What is the probability that a person with one combination of six numbers will win? What is the probability of winning if 100 different lottery tickets are purchased?
28. A state lottery is designed so that a player chooses six numbers from 1 to 30 on one lottery ticket. What is the probability that a player with one lottery ticket will win? What is the probability of winning if 100 different lottery tickets are purchased?

*Exercises 29–30 involve a deck of 52 cards. If necessary, refer to the picture of a deck of cards, **Figure 10.11** on page 1019.*

29. A poker hand consists of five cards.
    a. Find the total number of possible five-card poker hands.
    b. A diamond flush is a five-card hand consisting of all diamonds. Find the number of possible diamond flushes.
    c. Find the probability of being dealt a diamond flush.
30. If you are dealt 3 cards from a shuffled deck of 52 cards, find the probability that all 3 cards are picture cards.

*The table shows the educational attainment of the U.S. population, ages 25 and over. Use the data in the table, expressed in millions, to solve Exercises 31–36.*

### Educational Attainment, in Millions, of the United States Population, Ages 25 and Over

|  | Less Than 4 Years High School | 4 Years High School Only | Some College [Less than 4 years] | 4 Years College [or More] | Total |
|---|---|---|---|---|---|
| Male | 14 | 25 | 20 | 23 | 82 |
| Female | 15 | 31 | 24 | 22 | 92 |
| Total | 29 | 56 | 44 | 45 | 174 |

*Source:* U.S. Census Bureau

*Find the probability, expressed as a simplified fraction, that a randomly selected American, aged 25 or over,*

**31.** has not completed four years (or more) of college.

**32.** has not completed four years of high school.

**33.** has completed four years of high school only or less than four years of college.

**34.** has completed less than four years of high school or four years of high school only.

**35.** has completed four years of high school only or is a man.

**36.** has completed four years of high school only or is a woman.

*In Exercises 37–42, you are dealt one card from a 52-card deck. Find the probability that*

**37.** you are not dealt a king.

**38.** you are not dealt a picture card.

**39.** you are dealt a 2 or a 3.

**40.** you are dealt a red 7 or a black 8.

**41.** you are dealt a 7 or a red card.

**42.** you are dealt a 5 or a black card.

*In Exercises 43–44, it is equally probable that the pointer on the spinner shown will land on any one of the eight regions, numbered 1 through 8. If the pointer lands on a borderline, spin again.*

*Find the probability that the pointer will stop on*

**43.** an odd number or a number less than 6.

**44.** an odd number or a number greater than 3.

*Use this information to solve Exercises 45–46. The mathematics department of a college has 8 male professors, 11 female professors, 14 male teaching assistants, and 7 female teaching assistants. If a person is selected at random from the group, find the probability that the selected person is*

**45.** a professor or a male.

**46.** a professor or a female.

*In Exercises 47–50, a single die is rolled twice. Find the probability of rolling*

**47.** a 2 the first time and a 3 the second time.

**48.** a 5 the first time and a 1 the second time.

**49.** an even number the first time and a number greater than 2 the second time.

**50.** an odd number the first time and a number less than 3 the second time.

**51.** If you toss a fair coin six times, what is the probability of getting all heads?

**52.** If you toss a fair coin seven times, what is the probability of getting all tails?

**53.** The probability that South Florida will be hit by a major hurricane (category 4 or 5) in any single year is $\frac{1}{16}$. (*Source:* National Hurricane Center)

**a.** What is the probability that South Florida will be hit by a major hurricane two years in a row?

**b.** What is the probability that South Florida will be hit by a major hurricane in three consecutive years?

**c.** What is the probability that South Florida will not be hit by a major hurricane in the next ten years?

**d.** What is the probability that South Florida will be hit by a major hurricane at least once in the next ten years?

## Writing in Mathematics

**54.** Describe the difference between theoretical probability and empirical probability.

**55.** Give an example of an event whose probability must be determined empirically rather than theoretically.

**56.** Write a probability word problem whose answer is one of the following fractions: $\frac{1}{6}$ or $\frac{1}{4}$ or $\frac{1}{3}$.

**57.** Explain how to find the probability of an event not occurring. Give an example.

**58.** What are mutually exclusive events? Give an example of two events that are mutually exclusive.

**59.** Explain how to find *or* probabilities with mutually exclusive events. Give an example.

**60.** Give an example of two events that are not mutually exclusive.

**61.** Explain how to find *or* probabilities with events that are not mutually exclusive. Give an example.

**62.** Explain how to find *and* probabilities with independent events. Give an example.

**63.** The president of a large company with 10,000 employees is considering mandatory cocaine testing for every employee. The test that would be used is 90% accurate, meaning that it will detect 90% of the cocaine users who are tested, and that 90% of the nonusers will test negative. This also means that the test gives 10% false positive. Suppose that 1% of the employees actually use cocaine. Find the probability that someone who tests positive for cocaine use is, indeed, a user.

*Hint:* Find the following probability fraction:

$$\frac{\text{the number of employees who test positive}}{\text{the number of employees who test positive}}$$
and are cocaine users

This fraction is given by

$$\frac{90\% \text{ of } 1\% \text{ of } 10{,}000}{\text{the number who test positive who actually use}}.$$
cocaine plus the number who test positive
who do not use cocaine

What does this probability indicate in terms of the percentage of employees who test positive who are not actually users? Discuss these numbers in terms of the issue of mandatory drug testing. Write a paper either in favor of or against mandatory drug testing, incorporating the actual percentage accuracy for such tests.

## Critical Thinking Exercises

**Make Sense?** *In Exercises 64–67, determine whether each statement makes sense or does not make sense, and explain your reasoning.*

**64.** The probability that Jill will win the election is 0.7 and the probability that she will not win is 0.4.

**65.** Assuming the next U.S. president will be a Democrat or a Republican, the probability of a Republican president is 0.5.

**66.** The probability that I will go to graduate school is 1.5.

**67.** When I toss a coin, the probability of getting heads *or* tails is 1, but the probability of getting heads *and* tails is 0.

**68.** The target in the figure shown contains four squares. If a dart thrown at random hits the target, find the probability that it will land in a yellow region.

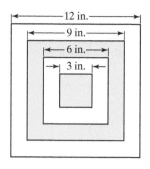

**69.** Suppose that it is a week in which the cash prize in Florida's LOTTO is promised to exceed $50 million. If a person purchases 22,957,480 tickets in LOTTO at $1 per ticket (all possible combinations), isn't this a guarantee of winning the lottery? Because the probability in this situation is 1, what's wrong with doing this?

**70.** Some three-digit numbers, such as 101 and 313, read the same forward and backward. If you select a number from all three-digit numbers, find the probability that it will read the same forward and backward.

**71.** In a class of 50 students, 29 are Democrats, 11 are business majors, and 5 of the business majors are Democrats. If one student is randomly selected from the class, find the probability of choosing

**a.** a Democrat who is not a business major.

**b.** a student who is neither a Democrat nor a business major.

**72.** On New Year's Eve, the probability of a person driving while intoxicated or having a driving accident is 0.35. If the probability of driving while intoxicated is 0.32 and the probability of having a driving accident is 0.09, find the probability of a person having a driving accident while intoxicated.

**73. a.** If two people are selected at random, the probability that they do not have the same birthday (day and month) is $\frac{365}{365} \cdot \frac{364}{365}$. Explain why this is so. (Ignore leap years and assume 365 days in a year.)

**b.** If three people are selected at random, find the probability that they all have different birthdays.

**c.** If three people are selected at random, find the probability that at least two of them have the same birthday.

**d.** If 20 people are selected at random, find the probability that at least 2 of them have the same birthday.

**e.** How large a group is needed to give a 0.5 chance of at least two people having the same birthday?

## Group Exercise

**74.** Research and present a group report on state lotteries. Include answers to some or all of the following questions: Which states do not have lotteries? Why not? How much is spent per capita on lotteries? What are some of the lottery games? What is the probability of winning top prize in these games? What income groups spend the greatest amount of money on lotteries? If your state has a lottery, what does it do with the money it makes? Is the way the money is spent what was promised when the lottery first began?

## Preview Exercises

*Exercises 75–77 will help you prepare for the material covered in the first section of the next chapter.*

**75.** Use the table to complete each statement.

| | *x* approaches 4 from the left. | | | | *x* approaches 4 from the right. | | |
|---|---|---|---|---|---|---|---|
| $x$ | 3.9 | 3.99 | 3.999 | 4 | 4.001 | 4.01 | 4.1 |
| $f(x) = \dfrac{x^2 - 6x + 8}{x - 4}$ | 1.9 | 1.99 | 1.999 | Undefined | 2.001 | 2.01 | 2.1 |

**a.** $f(4)$ is undefined because _____.

**b.** If $x$ is less than 4 and approaches 4 from the left, the values of $f(x)$ are getting closer to the integer _____.

**c.** If $x$ is greater than 4 and approaches 4 from the right, the values of $f(x)$ are getting closer to the integer _____.

**76.** Graph $f(x) = \dfrac{x^2 - 6x + 8}{x - 4}$, the function in Exercise 75. Begin by simplifying the function's equation. How does your graph illustrate the statement in Exercise 75(b) and the statement in Exercise 75(c)?

**77.** Graph the compound function:

$$f(x) = \begin{cases} 2x - 4 & \text{if} & x \neq 3 \\ -5 & \text{if} & x = 3. \end{cases}$$

# Chapter 10 Summary, Review, and Test

## Summary

| DEFINITIONS AND CONCEPTS | EXAMPLES |
|---|---|

### 10.1 Sequences and Summation Notation

**a.** An infinite sequence $\{a_n\}$ is a function whose domain is the set of positive integers. The function values, or terms, are represented by

$$a_1, a_2, a_3, a_4, \ldots, a_n, \ldots.$$

Ex. 1, p. 953

**b.** Sequences can be defined using recursion formulas that define the $n$th term as a function of the previous term.

Ex. 2, p. 954

**c.** Factorial Notation:

$$n! = n(n-1)(n-2)\cdots(3)(2)(1) \quad \text{and} \quad 0! = 1$$

Ex. 3, p. 955;
Ex. 4, p. 956

**d.** Summation Notation:

$$\sum_{i=1}^{n} a_i = a_1 + a_2 + a_3 + a_4 + \cdots + a_n$$

Ex. 5, p. 957;
Ex. 6, p. 959

### 10.2 Arithmetic Sequences

**a.** In an arithmetic sequence, each term after the first differs from the preceding term by a constant, the common difference. Subtract any term from the term that directly follows to find the common difference.

List of arithmetic sequences and common differences, p. 963;
Ex. 1, p. 964

**b.** General term or $n$th term: $a_n = a_1 + (n-1)d$. The first term is $a_1$ and the common difference is $d$.

Ex. 2, p. 965;
Ex. 3, p. 965

**c.** Sum of the first $n$ terms: $S_n = \dfrac{n}{2}(a_1 + a_n)$

Ex. 4, p. 967;
Ex. 5, p. 968;
Ex. 6, p. 968

### 10.3 Geometric Sequences and Series

**a.** In a geometric sequence, each term after the first is obtained by multiplying the preceding term by a nonzero constant, the common ratio. Divide any term after the first by the term that directly precedes it to find the common ratio.

List of geometric sequences and common ratios, p. 973;
Ex. 1, p. 973

**b.** General term or $n$th term: $a_n = a_1 r^{n-1}$. The first term is $a_1$ and the common ratio is $r$.

Ex. 2, p. 974;
Ex. 3, p. 974

**c.** Sum of the first $n$ terms: $S_n = \dfrac{a_1(1 - r^n)}{1 - r}, r \neq 1$

Ex. 4, p. 976;
Ex. 5, p. 976;
Ex. 6, p. 977

**d.** An annuity is a sequence of equal payments made at equal time periods. The value of an annuity, $A$, is the sum of all deposits made plus all interest paid, given by

$$A = \frac{P\left[\left(1 + \dfrac{r}{n}\right)^{nt} - 1\right]}{\dfrac{r}{n}}.$$

Ex. 7, p. 979

The deposit made at the end of each period is $P$, the annual interest rate is $r$, compounded $n$ times per year, and $t$ is the number of years deposits have been made.

| **DEFINITIONS AND CONCEPTS** | **EXAMPLES** |
|---|---|
| **e.** The sum of the infinite geometric series $a_1 + a_1r + a_1r^2 + a_1r^3 + \cdots$ is $S = \dfrac{a_1}{1 - r}$; $|r| < 1$. If $|r| \geq 1$, the infinite series does not have a sum. | Ex. 8, p. 981; Ex. 9, p. 982; Ex. 10, p. 982 |

## 10.4 Mathematical Induction

| | |
|---|---|
| To prove that $S_n$ is true for all positive integers $n$, <br> **1.** Show that $S_1$ is true. <br> **2.** Show that if $S_k$ is assumed true, then $S_{k+1}$ is also true, for every positive integer $k$. | Ex. 2, p. 991; Ex. 3, p. 992; Ex. 4, p. 993 |

## 10.5 The Binomial Theorem

| | |
|---|---|
| **a.** Binomial coefficient: $\dbinom{n}{r} = \dfrac{n!}{r!(n - r)!}$ | Ex. 1, p. 996 |
| **b.** Binomial Theorem: $$(a + b)^n = \binom{n}{0}a^n + \binom{n}{1}a^{n-1}b + \binom{n}{2}a^{n-2}b^2 + \cdots + \binom{n}{n}b^n$$ | Ex. 2, p. 998; Ex. 3, p. 998 |
| **c.** The $(r + 1)$st term in the expansion of $(a + b)^n$ is $$\binom{n}{r}a^{n-r}b^r.$$ | Ex. 4, p. 1000 |

## 10.6 Counting Principles, Permutations, and Combinations

| | |
|---|---|
| **a.** The Fundamental Counting Principle: The number of ways in which a series of successive things can occur is found by multiplying the number of ways in which each thing can occur. | Ex. 1, p. 1004; Ex. 2, p. 1005; Ex. 3, p. 1005 |
| **b.** A permutation from a group of items occurs when no item is used more than once and the order of arrangement makes a difference. | |
| **c.** Permutations Formula: The number of possible permutations if $r$ items are taken from $n$ items is $$_nP_r = \frac{n!}{(n - r)!}.$$ | Ex. 4, p. 1007; Ex. 5, p. 1007 |
| **d.** A combination from a group of items occurs when no item is used more than once and the order of items makes no difference. | Ex. 6, p. 1009 |
| **e.** Combinations Formula: The number of possible combinations if $r$ items are taken from $n$ items is $$_nC_r = \frac{n!}{(n - r)!r!}.$$ | Ex. 7, p. 1010; Ex. 8, p. 1011 |

## 10.7 Probability

| | |
|---|---|
| **a.** Empirical probability applies to situations in which we observe the frequency of the occurrence of an event. The empirical probability of event $E$ is $$P(E) = \frac{\text{observed number of times } E \text{ occurs}}{\text{total number of observed occurrences}}.$$ | Ex. 1, p. 1015 |
| **b.** Theoretical probability applies to situations in which the sample space of all equally likely outcomes is known. The theoretical probability of event $E$ is $$P(E) = \frac{\text{number of outcomes in event } E}{\text{number of outcomes in sample space } S} = \frac{n(E)}{n(S)}.$$ | Ex. 2, p. 1018; Ex. 3, p. 1018; Ex. 4, p. 1019; Ex. 5, p. 1020 |
| **c.** Probability of an event not occurring: $P(\text{not } E) = 1 - P(E)$. | Ex. 6, p. 1021 |
| **d.** If it is impossible for events $A$ and $B$ to occur simultaneously, the events are mutually exclusive. | |

**DEFINITIONS AND CONCEPTS**  **EXAMPLES**

**e.** If $A$ and $B$ are mutually exclusive events, then $P(A \text{ or } B) = P(A) + P(B)$.  Ex. 7, p. 1022

**f.** If $A$ and $B$ are not mutually exclusive events, then
$$P(A \text{ or } B) = P(A) + P(B) - P(A \text{ and } B).$$
Ex. 8, p. 1022;
Ex. 9, p. 1023

**g.** Two events are independent if the occurrence of either of them has no effect on the probability of the other.

**h.** If $A$ and $B$ are independent events, then
$$P(A \text{ and } B) = P(A) \cdot P(B).$$
Ex. 10, p. 1025

**i.** The probability of a succession of independent events is the product of each of their probabilities.  Ex. 11, p. 1025

## Review Exercises

### 10.1

*In Exercises 1–6, write the first four terms of each sequence whose general term is given.*

**1.** $a_n = 7n - 4$

**2.** $a_n = (-1)^n \dfrac{n + 2}{n + 1}$

**3.** $a_n = \dfrac{1}{(n - 1)!}$

**4.** $a_n = \dfrac{(-1)^{n+1}}{2^n}$

**5.** $a_1 = 9$ and $a_n = \dfrac{2}{3a_{n-1}}$ for $n \geq 2$

**6.** $a_1 = 4$ and $a_n = 2a_{n-1} + 3$ for $n \geq 2$

**7.** Evaluate: $\dfrac{40!}{4!38!}$.

*In Exercises 8–9, find each indicated sum.*

**8.** $\displaystyle\sum_{i=1}^{5} (2i^2 - 3)$

**9.** $\displaystyle\sum_{i=0}^{4} (-1)^{i+1} i!$

*In Exercises 10–11, express each sum using summation notation. Use i for the index of summation.*

**10.** $\dfrac{1}{3} + \dfrac{2}{4} + \dfrac{3}{5} + \cdots + \dfrac{15}{17}$

**11.** $4^3 + 5^3 + 6^3 + \cdots + 13^3$

### 10.2

*In Exercises 12–15, write the first six terms of each arithmetic sequence.*

**12.** $a_1 = 7, d = 4$

**13.** $a_1 = -4, d = -5$

**14.** $a_1 = \frac{3}{2}, d = -\frac{1}{2}$

**15.** $a_{n+1} = a_n + 5, a_1 = -2$

*In Exercises 16–18, find the indicated term of the arithmetic sequence with first term, $a_1$, and common difference, $d$.*

**16.** Find $a_6$ when $a_1 = 5, d = 3$.

**17.** Find $a_{12}$ when $a_1 = -8, d = -2$.

**18.** Find $a_{14}$ when $a_1 = 14, d = -4$.

*In Exercises 19–21, write a formula for the general term (the nth term) of each arithmetic sequence. Do not use a recursion formula. Then use the formula for $a_n$ to find $a_{20}$, the 20th term of the sequence.*

**19.** $-7, -3, 1, 5, \ldots$

**20.** $a_1 = 200, d = -20$

**21.** $a_n = a_{n-1} - 5, a_1 = 3$

**22.** Find the sum of the first 22 terms of the arithmetic sequence: $5, 12, 19, 26, \ldots$.

**23.** Find the sum of the first 15 terms of the arithmetic sequence: $-6, -3, 0, 3, \ldots$.

**24.** Find $3 + 6 + 9 + \cdots + 300$, the sum of the first 100 positive multiples of 3.

*In Exercises 25–27, use the formula for the sum of the first n terms of an arithmetic sequence to find the indicated sum.*

**25.** $\displaystyle\sum_{i=1}^{16} (3i + 2)$

**26.** $\displaystyle\sum_{i=1}^{25} (-2i + 6)$

**27.** $\displaystyle\sum_{i=1}^{30} (-5i)$

**28.** The graphic indicates that there are more eyes at school.

**Percentage of United States Students Ages 12–18 Seeing Security Cameras at School**

2005 58%

2001 39%

35 a

*Source:* Department of Education

In 2001, 39% of students ages 12–18 reported seeing one or more security cameras at their school. On average, this has increased by approximately 4.75% per year since then.

**a.** Write a formula for the $n$th term of the arithmetic sequence that describes the percentage of students ages 12–18 who reported seeing security cameras at school $n$ years after 2000.

**b.** Use the model to predict the percentage of students ages 12–18 who will report seeing security cameras at school by the year 2013.

**29.** A company offers a starting salary of $31,500 with raises of $2300 per year. Find the total salary over a ten-year period.

**30.** A theater has 25 seats in the first row and 35 rows in all. Each successive row contains one additional seat. How many seats are in the theater?

## 10.3

In Exercises 31–34, write the first five terms of each geometric sequence.

**31.** $a_1 = 3, r = 2$

**32.** $a_1 = \frac{1}{2}, r = \frac{1}{2}$

**33.** $a_1 = 16, r = -\frac{1}{2}$

**34.** $a_n = -5a_{n-1}, a_1 = -1$

In Exercises 35–37, use the formula for the general term (the nth term) of a geometric sequence to find the indicated term of each sequence.

**35.** Find $a_7$ when $a_1 = 2, r = 3$.

**36.** Find $a_6$ when $a_1 = 16, r = \frac{1}{2}$.

**37.** Find $a_5$ when $a_1 = -3, r = 2$.

In Exercises 38–40, write a formula for the general term (the nth term) of each geometric sequence. Then use the formula for $a_n$ to find $a_8$, the eighth term of the sequence.

**38.** $1, 2, 4, 8, \ldots$

**39.** $100, 10, 1, \frac{1}{10}, \ldots$

**40.** $12, -4, \frac{4}{3}, -\frac{4}{9}, \ldots$

**41.** Find the sum of the first 15 terms of the geometric sequence: $5, -15, 45, -135, \ldots$.

**42.** Find the sum of the first 7 terms of the geometric sequence: $8, 4, 2, 1, \ldots$.

In Exercises 43–45, use the formula for the sum of the first n terms of a geometric sequence to find the indicated sum.

**43.** $\sum_{i=1}^{6} 5^i$

**44.** $\sum_{i=1}^{7} 3(-2)^i$

**45.** $\sum_{i=1}^{5} 2\left(\frac{1}{4}\right)^{i-1}$

In Exercises 46–49, find the sum of each infinite geometric series.

**46.** $9 + 3 + 1 + \frac{1}{3} + \cdots$

**47.** $2 - 1 + \frac{1}{2} - \frac{1}{4} + \cdots$

**48.** $-6 + 4 - \frac{8}{3} + \frac{16}{9} - \cdots$

**49.** $\sum_{i=1}^{\infty} 5(0.8)^i$

In Exercises 50–51, express each repeating decimal as a fraction in lowest terms.

**50.** $0.\overline{6}$

**51.** $0.\overline{47}$

**52.** Projections for the U.S. population, ages 85 and older, are shown in the following table.

| Year | 2000 | 2010 | 2020 | 2030 | 2040 | 2050 |
|---|---|---|---|---|---|---|
| Projected Population in millions | 4.2 | 5.9 | 8.3 | 11.6 | 16.2 | 22.7 |

Actual 2000 population

*Source:* U.S. Census Bureau

**a.** Show that the U.S. population, ages 85 and older, is projected to increase geometrically.

**b.** Write the general term of the geometric sequence describing the U.S. population ages 85 and older, in millions, $n$ decades after 2000.

**c.** Use the model in part (b) to project the U.S. population, ages 85 and older, in 2080.

**53.** A job pays $32,000 for the first year with an annual increase of 6% per year beginning in the second year. What is the salary in the sixth year? What is the total salary paid over this six-year period? Round answers to the nearest dollar.

In Exercises 54–55, use the formula for the value of an annuity and round to the nearest dollar.

**54.** You spend $10 per week on lottery tickets, averaging $520 per year. Instead of buying tickets, if you deposited the $520 at the end of each year in an annuity paying 6% compounded annually,

**a.** How much would you have after 20 years?

**b.** Find the interest.

**55.** To save for retirement, you decide to deposit $100 at the end of each month in an IRA that pays 5.5% compounded monthly.

**a.** How much will you have from the IRA after 30 years?

**b.** Find the interest.

**56.** A factory in an isolated town has an annual payroll of $4 million. It is estimated that 70% of this money is spent within the town, that people in the town receiving this money will again spend 70% of what they receive in the town, and so on. What is the total of all this spending in the town each year?

## 10.4

In Exercises 57–61, use mathematical induction to prove that each statement is true for every positive integer n.

**57.** $5 + 10 + 15 + \cdots + 5n = \dfrac{5n(n+1)}{2}$

**58.** $1 + 4 + 4^2 + \cdots + 4^{n-1} = \dfrac{4^n - 1}{3}$

**59.** $2 + 6 + 10 + \cdots + (4n - 2) = 2n^2$

**60.** $1 \cdot 3 + 2 \cdot 4 + 3 \cdot 5 + \cdots + n(n+2) = \dfrac{n(n+1)(2n+7)}{6}$

**61.** 2 is a factor of $n^2 + 5n$.

## 10.5

In Exercises 62–63, evaluate the given binomial coefficient.

**62.** $\dbinom{11}{8}$

**63.** $\dbinom{90}{2}$

In Exercises 64–67, use the Binomial Theorem to expand each binomial and express the result in simplified form.

**64.** $(2x + 1)^3$

**65.** $(x^2 - 1)^4$

**66.** $(x + 2y)^5$

**67.** $(x - 2)^6$

*In Exercises 68–69, write the first three terms in each binomial expansion, expressing the result in simplified form.*

**68.** $(x^2 + 3)^8$          **69.** $(x - 3)^9$

*In Exercises 70–71, find the term indicated in each expansion.*

**70.** $(x + 2)^5$; fourth term     **71.** $(2x - 3)^6$; fifth term

## 10.6

*In Exercises 72–75, evaluate each expression.*

**72.** $_8P_3$             **73.** $_9P_5$

**74.** $_8C_3$             **75.** $_{13}C_{11}$

*In Exercises 76–82, solve by the method of your choice.*

**76.** A popular brand of pen comes in red, green, blue, or black ink. The writing tip can be chosen from extra bold, bold, regular, fine, or micro. How many different choices of pens do you have with this brand?

**77.** A stock can go up, go down, or stay unchanged. How many possibilities are there if you own five stocks?

**78.** A club with 15 members is to choose four officers—president, vice-president, secretary, and treasurer. In how many ways can these offices be filled?

**79.** How many different ways can a director select 4 actors from a group of 20 actors to attend a workshop on performing in rock musicals?

**80.** From the 20 CDs that you've bought during the past year, you plan to take 3 with you on vacation. How many different sets of three CDs can you take?

**81.** How many different ways can a director select from 20 male actors and cast the roles of Mark, Roger, Angel, and Collins in the musical *Rent*?

**82.** In how many ways can five airplanes line up for departure on a runway?

## 10.7

*Suppose that a survey of 350 college students is taken. Each student is asked the type of college attended (public or private) and the family's income level (low, middle, high). Use the data in the table to solve Exercises 83–88. Express probabilities as simplified fractions.*

|  | Public | Private | Total |
|---|---|---|---|
| Low | 120 | 20 | 140 |
| Middle | 110 | 50 | 160 |
| High | 22 | 28 | 50 |
| Total | 252 | 98 | 350 |

*Find the probability that a randomly selected student in the survey*

**83.** attends a public college.

**84.** is not from a high-income family.

**85.** is from a middle-income or a high-income family.

**86.** attends a private college or is from a high-income family.

**87.** Among people who attend a public college, find the probability that a randomly selected student is from a low-income family.

**88.** Among people from a middle-income family, find the probability that a randomly selected student attends a private college.

*In Exercises 89–90, a die is rolled. Find the probability of*

**89.** getting a number less than 5.

**90.** getting a number less than 3 or greater than 4.

*In Exercises 91–92, you are dealt one card from a 52-card deck. Find the probability of*

**91.** getting an ace or a king.

**92.** getting a queen or a red card.

*In Exercises 93–95, it is equally probable that the pointer on the spinner shown will land on any one of the six regions, numbered 1 through 6, and colored as shown. If the pointer lands on a borderline, spin again. Find the probability of*

**93.** not stopping on yellow.

**94.** stopping on red or a number greater than 3.

**95.** stopping on green on the first spin and stopping on a number less than 4 on the second spin.

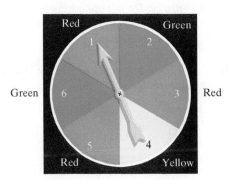

**96.** A lottery game is set up so that each player chooses five different numbers from 1 to 20. If the five numbers match the five numbers drawn in the lottery, the player wins (or shares) the top cash prize. What is the probability of winning the prize

  **a.** with one lottery ticket?

  **b.** with 100 different lottery tickets?

**97.** What is the probability of a family having five boys born in a row?

**98.** The probability of a flood in any given year in a region prone to floods is 0.2.

  **a.** What is the probability of a flood two years in a row?

  **b.** What is the probability of a flood for three consecutive years?

  **c.** What is the probability of no flooding for four consecutive years?

**Chapter 10   Test**

1. Write the first five terms of the sequence whose general term is $a_n = \dfrac{(-1)^{n+1}}{n^2}$.

*In Exercises 2–4, find each indicated sum.*

2. $\displaystyle\sum_{i=1}^{5} (i^2 + 10)$

3. $\displaystyle\sum_{i=1}^{20} (3i - 4)$

4. $\displaystyle\sum_{i=1}^{15} (-2)^i$

*In Exercises 5–7, evaluate each expression.*

5. $\dbinom{9}{2}$

6. $_{10}P_3$

7. $_{10}C_3$

8. Express the sum using summation notation. Use $i$ for the index of summation.
$$\frac{2}{3} + \frac{3}{4} + \frac{4}{5} + \cdots + \frac{21}{22}$$

*In Exercises 9–10, write a formula for the general term (the nth term) of each sequence. Do not use a recursion formula. Then use the formula to find the twelfth term of the sequence.*

9. $4, 9, 14, 19, \ldots$

10. $16, 4, 1, \frac{1}{4}, \ldots$

*In Exercises 11–12, use a formula to find the sum of the first ten terms of each sequence.*

11. $7, -14, 28, -56, \ldots$

12. $-7, -14, -21, -28, \ldots$

13. Find the sum of the infinite geometric series:
$$4 + \frac{4}{2} + \frac{4}{2^2} + \frac{4}{2^3} + \cdots.$$

14. Express $0.\overline{73}$ in fractional notation.

15. A job pays \$30,000 for the first year with an annual increase of 4% per year beginning in the second year. What is the total salary paid over an eight-year period? Round to the nearest dollar.

16. Use mathematical induction to prove that for every positive integer $n$,
$$1 + 4 + 7 + \cdots + (3n - 2) = \frac{n(3n - 1)}{2}.$$

17. Use the Binomial Theorem to expand and simplify: $(x^2 - 1)^5$.

18. Use the Binomial Theorem to write the first three terms in the expansion and simplify: $(x + y^2)^8$.

19. A human resource manager has 11 applicants to fill three different positions. Assuming that all applicants are equally qualified for any of the three positions, in how many ways can this be done?

20. From the ten books that you've recently bought but not read, you plan to take four with you on vacation. How many different sets of four books can you take?

21. How many seven-digit local telephone numbers can be formed if the first three digits are 279?

*A class is collecting data on eye color and gender. They organize the data they collected into the table shown. Numbers in the table represent the number of students from the class that belong to each of the categories. Use the data to solve Exercises 22–25. Express probabilities as simplified fractions.*

|        | Brown | Blue | Green |
|--------|-------|------|-------|
| Male   | 22    | 18   | 10    |
| Female | 18    | 20   | 12    |

*Find the probability that a randomly selected student from this class*

22. does not have brown eyes.

23. has brown eyes or blue eyes.

24. is female or has green eyes.

25. Among the students with blue eyes, find the probability of selecting a male.

26. A lottery game is set up so that each player chooses six different numbers from 1 to 15. If the six numbers match the six numbers drawn in the lottery, the player wins (or shares) the top cash prize. What is the probability of winning the prize with 50 different lottery tickets?

27. One card is randomly selected from a deck of 52 cards. Find the probability of selecting a black card or a picture card.

28. A group of students consists of 10 male freshmen, 15 female freshmen, 20 male sophomores, and 5 female sophomores. If one person is randomly selected from the group, find the probability of selecting a freshman or a female.

29. A quiz consisting of four multiple-choice questions has four available options (a, b, c, or d) for each question. If a person guesses at every question, what is the probability of answering all questions correctly?

30. If the spinner shown is spun twice, find the probability that the pointer lands on red on the first spin and blue on the second spin.

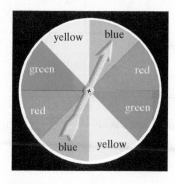

# Cumulative Review Exercises (Chapters P–10)

*The figure shows the graph of $y = f(x)$ and its vertical asymptote. Use the graph to solve Exercises 1–9.*

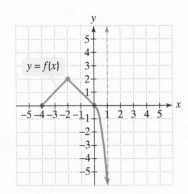

1. Find the domain and the range of $f$.
2. Does $f$ have a relative maximum or a relative minimum? What is this relative maximum or minimum and where does it occur?
3. Find the interval on which $f$ is decreasing.
4. Is $f$ even, odd, or neither?
5. For what value(s) of $x$ is $f(x) = 1$?
6. Find $(f \circ f)(-4)$.
7. Use arrow notation to complete this statement:
$$f(x) \to -\infty \quad \text{as} \quad \underline{\hspace{1.5cm}}.$$
8. Graph $g(x) = f(x - 2) + 1$.
9. Graph $h(x) = -f(2x)$.

*In Exercises 10–22, solve each equation, inequality, or system of equations.*

10. $-2(x - 5) + 10 = 3(x + 2)$
11. $3x^2 - 6x + 2 = 0$
12. $\log_2 x + \log_2(2x - 3) = 1$
13. $x^{\frac{1}{2}} - 6x^{\frac{1}{4}} + 8 = 0$
14. $e^{2x} - 6e^x + 8 = 0$
15. $|2x + 1| \le 1$
16. $6x^2 - 6 < 5x$
17. $\dfrac{x - 1}{x + 3} \le 0$
18. $30e^{0.7x} = 240$
19. $2x^3 + 3x^2 - 8x + 3 = 0$
20. $\begin{cases} 4x^2 + 3y^2 = 48 \\ 3x^2 + 2y^2 = 35 \end{cases}$
21. (Use matrices.)
$$\begin{cases} x - 2y + z = 16 \\ 2x - y - z = 14 \\ 3x + 5y - 4z = -10 \end{cases}$$
22. $\begin{cases} x - y = 1 \\ x^2 - x - y = 1 \end{cases}$

*In Exercises 23–29, graph each equation, function, or system in a rectangular coordinate system. If two functions are indicated, graph both in the same system.*

23. $100x^2 + y^2 = 25$
24. $4x^2 - 9y^2 - 16x + 54y - 29 = 0$
25. $f(x) = \dfrac{x^2 - 1}{x - 2}$
26. $\begin{cases} 2x - y \ge 4 \\ x \le 2 \end{cases}$
27. $f(x) = x^2 - 4x - 5$
28. $f(x) = \sqrt[3]{x + 4}$ and $f^{-1}$
29. $f(x) = \log_2 x$ and $g(x) = -\log_2(x + 1)$

*In Exercises 30–31, let $f(x) = -x^2 - 2x + 1$ and $g(x) = x - 1$.*

30. Find $(f \circ g)(x)$ and $(g \circ f)(x)$.
31. Find $\dfrac{f(x + h) - f(x)}{h}$ and simplify.
32. If $A = \begin{bmatrix} 4 & 2 \\ 1 & -1 \\ 0 & 5 \end{bmatrix}$ and $B = \begin{bmatrix} 2 & 4 \\ 3 & 1 \end{bmatrix}$, find $AB - 4A$.
33. Find the partial fraction decomposition for
$$\dfrac{2x^2 - 10x + 2}{(x - 2)(x^2 + 2x + 2)}.$$
34. Expand and simplify: $(x^3 + 2y)^5$.
35. Use the formula for the sum of the first $n$ terms of an arithmetic sequence to find $\displaystyle\sum_{i=1}^{50} (4i - 25)$.

*In Exercises 36–37, write the linear function in slope-intercept form satisfying the given conditions.*

36. Graph of $f$ passes through $(6, 3)$ and $(-2, 1)$.
37. Graph of $g$ passes through $(0, -2)$ and is perpendicular to the line whose equation is $x - 5y - 20 = 0$.
38. For a summer sales job, you are choosing between two pay arrangements: a weekly salary of $200 plus 5% commission on sales, or a straight 15% commission. For how many dollars of sales will the earnings be the same regardless of the pay arrangement?
39. The perimeter of a soccer field is 300 yards. If the length is 50 yards longer than the width, what are the field's dimensions?
40. If 10 pens and 12 pads cost $42, and 5 of the same pens and 10 of the same pads cost $29, find the cost of a pen and a pad.

**41.** A ball is thrown vertically upward from the top of a 96-foot-tall building with an initial velocity of 80 feet per second. The height of the ball above ground, $s(t)$, in feet, after $t$ seconds is modeled by the position function

$$s(t) = -16t^2 + 80t + 96.$$

   **a.** After how many seconds will the ball strike the ground?

   **b.** When does the ball reach its maximum height? What is the maximum height?

**42.** The current, $I$, in amperes, flowing in an electrical circuit varies inversely as the resistance, $R$, in ohms, in the circuit. When the resistance of an electric percolator is 22 ohms, it draws 5 amperes of current. How much current is needed when the resistance is 10 ohms?

**43.** The bar graph shows the decline in the percentage of the U.S. adult population that smokes cigarettes. Develop a linear function that models the data. Then use the function to make a projection about what might occur in the future.

**Butt Out: Percentage of Cigarette
Smokers Among U.S. Adults**

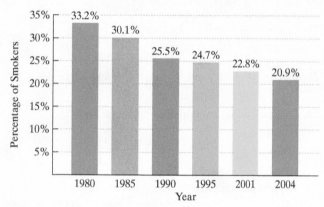

*Source:* Centers for Disease Control and Prevention

**44.** An object moves in simple harmonic motion described by $d = 10 \sin \frac{3\pi}{4} t$, where $t$ is measured in seconds and $d$ in inches. Find **a.** the maximum displacement; **b.** the frequency; and **c.** the time required for one oscillation.

*Verify each identity in Exercises 45–46.*

**45.** $\tan x + \dfrac{1}{\tan x} = \dfrac{1}{\sin x \cos x}$

**46.** $\dfrac{1 - \tan^2 x}{1 + \tan^2 x} = \cos 2x$

**47.** Graph one period: $y = -2 \cos(3x - \pi)$.

*In Exercises 48–49, solve each equation on the interval $[0, 2\pi)$.*

**48.** $4 \cos^2 x = 3$

**49.** $2 \sin^2 x + 3 \cos x - 3 = 0$

**50.** Find the exat value of $\cot\left[\cos^{-1}\left(-\frac{5}{6}\right)\right]$.

**51.** Graph the polar equation: $r = 1 + 2 \cos \theta$.

**52.** In oblique triangle $ABC$, $A = 34°$, $a = 22$, and $b = 32$. Solve the triangle(s). Round lengths to the nearest tenth and angle measures to the nearest degree.

**53.** Use the parametric equations

$$x = \sin t, \quad y = 1 + \cos^2 t, \quad -\frac{\pi}{2} < t < \frac{\pi}{2}$$

and eliminate the parameter. Graph the plane curve represented by the parametric equations. Use arrows to show the orientation of the curve.

# Introduction to Calculus

# 11

We revisit an idea introduced in an essay in Chapter 1. Take a rapid sequence of still photographs of a moving scene and project them onto a screen at thirty shots a second or faster. Our eyes see the result as continuous motion. The small difference between one frame and the next cannot be detected by the human visual system. The idea of calculus likewise regards continuous motion as made up of a sequence of still configurations. In this chapter, you will see how calculus uses a revolutionary concept called *limits* to master the mystery of movement by "freezing the frame" instant by instant.

*Using limits to describe instantaneous rates of change is introduced in the Section 11.4 opener and developed throughout the section.*

**Section 11.1 Finding Limits Using Tables and Graphs**

### Objectives

1. Understand limit notation.
2. Find limits using tables.
3. Find limits using graphs.
4. Find one-sided limits and use them to determine if a limit exists.

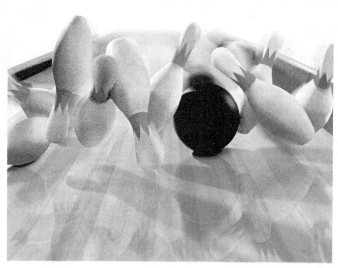

Motion and change are the very essence of life. Moving air brushes against our faces, rain falls on our heads, birds fly past us, plants spring from the earth, grow, and then die, and rocks thrown upward reach a maximum height before falling to the ground.

The tools of algebra and trigonometry are essentially static; numbers, points, lines, equations, functions, and graphs do not incorporate motion. The development of calculus in the middle of the seventeenth century provided a way to use these static tools to analyze motion and change. It took nearly two thousand years of effort for humankind to achieve this feat, made possible by a revolutionary concept called *limits*. The invention of limits marked a turning point in human history, having as dramatic an impact on our lives as the invention of the wheel and the printing press. In this section, we introduce this bold and dramatic style of thinking about mathematics.

① Understand limit notation.

### An Introduction to Limits

Suppose that you and a friend are walking along the graph of the function

$$f(x) = \frac{x^2 - 4}{x - 2}.$$

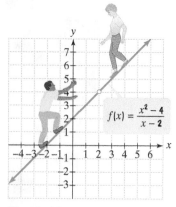

Figure 11.1  Walking along the graph of $f$, very close to 2

**Figure 11.1** illustrates that you are walking uphill and your friend is walking downhill. Because 2 is not in the domain of the function, there is a hole in the graph at $x = 2$. Warning signs along the graph might be appropriate: Caution: $f(2)$ is undefined! If you or your friend reach 2, you will fall through the hole and splatter onto the $x$-axis.

Obviously, there is a problem at $x = 2$. But what happens along the graph of $f(x) = \frac{x^2 - 4}{x - 2}$ as you and your friend walk very, very close to $x = 2$? What function value, $f(x)$, will each of you approach? One way to answer this question is to construct a table of function values to analyze numerically the behavior of $f$ as $x$ gets closer and closer to 2. Remember that you are walking uphill, approaching 2 from the left side of 2. Your friend is walking downhill, approaching 2 from the right side of 2. Thus, we must include values of $x$ that are less than 2 and values of $x$ that are greater than 2.

In **Table 11.1** at the top of the next page, we choose values of $x$ close to 2. As $x$ approaches 2 from the left, we arbitrarily start with $x = 1.99$. Then we select two additional values of $x$ that are closer to 2, but still less than 2. We choose 1.999 and 1.9999. As $x$ approaches 2 from the right, we arbitrarily start with $x = 2.01$. Then we select two additional values of $x$ that are closer to 2, but still greater than 2. We choose 2.001 and 2.0001. Finally, evaluate $f$ at each chosen value of $x$ to obtain **Table 11.1**.

## Technology

A graphing utility with a TABLE feature can be used to generate the entries in Table 11.1. In TBLSET, change Auto to Ask for Indpnt, the independent variable. Here is a typical screen that verifies **Table 11.1**.

| X | Y1 |
|------|-------|
| 1.99 | 3.99 |
| 1.999 | 3.999 |
| 1.9999 | 3.9999 |
| 2.0001 | 4.0001 |
| 2.001 | 4.001 |
| 2.01 | 4.01 |

Y1■(X²-4)/(X-2)

**Table 11.1**

| | | x approaches 2 from the left. | | | | x approaches 2 from the right. | | |
|---|---|---|---|---|---|---|---|---|
| $x$ | | 1.99 | 1.999 | 1.9999 | 2 | 2.0001 | 2.001 | 2.01 |
| $f(x) = \dfrac{x^2 - 4}{x - 2}$ | | 3.99 | 3.999 | 3.9999 | Undefined | 4.0001 | 4.001 | 4.01 |

| $f(x)$ gets closer to 4. | $f(x)$ gets closer to 4. |
|---|---|

From **Table 11.1**, it appears that as $x$ gets closer to 2, the values of $f(x) = \dfrac{x^2 - 4}{x - 2}$ get closer to 4. We say that

"The limit of $\dfrac{x^2 - 4}{x - 2}$ as $x$ approaches 2 equals the number 4."

We can express this sentence in a mathematical notation called **limit notation**. We use an arrow for the word *approaches*. Likewise, we use *lim* as shorthand for the word *limit*. Thus, the limit notation for the English sentence in quotations is

$$\lim_{x \to 2} \frac{x^2 - 4}{x - 2} = 4. \qquad \text{The limit of } \frac{x^2 - 4}{x - 2} \text{ as x approaches 2 equals the number 4.}$$

Calculus is the study of limits and their applications. Limits are the foundation of the concepts that you will encounter in calculus.

### Limit Notation and Its Description

Suppose that $f$ is a function defined on some open interval containing the number $a$. The function $f$ may or may not be defined at $a$. The **limit notation**

$$\lim_{x \to a} f(x) = L$$

is read "the limit of $f(x)$ as $x$ approaches $a$ equals the number $L$." This means that as $x$ gets closer to $a$, but remains unequal to $a$, the corresponding values of $f(x)$ get closer to $L$.

**2** Find limits using tables.

## Finding Limits Using Tables

To find $\lim_{x \to a} f(x)$, use a graphing utility with a TABLE feature or create a table by hand. Approach $a$ from the left, choosing values of $x$ that are close to $a$, but still less than $a$. Then approach $a$ from the right, choosing values of $x$ that are close to $a$, but still greater than $a$. Evaluate $f$ at each chosen value of $x$ to obtain the desired table.

Choose values of $x$ so that the table makes it obvious what the corresponding values of $f(x)$ are getting close to. If the values of $f(x)$ are getting close to the number $L$, we infer that

$$\lim_{x \to a} f(x) = L.$$

**EXAMPLE 1** Finding a Limit Using a Table

Find: $\lim\limits_{x \to 4} 3x^2$.

**Solution** As $x$ gets closer to 4, but remains unequal to 4, we must find the number that the corresponding values of $3x^2$ get closer to. The voice balloons shown below indicate that in this limit problem, $f(x) = 3x^2$ and $a = 4$.

$$\lim\limits_{x \to 4} 3x^2$$

| This is $a$ in $\lim\limits_{x \to a} f(x)$. | This is $f(x)$ in $\lim\limits_{x \to a} f(x)$. |
|---|---|

In making a table, we choose values of $x$ close to 4. As $x$ approaches 4 from the left, we arbitrarily start with $x = 3.99$. Then we select two additional values of $x$ that are closer to 4, but still less than 4. We choose 3.999 and 3.9999. As $x$ approaches 4 from the right, we arbitrarily start with $x = 4.01$. Then we select two additional numbers that are closer to 4, but still greater than 4. We choose 4.001 and 4.0001. Finally, we evaluate $f$ at each chosen value of $x$ to obtain **Table 11.2**. The values of $f(x)$ in the table are rounded to four decimal places.

**Table 11.2**

| | x approaches 4 from the left. | | | | x approaches 4 from the right. | | |
|---|---|---|---|---|---|---|---|
| $x$ | 3.99 | 3.999 | 3.9999 | $\longrightarrow \longleftarrow$ | 4.0001 | 4.001 | 4.01 |
| $f(x) = 3x^2$ | 47.7603 | 47.9760 | 47.9976 | $\longrightarrow \longleftarrow$ | 48.0024 | 48.0240 | 48.2403 |
| | $f(x)$ gets closer to 48. | | | | $f(x)$ gets closer to 48. | | |

From **Table 11.2**, it appears that as $x$ gets closer to 4, the values of $3x^2$ get closer to 48. We infer that

$$\lim\limits_{x \to 4} 3x^2 = 48.$$

⊘ Check Point **1** Find: $\lim\limits_{x \to 3} 4x^2$.

**EXAMPLE 2** Finding a Limit Using a Table

Find: $\lim\limits_{x \to 0} \dfrac{\sin x}{x}$.

**Solution** As $x$ gets closer to 0, but remains unequal to 0, we must find the number that the corresponding values of $\dfrac{\sin x}{x}$ get closer to. The voice balloons shown below indicate that in this limit problem, $f(x) = \dfrac{\sin x}{x}$ and $a = 0$.

$$\lim\limits_{x \to 0} \dfrac{\sin x}{x}$$

| This is $a$ in $\lim\limits_{x \to a} f(x)$. | This is $f(x)$ in $\lim\limits_{x \to a} f(x)$. |
|---|---|

Because division by 0 is undefined, the domain of $f(x) = \dfrac{\sin x}{x}$ is $\{x | x \neq 0\}$. Thus, $f$ is not defined at 0. However, in this limit problem, we do not care what is happening at $x = 0$. We are interested in the behavior of the function as $x$ gets close to 0. **Table 11.3** shows the values of $f(x)$, rounded to five decimal places, as $x$ approaches 0 from the left and from the right. Values of $x$ in the table are measured in radians.

**Table 11.3**

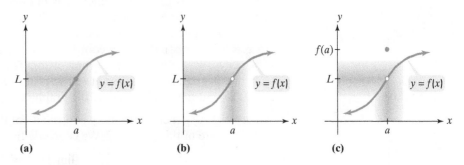

| | $x$ approaches 0 from the left. | | | | $x$ approaches 0 from the right. | | |
|---|---|---|---|---|---|---|---|
| $x$ | −0.03 | −0.02 | −0.01 | 0.01 | 0.02 | 0.03 |
| $f(x) = \dfrac{\sin x}{x}$ | 0.99985 | 0.99993 | 0.99998 | 0.99998 | 0.99993 | 0.99985 |
| | $f(x)$ gets closer to 1. | | | $f(x)$ gets closer to 1. | | | |

From **Table 11.3**, it appears that as $x$ gets closer to 0, the values of $\dfrac{\sin x}{x}$ get closer to 1. We infer that

$$\lim_{x \to 0} \frac{\sin x}{x} = 1.$$

✓ Check Point **2** Find: $\displaystyle\lim_{x \to 0} \frac{\cos x - 1}{x}$.

## Technology

**Graphic Connections**

The graph of $f(x) = \dfrac{\sin x}{x}$ illustrates that as $x$ gets closer to 0, the values of $f(x)$ are approaching 1. This supports our inference that

$$\lim_{x \to 0} \frac{\sin x}{x} = 1.$$

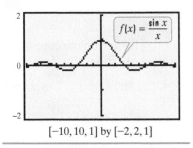

$[-10, 10, 1]$ by $[-2, 2, 1]$

**3** Find limits using graphs.

## Finding Limits Using Graphs

The limit statement

$$\lim_{x \to a} f(x) = L$$

is illustrated in **Figure 11.2**. In the three graphs, the number that $x$ is approaching, $a$, is shown on the $x$-axis. The limit, $L$, is shown on the $y$-axis. Take a few minutes to examine the graphs. Can you see that as $x$ approaches $a$ along the $x$-axis, $f(x)$ approaches $L$ along the $y$-axis? In each graph, as $x$ gets closer to $a$, the values of $f(x)$ get closer to $L$.

**Figure 11.2** In each graph, as $x$ gets closer to $a$, the values of $f$ get closer to $L$: $\displaystyle\lim_{x \to a} f(x) = L$.

In **Figure 11.2(a)**, as $x$ approaches $a$, $f(x)$ approaches $L$. At $a$, the value of the function is $L$: $f(a) = L$. In **Figure 11.2(b)**, as $x$ approaches $a$, $f(x)$ approaches $L$. This is true although $f$ is not defined at $a$, shown by the hole in the graph. In **Figure 11.2(c)**, we again see that as $x$ approaches $a$, $f(x)$ approaches $L$. Notice, however, that the value of the function at $a$, $f(a)$, shown by the blue dot, is not equal to the limit: $f(a) \neq L$. What you get as you approach $a$ is not the same as what you get at $a$.

Example 3 illustrates that the graph of a function can sometimes be helpful in finding limits.

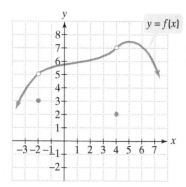

**Figure 11.3**

EXAMPLE 3 Finding a Limit Using a Graph

Use the graph in **Figure 11.3** to find each of the following:

**a.** $\lim_{x \to 4} f(x)$      **b.** $f(4)$.

**Solution**

**a.** To find $\lim_{x \to 4} f(x)$, examine the graph of $f$ *near* $x = 4$. As $x$ gets closer to 4, the values of $f(x)$ get closer to the $y$-coordinate of the point shown by the open dot on the right. The $y$-coordinate of this point is 7. Thus, as $x$ gets closer to 4, the values of $f(x)$ get closer to 7. We conclude from the graph that

$$\lim_{x \to 4} f(x) = 7.$$

**b.** To find $f(4)$, examine the graph of $f$ at $x = 4$. At $x = 4$, the open dot is not included in the graph of $f$. The graph of $f$ at 4 is shown by the closed dot with coordinates $(4, 2)$. Thus, $f(4) = 2$.

In Example 3, notice that the value of $f$ at 4 has nothing to do with the conclusion that $\lim_{x \to 4} f(x) = 7$. Regardless of how $f$ is defined at 4, it is still true that $\lim_{x \to 4} f(x) = 7$. Furthermore, if $f$ were undefined at 4, the limit of $f(x)$ as $x \to 4$ would still equal 7.

⌀ Check Point **3** Use the graph in **Figure 11.3** to find each of the following:

**a.** $\lim_{x \to -2} f(x)$      **b.** $f(-2)$.

EXAMPLE 4 Finding a Limit by Graphing a Function

Graph the function

$$f(x) = \begin{cases} 2x - 4 & \text{if } x \neq 3 \\ -5 & \text{if } x = 3. \end{cases}$$

Use the graph to find $\lim_{x \to 3} f(x)$.

**Solution** This piecewise function is defined by two equations. Graph the piece defined by the linear function, $f(x) = 2x - 4$, using the $y$-intercept, $-4$, and the slope, 2. Because $x = 3$ is not included, show an open dot on the line corresponding to $x = 3$. This open dot, with coordinates $(3, 2)$, is shown in **Figure 11.4**.

Now we complete the graph using $f(x) = -5$ if $x = 3$. This part of the function is graphed as the point $(3, -5)$, shown as a closed blue dot in **Figure 11.4**.

To find $\lim_{x \to 3} f(x)$, examine the graph of $f$ near $x = 3$. As $x$ gets closer to 3, the values of $f(x)$ get closer to the $y$-coordinate of the point shown by the open dot. The $y$-coordinate of this point is 2. We conclude from the graph that

$$\lim_{x \to 3} f(x) = 2.$$

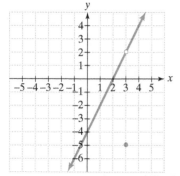

**Figure 11.4** As $x$ gets closer to 3, what number are the function values getting closer to?

⌀ Check Point **4** Graph the function

$$f(x) = \begin{cases} 3x - 2 & \text{if } x \neq 2 \\ 1 & \text{if } x = 2. \end{cases}$$

Use the graph to find $\lim_{x \to 2} f(x)$.

**④** Find one-sided limits and use them to determine if a limit exists.

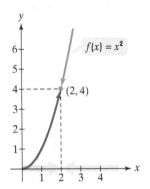

**Figure 11.5** As $x$ approaches 2 from the left (red arrow) or from the right (blue arrow), values of $f(x)$ get closer to 4.

## One-Sided Limits

The graph in **Figure 11.5** shows a portion of the graph of the function $f(x) = x^2$. The graph illustrates that

$$\lim_{x \to 2} x^2 = 4.$$

As $x$ gets closer to 2, but remains unequal to 2, the corresponding values of $f(x)$ get closer to 4. The values of $x$ near 2 fall into two categories: those that lie to the left of 2, shown by the red arrow on the $x$-axis, and those that lie to the right of 2, shown by the blue arrow on the $x$-axis.

The values of $x$ can get closer to 2 in two ways. The values of $x$ can approach 2 from the left, through numbers that are less than 2. **Table 11.4** shows some values of $x$ and the corresponding values of $f(x)$ rounded to four decimal places. The red portion of the graph in **Figure 11.5** shows that as $x$ approaches 2 from the left of 2, $f(x)$ approaches 4.

Table 11.4

| $x$ | 1.99 | 1.999 | 1.9999 $\to$ |
|---|---|---|---|
| $f(x) = x^2$ | 3.9601 | 3.9960 | 3.9996 $\to$ |

We say that "the limit of $x^2$ as $x$ approaches 2 from the left equals 4." The mathematical notation for this English sentence is

$$\lim_{x \to 2^-} x^2 = 4.$$

The notation $x \to 2^-$ indicates that $x$ is less than 2 and is approaching 2 from the left.

The values of $x$ can also approach 2 from the right, through numbers that are greater than 2. **Table 11.5** shows some values of $x$ and the corresponding values of $f(x)$ rounded to four decimal places. The blue portion of the graph in **Figure 11.5** shows that as $x$ approaches 2 from the right of 2, $f(x)$ approaches 4.

Table 11.5

| $x$ | $\leftarrow$ 2.0001 | 2.001 | 2.01 |
|---|---|---|---|
| $f(x) = x^2$ | $\leftarrow$ 4.0004 | 4.0040 | 4.0401 |

We say that "the limit of $x^2$ as $x$ approaches 2 from the right equals 4." The mathematical notation for this English sentence is

$$\lim_{x \to 2^+} x^2 = 4.$$

The notation $x \to 2^+$ indicates that $x$ is greater than 2 and is approaching 2 from the right.

In general, if $x$ approaches $a$ from one side, we have a **one-sided limit**.

### One-Sided Limits

**Left-Hand Limit** The limit notation

$$\lim_{x \to a^-} f(x) = L$$

is read "the limit of $f(x)$ as $x$ approaches $a$ from the left equals $L$" and is called the **left-hand limit**. This means that as $x$ gets closer to $a$, but remains less than $a$, the corresponding values of $f(x)$ get closer to $L$.

**Right-Hand Limit** The limit notation

$$\lim_{x \to a^+} f(x) = L$$

is read "the limit of $f(x)$ as $x$ approaches $a$ from the right equals $L$" and is called the **right-hand limit**. This means that as $x$ gets closer to $a$, but remains greater than $a$, the corresponding values of $f(x)$ get closer to $L$.

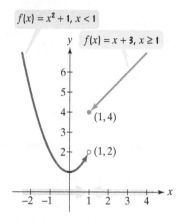

$f(x) = x^2 + 1, x < 1$

$f(x) = x + 3, x \geq 1$

(1, 4)

(1, 2)

**Figure 11.6** As $x$ approaches 1 from the left (red arrow) and from the right (blue arrow), values of $f(x)$ do not get closer to a single number.

A function's graph can be helpful in finding one-sided limits. For example, **Figure 11.6** shows the graph of the piecewise function

$$f(x) = \begin{cases} x^2 + 1 & \text{if } x < 1 \\ x + 3 & \text{if } x \geq 1. \end{cases}$$

The red portion of the graph, part of a parabola, illustrates that as $x$ approaches 1 from the left, the corresponding values of $f(x)$ get closer to 2. The left-hand limit is 2:

$$\lim_{x \to 1^-} f(x) = 2.$$

The blue portion of the graph, part of a line, illustrates that as $x$ approaches 1 from the right, the corresponding values of $f(x)$ get closer to 4. The right-hand limit is 4:

$$\lim_{x \to 1^+} f(x) = 4.$$

Because $\lim_{x \to 1^-} f(x) = 2$ and $\lim_{x \to 1^+} f(x) = 4$, there is no single number that the values of $f(x)$ are close to when $x$ is close to 1. In this case, we say that **$f$ has no limit as $x$ approaches 1** or that **$\lim_{x \to 1} f(x)$ does not exist**.

In general, a function $f$ has a limit as $x$ approaches $a$ if and only if the left-hand limit equals the right-hand limit.

### Equal and Unequal One-Sided Limits

- One-sided limits can be used to show that a function has a limit as $x$ approaches $a$.

$$\lim_{x \to a} f(x) = L \text{ if and only if both}$$

$$\lim_{x \to a^-} f(x) = L \quad \text{and} \quad \lim_{x \to a^+} f(x) = L.$$

- One-sided limits can be used to show that a function has no limit as $x$ approaches $a$.

If $\lim_{x \to a^-} f(x) = L$ and $\lim_{x \to a^+} f(x) = M$, where $L \neq M$,

$$\lim_{x \to a} f(x) \text{ does not exist.}$$

### Study Tip

The word *from* is helpful in distinguishing left- and right-hand limits. A left-hand limit means you approach the given $x$-value *from* the left. It does not mean that you approach toward the left on the graph. A right-hand limit means you approach the given $x$-value *from* the right. It does not mean you approach toward the right on the graph.

> **EXAMPLE 5** Finding One-Sided Limits Using a Graph

Use the graph of the piecewise function $f$ in **Figure 11.7** to find each of the following, or state that the limit or function value does not exist:

**a.** $\lim_{x \to -2^-} f(x)$     **b.** $\lim_{x \to -2^+} f(x)$     **c.** $\lim_{x \to -2} f(x)$     **d.** $f(-2)$.

### Solution

**a.** To find $\lim_{x \to -2^-} f(x)$, examine the portion of the graph shown in red that is near, but to the left of $x = -2$. As $x$ approaches $-2$ from the left, the values of $f(x)$ get close to the $y$-coordinate of the point shown by the red open dot. This point, $(-2, 0)$, has a $y$-coordinate of 0. Thus,

$$\lim_{x \to -2^-} f(x) = 0.$$

**b.** To find $\lim_{x \to -2^+} f(x)$, examine the portion of the graph shown in blue that is near, but to the right of $x = -2$. As $x$ approaches $-2$ from the right, the values of

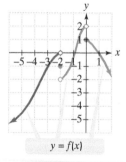

$y = f(x)$

**Figure 11.7**

$f(x)$ get close to the $y$-coordinate of the point shown by the blue open dot. This point, $(-2, -2)$, has a $y$-coordinate of $-2$. Thus,

$$\lim_{x \to -2^+} f(x) = -2.$$

**c.** We found that

$$\lim_{x \to -2^-} f(x) = 0 \quad \text{and} \quad \lim_{x \to -2^+} f(x) = -2.$$

> The limit as $x$ approaches $-2$ from the left equals 0.

> The limit as $x$ approaches $-2$ from the right equals $-2$.

Because the left- and right-hand limits are unequal, $\lim_{x \to -2} f(x)$ does not exist.

**d.** To find $f(-2)$, examine the graph of $f$ at $x = -2$. The graph of $f$ at $-2$ is shown by the blue closed dot with coordinates $(-2, -1)$. Thus, $f(-2) = -1$.

✓ Check Point **5** Use the graph of the piecewise function $f$ in **Figure 11.7** to find each of the following, or state that the limit or function value does not exist:

**a.** $\lim_{x \to 0^-} f(x)$     **b.** $\lim_{x \to 0^+} f(x)$     **c.** $\lim_{x \to 0} f(x)$     **d.** $f(0)$.

# Exercise Set 11.1

## Practice Exercises

*In Exercises 1–4, use each table to find the indicated limit.*

**1.** $\lim_{x \to 2} 2x^2$

| $x$ | 1.99 | 1.999 | 1.9999 → | ← 2.0001 | 2.001 | 2.01 |
|---|---|---|---|---|---|---|
| $f(x) = 2x^2$ | 7.9202 | 7.9920 | 7.9992 → | ← 8.0008 | 8.0080 | 8.0802 |

**2.** $\lim_{x \to 3} 5x^2$

| $x$ | 2.99 | 2.999 | 2.9999 → | ← 3.0001 | 3.001 | 3.01 |
|---|---|---|---|---|---|---|
| $f(x) = 5x^2$ | 44.701 | 44.970 | 44.997 → | ← 45.003 | 45.030 | 45.301 |

**3.** $\lim_{x \to 0} \dfrac{\sin 3x}{x}$

| $x$ | −0.03 | −0.02 | −0.01 → | ← 0.01 | 0.02 | 0.03 |
|---|---|---|---|---|---|---|
| $f(x) = \dfrac{\sin 3x}{x}$ | 2.9960 | 2.9982 | 2.9996 → | ← 2.9996 | 2.9982 | 2.9960 |

**4.** $\lim_{x \to 0} \dfrac{\sin 4x}{\sin 2x}$

| $x$ | −0.03 | −0.02 | −0.01 → | ← 0.01 | 0.02 | 0.03 |
|---|---|---|---|---|---|---|
| $f(x) = \dfrac{\sin 4x}{\sin 2x}$ | 1.9964 | 1.9984 | 1.9996 → | ← 1.9996 | 1.9984 | 1.9964 |

*In Exercises 5–18, construct a table to find the indicated limit.*

**5.** $\lim_{x \to 2} 5x^2$

**6.** $\lim_{x \to 2} (x^2 - 1)$

**7.** $\lim_{x \to 3} \dfrac{1}{x - 2}$

**8.** $\lim_{x \to 4} \dfrac{1}{x - 3}$

**9.** $\lim_{x \to 0} \dfrac{x}{x^2 + 1}$

**10.** $\lim_{x \to 0} \dfrac{x + 1}{x^2 + 1}$

**11.** $\lim_{x \to -2} \dfrac{x^3 + 8}{x + 2}$

**12.** $\lim_{x \to -5} \dfrac{x^2 - 25}{x + 5}$

**13.** $\lim_{x \to 0} \dfrac{2x^2 + x}{\sin x}$

**14.** $\lim_{x \to 0} \dfrac{\sin x^2}{x}$

**15.** $\lim_{x \to 0} \dfrac{\tan x}{x}$

**16.** $\lim_{x \to 0} \dfrac{x^2}{\sec x - 1}$

**17.** $\lim_{x \to 0} f(x)$, where $f(x) = \begin{cases} x + 1 & \text{if } x < 0 \\ 2x + 1 & \text{if } x \geq 0 \end{cases}$

**18.** $\lim_{x \to 0} f(x)$, where $f(x) = \begin{cases} x + 2 & \text{if } x < 0 \\ 3x + 2 & \text{if } x \geq 0 \end{cases}$

*In Exercises 19–22, use the graph of f to find the indicated limit and function value.*

**19.**

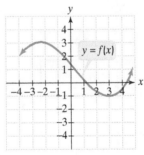

**a.** $\lim_{x \to 3} f(x)$        **b.** $f(3)$

**20.**

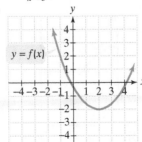

**a.** $\lim_{x \to 2} f(x)$        **b.** $f(2)$

**21.**

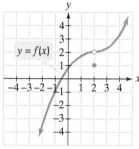

**a.** $\lim\limits_{x \to 2} f(x)$          **b.** $f(2)$

**22.**

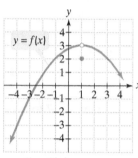

**a.** $\lim\limits_{x \to 1} f(x)$          **b.** $f(1)$

*In Exercises 23–26, use the graph and the viewing rectangle shown below the graph to find the indicated limit.*

**23.** $\lim\limits_{x \to 2}(1 - x^2)$

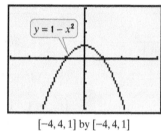

$[-4, 4, 1]$ by $[-4, 4, 1]$

**24.** $\lim\limits_{x \to -2} |2x|$

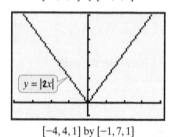

$[-4, 4, 1]$ by $[-1, 7, 1]$

**25.** $\lim\limits_{x \to -\frac{\pi}{2}} \sin x$

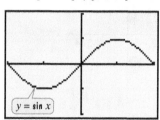

$\left[-\pi, \pi, \frac{\pi}{2}\right]$ by $[-2, 2, 1]$

**26.** $\lim\limits_{x \to -\frac{\pi}{2}} \cos x$

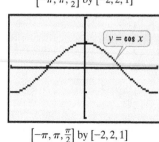

$\left[-\pi, \pi, \frac{\pi}{2}\right]$ by $[-2, 2, 1]$

*In Exercises 27–32, the graph of a function is given. Use the graph to find the indicated limits and function values, or state that the limit or function value does not exist.*

**27.**

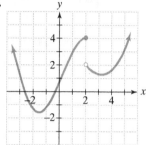

**a.** $\lim\limits_{x \to 2^-} f(x)$   **b.** $\lim\limits_{x \to 2^+} f(x)$   **c.** $\lim\limits_{x \to 2} f(x)$   **d.** $f(2)$

**28.**

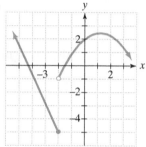

**a.** $\lim\limits_{x \to -2^-} f(x)$   **b.** $\lim\limits_{x \to -2^+} f(x)$   **c.** $\lim\limits_{x \to -2} f(x)$   **d.** $f(-2)$

**29.**

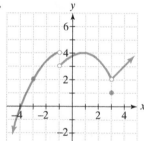

**a.** $\lim\limits_{x \to -3^-} f(x)$   **b.** $\lim\limits_{x \to -3^+} f(x)$   **c.** $\lim\limits_{x \to -3} f(x)$   **d.** $f(-3)$

**e.** $\lim\limits_{x \to -1^-} f(x)$   **f.** $\lim\limits_{x \to -1^+} f(x)$   **g.** $\lim\limits_{x \to -1} f(x)$   **h.** $f(-1)$

**i.** $\lim\limits_{x \to 3^-} f(x)$   **j.** $\lim\limits_{x \to 3^+} f(x)$   **k.** $\lim\limits_{x \to 3} f(x)$   **l.** $f(3)$

**30.**

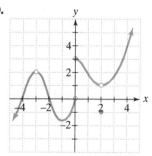

**a.** $\lim\limits_{x \to -3^-} f(x)$   **b.** $\lim\limits_{x \to -3^+} f(x)$   **c.** $\lim\limits_{x \to -3} f(x)$   **d.** $f(-3)$

**e.** $\lim\limits_{x \to 0^-} f(x)$   **f.** $\lim\limits_{x \to 0^+} f(x)$   **g.** $\lim\limits_{x \to 0} f(x)$   **h.** $f(0)$

**i.** $\lim\limits_{x \to 2^-} f(x)$   **j.** $\lim\limits_{x \to 2^+} f(x)$   **k.** $\lim\limits_{x \to 2} f(x)$   **l.** $f(2)$

**31.**

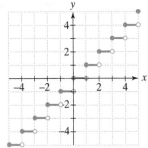

**a.** $\lim\limits_{x \to 2^-} f(x)$ **b.** $\lim\limits_{x \to 2^+} f(x)$ **c.** $\lim\limits_{x \to 2} f(x)$ **d.** $f(2)$

**e.** $\lim\limits_{x \to 2.5^-} f(x)$ **f.** $\lim\limits_{x \to 2.5^+} f(x)$ **g.** $\lim\limits_{x \to 2.5} f(x)$ **h.** $f(2.5)$

**32.**

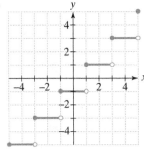

**a.** $\lim\limits_{x \to 3^-} f(x)$ **b.** $\lim\limits_{x \to 3^+} f(x)$ **c.** $\lim\limits_{x \to 3} f(x)$ **d.** $f(3)$

**e.** $\lim\limits_{x \to 3.5^-} f(x)$ **f.** $\lim\limits_{x \to 3.5^+} f(x)$ **g.** $\lim\limits_{x \to 3.5} f(x)$ **h.** $f(3.5)$

*In Exercises 33–54, graph each function. Then use your graph to find the indicated limit, or state that the limit does not exist.*

**33.** $f(x) = 2x + 1, \lim\limits_{x \to 3} f(x)$ **34.** $f(x) = 2x - 1, \lim\limits_{x \to 3} f(x)$

**35.** $f(x) = 4 - x^2, \lim\limits_{x \to -3} f(x)$ **36.** $f(x) = 9 - x^2, \lim\limits_{x \to -2} f(x)$

**37.** $f(x) = |x + 1|, \lim\limits_{x \to -1} f(x)$ **38.** $f(x) = |x + 2|, \lim\limits_{x \to -2} f(x)$

**39.** $f(x) = \dfrac{1}{x}, \lim\limits_{x \to -1} f(x)$ **40.** $f(x) = \dfrac{1}{x^2}, \lim\limits_{x \to -1} f(x)$

**41.** $f(x) = \dfrac{x^2 - 1}{x - 1}, \lim\limits_{x \to 1} f(x)$ **42.** $f(x) = \dfrac{x^2 - 100}{x - 10}, \lim\limits_{x \to 10} f(x)$

**43.** $f(x) = e^x, \lim\limits_{x \to 0} f(x)$ **44.** $f(x) = \ln x, \lim\limits_{x \to 1} f(x)$

**45.** $f(x) = \sin x, \lim\limits_{x \to \pi} f(x)$ **46.** $f(x) = \cos x, \lim\limits_{x \to \pi} f(x)$

**47.** $f(x) = \begin{cases} x + 1 & \text{if } x \neq 2 \\ 5 & \text{if } x = 2, \lim\limits_{x \to 2} f(x) \end{cases}$

**48.** $f(x) = \begin{cases} x - 1 & \text{if } x \neq 3 \\ 4 & \text{if } x = 3, \lim\limits_{x \to 3} f(x) \end{cases}$

**49.** $f(x) = \begin{cases} x + 3 & \text{if } x < 0 \\ 4 & \text{if } x \geq 0, \lim\limits_{x \to 0} f(x) \end{cases}$

**50.** $f(x) = \begin{cases} x + 4 & \text{if } x < 0 \\ 5 & \text{if } x \geq 0, \lim\limits_{x \to 0} f(x) \end{cases}$

**51.** $f(x) = \begin{cases} 2x & \text{if } x < 1 \\ x + 1 & \text{if } x \geq 1, \lim\limits_{x \to 1} f(x) \end{cases}$

**52.** $f(x) = \begin{cases} 3x & \text{if } x < 1 \\ x + 2 & \text{if } x \geq 1, \lim\limits_{x \to 1} f(x) \end{cases}$

**53.** $f(x) = \begin{cases} x + 1 & \text{if } x < 0 \\ \sin x & \text{if } x \geq 0, \lim\limits_{x \to 0} f(x) \end{cases}$

**54.** $f(x) = \begin{cases} x & \text{if } x < 0 \\ \cos x & \text{if } x \geq 0, \lim\limits_{x \to 0} f(x) \end{cases}$

## Practice Plus

*In Exercises 55–56, use the equations for the functions f and g to graph the function $y = (f \circ g)(x)$. Then use the graph of $f \circ g$ to find the indicated limit.*

**55.** $f(x) = x^2 - 5, g(x) = \sqrt{x}; \lim\limits_{x \to 2} (f \circ g)(x)$

**56.** $f(x) = x^2 + 3, g(x) = \sqrt{x}; \lim\limits_{x \to 1} (f \circ g)(x)$

*In Exercises 57–58, use the equation for the function f to find and graph the function $y = f^{-1}(x)$. Then use the graph of $f^{-1}$ to find the indicated limit.*

**57.** $f(x) = x^3 - 2; \lim\limits_{x \to 6} f^{-1}(x)$

**58.** $f(x) = x^3 - 4; \lim\limits_{x \to 4} f^{-1}(x)$

*In Exercises 59–66, use the graph of $y = f(x)$ to graph each function g. Then use the graph of g to find the indicated limit.*

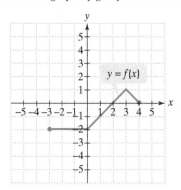

**59.** $g(x) = f(x) + 2; \lim\limits_{x \to 3} g(x)$ **60.** $g(x) = f(x) - 2; \lim\limits_{x \to 3} g(x)$

**61.** $g(x) = f(x + 3); \lim\limits_{x \to -1} g(x)$ **62.** $g(x) = f(x + 2); \lim\limits_{x \to -2^-} g(x)$

**63.** $g(x) = -f(x); \lim\limits_{x \to -3^+} g(x)$ **64.** $g(x) = -2f(x); \lim\limits_{x \to -3^+} g(x)$

**65.** $g(x) = f(2x); \lim\limits_{x \to 1} g(x)$ **66.** $g(x) = f(\tfrac{1}{2}x); \lim\limits_{x \to 1} g(x)$

## Application Exercises

**67.** You are approaching a fan located at 3 on the *x*-axis.

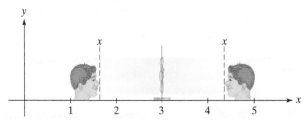

The function $f$ describes the breeze that you feel, $f(x)$, in miles per hour, when your nose is at position $x$ on the *x*-axis. Use the values in the table to solve this exercise.

| $x$ | 2.9 | 2.99 | 2.999 → ← 3.001 | 3.01 | 3.1 |
|---|---|---|---|---|---|
| $f(x)$ | 7.7 | 7.92 | 7.991 → ← 7.991 | 7.92 | 7.7 |

**a.** Find $\lim\limits_{x \to 3} f(x)$. Describe what this means in terms of the location of your nose and the breeze that you feel.

**b.** Would it be a good idea to move closer so that you actually reach $x = 3$? Describe the difference between what you feel for $\lim\limits_{x \to 3} f(x)$ and $f(3)$.

**68.** You are riding along an expressway traveling $x$ miles per hour. The function $f(x) = 0.015x^2 + x + 10$ describes the recommended safe distance, $f(x)$, in feet, between your car and other cars on the expressway. Use the values in the table below to find $\lim_{x \to 60} f(x)$. Describe what this means in terms of your car's speed and the recommended safe distance.

| $x$ | 59.9 | 59.99 | 59.999 → ← 60.001 | 60.01 | 60.1 |
|---|---|---|---|---|---|
| $f(x) = 0.015x^2 + x + 10$ | 123.72 | 123.972 | 123.997 → ← 124.003 | 124.028 | 124.28 |

*Functions can be used to model changes in intellectual abilities over one's life span. The graphs of f and g show mean scores on standardized tests measuring spatial orientation and verbal ability, respectively, as a function of age. Use the graphs of f and g to solve Exercises 69–70.*

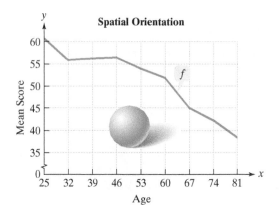

Spatial Orientation

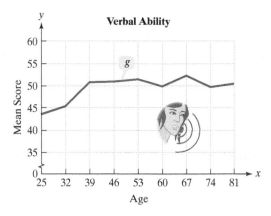

Verbal Ability

*Source:* Wade and Tavris, *Psychology Sixth Edition*, Prentice Hall, 2000

**69.** What mean score in spatial orientation is associated with a person whose age is close to 67? Use limit notation to express the answer.

**70.** What mean score in verbal ability is associated with a person whose age is close to 60? Use limit notation to express the answer.

**71.** You rent a car from a company that charges $20 per day plus $0.10 per mile. The car is driven 200 miles in the first day. The figure at the top of the next column shows the graph of the cost, $f(x)$, in dollars, as a function of the miles, $x$, that you drive the car.

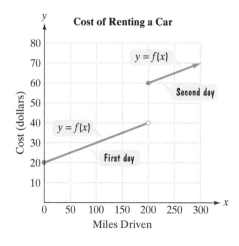

Cost of Renting a Car

**a.** Find $\lim_{x \to 100} f(x)$. Interpret the limit, referring to miles driven and cost.

**b.** For the first day only, what is the rental cost approaching as the mileage gets closer to 200?

**c.** What is the cost to rent the car at the start of the second day?

**72.** You are building a greenhouse next to your house, as shown in the figure. Because the house will be used for one side of the enclosure, only three sides will need to be enclosed. You have 60 feet of fiberglass to enclose the three walls.

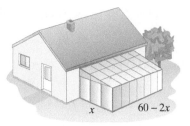

The function $f(x) = x(60 - 2x)$ describes the area of the greenhouse that you can enclose, $f(x)$, in square feet, if the width of the greenhouse is $x$ feet.

**a.** Use the table shown to find $\lim_{x \to 15} f(x)$.

| X | Y1 |
|---|---|
| 14.7 | 449.82 |
| 14.8 | 449.92 |
| 14.9 | 449.98 |
| 15 | |
| 15.1 | 449.98 |
| 15.2 | 449.92 |
| 15.3 | 449.82 |

Y1 ◙X*(60-2X)

**b.** Use the graph shown to find $\lim\limits_{x \to 15} f(x)$. Do you get the same limit as you did in part (a)? What information about the limit is shown by the graph that might not be obvious from the table?

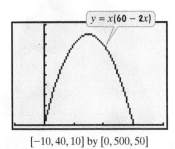

$y = x(60 - 2x)$

$[-10, 40, 10]$ by $[0, 500, 50]$

## Writing in Mathematics

**73.** Explain how to read $\lim\limits_{x \to a} f(x) = L$.

**74.** What does the limit notation $\lim\limits_{x \to a} f(x) = L$ mean?

**75.** Without showing the details, explain how to use a table to find $\lim\limits_{x \to 4} x^2$.

**76.** Explain how a graph can be used to find a limit.

**77.** When we find $\lim\limits_{x \to a} f(x)$, we do not care about the value of the function at $x = a$. Explain why this is so.

**78.** Explain how to read $\lim\limits_{x \to a^-} f(x) = L$.

**79.** What does the limit notation $\lim\limits_{x \to a^-} f(x) = L$ mean?

**80.** Explain how to read $\lim\limits_{x \to a^+} f(x) = L$.

**81.** What does the limit notation $\lim\limits_{x \to a^+} f(x) = L$ mean?

**82.** What does it mean if the limits in Exercises 79 and 81 are not both equal to the same number $L$?

## Technology Exercises

**83.** Use the $\boxed{\text{TABLE}}$ feature of your graphing utility to verify any five of the limits that you found in Exercises 5–16.

**84.** Use the $\boxed{\text{ZOOM IN}}$ feature of your graphing utility to verify any five of the limits that you found in Exercises 33–46. Zoom in on the graph of the given function, $f$, near $x = a$ to verify each limit.

*In Exercises 85–88, estimate $\lim\limits_{x \to a} f(x)$ by using the $\boxed{\text{TABLE}}$ feature of your graphing utility to create a table of values. Then use the $\boxed{\text{ZOOM IN}}$ feature to zoom in on the graph of $f$ near $x = a$ to justify or improve your estimate.*

**85.** $\lim\limits_{x \to 0} \dfrac{2^x - 1}{x}$

**86.** $\lim\limits_{x \to 4} \dfrac{\ln x - \ln 4}{x - 4}$

**87.** $\lim\limits_{x \to 1} \dfrac{x^{3/2} - 1}{x - 1}$

**88.** $\lim\limits_{x \to 0} \dfrac{x^2}{1 - \cos 2x}$

## Critical Thinking Exercises

**Make Sense?** *In Exercises 89–92, determine whether each statement makes sense or does not make sense, and explain your reasoning.*

**89.** Limits indicate that a graph can get really close to values without actually reaching them.

**90.** I'm working with a function that is undefined at 5, so $\lim\limits_{x \to 5} f(x)$ does not exist.

**91.** I'm working with a function that is undefined at 3, but defined at 2.99, 2.999, 2.9999, as well as at 3.01, 3.001, and 3.0001.

**92.** I'm working with a function for which $\lim\limits_{x \to a^-} f(x) \ne \lim\limits_{x \to a^+} f(x)$, so I cannot draw the graph of the function near $a$ without lifting my pencil off the paper.

**93.** Give an example of a function that is not defined at 2 for which $\lim\limits_{x \to 2} f(x) = 5$.

**94.** Consider the function $f(x) = 3x + 2$. As $x$ approaches 1, $f(x)$ approaches 5: $\lim\limits_{x \to 1} f(x) = 5$. Find the values of $x$ such that $f(x)$ is within 0.1 of 5 by solving

$$|f(x) - 5| < 0.1.$$

Then find the values of $x$ such that $f(x)$ is within 0.01 of 5.

**95.** Find an estimate of $3^{\pi}$ ($\pi \approx 3.14159265$) by taking a sequence of rational numbers, $x_1, x_2, x_3, \dots$ that approaches $\pi$. Obtain your estimate by evaluating $3^{x_1}, 3^{x_2}, 3^{x_3}, \dots$.

## Preview Exercises

*Exercises 96–98 will help you prepare for the material covered in the next section.*

**96. a.** Graph the piecewise function:

$$f(x) = \begin{cases} x^2 + 5 & \text{if } x < 2 \\ 3x + 1 & \text{if } x \ge 2. \end{cases}$$

**b.** Use your graph from part (a) to find each of the following limits, or indicate that the limit does not exist: $\lim\limits_{x \to 2^-} f(x)$; $\lim\limits_{x \to 2^+} f(x)$; $\lim\limits_{x \to 2} f(x)$.

**97.** Simplify: $\dfrac{x^2 - x - 6}{x - 3}$.

**98.** Rationalize the numerator: $\dfrac{\sqrt{4 + x} - 2}{x}$.

## Objectives

**1** Find limits of constant functions and the identity function.

**2** Find limits using properties of limits.

**3** Find one-sided limits using properties of limits.

**4** Find limits of fractional expressions in which the limit of the denominator is zero.

Isaac Newton

Gottfried Leibniz

Calculus was invented independently by British mathematician Isaac Newton (1642–1727) and German mathematician Gottfried Leibniz (1646–1716). Although Newton stated that limits were the basic concept in calculus, neither he nor Leibniz was able to express the idea of a limit in a precise mathematical fashion. In essence, Newton and Leibniz developed calculus into a powerful tool even though they could not fully understand why the tool worked.

A great triumph of calculus came with the work of German mathematician Karl Weierstrass (1815–1897). Weierstrass provided a precise definition of $\lim_{x \to a} f(x) = L$, placing calculus on a sound footing almost two hundred years after its invention. The properties of limits presented in this section are theorems that you will prove in calculus using this definition. In this section, you will learn to apply these properties to find limits.

**1** Find limits of constant functions and the identity function.

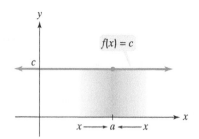

**Figure 11.8** The graph of the constant function $f(x) = c$. No matter how close $x$ is to $a$, the corresponding value of $f(x)$ is $c$.

## Limits Involving Constant Functions and the Identity Function

We frequently encounter the constant function, $f(x) = c$, and the identity function, $f(x) = x$. **Figure 11.8** shows the graph of the constant function. The graph is a horizontal line. What does this mean about the limit as $x$ approaches $a$? Regardless of how close $x$ is to $a$, the corresponding value of $f(x)$ is $c$. Thus, if $f(x) = c$, then $\lim_{x \to a} f(x) = c$.

### Limit of a Constant Function

For the constant function $f(x) = c$,

$$\lim_{x \to a} f(x) = \lim_{x \to a} c = c,$$

where $a$ is any number. In words, regardless of what number $x$ is approaching, the limit of any constant is that constant.

**EXAMPLE 1** **Finding Limits of Constant Functions**

Find the following limits:

**a.** $\lim_{x \to 4} 7$      **b.** $\lim_{x \to 0} (-5)$.

**Solution** Regardless of what number $x$ is approaching, the limit of any constant is that constant: $\lim\limits_{x \to a} c = c$. Using this formula, we find the given limits.

**a.** $\lim\limits_{x \to 4} 7 = 7$    **b.** $\lim\limits_{x \to 0} (-5) = -5$

✓ Check Point **1** Find the following limits:

**a.** $\lim\limits_{x \to 8} 11$    **b.** $\lim\limits_{x \to 0} (-9)$.

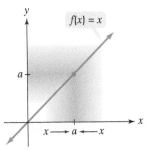

$f(x) = x$

$x \longrightarrow a \longleftarrow x$

**Figure 11.9** The graph of the identity function $f(x) = x$. No matter how close $x$ is to $a$, the corresponding value of $f(x)$ is just as close to $a$.

The graph of the identity function, $f(x) = x$, is shown in **Figure 11.9**. Each input for this function is associated with an identical output. What does this mean about the limit as $x$ approaches $a$? For any value of $a$, as $x$ gets closer to $a$, the corresponding value of $f(x)$ is just as close to $a$. Thus, if $f(x) = x$, then $\lim\limits_{x \to a} f(x) = a$.

### Limit of the Identity Function

For the identity function $f(x) = x$,

$$\lim_{x \to a} f(x) = \lim_{x \to a} x = a,$$

where $a$ is any number. In words, the limit of $x$ as $x$ approaches any number is that number.

(EXAMPLE 2) **Finding Limits of the Identity Function**

Find the following limits:

**a.** $\lim\limits_{x \to 7} x$    **b.** $\lim\limits_{x \to -\pi} x$.

**Solution** We use the formula $\lim\limits_{x \to a} x = a$. The number that $x$ is approaching is also the limit.

**a.** $\lim\limits_{x \to 7} x = 7$    **b.** $\lim\limits_{x \to -\pi} x = -\pi$

✓ Check Point **2** Find the following limits:

**a.** $\lim\limits_{x \to 19} x$    **b.** $\lim\limits_{x \to -\sqrt{2}} x$.

**②** Find limits using properties of limits.

## Properties of Limits

How do we find the limit of a sum, such as

$$\lim_{x \to 5} (x + 7)?$$

We find the limit of each function in the sum:

$$\lim_{x \to 5} x = 5 \quad \text{and} \quad \lim_{x \to 5} 7 = 7.$$

Use the formula $\lim\limits_{x \to a} x = a$.

Use the formula $\lim\limits_{x \to a} c = c$.

Then we add each of these limits. Thus,

$$\lim_{x \to 5} (x + 7) = \lim_{x \to 5} x + \lim_{x \to 5} 7 = 5 + 7 = 12.$$

This is an application of a limit property involving the limit of a sum.

## The Feud Over Who Invented Calculus

"How dare Leibniz publish a book on calculus!" fumed Isaac Newton. "He stole my ideas when he was in England. This will not pass easily."

Although Newton and Leibniz invented calculus independently, Newton's overwhelming fear of criticism kept him from publishing. Leibniz published his work on calculus in 1684; Newton waited over 20 years after he invented calculus and did not publish until 1687. Newton was dismayed that he did not publish his version first. Leibniz was accused of plagiarism in a report written by members of the Royal Society in England. The author of the report was not a matter of public record, for Newton himself had written most of it. Newton's accusations against Leibniz set off a bitter dispute between British mathematicians and mathematicians on Continental Europe that lasted over 100 years.

### The Limit of a Sum

If $\lim_{x \to a} f(x) = L$ and $\lim_{x \to a} g(x) = M$, then

$$\lim_{x \to a} [f(x) + g(x)] = \lim_{x \to a} f(x) + \lim_{x \to a} g(x) = L + M.$$

In words, the limit of the sum of two functions equals the sum of their limits.

**EXAMPLE 3** Finding the Limit of a Sum

Find: $\lim_{x \to -4} (x + 9)$.

**Solution**  The two functions in this limit problem are $f(x) = x$ and $g(x) = 9$. We seek the limit of the sum of these functions.

$$\lim_{x \to -4} (x + 9) = \lim_{x \to -4} x + \lim_{x \to -4} 9 \quad \text{The limit of a sum is the sum of the limits.}$$

$$= -4 + 9 \quad \lim_{x \to a} x = a \text{ and } \lim_{x \to a} c = c.$$

$$= 5$$

**Check Point 3** Find: $\lim_{x \to -3} (x + 16)$.

In calculus, you will prove the following property involving the limit of the difference of two functions:

### The Limit of a Difference

If $\lim_{x \to a} f(x) = L$ and $\lim_{x \to a} g(x) = M$, then

$$\lim_{x \to a} [f(x) - g(x)] = \lim_{x \to a} f(x) - \lim_{x \to a} g(x) = L - M.$$

In words, the limit of the difference of two functions equals the difference of their limits.

**EXAMPLE 4** Finding the Limit of a Difference

Find: $\lim_{x \to 5} (12 - x)$.

**Solution**  The two functions in this limit problem are $f(x) = 12$ and $g(x) = x$. We seek the limit of the difference of these functions.

$$\lim_{x \to 5} (12 - x) = \lim_{x \to 5} 12 - \lim_{x \to 5} x \quad \text{The limit of a difference is the difference of the limits.}$$

$$= 12 - 5 \quad \lim_{x \to a} c = c \text{ and } \lim_{x \to a} x = a.$$

$$= 7$$

**Check Point 4** Find: $\lim_{x \to 14} (19 - x)$.

Now we consider a property that will enable you to find the limit of the product of two functions.

## The Limit of a Product

If $\lim\limits_{x \to a} f(x) = L$ and $\lim\limits_{x \to a} g(x) = M$, then

$$\lim\limits_{x \to a}[f(x) \cdot g(x)] = \lim\limits_{x \to a} f(x) \cdot \lim\limits_{x \to a} g(x) = LM.$$

In words, the limit of the product of two functions equals the product of their limits.

---

( **EXAMPLE 5** )  **Finding the Limit of a Product**

Find:  $\lim\limits_{x \to 5}(-6x)$.

**Solution**  The two functions in this limit problem are $f(x) = -6$ and $g(x) = x$. We seek the limit of the product of these functions.

$$\lim\limits_{x \to 5}(-6x) = \lim\limits_{x \to 5}(-6) \cdot \lim\limits_{x \to 5} x \qquad \text{The limit of a product is the product of the limits.}$$

$$= -6 \cdot 5 \qquad \text{lim } c = c \text{ and } \lim\limits_{x \to a} x = a.$$

$$= -30$$

⊘ Check Point **5**  Find:  $\lim\limits_{x \to 7}(-10x)$.

---

( **EXAMPLE 6** )  **Finding Limits Using Properties of Limits**

Find the following limits:

**a.**  $\lim\limits_{x \to -3}(7x - 4)$    **b.**  $\lim\limits_{x \to 5} 6x^2$.

**Solution**

**a.**  $\lim\limits_{x \to -3}(7x - 4) = \lim\limits_{x \to -3}(7x) - \lim\limits_{x \to -3} 4$   The limit of a difference is the difference of the limits.

$$= \lim\limits_{x \to -3} 7 \cdot \lim\limits_{x \to -3} x - \lim\limits_{x \to -3} 4 \qquad \text{The limit of a product is the product of the limits.}$$

$$= 7(-3) - 4 \qquad \text{lim } c = c \text{ and } \lim\limits_{x \to a} x = a.$$

$$= -21 - 4$$

$$= -25$$

**b.**  $\lim\limits_{x \to 5} 6x^2 = \lim\limits_{x \to 5} 6 \cdot \lim\limits_{x \to 5} x^2$   The limit of a product is the product of the limits.

$$= 6 \cdot \lim\limits_{x \to 5}(x \cdot x) \qquad \text{lim } c = c$$

$$= 6 \cdot \lim\limits_{x \to 5} x \cdot \lim\limits_{x \to 5} x \qquad \text{The limit of a product is the product of the limits.}$$

$$= 6 \cdot 5 \cdot 5 \qquad \lim\limits_{x \to a} x = a$$

$$= 150$$

⊘ Check Point **6**  Find the following limits:

**a.**  $\lim\limits_{x \to -5}(3x - 7)$    **b.**  $\lim\limits_{x \to 3} 8x^2$.

The procedure used to find $\lim\limits_{x\to 5} 6x^2$ in Example 6(b) can be used to determine the limit of any monomial function in the form $f(x) = b_n x^n$, where $n$ is a positive integer and $b_n$ is a constant.

$$\lim_{x\to a} b_n x^n = \lim_{x\to a} b_n \cdot \lim_{x\to a} x^n \qquad \text{The limit of a product is the product of the limits.}$$

$$= b_n \cdot \lim_{x\to a} \underbrace{(x \cdot x \cdot x \cdot \cdots \cdot x)}_{} \qquad \lim_{x\to a} c = c$$

By definition, $x^n$ contains $n$ factors of $x$.

$$= b_n \cdot \underbrace{\lim_{x\to a} x \cdot \lim_{x\to a} x \cdot \lim_{x\to a} x \cdot \cdots \cdot \lim_{x\to a} x}_{} \qquad \text{The limit of the product containing } n \text{ factors is the product of the limits.}$$

There are $n$ factors of $\lim\limits_{x\to a} x$.

$$= b_n \cdot \underbrace{a \cdot a \cdot a \cdot \cdots \cdot a}_{} \qquad \lim_{x\to a} x = a$$

There are $n$ factors of $a$.

$$= b_n a^n$$

This is the monomial function $f(x) = b_n x^n$ evaluated at $a$.

## Limit of a Monomial

If $n$ is a positive integer and $b_n$ is a constant, then

$$\lim_{x\to a} b_n x^n = b_n a^n$$

for any number $a$. In words, the limit of a monomial as $x$ approaches $a$ is the monomial evaluated at $a$.

**(EXAMPLE 7) Finding the Limit of a Monomial**

Find: $\lim\limits_{x\to 2} (-6x^4)$.

**Solution** The limit of the monomial $-6x^4$ as $x$ approaches 2 is the monomial evaluated at 2. Thus, we find the limit by substituting 2 for $x$.

$$\lim_{x\to 2} (-6x^4) = -6 \cdot 2^4 = -6 \cdot 16 = -96 \qquad \bullet$$

⊘ Check Point **7** Find: $\lim\limits_{x\to 2} (-7x^3)$.

How do we find the limit of a polynomial function

$$f(x) = b_n x^n + b_{n-1} x^{n-1} + \cdots + b_1 x + b_0$$

as $x$ approaches $a$? A polynomial is a sum of monomials. Thus, the limit of a polynomial is the sum of the limits of its monomials.

$$\lim_{x\to a} f(x) = \lim_{x\to a} (b_n x^n + b_{n-1} x^{n-1} + \cdots + b_1 x + b_0) \qquad f \text{ is a polynomial function.}$$

$$= \lim_{x\to a} b_n x^n + \lim_{x\to a} b_{n-1} x^{n-1} + \cdots + \lim_{x\to a} b_1 x + \lim_{x\to a} b_0 \qquad \text{The limit of a sum is the sum of the limits.}$$

$$= b_n a^n + b_{n-1} a^{n-1} + \cdots + b_1 a + b_0 \qquad \text{Find limits by evaluating monomials at } a. \text{ Find the last limit in the sum using } \lim_{x\to a} c = c \text{ with } c = b_0.$$

This is the polynomial function $f(x) = b_n x^n + b_{n-1} x^{n-1} + \cdots + b_1 x + b_0$ evaluated at $a$.

$$= f(a)$$

### Limit of a Polynomial

If $f$ is a polynomial function, then

$$\lim_{x \to a} f(x) = f(a)$$

for any number $a$. In words, the limit of a polynomial as $x$ approaches $a$ is the polynomial evaluated at $a$.

( **EXAMPLE 8** ) **Finding the Limit of a Polynomial**

Find: $\lim\limits_{x \to 3}(4x^3 + 2x^2 - 6x + 5)$.

**Solution** The limit of the polynomial $4x^3 + 2x^2 - 6x + 5$ as $x$ approaches 3 is the polynomial evaluated at 3. Thus, we find the limit by substituting 3 for $x$.

$$\lim_{x \to 3}(4x^3 + 2x^2 - 6x + 5)$$
$$= 4 \cdot 3^3 + 2 \cdot 3^2 - 6 \cdot 3 + 5$$
$$= 4 \cdot 27 + 2 \cdot 9 - 6 \cdot 3 + 5$$
$$= 108 + 18 - 18 + 5$$
$$= 113$$

✓ Check Point **8** Find: $\lim\limits_{x \to 2}(7x^3 + 3x^2 - 5x + 3)$.

A linear function, $f(x) = mx + b$, is a polynomial function of degree one. This means that the limit of a linear function as $x$ approaches $a$ is the linear function evaluated at $a$:

$$\lim_{x \to a}(mx + b) = ma + b.$$

For example,

$$\lim_{x \to 4}(3x - 7) = 3 \cdot 4 - 7 = 12 - 7 = 5.$$

The next limit property involves the limit of a function to a power, such as

$$\lim_{x \to 2}(x^2 + 2x - 3)^4.$$

To find such a limit, first find $\lim\limits_{x \to 2}(x^2 + 2x - 3)$:

$$\lim_{x \to 2}(x^2 + 2x - 3) = 2^2 + 2 \cdot 2 - 3 = 4 + 4 - 3 = 5.$$

The limit that we seek is found by taking this limit, 5, and raising it to the fourth power. Thus,

$$\lim_{x \to 2}(x^2 + 2x - 3)^4 = \left[\lim_{x \to 2}(x^2 + 2x - 3)\right]^4 = 5^4 = 625.$$

### The Limit of a Power

If $\lim\limits_{x \to a} f(x) = L$ and $n$ is a positive integer, then

$$\lim_{x \to a}[f(x)]^n = \left[\lim_{x \to a} f(x)\right]^n = L^n.$$

In words, the limit of a function to a power is found by taking the limit of the function and then raising this limit to the power.

## Calculus in Japan

Mathematics was developed simultaneously in various cultures in all parts of the world. Seki Kowa, a 17th-century Japanese mathematician, is credited with the invention of calculus in Japan. The illustration shown below was drawn in 1670 by a pupil of Seki Kowa. It measures the circle's area with a series of rectangles.

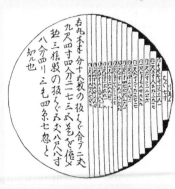

EXAMPLE 9 **Finding the Limit of a Power**

Find: $\lim\limits_{x \to 5} (2x - 7)^3$.

**Solution** The limit of the linear function $f(x) = 2x - 7$ as $x$ approaches 5 is the linear function evaluated at 5. Because this function is raised to the third power, the limit that we seek is the limit of the linear function raised to the third power.

$$\lim\limits_{x \to 5} (2x - 7)^3 = \left[ \lim\limits_{x \to 5} (2x - 7) \right]^3 = (2 \cdot 5 - 7)^3 = 3^3 = 27$$

Check Point **9** Find: $\lim\limits_{x \to 4} (3x - 5)^3$.

How do we find the limit of a root? Recall that if $\sqrt[n]{L}$ represents a real number and $n \geq 2$, then

$$\sqrt[n]{L} = L^{1/n}.$$

Because a root is a power, we find the limit of a root using a similar procedure for finding the limit of a power.

### The Limit of a Root

If $\lim\limits_{x \to a} f(x) = L$ and $n$ is a positive integer greater than or equal to 2, then

$$\lim\limits_{x \to a} \sqrt[n]{f(x)} = \sqrt[n]{\lim\limits_{x \to a} f(x)} = \sqrt[n]{L}$$

provided that all roots represent real numbers. In words, the limit of the $n$th root of a function is found by taking the limit of the function and then taking the $n$th root of this limit.

EXAMPLE 10 **Finding the Limit of a Root**

Find: $\lim\limits_{x \to -2} \sqrt{4x^2 + 5}$.

**Solution** The limit of the quadratic (polynomial) function $f(x) = 4x^2 + 5$ as $x$ approaches $-2$ is the function evaluated at $-2$. Because we have the square root of this function, the limit that we seek is the square root of the limit of the quadratic function.

$$\lim\limits_{x \to -2} \sqrt{4x^2 + 5} = \sqrt{\lim\limits_{x \to -2} (4x^2 + 5)} = \sqrt{4(-2)^2 + 5} = \sqrt{16 + 5} = \sqrt{21}$$

Check Point **10** Find: $\lim\limits_{x \to -1} \sqrt{6x^2 - 4}$.

We have considered limits of sums, differences, products, and roots. We conclude with a property that deals with the limit of a quotient.

### The Limit of a Quotient

If $\lim\limits_{x \to a} f(x) = L$ and $\lim\limits_{x \to a} g(x) = M, M \neq 0$, then

$$\lim\limits_{x \to a} \frac{f(x)}{g(x)} = \frac{\lim\limits_{x \to a} f(x)}{\lim\limits_{x \to a} g(x)} = \frac{L}{M}, M \neq 0.$$

In words, the limit of the quotient of two functions equals the quotient of their limits, **provided that the limit of the denominator is not zero.**

Before possibly applying the quotient property, begin by finding the limit of the denominator. If this limit is not zero, you can apply the quotient property. If this limit is zero, the quotient property cannot be used.

( **EXAMPLE 11** ) **Finding the Limit of a Quotient**

Find: $\lim\limits_{x \to 1} \dfrac{x^3 - 3x^2 + 7}{2x - 5}$.

**Solution** The two functions in this limit problem are $f(x) = x^3 - 3x^2 + 7$ and $g(x) = 2x - 5$. We seek the limit of the quotient of these functions. Can we use the quotient property for limits? We answer the question by finding the limit of the denominator, $g(x)$.

$$\lim\limits_{x \to 1} (2x - 5) = 2 \cdot 1 - 5 = -3$$

Because the limit of the denominator is not zero, we can apply the quotient property for limits. The limit of the quotient is the quotient of the limits.

$$\lim\limits_{x \to 1} \frac{x^3 - 3x^2 + 7}{2x - 5} = \frac{\lim\limits_{x \to 1}(x^3 - 3x^2 + 7)}{\lim\limits_{x \to 1}(2x - 5)} = \frac{1^3 - 3 \cdot 1^2 + 7}{2 \cdot 1 - 5} = \frac{5}{-3} = -\frac{5}{3} \quad \bullet$$

⊘ Check Point **11** Find: $\lim\limits_{x \to 2} \dfrac{x^2 - 4x + 1}{3x - 5}$.

We've considered a number of limit properties. Let's take a moment to summarize these properties.

## Properties of Limits

**Formulas for Finding Limits**

**1.** $\lim\limits_{x \to a} c = c$

**2.** $\lim\limits_{x \to a} x = a$

**3.** If $f$ is a polynomial (linear, quadratic, cubic, etc.) function, $\lim\limits_{x \to a} f(x) = f(a)$.

**Limits of Sums, Differences, Products, Powers, Roots, and Quotients**

If $\lim\limits_{x \to a} f(x) = L$ and $\lim\limits_{x \to a} g(x) = M$, then

**4.** $\lim\limits_{x \to a}[f(x) + g(x)] = \lim\limits_{x \to a} f(x) + \lim\limits_{x \to a} g(x) = L + M$.

**5.** $\lim\limits_{x \to a}[f(x) - g(x)] = \lim\limits_{x \to a} f(x) - \lim\limits_{x \to a} g(x) = L - M$.

**6.** $\lim\limits_{x \to a}[f(x) \cdot g(x)] = \lim\limits_{x \to a} f(x) \cdot \lim\limits_{x \to a} g(x) = LM$.

**7.** $\lim\limits_{x \to a}[f(x)]^n = [\lim\limits_{x \to a} f(x)]^n = L^n$, where $n \geq 2$ is an integer.

**8.** $\lim\limits_{x \to a} \sqrt[n]{f(x)} = \sqrt[n]{\lim\limits_{x \to a} f(x)} = \sqrt[n]{L}$, where $n \geq 2$ is an integer and all roots represent real numbers.

**9.** $\lim\limits_{x \to a} \dfrac{f(x)}{g(x)} = \dfrac{\lim\limits_{x \to a} f(x)}{\lim\limits_{x \to a} g(x)} = \dfrac{L}{M}, M \neq 0$.

③ Find one-sided limits using properties of limits.

## Properties of Limits and Piecewise Functions

In Section 11.1, we used graphs of piecewise functions to find one-sided limits. We can now find such limits by applying properties of limits to the appropriate part of a piecewise function's equation.

**EXAMPLE 12** **Using Limit Properties to Find One-Sided Limits**

Consider the piecewise function defined by

$$f(x) = \begin{cases} x^2 + 5 & \text{if} \quad x < 2 \\ 3x + 1 & \text{if} \quad x \geq 2. \end{cases}$$

Find each of the following limits, or state that the limit does not exist:

**a.** $\lim\limits_{x \to 2^-} f(x)$  **b.** $\lim\limits_{x \to 2^+} f(x)$  **c.** $\lim\limits_{x \to 2} f(x)$.

**Solution**

**a.** To find $\lim\limits_{x \to 2^-} f(x)$, we look at values of $f(x)$ when $x$ is close to 2, but less than 2. Because $x$ is less than 2, we use the first line of the piecewise function's equation, $f(x) = x^2 + 5$.

$$\lim_{x \to 2^-} f(x) = \lim_{x \to 2^-} (x^2 + 5) = 2^2 + 5 = 9$$

**b.** To find $\lim\limits_{x \to 2^+} f(x)$, we look at values of $f(x)$ when $x$ is close to 2, but greater than 2. Because $x$ is greater than 2, we use the second line of the piecewise function's equation, $f(x) = 3x + 1$.

$$\lim_{x \to 2^+} f(x) = \lim_{x \to 2^+} (3x + 1) = 3 \cdot 2 + 1 = 7$$

**c.** We found that

$$\lim_{x \to 2^-} f(x) = 9 \qquad \text{and} \qquad \lim_{x \to 2^+} f(x) = 7.$$

> The limit as x approaches 2 from the left equals 9.

> The limit as x approaches 2 from the right equals 7.

These one-sided limits are illustrated in **Figure 11.10**. Because the left- and right-hand limits are unequal, $\lim\limits_{x \to 2} f(x)$ does not exist. ●

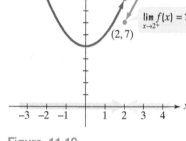

$f(x) = x^2 + 5, x < 2$

$f(x) = 3x + 1, x \geq 2$

$\lim\limits_{x \to 2^-} f(x) = 9$

$(2, 9)$

$\lim\limits_{x \to 2^+} f(x) = 7$

$(2, 7)$

**Figure 11.10**

✓ **Check Point 12** Consider the piecewise function defined by

$$f(x) = \begin{cases} -1 & \text{if} \quad x < 1 \\ \sqrt[3]{2x - 1} & \text{if} \quad x \geq 1. \end{cases}$$

Find each of the following limits, or state that the limit does not exist:

**a.** $\lim\limits_{x \to 1^-} f(x)$  **b.** $\lim\limits_{x \to 1^+} f(x)$  **c.** $\lim\limits_{x \to 1} f(x)$.

④ Find limits of fractional expressions in which the limit of the denominator is zero.

## Strategies for Finding Limits When the Limit of the Denominator is Zero

When taking the limit of a fractional expression in which the limit of the denominator is zero, the quotient property for limits cannot be used. In such cases, it is necessary to rewrite the expression before the limit can be found. Factoring is one technique that can be used to rewrite an expression.

**EXAMPLE 13** **Using Factoring to Find a Limit**

Find: $\lim\limits_{x \to 3} \dfrac{x^2 - x - 6}{x - 3}$.

**Solution** The limit of the denominator is zero:

$$\lim_{x \to 3} (x - 3) = 3 - 3 = 0.$$

## Study Tip

Avoid this common error:

**INCORRECT!**

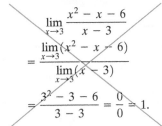

$$\lim_{x \to 3} \frac{x^2 - x - 6}{x - 3}$$

$$= \frac{\lim_{x \to 3}(x^2 - x - 6)}{\lim_{x \to 3}(x - 3)}$$

$$= \frac{3^2 - 3 - 6}{3 - 3} = \frac{0}{0} = 1.$$

Do not use the quotient property if the limit of the denominator is zero. Furthermore, division by zero is not permitted: $\frac{0}{0}$ is *not* equal to 1.

Thus, the quotient property for limits cannot be used. Instead, try simplifying the expression using factoring:

$$\frac{x^2 - x - 6}{x - 3} = \frac{(x - 3)(x + 2)}{x - 3}.$$

We seek the limit of this expression as $x$ approaches 3. Because $x$ is close to 3, but not equal to 3, the common factor in the numerator and denominator, $x - 3$, is not equal to zero. With $x - 3 \neq 0$, we can divide the numerator and denominator by $x - 3$. Cancel the common factor, $x - 3$, and then take the limit.

$$\lim_{x \to 3} \frac{x^2 - x - 6}{x - 3} = \lim_{x \to 3} \frac{\cancel{(x - 3)}(x + 2)}{\cancel{x - 3}} = \lim_{x \to 3}(x + 2) = 3 + 2 = 5 \quad \bullet$$

The graph of $f(x) = \dfrac{x^2 - x - 6}{x - 3}$ is shown in **Figure 11.11**. The hole in the graph at $x = 3$ shows that $f(3)$ is undefined. However, as $x$ approaches 3, the graph shows that the values of $f$ get closer to 5. This verifies the limit that we found in Example 13:

$$\lim_{x \to 3} \frac{x^2 - x - 6}{x - 3} = 5.$$

**Check Point 13** Find: $\lim_{x \to 1} \dfrac{x^2 + 2x - 3}{x - 1}$.

Rationalizing the numerator or denominator of a fractional expression is another technique that can be used to find a limit when the limit of the denominator is zero.

**EXAMPLE 14** Rationalizing a Numerator to Find a Limit

Find: $\lim_{x \to 0} \dfrac{\sqrt{4 + x} - 2}{x}$.

**Solution** As $x$ approaches 0, the denominator of the expression approaches zero. Thus, the quotient property for limits cannot be used. Instead, try rewriting the expression by rationalizing the numerator. If we multiply the numerator and denominator by $\sqrt{4 + x} + 2$, the numerator will not contain radicals.

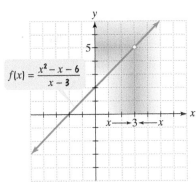

**Figure 11.11** As $x$ approaches 3, values of $f$ get closer to 5:

$$\lim_{x \to 3} \frac{x^2 - x - 6}{x - 3} = 5.$$

$$\lim_{x \to 0} \frac{\sqrt{4 + x} - 2}{x}$$

$$= \lim_{x \to 0} \frac{\sqrt{4 + x} - 2}{x} \cdot \frac{\sqrt{4 + x} + 2}{\sqrt{4 + x} + 2} \qquad \text{Rationalize the numerator.}$$

$$= \lim_{x \to 0} \frac{\left(\sqrt{4 + x}\right)^2 - 2^2}{x\left(\sqrt{4 + x} + 2\right)} \qquad \left(\sqrt{a} - \sqrt{b}\right)\left(\sqrt{a} + \sqrt{b}\right) = \left(\sqrt{a}\right)^2 - \left(\sqrt{b}\right)^2$$

$$= \lim_{x \to 0} \frac{4 + x - 4}{x\left(\sqrt{4 + x} + 2\right)} \qquad \left(\sqrt{4 + x}\right)^2 = 4 + x$$

$$= \lim_{x \to 0} \frac{x}{x\left(\sqrt{4 + x} + 2\right)} \qquad \text{Simplify: } 4 + x - 4 = x.$$

$$= \lim_{x \to 0} \frac{1}{\sqrt{4 + x} + 2} \qquad \begin{array}{l}\text{Divide both the numerator and denominator by } x. \\ \text{This is permitted because } x \text{ approaches 0, but is} \\ \text{not equal to 0.}\end{array}$$

$$= \frac{\lim_{x \to 0} 1}{\sqrt{\lim_{x \to 0}(4 + x)} + \lim_{x \to 0} 2} \qquad \text{Use limit properties.}$$

$$= \frac{1}{\sqrt{4 + 0} + 2} \qquad \text{Take the limits.}$$

$$= \frac{1}{2 + 2} = \frac{1}{4} \qquad \text{Simplify.}$$

⌀ Check Point 14 Find: $\lim_{x \to 0} \dfrac{\sqrt{9 + x} - 3}{x}$.

# Exercise Set 11.2

## Practice Exercises

*In Exercises 1–42, use properties of limits to find the indicated limit. It may be necessary to rewrite an expression before limit properties can be applied.*

**1.** $\lim_{x \to 2} 8$

**2.** $\lim_{x \to 3}(-6)$

**3.** $\lim_{x \to 2} x$

**4.** $\lim_{x \to 3} x$

**5.** $\lim_{x \to 6}(3x - 4)$

**6.** $\lim_{x \to 7}(4x - 3)$

**7.** $\lim_{x \to -2} 7x^2$

**8.** $\lim_{x \to -3} 5x^2$

**9.** $\lim_{x \to 5}(x^2 - 3x - 4)$

**10.** $\lim_{x \to 6}(x^2 - 4x - 7)$

**11.** $\lim_{x \to 2}(5x - 8)^3$

**12.** $\lim_{x \to 4}(6x - 21)^3$

**13.** $\lim_{x \to 1}(2x^2 - 3x + 5)^2$

**14.** $\lim_{x \to 2}(2x^2 + 3x - 1)^2$

**15.** $\lim_{x \to -4} \sqrt{x^2 + 9}$

**16.** $\lim_{x \to -1} \sqrt{5x^2 + 4}$

**17.** $\lim_{x \to 5} \dfrac{x}{x + 1}$

**18.** $\lim_{x \to 2} \dfrac{3x}{x - 4}$

**19.** $\lim_{x \to 2} \dfrac{x^2 - 1}{x - 1}$

**20.** $\lim_{x \to 3} \dfrac{x^2 - 4}{x - 2}$

**21.** $\lim_{x \to 1} \dfrac{x^2 - 1}{x - 1}$

**22.** $\lim_{x \to 2} \dfrac{x^2 - 4}{x - 2}$

**23.** $\lim_{x \to 2} \dfrac{2x - 4}{x - 2}$

**24.** $\lim_{x \to 3} \dfrac{4x - 12}{x - 3}$

**25.** $\lim_{x \to 1} \dfrac{x^2 + 2x - 3}{x^2 - 1}$

**26.** $\lim_{x \to 3} \dfrac{x^2 - x - 6}{x^2 - 9}$

**27.** $\lim_{x \to 2} \dfrac{x^3 - 2x^2 + 4x - 8}{x^4 - 2x^3 + x - 2}$

**28.** $\lim_{x \to -1} \dfrac{x^3 + 2x^2 + x}{x^4 + x^3 + 2x + 2}$

**29.** $\lim_{x \to 0} \dfrac{\sqrt{1 + x} - 1}{x}$

**30.** $\lim_{x \to 0} \dfrac{\sqrt{16 + x} - 4}{x}$

**31.** $\lim_{x \to 2}\left[(x + 1)^2(3x - 1)^3\right]$

**32.** $\lim_{x \to -1}\left[(x + 2)^3(3x + 2)\right]$

**33.** $\lim_{x \to 4} \dfrac{\sqrt{x} - 2}{x - 4}$

**34.** $\lim_{x \to 9} \dfrac{\sqrt{x} - 3}{x - 9}$

**35.** $\lim_{x \to 2} \dfrac{\dfrac{1}{x} - \dfrac{1}{2}}{x - 2}$

**36.** $\lim_{x \to 3} \dfrac{\dfrac{1}{x} - \dfrac{1}{3}}{x - 3}$

**37.** $\lim_{x \to 4} \dfrac{\sqrt{x} + 5}{x - 5}$

**38.** $\lim_{x \to 9} \dfrac{\sqrt{x} + 10}{x - 10}$

**39.** $\lim_{x \to 0} \dfrac{\dfrac{1}{x + 3} - \dfrac{1}{3}}{x}$

**40.** $\lim_{x \to 0} \dfrac{\dfrac{1}{x + 4} - \dfrac{1}{4}}{x}$

**41.** $\lim_{x \to 2} \dfrac{x^2 - 4}{x^3 - 8}$

**42.** $\lim_{x \to 1} \dfrac{x^2 - 1}{x^3 - 1}$

*In Exercises 43–50, a piecewise function is given. Use properties of limits to find the indicated limit, or state that the limit does not exist.*

**43.** $f(x) = \begin{cases} x + 5 & \text{if } x < 1 \\ x + 7 & \text{if } x \geq 1 \end{cases}$

   **a.** $\lim_{x \to 1^-} f(x)$    **b.** $\lim_{x \to 1^+} f(x)$    **c.** $\lim_{x \to 1} f(x)$

**44.** $f(x) = \begin{cases} x + 6 & \text{if } x < 1 \\ x + 9 & \text{if } x \geq 1 \end{cases}$

   **a.** $\lim_{x \to 1^-} f(x)$    **b.** $\lim_{x \to 1^+} f(x)$    **c.** $\lim_{x \to 1} f(x)$

**45.** $f(x) = \begin{cases} x^2 + 5 & \text{if } x < 2 \\ x^3 + 1 & \text{if } x \geq 2 \end{cases}$

   **a.** $\lim_{x \to 2^-} f(x)$    **b.** $\lim_{x \to 2^+} f(x)$    **c.** $\lim_{x \to 2} f(x)$

**46.** $f(x) = \begin{cases} x^2 + 6 & \text{if } x < 2 \\ x^3 + 2 & \text{if } x \geq 2 \end{cases}$

   **a.** $\lim_{x \to 2^-} f(x)$    **b.** $\lim_{x \to 2^+} f(x)$    **c.** $\lim_{x \to 2} f(x)$

**47.** $f(x) = \begin{cases} \dfrac{x^2 - 9}{x - 3} & \text{if } x \neq 3 \\ 5 & \text{if } x = 3 \end{cases}$

   **a.** $\lim_{x \to 3^-} f(x)$    **b.** $\lim_{x \to 3^+} f(x)$    **c.** $\lim_{x \to 3} f(x)$

**48.** $f(x) = \begin{cases} \dfrac{x^2 - 16}{x - 4} & \text{if } x \neq 4 \\ 7 & \text{if } x = 4 \end{cases}$

   **a.** $\lim_{x \to 4^-} f(x)$    **b.** $\lim_{x \to 4^+} f(x)$    **c.** $\lim_{x \to 4} f(x)$

**49.** $f(x) = \begin{cases} 1 - x & \text{if } x < 1 \\ 2 & \text{if } x = 1 \\ x^2 - 1 & \text{if } x > 1 \end{cases}$

   **a.** $\lim_{x \to 1^-} f(x)$    **b.** $\lim_{x \to 1^+} f(x)$    **c.** $\lim_{x \to 1} f(x)$

**50.** $f(x) = \begin{cases} 4 - x & \text{if } x < 1 \\ 2 & \text{if } x = 1 \\ x^2 + 2 & \text{if } x > 1 \end{cases}$

   **a.** $\lim_{x \to 1^-} f(x)$    **b.** $\lim_{x \to 1^+} f(x)$    **c.** $\lim_{x \to 1} f(x)$

## Practice Plus

**51.** Let $f(x) = x^3 - x^2 + 5x - 1$ and $g(x) = 2$. Find $\lim_{x \to 3}(f \circ g)(x)$ and $\lim_{x \to 3}(g \circ f)(x)$.

**52.** Let $f(x) = x^3 + x^2 - 6x - 1$ and $g(x) = 3$. Find $\lim_{x \to 4}(f \circ g)(x)$ and $\lim_{x \to 4}(g \circ f)(x)$.

**53.** Let $f(x) = \dfrac{2}{x}$ and $g(x) = \dfrac{3}{x-1}$.
Find $\lim\limits_{x \to 1}(f \circ g)(x)$ and $\lim\limits_{x \to 1}(g \circ f)(x)$.

**54.** Let $f(x) = \dfrac{4}{x-1}$ and $g(x) = \dfrac{1}{x+2}$.
Find $\lim\limits_{x \to 1}(f \circ g)(x)$ and $\lim\limits_{x \to 1}(g \circ f)(x)$.

**55.** Let $f(x) = x^2 + 4, x \geq 0$. Find $\lim\limits_{x \to 8} f^{-1}(x)$.

**56.** Let $f(x) = x^2 + 9, x \geq 0$. Find $\lim\limits_{x \to 25} f^{-1}(x)$.

**57.** Let $f(x) = \dfrac{2x+1}{x-1}$. Find $\lim\limits_{x \to 4} f^{-1}(x)$.

**58.** Let $f(x) = \dfrac{2x+3}{x+4}$. Find $\lim\limits_{x \to 5} f^{-1}(x)$.

## Application Exercises

*In Albert Einstein's special theory of relativity, time slows down and length in the direction of motion decreases from the point of view of an observer watching an object moving at velocities approaching the speed of light. (The speed of light is approximately 186,000 miles per second. At this speed, a beam of light can travel around the world about seven times in a single second.) Einstein's theory, verified with experiments in atomic physics, forms the basis of Exercises 59–60.*

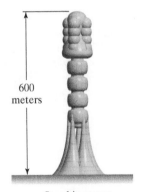

600 meters

Starship at rest

84 meters

Change in starship's length
when moving at 99% of light's speed
when viewed by an observer

**59.** The formula

$$L = L_0 \sqrt{1 - \dfrac{v^2}{c^2}}$$

expresses the length, $L$, of a starship moving at velocity $v$ with respect to an observer on Earth, where $L_0$ is the length of the starship at rest and $c$ is the speed of light.

  **a.** Find $\lim\limits_{v \to c^-} L$.

  **b.** If a starship is traveling at velocities approaching the speed of light, what does the limit in part (a) indicate about its length from the perspective of a stationary viewer on Earth?

  **c.** Explain why a left-hand limit is used in part (a).

**60.** The formula

$$R_a = R_f \sqrt{1 - \dfrac{v^2}{c^2}}$$

expresses the aging rate of an astronaut, $R_a$, relative to the aging rate of a friend on Earth, $R_f$, where $v$ is the astronaut's velocity and $c$ is the speed of light.

  **a.** Find $\lim\limits_{v \to c^-} R_a$.

  **b.** If you are traveling in a starship at velocities approaching the speed of light, what does the limit in part (a) indicate about your aging rate relative to a friend on Earth?

  **c.** Explain why a left-hand limit is used in part (a).

## Writing in Mathematics

**61.** Explain how to find the limit of a constant. Then express your written explanation using limit notation.

**62.** Explain how to find the limit of the identity function $f(x) = x$. Then express your written explanation using limit notation.

**63.** Explain how to find the limit of a sum. Then express your written explanation using limit notation.

**64.** Explain how to find the limit of a difference. Then express your written explanation using limit notation.

**65.** Explain how to find the limit of a product. Then express your written explanation using limit notation.

**66.** Describe how to find the limit of a polynomial function. Provide an example with your description.

**67.** Explain how to find the following limit: $\lim\limits_{x \to 2}(3x^2 - 10)^3$. Then use limit notation to write the limit property that supports your explanation.

**68.** Explain how to find the following limit: $\lim\limits_{x \to 2} \sqrt{5x - 6}$. Then use limit notation to write the limit property that supports your explanation.

**69.** Explain how to find the limit of a quotient if the limit of the denominator is not zero. Then express your written explanation using limit notation.

**70.** Write an example involving the limit of a quotient in which the quotient property for limits cannot be applied. Explain why the property cannot be applied to your limit problem.

**71.** Explain why

$$\lim\limits_{x \to 4} \dfrac{(x+4)(x-4)}{x-4}$$

can be found by first dividing the numerator and the denominator of the expression by $x - 4$. Division by zero is undefined. How can we be sure that we are not dividing the numerator and the denominator by zero?

## Technology Exercises

**72.** Use the $\boxed{\text{TABLE}}$ feature of your graphing utility to verify any five of the limits that you found in Exercises 1–42.

**73.** Use the $\boxed{\text{ZOOM IN}}$ feature of your graphing utility to verify any five of the limits that you found in Exercises 1–42. Zoom in on the graph of the given function, $f$, near $x = a$ to verify each limit.

# Critical Thinking Exercises

**Make Sense?** *In Exercises 74–77, determine whether each statement makes sense or does not make sense, and explain your reasoning.*

**74.** I evaluated a polynomial function $f$ at 3 and obtained 7, so 7 must be $\lim_{x \to 3} f(x)$.

**75.** I'm working with functions $f$ and $g$ for which $\lim_{x \to 4} f(x) = 0$, $\lim_{x \to 4} g(x) = -5$, and $\lim_{x \to 4} [f(x) - g(x)] = 5$.

**76.** I'm working with functions $f$ and $g$ for which

$$\lim_{x \to 4} f(x) = 0, \lim_{x \to 4} g(x) = -5, \text{ and } \lim_{x \to 4} \frac{f(x)}{g(x)} = 0.$$

**77.** I'm working with functions $f$ and $g$ for which

$$\lim_{x \to 4} f(x) = 0, \lim_{x \to 4} g(x) = -5, \text{ and } \lim_{x \to 4} \frac{g(x)}{f(x)} \neq 0.$$

*In Exercises 78–79, find the indicated limit.*

**78.** $\lim_{x \to 0} x\left(1 - \dfrac{1}{x}\right)$

**79.** $\lim_{x \to 4} \left(\dfrac{1}{x} - \dfrac{1}{4}\right)\left(\dfrac{1}{x-4}\right)$

*In Exercises 80–81, find* $\lim_{h \to 0} \dfrac{f(a+h) - f(a)}{h}$.

**80.** $f(x) = x^2 + 2x - 3, a = 1$
**81.** $f(x) = \sqrt{x}, a = 1$

*In Exercises 82–83, use properties of limits and the following limits*

$$\lim_{x \to 0} \frac{\sin x}{x} = 1, \quad \lim_{x \to 0} \frac{\cos x - 1}{x} = 0,$$

$$\lim_{x \to 0} \sin x = 0, \quad \lim_{x \to 0} \cos x = 1$$

*to find the indicated limit.*

**82.** $\lim_{x \to 0} \dfrac{\tan x}{x}$

**83.** $\lim_{x \to 0} \dfrac{2 \sin x + \cos x - 1}{3x}$

# Group Exercises

**84.** In the next column is a list of ten common errors involving algebra, trigonometry, and limits that students frequently make in calculus. Group members should examine each error and describe the mistake. Where possible, correct each error.

Finally, group members should offer suggestions for avoiding each error.

**a.** $(x + h)^3 - x^3 = x^3 + h^3 - x^3 = h^3$

**b.** $\dfrac{1}{a+b} = \dfrac{1}{a} + \dfrac{1}{b}$

**c.** $\dfrac{1}{a+b} = \dfrac{1}{a} + b$

**d.** $\sqrt{x+h} - \sqrt{x} = \sqrt{x} + \sqrt{h} - \sqrt{x} = \sqrt{h}$

**e.** $\dfrac{\sin 2x}{x} = \sin 2$

**f.** $\dfrac{a + bx}{a} = 1 + bx$

**g.** $\lim_{x \to 1} \dfrac{x^3 - 1}{x - 1} = \dfrac{1^3 - 1}{1 - 1} = \dfrac{0}{0} = 1$

**h.** $\sin(x + h) - \sin x = \sin x + \sin h - \sin x = \sin h$

**i.** $ax = bx$, so $a = b$

**j.** To find $\lim_{x \to 4} \dfrac{x^2 - 9}{x - 3}$, it is necessary to rewrite $\dfrac{x^2 - 9}{x - 3}$ by factoring $x^2 - 9$.

**85.** Research and present a group report about the history of the feud between Newton and Leibniz over who invented calculus. What other interests did these men have in addition to mathematics? What practical problems led them to the invention of calculus? What were their personalities like? Whose version established the notation and rules of calculus that we use today?

# Preview Exercises

*Exercises 86–88 will help you prepare for the material covered in the next section. In each exercise, use what occurs near 3 and at 3 to graph the function in an open interval about 3. (Graphs will vary.) Is it necessary to lift your pencil off the paper to obtain each graph? Explain your answer.*

**86.** $\lim_{x \to 3} f(x) = 5; f(3) = 5$

**87.** $\lim_{x \to 3} f(x) = 5; f(3) = 6$

**88.** $\lim_{x \to 3^-} f(x) = 5; \lim_{x \to 3^+} f(x) = 6; f(3) = 5$

---

**Section 11.3 Limits and Continuity**

## Objectives

1 Determine whether a function is continuous at a number.

2 Determine for what numbers a function is discontinuous.

Why you should not ski down discontinuous slopes

In everyday speech, a continuous process is one that goes on without interruption and without abrupt changes. In mathematics, a continuous function has much the same meaning. The graph of a continuous function does not have interrupting breaks, such as holes, gaps, or jumps. Thus, the graph of a continuous function can be drawn without lifting a pencil off the paper. In this section, you will learn how limits can be used to describe continuity.

①　Determine whether a function is continuous at a number.

# Limits and Continuity

**Figure 11.12** shows three graphs that cannot be drawn without lifting a pencil from the paper. In each case, there appears to be an interruption of the graph of $f$ at $x = a$.

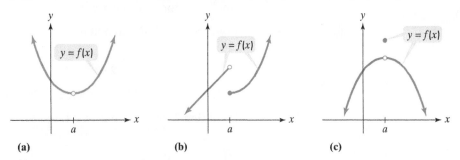

**(a)**　　　　　　　　　**(b)**　　　　　　　　　**(c)**

Figure 11.12　Each graph has an interruption at $x = a$.

Examine **Figure 11.12(a)**. The interruption occurs because the open dot indicates there is no point on the graph corresponding to $x = a$. This shows that $f(a)$ is not defined.

Now, examine **Figure 11.12(b)**. The closed blue dot at $x = a$ shows that $f(a)$ is defined. However, there is a jump at $a$. As $x$ approaches $a$ from the left, the values of $f$ get closer to the $y$-coordinate of the point shown by the open dot. By contrast, as $x$ approaches $a$ from the right, the values of $f$ get closer to the $y$-coordinate of the point shown by the closed dot. There is no single limit as $x$ approaches $a$. The jump in the graph reflects the fact that $\lim\limits_{x \to a} f(x)$ does not exist.

Finally, examine **Figure 11.12(c)**. The closed blue dot at $x = a$ shows that $f(a)$ is defined. Furthermore, as $x$ approaches $a$ from the left or from the right, the values of $f$ get closer to the $y$-coordinate of the point shown by the open dot. Thus, $\lim\limits_{x \to a} f(x)$ exists. However, there is still an interruption at $a$. Do you see why? The limit as $x$ approaches $a$, $\lim\limits_{x \to a} f(x)$, is the $y$-coordinate of the open dot. By contrast, the value of the function at $a$, $f(a)$, is the $y$-coordinate of the closed dot. The interruption in the graph reflects the fact that $\lim\limits_{x \to a} f(x)$ and $f(a)$ are not equal.

We now provide a precise definition of what it means for a function to be continuous at a number. Notice how each part of this definition avoids the interruptions that occurred in **Figure 11.12**.

## Definition of a Function Continuous at a Number

A function $f$ **is continuous at** $a$ when three conditions are satisfied.

**1.** $f$ is defined at $a$; that is, $a$ is in the domain of $f$, so that $f(a)$ is a real number.

**2.** $\lim\limits_{x \to a} f(x)$ exists.

**3.** $\lim\limits_{x \to a} f(x) = f(a)$

If $f$ is not continuous at $a$, we say that $f$ is **discontinuous at** $a$. Each of the functions whose graph is shown in **Figure 11.12** is discontinuous at $a$.

**EXAMPLE 1**　Determining Whether a Function Is Continuous at a Number

Determine whether the function

$$f(x) = \frac{2x + 1}{2x^2 - x - 1}$$

is continuous: **a.** at 2; **b.** at 1.

**Solution** According to the definition, three conditions must be satisfied to have continuity at $a$.

**a.** To determine whether $f(x) = \dfrac{2x + 1}{2x^2 - x - 1}$ is continuous at 2, we check the conditions for continuity with $a = 2$.

**Condition 1 $f$ is defined at $a$.** Is $f(2)$ defined?

$$f(2) = \frac{2 \cdot 2 + 1}{2 \cdot 2^2 - 2 - 1} = \frac{4 + 1}{8 - 2 - 1} = \frac{5}{5} = 1$$

Because $f(2)$ is a real number, 1, $f(2)$ is defined.

**Condition 2 $\lim\limits_{x \to a} f(x)$ exists.** Does $\lim\limits_{x \to 2} f(x)$ exist?

$$\lim_{x \to 2} f(x) = \lim_{x \to 2} \frac{2x + 1}{2x^2 - x - 1} = \frac{\lim\limits_{x \to 2}(2x + 1)}{\lim\limits_{x \to 2}(2x^2 - x - 1)}$$

$$= \frac{2 \cdot 2 + 1}{2 \cdot 2^2 - 2 - 1} = \frac{4 + 1}{8 - 2 - 1} = \frac{5}{5} = 1$$

Using properties of limits, we see that $\lim\limits_{x \to 2} f(x)$ exists.

**Condition 3 $\lim\limits_{x \to a} f(x) = f(a)$** Does $\lim\limits_{x \to 2} f(x) = f(2)$? We found that $\lim\limits_{x \to 2} f(x) = 1$ and $f(2) = 1$. Thus, as $x$ gets closer to 2, the corresponding values of $f(x)$ get closer to the function value at 2: $\lim\limits_{x \to 2} f(x) = f(2)$.

Because the three conditions are satisfied, we conclude that $f$ is continuous at 2.

**b.** To determine whether $f(x) = \dfrac{2x + 1}{2x^2 - x - 1}$ is continuous at 1, we check the conditions for continuity with $a = 1$.

**Condition 1 $f$ is defined at $a$.** Is $f(1)$ defined? Factor the denominator of the function's equation:

$$f(x) = \frac{2x + 1}{(x - 1)(2x + 1)}$$

Denominator is zero at $x = 1$.          Denominator is zero at $x = -\frac{1}{2}$.

Because division by zero is undefined, the domain of $f$ is $\left\{ x \mid x \neq 1, x \neq -\frac{1}{2} \right\}$. Thus, $f$ is not defined at 1.

Because one of the three conditions is not satisfied, we conclude that $f$ is not continuous at 1. Equivalently, we can say that $f$ is discontinuous at 1. ⬤

The graph of $f(x) = \dfrac{2x + 1}{2x^2 - x - 1}$ is shown in **Figure 11.13**. The graph verifies our work in Example 1. Can you see that $f$ is continuous at 2? By contrast, it is not continuous at 1, where the graph has a vertical asymptote.

The graph in **Figure 11.13** also reveals a discontinuity at $-\frac{1}{2}$. The open dot indicates that there is no point on the graph corresponding to $x = -\frac{1}{2}$. Can you see what is happening as $x$ approaches $-\frac{1}{2}$?

$$\lim_{x \to -\frac{1}{2}} \frac{2x + 1}{2x^2 - x - 1} = \lim_{x \to -\frac{1}{2}} \frac{2x + 1}{(x - 1)(2x + 1)} = \lim_{x \to -\frac{1}{2}} \frac{1}{x - 1} = \frac{1}{-\frac{1}{2} - 1} = -\frac{2}{3}$$

As $x$ gets closer to $-\frac{1}{2}$, the graph of $f$ gets closer to $-\frac{2}{3}$. Because $f$ is not defined at $-\frac{1}{2}$, the graph has a hole at $\left( -\frac{1}{2}, -\frac{2}{3} \right)$. This is shown by the open dot in **Figure 11.13**.

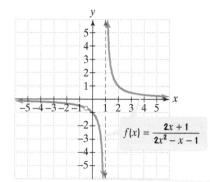

**Figure 11.13** $f$ is continuous at 2. It is not continuous at 1 or at $-\frac{1}{2}$.

⊘ Check Point | Determine whether the function

$$f(x) = \frac{x - 2}{x^2 - 4}$$

is continuous: **a.** at 1; **b.** at 2.

② Determine for what numbers a function is discontinuous.

## Determining Where Functions Are Discontinuous

We have seen that the limit of a polynomial function as $x$ approaches $a$ is the polynomial function evaluated at $a$. Thus, if $f$ is a polynomial function, then $\lim_{x \to a} f(x) = f(a)$ for any number $a$. This means that **a polynomial function is continuous at every number**.

Many of the functions discussed throughout this book are continuous at every number in their domain. For example, rational functions are continuous at every number, except any at which they are not defined. At numbers that are not in the domain of a rational function, a hole in the graph or an asymptote appears. Exponential, logarithmic, sine, and cosine functions are continuous at every number in their domain. Like rational functions, the tangent, cotangent, secant, and cosecant functions are continuous at every number, except any at which they are not defined. At numbers that are not in the domain of these trigonometric functions, an asymptote occurs.

### Study Tip

Most functions are always continuous at every number in their domain, including polynomial, rational, radical, exponential, logarithmic, and trigonometric functions. Most of the discontinuities you will encounter in calculus will be due to jumps in piecewise functions.

Example 2 illustrates how to determine where a piecewise function is discontinuous.

**EXAMPLE 2** Determining Where a Piecewise Function Is Discontinuous

Determine for what numbers $x$, if any, the following function is discontinuous:

$$f(x) = \begin{cases} x + 2 & \text{if } x \le 0 \\ 2 & \text{if } 0 < x \le 1. \\ x^2 + 2 & \text{if } x > 1 \end{cases}$$

**Solution**  First, let's determine whether each of the three pieces of $f$ is continuous. The first piece, $f(x) = x + 2$, is a linear function; it is continuous at every number $x$. The second piece, $f(x) = 2$, a constant function, is continuous at every number $x$. And the third piece, $f(x) = x^2 + 2$, a polynomial function, is also continuous at every number $x$. Thus, these three functions, a linear function, a constant function, and a polynomial function, can be graphed without lifting a pencil from the paper. However, the pieces change at $x = 0$ and at $x = 1$. Is it necessary to lift a pencil from the paper when graphing $f$ at these values? It appears that we must investigate continuity at 0 and at 1.

To determine whether the function is continuous at 0, we check the conditions for continuity with $a = 0$.

**Condition 1 $f$ is defined at $a$.** Is $f(0)$ defined? Because $a = 0$, we use the first line of the piecewise function, where $x \le 0$.

$f(x) = x + 2$   This is the function's equation for $x \le 0$, which includes $x = 0$.

$f(0) = 0 + 2$   Replace $x$ with 0.

$\qquad = 2$

Because $f(0)$ is a real number, 2, $f(0)$ is defined.

**Condition 2 $\lim_{x \to a} f(x)$ exists.** Does $\lim_{x \to 0} f(x)$ exist? To answer this question, we look at the values of $f(x)$ when $x$ is close to 0. Let us investigate the left- and right-hand limits. If these limits are equal, then $\lim_{x \to 0} f(x)$ exists. To find $\lim_{x \to 0^-} f(x)$,

$$f(x) = \begin{cases} x + 2 & \text{if } x \le 0 \\ 2 & \text{if } 0 < x \le 1 \\ x^2 + 2 & \text{if } x > 1 \end{cases}$$

The given piecewise function (repeated)

the left-hand limit, we look at the values of $f(x)$ when $x$ is close to 0, but less than 0. Because $x$ is less than 0, we use the first line of the piecewise function, $f(x) = x + 2$ if $x \le 0$. Thus,

$$\lim_{x \to 0^-} f(x) = \lim_{x \to 0^-} (x + 2) = 0 + 2 = 2.$$

To find $\lim_{x \to 0^+} f(x)$, the right-hand limit, we look at the values of $f(x)$ when $x$ is close to 0, but greater than 0. Because $x$ is greater than 0, we use the second line of the piecewise function, $f(x) = 2$ if $0 < x \le 1$. Thus,

$$\lim_{x \to 0^+} f(x) = \lim_{x \to 0^+} 2 = 2.$$

Because the left- and right-hand limits are both equal to 2, $\lim_{x \to 0} f(x) = 2$. Thus, we see that $\lim_{x \to 0} f(x)$ exists.

**Condition 3** $\lim_{x \to a} f(x) = f(a)$ Does $\lim_{x \to 0} f(x) = f(0)$? We found that $\lim_{x \to 0} f(x) = 2$ and $f(0) = 2$. This means that as $x$ gets closer to 0, the corresponding values of $f(x)$ get closer to the function value at 0: $\lim_{x \to 0} f(x) = f(0)$.

Because the three conditions are satisfied, we conclude that $f$ is continuous at 0.

Now we must determine whether the function is continuous at 1, the other value of $x$ where the pieces change. We check the conditions for continuity with $a = 1$.

**Condition 1** $f$ **is defined at** $a$. Is $f(1)$ defined? Because $a = 1$, we use the second line of the piecewise function, where $0 < x \le 1$.

$$f(x) = 2 \quad \text{\small This is the function's equation for } 0 < x \le 1, \text{ which includes } x = 1.$$
$$f(1) = 2 \quad \text{\small Replace } x \text{ with } 1.$$

Because $f(1)$ is a real number, 2, $f(1)$ is defined.

**Condition 2** $\lim_{x \to a} f(x)$ **exists.** Does $\lim_{x \to 1} f(x)$ exist? We investigate left- and right-hand limits as $x$ approaches 1. To find $\lim_{x \to 1^-} f(x)$, the left-hand limit, we look at values of $f(x)$ when $x$ is close to 1, but less than 1. Thus, we use the second line of the piecewise function, $f(x) = 2$ if $0 < x \le 1$. The left-hand limit is

$$\lim_{x \to 1^-} f(x) = \lim_{x \to 1^-} 2 = 2.$$

To find $\lim_{x \to 1^+} f(x)$, the right-hand limit, we look at values of $f(x)$ when $x$ is close to 1, but greater than 1. Thus, we use the third line of the piecewise function, $f(x) = x^2 + 2$ if $x > 1$. The right-hand limit is

$$\lim_{x \to 1^+} f(x) = \lim_{x \to 1^+} (x^2 + 2) = 1^2 + 2 = 3.$$

The left- and right-hand limits are not equal: $\lim_{x \to 1^-} f(x) = 2$ and $\lim_{x \to 1^+} f(x) = 3$. This means that $\lim_{x \to 1} f(x)$ does not exist.

Because one of the three conditions is not satisfied, we conclude that $f$ is not continuous at 1.

In summary, the given function is discontinuous at 1 only. The graph of $f$, shown in **Figure 11.14**, illustrates this conclusion. ●

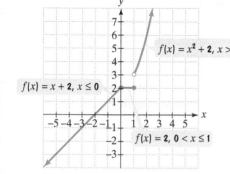

**Figure 11.14** This piecewise function is continuous at 0, where pieces change, and discontinuous at 1, where pieces change.

⬧ Check Point **2** Determine for what numbers $x$, if any, the following function is discontinuous:

$$f(x) = \begin{cases} 2x & \text{if } x \le 0 \\ x^2 + 1 & \text{if } 0 < x \le 2. \\ 7 - x & \text{if } x > 2 \end{cases}$$

# Exercise Set 11.3

## Practice Exercises

In Exercises 1–18, use the definition of continuity to determine whether f is continuous at a.

**1.** $f(x) = 2x + 5$
$a = 1$

**2.** $f(x) = 3x + 4$
$a = 1$

**3.** $f(x) = x^2 - 3x + 7$
$a = 4$

**4.** $f(x) = x^2 - 5x + 6$
$a = 4$

**5.** $f(x) = \dfrac{x^2 + 4}{x - 2}$
$a = 3$

**6.** $f(x) = \dfrac{x^2 + 6}{x - 5}$
$a = 6$

**7.** $f(x) = \dfrac{x + 5}{x - 5}$
$a = 5$

**8.** $f(x) = \dfrac{x + 7}{x - 7}$
$a = 7$

**9.** $f(x) = \dfrac{x - 5}{x + 5}$
$a = 5$

**10.** $f(x) = \dfrac{x - 7}{x + 7}$
$a = 7$

**11.** $f(x) = \dfrac{x^2 + 5x}{x^2 - 5x}$
$a = 0$

**12.** $f(x) = \dfrac{x^2 + 8x}{x^2 - 8x}$
$a = 0$

**13.** $f(x) = \begin{cases} \dfrac{x^2 - 4}{x - 2} & \text{if } x \neq 2 \\ 5 & \text{if } x = 2 \end{cases}$

$a = 2$

**14.** $f(x) = \begin{cases} \dfrac{x^2 - 36}{x - 6} & \text{if } x \neq 6 \\ 13 & \text{if } x = 6 \end{cases}$

$a = 6$

**15.** $f(x) = \begin{cases} x - 5 & \text{if } x \leq 0 \\ x^2 + x - 5 & \text{if } x > 0 \end{cases}$

$a = 0$

**16.** $f(x) = \begin{cases} x - 4 & \text{if } x \leq 0 \\ x^2 + x - 4 & \text{if } x > 0 \end{cases}$

$a = 0$

**17.** $f(x) = \begin{cases} 1 - x & \text{if } x < 1 \\ 0 & \text{if } x = 1 \\ x^2 - 1 & \text{if } x > 1 \end{cases}$

$a = 1$

**18.** $f(x) = \begin{cases} 2 - x & \text{if } x < 1 \\ 1 & \text{if } x = 1 \\ x^2 & \text{if } x > 1 \end{cases}$

$a = 1$

In Exercises 19–34, determine for what numbers, if any, the given function is discontinuous.

**19.** $f(x) = x^2 + 4x - 6$

**20.** $f(x) = x^2 + 8x - 10$

**21.** $f(x) = \dfrac{x + 1}{(x + 1)(x - 4)}$

**22.** $f(x) = \dfrac{x + 2}{(x + 2)(x - 5)}$

**23.** $f(x) = \dfrac{\sin x}{x}$

**24.** $f(x) = \dfrac{1 - \cos x}{x}$

**25.** $f(x) = \pi$

**26.** $f(x) = c$

**27.** $f(x) = \begin{cases} x - 1 & \text{if } x \leq 1 \\ x^2 & \text{if } x > 1 \end{cases}$

**28.** $f(x) = \begin{cases} x - 2 & \text{if } x \leq 2 \\ x^2 - 1 & \text{if } x > 2 \end{cases}$

**29.** $f(x) = \begin{cases} \dfrac{x^2 - 1}{x - 1} & \text{if } x \neq 1 \\ 2 & \text{if } x = 1 \end{cases}$

**30.** $f(x) = \begin{cases} \dfrac{x^2 - 9}{x - 3} & \text{if } x \neq 3 \\ 6 & \text{if } x = 3 \end{cases}$

**31.** $f(x) = \begin{cases} x + 6 & \text{if } x \leq 0 \\ 6 & \text{if } 0 < x \leq 2 \\ x^2 + 1 & \text{if } x > 2 \end{cases}$

**32.** $f(x) = \begin{cases} x + 7 & \text{if } x \leq 0 \\ 7 & \text{if } 0 < x \leq 3 \\ x^2 - 1 & \text{if } x > 3 \end{cases}$

**33.** $f(x) = \begin{cases} 5x & \text{if } x < 4 \\ 21 & \text{if } x = 4 \\ x^2 + 4 & \text{if } x > 4 \end{cases}$

**34.** $f(x) = \begin{cases} 7x & \text{if } x < 6 \\ 41 & \text{if } x = 6 \\ x^2 + 6 & \text{if } x > 6 \end{cases}$

## Practice Plus

In Exercises 35–38, graph each function. Then determine for what numbers, if any, the function is discontinuous.

**35.** $f(x) = \begin{cases} \sin x & \text{if } -\pi \leq x < 0 \\ -\sin x & \text{if } 0 \leq x < \pi \\ \cos x & \text{if } \pi \leq x \leq 2\pi \end{cases}$

**36.** $f(x) = \begin{cases} -\cos x & \text{if } -\pi \leq x < 0 \\ -\sin x & \text{if } 0 \leq x < \pi \\ \sin x & \text{if } \pi \leq x \leq 2\pi \end{cases}$

**37.** $f(x) = \begin{cases} -1 & \text{if } x \text{ is an integer.} \\ 1 & \text{if } x \text{ is not an integer.} \end{cases}$

**38.** $f(x) = \begin{cases} 2 & \text{if } x \text{ is an odd integer.} \\ -2 & \text{if } x \text{ is not an odd integer.} \end{cases}$

In Exercises 39–42, determine for what numbers, if any, the function is discontinuous. Construct a table to find any required limits.

**39.** $f(x) = \begin{cases} \dfrac{\sin 2x}{x} & \text{if } x \neq 0 \\ 2 & \text{if } x = 0 \end{cases}$

**40.** $f(x) = \begin{cases} \dfrac{\sin 3x}{x} & \text{if } x \neq 0 \\ 3 & \text{if } x = 0 \end{cases}$

**41.** $f(x) = \begin{cases} \dfrac{\cos x}{x - \dfrac{\pi}{2}} & \text{if } x \neq \dfrac{\pi}{2} \\ 1 & \text{if } x = \dfrac{\pi}{2} \end{cases}$

**42.** $f(x) = \begin{cases} \dfrac{\sin x}{x - \pi} & \text{if } x \neq \pi \\ 1 & \text{if } x = \pi \end{cases}$

## Application Exercises

**43.** The graph represents the percentage of required topics in a precalculus course, $p(t)$, that a student learned at various times, $t$, throughout the course. At time $t_2$, the student panicked for an instant during an exam. At time $t_3$, after working on a set of cumulative review exercises, a big jump in understanding suddenly took place.

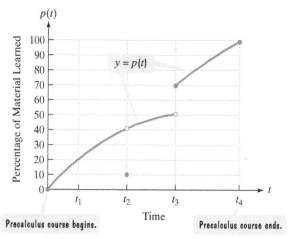

a. Find $\lim\limits_{t \to t_1} p(t)$ and $p(t_1)$.

b. Is $p$ continuous at $t_1$? Use the definition of continuity to explain your answer.

c. Find $\lim\limits_{t \to t_2} p(t)$ and $p(t_2)$.

d. Is $p$ continuous at $t_2$? Use the definition of continuity to explain your answer.

e. Find $\lim\limits_{t \to t_3} p(t)$ and $p(t_3)$.

f. Is $p$ continuous at $t_3$? Use the definition of continuity to explain your answer.

g. Find $\lim\limits_{t \to t_4^-} p(t)$ and $p(t_4)$.

h. Explain the meaning of both the limit and the function value in part (g) in terms of the time in the course and the percentage of topics learned.

**44.** The figure shows the cost of mailing a first-class letter, $f(x)$, as a function of its weight, $x$, in ounces, for weights not exceeding 3.5 ounces.

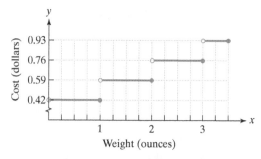

*Source:* Lynn E. Baring, Postmaster, Inverness, CA

a. Find $\lim\limits_{x \to 3^-} f(x)$.

b. Find $\lim\limits_{x \to 3^+} f(x)$.

c. What can you conclude about $\lim\limits_{x \to 3} f(x)$? How is this shown by the graph?

d. What aspect of costs for mailing a letter causes the graph to jump vertically by the same amount at its discontinuities?

**45.** The following piecewise function gives the tax owed, $T(x)$, by a single taxpayer in 2007 on a taxable income of $x$ dollars.

$$T(x) = \begin{cases} 0.10x & \text{if} & 0 < x \le 7825 \\ 782.50 + 0.15(x - 7825) & \text{if} & 7825 < x \le 31{,}850 \\ 4386.25 + 0.25(x - 31{,}850) & \text{if} & 31{,}850 < x \le 77{,}100 \\ 15{,}698.75 + 0.28(x - 77{,}100) & \text{if} & 77{,}100 < x \le 160{,}850 \\ 39{,}148.75 + 0.33(x - 160{,}850) & \text{if} & 160{,}850 < x \le 349{,}700 \\ 101{,}469.25 + 0.35(x - 349{,}700) & \text{if} & x > 349{,}700. \end{cases}$$

a. Determine whether $T$ is continuous at 7825.

b. Determine whether $T$ is continuous at 31,850.

c. If $T$ had discontinuities, use one of these discontinuities to describe a situation where it might be advantageous to earn less money in taxable income.

## Writing in Mathematics

**46.** Explain how to determine whether a function is continuous at a number.

**47.** If a function is not defined at $a$, how is this shown on the function's graph?

**48.** If a function is defined at $a$, but $\lim\limits_{x \to a} f(x)$ does not exist, how is this shown on the function's graph?

**49.** If a function is defined at $a$, $\lim\limits_{x \to a} f(x)$ exists, but $\lim\limits_{x \to a} f(x) \ne f(a)$, how is this shown on the function's graph?

**50.** In Exercises 43–44, functions that modeled learning in a precalculus course and the cost of mailing a letter had jumps in their graphs. Describe another situation that can be modeled by a function with discontinuities. What aspect of this situation causes the discontinuities?

**51.** Give two examples of the use of the word *continuous* in everyday English. Compare its use in your examples to its meaning in mathematics.

## Technology Exercises

**52.** Use your graphing utility to graph any five of the functions in Exercises 1–18 and verify whether $f$ is continuous at $a$.

**53.** Estimate $\lim\limits_{x \to 0^+} (1 + x)^{1/x}$ by using the $\boxed{\text{TABLE}}$ feature of your graphing utility to create a table of values. Then use the $\boxed{\text{ZOOM IN}}$ feature to zoom in on the graph of $f$ near and to the right of $x = 0$ to justify or improve your estimate.

## Critical Thinking Exercises

**Make Sense?** *In Exercises 54–57, determine whether each statement makes sense or does not make sense, and explain your reasoning.*

**54.** If $\lim\limits_{x \to a} f(x) \ne f(a)$ and $\lim\limits_{x \to a} f(x)$ exists, I can redefine $f(a)$ to make $f$ continuous at $a$.

**55.** If $\lim\limits_{x \to a^-} f(x) \ne f(a)$ and $\lim\limits_{x \to a^-} f(x) \ne \lim\limits_{x \to a^+} f(x)$, I can redefine $f(a)$ to make $f$ continuous at $a$.

**56.** $f$ and $g$ are both continuous at $a$, although $f + g$ is not.

**57.** $f$ and $g$ are both continuous at $a$, although $\dfrac{f}{g}$ is not.

**58.** Define $f(x) = \dfrac{x^2 - 81}{x - 9}$ at $x = 9$ so that the function becomes continuous at 9.

**59.** Is it possible to define $f(x) = \dfrac{1}{x - 9}$ at $x = 9$ so that the function becomes continuous at 9? How does this discontinuity differ from the discontinuity in Exercise 58?

**60.** For the function

$$f(x) = \begin{cases} x^2 & \text{if } x < 1 \\ Ax - 3 & \text{if } x \geq 1 \end{cases}$$

find $A$ so that the function is continuous at 1.

## Group Exercise

**61.** In this exercise, the group will define three piecewise functions. Each function should have three pieces and two values of $x$ at which the pieces change.

**a.** Define and graph a piecewise function that is continuous at both values of $x$ where the pieces change.

**b.** Define and graph a piecewise function that is continuous at one value of $x$ where the pieces change

and discontinuous at the other value of $x$ where the pieces change.

**c.** Define and graph a piecewise function that is discontinuous at both values of $x$ where the pieces change.

At the end of the activity, group members should turn in the functions and their graphs. Do not use any of the piecewise functions or graphs that appear anywhere in this book.

## Preview Exercises

*Exercises 62–64 will help you prepare for the material covered in the next section. In each exercise, find the indicated difference quotient and simplify.*

**62.** If $f(x) = x^2 + x$, find $\dfrac{f(2 + h) - f(2)}{h}$.

**63.** If $f(x) = x^3$, find $\dfrac{f(x + h) - f(x)}{h}$.

**64.** If $s(t) = -16t^2 + 48t + 160$, find $\dfrac{s(a + h) - s(a)}{h}$.

**Chapter 11** **Mid-Chapter Check Point**

**What you know:** We learned that $\lim\limits_{x \to a} f(x) = L$ means that as $x$ gets closer to $a$, but remains unequal to $a$, the corresponding values of $f(x)$ get closer to $L$. We found limits using tables, graphs, and properties of limits. The quotient property for limits did not apply to fractional expressions in which the limit of the denominator is zero. In these cases, rewriting the expression using factoring or rationalizing the numerator or denominator was helpful before finding the limit. We saw that if the left-hand limit, $\lim\limits_{x \to a^-} f(x)$, ($x$ approaches $a$ from the left) is not equal to the right-hand limit, $\lim\limits_{x \to a^+} f(x)$, ($x$ approaches $a$ from the right), then $\lim\limits_{x \to a} f(x)$ does not exist. Finally, we defined continuity in terms of limits. A function $f$ is continuous at $a$ when $f$ is defined at $a$, $\lim\limits_{x \to a} f(x)$ exists, and $\lim\limits_{x \to a} f(x) = f(a)$. If $f$ is not continuous at $a$, we say that $f$ is discontinuous at $a$.

*In Exercises 1–7, use the graphs of f and g to find the indicated limit or function value, or state that the limit or function value does not exist.*

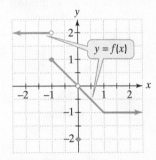
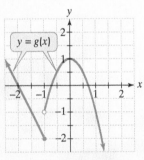

**1.** $\lim\limits_{x \to -1^-} f(x)$

**2.** $\lim\limits_{x \to -1^+} f(x)$

**3.** $\lim\limits_{x \to -1} f(x)$

**4.** $\lim\limits_{x \to 1}[f(x) + g(x)]$

**5.** $\lim\limits_{x \to 0}[f(x) - g(x)]$

**6.** $(f - g)(0)$

**7.** $\lim\limits_{x \to 1}\sqrt{10 + f(x)}$

**8.** Use the graph of $f$ shown above to determine for what numbers the function is discontinuous. Then use the definition of continuity to verify each discontinuity.

*In Exercises 9–11, use the table to find the indicated limit.*

| $x$ | $-0.03$ | $-0.02$ | $-0.01$ | $-0.007$ | $0.007$ | $0.01$ | $0.02$ | $0.03$ |
|---|---|---|---|---|---|---|---|---|
|  $f(x) = \dfrac{\sin x}{2x^2 - x}$ | $-0.9433$ | $-0.9615$ | $-0.9804$ | $-0.9862$ | $-1.014$ | $-1.02$ | $-1.042$ | $-1.064$ |
| $g(x) = \dfrac{e^x - \tan x}{\cos^2 x}$ | $1.0014$ | $1.0006$ | $1.0002$ | $1.0001$ | $1.0001$ | $1.0001$ | $1.0006$ | $1.0013$ |

*(In Exercises 9–11, be sure to refer to the table at the bottom of the previous page.)*

**9.** $\lim\limits_{x \to 0} f(x)$    **10.** $\lim\limits_{x \to 0} g(x)$    **11.** $\lim\limits_{x \to 0} \dfrac{4g(x)}{[f(x)]^2}$

*In Exercises 12–17, find the limits.*

**12.** $\lim\limits_{x \to -2} (x^3 - x + 5)$    **13.** $\lim\limits_{x \to 3} \sqrt{x^2 - 3x + 4}$

**14.** $\lim\limits_{x \to 5} \dfrac{2x^2 - x + 4}{x - 1}$    **15.** $\lim\limits_{x \to 5} \dfrac{2x^2 - 7x - 15}{x - 5}$

**16.** $\lim\limits_{x \to 0} \dfrac{\sqrt{x^2 + 9} - 3}{x^2}$    **17.** $\lim\limits_{x \to 0} \dfrac{\dfrac{1}{x + 10} - \dfrac{1}{x}}{x}$

*In Exercises 18–19, a piecewise function is given. Use the function to find the indicated limit, or state that the limit does not exist.*

**18.** $f(x) = \begin{cases} 9 - 2x & \text{if } x < 4 \\ \sqrt{x - 4} & \text{if } x \geq 4 \end{cases}$

    **a.** $\lim\limits_{x \to 4^-} f(x)$    **b.** $\lim\limits_{x \to 4^+} f(x)$    **c.** $\lim\limits_{x \to 4} f(x)$

**19.** $f(x) = \begin{cases} \dfrac{x^4 - 16}{x - 2} & \text{if } x \neq 2 \\ 32 & \text{if } x = 2 \end{cases}$

    **a.** $\lim\limits_{x \to 2^-} f(x)$    **b.** $\lim\limits_{x \to 2^+} f(x)$    **c.** $\lim\limits_{x \to 2} f(x)$

*In Exercises 20–21, use the definition of continuity to determine whether f is continuous at a.*

**20.** $f(x) = \begin{cases} \sqrt{3 - x} & \text{if } x \leq 3 \\ x^2 - 3x & \text{if } x > 3 \end{cases}$

    $a = 3$

**21.** $f(x) = \begin{cases} \dfrac{(x + 3)^2 - 9}{x} & \text{if } x \neq 0 \\ 6 & \text{if } x = 0 \end{cases}$

    $a = 0$

**22** Determine for what numbers, if any, the following function is discontinuous:

$$f(x) = \begin{cases} \dfrac{x^2 - 1}{x + 1} & \text{if } x < -1 \\ 2x & \text{if } -1 \leq x \leq 5. \\ 3x - 4 & \text{if } x > 5 \end{cases}$$

---

**Section 11.4 Introduction to Derivatives**

## Objectives

1. Find slopes and equations of tangent lines.
2. Find the derivative of a function.
3. Find average and instantaneous rates of change.
4. Find instantaneous velocity.

Things change over time and most changes occur at uneven rates. This is illustrated in the chapter opener (page 1037) with a sequence of photos of a young boy transforming into an adult. What does calculus have to say about this radical transformation?

In this section, we will see how calculus allows motion and change to be analyzed by "freezing the frame" of a continuously changing process, instant by instant. For example, **Figure 11.15** shows a male's changing height over intervals of time. Over the period of time from $P$ to $D$, his average rate of growth is his change in height—that is, his height at time $D$ minus his height at time $P$—divided by the change in time from $P$ to $D$.

The lines $PD, PC, PB,$ and $PA$ shown in **Figure 11.15** have slopes that show the man's average growth rates for successively shorter periods of time. Calculus makes these time frames so small that their limit approaches a single point—that is, a single instant in time. This point is shown as point $P$ in **Figure 11.15**. The slope of the line that touches the graph at $P$ gives the man's growth rate at one instant in time, $P$.

Keep this informal discussion of this man and his growth rate in mind as you read this section. We begin with the calculus that describes the slope of the line that touches the graph in **Figure 11.15** at $P$.

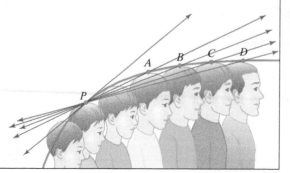

Figure 11.15

① Find slopes and equations of tangent lines.

## Slopes and Equations of Tangent Lines

In Chapter 1, we saw that if the graph of a function is not a straight line, the **average rate of change** between any two points is the slope of the line containing the two points. We called this line a **secant line**.

**Figure 11.16** shows the graph of a male's height, in inches, as a function of his age, in years. Two points on the graph are labeled: (13, 57) and (18, 76). At age 13, this person was 57 inches tall, and at age 18, he was 76 inches tall. The slope of the secant line containing these two point is

$$\frac{76 - 57}{18 - 13} = \frac{19}{5} = 3\frac{4}{5}.$$

Slope is the change in the $y$-coordinates divided by the change in the $x$-coordinates.

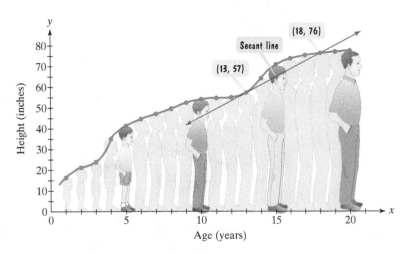

**Figure 11.16** Height as a function of age

The man's average rate of change, or average growth rate, from 13 to 18 was $3\frac{4}{5}$ inches per year.

How can we find this person's growth rate at the instant when he was 13? We can find this *instantaneous rate of change* by repeating the computation of slope from 13 to 17, then from 13 to 16, then from 13 to 15, again from 13 to 14, again from 13 to $13\frac{1}{2}$, and once again from 13 to 13.01. What limit is approached by these computations as the shrinking interval of time gets closer and closer to the instant when your cousin was 13?

We answer these questions by considering the graph of any function $f$, shown in **Figure 11.17**. We need to find the slope, or steepness, of this curve at the point $P = (a, f(a))$. This slope will reveal the function's instantaneous rate of change at $a$. We begin by choosing a second point, $Q$, whose $x$-coordinate is $a + h$, where $h \neq 0$. The point $Q = (a + h, f(a + h))$ is shown in **Figure 11.17**.

How do we find the average rate of change of $f$ between points $P$ and $Q$? We find the slope of the secant line, the line containing $P$ and $Q$.

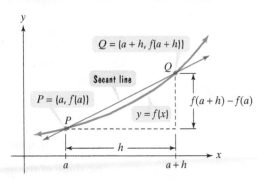

**Figure 11.17** Finding the average rate of change, or the slope of the secant line

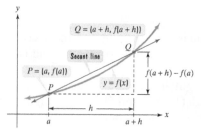

Figure 11.17 (repeated)

Slope of secant line

$$= \frac{f(a + h) - f(a)}{a + h - a}$$ Slope is the change in y-coordinates, $f(a + h) - f(a)$, divided by the change in x-coordinates, $(a + h) - a$.

$$= \frac{f(a + h) - f(a)}{h}$$ Simplify.

Do you recognize this expression as the difference quotient presented in Chapter 1? We will make use of this expression and our understanding of limits to find the slope of a graph at a specific point.

What happens if the distance labeled $h$ in **Figure 11.17** approaches 0? The value of the $x$-coordinate of point $Q$, $a + h$, will get closer and closer to $a$. Can you see that $a$ is the $x$-coordinate of point $P$? Thus, as $h$ approaches 0, point $Q$ approaches point $P$. Examine **Figure 11.18** to see how we visualize the changing position of point $Q$.

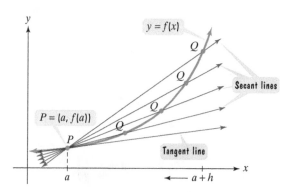

Figure 11.18 As $Q$ approaches $P$, the succession of secant lines approaches the tangent line.

**Figure 11.18** also shows how the secant line between points $P$ and $Q$ changes as $h$ approaches 0. Note how the position of the secant line changes as the position of $Q$ changes. The secant line between point $P$ and point $Q$ approaches the red line that touches the graph of $f$ at point $P$. This limiting position of the secant line is called the **tangent line** to the graph of $f$ at the point $P = (a, f(a))$.

According to our earlier derivation, the slope of each secant line in **Figure 11.18** is

$$\frac{f(a + h) - f(a)}{h}.$$ This difference quotient is also the average rate of change of $f$ from $x_1 = a$ to $x_2 = a + h$.

As $h$ approaches 0, this slope approaches the slope of the tangent line to the curve at $(a, f(a))$. Thus, the slope of the tangent line to the curve at $(a, f(a))$ is

$$\lim_{h \to 0} \frac{f(a + h) - f(a)}{h}.$$

This limit also represents the **instantaneous rate of change of $f$ with respect to $x$ at $a$**.

## Slope of the Tangent Line to a Curve at a Point

The **slope of the tangent line** to the graph of a function $y = f(x)$ at $(a, f(a))$ is given by

$$m_{\tan} = \lim_{h \to 0} \frac{f(a + h) - f(a)}{h}$$

provided that this limit exists. This limit also describes

• the **slope of the graph of $f$ at $(a, f(a))$**.

• the **instantaneous rate of change of $f$ with respect to $x$ at $a$**.

**EXAMPLE 1** Finding the Slope of a Tangent Line

Find the slope of the tangent line to the graph of $f(x) = x^2 + x$ at $(2, 6)$.

**Solution** The slope of the tangent line at $(a, f(a))$ is

$$m_{\tan} = \lim_{h \to 0} \frac{f(a + h) - f(a)}{h}.$$

We use this formula to find the slope of the tangent line at the given point. Because we are finding the slope of the tangent line at $(2, 6)$, we know that $a = 2$.

$$m_{\tan} = \lim_{h \to 0} \frac{f(2 + h) - f(2)}{h}$$   Because $a = 2$, substitute 2 into the formula for each occurrence of $a$.

$$= \lim_{h \to 0} \frac{[(2 + h)^2 + (2 + h)] - [2^2 + 2]}{h}$$   To find $f(2 + h)$, replace $x$ in $f(x) = x^2 + x$ with $2 + h$. To find $f(2)$ replace $x$ with 2.

$$= \lim_{h \to 0} \frac{[4 + 4h + h^2 + 2 + h] - 6}{h}$$   Square $2 + h$ using $(A + B)^2 = A^2 + 2AB + B^2$.

$$= \lim_{h \to 0} \frac{h^2 + 5h}{h}$$   Combine like terms in the numerator.

$$= \lim_{h \to 0} \frac{h(h + 5)}{h}$$   Factor the numerator.

$$= \lim_{h \to 0} (h + 5)$$   Divide both the numerator and denominator by $h$. This is permitted because $h$ approaches 0, but $h \neq 0$.

$$= 0 + 5$$   Use limit properties.

$$= 5$$

Thus, the slope of the tangent line to the graph of $f(x) = x^2 + x$ at $(2, 6)$ is 5. This is shown in **Figure 11.19**. We also say that the slope of the graph of $f(x) = x^2 + x$ at $(2, 6)$ is 5.

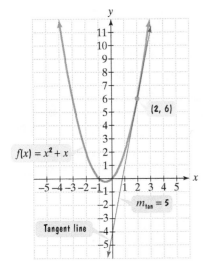

$f(x) = x^2 + x$

(2, 6)

$m_{\tan} = 5$

Tangent line

**Figure 11.19**

### Technology

Graphing utilities with a DRAW TANGENT feature will draw tangent lines to curves and display their slope-intercept equations. **Figure 11.20** shows the tangent line to the graph of $y = x^2 + x$ at the point whose $x$-coordinate is 2. Also displayed is the slope-intercept equation of the tangent line, $y = 5x - 4$.

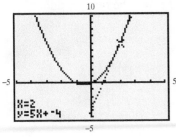

X=2
Y=5X+‑4

**Figure 11.20**

⊘ Check Point **1** Find the slope of the tangent line to the graph of $f(x) = x^2 - x$ at $(4, 12)$.

In Example 1, we found the *slope* of the tangent line shown in **Figure 11.19**. We can find an *equation* of this line using the point-slope form of the equation of a line

$$y - y_1 = m(x - x_1).$$

The tangent line passes through $(2, 6)$: $x_1 = 2$ and $y_1 = 6$. The slope of the tangent line is 5: $m = 5$. The point-slope equation of the tangent line is

$$y - 6 = 5(x - 2).$$

We can solve for $y$ and express the equation of the tangent line in slope-intercept form: $y = mx + b$. The slope-intercept equation of the tangent line is

$$y - 6 = 5x - 10$$   Apply the distributive property.

$$y = 5x - 4.$$   Add 6 to both sides and write in slope-intercept form.

**EXAMPLE 2** Finding the Slope-Intercept Equation of a Tangent Line

Find the slope-intercept equation of the tangent line to the graph of $f(x) = \sqrt{x}$ at $(4, 2)$.

**Solution** We begin by finding the slope of the tangent line to the graph of $f(x) = \sqrt{x}$ at $(4, 2)$.

$$m_{\tan} = \lim_{h \to 0} \frac{f(4 + h) - f(4)}{h}$$

The slope of the tangent line at $(a, f(a))$ is $\lim_{h \to 0} \dfrac{f(a + h) - f(a)}{h}$.

$$= \lim_{h \to 0} \frac{\sqrt{4 + h} - 2}{h}$$

To find $f(4 + h)$, replace $x$ in $f(x) = \sqrt{x}$ with $4 + h$. $f(4) = \sqrt{4} = 2$

$$= \lim_{h \to 0} \left[ \frac{\sqrt{4 + h} - 2}{h} \cdot \frac{\sqrt{4 + h} + 2}{\sqrt{4 + h} + 2} \right]$$

Rationalize the numerator.

$$= \lim_{h \to 0} \frac{4 + h - 4}{h(\sqrt{4 + h} + 2)}$$

Multiply the numerators.

$$= \lim_{h \to 0} \frac{h}{h(\sqrt{4 + h} + 2)}$$

Simplify the numerator.

$$= \lim_{h \to 0} \frac{1}{\sqrt{4 + h} + 2}$$

Divide both the numerator and the denominator by $h$. This is permitted because $h$ approaches 0, but $h \neq 0$.

$$= \frac{1}{\sqrt{4 + 0} + 2}$$

Use limit properties.

$$= \frac{1}{4}$$

Now that we have the slope of the tangent line, we can write the slope-intercept equation. Begin with the point-slope form

$$y - y_1 = m(x - x_1).$$

The tangent line is given to pass through $(4, 2)$: $x_1 = 4$ and $y_1 = 2$. We found the slope of the tangent line to be $\frac{1}{4}$: $m = \frac{1}{4}$. The point-slope equation of the tangent line is

$$y - 2 = \tfrac{1}{4}(x - 4).$$

Solving for $y$, we obtain the slope-intercept equation of the tangent line.

$y - 2 = \tfrac{1}{4}x - 1$   Apply the distributive property.

$y = \tfrac{1}{4}x + 1$   Add 2 to both sides. This is the slope-intercept form, $y = mx + b$, of the equation.

The slope-intercept equation of the tangent line to the graph of $f(x) = \sqrt{x}$ at $(4, 2)$ is $y = \tfrac{1}{4}x + 1$. **Figure 11.21** shows the graph of $f$ and the tangent line.

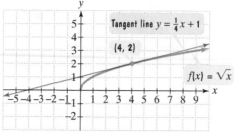

Figure 11.21

⊘ Check Point **2** Find the slope-intercept equation of the tangent line to the graph of $f(x) = \sqrt{x}$ at $(1, 1)$.

**②** Find the derivative of a function.

## The Derivative of a Function

In Examples 1 and 2, we found the slope of a tangent line to the graph of $f$ at $(a, f(a))$, where $a$ was a specific number. We can also find the slope of a tangent line at $(x, f(x))$, where $x$ can represent any number in the domain of $f'$. The resulting function is called the *derivative of f at x*.

### Definition of the Derivative of a Function

Let $y = f(x)$ denote a function $f$. The **derivative of f at x**, denoted by $f'(x)$, read "$f$ prime of $x$," is defined by

$$f'(x) = \lim_{h \to 0} \frac{f(x + h) - f(x)}{h}$$

provided that this limit exists. The derivative of a function $f$ gives the slope of $f$ for any value of $x$ in the domain of $f'$.

By evaluating the derivative, you can compute the slopes of various tangent lines to the graph of a function. Thus, the derivative gives you a way to analyze your moving world by revealing a function's instantaneous rate of change at any moment.

## The Seeds of Change

*Every shape that's born bears in its womb the seeds of change.*

—Ovid (Roman poet)

**Figure 11.22** shows a graph involving change, namely a male's height as a function of his age. The derivative of this function provides a formula for the slope of the tangent line to the function's graph at any point. The figure shows four tangent lines. The derivative of this function would reveal that the tangent line with the greatest slope touches the curve somewhere between $x = 3$ and $x = 4$. Thus, the instantaneous rate of change in the boy's growth is greatest at some moment in time between the ages of 3 and 4.

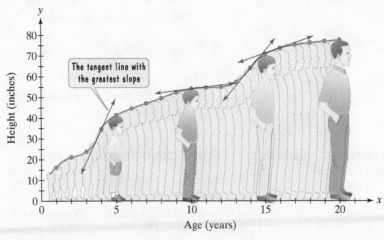

**Figure 11.22** Analyzing continuous change at an instant

$\boxed{\text{EXAMPLE 3}}$   **Finding the Derivative of a Function**

**a.** Find the derivative of $f(x) = x^2 + 3x$ at $x$. That is, find $f'(x)$.

**b.** Find the slope of the tangent line to the graph of $f(x) = x^2 + 3x$ at $x = -2$ and at $x = -\frac{3}{2}$.

**Solution**

**a.** We use the definition of the derivative of $f$ at $x$ to find the derivative of the given function.

$$f'(x) = \lim_{h \to 0} \frac{f(x + h) - f(x)}{h} \qquad \text{Use the definition of the derivative.}$$

$$= \lim_{h \to 0} \frac{[(x + h)^2 + 3(x + h)] - (x^2 + 3x)}{h} \qquad \begin{array}{l}\text{To find } f(x + h), \text{ replace } x \text{ in}\\ f(x) = x^2 + 3x \text{ with } x + h.\end{array}$$

$$= \lim_{h \to 0} \frac{x^2 + 2xh + h^2 + 3x + 3h - x^2 - 3x}{h} \qquad \begin{array}{l}\text{Perform the indicated operations}\\ \text{in the numerator.}\end{array}$$

$$= \lim_{h \to 0} \frac{2xh + h^2 + 3h}{h} \qquad \begin{array}{l}\text{Simplify the numerator:}\\ x^2 - x^2 = 0 \text{ and } 3x - 3x = 0.\end{array}$$

$$= \lim_{h \to 0} \frac{h(2x + h + 3)}{h} \qquad \text{Factor the numerator.}$$

$$= \lim_{h \to 0} (2x + h + 3) \qquad \begin{array}{l}\text{Divide the numerator and the}\\ \text{denominator by } h.\end{array}$$

$$= 2x + 0 + 3 \qquad \begin{array}{l}\text{Use limit properties. As } h\\ \text{approaches 0, only the term}\\ \text{containing } h \text{ is affected.}\end{array}$$

$$= 2x + 3$$

The derivative of $f(x) = x^2 + 3x$ is

$$f'(x) = 2x + 3.$$

**b.** The derivative gives the slope of the tangent line at any point. Thus, to find the slope of the tangent line to the graph of $f(x) = x^2 + 3x$ at $x = -2$, evaluate the derivative at $-2$. Similarly, to find the slope of the tangent line at $x = -\frac{3}{2}$, evaluate the derivative at $-\frac{3}{2}$.

$$f'(x) = 2x + 3$$
$$f'(-2) = 2(-2) + 3 = -4 + 3 = -1$$
$$f'\left(-\tfrac{3}{2}\right) = 2\left(-\tfrac{3}{2}\right) + 3 = -3 + 3 = 0$$

**Figure 11.23** shows the graph of $f(x) = x^2 + 3x$ and tangent lines at $x = -2$ and $x = -\frac{3}{2}$. The slope of the decreasing green tangent line at $x = -2$ is $-1$. The slope of the horizontal red tangent line at $x = -\frac{3}{2}$ is 0.   ⬤

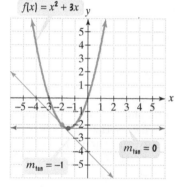

$f(x) = x^2 + 3x$

$m_{\tan} = 0$

$m_{\tan} = -1$

**Figure 11.23**   Two tangent lines to the graph of $f(x) = x^2 + 3x$ and their slopes

⊘ Check Point **3**

**a.** Find the derivative of $f(x) = x^2 - 5x$ at $x$. That is, find $f'(x)$.

**b.** Find the slope of the tangent line to the graph of $f(x) = x^2 - 5x$ at $x = -1$ and at $x = 3$.

③ Find average and instantaneous rates of change.

## Applications of the Derivative

Many applications of the derivative involve analyzing change by determining a function's instantaneous rate of change at any moment. How do we use the derivative of a function to reveal such changes? We know that the derivative of $f$ at $x$ is defined by

$$f'(x) = \lim_{h \to 0} \frac{f(x + h) - f(x)}{h}.$$

Thus, the derivative of $f$ at $a$ is

$$f'(a) = \lim_{h \to 0} \frac{f(a + h) - f(a)}{h}.$$

Do you recognize this limit? It describes the instantaneous rate of change of $f$ with respect to $x$ at $a$.

## Average and Instantaneous Rates of Change

**Average Rate of Change** The **average rate of change of $f$ from $x = a$ to $x = a + h$** is given by the difference quotient

$$\frac{f(a + h) - f(a)}{h}.$$

**Instantaneous Rate of Change** The **instantaneous rate of change of $f$ with respect to $x$ at $a$** is the derivative of $f$ at $a$:

$$f'(a) = \lim_{h \to 0} \frac{f(a + h) - f(a)}{h}.$$

( **EXAMPLE 4** ) **Finding Average and Instantaneous Rates of Change**

The function $f(x) = x^3$ describes the volume of a cube, $f(x)$, in cubic inches, whose length, width, and height each measure $x$ inches. If $x$ is changing,

**a.** Find the average rate of change of the volume with respect to $x$ as $x$ changes from 5 inches to 5.1 inches and from 5 inches to 5.01 inches.

**b.** Find the instantaneous rate of change of the volume with respect to $x$ at the moment when $x = 5$ inches.

## Solution

**a.** As $x$ changes from 5 to 5.1, $a = 5$ and $h = 0.1$. The average rate of change of the volume with respect to $x$ as $x$ changes from 5 to 5.1 is determined as follows.

$$\frac{f(a + h) - f(a)}{h}$$     The difference quotient gives the average rate of change from $a$ to $a + h$.

$$= \frac{f(5 + 0.1) - f(5)}{0.1}$$     This is the average rate of change from 5 to 5.1.

$$= \frac{f(5.1) - f(5)}{0.1}$$     Simplify.

$$= \frac{5.1^3 - 5^3}{0.1}$$     Use $f(x) = x^3$ and substitute 5.1 and 5, respectively, for $x$.

$$= 76.51$$

The average rate of change in the volume is 76.51 cubic inches per inch as $x$ changes from 5 to 5.1 inches.

As $x$ changes from 5 to 5.01, $a = 5$ and $h = 0.01$. The average rate of change of the volume with respect to $x$ as $x$ changes from 5 to 5.01 is determined as follows.

$$\frac{f(a + h) - f(a)}{h}$$     The difference quotient gives the average rate of change from $a$ to $a + h$.

$$= \frac{f(5 + 0.01) - f(5)}{0.01}$$     This is the average rate of change from 5 to 5.01.

$$= \frac{f(5.01) - f(5)}{0.01}$$     Simplify.

$$= \frac{5.01^3 - 5^3}{0.01}$$     Use $f(x) = x^3$ and substitute 5.01 and 5, respectively, for $x$.

$$= 75.1501$$

The average rate of change in the volume is 75.1501 cubic inches per inch as $x$ changes from 5 to 5.01 inches.

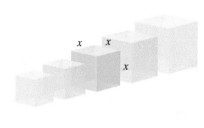

**b.** Instantaneous rates of change are given by the derivative. The derivative of $f$ at $a$, $f'(a)$, is the instantaneous rate of change of $f$ with respect to $x$ at $a$. We must find the instantaneous rate of change of the volume with respect to $x$ at the moment when $x = 5$ inches. This means that we must find $f'(5)$. We find $f'(5)$ by first finding $f'(x)$, the derivative, and then evaluating $f'$ at 5.

$$f'(x) = \lim_{h \to 0} \frac{f(x + h) - f(x)}{h}$$     Use the definition of the derivative.

$$= \lim_{h \to 0} \frac{(x + h)^3 - x^3}{h}$$     To find $f(x + h)$, replace x in $f(x) = x^3$ with $x + h$.

$$= \lim_{h \to 0} \frac{(x^3 + 3x^2h + 3xh^2 + h^3) - x^3}{h}$$     Use the Binomial Theorem to cube $x + h$.

$$= \lim_{h \to 0} \frac{3x^2h + 3xh^2 + h^3}{h}$$     Simplify the numerator: $x^3 - x^3 = 0$.

$$= \lim_{h \to 0} \frac{h(3x^2 + 3xh + h^2)}{h}$$     Factor the numerator.

$$= \lim_{h \to 0} (3x^2 + 3xh + h^2)$$     Divide the numerator and the denominator by h.

$$= 3x^2 + 3x \cdot 0 + 0^2$$     Use limit properties. As h approaches 0, only terms containing h are affected.

$$= 3x^2$$

## Technology

Graphing utilities have a feature that gives (or approximates) the derivative of a function evaluated at any number. Consult your manual for details. The screen below verifies that if $f(x) = x^3$, then $f'(5) = 75$.

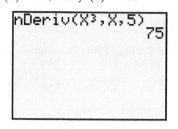

The derivative of $f(x) = x^3$ is $f'(x) = 3x^2$. To find the instantaneous change of $f$ at 5, evaluate the derivative at 5.

$$f'(x) = 3x^2$$
$$f'(5) = 3 \cdot 5^2 = 75$$

The instantaneous rate of change of the volume with respect to $x$ at the moment when $x = 5$ inches is 75 cubic inches per inch. Notice how the average rates of change that we computed in part (a), 76.51 and 75.1501, are approaching the instantaneous rate of change, 75. ●

⊘ Check Point **4** Use the function in Example 4, $f(x) = x^3$, to find each of the following:

**a.** the average rate of change of the volume with respect to $x$ as $x$ changes from 4 inches to 4.1 inches and from 4 inches to 4.01 inches.

**b.** the instantaneous rate of change of the volume with respect to $x$ at the moment when $x = 4$ inches.

**④** Find instantaneous velocity.

The ideas of calculus are frequently applied to position functions that express an object's position, $s(t)$, in terms of time, $t$. In the time interval from $t = a$ to $t = a + h$, the change in the object's position is

$$s(a + h) - s(a).$$

The **average velocity** over this time interval is

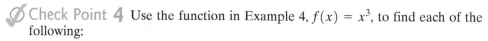

$$\frac{s(a + h) - s(a)}{h}.$$

The numerator is the change in position.

The denominator is the change in time from $t = a$ to $t = a + h$.

Now suppose that we compute the average velocities over shorter and shorter time intervals $[a, a + h]$. This means that we let $h$ approach 0. As in our previous discussion, we define the *instantaneous velocity* at time $t = a$ to be the limit of these average velocities. This limit is the derivative of $s$ at $a$.

## Instantaneous Velocity

Suppose that a function expresses an object's position, $s(t)$, in terms of time, $t$. The **instantaneous velocity** of the object at time $t = a$ is

$$s'(a) = \lim_{h \to 0} \frac{s(a + h) - s(a)}{h}.$$

Instantaneous velocity at time $a$ is also called **velocity** at time $a$.

---

( **EXAMPLE 5** ) **Finding Instantaneous Velocity**

A ball is thrown straight up from a rooftop 160 feet high with an initial velocity of 48 feet per second. The function

$$s(t) = -16t^2 + 48t + 160$$

describes the ball's height above the ground, $s(t)$, in feet, $t$ seconds after it is thrown. The ball misses the rooftop on its way down and eventually strikes the ground.

**a.** What is the instantaneous velocity of the ball 2 seconds after it is thrown?

**b.** What is the instantaneous velocity of the ball when it hits the ground?

**Solution** Instantaneous velocity is given by the derivative of a function that expresses an object's position, $s(t)$, in terms of time, $t$. The instantaneous velocity of the ball at $a$ seconds is $s'(a)$.

$$s'(a) = \lim_{h \to 0} \frac{s(a + h) - s(a)}{h} \quad \text{This derivative describes instantaneous velocity at time } a.$$

To find $s(a + h)$, replace $t$ in $s(t) = -16t^2 + 48t + 160$ with $a + h$. To find $s(a)$, replace $t$ with $a$. Thus,

$$s'(a) = \lim_{h \to 0} \frac{-16(a + h)^2 + 48(a + h) + 160 - (-16a^2 + 48a + 160)}{h}$$

Take a few minutes to simplify the numerator of the difference quotient and factor out $h$. You should obtain

$$s'(a) = \lim_{h \to 0} \frac{\not{h}(-32a - 16h + 48)}{\not{h}} = -32a - 16 \cdot 0 + 48 = -32a + 48.$$

The instantaneous velocity of the ball at $a$ seconds is

$$s'(a) = -32a + 48.$$

**a.** The instantaneous velocity of the ball at 2 seconds is found by replacing $a$ with 2.

$$s'(2) = -32 \cdot 2 + 48 = -64 + 48 = -16$$

Two seconds after the ball is thrown, its instantaneous velocity is $-16$ feet per second. The negative sign indicates that the ball is moving downward when $t = 2$ seconds.

**b.** To find the instantaneous velocity of the ball when it hits the ground, we need to know how many seconds elapse between the time the ball is thrown from the rooftop and the time it hits the ground. The ball hits the ground when $s(t)$, its height above the ground, is 0. Thus, we set $s(t)$ equal to 0.

$$-16t^2 + 48t + 160 = 0 \qquad \text{Set } s(t) = 0.$$
$$-16(t^2 - 3t - 10) = 0 \qquad \text{Factor out } -16.$$
$$-16(t - 5)(t + 2) = 0 \qquad \text{Factor completely.}$$
$$t - 5 = 0 \qquad t + 2 = 0 \qquad \text{Set each variable factor equal to 0.}$$
$$t = 5 \qquad\quad t = -2 \qquad \text{Solve for } t.$$

---

## Roller Coasters and Derivatives

Roller coaster rides give you the opportunity to spend a few hair-raising minutes plunging hundreds of feet, accelerating to 80 miles an hour in seven seconds, and enduring vertical loops that turn you upside-down. By finding a function that models your distance above the ground at every moment of the ride and taking its derivative, you can determine when the instantaneous velocity is the greatest. As you experience the glorious agony of the roller coaster, this is your moment of peak terror.

Because we are describing the ball's position for $t \geq 0$, we discard the solution $t = -2$. The ball hits the ground at 5 seconds. Its instantaneous velocity at 5 seconds is found by replacing $a$ with 5 in $s'(a)$.

$$s'(a) = -32a + 48 \qquad \text{This is the ball's instantaneous velocity after } a \text{ seconds.}$$
$$s'(5) = -32 \cdot 5 + 48 = -160 + 48 = -112$$

The instantaneous velocity of the ball when it hits the ground is $-112$ feet per second. The negative sign indicates that the ball is moving downward at the instant that it strikes the ground.

⊘ Check Point **5** A ball is thrown straight up from ground level with an initial velocity of 96 feet per second. The function

$$s(t) = -16t^2 + 96t$$

describes the ball's height above the ground, $s(t)$, in feet, $t$ seconds after it is thrown.

    **a.** What is the instantaneous velocity of the ball after 4 seconds?

    **b.** What is the instantaneous velocity of the ball when it hits the ground?

## Exercise Set 11.4

### Practice Exercises

*In Exercises 1–14,*

    **a.** *Find the slope of the tangent line to the graph of f at the given point.*

    **b.** *Find the slope-intercept equation of the tangent line to the graph of f at the given point.*

**1.** $f(x) = 2x + 3$ at $(1, 5)$      **2.** $f(x) = 4x + 2$ at $(1, 6)$

**3.** $f(x) = x^2 + 4$ at $(-1, 5)$      **4.** $f(x) = x^2 + 7$ at $(-1, 8)$

**5.** $f(x) = 5x^2$ at $(-2, 20)$      **6.** $f(x) = 4x^2$ at $(-2, 16)$

**7.** $f(x) = 2x^2 - x$ at $(2, 6)$      **8.** $f(x) = 3x^2 + x$ at $(1, 4)$

**9.** $f(x) = 2x^2 + x - 3$ at $(0, -3)$

**10.** $f(x) = 2x^2 - x + 5$ at $(0, 5)$

**11.** $f(x) = \sqrt{x}$ at $(9, 3)$      **12.** $f(x) = \sqrt{x}$ at $(16, 4)$

**13.** $f(x) = \dfrac{1}{x}$ at $(1, 1)$      **14.** $f(x) = \dfrac{2}{x}$ at $(1, 2)$

*In Exercises 15–28,*

    **a.** *Find the derivative of f at x. That is, find $f'(x)$.*

    **b.** *Find the slope of the tangent line to the graph of f at each of the two values of x given to the right of the function.*

**15.** $f(x) = -3x + 7; x = 1, x = 4$

**16.** $f(x) = -5x + 3; x = 1, x = 4$

**17.** $f(x) = x^2 - 6; x = -1, x = 3$

**18.** $f(x) = x^2 - 8; x = -1, x = 3$

**19.** $f(x) = x^2 - 3x + 5; x = \frac{3}{2}, x = 2$

**20.** $f(x) = x^2 - 4x + 7; x = \frac{3}{2}, x = 2$

**21.** $f(x) = x^3 + 2; x = -1, x = 1$

**22.** $f(x) = x^3 - 2; x = -1, x = 1$

**23.** $f(x) = \sqrt{x}; x = 1, x = 4$

**24.** $f(x) = \sqrt{x}; x = 25, x = 100$

**25.** $f(x) = \dfrac{4}{x}; x = -2, x = 1$

**26.** $f(x) = \dfrac{8}{x}; x = -2, x = 1$

**27.** $f(x) = 3.2x^2 + 2.1x; x = 0, x = 4$

**28.** $f(x) = 1.3x^2 - 1.4x; x = 0, x = 4$

### Practice Plus

*In Exercises 29–36,*

    **a.** *Use transformations of a common graph to obtain the graph of f.*

    **b.** *Find the slope-intercept equation of the tangent line to the graph of f at the point whose x-coordinate is given.*

    **c.** *Use the y-intercept and the slope to graph the tangent line in the same rectangular coordinate system as the graph of f.*

**29.** $f(x) = (x - 2)^2$; tangent line at 3

**30.** $f(x) = (x + 2)^2$; tangent line at $-1$

**31.** $f(x) = \sqrt{x + 1} - 2$; tangent line at 0

**32.** $f(x) = \sqrt{x - 1} + 2$; tangent line at 2

**33.** $f(x) = x^3 + 2$; tangent line at $-1$

**34.** $f(x) = x^3 - 2$; tangent line at 1

**35.** $f(x) = -\dfrac{1}{x + 3}$; tangent line at $-2$

**36.** $f(x) = -\dfrac{1}{x - 2}$; tangent line at 3

## Application Exercises

**37.** The function $f(x) = x^2$ describes the area of a square, $f(x)$, in square inches, whose sides each measure $x$ inches. If $x$ is changing,

    **a.** Find the average rate of change of the area with respect to $x$ as $x$ changes from 6 inches to 6.1 inches and from 6 inches to 6.01 inches.

    **b.** Find the instantaneous rate of change of the area with respect to $x$ at the moment when $x = 6$ inches.

**38.** The function $f(x) = x^2$ describes the area of a square, $f(x)$, in square inches, whose sides each measure $x$ inches. If $x$ is changing,

    **a.** Find the average rate of change of the area with respect to $x$ as $x$ changes from 10 inches to 10.1 inches and from 10 inches to 10.01 inches.

    **b.** Find the instantaneous rate of change of the area with respect to $x$ at the moment when $x = 10$ inches.

*In Exercises 39–42, express all answers in terms of $\pi$.*

**39.** The function $f(x) = \pi x^2$ describes the area of a circle, $f(x)$, in square inches, whose radius measures $x$ inches. If the radius is changing,

    **a.** Find the average rate of change of the area with respect to the radius as the radius changes from 2 inches to 2.1 inches and from 2 inches to 2.01 inches.

    **b.** Find the instantaneous rate of change of the area with respect to the radius when the radius is 2 inches.

**40.** The function $f(x) = \pi x^2$ describes the area of a circle, $f(x)$, in square inches, whose radius measures $x$ inches. If the radius is changing,

    **a.** Find the average rate of change of the area with respect to the radius as the radius changes from 4 inches to 4.1 inches and from 4 inches to 4.01 inches.

    **b.** Find the instantaneous rate of change of the area with respect to the radius when the radius is 4 inches.

**41.** The function $f(x) = 4\pi x^2$ describes the surface area, $f(x)$, of a sphere of radius $x$ inches. If the radius is changing, find the instantaneous rate of change of the surface area with respect to the radius when the radius is 6 inches.

**42.** The function $f(x) = 5\pi x^2$ describes the volume, $f(x)$, of a right circular cylinder of height 5 feet and radius $x$ feet. If the radius is changing, find the instantaneous rate of change of the volume with respect to the radius when the radius is 8 feet.

**43.** An explosion causes debris to rise vertically with an initial velocity of 64 feet per second. The function

$$s(t) = -16t^2 + 64t$$

describes the height of the debris above the ground, $s(t)$, in feet, $t$ seconds after the explosion.

    **a.** What is the instantaneous velocity of the debris 1 second after the explosion? 3 seconds after the explosion?

    **b.** What is the instantaneous velocity of the debris when it hits the ground?

**44.** An explosion causes debris to rise vertically with an initial velocity of 72 feet per second. The function

$$s(t) = -16t^2 + 72t$$

describes the height of the debris above the ground, $s(t)$, in feet, $t$ seconds after the explosion.

    **a.** What is the instantaneous velocity of the debris $\frac{1}{2}$ second after the explosion? 4 seconds after the explosion?

    **b.** What is the instantaneous velocity of the debris when it hits the ground?

**45.** A foul tip of a baseball is hit straight upward from a height of 4 feet with an initial velocity of 96 feet per second. The function

$$s(t) = -16t^2 + 96t + 4$$

describes the ball's height above the ground, $s(t)$, in feet, $t$ seconds after it is hit.

    **a.** What is the instantaneous velocity of the ball 2 seconds after it is hit? 4 seconds after it is hit?

    **b.** The ball reaches its maximum height above the ground when the instantaneous velocity is zero. After how many seconds does the ball reach its maximum height? What is its maximum height?

**46.** A foul tip of a baseball is hit straight upward from a height of 4 feet with an initial velocity of 64 feet per second. The function

$$s(t) = -16t^2 + 64t + 4$$

describes the ball's height above the ground, $s(t)$, in feet, $t$ seconds after it is hit.

    **a.** What is the instantaneous velocity of the ball 1 second after it is hit? 3 seconds after it is hit?

    **b.** The ball reaches its maximum height above the ground when the instantaneous velocity is zero. After how many seconds does the ball reach its maximum height? What is its maximum height?

## Writing in Mathematics

**47.** Explain how the tangent line to the graph of a function at point $P$ is related to the secant lines between points $P$ and $Q$ on the function's graph.

**48.** Explain what we mean by the slope of the graph of a function at a point.

**49.** Explain how to find the slope of $f(x) = x^2$ at $(2, 4)$.

**50.** Explain how to write an equation of the tangent line to the graph of $f(x) = x^2$ at $(2, 4)$.

**51.** If you are given $y = f(x)$, the equation of function $f$, describe how to find $f'(x)$.

**52.** Explain how to use the derivative to compute the slopes of various tangent lines to the graph of a function.

**53.** Explain how the instantaneous rate of change of a function at a point is related to its average rates of change.

**54.** If a function expresses an object's position in terms of time, how do you find the instantaneous velocity of the object at any time during its motion?

**55.** Use the concept of an interval of time to describe how calculus views a particular instant of time.

**56.** You are about to take a great picture of fog rolling into San Francisco from the middle of the Golden Gate Bridge, 400 feet above the water. Whoops! You accidently lean too far over the safety rail and drop your camera. Your friend quips, "Well at least you know calculus; you can figure out the velocity with which the camera is going to hit the water." If the camera's height, $s(t)$, in feet, over the water after $t$ seconds is $s(t) = 400 - 16t^2$, describe how to determine the camera's velocity at the instant of its demise.

**57.** A calculus professor introduced the derivative by saying that it could be summed up in one word: *slope*. Explain what this means.

**58.** For an unusual introduction to calculus by a poetic, quirky, and funny writer who loves the subject, read *A Tour of the Calculus* by David Berlinski (Vintage Books, 1995). Write a report describing two new things that you learned from the book about algebra, trigonometry, limits, or derivatives.

## Technology Exercises

**59.** Use the DRAW TANGENT feature of a graphing utility to graph the functions and tangent lines for any five exercises from Exercises 1–14. Use the equation that is displayed on the screen to verify the slope-intercept equation of the tangent line that you found in each exercise.

**60.** Without using the DRAW TANGENT feature of a graphing utility, graph the function and the tangent line whose equation you found for any five exercises from Exercises 1–14. Does the line appear to be tangent to the graph of $f$ at the point on $f$ that is given in the exercise?

**61.** Use the feature on a graphing utility that gives the derivative of a function evaluated at any number to verify part (b) for any five of your answers in Exercises 15–28.

*In Exercises 62–65, find, or approximate to two decimal places, the derivative of each function at the given number using a graphing utility.*

**62.** $f(x) = x^4 - x^3 + x^2 - x + 1$ at 1

**63.** $f(x) = \dfrac{x}{x-3}$ at 6

**64.** $f(x) = x^2 \cos x$ at $\dfrac{\pi}{4}$

**65.** $f(x) = e^x \sin x$ at 2

## Critical Thinking Exercises

**Make Sense?** *In Exercises 66–69, determine whether each statement makes sense or does not make sense, and explain your reasoning.*

**66.** Because I have two points to work with, I use the formula for slope, $\dfrac{y_2 - y_1}{x_2 - x_1}$, to find the slope of the tangent line to the graph of a function $y = f(x)$ at $(a, f(a))$.

**67.** I can find the slope of the tangent line to the graph of $f(x)$ at $(3, f(3))$ using $\lim\limits_{h \to 0} \dfrac{f(3+h) - f(3)}{h}$ or finding $f'(x)$ and then replacing $x$ with 3.

**68.** I obtained $f'(x)$ by finding $\lim\limits_{h \to 0}[f(x+h) - f(x)]$ and $\lim\limits_{h \to 0} h$, and then using the quotient rule for limits.

**69.** If $f(x) = \pi x^2$ describes the area of a circle, $f(x)$, with radius $x$, $f'(5) > f'(2)$ because the area increases more rapidly as the radius increases.

*In Exercises 70–75, graphs of functions are shown in $[-5, 5, 1]$ by $[-5, 5, 1]$ viewing rectangles. Match each function with the graph of its derivative. Graphs of derivatives are labeled (a)–(f) and are shown in $[-5, 5, 1]$ by $[-5, 5, 1]$ viewing rectangles.*

**70.** 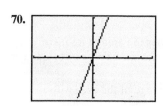   **71.**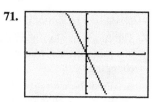

**72.** 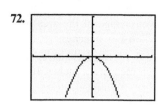   **73.**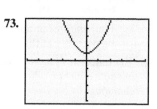

**74.** 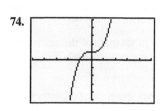   **75.**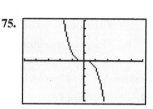

**a.** 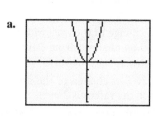   **b.**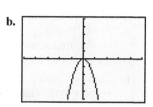

**c.** 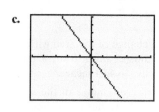   **d.**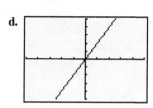

**e.** 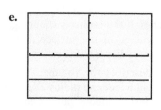   **f.**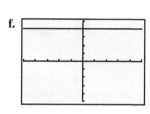

**76.** A ball is thrown straight up from a rooftop 96 feet high with an initial velocity of 80 feet per second. The function

$$s(t) = -16t^2 + 80t + 96$$

describes the ball's height above the ground, $s(t)$, in feet, $t$ seconds after it is thrown. The ball misses the rooftop on its way down and eventually strikes the ground. What is its instantaneous velocity as it passes the rooftop on the way down?

**77.** Show that the rate of change of the area of a circle with respect to its radius is equal to the circumference of the circle.

**78.** Show that the $x$-coordinate of the vertex of the parabola whose equation is $y = ax^2 + bx + c$ occurs when the derivative of the function is zero.

**79.** For any positive integer $n$, prove that if $f(x) = x^n$, then $f'(x) = nx^{n-1}$.

# Chapter 11  Summary, Review, and Test

## Summary

| DEFINITIONS AND CONCEPTS | EXAMPLES |
|---|---|
| **11.1 Finding Limits Using Tables and Graphs** | |
| **a.** Limit Notation and Its Description<br><br>$\lim\limits_{x \to a} f(x) = L$ is read "the limit of $f(x)$ as $x$ approaches $a$ equals the number $L$." This means that as $x$ gets closer to $a$, but remains unequal to $a$, the corresponding values of $f(x)$ get closer to $L$. | |
| **b.** Limits can be found using tables. | Ex. 1, p. 1040;<br>Ex. 2, p. 1040 |
| **c.** Limits can be found using graphs. | Ex. 3, p. 1042;<br>Ex. 4, p. 1042 |
| **d.** Left-Hand Limit<br><br>$\lim\limits_{x \to a^-} f(x) = L$ is read "the limit of $f(x)$ as $x$ approaches $a$ from the left equals $L$." This means that as $x$ gets closer to $a$, but remains less than $a$, the corresponding values of $f(x)$ get closer to $L$. | |
| **e.** Right-Hand Limit<br><br>$\lim\limits_{x \to a^+} f(x) = L$ is read "the limit of $f(x)$ as $x$ approaches $a$ from the right equals $L$." This means that as $x$ gets closer to $a$, but remains greater than $a$, the corresponding values of $f(x)$ get closer to $L$. | |
| **f.** If $\lim\limits_{x \to a^-} f(x) \neq \lim\limits_{x \to a^+} f(x)$, then $\lim\limits_{x \to a} f(x)$ does not exist. | Ex. 5, p. 1044 |
| **11.2 Finding Limits Using Properties of Limits** | |
| **a.** Properties of limits are given in the box on page 1057. | Ex. 1–Ex. 11,<br>pp. 1050–1057 |
| **b.** Properties of limits can be used to find one-sided limits. | Ex. 12, p. 1058 |
| **c.** When taking the limit of a fractional expression in which the limit of the denominator is zero, the quotient property for limits cannot be used. Rewriting the expression using factoring or rationalizing the numerator or denominator may be helpful before the limit is found. | Ex. 13, p. 1058;<br>Ex. 14, p. 1059 |
| **11.3 Limits and Continuity** | |
| **a.** A function $f$ is continuous at $a$ when $f$ is defined at $a$, $\lim\limits_{x \to a} f(x)$ exists, and $\lim\limits_{x \to a} f(x) = f(a)$.<br>If $f$ is not continuous at $a$, we say that $f$ is discontinuous at $a$. | Ex. 1, p. 1063;<br>Ex. 2, p. 1065 |
| **11.4 Introduction to Derivatives** | |
| **a.** The slope of the tangent line to the graph of a function $y = f(x)$ at $(a, f(a))$ is given by<br><br>$$m_{\tan} = \lim_{h \to 0} \frac{f(a + h) - f(a)}{h}$$<br><br>provided that this limit exists. The limit also describes the slope of the graph of $f$ at $(a, f(a))$. | Ex, 1, p. 1073;<br>Ex. 2, p. 1074 |
| **b.** The Derivative of a Function<br>The derivative of $f$ at $x$ is given by<br><br>$$f'(x) = \lim_{h \to 0} \frac{f(x + h) - f(x)}{h}$$<br><br>provided that this limit exists. The derivative gives the slope of $f$ for any value at $x$ in the domain of $f'$. | Ex. 3, p. 1076 |
| **c.** The derivative of $f$ at $a$, $f'(a) = \lim\limits_{h \to 0} \dfrac{f(a + h) - f(a)}{h}$, gives the instantaneous rate of change of $f$ with respect to $x$ at $a$. Expressions for average and instantaneous rates of change are given in the box on page 1077. | Ex. 4, p. 1077 |
| **d.** If a function expresses an object's position, $s(t)$, in terms of time, $t$, the instantaneous velocity of the object at time $t = a$ is<br><br>$$s'(a) = \lim_{h \to 0} \frac{s(a + h) - s(a)}{h}.$$ | Ex. 5, p. 1079 |

# Review Exercises

## 11.1

In Exercises 1–3, construct a table to find the indicated limit.

**1.** $\lim\limits_{x \to 1} \dfrac{x^3 - 1}{x - 1}$

**2.** $\lim\limits_{x \to 0} \dfrac{\sqrt{x + 1} - 1}{x}$

**3.** $\lim\limits_{x \to 0} \dfrac{\sin 2x}{x}$

In Exercises 4–8, use the graph of $f$ to find the indicated limit or function value.

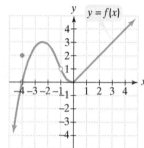

**4.** $\lim\limits_{x \to -4} f(x)$

**5.** $\lim\limits_{x \to -1} f(x)$

**6.** $\lim\limits_{x \to 3} f(x)$

**7.** $f(-4)$

**8.** $f(3)$

In Exercises 9–23, use the graph of function $f$ to find the indicated limit or function value, or state that the limit or function value does not exist.

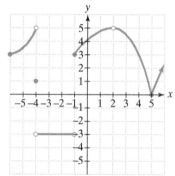

**9.** $\lim\limits_{x \to -6^+} f(x)$

**10.** $\lim\limits_{x \to -4^-} f(x)$

**11.** $\lim\limits_{x \to -4^+} f(x)$

**12.** $\lim\limits_{x \to -4} f(x)$

**13.** $f(-4)$

**14.** $\lim\limits_{x \to -1^+} f(x)$

**15.** $\lim\limits_{x \to -1^-} f(x)$

**16.** $\lim\limits_{x \to -1} f(x)$

**17.** $f(-1)$

**18.** $f(2)$

**19.** $\lim\limits_{x \to 2^-} f(x)$

**20.** $\lim\limits_{x \to 2^+} f(x)$

**21.** $\lim\limits_{x \to 2} f(x)$

**22.** $\lim\limits_{x \to 5} f(x)$

**23.** $f(5)$

In Exercises 24–26, graph each function. Then use your graph to find the indicated limit.

**24.** $f(x) = \dfrac{x^2 - 9}{x - 3}, \quad \lim\limits_{x \to 3} f(x)$

**25.** $f(x) = \sin x, \quad \lim\limits_{x \to \frac{3\pi}{2}} f(x)$

**26.** $f(x) = \begin{cases} 1 - x & \text{if } x < 0 \\ \cos x & \text{if } x \ge 0, \end{cases} \lim\limits_{x \to 0} f(x)$

## 11.2

In Exercises 27–37, find the limit.

**27.** $\lim\limits_{x \to 4} (2x^2 - 5x + 3)$

**28.** $\lim\limits_{x \to -1} (-2x^3 - x + 5)$

**29.** $\lim\limits_{x \to -3} (x^2 + 1)^3$

**30.** $\lim\limits_{x \to 4} \sqrt{x^2 + 9}$

**31.** $\lim\limits_{x \to 5} \dfrac{11x - 3}{x^2 + 1}$

**32.** $\lim\limits_{x \to -4} \dfrac{x^2 - 16}{x + 4}$

**33.** $\lim\limits_{x \to 7} \dfrac{5x - 35}{x - 7}$

**34.** $\lim\limits_{x \to 0} \dfrac{\sqrt{x + 100} - 10}{x}$

**35.** $\lim\limits_{x \to -1} \dfrac{x^2 - 1}{x^2 + x}$

**36.** $\lim\limits_{x \to 100} \dfrac{\sqrt{x} - 10}{x - 100}$

**37.** $\lim\limits_{x \to 0} \dfrac{\dfrac{1}{x + 5} - \dfrac{1}{5}}{x}$

In Exercises 38–40, a piecewise function is given. Use properties of limits to find the indicated limit, or state that the limit does not exist.

**38.** $f(x) = \begin{cases} x^2 + 1 & \text{if } x < 2 \\ 3x + 1 & \text{if } x \ge 2 \end{cases}$

   **a.** $\lim\limits_{x \to 2^-} f(x)$
   **b.** $\lim\limits_{x \to 2^+} f(x)$
   **c.** $\lim\limits_{x \to 2} f(x)$

**39.** $f(x) = \begin{cases} \sqrt[3]{x^2 + 7} & \text{if } x < 1 \\ 4x & \text{if } x \ge 1 \end{cases}$

   **a.** $\lim\limits_{x \to 1^-} f(x)$
   **b.** $\lim\limits_{x \to 1^+} f(x)$
   **c.** $\lim\limits_{x \to 1} f(x)$

**40.** $f(x) = \begin{cases} \dfrac{x^2 - 25}{x + 5} & \text{if } x \ne -5 \\ 13 & \text{if } x = -5 \end{cases}$

   **a.** $\lim\limits_{x \to -5^-} f(x)$
   **b.** $\lim\limits_{x \to -5^+} f(x)$
   **c.** $\lim\limits_{x \to -5} f(x)$

## 11.3

In Exercises 41–45, use the definition of continuity to determine whether $f$ is continuous at $a$.

**41.** $f(x) = 3x^2 - 2x + 1$
   $a = 4$

**42.** $f(x) = \dfrac{x^2 - 9}{x + 3}$
   $a = -3$

**43.** $f(x) = \begin{cases} \dfrac{x^2 + 5x}{x^2 - 5x} & \text{if } x \ne 0 \\ -2 & \text{if } x = 0 \end{cases}$
   $a = 0$

**44.** $f(x) = \begin{cases} \dfrac{x^2 + x}{x^2 - 3x - 4} & \text{if } x \ne -1 \\ \frac{1}{5} & \text{if } x = -1 \end{cases}$
   $a = -1$

**45.** $f(x) = \begin{cases} 3x & \text{if } x < 2 \\ 5 & \text{if } x = 2 \\ x + 4 & \text{if } x > 2 \end{cases}$
   $a = 2$

In Exercises 46–51, determine for what numbers, if any, the given function is discontinuous.

**46.** $f(x) = x^3 + 5x^2 - 1$

**47.** $f(x) = \dfrac{x - 1}{(x - 1)(x + 3)}$

**48.** $f(x) = \begin{cases} -1 & \text{if } x < 0 \\ 1 & \text{if } x \ge 0 \end{cases}$

**49.** $f(x) = \begin{cases} 4x & \text{if } x < 5 \\ x^2 - 5 & \text{if } x \ge 5 \end{cases}$

**50.** $f(x) = \begin{cases} \dfrac{x^2 - 4}{x + 2} & \text{if } x \neq -2 \\ 4 & \text{if } x = -2 \end{cases}$

**51.** $f(x) = \begin{cases} \dfrac{x^2 - 121}{x - 11} & \text{if } x \neq 11 \\ 20 & \text{if } x = 11 \end{cases}$

## 11.4

*In Exercises 52–53,*

    **a.** *Find the slope of the tangent line to the graph of f at the given point.*

    **b.** *Find the slope-intercept equation of the tangent line to the graph of f at the given point.*

**52.** $f(x) = 2x^2 + 5x$ at $(1, 7)$

**53.** $f(x) = x^2 - 7x - 4$ at $(-1, 4)$

*In Exercises 54–57,*

    **a.** *Find $f'(x)$.*

    **b.** *Find the slope of the tangent line to the graph of f at each of the two values of x given to the right of the function.*

**54.** $f(x) = 3x^2 + 12x - 1$; $x = -2$, $x = 1$

**55.** $f(x) = 2x^3 - x$; $x = -1$, $x = 1$

**56.** $f(x) = \dfrac{1}{x}$; $x = -2$, $x = 2$    **57.** $f(x) = \sqrt{x}$; $x = 36$, $x = 81$

**58.** The function $f(x) = 5x^2$ describes the volume of a rectangular box, $f(x)$, in cubic inches, whose square base has sides that each measure $x$ inches and whose height is 5 inches. If $x$ is changing,

    **a.** Find the average rate of change of the volume with respect to $x$ as $x$ changes from 2 inches to 2.1 inches and from 2 inches to 2.01 inches.

    **b.** Find the instantaneous rate of change of the volume with respect to $x$ at the moment when $x = 2$ inches.

**59.** The function $f(x) = \frac{4}{3}\pi x^3$ describes the volume, $f(x)$, of a sphere of radius $x$ inches. If the radius is changing, find the instantaneous rate of change of the volume with respect to the radius when the radius is 5 inches. Express the answer in terms of $\pi$.

**60.** A baseball is thrown straight upward from a height of 5 feet with an initial velocity of 80 feet per second. The function

$$s(t) = -16t^2 + 80t + 5$$

describes the ball's height above the ground, $s(t)$, in feet, $t$ seconds after it is thrown.

    **a.** What is the instantaneous velocity of the ball 2 seconds after it is thrown? 4 seconds after it is thrown?

    **b.** The ball reaches its maximum height above the ground when the instantaneous velocity is zero. After how many seconds does the ball reach its maximum height? What is the maximum height?

CHAPTER

## Test Prep
VIDEOS    **Chapter 11 Test**

**1.** Construct a table to find $\displaystyle\lim_{x \to 9} \dfrac{9 - x}{3 - \sqrt{x}}$.

*In Exercises 2–7, use the graph of function f to find the indicated limit or function value, or state that the limit or function value does not exist.*

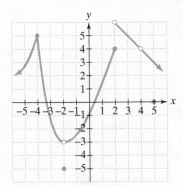

**2.** $\displaystyle\lim_{x \to -2} f(x)$          **3.** $f(-2)$

**4.** $\displaystyle\lim_{x \to 2^-} f(x)$       **5.** $\displaystyle\lim_{x \to 2^+} f(x)$

**6.** $\displaystyle\lim_{x \to 2} f(x)$         **7.** $\displaystyle\lim_{x \to 4} f(x)$

*In Exercises 8–10, find the limit.*

**8.** $\displaystyle\lim_{x \to -2}(x^2 + x + 1)^4$    **9.** $\displaystyle\lim_{x \to -1} \dfrac{x^2 - x - 2}{x + 1}$

**10.** $\displaystyle\lim_{x \to 9} \dfrac{\sqrt{x} - 3}{x - 9}$

*In Exercises 11–12, determine whether f is continuous at a.*

**11.** $f(x) = \begin{cases} \dfrac{x^2 - 1}{x + 1} & \text{if } x \neq -1 \\ 6 & \text{if } x = -1 \end{cases}$

    $a = -1$

**12.** $f(x) = \begin{cases} 2 - x & \text{if } x \leq 2 \\ x^2 - 2x & \text{if } x > 2 \end{cases}$

    $a = 2$

*In Exercises 13–14, find $f'(x)$.*

**13.** $f(x) = x^2 - 5x + 1$

**14.** $f(x) = \dfrac{10}{x}$

**15.** Find the slope-intercept equation of the tangent line to the graph of $f(x) = x^2$ at $(-3, 9)$.

**16.** A ball is thrown straight upward. The function

$$s(t) = -16t^2 + 72t$$

describes the ball's height above the ground, $s(t)$, in feet, $t$ seconds after it is thrown. What is the instantaneous velocity of the ball 3 seconds after it is thrown?

## Cumulative Review Exercises (Chapters P–11)

*Solve each equation or inequality in Exercises 1–5.*

1. $\dfrac{1}{x+2} > \dfrac{3}{x+1}$

2. $2x^3 + 11x^2 - 7x - 6 = 0$

3. $|2x + 4| > 3$

4. $\cos^2 x + \sin x + 1 = 0, 0 \le x < 2\pi$

5. $\log_4(x^2 - 9) - \log_4(x + 3) = 3$

*In Exercises 6–15, graph each equation, function, or system in a rectangular coordinate system.*

6. $f(x) = x^3 + x^2 - 12x$

7. $f(x) = \dfrac{2x^2 - 5x + 2}{x^2 - 4}$

8. $f(x) = \begin{cases} -x + 1 & \text{if } -1 \le x < 1 \\ 2 & \text{if } x = 1 \\ x^2 & \text{if } x > 1 \end{cases}$

9. $y = 2\sin\left(2x + \dfrac{\pi}{2}\right)$ (Graph one period.)

10. $y = \frac{1}{2}\sec 2\pi x, \quad 0 \le x \le 2$

11. $\begin{cases} x - 2y \le 4 \\ \quad\ x \ge 2 \end{cases}$

12. $x^2 - 4y^2 - 4x - 24y - 48 = 0$

13. $f(x) = \sqrt{x}, g(x) = \sqrt{x - 2} + 1$ (Graph $f$ and $g$ in the same rectangular coordinate system.)

14. $x = 3\sin t, y = 4\cos t + 2; 0 \le t \le 2\pi$

15. $2x^2 + 5xy + 2y^2 - \frac{9}{2} = 0$

16. Find $f'(x)$ if $f(x) = -2x^2 + 7x - 1$.

17. Find $f^{-1}(x)$ if $f(x) = 7x - 1$.

18. Find the limit: $\displaystyle\lim_{x \to -3} \dfrac{x^2 + x - 6}{x^2 + 2x - 3}$.

19. Expand and simplify: $(x^2 - 3y)^4$.

20. Write the slope-intercept form of the equation of the line passing through the point $(2, -3)$ and parallel to the line whose equation is $2x + y - 6 = 0$.

21. Find the dot product $\mathbf{v} \cdot \mathbf{w}$ and the angle between $\mathbf{v}$ and $\mathbf{w}$:

$$\mathbf{v} = -2\mathbf{i} + \mathbf{j}, \quad \mathbf{w} = 4\mathbf{i} - 3\mathbf{j}.$$

22. Find the partial fraction decomposition for

$$\dfrac{1}{x(x^2 + x + 1)}.$$

*Verify each identity in Exercises 23–24.*

23. $\tan\theta + \cot\theta = \sec\theta \csc\theta$    24. $\tan(\theta + \pi) = \tan\theta$

25. If $A = \begin{bmatrix} 2 & 1 & 3 \\ 1 & -1 & 0 \end{bmatrix}$ and $B = \begin{bmatrix} 1 & 0 \\ 3 & 2 \\ 2 & 1 \end{bmatrix}$, find $BA$.

26. Graph the polar equation: $r = 4\sin\theta$.

27. Express $h(x) = (x^2 - 3x + 7)^9$ as a composition of two functions $f$ and $g$ such that $h(x) = (f \circ g)(x)$.

28. Solve using matrices:

$$\begin{cases} 2x - y - 2z = -1 \\ x - 2y - z = 1 \\ x + y + z = 1. \end{cases}$$

29. Use the formula for the sum of the first $n$ terms of a geometric sequence to find $\displaystyle\sum_{i=1}^{6} 4(-2)^i$.

30. Use DeMoivre's Theorem to find

$$\left[\sqrt{2}(\cos 15° + i\sin 15°)\right]^4.$$

Write the answer in rectangular form.

31. A bank loaned out $120,000, part of it at 8% per year and the rest at 18% per year.

   a. Express the interest, $I$, on the two loans as a function of the amount loaned at 8%, $x$.

   b. If the interest received totaled $10,000, how much was loaned at each rate?

32. A machine produces open boxes using square sheets of metal. The machine cuts equal-sized squares measuring 9 centimeters on a side from each corner. Then the machine shapes the metal into an open box by turning up the sides. If each box must have a volume of 225 cubic centimeters, what should be the dimensions of the piece of sheet metal?

33. You have 200 feet of fencing to enclose a small rectangular garden with one side against a barn. If you do not fence the side along the barn, find the length and width of the garden that will maximize its area. What is the largest area that can be enclosed?

34. Use Newton's Law of Cooling, $T = C + (T_0 - C)e^{kt}$, to solve this exercise. You remove a pie that has a temperature of 375°F from the oven. You leave the pie in a room whose temperature is 72°F. After 60 minutes, the temperature of the pie is 75°F.

   a. Write a model for the temperature of the pie, $T$, after $t$ minutes.

   b. When will the temperature of the pie be 250°F?

35. You just purchased a rectangular waterfront lot along a river's edge. The area of the lot is 60,000 square feet. To create a sense of privacy, you decide to fence along three sides, excluding the side that fronts the river. An expensive fencing along the lot's front length costs $25 per foot. An inexpensive fencing along the two side widths costs only $5 per foot. Express the total cost, $C$, of fencing along the three sides as a function of the lot's length, $x$.

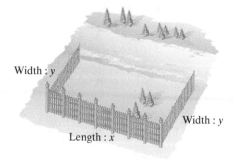

Width : $y$

Width : $y$

Length : $x$

**36.** Two ships leave a harbor at the same time. One ship travels at a bearing of N42°E for 23 miles. The other ship travels at a bearing of N38°W for 72 miles. After both ships are anchored, how far apart are they? Round to the nearest tenth of a mile.

**37.** At a fixed temperature, the volume of a given mass of gas varies inversely as the pressure applied to the gas. A certain mass of gas has a volume of 40 cubic inches when the pressure is 22 pounds. What is the volume of the gas when the pressure is 30 pounds?

**38.** A ball is thrown straight upward. The function

$$s(t) = -16t^2 + 40t$$

describes the ball's height above the ground, $s(t)$, in feet, $t$ seconds after it is thrown. What is the instantaneous velocity of the ball 2 seconds after it is thrown?

**39.** The figure shows an open box with a square base. The box is to have a volume of 4 cubic feet. Express the surface area of the box, $A$, as a function of the length of a side of its square base, $x$.

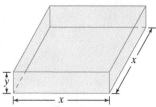

**40.** The function $f(x) = -2.32x^2 + 76.58x - 559.87$ models the percentage of U.S. students, $f(x)$, who are $x$ years old who say their school is not drug free, where $12 \le x \le 17$. At what age do 70% of U.S. students say that their school is not drug free? Round to the nearest tenth of a year.

# Appendix A

## Where Did That Come From?

## Selected Proofs

**Properties of Logarithms**

### The Product Rule

Let $b$, $M$, and $N$ be positive real numbers with $b \neq 1$.

$$\log_b(MN) = \log_b M + \log_b N$$

**Proof**

We begin by letting $\log_b M = R$ and $\log_b N = S$.
Now we write each logarithm in exponential form.

$$\log_b M = R \quad \text{means} \quad b^R = M.$$
$$\log_b N = S \quad \text{means} \quad b^S = N.$$

By substituting and using a property of exponents, we see that

$$MN = b^R b^S = b^{R+S}.$$

Now we change $MN = b^{R+S}$ to logarithmic form.

$$MN = b^{R+S} \quad \text{means} \quad \log_b(MN) = R + S.$$

Finally, substituting $\log_b M$ for $R$ and $\log_b N$ for $S$ gives us

$$\log_b(MN) = \log_b M + \log_b N,$$

the property that we wanted to prove.

The quotient and power rules for logarithms are proved using similar procedures.

### The Change-of-Base Property

For any logarithmic bases $a$ and $b$, and any positive number $M$,

$$\log_b M = \frac{\log_a M}{\log_a b}.$$

**Proof**

To prove the change-of-base property, we let $x$ equal the logarithm on the left side:

$$\log_b M = x.$$

Now we rewrite this logarithm in exponential form.

$$\log_b M = x \quad \text{means} \quad b^x = M.$$

Because $b^x$ and $M$ are equal, the logarithms with base $a$ for each of these expressions must be equal. This means that

$$\log_a b^x = \log_a M$$

$$x \log_a b = \log_a M \qquad \text{Apply the power rule for logarithms on the left side.}$$

$$x = \frac{\log_a M}{\log_a b} \qquad \text{Solve for x by dividing both sides by } \log_a b.$$

In our first step we let $x$ equal $\log_b M$. Replacing $x$ on the left side by $\log_b M$ gives us

$$\log_b M = \frac{\log_a M}{\log_a b},$$

which is the change-of-base property.

## Section 6.2 The Law of Cosines

### Heron's Formula for the Area of a Triangle

The area of a triangle with sides $a, b,$ and $c$ is

$$\text{Area} = \sqrt{s(s - a)(s - b)(s - c)},$$

where $s$ is one-half its perimeter: $s = \frac{1}{2}(a + b + c)$.

**Proof**

The proof of Heron's formula begins with a half-angle formula and the Law of Cosines.

$$\cos \frac{C}{2} = \sqrt{\frac{1 + \cos C}{2}} = \sqrt{\frac{1 + \frac{a^2 + b^2 - c^2}{2ab}}{2}} \qquad \begin{array}{l} \text{This is the Law of Cosines} \\ c^2 = a^2 + b^2 - 2ab \cos C \\ \text{solved for cos C.} \end{array}$$

$$= \sqrt{\frac{a^2 + 2ab + b^2 - c^2}{4ab}} = \sqrt{\frac{(a + b)^2 - c^2}{4ab}} = \sqrt{\frac{(a + b + c)(a + b - c)}{4ab}}$$

Multiply the numerator and denominator of the radicand by $2ab$.    Factor $a^2 + 2ab + b^2$.    Factor the numerator as the difference of two squares.

We now introduce the expression for one-half the perimeter: $s = \frac{1}{2}(a + b + c)$. We replace $a + b + c$ in the numerator by $2s$. We also find an expression for $a + b - c$ as follows:

$$a + b - c = a + b + c - 2c = 2s - 2c = 2(s - c).$$

Thus,

$$\cos \frac{C}{2} = \sqrt{\frac{(a + b + c)(a + b - c)}{4ab}} = \sqrt{\frac{2s \cdot 2(s - c)}{4ab}} = \sqrt{\frac{s(s - c)}{ab}}.$$

In a similar manner, we obtain

$$\sin \frac{C}{2} = \sqrt{\frac{1 - \cos C}{2}} = \sqrt{\frac{(s - a)(s - b)}{ab}}.$$

From our work in Section 6.1, we know that the area of a triangle is one-half the product of the length of two sides times the sine of their included angle.

$$\text{Area} = \frac{1}{2}ab \sin C$$

$$= \frac{1}{2}ab \cdot 2 \sin\frac{C}{2}\cos\frac{C}{2} \qquad \sin C = \sin 2\frac{C}{2} = 2\sin\frac{C}{2}\cos\frac{C}{2}$$

$$= ab\sqrt{\frac{(s-a)(s-b)}{ab}}\sqrt{\frac{s(s-c)}{ab}} \qquad \text{Use the expressions for } \sin\frac{C}{2} \text{ and}$$

$$\cos\frac{C}{2} \text{ on page A2.}$$

$$= ab\frac{\sqrt{s(s-a)(s-b)(s-c)}}{\sqrt{a^2b^2}} \qquad \text{Multiply the radicands.}$$

$$= \sqrt{s(s-a)(s-b)(s-c)} \qquad \text{Simplify: } \frac{ab}{\sqrt{a^2b^2}} = \frac{ab}{ab} = 1.$$

## Section 6.5  Complex Numbers in Polar Form; DeMoivre's Theorem

### The Quotient of Two Complex Numbers in Polar Form

Let $z_1 = r_1(\cos\theta_1 + i\sin\theta_1)$ and $z_2 = r_2(\cos\theta_2 + i\sin\theta_2)$ be two complex numbers in polar form. Their quotient, $\dfrac{z_1}{z_2}$, is

$$\frac{z_1}{z_2} = \frac{r_1}{r_2}[\cos(\theta_1 - \theta_2) + i\sin(\theta_1 - \theta_2)].$$

### Proof
We begin by multiplying the numerator and denominator of the quotient, $\dfrac{z_1}{z_2}$, by the conjugate of the expression in parentheses in the denominator. Then we simplify the quotient using the difference formulas for sine and cosine.

$$\frac{z_1}{z_2} = \frac{r_1(\cos\theta_1 + i\sin\theta_1)}{r_2(\cos\theta_2 + i\sin\theta_2)} \qquad \text{This is the given quotient.}$$

$$= \frac{r_1(\cos\theta_1 + i\sin\theta_1)(\cos\theta_2 - i\sin\theta_2)}{r_2(\cos\theta_2 + i\sin\theta_2)(\cos\theta_2 - i\sin\theta_2)} \qquad \text{Multiply the numerator and denominator by the conjugate of the expression in parentheses in the denominator. Recall that the conjugate of } a+bi \text{ is } a-bi.$$

$$= \frac{r_1(\cos\theta_1 + i\sin\theta_1)(\cos\theta_2 - i\sin\theta_2)}{r_2(\cos^2\theta_2 + \sin^2\theta_2)} \qquad \text{Multiply the conjugates in the denominator.}$$

$$= \frac{r_1(\cos\theta_1 + i\sin\theta_1)(\cos\theta_2 - i\sin\theta_2)}{r_2} \qquad \text{Use a Pythagorean identity: } \cos^2\theta_2 + \sin^2\theta_2 = 1.$$

$$= \frac{r_1}{r_2}(\cos\theta_1\cos\theta_2 - i\cos\theta_1\sin\theta_2 + i\sin\theta_1\cos\theta_2 - i^2\sin\theta_1\sin\theta_2) \qquad \text{Use the FOIL method.}$$

$$= \frac{r_1}{r_2}[\cos\theta_1\cos\theta_2 + i(\sin\theta_1\cos\theta_2 - \cos\theta_1\sin\theta_2) - i^2\sin\theta_1\sin\theta_2] \qquad \text{Factor } i \text{ from the second and third terms.}$$

$$= \frac{r_1}{r_2}[\cos\theta_1\cos\theta_2 + i(\sin\theta_1\cos\theta_2 - \cos\theta_1\sin\theta_2) - (-1)\sin\theta_1\sin\theta_2] \qquad i^2 = -1$$

$$= \frac{r_1}{r_2}[\cos\theta_1\cos\theta_2 + \sin\theta_1\sin\theta_2 + i(\sin\theta_1\cos\theta_2 - \cos\theta_1\sin\theta_2)] \qquad \text{Rearrange terms.}$$

This is $\cos(\theta_1 - \theta_2)$.　　　This is $\sin(\theta_1 - \theta_2)$.

$$= \frac{r_1}{r_2}[\cos(\theta_1 - \theta_2) + i\sin(\theta_1 - \theta_2)]$$

**Section 6.7** **The Dot Product**

### Properties of the Dot Product

If $\mathbf{u}$, $\mathbf{v}$, and $\mathbf{w}$ are vectors, and $c$ is a scalar, then

1. $\mathbf{u} \cdot \mathbf{v} = \mathbf{v} \cdot \mathbf{u}$
2. $\mathbf{u} \cdot (\mathbf{v} + \mathbf{w}) = \mathbf{u} \cdot \mathbf{v} + \mathbf{u} \cdot \mathbf{w}$
3. $\mathbf{0} \cdot \mathbf{v} = 0$
4. $\mathbf{v} \cdot \mathbf{v} = \|\mathbf{v}\|^2$
5. $(c\mathbf{u}) \cdot \mathbf{v} = c(\mathbf{u} \cdot \mathbf{v}) = \mathbf{u} \cdot (c\mathbf{v})$

### Proof

To prove the second property, let

$$\mathbf{u} = u_1\mathbf{i} + u_2\mathbf{j}, \quad \mathbf{v} = v_1\mathbf{i} + v_2\mathbf{j}, \quad \text{and} \quad \mathbf{w} = w_1\mathbf{i} + w_2\mathbf{j}.$$

Then,

$$\mathbf{u} \cdot (\mathbf{v} + \mathbf{w}) = (u_1\mathbf{i} + u_2\mathbf{j}) \cdot [(v_1\mathbf{i} + v_2\mathbf{j}) + (w_1\mathbf{i} + w_2\mathbf{j})]$$

These are the given vectors.

$$= (u_1\mathbf{i} + u_2\mathbf{j}) \cdot [(v_1 + w_1)\mathbf{i} + (v_2 + w_2)\mathbf{j}]$$

Add horizontal components and add vertical components.

$$= u_1(v_1 + w_1) + u_2(v_2 + w_2)$$

Multiply horizontal components and multiply vertical components.

$$= u_1v_1 + u_1w_1 + u_2v_2 + u_2w_2$$

Use the distributive property.

$$= u_1v_1 + u_2v_2 + u_1w_1 + u_2w_2$$

Rearrange terms.

This is the dot product of $\mathbf{u}$ and $\mathbf{v}$.        This is the dot product of $\mathbf{u}$ and $\mathbf{w}$.

$$= \mathbf{u} \cdot \mathbf{v} + \mathbf{u} \cdot \mathbf{w}.$$

To prove the third property, let

$$\mathbf{0} = 0\mathbf{i} + 0\mathbf{j} \quad \text{and} \quad \mathbf{v} = v_1\mathbf{i} + v_2\mathbf{j}.$$

Then,

$$\mathbf{0} \cdot \mathbf{v} = (0\mathbf{i} + 0\mathbf{j}) \cdot (v_1\mathbf{i} + v_2\mathbf{j})$$

These are the given vectors.

$$= 0 \cdot v_1 + 0 \cdot v_2$$

Multiply horizontal components and multiply vertical components.

$$= 0 + 0$$

$$= 0.$$

To prove the first part of the fifth property, let

$$\mathbf{u} = u_1\mathbf{i} + u_2\mathbf{j} \quad \text{and} \quad \mathbf{v} = v_1\mathbf{i} + v_2\mathbf{j}.$$

Then,

$$(c\mathbf{u}) \cdot \mathbf{v} = [c(u_1\mathbf{i} + u_2\mathbf{j})] \cdot (v_1\mathbf{i} + v_2\mathbf{j})$$

These are the given vectors.

$$= (cu_1\mathbf{i} + cu_2\mathbf{j}) \cdot (v_1\mathbf{i} + v_2\mathbf{j})$$

Multiply each component of $u_1\mathbf{i} + u_2\mathbf{j}$ by $c$.

$$= cu_1v_1 + cu_2v_2$$

Multiply horizontal components and multiply vertical components.

$$= c(u_1v_1 + u_2v_2)$$

Factor out $c$ from both terms.

This is the dot product of $\mathbf{u}$ and $\mathbf{v}$.

$$= c(\mathbf{u} \cdot \mathbf{v})$$

**Section 9.1 The Ellipse**

## The Standard Form of the Equation of an Ellipse with a Horizontal Major Axis Centered at the Origin

**Proof**
Refer to **Figure A.1**.

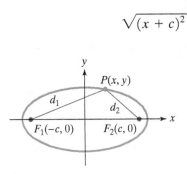

**Figure A.1**

$$d_1 + d_2 = 2a$$ The sum of the distances from $P$ to the foci equals a constant, $2a$.

$$\sqrt{(x+c)^2 + y^2} + \sqrt{(x-c)^2 + y^2} = 2a$$ Use the distance formula.

$$\sqrt{(x+c)^2 + y^2} = 2a - \sqrt{(x-c)^2 + y^2}$$ Isolate a radical.

$$(x+c)^2 + y^2 = 4a^2 - 4a\sqrt{(x-c)^2 + y^2}$$ Square both sides.
$$+ (x-c)^2 + y^2$$

$$x^2 + 2cx + c^2 + y^2 = 4a^2 - 4a\sqrt{(x-c)^2 + y^2}$$ Square $x+c$ and $x-c$.
$$+ x^2 - 2cx + c^2 + y^2$$

$$4cx - 4a^2 = -4a\sqrt{(x-c)^2 + y^2}$$ Simplify and isolate the radical.

$$cx - a^2 = -a\sqrt{(x-c)^2 + y^2}$$ Divide both sides by 4.

$$(cx - a^2)^2 = a^2[(x-c)^2 + y^2]$$ Square both sides.

$$c^2x^2 - 2a^2cx + a^4 = a^2(x^2 - 2cx + c^2 + y^2)$$ Square $cx - a^2$ and $x - c$.

$$c^2x^2 - 2a^2cx + a^4 = a^2x^2 - 2a^2cx + a^2c^2 + a^2y^2$$ Use the distributive property.

$$c^2x^2 + a^4 = a^2x^2 + a^2c^2 + a^2y^2$$ Add $2a^2cx$ to both sides.

$$c^2x^2 - a^2x^2 - a^2y^2 = a^2c^2 - a^4$$ Rearrange the terms.

$$(c^2 - a^2)x^2 - a^2y^2 = a^2(c^2 - a^2)$$ Factor out $x^2$ and $a^2$, respectively.

$$(a^2 - c^2)x^2 + a^2y^2 = a^2(a^2 - c^2)$$ Multiply both sides by $-1$.

Refer to the discussion on page 875 and let $b^2 = a^2 - c^2$ in the preceding equation.

$$b^2x^2 + a^2y^2 = a^2b^2$$

$$\frac{x^2}{a^2} + \frac{y^2}{b^2} = 1$$ Divide both sides by $a^2b^2$.

**Section 9.2 The Hyperbola**

## The Asymptotes of a Hyperbola Centered at the Origin

The hyperbola

$$\frac{x^2}{a^2} - \frac{y^2}{b^2} = 1$$

with a horizontal transverse axis has the two asymptotes

$$y = \frac{b}{a}x \quad \text{and} \quad y = -\frac{b}{a}x.$$

## Proof

Begin by solving the hyperbola's equation for $y$.

$$\frac{x^2}{a^2} - \frac{y^2}{b^2} = 1$$  *This is the standard form of the equation of a hyperbola.*

$$\frac{y^2}{b^2} = \frac{x^2}{a^2} - 1$$  *We isolate the term involving $y^2$ to solve for y.*

$$y^2 = \frac{b^2 x^2}{a^2} - b^2$$  *Multiply both sides by $b^2$.*

$$y^2 = \frac{b^2 x^2}{a^2}\left(1 - \frac{a^2}{x^2}\right)$$  *Factor out $\frac{b^2 x^2}{a^2}$ on the right. Verify that this result is correct by multiplying using the distributive property and obtaining the previous step.*

$$y = \pm\sqrt{\frac{b^2 x^2}{a^2}\left(1 - \frac{a^2}{x^2}\right)}$$  *Solve for y using the square root property: If $u^2 = d$, then $u = \pm\sqrt{d}$.*

$$y = \pm\frac{b}{a}x\sqrt{1 - \frac{a^2}{x^2}}$$  *Simplify.*

As $|x| \to \infty$, the value of $\frac{a^2}{x^2}$ approaches 0. Consequently, the value of $y$ can be approximated by

$$y = \pm\frac{b}{a}x.$$

This means that the lines whose equations are $y = \frac{b}{a}x$ and $y = -\frac{b}{a}x$ are asymptotes for the graph of the hyperbola.

# Appendix B
## The Transition from Precalculus to Calculus

Calculus is the study of limits and their applications. (Limits are introduced in Sections 11.1 and 11.2.)

| Precalculus | Calculus |
|---|---|
| Substitution: The value of function $f$ at $a$ <br><br> $f(a)$ | Limits: What occurs to the value of a function $f$ as $x$ gets closer to $a$, but remains unequal to $a$ <br><br> $\lim\limits_{x \to a} f(x)$ |

Calculus uses limits to extend ideas and topics from precalculus to more general situations.

| Precalculus Topic | Calculus Generalization |
|---|---|
| Slope of a line | Slope of a curve |
| Average rate of change; average velocity | Instantaneous rate of change; instantaneous velocity |
| Location of a quadratic function's $[f(x) = ax^2 + bx + c]$ maximum or minimum value | Location of any function's relative maxima and/or minima |
| Area of a rectangle | Area of a plane region bounded by curves |
| Length of a line segment | Length of a curve |
| Center of a circle | Center of gravity (the balance point) of a plane region |
| Work done by a constant force moving an object along a linear path | Work done by a variable force moving an object along a curved path |

The vast array of generalizations made possible by the invention of limits marked a turning point in human history, having as dramatic an impact on our lives as the invention of the wheel and the printing press.

# Answers to Selected Exercises

## CHAPTER P

### Section P.1

**Check Point Exercises**

**1.** 608  **2.** \$7567  **3.** $\{3, 7\}$  **4.** $\{3, 4, 5, 6, 7, 8, 9\}$  **5. a.** $\sqrt{9}$  **b.** $0, \sqrt{9}$  **c.** $-9, 0, \sqrt{9}$  **d.** $-9, -1.3, 0, 0.\overline{3}, \sqrt{9}$
**e.** $\frac{\pi}{2}, \sqrt{10}$  **f.** $-9, -1.3, 0, 0.\overline{3}, \frac{\pi}{2}, \sqrt{9}, \sqrt{10}$  **6. a.** $\sqrt{2} - 1$  **b.** $\pi - 3$  **c.** 1  **7.** 9  **8.** $38x^2 + 23x$  **9.** $42 - 4x$

**Exercise Set P.1**

**1.** 57  **3.** 10  **5.** 88  **7.** 10  **9.** 44  **11.** 46  **13.** 10  **15.** $-8$  **17.** 10°C  **19.** 60 ft  **21.** $\{2, 4\}$  **23.** $\{s, e, t\}$  **25.** $\varnothing$
**27.** $\varnothing$  **29.** $\{1, 2, 3, 4, 5\}$  **31.** $\{1, 2, 3, 4, 5, 6, 7, 8, 10\}$  **33.** $\{a, e, i, o, u\}$  **35. a.** $\sqrt{100}$  **b.** $0, \sqrt{100}$  **c.** $-9, 0, \sqrt{100}$

**d.** $-9, -\frac{4}{5}, 0, 0.25, 9.2, \sqrt{100}$  **e.** $\sqrt{3}$  **f.** $-9, -\frac{4}{5}, 0, 0.25, \sqrt{3}, 9.2, \sqrt{100}$  **37. a.** $\sqrt{64}$  **b.** $0, \sqrt{64}$  **c.** $-11, 0, \sqrt{64}$

**d.** $-11, -\frac{5}{6}, 0, 0.75, \sqrt{64}$  **e.** $\sqrt{5}, \pi$  **f.** $-11, -\frac{5}{6}, 0, 0.75, \sqrt{5}, \pi, \sqrt{64}$  **39.** 0  **41.** Answers may vary; an example is 2.
**43.** true  **45.** true  **47.** true  **49.** true  **51.** 300  **53.** $12 - \pi$  **55.** $5 - \sqrt{2}$  **57.** $-1$  **59.** 4  **61.** 3  **63.** 7  **65.** $-1$
**67.** $|17 - 2|$; 15  **69.** $|5 - (-2)|$; 7  **71.** $|-4 - (-19)|$; 15  **73.** $|-1.4 - (-3.6)|$; 2.2  **75.** commutative property of addition
**77.** associative property of addition  **79.** commutative property of addition  **81.** distributive property of multiplication over addition
**83.** inverse property of multiplication  **85.** $15x + 16$  **87.** $27x - 10$  **89.** $29y - 29$  **91.** $8y - 12$  **93.** $16y - 25$  **95.** $12x^2 + 11$

**97.** $14x$  **99.** $-2x + 3y + 6$  **101.** $x$  **103.** $>$  **105.** $=$  **107.** $<$  **109.** $=$  **111.** 45  **113.** $\frac{1}{121}$  **115.** 14  **117.** $-\frac{8}{3}$

**119.** $-\frac{1}{2}$  **121.** $x - (x + 4)$; $-4$  **123.** $6(-5x)$; $-30x$  **125.** $5x - 2x$; $3x$  **127.** $8x - (3x + 6)$; $5x - 6$  **129. a.** 140 beats per minute

**b.** 160 beats per minute  **131. a.** \$22,213  **b.** underestimates by \$5  **c.** \$25,075  **133. a.** $1200 - 0.07x$  **b.** \$780
**145.** does not make sense  **147.** makes sense  **149.** false  **151.** true  **153.** false  **155.** false  **157.** $<$  **159.** $>$  **160. a.** $b^7$
**b.** $b^{10}$  **c.** Add the exponents.  **161. a.** $b^4$  **b.** $b^6$  **c.** Subtract the exponents.  **162.** It moves the decimal point 3 places to the right.

### Section P.2

**Check Point Exercises**

**1. a.** $16x^{12}y^{24}$  **b.** $-18x^3y^8$  **c.** $\frac{5y^6}{x^4}$  **d.** $\frac{y^8}{25x^2}$  **2. a.** $-2,600,000,000$  **b.** $0.000003017$  **3. a.** $5.21 \times 10^9$  **b.** $-6.893 \times 10^{-8}$

**4.** $4.1 \times 10^9$  **5. a.** $3.55 \times 10^{-1}$  **b.** $4 \times 10^8$  **6.** \$2500  **7.** $2.5344 \times 10^3 = 2534.4$

**Exercise Set P.2**

**1.** 50  **3.** 64  **5.** $-64$  **7.** 1  **9.** $-1$  **11.** $\frac{1}{64}$  **13.** 32  **15.** 64  **17.** 16  **19.** $\frac{1}{9}$  **21.** $\frac{1}{16}$  **23.** $\frac{y}{x^2}$  **25.** $y^5$  **27.** $x^{10}$

**29.** $x^5$  **31.** $x^{21}$  **33.** $\frac{1}{x^{15}}$  **35.** $x^7$  **37.** $x^{21}$  **39.** $64x^6$  **41.** $-\frac{64}{x^3}$  **43.** $9x^4y^{10}$  **45.** $6x^{11}$  **47.** $18x^9y^5$  **49.** $4x^{16}$  **51.** $-5a^{11}b$

**53.** $\frac{2}{b^7}$  **55.** $\frac{1}{16x^6}$  **57.** $\frac{3y^{14}}{4x^4}$  **59.** $\frac{y^2}{25x^6}$  **61.** $-\frac{27\,b^{15}}{a^{18}}$  **63.** 1  **65.** 380  **67.** 0.0006  **69.** $-7,160,000$  **71.** 0.79  **73.** $-0.00415$

**75.** $-60,000,100,000$  **77.** $3.2 \times 10^4$  **79.** $6.38 \times 10^{17}$  **81.** $-5.716 \times 10^3$  **83.** $2.7 \times 10^{-3}$  **85.** $-5.04 \times 10^{-9}$  **87.** $6.3 \times 10^7$
**89.** $6.4 \times 10^4$  **91.** $1.22 \times 10^{-11}$  **93.** $2.67 \times 10^{13}$  **95.** $2.1 \times 10^3$  **97.** $4 \times 10^5$  **99.** $2 \times 10^{-8}$  **101.** $5 \times 10^3$  **103.** $4 \times 10^{15}$

**105.** $9 \times 10^{-3}$  **107.** 1  **109.** $\frac{y}{16x^8z^6}$  **111.** $\frac{1}{x^{12}y^{16}z^{20}}$  **113.** $\frac{x^{18}y^6}{4}$  **115. a.** $2.52 \times 10^{12}$  **b.** $3 \times 10^8$  **c.** \$8400  **117.** $\$9.57 \times 10^{12}$

**119.** $1.06 \times 10^{-18}$ g  **121.** $4.064 \times 10^9$  **131.** does not make sense  **133.** does not make sense  **135.** false  **137.** false  **139.** false

**141.** false  **143.** $\frac{1}{4}$  **145.** about $2.94 \times 10^9$ times  **147. a.** 8  **b.** 8  **c.** $\sqrt{16} \cdot \sqrt{4} = \sqrt{16 \cdot 4}$  **148. a.** 17.32  **b.** 17.32
**c.** $\sqrt{300} = 10\sqrt{3}$  **149. a.** $31x$  **b.** $31\sqrt{2}$

### Section P.3

**Check Point Exercises**

**1. a.** 9  **b.** $-3$  **c.** $\frac{1}{5}$  **d.** 10  **e.** 14  **2. a.** $5\sqrt{3}$  **b.** $5x\sqrt{2}$  **3. a.** $\frac{5}{4}$  **b.** $5x\sqrt{3}$  **4. a.** $17\sqrt{13}$  **b.** $-19\sqrt{17x}$

**5. a.** $17\sqrt{3}$  **b.** $10\sqrt{2x}$  **6. a.** $\frac{5\sqrt{3}}{3}$  **b.** $\sqrt{3}$  **7.** $\frac{8(4 - \sqrt{5})}{11}$ or $\frac{32 - 8\sqrt{5}}{11}$  **8. a.** $2\sqrt[3]{5}$  **b.** $2\sqrt[5]{2}$  **c.** $\frac{5}{3}$  **9.** $5\sqrt[3]{3}$

**10. a.** 5 **b.** 2 **c.** −3 **d.** −2 **e.** $\frac{1}{3}$ **11. a.** 81 **b.** 8 **c.** $\frac{1}{4}$ **12. a.** $10x^4$ **b.** $4x^{5/2}$ **13.** $\sqrt{x}$

## Exercise Set P.3

**1.** 6 **3.** −6 **5.** not a real number **7.** 3 **9.** 1 **11.** 13 **13.** $5\sqrt{2}$ **15.** $3|x|\sqrt{5}$ **17.** $2x\sqrt{3}$ **19.** $x\sqrt{x}$ **21.** $2x\sqrt{3x}$

**23.** $\frac{1}{9}$ **25.** $\frac{7}{4}$ **27.** $4x$ **29.** $5x\sqrt{2x}$ **31.** $2x^2\sqrt{5}$ **33.** $13\sqrt{3}$ **35.** $-2\sqrt{17x}$ **37.** $5\sqrt{2}$ **39.** $3\sqrt{2x}$ **41.** $34\sqrt{2}$

**43.** $20\sqrt{2} - 5\sqrt{3}$ **45.** $\frac{\sqrt{7}}{7}$ **47.** $\frac{\sqrt{10}}{5}$ **49.** $\frac{13(3 - \sqrt{11})}{-2}$ **51.** $7(\sqrt{5} + 2)$ **53.** $3(\sqrt{5} - \sqrt{3})$ **55.** 5 **57.** −2

**59.** not a real number **61.** 3 **63.** −3 **65.** $-\frac{1}{2}$ **67.** $2\sqrt[4]{4}$ **69.** $x\sqrt[3]{x}$ **71.** $3\sqrt[3]{2}$ **73.** $2x$ **75.** $7\sqrt[5]{2}$ **77.** $13\sqrt[3]{2}$

**79.** $-y\sqrt[3]{2x}$ **81.** $\sqrt{2} + 2$ **83.** 6 **85.** 2 **87.** 25 **89.** $\frac{1}{16}$ **91.** $14x^{7/12}$ **93.** $4x^{1/4}$ **95.** $x^2$ **97.** $5x^2|y|^3$ **99.** $27y^{2/3}$

**101.** $\sqrt{5}$ **103.** $x^2$ **105.** $\sqrt[3]{x^2}$ **107.** $\sqrt[6]{x^2y}$ **109.** 3 **111.** $\frac{x^2}{7y^{3/2}}$ **113.** $\frac{x^3}{y^2}$ **115. a.** 67.5%; underestimates by 0.5% **b.** 93.1%

**117.** $\frac{\sqrt{5} + 1}{2}$; 1.62 to 1 **119.** $P = 18\sqrt{5}$ ft; $A = 100$ ft² **129.** does not make sense **131.** does not make sense **133.** false **135.** false

**137.** Let □ = 3. **139.** 4 **141. a.** 8 **b.** $\frac{1}{4}$ **142.** $10x^7y^9$ **143.** $16x^8 + 6x^5$ **144.** $2x^3 + 11x^2 + 22x + 15$

## Section P.4

### Check Point Exercises

**1. a.** $-x^3 + x^2 - 8x - 20$ **b.** $20x^3 - 11x^2 - 2x - 8$ **2.** $15x^3 - 31x^2 + 30x - 8$ **3.** $28x^2 - 41x + 15$ **4. a.** $21x^2 - 25xy + 6y^2$
**b.** $4x^2 + 16xy + 16y^2$ **5. a.** $9x^2 + 12x + 4 - 25y^2$ **b.** $4x^2 + 4xy + y^2 + 12x + 6y + 9$

### Exercise Set P.4

**1.** yes; $3x^2 + 2x - 5$ **3.** no **5.** 2 **7.** 4 **9.** $11x^3 + 7x^2 - 12x - 4$; 3 **11.** $12x^3 + 4x^2 + 12x - 14$; 3 **13.** $6x^2 - 6x + 2$; 2
**15.** $x^3 + 1$ **17.** $2x^3 - 9x^2 + 19x - 15$ **19.** $x^2 + 10x + 21$ **21.** $x^2 - 2x - 15$ **23.** $6x^2 + 13x + 5$ **25.** $10x^2 - 9x - 9$
**27.** $15x^4 - 47x^2 + 28$ **29.** $8x^5 - 40x^3 + 3x^2 - 15$ **31.** $x^2 - 9$ **33.** $9x^2 - 4$ **35.** $25 - 49x^2$ **37.** $16x^4 - 25x^2$ **39.** $1 - y^{10}$
**41.** $x^2 + 4x + 4$ **43.** $4x^2 + 12x + 9$ **45.** $x^2 - 6x + 9$ **47.** $16x^4 - 8x^2 + 1$ **49.** $4x^2 - 28x + 49$ **51.** $x^3 + 3x^2 + 3x + 1$
**53.** $8x^3 + 36x^2 + 54x + 27$ **55.** $x^3 - 9x^2 + 27x - 27$ **57.** $27x^3 - 108x^2 + 144x - 64$ **59.** $7x^2 + 38xy + 15y^2$ **61.** $2x^2 + xy - 21y^2$
**63.** $15x^2y^2 + xy - 2$ **65.** $49x^2 + 70xy + 25y^2$ **67.** $x^4y^4 - 6x^2y^2 + 9$ **69.** $x^3 - y^3$ **71.** $9x^2 - 25y^2$ **73.** $x^2 + 2xy + y^2 - 9$
**75.** $9x^2 + 42x + 49 - 25y^2$ **77.** $25y^2 - 4x^2 - 12x - 9$ **79.** $x^2 + 2xy + y^2 + 2x + 2y + 1$ **81.** $4x^2 + 4xy + y^2 + 4x + 2y + 1$ **83.** $48xy$
**85.** $-9x^2 + 3x + 9$ **87.** $16x^4 - 625$ **89.** $4x^2 - 28x + 49$ **91. a.** \$56,995; underestimates by \$225
**b.** $M - W = -35x^3 + 1373x^2 - 15,995x + 63,210$ **c.** \$12,348 **d.** \$10,923; overestimates by \$1425 **93.** $4x^3 - 36x^2 + 80x$ **95.** $6x + 22$
**103.** makes sense **105.** makes sense **107.** $x^2 + 2x$ **109.** $2x^3 + 12x^2 + 12x + 10$ **111.** 4 **112.** 2 **113.** 3

## Section P.5

### Check Point Exercises

**1. a.** $2x^2(5x - 2)$ **b.** $(x - 7)(2x + 3)$ **2.** $(x + 5)(x^2 - 2)$ **3.** $(x + 8)(x + 5)$ or $(x + 5)(x + 8)$ **4.** $(x - 7)(x + 2)$ or $(x + 2)(x - 7)$
**5.** $(3x - 1)(2x + 7)$ or $(2x + 7)(3x - 1)$ **6.** $(3x - y)(x - 4y)$ or $(x - 4y)(3x - y)$ **7. a.** $(x + 9)(x - 9)$ **b.** $(6x + 5)(6x - 5)$
**8.** $(9x^2 + 4)(3x + 2)(3x - 2)$ **9. a.** $(x + 7)^2$ **b.** $(4x - 7)^2$ **10. a.** $(x + 1)(x^2 - x + 1)$ **b.** $(5x - 2)(25x^2 + 10x + 4)$ **11.** $3x(x - 5)^2$
**12.** $(x + 10 + 6a)(x + 10 - 6a)$ **13.** $\frac{2x - 1}{(x - 1)^{1/2}}$

### Exercise Set P.5

**1.** $9(2x + 3)$ **3.** $3x(x + 2)$ **5.** $9x^2(x^2 - 2x + 3)$ **7.** $(x + 5)(x + 3)$ **9.** $(x - 3)(x^2 + 12)$ **11.** $(x - 2)(x^2 + 5)$ **13.** $(x - 1)(x^2 + 2)$
**15.** $(3x - 2)(x^2 - 2)$ **17.** $(x + 2)(x + 3)$ **19.** $(x - 5)(x + 3)$ **21.** $(x - 5)(x - 3)$ **23.** $(3x + 2)(x - 1)$ **25.** $(3x - 28)(x + 1)$
**27.** $(2x - 1)(3x - 4)$ **29.** $(2x + 3)(2x + 5)$ **31.** $(3x - 2)(3x - 1)$ **33.** $(5x + 8)(4x - 1)$ **35.** $(2x + y)(x + y)$
**37.** $(3x + 2y)(2x - 3y)$ **39.** $(x + 10)(x - 10)$ **41.** $(6x + 7)(6x - 7)$ **43.** $(3x + 5y)(3x - 5y)$ **45.** $(x^2 + 4)(x + 2)(x - 2)$
**47.** $(4x^2 + 9)(2x + 3)(2x - 3)$ **49.** $(x + 1)^2$ **51.** $(x - 7)^2$ **53.** $(2x + 1)^2$ **55.** $(3x - 1)^2$ **57.** $(x + 3)(x^2 - 3x + 9)$
**59.** $(x - 4)(x^2 + 4x + 16)$ **61.** $(2x - 1)(4x^2 + 2x + 1)$ **63.** $(4x + 3)(16x^2 - 12x + 9)$ **65.** $3x(x + 1)(x - 1)$ **67.** $4(x + 2)(x - 3)$
**69.** $2(x^2 + 9)(x + 3)(x - 3)$ **71.** $(x - 3)(x + 3)(x + 2)$ **73.** $2(x - 8)(x + 7)$ **75.** $x(x - 2)(x + 2)$ **77.** prime **79.** $(x - 2)(x + 2)^2$
**81.** $y(y^2 + 9)(y + 3)(y - 3)$ **83.** $5y^2(2y + 3)(2y - 3)$ **85.** $(x - 6 + 7y)(x - 6 - 7y)$ **87.** $(x + y)(3b + 4)(3b - 4)$

**89.** $(y - 2)(x + 4)(x - 4)$ **91.** $2x(x + 6 + 2a)(x + 6 - 2a)$ **93.** $x^{1/2}(x - 1)$ **95.** $\frac{4(1 + 2x)}{x^{2/3}}$ **97.** $-(x + 3)^{1/2}(x + 2)$ **99.** $\frac{x + 4}{(x + 5)^{3/2}}$

**101.** $-\frac{4(4x - 1)^{1/2}(x - 1)}{3}$ **103.** $(x + 1)(5x - 6)(2x + 1)$ **105.** $(x^2 + 6)(6x^2 - 1)$ **107.** $y(y^2 + 1)(y^4 - y^2 + 1)$

**109.** $(x + 2y)(x - 2y)(x + y)(x - y)$ **111.** $(x - y)^2(x - y + 2)(x - y - 2)$ **113.** $(2x - y^2)(x - 3y^2)$

**115. a.** $(x - 0.4x)(1 - 0.4) = (0.6x)(0.6) = 0.36x$ **b.** no; 36% **117. a.** $9x^2 - 16$ **b.** $(3x + 4)(3x - 4)$ **119. a.** $x(x + y) - y(x + y)$

**b.** $(x + y)(x - y)$    **121.** $4a^3 - 4ab^2 = 4a(a + b)(a - b)$    **131.** makes sense    **133.** makes sense    **135.** true    **137.** false

**139.** $-(x + 5)(x - 1)$    **141.** $-\dfrac{10}{(x - 5)^{3/2}(x + 5)^{1/2}}$    **143.** $b = 0, 3, 4, -c(c + 4)$, where $c > 0$ is an integer    **144.** $\dfrac{(x + 5)(x + 1)}{(x + 5)(x - 5)} = \dfrac{x + 1}{x - 5}$

**145.** $\dfrac{2}{3}$    **146.** $\dfrac{7}{6}$

## Mid-Chapter P Check Point

**1.** $12x^2 - x - 35$    **2.** $-x + 12$    **3.** $10\sqrt{6}$    **4.** $3\sqrt{3}$    **5.** $x + 45$    **6.** $64x^2 - 48x + 9$    **7.** $\dfrac{x^2}{y^3}$    **8.** $\dfrac{3}{4}$    **9.** $-x^2 + 5x - 6$

**10.** $2x^3 - 11x^2 + 17x - 5$    **11.** $-x^6 + 2x^3$    **12.** $18a^2 - 11ab - 10b^2$    **13.** $\{a, c, d, e, f, h\}$    **14.** $\{c, d\}$    **15.** $5x^2y^3 + 2xy - y^2$

**16.** $-\dfrac{12y^{15}}{x^3}$    **17.** $\dfrac{6y^3}{x^7}$    **18.** $|\sqrt[3]{x}|$    **19.** $16y^2 - 9x^2 - 12x - 4$    **20.** $x^2 - 4xy + 4y^2 - 2x + 4y + 1$    **21.** $1.2 \times 10^{-2}$    **22.** $2\sqrt[3]{2}$

**23.** $x^6 - 4$    **24.** $x^4 + 4x^2 + 4$    **25.** $10\sqrt{3}$    **26.** $\dfrac{77 + 11\sqrt{3}}{46}$    **27.** $\dfrac{11\sqrt{3}}{3}$    **28.** $(7x - 1)(x - 3)$    **29.** prime    **30.** $(x^2 + 3)(x + 5)$

**31.** $(3x - 7y)(x + y)$    **32.** $y(4 - y)(16 + 4y + y^2)$    **33.** $2x(5x + 1)^2$    **34.** $(x - 3 - 7y)(x - 3 + 7y)$    **35.** $\dfrac{(1 - x)^2}{x^{3/2}}$    **36.** $\dfrac{(x - 3)(x + 3)}{(x^2 + 1)^{1/2}}$

**37.** $-11, -\dfrac{3}{7}, 0, 0.45, \sqrt{25}$    **38.** $\sqrt{13} - 2$    **39.** $-x^3$    **40.** $\$4.2 \times 10^{10}$    **41.** 4 times    **42. a.** model 2    **b.** underestimates by 3 channels
**c.** 132

## Section P.6

### Check Point Exercises

**1. a.** $-5$    **b.** $6, -6$    **2. a.** $x^2, x \neq -3$    **b.** $\dfrac{x - 1}{x + 1}, x \neq -1$    **3.** $\dfrac{x - 3}{(x - 2)(x + 3)}, x \neq 2, x \neq -2, x \neq -3$    **4.** $\dfrac{3(x - 1)}{x(x + 2)}, x \neq 1, x \neq 0, x \neq -2$

**5.** $-2, x \neq -1$    **6.** $\dfrac{2(4x + 1)}{(x + 1)(x - 1)}, x \neq 1, x \neq -1$    **7.** $(x - 3)(x - 3)(x + 3)$ or $(x - 3)^2(x + 3)$    **8.** $\dfrac{-x^2 + 11x - 20}{2(x - 5)^2}, x \neq 5$

**9.** $\dfrac{2(2 - 3x)}{4 + 3x}, x \neq 0, x \neq -\dfrac{4}{3}$    **10.** $-\dfrac{1}{x(x + 7)}, x \neq 0, x \neq -7$    **11.** $\dfrac{x + 1}{x^{3/2}}$    **12.** $\dfrac{1}{\sqrt{x + 3} + \sqrt{x}}$

### Exercise Set P.6

**1.** 3    **3.** $5, -5$    **5.** $-1, -10$    **7.** $\dfrac{3}{x - 3}, x \neq 3$    **9.** $\dfrac{x - 6}{4}, x \neq 6$    **11.** $\dfrac{y + 9}{y - 1}, y \neq 1, 2$    **13.** $\dfrac{x + 6}{x - 6}, x \neq 6, -6$    **15.** $\dfrac{1}{3}, x \neq 2, -3$

**17.** $\dfrac{(x - 3)(x + 3)}{x(x + 4)}, x \neq 0, -4, 3$    **19.** $\dfrac{x - 1}{x + 2}, x \neq -2, -1, 2, 3$    **21.** $\dfrac{x^2 + 2x + 4}{3x}, x \neq -2, 0, 2$    **23.** $\dfrac{7}{9}, x \neq -1$

**25.** $\dfrac{(x - 2)^2}{x}, x \neq 0, -2, 2$    **27.** $\dfrac{2(x + 3)}{3}, x \neq 3, -3$    **29.** $\dfrac{x - 5}{2}, x \neq 1, -5$    **31.** $\dfrac{(x + 2)(x + 4)}{x - 5}, x \neq -6, -3, -1, 3, 5$    **33.** $2, x \neq -\dfrac{5}{6}$

**35.** $\dfrac{2x - 1}{x + 3}, x \neq 0, -3$    **37.** $3, x \neq 2$    **39.** $\dfrac{3}{x - 3}, x \neq 3, -4$    **41.** $\dfrac{9x + 39}{(x + 4)(x + 5)}, x \neq -4, -5$    **43.** $-\dfrac{3}{x(x + 1)}, x \neq -1, 0$

**45.** $\dfrac{3x^2 + 4}{(x + 2)(x - 2)}, x \neq -2, 2$    **47.** $\dfrac{2x^2 + 50}{(x - 5)(x + 5)}, x \neq -5, 5$    **49.** $\dfrac{13}{6(x + 2)}, x \neq -2$    **51.** $\dfrac{4x + 16}{(x + 3)^2}, x \neq -3$

**53.** $\dfrac{x^2 - x}{(x + 5)(x - 2)(x + 3)}, x \neq -5, 2, -3$    **55.** $\dfrac{-x^2 - 2x + 1}{(x + 1)(x - 1)}, x \neq -1, 1$    **57.** $\dfrac{x - 1}{x + 2}, x \neq -2, -1$    **59.** $\dfrac{1}{3}, x \neq 3$    **61.** $\dfrac{x + 1}{3x - 1}, x \neq 0, \dfrac{1}{3}$

**63.** $\dfrac{1}{xy}, x \neq 0, y \neq 0, x \neq -y$    **65.** $\dfrac{x}{x + 3}, x \neq -2, -3$    **67.** $-\dfrac{x - 14}{7}, x \neq -2, 2$    **69.** $\dfrac{x - 3}{x + 2}, x \neq -2, -1, 3$

**71.** $-\dfrac{2x + h}{x^2(x + h)^2}, x \neq 0, h \neq 0, x \neq -h$    **73.** $1 - \dfrac{1}{3x}; x > 0$    **75.** $-\dfrac{2}{x^2\sqrt{x^2 + 2}}$    **77.** $\dfrac{\sqrt{x} - \sqrt{x + h}}{h\sqrt{x}\sqrt{x + h}}$    **79.** $\dfrac{1}{\sqrt{x + 5} + \sqrt{x}}$

**81.** $\dfrac{1}{(x + y)(\sqrt{x} - \sqrt{y})}$    **83.** $\dfrac{x^2 + 5x + 8}{(x + 2)(x + 1)}$    **85.** 2    **87.** $\dfrac{1}{y(y + 5)}$    **89.** $\dfrac{2d}{a^2 + ab + b^2}$    **91. a.** $86.67, 520, 1170$; It costs $\$86,670,000$ to

inoculate 40% of the population against this strain of flu, $\$520,000,000$ to inoculate 80% of the population, and $\$1,170,000,000$ to inoculate 90% of the
population.    **b.** $x = 100$    **c.** The cost increases rapidly; it is impossible to inoculate 100% of the population.

**93. a.** 2078; underestimates by 22 calories    **b.** 2662; underestimates by 38 calories    **c.** $\dfrac{-33x^2 + 263x + 515}{-60x^2 + 499x + 295}$    **95.** $\dfrac{4x^2 + 14x}{(x + 3)(x + 4)}$

**109.** does not make sense    **111.** does not make sense    **113.** false    **115.** true    **117.** $\dfrac{1}{x^{2n} - 1}$    **119.** $\dfrac{x - y + 1}{(x - y)(x - y)}$    **121.** true

**122.** $-x + 10$    **123.** $-5$

## Section P.7

**Check Point Exercises**

**1.** $\{5\}$  **2.** $\{1\}$  **3.** $\{7\}$  **4.** $\varnothing$  **5.** $q = \dfrac{pf}{p - f}$  **6.** $\{-2, 3\}$  **7. a.** $\{0, 3\}$  **b.** $\left\{\dfrac{1}{2}, -1\right\}$  **8. a.** $\{-\sqrt{7}, \sqrt{7}\}$

**b.** $\{-5 + \sqrt{11}, -5 - \sqrt{11}\}$  **9.** $\{-2 + \sqrt{5}, -2 - \sqrt{5}\}$  **10.** $\left\{\dfrac{-1 + \sqrt{3}}{2}, \dfrac{-1 - \sqrt{3}}{2}\right\}$  **11.** $-56$; no real solutions  **12.** $\{6\}$

**Exercise Set P.7**

**1.** $\{11\}$  **3.** $\{7\}$  **5.** $\{13\}$  **7.** $\{2\}$  **9.** $\{9\}$  **11.** $\left\{\dfrac{33}{2}\right\}$  **13.** $\{-12\}$  **15.** $\left\{\dfrac{46}{5}\right\}$  **17. a.** 1  **b.** $\{3\}$  **19. a.** $-1$  **b.** $\varnothing$

**21. a.** 1  **b.** $\{2\}$  **23. a.** $-1, 1$  **b.** $\{-3\}$  **25. a.** $-2, 4$  **b.** $\varnothing$  **27.** $P = \dfrac{I}{rt}$  **29.** $p = \dfrac{T - D}{m}$  **31.** $a = \dfrac{2A}{h} - b$

**33.** $r = \dfrac{S - P}{Pt}$  **35.** $S = \dfrac{F}{B} + V$  **37.** $I = \dfrac{E}{R + r}$  **39.** $f = \dfrac{pq}{p + q}$  **41.** $f_1 = -\dfrac{ff_2}{f - f_2}$ or $f_1 = \dfrac{ff_2}{f_2 - f}$  **43.** $\{-5, 9\}$  **45.** $\{-2, 3\}$

**47.** $\left\{-\dfrac{5}{3}, 3\right\}$  **49.** $\left\{-\dfrac{4}{5}, 4\right\}$  **51.** $\varnothing$  **53.** $\left\{\dfrac{1}{2}\right\}$  **55.** $\{-2, 5\}$  **57.** $\{3, 5\}$  **59.** $\{0, 4\}$  **61.** $\{\pm 3\}$  **63.** $\{\pm\sqrt{10}\}$  **65.** $\{4 \pm \sqrt{5}\}$

**67.** $\{-7, 1\}$  **69.** $\{1 + \sqrt{3}, 1 - \sqrt{3}\}$  **71.** $\{3 + 2\sqrt{5}, 3 - 2\sqrt{5}\}$  **73.** $\{-2 + \sqrt{3}, -2 - \sqrt{3}\}$  **75.** $\{-5, -3\}$

**77.** $\left\{\dfrac{-5 + \sqrt{13}}{2}, \dfrac{-5 - \sqrt{13}}{2}\right\}$  **79.** $\left\{\dfrac{3 + \sqrt{57}}{6}, \dfrac{3 - \sqrt{57}}{6}\right\}$  **81.** $\left\{\dfrac{1 + \sqrt{29}}{4}, \dfrac{1 - \sqrt{29}}{4}\right\}$  **83.** 36; 2 unequal real solutions

**85.** 97; 2 unequal real solutions  **87.** 0; 1 real solution  **89.** 37; 2 unequal real solutions  **91.** $\left\{-\dfrac{1}{2}, 1\right\}$  **93.** $\left\{\dfrac{1}{5}, 2\right\}$  **95.** $\{-2\sqrt{5}, 2\sqrt{5}\}$

**97.** $\{1 + \sqrt{2}, 1 - \sqrt{2}\}$  **99.** $\left\{\dfrac{-11 + \sqrt{33}}{4}, \dfrac{-11 - \sqrt{33}}{4}\right\}$  **101.** $\left\{0, \dfrac{8}{3}\right\}$  **103.** $\{2\}$  **105.** $\{-2, 2\}$  **107.** $\{2 \pm \sqrt{2}\}$  **109.** $\left\{0, \dfrac{7}{2}\right\}$

**111.** $\{2 + \sqrt{10}, 2 - \sqrt{10}\}$  **113.** $\{-5, -1\}$  **115.** $\{6\}$  **117.** $\{6\}$  **119.** $\{-6\}$  **121.** $\{10\}$  **123.** $\{-5\}$  **125.** $\{-2\}$

**127.** $\{-3, 1\}$  **129.** $\{-8, -6, 4, 6\}$  **131.** $\left\{\dfrac{-1 \pm \sqrt{21}}{2}\right\}$  **133.** $\{8\}$  **135.** $\dfrac{-2 - \sqrt{22}}{2}$ and $\dfrac{-2 + \sqrt{22}}{2}$  **137.** 142 pounds; 13 pounds

**139.** 125 liters  **141.** 33-year-olds and 58-year-olds; The formula models the actual data well.  **143.** 14 years after 1996, or 2010

**159.** does not make sense  **161.** does not make sense  **163.** false  **165.** true  **167.** 2  **169.** $C = \dfrac{LV - SN}{L - N}$  **171.** $x + 150$

**172.** $20 + 0.05x$  **173.** $4x + 400$

## Section P.8

**Check Point Exercises**

**1.** women: \$57,989; men: \$72,026  **2.** by 50 years after 1969, or in 2019  **3.** \$1200  **4.** 50 ft by 94 ft  **5.** 2 ft  **6.** 120 yd  **7.** 5 people

**Exercise Set P.8**

**1.** radio: 974 hr; TV: 1555 hr  **3.** carpenters: \$35,580; computer programmers: \$63,420  **5.** by 38 years after 1983, or in 2021
**7. a.** $y = 24,000 - 3000x$  **b.** after 5 years  **9.** 9 years after 2005, or in 2014; 22,300  **11.** \$420  **13.** \$150  **15.** \$467.20
**17.** 50 yd by 100 yd  **19.** 36 ft by 78 ft  **21.** 2 in.  **23.** length: 9 ft; width: 6 ft  **25.** 5 in.  **27.** 5 m  **29.** 3 ft  **31.** 13.2 ft  **33.** 13 ft
**35.** 21.9 yd  **37.** 8 people  **39.** car: 50 miles per hour; bus: 30 miles per hour  **41.** 6 miles per hour  **43.** 11 hr  **45.** 5 ft 7 in.  **47.** 10
**53.** does not make sense  **55.** does not make sense  **57.** 3 miles, 4 miles, 5 miles  **59.** Coburn = 60 years old; woman = 20 years old
**61.** \$4000 for the mother; \$8000 for the boy; \$2000 for the girl  **64.** yes  **65.** $\{-3\}$  **66.** $\{14\}$

## Section P.9

**Check Point Exercises**

**1. a.** $\{x \mid -2 \le x < 5\}$  **b.** $\{x \mid 1 \le x \le 3.5\}$  **c.** $\{x \mid x < -1\}$  **2. a.** $(2, 3]$  **b.** $[1, 6)$

**3.** $[-1, \infty)$ or $\{x \mid x \ge -1\}$  **4.** $\{x \mid x < 4\}$ or $(-\infty, 4)$  **5.** $\{x \mid x \ge 13\}$ or $[13, \infty)$

**6.** $[-1, 4)$ or $\{x \mid -1 \le x < 4\}$  **7.** $(-3, 7)$ or $\{x \mid -3 < x < 7\}$  **8.** $\left\{x \mid -\dfrac{11}{5} \le x \le 3\right\}$ or $\left[-\dfrac{11}{5}, 3\right]$

**9.** $\{x \mid x < -4 \text{ or } x > 8\}$ or $(-\infty, -4) \cup (8, \infty)$  **10.** more than 720 mi per week

## Exercise Set P.9

**1.** $\{x \mid 1 < x \le 6\}$

**3.** $\{x \mid -5 \le x < 2\}$

**5.** $\{x \mid -3 \le x \le 1\}$

**7.** $\{x \mid x > 2\}$

**9.** $\{x \mid x \ge -3\}$

**11.** $\{x \mid x < 3\}$

**13.** $\{x \mid x < 5.5\}$

**15.** $[-1, 0)$    **17.** $(-3, 2]$    **19.** $[1, 5)$
**21.** $(-\infty, 8)$    **23.** $(6, \infty)$    **25.** $[3, \infty)$

**27.** $(-\infty, 3)$

**29.** $\left[\dfrac{20}{3}, \infty\right)$

**31.** $(-\infty, -4]$

**33.** $\left(-\infty, -\dfrac{2}{5}\right]$

**35.** $[0, \infty)$

**37.** $(-\infty, 1)$

**39.** $[6, \infty)$

**41.** $[-10, \infty)$

**43.** $(-\infty, -6)$

**45.** $[13, \infty)$

**47.** $(-\infty, 2)$

**49.** $(3, 5)$    **51.** $[-1, 3)$    **53.** $(-5, -2]$    **55.** $[3, 6)$    **57.** $(-3, 3)$    **59.** $[-1, 3]$    **61.** $(-1, 7)$    **63.** $[-5, 3]$    **65.** $(-6, 0)$

**67.** $(-\infty, -3) \cup (3, \infty)$    **69.** $(-\infty, -1] \cup [3, \infty)$    **71.** $\left(-\infty, \dfrac{1}{3}\right) \cup (5, \infty)$    **73.** $(-\infty, -5] \cup [3, \infty)$    **75.** $(-\infty, -3) \cup (12, \infty)$

**77.** $(-\infty, -1] \cup [3, \infty)$    **79.** $[2, 6]$    **81.** $(-\infty, -3) \cup (5, \infty)$    **83.** $(-\infty, -1] \cup [2, \infty)$    **85.** $(-1, 9)$    **87.** $\left(-\infty, \dfrac{1}{3}\right) \cup (1, \infty)$

**89.** $\left(-\infty, -\dfrac{75}{14}\right) \cup \left(\dfrac{87}{14}, \infty\right)$    **91.** $(-\infty, -6]$ or $[24, \infty)$    **93.** $[6, \infty)$    **95.** $(-\infty, -10] \cup [2, \infty)$    **97.** $\left(-\infty, -\dfrac{1}{3}\right] \cup [3, \infty)$
**99.** $(0, 4)$    **101.** intimacy $\ge$ passion or passion $\le$ intimacy    **103.** commitment $>$ passion or passion $<$ commitment
**105.** 9; after 3 years    **107.** voting years after 2006    **109.** between 80 and 110 minutes, inclusive    **111.** $h \le 41$ or $h \ge 59$
**113.** $15 + 0.08x < 3 + 0.12x$; more than 300 min    **115.** $2 + 0.08x < 8 + 0.05x$; 199 checks or less
**117.** $5.50x > 3000 + 3x$; more than 1200 packages    **119.** $245 + 95x \le 3000$; at most 29 bags    **121. a.** $\dfrac{86 + 88 + x}{3} \ge 90$; at least a 96
**b.** $\dfrac{86 + 88 + x}{3} < 80$; a grade less than 66    **123.** $7.50 + 0.50x \le 3.00x$ and $7.50 + 0.50x \le 15.00$; more than 3 and less than 15 crossings per three-
month period    **133.** makes sense    **135.** makes sense    **137.** false    **139.** true    **141. a.** $|x - 4| < 3$    **b.** $|x - 4| \ge 3$
**143.** 7; 6; 5; 4; 3; 2; 1    **144.** $-5$; 0; 3; 4; 3; 0; $-5$    **145.** 3; 2; 1; 0; 1; 2; 3

## Chapter P Review Exercises

**1.** 51    **2.** 16    **3.** 124 ft    **4.** $\{a, c\}$    **5.** $\{a, b, c, d, e\}$    **6.** $\{a, b, c, d, f, g\}$    **7.** $\{a\}$    **8. a.** $\sqrt{81}$    **b.** $0, \sqrt{81}$    **c.** $-17, 0, \sqrt{81}$
**d.** $-17, -\dfrac{9}{13}, 0, 0.75, \sqrt{81}$    **e.** $\sqrt{2}, \pi$    **f.** $-17, -\dfrac{9}{13}, 0, 0.75, \sqrt{2}, \pi, \sqrt{81}$    **9.** 103    **10.** $\sqrt{2} - 1$    **11.** $\sqrt{17} - 3$    **12.** $|4 - (-17)|$; 21
**13.** commutative property of addition    **14.** associative property of multiplication    **15.** distributive property of multiplication over addition
**16.** commutative property of multiplication    **17.** commutative property of multiplication    **18.** commutative property of addition
**19.** $17x - 15$    **20.** $2x$    **21.** $5y - 17$    **22.** $10x$    **23.** 38.55%; overestimates by 3.55%    **24.** $-108$    **25.** $\dfrac{5}{16}$    **26.** $\dfrac{1}{25}$    **27.** $\dfrac{1}{27}$
**28.** $-8x^{12}y^9$    **29.** $\dfrac{10}{x^8}$    **30.** $\dfrac{1}{16x^{12}}$    **31.** $\dfrac{y^8}{4x^{10}}$    **32.** 37,400    **33.** 0.0000745    **34.** $3.59 \times 10^6$    **35.** $7.25 \times 10^{-3}$    **36.** 390,000
**37.** 0.023    **38. a.** $2.57 \times 10^{11}$    **b.** $1.75 \times 10^8$    **39.** \$1469    **40.** $10\sqrt{3}$    **41.** $2|x|\sqrt{3}$    **42.** $2x\sqrt{5}$    **43.** $r\sqrt{r}$    **44.** $\dfrac{11}{2}$    **45.** $4x\sqrt{3}$
**46.** $20\sqrt{5}$    **47.** $16\sqrt{2}$    **48.** $24\sqrt{2} - 8\sqrt{3}$    **49.** $6\sqrt{5}$    **50.** $\dfrac{\sqrt{6}}{3}$    **51.** $\dfrac{5(6 - \sqrt{3})}{33}$    **52.** $7(\sqrt{7} + \sqrt{5})$    **53.** 5    **54.** $-2$
**55.** not a real number    **56.** 5    **57.** $3\sqrt[3]{3}$    **58.** $y\sqrt[3]{y^2}$    **59.** $2\sqrt[4]{5}$    **60.** $13\sqrt[3]{2}$    **61.** $x\sqrt[4]{2}$    **62.** 4    **63.** $\dfrac{1}{5}$    **64.** 5    **65.** $\dfrac{1}{3}$
**66.** 16    **67.** $\dfrac{1}{81}$    **68.** $20x^{11/12}$    **69.** $3x^{1/4}$    **70.** $25x^4$    **71.** $\sqrt{y}$    **72.** $8x^3 + 10x^2 - 20x - 4$; degree 3    **73.** $8x^4 - 5x^3 + 6$; degree 4
**74.** $12x^3 + x^2 - 21x + 10$    **75.** $6x^2 - 7x - 5$    **76.** $16x^2 - 25$    **77.** $4x^2 + 20x + 25$    **78.** $9x^2 - 24x + 16$    **79.** $8x^3 + 12x^2 + 6x + 1$
**80.** $125x^3 - 150x^2 + 60x - 8$    **81.** $3x^2 + 16xy - 35y^2$    **82.** $9x^2 - 30xy + 25y^2$    **83.** $9x^4 + 12x^2y + 4y^2$    **84.** $49x^2 - 16y^2$    **85.** $a^3 - b^3$
**86.** $25y^2 - 4x^2 - 8x - 1$    **87.** $x^2 + 4xy + 4y^2 + 8x + 16y + 16$    **88.** $3x^2(5x + 1)$    **89.** $(x - 4)(x - 7)$    **90.** $(3x + 1)(5x - 2)$
**91.** $(8 - x)(8 + x)$    **92.** prime    **93.** $3x^2(x - 5)(x + 2)$    **94.** $4x^3(5x^4 - 9)$    **95.** $(x + 3)(x - 3)^2$    **96.** $(4x - 5)^2$
**97.** $(x^2 + 4)(x + 2)(x - 2)$    **98.** $(y - 2)(y^2 + 2y + 4)$    **99.** $(x + 4)(x^2 - 4x + 16)$    **100.** $3x^2(x - 2)(x + 2)$
**101.** $(3x - 5)(9x^2 + 15x + 25)$    **102.** $x(x - 1)(x + 1)(x^2 + 1)$    **103.** $(x^2 - 2)(x + 5)$    **104.** $(x + 9 + y)(x + 9 - y)$    **105.** $\dfrac{16(1 + 2x)}{x^{3/4}}$
**106.** $(x + 2)(x - 2)(x^2 + 3)^{1/2}(-x^4 + x^2 + 13)$    **107.** $\dfrac{6(2x + 1)}{x^{3/2}}$    **108.** $x^2, x \ne -2$    **109.** $\dfrac{x - 3}{x - 6}, x \ne -6, 6$    **110.** $\dfrac{x}{x + 2}, x \ne -2$

**111.** $\dfrac{(x+3)^3}{(x-2)^2(x+2)}, x \neq 2, -2$ **112.** $\dfrac{2}{x(x+1)}, x \neq 0, 1, -1, -\dfrac{1}{3}$ **113.** $\dfrac{x+3}{x-4}, x \neq -3, 4, 2, 8$ **114.** $\dfrac{1}{x-3}, x \neq 3, -3$

**115.** $\dfrac{4x(x-1)}{(x+2)(x-2)}, x \neq 2, -2$ **116.** $\dfrac{2x^2-3}{(x-3)(x+3)(x-2)}, x \neq 3, -3, 2$ **117.** $\dfrac{11x^2-x-11}{(2x-1)(x+3)(3x+2)}, x \neq \dfrac{1}{2}, -3, -\dfrac{2}{3}$ **118.** $\dfrac{3}{x}, x \neq 0, 2$

**119.** $\dfrac{3x}{x-4}, x \neq 0, 4, -4$ **120.** $\dfrac{3x+8}{3x+10}, x \neq -3, -\dfrac{10}{3}$ **121.** $\dfrac{25\sqrt{25-x^2}}{(5-x)^2(5+x)^2}$ **122.** $\{-13\}$ **123.** $\{-3\}$ **124.** $\{-1\}$

**125.** all real numbers except 1 and −1 **126.** $\{7\}$ **127.** $\{-2, 1\}$ **128.** $\left\{\dfrac{1}{2}, 5\right\}$ **129.** $\left\{-2, \dfrac{10}{3}\right\}$ **130.** $\left\{\dfrac{7+\sqrt{37}}{6}, \dfrac{7-\sqrt{37}}{6}\right\}$

**131.** $\{-3, 3\}$ **132.** $\{3 \pm 2\sqrt{6}\}$ **133.** $\{4\}$ **134.** $\{2\}$ **135.** $\{2\}$ **136.** $g = \dfrac{s-vt}{t^2}$ **137.** $P = \dfrac{A}{1+rT}$ **138.** no real solutions

**139.** one repeated real solution **140.** U.S.: 20.5 million barrels; China: 6.3 million barrels; Japan: 5.5 million barrels

**141.** by 19 years after 2000, or in 2019 **142.** $60 **143.** $10,000 in sales **144.** 44 yd by 126 yd **145.** 2021; 32,100

**146.** length: 5 yd; width: 3 yd **147.** approximately 134 m **148.** 2 in. **149.** 10 people

**150.** $\{x \mid -3 \leq x < 5\}$ **151.** $\{x \mid x > -2\}$ **152.** $\{x \mid x \leq 0\}$ **153.** $[-1, 1]$ **154.** $(-2, 3)$

**155.** $[1, 3)$ **156.** $(0, 4)$

**157.** $[-2, \infty)$ **158.** $\left[\dfrac{3}{5}, \infty\right)$ **159.** $\left(-\infty, -\dfrac{21}{2}\right)$ **160.** $(-3, \infty)$

**161.** $(-\infty, -2]$ **162.** $(2, 3]$ **163.** $[-9, 6]$ **164.** $(-\infty, -6)$ or $(0, \infty)$

**165.** $(-\infty, -3]$ or $[-2, \infty)$ **166.** $(-\infty, -5] \cup [1, \infty)$ **167.** no more than 80 miles per day **168.** $[49\%, 99\%)$

# Chapter P Test

**1.** $6x^2 - 27x$ **2.** $-6x + 17$ **3.** $\{5\}$ **4.** $\{1, 2, 5, a\}$ **5.** $\dfrac{5y^8}{x^6}$ **6.** $3r\sqrt{2}$ **7.** $11\sqrt{2}$ **8.** $\dfrac{3(5-\sqrt{2})}{23}$

**9.** $2x\sqrt[3]{2x}$ **10.** $\dfrac{x+3}{x-2}, x \neq 2, 1$ **11.** $2.5 \times 10^1$ **12.** $2x^3 - 13x^2 + 26x - 15$ **13.** $25x^2 + 30xy + 9y^2$ **14.** $\dfrac{2(x+3)}{x+1}, x \neq 3, -1, -4, -3$

**15.** $\dfrac{x^2+2x+15}{(x+3)(x-3)}, x \neq 3, -3$ **16.** $\dfrac{11}{(x-3)(x-4)}, x \neq 3, 4$ **17.** $\dfrac{2x}{(x+2)(x+1)}$ **18.** $\dfrac{10x}{\sqrt{(x^2+5)^3}}$ **19.** $(x-3)(x-6)$

**20.** $(x^2+3)(x+2)$ **21.** $(5x-3)(5x+3)$ **22.** $(6x-7)^2$ **23.** $(y-5)(y^2+5y+25)$ **24.** $(x+5+3y)(x+5-3y)$ **25.** $\dfrac{2x+3}{(x+3)^{3/5}}$

**26.** $-7, -\dfrac{4}{5}, 0, 0.25, \sqrt{4}, \dfrac{22}{7}$ **27.** commutative property of addition **28.** distributive property of multiplication over addition **29.** $7.6 \times 10^{-4}$

**30.** $\dfrac{1}{243}$ **31.** $1.32 \times 10^{10}$ **32. a.** 43.08%; overestimates by 0.08% **b.** $R = \dfrac{-0.28n + 47}{0.28n + 53}$ **c.** $\dfrac{2}{3}$; Three women will receive bachelor's degrees

for every two men.; It describes the projections exactly. **33.** $\{-1\}$ **34.** $\{-6\}$ **35.** $\{5\}$ **36.** $\left\{-\dfrac{1}{2}, 2\right\}$ **37.** $\left\{\dfrac{1-5\sqrt{3}}{3}, \dfrac{1+5\sqrt{3}}{3}\right\}$

**38.** $\{1-\sqrt{5}, 1+\sqrt{5}\}$ **39.** $\{7\}$ **40.** $\{2\}$ **41.** $\{6, 12\}$ **42.** $\left\{\dfrac{1}{2}, 3\right\}$ **43.** $\{4\}$

**44.** $(-\infty, 12]$ **45.** $\left[\dfrac{21}{8}, \infty\right)$ **46.** $\left[-7, \dfrac{13}{2}\right)$ **47.** $\left(-\infty, -\dfrac{5}{3}\right]$ or $\left[\dfrac{1}{3}, \infty\right)$

**48.** $h = \dfrac{3V}{lw}$ **49.** $x = \dfrac{y-y_1}{m} + x_1$ **50.** $a = -\dfrac{Rs}{R-s}$ or $a = \dfrac{Rs}{s-R}$ **51.** 2018 **52.** 2018 **53.** quite well

**54.** drive-in theaters: 1; movie theaters: 17; video rental stores: 65 **55.** 26 yr; $33,600 **56.** length: 12 ft; width: 4 ft **57.** 10 ft **58.** $50
**59.** 20 people **60.** more than 200 calls

# CHAPTER 1

## Section 1.1

### Check Point Exercises

**1.**

**2.**
$y = 4 - x$

**3.**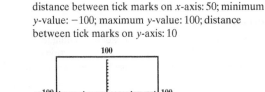
$y = |x + 1|$

**4.** minimum $x$-value: $-100$; maximum $x$-value: 100; distance between tick marks on $x$-axis: 50; minimum $y$-value: $-100$; maximum $y$-value: 100; distance between tick marks on $y$-axis: 10

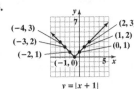

**5. a.** $x$-intercept: $-3$; $y$-intercept: 5
**b.** no $x$-intercept; $y$-intercept: 4
**c.** $x$-intercept: 0; $y$-intercept: 0
**6. a.** 65%   **b.** 60%   **c.** overestimates by 5%

## Exercise Set 1.1

**1.**

**3.**

**5.**

**7.**

**9.**

**11.**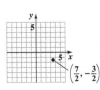

**13.**
$y = x^2 - 2$

**15.**
$y = x - 2$

**17.**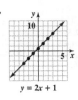
$y = 2x + 1$

**19.**
$y = -\frac{1}{2}x$

**21.**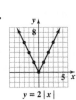
$y = 2|x|$

**23.**
$y = |x| + 1$

**25.**
$y = 9 - x^2$

**27.**
$y = x^3$

**29.** c   **31.** b   **33.** c   **35.** no   **37.** $(2, 0)$   **39.** $(-2, 4)$ and $(1, 1)$   **41. a.** 2   **b.** $-4$   **43. a.** $1, -2$   **b.** 2   **45. a.** $-1$   **b.** none

**47.** $y = 2x + 4$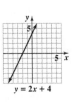
$y = 2x + 4$

**49.** $y = 3 - x^2$
$y = 3 - x^2$

**51.**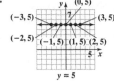
$y = 5$

**53.**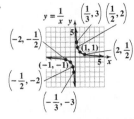

**55. a.** 20%   **b.** 18%; underestimates by 2%   **c.** Answers will vary.; approximately 45%   **d.** 44%; It's less than the estimate.   **e.** 1990; 14%
**57.** 8; 1   **59.** about 1.9   **67.** makes sense   **69.** does not make sense   **71.** false   **73.** true   **75.** a   **77.** b   **79.** b   **81.** c
**83.** set 1
**84.**
$y = 2x$
$y = 2x + 4$

**85. a.** 3   **b.** $-3$ and 3   **c.** all real numbers   **d.** all real numbers greater than or equal to 1

## Section 1.2

### Check Point Exercises

**1.** domain: $\{0, 10, 20, 30, 36\}$; range: $\{9.1, 6.7, 10.7, 13.2, 17.4\}$   **2. a.** not a function   **b.** function   **3. a.** $y = 6 - 2x$; function
**b.** $y = \pm\sqrt{1 - x^2}$; not a function   **4. a.** 42   **b.** $x^2 + 6x + 15$   **c.** $x^2 + 2x + 7$

**5.**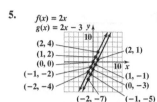

$f(x) = 2x$
$g(x) = 2x - 3$

$(2, 4)$ $(2, 1)$
$(1, 2)$
$(0, 0)$
$(-1, -2)$ $(1, -1)$
$(-2, -4)$ $(0, -3)$
$(-2, -7)$ $(-1, -5)$

; The graph of $g$ is the graph of $f$ shifted down by 3 units.

**6. a.** function    **b.** function    **c.** not a function    **7. a.** 400    **b.** 9    **c.** approximately 425
**8. a.** domain: $\{x | -2 \le x \le 1\}$; range: $\{y | 0 \le y \le 3\}$
   **b.** domain: $\{x | -2 < x \le 1\}$; range: $\{y | -1 \le y < 2\}$
   **c.** domain: $\{x | -3 \le x < 0\}$; range: $\{-3, -2, -1\}$

## Exercise Set 1.2

**1.** function; $\{1, 3, 5\}$; $\{2, 4, 5\}$    **3.** not a function; $\{3, 4\}$; $\{4, 5\}$    **5.** function; $\{3, 4, 5, 7\}$; $\{-2, 1, 9\}$    **7.** function; $\{-3, -2, -1, 0\}$; $\{-3, -2, -1, 0\}$
**9.** not a function; $\{1\}$; $\{4, 5, 6\}$    **11.** $y$ is a function of $x$.    **13.** $y$ is a function of $x$.    **15.** $y$ is not a function of $x$.    **17.** $y$ is not a function of $x$.
**19.** $y$ is a function of $x$.    **21.** $y$ is a function of $x$.    **23.** $y$ is a function of $x$.    **25.** $y$ is a function of $x$.    **27. a.** 29    **b.** $4x + 9$    **c.** $-4x + 5$
**29. a.** 2    **b.** $x^2 + 12x + 38$    **c.** $x^2 - 2x + 3$    **31. a.** 13    **b.** 1    **c.** $x^4 - x^2 + 1$    **d.** $81a^4 - 9a^2 + 1$    **33. a.** 3    **b.** 7    **c.** $\sqrt{x} + 3$
**35. a.** $\dfrac{15}{4}$    **b.** $\dfrac{15}{4}$    **c.** $\dfrac{4x^2 - 1}{x^2}$    **37. a.** 1    **b.** $-1$    **c.** 1

**39.**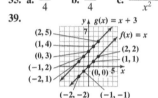

$g(x) = x + 3$
$f(x) = x$
$(2, 5)$
$(1, 4)$
$(2, 2)$
$(0, 3)$
$(1, 1)$
$(-1, 2)$
$(0, 0)$
$(-2, 1)$
$(-2, -2)$ $(-1, -1)$

**41.**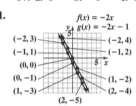

$f(x) = -2x$
$g(x) = -2x - 1$
$(-2, 3)$ $(-2, 4)$
$(-1, 1)$ $(-1, 2)$
$(0, 0)$
$(0, -1)$
$(1, -3)$ $(1, -2)$
$(2, -4)$
$(2, -5)$

**43.**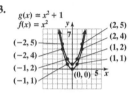

$g(x) = x^2 + 1$
$f(x) = x^2$
$(2, 5)$
$(-2, 5)$ $(2, 4)$
$(-2, 4)$ $(1, 2)$
$(-1, 2)$ $(1, 1)$
$(-1, 1)$ $(0, 0)$

**45.**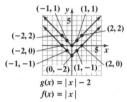

$(-1, 1)$ $(1, 1)$
$(-2, 2)$ $(2, 2)$
$(-2, 0)$ $(2, 0)$
$(-1, -1)$ $(0, -2)$ $(1, -1)$
$g(x) = |x| - 2$
$f(x) = |x|$

The graph of $g$ is the graph of $f$ shifted up by 3 units.    The graph of $g$ is the graph of $f$ shifted down by 1 unit.    The graph of $g$ is the graph of $f$ shifted up by 1 unit.    The graph of $g$ is the graph of $f$ shifted down by 2 units.

**47.**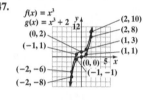

$f(x) = x^3$
$g(x) = x^3 + 2$
$(2, 10)$
$(0, 2)$ $(2, 8)$
$(-1, 1)$ $(1, 3)$
$(1, 1)$
$(0, 0)$
$(-2, -6)$ $(-1, -1)$
$(-2, -8)$

**49.**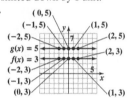

$(0, 5)$
$(-1, 5)$ $(1, 5)$
$(-2, 5)$ $(2, 5)$
$g(x) = 5$
$(2, 3)$
$f(x) = 3$
$(-2, 3)$
$(-1, 3)$
$(0, 3)$ $(1, 3)$

**51.**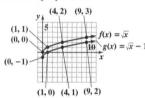

$(4, 2)$ $(9, 3)$
$(1, 1)$
$(0, 0)$
$f(x) = \sqrt{x}$
$g(x) = \sqrt{x} - 1$
$(0, -1)$
$(1, 0)$ $(4, 1)$ $(9, 2)$

**53.**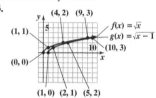

$(4, 2)$ $(9, 3)$
$(1, 1)$
$f(x) = \sqrt{x}$
$g(x) = \sqrt{x - 1}$
$(10, 3)$
$(0, 0)$
$(1, 0)$ $(2, 1)$ $(5, 2)$

The graph of $g$ is the graph of $f$ shifted up by 2 units.    The graph of $g$ is the graph of $f$ shifted up by 2 units.    The graph of $g$ is the graph of $f$ shifted down by 1 unit.    The graph of $g$ is the graph of $f$ shifted to the right by 1 unit.

**55.** function    **57.** function    **59.** not a function    **61.** function    **63.** function    **65.** $-4$    **67.** 4    **69.** 0    **71.** 2    **73.** 2
**75.** $-2$    **77. a.** $(-\infty, \infty)$    **b.** $[-4, \infty)$    **c.** $-3$ and 1    **d.** $-3$    **e.** $f(-2) = -3$ and $f(2) = 5$    **79. a.** $(-\infty, \infty)$    **b.** $[1, \infty)$    **c.** none
**d.** 1    **e.** $f(-1) = 2$ and $f(3) = 4$    **81. a.** $[0, 5)$    **b.** $[-1, 5)$    **c.** 2    **d.** $-1$    **e.** $f(3) = 1$    **83. a.** $[0, \infty)$    **b.** $[1, \infty)$    **c.** none
**d.** 1    **e.** $f(4) = 3$    **85. a.** $[-2, 6]$    **b.** $[-2, 6]$    **c.** 4    **d.** 4    **e.** $f(-1) = 5$    **87. a.** $(-\infty, \infty)$    **b.** $(-\infty, -2]$    **c.** none
**d.** $-2$    **e.** $f(-4) = -5$ and $f(4) = -2$    **89. a.** $(-\infty, \infty)$    **b.** $(0, \infty)$    **c.** none    **d.** 1.5    **e.** $f(4) = 6$    **91. a.** $\{-5, -2, 0, 1, 3\}$
**b.** $\{2\}$    **c.** none    **d.** 2    **e.** $f(-5) + f(3) = 4$    **93.** $-2; 10$    **95.** $-38$    **97.** $-2x^3 - 2x$
**99. a.** $\{(\text{Iceland}, 9.7), (\text{Finland}, 9.6), (\text{New Zealand}, 9.6), (\text{Denmark}, 9.5)\}$    **b.** Yes, each country is paired with only one corruption rating.
**c.** $\{(9.7, \text{Iceland}), (9.6, \text{Finland}), (9.6, \text{New Zealand}), (9.5, \text{Denmark})\}$    **d.** No, the corruption rating 9.6 is paired with two different countries,
Finland and New Zealand.    **101. a.** 83; The chance that a 60-year-old will survive to age 70 is 83%.    **b.** 76; The chance that a 60-year-old
will survive to age 70 is 76%.    **c.** $f$    **103. a.** 127; In 2004, Americans ordered an average of 127 takeout meals per person.; by the point $(20, 127)$
**b.** 94; In 1984, Americans ordered an average of 94 meals in restaurants per person.; by the point $(0, 94)$    **c.** 1988; 91 takeout meals and 91.6 meals
in restaurants    **105.** $C = 100{,}000 + 100x$, where $x$ is the number of bicycles produced; $C(90) = 109{,}000$; It costs \$109,000 to produce 90 bicycles.
**107.** $T = \dfrac{40}{x} + \dfrac{40}{x + 30}$, where $x$ is the rate on the outgoing trip; $T(30) = 2$; It takes 2 hours, traveling 30 mph outgoing and 60 mph returning.
**119.** does not make sense    **121.** does not make sense    **123.** false    **125.** false    **127.** Answers will vary; an example is $\{(1, 1), (2, 1)\}$.
**129.** 36; For 100 calling minutes, the monthly cost is \$36.
**130.**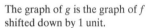

$f(x) = x + 2, x \le 1$

   **131.** $4xh + 2h^2 + 3h$

## Section 1.3

### Check Point Exercises

**1.** increasing on $(-\infty, -1)$, decreasing on $(-1, 1)$, increasing on $(1, \infty)$    **2. a.** even    **b.** odd    **c.** neither
**3. a.** 20; With 40 calling minutes, the cost is \$20.; $(40, 20)$    **b.** 28; With 80 calling minutes, the cost is \$28.; $(80, 28)$

**4.**

$$f(x) = \begin{cases} 3 & \text{if } x \le -1 \\ x - 2 & \text{if } x > -1 \end{cases}$$

**5. a.** $-2x^2 - 4xh - 2h^2 + x + h + 5$ **b.** $-4x - 2h + 1, h \ne 0$

## Exercise Set 1.3

**1. a.** $(-1, \infty)$ **b.** $(-\infty, -1)$ **c.** none **3. a.** $(0, \infty)$ **b.** none **c.** none **5. a.** none **b.** $(-2, 6)$ **c.** none **7. a.** $(-\infty, -1)$
**b.** none **c.** $(-1, \infty)$ **9. a.** $(-\infty, 0)$ or $(1.5, 3)$ **b.** $(0, 1.5)$ or $(3, \infty)$ **c.** none **11. a.** $(-2, 4)$ **b.** none **c.** $(-\infty, -2)$ or $(4, \infty)$
**13. a.** $0; f(0) = 4$ **b.** $-3, 3; f(-3) = f(3) = 0$ **15. a.** $-2; f(-2) = 21$ **b.** $1; f(1) = -6$ **17.** odd **19.** neither **21.** even **23.** even
**25.** even **27.** odd **29.** even **31.** odd **33. a.** $(-\infty, \infty)$ **b.** $[-4, \infty)$ **c.** 1 and 7 **d.** 4 **e.** $(4, \infty)$ **f.** $(0, 4)$ **g.** $(-\infty, 0)$
**h.** 4 **i.** $-4$ **j.** 4 **k.** 2 and 6 **l.** neither **35. a.** $(-\infty, 3]$ **b.** $(-\infty, 4]$ **c.** $-3$ and 3 **d.** 3 **e.** $(-\infty, 1)$ **f.** $(1, 3)$
**g.** $(-\infty, -3]$ **h.** A relative maximum of 4 occurs at 1. **i.** 1 **j.** positive **37. a.** $-1$ **b.** 7 **c.** 19 **41. a.** 8 **b.** 3 **c.** 6
**43. a.**

$$f(x) = \begin{cases} -x & \text{if } x < 0 \\ x & \text{if } x \ge 0 \end{cases}$$

**b.** $[0, \infty)$

**45. a.**

$$f(x) = \begin{cases} 2x & \text{if } x \le 0 \\ 2 & \text{if } x > 0 \end{cases}$$

**b.** $(-\infty, 0] \cup \{2\}$

**47. a.**

$$f(x) = \begin{cases} x + 3 & \text{if } x < -2 \\ x - 3 & \text{if } x \ge -2 \end{cases}$$

**b.** $(-\infty, \infty)$

**49. a.**

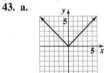

$$f(x) = \begin{cases} 3 & \text{if } x \le -1 \\ -3 & \text{if } x > -1 \end{cases}$$

**b.** $\{-3, 3\}$

**51. a.**

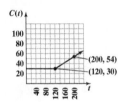

$$f(x) = \begin{cases} \frac{1}{2}x^2 & \text{if } x < 1 \\ 2x - 1 & \text{if } x \ge 1 \end{cases}$$

**b.** $[0, \infty)$

**53. a.**

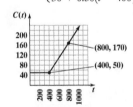

$$f(x) = \begin{cases} 0 & \text{if } x < -4 \\ -x & \text{if } -4 \le x < 0 \\ x^2 & \text{if } x \ge 0 \end{cases}$$

**b.** $[0, \infty)$

**55.** $4, h \ne 0$ **57.** $3, h \ne 0$ **59.** $2x + h, h \ne 0$ **61.** $2x + h - 4, h \ne 0$ **63.** $4x + 2h + 1, h \ne 0$ **65.** $-2x - h + 2, h \ne 0$

**67.** $-4x - 2h + 5, h \ne 0$ **69.** $-4x - 2h - 1, h \ne 0$ **71.** $0, h \ne 0$ **73.** $-\dfrac{1}{x(x + h)}, h \ne 0$ **75.** $\dfrac{1}{\sqrt{x + h} + \sqrt{x}}, h \ne 0$ **77.** $-18$

**79.** $0.30t - 6$ **81.** $C(t) = \begin{cases} 50 & \text{if } 0 \le t \le 400 \\ 50 + 0.30(t - 400) & \text{if } t > 400 \end{cases}$

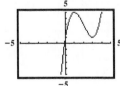

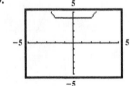

**83.** increasing: $(25, 55)$; decreasing: $(55, 75)$ **85.** 55 years old; 38% **87.** domain: $[25, 75]$; range: $[34, 38]$ **89.** men
**91.** 2608.75; A single taxpayer with taxable income of \$20,000 owes \$2608.75. **93.** $39,148.75 + 0.33(x - 160,850)$
**95.** 0.76; It costs \$0.76 to mail a 3-ounce first-class letter. **97.** \$0.59
**99.**

**107.**

increasing: $(-\infty, 1)$ or $(3, \infty)$
decreasing: $(1, 3)$

**109.**

increasing: $(2, \infty)$
decreasing: $(-\infty, -2)$
constant: $(-2, 2)$

**111.**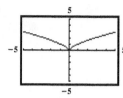

increasing: $(0, \infty)$
decreasing: $(-\infty, 0)$

**113. a.**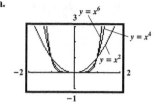

**b.**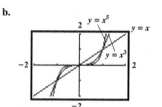

**c.** increasing: $(0, \infty)$; decreasing: $(-\infty, 0)$

**d.** $f(x) = x^n$ is increasing for $(-\infty, \infty)$ when $n$ is positive and odd.

**e.**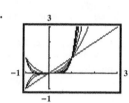

As $n$ increases the steepness increases.

**115.** makes sense     **117.** makes sense     **122.** 3     **123.** $\left(\dfrac{3}{2}, 0\right)$ and $(0, -2)$     **124.** $y = \dfrac{-3x + 4}{2}$ or $y = -\dfrac{3}{2}x + 2$

## Section 1.4

### Check Point Exercises

**1. a.** 6     **b.** $-\dfrac{7}{5}$     **2.** $y + 5 = 6(x - 2)$; $y = 6x - 17$     **3.** $y + 1 = -5(x + 2)$ or $y + 6 = -5(x + 1)$; $y = -5x - 11$

**4.**

$f(x) = \dfrac{3}{5}x + 1$

**5.**

**6.**

**7.** slope: $-\dfrac{1}{2}$; $y$-intercept: 2     **8.**

$3x + 6y - 12 = 0$

$(0, -3)$ $(2, 0)$
$3x - 2y - 6 = 0$

**9.** $f(x) = 0.016x + 52.0$; $61.6°$F

### Exercise Set 1.4

**1.** $\dfrac{3}{4}$; rises     **3.** $\dfrac{1}{4}$; rises     **5.** 0; horizontal     **7.** $-5$; falls     **9.** undefined; vertical     **11.** $y - 5 = 2(x - 3)$; $y = 2x - 1$

**13.** $y - 5 = 6(x + 2)$; $y = 6x + 17$     **15.** $y + 3 = -3(x + 2)$; $y = -3x - 9$     **17.** $y - 0 = -4(x + 4)$; $y = -4x - 16$

**19.** $y + 2 = -1\left(x + \dfrac{1}{2}\right)$; $y = -x - \dfrac{5}{2}$     **21.** $y - 0 = \dfrac{1}{2}(x - 0)$; $y = \dfrac{1}{2}x$     **23.** $y + 2 = -\dfrac{2}{3}(x - 6)$; $y = -\dfrac{2}{3}x + 2$

**25.** using $(1, 2)$, $y - 2 = 2(x - 1)$; $y = 2x$     **27.** using $(-3, 0)$, $y - 0 = 1(x + 3)$; $y = x + 3$     **29.** using $(-3, -1)$, $y + 1 = 1(x + 3)$; $y = x + 2$

**31.** using $(-3, -2)$, $y + 2 = \dfrac{4}{3}(x + 3)$; $y = \dfrac{4}{3}x + 2$     **33.** using $(-3, -1)$, $y + 1 = 0(x + 3)$; $y = -1$     **35.** using $(2, 4)$, $y - 4 = 1(x - 2)$; $y = x + 2$

**37.** using $(0, 4)$, $y - 4 = 8(x - 0)$; $y = 8x + 4$

**39.** $m = 2$; $b = 1$     **41.** $m = -2$; $b = 1$     **43.** $m = \dfrac{3}{4}$; $b = -2$     **45.** $m = -\dfrac{3}{5}$; $b = 7$

$y = 2x + 1$     $f(x) = -2x + 1$     $f(x) = \dfrac{3}{4}x - 2$     $y = -\dfrac{3}{5}x + 7$

**47.** $m = -\dfrac{1}{2}$; $b = 0$     **49.** $y = -2$     **51.** $x = -3$     **53.** $y = 0$     **55.** $f(x) = 1$

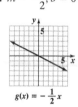
$g(x) = -\dfrac{1}{2}x$

**57.**

**59. a.** $y = -3x + 5$
**b.** $m = -3; b = 5$
**c.**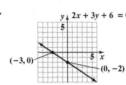
$3x + y - 5 = 0$

**61. a.** $y = -\frac{2}{3}x + 6$
**b.** $m = -\frac{2}{3}; b = 6$
**c.**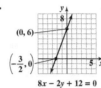
$2x + 3y - 18 = 0$

**63. a.** $y = 2x - 3$
**b.** $m = 2; b = -3$
**c.**
$8x - 4y - 12 = 0$

**65. a.** $y = 3$
**b.** $m = 0; b = 3$
**c.**

**67.**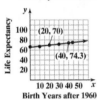
$(2, 0)$
$(0, -6)$
$6x - 2y - 12 = 0$

**69.**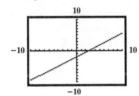
$2x + 3y + 6 = 0$
$(-3, 0)$
$(0, -2)$

**71.**
$(0, 6)$
$\left(-\frac{3}{2}, 0\right)$
$8x - 2y + 12 = 0$

**73.** $m = -\frac{a}{b}$; falls
**75.** undefined slope; vertical
**77.** $m = -\frac{A}{B}; b = \frac{C}{B}$
**79.** $-2$

**81.**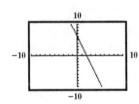
$3x - 4f(x) - 6 = 0$
$\left(0, -\frac{3}{2}\right)$

**83.** 5
**85.** $m_1, m_3, m_2, m_4$
**87. a.** $y - 31.1 = 0.78(x - 10)$ or $y - 38.9 = 0.78(x - 20)$ **b.** $f(x) = 0.78x + 23.3$ **c.** 54.5%

**89. a &b.**  ; $E(x) = 0.215x + 65.7$

Life Expectancy for United States Males, by Year of Birth
$(20, 70)$
$(40, 74.3)$
Life Expectancy
Birth Years after 1960

**c.** 78.6 yr

**91.** Answers will vary; an example is $y = -2.3x + 255$, where $x$ is the percentage of adult females who are literate and $y$ is under-five mortality per thousand.; Predictions will vary.

**101.** $m = -3$

**103.** $m = \frac{3}{4}$

**105.** does not make sense   **107.** does not make sense
**109.** false   **111.** true
**113.** coefficient of $x$: $-6$; coefficient of $y$: 3
**118.** $y = 2x + 7$ or $f(x) = 2x + 7$
**119.** $4x - y - 17 = 0$   **120.** 5

## Section 1.5

### Check Point Exercises

**1.** $y - 5 = 3(x + 2); y = 3x + 11$ or $f(x) = 3x + 11$   **2. a.** 3   **b.** $3x - y = 0$   **3.** $m \approx 0.25$; The number of men living alone increased at a rate of 0.25 million per year. The rate of change is 0.25 million men per year.   **4. a.** 1   **b.** 7   **c.** 4   **5.** 0.01 mg per 100 ml per hr
**6. a.** 12 ft/sec   **b.** 10 ft/sec   **c.** 8.04 ft/sec

### Exercise Set 1.5

**1.** $y - 2 = 2(x - 4); y = 2x - 6$ or $f(x) = 2x - 6$   **3.** $y - 4 = -\frac{1}{2}(x - 2); y = -\frac{1}{2}x + 5$ or $f(x) = -\frac{1}{2}x + 5$

**5.** $y + 10 = -4(x + 8); y = -4x - 42$   **7.** $y + 3 = -5(x - 2); y = -5x + 7$   **9.** $y - 2 = \frac{2}{3}(x + 2); 2x - 3y + 10 = 0$

**11.** $y + 7 = -2(x - 4); 2x + y - 1 = 0$   **13.** 3   **15.** 10   **17.** $\frac{1}{5}$   **19. a.** 70 ft/sec   **b.** 65 ft/sec   **c.** 60.1 ft/sec   **d.** 60.01 ft/sec

**21.** $f(x) = 5$   **23.** $f(x) = -\frac{1}{2}x + 1$   **25.** $f(x) = -\frac{2}{3}x - 2$   **27.** $P(x) = -1.2x + 47$   **29.** 137; There was an average increase of

approximately 137 discharges per year.   **31. a.** 142   **b.** overestimates by 5 discharges per year

**39. a.** The product of their slopes is −1.

**b.** 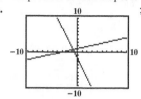 ; no   **c.** 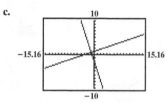 ; The lines now appear to be perpendicular.

**41.** makes sense   **43.** makes sense   **45.** $-\dfrac{3}{7}$

**46. a.** 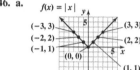   **b.** 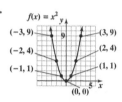   **c.** The graph in part (b) is the graph in part (a) shifted down 4 units.

**47. a.** 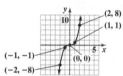   **b.** 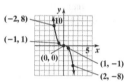   **c.** The graph in part (b) is the graph in part (a) shifted to the right 2 units.

**48. a.** 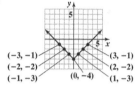   **b.**    **c.** The graph in part (b) is the graph in part (a) reflected across the $y$-axis.

## Mid-Chapter I Check Point

**1.** not a function; domain: $\{1, 2\}$; range: $\{-6, 4, 6\}$   **2.** function; domain: $\{0, 2, 3\}$; range: $\{1, 4\}$   **3.** function; domain: $\{x \mid -2 \le x < 2\}$ or $[-2, 2)$; range: $\{y \mid 0 \le y \le 3\}$ or $[0, 3]$   **4.** not a function; domain: $\{x \mid -3 < x \le 4\}$ or $(-3, 4]$; range: $\{y \mid -1 \le y \le 2\}$ or $[-1, 2]$

**5.** not a function; domain: $\{-2, -1, 0, 1, 2\}$; range: $\{-2, -1, 1, 3\}$   **6.** function; domain: $\{x \mid x \le 1\}$ or $(-\infty, 1]$; range: $\{y \mid y \ge -1\}$ or $[-1, \infty)$

**7.** $y$ is a function of $x$.   **8.** $y$ is not a function of $x$.   **9.** No vertical line intersects the graph in more than one point.   **10.** $(-\infty, \infty)$

**11.** $(-\infty, 4]$   **12.** −6 and 2   **13.** 3   **14.** $(-\infty, -2)$   **15.** $(-2, \infty)$   **16.** −2   **17.** 4   **18.** 3   **19.** −7 and 3   **20.** −6 and 2

**21.** $(-6, 2)$   **22.** negative   **23.** neither   **24.** −1

**25.** $y = -2x$    **26.** $y = -2$    **27.** $x + y = -2$    **28.** $y = \dfrac{1}{3}x - 2$    **29.** $x = 3.5$

**30.**  $4x - 2y = 8$   **31.**  $f(x) = x^2 - 4$   **32.**  $f(x) = x - 4$   **33.** $f(x) = |x| - 4$   **34.**  $5y = -3x$

**35.**  $5y = 20$   **36.**  $f(x) = \begin{cases} -1 & \text{if } x \le 0 \\ 2x + 1 & \text{if } x > 0 \end{cases}$

**37. a.** $f(-x) = -2x^2 - x - 5$; neither   **b.** $-4x - 2h + 1, h \ne 0$   **38. a.** 30   **b.** 50

**39.** $f(x) = -2x - 5$   **40.** $f(x) = 2x - 3$   **41.** $f(x) = 3x - 13$

**42.** $f(x) = -\dfrac{5}{2}x - 13$   **43.** The lines are parallel.

**44. a.** 0.16   **b.** 0.16; 0.16; minute of brisk walking   **45.** 2

## Section 1.6

**Check Point Exercises**

**1.**

**2.**

**3.**

**4.**

**5.**

**6.**

**7. a.**
$$g(x) = f(2x)$$

**b.**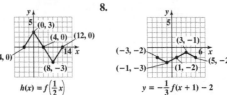
$$h(x) = f\left(\frac{1}{2}x\right)$$

**8.**
$$y = -\frac{1}{3}f(x+1) - 2$$

**9.**
$$g(x) = 2(x-1)^2 + 3$$

## Exercise Set 1.6

**1.**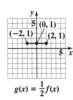
$$g(x) = f(x) + 1$$

**3.**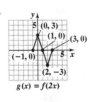
$$g(x) = f(x+1)$$

**5.**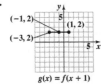
$$g(x) = f(x-1) - 2$$

**7.**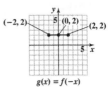
$$g(x) = f(-x)$$

**9.**
$$g(x) = -f(x) + 3$$

**11.**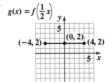
$$g(x) = \frac{1}{2}f(x)$$

**13.** $g(x) = f\left(\frac{1}{2}x\right)$

**15.**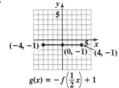
$$g(x) = -f\left(\frac{1}{2}x\right) + 1$$

**17.**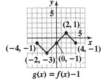
$$g(x) = f(x) - 1$$

**19.**
$$g(x) = f(x-1)$$

**21.**
$$g(x) = f(x-1) + 2$$

**23.**
$$g(x) = -f(x)$$

**25.**
$$g(x) = f(-x) + 1$$

**27.**
$$g(x) = 2f(x)$$

**29.**
$$g(x) = f(2x)$$

**31.**
$$g(x) = 2f(x+2) + 1$$

**33.**
$$g(x) = f(x) + 2$$

**35.**
$$g(x) = f(x+2)$$

**37.**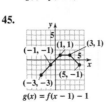
$$g(x) = -f(x+2)$$

**39.**
$$g(x) = -\frac{1}{2}f(x+2)$$

**41.**
$$g(x) = -\frac{1}{2}f(x+2) - 2$$

**43.**
$$g(x) = \frac{1}{2}f(2x)$$

**45.**
$$g(x) = f(x-1) - 1$$

**47.**
$$g(x) = -f(x-1) + 1$$

**49.**
$$g(x) = 2f\left(\frac{1}{2}x\right)$$

**51.**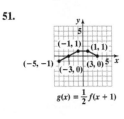
$$g(x) = \frac{1}{2}f(x+1)$$

**53.**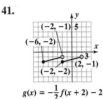

**55.**

**57.**

**59.**

**61.**    **63.**    **65.**    **67.**    **69.**

**71.**    **73.**    **75.**    **77.**    **79.**

**81.**    **83.**    **85.**    **87.**    **89.**

**91.**    **93.**    **95.**    **97.**    **99.**

**101.**    **103.**    **105.**    **107.**    **109.**

**111.**    **113.**    **115.**    **117.**    **119.**

$g(x) = 2 \text{ int } (x + 1)$

**121.**    **123.** $y = \sqrt{x - 2}$   **125.** $y = (x + 1)^2 - 4$
**127. a.** First, vertically stretch the graph of $f(x) = \sqrt{x}$
by the factor 2.9; then, shift the result up 20.1 units.   **b.** 40.2 in.; very well
**c.** 0.9 in. per month   **d.** 0.2 in. per month; This is a much smaller rate of change;
The graph is not as steep between 50 and 60 as it is between 0 and 10.

$h(x) = \text{int } (-x) + 1$

**135. a.** 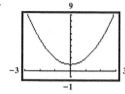   **b.**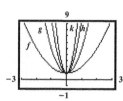

**137.** makes sense   **139.** does not make sense   **141.** false   **143.** false   **145.** $g(x) = -(x + 4)^2$   **147.** $g(x) = -\sqrt{x - 2} + 2$

**149.** $(-a, b)$   **151.** $(a + 3, b)$   **153.** $2x^3 + x^2 - 5x + 2$   **154.** $9x^2 - 30x + 30$   **155.** $\dfrac{2x}{3 - x}$

## Section 1.7

### Check Point Exercises

**1. a.** $(-\infty, \infty)$   **b.** $(-\infty, -7) \cup (-7, 7) \cup (7, \infty)$   **c.** $[3, \infty)$   **2. a.** $(f + g)(x) = x^2 + x - 6; (-\infty, \infty)$   **b.** $(f - g)(x) = -x^2 + x - 4; (-\infty, \infty)$

**c.** $(fg)(x) = x^3 - 5x^2 - x + 5; (-\infty, \infty)$   **d.** $\left(\dfrac{f}{g}\right)(x) = \dfrac{x - 5}{x^2 - 1}; (-\infty, -1) \cup (-1, 1) \cup (1, \infty)$   **3. a.** $(f + g)(x) = \sqrt{x - 3} + \sqrt{x + 1}$   **b.** $[3, \infty)$

**4. a.** $(f \circ g)(x) = 10x^2 - 5x + 1$   **b.** $(g \circ f)(x) = 50x^2 + 115x + 65$   **c.** 16   **5. a.** $(f \circ g)(x) = \dfrac{4x}{1 + 2x}$   **b.** $\left(-\infty, -\dfrac{1}{2}\right) \cup \left(-\dfrac{1}{2}, 0\right) \cup (0, \infty)$

**6.** If $f(x) = \sqrt{x}$ and $g(x) = x^2 + 5$, then $h(x) = (f \circ g)(x)$.

## Exercise Set 1.7

**1.** $(-\infty, \infty)$   **3.** $(-\infty, 4) \cup (4, \infty)$   **5.** $(-\infty, \infty)$   **7.** $(-\infty, -3) \cup (-3, 5) \cup (5, \infty)$   **9.** $(-\infty, -7) \cup (-7, 9) \cup (9, \infty)$
**11.** $(-\infty, -1) \cup (-1, 1) \cup (1, \infty)$   **13.** $(-\infty, 0) \cup (0, 3) \cup (3, \infty)$   **15.** $(-\infty, 1) \cup (1, 3) \cup (3, \infty)$   **17.** $[3, \infty)$   **19.** $(3, \infty)$   **21.** $[-7, \infty)$
**23.** $(-\infty, 12]$   **25.** $[2, \infty)$   **27.** $[2, 5) \cup (5, \infty)$   **29.** $(-\infty, -2) \cup (-2, 2) \cup (2, 5) \cup (5, \infty)$

**31.** $(f + g)(x) = 3x + 2$; domain: $(-\infty, \infty)$; $(f - g)(x) = x + 4$; domain: $(-\infty, \infty)$; $(fg)(x) = 2x^2 + x - 3$; domain: $(-\infty, \infty)$; $\left(\dfrac{f}{g}\right)(x) = \dfrac{2x + 3}{x - 1}$;
domain: $(-\infty, 1) \cup (1, \infty)$   **33.** $(f + g)(x) = 3x^2 + x - 5$; domain: $(-\infty, \infty)$; $(f - g)(x) = -3x^2 + x - 5$; domain: $(-\infty, \infty)$; $(fg)(x) = 3x^3 - 15x^2$;
domain: $(-\infty, \infty)$; $\left(\dfrac{f}{g}\right)(x) = \dfrac{x - 5}{3x^2}$; domain: $(-\infty, 0) \cup (0, \infty)$   **35.** $(f + g)(x) = 2x^2 - 2$; domain: $(-\infty, \infty)$; $(f - g)(x) = 2x^2 - 2x - 4$;
domain: $(-\infty, \infty)$; $(fg)(x) = 2x^3 + x^2 - 4x - 3$; domain: $(-\infty, \infty)$; $\left(\dfrac{f}{g}\right)(x) = 2x - 3$; domain: $(-\infty, -1) \cup (-1, \infty)$

**37.** $(f + g)(x) = 2x - 12$; domain: $(-\infty, \infty)$; $(f - g)(x) = -2x^2 - 2x + 18$; domain: $(-\infty, \infty)$; $(fg)(x) = -x^4 - 2x^3 + 18x^2 + 6x - 45$;
domain: $(-\infty, \infty)$; $\left(\dfrac{f}{g}\right)(x) = \dfrac{3 - x^2}{x^2 + 2x - 15}$; domain: $(-\infty, -5) \cup (-5, 3) \cup (3, \infty)$

**39.** $(f + g)(x) = \sqrt{x} + x - 4$; domain: $[0, \infty)$; $(f - g)(x) = \sqrt{x} - x + 4$; domain: $[0, \infty)$; $(fg)(x) = \sqrt{x}(x - 4)$; domain: $[0, \infty)$; $\left(\dfrac{f}{g}\right)(x) = \dfrac{\sqrt{x}}{x - 4}$;
domain: $[0, 4) \cup (4, \infty)$   **41.** $(f + g)(x) = \dfrac{2x + 2}{x}$; domain: $(-\infty, 0) \cup (0, \infty)$; $(f - g)(x) = 2$; domain: $(-\infty, 0) \cup (0, \infty)$; $(fg)(x) = \dfrac{2x + 1}{x^2}$;
domain: $(-\infty, 0) \cup (0, \infty)$; $\left(\dfrac{f}{g}\right)(x) = 2x + 1$; domain: $(-\infty, 0) \cup (0, \infty)$   **43.** $(f + g)(x) = \dfrac{9x - 1}{x^2 - 9}$; domain:
$(-\infty, -3) \cup (-3, 3) \cup (3, \infty)$; $(f - g)(x) = \dfrac{x + 3}{x^2 - 9} = \dfrac{1}{x - 3}$; domain: $(-\infty, -3) \cup (-3, 3) \cup (3, \infty)$; $(fg)(x) = \dfrac{20x^2 - 6x - 2}{(x^2 - 9)^2}$;
domain: $(-\infty, -3) \cup (-3, 3) \cup (3, \infty)$; $\left(\dfrac{f}{g}\right)(x) = \dfrac{5x + 1}{4x - 2}$; domain: $(-\infty, -3) \cup \left(-3, \dfrac{1}{2}\right) \cup \left(\dfrac{1}{2}, 3\right) \cup (3, \infty)$

**45.** $(f + g)(x) = \sqrt{x + 4} + \sqrt{x - 1}$; domain: $[1, \infty)$; $(f - g)(x) = \sqrt{x + 4} - \sqrt{x - 1}$; domain: $[1, \infty)$; $(fg)(x) = \sqrt{x^2 + 3x - 4}$;
domain: $[1, \infty)$; $\left(\dfrac{f}{g}\right)(x) = \dfrac{\sqrt{x + 4}}{\sqrt{x - 1}}$; domain: $(1, \infty)$   **47.** $(f + g)(x) = \sqrt{x - 2} + \sqrt{2 - x}$; domain: $\{2\}$; $(f - g)(x) = \sqrt{x - 2} - \sqrt{2 - x}$;
domain: $\{2\}$; $(fg)(x) = \sqrt{x - 2} \cdot \sqrt{2 - x}$; domain: $\{2\}$; $\left(\dfrac{f}{g}\right)(x) = \dfrac{\sqrt{x - 2}}{\sqrt{2 - x}}$; domain: $\varnothing$   **49. a.** $(f \circ g)(x) = 2x + 14$   **b.** $(g \circ f)(x) = 2x + 7$
**c.** $(f \circ g)(2) = 18$   **51. a.** $(f \circ g)(x) = 2x + 5$   **b.** $(g \circ f)(x) = 2x + 9$   **c.** $(f \circ g)(2) = 9$   **53. a.** $(f \circ g)(x) = 20x^2 - 11$
**b.** $(g \circ f)(x) = 80x^2 - 120x + 43$   **c.** $(f \circ g)(2) = 69$   **55. a.** $(f \circ g)(x) = x^4 - 4x^2 + 6$   **b.** $(g \circ f)(x) = x^4 + 4x^2 + 2$   **c.** $(f \circ g)(2) = 6$
**57. a.** $(f \circ g)(x) = -2x^2 - x - 1$   **b.** $(g \circ f)(x) = 2x^2 - 17x + 41$   **c.** $-11$   **59. a.** $(f \circ g)(x) = \sqrt{x - 1}$   **b.** $(g \circ f)(x) = \sqrt{x} - 1$
**c.** $(f \circ g)(2) = 1$   **61. a.** $(f \circ g)(x) = x$   **b.** $(g \circ f)(x) = x$   **c.** $(f \circ g)(2) = 2$   **63. a.** $(f \circ g)(x) = x$   **b.** $(g \circ f)(x) = x$   **c.** 2
**65. a.** $(f \circ g)(x) = \dfrac{2x}{1 + 3x}$   **b.** $\left(-\infty, -\dfrac{1}{3}\right) \cup \left(-\dfrac{1}{3}, 0\right) \cup (0, \infty)$   **67. a.** $(f \circ g)(x) = \dfrac{4}{4 + x}$   **b.** $(-\infty, -4) \cup (-4, 0) \cup (0, \infty)$
**69. a.** $(f \circ g)(x) = \sqrt{x - 2}$   **b.** $[2, \infty)$   **71. a.** $(f \circ g)(x) = 5 - x$   **b.** $(-\infty, 1]$   **73.** $f(x) = x^4, g(x) = 3x - 1$
**75.** $f(x) = \sqrt[3]{x}, g(x) = x^2 - 9$   **77.** $f(x) = |x|, g(x) = 2x - 5$   **79.** $f(x) = \dfrac{1}{x}, g(x) = 2x - 3$   **81.** 5   **83.** $-1$   **85.** $[-4, 3]$

**87.**   **89.** 1   **91.** $-6$   **93.** 1 and 2
**95. a.** $(B - D)(x) = 10.9x^2 - 35x + 1641$
   **b.** 1634.1 thousand   **c.** overestimates by 0.1 thousand

**97.** $(R - C)(20,000) = -200,000$; The company loses \$200,000 when 20,000 radios are sold.; $(R - C)(30,000) = 0$; The company breaks even when
30,000 radios are sold.; $(R - C)(40,000) = 200,000$; The company makes a profit of \$200,000 when 40,000 radios are sold.   **99. a.** $f$ gives the price
of the computer after a \$400 discount. $g$ gives the price of the computer after a 25% discount.   **b.** $(f \circ g)(x) = 0.75x - 400$; This models the price
of a computer after first a 25% discount and then a \$400 discount.   **c.** $(g \circ f)(x) = 0.75(x - 400)$; This models the price of a computer after first a
\$400 discount and then a 25% discount.   **d.** $f \circ g$ because $0.75x - 400 < 0.75(x - 400)$
**107.**   **109.** makes sense   **111.** does not make sense   **113.** false   **115.** true
   **117.** Answers will vary; One possible answer is $f(x) = x + 1$ and $g(x) = x - 1$.

   **118.** $\{(4, -2), (1, -1), (1, 1), (4, 2)\}$; no   **119.** $y = \dfrac{5}{x - 4}$   **120.** $y = \sqrt{x + 1}$

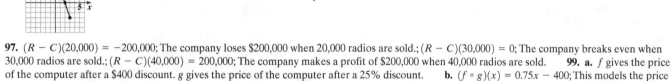

Domain: $[0, 4]$

## Section 1.8

### Check Point Exercises

**1.** $f(g(x)) = 4\left(\dfrac{x+7}{4}\right) - 7 = x + 7 - 7 = x$; $g(f(x)) = \dfrac{(4x-7)+7}{4} = \dfrac{4x}{4} = x$  **2.** $f^{-1}(x) = \dfrac{x-7}{2}$  **3.** $f^{-1}(x) = \sqrt[3]{\dfrac{x+1}{4}}$

**4.** $f^{-1}(x) = \dfrac{3}{x+1}$  **5.** (b) and (c)

**6.** 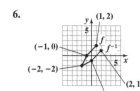  **7.** $f^{-1}(x) = \sqrt{x-1}$

### Exercise Set 1.8

**1.** $f(g(x)) = x$; $g(f(x)) = x$; $f$ and $g$ are inverses.  **3.** $f(g(x)) = x$; $g(f(x)) = x$; $f$ and $g$ are inverses.

**5.** $f(g(x)) = \dfrac{5x-56}{9}$; $g(f(x)) = \dfrac{5x-4}{9}$; $f$ and $g$ are not inverses.  **7.** $f(g(x)) = x$; $g(f(x)) = x$; $f$ and $g$ are inverses.

**9.** $f(g(x)) = x$; $g(f(x)) = x$; $f$ and $g$ are inverses.  **11.** $f^{-1}(x) = x - 3$  **13.** $f^{-1}(x) = \dfrac{x}{2}$  **15.** $f^{-1}(x) = \dfrac{x-3}{2}$  **17.** $f^{-1}(x) = \sqrt[3]{x-2}$

**19.** $f^{-1}(x) = \sqrt[3]{x} - 2$  **21.** $f^{-1}(x) = \dfrac{1}{x}$  **23.** $f^{-1}(x) = x^2$, $x \geq 0$  **25.** $f^{-1}(x) = \dfrac{7}{x+3}$  **27.** $f^{-1}(x) = \dfrac{3x+1}{x-2}$; $x \neq 2$

**29.** The function is not one-to-one, so it does not have an inverse function.  **31.** The function is not one-to-one, so it does not have an inverse function.
**33.** The function is one-to-one, so it does have an inverse function.
**35.**   **37.**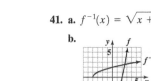

**39. a.** $f^{-1}(x) = \dfrac{x+1}{2}$  **41. a.** $f^{-1}(x) = \sqrt{x+4}$  **43. a.** $f^{-1}(x) = -\sqrt{x} + 1$

**b.** 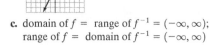  **b.**   **b.**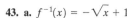

**c.** domain of $f$ = range of $f^{-1} = (-\infty, \infty)$; range of $f$ = domain of $f^{-1} = (-\infty, \infty)$  **c.** domain of $f$ = range of $f^{-1} = [0, \infty)$; range of $f$ = domain of $f^{-1} = [-4, \infty)$  **c.** domain of $f$ = range of $f^{-1} = (-\infty, 1]$; range of $f$ = domain of $f^{-1} = [0, \infty)$

**45. a.** $f^{-1}(x) = \sqrt[3]{x+1}$  **47. a.** $f^{-1}(x) = \sqrt[3]{x} - 2$  **49. a.** $f^{-1}(x) = x^2 + 1$, $x \geq 0$

**b.** 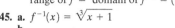  **b.**   **b.**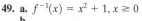

**c.** domain of $f$ = range of $f^{-1} = (-\infty, \infty)$; range of $f$ = domain of $f^{-1} = (-\infty, \infty)$  **c.** domain of $f$ = range of $f^{-1} = (-\infty, \infty)$; range of $f$ = domain of $f^{-1} = (-\infty, \infty)$  **c.** domain of $f$ = range of $f^{-1} = [1, \infty)$; range of $f$ = domain of $f^{-1} = [0, \infty)$

**51. a.** $f^{-1}(x) = (x-1)^3$  **53.** 5  **55.** 1  **57.** 2  **59.** –7  **61.** 3  **63.** 11
**b.** 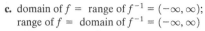  **65. a.** $\{(17, 9.7), (22, 8.7), (30, 8.4), (40, 8.3), (50, 8.2), (60, 8.3)\}$
**b.** $\{(9.7, 17), (8.7, 22), (8.4, 30), (8.3, 40), (8.2, 50), (8.3, 60)\}$; no; The inverse of $f$ is not a function.
**67. a.** $f$ is a one-to-one function.  **b.** $f^{-1}(0.25)$ is the number of people in a room for a 25% probability of two people sharing a birthday. $f^{-1}(0.5)$ is the number of people in a room for a 50% probability of two people sharing a birthday. $f^{-1}(0.7)$ is the number of people in a room for a 70% probability of two people sharing a birthday.

**c.** domain of $f$ = range of $f^{-1} = (-\infty, \infty)$; range of $f$ = domain of $f^{-1} = (-\infty, \infty)$

**69.** $f(g(x)) = \dfrac{9}{5}\left[\dfrac{5}{9}(x - 32)\right] + 32 = x$ and $g(f(x)) = \dfrac{5}{9}\left[\left(\dfrac{9}{5}x + 32\right) - 32\right] = x$

**77.**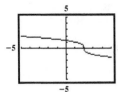

one-to-one

**79.**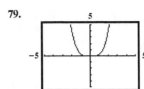

not one-to-one

**81.**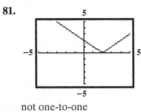

not one-to-one

**83.**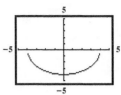

not one-to-one

**85.**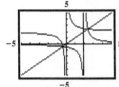

$f$ and $g$ are inverses.

**87.** makes sense **89.** makes sense **91.** false **93.** false

**95.** $(f \circ g)^{-1}(x) = \dfrac{x - 15}{3}$; $(g^{-1} \circ f^{-1})(x) = \dfrac{x}{3} - 5 = \dfrac{x - 15}{3}$

**97.** No; The space craft was at the same height, $s(t)$, for two different values of $t$-once during the ascent and once again during the descent.

**100.** $3\sqrt{5}$ **101.** (1, −1) **102.** $\{3 \pm \sqrt{13}\}$

# Section 1.9

## Check Point Exercises

**1.** 13 **2.** $\left(4, -\dfrac{1}{2}\right)$ **3.** $x^2 + y^2 = 16$ **4.** $x^2 + (y + 6)^2 = 100$

**5. a.** center: $(-3, 1)$; radius: 2 **6.** $(x + 2)^2 + (y - 2)^2 = 9$

**b.**
$(x + 3)^2 + (y - 1)^2 = 4$

$x^2 + y^2 + 4x - 4y - 1 = 0$

**c.** domain: $[-5, -1]$
range: $[-1, 3]$

## Exercise Set 1.9

**1.** 13 **3.** $2\sqrt{29} \approx 10.77$ **5.** 5 **7.** $\sqrt{29} \approx 5.39$ **9.** $4\sqrt{2} \approx 5.66$ **11.** $2\sqrt{5} \approx 4.47$ **13.** $2\sqrt{2} \approx 2.83$ **15.** $\sqrt{93} \approx 9.64$

**17.** $\sqrt{5} \approx 2.24$ **19.** $(4, 6)$ **21.** $(-4, -5)$ **23.** $\left(\dfrac{3}{2}, -6\right)$ **25.** $(-3, -2)$ **27.** $(1, 5\sqrt{5})$ **29.** $(2\sqrt{2}, 0)$ **31.** $x^2 + y^2 = 49$

**33.** $(x - 3)^2 + (y - 2)^2 = 25$ **35.** $(x + 1)^2 + (y - 4)^2 = 4$ **37.** $(x + 3)^2 + (y + 1)^2 = 3$ **39.** $(x + 4)^2 + y^2 = 100$

**41.** center: $(0, 0)$
radius: 4
domain: $[-4, 4]$
range: $[-4, 4]$

$x^2 + y^2 = 16$

**43.** center: $(3, 1)$
radius: 6
domain: $[-3, 9]$
range: $[-5, 7]$

$(x - 3)^2 + (y - 1)^2 = 36$

**45.** center: $(-3, 2)$
radius: 2
domain: $[-5, -1]$
range: $[0, 4]$

$(x + 3)^2 + (y - 2)^2 = 4$

**47.** center: $(-2, -2)$
radius: 2
domain: $[-4, 0]$
range: $[-4, 0]$

$(x + 2)^2 + (y + 2)^2 = 4$

**49.** center: $(0, 1)$
radius: 1
domain: $[-1, 1]$
range: $[0, 2]$

$x^2 + (y - 1)^2 = 1$

**51.** center: $(-1, 0)$
radius: 5
domain: $[-6, 4]$
range: $[-5, 5]$

$(x + 1)^2 + y^2 = 25$

**53.** $(x + 3)^2 + (y + 1)^2 = 4$
center: $(-3, -1)$
radius: 2

$x^2 + y^2 + 6x + 2y + 6 = 0$

**55.** $(x - 5)^2 + (y - 3)^2 = 64$
center: $(5, 3)$
radius: 8

$x^2 + y^2 - 10x - 6y - 30 = 0$

**57.** $(x + 4)^2 + (y - 1)^2 = 25$
center: $(-4, 1)$
radius: 5

$x^2 + y^2 + 8x - 2y - 8 = 0$

**59.** $(x - 1)^2 + y^2 = 16$

center: $(1, 0)$

radius: 4

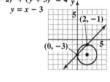

$x^2 - 2x + y^2 - 15 = 0$

**61.** $\left(x - \dfrac{1}{2}\right)^2 + (y + 1)^2 = \dfrac{1}{4}$

center: $\left(\dfrac{1}{2}, -1\right)$

radius: $\dfrac{1}{2}$

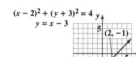

$x^2 + y^2 - x + 2y + 1 = 0$

**63.** $\left(x + \dfrac{3}{2}\right)^2 + (y - 1)^2 = \dfrac{17}{4}$

center: $\left(-\dfrac{3}{2}, 1\right)$

radius: $\dfrac{\sqrt{17}}{2}$

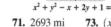

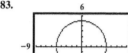

$x^2 + y^2 + 3x - 2y - 1 = 0$

**65. a.** $(5, 10)$　**b.** $\sqrt{5}$
**c.** $(x - 5)^2 + (y - 10)^2 = 5$

**67.** $\{(0, -4), (4, 0)\}$

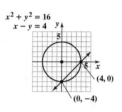

$x^2 + y^2 = 16$
$x - y = 4$

$(4, 0)$
$(0, -4)$

**69.** $\{(0, -3), (2, -1)\}$

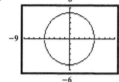

$(x - 2)^2 + (y + 3)^2 = 4$
$y = x - 3$

$(2, -1)$

$(0, -3)$

**71.** 2693 mi　**73.** $(x + 2.4)^2 + (y + 2.7)^2 = 900$

**83.**

**85.**

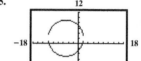

**87.** makes sense
**89.** makes sense
**91.** false
**93.** false

**95. a.** Distance between $(x_1, y_1)$ and $\left(\dfrac{x_1 + x_2}{2}, \dfrac{y_1 + y_2}{2}\right)$

$= \sqrt{\left(\dfrac{x_1 + x_2}{2} - x_1\right)^2 + \left(\dfrac{y_1 + y_2}{2} - y_1\right)^2}$

$= \sqrt{\left(\dfrac{x_1 + x_2 - 2x_1}{2}\right)^2 + \left(\dfrac{y_1 + y_2 - 2y_1}{2}\right)^2}$

$= \sqrt{\left(\dfrac{x_2 - x_1}{2}\right)^2 + \left(\dfrac{y_2 - y_1}{2}\right)^2}$

$= \sqrt{\dfrac{x_2^2 - 2x_1x_2 + x_1^2}{4} + \dfrac{y_2^2 - 2y_1y_2 + y_1^2}{4}}$

$= \sqrt{\dfrac{x_1^2 - 2x_1x_2 + x_2^2}{4} + \dfrac{y_1^2 - 2y_1y_2 + y_2^2}{4}}$

$= \sqrt{\left(\dfrac{x_1 - x_2}{2}\right)^2 + \left(\dfrac{y_1 - y_2}{2}\right)^2}$

$= \sqrt{\left(\dfrac{x_1 + x_2 - 2x_2}{2}\right)^2 + \left(\dfrac{y_1 + y_2 - 2y_2}{2}\right)^2}$

$= \sqrt{\left(\dfrac{x_1 + x_2}{2} - x_2\right)^2 + \left(\dfrac{y_1 + y_2}{2} - y_2\right)^2}$

$=$ Distance between $(x_2, y_2)$ and $\left(\dfrac{x_1 + x_2}{2}, \dfrac{y_1 + y_2}{2}\right)$

**b.** $\sqrt{\left(\dfrac{x_2 - x_1}{2}\right)^2 + \left(\dfrac{y_2 - y_1}{2}\right)^2} + \sqrt{\left(\dfrac{x_2 - x_1}{2}\right)^2 + \left(\dfrac{y_2 - y_1}{2}\right)^2}$

$= 2\sqrt{\left(\dfrac{x_2 - x_1}{2}\right)^2 + \left(\dfrac{y_2 - y_1}{2}\right)^2}$

$= 2\sqrt{\dfrac{(x_2 - x_1)^2 + (y_2 - y_1)^2}{4}}$

$= \sqrt{(x_2 - x_1)^2 + (y_2 - y_1)^2}$

$=$ Distance from $(x_1, y_1)$ to $(x_2, y_2)$

**97.** $y + 4 = \dfrac{3}{4}(x - 3)$　**98.** $x - 200$　**99. a.** perimeter: 140 yd; area: 1200 yd$^2$　**b.** perimeter: 140 yd; area: 1000 yd$^2$　**100.** $h = \dfrac{22}{\pi r^2}; 2\pi r^2 + \dfrac{44}{r}$

## Section 1.10

### Check Point Exercises

**1. a.** $f(x) = 0.08x + 15$　**b.** $g(x) = 0.12x + 3$　**c.** 300 min　**2. a.** $N(x) = -100x + 18{,}000$　**b.** $R(x) = -100x^2 + 18{,}000x$
**3. a.** $V(x) = x(15 - 2x)(8 - 2x)$　**b.** $\{x \mid 0 < x < 4\}$ or $(0, 4)$　**4.** $x(100 - x) = 100x - x^2 \text{ ft}^2$　**5.** $A(r) = 2\pi r^2 + \dfrac{2000}{r}$
**6.** $I(x) = 0.07x + 0.09(25{,}000 - x)$　**7.** $d = \sqrt{x^6 + x^2}$

### Exercise Set 1.10

**1. a.** $f(x) = 200 + 0.15x$　**b.** 800 mi　**3. a.** $M(x) = 239.4 - 0.3x$　**b.** 2152　**5. a.** $f(x) = 1.25x$　**b.** $g(x) = 21 + 0.5x$　**c.** 28 times;
$35　**7. a.** $f(x) = 100 + 0.8x$　**b.** $g(x) = 40 + 0.9x$　**c.** $600; $580　**9. a.** $N(x) = -500x + 40{,}000$　**b.** $R(x) = -500x^2 + 40{,}000x$
**11. a.** $N(x) = -50x + 16{,}500$　**b.** $R(x) = -50x^2 + 16{,}500x$　**13. a.** $Y(x) = -4x + 520$　**b.** $T(x) = -4x^2 + 520x$
**15. a.** $V(x) = x(24 - 2x)^2$　**b.** $V(2) = 800$; If a 2-in. square is cut from each corner, the volume is 800 cubic in.; $V(3) = 972$; if a 3-in. square is cut
from each corner, the volume is 972 cubic in.; $V(4) = 1024$; if a 4-in. square is cut from each corner, the volume is 1024 cubic in.; $V(5) = 980$; if a 5-in.
square is cut from each corner, the volume is 980 cubic in.; $V(6) = 864$; if a 6-in. square is cut from each corner, the volume is 864 cubic in. Initially, as $x$
increases, $V$ increases. When $x = 4$, $V$ is a maximum. As $x$ increases beyond 4, $V$ decreases.　**c.** $(0, 12)$　**17.** $A(x) = x(20 - 2x)$

**19.** $P(x) = x(66 - x)$　**21.** $A(x) = x(400 - x)$　**23.** Let $x$ be the length of the side perpendicular to the canal. $A(x) = x(800 - 2x)$
**25.** $A(x) = \dfrac{x(1000 - 2x)}{3}$　**27.** $A(r) = r(440 - \pi r)$　**29.** Let $x$ be the length of the interior wall. $C(x) = 475x + \dfrac{1{,}400{,}000}{x}$

**31.** $A(x) = \dfrac{40}{x} + x^2$    **33.** $V(x) = 300x^2 - 4x^3$    **35. a.** $I(x) = 0.15x + 0.07(50{,}000 - x)$    **b.** \$31,250 at 15%, \$18,750 at 7%

**37.** $I(x) = 0.12x - 0.05(8000 - x)$    **39.** $d(x) = \sqrt{x^4 - 7x^2 + 16}$    **41.** $d(x) = \sqrt{x^2 - x + 1}$    **43. a.** $A(x) = 2x\sqrt{4 - x^2}$

**b.** $P(x) = 4x + 2\sqrt{4 - x^2}$    **45.** $f(x) = \sqrt{x^2 + 36} + \sqrt{x^2 - 20x + 164}$    **47.** $A(x) = 3x^2 + x - 4$    **49.** $V(x) = 2x^3 + 12x^2 + 12x + 10$

**63.** does not make sense    **65.** does not make sense    **67.** $T(x) = \dfrac{\sqrt{x^2 + 4}}{2} + \dfrac{6 - x}{5}$    **69.** $A(r) = 12r - \dfrac{4 + \pi}{2}r^2$    **71.** $15x^2 - 29x - 14$

**72.** $\sqrt{2}$    **73.** $-\dfrac{54 + 43\sqrt{2}}{46}$

## Chapter 1 Review Exercises

**1.**     **2.**     **3.** 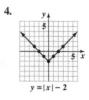    **4.** 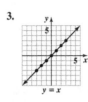    **5.**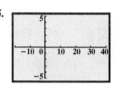

$y = 2x - 2$    $y = x^2 - 3$    $y = x$    $y = |x| - 2$

**6.** $x$-intercept: $-2$; $y$-intercept: $2$    **7.** $x$-intercepts: $-2, 2$; $y$-intercept: $-4$    **8.** $x$-intercept: $5$; no $y$-intercept    **9.** $(1985, 50\%)$    **10.** $35\%$
**11.** $1945; 94\%$    **12.** $1990; 28\%$    **13.** $1950$–$1960; 91\%$    **14.** $1930$–$1935; 38\%$
**15.** function; domain: $\{2, 3, 5\}$; range: $\{7\}$    **16.** function; domain: $\{1, 2, 13\}$; range: $\{10, 500, \pi\}$    **17.** not a function; domain: $\{12, 14\}$; range: $\{13, 15, 19\}$
**18.** $y$ is a function of $x$.    **19.** $y$ is a function of $x$.    **20.** $y$ is not a function of $x$.    **21. a.** $f(4) = -23$    **b.** $f(x + 3) = -7x - 16$
**c.** $f(-x) = 5 + 7x$    **22. a.** $g(0) = 2$    **b.** $g(-2) = 24$    **c.** $g(x - 1) = 3x^2 - 11x + 10$    **d.** $g(-x) = 3x^2 + 5x + 2$    **23. a.** $g(13) = 3$
**b.** $g(0) = 4$    **c.** $g(-3) = 7$    **24. a.** $f(-2) = -1$    **b.** $f(1) = 12$    **c.** $f(2) = 3$    **25.** not a function    **26.** function    **27.** function
**28.** not a function    **29.** not a function    **30.** function    **31. a.** $[-3, 5)$    **b.** $[-5, 0]$    **c.** $-3$    **d.** $-2$    **e.** increasing: $(-2, 0)$ or $(3, 5)$;
decreasing: $(-3, -2)$ or $(0, 3)$    **f.** $f(-2) = -3$ and $f(3) = -5$    **32. a.** $(-\infty, \infty)$    **b.** $(-\infty, 3)$    **c.** $-2$ and $3$    **d.** $3$    **e.** increasing:
$(\infty, 0)$; decreasing: or $(0, \infty)$    **f.** $f(-2) = 0$ and $f(6) = -3$    **33. a.** $(-\infty, \infty)$    **b.** $[-2, 2]$    **c.** $0$    **d.** $0$    **e.** increasing: $(-2, 2)$; constant:
$(-\infty, -2)$ or $(2, \infty)$    **f.** $f(-9) = -2$ and $f(14) = 2$    **34. a.** $0; f(0) = -2$    **b.** $-2, 3; f(-2) = -3, f(3) = -5$
**35. a.** $0; f(0) = 3$    **b.** none    **36.** odd; symmetric with respect to the origin    **37.** even; symmetric with respect to the $y$-axis
**38.** odd; symmetric with respect to the origin
**39.** 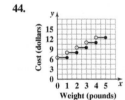    $; \{-3, 5\}$    **40.**     $; (-\infty, 0]$

$f(x) = \begin{cases} 5 \text{ if } x \le -1 \\ -3 \text{ if } x > -1 \end{cases}$    $f(x) = \begin{cases} 2x \text{ if } x < 0 \\ -x \text{ if } x \ge 0 \end{cases}$

**41.** $8$    **42.** $-4x - 2h + 1$    **43. a.** yes; The graph passes the vertical line test.    **b.** $(3, 12)$; The eagle descended.
**c.** $(0, 3)$ and $(12, 17)$; The eagle's height held steady during the first 3 seconds and the eagle was on the ground for 5 seconds.
**d.** $(17, 30)$; The eagle was ascending.

**44.**

**45.** $-\dfrac{1}{2}$; falls    **46.** $1$; rises    **47.** $0$; horizontal    **48.** undefined; vertical
**49.** $y - 2 = -6(x + 3); y = -6x - 16$    **50.** using $(1, 6), y - 6 = 2(x - 1); y = 2x + 4$
**51.** $y + 7 = -3(x - 4); y = -3x + 5$    **52.** $y - 6 = -3(x + 3); y = -3x - 3$    **53.** $x + 6y + 18 = 0$

**54.** Slope: $\dfrac{2}{5}$; $y$-intercept: $-1$    **55.** Slope: $-4$; $y$-intercept: $5$    **56.** Slope: $-\dfrac{2}{3}$; $y$-intercept: $-2$    **57.** Slope: $0$; $y$-intercept: $4$

$y = \dfrac{2}{5}x - 1$    $f(x) = -4x + 5$    $2x + 3y + 6 = 0$    $2y - 8 = 0$

**58.** 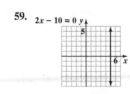    **59.**

$2x - 5y - 10 = 0$

**60. a.** $y - 2.3 = 0.116(x - 15)$ or $y - 11 = 0.116(x - 90)$ **b.** $f(x) = 0.116x + 0.56$ **c.** approximately 5 deaths per 100,000 persons
**d.** 4.3 deaths per 100,000 persons; underestimates by 0.7 death per 100,000 persons; The line passes below the point for France.
**61.** 182.5; Corporate profits increased at a rate of \$182.5 billion per year. The rate of change is \$182.5 billion per year. **62.** 10
**63. a.** 32 ft/sec **b.** −32 ft/sec **c.** The positive sign in part (a) means that the ball is moving up on $(0, 2)$. The negative sign in part (b) means that the ball is moving down on $(2, 4)$.

**64.** 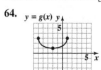　**65.** 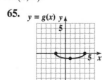　**66.** 　**67.** 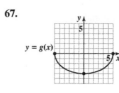　**68.**

**69.** 　**70.** 　**71.** 　**72.** 　**73.**

**74.** 　**75.** 　**76.** 　**77.** 　**78.**

**79.** 　**80.** 　**81.** 　**82.** 　**83.**

**84.**
**85.** $(-\infty, \infty)$ **86.** $(-\infty, 7)\cup(7, \infty)$ **87.** $(-\infty, 4]$ **88.** $(-\infty, -7)\cup(-7, 3)\cup(3, \infty)$
**89.** $[2, 5)\cup(5, \infty)$ **90.** $[1, \infty)$ **91.** $(f + g)(x) = 4x - 6$; domain: $(-\infty, \infty)$; $(f - g)(x) = 2x + 4$;
domain: $(-\infty, \infty)$; $(fg)(x) = 3x^2 - 16x + 5$; domain: $(-\infty, \infty)$; $\left(\dfrac{f}{g}\right)(x) = \dfrac{3x - 1}{x - 5}$; domain: $(-\infty, 5)\cup(5, \infty)$
**92.** $(f + g)(x) = 2x^2 + x$; domain: $(-\infty, \infty)$; $(f - g)(x) = x + 2$; domain: $(-\infty, \infty)$; $(fg)(x) = x^4 + x^3 - x - 1$;
domain: $(-\infty, \infty)$; $\left(\dfrac{f}{g}\right)(x) = \dfrac{x^2 + x + 1}{x^2 - 1}$; domain: $(-\infty, -1)\cup(-1, 1)\cup(1, \infty)$
**93.** $(f + g)(x) = \sqrt{x + 7} + \sqrt{x - 2}$; domain: $[2, \infty)$; $(f - g)(x) = \sqrt{x + 7} - \sqrt{x - 2}$; domain: $[2, \infty)$; $(fg)(x) = \sqrt{x^2 + 5x - 14}$; domain:
$[2, \infty)$; $\left(\dfrac{f}{g}\right)(x) = \dfrac{\sqrt{x + 7}}{\sqrt{x - 2}}$; domain: $(2, \infty)$ **94. a.** $(f \circ g)(x) = 16x^2 - 8x + 4$ **b.** $(g \circ f)(x) = 4x^2 + 11$ **c.** $(f \circ g)(3) = 124$
**95. a.** $(f \circ g)(x) = \sqrt{x + 1}$ **b.** $(g \circ f)(x) = \sqrt{x} + 1$ **c.** $(f \circ g)(3) = 2$ **96. a.** $(f \circ g)(x) = \dfrac{1 + x}{1 - 2x}$ **b.** $(-\infty, 0)\cup\left(0, \dfrac{1}{2}\right)\cup\left(\dfrac{1}{2}, \infty\right)$
**97. a.** $(f \circ g)(x) = \sqrt{x + 2}$ **b.** $[-2, \infty)$ **98.** $f(x) = x^4, g(x) = x^2 + 2x - 1$ **99.** $f(x) = \sqrt[3]{x}, g(x) = 7x + 4$ **100.** $f(g(x)) = x - \dfrac{7}{10}$;
$g(f(x)) = x - \dfrac{7}{6}$; $f$ and $g$ are not inverses of each other. **101.** $f(g(x)) = x$; $g(f(x)) = x$; $f$ and $g$ are inverses of each other. **102.** $f^{-1}(x) = \dfrac{x + 3}{4}$
**103.** $f^{-1}(x) = \sqrt[3]{\dfrac{x - 1}{8}}$ or $\dfrac{\sqrt[3]{x - 1}}{2}$ **104.** $f^{-1}(x) = \dfrac{2}{x - 5}$ **105.** Inverse function exists. **106.** Inverse function does not exist.
**107.** Inverse function exists. **108.** Inverse function does not exist.
**109.**  **110.** $f^{-1}(x) = \sqrt{1 - x}$ **111.** $f^{-1}(x) = (x - 1)^2, x \geq 1$ **112.** 13 **113.** $2\sqrt{2} \approx 2.83$ **114.** $(-5, 5)$
  **115.** $\left(-\dfrac{11}{2}, -2\right)$ **116.** $x^2 + y^2 = 9$
**117.** $(x + 2)^2 + (y - 4)^2 = 36$

**118.** center: $(0, 0)$; radius: 1 **119.** center: $(-2, 3)$; radius: 3 **120.** center: $(2, -1)$; radius: 3
domain: $[-1, 1]$; range: $[-1, 1]$ domain: $[-5, 1]$; range: $[0, 6]$ domain: $[-1, 5]$; range: $[-4, 2]$

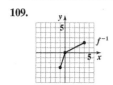 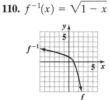 

$x^2 + y^2 = 1$ $(x + 2)^2 + (y - 3)^2 = 9$ $x^2 + y^2 - 4x + 2y - 4 = 0$

**121. a.** $W(x) = 15x + 567$ **b.** 2009 **122. a.** $f(x) = 0.05x + 15$ **b.** $g(x) = 0.07x + 5$ **c.** 500 min

**123. a.** $N(x) = 640 - 2x$ **b.** $R(x) = x(640 - 2x)$ **124. a.** $V(x) = x(16 - 2x)(24 - 2x)$ **b.** $(0, 8)$

**125.** $A(x) = x\left(\dfrac{400 - 3x}{2}\right)$ **126.** $A(x) = 2x^2 + \dfrac{32}{x}$ **127.** $T(x) = 0.08x + 0.12(10{,}000 - x)$

## Chapter 1 Test

**1.** b, c, d **2. a.** $f(4) - f(-3) = 5$ **b.** $(-5, 6]$ **c.** $[-4, 5]$ **d.** $(-1, 2)$ **e.** $(-5, -1)$ or $(2, 6)$ **f.** $2; f(2) = 5$ **g.** $-1; f(-1) = -4$

**h.** $-4, 1,$ and $5$ **i.** $-3$ **3. a.** $-2$ and $2$ **b.** $-1$ and $1$ **c.** $0$ **d.** even **e.** no **f.** relative minimum

**g.** 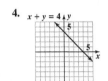 **h.**  **i.** 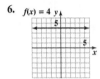  **j.** $-\dfrac{1}{3}$

**4.**  **5.** 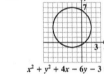 **6.**  **7.**  **8.**

domain: $(-\infty, \infty)$    domain: $[-2, 2]$    domain: $(-\infty, \infty)$    domain: $(-\infty, \infty)$    domain: $[-5, 1]$

range: $(-\infty, \infty)$    range: $[-2, 2]$    range: $\{4\}$    range: $(-\infty, \infty)$    range: $[-2, 4]$

$f(x) = -\dfrac{1}{3}x + 2$    $(x + 2)^2 + (y - 1)^2 = 9$

**9.**  **10.**  **11.**

$f(x) = \begin{cases} 2 \text{ if } x \le 0 \\ -1 \text{ if } x > 0 \end{cases}$    $x^2 + y^2 + 4x - 6y - 3 = 0$

domain: $(-\infty, \infty)$    domain: $[-6, 2]$    domain of $f =$ domain of $g = (-\infty, \infty)$

range: $\{-1, 2\}$    range: $[-1, 7]$    range of $f = [0, \infty)$; range of $g = [-2, \infty)$

**12.**  **13.**  **14.**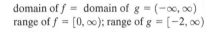

domain of $f =$ domain of $g = (-\infty, \infty)$    domain of $f =$ range of $f^{-1} = (-\infty, \infty)$    domain of $f =$ range of $f^{-1} = (-\infty, \infty)$

range of $f = [0, \infty)$; range of $g = (-\infty, 4]$    range of $f =$ domain of $f^{-1} = (-\infty, \infty)$    range of $f =$ domain of $f^{-1} = (-\infty, \infty)$

**15.** 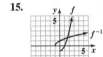 **16.** $f(x - 1) = x^2 - 3x - 2$ **17.** $2x + h - 1$ **18.** $(g - f)(x) = -x^2 + 3x - 2$

**19.** $\left(\dfrac{f}{g}\right)(x) = \dfrac{x^2 - x - 4}{2x - 6}; (-\infty, 3) \cup (3, \infty)$ **20.** $(f \circ g)(x) = 4x^2 - 26x + 38$ **21.** $(g \circ f)(x) = 2x^2 - 2x - 14$

**22.** $-10$ **23.** $f(-x) = x^2 + x - 4$; neither **24.** using $(2, 1)$, $y - 1 = 3(x - 2)$; $y = 3x - 5$

**25.** $y - 6 = 4(x + 4)$; $y = 4x + 22$ **26.** $2x + y + 24 = 0$ **27. a.** $y - 476 = 5(x - 2)$ or $y - 486 = 5(x - 4)$

**b.** $f(x) = 5x + 466$ **c.** 516 per 100,000 residents **28.** 48 **29.** $g(-1) = 4; g(7) = 2$ **30.** $(-\infty, -5) \cup (-5, 1) \cup (1, \infty)$

domain of $f =$ range of $f^{-1} = [0, \infty)$

range of $f =$ domain of $f^{-1} = [-1, \infty)$

**31.** $[1, \infty)$ **32.** $\dfrac{7x}{2 - 4x}$; domain: $(-\infty, 0) \cup \left(0, \dfrac{1}{2}\right) \cup \left(\dfrac{1}{2}, \infty\right)$ **33.** $f(x) = x^7, g(x) = 2x + 3$ **34.** $5; (3.5, 0)$ **35. a.** $T(x) = 41.78 - 0.19x$

**b.** 2012 **36. a.** $Y(x) = 50 - 1.5(x - 30)$ **b.** $T(x) = x(50 - 1.5(x - 30))$ **37.** $A(x) = x(300 - x)$ **38.** $A(x) = 2x^2 + \dfrac{32{,}000}{x}$

# CHAPTER 2

## Section 2.1

### Check Point Exercises

**1. a.** $8 + i$ **b.** $-10 + 7i$ **2. a.** $63 + 14i$ **b.** $58 - 11i$ **3.** $\frac{16}{17} + \frac{21}{17}i$ **4. a.** $7i\sqrt{3}$ **b.** $1 - 4i\sqrt{3}$ **c.** $-7 + i\sqrt{3}$
**5.** $\{1 + i, 1 - i\}$

### Exercise Set 2.1

**1.** $8 - 2i$ **3.** $-2 + 9i$ **5.** $24 - 3i$ **7.** $-14 + 17i$ **9.** $21 + 15i$ **11.** $-19 + 7i$ **13.** $-29 - 11i$ **15.** $34$ **17.** $26$ **19.** $-5 + 12i$

**21.** $\frac{3}{5} + \frac{1}{5}i$ **23.** $1 + i$ **25.** $-\frac{24}{25} + \frac{32}{25}i$ **27.** $\frac{7}{5} + \frac{4}{5}i$ **29.** $3i$ **31.** $47i$ **33.** $-8i$ **35.** $2 + 6i\sqrt{7}$ **37.** $-\frac{1}{3} + i\frac{\sqrt{2}}{6}$

**39.** $-\frac{1}{8} - i\frac{\sqrt{3}}{24}$ **41.** $-2\sqrt{6} - 2i\sqrt{10}$ **43.** $24\sqrt{15}$ **45.** $\{3 + i, 3 - i\}$ **47.** $\left\{-1 + \frac{3}{2}i, -1 - \frac{3}{2}i\right\}$ **49.** $\left\{\frac{4}{3} + i\frac{\sqrt{5}}{3}, \frac{4}{3} - i\frac{\sqrt{5}}{3}\right\}$

**51.** $-11 - 5i$ **53.** $-5 + 10i$ **55.** $0 + 47i$ or $47i$ **57.** $0$ **59.** $\frac{20}{13} + \frac{30}{13}i$ **61.** $(47 + 13i)$ volts **63.** $(5 + i\sqrt{15}) + (5 - i\sqrt{15}) = 10$;

$(5 + i\sqrt{15})(5 - i\sqrt{15}) = 25 - 15i^2 = 25 + 15 = 40$ **73.** makes sense **75.** does not make sense **77.** false **79.** false

**81.** $\frac{14}{25} - \frac{2}{25}i$ **83.** $\frac{8}{5} + \frac{16}{5}i$ **84.** $\{1, 5\}$ **85.** $\{-1 \pm \sqrt{2}\}$ **86.**

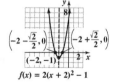

$f(x) = x^2$
$g(x) = (x + 3)^2 + 1$

## Section 2.2

### Check Point Exercises

**1.**

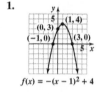

$f(x) = -(x - 1)^2 + 4$

**2.**

$f(x) = (x - 2)^2 + 1$

**3.**

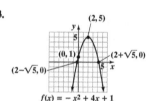

$f(x) = -x^2 + 4x + 1$
domain: $(-\infty, \infty)$; range: $(-\infty, 5]$

**4. a.** minimum **b.** Minimum is 984 at $x = 2$.
**c.** domain: $(-\infty, \infty)$; range: $[984, \infty)$
**5. a.** 205 ft; 200 ft **b.** 402 ft
**c.**

Arrow's Horizontal Distance (feet)

**6.** $4, -4; -16$ **7.** 30 ft by 30 ft; 900 sq ft

### Exercise Set 2.2

**1.** $h(x) = (x - 1)^2 + 1$ **3.** $j(x) = (x - 1)^2 - 1$ **5.** $h(x) = x^2 - 1$
**7.** $g(x) = x^2 - 2x + 1$ **9.** $(3, 1)$ **11.** $(-1, 5)$
**13.** $(2, -5)$ **15.** $(-1, 9)$
**17.** domain: $(-\infty, \infty)$
range: $[-1, \infty)$
axis of symmetry: $x = 4$

$f(x) = (x - 4)^2 - 1$

**19.** domain: $(-\infty, \infty)$
range: $[2, \infty)$
axis of symmetry: $x = 1$

$f(x) = (x - 1)^2 + 2$

**21.** domain: $(-\infty, \infty)$
range: $[1, \infty)$
axis of symmetry: $x = 3$

$y - 1 = (x - 3)^2$

**23.** domain: $(-\infty, \infty)$
range: $[-1, \infty)$
axis of symmetry: $x = -2$

$\left(-2 - \frac{\sqrt{2}}{2}, 0\right)$ $\left(-2 + \frac{\sqrt{2}}{2}, 0\right)$
$(-2, -1)$

$f(x) = 2(x + 2)^2 - 1$

**25.** domain: $(-\infty, \infty)$

range: $(-\infty, 4]$

axis of symmetry: $x = 1$

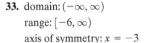

$f(x) = 4 - (x-1)^2$

**27.** domain: $(-\infty, \infty)$

range: $[-4, \infty)$

axis of symmetry: $x = 1$

$f(x) = x^2 - 2x - 3$

**29.** domain: $(-\infty, \infty)$

range: $\left[-\dfrac{49}{4}, \infty\right)$

axis of symmetry: $x = -\dfrac{3}{2}$

$f(x) = x^2 + 3x - 10$

**31.** domain: $(-\infty, \infty)$

range: $(-\infty, 4]$

axis of symmetry: $x = 1$

$f(x) = 2x - x^2 + 3$

**33.** domain: $(-\infty, \infty)$
range: $[-6, \infty)$
axis of symmetry: $x = -3$

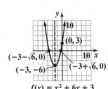

$f(x) = x^2 + 6x + 3$

**35.** domain: $(-\infty, \infty)$
range: $[-5, \infty)$
axis of symmetry: $x = -1$

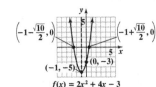

$f(x) = 2x^2 + 4x - 3$

**37.** domain: $(-\infty, \infty)$
range: $(-\infty, -1]$
axis of symmetry: $x = 1$

$f(x) = 2x - x^2 - 2$

**39. a.** minimum  **b.** Minimum is $-13$ at $x = 2$.  **c.** domain: $(-\infty, \infty)$; range: $[-13, \infty)$
**41. a.** maximum  **b.** Maximum is 1 at $x = 1$.  **c.** domain: $(-\infty, \infty)$; range: $(-\infty, 1]$

**43. a.** minimum  **b.** Minimum is $-\dfrac{5}{4}$ at $x = \dfrac{1}{2}$.  **c.** domain: $(-\infty, \infty)$; range: $\left[-\dfrac{5}{4}, \infty\right)$

**45.** domain: $(-\infty, \infty)$; range: $[-2, \infty)$   **47.** domain: $(-\infty, \infty)$; range: $(-\infty, -6]$   **49.** $f(x) = 2(x - 5)^2 + 3$   **51.** $f(x) = 2(x + 10)^2 - 5$
**53.** $f(x) = -3(x + 2)^2 + 4$   **55.** $f(x) = 3(x - 11)^2$   **57. a.** 18.35 ft; 35 ft   **b.** 77.8 ft   **c.** 6.1 ft   **59. a.** 2.75 gal per person;
underestimates by 0.05 gal   **b.** 1992; 2.048 gal; seems reasonable   **61.** 8 and 8; 64   **63.** 8, $-8$; $-64$   **65.** length: 300 ft; width: 150 ft; maximum
area: 45,000 sq ft   **67.** 12.5 yd by 12.5 yd; 156.25 sq yd   **69.** 150 ft by 100 ft; 15,000 sq ft   **71.** 5 in.; 50 sq in.   **73.** \$65; \$422,500
**75.** 25; 1250 lb   **85.** (80, 1600)   **87.** $(-4, 520)$

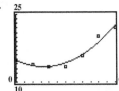

**89. a & d.**

**a.** The values of $y$ increase, then decrease.
**b.** $y = 0.005x^2 - 0.170x + 14.817$
**c.** 1957; about 13.372 miles/gal
**91.** makes sense   **93.** does not make sense   **95.** false
**97.** false   **99.** $x = 3$; (0, 11)   **101.** $f(x) = -2(x + 3)^2 - 1$
**103.** \$95; \$21,675   **106.** $(x + 3)(x + 1)(x - 1)$

**107.** $f(2) = -1$; $f(3) = 16$; The graph passes through $(2, -1)$, which is below the $x$-axis, and $(3, 16)$, which is above the $x$-axis. Since the graph of $f$ is
continuous, it must cross the $x$-axis somewhere between 2 and 3 to get from one of these points to the other.
**108.** even; symmetric with respect to the $y$-axis

## Section 2.3

### Check Point Exercises

**1.** The graph rises to the left and to the right.   **2.** The graph falls to the left and rises to the right.   **3.** Since $n$ is odd and the leading coefficient is
negative, the function falls to the right. Since the ratio cannot be negative, the model won't be appropriate.   **4.** No; the graph should fall to the left,
but doesn't appear to.   **5.** $\{-2, 2\}$   **6.** $\{-2, 0, 2\}$   **7.** $-\dfrac{1}{2}$ with multiplicity 2 and 5 with multiplicity 3; touches and turns at $-\dfrac{1}{2}$ and crosses at 5
**8.** $f(-3) = -42$; $f(-2) = 5$   **9.**

$f(x) = x^3 - 3x^2$

## Exercise Set 2.3

**1.** polynomial function; degree: 3    **3.** polynomial function; degree: 5    **5.** not a polynomial function    **7.** not a polynomial function
**9.** not a polynomial function    **11.** could be polynomial function    **13.** not a polynomial function    **15.** b    **17.** a
**19.** falls to the left and rises to the right    **21.** rises to the left and to the right    **23.** falls to the left and to the right
**25.** $x = 5$ has multiplicity 1; The graph crosses the $x$-axis; $x = -4$ has multiplicity 2; The graph touches the $x$-axis and turns around.
**27.** $x = 3$ has multiplicity 1; The graph crosses the $x$-axis; $x = -6$ has multiplicity 3; The graph crosses the $x$-axis.
**29.** $x = 0$ has multiplicity 1; The graph crosses the $x$-axis; $x = 1$ has multiplicity 2; The graph touches the $x$-axis and turns around.
**31.** $x = 2$, $x = -2$ and $x = -7$ have multiplicity 1; The graph crosses the $x$-axis.    **33.** $f(1) = -1$; $f(2) = 5$; 1.3    **35.** $f(-1) = -1$; $f(0) = 1$; $-0.5$
**37.** $f(-3) = -11$; $f(-2) = 1$; $-2.1$    **39.** $f(-3) = -42$; $f(-2) = 5$; $-2.2$

**41. a.** $f(x)$ rises to the right and falls to the left.
   **b.** $x = -2$, $x = 1$, $x = -1$;
     $f(x)$ crosses the $x$-axis at each.
   **c.** The $y$-intercept is $-2$.
   **d.** neither
   **e.**

$f(x) = x^3 + 2x^2 - x - 2$

**43. a.** $f(x)$ rises to the left and the right.
   **b.** $x = 0$, $x = 3$, $x = -3$;
     $f(x)$ crosses the $x$-axis at $-3$ and 3;
     $f(x)$ touches the $x$-axis at 0.
   **c.** The $y$-intercept is 0.
   **d.** $y$-axis symmetry
   **e.**

$f(x) = x^4 - 9x^2$

**45. a.** $f(x)$ falls to the left and the right.
   **b.** $x = 0$, $x = 4$, $x = -4$;
     $f(x)$ crosses the $x$-axis at $-4$ and 4;
     $f(x)$ touches the $x$-axis at 0.
   **c.** The $y$-intercept is 0.
   **d.** $y$-axis symmetry
   **e.**

$f(x) = -x^4 + 16x^2$

**47. a.** $f(x)$ rises to the left and the right.
   **b.** $x = 0$, $x = 1$;
     $f(x)$ touches the $x$-axis at 0 and 1.
   **c.** The $y$-intercept is 0.
   **d.** neither
   **e.**

$f(x) = x^4 - 2x^3 + x^2$

**49. a.** $f(x)$ falls to the left and the right.
   **b.** $x = 0$, $x = 2$;
     $f(x)$ crosses the $x$-axis at 0 and 2.
   **c.** The $y$-intercept is 0.
   **d.** neither
   **e.**

$f(x) = -2x^4 + 4x^3$

**51. a.** $f(x)$ rises to the left and falls to the right.
   **b.** $x = 0$, $x = \pm\sqrt{3}$;
     $f(x)$ crosses the $x$-axis at 0;
     $f(x)$ touches the $x$-axis at $\sqrt{3}$ and $-\sqrt{3}$.
   **c.** The $y$-intercept is 0.
   **d.** origin symmetry
   **e.**

$f(x) = 6x^3 - 9x - x^5$

**53. a.** $f(x)$ rises to the left and falls to the right.
   **b.** $x = 0$, $x = 3$;
     $f(x)$ crosses the $x$-axis at 3;
     $f(x)$ touches the $x$-axis at 0.
   **c.** The $y$-intercept is 0.
   **d.** neither
   **e.**

$f(x) = 3x^2 - x^3$

**55. a.** $f(x)$ falls to the left and the right.
   **b.** $x = 1$, $x = -2$, $x = 2$;
     $f(x)$ crosses the $x$-axis at $-2$ and 2;
     $f(x)$ touches the $x$-axis at 1.
   **c.** The $y$-intercept is 12.
   **d.** neither
   **e.**

$f(x) = -3(x - 1)^2 (x^2 - 4)$

**57. a.** $f(x)$ rises to the left and the right.
**b.** $x = -2, x = 0, x = 1$;
$f(x)$ crosses the $x$-axis at $-2$ and 1;
$f(x)$ touches the $x$-axis at 0.
**c.** The $y$-intercept is 0.
**d.** neither
**e.**

$f(x) = x^2 (x - 1)^3 (x + 2)$

**59. a.** $f(x)$ falls to the left and the right.
**b.** $x = -3, x = 0, x = 1$;
$f(x)$ crosses the $x$-axis at $-3$ and 1;
$f(x)$ touches the $x$-axis at 0.
**c.** The $y$-intercept is 0.
**d.** neither
**e.**

$f(x) = -x^2 (x - 1)(x + 3)$

**61. a.** $f(x)$ falls to the left and the right.
**b.** $x = -5, x = 0, x = 1$;
$f(x)$ crosses the $x$-axis at $-5$ and 0;
$f(x)$ touches the $x$-axis at 1.
**c.** The $y$-intercept is 0.
**d.** neither
**e.**

$f(x) = -2x^3 (x - 1)^2 (x + 5)$

**63. a.** $f(x)$ rises to the left and the right.
**b.** $x = -4, x = 1, x = 2$;
$f(x)$ crosses the $x$-axis at $-4$ and 1;
$f(x)$ touches the $x$-axis at 2.
**c.** The $y$-intercept is $-16$.
**d.** neither
**e.**

$f(x) = (x - 2)^2 (x + 4)(x - 1)$

**65. a.** $-2$, odd; 1, odd; 4, odd    **b.** $f(x) = (x + 2)(x - 1)(x - 4)$    **c.** 8    **67. a.** $-1$, odd; 3, even    **b.** $f(x) = (x + 1)(x - 3)^2$    **c.** 9
**69. a.** $-3$, even; 2, even    **b.** $f(x) = -(x + 3)^2(x - 2)^2$    **c.** $-36$    **71. a.** $-2$, even; $-1$, odd; 1, odd    **b.** $f(x) = (x + 2)^2(x + 1)(x - 1)^3$
**c.** $-4$    **73. a.** $f(3) = 404{,}444$; $g(3) = 404{,}443$; function $f$    **b.** falls to the right; No, since the graph falls to the right, the number of people living with HIV and AIDS will eventually be negative; model breakdown will occur.    **75. a.** from 1 through 4 min and from 8 through 10 min
**b.** from 4 through 8 min and from 10 through 12 min    **c.** 3    **d.** 4    **e.** negative; The graph falls to the left and falls to the right.
**f.** $116 \pm 1$ beats per min; 10 min    **g.** $64 \pm 1$ beats per min; 8 min

**95.**

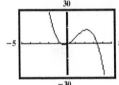

**97.**

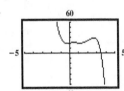

**99.**

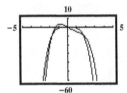

**101.** does not make sense    **103.** makes sense    **105.** false    **107.** false    **109.** $f(x) = x^3 - 2x^2$    **110.** $35\frac{2}{21}$

**111.** $6x^3 - x^2 - 5x + 4$    **112.** $(x - 3)(2x - 1)(x + 2)$

## Section 2.4

### Check Point Exercises

**1.** $x + 5$    **2.** $2x^2 + 3x - 2 + \dfrac{1}{x - 3}$    **3.** $2x^2 + 7x + 14 + \dfrac{21x - 10}{x^2 - 2x}$    **4.** $x^2 - 2x - 3$    **5.** $-105$    **6.** $\left\{-1, -\dfrac{1}{3}, \dfrac{2}{5}\right\}$

### Exercise Set 2.4

**1.** $x + 3$    **3.** $x^2 + 3x + 1$    **5.** $2x^2 + 3x + 5$    **7.** $4x + 3 + \dfrac{2}{3x - 2}$    **9.** $2x^2 + x + 6 - \dfrac{38}{x + 3}$    **11.** $4x^3 + 16x^2 + 60x + 246 + \dfrac{984}{x - 4}$

**13.** $2x + 5$    **15.** $6x^2 + 3x - 1 - \dfrac{3x - 1}{3x^2 + 1}$    **17.** $2x + 5$    **19.** $3x - 8 + \dfrac{20}{x + 5}$    **21.** $4x^2 + x + 4 + \dfrac{3}{x - 1}$

**23.** $6x^4 + 12x^3 + 22x^2 + 48x + 93 + \dfrac{187}{x - 2}$    **25.** $x^3 - 10x^2 + 51x - 260 + \dfrac{1300}{x + 5}$    **27.** $x^4 + x^3 + 2x^2 + 2x + 2$    **29.** $x^3 + 4x^2 + 16x + 64$

**31.** $2x^4 - 7x^3 + 15x^2 - 31x + 64 - \dfrac{129}{x + 2}$    **33.** $-25$    **35.** $-133$    **37.** 240    **39.** 1    **41.** $x^2 - 5x + 6$; $x = -1, x = 2, x = 3$

**43.** $\left\{-\dfrac{1}{2}, 1, 2\right\}$    **45.** $\left\{-\dfrac{3}{2}, -\dfrac{1}{3}, \dfrac{1}{2}\right\}$    **47.** 2; The remainder is zero; $\{-3, -1, 2\}$    **49.** 1; The remainder is zero; $\left\{\dfrac{1}{3}, \dfrac{1}{2}, 1\right\}$

**51. a.** The remainder is 0.    **b.** 3 mm    **53.** $0.5x^2 - 0.4x + 0.3$    **55. a.** 70; When the tax rate is 30%, tax revenue is \$700 billion.; (30, 70)

**b.** $80 + \dfrac{800}{x - 110}$; $f(30) = 70$; yes    **c.** No, $f$ is a rational function because it is a quotient of two polynomials.    **67.** makes sense

**69.** does not make sense    **71.** true    **73.** false    **75.** $x - 2$    **79.** $\{-2 \pm \sqrt{5}\}$    **80.** $\{-2 \pm i\sqrt{2}\}$    **81.** $-3$

## Section 2.5

**Check Point Exercises**

**1.** $\pm 1, \pm 2, \pm 3, \pm 6$　**2.** $\pm 1, \pm 3, \pm \dfrac{1}{2}, \pm \dfrac{1}{4}, \pm \dfrac{3}{2}, \pm \dfrac{3}{4}$　**3.** $\{-5, -4, 1\}$　**4.** $\left\{2, \dfrac{-3 - \sqrt{5}}{2}, \dfrac{-3 + \sqrt{5}}{2}\right\}$　**5.** $\{1, 2 - 3i, 2 + 3i\}$

**6.** $f(x) = x^3 + 3x^2 + x + 3$　**7.** 4, 2, or 0 positive zeros, no possible negative zeros

**Exercise Set 2.5**

**1.** $\pm 1, \pm 2, \pm 4$　**3.** $\pm 1, \pm 2, \pm 3, \pm 6, \pm \dfrac{1}{3}, \pm \dfrac{2}{3}$　**5.** $\pm 1, \pm 2, \pm 3, \pm 6, \pm \dfrac{1}{2}, \pm \dfrac{1}{4}, \pm \dfrac{3}{2}, \pm \dfrac{3}{4}$　**7.** $\pm 1, \pm 2, \pm 3, \pm 4, \pm 6, \pm 12$　**9. a.** $\pm 1, \pm 2, \pm 4$

**b.** $-2, -1,$ or $2$　**c.** $\{-2, -1, 2\}$　**11. a.** $\pm 1, \pm 2, \pm 3, \pm 6, \pm \dfrac{1}{2}, \pm \dfrac{3}{2}$　**b.** $-2, \dfrac{1}{2},$ or $3$　**c.** $\left\{-2, \dfrac{1}{2}, 3\right\}$　**13. a.** $\pm 1, \pm 2, \pm 3, \pm 6$

**b.** $-1$　**c.** $\left\{-1, \dfrac{-3 - \sqrt{33}}{2}, \dfrac{-3 + \sqrt{33}}{2}\right\}$　**15. a.** $\pm 1, \pm \dfrac{1}{2}, \pm 2$　**b.** $-2$　**c.** $\left\{-2, \dfrac{-1 + i}{2}, \dfrac{-1 - i}{2}\right\}$　**17. a.** $\pm 1, \pm 2, \pm 3, \pm 4, \pm 6, \pm 12$

**b.** $-3, 1,$ or $4$　**c.** $\{-3, 1, 4\}$　**19. a.** $\pm 1, \pm 2, \pm 3, \pm 4, \pm 6, \pm 12$　**b.** $-2$　**c.** $\{-2, 1 + \sqrt{7}, 1 - \sqrt{7}\}$　**21. a.** $\pm 1, \pm 5, \pm \dfrac{1}{2}, \pm \dfrac{5}{2}, \pm \dfrac{1}{3}, \pm \dfrac{5}{3}, \pm \dfrac{1}{6}, \pm \dfrac{5}{6}$

**b.** $-5, \dfrac{1}{3},$ or $\dfrac{1}{2}$　**c.** $\left\{-5, \dfrac{1}{3}, \dfrac{1}{2}\right\}$　**23. a.** $\pm 1, \pm 2, \pm 4$　**b.** $-2$ or $2$　**c.** $\{-2, 2, 1 + \sqrt{2}, 1 - \sqrt{2}\}$　**25.** $f(x) = 2x^3 - 2x^2 + 50x - 50$

**27.** $f(x) = x^3 - 3x^2 - 15x + 125$　**29.** $f(x) = x^4 + 10x^2 + 9$　**31.** $f(x) = x^4 - 9x^3 + 21x^2 + 21x - 130$　**33.** no positive real roots; 3 or 1 negative real roots　**35.** 3 or 1 positive real roots; no negative real roots　**37.** 2 or 0 positive real roots; 2 or 0 negative real roots

**39.** $x = -2, x = 5, x = 1$　**41.** $\left\{-\dfrac{1}{2}, \dfrac{1 + \sqrt{17}}{2}, \dfrac{1 - \sqrt{17}}{2}\right\}$　**43.** $-1, 2 + 2i,$ and $2 - 2i$　**45.** $\{-1, -2, 3 + \sqrt{13}, 3 - \sqrt{13}\}$

**47.** $x = -1, x = 2, x = -\dfrac{1}{3}, x = 3$　**49.** $\left\{1, -\dfrac{3}{4}, i\sqrt{2}, -i\sqrt{2}\right\}$　**51.** $\left\{-2, \dfrac{1}{2}, \sqrt{2}, -\sqrt{2}\right\}$

**53. a.** $-4, 1,$ and $4$　**55. a.** $-1$ and $\dfrac{3}{2}$　**57. a.** $\dfrac{1}{2}, 3, -1 \pm i$　**59. a.** $-2, -1, -\dfrac{2}{3}, 1,$ and $2$

**b.**

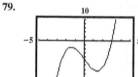

$f(x) = -x^3 + x^2 + 16x - 16$

**b.**

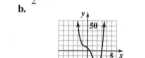

$f(x) = 4x^3 - 8x^2 - 3x + 9$

**b.**

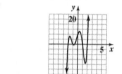

$f(x) = 2x^4 - 3x^3 - 7x^2 - 8x + 6$

**b.**

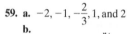

$f(x) = 3x^5 + 2x^4 - 15x^3 - 10x^2 + 12x + 8$

**61.** 7.8 in., 10 in.　**63. a.** $(7.8, 2000), (10, 2000)$　**b.** $(0, 15)$　**73.** $\left\{\dfrac{1}{2}, \dfrac{2}{3}, 2\right\}$　**75.** $\left\{\pm \dfrac{1}{2}\right\}$　**77.** 5, 3, or 1 positive real zeros; no negative real zeros

**79.**

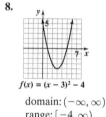

1 real zero, 2 nonreal complex zeros

**81.**

2 real zeros, 2 nonreal complex zeros

**83.** makes sense　**85.** makes sense　**87.** false

**89.** true　**91.** 3 in.　**93.** 3　**95.** 5

**98.** $x = 1$ and $x = 2$　**99.** $x = 1$　**100.** $y = 0$

## Mid-Chapter 2 Check Point

**1.** $-1 - i$　**2.** $-3 + 6i$　**3.** $7 + i$　**4.** $i$　**5.** $3i\sqrt{3}$　**6.** $1 - 4i\sqrt{3}$　**7.** $\dfrac{3}{4} \pm i \dfrac{\sqrt{23}}{4}$

**8.**

$f(x) = (x - 3)^2 - 4$

domain: $(-\infty, \infty)$
range: $[-4, \infty)$

**9.**

$f(x) = 5 - (x + 2)^2$

domain: $(-\infty, \infty)$
range: $(-\infty, 5]$

**10.**

$f(x) = -x^2 - 4x + 5$

domain: $(-\infty, \infty)$
range: $(-\infty, 9]$

**11.**

$f(x) = 3x^2 - 6x + 1$

domain: $(-\infty, \infty)$
range: $[-2, \infty)$

**12.** $-1$ and $2$

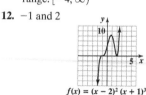

$f(x) = (x - 2)^2 (x + 1)^3$

**13.** $-1$ and $2$

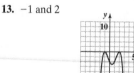

$f(x) = -(x - 2)^2 (x + 1)^2$

**14.** $-2, 1,$ and $2$

$f(x) = x^3 - x^2 - 4x + 4$

**15.** $-2, -1, 1,$ and $2$

$f(x) = x^4 - 5x^2 + 4$

**16.** $-1$

$f(x) = -(x + 1)^6$

**17.** $-\dfrac{1}{3}, \dfrac{1}{2},$ and $1$

$f(x) = -6x^3 + 7x^2 - 1$

**18.** $-1, 0,$ and $1$

$f(x) = 2x^3 - 2x$

**19.** $0, 1 \pm 5i$

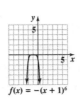

$f(x) = x^3 - 2x^2 + 26x$

**20.** $3, 1 \pm \sqrt{2}$

$f(x) = -x^3 + 5x^2 - 5x - 3$

**21.** $\{-2, 1\}$   **22.** $\left\{\dfrac{1}{3}, \dfrac{1}{2}, 1\right\}$   **23.** $\left\{-\dfrac{1}{2}, \dfrac{2}{3}, \dfrac{7}{2}\right\}$   **24.** $\left\{-10, -\dfrac{5}{2}, 10\right\}$   **25.** $\{-3, 4, \pm i\}$   **26.** $\left\{-3, \dfrac{1}{2}, 1 \pm \sqrt{3}\right\}$

**27.** 75 cabinets per day; \$1200   **28.** $-9, -9; 81$   **29.** 10 in.; 100 sq in.   **30.** $2x^2 - x - 3 + \dfrac{x + 1}{3x^2 - 1}$   **31.** $2x^3 - 5x^2 - 3x + 6$

**32.** $f(x) = -2x^3 + 2x^2 - 2x + 2$   **33.** $f(x) = x^4 - 4x^3 + 13x^2 - 36x + 36$   **34.** yes

## Section 2.6

### Check Point Exercises

**1. a.** $\{x | x \neq 5\}$   **b.** $\{x | x \neq -5, x \neq 5\}$   **c.** all real numbers   **2. a.** $x = 1, x = -1$   **b.** $x = -1$   **c.** none
**3. a.** $y = 3$   **b.** $y = 0$   **c.** none
**4.**

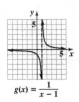

$g(x) = \dfrac{1}{x + 2} - 1$

**5.**

$f(x) = \dfrac{3x - 3}{x - 2}$

**6.**

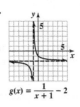

$f(x) = \dfrac{2x^2}{x^2 - 9}$

**7.**

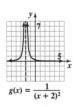

$f(x) = \dfrac{x^4}{x^2 + 2}$

**8.** $y = 2x - 1$   **9. a.** $C(x) = 500,000 + 400x$   **b.** $\overline{C}(x) = \dfrac{500,000 + 400x}{x}$   **c.** $\overline{C}(1000) = 900$: The average cost per wheelchair of producing 1000 wheelchairs per month is \$900.; $\overline{C}(10,000) = 450$: The average cost per wheelchair of producing 10,000 wheelchairs per month is \$450.; $\overline{C}(100,000) = 405$: The average cost per wheelchair of producing 100,000 wheelchairs per month is \$405.   **d.** $y = 400$; The cost per wheelchair approaches \$400 as more wheelchairs are produced.   **10.** $T(x) = \dfrac{20}{x} + \dfrac{20}{x - 10}$

### Exercise Set 2.6

**1.** $\{x | x \neq 4\}$   **3.** $\{x | x \neq 5, x \neq -4\}$   **5.** $\{x | x \neq 7, x \neq -7\}$   **7.** all real numbers   **9.** $-\infty$   **11.** $-\infty$   **13.** $0$   **15.** $+\infty$
**17.** $-\infty$   **19.** $1$   **21.** $x = -4$   **23.** $x = 0, x = -4$   **25.** $x = -4$   **27.** no vertical asymptotes   **29.** $y = 0$   **31.** $y = 4$
**33.** no horizontal asymptote   **35.** $y = -\dfrac{2}{3}$

**37.**

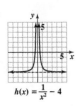

$g(x) = \dfrac{1}{x - 1}$

**39.**

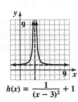

$h(x) = \dfrac{1}{x} + 2$

**41.**

$g(x) = \dfrac{1}{x + 1} - 2$

**43.**

$g(x) = \dfrac{1}{(x + 2)^2}$

**45.**

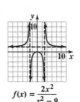

$h(x) = \dfrac{1}{x^2} - 4$

**47.**

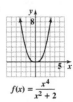

$h(x) = \dfrac{1}{(x - 3)^2} + 1$

**49.**

$f(x) = \dfrac{4x}{x - 2}$

**51.**

$f(x) = \dfrac{2x}{x^2 - 4}$

**53.**

$$f(x) = \frac{2x^2}{x^2 - 1}$$

**55.**

$$f(x) = \frac{-x}{x + 1}$$

**57.**

$$f(x) = -\frac{1}{x^2 - 4}$$

**59.**

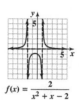

$$f(x) = \frac{2}{x^2 + x - 2}$$

**61.**

$$f(x) = \frac{2x^2}{x^2 + 4}$$

**63.**

$$f(x) = \frac{x + 2}{x^2 + x - 6}$$

**65.**

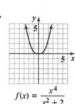

$$f(x) = \frac{x^4}{x^2 + 2}$$

**67.**

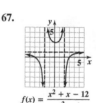

$$f(x) = \frac{x^2 + x - 12}{x^2 - 4}$$

**69.**

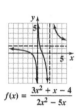

$$f(x) = \frac{3x^2 + x - 4}{2x^2 - 5x}$$

**71. a.** Slant asymptote: $y = x$
**b.**

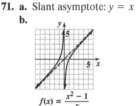

$$f(x) = \frac{x^2 - 1}{x}$$

**73. a.** Slant asymptote: $y = x$
**b.**

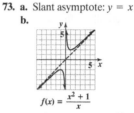

$$f(x) = \frac{x^2 + 1}{x}$$

**75. a.** Slant asymptote: $y = x + 4$
**b.**

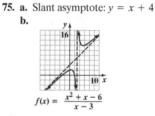

$$f(x) = \frac{x^2 + x - 6}{x - 3}$$

**77. a.** Slant asymptote: $y = x - 2$
**b.**

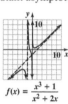

$$f(x) = \frac{x^3 + 1}{x^2 + 2x}$$

**79.**

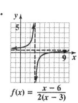

$$f(x) = \frac{x + 2}{2x(x - 2)}$$

**81.**

$$f(x) = \frac{x - 6}{2(x - 3)}$$

**83.**

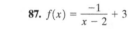

$$f(x) = \frac{x - 2}{x + 2}$$

**85.** $f(x) = \dfrac{1}{x + 3} + 2$

$$g(x) = \frac{1}{x + 3} + 2$$

**87.** $f(x) = \dfrac{-1}{x - 2} + 3$

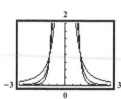

$$g(x) = \frac{-1}{x - 2} + 3$$

**89. a.** $C(x) = 100x + 100{,}000$ **b.** $\overline{C}(x) = \dfrac{100x + 100{,}000}{x}$

**c.** $\overline{C}(500) = 300$, when 500 bicycles are produced, it costs \$300 to produce each bicycle; $\overline{C}(1000) = 200$, when 1000 bicycles are produced, it costs \$200 to produce each bicycle; $\overline{C}(2000) = 150$, when 2000 bicycles are produced, it costs \$150 to produce each bicycle; $\overline{C}(4000) = 125$, when 4000 bicycles are produced, it costs \$125 to produce each bicycle.

**d.** $y = 100$; The cost per bicycle approaches \$100 as more bicycles are produced.
**91. a.** 6.0 **b.** after 6 minutes; about 4.8 **c.** 6.5 **d.** $y = 6.5$; Over time, the pH level rises back to normal. **e.** It quickly drops below normal and then slowly begins to approach the normal level. **93.** 90; An incidence ratio of 10 means 90% of the deaths are smoking related.

**95.** $y = 100$; The percentage of deaths cannot exceed 100% as the incidence ratios increase. **97. a.** $f(x) = \dfrac{11x^2 + 40x + 1040}{12x^2 + 230x + 2190}$ **b.** 63%

**c.** 64%; overestimates by 1% **d.** $y = \dfrac{11}{12}$; 92%; Answers may vary. **99.** $T(x) = \dfrac{10}{x} + \dfrac{5}{x}$ **101.** $A(x) = 2x + \dfrac{50}{x} + 52$

**113.**

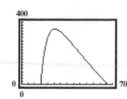

The graph approaches the horizontal asymptote faster and the vertical asymptote slower as $n$ increases.

**115. a.**

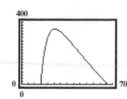

**b.** The graph increases and reaches a maximum of about 356 arrests per 100,000 drivers at age 25.
**c.** at age 25, about 356 arrests

**117.** does not make sense    **119.** does not make sense    **121.** true    **123.** true

**128.** $\left\{-3, \dfrac{5}{2}\right\}$    **129.** $\{-2, -1, 2\}$    **130.** $\dfrac{-x-5}{x+3}$ or $-\dfrac{x+5}{x+3}$

## Section 2.7

### Check Point Exercises

**1.** $\{x \mid x < -4 \text{ or } x > 5\}$ or $(-\infty, -4) \cup (5, \infty)$

**2.** $\{x \mid x \le -3 \text{ or } -1 \le x \le 1\}$ or $(-\infty, -3] \cup [-1, 1]$

**3.** $\{x \mid x < -1 \text{ or } x \ge 1\}$ or $(-\infty, -1) \cup [1, \infty)$

**4.** between 1 and 4 seconds, excluding $t = 1$ and $t = 4$

### Exercise Set 2.7

**1.** $(-\infty, -2)$ or $(4, \infty)$

**3.** $[-3, 7]$

**5.** $(-\infty, 1)$ or $(4, \infty)$

**7.** $(-\infty, -4)$ or $(-1, \infty)$

**9.** $\varnothing$

**11.** $\left[-4, \dfrac{2}{3}\right]$

**13.** $\left(-3, \dfrac{5}{2}\right)$

**15.** $\left(-1, -\dfrac{3}{4}\right)$

**17.** $\left[-2, \dfrac{1}{3}\right]$

**19.** $(-\infty, 0]$ or $[4, \infty)$

**21.** $\left(-\infty, -\dfrac{3}{2}\right)$ or $(0, \infty)$

**23.** $[0, 1]$

**25.** $[2 - \sqrt{2}, 2 + \sqrt{2}]$

**27.** $\varnothing$

**29.** $[1, 2]$ or $[3, \infty)$

**31.** $[0, 3] \cup [5, \infty)$

**33.** $(-\infty, 2) \cup \left(2, \dfrac{7}{2}\right)$

**35.** $[-2, -1]$ or $[1, \infty)$

**37.** $(-\infty, -3)$

**39.** $(-1, \infty)$

**41.** $\{0\}$ or $[9, \infty)$

**43.** $(-\infty, -3)$ or $(4, \infty)$

**45.** $(-4, -3)$

**47.** $[2, 4)$

**49.** $\left(-\infty, -\dfrac{4}{3}\right)$ or $[2, \infty)$

**51.** $(-\infty, 0)$ or $(3, \infty)$

**53.** $(-\infty, -4] \cup (-2, 1]$

**55.** $(-\infty, -5)$ or $(-3, \infty)$

**57.** $\left(-\infty, \dfrac{1}{2}\right)$ or $\left[\dfrac{7}{5}, \infty\right)$

**59.** $(-\infty, -6]$ or $(-2, \infty)$

**61.** $\left(-\infty, \dfrac{1}{2}\right] \cup [2, \infty)$    **63.** $(-\infty, -1) \cup [1, \infty)$

**65.** $(-\infty, -8) \cup (-6, 4) \cup (6, \infty)$

**67.** $(-3, 2)$

**69.** $(-\infty, -1) \cup (1, 2) \cup (3, \infty)$

**71.** $\left[-6, -\dfrac{1}{2}\right] \cup [1, \infty)$    **73.** $(-\infty, -2) \cup [-1, 2)$    **75.** between 0 and $\dfrac{1}{2}$ second    **77. a.** dry: 160 ft; wet: 185 ft    **b.** dry pavement: graph (b); wet pavement: graph (a)    **c.** extremely well; Function values and data are identical    **d.** speeds exceeding 76 miles per hour; points on (b) to the right of $(76, 540)$

**79.** The sides (in feet) are in $(0, 6]$ or $[19, 25)$.    **87.** $\left[-3, \dfrac{1}{2}\right]$    **89.** $(1, 4]$    **91.** $(-4, -1) \cup [2, \infty)$    **93. a.** $f(x) = 0.1375x^2 - 0.7x + 37.8$

**b.** speeds exceeding 52 miles per hour    **95.** does not make sense    **97.** does not make sense    **99.** false    **101.** true

**103.** Answers may vary. One possible solution is $\dfrac{x-3}{x+4} \ge 0$.    **105.** $\{2\}$    **107.** $(-\infty, 2) \cup (2, \infty)$

**109.**
$$27 - 3x^2 \ge 0$$
$$3x^2 \le 27$$
$$x^2 \le 9$$
$$-3 \le x \le 3$$

**110. a.** 16    **b.** $y = 16x^2$    **c.** 400    **111. a.** 96    **b.** $y = \dfrac{96}{x}$    **c.** 32    **112.** 8

## Section 2.8

### Check Point Exercises

**1.** 66 gal    **2.** 9375 lb    **3.** 512 cycles per second    **4.** 24 min    **5.** $96\pi$ cubic feet

### Exercise Set 2.8

**1.** 156    **3.** 30    **5.** $\dfrac{5}{6}$    **7.** 240    **9.** 50    **11.** $x = kyz;\ y = \dfrac{x}{kz}$    **13.** $x = \dfrac{kz^3}{y};\ y = \dfrac{kz^3}{x}$    **15.** $x = \dfrac{kyz}{\sqrt{w}};\ y = \dfrac{x\sqrt{w}}{kz}$

**17.** $x = kz(y + w);\ y = \dfrac{x - kzw}{kz}$    **19.** $x = \dfrac{kz}{y - w};\ y = \dfrac{xw + kz}{x}$    **21.** 5.4 ft    **23.** 80 in.    **25.** about 607 lb    **27.** 32°

**29.** 90 milliroentgens per hour    **31.** This person has a BMI of 24.4 and is not overweight.    **33.** 1800 Btu per hour

**35.** $\dfrac{1}{4}$ of what it was originally    **37. a.** $C = \dfrac{kP_1P_2}{d^2}$    **b.** $k \approx 0.02;\ C = \dfrac{0.02\,P_1P_2}{d^2}$    **c.** 17,875 daily phone calls

**39. a.**

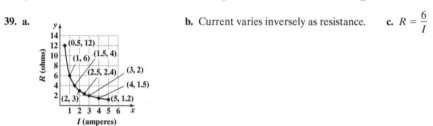

**b.** Current varies inversely as resistance.    **c.** $R = \dfrac{6}{I}$

**49.** does not make sense    **51.** makes sense    **53.** The destructive power is four times as much.    **55.** Reduce the resistance by a factor of $\dfrac{1}{3}$.

**58.**      **59.**      **60.**

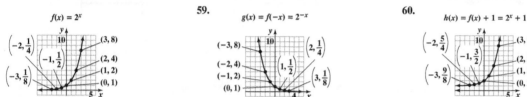

## Chapter 2 Review Exercises

**1.** $-9 + 4i$    **2.** $-12 - 8i$    **3.** $17 + 19i$    **4.** $-7 - 24i$    **5.** 113    **6.** $\dfrac{15}{13} - \dfrac{3}{13}i$    **7.** $\dfrac{1}{5} + \dfrac{11}{10}i$    **8.** $i\sqrt{2}$    **9.** $-96 - 40i$

**10.** $2 + i\sqrt{2}$    **11.** $\{1 + i\sqrt{3}, 1 - i\sqrt{3}\}$    **12.** $\left\{\dfrac{3}{2} + \dfrac{1}{2}i, \dfrac{3}{2} - \dfrac{1}{2}i\right\}$

**13.**      **14.**      **15.**      **16.**

     axis of symmetry; $x = -1$      axis of symmetry: $x = -4$      axis of symmetry: $x = 1$      axis of symmetry: $x = 1$

     domain: $(-\infty, \infty)$; range: $(-\infty, 4]$      domain: $(-\infty, \infty)$; range: $[-2, \infty)$      domain: $(-\infty, \infty)$; range: $(-\infty, 4]$      domain: $(-\infty, \infty)$; range: $[-8, \infty)$

**17. a.** maximum is $-57$ at $x = 7$    **b.** domain: $(-\infty, \infty)$; range: $(-\infty, -57]$    **18. a.** minimum is 685 at $x = -3$    **b.** domain: $(-\infty, \infty)$; range: $[685, \infty)$

**19. a.** 16 ft; 20 yd    **b.** 6 ft    **c.** 45.3 yd    **d.**      **20.** 250 yd by 500 yd; 125,000 sq yard    **21.** $-7$ and 7; $-49$

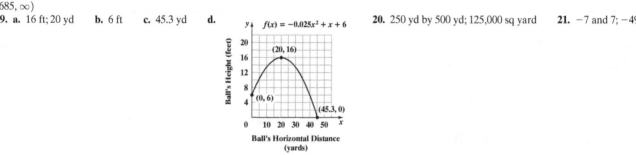

**22.** $x = 166\dfrac{2}{3}$ ft by $y = 125$ ft    **23.** 36; 5256 lb    **24.** c    **25.** b    **26.** a    **27.** d    **28.** No; the graph falls to the right, so eventually there would be a negative number of thefts, which is not possible.    **29.** The graph falls to the right; eventually the elk population will be extinct.

**30.** $x = 1$, multiplicity 1, crosses; $x = -2$, multiplicity 2, touches; $x = -5$, multiplicity 3, crosses

**31.** $x = -5$, multiplicity 1, crosses; $x = 5$, multiplicity 2, touches

**32.** $f(1)$ is negative and $f(2)$ is positive, so by the Intermediate Value Theorem, $f$ has a real zero between 1 and 2.

**33. a.** The graph falls to the
left and rises to the right.
**b.** no symmetry
**c.**

$f(x) = x^3 - x^2 - 9x + 9$

**34. a.** The graph rises to the
left and falls to the right.
**b.** origin symmetry
**c.**
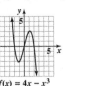
$f(x) = 4x - x^3$

**35. a.** The graph falls to the
left and rises to the right.
**b.** no symmetry
**c.**
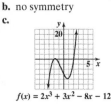
$f(x) = 2x^3 + 3x^2 - 8x - 12$

**36. a.** The graph falls to the
left and to the right.
**b.** $y$-axis symmetry
**c.**

$f(x) = -x^4 + 25x^2$

**37. a.** The graph falls to the
left and to the right.
**b.** no symmetry
**c.**

$f(x) = -x^4 + 6x^3 - 9x^2$

**38. a.** The graph rises to the
left and to the right.
**b.** no symmetry
**c.**

$f(x) = 3x^4 - 15x^3$

**39.**

$f(x) = 2x^2(x-1)^3(x+2)$

**40.**

$f(x) = -x^3(x+4)^2(x-1)$

**41.** $4x^2 - 7x + 5 - \dfrac{4}{x+1}$

**42.** $2x^2 - 4x + 1 - \dfrac{10}{5x-3}$

**43.** $2x^2 + 3x - 1$      **44.** $3x^3 - 4x^2 + 7$

**45.** $3x^3 + 6x^2 + 10x + 10 + \dfrac{20}{x-2}$      **46.** $-5697$

**47.** $2, \dfrac{1}{2}, -3$      **48.** $\{4, -2\pm\sqrt{5}\}$      **49.** $\pm1, \pm5$      **50.** $\pm1, \pm2, \pm4, \pm8, \dfrac{8}{3}, \dfrac{4}{3}, \dfrac{2}{3}, \dfrac{1}{3}$      **51.** 2 or 0 positive real zeros; no negative real zeros

**52.** 3 or 1 positive real zeros; 2 or 0 negative real zeros      **53.** No sign variations exist for either $f(x)$ or $f(-x)$, so no real roots exist.

**54. a.** $\pm1, \pm2, \pm4$      **b.** 1 positive real zero; 2 or no negative real zeros      **c.** $-2$ or $1$      **d.** $-2, 1$

**55. a.** $\pm1, \pm\dfrac{1}{2}, \pm\dfrac{1}{3}, \pm\dfrac{1}{6}$      **b.** 2 or 0 positive real zeros; 1 negative real zero      **c.** $-1, \dfrac{1}{3},$ or $\dfrac{1}{2}$      **d.** $-1, \dfrac{1}{3}, \dfrac{1}{2}$

**56. a.** $\pm1, \pm3, \pm5, \pm15, \pm\dfrac{1}{2}, \pm\dfrac{1}{4}, \pm\dfrac{1}{8}, \pm\dfrac{3}{2}, \pm\dfrac{3}{4}, \pm\dfrac{3}{8}, \pm\dfrac{5}{2}, \pm\dfrac{5}{4}, \pm\dfrac{5}{8}, \pm\dfrac{15}{2}, \pm\dfrac{15}{4}, \pm\dfrac{15}{8}$      **b.** 3 or 1 positive real solutions; no negative real solutions

**c.** $\dfrac{1}{2}, \dfrac{3}{2},$ or $\dfrac{5}{2}$      **d.** $\left\{\dfrac{1}{2}, \dfrac{3}{2}, \dfrac{5}{2}\right\}$      **57. a.** $\pm1, \pm\dfrac{1}{2}$      **b.** 2 or 0 positive real solutions; 1 negative solution      **c.** $\dfrac{1}{2}$      **d.** $\left\{\dfrac{1}{2}, \dfrac{-5-\sqrt{29}}{2}, \dfrac{-5+\sqrt{29}}{2}\right\}$

**58. a.** $\pm1, \pm2, \pm3, \pm6$      **b.** 2 or zero positive real solutions; 2 or zero negative real solutions      **c.** $-2, -1, 1,$ or $3$      **d.** $\{-2, -1, 1, 3\}$

**59. a.** $\pm1, \pm2, \pm\dfrac{1}{2}, \pm\dfrac{1}{4}$      **b.** 1 positive real root; 1 negative real root      **c.** $-\dfrac{1}{2}$ or $\dfrac{1}{2}$      **d.** $\left\{-\dfrac{1}{2}, \dfrac{1}{2}, i\sqrt{2}, -i\sqrt{2}\right\}$

**60. a.** $\pm1, \pm2, \pm4, \pm\dfrac{1}{2}$      **b.** 2 or no positive zeros; 2 or no negative zeros      **c.** $-2, -1, \dfrac{1}{2},$ or $2$      **d.** $\left\{-2, -1, \dfrac{1}{2}, 2\right\}$

**61.** $f(x) = x^3 - 6x^2 + 21x - 26$      **62.** $f(x) = 2x^4 + 12x^3 + 20x^2 + 12x + 18$      **63.** $-2, \dfrac{1}{2}, \pm i; f(x) = (x-i)(x+i)(x+2)(2x-1)$

**64.** $-1, 4; g(x) = (x+1)^2(x-4)^2$      **65.** 4 real zeros, one with multiplicity two      **66.** 3 real zeros; 2 nonreal complex zeros
**67.** 2 real zeros, one with multiplicity two; 2 nonreal complex zeros      **68.** 1 real zero; 4 nonreal complex zeros

**69.**

$g(x) = \dfrac{1}{(x+2)^2} - 1$

**70.**

$h(x) = \dfrac{1}{x-1} + 3$

**71.** Vertical asymptote: $x = 3$ and $x = -3$
horizontal asymptote: $y = 0$
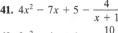
$f(x) = \dfrac{2x}{x^2 - 9}$

**72.** Vertical asymptote: $x = -3$
horizontal asymptote: $y = 2$
$f(x) = \dfrac{2x - 4}{x + 3}$

**73.** Vertical asymptotes: $x = 3, -2$
horizontal asymptote: $y = 1$

$h(x) = \dfrac{x^2 - 3x - 4}{x^2 - x - 6}$

**74.** Vertical asymptote: $x = -2$
horizontal asymptote: $y = 1$

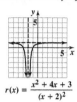

$r(x) = \dfrac{x^2 + 4x + 3}{(x + 2)^2}$

**75.** Vertical asymptote: $x = -1$
no horizontal asymptote
slant asymptote: $y = x - 1$

$y = \dfrac{x^2}{x + 1}$

**76.** Vertical asymptote: $x = 3$
no horizontal asymptote
slant asymptote: $y = x + 5$

$y = \dfrac{x^2 + 2x - 3}{x - 3}$

**77.** No vertical asymptote

no horizontal asymptote

slant asymptote: $y = -2x$

$f(x) = \dfrac{-2x^3}{x^2 + 1}$

**78.** Vertical asymptote: $x = \dfrac{3}{2}$

no horizontal asymptote

slant asymptote: $y = 2x - 5$

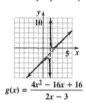

$g(x) = \dfrac{4x^2 - 16x + 16}{2x - 3}$

**79. a.** $C(x) = 25x + 50,000$

**b.** $\overline{C}(x) = \dfrac{25x + 50,000}{x}$

**c.** $\overline{C}(50) = 1025$, when 50 calculators are manufactured, it costs \$1025 to manufacture each; $\overline{C}(100) = 525$, when 100 calculators are manufactured, it costs \$525 to manufacture each; $\overline{C}(1000) = 75$, when 1000 calculators are manufactured, it costs \$75 to manufacture each; $\overline{C}(100,000) = 25.5$, when 100,000 calculators are manufactured, it costs \$25.50 to manufacture each.

**d.** $y = 25$; costs will approach \$25.

**80.** $y = 3000$; The number of fish in the pond approaches 3000.
**81.** $y = 0$; As the number of years of education increases the percentage rate of unemployment approaches zero.
**82. a.** $P(x) = 3.06x + 235$   **b.** $R(x) = \dfrac{1.58x + 114.4}{3.06x + 235}$   **c.** $y = 0.52$; Over time the percentage of men in the U.S. population will approach 52%.

**83.** $T(x) = \dfrac{4}{x + 3} + \dfrac{2}{x}$   **84.** $P(x) = 2x + \dfrac{2000}{x}$

**85.** $\left(-3, \dfrac{1}{2}\right)$

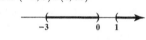

**86.** $(-\infty, -4] \cup \left[-\dfrac{1}{2}, \infty\right)$

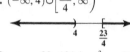

**87.** $(-3, 0) \cup (1, \infty)$

**88.** $(-\infty, -2) \cup (6, \infty)$

**89.** $[-1, 1) \cup [2, \infty)$

**90.** $(-\infty, 4) \cup \left[\dfrac{23}{4}, \infty\right)$

**91. a.** 261 ft; overestimates by 1 ft   **b.** speeds exceeding 40 miles per hour   **92.** from 1 to 2 sec   **93.** 134.4 cm³   **94.** 1600 ft
**95.** 440 vibrations per second   **96.** 112 decibels   **97.** 16 hr   **98.** 800 ft³   **99. a.** $L = \dfrac{1890}{R}$   **b.** an approximate model   **c.** 70 yr

## Chapter 2 Test

**1.** $47 + 16i$   **2.** $2 + i$   **3.** $38i$   **4.** $\{2 + i, 2 - i\}$
**5.**

$f(x) = (x + 1)^2 + 4$

axis of symmetry: $x = -1$
domain: $(-\infty, \infty)$; range: $[4, \infty)$
**10. a.** $5, 2, -2$
**b.**

$f(x) = x^3 - 5x^2 - 4x + 20$

**6.**

$f(x) = x^2 - 2x - 3$

axis of symmetry: $x = 1$
domain: $(-\infty, \infty)$; range: $[-4, \infty)$

**7. a.** maximum of 2 at $x = 3$;
**b.** domain: $(-\infty, \infty)$; range: $(-\infty, 2]$
**8.** 23 computers;
maximum daily profit = \$16,900
**9.** 7 and 7; 49

**11.** Since the degree of the polynomial is odd and the leading coefficient is positive, the graph of $f$ should fall to the left and rise to the right. The $x$-intercepts should be $-1, 0$, and 1.
**12. a.** 2   **b.** $\dfrac{1}{2}, \dfrac{2}{3}$   **13.** $\pm 1, \pm 2, \pm 3, \pm 6, \pm \dfrac{1}{2}, \pm \dfrac{3}{2}$
**14.** 3 or 1 positive real zeros; no negative real zeros.

**15.** $\{-3, -3 - \sqrt{11}, -3 + \sqrt{11}\}$   **16. a.** $\pm 1, \pm 3, \pm 5, \pm 15, \pm \dfrac{1}{2}, \pm \dfrac{3}{2}, \pm \dfrac{5}{2}, \pm \dfrac{15}{2}$   **b.** $-\sqrt{5}, -1, \dfrac{3}{2}$, and $\sqrt{5}$   **17.** $(x - 1)(x + 2)^2$

**18.** $f(x) = 2x^4 - 2$   **19.** $-1$ and $\dfrac{2}{3}$   **20.** $(-\infty, -3)\cup(-3, \infty)$   **21.** $(-\infty, 1)\cup(1, \infty)$

$f(x) = -3x^3 - 4x^2 + x + 2$

$f(x) = \dfrac{1}{(x+3)^2}$

$f(x) = \dfrac{1}{x-1} + 2$

**22.** domain: $\{x | x \neq 4, x \neq -4\}$   **23.** domain: $\{x | x \neq 2\}$   **24.** domain: $\{x | x \neq -3, x \neq 1\}$   **25.** domain: all real numbers

$f(x) = \dfrac{x}{x^2 - 16}$

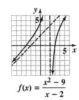
$f(x) = \dfrac{x^2 - 9}{x - 2}$

$f(x) = \dfrac{x + 1}{x^2 + 2x - 3}$

$f(x) = \dfrac{4x^2}{x^2 + 3}$

**26. a.** $\overline{C}(x) = \dfrac{300,000 + 10x}{x}$   **b.** $y = 10$; As the number of satellite radio players increases, the average cost approaches \$10.

**27.** $(-3, 4)$   **28.** $(-\infty, 3)\cup[10, \infty)$   **29.** 45 foot-candles

## Cumulative Review Exercises (Chapters P–2)

**1.** domain: $(-2, 2)$; range: $[0, \infty)$   **2.** $-1$ and $1$, both of multiplicity 2   **3.** 0   **4.** 3   **5.** $x \to -2^+; x \to 2^-$

**6.**

$g(x) = f(x + 2) + 1$

**7.** $\{2, -1\}$   **8.** $\left\{\dfrac{5 + \sqrt{13}}{6}, \dfrac{5 - \sqrt{13}}{6}\right\}$   **9.** $\left\{\dfrac{1}{3}, -\dfrac{2}{3}\right\}$   **10.** $\{-3, -1, 2\}$   **11.** $(-\infty, 1) \cup (4, \infty)$

**12.** $(-\infty, -1) \cup \left(\dfrac{5}{3}, \infty\right)$   **13.**

$f(x) = x^3 - 4x^2 - x + 4$

**14.**

$f(x) = x^2 + 2x - 8$

**15.**

$f(x) = x^2(x - 3)$

**16.**
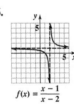
$f(x) = \dfrac{x - 1}{x - 2}$

**17.**

**18.**
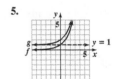
$x^2 + y^2 - 2x + 4y - 4 = 0$

**19.** $(f \circ g)(x) = 32x^2 - 20x + 2$   **20.** $4x + 2h - 1$

# CHAPTER 3

## Section 3.1

### Check Point Exercises

**1.** approximately \$160; overestimates by \$11

**2.**

$f(x) = 3^x$

**3.**

$f(x) = \left(\dfrac{1}{3}\right)^x$

**4.**

$f(x) = 3^x$
$g(x) = 3^{x-1}$

**5.**
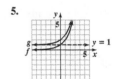
$f(x) = 2^x$
$g(x) = 2^x + 1$

**6.** approximately 4446   **7. a.** \$14,859.47   **b.** \$14,918.25

## Exercise Set 3.1

**1.** 10.556   **3.** 11.665   **5.** 0.125   **7.** 9.974   **9.** 0.387

**11.**

$f(x) = 4^x$

**13.**

$g(x) = \left(\dfrac{3}{2}\right)^x$

**15.**

$h(x) = \left(\dfrac{1}{2}\right)^x$

**17.**

$f(x) = (0.6)^x$

**19.** $H(x) = -3^{-x}$
**21.** $F(x) = -3^x$
**23.** $h(x) = 3^x - 1$

**25.**

$f(x) = 2^x$
$g(x) = 2^{x+1}$

asymptote: $y = 0$
domain: $(-\infty, \infty)$
range: $(0, \infty)$

**27.**

$f(x) = 2^x$
$g(x) = 2^x - 1$

asymptote: $y = -1$
domain: $(-\infty, \infty)$
range: $(-1, \infty)$

**29.**

$f(x) = 2^x$
$h(x) = 2^{x+1} - 1$

asymptote: $y = -1$
domain: $(-\infty, \infty)$
range: $(-1, \infty)$

**31.**

$f(x) = 2^x$
$g(x) = -2^x$

asymptote: $y = 0$
domain: $(-\infty, \infty)$
range: $(-\infty, 0)$

**33.**

$f(x) = 2^x$
$g(x) = 2 \cdot 2^x$

asymptote: $y = 0$
domain: $(-\infty, \infty)$
range: $(0, \infty)$

**35.**

$g(x) = e^x - 1$

asymptote: $y = 0$
domain: $(-\infty, \infty)$
range: $(0, \infty)$

**37.**

$g(x) = e^x + 2$

asymptote: $y = 2$
domain: $(-\infty, \infty)$
range: $(2, \infty)$

**39.**

$h(x) = e^{x-1} + 2$

asymptote: $y = 2$
domain: $(-\infty, \infty)$
range: $(2, \infty)$

**41.**

$h(x) = e^{-x}$

asymptote: $y = 0$
domain: $(-\infty, \infty)$
range: $(0, \infty)$

**43.**

$g(x) = 2e^x$

asymptote: $y = 0$
domain: $(-\infty, \infty)$
range: $(0, \infty)$

**45.**

$h(x) = e^{2x} + 1$

asymptote: $y = 1$
domain: $(-\infty, \infty)$
range: $(1, \infty)$

**47.**

$f(x) = 3^x$
$g(x) = 3^{-x}$

asymptote of $f$: $y = 0$
asymptote of $g$: $y = 0$

**49.**

$f(x) = 3^x$
$g(x) = \dfrac{1}{3} \cdot 3^x$

asymptote of $f$: $y = 0$
asymptote of $g$: $y = 0$

**51.**

$f(x) = \left(\dfrac{1}{2}\right)^x$
$g(x) = \left(\dfrac{1}{2}\right)^{x-1} + 1$

asymptote of $f$: $y = 0$
asymptote of $g$: $y = 1$

**53.** **a.** \$13,116.51
**b.** \$13,140.67
**c.** \$13,157.04
**d.** \$13,165.31
**55.** 7% compounded monthly

**57.** $(0, 1)$

$g(x) = 2^{-x}$   $f(x) = 2^x$

**59.**

$y = 2^x$

$x = 2^y$

**61.** $y = 4^x$   **63.** $y = -e^x$   **65. a.** 574 million   **b.** 1148 million   **c.** 2295 million   **d.** 4590 million   **e.** It appears to double.
**67.** \$832,744   **69.** 3.249009585; 3.317278183; 3.321880096; 3.321995226; 3.321997068; $2^{\sqrt{3}} \approx 3.321997085$; The closer the exponent is to $\sqrt{3}$, the closer the value is to $2^{\sqrt{3}}$.   **71. a.** approximately 8.9 million words   **b.** approximately 10.4 million words   **c.** linear model
**73. a.** 100%   **b.** $\approx 68.5\%$   **c.** $\approx 30.8\%$   **d.** $\approx 20\%$   **75.** the function $g$

**81. a.** $A = 10{,}000\left(1 + \dfrac{0.05}{4}\right)^{4t}$; $A = 10{,}000\left(1 + \dfrac{0.045}{12}\right)^{12t}$   **83.** does not make sense   **85.** does not make sense   **87.** false   **89.** false

**b.**

24,000

0          20
8000

5% interest compounded quarterly

**91.** $y = 3^x$ is (d); $y = 5^x$ is (c); $y = \left(\dfrac{1}{3}\right)^x$ is (a); $y = \left(\dfrac{1}{5}\right)^x$ is (b).

**93. a.** $\cosh(-x) = \dfrac{e^{-x} + e^{-(-x)}}{2} = \dfrac{e^{-x} + e^{x}}{2} = \dfrac{e^{x} + e^{-x}}{2} = \cosh x$     **c.** $\left(\dfrac{e^{x} + e^{-x}}{2}\right)^{2} - \left(\dfrac{e^{x} - e^{-x}}{2}\right)^{2} \overset{?}{=} 1$

**b.** $\sinh(-x) = \dfrac{e^{-x} - e^{-(-x)}}{2} = \dfrac{e^{-x} - e^{x}}{2} = -\dfrac{e^{x} - e^{-x}}{2} = -\sinh x$     $\dfrac{e^{2x} + 2 + e^{-2x}}{4} - \dfrac{e^{2x} - 2 + e^{-2x}}{4} \overset{?}{=} 1$

$\dfrac{e^{2x} + 2 + e^{-2x} - e^{2x} + 2 - e^{-2x}}{4} \overset{?}{=} 1$

$\dfrac{4}{4} \overset{?}{=} 1$

$1 = 1$

**94.** We don't know how to solve $x = 2^{y}$ for $y$.     **95.** $\dfrac{1}{2}$     **96.** $(-\infty, 3) \cup (3, \infty)$

## Section 3.2

### Check Point Exercises

**1. a.** $7^{3} = x$     **b.** $b^{2} = 25$     **c.** $4^{y} = 26$     **2. a.** $5 = \log_{2} x$     **b.** $3 = \log_{b} 27$     **c.** $y = \log_{e} 33$     **3. a.** $2$     **b.** $-3$     **c.** $\dfrac{1}{2}$     **d.** $\dfrac{1}{7}$
**4. a.** $1$     **b.** $0$     **5. a.** $8$     **b.** $17$     **6.**     **7.** $(5, \infty)$     **8.** $80\%$     **9.** $4.0$     **10. a.** $(-\infty, 4)$     **b.** $(-\infty, 0) \cup (0, \infty)$
**11.** $34°$; quite well

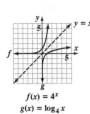

$f(x) = 3^{x}$
$g(x) = \log_{3} x$

### Exercise Set 3.2

**1.** $2^{4} = 16$     **3.** $3^{2} = x$     **5.** $b^{5} = 32$     **7.** $6^{y} = 216$     **9.** $\log_{2} 8 = 3$     **11.** $\log_{2} \dfrac{1}{16} = -4$     **13.** $\log_{8} 2 = \dfrac{1}{3}$     **15.** $\log_{13} x = 2$

**17.** $\log_{b} 1000 = 3$     **19.** $\log_{7} 200 = y$     **21.** $2$     **23.** $6$     **25.** $-1$     **27.** $-3$     **29.** $\dfrac{1}{2}$     **31.** $-\dfrac{1}{2}$     **33.** $\dfrac{1}{2}$     **35.** $1$     **37.** $0$     **39.** $7$     **41.** $19$

**43.**          **45.**          **47.** $H(x) = 1 - \log_{3} x$     **49.** $h(x) = \log_{3} x - 1$     **51.** $g(x) = \log_{3}(x - 1)$

$f(x) = 4^{x}$
$g(x) = \log_{4} x$

$f(x) = \left(\dfrac{1}{2}\right)^{x}$
$g(x) = \log_{1/2} x$

**53.**          **55.**          **57.**          **59.**

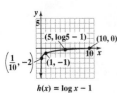

$f(x) = \log_{2} x$
$g(x) = \log_{2}(x+1)$

vertical asymptote: $x = -1$
domain: $(-1, \infty)$
range: $(-\infty, \infty)$

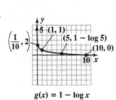

$f(x) = \log_{2} x$
$h(x) = 1 + \log_{2} x$

vertical asymptote: $x = 0$
domain: $(0, \infty)$
range: $(-\infty, \infty)$

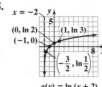

$f(x) = \log_{2} x$
$g(x) = \dfrac{1}{2} \log_{2} x$

vertical asymptote: $x = 0$
domain: $(0, \infty)$
range: $(-\infty, \infty)$

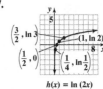

$g(x) = \log(x - 1)$

asymptote: $x = 1$
domain: $(1, \infty)$
range: $(-\infty, \infty)$

**61.**          **63.**          **65.**          **67.**

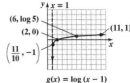

$h(x) = \log x - 1$

asymptote: $x = 0$
domain: $(0, \infty)$
range: $(-\infty, \infty)$

$g(x) = 1 - \log x$

asymptote: $x = 0$
domain: $(0, \infty)$
range: $(-\infty, \infty)$

$g(x) = \ln(x + 2)$

asymptote: $x = -2$
domain: $(-2, \infty)$
range: $(-\infty, \infty)$

$h(x) = \ln(2x)$

asymptote: $x = 0$
domain: $(0, \infty)$
range: $(-\infty, \infty)$

**69.**

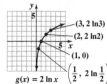

$g(x) = 2 \ln x$

**71.**

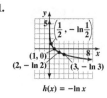

$h(x) = -\ln x$

**73.**

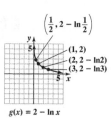

$g(x) = 2 - \ln x$

asymptote: $x = 0$
domain: $(0, \infty)$
range: $(-\infty, \infty)$

asymptote: $x = 0$
domain: $(0, \infty)$
range: $(-\infty, \infty)$

asymptote: $x = 0$
domain: $(0, \infty)$
range: $(-\infty, \infty)$

**75.** $(-4, \infty)$     **77.** $(-\infty, 2)$     **79.** $(-\infty, 2) \cup (2, \infty)$     **81.** 2     **83.** 7     **85.** 33     **87.** 0     **89.** 6     **91.** $-6$     **93.** 125     **95.** $9x$

**97.** $5x^2$     **99.** $\sqrt{x}$     **101.** $3^2 = x - 1; \{10\}$     **103.** $4^{-3} = x; \left\{\dfrac{1}{64}\right\}$     **105.** 0     **107.** 2     **109.** $(-\infty, -1) \cup (2, \infty)$     **111.** $(-\infty, -1) \cup (5, \infty)$

**113.** 95.4%     **115. a.** 26.4%; underestimates by 1%     **b.** 25.2%     **117.** $\approx 188$ db; yes

**119. a.** 88     **129.**     **131.**
**b.** 71.5; 63.9; 58.8; 55; 52; 49.5
**c.**

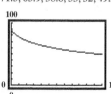

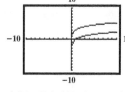

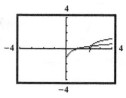

Material retention decreases
as time passes.

$g(x)$ is $f(x)$ shifted upward
3 units.

$g(x)$ is $f(x)$ shifted right 2 units
and upward 1 unit.

**133. a.**     **b.**

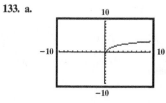

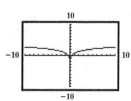

**c.**

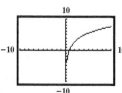

**d.** They are the same.
$\log_b M + \log_b N$
**e.** the sum of the logarithms
of its factors

**135.** makes sense     **137.** makes sense     **139.** false     **141.** false     **143.** $\dfrac{4}{5}$     **145.** $\log_3 40 > \log_4 60$     **147. a.** 5     **b.** 5

**c.** $\log_2(8 \cdot 4) = \log_2 8 + \log_2 2$     **148. a.** 4     **b.** 4     **c.** $\log_2\left(\dfrac{32}{2}\right) = \log_2 32 - \log_2 2$     **149. a.** 4     **b.** 4     **c.** $\log_3 9^2 = 2\log_3 9$

## Section 3.3

### Check Point Exercises

**1. a.** $\log_6 7 + \log_6 11$     **b.** $2 + \log x$     **2. a.** $\log_8 23 - \log_8 x$     **b.** $5 - \ln 11$     **3. a.** $9 \log_6 3$     **b.** $\dfrac{1}{3} \ln x$     **c.** $2 \log(x + 4)$

**4. a.** $4 \log_b x + \dfrac{1}{3} \log_b y$     **b.** $\dfrac{1}{2} \log_5 x - 2 - 3 \log_5 y$     **5. a.** $\log 100 = 2$     **b.** $\log\dfrac{7x + 6}{x}$     **6. a.** $\ln x^2 \sqrt[3]{x + 5}$     **b.** $\log\dfrac{(x - 3)^2}{x}$

**c.** $\log_b \dfrac{\sqrt[4]{x}}{25y^{10}}$     **7.** 4.02     **8.** 4.02

### Exercise Set 3.3

**1.** $\log_5 7 + \log_5 3$     **3.** $1 + \log_7 x$     **5.** $3 + \log x$     **7.** $1 - \log_7 x$     **9.** $\log x - 2$     **11.** $3 - \log_4 y$     **13.** $2 - \ln 5$     **15.** $3 \log_b x$

**17.** $-6 \log N$     **19.** $\dfrac{1}{5} \ln x$     **21.** $2 \log_b x + \log_b y$     **23.** $\dfrac{1}{2} \log_4 x - 3$     **25.** $2 - \dfrac{1}{2} \log_6(x + 1)$     **27.** $2 \log_b x + \log_b y - 2 \log_b z$

**29.** $1 + \dfrac{1}{2} \log x$     **31.** $\dfrac{1}{3} \log x - \dfrac{1}{3} \log y$     **33.** $\dfrac{1}{2}\log_b x + 3\log_b y - 3\log_b z$     **35.** $\dfrac{2}{3}\log_5 x + \dfrac{1}{3}\log_5 y - \dfrac{2}{3}$     **37.** $3\ln x + \dfrac{1}{2}\ln(x^2 + 1) - 4\ln(x + 1)$

**39.** $1 + 2\log x + \dfrac{1}{3}\log(1 - x) - \log 7 - 2\log(x + 1)$     **41.** 1     **43.** $\ln(7x)$     **45.** 5     **47.** $\log\left(\dfrac{2x + 5}{x}\right)$     **49.** $\log(xy^3)$

**51.** $\ln(x^{1/2}y)$ or $\ln(y\sqrt{x})$     **53.** $\log_b(x^2 y^3)$     **55.** $\ln\left(\dfrac{x^5}{y^2}\right)$     **57.** $\ln\left(\dfrac{x^3}{y^{1/3}}\right)$ or $\ln\left(\dfrac{x^3}{\sqrt[3]{y}}\right)$     **59.** $\ln\dfrac{(x + 6)^4}{x^3}$     **61.** $\ln\left(\dfrac{x^3 y^5}{z^6}\right)$     **63.** $\log\sqrt{xy}$

**65.** $\log_5\left(\dfrac{\sqrt{xy}}{(x+1)^2}\right)$  **67.** $\ln\sqrt[3]{\dfrac{(x+5)^2}{x(x^2-4)}}$  **69.** $\log\dfrac{x(x^2-1)}{7(x+1)} = \log\dfrac{x(x-1)}{7}$  **71.** 1.5937  **73.** 1.6944  **75.** $-1.2304$  **77.** 3.6193

**79.** 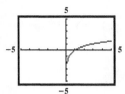  **81.**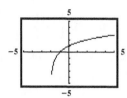

**83.** $C - A$  **85.** $3A$  **87.** $\dfrac{1}{2}A - \dfrac{3}{2}C$  **89.** false; $\ln e = 1$  **91.** false; $\log_4(2x)^3 = 3\log_4(2x)$  **93.** true  **95.** true

**97.** false; $\log(x+3) - \log(2x) = \log\left(\dfrac{x+3}{2x}\right)$  **99.** true  **101.** true  **103. a.** $D = 10\log\dfrac{I}{I_0}$  **b.** 20 decibels louder

**113. a.** 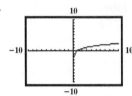  **b.** 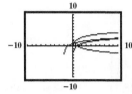  $y = 2 + \log_3 x$ shifts the graph of $y = \log_3 x$ two units upward; $y = \log_3(x+2)$ shifts the graph of $y = \log_3 x$ two units left; $y = -\log_3 x$ reflects the graph of $y = \log_3 x$ about the $x$-axis.

**115.** 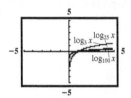  **a.** top graph: $y = \log_{100} x$; bottom graph: $y = \log_3 x$
**b.** top graph: $y = \log_3 x$; bottom graph: $y = \log_{100} x$
**c.** The graph of the equation with the largest $b$ will be on the top in the interval $(0, 1)$ and on the bottom in the interval $(1, \infty)$.

**121.** makes sense  **123.** makes sense

**125.** true  **127.** false  **129.** $\log e = \log_{10} e = \dfrac{\ln e}{\ln 10} = \dfrac{1}{\ln 10}$  **131.** $4x^3$  **133.** $x = \dfrac{2a + 3b}{a - 2b}$  **134.** $\left\{\dfrac{7 \pm \sqrt{61}}{2}\right\}$  **135.** $\{-1, 3\}$

## Mid-Chapter 3 Check Point

**1.**
$f(x) = 2^x$
$g(x) = 2^x - 3$

asymptote of $f$: $y = 0$
asymptote of $g$: $y = -3$
domain of $f$ = domain of $g = (-\infty, \infty)$
range of $f = (0, \infty)$; range of $g = (-3, \infty)$

**2.**
$f(x) = \left(\dfrac{1}{2}\right)^x$
$g(x) = \left(\dfrac{1}{2}\right)^{x-1}$

asymptote of $f$: $y = 0$
asymptote of $g$: $y = 0$
domain of $f$ = domain of $g = (-\infty, \infty)$
range of $f$ = range of $g = (0, \infty)$

**3.**
$f(x) = e^x$
$g(x) = \ln x$

asymptote of $f$: $y = 0$
asymptote of $g$: $x = 0$
domain of $f$ = range of $g = (-\infty, \infty)$
range of $f$ = domain of $g = (0, \infty)$

**4.**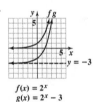
$f(x) = \log_2 x$
$g(x) = \log_2(x - 1) + 1$

asymptote of $f$: $x = 0$
asymptote of $g$: $x = 1$
domain of $f = (0, \infty)$; domain of $g = (1, \infty)$
range of $f$ = range of $g = (-\infty, \infty)$

**5.**
$f(x) = \log_{1/2} x$
$g(x) = -2\log_{1/2} x$

asymptote of $f$: $x = 0$
asymptote of $g$: $x = 0$
domain of $f$ = domain of $g = (0, \infty)$
range of $f$ = range of $g = (-\infty, \infty)$

**6.** $(-6, \infty)$  **7.** $(0, \infty)$  **8.** $(-\infty, -6) \cup (-6, \infty)$  **9.** $(-\infty, \infty)$  **10.** 5  **11.** $-2$  **12.** $\dfrac{1}{2}$  **13.** $\dfrac{1}{3}$  **14.** 2

**15.** Evaluation not possible; $\log_2\dfrac{1}{8} = -3$ and $\log_3(-3)$ is undefined.  **16.** 5  **17.** $\sqrt{7}$  **18.** 13  **19.** $-\dfrac{1}{2}$  **20.** $\sqrt{\pi}$

**21.** $\dfrac{1}{2}\log x + \dfrac{1}{2}\log y - 3$  **22.** $19 + 20\ln x$  **23.** $\log_7\left(\dfrac{x^8}{\sqrt[4]{y}}\right)$  **24.** $\log_5 x^9$  **25.** $\ln\left[\dfrac{\sqrt{x}}{y^3(z-2)}\right]$  **26.** $\$8$

## Section 3.4

**Check Point Exercises**

**1. a.** {3}  **b.** {−12}  **2. a.** $\left\{\dfrac{\ln 134}{\ln 5}\right\}$; ≈ 3.04  **b.** {log 8000}; ≈ 3.90  **3.** $\left\{\dfrac{\ln 9}{2}\right\}$; ≈ 1.10  **4.** $\left\{\dfrac{\ln 3 + \ln 7}{2\ln 3 - \ln 7}\right\}$; ≈ 12.11

**5.** {0, ln 7}; ln 7 ≈ 1.95  **6. a.** {12}  **b.** $\left\{\dfrac{e^2}{3}\right\}$  **7.** {5}  **8.** {4, 5}  **9.** 0.01  **10.** 16.2 yr  **11.** $11,000

**Exercise Set 3.4**

**1.** {6}  **3.** {3}  **5.** {3}  **7.** {2}  **9.** $\left\{\dfrac{3}{5}\right\}$  **11.** $\left\{\dfrac{3}{2}\right\}$  **13.** {4}  **15.** {5}  **17.** $\left\{-\dfrac{1}{4}\right\}$  **19.** {13}  **21.** {−2}

**23.** $\left\{\dfrac{\ln 3.91}{\ln 10}\right\}$; ≈ 0.59  **25.** {ln 5.7}; ≈ 1.74  **27.** $\left\{\dfrac{\ln 17}{\ln 5}\right\}$; ≈ 1.76  **29.** $\left\{\ln\dfrac{23}{5}\right\}$; ≈ 1.53  **31.** $\left\{\dfrac{\ln 659}{5}\right\}$; ≈ 1.30

**33.** $\left\{\dfrac{\ln 793 - 1}{-5}\right\}$; ≈ −1.14  **35.** $\left\{\dfrac{\ln 10{,}478 + 3}{5}\right\}$; ≈ 2.45  **37.** $\left\{\dfrac{\ln 410}{\ln 7} - 2\right\}$; ≈ 1.09  **39.** $\left\{\dfrac{\ln 813}{0.3 \ln 7}\right\}$; ≈ 11.48  **41.** $\left\{\dfrac{3\ln 5 + \ln 3}{\ln 3 - 2\ln 5}\right\}$; ≈ −2.80

**43.** {0, ln 2}; ln 2 ≈ 0.69  **45.** $\left\{\dfrac{\ln 3}{2}\right\}$; ≈ 0.55  **47.** {0}  **49.** {81}  **51.** {$e^2$}; ≈ 7.39  **53.** {59}  **55.** $\left\{\dfrac{109}{27}\right\}$  **57.** $\left\{\dfrac{62}{3}\right\}$

**59.** $\left\{\dfrac{e^4}{2}\right\}$; ≈ 27.30  **61.** {$e^{-1/2}$}; ≈ 0.61  **63.** {$e^2 - 3$}; ≈ 4.39  **65.** $\left\{\dfrac{5}{4}\right\}$  **67.** {6}  **69.** {6}  **71.** {5}  **73.** {12}  **75.** $\left\{\dfrac{4}{3}\right\}$  **77.** ∅

**79.** {5}  **81.** $\left\{\dfrac{2}{9}\right\}$  **83.** {28}  **85.** {2}  **87.** ∅  **89.** $\left\{\dfrac{11}{3}\right\}$  **91.** $\left\{\dfrac{1}{2}\right\}$  **93.** {$e^3, e^{-3}$}  **95.** $\left\{\pm\sqrt{\dfrac{\ln 45}{\ln 3}}\right\}$  **97.** $\left\{\dfrac{5 + \sqrt{37}}{2}\right\}$

**99.** {−2, 6}  **101. a.** 36.1 million  **b.** 2013  **103.** 118 ft; by the point (118, 1)  **105.** 8.2 yr  **107.** 16.8%  **109.** 8.7 yr  **111.** 15.7%
**113. a.** 69%; overestimates by 1%  **b.** 2010  **115.** 2.8 days; (2.8, 50)  **117. a.** $10^{-5.6}$ mole per liter  **b.** $10^{-2.4}$ mole per liter  **c.** $10^{3.2}$ times greater
**123.** {2}  **125.** {4}  **127.** {2}  **129.** {−1.391606, 1.6855579}

**131.**
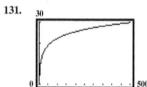

As distance from eye increases, barometric
air pressure increases.

**133.**
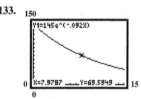

about 7.9 min

**135.** does not make sense  **137.** makes sense  **139.** false  **141.** true  **143.** after 36 yr  **145.** {$10^{-2}, 10^{3/2}$}, $10^{3/2} = 10\sqrt{10} ≈ 31.62$
**148. a.** 10 million; 9.97 million; 9.94 million; 9.91 million  **b.** decreasing
**149.**
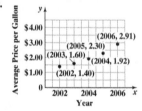
; exponential function  **150. a.** 3  **b.** $e^{(\ln 3)x}$

## Section 3.5

**Check Point Exercises**

**1. a.** $A = 643\,e^{0.021t}$  **b.** 2044  **2. a.** $A = A_0 e^{-0.0248t}$  **b.** about 72 yr  **3. a.** 0.4 correct responses  **b.** 0.7 correct responses
**c.** 0.8 correct responses  **4. a.** $T = 30 + 70e^{-0.0673t}$  **b.** 48°C  **c.** 39 min

**5.**
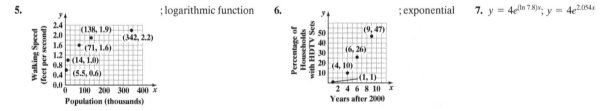
; logarithmic function  **6.** ; exponential  **7.** $y = 4e^{(\ln 7.8)x}$; $y = 4e^{2.054x}$

**Exercise Set 3.5**

**1.** 127.5 million  **3.** Iraq; 2.7%  **5.** 2015  **7. a.** $A = 6.04e^{0.01t}$  **b.** 2040  **9.** 118.7 million  **11.** 0.0121  **13.** −0.0053
**15.** approximately 8 grams  **17.** 8 grams after 10 seconds; 4 grams after 20 seconds; 2 grams after 30 seconds; 1 gram after 40 seconds; 0.5 gram after
50 seconds  **19.** approximately 15,679 years old  **21.** 12.6 yr  **23.** −0.000428; 0.0428% per year  **25.** −0.039608; 3.9608% per day

**27. a.** $\dfrac{1}{2} = e^{1.31k}$ yields $k = \dfrac{\ln\left(\dfrac{1}{2}\right)}{1.31} ≈ -0.52912.$  **b.** about 0.1069 billion or 106,900,000 years old  **29.** 7.1 yr  **31.** 5.5 hr

**33.** $2A_0 = A_0 e^{kt}$; $2 = e^{kt}$; $\ln 2 = \ln e^{kt}$; $\ln 2 = kt$; $\dfrac{\ln 2}{k} = t$    **35. a.** 1%    **b.** about 69 yr    **37. a.** about 20 people    **b.** about 1080 people

**c.** 100,000 people    **39.** quite well    **41.** 2026    **43.** about 3.7%    **45.** about 48 years old    **47. a.** $T = 45 + 25e^{-0.0916t}$    **b.** 51°F

**c.** 18 min    **49.** 26 min    **50.** 45 min

**51. a.**

Percent of Miscarriages vs Woman's Age with points (22, 9), (27, 10), (47, 52), (42, 38), (37, 20), (32, 13)

**b.** exponential function

**53. a.**

Loudness Level (decibels) vs Intensity (watts per meter²) with points (100, 140), (10, 130), (1, 120), (0.1, 110)

**b.** logarithmic function

**55.** $y = 100e^{(\ln 4.6)x}$; $y = 100e^{1.526x}$

**57.** $y = 2.5e^{(\ln 0.7)x}$; $y = 2.5e^{-0.357x}$

**69.** $y = 193.1 + 23.574 \ln x$; $r \approx 0.878$; Fit is ok, but not great.

**71.** $y = 195.871x^{0.097}$; $r \approx 0.901$; Fits data fairly well.

**73. a.** $y = 3.46(1.02)^x$
**b.** $y = 3.46e^{(\ln 1.02)x}$; $y = 3.46e^{0.02x}$; by approximately 2%

**75.** does not make sense    **77.** makes sense    **79.** true    **81.** true    **83.** about 8:02 a.m.    **85.** $\left\{\dfrac{5}{8}\right\}$    **86.** $\dfrac{5\pi}{6}$    **87.** $\dfrac{23\pi}{12}$

## Chapter 3 Review Exercises

**1.** $g(x) = 4^{-x}$    **2.** $h(x) = -4^{-x}$    **3.** $r(x) = -4^{-x} + 3$    **4.** $f(x) = 4^x$

**5.**

$f(x) = 2^x$
$g(x) = 2^{x-1}$

asymptote of $f$: $y = 0$
asymptote of $g$: $y = 0$
domain of $f$ = domain of $g$ = $(-\infty, \infty)$
range of $f$ = range of $g$ = $(0, \infty)$

**6.**

$f(x) = 3^x$
$g(x) = 3^x - 1$

asymptote of $f$: $y = 0$
asymptote of $g$: $y = -1$
domain of $f$ = domain of $g$ = $(-\infty, \infty)$
range of $f$ = $(0, \infty)$; range of $g$ = $(-1, \infty)$

**7.**

$f(x) = 3^x$
$g(x) = -3^x$

asymptote of $f$: $y = 0$
asymptote of $g$: $y = 0$
domain of $f$ = domain of $g$ = $(-\infty, \infty)$
range of $f$ = $(0, \infty)$; range of $g$ = $(-\infty, 0)$

**8.**

$f(x) = \left(\dfrac{1}{2}\right)^x$

$g(x) = \left(\dfrac{1}{2}\right)^{-x}$

asymptote of $f$: $y = 0$
asymptote of $g$: $y = 0$
domain of $f$ = domain of $g$ = $(-\infty, \infty)$
range of $f$ = range of $g$ = $(0, \infty)$

**9.**

$f(x) = e^x$
$g(x) = 2e^{x/2}$

asymptote of $f$: $y = 0$
asymptote of $g$: $y = 0$
domain of $f$ = domain of $g$ = $(-\infty, \infty)$
range of $f$ = range of $g$ = $(0, \infty)$

**10.** 5.5% compounded semiannually    **11.** 7% compounded monthly    **12. a.** 200°    **b.** 120°; 119°    **c.** 70°; The temperature in the room is 70°.
**13.** $49^{1/2} = 7$    **14.** $4^3 = x$    **15.** $3^y = 81$    **16.** $\log_6 216 = 3$    **17.** $\log_b 625 = 4$    **18.** $\log_{13} 874 = y$    **19.** 3    **20.** $-2$    **21.** undefined; $\log_b x$ is defined only for $x > 0$.    **22.** $\dfrac{1}{2}$    **23.** 1    **24.** 8    **25.** 5    **26.** $-\dfrac{1}{2}$    **27.** $-2$    **28.** $-3$    **29.** 0

**30.**

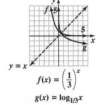

$f(x) = 2^x$
$g(x) = \log_2 x$

domain of $f$ = range of $g$ = $(-\infty, \infty)$
range of $f$ = domain of $g$ = $(0, \infty)$

**31.**

$f(x) = \left(\dfrac{1}{3}\right)^x$
$g(x) = \log_{1/3} x$

domain of $f$ = range of $g$ = $(-\infty, \infty)$
range of $f$ = domain of $g$ = $(0, \infty)$

**32.** $g(x) = \log(-x)$
**33.** $r(x) = 1 + \log(2 - x)$
**34.** $h(x) = \log(2 - x)$
**35.** $f(x) = \log x$

**36.**

$x = 2$

$f(x) = \log_2 x$
$g(x) = \log_2(x - 2)$

*x*-intercept: $(3, 0)$
vertical asymptote: $x = 2$
domain: $(2, \infty)$; range: $(-\infty, \infty)$

**37.**

$f(x) = \log_2 x$
$h(x) = -1 + \log_2 x$

*x*-intercept: $(2, 0)$
vertical asymptote: $x = 0$
domain: $(0, \infty)$; range: $(-\infty, \infty)$

**38.**

$f(x) = \log_2 x$
$r(x) = \log_2(-x)$

*x*-intercept: $(-1, 0)$
vertical asymptote: $x = 0$
domain: $(-\infty, 0)$; range: $(-\infty, \infty)$

**39.**

$x = -3$

$f(x) = \log x$
$g(x) = -\log(x + 3)$

asymptote of $f$: $x = 0$
asymptote of $g$: $x = -3$
domain of $f = (0, \infty)$; domain of $g = (-3, \infty)$
range of $f$ = range of $g = (-\infty, \infty)$

**40.**

$f(x) = \ln x$
$g(x) = -\ln(2x)$

asymptote of $f$: $x = 0$
asymptote of $g$: $x = 0$
domain of $f$ = domain of $g = (0, \infty)$
range of $f$ = range of $g = (-\infty, \infty)$

**41.** $(-5, \infty)$
**42.** $(-\infty, 3)$
**43.** $(-\infty, 1) \cup (1, \infty)$
**44.** $6x$
**45.** $\sqrt{x}$
**46.** $4x^2$
**47.** $3.0$

**48. a.** $76$   **b.** $\approx 67, \approx 63, \approx 61, \approx 59, \approx 56$
**c.**

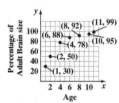

$f(t) = 76 - 18 \log(t + 1)$

**49.** about 9 weeks   **50.** $2 + 3 \log_6 x$   **51.** $\dfrac{1}{2}\log_4 x - 3$

**52.** $\log_2 x + 2 \log_2 y - 6$   **53.** $\dfrac{1}{3}\ln x - \dfrac{1}{3}$   **54.** $\log_b 21$   **55.** $\log \dfrac{3}{x^3}$

**56.** $\ln(x^3 y^4)$   **57.** $\ln \dfrac{\sqrt{x}}{y}$   **58.** $6.2448$   **59.** $-0.1063$

**60.** true   **61.** false; $\log(x + 9) - \log(x + 1) = \log\left(\dfrac{x + 9}{x + 1}\right)$

**62.** false; $4 \log_2 x = \log_2 x^4$   **63.** true   **64.** $\{2\}$   **65.** $\left\{\dfrac{2}{3}\right\}$   **66.** $\{\log 7000\}; \approx 3.85$

**67.** $\left\{-\dfrac{4}{5}\right\}$   **68.** $\left\{\dfrac{\ln 12{,}143}{\ln 8}\right\}; \approx 4.52$   **69.** $\left\{\dfrac{1}{5}\ln 141\right\}; \approx 0.99$   **70.** $\left\{\dfrac{12 - \ln 130}{5}\right\}; \approx 1.43$   **71.** $\left\{\dfrac{\ln 37{,}500 - 2 \ln 5}{4 \ln 5}\right\}; \approx 1.14$

**72.** $\left\{\dfrac{\ln 7 + 4 \ln 3}{2 \ln 7 - \ln 3}\right\}; \approx 2.27$   **73.** $\{\ln 3\}; \approx 1.10$   **74.** $\{23\}$   **75.** $\left\{\dfrac{e^3}{2}\right\}; \approx 10.04$   **76.** $\{5\}$   **77.** $\varnothing$   **78.** $\{2\}$   **79.** $\{4\}$

**80.** 5.5 mi   **81.** approximately 2086   **82.** approximately 8103 thousand or 8,103,000   **83.** 7.3 yr   **84.** 14.6 yr   **85.** about 22%
**86. a.** 0.045   **b.** 55.1 million   **c.** 2012   **87.** 325 days   **88. a.** 200 people   **b.** about 45,411 people   **c.** 500,000 people
**89. a.** $T = 65 + 120e^{-0.144t}$   **b.** 8 min
**90. a.**

**b.** logarithmic function

**91. a.**

**b.** exponential function

**92.** $y = 73e^{(\ln 2.6)x}; y = 73e^{0.956x}$   **93.** $y = 6.5e^{(\ln 0.43)x}; y = 6.5e^{-0.844x}$

## Chapter 3 Test

**1.**

$f(x) = 2^x$
$g(x) = 2^{x+1}$

**2.**

$x = 1$

$f(x) = \log_2 x$
$g(x) = \log_2(x - 1)$

**3.** $5^3 = 125$   **4.** $\log_{36} 6 = \dfrac{1}{2}$   **5.** $(-\infty, 3)$   **6.** $3 + 5 \log_4 x$

**7.** $\dfrac{1}{3}\log_3 x - 4$   **8.** $\log(x^6 y^2)$   **9.** $\ln \dfrac{7}{x^3}$   **10.** 1.5741   **11.** $\{-10\}$

**12.** $\left\{\dfrac{\ln 1.4}{\ln 5}\right\}$   **13.** $\left\{\dfrac{\ln 4}{0.005}\right\}$   **14.** $\{0, \ln 5\}$   **15.** $\{54.25\}$

**16.** $\left\{\dfrac{e^4}{3}\right\}$   **17.** $\{5\}$   **18.** $\varnothing$   **19.** 120 db   **20.** $5x$   **21.** 1   **22.** 0

**23.** 6.5% compounded semiannually; $221 more   **24.** 13.9 years   **25.** about 6.9%

**26. a.** 82.3 million   **b.** decreasing; The growth rate, $-0.002$, is negative.   **c.** 2008   **27.** $A = 509e^{0.036t}$   **28.** 12.5 days   **29. a.** 14 elk
**b.** about 51 elk   **c.** 140 elk   **30.** linear   **31.** logarithmic   **32.** exponential   **33.** quadratic   **34.** $y = 96e^{(\ln 0.38)x}; y = 96e^{-0.968x}$

## Cumulative Review Exercises (Chapters P–3)

**1.** $\left\{\dfrac{2}{3}, 2\right\}$    **2.** $\{-1 \pm 2i\}$    **3.** $\{-2, -1, 1\}$    **4.** $\left\{\dfrac{\ln 128}{5}\right\}$    **5.** $\{3\}$    **6.** $\varnothing$    **7.** $(-\infty, 4]$    **8.** $[1, 3]$

**9.**

$(x - 3)^2 + (y + 2)^2 = 4$

**10.**

$f(x) = (x - 2)^2 - 1$

**11.**
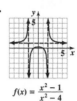
$f(x) = \dfrac{x^2 - 1}{x^2 - 4}$

**12.**

$f(x) = (x - 2)^2(x + 1)$

**13.**
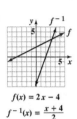
$f(x) = 2x - 4$
$f^{-1}(x) = \dfrac{x + 4}{2}$

**14.**
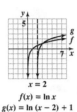
$x = 2$
$f(x) = \ln x$
$g(x) = \ln(x - 2) + 1$

**15.** using $(1, 3)$, $y - 3 = -3(x - 1)$; $y = -3x + 6$
**16.** $(f \circ g)(x) = (x + 2)^2$; $(g \circ f)(x) = x^2 + 2$
**17.** You can expect to sleep 2 hours.
**18.** after 2 sec; 69 ft
**19.** 4.1 sec
**20.** $12 per hr

# CHAPTER 4

## Section 4.1

### Check Point Exercises

**1.** 3.5 radians    **2. a.** $\dfrac{\pi}{3}$ radians   **b.** $\dfrac{3\pi}{2}$ radians   **c.** $-\dfrac{5\pi}{3}$ radians    **3. a.** 45°   **b.** $-240°$   **c.** 343.8°

**4. a.**

$-\dfrac{\pi}{4}$

**b.**

$\dfrac{3\pi}{4}$

**c.**

$-\dfrac{7\pi}{4}$

**d.**

$\dfrac{13\pi}{4}$

**5. a.** 40°   **b.** 225°    **6. a.** $\dfrac{3\pi}{5}$   **b.** $\dfrac{29\pi}{15}$    **7. a.** 135°   **b.** $\dfrac{5\pi}{3}$   **c.** $\dfrac{11\pi}{6}$    **8.** $\dfrac{3\pi}{2}$ in. $\approx 4.71$ in.    **9.** $135\pi$ in./min $\approx 424$ in./min

### Exercise Set 4.1

**1.** obtuse    **3.** acute    **5.** straight    **7.** 4 radians    **9.** $\dfrac{4}{3}$ radians    **11.** 4 radians    **13.** $\dfrac{\pi}{4}$ radians    **15.** $\dfrac{3\pi}{4}$ radians    **17.** $\dfrac{5\pi}{3}$ radians

**19.** $-\dfrac{5\pi}{4}$ radians    **21.** 90°    **23.** 120°    **25.** 210°    **27.** $-540°$    **29.** 0.31 radians    **31.** $-0.70$ radians    **33.** 3.49 radians    **35.** 114.59°

**37.** 13.85°    **39.** $-275.02°$

**41.**

; quadrant III

**43.**

; quadrant II

**45.**
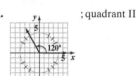
; quadrant III

**47.**

; quadrant II

**49.**

; quadrant III

**51.**
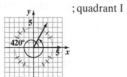
; quadrant II

**53.**
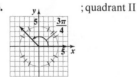
; quadrant II

**55.**
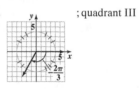
; quadrant I    **57.** 35°    **59.** 210°    **61.** 315°    **63.** $\dfrac{7\pi}{6}$    **65.** $\dfrac{3\pi}{5}$

**67.** $\dfrac{99\pi}{50}$    **69.** $\dfrac{11\pi}{7}$    **71.** $3\pi$ in. $\approx 9.42$ in.    **73.** $10\pi$ ft $\approx 31.42$ ft    **75.** $\dfrac{12\pi \text{ radians}}{\text{second}}$    **77.** $-\dfrac{4\pi}{3}$ and $\dfrac{2\pi}{3}$    **79.** $-\dfrac{3\pi}{4}$ and $\dfrac{5\pi}{4}$

**81.** $-\dfrac{\pi}{2}$ and $\dfrac{3\pi}{2}$  **83.** $\dfrac{11\pi}{6}$  **85.** $\dfrac{22\pi}{3}$  **87.** $60°; \dfrac{\pi}{3}$ radians  **89.** $\dfrac{8\pi}{3}$ in. $\approx 8.38$ in.  **91.** $12\pi$ in. $\approx 37.70$ in.

**93.** 2 radians; 114.59°  **95.** 2094 mi  **97.** 1047 mph  **99.** 1508 ft/min  **113.** 30.25°  **115.** 30°25′12″  **117.** does not make sense

**119.** makes sense  **121.** smaller than a right angle  **123.** 1815 mi

**124.**

**125.** domain: $\{x | -1 \le x \le 1\}$ or $[-1, 1]$; range: $\{y | -1 \le y \le 1\}$ or $[-1, 1]$

**126.** $-\dfrac{\sqrt{3}}{3}$

## Section 4.2

### Check Point Exercises

**1.** $\sin t = \dfrac{1}{2}$; $\cos t = \dfrac{\sqrt{3}}{2}$; $\tan t = \dfrac{\sqrt{3}}{3}$; $\csc t = 2$; $\sec t = \dfrac{2\sqrt{3}}{3}$; $\cot t = \sqrt{3}$  **2.** $\sin \pi = 0$; $\cos \pi = -1$; $\tan \pi = 0$; $\csc \pi$ is undefined;

$\sec \pi = -1$; $\cot \pi$ is undefined  **3.** $\sqrt{2}$; $\sqrt{2}$; 1  **4. a.** $\sqrt{2}$  **b.** $-\dfrac{\sqrt{2}}{2}$  **5.** $\tan \theta = \dfrac{2\sqrt{5}}{5}$; $\csc \theta = \dfrac{3}{2}$; $\sec \theta = \dfrac{3\sqrt{5}}{5}$; $\cot \theta = \dfrac{\sqrt{5}}{2}$  **6.** $\dfrac{\sqrt{3}}{2}$

**7. a.** 1  **b.** $\dfrac{\sqrt{2}}{2}$  **8. a.** 0.7071  **b.** 1.0025

### Exercise Set 4.2

**1.** $\sin t = \dfrac{8}{17}$; $\cos t = -\dfrac{15}{17}$; $\tan t = -\dfrac{8}{15}$; $\csc t = \dfrac{17}{8}$; $\sec t = -\dfrac{17}{15}$; $\cot t = -\dfrac{15}{8}$

**3.** $\sin t = -\dfrac{\sqrt{2}}{2}$; $\cos t = \dfrac{\sqrt{2}}{2}$; $\tan t = -1$; $\csc t = -\sqrt{2}$; $\sec t = \sqrt{2}$; $\cot t = -1$  **5.** $\dfrac{1}{2}$  **7.** $-\dfrac{\sqrt{3}}{2}$  **9.** 0  **11.** $-2$  **13.** $\dfrac{2\sqrt{3}}{3}$  **15.** $-1$

**17.** undefined  **19. a.** $\dfrac{\sqrt{3}}{2}$  **b.** $\dfrac{\sqrt{3}}{2}$  **21. a.** $\dfrac{1}{2}$  **b.** $-\dfrac{1}{2}$  **23. a.** $-\sqrt{3}$  **b.** $\sqrt{3}$

**25.** $\tan t = \dfrac{8}{15}$; $\csc t = \dfrac{17}{8}$; $\sec t = \dfrac{17}{15}$; $\cot t = \dfrac{15}{8}$  **27.** $\tan t = \dfrac{\sqrt{2}}{4}$; $\csc t = 3$; $\sec t = \dfrac{3\sqrt{2}}{4}$; $\cot t = 2\sqrt{2}$  **29.** $\dfrac{\sqrt{13}}{7}$  **31.** $\dfrac{5}{8}$  **33.** 1  **35.** 1

**37.** 1  **39.** $\dfrac{\sqrt{2}}{2}$  **41.** $-\dfrac{\sqrt{2}}{2}$  **43.** 1  **45.** $-1$  **47.** $-1$  **49.** $-\dfrac{\sqrt{2}}{2}$  **51.** $\dfrac{\sqrt{2}}{2}$  **53. a.** $\dfrac{\sqrt{2}}{2}$  **b.** $\dfrac{\sqrt{2}}{2}$  **55. a.** 0  **b.** 0

**57. a.** 0  **b.** 0  **59. a.** $-\dfrac{\sqrt{2}}{2}$  **b.** $-\dfrac{\sqrt{2}}{2}$  **61.** 0.7174  **63.** 0.2643  **65.** 1.1884  **67.** 0.9511  **69.** 3.7321  **71.** $-2a$  **73.** $3b$

**75.** $a - b + c$  **77.** $-a - b + c$  **79.** $3a + 2b - 2c$  **81. a.** 12 hr  **b.** 20.3 hr  **c.** 3.7 hr  **83. a.** 1; 0; −1; 0; 1  **b.** 28 days

**97.** makes sense  **99.** does not make sense  **101.** c  **103.** $-\dfrac{1}{4}$  **105.** $\dfrac{5}{13}$  **106.** $\dfrac{\sqrt{2}}{2}$  **107.** 1

## Section 4.3

### Check Point Exercises

**1.** $\sin \theta = \dfrac{3}{5}$; $\cos \theta = \dfrac{4}{5}$; $\tan \theta = \dfrac{3}{4}$; $\csc \theta = \dfrac{5}{3}$; $\sec \theta = \dfrac{5}{4}$; $\cot \theta = \dfrac{4}{3}$  **2.** $\sin \theta = \dfrac{1}{5}$; $\cos \theta = \dfrac{2\sqrt{6}}{5}$; $\tan \theta = \dfrac{\sqrt{6}}{12}$; $\csc \theta = 5$; $\sec \theta = \dfrac{5\sqrt{6}}{12}$; $\cot \theta = 2\sqrt{6}$

**3.** $\sqrt{2}$; $\sqrt{2}$; 1  **4.** $\sqrt{3}$; $\dfrac{\sqrt{3}}{3}$  **5. a.** $\cos 44°$  **b.** $\tan \dfrac{5\pi}{12}$  **6.** 333.9 yd  **7.** 54°

### Exercise Set 4.3

**1.** 15; $\sin \theta = \dfrac{3}{5}$; $\cos \theta = \dfrac{4}{5}$; $\tan \theta = \dfrac{3}{4}$; $\csc \theta = \dfrac{5}{3}$; $\sec \theta = \dfrac{5}{4}$; $\cot \theta = \dfrac{4}{3}$

**3.** 20; $\sin \theta = \dfrac{20}{29}$; $\cos \theta = \dfrac{21}{29}$; $\tan \theta = \dfrac{20}{21}$; $\csc \theta = \dfrac{29}{20}$; $\sec \theta = \dfrac{29}{21}$; $\cot \theta = \dfrac{21}{20}$

**5.** 24; $\sin \theta = \dfrac{5}{13}$; $\cos \theta = \dfrac{12}{13}$; $\tan \theta = \dfrac{5}{12}$; $\csc \theta = \dfrac{13}{5}$; $\sec \theta = \dfrac{13}{12}$; $\cot \theta = \dfrac{12}{5}$  **7.** 28; $\sin \theta = \dfrac{4}{5}$; $\cos \theta = \dfrac{3}{5}$; $\tan \theta = \dfrac{4}{3}$; $\csc \theta = \dfrac{5}{4}$; $\sec \theta = \dfrac{5}{3}$; $\cot \theta = \dfrac{3}{4}$

**9.** $\dfrac{\sqrt{3}}{2}$  **11.** $\sqrt{2}$  **13.** $\sqrt{3}$  **15.** 0  **17.** $\dfrac{\sqrt{6} - 4}{4}$  **19.** $\dfrac{12\sqrt{3} + \sqrt{6}}{6}$  **21.** $\cos 83°$  **23.** $\sec 65°$  **25.** $\cot \dfrac{7\pi}{18}$  **27.** $\sin \dfrac{\pi}{10}$

**29.** 188 cm  **31.** 182 in.  **33.** 41 m  **35.** 17°  **37.** 78°  **39.** 1.147 radians  **41.** 0.395 radians  **43.** 0  **45.** 2  **47.** 1

**49.** $\dfrac{2\sqrt{3} - 1}{2}$  **51.** $\dfrac{1}{4}$  **53.** 529 yd  **55.** 36°  **57.** 2879 ft  **59.** 37°  **69.** 0.92106, −0.19735; 0.95534, −0.148878; 0.98007, −0.099667;

0.99500, −0.04996; 0.99995, −0.005; 0.9999995, −0.0005; 0.999999995, −0.00005; 0.99999999995, −0.000005; $\dfrac{\cos \theta - 1}{\theta}$ approaches 0 as $\theta$ approaches 0.

**71.** does not make sense  **73.** makes sense  **75.** true  **77.** true  **79.** As $\theta$ approaches 90°, $\tan \theta$ increases without bound. At 90°, $\tan \theta$ is

undefined.  **81. a.** $\dfrac{y}{r}$  **b.** $\dfrac{4}{5}$; positive  **82. a.** $\dfrac{x}{r}$  **b.** $-\dfrac{3\sqrt{34}}{34}$; negative  **83. a.** 15°  **b.** $\dfrac{\pi}{6}$

## Section 4.4

### Check Point Exercises

**1.** $\sin \theta = -\frac{3\sqrt{10}}{10}$; $\cos \theta = \frac{\sqrt{10}}{10}$; $\tan \theta = -3$; $\csc \theta = -\frac{\sqrt{10}}{3}$; $\sec \theta = \sqrt{10}$; $\cot \theta = -\frac{1}{3}$  **2. a.** 1; undefined  **b.** 0; 1  **c.** $-1$; undefined

**d.** 0; $-1$  **3.** quadrant III  **4.** $\frac{\sqrt{10}}{10}$; $-\frac{\sqrt{10}}{3}$  **5. a.** 30°  **b.** $\frac{\pi}{4}$  **c.** 60°  **d.** 0.46  **6. a.** 55°  **b.** $\frac{\pi}{4}$  **c.** $\frac{\pi}{3}$

**7. a.** $-\frac{\sqrt{3}}{2}$  **b.** 1  **c.** $\frac{2\sqrt{3}}{3}$  **8. a.** $-\frac{\sqrt{3}}{2}$  **b.** $\frac{\sqrt{3}}{2}$

### Exercise Set 4.4

**1.** $\sin \theta = \frac{3}{5}$; $\cos \theta = -\frac{4}{5}$; $\tan \theta = -\frac{3}{4}$; $\csc \theta = \frac{5}{3}$; $\sec \theta = -\frac{5}{4}$; $\cot \theta = -\frac{4}{3}$

**3.** $\sin \theta = \frac{3\sqrt{13}}{13}$; $\cos \theta = \frac{2\sqrt{13}}{13}$; $\tan \theta = \frac{3}{2}$; $\csc \theta = \frac{\sqrt{13}}{3}$; $\sec \theta = \frac{\sqrt{13}}{2}$; $\cot \theta = \frac{2}{3}$  **5.** $\sin \theta = -\frac{\sqrt{2}}{2}$; $\cos \theta = \frac{\sqrt{2}}{2}$; $\tan \theta = -1$; $\csc \theta = -\sqrt{2}$;

$\sec \theta = \sqrt{2}$; $\cot \theta = -1$  **7.** $\sin \theta = -\frac{5\sqrt{29}}{29}$; $\cos \theta = -\frac{2\sqrt{29}}{29}$; $\tan \theta = \frac{5}{2}$; $\csc \theta = -\frac{\sqrt{29}}{5}$; $\sec \theta = -\frac{\sqrt{29}}{2}$; $\cot \theta = \frac{2}{5}$  **9.** $-1$  **11.** $-1$

**13.** undefined  **15.** 0  **17.** quadrant I  **19.** quadrant III  **21.** quadrant II

**23.** $\sin \theta = -\frac{4}{5}$; $\tan \theta = \frac{4}{3}$; $\csc \theta = -\frac{5}{4}$; $\sec \theta = -\frac{5}{3}$; $\cot \theta = \frac{3}{4}$  **25.** $\cos \theta = -\frac{12}{13}$; $\tan \theta = -\frac{5}{12}$; $\csc \theta = \frac{13}{5}$; $\sec \theta = -\frac{13}{12}$; $\cot \theta = -\frac{12}{5}$

**27.** $\sin \theta = -\frac{15}{17}$; $\tan \theta = -\frac{15}{8}$; $\csc \theta = -\frac{17}{15}$; $\sec \theta = \frac{17}{8}$; $\cot \theta = -\frac{8}{15}$  **29.** $\sin \theta = \frac{2\sqrt{13}}{13}$; $\cos \theta = -\frac{3\sqrt{13}}{13}$; $\csc \theta = \frac{\sqrt{13}}{2}$; $\sec \theta = -\frac{\sqrt{13}}{3}$; $\cot \theta = -\frac{3}{2}$

**31.** $\sin \theta = -\frac{4}{5}$; $\cos \theta = -\frac{3}{5}$; $\csc \theta = -\frac{5}{4}$; $\sec \theta = -\frac{5}{3}$; $\cot \theta = \frac{3}{4}$  **33.** $\sin \theta = -\frac{2\sqrt{2}}{3}$; $\cos \theta = -\frac{1}{3}$; $\tan \theta = 2\sqrt{2}$; $\csc \theta = -\frac{3\sqrt{2}}{4}$; $\cot \theta = \frac{\sqrt{2}}{4}$

**35.** 20°  **37.** 25°  **39.** 5°  **41.** $\frac{\pi}{4}$  **43.** $\frac{\pi}{6}$  **45.** 30°  **47.** 25°  **49.** 1.56  **51.** 25°  **53.** $\frac{\pi}{6}$  **55.** $\frac{\pi}{4}$  **57.** $\frac{\pi}{4}$  **59.** $\frac{\pi}{6}$

**61.** $-\frac{\sqrt{2}}{2}$  **63.** $\frac{\sqrt{3}}{3}$  **65.** $\sqrt{3}$  **67.** $\frac{\sqrt{3}}{2}$  **69.** $-2$  **71.** 1  **73.** $\frac{\sqrt{3}}{2}$  **75.** $-1$  **77.** $-\sqrt{2}$  **79.** $\sqrt{3}$  **81.** $\frac{\sqrt{2}}{2}$  **83.** $\frac{\sqrt{3}}{3}$

**85.** $\frac{\sqrt{3}}{2}$  **87.** $\frac{1-\sqrt{3}}{2}$  **89.** $\frac{-\sqrt{6}-\sqrt{2}}{4}$ or $-\frac{\sqrt{6}+\sqrt{2}}{4}$  **91.** $-\frac{3}{2}$  **93.** $\frac{-1-\sqrt{3}}{2}$ or $-\frac{1+\sqrt{3}}{2}$  **95.** 1  **97.** $\frac{2\sqrt{2}-4}{\pi}$  **99.** $\frac{\pi}{4}$ and $\frac{3\pi}{4}$

**101.** $\frac{5\pi}{4}$ and $\frac{7\pi}{4}$  **103.** $\frac{2\pi}{3}$ and $\frac{5\pi}{3}$  **111.** does not make sense  **113.** makes sense  **114.** $\frac{1}{2}$; 0; $-\frac{1}{2}$; 0; $\frac{1}{2}$  **115.** 0; 4; 0; $-4$; 0

**116.** 0; $\frac{3}{2}$; 3; $\frac{3}{2}$; 0; $-\frac{3}{2}$; $-3$; $-\frac{3}{2}$; 0

## Mid-Chapter 4 Check Point

**1.** $\frac{\pi}{18}$  **2.** $-\frac{7\pi}{12}$  **3.** 75°  **4.** $-117°$

**5. a.** $\frac{5\pi}{3}$  **6. a.** $\frac{5\pi}{4}$  **7. a.** 150°

**b.**

**b.**

**b.**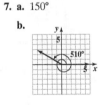

**c.** $\frac{\pi}{3}$  **c.** $\frac{\pi}{4}$  **c.** 30°

**8.** $\sin t = -\frac{4}{5}$; $\cos t = -\frac{3}{5}$; $\tan t = \frac{4}{3}$; $\csc t = -\frac{5}{4}$; $\sec t = -\frac{5}{3}$; $\cot t = \frac{3}{4}$  **9.** $\sin \theta = \frac{5}{6}$; $\cos \theta = \frac{\sqrt{11}}{6}$; $\tan \theta = \frac{5\sqrt{11}}{11}$; $\csc \theta = \frac{6}{5}$; $\sec \theta = \frac{6\sqrt{11}}{11}$;

$\cot \theta = \frac{\sqrt{11}}{5}$  **10.** $\sin \theta = -\frac{2\sqrt{13}}{13}$; $\cos \theta = \frac{3\sqrt{13}}{13}$; $\tan \theta = -\frac{2}{3}$; $\csc \theta = -\frac{\sqrt{13}}{2}$; $\sec \theta = \frac{\sqrt{13}}{3}$; $\cot \theta = -\frac{3}{2}$  **11.** $\sin \theta = \frac{3}{5}$; $\cos \theta = -\frac{4}{5}$; $\csc \theta = \frac{5}{3}$;

$\sec \theta = -\frac{5}{4}$; $\cot \theta = -\frac{4}{3}$  **12.** $\sin \theta = -\frac{2\sqrt{10}}{7}$; $\tan \theta = -\frac{2\sqrt{10}}{3}$; $\csc \theta = -\frac{7\sqrt{10}}{20}$; $\sec \theta = \frac{7}{3}$; $\cot \theta = -\frac{3\sqrt{10}}{20}$  **13.** 52 cm  **14.** 809 m

**15.** $\sqrt{35}$  **16.** $\frac{\sqrt{3}}{3}$  **17.** $-\frac{\sqrt{3}}{3}$  **18.** $-\frac{1}{2}$  **19.** $\frac{2\sqrt{3}}{3}$  **20.** 1  **21.** $-\frac{\sqrt{3}}{2}$  **22.** $-\frac{2\sqrt{3}}{3}$  **23.** $-\frac{\sqrt{2}}{2}$  **24.** $\frac{\sqrt{3}}{3}$  **25.** 2

**26.** $-\frac{5\sqrt{3}}{6}$  **27.** $8\pi$ cm $\approx 25.13$ cm  **28.** $160\pi$ ft/min $\approx 502$ ft/min  **29.** 551.9 ft  **30.** 40°

## Section 4.5

### Check Point Exercises

**1.** 3

**2.** $\frac{1}{2}$

**3.** $2; 4\pi$

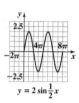

$y = 2 \sin \frac{1}{2} x$

**4.** $3; \pi; \frac{\pi}{6}$

$y = 3 \sin \left(2x - \frac{\pi}{3}\right)$

**5.** $4; 2$

$y = -4 \cos \pi x$

**6.** $\frac{3}{2}; \pi; -\frac{\pi}{2}$

$y = \frac{3}{2} \cos(2x + \pi)$

**7.**

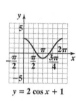

$y = 2 \cos x + 1$

**8.** $y = 4 \sin 4x$

**9.** $y = 2 \sin \left(\frac{\pi}{6} x - \frac{\pi}{2}\right) + 12$

## Exercise Set 4.5

**1.** 4

**3.** $\frac{1}{3}$

**5.** 3

$y = -3 \sin x$

**7.** $1; \pi$

$y = \sin 2x$

**9.** $3; 4\pi$

$y = 3 \sin \frac{1}{2} x$

**11.** $4; 2$

$y = 4 \sin \pi x$

**13.** $3; 1$

$y = -3 \sin 2\pi x$

**15.** $1; 3\pi$

$y = -\sin \frac{2}{3} x$

**17.** $1; 2\pi; \pi$

$y = \sin (x - \pi)$

**19.** $1; \pi; \frac{\pi}{2}$

$y = \sin (2x - \pi)$

**21.** $3; \pi; \frac{\pi}{2}$

$y = 3 \sin (2x - \pi)$

**23.** $\frac{1}{2}; 2\pi; -\frac{\pi}{2}$

$y = \frac{1}{2} \sin \left(x + \frac{\pi}{2}\right)$

**25.** $2; \pi; -\frac{\pi}{4}$

$y = -2 \sin \left(2x + \frac{\pi}{2}\right)$

**27.** $3; 2; -\frac{2}{\pi}$

$y = 3 \sin (\pi x + 2)$

**29.** $2; 1; -2$

$y = -2 \sin (2\pi x + 4\pi)$

**31.** 2

$y = 2 \cos x$ / $y = \cos x$

**33.** 2

$y = \cos x$ / $y = -2 \cos x$

**35.** $1; \pi$

$y = \cos 2x$

**37.** $4; 1$

$y = 4 \cos 2\pi x$

**39.** $4; 4\pi$

$y = -4 \cos \frac{1}{2} x$

**41.** $\frac{1}{2}$; 6

$$y = -\frac{1}{2}\cos\frac{\pi}{3}x$$

**43.** $1; 2\pi, \frac{\pi}{2}$

$$y = \cos\left(x - \frac{\pi}{2}\right)$$

**45.** $3; \pi; \frac{\pi}{2}$

$$y = 3\cos(2x - \pi)$$

**47.** $\frac{1}{2}; \frac{2\pi}{3}; -\frac{\pi}{6}$

$$y = \frac{1}{2}\cos\left(3x + \frac{\pi}{2}\right)$$

**49.** $3; \pi; \frac{\pi}{4}$

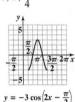

$$y = -3\cos\left(2x - \frac{\pi}{2}\right)$$

**51.** $2; 1; -4$

$$y = 2\cos(2\pi x + 8\pi)$$

**53.**

$$y = \sin x + 2$$

**55.**

$$y = \cos x - 3$$

**57.**

$$y = 2\sin\frac{1}{2}x + 1$$

**59.**

$$y = -3\cos 2\pi x + 2$$

**61.** One possibility: $y = 3\cos\left(\frac{1}{2}x\right)$

**63.** One possibility: $y = -2\sin(2x)$

**65.** One possibility: $y = 2\sin\left(\frac{\pi}{2}x\right)$

**67.**

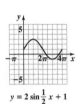

$$y = \left|2\cos\frac{x}{2}\right|$$

**69.**

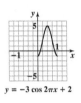

$$y = -|3\sin \pi x|$$

**71.**

**73.**

**75.** 33 days    **77.** 23 days    **79.** March 21    **81.** No

**83.**

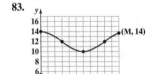

**85. a.** 3    **b.** 365 days    **c.** 15 hours of daylight    **87.** $y = 3\cos\frac{\pi x}{6} + 9$

**d.** 9 hours of daylight

**e.**

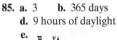

**101.**

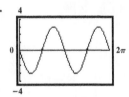

**103.**

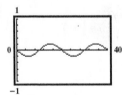

**105.**

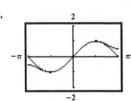

**107.**

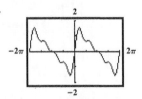

The graph is similar to $y = \sin x$, except the amplitude is greater and the curve is less smooth.

**109. a.**

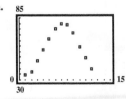

**b.** $y = 22.61 \sin(0.50x - 2.04) + 57.17$    **111.** makes sense    **113.** makes sense

**c.**

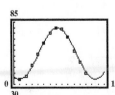

**115. a.** range: $[-5, 1]$; $\left[-\frac{\pi}{6}, \frac{23\pi}{6}, \frac{\pi}{6}\right]$ by $[-5, 1, 1]$

**b.** range: $[-3, -1]$; $\left[-\frac{\pi}{6}, \frac{7\pi}{6}, \frac{\pi}{6}\right]$ by $[-3, -1, 1]$

**117.**

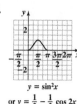

$y = \sin^2 x$

or $y = \frac{1}{2} - \frac{1}{2}\cos 2x$

**120.** $\left\{ x \Big| -\frac{3\pi}{4} < x < \frac{\pi}{4} \right\}$ or $\left( -\frac{3\pi}{4}, \frac{\pi}{4} \right)$    **121.** $-\frac{\pi}{4}$

**122. a.**

$y = -3\cos\frac{x}{2}$

**b.** The reciprocal function is undefined.

## Section 4.6

### Check Point Exercises

**1.**

$y = 3\tan 2x$

**2.**

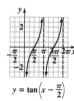

$y = \tan\left(x - \frac{\pi}{2}\right)$

**3.**

$y = \frac{1}{2}\cot\frac{\pi}{2}x$

**4.**

$y = \csc\left(x + \frac{\pi}{4}\right)$

**5.**

$y = 2\sec 2x$

### Exercise Set 4.6

**1.** $y = \tan(x + \pi)$    **3.** $y = -\tan\left(x - \frac{\pi}{2}\right)$

**5.**

$y = 3\tan\frac{x}{4}$

**7.**

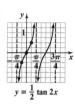

$y = \frac{1}{2}\tan 2x$

**9.**

$y = -2\tan\frac{1}{2}x$

**11.**

$y = \tan(x - \pi)$

**13.** $y = -\cot x$

**15.** $y = \cot\left(x + \frac{\pi}{2}\right)$

**17.**

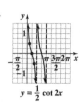

$y = 2\cot x$

**19.**

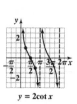

$y = \frac{1}{2}\cot 2x$

**21.**

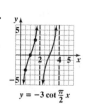

$y = -3\cot\frac{\pi}{2}x$

**23.**

$y = 3\cot\left(x + \frac{\pi}{2}\right)$

**25.** $y = -\frac{1}{2}\csc\frac{x}{2}$

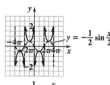

$y = -\frac{1}{2}\sin\frac{x}{2}$

$y = -\frac{1}{2}\csc\frac{x}{2}$

**27.** $y = \frac{1}{2}\sec 2\pi x$

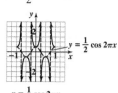

$y = \frac{1}{2}\cos 2\pi x$

$y = \frac{1}{2}\sec 2\pi x$

**29.**

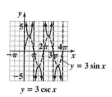

$y = 3\sin x$

$y = 3\csc x$

**31.**

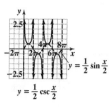

$y = \frac{1}{2}\sin\frac{x}{2}$

$y = \frac{1}{2}\csc\frac{x}{2}$

**33.**

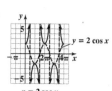

$y = 2\cos x$

$y = 2\sec x$

**35.**

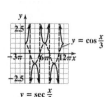

$y = \cos\frac{x}{3}$

$y = \sec\frac{x}{3}$

**37.**

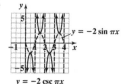

$y = -2\sin \pi x$

$y = -2\csc \pi x$

**39.**

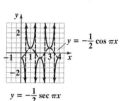

$y = -\frac{1}{2}\cos \pi x$

$y = -\frac{1}{2}\sec \pi x$

**41.**

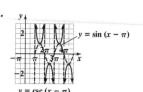

$y = \sin(x - \pi)$

$y = \csc(x - \pi)$

**43.**

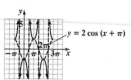

$y = 2\cos(x + \pi)$

$y = 2\sec(x + \pi)$

**45.**

$y = 2\tan\left(x - \frac{\pi}{6}\right) + 1$

**47.**

$y = \sec\left(2x + \frac{\pi}{2}\right) - 1$

**49.**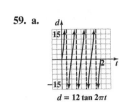

**51.**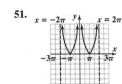

**53.**

**55.** $\left\{ -\dfrac{5\pi}{4}, -\dfrac{\pi}{4}, \dfrac{3\pi}{4}, \dfrac{7\pi}{4} \right\}$

**57.** $\left\{ -\dfrac{3\pi}{2}, \dfrac{\pi}{2} \right\}$

**59. a.**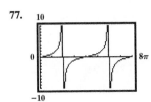

**b.** $0.25, 0.75, 1.25, 1.75$;
The beam of light is shining parallel to the wall at these times.

**61.** $d = 10 \sec x$

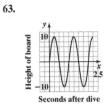

**63.**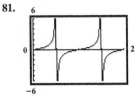

**77.**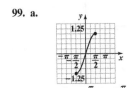

**79.**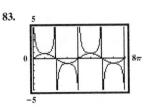

**81.**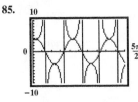

**83.**

**85.**

**87.**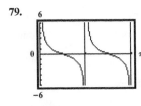

**89.** makes sense **91.** does not make sense **93.** $y = \cot \dfrac{3}{2}x$ **95.** $y = 2\csc \dfrac{3x}{2}$ **97. a.** range: $(-\infty, -1] \cup [1, \infty)$; $\left[ -\dfrac{\pi}{6}, \pi, \dfrac{7\pi}{6} \right]$ by $[-3, 3, 1]$

**b.** range: $(-\infty, -3] \cup [3, \infty)$; $\left[ -\dfrac{1}{2}, \dfrac{7}{2}, 1 \right]$ by $[-6, 6, 1]$

**99. a.**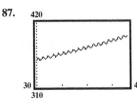

**b.** yes **c.** $-\dfrac{\pi}{6}, \left( -\dfrac{\pi}{6}, -\dfrac{1}{2} \right)$ **100. a.**  **b.** yes **c.** $\dfrac{5\pi}{6}, \left( \dfrac{5\pi}{6}, -\dfrac{\sqrt{3}}{2} \right)$

**101. a.**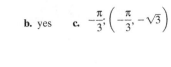

**b.** yes **c.** $-\dfrac{\pi}{3}, \left( -\dfrac{\pi}{3}, -\sqrt{3} \right)$

## Section 4.7

**Check Point Exercises**

**1.** $\dfrac{\pi}{3}$ **2.** $-\dfrac{\pi}{4}$ **3.** $\dfrac{2\pi}{3}$ **4.** $-\dfrac{\pi}{4}$ **5. a.** $1.2310$ **b.** $-1.5429$ **6. a.** $0.7$ **b.** $0$ **c.** not defined **7.** $\dfrac{3}{5}$ **8.** $\dfrac{\sqrt{3}}{2}$ **9.** $\sqrt{x^2 + 1}$

**Exercise Set 4.7**

**1.** $\dfrac{\pi}{6}$ **3.** $\dfrac{\pi}{4}$ **5.** $-\dfrac{\pi}{6}$ **7.** $\dfrac{\pi}{6}$ **9.** $\dfrac{3\pi}{4}$ **11.** $\dfrac{\pi}{2}$ **13.** $\dfrac{\pi}{6}$ **15.** $0$ **17.** $-\dfrac{\pi}{3}$ **19.** $0.30$ **21.** $-0.33$ **23.** $1.19$ **25.** $1.25$

**27.** $-1.52$ **29.** $-1.52$ **31.** $0.9$ **33.** $\dfrac{\pi}{3}$ **35.** $\dfrac{\pi}{6}$ **37.** $125$ **39.** $-\dfrac{\pi}{6}$ **41.** $-\dfrac{\pi}{3}$ **43.** $0$ **45.** not defined **47.** $\dfrac{3}{5}$ **49.** $\dfrac{12}{5}$

**51.** $-\dfrac{3}{4}$   **53.** $\dfrac{\sqrt{2}}{2}$   **55.** $\dfrac{4\sqrt{15}}{15}$   **57.** $-2\sqrt{2}$   **59.** $2$   **61.** $\dfrac{3\sqrt{13}}{13}$   **63.** $\dfrac{\sqrt{1-x^2}}{x}$   **65.** $\sqrt{1-4x^2}$   **67.** $\dfrac{\sqrt{x^2-1}}{x}$   **69.** $\dfrac{\sqrt{3}}{x}$

**71.** $\dfrac{\sqrt{x^2+4}}{2}$   **73. a.**

$y = \sec x$

**b.** No horizontal line intersects the graph of $y = \sec x$ more than once, so the function is one-to-one and has an inverse function.

**c.**

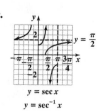

$y = \sec x$
$y = \sec^{-1} x$

**75.**

$f(x) = \sin^{-1} x + \dfrac{\pi}{2}$

domain: $[-1, 1]$;

range: $[0, \pi]$

**77.**

$g(x) = \cos^{-1}(x + 1)$

domain: $[-2, 0]$;

range: $[0, \pi]$

**79.**

$f(x) = -2\tan^{-1} x$

domain: $(-\infty, \infty)$;

range: $(-\pi, \pi)$

**81.**

$f(x) = \sin^{-1}(x - 2) - \dfrac{\pi}{2}$

domain: $[1, 3]$;

range: $[-\pi, 0]$

**83.**

$g(x) = \cos^{-1}\dfrac{x}{2}$

domain: $[-2, 2]$;

range: $[0, \pi]$

**85.** domain: $[-1, 1]$; range: $[-1, 1]$   **87.** domain: $(-\infty, \infty)$; range: $[0, \pi]$

**89.** domain: $(-\infty, \infty)$; range: $\left[-\dfrac{\pi}{2}, \dfrac{\pi}{2}\right]$   **91.** domain: $[-1, 1]$; range: $\left\{\dfrac{\pi}{2}\right\}$

**93.** 0.408 radians; 0.602 radians; 0.654 radians; 0.645 radians; 0.613 radians

**95.** 1.3157 radians or 75.4°

**97.** 1.1071 sq units   **111.**

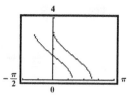

**113.**

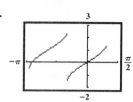

Shifted left 2 units and up 1 unit

**115.**

It seems
$$\sin^{-1} x + \cos^{-1} x = \dfrac{\pi}{2} \text{ for } -1 \le x \le 1.$$

**117.** does not make sense   **119.** does not make sense   **121.** $x = \sin\dfrac{\pi}{8}$

**123.** $\tan\alpha = \dfrac{8}{x}$, so $\tan^{-1}\dfrac{8}{x} = \alpha$. $\tan(\alpha + \theta) = \dfrac{33}{x}$, so $\tan^{-1}\dfrac{33}{x} = \alpha + \theta$. $\theta = \alpha + \theta - \alpha = \tan^{-1}\dfrac{33}{x} - \tan^{-1}\dfrac{8}{x}$.   **124.** $a \approx 4.96$; $c \approx 13.08$

**125.** 35.8°   **126.** amplitude: 10; period: 12

# Section 4.8

## Check Point Exercises

**1.** $B = 27.3°$; $b \approx 4.34$; $c \approx 9.45$   **2.** 994 ft   **3.** 29.0°   **4.** 60.3 ft   **5. a.** S 25°E   **b.** S 15°W   **6. a.** 4.2 m   **b.** S87.7°W

**7.** $d = -6\cos\dfrac{\pi}{2}t$   **8. a.** 12 cm   **b.** $\dfrac{1}{8}$ cm per sec   **c.** 8 sec

## Exercise Set 4.8

**1.** $B = 66.5°$; $a \approx 4.35$; $c \approx 10.90$   **3.** $B = 37.4°$; $a \approx 42.90$; $b \approx 32.80$   **5.** $A = 73.2°$; $a \approx 101.02$; $c \approx 105.52$
**7.** $b \approx 39.95$; $A \approx 37.3°$; $B \approx 52.7°$   **9.** $c \approx 26.96$; $A \approx 23.6°$; $B \approx 66.4°$   **11.** $a \approx 6.71$; $B \approx 16.6°$; $A \approx 73.4°$   **13.** N 15° E

**15.** S 80° W   **17.** $d = -6\cos\dfrac{\pi}{2}t$   **19.** $d = -3\sin\dfrac{4\pi}{3}t$

**21. a.** 5 in.   **b.** $\dfrac{1}{4}$ in. per sec   **c.** 4 sec   **23. a.** 6 in.   **b.** 1 in. per sec   **c.** 1 sec   **25. a.** $\dfrac{1}{2}$ in.   **b.** 0.32 in. per sec   **c.** 3.14 sec

**27. a.** 5 in.   **b.** $\dfrac{1}{3}$ in. per sec   **c.** 3 sec   **29.** 653 units   **31.** 39 units   **33.** 298 units   **35.** 257 units

**37.**

$$d = 4\cos\left(\pi t - \frac{\pi}{2}\right)$$

**39.**

$$d = -2\sin\left(\frac{\pi}{4}t + \frac{\pi}{2}\right)$$

**41.** 2059 ft    **43.** 695 ft    **45.** 1376 ft    **47.** 15.1°    **49.** 33.7 ft
**51.** 90 mi north and 120 mi east    **53.** 13.2 mi    **55.** N 53° W
**57.** N 89.5° E    **59.** $d = 6\sin \pi t$    **61.** $d = \sin 528\,\pi t$

**a.** 4 in.    **b.** $\frac{1}{2}$ in. per sec       **a.** 2 in.    **b.** $\frac{1}{8}$ in. per sec
**c.** 2 sec    **d.** $\frac{1}{2}$                   **c.** 8 sec    **d.** $-2$

**71.**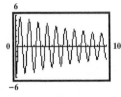

10 complete oscillations

**73.** does not make sense
**75.** does not make sense
**77.** 48 ft
**79.** csc $x$
**80.** 1
**81.** $\dfrac{1 + \sin x}{\cos x}$

## Chapter 4 Review Exercises

**1.** 4.5 radians    **2.** $\frac{\pi}{12}$ radians    **3.** $\frac{2\pi}{3}$ radians    **4.** $\frac{7\pi}{4}$ radians    **5.** 300°    **6.** 252°    **7.** $-150°$

**8.**     **9.**     **10.**     **11.**     **12.**

**13.** 40°    **14.** 275°    **15.** $\frac{5\pi}{4}$    **16.** $\frac{7\pi}{6}$    **17.** $\frac{4\pi}{3}$    **18.** $\frac{15\pi}{2}$ ft $\approx$ 23.56 ft    **19.** 20.6$\pi$ radians per min    **20.** 42,412 ft per min

**21.** $\sin t = -\frac{3}{5}; \cos t = -\frac{4}{5}; \tan t = \frac{3}{4}; \csc t = -\frac{5}{3}; \sec t = -\frac{5}{4}; \cot t = \frac{4}{3}$

**22.** $\sin t = -\frac{15}{17}; \cos t = \frac{8}{17}; \tan t = -\frac{15}{8}; \csc t = -\frac{17}{15}; \sec t = \frac{17}{8}; \cot t = -\frac{8}{15}$

**23.** $-\frac{2\sqrt{3}}{3}$    **24.** $\sqrt{3}$    **25.** undefined    **26.** undefined    **27.** $\cos t = \frac{\sqrt{21}}{7}; \tan t = \frac{2\sqrt{3}}{3}; \csc t = \frac{\sqrt{7}}{2}; \sec t = \frac{\sqrt{21}}{3}; \cot t = \frac{\sqrt{3}}{2}$    **28.** 1

**29.** 1    **30.** $-1$    **31.** $\sin \theta = \frac{5\sqrt{89}}{89}; \cos \theta = \frac{3\sqrt{89}}{89}; \tan \theta = \frac{5}{8}; \csc \theta = \frac{\sqrt{89}}{5}; \sec \theta = \frac{\sqrt{89}}{8}; \cot \theta = \frac{3}{5}$    **32.** $\frac{7}{2}$    **33.** $-\frac{1}{2}$    **34.** 1    **35.** 1

**36.** $\cos 20°$    **37.** $\sin 0$    **38.** 42 mm    **39.** 23 cm    **40.** 37 in.    **41.** $\sqrt{15}$    **42.** 772 ft    **43.** 31 m    **44.** 56°    **45.** $\sin \theta = -\frac{5\sqrt{26}}{26};$

$\cos \theta = -\frac{\sqrt{26}}{26}; \tan \theta = 5; \csc \theta = -\frac{\sqrt{26}}{5}; \sec \theta = -\sqrt{26}; \cot \theta = \frac{1}{5}$    **46.** $\sin \theta = -1; \cos \theta = 0; \tan \theta$ is undefined; $\csc \theta = -1; \sec \theta$ is undefined;

$\cot \theta = 0$    **47.** quadrant I    **48.** quadrant III    **49.** $\sin \theta = -\frac{\sqrt{21}}{5}; \tan \theta = -\frac{\sqrt{21}}{2}; \csc \theta = -\frac{5\sqrt{21}}{21}; \sec \theta = \frac{5}{2}; \cot \theta = -\frac{2\sqrt{21}}{21}$

**50.** $\sin \theta = \frac{\sqrt{10}}{10}; \cos \theta = -\frac{3\sqrt{10}}{10}; \csc \theta = \sqrt{10}; \sec \theta = -\frac{\sqrt{10}}{3}; \cot \theta = -3$    **51.** $\sin \theta = -\frac{\sqrt{10}}{10}; \cos \theta = -\frac{3\sqrt{10}}{10}; \tan \theta = \frac{1}{3}; \csc \theta = -\sqrt{10};$

$\sec \theta = -\frac{\sqrt{10}}{3}$    **52.** 85°    **53.** $\frac{3\pi}{8}$    **54.** 50°    **55.** $\frac{\pi}{6}$    **56.** $\frac{\pi}{3}$    **57.** $-\frac{\sqrt{3}}{2}$    **58.** $-\sqrt{3}$    **59.** $\sqrt{2}$    **60.** $\frac{\sqrt{3}}{2}$    **61.** $-\sqrt{3}$

**62.** $-\frac{2\sqrt{3}}{3}$    **63.** $-\frac{\sqrt{3}}{2}$    **64.** $\frac{\sqrt{2}}{2}$    **65.** 1    **66.** $-\frac{\sqrt{3}}{2}$    **67.** $\frac{\sqrt{3}}{2}$

**68.**

$y = 3 \sin 4x$

**69.**

$y = -2 \cos 2x$

**70.**

$y = 2 \cos \frac{1}{2}x$

**71.**

$y = \frac{1}{2} \sin \frac{\pi}{3}x$

**72.**

$y = -\sin \pi x$

**73.**

$y = 3 \cos \frac{x}{3}$

**74.**

$y = 2 \sin (x - \pi)$

**75.**

$y = -3 \cos (x + \pi)$

**76.**

$y = \frac{3}{2} \cos\left(2x + \frac{\pi}{4}\right)$

**77.**

$y = \frac{5}{2} \sin\left(2x + \frac{\pi}{2}\right)$

**78.**

$y = -3 \sin\left(\frac{\pi}{3}x - 3\pi\right)$

**79.**

$y = \sin 2x + 1$

**80.**
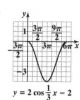
$y = 2 \cos\frac{1}{3}x - 2$

**81. a.** $\approx 98.52°$   **b.** 24 hr   **c.** 5:00 p.m.; 98.9°   **d.** 5:00 a.m.; 98.3°
**e.**
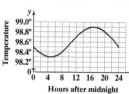

**82.** blue: $y = \sin\frac{\pi}{240}x$; red: $y = \sin\frac{\pi}{320}x$

**83.**

$y = 4 \tan 2x$

**84.**

$y = -2 \tan\frac{\pi}{4}x$

**85.**

$y = \tan(x + \pi)$

**86.**
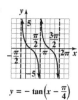
$y = -\tan\left(x - \frac{\pi}{4}\right)$

**87.**
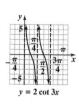
$y = 2 \cot 3x$

**88.**
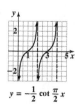
$y = -\frac{1}{2} \cot\frac{\pi}{2}x$

**89.**
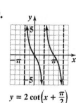
$y = 2 \cot\left(x + \frac{\pi}{2}\right)$

**90.**
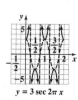
$y = 3 \sec 2\pi x$

**91.**

$y = -2 \csc \pi x$

**92.**
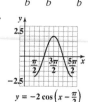
$y = 3 \sec(x + \pi)$

**93.**

$y = \frac{5}{2} \csc(x - \pi)$

**94.** $\frac{\pi}{2}$   **95.** 0   **96.** $\frac{\pi}{4}$

**97.** $-\frac{\pi}{3}$   **98.** $\frac{2\pi}{3}$   **99.** $-\frac{\pi}{6}$

**100.** $\frac{\sqrt{2}}{2}$   **101.** 1   **102.** $-\frac{\sqrt{3}}{3}$

**103.** $-\frac{\sqrt{3}}{3}$   **104.** 2   **105.** $\frac{4}{5}$   **106.** $\frac{4}{5}$

**107.** $-\frac{3}{4}$   **108.** $-\frac{3}{4}$   **109.** $-\frac{\sqrt{10}}{10}$   **110.** $\frac{\pi}{3}$   **111.** $\frac{\pi}{3}$   **112.** $-\frac{\pi}{6}$   **113.** $\frac{2\sqrt{x^2 + 4}}{x^2 + 4}$   **114.** $\frac{x\sqrt{x^2 - 1}}{x^2 - 1}$

**115.** $B \approx 67.7°$; $a \approx 37.9$; $b \approx 9.25$   **116.** $A \approx 52.6°$; $a \approx 7.85$; $c \approx 9.88$   **117.** $A \approx 16.6°$; $B \approx 73.4°$; $b \approx 6.71$

**118.** $A \approx 21.3°$; $B \approx 68.7°$; $c \approx 3.86$   **119.** 38 ft   **120.** 90 yd   **121.** 21.7 ft   **122.** N 35° E   **123.** S 35° W   **124.** 24.6 mi

**125. a.** 1282.2 mi   **b.** S 74° E   **126. a.** 20 cm   **b.** $\frac{1}{8}$ cm per sec   **c.** 8 sec   **127. a.** $\frac{1}{2}$ cm   **b.** 0.64 cm per sec   **c.** 1.57 sec

**128.** $d = -30 \cos \pi t$   **129.** $d = -\frac{1}{4} \sin\frac{2\pi}{5}t$

## Chapter 4 Test

**1.** $\frac{3\pi}{4}$ radians   **2.** $\frac{25\pi}{3}$ ft $\approx 26.18$ ft   **3. a.** $\frac{4\pi}{3}$   **b.** $\frac{\pi}{3}$

**4.** $\sin\theta = \frac{5\sqrt{29}}{29}$; $\cos\theta = -\frac{2\sqrt{29}}{29}$; $\tan\theta = -\frac{5}{2}$; $\csc\theta = \frac{\sqrt{29}}{5}$; $\sec\theta = -\frac{\sqrt{29}}{2}$; $\cot\theta = -\frac{2}{5}$   **5.** quadrant III

**6.** $\sin\theta = -\frac{2\sqrt{2}}{3}$; $\tan\theta = -2\sqrt{2}$; $\csc\theta = -\frac{3\sqrt{2}}{4}$; $\sec\theta = 3$; $\cot\theta = -\frac{\sqrt{2}}{4}$   **7.** $\frac{\sqrt{3}}{6}$   **8.** $-\sqrt{3}$   **9.** $-\frac{\sqrt{2}}{2}$   **10.** $-2$   **11.** $\frac{\sqrt{3}}{3}$

**12.** $\sqrt{3}$   **13. a.** $-a + b$ or $b - a$   **b.** $\frac{a}{b} - \frac{1}{b}$ or $\frac{a - 1}{b}$

**14.**

$y = 3 \sin 2x$

**15.**
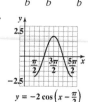
$y = -2 \cos\left(x - \frac{\pi}{2}\right)$

**16.**

$y = 2 \tan\frac{x}{2}$

**17.**

$y = -\frac{1}{2} \csc \pi x$

**18.** $-\sqrt{3}$   **19.** $\dfrac{\sqrt{9-x^2}}{3}$   **20.** $B = 69°; a = 4.7; b = 12.1$   **21.** 23 yd   **22.** 36.1°   **23.** N 80° W   **24. a.** 6 in.   **b.** $\dfrac{1}{2}$ in. per sec
**c.** 2 sec   **25.** Trigonometric functions are periodic.

## Cumulative Review Exercises (Chapters P–4)

**1.** $\{-3, 6\}$   **2.** $\{-5, -2, 2\}$   **3.** $\{4\}$   **4.** $\{7\}$   **5.** $\{-1, 2, 3\}$   **6.** $-3 \le x \le 8$   **7.** $f^{-1}(x) = x^2 + 6$
**8.** $4x^2 - \dfrac{14}{5}x - \dfrac{17}{25} + \dfrac{284}{125x + 50}$   **9.** $\log 1000 = 3$   **10.** 280°   **11.** 3 positive real roots; 1 negative real root

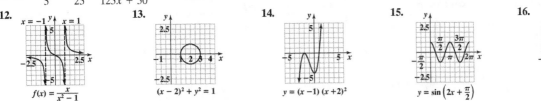

**17.** 48 performances   **18. a.** $A = 110e^{0.1251t}$ where $t$ is the number of years after 2000   **b.** 8 years after 2000, or 2008   **19.** 1540 Btu per hr
**20.** 76°

# CHAPTER 5

## Section 5.1

### Check Point Exercises

**1.** $\csc x \tan x = \dfrac{1}{\sin x} \cdot \dfrac{\sin x}{\cos x} = \dfrac{1}{\cos x} = \sec x$

**2.** $\cos x \cot x + \sin x = \cos x \cdot \dfrac{\cos x}{\sin x} + \sin x = \dfrac{\cos^2 x}{\sin x} + \sin x \cdot \dfrac{\sin x}{\sin x} = \dfrac{\cos^2 x + \sin^2 x}{\sin x} = \dfrac{1}{\sin x} = \csc x$

**3.** $\sin x - \sin x \cos^2 x = \sin x(1 - \cos^2 x) = \sin x \cdot \sin^2 x = \sin^3 x$   **4.** $\dfrac{1 + \cos\theta}{\sin\theta} = \dfrac{1}{\sin\theta} + \dfrac{\cos\theta}{\sin\theta} = \csc\theta + \cot\theta$

**5.** $\dfrac{\sin x}{1 + \cos x} + \dfrac{1 + \cos x}{\sin x} = \dfrac{\sin x(\sin x)}{(1 + \cos x)(\sin x)} + \dfrac{(1 + \cos x)(1 + \cos x)}{(\sin x)(1 + \cos x)} = \dfrac{\sin^2 x + 1 + 2\cos x + \cos^2 x}{(1 + \cos x)(\sin x)}$
$= \dfrac{\sin^2 x + \cos^2 x + 1 + 2\cos x}{(1 + \cos x)(\sin x)} = \dfrac{1 + 1 + 2\cos x}{(1 + \cos x)(\sin x)} = \dfrac{2 + 2\cos x}{(1 + \cos x)(\sin x)} = \dfrac{2(1 + \cos x)}{(1 + \cos x)(\sin x)} = \dfrac{2}{\sin x} = 2\csc x$

**6.** $\dfrac{\cos x}{1 + \sin x} = \dfrac{\cos x(1 - \sin x)}{(1 + \sin x)(1 - \sin x)} = \dfrac{\cos x(1 - \sin x)}{1 - \sin^2 x} = \dfrac{\cos x(1 - \sin x)}{\cos^2 x} = \dfrac{1 - \sin x}{\cos x}$   **7.** $\dfrac{\sec x + \csc(-x)}{\sec x \csc x} = \dfrac{\sec x - \csc x}{\sec x \csc x}$

$= \dfrac{\dfrac{1}{\cos x} - \dfrac{1}{\sin x}}{\dfrac{1}{\cos x} \cdot \dfrac{1}{\sin x}} = \dfrac{\dfrac{\sin x}{\cos x \cdot \sin x} - \dfrac{\cos x}{\cos x \cdot \sin x}}{\dfrac{1}{\cos x \cdot \sin x}} = \dfrac{\dfrac{\sin x - \cos x}{\cos x \cdot \sin x}}{\dfrac{1}{\cos x \cdot \sin x}} = \dfrac{\sin x - \cos x}{\cos x \cdot \sin x} \cdot \dfrac{\cos x \cdot \sin x}{1} = \sin x - \cos x$

**8.** Left side: $\dfrac{1}{1 + \sin\theta} + \dfrac{1}{1 - \sin\theta} = \dfrac{1(1 - \sin\theta)}{(1 + \sin\theta)(1 - \sin\theta)} + \dfrac{1(1 + \sin\theta)}{(1 - \sin\theta)(1 + \sin\theta)} = \dfrac{1 - \sin\theta + 1 + \sin\theta}{(1 + \sin\theta)(1 - \sin\theta)} = \dfrac{2}{1 - \sin^2\theta}$;

Right side: $2 + 2\tan^2\theta = 2 + 2\left(\dfrac{\sin^2\theta}{\cos^2\theta}\right) = \dfrac{2\cos^2\theta}{\cos^2\theta} + \dfrac{2\sin^2\theta}{\cos^2\theta} = \dfrac{2\cos^2\theta + 2\sin^2\theta}{\cos^2\theta} = \dfrac{2(\cos^2\theta + \sin^2\theta)}{\cos^2\theta} = \dfrac{2}{\cos^2\theta} = \dfrac{2}{1 - \sin^2\theta}$

### Exercise Set 5.1

For Exercises 1–59, proofs may vary.
**61.** $\cos x$; Proofs may vary.   **63.** $2\sin x$; Proofs may vary.   **65.** $2\sec x$; Proofs may vary.   **67.** $\dfrac{1}{\cos x}$   **69.** $\dfrac{1}{\cos x}$   **71.** $2\csc^2 x - 1$

**73.** $\sec x \tan x$

**79.**

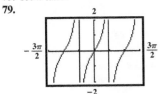

Proofs may vary.

**81.**

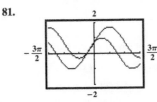

Values for $x$ may vary.

**83.**

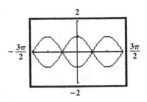

Values for $x$ may vary.

**85.**

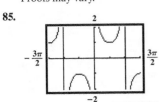

Proofs may vary.

**87.**

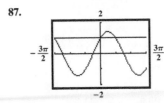

Values for $x$ may vary.

**89.** makes sense   **91.** does not make sense

For Exercises 92–95, proofs may vary.

**98.** $\dfrac{\sqrt{3}}{2}; \dfrac{1}{2}; \dfrac{1}{2}; \dfrac{\sqrt{3}}{2}; 0; 1$   **99. a.** no   **b.** yes   **100. a.** no   **b.** yes

## Section 5.2

### Check Point Exercises

**1.** $\dfrac{\sqrt{3}}{2}$   **2.** $\dfrac{\sqrt{3}}{2}$   **3.** $\dfrac{\cos(\alpha - \beta)}{\cos \alpha \cos \beta} = \dfrac{\cos \alpha \cos \beta + \sin \alpha \sin \beta}{\cos \alpha \cos \beta} = \dfrac{\cos \alpha}{\cos \alpha} \cdot \dfrac{\cos \beta}{\cos \beta} + \dfrac{\sin \alpha}{\cos \alpha} \cdot \dfrac{\sin \beta}{\cos \beta} = 1 + \tan \alpha \tan \beta$

**4.** $\dfrac{\sqrt{2} + \sqrt{6}}{4}$   **5. a.** $\cos \alpha = -\dfrac{3}{5}$   **b.** $\cos \beta = \dfrac{\sqrt{3}}{2}$   **c.** $\dfrac{-3\sqrt{3} - 4}{10}$   **d.** $\dfrac{4\sqrt{3} - 3}{10}$   **6. a.** $y = \sin x$

**b.** $\cos\left(x + \dfrac{3\pi}{2}\right) = \cos x \cos \dfrac{3\pi}{2} - \sin x \sin \dfrac{3\pi}{2} = \cos x \cdot 0 - \sin x \cdot (-1) = \sin x$

**7.** $\tan(x + \pi) = \dfrac{\tan x + \tan \pi}{1 - \tan x \tan \pi} = \dfrac{\tan x + 0}{1 - \tan x \cdot 0} = \dfrac{\tan x}{1} = \tan x$

### Exercise Set 5.2

**1.** $\dfrac{\sqrt{6} + \sqrt{2}}{4}$   **3.** $\dfrac{\sqrt{2} - \sqrt{6}}{4}$   **5. a.** $\alpha = 50°, \beta = 20°$   **b.** $\cos 30°$   **c.** $\dfrac{\sqrt{3}}{2}$   **7. a.** $\alpha = \dfrac{5\pi}{12}, \beta = \dfrac{\pi}{12}$   **b.** $\cos \dfrac{\pi}{3}$   **c.** $\dfrac{1}{2}$

For Exercises 9 and 11, proofs may vary.   **13.** $\dfrac{\sqrt{6} - \sqrt{2}}{4}$   **15.** $\dfrac{\sqrt{6} + \sqrt{2}}{4}$   **17.** $-\dfrac{\sqrt{6} + \sqrt{2}}{4}$   **19.** $\dfrac{\sqrt{6} - \sqrt{2}}{4}$   **21.** $\dfrac{\sqrt{3} + 1}{\sqrt{3} - 1}$   **23.** $\dfrac{\sqrt{3} - 1}{\sqrt{3} + 1}$

**25.** $\sin 30°; \dfrac{1}{2}$   **27.** $\tan 45°; 1$   **29.** $\sin \dfrac{\pi}{6}; \dfrac{1}{2}$   **31.** $\tan \dfrac{\pi}{6}; \dfrac{\sqrt{3}}{3}$

For Exercises 33–55, proofs may vary.

**57. a.** $-\dfrac{63}{65}$   **b.** $-\dfrac{16}{65}$   **c.** $\dfrac{16}{63}$   **59. a.** $-\dfrac{4 + 6\sqrt{2}}{15}$   **b.** $\dfrac{3 - 8\sqrt{2}}{15}$   **c.** $\dfrac{54 - 25\sqrt{2}}{28}$

**61. a.** $-\dfrac{8\sqrt{3} + 15}{34}$   **b.** $\dfrac{15\sqrt{3} - 8}{34}$   **c.** $\dfrac{480 - 289\sqrt{3}}{33}$   **63. a.** $-\dfrac{4 + 3\sqrt{15}}{20}$   **b.** $\dfrac{-3 + 4\sqrt{15}}{20}$   **c.** $\dfrac{3 - 4\sqrt{15}}{4 + 3\sqrt{15}}$

**65. a.** $y = \sin x$   **b.** $\sin(\pi - x) = \sin \pi \cos x - \cos \pi \sin x = 0 \cdot \cos x - (-1) \sin x = \sin x$   **67. a.** $y = 2 \cos x$

**b.** $\sin\left(x + \dfrac{\pi}{2}\right) + \sin\left(\dfrac{\pi}{2} - x\right) = \sin x \cos \dfrac{\pi}{2} + \cos x \sin \dfrac{\pi}{2} + \sin \dfrac{\pi}{2} \cos x - \cos \dfrac{\pi}{2} \sin x = \sin x \cdot 0 + \cos x \cdot 1 + 1 \cdot \cos x - 0 \cdot \sin x$

$= \cos x + \cos x = 2 \cos x$   **69.** $\cos \alpha$   **71.** $\tan \beta$   **73.** $\cos \dfrac{\pi}{3} = \dfrac{1}{2}$   **75.** $\cos 3x$; Proofs may vary.   **77.** $\sin \dfrac{x}{2}$; Proofs may vary.

**79.** Proofs may vary.; amplitude is $\sqrt{13}$; period is $2\pi$

**89.**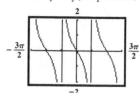

Proofs may vary.

**91.**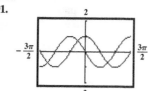

Values for $x$ may vary.

**93.**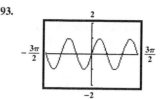

Proofs may vary.

**95.** makes sense   **97.** makes sense.   **99.** $\dfrac{4\sqrt{3} + 3}{10}$   **101.** $-\dfrac{33}{65}$   **103.** $y\sqrt{1 - x^2} + x\sqrt{1 - y^2}$   **105.** $\dfrac{xy + \left(\sqrt{1 - x^2}\right)\left(\sqrt{1 - y^2}\right)}{y\sqrt{1 - x^2} - x\sqrt{1 - y^2}}$

**107.** $\dfrac{\sqrt{3}}{2}; \dfrac{1}{2}; \dfrac{1}{2}; \dfrac{\sqrt{3}}{2}$   **108. a.** no   **b.** yes   **109. a.** no   **b.** yes

## Section 5.3

### Check Point Exercises

**1. a.** $-\dfrac{24}{25}$   **b.** $-\dfrac{7}{25}$   **c.** $\dfrac{24}{7}$   **2.** $\dfrac{\sqrt{3}}{2}$   **3.** $\sin 3\theta = \sin(2\theta + \theta) = \sin 2\theta \cos \theta + \cos 2\theta \sin \theta = 2 \sin \theta \cos \theta \cos \theta$

$+ (2\cos^2 \theta - 1)\sin \theta = 2 \sin \theta \cos^2 \theta + 2 \sin \theta \cos^2 \theta - \sin \theta = 4 \sin \theta \cos^2 \theta - \sin \theta = 4 \sin \theta (1 - \sin^2 \theta) - \sin \theta = 4 \sin \theta - 4 \sin^3 \theta$

$- \sin \theta = 3 \sin \theta - 4 \sin^3 \theta$   **4.** $\sin^4 x = (\sin^2 x)^2 = \left(\dfrac{1 - \cos 2x}{2}\right)^2 = \dfrac{1 - 2 \cos 2x + \cos^2 2x}{4} = \dfrac{1}{4} - \dfrac{1}{2} \cos 2x + \dfrac{1}{4} \cos^2 2x$

$= \dfrac{1}{4} - \dfrac{1}{2} \cos 2x + \dfrac{1}{4}\left(\dfrac{1 + \cos 2(2x)}{2}\right) = \dfrac{1}{4} - \dfrac{1}{2}\cos 2x + \dfrac{1}{8} + \dfrac{1}{8}\cos 4x = \dfrac{3}{8} - \dfrac{1}{2}\cos 2x + \dfrac{1}{8}\cos 4x$   **5.** $-\dfrac{\sqrt{2 - \sqrt{3}}}{2}$

**6.** $\dfrac{\sin 2\theta}{1 + \cos 2\theta} = \dfrac{2 \sin \theta \cos \theta}{1 + (1 - 2 \sin^2 \theta)} = \dfrac{2 \sin \theta \cos \theta}{2 - 2 \sin^2 \theta} = \dfrac{2 \sin \theta \cos \theta}{2(1 - \sin^2 \theta)} = \dfrac{2 \sin \theta \cos \theta}{2 \cos^2 \theta} = \dfrac{\sin \theta}{\cos \theta} = \tan \theta$

**7.** $\dfrac{\sec \alpha}{\sec \alpha \csc \alpha + \csc \alpha} = \dfrac{\dfrac{1}{\cos \alpha}}{\dfrac{1}{\cos \alpha} \cdot \dfrac{1}{\sin \alpha} + \dfrac{1}{\sin \alpha}} = \dfrac{\dfrac{1}{\cos \alpha}}{\dfrac{1}{\cos \alpha \sin \alpha} + \dfrac{\cos \alpha}{\cos \alpha \sin \alpha}} = \dfrac{\dfrac{1}{\cos \alpha}}{\dfrac{1 + \cos \alpha}{\cos \alpha \sin \alpha}} = \dfrac{1}{\cos \alpha} \cdot \dfrac{\cos \alpha \sin \alpha}{1 + \cos \alpha} = \dfrac{\sin \alpha}{1 + \cos \alpha} = \tan \dfrac{\alpha}{2}$

## Exercise Set 5.3

**1.** $\frac{24}{25}$  **3.** $\frac{24}{7}$  **5.** $\frac{527}{625}$  **7. a.** $-\frac{240}{289}$  **b.** $-\frac{161}{289}$  **c.** $\frac{240}{161}$  **9. a.** $-\frac{336}{625}$  **b.** $\frac{527}{625}$  **c.** $-\frac{336}{527}$

**11. a.** $\frac{4}{5}$  **b.** $\frac{3}{5}$  **c.** $\frac{4}{3}$  **13. a.** $\frac{720}{1681}$  **b.** $\frac{1519}{1681}$  **c.** $\frac{720}{1519}$  **15.** $\frac{1}{2}$  **17.** $-\frac{\sqrt{3}}{2}$  **19.** $\frac{\sqrt{2}}{2}$  **21.** $\frac{\sqrt{3}}{3}$

For Exercises 23–33, proofs may vary.  **35.** $\frac{9}{4} - 3\cos 2x + \frac{3}{4}\cos 4x$  **37.** $\frac{1}{8} - \frac{1}{8}\cos 4x$  **39.** $\frac{\sqrt{2 - \sqrt{3}}}{2}$  **41.** $-\frac{\sqrt{2 + \sqrt{2}}}{2}$

**43.** $2 + \sqrt{3}$  **45.** $-\sqrt{2} + 1$  **47.** $\frac{\sqrt{10}}{10}$  **49.** $\frac{1}{3}$  **51.** $\frac{7\sqrt{2}}{10}$  **53.** $\frac{3}{5}$  **55. a.** $\frac{2\sqrt{5}}{5}$  **b.** $-\frac{\sqrt{5}}{5}$  **c.** $-2$  **57. a.** $\frac{3\sqrt{13}}{13}$  **b.** $\frac{2\sqrt{13}}{13}$  **c.** $\frac{3}{2}$

For Exercises 59–67, proofs may vary.

**69.** $\cos 2x$; Proofs may vary.  **71.** $1 + \sin x$; Proofs may vary.  **73.** $\sec x$; Proofs may vary.  **75.** $2\csc 2x$; Proofs may vary.

**77.** $\sin 3x$; Proofs may vary.  **79. a.** $\frac{v_0^2}{32} \cdot \sin 2\theta$  **b.** $\theta = \frac{\pi}{4}$  **81.** $\sqrt{2 - \sqrt{2}} \cdot (2 + \sqrt{2}) \approx 2.6$

**95.**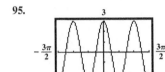

Proofs may vary.

**97.**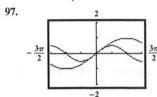

Values for $x$ may vary.

**99.**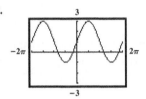

**a.** $y = 1 + 2\sin x$
**b.** Proofs may vary.

**101.**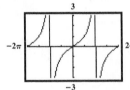

**a.** $y = \tan\frac{x}{2}$  **b.** Proofs may vary.  **103.** does not make sense  **105.** does not makes sense

**107.** $\frac{\sqrt{3}}{2}$  **109.** $\frac{9}{10}$  **111.** $2x\sqrt{1 - x^2}$  **113.** Both sides equal $\frac{\sqrt{3}}{4}$.  **114.** Both sides equal 0.

**115.** Both sides equal 0.

## Mid-Chapter 5 Check Point

For Exercises 1–18, proofs may vary.

**19.** $\frac{33}{65}$  **20.** $-\frac{16}{63}$  **21.** $-\frac{24}{25}$  **22.** $-\frac{\sqrt{26}}{26}$  **23.** $-\frac{\sqrt{6} + \sqrt{2}}{4}$  **24.** $\frac{\sqrt{3}}{2}$  **25.** $\frac{1}{2}$  **26.** $\sqrt{\frac{\sqrt{2} - 1}{\sqrt{2} + 1}}$

## Section 5.4

### Check Point Exercises

**1. a.** $\frac{1}{2}[\cos 3x - \cos 7x]$  **b.** $\frac{1}{2}[\cos 6x + \cos 8x]$  **2. a.** $2\sin 5x \cos 2x$  **b.** $2\cos\frac{5x}{2}\cos\frac{x}{2}$

**3.** $\dfrac{\cos 3x - \cos x}{\sin 3x + \sin x} = \dfrac{-2\sin\left(\dfrac{3x + x}{2}\right)\sin\left(\dfrac{3x - x}{2}\right)}{2\sin\left(\dfrac{3x + x}{2}\right)\cos\left(\dfrac{3x - x}{2}\right)} = \dfrac{-2\sin\left(\dfrac{4x}{2}\right)\sin\left(\dfrac{2x}{2}\right)}{2\sin\left(\dfrac{4x}{2}\right)\cos\left(\dfrac{2x}{2}\right)} = \dfrac{-2\sin 2x \sin x}{2\sin 2x \cos x} = -\dfrac{\sin x}{\cos x} = -\tan x$

### Exercise Set 5.4

**1.** product; difference  **3.** product; sum  **5.** $\frac{1}{2}[\cos 4x - \cos 8x]$  **7.** $\frac{1}{2}[\cos 4x + \cos 10x]$  **9.** $\frac{1}{2}[\sin 3x - \sin x]$  **11.** $\frac{1}{2}[\sin 2x - \sin x]$

**13.** sum; product  **15.** sum; product  **17.** $2\sin 4x \cos 2x$  **19.** $2\sin 2x \cos 5x$  **21.** $2\cos 3x \cos x$  **23.** $2\sin\frac{3x}{2}\cos\frac{x}{2}$

**25.** $2\cos x \cos\frac{x}{2}$  **27.** $\frac{\sqrt{6}}{2}$  **29.** $-\frac{\sqrt{2}}{2}$  For Exercises 31–37, proofs may vary.

**39. a.** $y = \cos x$  **b.** Proofs may vary.  **41. a.** $y = \tan 2x$  **b.** Proofs may vary.

**43. a.** $y = -\cot 2x$  **b.** Proofs may vary.  **45. a.** $y = \sin 1704\pi t + \sin 2418\pi t$  **b.** $2\sin 2061\pi t \cdot \cos 357\pi t$

**53.**

Values for $x$ may vary.

**55.**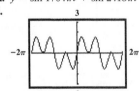

Proofs may vary.

**57.**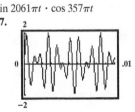

**59. a.** 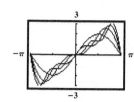    **b.** 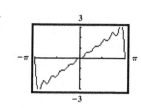    **c.** $\pi = 4 - \dfrac{4}{3} + \dfrac{4}{5} - \dfrac{4}{7} + \cdots$

**61.** makes sense    **63.** makes sense

For Exercises 65–69, proofs may vary.    **71.** $\left\{-\dfrac{1}{2}, 2\right\}$    **72.** $\{-\sqrt{3}, 0, \sqrt{3}\}$    **73.** $\left\{\dfrac{1 - \sqrt{5}}{2}, \dfrac{1 + \sqrt{5}}{2}\right\}$

## Section 5.5

### Check Point Exercises

**1.** $x = \dfrac{\pi}{3} + 2n\pi$ or $x = \dfrac{2\pi}{3} + 2n\pi$, where $n$ is any integer.    **2.** $\dfrac{\pi}{6}, \dfrac{2\pi}{3}, \dfrac{7\pi}{6}, \dfrac{5\pi}{3}$    **3.** $\dfrac{\pi}{2}$    **4.** $\dfrac{\pi}{6}, \dfrac{\pi}{2}, \dfrac{5\pi}{6}$    **5.** $\dfrac{\pi}{6}, \dfrac{5\pi}{6}, \dfrac{7\pi}{6}, \dfrac{11\pi}{6}$    **6.** $0, \dfrac{\pi}{4}, \pi, \dfrac{5\pi}{4}$

**7.** $\dfrac{\pi}{3}, \dfrac{5\pi}{3}$    **8.** $\dfrac{\pi}{2}, \dfrac{7\pi}{6}, \dfrac{11\pi}{6}$    **9.** $\dfrac{3\pi}{4}, \dfrac{7\pi}{4}$    **10.** $\dfrac{\pi}{2}, \pi$    **11. a.** $1.2592, 4.4008$    **b.** $3.3752, 6.0496$    **12.** $2.3423, 3.9409$

### Exercise Set 5.5

**1.** Solution    **3.** Not a solution    **5.** Solution    **7.** Solution    **9.** Not a solution    **11.** $x = \dfrac{\pi}{3} + 2n\pi$ or $x = \dfrac{2\pi}{3} + 2n\pi$, where $n$ is any integer.

**13.** $x = \dfrac{\pi}{4} + n\pi$, where $n$ is any integer.    **15.** $x = \dfrac{2\pi}{3} + 2n\pi$ or $x = \dfrac{4\pi}{3} + 2n\pi$, where $n$ is any integer.    **17.** $x = n\pi$, where $n$ is any integer.

**19.** $x = \dfrac{5\pi}{6} + 2n\pi$ or $x = \dfrac{7\pi}{6} + 2n\pi$, where $n$ is any integer.    **21.** $\theta = \dfrac{\pi}{6} + 2n\pi$ or $\theta = \dfrac{5\pi}{6} + 2n\pi$, where $n$ is any integer.

**23.** $\theta = \dfrac{3\pi}{2} + 2n\pi$, where $n$ is any integer.    **25.** $\dfrac{\pi}{6}, \dfrac{\pi}{3}, \dfrac{7\pi}{6}, \dfrac{4\pi}{3}$    **27.** $\dfrac{5\pi}{24}, \dfrac{7\pi}{24}, \dfrac{17\pi}{24}, \dfrac{19\pi}{24}, \dfrac{29\pi}{24}, \dfrac{31\pi}{24}, \dfrac{41\pi}{24}, \dfrac{43\pi}{24}$    **29.** $\dfrac{\pi}{18}, \dfrac{7\pi}{18}, \dfrac{13\pi}{18}, \dfrac{19\pi}{18}, \dfrac{25\pi}{18}, \dfrac{31\pi}{18}$

**31.** $0$    **33.** no solution    **35.** $\dfrac{4\pi}{9}, \dfrac{8\pi}{9}, \dfrac{16\pi}{9}$    **37.** $0, \dfrac{\pi}{3}, \pi, \dfrac{4\pi}{3}$    **39.** $\dfrac{\pi}{2}, \dfrac{7\pi}{6}, \dfrac{11\pi}{6}$    **41.** $\dfrac{2\pi}{3}, \pi, \dfrac{4\pi}{3}$    **43.** $\dfrac{3\pi}{2}$    **45.** $\dfrac{\pi}{2}, \dfrac{3\pi}{2}$

**47.** $\dfrac{\pi}{3}, \dfrac{2\pi}{3}, \dfrac{4\pi}{3}, \dfrac{5\pi}{3}$    **49.** $\dfrac{\pi}{6}, \dfrac{5\pi}{6}, \dfrac{7\pi}{6}, \dfrac{11\pi}{6}$    **51.** $\dfrac{\pi}{4}, \dfrac{3\pi}{4}, \dfrac{5\pi}{4}, \dfrac{7\pi}{4}$    **53.** $\dfrac{\pi}{4}, \pi, \dfrac{5\pi}{4}$    **55.** $\dfrac{5\pi}{6}, \dfrac{7\pi}{6}, \dfrac{11\pi}{6}$    **57.** $\dfrac{\pi}{4}, \dfrac{5\pi}{4}$    **59.** $0, \dfrac{2\pi}{3}, \pi, \dfrac{4\pi}{3}$

**61.** $0, \pi$    **63.** $\dfrac{\pi}{2}, \dfrac{7\pi}{6}, \dfrac{11\pi}{6}$    **65.** $\pi$    **67.** $\dfrac{\pi}{6}, \dfrac{5\pi}{6}$    **69.** $\dfrac{\pi}{6}, \dfrac{\pi}{2}, \dfrac{5\pi}{6}, \dfrac{3\pi}{2}$    **71.** $0, \dfrac{2\pi}{3}, \dfrac{4\pi}{3}$    **73.** $\dfrac{2\pi}{3}, \dfrac{4\pi}{3}$    **75.** $\dfrac{\pi}{8}, \dfrac{3\pi}{8}, \dfrac{9\pi}{8}, \dfrac{11\pi}{8}$    **77.** $0, \dfrac{\pi}{2}$

**79.** $\dfrac{\pi}{4}, \dfrac{3\pi}{4}$    **81.** $\dfrac{\pi}{12}, \dfrac{\pi}{4}, \dfrac{3\pi}{4}, \dfrac{11\pi}{12}, \dfrac{17\pi}{12}, \dfrac{19\pi}{12}$    **83.** $0$    **85.** $0.9695, 2.1721$    **87.** $1.9823, 4.3009$    **89.** $1.8925, 5.0341$    **91.** $2.2370, 4.0461$

**93.** $0.4636, 0.9828, 3.6052, 4.1244$    **95.** $0.3876, 2.7540, 3.5292, 5.8956$    **97.** $\dfrac{\pi}{3}, \dfrac{2\pi}{3}, \dfrac{4\pi}{3}, \dfrac{5\pi}{3}$    **99.** $0, \dfrac{2\pi}{3}, \pi, \dfrac{4\pi}{3}$    **101.** $\dfrac{\pi}{6}, \dfrac{11\pi}{6}$

**103.** $1.7798, 4.9214$    **105.** $\dfrac{\pi}{2}$    **107.** $\dfrac{\pi}{6}, \dfrac{\pi}{2}, \dfrac{5\pi}{6}, \dfrac{3\pi}{2}$    **109.** $\dfrac{\pi}{6}, \dfrac{5\pi}{6}, \dfrac{7\pi}{6}, \dfrac{11\pi}{6}$    **111.** $0.7495, 5.5337$    **113.** $\dfrac{7\pi}{6}, \dfrac{11\pi}{6}$

**115.** $2.1588, \dfrac{3\pi}{4}, 5.3004, \dfrac{7\pi}{4}$    **117.** $\left(\dfrac{2\pi}{3}, -\dfrac{3}{2}\right), \left(\dfrac{4\pi}{3}, -\dfrac{3}{2}\right)$    **119.** $(3.5163, 0.7321), (5.9085, 0.7321)$    **121.** $\dfrac{\pi}{6}, \dfrac{5\pi}{6}, \dfrac{7\pi}{6}, \dfrac{11\pi}{6}$

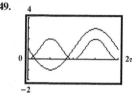

$\left(\dfrac{2\pi}{3}, -\dfrac{3}{2}\right)$    $\left(\dfrac{4\pi}{3}, -\dfrac{3}{2}\right)$

$f(x) = 3\cos x$
$g(x) = \cos x - 1$

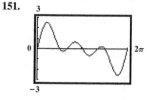

(3.5163, 0.7321)    (5.9085, 0.7321)

$f(x) = \cos 2x$
$g(x) = -2\sin x$

**123.** $\dfrac{\pi}{6}, \dfrac{5\pi}{6}, 3.3430, 6.0818$

**125.** $0, \dfrac{2\pi}{3}, \pi, \dfrac{4\pi}{3}$

**127.** $0.3649, 1.2059, 3.5064, 4.3475$; a

**129.** $0.4$ sec and $2.1$ sec    **131.** $49$ days and $292$ days    **133.** $t = 2 + 6n$ or $t = 4 + 6n$ where $n$ is any nonnegative integer.    **135.** $21°$ or $69°$.

**147.** 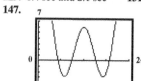    **149.** (graph)    **151.** (graph)

$x = 1.37, x = 2.30, x = 3.98,$
or $x = 4.91$

$x = 0.37$ or $x = 2.77$

$x = 0, x = 1.57, x = 2.09, x = 3.14, x = 4.19,$ or $x = 4.71$

**153.** makes sense    **155.** does not make sense    **157.** false    **159.** false    **161.** $\dfrac{\pi}{2}, \dfrac{3\pi}{2}, \dfrac{7\pi}{12}, \dfrac{11\pi}{12}, \dfrac{19\pi}{12}, \dfrac{23\pi}{12}$    **163.** $a \approx 45.2$

**164.** $B \approx 31.5°$    **165.** no solution or $\varnothing$

## Chapter 5 Review Exercises

For Exercises 1–13, proofs may vary.

**14.** $\dfrac{\sqrt{6} - \sqrt{2}}{4}$    **15.** $\dfrac{\sqrt{2} - \sqrt{6}}{4}$    **16.** $2 - \sqrt{3}$    **17.** $\sqrt{3} + 2$    **18.** $\dfrac{1}{2}$    **19.** $\dfrac{1}{2}$

For Exercises 19–31, proofs may vary.

**32. a.** $y = \cos x$   **b.** $\sin\left(x - \dfrac{3\pi}{2}\right) = \sin x \cos \dfrac{3\pi}{2} - \cos x \sin \dfrac{3\pi}{2} = \sin x \cdot 0 - \cos x \cdot -1 = \cos x$

**33. a.** $y = -\sin x$   **b.** $\cos\left(x + \dfrac{\pi}{2}\right) = \cos x \cos \dfrac{\pi}{2} - \sin x \sin \dfrac{\pi}{2} = \cos x \cdot 0 - \sin x \cdot 1 = -\sin x$

**34. a.** $y = \tan x$   **b.** $y = \dfrac{\tan x - 1}{1 - \cot x} = \dfrac{\dfrac{\sin x}{\cos x} - 1}{1 - \dfrac{\cos x}{\sin x}} = \dfrac{\dfrac{\sin x - \cos x}{\cos x}}{\dfrac{\sin x - \cos x}{\sin x}} = \dfrac{\sin x - \cos x}{\cos x} \cdot \dfrac{\sin x}{\sin x - \cos x} = \dfrac{\sin x}{\cos x} = \tan x$

**35. a.** $\dfrac{33}{65}$   **b.** $\dfrac{16}{65}$   **c.** $-\dfrac{33}{56}$   **d.** $\dfrac{24}{25}$   **e.** $\dfrac{2\sqrt{13}}{13}$   **36. a.** $-\dfrac{63}{65}$   **b.** $-\dfrac{56}{65}$   **c.** $\dfrac{63}{16}$   **d.** $\dfrac{24}{25}$   **e.** $\dfrac{5\sqrt{26}}{26}$

**37. a.** 1   **b.** $-\dfrac{3}{5}$   **c.** undefined   **d.** $-\dfrac{3}{5}$   **e.** $\dfrac{\sqrt{10 + 3\sqrt{10}}}{2\sqrt{5}}$   **38. a.** 1   **b.** $\dfrac{4\sqrt{2}}{9}$   **c.** undefined   **d.** $\dfrac{4\sqrt{2}}{9}$   **e.** $-\dfrac{\sqrt{3}}{3}$

**39.** $\dfrac{\sqrt{3}}{2}$   **40.** $-\dfrac{\sqrt{3}}{3}$   **41.** $\dfrac{\sqrt{2 - \sqrt{2}}}{2}$   **42.** $2 - \sqrt{3}$   **43.** $\dfrac{1}{2}[\cos 2x - \cos 10x]$   **44.** $\dfrac{1}{2}[\sin 10x + \sin 4x]$   **45.** $-2\sin x \cos 3x$

**46.** $\dfrac{\sqrt{6}}{2}$   **47.** Proofs may vary.   **48.** Proofs may vary.   **49. a.** $y = \cot x$   **b.** Proofs may vary.

**50.** $x = \dfrac{2\pi}{3} + 2n\pi$ or $x = \dfrac{4\pi}{3} + 2n\pi$, where $n$ is any integer.   **51.** $x = \dfrac{\pi}{4} + 2n\pi$ or $x = \dfrac{3\pi}{4} + 2n\pi$, where $n$ is any integer.

**52.** $x = \dfrac{7\pi}{6} + 2n\pi$ or $x = \dfrac{11\pi}{6} + 2n\pi$, where $n$ is any integer.   **53.** $x = \dfrac{\pi}{6} + n\pi$, where $n$ is any integer.   **54.** $\dfrac{\pi}{2}, \dfrac{3\pi}{2}$   **55.** $\dfrac{\pi}{6}, \dfrac{5\pi}{6}, \dfrac{9\pi}{6}$

**56.** $\dfrac{3\pi}{2}$   **57.** $0, \dfrac{\pi}{3}, \pi, \dfrac{5\pi}{3}$   **58.** $\pi$   **59.** $\dfrac{\pi}{6}, \dfrac{5\pi}{6}, \dfrac{3\pi}{2}$   **60.** $\dfrac{\pi}{6}, \dfrac{5\pi}{6}, \dfrac{7\pi}{6}, \dfrac{11\pi}{6}$   **61.** $0, \pi, \dfrac{7\pi}{6}, \dfrac{11\pi}{6}$   **62.** $0, \dfrac{\pi}{6}, \pi, \dfrac{11\pi}{6}$   **63.** $0, \pi$

**64.** $3.7890, 5.6358$   **65.** $0.6847, 2.4569, 3.8263, 5.5985$   **66.** $\dfrac{\pi}{4}, 1.2490, \dfrac{5\pi}{4}, 4.3906$   **67.** $0.8959, 2.2457$

**68.** $t = \dfrac{2}{3} + 4n$ or $t = \dfrac{10}{3} + 4n$, where $n$ is any integer.   **69.** $12°$ or $78°$

## Chapter 5 Test

**1.** $-\dfrac{63}{65}$   **2.** $\dfrac{56}{33}$   **3.** $-\dfrac{24}{25}$   **4.** $\dfrac{3\sqrt{13}}{13}$   **5.** $\dfrac{\sqrt{6} + \sqrt{2}}{4}$   **6.** $\cos x \csc x = \cos x \cdot \dfrac{1}{\sin x} = \dfrac{\cos x}{\sin x} = \cot x$

**7.** $\dfrac{\sec x}{\cot x + \tan x} = \dfrac{\dfrac{1}{\cos x}}{\dfrac{\cos x}{\sin x} + \dfrac{\sin x}{\cos x}} = \dfrac{\dfrac{1}{\cos x}}{\dfrac{\cos^2 x + \sin^2 x}{\sin x \cos x}} = \dfrac{1}{\cos x} \cdot \dfrac{\sin x \cos x}{1} = \sin x$

**8.** $1 - \dfrac{\cos^2 x}{1 + \sin x} = 1 - \dfrac{(1 - \sin^2 x)}{1 + \sin x} = 1 - \dfrac{(1 + \sin x)(1 - \sin x)}{1 + \sin x} = 1 - (1 - \sin x) = \sin x$

**9.** $\cos\left(\theta + \dfrac{\pi}{2}\right) = \cos \theta \cos \dfrac{\pi}{2} - \sin \theta \sin \dfrac{\pi}{2} = \cos \theta \cdot 0 - \sin \theta \cdot 1 = -\sin \theta$

**10.** $\dfrac{\sin(\alpha - \beta)}{\sin \alpha \cos \beta} = \dfrac{\sin \alpha \cos \beta - \cos \alpha \sin \beta}{\sin \alpha \cos \beta} = \dfrac{\sin \alpha \cos \beta}{\sin \alpha \cos \beta} - \dfrac{\cos \alpha \sin \beta}{\sin \alpha \cos \beta} = 1 - \cot \alpha \tan \beta$

**11.** $\sin t \cos t(\tan t + \cot t) = \sin t \cos t\left(\dfrac{\sin t}{\cos t} + \dfrac{\cos t}{\sin t}\right) = \sin^2 t + \cos^2 t = 1$   **12.** $\dfrac{7\pi}{18}, \dfrac{11\pi}{18}, \dfrac{19\pi}{18}, \dfrac{23\pi}{18}, \dfrac{31\pi}{18},$ and $\dfrac{35\pi}{18}$

**13.** $\dfrac{\pi}{2}, \dfrac{7\pi}{6}, \dfrac{3\pi}{2}, \dfrac{11\pi}{6}$   **14.** $0, \dfrac{\pi}{3}, \dfrac{5\pi}{3}$   **15.** $0, \dfrac{2\pi}{3}, \dfrac{4\pi}{3}$   **16.** $2.5136, 3.7696$   **17.** $1.2340, \dfrac{\pi}{2}, \dfrac{3\pi}{2}, 5.0522$   **18.** $1.2971, 2.6299, 4.4387, 5.7715$

## Cumulative Review Exercises (Chapters P–5)

**1.** $-3, 1 + 2i,$ and $1 - 2i$   **2.** $x = \dfrac{\log 125}{\log 11} + 1$ or $x \approx 3.01$   **3.** $(-\infty, -4] \cup [2, \infty)$   **4.** $\dfrac{\pi}{3}, \dfrac{5\pi}{3}$   **5.** $\dfrac{\pi}{4}, 2.0344, \dfrac{5\pi}{4}, 5.1760$

**6.**

$y = \sqrt{x + 2} - 1$

**7.**

$(x - 1)^2 + (y + 2)^2 = 9$

**8.**
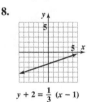
$y + 2 = \dfrac{1}{3}(x - 1)$

**9.**

$y = 3\cos 2x$

**10.**
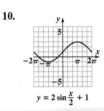
$y = 2\sin \dfrac{x}{2} + 1$

**11.**
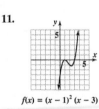
$f(x) = (x - 1)^2(x - 3)$

**12.** $2a + h + 3$   **13.** $-\dfrac{\sqrt{2}}{2}$   **14.** Proofs may vary.

**15.** $\dfrac{16\pi}{9}$ radians   **16.** $t \approx 19.1$ yr

**17.** $f^{-1}(x) = \dfrac{3x + 1}{x - 2}$   **18.** $B = 67°, b = 28.27, c = 30.71$

**19.** 106 mg   **20.** $h \approx 15.9$ ft

# CHAPTER 6

## Section 6.1

**Check Point Exercises**

**1.** $B = 34°, a \approx 12.7$ cm, $b \approx 7.4$ cm **2.** $B = 117.5°, a \approx 8.7, c \approx 5.2$ **3.** $B \approx 41°, C \approx 82°, c \approx 39.0$ **4.** no triangle
**5.** two triangles; $B_1 \approx 50°, C_1 \approx 95°, c_1 = 20.8; B_2 \approx 130°, C_2 \approx 15°, c_2 \approx 5.4$ **6.** approximately 34 sq m **7.** approximately 11 mi

## Exercise Set 6.1

**1.** $B = 42°, a \approx 8.1, b \approx 8.1$ **3.** $A = 44°, b \approx 18.6, c \approx 22.8$ **5.** $C = 95°, b \approx 81.0, c \approx 134.1$ **7.** $B = 40°, b \approx 20.9, c \approx 31.8$
**9.** $C = 111°, b \approx 7.3, c \approx 16.1$ **11.** $A = 80°, a \approx 39.5, c \approx 10.4$ **13.** $B = 30°, a \approx 316.0, b \approx 174.3$ **15.** $C = 50°, a \approx 7.1, b \approx 7.1$
**17.** one triangle; $B \approx 29°, c \approx 111°, c \approx 29.0$ **19.** one triangle; $C \approx 52°, B \approx 65°, b \approx 10.2$ **21.** one triangle; $C \approx 55°, B \approx 13°, b \approx 10.2$
**23.** no triangle **25.** two triangles; $B_1 \approx 77°, C_1 \approx 43°, c_1 \approx 12.6; B_2 \approx 103°, C_2 \approx 17°, c_2 \approx 5.4$
**27.** two triangles; $B_1 \approx 54°, C_1 \approx 89°, c_1 \approx 19.9; B_2 \approx 126°, C_2 \approx 17°, c_2 \approx 5.8$
**29.** two triangles; $C_1 \approx 68°, B_1 \approx 54°, b_1 \approx 21.0; C_2 \approx 112°, B_2 \approx 10°, b_2 \approx 4.5$ **31.** no triangle **33.** 297 sq ft **35.** 5 sq yd **37.** 10 sq m
**39.** 481.6 **41.** 64.4 **43.** $A \approx 82°, B \approx 41°, C \approx 57°, c \approx 255.7$ **45.** 10
**47.** Station A is about 6 miles from the fire, station B is about 9 miles from the fire. **49.** The platform is about 3672 yards from one end of the beach and 3576 yards from the other. **51.** about 184 ft **53.** about 56 ft **55.** about 30 ft **57. a.** $a \approx 494$ ft **b.** about 343 ft
**59.** either 9.9 mi or 2.4 mi **71.** does not make sense **73.** does not make sense **75.** no **77.** 41 ft **78.** 127°
**79.** $\sqrt{7280} = 4\sqrt{455} \approx 85$ **80.**

## Section 6.2

**Check Point Exercises**

**1.** $a = 13, B \approx 28°, C \approx 32°$ **2.** $A \approx 52°, B \approx 98°, C \approx 30°$ **3.** approximately 917 mi apart **4.** approximately 47 sq m

## Exercise Set 6.2

**1.** $a \approx 6.0, B \approx 29°, C \approx 105°$ **3.** $c \approx 7.6, A \approx 52°, B \approx 32°$ **5.** $A \approx 44°, B \approx 68°, C \approx 68°$ **7.** $A \approx 117°, B \approx 36°, C \approx 27°$
**9.** $c \approx 4.7, A \approx 46°, B \approx 92°$ **11.** $a \approx 6.3, C \approx 28°, B \approx 50°$ **13.** $b \approx 4.7, C \approx 54°, A \approx 76°$ **15.** $b \approx 5.4, C \approx 22°, A \approx 68°$
**17.** $C \approx 112°, A \approx 28°, B \approx 40°$ **19.** $B \approx 100°, A \approx 19°, C \approx 61°$ **21.** $A = 60°, B = 60°, C = 60°$ **23.** $A \approx 117°, B \approx 18°, C \approx 45°$
**25.** 4 sq ft **27.** 22 sq m **29.** 31 sq yd **31.** $A \approx 31°, B \approx 19°, C \approx 130°, c \approx 19.1$
**33.** $A \approx 51°, B \approx 61°, C \approx 68°, AB = 9, AC = 8.5, BC = 7.5$ **35.** $A \approx 145°, B \approx 13°, C \approx 22°, a = \sqrt{61} \approx 7.8, b = \sqrt{10} \approx 3.2, c = 5$
**37.** 157° **39.** about 61.7 mi apart **41.** about 193 yd **43.** N12°E **45. a.** about 19.3 mi **b.** S58°E
**47.** The guy wire anchored downhill is about 417.4 feet. The one anchored uphill is about 398.2 feet. **49.** about 63.7 ft **51.** $123,454
**61.** makes sense **63.** makes sense **65.** $A \approx 29°, B \approx 87°, C \approx 64°, a \approx 11.6, b \approx 23.9$

**68.**

$y = 3$

**69.**

$x^2 + (y-1)^2 = 1$

**70.** $(x + 3)^2 + y^2 = 9$; center: $(-3, 0)$; radius: 3;

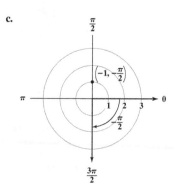

$x^2 + 6x + y^2 = 0$

## Section 6.3

**Check Point Exercises**

**1. a.**

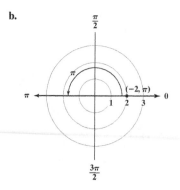

**2. a.** $\left(5, \dfrac{9\pi}{4}\right)$    **b.** $\left(-5, \dfrac{5\pi}{4}\right)$    **c.** $\left(5, -\dfrac{7\pi}{4}\right)$    **3. a.** $(-3, 0)$    **b.** $(-5\sqrt{3}, -5)$    **4.** $\left(2, \dfrac{5\pi}{3}\right)$    **5.** $\left(4, \dfrac{3\pi}{2}\right)$

**6. a.** $r = \dfrac{6}{3\cos\theta - \sin\theta}$    **b.** $r = -2\sin\theta$    **7. a.** $x^2 + y^2 = 16$    **b.** $y = -x$    **c.** $x = -2$    **d.** $x^2 + (y-5)^2 = 25$

## Exercise Set 6.3

**1.** *C*    **3.** *A*    **5.** *B*    **7.** *C*    **9.** *A*

**11.**

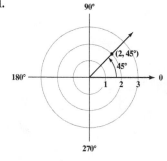

**13.**

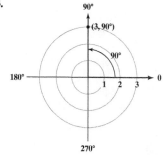

**15.**

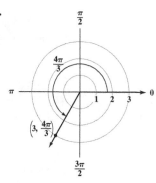

**17.**

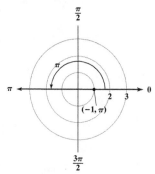

**19.**

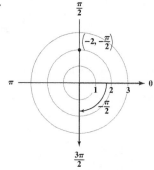

**21.**

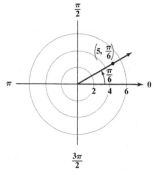

**a.** $\left(5, \dfrac{13\pi}{6}\right)$    **b.** $\left(-5, \dfrac{7\pi}{6}\right)$

**c.** $\left(5, -\dfrac{11\pi}{6}\right)$

**23.**

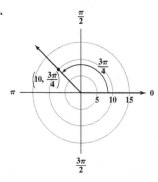

**25.**

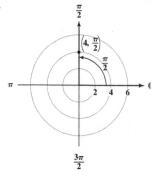

**a.** $\left(10, \dfrac{11\pi}{4}\right)$    **b.** $\left(-10, \dfrac{7\pi}{4}\right)$

**c.** $\left(10, -\dfrac{5\pi}{4}\right)$

**a.** $\left(4, \dfrac{5\pi}{2}\right)$    **b.** $\left(-4, \dfrac{3\pi}{2}\right)$

**c.** $\left(4, -\dfrac{3\pi}{2}\right)$

**27.** a, b, d    **29.** b, d    **31.** a, b    **33.** $(0, 4)$    **35.** $(1, \sqrt{3})$    **37.** $(0, -4)$    **39.** approximately $(-5.9, 4.4)$    **41.** $\left(\sqrt{8}, \dfrac{3\pi}{4}\right)$

**43.** $\left(4, \dfrac{5\pi}{3}\right)$    **45.** $\left(2, \dfrac{7\pi}{6}\right)$    **47.** $(5, 0)$    **49.** $r = \dfrac{7}{3\cos\theta + \sin\theta}$    **51.** $r = \dfrac{7}{\cos\theta}$    **53.** $r = 3$    **55.** $r = 4\cos\theta$    **57.** $r = \dfrac{6\cos\theta}{\sin^2\theta}$

**59.** $x^2 + y^2 = 64$

$x^2 + y^2 = 64$

**61.** $x = 0$

$x = 0$

**63.** $y = 3$

$y = 3$

**65.** $y = 4$

$y = 4$

**67.** $x^2 + y^2 = y$

$x^2 + y^2 = y$

**69.** $(x - 6)^2 + y^2 = 36$

$(x - 6)^2 + y^2 = 36$

**71.** $x^2 + y^2 = 6x + 4y$

$x^2 + y^2 = 6x + 4y$

**73.** $y = \dfrac{1}{x}$

$y = \dfrac{1}{x}$

**75.** $r = a \sec \theta; r \cos \theta = a; x = a; x = a$ is a vertical line $a$ units to the right of the $y$-axis when $a > 0$ and $|a|$ to the left of the $y$-axis when $a < 0$.

**77.** $r = a \sin \theta; r^2 = ar \sin \theta; x^2 + y^2 = ay; x^2 + y^2 - ay = 0; x^2 + \left(y - \dfrac{a}{2}\right)^2 = \left(\dfrac{a}{2}\right)^2$    **79.** $y = x + 2\sqrt{2}$; slope: 1; $y$-intercept: $2\sqrt{2}$

**81.** $(-1, \sqrt{3}), (2\sqrt{3}, 2); 2\sqrt{5}$    **83.** $\left(15, \dfrac{4\pi}{3}\right)$    **85.** 6.3 knots at an angle of 50° to the wind    **87.** Answers may vary.    **97.** $(-2, 3.464)$

**99.** $(-1.857, -3.543)$    **101.** $(3, 0.730)$    **103.** does not make sense    **105.** makes sense
**109.** 0; 0.13; 0.5; 1; 1.5; 1.87; 2    **110.** 1; 2; 2.73; 3; 2.73; 2; 1; 0; −0.73; −1    **111.** 0; 3.46; 4; 3; 3.46; 0; −3.46; −4; −3.46; 0

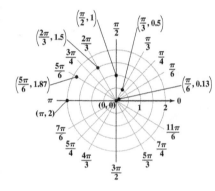

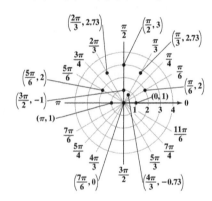

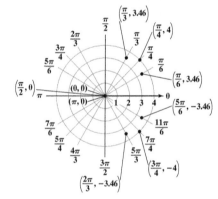

## Section 6.4

### Check Point Exercises

**1.**

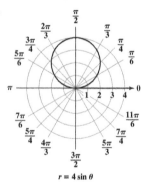

$r = 4 \sin \theta$

**2.**

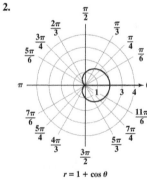

$r = 1 + \cos \theta$

**3.**

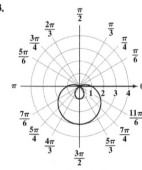

$r = 1 - 2 \sin \theta$

**4.**

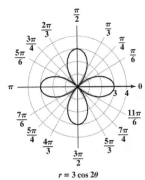

$r = 3 \cos 2\theta$

**5.**

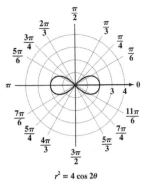

$r^2 = 4 \cos 2\theta$

## Exercise Set 6.4

**1.** $r = 1 - \sin \theta$   **3.** $r = 2 \cos \theta$   **5.** $r = 3 \sin 3\theta$   **7. a.** May or may not have symmetry with respect to polar axis.   **b.** Has symmetry with respect to the line $\theta = \dfrac{\pi}{2}$.   **c.** May or may not have symmetry about the pole.   **9. a.** Has symmetry with respect to polar axis.   **b.** May or may not have symmetry with respect to the line $\theta = \dfrac{\pi}{2}$.   **c.** May or may not have symmetry about pole.   **11. a.** Has symmetry with respect to polar axis.   **b.** Has symmetry with respect to the line $\theta = \dfrac{\pi}{2}$.   **c.** Has symmetry about the pole.

**13.**

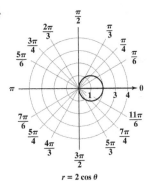

$r = 2 \cos \theta$

**15.**

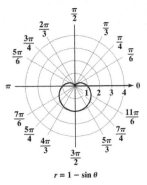

$r = 1 - \sin \theta$

**17.**

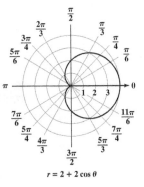

$r = 2 + 2 \cos \theta$

**19.**

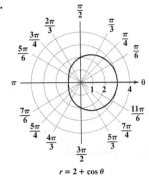

$r = 2 + \cos \theta$

**21.**

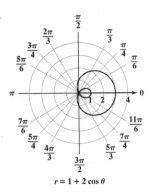

$r = 1 + 2 \cos \theta$

**23.**

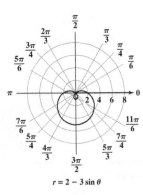

$r = 2 - 3 \sin \theta$

**25.**

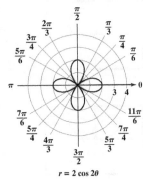

$r = 2 \cos 2\theta$

**27.**

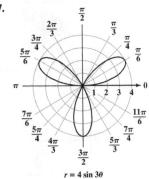

$r = 4 \sin 3\theta$

**29.**

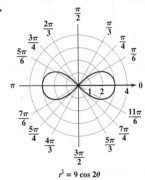

$r^2 = 9 \cos 2\theta$

**31.**

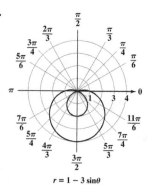

$r = 1 - 3 \sin\theta$

**33.**

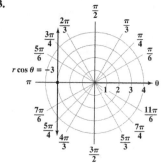

$r \cos\theta = -3$

**35.**

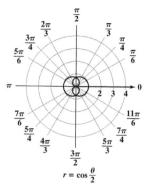

$r = \cos\dfrac{\theta}{2}$

**37.**

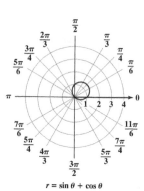

$r = \sin\theta + \cos\theta$

**39.**

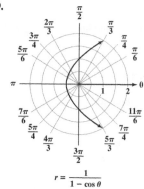

$r = \dfrac{1}{1 - \cos\theta}$

**41.**

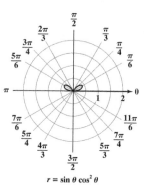

$r = \sin\theta \cos^2\theta$

**43.**

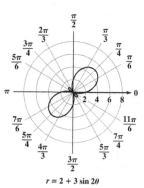

$r = 2 + 3 \sin 2\theta$

**45.** 6 knots

**47.** 8 knots

**49.** 90°; about $7\frac{1}{2}$ knots

**59.**

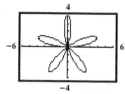

**61.**

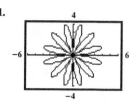

**63.**

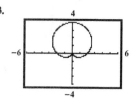

**65.**

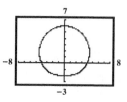

**67.**

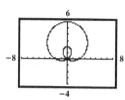

**69.**

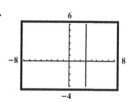

**71.**

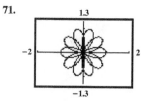

**73.**

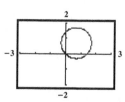

**75.**

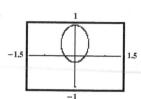

**77.** $2\pi$

**79.**

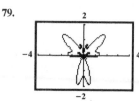

**81.**

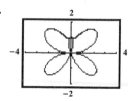

**83.** If $n$ is odd, there are $n$ loops and $\theta$max $= \pi$ traces the graph once; while if $n$ is even, there are $2n$ loops and $\theta$max $= 2\pi$ traces the graph once. In each separate case, as $n$ increases, $\sin n\theta$ increases its number of loops.     **85.** There are $n$ small petals and $n$ large petals for each value of $n$. For odd values of $n$, the small petals are inside the large petals. For even $n$, they are between the large petals.

**87.**

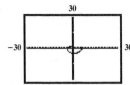

**89.** does not make sense **91.** makes sense

**93.**

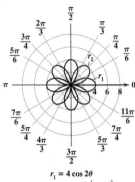

**96.** $4i$ **97.** 8 **98.** 2

$r_1 = 4 \cos 2\theta$
$r_2 = 4 \cos 2\left(\theta - \frac{\pi}{4}\right)$

The graph of $r_2$ is the

graph of $r_1$ rotated $\frac{\pi}{4}$ or 45°.

## Mid-Chapter 6 Check Point

**1.** $C = 107°, b \approx 24.8, c \approx 36.1$ **2.** $B \approx 37°, C \approx 101°, c \approx 92.4$ **3.** no triangle **4.** $A \approx 26°, C \approx 44°, b \approx 21.6$ **5.** Two triangles:
$A_1 \approx 55°, B_1 \approx 83°, b_1 \approx 19.3; A_2 \approx 125°, B_2 \approx 13°, b_2 \approx 4.4$ **6.** $A \approx 28°, B \approx 42°, C \approx 110°$ **7.** 10 ft² **8.** $14\sqrt{5} \approx 31$ m² **9.** 148 miles

**10.** 15.0 miles **11.** 327 ft **12.** $\left(\frac{3\sqrt{2}}{2}, \frac{3\sqrt{2}}{2}\right)$ **13.** $(0, -6)$ **14.** $\left(4, -\frac{\pi}{3}\right)$ **15.** $(6, \pi)$

**16.**

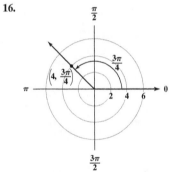

**a.** $\left(4, \frac{11\pi}{4}\right)$ **b.** $\left(-4, \frac{7\pi}{4}\right)$

**c.** $\left(4, -\frac{5\pi}{4}\right)$

**17.**

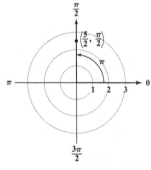

**a.** $\left(\frac{5}{2}, \frac{5\pi}{2}\right)$ **b.** $\left(-\frac{5}{2}, \frac{3\pi}{2}\right)$

**c.** $\left(\frac{5}{2}, -\frac{3\pi}{2}\right)$

**18.** $r = \dfrac{7}{5 \cos \theta - \sin \theta}$ **19.** $r = -7 \csc \theta$
**20.** $r = -2 \cos \theta$

**21.** $x^2 + y^2 = 36$

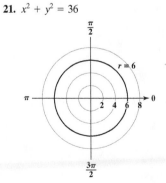

**22.** $y = \sqrt{3}x$

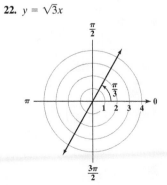

**23.** $y = -3$

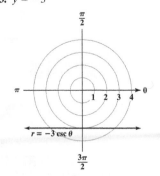

**24.** $(x + 5)^2 + y^2 = 25$       **25.** $y = \dfrac{1}{4}x^2$

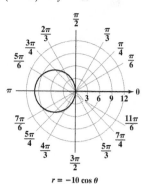

$r = -10 \cos \theta$

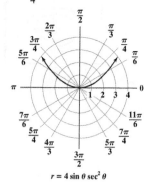

$r = 4 \sin \theta \sec^2 \theta$

**26. a.** Has symmetry with respect to the polar axis.    **b.** May or may not have symmetry with respect to the line $\theta = \dfrac{\pi}{2}$.    **c.** May or may not have symmetry with respect to the pole.    **27. a.** Has symmetry with respect to the polar axis.    **b.** Has symmetry with respect to the line $\theta = \dfrac{\pi}{2}$. **c.** Has symmetry with respect to the pole.

**28.**

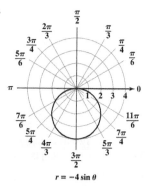

$r = -4 \sin \theta$

**29.**

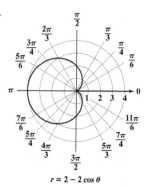

$r = 2 - 2 \cos \theta$

**30.**

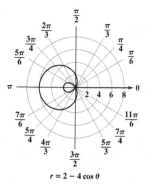

$r = 2 - 4 \cos \theta$

**31.**

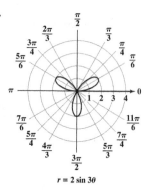

$r = 2 \sin 3\theta$

**32.**

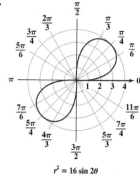

$r^2 = 16 \sin 2\theta$

## Section 6.5

**Check Point Exercises**

**1. a.**

**b.**

$z = -3 - 5i$

**c.**

**d.**

**2. a.** 13    **b.** $\sqrt{13}$    **3.**

$z = -1 - i\sqrt{3}$

$; 2\left(\cos \dfrac{4\pi}{3} + i \sin \dfrac{4\pi}{3}\right)$

**4.** $z = 2\sqrt{3} + 2i$    **5.** $30(\cos 60° + i \sin 60°)$

**6.** $10(\cos \pi + i \sin \pi)$    **7.** $-16\sqrt{3} + 16i$    **8.** $-4$

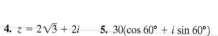

**9.** $2(\cos 15° + i \sin 15°); 2(\cos 105° + i \sin 105°); 2(\cos 195° + i \sin 195°); 2(\cos 285° + i \sin 285°)$    **10.** $3; -\dfrac{3}{2} + \dfrac{3\sqrt{3}}{2}i; -\dfrac{3}{2} - \dfrac{3\sqrt{3}}{2}i$

## Exercise Set 6.5

**1.**
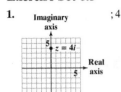 ;4

**3.**
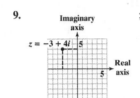 ;3

**5.**
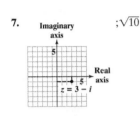 ;$\sqrt{13}$

**7.**
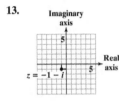 ;$\sqrt{10}$

**9.**
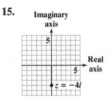 ;5

**11.**
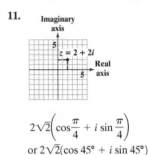

$$2\sqrt{2}\left(\cos\frac{\pi}{4} + i\sin\frac{\pi}{4}\right)$$
or $2\sqrt{2}(\cos 45° + i \sin 45°)$

**13.**
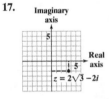

$$\sqrt{2}\left(\cos\frac{5\pi}{4} + i\sin\frac{5\pi}{4}\right) \text{ or } \sqrt{2}(\cos 225° + i \sin 225°)$$

**15.**
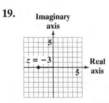

$$4\left(\cos\frac{3\pi}{2} + i\sin\frac{3\pi}{2}\right) \text{ or } 4(\cos 270° + i \sin 270°)$$

**17.**
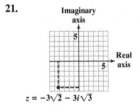

$$4\left(\cos\frac{11\pi}{6} + i\sin\frac{11\pi}{6}\right) \text{ or } 4(\cos 330° + i \sin 330°)$$

**19.**
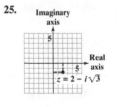

$$3(\cos\pi + i \sin\pi) \text{ or } 3(\cos 180° + i \sin 180°)$$

**21.**
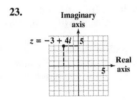
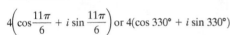

$\approx 3\sqrt{5}(\cos 230.8° + i \sin 230.8°)$

**23.**

$z = -3 + 4i$

$\approx 5(\cos 126.9° + i \sin 126.9°)$

**25.**

$z = 2 - i\sqrt{3}$

$\approx \sqrt{7}(\cos 319.1° + i \sin 319.1°)$

**27.** $3\sqrt{3} + 3i$    **29.** $-2 - 2i\sqrt{3}$    **31.** $4\sqrt{2} - 4i\sqrt{2}$    **33.** $5i$    **35.** $z \approx -18.1 - 8.5i$    **37.** $30(\cos 70° + i \sin 70°)$

**39.** $12\left(\cos\dfrac{3\pi}{10} + i\sin\dfrac{3\pi}{10}\right)$    **41.** $\cos\dfrac{7\pi}{12} + i\sin\dfrac{7\pi}{12}$    **43.** $2(\cos\pi + i\sin\pi)$    **45.** $5(\cos 50° + i \sin 50°)$    **47.** $\dfrac{3}{4}\left(\cos\dfrac{\pi}{10} + i\sin\dfrac{\pi}{10}\right)$

**49.** $\cos 240° + i \sin 240°$    **51.** $2(\cos 0° + i \sin 0°)$    **53.** $32\sqrt{2} + 32i\sqrt{2}$    **55.** $-4 - 4i\sqrt{3}$    **57.** $\dfrac{1}{64}i$    **59.** $-2 - 2i\sqrt{3}$    **61.** $-4 - 4i$

**63.** $-64$    **65.** $3(\cos 15° + i \sin 15°); 3(\cos 195° + i \sin 195°)$    **67.** $2(\cos 70° + i \sin 70°); 2(\cos 190° + i \sin 190°); 2(\cos 310° + i \sin 310°)$

**69.** $\dfrac{3}{2} + \dfrac{3\sqrt{3}}{2}i; -\dfrac{3\sqrt{3}}{2} + \dfrac{3}{2}i; -\dfrac{3}{2} - \dfrac{3\sqrt{3}}{2}i; \dfrac{3\sqrt{3}}{2} - \dfrac{3}{2}i$    **71.** $2; \approx 0.6 + 1.9i; \approx -1.6 + 1.2i; \approx -1.6 - 1.2i; \approx 0.6 - 1.9i$

**73.** $1; -\dfrac{1}{2} + \dfrac{\sqrt{3}}{2}i; -\dfrac{1}{2} - \dfrac{\sqrt{3}}{2}i$    **75.** $\approx 1.1 + 0.2i; \approx -0.2 + 1.1i; \approx -1.1 - 0.2i; \approx 0.2 - 1.1i$

**77.** $[1(\cos 90° + i \sin 90°)][2\sqrt{2}(\cos 45° + i \sin 45°)][2(\cos 150° + i \sin 150°)]; 4\sqrt{2}(\cos 285° + i \sin 285°); \approx 1.4641 - 5.4641i$

**79.** $\dfrac{[2(\cos 60° + i \sin 60°)][\sqrt{2}(\cos(-45°) + i \sin(-45°))]}{8(\cos(-30°) + i \sin(-30°))}; \dfrac{\sqrt{2}}{2}(\cos 45° + i \sin 45°); \dfrac{1}{2} + \dfrac{1}{2}i$

**81.** $\cos 0° + i \sin 0°$, $\cos 60° + i \sin 60°$, $\cos 120° + i \sin 120°$, $\cos 180° + i \sin 180°$, $\cos 240° + i \sin 240°$, $\cos 300° + i \sin 300°$;

$1, \dfrac{1}{2} + \dfrac{\sqrt{3}}{2}i, -\dfrac{1}{2} + \dfrac{\sqrt{3}}{2}i, -1, -\dfrac{1}{2} - \dfrac{\sqrt{3}}{2}i, \dfrac{1}{2} - \dfrac{\sqrt{3}}{2}i$

**83.** $2(\cos 67.5° + i \sin 67.5°)$, $2(\cos 157.5° + i \sin 157.5°)$, $2(\cos 247.5° + i \sin 247.5°)$, $2(\cos 337.5° + i \sin 337.5°)$;
$0.7654 + 1.8478i$, $-1.8478 + 0.7654i$, $-0.7654 - 1.8478i$, $1.8478 - 0.7654i$

**85.** $\sqrt[3]{2}(\cos 20° + i \sin 20°)$, $\sqrt[3]{2}(\cos 140° + i \sin 140°)$, $\sqrt[3]{2}(\cos 260° + i \sin 260°)$; $1.1839 + 0.4309i$, $-0.9652 + 0.8099i$, $-0.2188 - 1.2408i$

**87.** 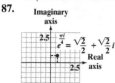      **89.**

**91. a.** $i; -1 + i; -i; -1 + i; -i; -1 + i$    **b.** Complex numbers may vary.
**107.** does not make sense    **109.** does not make sense
**111.** 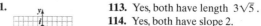    **113.** Yes, both have length $3\sqrt{5}$.
**114.** Yes, both have slope 2.
**115.** $8x + 34y$

## Section 6.6

### Check Point Exercises

**1.** $\|\mathbf{u}\| = 5 = \|\mathbf{v}\|$ and $m_u = \dfrac{4}{3} = m_v$    **2.**  $; \|\mathbf{v}\| = 3\sqrt{2}$    **3.** $\mathbf{v} = 3\mathbf{i} + 4\mathbf{j}$    **4. a.** $11\mathbf{i} - 2\mathbf{j}$    **b.** $3\mathbf{i} + 8\mathbf{j}$

**5. a.** $56\mathbf{i} + 80\mathbf{j}$    **b.** $-35\mathbf{i} - 50\mathbf{j}$    **6.** $30\mathbf{i} + 33\mathbf{j}$

**7.** $\dfrac{4}{5}\mathbf{i} - \dfrac{3}{5}\mathbf{j}; \sqrt{\left(\dfrac{4}{5}\right)^2 + \left(-\dfrac{3}{5}\right)^2} = \sqrt{\dfrac{16}{25} + \dfrac{9}{25}} = \sqrt{\dfrac{25}{25}} = 1$    **8.** $30\sqrt{2}\mathbf{i} + 30\sqrt{2}\mathbf{j}$    **9.** 82.55 lb; 46.2°

### Exercise Set 6.6

**1. a.** $\sqrt{41}$   **b.** $\sqrt{41}$   **c.** $\mathbf{u} = \mathbf{v}$    **3. a.** 6   **b.** 6   **c.** $\mathbf{u} = \mathbf{v}$
**5.**        **7.**        **9.**        **11.**

$\sqrt{10}$                $\sqrt{2}$                $2\sqrt{10}$                4

**13.** $10\mathbf{i} + 6\mathbf{j}$   **15.** $6\mathbf{i} - 3\mathbf{j}$   **17.** $-6\mathbf{i} - 14\mathbf{j}$   **19.** $9\mathbf{i}$   **21.** $-\mathbf{i} + 2\mathbf{j}$   **23.** $5\mathbf{i} - 12\mathbf{j}$   **25.** $-5\mathbf{i} + 12\mathbf{j}$   **27.** $-15\mathbf{i} + 35\mathbf{j}$   **29.** $4\mathbf{i} + 24\mathbf{j}$

**31.** $-9\mathbf{i} - 4\mathbf{j}$   **33.** $-5\mathbf{i} + 45\mathbf{j}$   **35.** $2\sqrt{29}$   **37.** $\sqrt{10}$   **39.** $\mathbf{i}$   **41.** $\dfrac{3}{5}\mathbf{i} - \dfrac{4}{5}\mathbf{j}$   **43.** $\dfrac{3\sqrt{13}}{13}\mathbf{i} - \dfrac{2\sqrt{13}}{3}\mathbf{j}$   **45.** $\dfrac{\sqrt{2}}{2}\mathbf{i} + \dfrac{\sqrt{2}}{2}\mathbf{j}$

**47.** $3\sqrt{3}\mathbf{i} + 3\mathbf{j}$   **49.** $-6\sqrt{2}\mathbf{i} - 6\sqrt{2}\mathbf{j}$   **51.** $\approx -0.20\mathbf{i} + 0.46\mathbf{j}$   **53.** $-23\mathbf{i} + 14\mathbf{j}$   **55.** $-60$   **57.** commutative property
**59.** distributive property   **61.** 18.03; 123.7°   **63.** 6; 90°   **65.** $22\sqrt{3}\mathbf{i} + 22\mathbf{j}$   **67.** $148.5\mathbf{i} + 20.9\mathbf{j}$   **69.** $\approx 1.4\mathbf{i} + 0.6\mathbf{j}$; 1.4 in.
**71.** $\approx 108.21$ lbs; S 77.4° E   **73.** 2038.28 lb; 162.8°   **75.** $\approx 30.9$ lbs   **77. a.** 335 lb   **b.** 3484 lb   **79. a.** $\mathbf{F} = 9\mathbf{i} - 3\mathbf{j}$   **b.** $\mathbf{F}_3 = -9\mathbf{i} + 3\mathbf{j}$
**81. a.** $\mathbf{F} = -2\mathbf{j}$   **b.** $\mathbf{F}_5 = 2\mathbf{j}$
**83. a.** $\mathbf{v} = 180 \cos 40°\mathbf{i} + 180 \sin 40°\mathbf{j} \approx 137.89\mathbf{i} + 115.70\mathbf{j}$,    $\mathbf{w} = 40 \cos 0°\mathbf{i} + 40 \sin 0°\mathbf{j} = 40\mathbf{i}$   **b.** $\mathbf{v} + \mathbf{w} \approx 177.89\mathbf{i} + 115.70\mathbf{j}$
**c.** 212 mph    **d.** 33.0°; N 57°E    **85.** 78 mph, 75.4°    **105.** does not make sense    **107.** does not make sense    **109.** true    **111.** true
**113.** The plane's true speed relative to the ground is about 269 miles per hour.; The compass heading relative to the ground is 278.3°.

**115. a.** 76°    **b.** increase    **116.** 137.7°    **117.** $\dfrac{7}{5}\mathbf{i} - \dfrac{21}{5}\mathbf{j}$

**118. a.** $\|\mathbf{u}\|^2 = \|\mathbf{v}\|^2 + \|\mathbf{w}\|^2 - 2\|\mathbf{v}\|\|\mathbf{w}\|\cos\theta$    **b.** $\|\mathbf{u}\| = \sqrt{(a_1 - a_2)^2 + (b_1 - b_2)^2}; \|\mathbf{u}\|^2 = (a_1 - a_2)^2 + (b_1 - b_2)^2; \|\mathbf{v}\| = \sqrt{a_1^2 + b_1^2};$

$\|\mathbf{v}\|^2 = a_1^2 + b_1^2; \|\mathbf{w}\| = \sqrt{a_2^2 + b_2^2}; \quad \|\mathbf{w}\|^2 = a_2^2 + b_2^2$

## Section 6.7

### Check Point Exercises

**1. a.** 18   **b.** 18   **c.** 5    **2.** 100.3°    **3.** orthogonal    **4.** $\dfrac{7}{2}\mathbf{i} - \dfrac{7}{2}\mathbf{j}$    **5.** $\mathbf{v}_1 = \dfrac{7}{2}\mathbf{i} - \dfrac{7}{2}\mathbf{j}; \mathbf{v}_2 = -\dfrac{3}{2}\mathbf{i} - \dfrac{3}{2}\mathbf{j}$    **6.** approximately 2598 ft-lb

### Exercise Set 6.7

**1.** 6; 10    **3.** $-6$; 41    **5.** 100; 61    **7.** 0; 25    **9.** 3    **11.** 3    **13.** 20    **15.** 20    **17.** 79.7°    **19.** 160.3°    **21.** 38.7°    **23.** orthogonal

**25.** orthogonal    **27.** not orthogonal    **29.** not orthogonal    **31.** orthogonal    **33.** $\mathbf{v}_1 = \text{proj}_w\mathbf{v} = \dfrac{5}{2}\mathbf{i} - \dfrac{5}{2}\mathbf{j}; \mathbf{v}_2 = \dfrac{1}{2}\mathbf{i} + \dfrac{1}{2}\mathbf{j}$
**35.** $\mathbf{v}_1 = \text{proj}_w\mathbf{v} = -\dfrac{26}{29}\mathbf{i} + \dfrac{65}{29}\mathbf{j}; \mathbf{v}_2 = \dfrac{55}{29}\mathbf{i} + \dfrac{22}{29}\mathbf{j}$    **37.** $\mathbf{v}_1 = \text{proj}_w\mathbf{v} = \mathbf{i} + 2\mathbf{j}; \mathbf{v}_2 = 0$    **39.** 25    **41.** $5\mathbf{i} - 5\mathbf{j}$    **43.** 30°    **45.** parallel

**47.** neither    **49.** orthogonal    **51.** 1617; $\mathbf{v} \cdot \mathbf{w} = 1617$ means that \$1617 in revenue is generated when 240 gallons of regular gasoline are sold at \$2.90 per gallon and 300 gallons of premium gasoline are sold at \$3.09 per gallon.    **53.** 7600 foot-pounds    **55.** 3392 foot-pounds

**57.** 1079 foot-pounds    **59.** 40 foot-pounds    **61.** 22.05 foot-pounds    **63. a.** $\frac{\sqrt{3}}{2}\mathbf{i} + \frac{1}{2}\mathbf{j}$    **b.** $-175\sqrt{3}\mathbf{i} - 175\mathbf{j}$    **c.** 350; A force of 350

pounds is required to keep the boat from rolling down the ramp.    **75.** makes sense    **77.** makes sense

**79.** $\mathbf{u} \cdot \mathbf{w} = (a_1\mathbf{i} + b_1\mathbf{j}) \cdot (a_2\mathbf{i} + b_2\mathbf{j})$

$\qquad = a_1a_2 + b_1b_2$

$\qquad = a_2a_1 + b_2b_1$

$\qquad = (a_2\mathbf{i} + b_2\mathbf{j}) \cdot (a_1\mathbf{i} + b_1\mathbf{j})$

$\qquad = \mathbf{v} \cdot \mathbf{u}$

**81.** $\mathbf{u} \cdot (\mathbf{v} + \mathbf{w}) = (a_1\mathbf{i} + b_1\mathbf{j}) \cdot [(a_2\mathbf{i} + b_2\mathbf{j}) + (a_3\mathbf{i} + b_3\mathbf{j})]$

$\qquad = (a_1\mathbf{i} + b_1\mathbf{j}) \cdot [(a_2 + a_3)\mathbf{i} + (b_2 + b_3)\mathbf{j}]$

$\qquad = a_1(a_2 + a_3) + b_1(b_2 + b_3)$

$\qquad = a_1a_2 + a_1a_3 + b_1b_2 + b_1b_3$

$\qquad = a_1a_2 + b_1b_2 + a_1a_3 + b_1b_3$

$\qquad = (a_1\mathbf{i} + b_1\mathbf{j}) \cdot (a_2\mathbf{i} + b_2\mathbf{j}) + (a_1\mathbf{i} + b_1\mathbf{j}) \cdot (a_3\mathbf{i} + b_3\mathbf{j})$

$\qquad = \mathbf{u} \cdot \mathbf{v} + \mathbf{u} \cdot \mathbf{w}$

**83.** $b = -20$    **85.** any two vectors, $\mathbf{v}$ and $\mathbf{w}$, having the same direction    **87. a.** yes    **b.** yes

**88.** $(4, -1)$;    **89.** $\{4\}$

## Chapter 6 Review Exercises

**1.** $C = 55°$, $b \approx 10.5$, and $c \approx 10.5$    **2.** $A = 43°$, $a \approx 171.9$, and $b \approx 241.0$    **3.** $b \approx 16.3$, $A \approx 72°$, and $C \approx 42°$

**4.** $C \approx 98°$, $A \approx 55°$, and $B \approx 27°$    **5.** $C = 120°$, $a \approx 45.0$, and $b \approx 33.2$    **6.** two triangles; $B_1 \approx 55°$, $C_1 \approx 86°$, and $c_1 \approx 31.7$;

$B_2 \approx 125°$, $C_2 \approx 16°$, and $c_2 \approx 8.8$    **7.** no triangle    **8.** $a \approx 59.0$, $B \approx 3°$, and $C \approx 15°$    **9.** $B \approx 78°$, $A \approx 39°$, and $C \approx 63°$

**10.** $B \approx 25°$, $C \approx 115°$, and $c \approx 8.5$    **11.** two triangles; $A_1 \approx 59°$, $C_1 \approx 84°$, $c_1 \approx 14.4$; $A_2 \approx 121°$, $C_2 \approx 22°$, $c_2 \approx 5.4$

**12.** $B \approx 9°$, $C \approx 148°$, and $c \approx 73.6$    **13.** 8 sq ft    **14.** 4 sq ft    **15.** 4 sq m    **16.** 2 sq m    **17.** 35 ft    **18.** 35.6 mi

**19.** 861 mi    **20.** 404 ft; 551 ft    **21.** \$214,194

**22.**

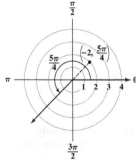

$(2, 2\sqrt{3})$

**23.**

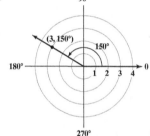

$\left(-\dfrac{3\sqrt{3}}{2}, \dfrac{3}{2}\right)$

**24.**

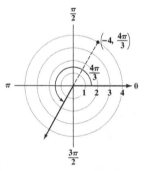

$(2, 2\sqrt{3})$

**25.**

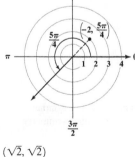

$(\sqrt{2}, \sqrt{2})$

**26.**

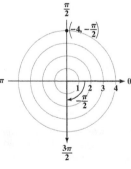

$(0, 4)$

**27.**

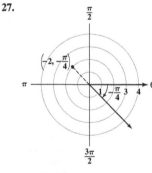

$(-\sqrt{2}, \sqrt{2})$

**28.**

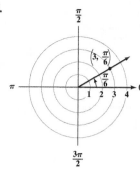

**a.** $\left(3, \dfrac{13\pi}{6}\right)$   **b.** $\left(-3, \dfrac{7\pi}{6}\right)$

**c.** $\left(3, -\dfrac{11\pi}{6}\right)$

**29.**

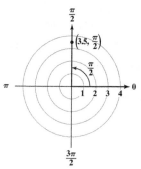

**a.** $\left(2, \dfrac{8\pi}{3}\right)$   **b.** $\left(-2, \dfrac{5\pi}{3}\right)$

**c.** $\left(2, -\dfrac{4\pi}{3}\right)$

**30.**

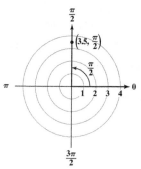

**a.** $\left(3.5, \dfrac{5\pi}{2}\right)$   **b.** $\left(-3.5, \dfrac{3\pi}{2}\right)$

**c.** $\left(3.5, -\dfrac{3\pi}{2}\right)$

**31.** $\left(4\sqrt{2}, \dfrac{3\pi}{4}\right)$   **32.** $\left(3\sqrt{2}, \dfrac{7\pi}{4}\right)$   **33.** approximately $(13, 67°)$   **34.** approximately $(5, 127°)$   **35.** $\left(5, \dfrac{3\pi}{2}\right)$   **36.** $(1, 0)$

**37.** $r = \dfrac{8}{2 \cos \theta + 3 \sin \theta}$   **38.** $r = 10$   **39.** $r = 12 \cos \theta$

**40.** $x^2 + y^2 = 9$

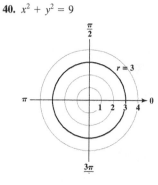

**41.** $y = -x$

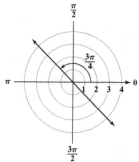

**42.** $x = -1$

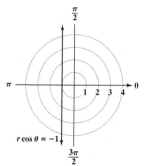

**43.** $y = 5$

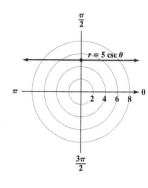

**44.** $\left(x - \dfrac{3}{2}\right)^2 + y^2 = \dfrac{9}{4}$

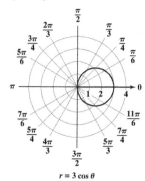

$r = 3 \cos \theta$

**45.** $y = -4x + 8$

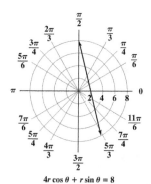

$4r \cos \theta + r \sin \theta = 8$

**46.** $y = -\dfrac{1}{x}$

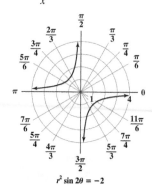

$r^2 \sin 2\theta = -2$

**47. a.** has symmetry   **b.** may or may not have symmetry   **c.** may or may not have symmetry
**48. a.** may or may not have symmetry   **b.** has symmetry   **c.** may or may not have symmetry
**49. a.** has symmetry   **b.** has symmetry   **c.** has symmetry

**50.**

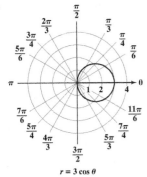

$r = 3 \cos \theta$

**51.**

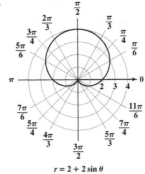

$r = 2 + 2 \sin \theta$

**52.**

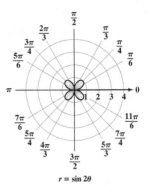

$r = \sin 2\theta$

**53.**

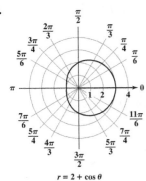

$r = 2 + \cos \theta$

**54.**

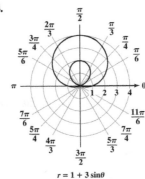

$r = 1 + 3 \sin\theta$

**55.**

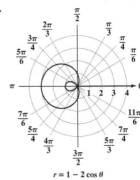

$r = 1 - 2 \cos \theta$

**56.**

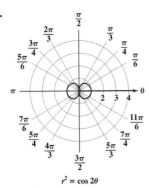

$r^2 = \cos 2\theta$

**57.**

$\sqrt{2}\left(\cos \dfrac{7\pi}{4} + i \sin \dfrac{7\pi}{4}\right)$ or

$\sqrt{2}(\cos 315° + i \sin 315°)$

**58.**

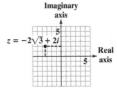

$4(\cos 150° + i \sin 150°)$ or

$4\left(\cos \dfrac{5\pi}{6} + i \sin \dfrac{5\pi}{6}\right)$

**59.**

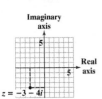

$z = -3 - 4i \approx 5(\cos 233° + i \sin 233°)$

**60.**

$5\left(\cos \dfrac{3\pi}{2} + i \sin \dfrac{3\pi}{2}\right)$ or

$5(\cos 270° + i \sin 270°)$

**61.** $z = 4 + 4\sqrt{3}i$
**62.** $z = -2\sqrt{3} - 2i$
**63.** $z = -3 + 3\sqrt{3}i$
**64.** $z \approx -0.1 + 0.6i$
**65.** $15(\cos 110° + i \sin 110°)$
**66.** $\cos 265° + i \sin 265°$
**67.** $40(\cos \pi + i \sin \pi)$
**68.** $2(\cos 5° + i \sin 5°)$

**69.** $\dfrac{1}{2}(\cos \pi + i \sin \pi)$  **70.** $2\left(\cos\dfrac{7\pi}{6} + i \sin\dfrac{7\pi}{6}\right)$  **71.** $4 + 4i\sqrt{3}$  **72.** $-32\sqrt{3} + 32i$  **73.** $\dfrac{1}{128}i$  **74.** $64 - 64i\sqrt{3}$  **75.** $128 + 128i$

**76.** $7(\cos 25° + i \sin 25°)$; $7(\cos 205° + i \sin 205°)$  **77.** $5(\cos 55° + i \sin 55°)$; $5(\cos 175° + i \sin 175°)$; $5(\cos 295° + i \sin 295°)$

**78.** $\sqrt{3} + i$; $-1 + i\sqrt{3}$; $-\sqrt{3} - i$; $1 - i\sqrt{3}$  **79.** $\sqrt{3} + i$; $-\sqrt{3} + i$; $-2i$  **80.** $\dfrac{1}{2} + \dfrac{\sqrt{3}}{2}i$; $-1$; $\dfrac{1}{2} - \dfrac{\sqrt{3}}{2}i$

**81.** $\dfrac{\sqrt[5]{8}}{2} + \dfrac{\sqrt[5]{8}}{2}i$; $\approx -0.49 + 0.95i$; $\approx -1.06 - 0.17i$; $\approx -0.17 - 1.06i$; $\approx 0.95 - 0.49i$

**82.**

; 5

**83.**

; $\sqrt{29}$

**84.**

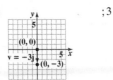

; 3

**85.** $3\mathbf{i} - 2\mathbf{j}$   **86.** $\mathbf{i} - 2\mathbf{j}$   **87.** $-\mathbf{i} + 2\mathbf{j}$   **88.** $-3\mathbf{i} + 12\mathbf{j}$   **89.** $12\mathbf{i} - 51\mathbf{j}$   **90.** $2\sqrt{26}$   **91.** $\dfrac{4}{5}\mathbf{i} - \dfrac{3}{5}\mathbf{j}$   **92.** $-\dfrac{1}{\sqrt{5}}\mathbf{i} + \dfrac{2}{\sqrt{5}}\mathbf{j}$

**93.** $6i + 6\sqrt{3}j$    **94.** 270 lb; 27.7°    **95. a.** $13.59i + 6.34j$    **b.** 14.0 mph    **c.** 13.9°    **96.** 4    **97.** 2; 86.1°    **98.** $-32$; 124.8°

**99.** 1; 71.6°    **100.** orthogonal    **101.** not orthogonal    **102.** $v_1 = \text{proj}_w v = \dfrac{50}{41}i + \dfrac{40}{41}j; v_2 = -\dfrac{132}{41}i + \dfrac{165}{41}j$

**103.** $v_1 = \text{proj}_w v = -\dfrac{3}{2}i + \dfrac{1}{2}j; v_2 = \dfrac{1}{2}i + \dfrac{3}{2}j$    **104.** 1115 ft-lb    **105.** Answers may vary.

## Chapter 6 Test

**1.** 8.0    **2.** 6.2    **3.** 206 sq in.

**4.**

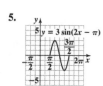

; Ordered pairs may vary.    **5.** $\left(\sqrt{2}, \dfrac{7\pi}{4}\right)$    **7.** $x = -4$

**6.** $r = -16 \sin \theta$

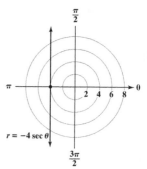

$r = -4 \sec \theta$

**8.**

$r = 1 + \sin \theta$

**9.**

$r = 1 + 3 \cos \theta$

**10.** $2(\cos 150° + i \sin 150°)$ or $2\left(\cos\dfrac{5\pi}{6} + i \sin\dfrac{5\pi}{6}\right)$

**11.** $50(\cos 20° + i \sin 20°)$

**12.** $\dfrac{1}{2}\left(\cos\dfrac{\pi}{6} + i \sin\dfrac{\pi}{6}\right)$

**13.** $32(\cos 50° + i \sin 50°)$

**14.** $3; -\dfrac{3}{2} + \dfrac{\sqrt{3}}{2}i; -\dfrac{3}{2} - \dfrac{\sqrt{3}}{2}i$

**15. a.** $i + 2j$    **b.** $\sqrt{5}$

**16.** $-23i + 22j$

**17.** $-18$

**18.** 138°    **19.** $-\dfrac{9}{5}i + \dfrac{18}{5}j$

**20.** 1.0 mi    **21.** 323 pounds; 3.4°    **22.** 1966 ft-lb

## Cumulative Review Exercises (Chapters P–6)

**1.** $\{-1, 2, i, -i\}$    **2.** $\dfrac{\pi}{6}, \dfrac{5\pi}{6}, \dfrac{\pi}{2}$    **3.** $\{x | x < -4 \text{ or } x > 2\}$    **4.** $\dfrac{3\pi}{4}, \dfrac{7\pi}{4}$

**5.**

**6.**

**7.** $\sin \theta \csc \theta - \cos^2 \theta = \sin \theta\left(\dfrac{1}{\sin \theta}\right) - \cos^2 \theta$
$= 1 - \cos^2 \theta = \sin^2 \theta$

**8.** $\cos\left(\theta + \dfrac{3\pi}{2}\right) = \cos \theta \cos\dfrac{3\pi}{2} - \sin \theta \sin\dfrac{3\pi}{2}$
$= \cos \theta(0) - \sin \theta(-1) = \sin \theta$

**9.** slope is $-\dfrac{1}{2}$; y-intercept is 2.    **10.** 0    **11.** $\dfrac{\sqrt{5}}{5}$    **12.** $\{x | x \le 5\}$    **13.** $\{x | x \ne 3, x \ne -3\}$    **14.** 1.5 sec; 44 ft

**15. a.** 4 m    **b.** $\dfrac{5}{2\pi}$    **c.** $\dfrac{2\pi}{5}$ sec    **16.** $\dfrac{\sqrt{\sqrt{2} + 2}}{2}$    **17. a.** $5i + 23j$    **b.** $-12$    **18.** $\log_b \dfrac{\sqrt{x}}{x^2 + 1}$    **19.** $y = -\dfrac{1}{2}x + 1$

**20. a.** 0.014    **b.** 73 words    **c.** about 144 min

# CHAPTER 7

## Section 7.1

### Check Point Exercises

**1. a.** solution    **b.** not a solution    **2.** $\{(-2, 5)\}$    **3.** $\{(2, -1)\}$    **4.** $\left\{\left(\dfrac{60}{17}, -\dfrac{11}{17}\right)\right\}$    **5.** no solution or $\varnothing$

**6.** $\{(x, y) | x = 4y - 8\}$ or $\{(x, y) | 5x - 20y = -40\}$    **7.** 4 l of 18% solution; 8 l of 45% solution    **8.** boat: 35 mph; current: 7 mph

**9. a.** $C(x) = 300,000 + 30x$    **b.** $R(x) = 80x$    **c.** (6000, 480,000); The company will break even if it produces and sells 6000 pairs of shoes.

### Exercise Set 7.1

**1.** solution    **3.** not a solution    **5.** $\{(1, 3)\}$    **7.** $\{(5, 1)\}$    **9.** $\{(-22, -5)\}$    **11.** $\{(0, 0)\}$    **13.** $\{(3, -2)\}$    **15.** $\{(5, 4)\}$    **17.** $\{(7, 3)\}$

**19.** $\{(2, -1)\}$    **21.** $\{(3, 0)\}$    **23.** $\{(-4, 3)\}$    **25.** $\{(3, 1)\}$    **27.** $\{(1, -2)\}$    **29.** $\left\{\left(\dfrac{7}{25}, -\dfrac{1}{25}\right)\right\}$    **31.** $\varnothing$    **33.** $\{(x, y) | y = 3x - 5\}$

**35.** $\{(1, 4)\}$ **37.** $\{(x, y) | x + 3y = 2\}$ **39.** $\{(-5, -1)\}$ **41.** $\left\{\left(\dfrac{29}{22}, -\dfrac{5}{11}\right)\right\}$ **43.** $x + y = 7; x - y = -1$; 3 and 4

**45.** $3x - y = 1; x + 2y = 12$; 2 and 5 **47.** $\{(6, -1)\}$ **49.** $\left\{\left(\dfrac{1}{a}, 3\right)\right\}$ **51.** $m = -4, b = 3$ **53.** $y = x - 4; y = -\dfrac{1}{3}x + 4$

**55.** California: 100 gal; French: 100 gal **57.** 18-karat gold: 96 g; 12-karat gold: 204 g **59.** cheaper candy: 30 lb; more expensive candy: 45 lb
**61.** plane: 130 mph; wind: 30 mph **63.** crew: 6 km/hr; current: 2 km/hr **65.** velocity in still water: 4.5 mph; current: 1.5 mph
**67.** 500 radios **69.** $-6000$; When the company produces and sells 200 radios, the loss is $6000. **71. a.** $P(x) = 20x - 10,000$ **b.** $190,000
**73. a.** $C(x) = 18,000 + 20x$ **b.** $R(x) = 80x$ **c.** $(300, 24,000)$; When 300 canoes are produced and sold, both revenue and cost are $24,000.
**75. a.** $C(x) = 30,000 + 2500x$ **b.** $R(x) = 3125x$ **c.** $(48, 150,000)$; For 48 sold-out performances, both cost and revenue are $150,000.
**77. a.** 4 million workers; $4.50 per hour **b.** $4.50; 4; 4 **c.** 2 million **d.** 5.7 million **e.** 3.7 million **79.** 2009; 18.5% pro-choice and 18.5%
pro-life **81. a.** $y = 0.45x + 0.8$ **b.** $y = 0.15x + 2.6$ **c.** week 6; 3.5 symptoms; by the intersection point (6, 3.5) **83. a.** $y = -0.54x + 38$
**b.** $y = -0.79x + 40$ **c.** 1993; 33.68% **85.** Mr. Goodbar: 264 cal; Mounds: 258 cal **87.** 3 Mr. Goodbars and 2 Mounds bars **89.** 50 rooms
with kitchen facilities, 150 rooms without kitchen facilities **91.** 100 ft long by 80 ft wide **93.** 80°, 50°, 50° **105.** does not make sense

**107.** makes sense **109.** $y = \dfrac{a_1c_2 - a_2c_1}{a_1b_2 - a_2b_1}; x = \dfrac{b_2c_1 - b_1c_2}{a_1b_2 - a_2b_1}$ **111.** Yes; 8 hexagons and 4 squares **113.** yes **114.** $11x + 4y = -3$

**115.** $1682 = 16a + 4b + c$

## Section 7.2

### Check Point Exercises

**1.** $(-1) - 2(-4) + 3(5) = 22; 2(-1) - 3(-4) - 5 = 5; 3(-1) + (-4) - 5(5) = -32$ **2.** $\{(1, 4, -3)\}$ **3.** $\{(4, 5, 3)\}$ **4.** $y = 3x^2 - 12x + 13$

### Exercise Set 7.2

**1.** solution **3.** solution **5.** $\{(2, 3, 3)\}$ **7.** $\{(2, -1, 1)\}$ **9.** $\{(1, 2, 3)\}$ **11.** $\{(3, 1, 5)\}$ **13.** $\{(1, 0, -3)\}$ **15.** $\{(1, -5, -6)\}$

**17.** $\left\{\left(\dfrac{1}{2}, \dfrac{1}{3}, -1\right)\right\}$ **19.** $y = 2x^2 - x + 3$ **21.** $y = 2x^2 + x - 5$ **23.** 7, 4, and 5 **25.** $\{(4, 8, 6)\}$ **27.** $y = -\dfrac{3}{4}x^2 + 6x - 11$

**29.** $\left\{\left(\dfrac{8}{a}, -\dfrac{3}{b}, -\dfrac{5}{c}\right)\right\}$ **31. a.** $y = -16x^2 + 40x + 200$ **b.** $y = 0$ when $x = 5$; The ball hits the ground after 5 seconds.

**33.** water: 58%; fat: 23%; protein: 14% **35.** 200 $8 tickets; 150 $10 tickets; 50 $12 tickets **37.** $1200 at 8%, $2000 at 10%, and $3500 at 12%
**39.** $x = 60, y = 55, z = 65$ **47.** does not make sense **49.** makes sense **51.** 13 triangles, 21 rectangles, and 6 pentagons

**53.** $\dfrac{x + 14}{(x - 4)(x + 2)}$ **54.** $\dfrac{5x^3 - 3x^2 + 7x - 3}{(x^2 + 1)^2}$ **55.** $\{(5, -2, 3)\}$

## Section 7.3

### Check Point Exercises

**1.** $\dfrac{2}{x - 3} + \dfrac{3}{x + 4}$ **2.** $\dfrac{2}{x} - \dfrac{2}{x - 1} + \dfrac{3}{(x - 1)^2}$ **3.** $\dfrac{2}{x + 3} + \dfrac{6x - 8}{x^2 + x + 2}$ **4.** $\dfrac{2x}{x^2 + 1} + \dfrac{-x + 3}{(x^2 + 1)^2}$

### Exercise Set 7.3

**1.** $\dfrac{A}{x - 2} + \dfrac{B}{x + 1}$ **3.** $\dfrac{A}{x + 2} + \dfrac{B}{x - 3} + \dfrac{C}{(x - 3)^2}$ **5.** $\dfrac{A}{x - 1} + \dfrac{Bx + C}{x^2 + 1}$ **7.** $\dfrac{Ax + B}{x^2 + 4} + \dfrac{Cx + D}{(x^2 + 4)^2}$ **9.** $\dfrac{3}{x - 3} - \dfrac{2}{x - 2}$

**11.** $\dfrac{7}{x - 9} - \dfrac{4}{x + 2}$ **13.** $\dfrac{24}{7(x - 4)} + \dfrac{25}{7(x + 3)}$ **15.** $\dfrac{4}{7(x - 3)} - \dfrac{8}{7(2x + 1)}$ **17.** $\dfrac{3}{x} + \dfrac{2}{x - 1} - \dfrac{1}{x + 3}$ **19.** $\dfrac{3}{x} + \dfrac{4}{x + 1} - \dfrac{3}{x - 1}$

**21.** $\dfrac{6}{x - 1} - \dfrac{5}{(x - 1)^2}$ **23.** $\dfrac{1}{x - 2} - \dfrac{2}{(x - 2)^2} - \dfrac{5}{(x - 2)^3}$ **25.** $\dfrac{7}{x} - \dfrac{6}{x - 1} + \dfrac{10}{(x - 1)^2}$ **27.** $\dfrac{1}{4(x + 1)} + \dfrac{3}{4(x - 1)} + \dfrac{1}{2(x - 1)^2}$

**29.** $\dfrac{3}{x - 1} + \dfrac{2x - 4}{x^2 + 1}$ **31.** $\dfrac{2}{x + 1} + \dfrac{3x - 1}{x^2 + 2x + 2}$ **33.** $\dfrac{1}{4x} + \dfrac{1}{x^2} - \dfrac{x + 4}{4(x^2 + 4)}$ **35.** $\dfrac{4}{x + 1} + \dfrac{2x - 3}{x^2 + 1}$ **37.** $\dfrac{x + 1}{x^2 + 2} - \dfrac{2x}{(x^2 + 2)^2}$

**39.** $\dfrac{x - 2}{x^2 - 2x + 3} + \dfrac{2x + 1}{(x^2 - 2x + 3)^2}$ **41.** $\dfrac{3}{x - 2} + \dfrac{x - 1}{x^2 + 2x + 4}$ **43.** $x^3 + x - \dfrac{1}{2(x + 1)} + \dfrac{3}{2(x - 1)}$ **45.** $x + 1 - \dfrac{2}{x} - \dfrac{2}{x^2} + \dfrac{2}{x - 1}$

**47.** $\dfrac{\frac{1}{2c}}{x - c} - \dfrac{\frac{1}{2c}}{x + c}$ **49.** $\dfrac{a}{x - c} + \dfrac{ac + b}{(x - c)^2}$ **51.** $\dfrac{1}{x} - \dfrac{1}{x + 1}; \dfrac{99}{100}$ **61.** does not make sense **63.** does not make sense

**65.** $\dfrac{2}{x - 3} + \dfrac{2x + 5}{x^2 + 3x + 3}$ **66.** $\{(2.5, -2)\}$ **67.** $\{(4, -3)\}$

**68.** ; $(0, -3)$ and $(2, -1); 0 - (-3) = 3$ and $(0 - 2)^2 + (-3 + 3)^2 = 4$ are true;
$2 - (-1) = 3$ and $(2 - 2)^2 + (-1 + 3)^2 = 4$ are true.

## Section 7.4

**Check Point Exercises**

**1.** $\{(0, 1), (4, 17)\}$  **2.** $\left\{\left(-\frac{6}{5}, \frac{3}{5}\right), (2, -1)\right\}$  **3.** $\{(3, 2), (3, -2), (-3, 2), (-3, -2)\}$  **4.** $\{(0, 5)\}$  **5.** length: 7 ft; width: 3 ft or length: 3 ft; width: 7 ft

**Exercise Set 7.4**

**1.** $\{(-3, 5), (2, 0)\}$  **3.** $\{(1, 1), (2, 0)\}$  **5.** $\{(4, -10), (-3, 11)\}$  **7.** $\{(4, 3), (-3, -4)\}$  **9.** $\left\{\left(-\frac{3}{2}, -4\right), (2, 3)\right\}$  **11.** $\{(-5, -4), (3, 0)\}$

**13.** $\{(3, 1), (-3, -1), (1, 3), (-1, -3)\}$  **15.** $\{(4, -3), (-1, 2)\}$  **17.** $\{(0, 1), (4, -3)\}$  **19.** $\{(3, 2), (3, -2), (-3, 2), (-3, -2)\}$

**21.** $\{(3, 2), (3, -2), (-3, 2), (-3, -2)\}$  **23.** $\{(2, 1), (2, -1), (-2, 1), (-2, -1)\}$  **25.** $\{(3, 4), (3, -4)\}$

**27.** $\{(0, 2), (0, -2), (-1, \sqrt{3}), (-1, -\sqrt{3})\}$  **29.** $\{(2, 1), (2, -1), (-2, 1), (-2, -1)\}$  **31.** $\{(-2\sqrt{2}, -\sqrt{2}), (-1, -4), (1, 4), (2\sqrt{2}, \sqrt{2})\}$

**33.** $\{(2, 2), (4, 1)\}$  **35.** $\{(0, 0), (-1, 1)\}$  **37.** $\{(0, 0), (-2, 2), (2, 2)\}$  **39.** $\left\{(-4, 1), \left(-\frac{5}{2}, \frac{1}{4}\right)\right\}$  **41.** $\left\{\left(\frac{12}{5}, -\frac{29}{5}\right), (-2, 3)\right\}$

**43.** 4 and 6  **45.** 2 and 1, 2 and −1, −2 and 1, or −2 and −1

**47.** $\{(2, -1), (-2, 1)\}$  **49.** $\{(2, 20), (-2, 4), (-3, 0)\}$  **51.** $\left\{\left(-1, -\frac{1}{2}\right), \left(-1, \frac{1}{2}\right), \left(1, -\frac{1}{2}\right), \left(1, \frac{1}{2}\right)\right\}$

**53.** 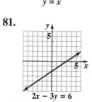  **55.** $(0, -4), (-2, 0), (2, 0)$  **57.** 11 ft and 7 ft  **59.** width: 6 in.; length: 8 in.
**61.** $x = 5$ m, $y = 2$ m  **63. a.** between the 1940s and the 1960s  **b.** 1949; 43%; 43%  **c.** 1920; 28%
**d.** 1919; white collar: 27.5%; farmers: 27.4%; fairly well, although answers may vary.
**69.** makes sense  **71.** makes sense  **73.** false  **75.** false  **77.** 18 sq units  **79.** $\{(8, 2)\}$

$y = x^2 - 4$
$y = x$

**81.**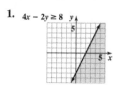

$2x - 3y = 6$

**82.** 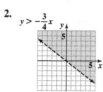  $f(x) = -\frac{2}{3}x$

**83.** $f(x) = -2$

## Mid-Chapter 7 Check Point

**1.** $\{(-1, 2)\}$  **2.** $\{(1, -2)\}$  **3.** $\{(6, 10)\}$  **4.** $\{(x, y)\,|\,y = 4x - 5\}$ or $\{(x, y)\,|\,8x - 2y = 10\}$  **5.** $\left\{\left(\frac{11}{19}, \frac{7}{19}\right)\right\}$  **6.** $\varnothing$  **7.** $\{(-1, 2, -2)\}$

**8.** $\{(4, -2, 3)\}$  **9.** $\left\{\left(-\frac{9}{5}, \frac{12}{5}\right), (3, 0)\right\}$  **10.** $\{(-2, -1), (-2, 1), (2, -1), (2, 1)\}$  **11.** $\{(-\sqrt{7}, 1), (-2, -2), (2, -2), (\sqrt{7}, 1)\}$

**12.** $\{(0, -2), (6, 1)\}$  **13.** $\frac{1}{x - 2} - \frac{2}{(x - 2)^2} - \frac{5}{(x - 2)^3}$  **14.** $\frac{5}{x + 2} + \frac{3}{x + 1} + \frac{2}{x - 1}$  **15.** $-\frac{2}{x + 3} + \frac{3x - 5}{x^2 + 4}$  **16.** $\frac{x}{x^2 + 4} - \frac{4x}{(x^2 + 4)^2}$

**17. a.** $C(x) = 400{,}000 + 20x$  **b.** $R(x) = 100x$  **c.** $P(x) = 80x - 400{,}000$  **d.** $(5000, 500{,}000)$; The company will break even when it
produces and sells 5000 PDAs. At this level, both revenue and cost are $500,000.  **18.** 6 roses and 14 carnations  **19.** north campus: 300 students;
south campus: 900 students  **20.** rowing rate in still water: 3 mph; current: 1.5 mph  **21.** $x = 55°$, $y = 35°$  **22.** $y = -x^2 + 2x + 3$
**23.** length: 8 m; width: 2.5 m

## Section 7.5

**Check Point Exercises**

**1.** $4x - 2y \geq 8$  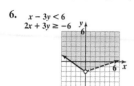  **2.** $y > -\frac{3}{4}x$  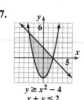  **3. a.** $y > 1$  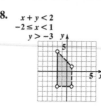  **b.** $x \leq -2$  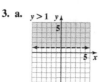  **4.**   $x^2 + y^2 \geq 16$

**5.** Point $B = (66, 130)$; $4.9(66) - 130 \geq 165$, or $193.4 \geq 165$, is true; $3.7(66) - 130 \leq 125$, or $114.2 \leq 125$, is true.

**6.** $x - 3y < 6$
$2x + 3y \geq -6$  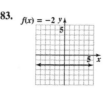  **7.**  **8.** $x + y < 2$
$-2 \leq x < 1$
$y > -3$

$y \geq x^2 - 4$
$x + y \leq 2$

## Exercise Set 7.5

**1.**

$x + 2y \leq 8$

**3.**

$x - 2y > 10$

**5.**

$y \leq \frac{1}{3}x$

**7.**

$y > 2x - 1$

**9.**

$x \leq 1$

**11.**

$y > 1$

**13.**

$x^2 + y^2 \leq 1$

**15.**

$x^2 + y^2 > 25$

**17.**

$(x - 2)^2 + (y + 1)^2 < 9$

**19.**

$y < x^2 - 1$

**21.**

$y \geq x^2 - 9$

**23.**

$y > 2^x$

**25.** $x = -1$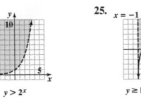

$y \geq \log_2(x + 1)$

**27.** $3x + 6y \leq 6$
$2x + y \leq 8$

**29.** $2x - 5y \leq 10$
$3x - 2y > 6$

**31.** $y > 2x - 3$
$y < -x + 6$

**33.** $x + 2y \leq 4$
$y \geq x - 3$

**35.** $x \leq 2$
$y \geq -1$

**37.** $-2 \leq x < 5$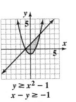

**39.** $x - y \leq 1$
$x \geq 2$

**41.** $\varnothing$

**43.** $x + y > 4$
$x + y > -1$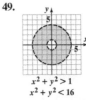

**45.**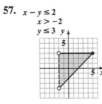

$y \geq x^2 - 1$
$x - y \geq -1$

**47.**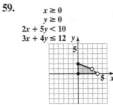

$x^2 + y^2 \leq 16$
$x + y > 2$

**49.**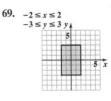

$x^2 + y^2 > 1$
$x^2 + y^2 < 16$

**51.**

$(x - 1)^2 + (y + 1)^2 < 25$
$(x - 1) + (y + 1)^2 \geq 16$

**53.**

$x^2 + y^2 \leq 1$
$y - x^2 > 0$

**55.**

$x^2 + y^2 < 16$
$y \geq 2^x$

**57.** $x - y \leq 2$
$x > -2$
$y \leq 3$

**59.** $x \geq 0$
$y \geq 0$
$2x + 5y < 10$
$3x + 4y \leq 12$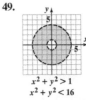

**61.** $3x + y \leq 6$
$2x - y \leq -1$
$x > -2$
$y < 4$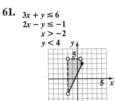

**63.** $y \geq -2x + 4$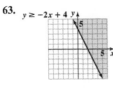

**65.** $x + y \leq 4$
$3x + y \leq 6$

**67.**

$x + y \leq 2$
$y \geq x^2 - 4$

**69.** $-2 \leq x \leq 2$
$-3 \leq y \leq 3$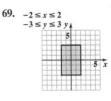

**71.** $y > \frac{3}{2}x - 2$ or $y < 4$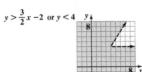

**73.** no solution

**75.** infinitely many solutions

**77.** Point $A = (66, 160)$; $5.3(66) - 160 \geq 180$, or $189.8 \geq 180$, is true; $4.1(66) - 160 \leq 140$, or $110.6 \leq 140$, is true.

**79.** no

**81. a.** $50x + 150y > 2000$

**b.**

$50x + 150y > 2000$

**c.** Answers may vary. Example:
(20, 20): 20 children and 20 adults
will cause the elevator to be overloaded.

**83. a.** $y \geq 0$; $x + y \geq 5$; $x \geq 1$; $200x + 100y \leq 700$

**b.**
$y \geq 0$
$x + y \geq 5$
$x \geq 1$
$200x + 100y \leq 700$

**c.** 2 nights

**85. a.** 27.1    **b.** overweight

**97.**

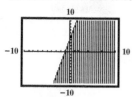

**99.**

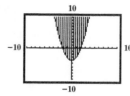

**101.**

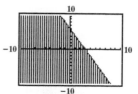

**107.** does not make sense    **109.** makes sense    **111.** $y > x - 3$; $y \leq x$    **113.** $x + 2y \leq 6$ or $2x + y \leq 6$

**115.**
$y \geq nx + b$
$y \leq mx + b$

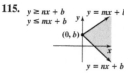

**116. a.**

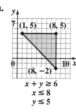

**b.** $(1, 5), (8, 5), (8, -2)$

$x + y \geq 6$
$x \leq 8$
$y \leq 5$

**c.** at $(1, 5)$: 13; at $(8, 5)$: 34; at $(8, -2)$: 20

**117. a.**

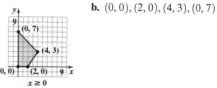

**b.** $(0, 0), (2, 0), (4, 3), (0, 7)$

$x \geq 0$
$y \geq 0$
$3x - 2y \leq 6$
$y \leq -x + 7$

**c.** at $(0, 0)$: 0; at $(2, 0)$: 4; at $(4, 3)$: 23; $(0, 7)$: 35

**118.** $20x + 10y \leq 80,000$

## Section 7.6

### Check Point Exercises

**1.** $z = 25x + 55y$    **2.** $x + y \leq 80$    **3.** $30 \leq x \leq 80$; $10 \leq y \leq 30$; objective function: $z = 25x + 55y$; constraints: $x + y \leq 80$; $30 \leq x \leq 80$; $10 \leq y \leq 30$    **4.** 50 bookshelves and 30 desks; $2900    **5.** 30

### Exercise Set 7.6

**1.** $(1, 2)$: 17; $(2, 10)$: 70; $(7, 5)$: 65; $(8, 3)$: 58; maximum: $z = 70$; minimum: $z = 17$
**3.** $(0, 0)$: 0; $(0, 8)$: 400; $(4, 9)$: 610; $(8, 0)$: 320; maximum: $z = 610$; minimum: $z = 0$

**5. a.**

**b.** $(0, 8)$: 16; $(0, 4)$: 8; $(4, 0)$: 12
**c.** maximum value: 16 at $x = 0$ and $y = 8$

**7. a.**

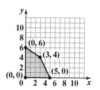

**b.** $(0, 4)$: 4; $(0, 3)$: 3; $(3, 0)$: 12; $(6, 0)$: 24
**c.** maximum value: 24 at $x = 6$ and $y = 0$

**9. a.**

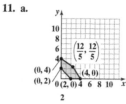

**b.** $(1, 2)$: $-1$; $(1, 4)$: $-5$; $(5, 8)$: $-1$; $(5, 2)$: 11

**c.** maximum value: 11 at $x = 5$ and $y = 2$

**11. a.**

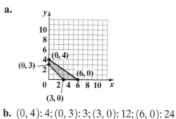

**b.** $(0, 4)$: 8; $(0, 2)$: 4; $(2, 0)$: 8; $(4, 0)$: 16;
$\left(\frac{12}{5}, \frac{12}{5}\right)$: $\frac{72}{5}$

**c.** maximum value: 16 at $x = 4$ and $y = 0$

**13. a.**

**b.** $(0, 6)$: 72; $(0, 0)$: 0; $(5, 0)$: 50; $(3, 4)$: 78

**c.** maximum value: 78 at $x = 3$ and $y = 4$

**15. a.** $z = 125x + 200y$     **b.** $x \leq 450;\ y \leq 200;\ 600x + 900y \leq 360,000$

**c.**      **d.** $(0, 0): 0;\ (0, 200): 40,000;$
$(300, 200): 77,500;\ (450, 100): 76,250;$
$(450, 0): 56,250$

**e.** $300; 200; \$77,500$

**17.** 40 model A bicycles and no model B bicycles
**19.** 300 cartons of food and 200 cartons of clothing
**21.** 50 students and 100 parents
**23.** 10 Boeing 727s and 42 Falcon 20s
**29.** does not make sense     **31.** makes sense
**33.** \$5000 in stocks and \$5000 in bonds
**37.** $\{(6, 3, 5)\}$; Answers may vary.

**38.** $\{(-2, 1, 4, 3)\}$; Answers may vary.     **39.** $\begin{bmatrix} 1 & 2 & -1 \\ 0 & -11 & -11 \end{bmatrix}$

## Chapter 7 Review Exercises

**1.** $\{(1, 5)\}$     **2.** $\{(2, 3)\}$     **3.** $\{(2, -3)\}$     **4.** $\varnothing$     **5.** $\{(x, y) | 3x - 6y = 12\}$     **6. a.** $C(x) = 60,000 + 200x$     **b.** $R(x) = 450x$

**c.** $(240, 108,000)$; This means the company will break even if it produces and sells 240 desks.     **7.** Klimt: \$135 million; Picasso: \$104 million

**8. a.** Answers will vary; approximately $(2004, 180)$; 2004; 180 million     **b.** $y = 19.8x + 98$     **c.** 2004; 180 million     **d.** Answers will vary from

"quite well" to "extremely well."     **9.** \$80 per day for the room, \$60 per day for the car     **10.** 10 ml of 34%; 90 ml of 4%     **11.** plane: 630 mph;

wind: 90 mph     **12.** $\{(0, 1, 2)\}$     **13.** $\{(2, 1, -1)\}$     **14.** $y = 3x^2 - 4x + 5$     **15.** 18–29: \$8300; 30–39: \$16,400; 40–49: \$19,500

**16.** $\dfrac{3}{5(x-3)} + \dfrac{2}{5(x+2)}$     **17.** $\dfrac{6}{x-4} + \dfrac{5}{x+3}$     **18.** $\dfrac{2}{x} + \dfrac{3}{x+2} - \dfrac{1}{x-1}$     **19.** $\dfrac{2}{x-2} + \dfrac{5}{(x-2)^2}$     **20.** $-\dfrac{4}{x-1} + \dfrac{4}{x-2} - \dfrac{2}{(x-2)^2}$

**21.** $\dfrac{6}{5(x-2)} + \dfrac{-6x+3}{5(x^2+1)}$     **22.** $\dfrac{5}{x-3} + \dfrac{2x-1}{x^2+4}$     **23.** $\dfrac{x}{x^2+4} - \dfrac{4x}{(x^2+4)^2}$     **24.** $\dfrac{4x+1}{x^2+x+1} + \dfrac{2x-2}{(x^2+x+1)^2}$     **25.** $\{(4, 3), (1, 0)\}$

**26.** $\{(0, 1), (-3, 4)\}$     **27.** $\{(1, -1), (-1, 1)\}$     **28.** $\{(3, \sqrt{6}), (3, -\sqrt{6}), (-3, \sqrt{6}), (-3, -\sqrt{6})\}$     **29.** $\{(2, 2), (-2, -2)\}$     **30.** $\{(9, 6), (1, 2)\}$

**31.** $\{(-3, -1), (1, 3)\}$     **32.** $\left\{\left(\dfrac{1}{2}, 2\right), (-1, -1)\right\}$     **33.** $\left\{\left(\dfrac{5}{2}, -\dfrac{7}{2}\right), (0, -1)\right\}$     **34.** $\{(2, -3), (-2, -3), (3, 2), (-3, 2)\}$

**35.** $\{(3, 1), (3, -1), (-3, 1), (-3, -1)\}$     **36.** 8 m and 5 m     **37.** $(1, 6), (3, 2)$     **38.** $x = 46$ and $y = 28$ or $x = 50$ and $y = 20$

**39.**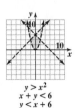
$3x - 4y > 12$

**40.**
$y \leq -\dfrac{1}{2}x + 2$

**41.**
$x < -2$

**42.**
$y \geq 3$

**43.**
$x^2 + y^2 > 4$

**44.**
$y \leq x^2 - 1$

**45.**
$y \leq 2^x$

**46.**
$3x + 2y \geq 6$
$2x + y \geq 6$

**47.**
$2x - y \geq 4$
$x + 2y < 2$

**48.**
$y < x$
$y \leq 2$

**49.**
$x + y \leq 6$
$y \geq 2x - 3$

**50.**
$0 \leq x \leq 3$
$y > 2$

**51.** no solution

**52.**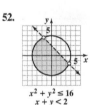
$x^2 + y^2 \leq 16$
$x + y < 2$

**53.**
$x^2 + y^2 \leq 9$
$y < -3x + 1$

**54.**
$y > x^2$
$x + y < 6$
$y < x + 6$

**55.**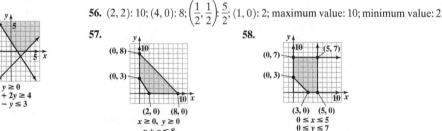
$y \geq 0$
$3x + 2y \geq 4$
$x - y \leq 3$

**56.** $(2, 2): 10;\ (4, 0): 8;\ \left(\dfrac{1}{2}, \dfrac{1}{2}\right): \dfrac{5}{2};\ (1, 0): 2$; maximum value: 10; minimum value: 2

**57.**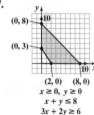
$x \geq 0,\ y \geq 0$
$x + y \leq 8$
$3x + 2y \geq 6$

**58.**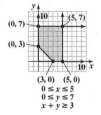
$0 \leq x \leq 5$
$0 \leq y \leq 7$
$x + y \geq 3$

Maximum is 24 at $x = 0, y = 8$.     Maximum is 33 at $x = 5, y = 7$.

**59.**

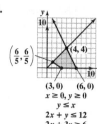

$\left(\frac{6}{5}, \frac{6}{5}\right)$ (4, 4)

(3, 0)  (6, 0)
$x \geq 0, y \geq 0$
$y \leq x$
$2x + y \leq 12$
$2x + 3y \geq 6$

**60. a.** $z = 500x + 350y$
**b.** $x + y \leq 200; x \geq 10; y \geq 80$
**c.**

(10, 190)
200
(120, 80)
(10, 80)
200 x
$x + y \leq 200$
$x \geq 10, y \geq 80$

**d.** (10, 80): 33,000; (10, 190): 71,500; (120, 80): 88,000
**e.** 120; 80; 88,000

Maximum is 44 at $x = y = 4$.
**61.** 480 of model A and 240 of model B

## Chapter 7 Test

**1.** $\{(1, -3)\}$    **2.** $\{(4, -2)\}$    **3.** $\{(1, 3, 2)\}$    **4.** $\{(4, -3), (-3, 4)\}$    **5.** $\{(3, 2), (3, -2), (-3, 2), (-3, -2)\}$    **6.** $\dfrac{-1}{10(x + 1)} + \dfrac{x + 9}{10(x^2 + 9)}$

**7.**

$x - 2y < 8$

**8.**

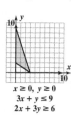

$x \geq 0, y \geq 0$
$3x + y \leq 9$
$2x + 3y \geq 6$

**9.**

$x^2 + y^2 > 1$
$x^2 + y^2 < 4$

**10.**

$y \leq 1 - x^2$
$x^2 + y^2 \leq 9$

**11.** 26    **12.** shrimp: 42 mg; scallops: 15mg    **13. a.** $C(x) = 360,000 + 850x$    **b.** $R(x) = 1150x$    **c.** (1200, 1,380,000); The company will break even if it produces and sells 1200 computers.    **14.** 40 oz of 20%; 20 oz of 50%    **15.** plane: 725 km/hr; wind: 75 km/hr    **16.** $y = x^2 - 3$    **17.** $x = 7.5$ ft and $y = 24$ ft or $x = 12$ ft and $y = 15$ ft    **18.** 50 regular and 100 deluxe jet skis; $35,000

## Cumulative Review Exercises (Chapters P–7)

**1.** domain: $(-2, 2)$; range: $(-\infty, 3]$    **2.** $-1$ and 1    **3.** maximum of 3 at $x = 0$    **4.** $(0, 2)$
**5.** positive    **6.** 3    **7.** $x \to -2^+; x \to 2^-$    **8.** even

**9.**

$g(x) = f(x + 2) - 1$

**10.**

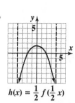

$h(x) = \frac{1}{2} f(\frac{1}{2} x)$

**11.** $\{3, 4\}$    **12.** $\left\{\dfrac{2 + i\sqrt{3}}{2}, \dfrac{2 - i\sqrt{3}}{2}\right\}$
**13.** $(-18, 6)$    **14.** $(1, 7)$
**15.** $\left\{-3, \dfrac{1}{2}, 2\right\}$    **16.** $\{-2\}$
**17.** $\{2\}$    **18.** $\{-2 + \log_3 11\}$
**19.** $\{625\}$    **20.** $\left\{\left(-\dfrac{1}{2}, \dfrac{1}{2}\right), (2, 8)\right\}$    **21.** $\{(8, -2, -2)\}$

**22.**

$f(x) = (x + 2)^2 - 4$

**23.**

$2x - 3y \leq 6$

**24.**

$y = 3^{x-2}$

**25.**

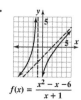

$f(x) = \dfrac{x^2 - x - 6}{x + 1}$

**26.**

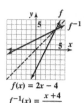

$f(x) = 2x - 4$
$f^{-1}(x) = \dfrac{x + 4}{2}$

**27.**

$(x - 2)^2 + (y - 4)^2 > 9$

**28.**

$f(x) = |x|$
$g(x) = -|x - 2|$

**29.** $(f \circ g)(x) = 2x^2 - 3x$;
$(g \circ f)(x) = -2x^2 + x + 2$
**30.** $4x + 2h - 1$
**31.** $y = -3x + 10$
**32.** $y = 3x + 3$
**33.** $2600 at 12%; $1400 at 14%
**34.** 4 m by 9 m
**35.** 10.99%

**36.** $\sec \theta - \cos \theta = \dfrac{1}{\cos \theta} - \cos \theta = \dfrac{1 - \cos^2 \theta}{\cos \theta} = \dfrac{\sin^2 \theta}{\cos \theta} = \dfrac{\sin \theta}{\cos \theta} \sin \theta = \tan \theta \sin \theta$

**37.** $\tan x + \tan y = \dfrac{\sin x}{\cos x} + \dfrac{\sin y}{\cos y} = \dfrac{\sin x \cos y + \sin y \cos x}{\cos x \cos y} = \dfrac{\sin(x + y)}{\cos x \cos y}$    **38.** $\{0, \pi\}$    **39.** $\left\{0, \dfrac{\pi}{3}, \dfrac{5\pi}{3}\right\}$    **40.** 92.9

# CHAPTER 8

## Section 8.1

### Check Point Exercises

**1. a.** $\begin{bmatrix} 1 & 6 & -3 & | & 7 \\ 4 & 12 & -20 & | & 8 \\ -3 & -2 & 1 & | & -9 \end{bmatrix}$  **b.** $\begin{bmatrix} 1 & 3 & -5 & | & 2 \\ 1 & 6 & -3 & | & 7 \\ -3 & -2 & 1 & | & -9 \end{bmatrix}$  **c.** $\begin{bmatrix} 4 & 12 & -20 & | & 8 \\ 1 & 6 & -3 & | & 7 \\ 0 & 16 & -8 & | & 12 \end{bmatrix}$  **2.** $\{(5,2,3)\}$  **3.** $\{(1,-1,2,-3)\}$  **4.** $\{(5,2,3)\}$

### Exercise Set 8.1

**1.** $\begin{bmatrix} 2 & 1 & 2 & | & 2 \\ 3 & -5 & -1 & | & 4 \\ 1 & -2 & -3 & | & -6 \end{bmatrix}$  **3.** $\begin{bmatrix} 1 & -1 & 1 & | & 8 \\ 0 & 1 & -12 & | & -15 \\ 0 & 0 & 1 & | & 1 \end{bmatrix}$  **5.** $\begin{bmatrix} 5 & -2 & -3 & | & 0 \\ 1 & 1 & 0 & | & 5 \\ 2 & 0 & -3 & | & 4 \end{bmatrix}$

**7.** $\begin{bmatrix} 2 & 5 & -3 & 1 & | & 2 \\ 0 & 3 & 1 & 0 & | & 4 \\ 1 & -1 & 5 & 0 & | & 9 \\ 5 & -5 & -2 & 0 & | & 1 \end{bmatrix}$  **9.** $\begin{aligned} 5x + 3z &= -11 \\ y - 4z &= 12 \\ 7x + 2y &= 3 \end{aligned}$  **11.** $\begin{aligned} w + x + 4y + z &= 3 \\ -w + x - y &= 7 \\ 2w + 5z &= 11 \\ 12y + 4z &= 5 \end{aligned}$

**13.** $\begin{bmatrix} 1 & -3 & 2 & | & 5 \\ 1 & 5 & -5 & | & 0 \\ 3 & 0 & 4 & | & 7 \end{bmatrix}$  **15.** $\begin{bmatrix} 1 & -3 & 2 & | & 0 \\ 0 & 10 & -7 & | & 7 \\ 2 & -2 & 1 & | & 3 \end{bmatrix}$  **17.** $\begin{bmatrix} 1 & -1 & 1 & 1 & | & 3 \\ 0 & 1 & -2 & -1 & | & 0 \\ 0 & 2 & 1 & 2 & | & 5 \\ 0 & 6 & -3 & -1 & | & -9 \end{bmatrix}$

**19.** $R_2$: $-3, -18$; $R_3$: $-12, -15$; $R_2$: $-\dfrac{3}{5}, -\dfrac{18}{5}$; $R_3$: $-12, -15$  **21.** $\{(1,-1,2)\}$  **23.** $\{(3,-1,-1)\}$  **25.** $\{(2,-1,1)\}$  **27.** $\{(2,1,1)\}$

**29.** $\{(2,-1,1)\}$  **31.** $\{(-1,2,-2)\}$  **33.** $\{(1,2,-1)\}$  **35.** $\{(1,2,3,-2)\}$  **37.** $\{(0,-3,0,-3)\}$  **39.** $f(x) = -x^2 + x + 2$

**41.** $f(x) = x^3 - 2x^2 + 3$  **43.** $\{(e^{-1}, e, e^{-3}, e^{-2})\}$  **45. a.** $a = -32, v_0 = 56, s_0 = 0$  **b.** 0; The ball hits the ground 3.5 seconds after it is thrown.
**c.** 1.75 sec; 49 ft

**47.** $\begin{aligned} 40x + 200y + 400z &= 660; \text{4 oz of Food } A; \dfrac{1}{2} \text{ oz of Food } B; 1 \text{ oz of Food } C \\ 5x + 2y + 4z &= 25 \\ 30x + 10y + 300z &= 425 \end{aligned}$

**49.** Asians: 122; Africans: 28; Europeans: 24; Americans: 9  **59.** makes sense  **61.** makes sense  **63.** false  **65.** false  **67.** 60 units: $7700
**68.** For $z = 0$, $(12z + 1, 10z - 1, z)$ is $(1, -1, 0)$; $3(1) - 4(-1) + 4(0) = 7$ is true; $1 - (-1) - 2(0) = 2$ is true; $2(1) - 3(-1) + 6(0) = 5$ is true.
**69.** For $z = 1$, $(12z + 1, 10z - 1, z)$ is $(13, 9, 1)$; $3(13) - 4(9) + 4(1) = 7$ is true; $13 - 9 - 2(1) = 2$ is true; $2(13) - 3(9) + 6(1) = 5$ is true.
**70. a.** Answers may vary.  **b.** This system has more than one solution.

## Section 8.2

### Check Point Exercises

**1.** $\varnothing$  **2.** $\{(11t + 13, 5t + 4, t)\}$  **3.** $\{(t + 50, -2t + 10, t)\}$
**4. a.** $\begin{aligned} w + z &= 15 \\ w + x &= 30 \\ x + y &= 45 \\ y + z &= 30 \end{aligned}$  **b.** $\{(-t + 15, t + 15, -t + 30, t)\}$  **c.** $w = 5; x = 25; y = 20$

### Exercise Set 8.2

**1.** $\varnothing$  **3.** $\left\{\left(-2t + 2, 2t + \dfrac{1}{2}, t\right)\right\}$  **5.** $\{(-3, 4, -2)\}$  **7.** $\{(5 - 2t, -2 + t, t)\}$  **9.** $\{(-1, 2, 1, 1)\}$  **11.** $\{(1, 3, 2, 1)\}$

**13.** $\{(1, -2, 1, 1)\}$  **15.** $\left\{\left(1 + \dfrac{1}{3}t, \dfrac{1}{3}t, t\right)\right\}$  **17.** $\{(-13t + 5, 5t, t)\}$  **19.** $\left\{\left(2t - \dfrac{5}{4}, \dfrac{13}{4}, t\right)\right\}$  **21.** $\{(1, -t - 1, 2, t)\}$

**23.** $\left\{\left(-\dfrac{2}{11}t + \dfrac{81}{11}, \dfrac{1}{22}t + \dfrac{10}{11}, \dfrac{4}{11}t - \dfrac{8}{11}, t\right)\right\}$

**25. a.** $4w - 2x + 2y - 3z = 0; 7w - x - y - 3z = 0; w + x + y - z = 0$  **b.** $\{(0.5t, 0, 0.5t, t)\}$
**27. a.** $w + 2x + 5y + 5z = -3; w + x + 3y + 4z = -1; w - x - y + 2z = 3$  **b.** $\{(1 - 3s - t, -2 - s - 2t, t, s)\}$
**29.** $z + 12 = x + 6$  **31.** $\{(t + 6, t + 2, t)\}$
**33. a.** $\begin{aligned} w + z &= 380 \\ w + x &= 600 \\ x - y &= 170 \\ y - z &= 50 \end{aligned}$  **b.** $\{(380 - t, 220 + t, 50 + t, t)\}$  **c.** $w = 330, x = 270, y = 100$
**35. a.** The system has no solution, so there is no way to satisfy these dietary requirements with no Food 1 available.
  **b.** 4 oz of Food 1, 0 oz of Food 2, 10 oz of Food 3; 2 oz of Food 1, 5 oz of Food 2, 9 oz of Food 3 (other answers are possible).
**41.** does not make sense  **43.** does not make sense  **45.** $a = 1$ or $a = 3$  **47.** $-1$  **48.** $-12$  **49.** 8

## Section 8.3

**Check Point Exercises**

**1. a.** $3 \times 2$   **b.** $a_{12} = -2; a_{31} = 1$   **2. a.** $\begin{bmatrix} 2 & 0 \\ 9 & -10 \end{bmatrix}$   **b.** $\begin{bmatrix} 9 & -4 \\ -9 & 7 \\ 5 & -2 \end{bmatrix}$   **3. a.** $\begin{bmatrix} 6 & 12 \\ -48 & -30 \end{bmatrix}$   **b.** $\begin{bmatrix} -14 & -1 \\ 25 & 10 \end{bmatrix}$   **4.** $\begin{bmatrix} -4 & 3 \\ -3 & \frac{13}{3} \end{bmatrix}$

**5.** $\begin{bmatrix} 7 & 6 \\ 13 & 12 \end{bmatrix}$   **6.** $[30]$; $\begin{bmatrix} 2 & 0 & 4 \\ 6 & 0 & 12 \\ 14 & 0 & 28 \end{bmatrix}$   **7. a.** $\begin{bmatrix} 2 & 18 & 11 & 9 \\ 0 & 10 & 8 & 2 \end{bmatrix}$   **b.** The product is undefined.

**8.** $\begin{bmatrix} 2 & 1 & 1 \\ 2 & 1 & 1 \\ 2 & 2 & 1 \end{bmatrix} + \begin{bmatrix} -1 & 2 & 2 \\ -1 & 2 & 2 \\ -1 & -1 & 2 \end{bmatrix} = \begin{bmatrix} 1 & 3 & 3 \\ 1 & 3 & 3 \\ 1 & 1 & 3 \end{bmatrix}$

**9. a.** $\begin{bmatrix} 0 & 3 & 4 \\ 0 & 5 & 2 \end{bmatrix} + \begin{bmatrix} -3 & -3 & -3 \\ -1 & -1 & -1 \end{bmatrix} = \begin{bmatrix} -3 & 0 & 1 \\ -1 & 4 & 1 \end{bmatrix}$   **b.** $2\begin{bmatrix} 0 & 3 & 4 \\ 0 & 5 & 2 \end{bmatrix} = \begin{bmatrix} 0 & 6 & 8 \\ 0 & 10 & 4 \end{bmatrix}$

**c.** $\begin{bmatrix} 0 & 3 & 4 \\ 0 & -5 & -2 \end{bmatrix}$; Multiplying by $B$ reflects the triangle over the $x$-axis.

## Exercise Set 8.3

**1. a.** $2 \times 3$   **b.** $a_{32}$ does not exist; $a_{23} = -1$   **3. a.** $3 \times 4$   **b.** $a_{32} = \frac{1}{2}; a_{23} = -6$   **5.** $x = 6; y = 4$   **7.** $x = 4; y = 6; z = 3$

**9. a.** $\begin{bmatrix} 9 & 10 \\ 3 & 9 \end{bmatrix}$   **b.** $\begin{bmatrix} -1 & -8 \\ 3 & -5 \end{bmatrix}$   **c.** $\begin{bmatrix} -16 & -4 \\ -12 & -8 \end{bmatrix}$   **d.** $\begin{bmatrix} 22 & 21 \\ 9 & 20 \end{bmatrix}$   **11. a.** $\begin{bmatrix} 3 & 2 \\ 6 & 2 \\ 5 & 7 \end{bmatrix}$   **b.** $\begin{bmatrix} -1 & 4 \\ 0 & 6 \\ 5 & 5 \end{bmatrix}$   **c.** $\begin{bmatrix} -4 & -12 \\ -12 & -16 \\ -20 & -24 \end{bmatrix}$   **d.** $\begin{bmatrix} 7 & 7 \\ 15 & 8 \\ 15 & 20 \end{bmatrix}$

**13. a.** $\begin{bmatrix} -3 \\ -1 \\ 0 \end{bmatrix}$   **b.** $\begin{bmatrix} 7 \\ -7 \\ 2 \end{bmatrix}$   **c.** $\begin{bmatrix} -8 \\ 16 \\ -4 \end{bmatrix}$   **d.** $\begin{bmatrix} -4 \\ -6 \\ 1 \end{bmatrix}$   **15. a.** $\begin{bmatrix} 8 & 0 & -4 \\ 14 & 0 & 6 \\ -1 & 0 & 0 \end{bmatrix}$   **b.** $\begin{bmatrix} -4 & -20 & 0 \\ 14 & 24 & 14 \\ 9 & -4 & 4 \end{bmatrix}$   **c.** $\begin{bmatrix} -8 & 40 & 8 \\ -56 & -48 & -40 \\ -16 & 8 & -8 \end{bmatrix}$   **d.** $\begin{bmatrix} 18 & -10 & -10 \\ 42 & 12 & 22 \\ 2 & -2 & 2 \end{bmatrix}$

**17.** $\begin{bmatrix} -8 & -8 \\ 2 & -9 \\ 8 & -4 \end{bmatrix}$   **19.** $\begin{bmatrix} -1 & 3 \\ -1 & \frac{9}{2} \\ -1 & -2 \end{bmatrix}$   **21.** $\begin{bmatrix} \frac{1}{3} & \frac{13}{3} \\ -\frac{4}{3} & 6 \\ -\frac{7}{3} & -\frac{4}{3} \end{bmatrix}$   **23.** $\begin{bmatrix} 7 & 27 \\ -8 & 36 \\ -17 & -4 \end{bmatrix}$   **25.** $\begin{bmatrix} \frac{27}{2} & \frac{31}{2} \\ -4 & 18 \\ -\frac{29}{2} & 6 \end{bmatrix}$   **27. a.** $\begin{bmatrix} 0 & 16 \\ 12 & 8 \end{bmatrix}$   **b.** $\begin{bmatrix} -7 & 3 \\ 29 & 15 \end{bmatrix}$

**29. a.** $[30]$   **b.** $\begin{bmatrix} 1 & 2 & 3 & 4 \\ 2 & 4 & 6 & 8 \\ 3 & 6 & 9 & 12 \\ 4 & 8 & 12 & 16 \end{bmatrix}$   **31. a.** $\begin{bmatrix} 4 & -5 & 8 \\ 6 & -1 & 5 \\ 0 & 4 & -6 \end{bmatrix}$   **b.** $\begin{bmatrix} 5 & -2 & 7 \\ 17 & -3 & 2 \\ 3 & 0 & -5 \end{bmatrix}$   **33. a.** $\begin{bmatrix} 6 & 8 & 16 \\ 11 & 16 & 24 \\ 1 & -1 & 12 \end{bmatrix}$   **b.** $\begin{bmatrix} 38 & 27 \\ -16 & -4 \end{bmatrix}$

**35. a.** $\begin{bmatrix} 0 & 0 \\ 0 & 0 \end{bmatrix}$   **b.** $\begin{bmatrix} 4 & -1 & -3 & 1 \\ -1 & 4 & -3 & 2 \\ 14 & -11 & -3 & -1 \\ 25 & -25 & 0 & -5 \end{bmatrix}$   **37.** $\begin{bmatrix} 17 & 7 \\ -5 & -11 \end{bmatrix}$   **39.** $\begin{bmatrix} 11 & -1 \\ -7 & -3 \end{bmatrix}$

**41.** $A - C$ is not defined because $A$ is $3 \times 2$ and $C$ is $2 \times 2$.   **43.** $\begin{bmatrix} 16 & -16 \\ -12 & 12 \\ 0 & 0 \end{bmatrix}$   **45.** $\begin{bmatrix} 0 & 0 \\ 0 & 0 \end{bmatrix}$

**47.** Answers will vary.; Example:

$A(B + C) = \begin{bmatrix} 1 & 0 \\ 0 & 1 \end{bmatrix}\left(\begin{bmatrix} 1 & 0 \\ 0 & -1 \end{bmatrix} + \begin{bmatrix} -1 & 0 \\ 0 & 1 \end{bmatrix}\right) = \begin{bmatrix} 1 & 0 \\ 0 & 1 \end{bmatrix}\begin{bmatrix} 0 & 0 \\ 0 & 0 \end{bmatrix} = \begin{bmatrix} 0 & 0 \\ 0 & 0 \end{bmatrix}$

$AB + AC = \begin{bmatrix} 1 & 0 \\ 0 & 1 \end{bmatrix}\begin{bmatrix} 1 & 0 \\ 0 & -1 \end{bmatrix} + \begin{bmatrix} 1 & 0 \\ 0 & 1 \end{bmatrix}\begin{bmatrix} -1 & 0 \\ 0 & 1 \end{bmatrix} = \begin{bmatrix} 1 & 0 \\ 0 & -1 \end{bmatrix} + \begin{bmatrix} -1 & 0 \\ 0 & 1 \end{bmatrix} = \begin{bmatrix} 0 & 0 \\ 0 & 0 \end{bmatrix}$

So, $A(B + C) = AB + AC$.

**49.** $\begin{bmatrix} x \\ -y \end{bmatrix}$; It changes the sign of the $y$-coordinate.

**51. a.** $\begin{bmatrix} 1 & 3 & 1 \\ 3 & 3 & 3 \\ 1 & 3 & 1 \end{bmatrix}$   **b.** $\begin{bmatrix} 1 & 3 & 1 \\ 3 & 3 & 3 \\ 1 & 3 & 1 \end{bmatrix} + \begin{bmatrix} -1 & -1 & -1 \\ -1 & -1 & -1 \\ -1 & -1 & -1 \end{bmatrix} = \begin{bmatrix} 0 & 2 & 0 \\ 2 & 2 & 2 \\ 0 & 2 & 0 \end{bmatrix}$   **c.** $\begin{bmatrix} 1 & 3 & 1 \\ 3 & 3 & 3 \\ 1 & 3 & 1 \end{bmatrix} + \begin{bmatrix} 1 & -2 & 1 \\ -2 & -2 & -2 \\ 1 & -2 & 1 \end{bmatrix} = \begin{bmatrix} 2 & 1 & 2 \\ 1 & 1 & 1 \\ 2 & 1 & 2 \end{bmatrix}$

**53.** $\begin{bmatrix} -2 & 1 & 1 & -1 & -1 & -2 \\ -3 & -3 & -2 & -2 & 2 & 2 \end{bmatrix}$

**55.** $\begin{bmatrix} 0 & \frac{3}{2} & \frac{3}{2} & \frac{1}{2} & \frac{1}{2} & 0 \\ 1 & 1 & \frac{3}{2} & \frac{3}{2} & \frac{7}{2} & \frac{7}{2} \end{bmatrix}$

**57. a.** $\begin{bmatrix} 0 & 3 & 3 & 1 & 1 & 0 \\ 0 & 0 & -1 & -1 & -5 & -5 \end{bmatrix}$

**b.** The effect is a reflection across the $x$-axis.

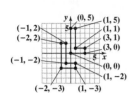

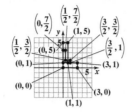

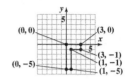

**59. a.** $\begin{bmatrix} 0 & 0 & -1 & -1 & -5 & -5 \\ 0 & 3 & 3 & 1 & 1 & 0 \end{bmatrix}$

**b.**

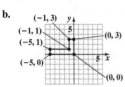

The effect is a 90° counterclockwise rotation about the origin.

**61. a.** $A = \begin{bmatrix} 2 & 6 \\ 31 & 46 \end{bmatrix}$  **b.** $B = \begin{bmatrix} 9 & 29 \\ 65 & 77 \end{bmatrix}$

**c.** $B - A = \begin{bmatrix} 7 & 23 \\ 34 & 31 \end{bmatrix}$

The difference between the percentage of people completing the transition to adulthood in 1960 and 2000 by age and gender

**63. a.** System 1: The midterm and final both count for 50% of the course grade.  System 2: The midterm counts for 30% of the course grade and the final counts for 70%.

**b.** $\begin{bmatrix} 84 & 87.2 \\ 79 & 81 \\ 90 & 88.4 \\ 73 & 68.6 \\ 69 & 73.4 \end{bmatrix}$ System 1 grades are listed first (if different).  Student 1: B; Student 2: C or B; Student 3: A or B; Student 4: C or D; Student 5: D or C

**77.** makes sense   **79.** makes sense   **83.** $AB = -BA$ so they are anticommutative.

**85.** $\begin{bmatrix} a_{11} & a_{12} \\ a_{21} & a_{22} \end{bmatrix}$; Nothing happens to the elements in the first matrix.   **86.** $\{(15, -12, -4)\}$   **87.** $\begin{cases} a_1x + b_1y + c_1z = d_1 \\ a_2x + b_2y + c_2z = d_2 \\ a_3x + b_3y + c_3z = d_3 \end{cases}$

## Mid-Chapter 8 Check Point

**1.** $\{(1, -1, 2)\}$   **2.** $\varnothing$   **3.** $\left\{\left(-\frac{4}{7} - \frac{4}{7}t, \frac{5}{7} + \frac{5}{7}t, t\right)\right\}$   **4.** $\{(3, 6, -4, 1)\}$   **5.** $\varnothing$   **6.** $\begin{bmatrix} -4 & -\frac{1}{2} \\ 3 & 3 \end{bmatrix}$   **7.** $\begin{bmatrix} -12 & -2 \\ -21 & -4 \\ 3 & 1 \end{bmatrix}$   **8.** $\begin{bmatrix} 12 & -4 \\ 22 & -7 \\ -4 & 1 \end{bmatrix}$

**9.** $A + C$ does not exist because $A$ is $3 \times 2$ and $C$ is $2 \times 2$.   **10.** $\begin{bmatrix} \frac{1}{2} & \frac{1}{2} \\ -3 & \frac{1}{2} \end{bmatrix}$

## Section 8.4

### Check Point Exercises

**1.** $AB = I_2$; $BA = I_2$   **2.** $\begin{bmatrix} 3 & -7 \\ -2 & 5 \end{bmatrix}$   **3.** $\begin{bmatrix} 1 & 2 \\ 1 & 3 \end{bmatrix}$   **4.** $\begin{bmatrix} 3 & -2 & -4 \\ 3 & -2 & -5 \\ -1 & 1 & 2 \end{bmatrix}$   **5.** $\{(4, -2, 1)\}$   **6.** The encoded message is $-7, 10, -53, 77$.

**7.** The decoded message is $2, 1, 19, 5$ or BASE.

### Exercise Set 8.4

**1.** $AB = I_2$; $BA = I_2$; $B = A^{-1}$   **3.** $AB = \begin{bmatrix} 8 & -16 \\ -2 & 7 \end{bmatrix}$; $BA = \begin{bmatrix} 12 & 12 \\ 1 & 3 \end{bmatrix}$; $B \neq A^{-1}$   **5.** $AB = I_2$; $BA = I_2$; $B = A^{-1}$

**7.** $AB = I_3$; $BA = I_3$; $B = A^{-1}$   **9.** $AB = I_3$; $BA = I_3$; $B = A^{-1}$   **11.** $AB = I_4$; $BA = I_4$; $B = A^{-1}$

**13.** $\begin{bmatrix} \frac{2}{7} & -\frac{3}{7} \\ \frac{1}{7} & \frac{2}{7} \end{bmatrix}$   **15.** $\begin{bmatrix} 1 & \frac{1}{2} \\ 2 & \frac{3}{2} \end{bmatrix}$   **17.** $A$ does not have an inverse.   **19.** $\begin{bmatrix} \frac{1}{2} & 0 & 0 \\ 0 & \frac{1}{4} & 0 \\ 0 & 0 & \frac{1}{6} \end{bmatrix}$   **21.** $\begin{bmatrix} 1 & 1 & 2 \\ 1 & 1 & 1 \\ 2 & 3 & 4 \end{bmatrix}$   **23.** $\begin{bmatrix} 1 & 0 & 1 \\ 1 & 1 & 2 \\ 3 & 2 & 6 \end{bmatrix}$

**25.** $\begin{bmatrix} -3 & 2 & -4 \\ -1 & 1 & -1 \\ 8 & -5 & 10 \end{bmatrix}$  **27.** $\begin{bmatrix} 1 & 0 & 0 & 0 \\ 0 & -1 & 0 & 0 \\ 0 & 0 & \frac{1}{3} & 0 \\ -1 & 0 & 0 & 1 \end{bmatrix}$  **29.** $\begin{bmatrix} 6 & 5 \\ 5 & 4 \end{bmatrix}\begin{bmatrix} x \\ y \end{bmatrix} = \begin{bmatrix} 13 \\ 10 \end{bmatrix}$  **31.** $\begin{bmatrix} 1 & 3 & 4 \\ 1 & 2 & 3 \\ 1 & 4 & 3 \end{bmatrix}\begin{bmatrix} x \\ y \\ z \end{bmatrix} = \begin{bmatrix} -3 \\ -2 \\ -6 \end{bmatrix}$  **33.** $4x - 7y = -3$ $2x - 3y = 1$

**35.** $\begin{array}{r} 2x - z = 6 \\ 3y = 9 \\ x + y = 5 \end{array}$  **37. a.** $\begin{bmatrix} 2 & 6 & 6 \\ 2 & 7 & 6 \\ 2 & 7 & 7 \end{bmatrix}\begin{bmatrix} x \\ y \\ z \end{bmatrix} = \begin{bmatrix} 8 \\ 10 \\ 9 \end{bmatrix}$  **b.** $\{(1, 2, -1)\}$  **39. a.** $\begin{bmatrix} 1 & -1 & 1 \\ 0 & 2 & -1 \\ 2 & 3 & 0 \end{bmatrix}\begin{bmatrix} x \\ y \\ z \end{bmatrix} = \begin{bmatrix} 8 \\ -7 \\ 1 \end{bmatrix}$  **b.** $\{(2, -1, 5)\}$

**41. a.** $\begin{bmatrix} 1 & -1 & 2 & 0 \\ 0 & 1 & -1 & 1 \\ -1 & 1 & -1 & 2 \\ 0 & -1 & 1 & -2 \end{bmatrix}\begin{bmatrix} w \\ x \\ y \\ z \end{bmatrix} = \begin{bmatrix} -3 \\ 4 \\ 2 \\ -4 \end{bmatrix}$  **b.** $\{(2, 3, -1, 0)\}$  **43.** $\begin{bmatrix} \frac{1}{2}e^{-x} & -\frac{1}{2}e^{-3x} \\ \frac{1}{2}e^{-3x} & \frac{1}{2}e^{-5x} \end{bmatrix}$  **45.** $\begin{bmatrix} \frac{1}{8} & \frac{5}{8} \\ \frac{3}{8} & \frac{7}{8} \end{bmatrix}$

**47.** $(AB)^{-1} = \begin{bmatrix} -23 & 16 \\ 13 & -9 \end{bmatrix}; A^{-1}B^{-1} = \begin{bmatrix} -3 & 11 \\ 8 & -29 \end{bmatrix}; B^{-1}A^{-1} = \begin{bmatrix} -23 & 16 \\ 13 & -9 \end{bmatrix}; (AB)^{-1} = B^{-1}A^{-1}$  **49.** $AA^{-1} = I_3$ and $A^{-1}A = I_3$

**51.** The encoded message is $27, -19, 32, -20.$; The decoded message is $8, 5, 12, 16$ or HELP.
**53.** The encoded message is $14, 85, -33, 4, 18, -7, -18, 19, -9.$

**65.** $\begin{bmatrix} 1 & 1 \\ 2 & 3 \end{bmatrix}$  **67.** $\begin{bmatrix} 1 & 0 & 1 \\ 2 & 1 & 3 \\ -1 & 1 & 1 \end{bmatrix}$  **69.** $\begin{bmatrix} 0 & -1 & 0 & 1 \\ -1 & -5 & 0 & 3 \\ -2 & -4 & 1 & -2 \\ -1 & -4 & 0 & 1 \end{bmatrix}$  **71.** $\{(2, 3, -5)\}$  **73.** $\{(1, 2, -1)\}$  **75.** $\{(2, 1, 3, -2, 4)\}$

**79.** does not make sense  **81.** makes sense  **83.** false  **85.** false  **87.** false  **91.** $a = 3$ or $a = -2$  **93.** 2  **94.** 6  **95.** $-31$

## Section 8.5

### Check Point Exercises

**1. a.** $-4$  **b.** $-17$  **2.** $\{(4, -2)\}$  **3.** 80  **4.** $-24$  **5.** $\{(2, -3, 4)\}$  **6.** $-250$

### Exercise Set 8.5

**1.** 1  **3.** $-29$  **5.** 0  **7.** 33  **9.** $-\frac{7}{16}$  **11.** $\{(5, 2)\}$  **13.** $\{(2, -3)\}$  **15.** $\{(3, -1)\}$  **17.** The system is dependent.  **19.** $\{(4, 2)\}$
**21.** $\{(7, 4)\}$  **23.** The system is inconsistent.  **25.** The system is dependent.  **27.** 72  **29.** $-75$  **31.** 0  **33.** $\{(-5, -2, 7)\}$
**35.** $\{(2, -3, 4)\}$  **37.** $\{(3, -1, 2)\}$  **39.** $\{(2, 3, 1)\}$  **41.** $-200$  **43.** 195  **45.** $-42$  **47.** $2x - 4y = 8; 3x + 5y = -10$
**49.** $-11$  **51.** 4  **53.** 28 sq units  **55.** yes  **57.** The equation of the line is $y = -\frac{11}{5}x + \frac{8}{5}$.  **69.** 13,200  **71.** does not make sense
**73.** does not make sense  **75. a.** $a^2$  **b.** $a^3$  **c.** $a^4$  **d.** Each determinant has zeros below the main diagonal and $a$'s everywhere else.
**e.** Each determinant equals $a$ raised to the power equal to the order of the determinant.  **77.** The sign of the value is changed when
2 columns are interchanged in a 2nd order determinant.

**79.** $\begin{vmatrix} x & y & 1 \\ x_1 & y_1 & 1 \\ x_2 & y_2 & 1 \end{vmatrix} = x(y_1 - y_2) - y(x_1 - x_2) + (x_1y_2 - x_2y_1) = 0$; solving for $y$, $y = \frac{y_1 - y_2}{x_1 - x_2}x + \frac{x_1y_2 - x_2y_1}{x_1 - x_2}$, and $m = \frac{y_1 - y_2}{x_1 - x_2}$ and $b = \frac{x_1y_2 - x_2y_1}{x_1 - x_2}$.

**81. a.** $-3$ and 3  **b.** $-2$ and 2  **82.** $\frac{x^2}{16} + \frac{y^2}{25} = 1$  **83.** $(x - 1)^2 + (y + 2)^2 = 9$; center: $(1, -2)$; radius: 3;

$x^2 + y^2 - 2x + 4y = 4$

## Chapter 8 Review Exercises

**1.** $\begin{bmatrix} 1 & 2 & 2 & | & 2 \\ 0 & 1 & -1 & | & 2 \\ 0 & 0 & 9 & | & -9 \end{bmatrix}$  **2.** $\begin{bmatrix} 1 & -1 & \frac{1}{2} & | & -\frac{1}{2} \\ 1 & 2 & -1 & | & 2 \\ 6 & 4 & 3 & | & 5 \end{bmatrix}$  **3.** $\{(1, 3, -4)\}$  **4.** $\{(-2, -1, 0)\}$  **5.** $\{(2, -2, 3, 4)\}$

**6. a.** $a = -2; b = 32; c = 42$  **b.** 2:00 p.m.; 170 parts per million  **7.** capitalist: 1%; upper middle: 15%; lower middle: 34%; working: 30%
**8.** $\varnothing$  **9.** $\{(2t + 4, t + 1, t)\}$  **10.** $\{(-37t + 2, 16t, -7t + 1, t)\}$  **11.** $\{(7t + 18, -3t - 7, t)\}$

**12. a.** $x + z = 750$
$y - z = -250$
$x + y = 500$
**b.** $\{(-t + 750, t - 250, t)\}$ **c.** $x = 350; y = 150$ **13.** $x = -5; y = 6; z = 6$ **14.** $\begin{bmatrix} 0 & 2 & 3 \\ 8 & 1 & 3 \end{bmatrix}$ **15.** $\begin{bmatrix} 0 & -4 \\ 6 & 4 \\ 2 & -10 \end{bmatrix}$

**16.** $\begin{bmatrix} -4 & 4 & -1 \\ -2 & -5 & 5 \end{bmatrix}$ **17.** Not possible since $B$ is $3 \times 2$ and $C$ is $3 \times 3$. **18.** $\begin{bmatrix} 2 & 3 & 8 \\ 21 & 5 & 5 \end{bmatrix}$ **19.** $\begin{bmatrix} -12 & 14 & 0 \\ 2 & -14 & 18 \end{bmatrix}$ **20.** $\begin{bmatrix} 0 & -10 & -15 \\ -40 & -5 & -15 \end{bmatrix}$

**21.** $\begin{bmatrix} -1 & -16 \\ 8 & 1 \end{bmatrix}$ **22.** $\begin{bmatrix} -10 & -6 & 2 \\ 16 & 3 & 4 \\ -23 & -16 & 7 \end{bmatrix}$ **23.** $\begin{bmatrix} -6 & 4 & -8 \\ 0 & 5 & 11 \\ -17 & 13 & -19 \end{bmatrix}$ **24.** $\begin{bmatrix} 10 & 5 \\ -2 & -30 \end{bmatrix}$ **25.** Not possible since $AB$ is $2 \times 2$ and $BA$ is $3 \times 3$.

**26.** $\begin{bmatrix} 7 & 6 & 5 \\ 2 & -1 & 11 \end{bmatrix}$ **27.** $\begin{bmatrix} -6 & -22 & -40 \\ 9 & 43 & 58 \\ -14 & -48 & -94 \end{bmatrix}$ **28.** $\begin{bmatrix} -2 & -6 \\ 3 & \frac{1}{3} \end{bmatrix}$ **29.** $\begin{bmatrix} 2 & 2 & 2 \\ 1 & 2 & 1 \\ 1 & 2 & 1 \end{bmatrix}$ **30.** $\begin{bmatrix} 1 & 1 & 1 \\ -1 & 1 & -1 \\ -1 & 1 & -1 \end{bmatrix}$

**31.** $\begin{bmatrix} -2 & 0 & 0 \\ 1 & 1 & -3 \end{bmatrix}$ **32.** $\begin{bmatrix} 0 & 1 & 1 \\ -2 & -2 & -4 \end{bmatrix}$ **33.** $\begin{bmatrix} 0 & 2 & 2 \\ 0 & 0 & 4 \end{bmatrix}$

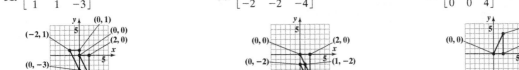

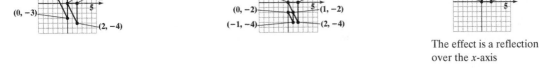

The effect is a reflection
over the $x$-axis

**34.** $\begin{bmatrix} 0 & -2 & -2 \\ 0 & 0 & -4 \end{bmatrix}$ **35.** $\begin{bmatrix} 0 & 0 & 4 \\ 0 & 2 & 2 \end{bmatrix}$ **36.** $\begin{bmatrix} 0 & 4 & 4 \\ 0 & 0 & -4 \end{bmatrix}$

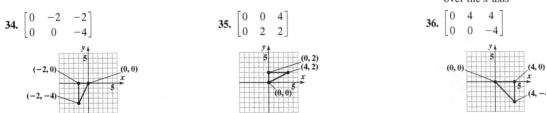

The effect is a reflection
over the $y$-axis

The effect is a 90° counterclockwise
rotation about the origin

The effect is a horizontal stretch
by a factor of 2.

**37.** $AB = \begin{bmatrix} 1 & 7 \\ 0 & 5 \end{bmatrix}; BA = \begin{bmatrix} 1 & 0 \\ 1 & 5 \end{bmatrix}; B \neq A^{-1}$ **38.** $AB = I_3; BA = I_3; B = A^{-1}$ **39.** $\begin{bmatrix} 3 & 1 \\ 2 & 1 \end{bmatrix}$ **40.** $\begin{bmatrix} -\frac{3}{5} & \frac{1}{5} \\ 1 & 0 \end{bmatrix}$ **41.** $\begin{bmatrix} 3 & 0 & -2 \\ -6 & 1 & 4 \\ 1 & 0 & -1 \end{bmatrix}$

**42.** $\begin{bmatrix} 8 & -8 & 5 \\ -3 & 2 & -1 \\ -1 & -1 & 1 \end{bmatrix}$ **43. a.** $\begin{bmatrix} 1 & 1 & 2 \\ 0 & 1 & 3 \\ 3 & 0 & -2 \end{bmatrix}\begin{bmatrix} x \\ y \\ z \end{bmatrix} = \begin{bmatrix} 7 \\ -2 \\ 0 \end{bmatrix}$ **b.** $\{(-18, 79, -27)\}$ **44. a.** $\begin{bmatrix} 1 & -1 & 2 \\ 0 & 1 & -1 \\ 1 & 0 & 2 \end{bmatrix}\begin{bmatrix} x \\ y \\ z \end{bmatrix} = \begin{bmatrix} 12 \\ -5 \\ 10 \end{bmatrix}$

**b.** $\{(4, -2, 3)\}$ **45.** The encoded message is $96, 135, 46, 63$; The decoded message is $18, 21, 12, 5$ or RULE. **46.** 17 **47.** 4

**48.** $-86$ **49.** $-236$ **50.** 4 **51.** 16 **52.** $\left\{\left(\frac{7}{4}, -\frac{25}{8}\right)\right\}$ **53.** $\{(2, -7)\}$ **54.** $\{(23, -12, 3)\}$ **55.** $\{(-3, 2, 1)\}$

**56.** $a = \frac{5}{8}; b = -50; c = 1150$; 30- and 50-year-olds are involved in an average of 212.5 automobile accidents per day.

## Chapter 8 Test

**1.** $\left\{\left(-3, \frac{1}{2}, 1\right)\right\}$ **2.** $\{(t, t - 1, t)\}$ **3.** $\begin{bmatrix} 5 & 4 \\ 1 & 11 \end{bmatrix}$ **4.** $\begin{bmatrix} 5 & -2 \\ 1 & -1 \\ 4 & -1 \end{bmatrix}$ **5.** $\begin{bmatrix} \frac{3}{5} & -\frac{2}{5} \\ \frac{1}{5} & \frac{1}{5} \end{bmatrix}$ **6.** $\begin{bmatrix} -1 & 2 \\ -5 & 4 \end{bmatrix}$ **7.** $AB = I_3; BA = I_3$

**8. a.** $\begin{bmatrix} 3 & 5 \\ 2 & -3 \end{bmatrix}\begin{bmatrix} x \\ y \end{bmatrix} = \begin{bmatrix} 9 \\ -13 \end{bmatrix}$ **b.** $\begin{bmatrix} \frac{3}{19} & \frac{5}{19} \\ \frac{2}{19} & -\frac{3}{19} \end{bmatrix}$ **c.** $\{(-2, 3)\}$ **9.** 18 **10.** $x = 2$

## Cumulative Review Exercises (Chapters P–8)

**1.** $\left\{\frac{-1 + \sqrt{33}}{4}, \frac{-1 - \sqrt{33}}{4}\right\}$ **2.** $\left[\frac{1}{2}, \infty\right)$ **3.** $[-2, -1] \cup [2, \infty)$ **4.** $\left\{-4, \frac{1}{3}, 1\right\}$ **5.** $\{\ln 5, \ln 9\}$ **6.** $\{1\}$ **7.** $\{(7, -4, 6)\}$

**8.** $y = -1$ **9.** $f^{-1}(x) = \frac{x^2 + 7}{4}(x \geq 0)$

**10.**

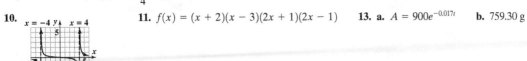

$f(x) = \dfrac{x}{x^2 - 16}$

**11.** $f(x) = (x + 2)(x - 3)(2x + 1)(2x - 1)$ **13. a.** $A = 900e^{-0.017t}$ **b.** 759.30 g

**12.**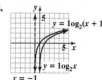

**14.** $\begin{bmatrix} 2 & -1 \\ 13 & 1 \end{bmatrix}$   **15.** $\dfrac{8}{x-3} + \dfrac{-2}{x-2} + \dfrac{-3}{x+2}$

**16.**
$y = -\frac{2}{3}x - 1$

**17.**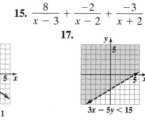
$3x - 5y < 15$

**18.**
$f(x) = x^2 - 2x - 3$

**19.**
$(x-1)^2 + (y+1)^2 = 9$

**20.** $x^2 + 2x - 2$

**21.**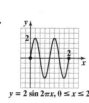
$y = 2 \sin 2\pi x, \ 0 \le x \le 2$

**22.** $\dfrac{3}{5}$

**23.** $\dfrac{\cos 2x}{\cos x - \sin x} = \dfrac{\cos^2 x - \sin^2 x}{\cos x - \sin x} = \dfrac{(\cos x + \sin x)(\cos x - \sin x)}{\cos x - \sin x} = \cos x + \sin x$

**24.** $\dfrac{3\pi}{2}$   **25.** $2i - 13j$

# CHAPTER 9

## Section 9.1

### Check Point Exercises

**1.** foci at $(-3\sqrt{3}, 0)$ and $(3\sqrt{3}, 0)$   **2.** foci at $(0, -\sqrt{7})$ and $(0, \sqrt{7})$   **3.** $\dfrac{x^2}{9} + \dfrac{y^2}{5} = 1$   **4.** foci at $(-1 - \sqrt{5}, 2)$ and $(-1 + \sqrt{5}, 2)$

$\dfrac{x^2}{36} + \dfrac{y^2}{9} = 1$

$16x^2 + 9y^2 = 144$

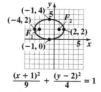
$\dfrac{(x+1)^2}{9} + \dfrac{(y-2)^2}{4} = 1$

**5.** Yes

### Exercise Set 9.1

**1.** foci at $(-2\sqrt{3}, 0)$ and $(2\sqrt{3}, 0)$   **3.** foci at $(0, -3\sqrt{3})$ and $(0, 3\sqrt{3})$   **5.** foci at $(0, -\sqrt{39})$ and $(0, \sqrt{39})$

$\dfrac{x^2}{16} + \dfrac{y^2}{4} = 1$

$\dfrac{x^2}{9} + \dfrac{y^2}{36} = 1$

$\dfrac{x^2}{25} + \dfrac{y^2}{64} = 1$

**7.** foci at $(0, -4\sqrt{2})$ and $(0, 4\sqrt{2})$   **9.** foci at $(0, -2)$ and $(0, 2)$   **11.** foci at $\left(-\dfrac{\sqrt{3}}{2}, 0\right)$ and $\left(\dfrac{\sqrt{3}}{2}, 0\right)$

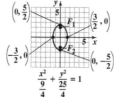
$\dfrac{x^2}{49} + \dfrac{y^2}{81} = 1$

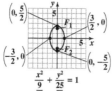
$\dfrac{x^2}{\frac{9}{4}} + \dfrac{y^2}{\frac{25}{4}} = 1$

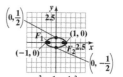
$x^2 = 1 - 4y^2$

**13.** foci at $(0, -\sqrt{21})$ and $(0, \sqrt{21})$   **15.** foci at $(-2\sqrt{3}, 0)$ and $(2\sqrt{3}, 0)$   **17.** foci at $(0, -\sqrt{2})$ and $(0, \sqrt{2})$

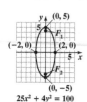
$25x^2 + 4y^2 = 100$

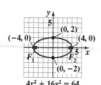
$4x^2 + 16y^2 = 64$

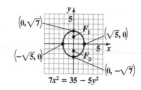
$7x^2 = 35 - 5y^2$

**19.** $\frac{x^2}{4} + \frac{y^2}{1} = 1$; foci at $(-\sqrt{3}, 0)$ and $(\sqrt{3}, 0)$　**21.** $\frac{x^2}{1} + \frac{y^2}{4} = 1$; foci at $(0, \sqrt{3})$ and $(0, -\sqrt{3})$

**23.** $\frac{(x + 1)^2}{4} + \frac{(y - 1)^2}{1} = 1$; foci at $(-1 - \sqrt{3}, 1)$ and $(-1 + \sqrt{3}, 1)$　**25.** $\frac{x^2}{64} + \frac{y^2}{39} = 1$　**27.** $\frac{x^2}{33} + \frac{y^2}{49} = 1$

**29.** $\frac{x^2}{13} + \frac{y^2}{9} = 1$　**31.** $\frac{x^2}{16} + \frac{y^2}{4} = 1$　**33.** $\frac{(x + 2)^2}{4} + \frac{(y - 3)^2}{25} = 1$　**35.** $\frac{(x - 7)^2}{4} + \frac{(y - 6)^2}{9} = 1$

**37.** foci at $(2 - \sqrt{5}, 1)$ and $(2 + \sqrt{5}, 1)$　**39.** foci at $(-3 - 2\sqrt{3}, 2)$ and $(-3 + 2\sqrt{3}, 2)$　**41.** foci at $(4, 2)$ and $(4, -6)$

$\frac{(x - 2)^2}{9} + \frac{(y - 1)^2}{4} = 1$

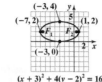

$(x + 3)^2 + 4(y - 2)^2 = 16$

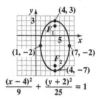

$\frac{(x - 4)^2}{9} + \frac{(y + 2)^2}{25} = 1$

**43.** foci at $(0, 2 + \sqrt{11}), (0, 2 - \sqrt{11})$　**45.** foci at $(-3 - 2\sqrt{2}, 2)$ and $(-3 + 2\sqrt{2}, 2)$　**47.** foci at $(1, -3 + \sqrt{3})$ and $(1, -3 - \sqrt{3})$

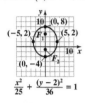

$\frac{x^2}{25} + \frac{(y - 2)^2}{36} = 1$

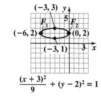

$\frac{(x + 3)^2}{9} + (y - 2)^2 = 1$

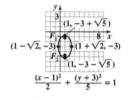

$\frac{(x - 1)^2}{2} + \frac{(y + 3)^2}{5} = 1$

**49.** foci at $(1, -3 + \sqrt{5})$ and $(1, -3 - \sqrt{5})$　**51.** $\frac{(x - 2)^2}{25} + \frac{(y + 1)^2}{9} = 1$　**53.** $\frac{(x - 1)^2}{16} + \frac{(y + 2)^2}{9} = 1$

foci at $(-2, -1)$ and $(6, -1)$　foci at $(1 - \sqrt{7}, -2)$ and $(1 + \sqrt{7}, -2)$

$9(x - 1)^2 + 4(y + 3)^2 = 36$

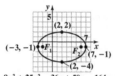

$9x^2 + 25y^2 - 36x + 50y - 164 = 0$

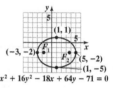

$9x^2 + 16y^2 - 18x + 64y - 71 = 0$

**55.** $\frac{(x + 2)^2}{16} + \frac{(y - 3)^2}{64} = 1$

foci at $(-2, 3 + 4\sqrt{3})$ and $(-2, 3 - 4\sqrt{3})$　**57.** $\{(0, -1), (0, 1)\}$　**59.** $\{(0, 3)\}$　**61.** $\{(0, -2), (1, 0)\}$　**63.**

$4x^2 + y^2 + 16x - 6y - 39 = 0$

$y = -\sqrt{16 - 4x^2}$

**65.** Yes　**67. a.** $\frac{x^2}{2304} + \frac{y^2}{529} = 1$　**b.** about 42 feet　**79.** does not make sense　**81.** does not make sense　**83.** $\frac{x^2}{\frac{36}{5}} + \frac{y^2}{36} = 1$

**85.** large circle: $x^2 + y^2 = 25$; small circle: $x^2 + y^2 = 9$　**87.** $\frac{x^2}{9} - \frac{y^2}{4} = 1$; Terms are separated by subtraction rather than addition.

**88. a.** $-4$ and $4$　**b.** The equation $y^2 = -9$ has no real solutions.　**89. a.** $-3$ and $3$　**b.** The equation $x^2 = -16$ has no real solutions.

## Section 9.2

### Check Point Exercises

**1. a.** vertices at $(5, 0)$ and $(-5, 0)$; foci at $(\sqrt{41}, 0)$ and $(-\sqrt{41}, 0)$　**b.** vertices at $(0, 5)$ and $(0, -5)$; foci at $(0, \sqrt{41})$ and $(0, -\sqrt{41})$　**2.** $\frac{y^2}{9} - \frac{x^2}{16} = 1$

**3.** foci at $(-3\sqrt{5}, 0)$ and $(3\sqrt{5}, 0)$　**4.** foci at $(0, \sqrt{5})$ and $(0, -\sqrt{5})$　**5.** foci at $(3 - \sqrt{5}, 1)$ and $(3 + \sqrt{5}, 1)$

asymptotes: $y = \pm\frac{1}{2}x$　asymptotes: $y = \pm 2x$　asymptotes: $(y - 1) = \pm\frac{1}{2}(x - 3)$

$\frac{x^2}{36} - \frac{y^2}{9} = 1$

$y^2 - 4x^2 = 4$

$\frac{(x - 3)^2}{4} - \frac{(y - 1)^2}{1} = 1$

**6.** foci at $(3, -5 + \sqrt{13})$ and $(3, -5 - \sqrt{13})$   **7.** $\dfrac{x^2}{2,722,500} - \dfrac{y^2}{25,155,900} = 1$

asymptotes: $(y + 5) = \pm\dfrac{2}{3}(x - 3)$

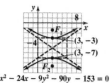

$4x^2 - 24x - 9y^2 - 90y - 153 = 0$

## Exercise Set 9.2

**1.** vertices at $(2, 0)$ and $(-2, 0)$; foci at $(\sqrt{5}, 0)$ and $(-\sqrt{5}, 0)$; graph (b)   **3.** vertices at $(0, 2)$ and $(0, -2)$; foci at $(0, \sqrt{5})$ and $(0, -\sqrt{5})$; graph (a)

**5.** $y^2 - \dfrac{x^2}{8} = 1$   **7.** $\dfrac{x^2}{9} - \dfrac{y^2}{7} = 1$   **9.** $\dfrac{y^2}{36} - \dfrac{x^2}{9} = 1$   **11.** $\dfrac{(x - 4)^2}{4} - \dfrac{(y + 2)^2}{5} = 1$

**13.** foci: $(\pm\sqrt{34}, 0)$

asymptotes: $y = \pm\dfrac{5}{3}x$

$\dfrac{x^2}{9} - \dfrac{y^2}{25} = 1$

**15.** foci: $(\pm 2\sqrt{41}, 0)$

asymptotes: $y = \pm\dfrac{4}{5}x$

$\dfrac{x^2}{100} - \dfrac{y^2}{64} = 1$

**17.** foci: $(0, \pm 2\sqrt{13})$

asymptotes: $y = \pm\dfrac{2}{3}x$

$\dfrac{y^2}{16} - \dfrac{x^2}{36} = 1$

**19.** foci: $\left(0, \pm\dfrac{\sqrt{5}}{2}\right)$

asymptotes: $y = \pm\dfrac{1}{2}x$

$4y^2 - x^2 = 1$

**21.** foci: $(\pm\sqrt{13}, 0)$

asymptotes: $y = \pm\dfrac{3}{2}x$

$9x^2 - 4y^2 = 36$

**23.** foci: $(0, \pm\sqrt{34})$

asymptotes: $y = \pm\dfrac{5}{3}x$

$9y^2 - 25x^2 = 225$

**25.** foci: $(\pm 2, 0)$

asymptotes: $y = \pm x$

$y = \pm\sqrt{x^2 - 2}$

**27.** $\dfrac{x^2}{9} - \dfrac{y^2}{25} = 1$

**29.** $\dfrac{y^2}{4} - \dfrac{x^2}{9} = 1$

**31.** $\dfrac{(x - 2)^2}{4} - \dfrac{(y + 3)^2}{9} = 1$

**33.** foci: $(-9, -3), (1, -3)$

asymptotes: $(y + 3) = \pm\dfrac{4}{3}(x + 4)$

$\dfrac{(x + 4)^2}{9} - \dfrac{(y + 3)^2}{16} = 1$

**35.** foci: $(-3 \pm \sqrt{41}, 0)$

asymptotes: $y = \pm\dfrac{4}{5}(x + 3)$

$\dfrac{(x + 3)^2}{25} - \dfrac{y^2}{16} = 1$

**37.** foci: $(1, -2 \pm 2\sqrt{5})$

asymptotes: $(y + 2) = \pm\dfrac{1}{2}(x - 1)$

$\dfrac{(y + 2)^2}{4} - \dfrac{(x - 1)^2}{16} = 1$

**39.** foci: $(3 \pm \sqrt{5}, -3)$

asymptotes: $(y + 3) = \pm\dfrac{1}{2}(x - 3)$

$(x - 3)^2 - 4(y + 3)^2 = 4$

**41.** foci: $(1 \pm \sqrt{6}, 2)$

asymptotes: $(y - 2) = \pm(x - 1)$

$(x - 1)^2 - (y - 2)^2 = 3$

**43.** $(x - 1)^2 - (y + 2)^2 = 1$

foci: $(1 \pm \sqrt{2}, -2)$

asymptotes: $(y + 2) = \pm(x - 1)$

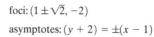

$x^2 - y^2 - 2x - 4y - 4 = 0$

**45.** $\dfrac{(y+1)^2}{4} - \dfrac{(x+2)^2}{0.25} = 1$
foci: $(-2, -1 \pm \sqrt{4.25})$

asymptotes: $(y+1) = \pm 4(x+2)$

$16x^2 - y^2 + 64x - 2y + 67 = 0$

**47.** $\dfrac{(x-2)^2}{9} - \dfrac{(y-3)^2}{4} = 1$
foci: $(2 \pm \sqrt{13}, 3)$

asymptotes: $(y-3) = \pm\dfrac{2}{3}(x-2)$

$4x^2 - 9y^2 - 16x + 5y - 101 = 0$

**49.** $\dfrac{y^2}{4} - \dfrac{(x-4)^2}{25} = 1$
foci: $(4, \pm\sqrt{29})$

asymptotes: $y = \pm\dfrac{2}{5}(x-4)$

$4x^2 - 25y^2 - 32x + 164 = 0$

**51.** domain: $(-\infty, -3] \cup [3, \infty)$
range: $(-\infty, \infty)$

$\dfrac{x^2}{9} - \dfrac{y^2}{16} = 1$

**53.** domain: $[-3, 3]$
range: $[-4, 4]$

$\dfrac{x^2}{9} + \dfrac{y^2}{16} = 1$

**55.** domain: $(-\infty, \infty)$
range: $(-\infty, -4] \cup [4, \infty)$

$\dfrac{y^2}{16} - \dfrac{x^2}{9} = 1$

**57.** $\{(-2, 0), (2, 0)\}$   **59.** $\{(0, -3), (0, 3)\}$

**61.** If $M_1$ is located 2640 feet to the right of the origin on the x-axis, the explosion is located on the right branch of the hyperbola given by the equation $\dfrac{x^2}{1,210,000} - \dfrac{y^2}{5,759,600} = 1$.

**63.** 40 yd    **65. a.** ellipse    **b.** $x^2 + 4y^2 = 4$

**77.** 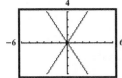 ; no; two intersecting lines

**79.** $2y^2 + (10 - 6x)y + (4x^2 - 3x - 6) = 0$
$y = \dfrac{3x - 5 \pm \sqrt{x^2 - 24x + 37}}{2}$

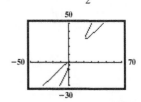

The xy-term rotates the hyperbola.

**81.** does not make sense    **83.** makes sense    **85.** false    **87.** true    **89.** $\dfrac{c}{a}$ will be large when $a$ is small. When this happens, the asymptotes will be nearly vertical.    **91.** Any hyperbola where $a = b$, such as $\dfrac{x^2}{4} - \dfrac{y^2}{4} = 1$, has perpendicular asymptotes.

**92.**

**93.**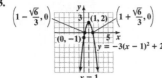

**94.** $(y+1)^2 = -12x + 24$

## Section 9.3

### Check Point Exercises

**1.** focus: $(2, 0)$
directrix: $x = -2$

$y^2 = 8x$

**2.** focus: $(0, -3)$
directrix: $y = 3$

**3.** $y^2 = 32x$

**4.** vertex: $(2, -1)$; focus: $(2, 0)$
directrix: $y = -2$

$(x-2)^2 = 4(y+1)$

**5.** vertex: $(2, -1)$; focus: $(1, -1)$
directrix: $x = 3$

$y^2 + 2y + 4x - 7 = 0$

**6.** $x^2 = \dfrac{9}{4}y$; The light should be placed at $\left(0, \dfrac{9}{16}\right)$, or $\dfrac{9}{16}$ inch above the vertex.

### Exercise Set 9.3

**1.** focus: $(1, 0)$; directrix: $x = -1$; graph (c)    **3.** focus: $(0, -1)$, directrix: $y = 1$; graph (b)

**5.** focus: $(4, 0)$; directrix: $x = -4$

$y^2 = 16x$

**7.** focus: $(-2, 0)$; directrix: $x = 2$

$y^2 = -8x$

**9.** focus: $(0, 3)$; directrix: $y = -3$

$x^2 = 12y$

**11.** focus: $(0, -4)$; directrix: $y = 4$

$x^2 = -16y$

**13.** focus: $\left(\dfrac{3}{2}, 0\right)$; directrix: $x = -\dfrac{3}{2}$

$y^2 - 6x = 0$

**15.** focus: $\left(0, -\dfrac{1}{8}\right)$; directrix: $y = \dfrac{1}{8}$

$8x^2 + 4y = 0$

**17.** $y^2 = 28x$    **19.** $y^2 = -20x$    **21.** $x^2 = 60y$    **23.** $x^2 = -100y$    **25.** $(x - 2)^2 = -8(y + 3)$    **27.** $(y - 2)^2 = 8(x - 1)$

**29.** $(x + 3)^2 = 4(y - 3)$    **31.** vertex: $(1, 1)$; focus: $(2, 1)$; directrix: $x = 0$; graph (c)    **33.** vertex: $(-1, -1)$; focus: $(-1, -2)$; directrix: $y = 0$; graph (d)

**35.** vertex: $(2, 1)$; focus: $(2, 3)$
    directrix: $y = -1$

$(x - 2)^2 = 8(y - 1)$

**37.** vertex: $(-1, -1)$; focus: $(-1, -3)$
    directrix: $y = 1$

$(x + 1)^2 = -8(y + 1)$

**39.** vertex: $(-1, -3)$; focus: $(2, -3)$
    directrix: $x = -4$

$(y + 3)^2 = 12(x + 1)$

**41.** vertex: $(0, -1)$; focus: $(-2, -1)$
    directrix: $x = 2$

$(y + 1)^2 = -8x$

**43.** $(x - 1)^2 = 4(y - 2)$; vertex: $(1, 2)$
    focus: $(1, 3)$; directrix: $y = 1$

$x^2 - 2x - 4y + 9 = 0$

**45.** $(y - 1)^2 = -12(x - 3)$
    vertex: $(3, 1)$; focus: $(0, 1)$   directrix: $x = 6$

$y^2 - 2y + 12x - 35 = 0$

**47.** $(x + 3)^2 = 4(y + 2)$
    vertex: $(-3, -2)$; focus: $(-3, -1)$
    directrix: $y = -3$

$x^2 + 6x - 4y + 1 = 0$

**49.** domain: $[-4, \infty)$
    range: $(-\infty, \infty)$; not a function
**51.** domain: $(-\infty, \infty)$
    range: $(-\infty, 1]$; function
**53.** domain: $(-\infty, 3]$
    range: $(-\infty, \infty)$; not a function

**55.** $\{(-4, 2), (0, 0)\}$

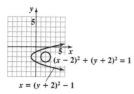

$x = (y - 2)^2 - 4$ ; $(-4, 2)$ ; $(0, 0)$ ; $y = -\dfrac{1}{2}x$

**57.** $\{(-2, 1)\}$

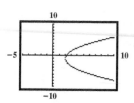

$x = y^2 - 3y$ ; $(-2, 1)$ ; $x = y^2 - 3$

**59.** $\varnothing$

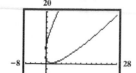

$(x - 2)^2 + (y + 2)^2 = 1$ ; $x = (y + 2)^2 - 1$

**61.** 1 inch above the vertex
**63.** 4.5 feet from the base of the dish
**65.** 76 m    **67.** yes

**77.** $y = -1 \pm \sqrt{6x - 12}$

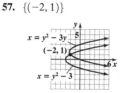

**79.** $9y^2 + (-24x - 80)y + 16x^2 - 60x + 100 = 0$
$$y = \frac{12x + 40 \pm 10\sqrt{15x + 7}}{9}$$

**81.** does not make sense
**83.** makes sense
**85.** false
**87.** false
**89.** focus: $\left(0, -\dfrac{E}{4A}\right)$; directrix: $y = \dfrac{E}{4A}$

**92.** $(x')^2 - (y')^2 = 2$

**93. a.**

(-7, 24)  2θ

**b.** $-\dfrac{7}{25}$    **c.** $\sin\theta = 0.8; \cos\theta = 0.6$

**d.** Since $90° < 2\theta < 180°$, we have $45° < \theta < 90°$. Both $\cos\theta$ and $\sin\theta$ are positive when $45° < \theta < 90°$.

**94.** 0

## Mid-Chapter 9 Check Point

**1.** foci: $(\pm\sqrt{21}, 0)$

$\dfrac{x^2}{25} + \dfrac{y^2}{4} = 1$

**2.** foci: $(0, \pm\sqrt{5})$

$9x^2 + 4y^2 = 36$

**3.** foci: $(2, 2), (2, -4)$

$\dfrac{(x-2)^2}{16} + \dfrac{(y+1)^2}{25} = 1$

**4.** foci: $(-5, 1), (1, 1)$

$\dfrac{(x+2)^2}{25} + \dfrac{(y-1)^2}{16} = 1$

**5.** foci: $(2 \pm 4\sqrt{2}, -3)$

$x^2 + 9y^2 - 4x + 54y + 49 = 0$

**6.** foci: $(\pm\sqrt{10}, 0)$
asymptotes: $y = \pm\dfrac{1}{3}x$

$\dfrac{x^2}{9} - y^2 = 1$

**7.** foci: $(0, \pm\sqrt{10})$
asymptotes: $y = \pm 3x$

$\dfrac{y^2}{9} - x^2 = 1$

**8.** foci: $(0, \pm 2\sqrt{5})$
asymptotes: $y = \pm 2x$

$y^2 - 4x^2 = 16$

**9.** foci: $(\pm\sqrt{53}, 0)$
asymptotes: $y = \pm\dfrac{2}{7}x$

$4x^2 - 49y^2 = 196$

**10.** foci: $(-3, -2), (7, -2)$
asymptotes:
$(y + 2) = \pm\dfrac{4}{3}(x - 2)$

$\dfrac{(x-2)^2}{9} - \dfrac{(y+2)^2}{16} = 1$

**11.** foci: $(-1, 3 \pm 2\sqrt{5})$;
asymptotes:
$(y - 3) = \pm 2(x + 1)$

$4x^2 - y^2 + 8x + 6y + 11 = 0$

**12.** focus: $(2, -4)$;
directrix: $y = 2$;

$(x - 2)^2 = -12(y + 1)$

**13.** focus: $\left(-\dfrac{5}{2}, 1\right)$;
directrix: $x = -\dfrac{7}{2}$;

**14.**

$x^2 + y^2 = 4$

**15.**

$x + y = 4$

**16.**

$x^2 - y^2 = 4$

**17.**

$x^2 + 4y^2 = 4$

**18.**

$(x + 1)^2 + (y - 1)^2 = 4$

**19.**

$x^2 + 4(y - 1)^2 = 4$

**20.**

$(x - 1)^2 - (y - 1)^2 = 4$

**21.**

**22.** $\dfrac{x^2}{25} + \dfrac{y^2}{9} = 1$    **23.** $\dfrac{(x-1)^2}{81} + \dfrac{(y-2)^2}{56} = 1$

**24.** $\dfrac{y^2}{4} - \dfrac{x^2}{5} = 1$    **25.** $\dfrac{(x+1)^2}{4} - \dfrac{(y-5)^2}{5} = 1$

**26.** $(x - 4)^2 = 12(y - 2)$    **27.** $(y - 6)^2 = -20(x - 3)$

**28.** no    **29.** $20\sqrt{3}$ cm

**30. a.** $\dfrac{x^2}{1.1025} - \dfrac{y^2}{7.8975} = 1$    **b.**

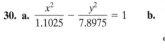

outpost  (3, 0)
(-3, 0)  primary station

**31.** 1.4 m

## Section 9.4

### Check Point Exercises

**1. a.** ellipse    **b.** circle    **c.** parabola    **d.** hyperbola

**2.** $\dfrac{x'^2}{4} - \dfrac{y'^2}{4} = 1$

**3.** $\dfrac{x'^2}{\frac{4}{5}} + \dfrac{y'^2}{4} = 1$

**4.**

**5.** parabola

## Exercise Set 9.4

**1.** parabola    **3.** hyperbola    **5.** circle    **7.** hyperbola    **9.** $\dfrac{y'^2}{2} - \dfrac{x'^2}{2} = 1$    **11.** $\dfrac{y'^2}{1} - \dfrac{x'^2}{3} = 1$    **13.** $\dfrac{x'^2}{4} - \dfrac{y'^2}{9} = 1$

**15.** $x = \dfrac{\sqrt{2}}{2}(x' - y');\ y = \dfrac{\sqrt{2}}{2}(x' + y')$    **17.** $x = \dfrac{\sqrt{2}}{2}(x' - y');\ y = \dfrac{\sqrt{2}}{2}(x' + y')$    **19.** $x = \dfrac{\sqrt{3}x' - y'}{2};\ y = \dfrac{x' + \sqrt{3}y'}{2}$

**21.** $x = \dfrac{3x' - 4y'}{5};\ y = \dfrac{4x' + 3y'}{5}$    **23.** $x = \sqrt{5}\left(\dfrac{2x' - y'}{5}\right);\ y = \sqrt{5}\left(\dfrac{x' + 2y'}{5}\right)$    **25.** $x = \dfrac{4x' - 3y'}{5};\ y = \dfrac{3x' + 4y'}{5}$

**27. a.** $3x'^2 + y'^2 = 20$
**b.** $\dfrac{x'^2}{\frac{20}{3}} + \dfrac{y'^2}{20} = 1$
**c.**

**29. a.** $-4x'^2 + 16y'^2 = 64$
**b.** $\dfrac{y'^2}{4} - \dfrac{x'^2}{16} = 1$
**c.**

**31. a.** $64x'^2 - 16y'^2 = 16$
**b.** $\dfrac{x'^2}{\frac{1}{4}} - \dfrac{y'^2}{1} = 1$
**c.**

**33. a.** $650x'^2 + 25y'^2 = 225$
**b.** $\dfrac{x'^2}{\frac{9}{26}} + \dfrac{y'^2}{9} = 1$
**c.**

**35. a.** $50x'^2 - 75y'^2 = 25$
**b.** $\dfrac{x'^2}{\frac{1}{2}} - \dfrac{y'^2}{\frac{1}{3}} = 1$
**c.**

**37. a.** $625x'^2 + 1250y'^2 = 625$
**b.** $\dfrac{x'^2}{1} + \dfrac{y'^2}{\frac{1}{2}} = 1$
**c.**

**39.** ellipse or circle    **41.** parabola    **43.** hyperbola    **45.** ellipse; $(0, 1), (0, -1)$    **47.** parabola; $(3, -1)$

**55.**

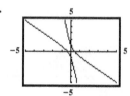

**57.**

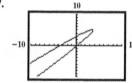

**59.**

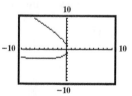

**61.** does not make sense    **63.** makes sense    **65.** There are no solutions to this equation just as there is no such sound.

**67.**    $A' = A\cos^2\theta + B\sin\theta\cos\theta + C\sin^2\theta$
    $C' = A\sin^2\theta - B\sin\theta\cos\theta + C\cos^2\theta$
$A' + C' = A\cos^2\theta + B\sin\theta\cos\theta + C\sin^2\theta + A\sin^2\theta - B\sin\theta\cos\theta + C\cos^2\theta$
    $= A(\cos^2\theta + \sin^2\theta) + B(\sin\theta\cos\theta - \sin\theta\cos\theta) + C(\sin^2\theta + \cos^2\theta)$
    $= A(1) + B(0) + C(1)$
    $= A + C$

**70.**

$y^2 = 4(x + 1)$

**71.**

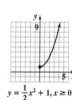

$y = \dfrac{1}{2}x^2 + 1, x \ge 0$

**72.**

$\dfrac{x^2}{25} + \dfrac{y^2}{4} = 1$

## Section 9.5

### Check Point Exercises

**1.**    **2.**    **3.**    **4.** $x = t$ and $y = t^2 - 25$

### Exercise Set 9.5

**1.** $(-2, 6)$   **3.** $(5, -3)$   **5.** $(4, 8)$   **7.** $(60\sqrt{3}, 1)$

**9.**    **11.**    **13.**    **15.**    **17.**

**19.**    **21.** $y = 2x$    **23.** $y = (x + 4)^2$    **25.** $y = x^2 - 1, x \ge 0$    **27.** $\dfrac{x^2}{4} + \dfrac{y^2}{4} = 1$

**29.** $\dfrac{(x - 1)^2}{9} + \dfrac{(y - 2)^2}{9} = 1$    **31.** $\dfrac{x^2}{4} + \dfrac{y^2}{9} = 1$    **33.** $\dfrac{(x - 1)^2}{9} + \dfrac{(y + 1)^2}{4} = 1, -2 \le x \le 4, -1 \le y \le 1$

**35.** $x^2 - y^2 = 1$    **37.** $y = x - 4, x \ge 2, y \ge -2$ 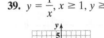   **39.** $y = \dfrac{1}{x}, x \ge 1, y \ge 0$ 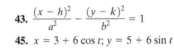   **41.** $(x - h)^2 + (y - k)^2 = r^2$

**43.** $\dfrac{(x - h)^2}{a^2} - \dfrac{(y - k)^2}{b^2} = 1$

**45.** $x = 3 + 6 \cos t; y = 5 + 6 \sin t$

**47.** $x = -2 + 5 \cos t; y = 3 + 2 \sin t$

**49.** $x = 4 \sec t; y = \sqrt{20} \tan t$   **51.** $x = -2 + 3t; y = 4 + 3t$   **53.** Answers may vary. Sample answer: $x = t$ and $y = 4t - 3; x = t + 1$ and

$y = 4t + 1$   **55.** Answers may vary. Sample answer: $x = t$ and $y = t^2 + 4; x = t + 1$ and $y = t^2 + 2t + 5$

**57. a.**    **b.**    **c.**    **d.**

**59.**    **61.**    **63.**    **65.**

domain: $[-2, 6]$         domain: $\left[\dfrac{3}{4}, \infty\right)$         **a.** increasing: $(-\infty, \infty)$     **a.** decreasing: $(-\infty, 1)$; increasing: $(1, \infty)$

range: $[-5, 3]$         range: $(-\infty, \infty)$         **b.** no maximum or minimum   **b.** minimum of $-5$ at $x = 1$

**67.**

**a.** increasing: $(0, 2\pi)$; decreasing: $(2\pi, 4\pi)$
**b.** maximum of 4 at $x = 2\pi$
minimum of 0 at $x = 0$ and $x = 4\pi$

**69. a.** $x = (180 \cos 40°)t;\ y = 3 + (180 \sin 40°)t - 16t^2$
**b.** After 1 second: 137.9 feet in distance, 102.7 feet in height;
After 2 seconds: 275.8 feet in distance, 170.4 feet in height;
After 3 seconds: 413.7 feet in distance, 206.1 feet in height
**c.** $t = 7.3$ sec; total horizontal distance: 1006.6 ft; yes

**79.**

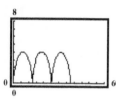

**81.**

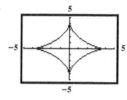

**83.**

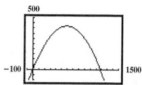

Window: $[-100, 1500] \times [-100, 500]$;
The maximum height is 419.4 feet at a time of 5.1 seconds.
The range of the projectile is 1174.6 feet horizontally.
It hits the ground at 10.2 seconds.

**85. a.** $x = (140 \cos 22°)t;\ y = 5 + (140 \sin 22°)t - 16t^2$
**b.**

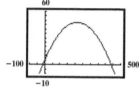

Window: $[-100, 500] \times [-10, 60]$

**c.** The maximum height is 48.0 feet. It occurs at 1.6 seconds.   **d.** 3.4 sec   **e.** 437.5 ft

**87.** makes sense   **89.** makes sense

**91.** $x = 3 \sin t;\ y = 3 \cos t$

**93.** $r = \dfrac{2}{1 + \frac{1}{2}\cos\theta}$

**94.** $\dfrac{4}{3} \approx 1.33;\ 2;\ \dfrac{8}{3} \approx 2.66;\ 3.09;\ 3.53;\ 4;$

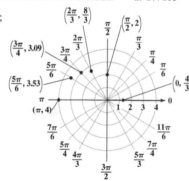

**95. a.** $r = \dfrac{1}{3 - 3\cos\theta}$

$r(3 - 3\cos\theta) = 1$

$3r - 3r\cos\theta = 1$

$3r = 1 + 3r\cos\theta$

$(3r)^2 = (1 + 3r\cos\theta)^2$

$9r^2 = (1 + 3r\cos\theta)^2$

**b.** $9y^2 = 1 + 6x$; parabola

# Section 9.6

## Check Point Exercises

**1.**

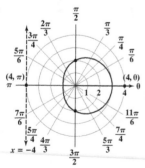

**2.**

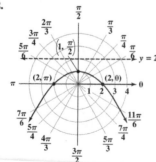

**3.**

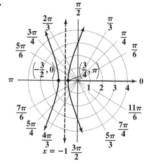

## Exercise Set 9.6

**1. a.** parabola   **b.** The directrix is 3 units above the pole, at $y = 3$.   **3. a.** ellipse   **b.** The directrix is 3 units to the left of the pole, at $x = -3$.
**5. a.** parabola   **b.** The directrix is 4 units above the pole, at $y = 4$.   **7. a.** hyperbola   **b.** The directrix is 3 units to the left of the pole, at $x = -3$.

**9.**

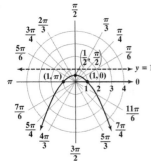

**11.**

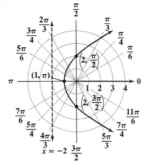

**13.**

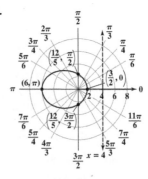

**15.**

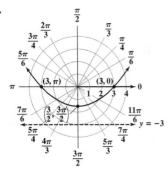

**17.**

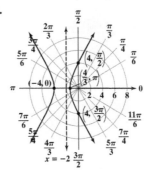

**19.**

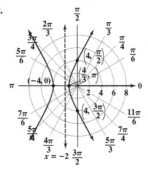

**21.** $[-3, 15, 1]$ by $[-7, 7, 1]$    **23.** $[-4, 2, 1]$ by $[-10, 10, 1]$    **25.** $[-2, 5, 1]$ by $[-10, 10, 1]$    **27.** $[-4, 4, 1]$ by $[-10, 0.4, 1]$

**29.** 0.54 astronomical units or 51 million miles    **31.** 4122 miles from the center of the earth; 162 miles from the surface of the earth

**41.** hyperbola

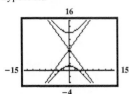

**43.**

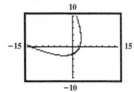

The graph appears to be rotated counterclockwise through an angle of $\frac{\pi}{4}$ radians.

**45.** Mercury: $r = \dfrac{(1 - 0.2056^2)(36.0 \times 10^6)}{1 - 0.2056 \cos \theta}$

Earth: $r = \dfrac{(1 - 0.0167^2)(92.96 \times 10^6)}{1 - 0.0167 \cos \theta}$

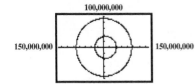

**47.** does not make sense    **49.** does not make sense

**51.** $r = \dfrac{2}{1 - \frac{1}{2}\cos \theta}$ or $r = \dfrac{6}{1 + \frac{1}{2}\cos \theta}$

**53.** parabola; using the relationships between rectangular and polar coordinates,

$$x^2 + y^2 = r^2 \text{ and } x = r \cos \theta: y^2 = x + \frac{1}{4}$$

**55.** $-\dfrac{1}{2}, \dfrac{1}{8}, -\dfrac{1}{26}, \dfrac{1}{80}$    **56.** 120    **57.** 2; 5; 10; 17; 26; 37; Sum is 97.

## Chapter 9 Review Exercises

**1.** foci: $(\pm\sqrt{11}, 0)$

$\dfrac{x^2}{36} + \dfrac{y^2}{25} = 1$

**2.** foci: $(0, \pm 3)$

$\dfrac{y^2}{25} + \dfrac{x^2}{16} = 1$

**3.** foci: $(0, \pm 2\sqrt{3})$

$4x^2 + y^2 = 16$

**4.** foci: $(\pm\sqrt{5}, 0)$

$4x^2 + 9y^2 = 36$

**5.** foci: $(1 \pm \sqrt{7}, -2)$

$$\frac{(x-1)^2}{16} + \frac{(y+2)^2}{9} = 1$$

**6.** foci: $(-1, 2 \pm \sqrt{7})$

$$\frac{(x+1)^2}{9} + \frac{(y-2)^2}{16} = 1$$

**7.** foci: $(-3 \pm \sqrt{5}, 2)$

$$4x^2 + 9y^2 + 24x - 36y + 36 = 0$$

**8.** foci: $(1, -1 \pm \sqrt{5})$

$$9x^2 + 4y^2 - 18x + 8y - 23 = 0$$

**9.** $\dfrac{x^2}{25} + \dfrac{y^2}{9} = 1$   **10.** $\dfrac{x^2}{27} + \dfrac{y^2}{36} = 1$   **11.** $\dfrac{(x+3)^2}{36} + \dfrac{(y-5)^2}{4} = 1$   **12.** $\dfrac{x^2}{100} + \dfrac{y^2}{36} = 1$   **13.** yes

**14.** The hit ball will collide with the other ball.

**15.** foci: $(\pm\sqrt{17}, 0)$; $y = \pm\dfrac{1}{4}x$   **16.** foci: $(0, \pm\sqrt{17})$; $y = \pm 4x$   **17.** foci: $(\pm 5, 0)$; $y = \pm\dfrac{3}{4}x$   **18.** foci: $(0, \pm 2\sqrt{5})$; $y = \pm\dfrac{1}{2}x$

$$\frac{x^2}{16} - y^2 = 1$$

$$\frac{y^2}{16} - x^2 = 1$$

$$9x^2 - 16y^2 = 144$$

$$4y^2 - x^2 = 16$$

**19.** foci: $(2 \pm \sqrt{41}, -3)$
$y + 3 = \pm\dfrac{4}{5}(x - 2)$

**20.** foci: $(3, -2 \pm \sqrt{41})$
$y + 2 = \pm\dfrac{5}{4}(x - 3)$

**21.** foci: $(1, 2 \pm \sqrt{5})$
$y - 2 = \pm 2(x - 1)$

**22.** foci: $(1 \pm \sqrt{2}, -1)$
$y + 1 = \pm(x - 1)$

$$\frac{(x-2)^2}{25} - \frac{(y+3)^2}{16} = 1$$

$$\frac{(y+2)^2}{25} - \frac{(x-3)^2}{16} = 1$$

$$y^2 - 4y - 4x^2 + 8x - 4 = 0$$

$$x^2 - y^2 - 2x - 2y - 1 = 0$$

**23.** $\dfrac{y^2}{4} - \dfrac{x^2}{12} = 1$   **24.** $\dfrac{x^2}{9} - \dfrac{y^2}{55} = 1$   **25.** $c$ must be greater than $a$.   **26.** $\dfrac{x^2}{2162.25} - \dfrac{y^2}{7837.75} = 1$

**27.** vertex: $(0, 0)$; focus: $(2, 0)$
directrix: $x = -2$

**28.** vertex: $(0, 0)$; focus: $(0, -4)$
directrix: $y = 4$

**29.** vertex: $(0, 2)$; focus: $(-4, 2)$
directrix: $x = 4$

**30.** vertex: $(4, -1)$; focus: $(4, 0)$
directrix: $y = -2$

$$y^2 = 8x$$

$$x^2 + 16y = 0$$

$$(y - 2)^2 = -16x$$

$$(x - 4)^2 = 4(y + 1)$$

**31.** vertex: $(0, 1)$; focus: $(0, 0)$
directrix: $y = 2$

**32.** vertex: $(-1, 5)$; focus: $(0, 5)$
directrix: $x = -2$

**33.** vertex: $(2, -2)$; focus: $\left(2, -\dfrac{3}{2}\right)$; directrix: $y = -\dfrac{5}{2}$

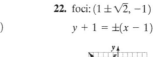

$$x^2 + 4y = 4$$

$$y^2 - 4x - 10y + 21 = 0$$

$$x^2 - 4x - 2y = 0$$

**34.** $y^2 = 48x$   **35.** $x^2 = -44y$   **36.** $x^2 = 12y$; Place the light 3 inches from the vertex at $(0, 3)$.   **37.** approximately 58 ft
**38.** approximately 128 ft   **39.** parabola   **40.** ellipse   **41.** ellipse   **42.** hyperbola   **43.** ellipse or circle   **44.** ellipse or circle
**45.** parabola   **46.** ellipse or circle

**47. a.** $x'^2 - y'^2 = 8$
**b.** $\dfrac{x'^2}{8} - \dfrac{y'^2}{8} = 1$
**c.**

**48. a.** $3x'^2 + y'^2 = 2$
**b.** $\dfrac{x'^2}{\frac{2}{3}} + \dfrac{y'^2}{2} = 1$
**c.**

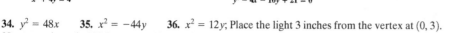

**49. a.** $18x'^2 - 2y'^2 = 18$
**b.** $\dfrac{x'^2}{1} - \dfrac{y'^2}{9} = 1$
**c.**

**50. a.** $50x'^2 + 150y'^2 = 450$

**b.** $\dfrac{x'^2}{9} + \dfrac{y'^2}{3} = 1$

**c.**

**51. a.** $16x'^2 + 96y' = 0$

**b.** $x'^2 = -6y'$

**c.**

**52.** $y = -\dfrac{1}{2}x + \dfrac{1}{2}$

**53.** $(y + 1)^2 = x, 0 \le x \le 9,$
$-2 \le y \le 2$

**54.** $(y - 1)^2 = \dfrac{1}{4}x$

**55.** $\dfrac{x^2}{16} + \dfrac{y^2}{9} = 1, 0 \le x \le 4,$
$-3 < y \le 3$

**56.** $\dfrac{(x - 3)^2}{4} + \dfrac{(y - 1)^2}{4} = 1$
or $(x - 3)^2 + (y - 1)^2 = 4$

 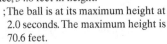

**57.** $\dfrac{x^2}{9} - \dfrac{y^2}{9} = 1,$
$3 \le x \le 3\sqrt{2}, 0 \le y \le 3$

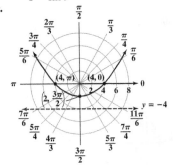

**58.** Answers may vary. Sample answer: $x = t$ and $y = t^2 + 6$; $x = t + 1$ and $y = t^2 + 2t + 7$

**59. a.** $x = (100 \cos 40°)t; y = 6 + (100 \sin 40°)t - 16t^2$

**b.** After 1 second: 76.6 feet in distance, 54.3 feet in height; after 2 seconds: 153.2 feet in distance, 70.6 feet in height; after 3 seconds: 229.8 feet in distance, 54.8 feet in height.

**c.** 4.1 sec; 314.1 ft  **d.**

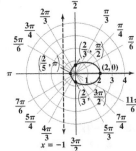

; The ball is at its maximum height at 2.0 seconds. The maximum height is 70.6 feet.

**60. a.** $r = \dfrac{4}{1 - \sin \theta}$  **b.** $e = 1$; $p = 4$; parabola

**c.**

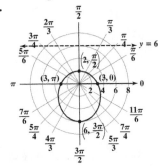

**61. a.** $r = \dfrac{6}{1 + \cos \theta}$  **b.** $e = 1$; $p = 6$; parabola

**c.**

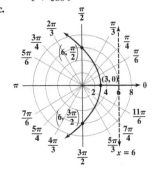

**62. a.** $r = \dfrac{3}{1 + \frac{1}{2}\sin \theta}$  **b.** $e = \dfrac{1}{2}$; $p = 6$; ellipse

**c.**

**63. a.** $r = \dfrac{\frac{2}{3}}{1 - \frac{2}{3}\cos \theta}$  **b.** $e = \dfrac{2}{3}$; $p = 1$; ellipse

**c.**

**64. a.** $r = \dfrac{2}{1 + 2\sin\theta}$  **b.** $e = 2$; $p = 1$; hyperbola

**c.**

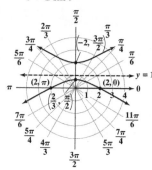

**65. a.** $r = \dfrac{2}{1 + 4\cos\theta}$  **b.** $e = 4$; $p = \dfrac{1}{2}$; hyperbola

**c.**

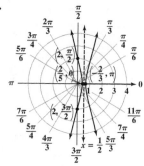

## Chapter 9 Test

**1.** foci: $(\pm\sqrt{13}, 0)$
asymptotes: $y = \pm\dfrac{3}{2}x$

$9x^2 - 4y^2 = 36$

**2.** vertex: $(0, 0)$; focus: $(0, -2)$
directrix: $y = 2$

$x^2 = -8y$

**3.** foci: $(-6, 5), (2, 5)$

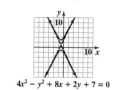

$\dfrac{(x+2)^2}{25} + \dfrac{(y-5)^2}{9} = 1$

**4.** foci: $(-1, 1\pm\sqrt{5})$
asymptotes: $y - 1 = \pm 2(x + 1)$

$4x^2 - y^2 + 8x + 2y + 7 = 0$

**5.** vertex: $(-5, 1)$; focus: $(-5, 3)$
directrix: $y = -1$

$(x + 5)^2 = 8(y - 1)$

**6.** $\dfrac{x^2}{100} + \dfrac{y^2}{51} = 1$  **7.** $\dfrac{y^2}{49} - \dfrac{x^2}{51} = 1$  **8.** $y^2 = 200x$  **9.** 32 ft

**10. a.** $x^2 = 3y$  **b.** Light is placed $\dfrac{3}{4}$ inch above the vertex.  **11.** ellipse  **12.** ellipse or circle

**13.** $\theta = 30°$

**14.** $(y + 1)^2 = x$

**15.** $\dfrac{(x-1)^2}{9} + \dfrac{y^2}{4} = 1$

**16.** parabola

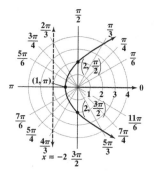

$x = -2$

**17.** ellipse

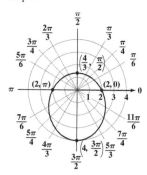

## Cumulative Review Exercises (Chapters P–9)

**1.** $\{2\}$  **2.** $\{x\,|\,x < 2\}$ or $(-\infty, 2)$  **3.** $\{9\}$  **4.** $\{2 + 2\sqrt{5}, 2 - 2\sqrt{5}\}$  **5.** $\{x\,|\,x \geq 4$ or $x \leq -3\}$ or $(-\infty, -3]\cup[4, \infty)$  **6.** $\left\{\dfrac{2}{3}, -1\pm\sqrt{2}\right\}$

**7.** $\{3\}$  **8.** $\{(2, -1)\}$  **9.** $\{(2, -4), (-14, -20)\}$  **10.** $\{(7, -4, 6)\}$

**11.**

$f(x) = (x-1)^2 - 4$

**12.**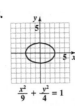

$\frac{x^2}{9} + \frac{y^2}{4} = 1$

**13.**

**14. a.** $\pm 1, \pm 3, \pm\frac{1}{2}, \pm\frac{3}{2}, \pm\frac{1}{4}, \pm\frac{3}{4}, \pm\frac{1}{8}, \pm\frac{3}{8}, \pm\frac{1}{16}, \pm\frac{3}{16}, \pm\frac{1}{32}, \pm\frac{3}{32}$

**b.** $\left\{ -\frac{1}{8}, \frac{3}{4}, 1 \right\}$

**15. a.** domain: $(-2, 2)$; range: $[-3, \infty)$

**b.** minimum of $-3$ at $x = 0$    **c.** $(0, 2)$

**d.** 3    **e.** $-3$    **f.** $x \to -2^+; x \to 2^-$

**g.**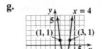

$g(x) = f(x - 2) + 1$

**h.**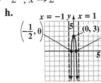

$h(x) = -f(2x)$

**16.** $(g \circ f)(x) = x^2 - 2$    **17.** $3 \log_5 x + \frac{1}{2} \log_5 y - 3$    **18.** $y = -2x - 2$

**19.** The costs will be the same when the number of miles driven is 175 miles. The cost will be $67.    **20.** $25 for basic cable service and $10 for each movie channel

**21.** $\dfrac{\csc\theta - \sin\theta}{\sin\theta} = \dfrac{\csc\theta}{\sin\theta} - \dfrac{\sin\theta}{\sin\theta} = \dfrac{\frac{1}{\sin\theta}}{\sin\theta} - 1 = \dfrac{1}{\sin^2\theta} - 1 = \dfrac{1 - \sin^2\theta}{\sin^2\theta} = \dfrac{\cos^2\theta}{\sin^2\theta} = \cot^2\theta$

**22.**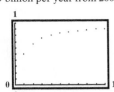

**23.** $-3\mathbf{i} - 3\mathbf{j}$    **24.** $\theta = 0, \theta = \pi, \theta = \frac{\pi}{3}, \text{ or } \theta = \frac{5\pi}{3}$    **25.** $b \approx 14.4, C = 44°, c \approx 10.5$

# CHAPTER 10

## Section 10.1

### Check Point Exercises

**1. a.** $7, 9, 11, 13$    **b.** $-\frac{1}{3}, \frac{1}{5}, -\frac{1}{9}, \frac{1}{17}$    **2.** $3, 11, 27, 59$    **3.** $10, \frac{10}{3}, \frac{5}{6}, \frac{1}{6}$    **4. a.** 91    **b.** $n$    **5. a.** 182    **b.** 47    **c.** 20

**6. a.** $\sum_{i=1}^{9} i^2$    **b.** $\sum_{i=1}^{n} \frac{1}{2^{i-1}}$

### Exercise Set 10.1

**1.** $5, 8, 11, 14$    **3.** $3, 9, 27, 81$    **5.** $-3, 9, -27, 81$    **7.** $-4, 5, -6, 7$    **9.** $\frac{2}{5}, \frac{2}{3}, \frac{6}{7}, 1$    **11.** $1, -\frac{1}{3}, \frac{1}{7}, -\frac{1}{15}$    **13.** $7, 12, 17, 22$

**15.** $3, 12, 48, 192$    **17.** $4, 11, 25, 53$    **19.** $1, 2, \frac{3}{2}, \frac{2}{3}$    **21.** $4, 12, 48, 240$    **23.** 272    **25.** 120    **27.** $(n+2)(n+1)$    **29.** 105    **31.** 60

**33.** 115    **35.** $-\frac{5}{16}$    **37.** 55    **39.** $\frac{3}{8}$    **41.** 15    **43.** $\sum_{i=1}^{15} i^2$    **45.** $\sum_{i=1}^{11} 2^i$    **47.** $\sum_{i=1}^{30} i$    **49.** $\sum_{i=1}^{14} \frac{i}{i+1}$    **51.** $\sum_{i=1}^{n} \frac{4^i}{i}$    **53.** $\sum_{i=1}^{n} (2i - 1)$

**55.** $\sum_{k=1}^{14} (2k + 3)$    **57.** $\sum_{k=0}^{12} ar^k$    **59.** $\sum_{k=0}^{n} (a + kd)$    **61.** 45    **63.** 0    **65.** 2    **67.** 80    **69. a.** 9.9; Online ad spending averaged

$9.9 billion per year from 2000 through 2006.    **71.** $8081.13    **81.** 39,800    **83.** 8.109673361 E15    **85.** 24,804

**89.**     **91.**

As $n$ gets larger, $a_n$ approaches 1.      As $n$ gets larger, $a_n$ approaches 0.

**93.** does not make sense    **95.** makes sense    **97.** false    **99.** false    **101.** $9, 32, 16, 8, 4$    **103.** $-5; -5; -5; -5;$ The difference between consecutive terms is always $-5$.    **104.** $4; 4; 4; 4;$ The difference between consecutive terms is always 4.    **105.** $-45$

## Section 10.2

### Check Point Exercises

**1.** $100, 70, 40, 10, -20, -50$    **2.** $-34$    **3. a.** $a_n = 0.7n + 31.3$    **b.** 39    **4.** 360    **5.** 2460    **6.** $740,300

### Exercise Set 10.2

**1.** $200, 220, 240, 260, 280, 300$    **3.** $-7, -3, 1, 5, 9, 13$    **5.** $300, 210, 120, 30, -60, -150$    **7.** $\frac{5}{2}, 2, \frac{3}{2}, 1, \frac{1}{2}, 0$    **9.** $-9, -3, 3, 9, 15, 21$

**11.** $30, 20, 10, 0, -10, -20$    **13.** $1.6, 1.2, 0.8, 0.4, 0, -0.4$    **15.** 33    **17.** 252    **19.** 955    **21.** $-142$    **23.** $a_n = 4n - 3; a_{20} = 77$

**25.** $a_n = 11 - 4n$; $a_{20} = -69$   **27.** $a_n = 7 + 2n$; $a_{20} = 47$   **29.** $a_n = -16 - 4n$; $a_{20} = -96$   **31.** $a_n = 1 + 3n$; $a_{20} = 61$
**33.** $a_n = 40 - 10n$; $a_{20} = -160$   **35.** 1220   **37.** 4400   **39.** 5050   **41.** 3660   **43.** 396   **45.** $8 + 13 + 18 + \cdots + 88$; 816
**47.** $2 - 1 - 4 - \cdots - 85$; $-1245$   **49.** $4 + 8 + 12 + \cdots + 400$; 20,200   **51.** 7   **53.** 22   **55.** 847   **57.** $f(x) = -4x + 5$
**59.** $a_n = 3n - 2$   **61. a.** $a_n = 0.77n + 9.23$   **b.** 30.0%   **63.** Company A will pay \$1400 more in year 10.   **65. a.** \$21,153
**b.** \$21,158; overestimates by \$5   **69.** Company A: \$307,000; Company B: \$324,000; Company B pays the greater total amount.
**71.** 2869 seats   **79.** makes sense   **81.** makes sense   **83.** 320 degree-days   **85.** $-2$; $-2$; $-2$; $-2$; The ratio of a term to the term that directly precedes it is always $-2$.   **86.** 5; 5; 5; 5; The ratio of a term to the term that directly precedes it is always 5.   **87.** 8019

## Section 10.3

### Check Point Exercises

**1.** $12, 6, 3, \dfrac{3}{2}, \dfrac{3}{4}, \dfrac{3}{8}$   **2.** 3645   **3.** $a_n = 3(2)^{n-1}$; $a_8 = 384$   **4.** 9842   **5.** 19,680   **6.** \$2,371,746   **7. a.** \$333,946   **b.** \$291,946
**8.** 9   **9.** 1   **10.** \$4000

### Exercise Set 10.3

**1.** $5, 15, 45, 135, 405$   **3.** $20, 10, 5, \dfrac{5}{2}, \dfrac{5}{4}$   **5.** $10, -40, 160, -640, 2560$   **7.** $-6, 30, -150, 750, -3750$   **9.** $a_8 = 768$   **11.** $a_{12} = -10,240$
**13.** $a_{40} \approx -0.000000002$   **15.** $a_8 = 0.1$   **17.** $a_n = 3(4)^{n-1}$; $a_7 = 12,288$   **19.** $a_n = 18\left(\dfrac{1}{3}\right)^{n-1}$; $a_7 = \dfrac{2}{81}$   **21.** $a_n = 1.5(-2)^{n-1}$; $a_7 = 96$
**23.** $a_n = 0.0004(-10)^{n-1}$; $a_7 = 400$   **25.** 531,440   **27.** 2049   **29.** $\dfrac{16,383}{2}$   **31.** 9840   **33.** 10,230   **35.** $\dfrac{63}{128}$   **37.** $\dfrac{3}{2}$   **39.** 4
**41.** $\dfrac{2}{3}$   **43.** $\dfrac{80}{13} \approx 6.15385$   **45.** $\dfrac{5}{9}$   **47.** $\dfrac{47}{99}$   **49.** $\dfrac{257}{999}$   **51.** arithmetic, $d = 1$   **53.** geometric, $r = 2$   **55.** neither
**57.** 2435   **59.** 2280   **61.** $-140$   **63.** $a_2 = 12, a_3 = 18$   **65.** \$16,384   **67.** \$3,795,957   **69. a.** approximately 1.01 for each division
**b.** $a_n = 35.48(1.01)^{n-1}$   **c.** approximately 38.04 million   **71.** \$32,767   **73.** \$793,583   **75.** 130.26 in.   **77. a.** \$11,617   **b.** \$1617
**79. a.** \$87,052   **b.** \$63,052   **81. a.** \$693,031   **b.** \$293,031   **83.** \$30,000   **85.** \$9 million   **87.** $\dfrac{1}{3}$   **99.**
**101.** makes sense   **103.** makes sense   **105.** false   **107.** false   **109.** Release 2000 flies each day.
**112.** $6 = 6$   **113.** $15 = 15$   **114.** $\dfrac{(k+1)(k+2)(2k+3)}{6}$

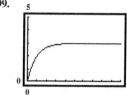

horizontal asymptote: $y = 3$;
sum of series: 3

## Mid-Chapter 10 Check Point

**1.** $1, -2, \dfrac{3}{2}, -\dfrac{2}{3}, \dfrac{5}{24}$   **2.** $5, 2, -1, -4, -7$   **3.** $5, -15, 45, -135, 405$   **4.** $3, 1, 3, 1, 3$   **5.** $a_n = 4n - 2$; $a_{20} = 78$
**6.** $a_n = 3(2)^{n-1}$; $a_{10} = 1536$   **7.** $a_n = -\dfrac{1}{2}n + 2$; $a_{30} = -13$   **8.** 5115   **9.** 2350   **10.** 6820   **11.** $-29,300$   **12.** 44   **13.** 3725
**14.** $\dfrac{1995}{64}$   **15.** $\dfrac{5}{7}$   **16.** $\dfrac{5}{11}$   **17.** Answers will vary. An example is $\displaystyle\sum_{i=1}^{18} \dfrac{i}{i+2}$.   **18.** 464 ft; 3600 ft   **19.** \$311,249

## Section 10.4

### Check Point Exercises

**1. a.** $S_1$: $2 = 1(1 + 1)$; $S_k$: $2 + 4 + 6 + \cdots + 2k = k(k + 1)$; $S_{k+1}$: $2 + 4 + 6 + \cdots + 2(k + 1) = (k + 1)(k + 2)$
  **b.** $S_1$: $1^3 = \dfrac{1^2(1 + 1)^2}{4}$; $S_k$: $1^3 + 2^3 + 3^3 + \cdots + k^3 = \dfrac{k^2(k + 1)^2}{4}$; $S_{k+1}$: $1^3 + 2^3 + 3^3 + \cdots + (k + 1)^3 = \dfrac{(k + 1)^2(k + 2)^2}{4}$
**2.** $S_1$: $2 = 1(1 + 1)$; $S_k$: $2 + 4 + 6 + \cdots + 2k = k(k + 1)$; $S_{k+1}$: $2 + 4 + 6 + \cdots + 2k + 2(k + 1) = (k + 1)(k + 2)$; $S_{k+1}$ can be obtained by adding $2k + 2$ to both sides of $S_k$.
**3.** $S_1$: $1^3 = \dfrac{1^2(1 + 1)^2}{4}$; $S_k$: $1^3 + 2^3 + 3^3 + \cdots + k^3 = \dfrac{k^2(k + 1)^2}{4}$; $S_{k+1}$: $1^3 + 2^3 + 3^3 + \cdots + k^3 + (k + 1)^3 = \dfrac{(k + 1)^2(k + 2)^2}{4}$; $S_{k+1}$ can
  be obtained by adding $k^3 + 3k^2 + 3k + 1$ to both sides of $S_k$.
**4.** $S_1$: 2 is a factor of $1^2 + 1$; $S_k$: 2 is a factor of $k^2 + k$; $S_{k+1}$: 2 is a factor of $(k + 1)^2 + (k + 1) = k^2 + 3k + 2$; $S_{k+1}$ can be obtained from $S_k$ by writing $k^2 + 3k + 2$ as $(k^2 + k) + 2(k + 1)$.

### Exercise Set 10.4

**1.** $S_1$: $1 = 1^2$; $S_2$: $1 + 3 = 2^2$; $S_3$: $1 + 3 + 5 = 3^2$   **3.** $S_1$: 2 is a factor of $1 - 1 = 0$; $S_2$: 2 is a factor of $2^2 - 2 = 2$; $S_3$: 2 is a factor of $3^2 - 3 = 6$.
**5.** $S_k$: $4 + 8 + 12 + \cdots + 4k = 2k(k + 1)$; $S_{k+1}$: $4 + 8 + 12 + \cdots + (4k + 4) = 2(k + 1)(k + 2)$
**7.** $S_k$: $3 + 7 + 11 + \cdots + (4k - 1) = k(2k + 1)$; $S_{k+1}$: $3 + 7 + 11 + \cdots + (4k + 3) = (k + 1)(2k + 3)$
**9.** $S_k$: 2 is a factor of $k^2 - k + 2$; $S_{k+1}$: 2 is a factor of $k^2 + k + 2$.
**11.** $S_1$: $4 = 2(1)(1 + 1)$; $S_k$: $4 + 8 + 12 + \cdots + 4k = 2k(k + 1)$; $S_{k+1}$: $4 + 8 + 12 + \cdots + 4(k + 1) = 2(k + 1)(k + 2)$; $S_{k+1}$ can be obtained by adding $4k + 4$ to both sides of $S_k$.

**13.** $S_1: 1 = 1^2$; $S_k: 1 + 3 + 5 + \cdots + (2k - 1) = k^2$; $S_{k+1}: 1 + 3 + 5 + \cdots + (2k + 1) = (k + 1)^2$; $S_{k+1}$ can be obtained by adding $2k + 1$ to both sides of $S_k$.

**15.** $S_1: 3 = 1[2(1) + 1]$; $S_k: 3 + 7 + 11 + \cdots + (4k - 1) = k(2k + 1)$; $S_{k+1}: 3 + 7 + 11 + \cdots + (4k + 3) = (k + 1)(2k + 3)$; $S_{k+1}$ can be obtained by adding $4k + 3$ to both sides of $S_k$.

**17.** $S_1: 1 = 2^1 - 1$; $S_k: 1 + 2 + 2^2 + \cdots + 2^{k-1} = 2^k - 1$; $S_{k+1}: 1 + 2 + 2^2 + \cdots + 2^k = 2^{k+1} - 1$; $S_{k+1}$ can be obtained by adding $2^k$ to both sides of $S_k$.

**19.** $S_1: 2 = 2^{1+1} - 2$; $S_k: 2 + 4 + 8 + \cdots + 2^k = 2^{k+1} - 2$; $S_{k+1}: 2 + 4 + 8 + \cdots + 2^{k+1} = 2^{k+2} - 2$; $S_{k+1}$ can be obtained by adding $2^{k+1}$ to both sides of $S_k$.

**21.** $S_1: 1 \cdot 2 = \dfrac{1(1 + 1)(1 + 2)}{3}$; $S_k: 1 \cdot 2 + 2 \cdot 3 + 3 \cdot 4 + \cdots + k(k + 1) = \dfrac{k(k + 1)(k + 2)}{3}$;

$S_{k+1}: 1 \cdot 2 + 2 \cdot 3 + 3 \cdot 4 + \cdots + (k + 1)(k + 2) = \dfrac{(k + 1)(k + 2)(k + 3)}{3}$; $S_{k+1}$ can be obtained by adding $(k + 1)(k + 2)$ to both sides of $S_k$.

**23.** $S_1: \dfrac{1}{1 \cdot 2} = \dfrac{1}{1 + 1}$; $S_k: \dfrac{1}{1 \cdot 2} + \dfrac{1}{2 \cdot 3} + \dfrac{1}{3 \cdot 4} + \cdots + \dfrac{1}{k(k + 1)} = \dfrac{k}{k + 1}$; $S_{k+1}: \dfrac{1}{1 \cdot 2} + \dfrac{1}{2 \cdot 3} + \dfrac{1}{3 \cdot 4} + \cdots + \dfrac{1}{(k + 1)(k + 2)} = \dfrac{k + 1}{k + 2}$; $S_{k+1}$ can be obtained by adding $\dfrac{1}{(k + 1)(k + 2)}$ to both sides of $S_k$.

**25.** $S_1: 2$ is a factor of $0$; $S_k: 2$ is a factor of $k^2 - k$; $S_{k+1}: 2$ is a factor of $k^2 + k$; $S_{k+1}$ can be obtained from $S_k$ by rewriting $k^2 + k$ as $(k^2 - k) + 2k$.

**27.** $S_1: 6$ is a factor of $6$; $S_k: 6$ is a factor of $k(k + 1)(k + 2)$; $S_{k+1}: 6$ is a factor of $(k + 1)(k + 2)(k + 3)$; $S_{k+1}$ can be obtained from $S_k$ by rewriting $(k + 1)(k + 2)(k + 3)$ as $k(k + 1)(k + 2) + 3(k + 1)(k + 2)$ and noting that either $k + 1$ or $k + 2$ is even, so $6$ is a factor of $3(k + 1)(k + 2)$.

**29.** $S_1: 5 \cdot 6^1 = 6(6^1 - 1)$; $S_k: \sum_{i=1}^{k} 5 \cdot 6^i = 6(6^k - 1)$; $S_{k+1}: \sum_{i=1}^{k+1} 5 \cdot 6^i = 6(6^{k+1} - 1)$; $S_{k+1}$ can be obtained by adding $5 \cdot 6^{k+1}$ to both sides of $S_k$.

**31.** $S_1: 1 + 2 > 1$; $S_k: k + 2 > k$; $S_{k+1}: k + 3 > k + 1$; $S_{k+1}$ can be obtained by adding $1$ to both sides of $S_k$.

**33.** $S_1: (ab)^1 = a^1 b^1$; $S_k: (ab)^k = a^k b^k$; $S_{k+1}: (ab)^{k+1} = a^{k+1} b^{k+1}$; $S_{k+1}$ can be obtained by multiplying both sides of $S_k$ by $(ab)$.

**37.** does not make sense    **39.** does not make sense

**41.** $S_3: 3^2 > 2(3) + 1$; $S_k: k^2 > 2k + 1$ for $k \geq 3$; $S_{k+1}: (k + 1)^2 > 2(k + 1) + 1$ or $k^2 + 2k + 1 > 2k + 3$; $S_{k+1}$ can be obtained from $S_k$ by noting that $S_{k+1}$ is the same as $k^2 > 2$ which is true for $k \geq 3$.

**43.** $S_1: \dfrac{1}{4}$; $S_2: \dfrac{1}{3}$; $S_3: \dfrac{3}{8}$; $S_4: \dfrac{2}{5}$; $S_5: \dfrac{5}{12}$; $S_n: \dfrac{n}{2n + 2}$; Use $S_k$ to obtain the conjectured formula.

**46.** The exponents begin with the exponent on $a + b$ and decrease by 1 in each successive term.    **47.** The exponents begin with 0, increase by 1 in each successive term, and end with the exponent on $a + b$.    **48.** The sum of the exponents is the exponent on $a + b$.

## Section 10.5

### Check Point Exercises

**1. a.** 20    **b.** 1    **c.** 28    **d.** 1    **2.** $x^4 + 4x^3 + 6x^2 + 4x + 1$    **3.** $x^5 - 10x^4 y + 40x^3 y^2 - 80x^2 y^3 + 80xy^4 - 32y^5$    **4.** $4032x^5 y^4$

### Exercise Set 10.5

**1.** 56    **3.** 12    **5.** 1    **7.** 4950    **9.** $x^3 + 6x^2 + 12x + 8$    **11.** $27x^3 + 27x^2 y + 9xy^2 + y^3$    **13.** $125x^3 - 75x^2 + 15x - 1$
**15.** $16x^4 + 32x^3 + 24x^2 + 8x + 1$    **17.** $x^8 + 8x^6 y + 24x^4 y^2 + 32x^2 y^3 + 16y^4$    **19.** $y^4 - 12y^3 + 54y^2 - 108y + 81$
**21.** $16x^{12} - 32x^9 + 24x^6 - 8x^3 + 1$    **23.** $c^5 + 10c^4 + 40c^3 + 80c^2 + 80c + 32$    **25.** $x^5 - 5x^4 + 10x^3 - 10x^2 + 5x - 1$
**27.** $243x^5 - 405x^4 y + 270x^3 y^2 - 90x^2 y^3 + 15xy^4 - y^5$    **29.** $64a^6 + 192a^5 b + 240a^4 b^2 + 160a^3 b^3 + 60a^2 b^4 + 12ab^5 + b^6$
**31.** $x^8 + 16x^7 + 112x^6 + \cdots$    **33.** $x^{10} - 20x^9 y + 180x^8 y^2 - \cdots$    **35.** $x^{32} + 16x^{30} + 120x^{28} + \cdots$    **37.** $y^{60} - 20y^{57} + 190y^{54} - \cdots$
**39.** $240x^4 y^2$    **41.** $126x^5$    **43.** $56x^6 y^{15}$    **45.** $-\dfrac{21}{2}x^6$    **47.** $319{,}770x^{16} y^{14}$    **49.** $x^{12} + 4x^7 + 6x^2 + \dfrac{4}{x^3} + \dfrac{1}{x^8}$    **51.** $x - 3x^{1/3} + \dfrac{3}{x^{1/3}} - \dfrac{1}{x}$
**53.** $4x^3 + 6x^2 h + 4xh^2 + h^3$    **55.** 252    **57.** 0.1138    **69.**    **71.** $f_1(x) = x^4 - 8x^3 + 24x^2 - 32x + 16$
**73.** makes sense    **75.** does not make sense
**77.** false    **79.** false
**81.** $x^6 + 3x^5 + 6x^4 + 7x^3 + 6x^2 + 3x + 1$

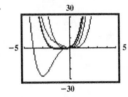

$f_2, f_3, f_4,$ and $f_5$ are approaching $f_1 = f_6$.

**83.** $\dbinom{n}{r} = \dfrac{n!}{r!(n - r)!} = \dfrac{n!}{(n - r)!r!} = \dfrac{n!}{(n - r)![n - (n - r)]!} = \dbinom{n}{n - r}$

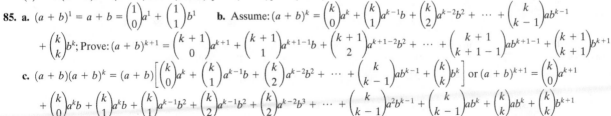

**85. a.** $(a + b)^1 = a + b = \dbinom{1}{0}a^1 + \dbinom{1}{1}b^1$    **b.** Assume: $(a + b)^k = \dbinom{k}{0}a^k + \dbinom{k}{1}a^{k-1}b + \dbinom{k}{2}a^{k-2}b^2 + \cdots + \dbinom{k}{k-1}ab^{k-1}$

$+ \dbinom{k}{k}b^k$; Prove: $(a + b)^{k+1} = \dbinom{k + 1}{0}a^{k+1} + \dbinom{k + 1}{1}a^{k+1-1}b + \dbinom{k + 1}{2}a^{k+1-2}b^2 + \cdots + \dbinom{k + 1}{k + 1 - 1}ab^{k+1-1} + \dbinom{k + 1}{k + 1}b^{k+1}$

**c.** $(a + b)(a + b)^k = (a + b)\left[\dbinom{k}{0}a^k + \dbinom{k}{1}a^{k-1}b + \dbinom{k}{2}a^{k-2}b^2 + \cdots + \dbinom{k}{k-1}ab^{k-1} + \dbinom{k}{k}b^k\right]$ or $(a + b)^{k+1} = \dbinom{k}{0}a^{k+1}$

$+ \dbinom{k}{0}a^k b + \dbinom{k}{1}a^k b + \dbinom{k}{1}a^{k-1}b^2 + \dbinom{k}{2}a^{k-1}b^2 + \dbinom{k}{2}a^{k-2}b^3 + \cdots + \dbinom{k}{k-1}a^2 b^{k-1} + \dbinom{k}{k-1}ab^k + \dbinom{k}{k}ab^k + \dbinom{k}{k}b^{k+1}$

**d.** $(a + b)^{k+1} = \binom{k}{0}a^{k+1} + \left[\binom{k}{0} + \binom{k}{1}\right]a^k b + \left[\binom{k}{1} + \binom{k}{2}\right]a^{k-1}b^2 + \left[\binom{k}{2} + \binom{k}{3}\right]a^{k-2}b^3 + \cdots + \left[\binom{k}{k-1} + \binom{k}{k}\right]ab^k + \binom{k}{k}b^{k+1}$

**e.** $(a + b)^{k+1} = \binom{k}{0}a^{k+1} + \binom{k+1}{1}a^k b + \binom{k+1}{2}a^{k-1}b^2 + \binom{k+1}{3}a^{k-2}b^3 + \cdots + \binom{k+1}{k}ab^k + \binom{k}{k}b^{k+1}$

**f.** $(a + b)^{k+1} = \binom{k+1}{0}a^{k+1} + \binom{k+1}{1}a^k b + \binom{k+1}{2}a^{k-1}b^2 + \binom{k+1}{3}a^{k-2}b^3 + \cdots + \binom{k+1}{k}ab^k + \binom{k+1}{k+1}b^{k+1}$

**86.** 6840 **87.** 56 **88.** true

## Section 10.6

### Check Point Exercises

**1.** 72 **2.** 729 **3.** 676,000 **4.** 840 **5.** 720 **6. a.** combinations **b.** permutations **7.** 210 **8.** 1820

### Exercise Set 10.6

**1.** 3024 **3.** 6720 **5.** 720 **7.** 1 **9.** 126 **11.** 330 **13.** 1 **15.** 1 **17.** combinations **19.** permutations **21.** 0 **23.** $\frac{3}{4}$
**25.** −9499 **27.** $\frac{3}{68}$ **29.** 27 ways **31.** 40 ways **33.** 243 ways **35.** 144 area codes **37.** 120 ways **39.** 6 paragraphs
**41.** 720 ways **43.** 8,648,640 ways **45.** 120 ways **47.** 15,120 lineups **49.** 20 ways **51.** 495 collections **53.** 24,310 groups
**55.** 22,957,480 selections **57.** 360 ways **59.** 1716 ways **61.** 1140 ways **63.** 840 passwords **65.** 2730 cones **67.** 720 **69.** 20
**71.** 24 **83.** makes sense **85.** does not make sense **87.** false **89.** true **91.** 14,400 ways **93.** 450 ways **95.** $\frac{2}{3}$ **96.** $\frac{1}{3}$ **97.** $\frac{2}{3}$

## Section 10.7

### Check Point Exercises

**1. a.** $\frac{7664}{100,000}$ or $\frac{479}{6250} \approx 0.077$ **b.** $\frac{720}{800}$ or $\frac{9}{10} = 0.9$ **c.** $\frac{720}{7664}$ or $\frac{45}{479} \approx 0.094$ **2.** $\frac{1}{3}$ **3.** $\frac{1}{9}$ **4.** $\frac{1}{13}$ **5.** $\frac{1}{13,983,816} \approx 0.0000000715$
**6.** $\frac{160}{191}$ **7.** $\frac{1}{3}$ **8.** $\frac{3}{4}$ **9. a.** 0.99 **b.** 0.64 **10.** $\frac{1}{361} \approx 0.00277$ **11.** $\frac{1}{16}$

### Exercise Set 10.7

**1.** 0.10 **3.** 0.52 **5.** 0.01 **7.** 0.59 **9.** 0.61 **11.** $\frac{1}{6}$ **13.** $\frac{1}{2}$ **15.** $\frac{1}{3}$ **17.** $\frac{1}{13}$ **19.** $\frac{3}{13}$ **21.** $\frac{1}{4}$ **23.** $\frac{7}{8}$ **25.** $\frac{1}{12}$
**27.** $\frac{1}{18,009,460}; \frac{5}{900,473}$ **29. a.** 2,598,960 **b.** 1287 **c.** $\frac{1287}{2,598,960} \approx 0.0005$ **31.** $\frac{43}{58}$ **33.** $\frac{50}{87}$ **35.** $\frac{113}{174}$ **37.** $\frac{12}{13}$ **39.** $\frac{2}{13}$
**41.** $\frac{7}{13}$ **43.** $\frac{3}{4}$ **45.** $\frac{33}{40}$ **47.** $\frac{1}{36}$ **49.** $\frac{1}{3}$ **51.** $\frac{1}{64}$ **53. a.** $\frac{1}{256}$ **b.** $\frac{1}{4096}$ **c.** $\left(\frac{15}{16}\right)^{10} \approx 0.524$ **d.** $1 - \left(\frac{15}{16}\right)^{10} \approx 0.476$
**65.** does not make sense **67.** makes sense **71. a.** $\frac{12}{25}$ **b.** $\frac{3}{10}$ **73. a.** The first person can have any birthday in the year. The second
person can have all but one birthday. **b.** $\frac{365}{365} \cdot \frac{364}{365} \cdot \frac{363}{365} \approx 0.99$ **c.** $\approx 0.01$ **d.** $\approx 0.41$ **e.** 23 people

**75. a.** The denominator is zero when $x = 4$. **b.** 2 **c.** 2 **76.**

; The two pieces of the graph approach the point $(4, 2)$

$$f(x) = \frac{x^2 - 6x + 8}{x - 4}$$

**77.**

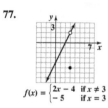

$$f(x) = \begin{cases} 2x - 4 & \text{if } x \ne 3 \\ -5 & \text{if } x = 3 \end{cases}$$

## Chapter 10 Review Exercises

**1.** $a_1 = 3; a_2 = 10; a_3 = 17; a_4 = 24$ **2.** $a_1 = -\frac{3}{2}; a_2 = \frac{4}{3}; a_3 = -\frac{5}{4}; a_4 = \frac{6}{5}$ **3.** $a_1 = 1; a_2 = 1; a_3 = \frac{1}{2}; a_4: \frac{1}{6}$
**4.** $a_1 = \frac{1}{2}; a_2 = -\frac{1}{4}; a_3 = \frac{1}{8}; a_4 = -\frac{1}{16}$ **5.** $a_1 = 9; a_2 = \frac{2}{27}; a_3 = 9; a_4 = \frac{2}{27}$ **6.** $a_1 = 4; a_2 = 11; a_3 = 25; a_4 = 53$ **7.** 65 **8.** 95
**9.** −20 **10.** $\sum_{i=1}^{15} \frac{i}{i+2}$ **11.** $\sum_{i=4}^{13} i^3$ or $\sum_{i=1}^{10}(i + 3)^3$ **12.** 7, 11, 15, 19, 23, 27 **13.** −4, −9, −14, −19, −24, −29 **14.** $\frac{3}{2}, 1, \frac{1}{2}, 0, -\frac{1}{2}, -1$
**15.** −2, 3, 8, 13, 18, 23 **16.** $a_6 = 20$ **17.** $a_{12} = -30$ **18.** $a_{14} = -38$ **19.** $a_n = 4n - 11; a_{20} = 69$ **20.** $a_n = 220 - 20n; a_{20} = -180$
**21.** $a_n = 8 - 5n; a_{20} = -92$ **22.** 1727 **23.** 225 **24.** 15,150 **25.** 440 **26.** −500 **27.** −2325 **28. a.** $a_n = 4.75n + 34.25$ **b.** 96%
**29.** $418,500 **30.** 1470 seats **31.** 3, 6, 12, 24, 48 **32.** $\frac{1}{2}, \frac{1}{4}, \frac{1}{8}, \frac{1}{16}, \frac{1}{32}$ **33.** 16, −8, 4, −2, 1 **34.** −1, 5, −25, 125, −625
**35.** $a_7 = 1458$ **36.** $a_6 = \frac{1}{2}$ **37.** $a_5 = -48$ **38.** $a_n = 2^{n-1}; a_8 = 128$ **39.** $a_n = 100\left(\frac{1}{10}\right)^{n-1}; a_8 = \frac{1}{100,000}$

**40.** $a_n = 12\left(-\dfrac{1}{3}\right)^{n-1}$; $a_8 = -\dfrac{4}{729}$ **41.** 17,936,135 **42.** $\dfrac{127}{8}$ **43.** 19,530 **44.** $-258$ **45.** $\dfrac{341}{128}$ **46.** $\dfrac{27}{2}$ **47.** $\dfrac{4}{3}$ **48.** $-\dfrac{18}{5}$

**49.** 20 **50.** $\dfrac{2}{3}$ **51.** $\dfrac{47}{99}$ **52. a.** $\dfrac{5.9}{4.2} \approx 1.4$; $\dfrac{8.3}{5.9} \approx 1.4$; $\dfrac{11.6}{8.3} \approx 1.4$; $\dfrac{16.2}{11.6} \approx 1.4$; $\dfrac{22.7}{16.2} \approx 1.4$ **b.** $a_n = 4.2(1.4)^n$ **c.** 62.0 million

**53.** \$42,823; \$223,210 **54. a.** \$19,129 **b.** \$8729 **55. a.** \$91,361 **b.** \$55,361 **56.** $\$9\dfrac{1}{3}$ million

**57.** $S_1\colon 5 = \dfrac{5(1)(1+1)}{2}$; $S_k\colon 5 + 10 + 15 + \cdots + 5k = \dfrac{5k(k+1)}{2}$; $S_{k+1}\colon 5 + 10 + 15 + \cdots + 5(k+1) = \dfrac{5(k+1)(k+2)}{2}$; $S_{k+1}$

can be obtained by adding $5(k+1)$ to both sides of $S_k$.

**58.** $S_1\colon 1 = \dfrac{4^1 - 1}{3}$; $S_k\colon 1 + 4 + 4^2 + \cdots + 4^{k-1} = \dfrac{4^k - 1}{3}$; $S_{k+1}\colon 1 + 4 + 4^2 + \cdots + 4^k = \dfrac{4^{k+1} - 1}{3}$; $S_{k+1}$ can be obtained by adding $4^k$

to both sides of $S_k$.

**59.** $S_1\colon 2 = 2(1)^2$; $S_k\colon 2 + 6 + 10 + \cdots + (4k - 2) = 2k^2$; $S_{k+1}\colon 2 + 6 + 10 + \cdots + (4k + 2) = 2k^2 + 4k + 2$; $S_{k+1}$ can be obtained by adding $4k + 2$ to both sides of $S_k$.

**60.** $S_1\colon 1 \cdot 3 = \dfrac{1(1+1)[2(1)+7]}{6}$; $S_k\colon 1 \cdot 3 + 2 \cdot 4 + 3 \cdot 5 + \cdots + k(k+2) = \dfrac{k(k+1)(2k+7)}{6}$;

$S_{k+1}\colon 1 \cdot 3 + 2 \cdot 4 + 3 \cdot 5 + \cdots + (k+1)(k+3) = \dfrac{(k+1)(k+2)(2k+9)}{6}$; $S_{k+1}$ can be obtained by adding $(k+1)(k+3)$ to both sides of $S_k$.

**61.** $S_1\colon 2$ is a factor of 6; $S_k\colon 2$ is a factor of $k^2 + 5k$; $S_{k+1}\colon 2$ is a factor of $k^2 + 7k + 6$; $S_{k+1}$ can be obtained from $S_k$ by rewriting $k^2 + 7k + 6$ as $(k^2 + 5k) + 2(k + 3)$.

**62.** 165 **63.** 4005 **64.** $8x^3 + 12x^2 + 6x + 1$ **65.** $x^8 - 4x^6 + 6x^4 - 4x^2 + 1$ **66.** $x^5 + 10x^4y + 40x^3y^2 + 80x^2y^3 + 80xy^4 + 32y^5$

**67.** $x^6 - 12x^5 + 60x^4 - 160x^3 + 240x^2 - 192x + 64$ **68.** $x^{16} + 24x^{14} + 252x^{12} + \cdots$ **69.** $x^9 - 27x^8 + 324x^7 - \cdots$ **70.** $80x^2$

**71.** $4860x^2$ **72.** 336 **73.** 15,120 **74.** 56 **75.** 78 **76.** 20 choices **77.** 243 possibilities **78.** 32,760 ways **79.** 4845 ways

**80.** 1140 sets **81.** 116,280 ways **82.** 120 ways **83.** $\dfrac{18}{25}$ **84.** $\dfrac{6}{7}$ **85.** $\dfrac{3}{5}$ **86.** $\dfrac{12}{35}$ **87.** $\dfrac{10}{21}$ **88.** $\dfrac{5}{16}$ **89.** $\dfrac{2}{3}$ **90.** $\dfrac{2}{3}$

**91.** $\dfrac{2}{13}$ **92.** $\dfrac{7}{13}$ **93.** $\dfrac{5}{6}$ **94.** $\dfrac{5}{6}$ **95.** $\dfrac{1}{6}$ **96. a.** $\dfrac{1}{15,504}$ **b.** $\dfrac{25}{3876}$ **97.** $\dfrac{1}{32}$ **98. a.** 0.04 **b.** 0.008 **c.** 0.4096

## Chapter 10 Test

**1.** $a_1 = 1$; $a_2 = -\dfrac{1}{4}$; $a_3 = \dfrac{1}{9}$; $a_4 = -\dfrac{1}{16}$; $a_5 = \dfrac{1}{25}$ **2.** 105 **3.** 550 **4.** $-21,846$ **5.** 36 **6.** 720 **7.** 120 **8.** $\displaystyle\sum_{i=1}^{20} \dfrac{i+1}{i+2}$

**9.** $a_n = 5n - 1$; $a_{12} = 59$ **10.** $a_n = 16\left(\dfrac{1}{4}\right)^{n-1}$; $a_{12} = \dfrac{1}{262,144}$ **11.** $-2387$ **12.** $-385$ **13.** 8 **14.** $\dfrac{73}{99}$ **15.** \$276,427

**16.** $S_1\colon 1 = \dfrac{1[3(1)-1]}{2}$; $S_k\colon 1 + 4 + 7 + \cdots + (3k-2) = \dfrac{k(3k-1)}{2}$; $S_{k+1}\colon 1 + 4 + 7 + \cdots + (3k+1) = \dfrac{(k+1)(3k+2)}{2}$; $S_{k+1}$

can be obtained by adding $3k + 1$ to both sides of $S_k$.

**17.** $x^{10} - 5x^8 + 10x^6 - 10x^4 + 5x^2 - 1$ **18.** $x^8 + 8x^7y^2 + 28x^6y^4$ **19.** 990 ways **20.** 210 sets **21.** $10^4 = 10,000$ **22.** $\dfrac{3}{5}$ **23.** $\dfrac{39}{50}$

**24.** $\dfrac{3}{5}$ **25.** $\dfrac{9}{19}$ **26.** $\dfrac{10}{1001}$ **27.** $\dfrac{8}{13}$ **28.** $\dfrac{3}{5}$ **29.** $\dfrac{1}{256}$ **30.** $\dfrac{1}{16}$

## Cumulative Review Exercises (Chapters P–10)

**1.** domain: $[-4, 1)$; range: $(-\infty, 2]$ **2.** maximum of 2 at $x = -2$ **3.** $(-2, 1)$ **4.** neither **5.** $-3$ and $-1$ **6.** 0 **7.** $x \to 1^-$

**8.**

$g(x) = f(x - 2) + 1$

**9.**

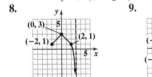

$h(x) = -f(2x)$

**10.** $\left\{\dfrac{14}{5}\right\}$ **11.** $\left\{\dfrac{3+\sqrt{3}}{3}, \dfrac{3-\sqrt{3}}{3}\right\}$ **12.** $\{2\}$

**13.** $\{16,256\}$ **14.** $\{\ln 2, \ln 4\}$ **15.** $-1 \le x \le 0$ or $[-1, 0]$

**16.** $\left(-\dfrac{2}{3}, \dfrac{3}{2}\right)$ **17.** $(-3, 1]$ **18.** $\{2.9706\}$ **19.** $\left\{1, \dfrac{1}{2}, -3\right\}$

**20.** $\{(3, 2), (3, -2), (-3, 2), (-3, -2)\}$ **21.** $\{(6, -4, 2)\}$

**22.** $\{(0, -1), (2, 1)\}$

**23.**

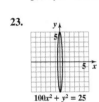

$100x^2 + y^2 = 25$

**24.**

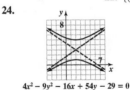

$4x^2 - 9y^2 - 16x + 54y - 29 = 0$

**25.**

$f(x) = \dfrac{x^2 - 1}{x - 2}$

**26.**

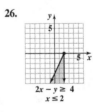

$2x - y \ge 4$
$x \le 2$

**27.**

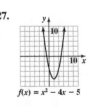

$f(x) = x^2 - 4x - 5$

**28.**

**29.**

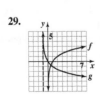

**30.** $(f \circ g)(x) = -x^2 + 2$; $(g \circ f)(x) = -x^2 - 2x$

**31.** $-2x - h - 2$

**32.** $\begin{bmatrix} -2 & 10 \\ -5 & 7 \\ 15 & -15 \end{bmatrix}$ **33.** $\dfrac{-1}{x-2} + \dfrac{3x-2}{x^2 + 2x + 2}$

**34.** $x^{15} + 10x^{12}y + 40x^9y^2 + 80x^6y^3 + 80x^3y^4 + 32y^5$ **35.** 3850

**36.** $y = \dfrac{1}{4}x + \dfrac{3}{2}$ **37.** $y = -5x - 2$ **38.** \$2000 **39.** length: 100 yd; width: 50 yd **40.** pen: \$1.80; pad: \$2

**41. a.** 6 sec **b.** 2.5 sec; 196 ft **42.** 11 amps

**43.** Answer will vary. An example is: $y = -0.88x + 33.2$ where $x$ is the number of years after 1980. Eventually there may be no smokers among U.S. adults.

**44. a.** 20 in.  **b.** $\dfrac{3}{8}$ cycles/sec  **c.** $\dfrac{8}{3}$ sec

**45.** $\tan x + \dfrac{1}{\tan x} = \dfrac{\sin x}{\cos x} + \dfrac{1}{\dfrac{\sin x}{\cos x}} = \dfrac{\sin x}{\cos x} + \dfrac{\cos x}{\sin x} = \dfrac{\sin^2 x + \cos^2 x}{\cos x \sin x} = \dfrac{1}{\cos x \sin x}$

**46.** $\dfrac{1 - \tan^2 x}{1 + \tan^2 x} = \dfrac{1 - \dfrac{\sin^2 x}{\cos^2 x}}{1 + \dfrac{\sin^2 x}{\cos^2 x}} \cdot \dfrac{\cos^2 x}{\cos^2 x} = \dfrac{\cos^2 x - \sin^2 x}{\cos^2 x + \sin^2 x} = \dfrac{\cos 2x}{1} = \cos 2x$

**47.**
$y = -2 \cos(3x - \pi)$

**48.** $\dfrac{\pi}{6}, \dfrac{5\pi}{6}, \dfrac{7\pi}{6}, \dfrac{11\pi}{6}$  **49.** $0, \dfrac{\pi}{3}, \dfrac{5\pi}{3}$  **50.** $-\dfrac{5}{\sqrt{11}}$

**51.**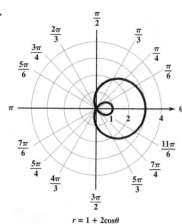
$r = 1 + 2\cos\theta$

**52.** $B \approx 54°, C \approx 92°, c \approx 39.5$ or $B \approx 126°, C \approx 20°, c \approx 13.7$

**53.** $y = 2 - x^2$;

# CHAPTER 11

## Section 11.1

### Check Point Exercises

**1.** 36  **2.** 0  **3. a.** 5  **b.** 3  **4.**  ; 4  **5. a.** 2  **b.** 1  **c.** does not exist  **d.** 1

$f(x) = \begin{cases} 3x - 2 & \text{if } x \neq 2 \\ 1 & \text{if } x = 2 \end{cases}$

### Exercise Set 11.1

**1.** 8  **3.** 3  **5.** 20  **7.** 1  **9.** 0  **11.** 12  **13.** 1  **15.** 1  **17.** 1  **19. a.** $-1$  **b.** $-1$  **21. a.** 2  **b.** 1  **23.** $-3$  **25.** $-1$
**27. a.** 4  **b.** 2  **c.** does not exist  **d.** 4  **29. a.** 2  **b.** 2  **c.** 2  **d.** 2  **e.** 4  **f.** 3  **g.** does not exist  **h.** does not exist
**i.** 2  **j.** 2  **k.** 2  **l.** 1  **31. a.** 1  **b.** 2  **c.** does not exist  **d.** 2  **e.** 2  **f.** 2  **g.** 2  **h.** 2  **33.** 7  **35.** $-5$  **37.** 0
**39.** $-1$  **41.** 2  **43.** 1  **45.** 0  **47.** 3  **49.** does not exist  **51.** 2  **53.** does not exist  **55.** $-3$  **57.** 2  **59.** 3  **61.** 0
**63.** 2  **65.** 0  **67. a.** 8; As your nose approaches the fan, the speed of the breeze that your nose feels approaches 8 miles per hour.  **b.** Answers
may vary.  **69.** $\lim\limits_{x \to 67} f(x) = 45$  **71. a.** 30; The cost to rent the car one day and drive it 100 miles is \$30.  **b.** \$40  **c.** \$60  **85.** 0.69315;
0.693147  **87.** 1.5000; 1.50000  **89.** makes sense  **91.** makes sense  **95.** 31.544281

**96. a.**

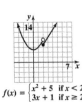

$$f(x) = \begin{cases} x^2 + 5 & \text{if } x < 2 \\ 3x + 1 & \text{if } x \geq 2 \end{cases}$$

**b.** $\lim_{x \to 2^-} f(x) = 9$; $\lim_{x \to 2^+} f(x) = 7$; $\lim_{x \to 2} f(x)$ does not exist.

**97.** $x + 2$    **98.** $\dfrac{1}{\sqrt{4 + x} + 2}$

## Section 11.2

**Check Point Exercises**

**1. a.** 11    **b.** $-9$    **2. a.** 19    **b.** $-\sqrt{2}$    **3.** 13    **4.** 5    **5.** $-70$    **6. a.** $-22$    **b.** 72    **7.** $-56$    **8.** 61    **9.** 343    **10.** $\sqrt{2}$
**11.** $-3$    **12. a.** $-1$    **b.** 1    **c.** does not exist    **13.** 4    **14.** $\dfrac{1}{6}$

**Exercise Set 11.2**

**1.** 8    **3.** 2    **5.** 14    **7.** 28    **9.** 6    **11.** 8    **13.** 16    **15.** 5    **17.** $\dfrac{5}{6}$    **19.** 3    **21.** 2    **23.** 2    **25.** 2    **27.** $\dfrac{8}{9}$    **29.** $\dfrac{1}{2}$
**31.** 1125    **33.** $\dfrac{1}{4}$    **35.** $-\dfrac{1}{4}$    **37.** $-7$    **39.** $-\dfrac{1}{9}$    **41.** $\dfrac{1}{3}$    **43. a.** 6    **b.** 8    **c.** does not exist    **45. a.** 9    **b.** 9    **c.** 9
**47. a.** 6    **b.** 6    **c.** 6    **49. a.** 0    **b.** 0    **c.** 0    **51.** 13; 2    **53.** 0; 3    **55.** 2    **57.** $\dfrac{5}{2}$    **59. a.** 0    **b.** The length of the starship
appears to approach 0.    **c.** It is not possible to exceed the speed of light.    **75.** makes sense    **77.** makes sense    **79.** $-\dfrac{1}{16}$    **81.** $\dfrac{1}{2}$
**83.** $\dfrac{2}{3}$    **86.**

$$\lim_{x \to 3} f(x) = 5; f(3) = 5$$

No, it is not necessary to lift
your pencil off the paper.

**87.**

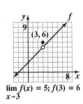

$$\lim_{x \to 3} f(x) = 5; f(3) = 6$$

Yes, it is necessary to lift
your pencil off the paper.

**88.**

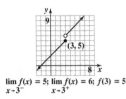

$$\lim_{x \to 3^-} f(x) = 5; \lim_{x \to 3^+} f(x) = 6; f(3) = 5$$

Yes, it is necessary to lift
your pencil off the paper.

## Section 11.3

**Check Point Exercises**

**1. a.** continuous    **b.** discontinuous    **2.** discontinuous at 0

**Exercise Set 11.3**

**1.** continuous    **3.** continuous    **5.** continuous    **7.** discontinuous    **9.** continuous    **11.** discontinuous    **13.** discontinuous
**15.** continuous    **17.** continuous    **19.** continuous for every number $x$    **21.** $-1$ and 4    **23.** 0    **25.** continuous for every number $x$
**27.** 1    **29.** continuous for every number $x$    **31.** 2    **33.** 4    **35.** discontinuous at $\pi$    **37.** discontinuous at each integer
**39.** continuous for every number $x$    **41.** discontinuous at $\dfrac{\pi}{2}$    **43. a.** 20; 20    **b.** yes    **c.** 40; 10    **d.** no    **e.** does not exist; 70    **f.** no
**g.** 100    **h.** As the end of the course approached, the percentage of material learned by the student approached 100%    **45. a.** continuous
**b.** continuous    **c.** Answers may vary.    **53.** 2.7183; 2.71828    **55.** does not make sense    **57.** makes sense    **59.** No. In Exercise 58, $\lim_{x \to 9} f(x)$
exists. In this exercise, however, $\lim_{x \to 9} \dfrac{1}{x - 9}$ does not exist.    **62.** $5 + h$    **63.** $3x^2 + 3xh + h^2$    **64.** $-32a - 16h + 48$

## Mid-Chapter 11 Check Point

**1.** 2    **2.** 1    **3.** does not exist    **4.** $-2$    **5.** $-1$    **6.** $-3$    **7.** 3    **8.** discontinuous at $-1$ and 0    **9.** $-1$    **10.** 1    **11.** 4
**12.** $-1$    **13.** 2    **14.** $\dfrac{49}{4}$    **15.** 13    **16.** $\dfrac{1}{6}$    **17.** does not exist    **18. a.** 1    **b.** 0    **c.** does not exist    **19. a.** 32    **b.** 32    **c.** 32
**20.** yes    **21.** yes    **22.** discontinuous at 5

## Section 11.4

**Check Point Exercises**

**1.** 7    **2.** $y = \dfrac{1}{2}x + \dfrac{1}{2}$    **3. a.** $2x - 5$    **b.** $-7; 1$    **4. a.** 49.21 cubic inches per inch; 48.1201 cubic inches per inch
**b.** 48 cubic inches per inch    **5. a.** $-32$ ft/sec    **b.** $-96$ ft/sec

## Exercise Set 11.4

**1. a.** 2 **b.** $y = 2x + 3$ **3. a.** $-2$ **b.** $y = -2x + 3$ **5. a.** $-20$ **b.** $y = -20x - 20$ **7. a.** 7 **b.** $y = 7x - 8$

**9. a.** 1 **b.** $y = x - 3$ **11. a.** $\frac{1}{6}$ **b.** $y = \frac{1}{6}x + \frac{3}{2}$ **13. a.** $-1$ **b.** $y = -x + 2$ **15. a.** $-3$ **b.** $-3; -3$ **17. a.** $2x$ **b.** $-2; 6$

**19. a.** $2x - 3$ **b.** $0; 1$ **21. a.** $3x^2$ **b.** $3; 3$ **23. a.** $\frac{1}{2\sqrt{x}}$ **b.** $\frac{1}{2}; \frac{1}{4}$ **25. a.** $-\frac{4}{x^2}$ **b.** $-1; -4$ **27. a.** $6.4x + 2.1$ **b.** $2.1; 27.7$

**29. a. & c.** **b.** $y = 2x - 5$ **31. a. & c.** **b.** $y = \frac{1}{2}x - 1$ **33. a. & c.** **b.** $y = 3x + 4$ **35. a. & c.** **b.** $y = x + 1$

**37. a.** 12.1 square inches per inch; 12.01 square inches per inch **b.** 12 square inches per inch **39. a.** $4.1\pi$ square inches per inch; $4.01\pi$ square inches per inch **b.** $4\pi$ square inches per inch **41.** $48\pi$ square inches per inch **43. a.** 32 feet per second; $-32$ feet per second **b.** $-64$ feet per second **45. a.** 32 feet per second; $-32$ feet per second **b.** 3 sec; 148 ft **63.** $-0.33$ **65.** 3.64 **67.** makes sense **69.** makes sense **71.** e **73.** d **75.** b

**77.**
$$A'(r) = \lim_{h \to 0} \frac{A(r + h) - A(r)}{h}$$
$$= \lim_{h \to 0} \frac{\pi(r + h)^2 - \pi r^2}{h}$$
$$= \lim_{h \to 0} \frac{\pi(r^2 + 2rh + h^2) - \pi r^2}{h}$$
$$= \lim_{h \to 0} \frac{\pi r^2 + 2\pi rh + \pi h^2 - \pi r^2}{h}$$
$$= \lim_{h \to 0} \frac{h(2\pi r + \pi h)}{h}$$
$$= \lim_{h \to 0} (2\pi r + \pi h) = 2\pi r + 0 = 2\pi r$$

## Chapter 11 Review Exercises

**1.** 3 **2.** $\frac{1}{2}$ **3.** 2 **4.** 0 **5.** 1 **6.** 3 **7.** 2 **8.** 3 **9.** 3 **10.** 5 **11.** $-3$ **12.** does not exist **13.** 1 **14.** 3 **15.** $-3$ **16.** does not exist **17.** 3 **18.** does not exist **19.** 5 **20.** 5 **21.** 5 **22.** 0 **23.** 0 **24.** 6 **25.** $-1$ **26.** 1 **27.** 15 **28.** 8 **29.** 1000 **30.** 5 **31.** 2 **32.** $-8$ **33.** 5 **34.** $\frac{1}{20}$ **35.** 2 **36.** $\frac{1}{20}$ **37.** $-\frac{1}{25}$ **38. a.** 5 **b.** 7 **c.** does not exist **39. a.** 2 **b.** 4 **c.** does not exist **40. a.** $-10$ **b.** $-10$ **c.** $-10$ **41.** continuous **42.** discontinuous **43.** discontinuous **44.** continuous **45.** discontinuous **46.** continuous for every number $x$ **47.** 1 and $-3$ **48.** 0 **49.** continuous for every number $x$ **50.** $-2$ **51.** 11 **52. a.** 9 **b.** $y = 9x - 2$ **53. a.** $-9$ **b.** $y = -9x - 5$ **54. a.** $6x + 12$ **b.** $0; 18$ **55. a.** $6x^2 - 1$ **b.** $5; 5$ **56. a.** $-\frac{1}{x^2}$ **b.** $-\frac{1}{4}; -\frac{1}{4}$ **57. a.** $\frac{1}{2\sqrt{x}}$ **b.** $\frac{1}{12}; \frac{1}{18}$ **58. a.** 20.5 cubic inches per inch; 20.05 cubic inches per inch **b.** 20 cubic inches per inch **59.** $100\pi$ cubic inches per inch **60. a.** 16 feet per second; $-48$ feet per second **b.** 2.5 sec; 105 ft

## Chapter 11 Test

**1.** 6 **2.** $-3$ **3.** $-5$ **4.** 4 **5.** 6 **6.** does not exist **7.** 4 **8.** 81 **9.** $-3$ **10.** $\frac{1}{6}$ **11.** discontinuous **12.** continuous **13.** $2x - 5$ **14.** $-\frac{10}{x^2}$ **15.** $y = -6x - 9$ **16.** $-24$ feet per second

## Cumulative Review Exercises (Chapters P–11)

**1.** $\left\{ x \mid x < -\frac{5}{2} \text{ or } -2 < x < -1 \right\}$ **2.** $\left\{ 1, -\frac{1}{2}, -6 \right\}$ **3.** $\left\{ x \mid x < -\frac{7}{2} \text{ or } x > -\frac{1}{2} \right\}$ **4.** $\left\{ \frac{3\pi}{2} \right\}$ **5.** $\{67\}$

**6.**  **7.**  **8.**  **9.**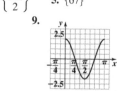

**10.**

**11.**

**12.**

**13.**

**14.**

**15.**

**16.** $-4x + 7$

**17.** $\dfrac{1}{7}x + \dfrac{1}{7}$

**18.** $\dfrac{5}{4}$

**19.** $x^8 - 12x^6y + 54x^4y^2 - 108x^2y^3 + 81y^4$

**20.** $y = -2x + 1$   **21.** $-11; 170°$   **22.** $\dfrac{1}{x} - \dfrac{x+1}{x^2+x+1}$

**23.** $\tan\theta + \cot\theta = \dfrac{\sin\theta}{\cos\theta} + \dfrac{\cos\theta}{\sin\theta}$

$\qquad = \dfrac{\sin^2\theta + \cos^2\theta}{\cos\theta\sin\theta}$

$\qquad = \dfrac{1}{\cos\theta\sin\theta}$

$\qquad = \sec\theta\csc\theta$

**24.** $\tan(\theta + \pi) = \dfrac{\tan\theta + \tan\pi}{1 - \tan\theta\tan\pi}$

$\qquad = \dfrac{\tan\theta + 0}{1 - \tan\theta(0)}$

$\qquad = \tan\theta$

**25.** $\begin{bmatrix} 2 & 1 & 3 \\ 8 & 1 & 9 \\ 5 & 1 & 6 \end{bmatrix}$

**26.**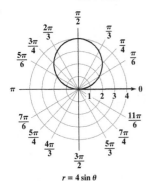

$r = 4\sin\theta$

**27.** $f(x) = x^9; g(x) = x^2 - 3x + 7$   **28.** $\{(2, -1, 3)\}$

**29.** 168   **30.** $2 + 2\sqrt{3}i$

**31. a.** $I(x) = 21,600 - 0.1x$

**b.** $116,000 at 8\%; $4000 at 18\%$

**32.** 23 cm $\times$ 23 cm

**33.** 100 ft by 50 ft; 5000 sq ft

**34. a.** $T = 72 + 303e^{-0.0769t}$

**b.** after 6.9 min

**35.** $C(x) = 25x + \dfrac{600,000}{x}$   **36.** 71.6 mi

**37.** $29\dfrac{1}{3}$ cu in.   **38.** $-24$ feet per second

**39.** $A(x) = x^2 + \dfrac{16}{x}$   **40.** 15.6 years old

# Applications Index

## A

Abortion polars as a percentage of voters, 744–45 (Exercise 79)
Acid rain, 435 (Exercise 117)
Actor selection, 1013 (Exercise 46), 1033 (Exercises 79, 81)
Adult residential community costs, 963, 968–69
Advertising
  online ad spending, U.S., 961 (Exercise 69)
  spending for consumer drug ads, 961 (Exercise 70)
Advertising budget, sales and price and, 374–75
African life span, AIDS and, 755 (Exercise 43)
Age. *See also* Marriage age
  average debt by, 800 (Exercise 15)
  awakenings at night by, 145 (Exercises 57–60)
  body-mass index and, 789 (Exercises 85–86)
  driver's. *See* Driver's age
  height as function of, 196–97, 1070–71, 1075
  hours slept per day by, 241–42 (Exercises 65–66)
  number of U.S. car drivers, by age group, 1021
  percent body fat in adults by, 176 (Exercises 83–90)
  preferred age in a mate, 232–33
  spatial orientation and, 1048 (Exercise 69)
  verbal ability and, 1048 (Exercise 70)
Aging rate, space travel and, 30, 42, 44 (Exercise 118), 1061 (Exercise 60)
AIDS
  African life span and, 755 (Exercise 43)
  cases diagnosed (U.S.), 302, 303, 305
  number of Americans living with, 313 (Exercises 73–74)
Aircraft, Mach speed of, 617 (Exercises 80–81)
Airline revenue, number of customers and, 255–56, 262 (Exercises 11–12)
Airplanes. *See* Plane(s)
Airports, distance between, 662 (Exercise 40)
Alcohol and risk of accident, 430–31, 435 (Exercise 122)
  arrests and drunk driving, 358 (Exercise 115)
Alcohol content of wines, mixture based on, 743 (Exercise 55)
Alcohol use
  moderate wine consumption and heart disease, 191 (Exercise 104)
  by U.S. high school seniors, 144–45 (Exercises 55–56)
Alligator's tail length given body length, 377 (Exercise 21)
Altitude
  and atmospheric pressure, 455 (Exercise 80)
  gained by hiker climbing incline, 581 (Exercise 42)
  increase on inclined road of, 500 (Exercise 58)
Amusia (tone deafness), 596
  sound quality and, 596, 598
Angle of depression, 495, 575 (Exercises 45–46)
Angle of elevation, 495–98, 499 (Exercises 54–56), 501 (Exercise 80), 515 (Exercise 30), 548 (Exercise 60), 575 (Exercises 41–44, 47–50), 576 (Exercise 77), 581 (Exercise 44), 584 (Exercise 20), 638 (Exercises 135–136, 145), 641 (Exercise 69), 653–54 (Exercises 51–52), 654 (Exercises 55–56)
Angles
  in architecture, 460
  clock hands forming, 460, 461
Angular speed
  of carousel, 471
  of propeller on wind generator, 580
Annuities, 978–80, 1032 (Exercise 54)
  value of, 984–85 (Exercises 77–84)

Antenna on top of building, height of, 582 (Exercise 121)
Apologizing to friend, formula for deciding about, 15
Arch, height of, 501 (Exercise 73)
Arch bridge, 907, 946 (Exercises 12–13)
Architecture
  angles in, 460
  conic sections in, 886
Area
  of circle with changing radius, 1081 (Exercises 39–40)
  of greenhouse, 1048–49 (Exercise 72)
  maximum, 297, 300 (Exercises 65–72), 301 (Exercise 104), 339 (Exercise 29), 382 (Exercises 20, 22), 1086 (Exercise 33)
  of page, as function of width of rectangle containing print on, 357 (Exercise 101)
  of plane figure, 55 (Exercise 107)
  of rectangular garden/field, 257–59, 276 (Exercise 37)
  of region under curve, 564 (Exercises 97–98)
  of shaded region, 55 (Exercises 95–96), 66 (Exercises 117–120)
  of square with changing side, 1081 (Exercises 37–38)
  of triangle, 660, 866–67 (Exercises 53–54)
Area code possibilities, 1012 (Exercise 35)
Arrests and drunk driving, 358 (Exercise 115)
Arrow, parabolic path of archer's, 295
Artistic development, carbon dating and, 439
Artists in documentary, 1008
Asteroid detection, 767
Atmospheric pressure and altitude, 455 (Exercise 80)
Attitudes in U.S., changing, 111–12 (Exercises 5–6)
Automobile accidents per day, age of driver and, 871 (Exercise 56)
Automobile race finishes, possible, 1013 (Exercises 45, 57)
Automobile repair estimate, 128 (Exercise 122)
Automobiles. *See* Car(s)
Average cost, 352
Average cost function, 352, 353, 356 (Exercises 89–90), 383 (Exercise 79), 386 (Exercise 26)
Average growth rates, 1070–71
Average rate of change, 196–99
  of area of square, 1081 (Exercises 37–38)
  in boys' and girls' height, 199, 218 (Exercises 127–128)
  of volume, 1077–78, 1085 (Exercise 58)
Average velocity, 113 (Exercises 39–42), 199, 353–54, 357 (Exercises 98–99), 384 (Exercise 83), 1078
  of airplane, 738–39, 743 (Exercises 61–62)
  of ball rolling down ramp, 199–200
  of boat, 739, 743 (Exercises 63–66), 777 (Exercise 20)
  of current, rowing time and, 777 (Exercise 20)
  of plane, 738–39, 743 (Exercises 61–62), 800 (Exercise 11), 803 (Exercise 15)
  of wind, 747 (Exercise 107), 800 (Exercise 11), 803 (Exercise 15)

## B

Babies born out of wedlock, 261 (Exercise 4)
Bachelor degrees awarded, by gender, 133 (Exercise 32)
Ball. *See also* Baseball; Football
  angle of elevation and throwing distance of, 641 (Exercise 69)
  location of thrown, 925–26
  rolling down ramp, average velocity of, 199–200
  thrown straight up, instantaneous velocity of, 1079–80, 1082 (Exercise 76), 1085 (Exercises 16, 60), 1087 (Exercise 38)
  thrown straight up, maximum height of, 1085 (Exercise 60)

Ball attached to spring
  finding amplitude and period of motion of, 606 (Exercise 79)
  simple harmonic motion of, 570–72, 638 (Exercises 133–134), 641 (Exercise 68)
Ball's height above ground, 272 (Exercise 63), 364–65, 367 (Exercise 76), 754 (Exercise 31), 1036 (Exercise 41)
  baseball, 458 (Exercises 18–19)
  bounce height, 377 (Exercise 23)
  football, 16 (Exercises 19–20), 816 (Exercise 46)
  maximum height, 726 (Exercise 14), 816 (Exercises 45–46), 1085 (Exercise 60)
Bank and credit union charges, 127 (Exercise 115)
Banking angle and turning radius of bicycle, 377 (Exercise 27)
Bank loans, interest on, 1086 (Exercise 31)
Baseball
  angle of elevation and throwing distance of, 638 (Exercises 135–136)
  height above ground, 458 (Exercises 18–19)
  hit straight upward, instantaneous velocity of, 1081 (Exercises 45–46)
  path of, 925, 933–34 (Exercises 69–70), 934 (Exercise 85)
  position as function of time, 933–34 (Exercises 69–70), 934 (Exercise 85)
Baseball contract, 951, 984 (Exercise 67), 986 (Exercise 111)
Baseball diamond, distance from pitcher's mound to bases on, 663 (Exercises 49–50)
Baseball game attendance, ticket price and, 262 (Exercise 10)
Basketball court dimensions, 107
Bass in lake over time, 383 (Exercise 80)
Batting average, 113 (Exercises 47–48)
Bearings, finding, 569–70, 576 (Exercises 55–58), 583 (Exercise 23)
  of boat, 570, 575 (Exercises 51–52), 576 (Exercises 56, 58), 662–63 (Exercises 45–46)
  distance at certain bearing, 575–76 (Exercises 51–54), 582–83 (Exercises 124–125)
  distance between lighthouse and boat, 655 (Exercise 59)
  distance between ships traveling at different bearings, 1087 (Exercise 36)
  of fire from two fire stations, locating fire using, 651, 653 (Exercise 47)
  of jet from control tower, 576 (Exercise 57)
  true, of plane, 711 (Exercises 83–84)
  between two cities, 583 (Exercise 125)
Beauty, symmetry and, 167
Benefit concert lineup possibilities, 1013 (Exercise 47)
Berlin Airlift, 790–91, 797 (Exercise 20)
Bike ride, graphs describing, 146 (Exercise 82)
Biorhythms, 459, 475, 488 (Exercise 83), 534 (Exercises 75–82), 536 (Exercise 119)
Birthday, probability of same, 1028 (Exercise 73)
Birthday cake, 45 (Exercise 141)
Birthday date sharing, 242 (Exercise 67), 619
Births and deaths in U.S. from 2000 through 2005, 220, 231 (Exercise 96)
Black holes, formation of, 26–27
Blood
  body weight and volume of, 370–71
  speed of, 27
Blood alcohol concentration, 430–31, 435 (Exercise 122)
Boat
  average velocity of, 739, 743 (Exercises 63–66), 777 (Exercise 20)
  direction angle of, 725 (Exercise 95)
  distance from lighthouse, 655 (Exercise 59)
  ground speed, 725 (Exercise 95)
  on tilted ramp, vector components of force on, 716, 720 (Exercises 63–64)
  velocity of, 725 (Exercise 95)
  velocity vector of, 708
Boat/ship, finding bearing of, 570, 576 (Exercise 58)

changing bearings, 662–63 (Exercises 45–46)
distance traveled at certain bearing, 575 (Exercises 51–52)
to sail into harbor, 576 (Exercise 56)
traveling at different bearings, distance between, 1087 (Exercise 36)
Body composition of adult male and female, 754–55 (Exercises 33–34)
Body fat in adults, percent, 176 (Exercises 83–90)
Body-mass index, 377 (Exercise 31)
  age and, 789 (Exercises 85–86)
Body temperature, variation in, 582 (Exercise 81)
Book club selections, 1013 (Exercise 58)
Book selections, 1013 (Exercise 51), 1034 (Exercise 20)
Books on shelf, arranging, 1007–8
Bouquet, mixture of flowers in, 777 (Exercise 18)
Box dimensions, 325 (Exercise 52). *See also* Open boxes
Brain
  growth of the human, 456 (Exercise 90)
  modeling brain activity, 548 (Exercise 72)
Break-even analysis, 739–41, 743 (Exercise 67), 744 (Exercises 73–76), 777 (Exercise 17)
  of play production, 584 (Exercise 17)
Breathing, graphs describing, 146 (Exercise 80)
Breathing cycle, 515
  modeling, 530–31
  velocity of air flow in, 637 (Exercises 129–130)
Breeze from fan, location and feeling, 1047 (Exercise 67)
Bridge
  arch, 907, 946 (Exercises 12–13)
  suspension, 907, 911 (Exercises 65–66)
Bridge coupon book/toll passes, 128 (Exercise 123), 262 (Exercise 6)
Building, finding height of, 496, 497, 575 (Exercise 42), 576 (Exercise 77), 582 (Exercises 119–120), 583 (Exercise 21), 655 (Exercise 76)
Building's shadow, 132 (Exercise 147)
Bus fares, 261 (Exercise 5)
Business ventures, 744 (Exercises 73–76)
Butterfat content in cream, 743 (Exercise 58)
Butterflies, symmetry of, 664

## C

Cable car, distance covered by, 654–55 (Exercise 58)
Cable lengths between vertical poles, 264 (Exercise 45)
Cable television deals, 950 (Exercise 20)
Calculator manufacturing costs, 383 (Exercise 79)
Calories
  daily caloric needs, 841 (Exercise 62)
  needed to maintain energy balance for moderately active lifestyles, 81 (Exercise 93)
Camera(s)
  instantaneous velocity when dropped into water, 1081 (Exercise 56)
  percentage of new cellphones with, 434 (Exercises 113–114)
  price reduction on digital, 105
  viewing angle for, 564 (Exercises 95–96)
Candy bars with highest fat content, 746 (Exercises 85–88)
Candy mixtures, 743 (Exercise 59)
Car(s)
  computing work of pushing, 718, 720 (Exercise 53)
  distance traveled after brakes applied, 754 (Exercise 32)
  leaving city at same time, distance between, 724 (Exercise 18)
  purchase options, 1012 (Exercise 29)
  stopping distances for, at selected speeds, 359, 367 (Exercises 77–78)
  value over time, 163 (Exercise 106), 961 (Exercise 80)

Carbon-14 dating, 439–40, 448 (Exercises 15–16)
  decay model, 448 (Exercises 15–16, 19–20)
Carbon dioxide concentration in atmosphere
  global temperature and, 135, 187–88
  patterns of, 537, 549 (Exercise 87)
Cardboard length/width for box, 776 (Exercise 62)
Car depreciation, 112 (Exercises 7–8)
Car meals, 966
Carousel, linear speed and angular speed of animals on, 471, 474 (Exercises 100, 110)
Car rentals, 114, 118, 125, 132 (Exercise 167), 261 (Exercises 1–2), 1048 (Exercise 71)
CD selection for vacation trip, 1033 (Exercise 80)
Cellphones
  with cameras, percentage of new, 434 (Exercises 113–114)
  number of cellphone and land-line customers in U.S., 800 (Exercise 8)
Cellular phone plan, 127 (Exercise 109), 169–70, 176 (Exercises 79–82), 178 (Exercise 121)
Centrifugal force, 376
Chaos, patterns of, 643, 686
Chernobyl nuclear power plant accident, 398 (Exercise 66)
Cherry tree yield, maximum, 300 (Exercise 76)
Chess moves, 1005
Chickens eaten per year, 29 (Exercise 121)
Child born in U.S., cost of raising, 956–57
Children's height modeled, 407
Cholesterol
  and dietary restrictions, 788 (Exercise 82)
  intake, 803 (Exercise 12)
Cigarette consumption of U.S. adults
  by ethnicity, 745–46 (Exercises 83–84)
  percentage of adult smokers, 1036 (Exercise 43)
  probability of smokers suffering from some ailments, 1001–2 (Exercises 57–58)
Circle
  with changing radius, area of, 1081 (Exercises 39–40)
  finding length of arc on, 583 (Exercise 2)
Class structure of U.S., 869–70 (Exercise 7)
Cliff, distance of ship from base of, 575 (Exercise 44)
Clock
  angles formed by hands of, 460, 461
  degrees moved by minute hand on, 473–74 (Exercises 87–88)
  distance between tip of hour hand and ceiling, 535 (Exercise 84)
  distance between tips of hands at 10:00, 663 (Exercise 62)
  minute hand movement in term of $\pi$, 474 (Exercise 89–90)
Club officers, choosing, 1012 (Exercise 41), 1033 (Exercise 78)
Coding, 842, 851–53, 854–55 (Exercises 51–54), 855 (Exercises 63–64, 77–78), 856 (Exercise 92), 871 (Exercise 45)
Coffee consumption, sleep and, 458 (Exercise 17)
Coin tosses, 127 (Exercise 111), 1017–18, 1024, 1026 (Exercises 21–22), 1027 (Exercises 51–52), 1028 (Exercise 67)
College campuses, number of students before merger, 777 (Exercise 19)
College education
  bachelor's degrees awarded, by gender, 133 (Exercise 32)
  cost of, 2, 4–5, 17–18 (Exercises 131–132), 970–71 (Exercises 65–67)
  percentage of college graduates among people ages 25 and older, in U.S., 399 (Exercises 75–76)
College enrollment, projected, 112 (Exercise 9), 132 (Exercise 145)
College students
  attitudes of freshmen, 104–5
  claiming no religious affiliation, 148
  Harvard students with B+ averages or better, 314 (Exercise 76)
  high school grades for college freshmen, 970 (Exercise 62)
  opposition to feminism among first-year (1970-2004), 412 (Exercises 115–116)
  survey of type of college attended and family income, 1033 (Exercises 83–88)

symptoms of physical illness among, procrastination and, 728, 745 (Exercise 81)
Collinear points, 867 (Exercises 55–56)
Comedy act schedule, 1012 (Exercise 37)
Comets
  Halley's Comet, 882, 896, 907, 943 (Exercises 29–30)
  intersection of planet paths and, 775 (Exercise 55)
Committee formation, 1009, 1010–11, 1013 (Exercises 50, 54)
Commuter, average velocity and time required for round trip of, 354
Compound interest, 395–96, 397 (Exercises 53–56), 398 (Exercise 74), 399 (Exercises 81, 87), 431, 434 (Exercises 105–112), 436 (Exercise 143), 454 (Exercises 10–11), 455 (Exercises 83–85), 457 (Exercises 23–25), 961 (Exercises 71–72), 1032 (Exercise 54)
  on annuity, 978–80, 984–85 (Exercises 77–84)
  continuously compounded, 395, 423 (Exercise 26), 455 (Exercises 84–85), 457 (Exercise 25), 804 (Exercise 35)
  on IRA, 986 (Exercise 110)
Computer(s)
  angular speed of hard drive in, 471 (Exercises 95–99)
  assembly, time required for, 385 (Exercise 97)
  discounts, 224–26, 231 (Exercise 99)
  invention of, 856
  price before reduction, 105
  prices, 233–34
  sale, 66 (Exercise 115)
  visualizations of chaos, 643
Computer-generated animation, 204
Computer graphics, 837–38, 839 (Exercises 49–50)
Computer images, 805
Concentration of mixture, 100 (Exercises 139–140). See also Mixture problems
Cone volume, 266 (Exercise 70), 376
Conference attendees, choosing, 1011, 1013 (Exercise 61)
Constraints, 791–95, 796 (Exercises 15–16), 796–97 (Exercises 19–21), 797 (Exercise 23), 802 (Exercise 60)
Continuously compounded interest, 395, 423 (Exercise 26), 455 (Exercises 84–85), 457 (Exercise 25), 804 (Exercise 35)
Cooling, Newton's Law of, 442–43, 449 (Exercises 47–50), 451 (Exercise 83), 456 (Exercise 89)
Cooling pie, modeling temperature of, 1086 (Exercise 34)
Coronary heart disease, 449 (Exercises 43–46)
Corporate profits from 2002 through 2006, 272 (Exercise 61)
Corporation officers, choosing, 1007, 1012 (Exercise 42)
Corruption Perceptions Index, rating countries on, 162 (Exercises 99–100)
Cost(s). See also Manufacturing costs
  average, 352
  of college education, 2, 4–5, 17–18 (Exercises 131–132), 970–71 (Exercises 65–67)
  mailing, 177 (Exercises 95–99), 271 (Exercise 44), 1068 (Exercise 44)
  minimizing, 796 (Exercise 18)
  of raising child born in U.S., 956–57
Cost and revenue functions, 739, 740, 743–44 (Exercises 67–72)
  for PDA manufacturing, 777 (Exercise 17)
Cost and revenue functions/break-even points, 744 (Exercises 73–76), 799 (Exercise 6), 803 (Exercise 13)
Cost function, 383 (Exercise 79). See also Cost and revenue functions
  bike manufacturing, 356 (Exercise 89)
  robotic exoskeleton manufacturing, 352–53
  running shoe manufacturing, 356 (Exercise 90)
  wheelchair manufacturing, 353
Course schedule, options in planning, 1004–5
Crane lifting boulder, computing work of, 720 (Exercise 54)
Crate, computing work of dragging, 725 (Exercise 104)
Cryptograms, 851–53, 855 (Exercises 77–78). See also Coding

Culture, standards of attractiveness and, 727
Cycles, modeling, 501
Cycloid, 932, 934 (Exercises 78–79, 92)

**D**

Daylight, number of hours of, 475, 488 (Exercises 81–82), 637 (Exercises 131–132)
  modeling, 533, 535 (Exercises 83, 85), 548 (Exercise 62)
Dead Sea Scrolls, age of, 439–40
Death penalty, percentage of Americans in favor of, 745 (Exercise 80)
Death rate
  firearms and, for industrialized countries, 272 (Exercise 60)
  and hours of sleep, 748, 752–53
Debris from explosion, instantaneous velocity of, 1081 (Exercises 43–44)
Debt
  average debt by age, 800 (Exercise 15)
  national, 19, 23, 26
Decay model for carbon–14, 448 (Exercises 15–16, 19–20)
Deck of 52 cards, probability and, 1019, 1021–22, 1026 (Exercises 17–20, 29–30), 1027 (Exercises 37–42), 1033 (Exercises 91–92), 1034 (Exercise 27)
Decoding a word or message, 852–53, 854–55 (Exercises 51–54), 855 (Exercises 77–78), 856 (Exercise 92), 871 (Exercise 45)
Degree-days, 971 (Exercise 83)
Depreciation, car, 112 (Exercises 7–8)
Depression
  probability of U.S. adult suffering from, 1001–2 (Exercises 57–58)
  in remission, exercise and, 204 (Exercise 44)
Depression, angle of, 495, 575 (Exercises 45–46)
Depth reached by sunlight beneath ocean's surface, 433 (Exercises 103–104)
Desk manufacturing, 816 (Exercise 48)
Die rolling outcomes, 1018–19, 1026 (Exercises 11–16, 25–26), 1027 (Exercises 47–50), 1033 (Exercises 89–90)
Digital photography, 827, 840 (Exercises 51–52), 841 (Exercise 75), 870 (Exercise 29)
Dinosaur bones and potassium-40 dating, 448 (Exercise 27)
Dinosaur footprints, pace angle and stride indicated by, 656, 662 (Exercises 37–38)
Direction, magnitude and, 698–99. See also Resultant forces
Discount warehouse membership plans, 262 (Exercises 7–8)
Distance
  from base to top of Leaning Tower of Pisa, 653 (Exercise 51)
  between cars leaving city at same time, 724 (Exercise 18)
  between cars on expressway, speed and recommended, 1048 (Exercise 68)
  of forest ranger from fire, 575 (Exercise 53)
  between houses at closest point, 899 (Exercise 63)
  of island from coast, 575 (Exercise 45)
  across lake, 496, 499 (Exercise 53), 581 (Exercise 43), 662 (Exercises 41–42)
  of marching band from person filming it, 548 (Exercise 61)
  of oil platform from ends of beach, 653 (Exercise 49)
  between pair of cities, 251 (Exercises 71–72)
  of rotating beam of light from point, 547 (Exercise 59), 548 (Exercise 64)
  of ship from base of cliff, 575 (Exercise 44)
  of ship from base of Statue of Liberty, 575 (Exercise 43)
  of ship from lighthouse, 501 (Exercise 80), 582 (Exercise 124)
  of ship from radio towers on coast, 899 (Exercise 62)
  of skydiver's fall, time and, 372, 384 (Exercise 94), 987 (Exercise 18)
  of stolen car from point directly below helicopter, 575 (Exercise 46)
  that skydiver falls in given time, 987 (Exercise 18)
  throwing. See Throwing distance

time traveled as function of, 266 (Exercise 67)
  between two points on Earth, 474 (Exercises 93–96)
  between two points on opposite banks of river, 653 (Exercise 50)
  between two trains leaving station at same time, 685 (Exercise 9)
Distance traveled, 18 (Exercise 134)
  by car after brakes applied, 754 (Exercise 32)
  by plane, 500 (Exercise 57)
Diver's height above water, 367 (Exercise 75)
Diving board motion, modeling, 548 (Exercise 63)
Divorce
  by number of years of marriage, 164
  wife's age at marriage and probability of, 142–43
DNA, structure of, 489, 931
Domed ceiling, light source placement in, 912 (Exercise 31)
Dominoes, falling, 989, 995 (Exercise 36)
Drink order possibilities, 1012 (Exercise 31)
Driver's age
  and accidents, 871 (Exercise 56)
  arrests and drunk driving as function of, 358 (Exercise 115)
  fatal crashes and, 100 (Exercises 141–142)
  number of U.S. car drivers by, 1021
Driving accident while intoxicated, probability of, 1028 (Exercise 72)
Driving rate and time for trip, 372–73
Drug ads, spending for consumer, 961 (Exercise 70)
Drug concentration, 198–99, 356 (Exercise 92)
Drug dosage, child vs. adult, 642 (Exercise 19)
Drug experiment volunteer selection, 1012 (Exercise 17), 1013 (Exercise 59)
Drug tests, probability of accurate results of mandatory, 1027–28 (Exercise 63)
Dual investments, 260, 264 (Exercises 35–38), 274 (Exercise 127), 804 (Exercise 33)

**E**

Eagle's height and time in flight, 271 (Exercise 43)
Earth
  angular velocity of point on, 474 (Exercise 111)
  distance between two points on, 474 (Exercises 93–96)
  finding radius of, 576 (Exercise 76)
  motion of Moon relative to, 489
Earthquake, simple harmonic motion from, 573
Earthquake epicenter, 251 (Exercise 73)
Earthquake intensity, 400, 408, 413 (Exercise 138), 455 (Exercise 47)
Earthquake relief, 790 (Exercise 118), 791–94
Educational attainment
  median annual income by, 54 (Exercises 91–92)
  of U.S. population, 1027 (Exercises 31–36)
Election, probability of winning, 1028 (Exercise 64)
Election ballot, 1013 (Exercise 49)
Electrical resistance, 81 (Exercise 94), 378 (Exercise 39), 1036 (Exercise 42)
Elephant's weight, 435 (Exercise 134)
Elevation, angle of, 495–98, 499 (Exercises 54–56), 501 (Exercises 73, 80), 515 (Exercise 30), 548 (Exercise 60), 575 (Exercises 41–44, 47–50), 576 (Exercise 77), 581 (Exercise 44), 584 (Exercise 20), 638 (Exercises 135–136, 145), 641 (Exercise 69), 653–54 (Exercises 52), 654 (Exercises 55–56)
Elevator capacity, 127–28 (Exercises 118–119), 788 (Exercise 81)
Elk population, 382 (Exercise 29), 457 (Exercise 29)
Elliptipool, 885 (Exercise 74)
E-mail, spam as percentage of, 44 (Exercise 115)
Encoding a message, 842, 851–52, 854–55 (Exercises 51–54), 855 (Exercises 63–64), 856 (Exercise 92), 871 (Exercise 45)
Endangered species, 448 (Exercise 32)

Equator, linear velocity of point on, 474 (Exercise 97)

Equilibrium, forces in, 711 (Exercises 79–80)

Exam grades, 128 (Exercises 120–121), 132 (Exercise 168), 841 (Exercise 63)

Exercise
depression in remission and, 204 (Exercise 44)
heart rate and, 3, 17 (Exercises 129–130)

Explosion recorded by two microphones, location of, 896–97, 898 (Exercise 61), 912 (Exercise 30)

Exponential decay model, 448 (Exercises 19–20, 28–31), 456 (Exercise 87), 457 (Exercise 28), 872 (Exercise 13)

Exponential growth model, 448–49 (Exercises 33–36), 584 (Exercise 18)

Expressway speeds and safe distances, 129 (Exercise 3)

Eye color and gender, 1034 (Exercises 22–25)

## F

Fahrenheit/Celsius temperature interconversions, 16 (Exercises 17–18), 127 (Exercise 110), 242 (Exercise 69)

Families, independent events in, 1025, 1026 (Exercises 23–24), 1033 (Exercise 97)

Fat content, candy bars with the highest, 746 (Exercises 85–88)

Federal budget expenditures on human resources, 357 (Exercise 97)

Federal Express aircraft purchase decisions, 797 (Exercise 23)

Fencing
cost of, 1086 (Exercise 35)
for enclosure, 263 (Exercises 21–26), 274 (Exercise 125), 773–74, 1086 (Exercise 33)
maximum area inside, 297, 382 (Exercises 20, 22), 1086 (Exercise 33)

Ferris wheel, 251 (Exercise 74)
height above ground when riding, 489 (Exercise 104)
linear speed of, 474 (Exercise 98)

Field's dimensions, 801 (Exercise 38), 1035 (Exercise 39)

Fire
distance of forest ranger from, 575 (Exercise 53)
locating potentially devastating, 644, 651, 653 (Exercise 47), 685 (Exercise 10), 726 (Exercise 20)

Firearms, death rates for industrialized countries and, 272 (Exercise 60)

Fishing trip, shared cost per club member, 132 (Exercise 149)

Flagpole
height of, finding, 642 (Exercise 20)
leaning, angle made with ground, 655 (Exercise 60)
on top of building, height of, 575 (Exercise 50)

Flashlight using parabolic reflecting mirror, 908–9, 910 (Exercises 61–62)

Flood, probability of, 1033 (Exercise 98)

Floor dimensions/area for pool and fountain, 775 (Exercise 61)

Flu
epidemic, 441, 449 (Exercise 37), 456 (Exercise 88)
inoculation costs, 80–81 (Exercise 91)
outbreak on campus, 985 (Exercise 96)
time-temperature flu scenario, 164–65
vaccine, 163 (Exercise 108), 736–38

Flying time from one city to another, 251 (Exercise 92)

Focal length of glasses lens, 88

Football
height above ground, 16 (Exercises 19–20), 816 (Exercise 46)
maximum height of, 382 (Exercise 19), 948 (Exercise 59)
parabolic path of, 293–95, 382 (Exercise 19)
position as function of time, 948 (Exercise 59)
vector describing thrown, 710 (Exercise 65)

Football field dimensions, 106–7

Football game attendance, ticket price and, 262 (Exercise 9)

Force(s)
acting against body leaning against wall, 698, 701
in equilibrium, 711 (Exercises 79–80)
exerted on held package, 707

gravitational, 375
required to stretch spring, 377 (Exercise 24)
resultant, 707–8, 710 (Exercises 71–74), 711 (Exercises 79–80), 725 (Exercise 94), 726 (Exercise 21)

Frame dimensions, 112 (Exercise 21), 132 (Exercise 148)

*Freedom 7* spacecraft flight, 243 (Exercise 97)

Free-falling object's position, 364–65, 366, 367 (Exercise 76), 1036 (Exercise 41)

Friends
apologizing to, formula for deciding about, 15
percentage of Americans with no close, 970 (Exercise 61)

*Friendship 7*, distance from Earth's center, 943 (Exercises 31–32)

Fruit tree yield, 262 (Exercises 13–14)
maximum, 382 (Exercise 23)

Fuel efficiency, 301 (Exercise 89)

## G

Galaxies, elliptical, 996

Gasoline sold, gallons of regular and premium, 719 (Exercise 51)

Gas pressure in can, 373–74

Gas price in U.S., average, 436 (Exercise 149)

Gas under pressure, volume of, 1087 (Exercise 37)

Gay service members discharged from military, 201 (Exercises 29–32)

Gender
attitudes of college freshmen and, 104–5
awakenings at night by, 145 (Exercises 57–60)
bachelor's degrees awarded by, 133 (Exercise 32)
college students claiming no religious affiliation and, 148
eye color and, 1034 (Exercises 22–25)
teaching salaries at private colleges and, 103

George Washington Bridge, height of cable between towers of, 947 (Exercise 37)

Global warming, 135, 187, 537

Gold alloys/karats, 743 (Exercises 56–57)

Golden Gate Bridge, 911 (Exercise 65)

Golden rectangles, 44 (Exercise 117)

Granola and raisin mixture, 743 (Exercise 60)

Gravitational force, 375

Greenhouse, area enclosed for, 1048–49 (Exercise 72)

Greenhouse effect, 455 (Exercise 81)

Grooming, average number of minutes per day spent on, 806

Ground speed, 711 (Exercises 83–84), 712 (Exercise 113)

Groups fitting into van, 1013 (Exercise 53)

Growth rates
average, 1070–71
instantaneous, 1075

Guy wire attached to pole, angle made with ground and, 568

## H

Half-life of radioactive element, 448 (Exercises 17–18, 21–26), 872 (Exercise 13)

Halley's Comet, 882, 896, 907
distance from Sun, 943 (Exercises 29–30)

Happiness
average level of, at different times of day, 242 (Exercise 68)
per capita income and national, 191

Harvard students with B+ averages or better, 314 (Exercise 76)

Headlight, parabolic surface of, 947 (Exercise 36), 948–49 (Exercise 10)

Health, annual income and, 432

Health-care expenses after retirement, savings needed for, 450 (Exercise 52)

Heart beats over lifetime, 30 (Exercise 145)

Heart disease
coronary, 449 (Exercises 43–46)
moderate wine consumption and, 191 (Exercise 104)

Heart rate
exercise and, 3, 17 (Exercises 129–130)
life span, 385 (Exercise 99)
before and during panic attack, 314 (Exercise 75)

Heat generated by stove, 378 (Exercise 55)

Heating systems, cost comparison for, 134 (Exercise 55)

Heat loss of a glass window, 378 (Exercise 33)

Height. *See also* Ball's height above ground
of antenna on top of building, 582 (Exercise 121)
of arch, 501 (Exercise 73)
average rate of growth, 199, 218 (Exercises 127–128)
of building, finding, 496, 497, 575 (Exercise 42), 576 (Exercise 77), 582 (Exercises 119–120), 583 (Exercise 21), 655 (Exercise 76)
child's height modeled, 407
diver's height above water, 367 (Exercise 75)
of eagle, in terms of time in flight, 271 (Exercise 43)
on ferris wheel while riding, 489 (Exercise 104)
of flagpole, finding, 642 (Exercise 20)
of flagpole on top of building, 575 (Exercise 50)
as a function of age, 196–97, 1070–71, 1075
of leaning wall, finding, 654 (Exercise 56)
over lifetime, graphs describing, 146 (Exercise 91)
maximum, 382 (Exercise 19), 726 (Exercise 14), 948 (Exercise 59), 1036 (Exercise 41)
maximum, of ball, 726 (Exercise 14), 816 (Exercises 45–46), 1085 (Exercise 60)
maximum, of shot put, 299 (Exercises 57–58)
median, of boys, 217–18 (Exercise 127)
median, of girls, 218 (Exercise 128)
of Mt. Rushmore sculpture, 568
percentage of adult height attained by girl of given age, 411 (Exercises 113–114), 413 (Exercise 146)
of plane, 501 (Exercise 80), 515 (Exercise 29)
of tower, finding, 109, 567, 575 (Exercise 41)
of tree, finding, 654 (Exercises 52, 57), 685 (Exercise 11)
weight and height recommendations/calculations, 99–100 (Exercises 137–138), 113 (Exercise 45), 377 (Exercise 25), 778, 783, 788 (Exercises 77–80)

Higher education. *See* College education

Hiking trails, finding bearings on, 570

HIV infection. *See also* AIDS
number of Americans living with, 313 (Exercises 73–74)
percentage of U.S. adults tested for, by age, 130 (Exercise 23)
T cell count and progression of, 147, 155–57

Hot-air balloon, distance traveled by ascending, 568, 575 (Exercise 49)

Hotel room cost, revenue and, 274 (Exercise 123)

Hotel room types, 746 (Exercise 89)

Households with HDTV sets, 446

House value
inflation rate and, 398 (Exercises 67–68)
sales prices and appreciation of, 987 (Exercise 19)

Hubble Space Telescope, 379 (Exercise 55), 873, 900, 908

Human resources, federal budget expenditures on, 357 (Exercise 97)

Hurricane probability, 1027 (Exercise 53)

Hurricanes and barometric air pressure, 435 (Exercises 131–132)

Hybrid Assistive Limb (HAL), 340

Hydrogen atom, mass of, 29 (Exercise 120)

Hypocycloid, 934 (Exercise 81)

## I

Ice cream, total annual spending on, 68 (Exercise 40)

Ice cream flavor combinations, 1009, 1013 (Exercises 65–66)

Identical twins, distinguishing between, 747 (Exercise 110)

Illumination intensity, 377 (Exercise 30), 378 (Exercise 54)

Imaginary number joke, 285 (Exercise 70)

Income
health by annual, 432
median annual, by level of education, 54 (Exercises 91–92)

Individual Retirement Account (IRA), 978, 979–80, 984–85 (Exercises 79–80), 986 (Exercise 110), 1032 (Exercise 55)

Inflation rate, 398 (Exercises 67–68)

Inn's nightly cost before the tax, 112 (Exercises 13–14)

Inoculation costs for flu, 80–81 (Exercise 91)

Instantaneous rate of change, 1075
of area of square with changing side, 1081 (Exercises 37–38)
of volume, 1077–78, 1081 (Exercise 42), 1085 (Exercises 58–59)

Instantaneous velocity, 1078–80, 1081 (Exercises 43–46)
of ball thrown straight up, 1079–80, 1082 (Exercise 76), 1085 (Exercises 16, 60), 1087 (Exercise 38)
of baseball hit straight upward, 1081 (Exercises 45–46)
of debris from explosions, 1081 (Exercises 43–44)

Insulation, rate of heat lost through, 584 (Exercise 19)

Intelligence quotient (IQ) and mental/chronological age, 377 (Exercise 32)

Interest
on bank loans, 1086 (Exercise 31)
compound. *See* Compound interest
simple, 260

Investment(s)
accumulated value of, 395, 397 (Exercises 53–54), 431
amounts invested per rate, 755 (Exercises 37–38)
choosing between, 396
comparing lump-sum vs. annuity, 985 (Exercises 83–84)
compound interest, 395–96, 397 (Exercises 53–56), 398 (Exercise 74), 399 (Exercises 81, 87), 431, 434 (Exercises 105–112), 436 (Exercise 143), 454 (Exercises 10–11), 455 (Exercises 83–85), 457 (Exercises 23–25), 804 (Exercise 35)
doubling time, 431
dual, 260, 264 (Exercises 35–38), 274 (Exercise 127), 804 (Exercise 33)
and interest rates, 18 (Exercise 133)
maximizing expected returns, 797 (Exercise 33)
money divided between high- and low-risk, 788 (Exercise 84)
possibility of stock changes, 1033 (Exercise 77)

Island, distance from coast of, 575 (Exercise 45)

## J

Jeans price, 231 (Exercise 100)

Job applicants, filling positions with, 1034 (Exercise 19)

Job offers, 971 (Exercise 69), 972, 984 (Exercise 68)

Jokes about books, 1013 (Exercises 67–72)

## K

Kidney stone disintegration, 873, 882, 912 (Exercise 29)

Kinetic energy, 378 (Exercise 34)

Kite, angle made with ground of flying, 567–68

## L

Labrador retrievers, color of, 53

Ladder's reach, 113 (Exercises 31–32)

Lake, distance across, 496, 499 (Exercise 53), 581 (Exercise 43), 662 (Exercises 41–42)

Land, triangular piece of
cost of, 663 (Exercises 51–52), 724 (Exercise 21)
length of sides of, 724 (Exercise 20)
right triangular piece of land, 114 (Exercise 57)

Landscape design, 107–8

Language other than English, percentage of people at home in U.S. speaking, 132 (Exercise 141)

Last names, top five U.S., 147–48, 149

Leaning Tower of Pisa, distance from base to top of, 653 (Exercise 51)

Leaning wall, finding height of, 654 (Exercise 56)

Learning
measuring rate and amount learned, 726 (Exercise 20)
in precalculus course, 1068 (Exercise 43)

Learning theory project, 441
Length
  alligator's tail and body, 377
  of great white shark, weight and, 372
  of moving starship with respect to
    observer on Earth, 1061 (Exercise 59)
  of violin string and frequency, 374
Letter arrangements, 1013 (Exercise 48)
License plates, 1006
Life expectancy, 162 (Exercises 101–102),
  190 (Exercises 89–90)
Life span, heart rate and, 385 (Exercise 99)
Light intensity, 386 (Exercise 29)
Light reflectance and parabolic surface,
  908–9
Light waves, modeling, 582 (Exercise 82)
Linear speed, 474 (Exercises 97–100)
  of airplane propeller, 580 (Exercise 20)
  of animals on carousel, 471, 474
    (Exercises 100, 110)
  of wind machine propeller, 472
Line formation, 1014 (Exercise 91)
Lissajous Curve, 934 (Exercise 82)
Literacy and child mortality, 178–79, 190
  (Exercise 91)
Little league baseball team batting order,
  1006–7
Living alone, number of Americans,
  192–93, 196
Local telephone plans, 134 (Exercise 60)
Long-distance carriers/plans, 101 (Exercise
  172), 127 (Exercise 113), 253–55, 266
  (Exercise 63), 274 (Exercise 122)
Lottery
  number of winners sharing winnings,
    111, 113 (Exercise 37)
  numbers selection, 1013 (Exercise 56)
  probability of winning, 1003, 1019–20,
    1026 (Exercises 27–28), 1033
    (Exercise 96), 1034 (Exercise 26)
LOTTO
  numbers selection, 1013 (Exercise 55)
  probability of winning, 1020, 1028
    (Exercise 69)
Love over time, course of, 127 (Exercises
  99–106)
Luggage, volume of carry-on, 337
  (Exercises 61–64)
Lunch menus, 796 (Exercise 18), 1012
  (Exercise 32)

## M

Mach speed of aircraft, 617 (Exercises
  80–81)
Magnitude, direction and, 698–99. See also
  Resultant forces
Mailing costs, 177 (Exercises 95–99), 271
  (Exercise 44), 1068 (Exercise 44)
Mall browsing time and average amount
  spent, 388, 389
Mammals, heart rates and life spans of, 385
  (Exercise 99)
Mammography screening data, 1015–17
Mandatory drug testing, probability of
  accurate results, 1027–28 (Exercise 63)
Mandelbrot set, 686, 695, 697 (Exercises
  91–92, 103)
Manufacturing and testing, hours needed
  for, 825 (Exercise 36)
Manufacturing constraints, 792, 796
  (Exercise 15), 802 (Exercise 60)
Manufacturing costs. See also Cost
  function
  bicycles, 163 (Exercise 105)
  calculator, 383 (Exercise 79)
  PDAs, 777 (Exercise 17)
  robotic exoskeleton, 340, 352–53
  satellite radio players, 386 (Exercise 26)
  wheelchair, 353
Maps, making, 498
Marching band, 747 (Exercise 111)
Marijuana use by U.S. high school seniors,
  144 (Exercises 55–56)
Markup, 112 (Exercises 15–16)
Marriage
  divorce by number of years of, 164
  percentage of never-married population,
    ages 25–29 (U.S.), 189–90 (Exercises
    87–88)
Marriage age
  difference within couple, 114
    (Exercise 59)
  preferred age in a mate, 232–33
  women's age of first marriage,
    probability of divorce and, 142–43
Mass attached to spring, simple harmonic
  motion of, 572–73. See also Ball
    attached to spring

Mathematics department personnel,
  random selection from, 1027
    (Exercises 45–46)
Mathematics exam problems, 1014
  (Exercise 93)
Maximum area, 297, 300 (Exercises 65–72),
  301 (Exercise 104), 339 (Exercise 29),
  382 (Exercises 20, 22), 1086
    (Exercise 33)
Maximum height, 382 (Exercise 19), 726
  (Exercise 14), 948 (Exercise 59), 1036
    (Exercise 41)
  of football, 382 (Exercise 19), 948
    (Exercise 59)
  of shot put, 299 (Exercises 57–58)
  of thrown ball, 726 (Exercise 14), 816
    (Exercises 45–46), 1085 (Exercise 60)
Maximum product, 299 (Exercises 61–62),
  339 (Exercise 28), 385 (Exercise 9)
Maximum scores, 797 (Exercise 22)
Maximum yield, 300 (Exercises 75–76)
Media, average number of hours
  Americans used various, 111
    (Exercise 1)
Median age. See under Age
Medical care, number of Americans
  traveling abroad for, 399 (Exercise 85)
Medication dosage, adult vs. child/infant,
  642 (Exercise 19)
Memory retention, 398 (Exercise 73), 412
  (Exercises 119, 132), 434 (Exercises
  115–116), 455 (Exercise 48)
Merry-go-round
  linear speed of horse on, 515 (Exercise
    28)
  polar coordinates of horses on, 674
    (Exercises 83–84)
Miles per gallon, 301 (Exercise 89)
Military, gay service members discharged
  from, 201 (Exercises 29–32)
Minimum product, 300 (Exercises 63–64),
  382 (Exercise 21)
Miscarriages, by age, 449 (Exercise 51)
Mixture problems, 743 (Exercises 55–60),
  777 (Exercise 18), 800 (Exercise
  10), 803
  alcohol content of wines, 743
    (Exercise 55)
  butterfat in cream, 743 (Exercise 58)
  candy, 743 (Exercise 59)
  concentration, 100 (Exercises 139–140)
  flu vaccine, 163 (Exercise 108), 736–38
  gold alloys/karats, 743 (Exercises 56–57)
  raisins in granola, 743 (Exercise 60)
Modernistic painting consisting of
  geometric figures, 756 (Exercise 51)
Moiré patterns, 899 (Exercises 65–66)
Moon weight of person given Earth
  weight, 377 (Exercise 22)
Moth eggs and abdominal width, 316, 325
  (Exercise 51)
Motion, uniform. See Uniform motion
Motorcycles, stopping distances for, at
  selected speeds, 384 (Exercise 91)
Mountain, measuring height of, 489, 498,
  655 (Exercise 58)
Mt. Rushmore sculpture, height of, 568
Movie attendance, U.S., 299 (Exercise 60)
Movie ranking, 1012 (Exercise 44)
Movie theater(s)
  finding best viewing angle in, 550, 564
    (Exercises 93–94), 565 (Exercises 109,
    123)
  number of, 134 (Exercise 54)
Multiple-choice test, 1005, 1012 (Exercises
  33–34), 1034 (Exercise 29)
Multiplier effect, 982
Music
  amplitude and frequency of note's sine
    wave, 622
  amusia and, 596, 598
  modeling musical sounds, 572, 576
    (Exercise 61)

## N

National debt, 19, 23, 26
Natural disaster relief, 796 (Exercise 19)
Nature, Fibonacci numbers found in, 952
Navajo sand painting, 488 (Exercise 97)
Navigation, 489
  bearings in, 570
  bearings needed to visit three islands,
    662 (Exercises 43–44)
  changing bearings, 662–63 (Exercises
    45–46)
Negative square roots, 284 (Exercise 63)
Neurons in human vs. gorilla brain, 68
  (Exercise 41)

News media, percentage of Americans
  regularly using, 201 (Exercises 27–28)
Newton's Law of Cooling, 442–43, 449
  (Exercises 47–50), 451 (Exercise 83),
  456 (Exercise 89), 1086 (Exercise 34)
Norman window, area of, 266 (Exercise 69)
Nutritional content, 816 (Exercise 47), 825
  (Exercise 35)

## O

Ocean's surface, intensity of sunlight
  beneath, 433 (Exercises 103–104)
Officers for Internet marketing consulting
  firm, choosing, 1007
Ohm's law, 284 (Exercises 61–62)
Oil consumption, countries with the
  greatest, 132 (Exercise 140)
Online ad spending, U.S., 961 (Exercise 69)
Open boxes
  dimensions of sheet metal forming, 1086
    (Exercise 32)
  lengths and widths, 262 (Exercises
    15–16), 263–64 (Exercises 31–32), 274
    (Exercise 124)
  with square base, surface area of, 1087
    (Exercise 39)
  volume of, 55 (Exercises 93–94), 256–57,
    262 (Exercises 15–16)
Orbit(s)
  of comets, 775 (Exercise 55), 882, 896,
    899 (Exercise 73), 907
  of Halley's comet, 943 (Exercises 29–30)
  modeling, 935
  perigee/apogee of satellite's orbit, 885
    (Exercise 80)
  of planets, 775 (Exercise 55), 881, 885
    (Exercise 78), 944 (Exercise 45)
  of planets, eccentricities of, 942
Oxygen molecule, mass of, 29
  (Exercise 119)

## P

Package, forces exerted on held, 707
Paintings, amount paid for, 800
  (Exercise 7)
Panic attack, heart rate before and during,
  314 (Exercise 75)
Parabolic arch and boat clearance, 911
  (Exercise 67)
Paragraph formation, 1012 (Exercise 39)
Parking lot dimensions, 112 (Exercise 24)
Passwords formed, 1012 (Exercise 19),
  1013 (Exercise 63)
Path around pool, dimensions of, 112
  (Exercises 22, 27), 266 (Exercise 68)
Payroll spent in town, 1032 (Exercise 55)
PDA manufacturing costs and revenues,
  777 (Exercise 17)
Peanuts cartoon, 45 (Exercise 129)
Pen and pad, cost of, 1035 (Exercise 40)
Pen choices, 1012 (Exercise 30), 1033
  (Exercise 76)
Perceived length of time period and age,
  378 (Exercise 36)
Percentage of adult height attained by girl
  of given age, 411 (Exercises 113–114),
  413 (Exercise 146)
Perigee/apogee of satellite's orbit, 885
  (Exercise 80)
Perimeter of rectangular floor, as function
  of width of rectangle, 357
  (Exercise 100)
Periodic rhythms, 626
Pest-eradication program, 986
pH level of human mouth after eating, 356
  (Exercise 91)
Phone calls between cities, 369, 378
  (Exercises 37, 47)
pH scale, hydrogen ion concentration and,
  435 (Exercises 117–118)
Physical attractiveness, cultural values
  of, 727
Physical illness among college students,
  procrastination and symptoms of, 728,
  745 (Exercise 81)
Physician visits, 177 (Exercise 106)
Piano keyboard, Fibonacci numbers
  on, 952
Pier, finding length of, 654 (Exercise 54)
Pitch of musical tone, wavelength and, 385
  (Exercise 95)
Pizza choices, 1005
Plane(s)
  approaching runway, vector describing,
    710 (Exercise 67)

average velocity of, 738–39, 743
  (Exercises 61–62), 800 (Exercise 11),
  803 (Exercise 15)
direction angle of, given speed, 712
  (Exercise 115)
distance and angle of elevation of, 548
  (Exercise 60)
distance flown by, 500 (Exercise 57)
graphs describing flight, 146
  (Exercise 79)
ground speed of, 711 (Exercises 83–84),
  712 (Exercise 113)
height of, 501 (Exercise 80), 515
  (Exercise 29)
leaving airport at same time, distance
  between, 655, 724 (Exercise 19)
linear speed of propeller, 580
  (Exercise 20)
line up for departure on runway, 1033
  (Exercise 82)
true bearing of, 711 (Exercises 83–84)
vector describing flight of, 710
  (Exercise 68)
velocity vector of, 708
weight/volume constraints, 791–92
wind speed and direction angle exerted
  on, 711 (Exercises 85–86)
Planetary motion, modeling, 942, 944
Planets, elliptical orbits of, 775 (Exercise
  55), 881, 885 (Exercise 78), 942, 944
  (Exercise 45)
Play production, break-even analysis of,
  584 (Exercise 17)
Poker hands, 1011
Pole, angle made by rope anchoring circus
  tent and, 583 (Exercise 22)
Pollutants in the air, 869 (Exercise 8)
Pollution removal costs, 68–69
Pool dimensions, 112 (Exercises 18, 20)
  path around, 112 (Exercises 22, 27), 266
    (Exercise 68)
Pool table, elliptical, 946 (Exercise 14)
Population, 447–48 (Exercises 1–14)
  Africa, 439
  over age 65 (U.S.), 44 (Exercise 116), 451
    (Exercise 73)
  bird species in danger of extinction, 448
    (Exercise 32)
  Bulgaria, 448 (Exercise 14)
  California, 433 (Exercise 101), 984
    (Exercise 69)
  Canada, 451 (Exercises 79–82)
  of cities, walking speed and, 444, 455
    (Exercise 82)
  Colombia, 448 (Exercise 11)
  elk, 382 (Exercise 29), 457 (Exercise 29)
  Europe, 457 (Exercise 27)
  exponential growth modeling, 448–49
    (Exercises 33–36)
  foreign-born (U.S.), 755 (Exercise 49)
  geometric growth in, 974
  Germany, 457 (Exercise 26)
  global, as village of 200 people, 816
    (Exercise 49)
  gray wolf, 394
  Hispanic, 456 (Exercise 86)
  Hungary, 436 (Exercise 148)
  India, 398 (Exercise 65), 447
    (Exercises 5–6)
  Iraq, 447 (Exercise 2)
  Israel, 447 (Exercise 7)
  Japan, 447 (Exercise 1)
  Madagascar, 448 (Exercise 12)
  Mexico, 449 (Exercise 36)
  New Zealand, 448 (Exercise 35)
  Nigeria, 450 (Exercise 59)
  Pakistan, 448 (Exercise 10)
  Palestinian, 447 (Exercise 8)
  percentage of never-married, ages 25-29
    (U.S.), 189–90 (Exercises 87–88)
  Philippines, 448 (Exercise 9)
  in scientific notation, 24–25
  single, 192–93, 196
  South Africa, 448 (Exercise 13)
  Texas, 433 (Exercise 102), 984
    (Exercise 70)
  Uganda, 451 (Exercises 79–82)
  United States, 24–25, 384 (Exercise 82),
    437–39, 450 (Exercises 68–72), 974–75
  United States, ages 85 and older, 1032
    (Exercise 52)
  United States, from 2000 through 2005,
    231 (Exercises 95–96)
  United States, total tax collections and,
    29 (Exercises 115–116)
  world, 133 (Exercise 31), 436–37, 445,
    446–47, 449 (Exercises 38–42), 456
    (Exercise 94)

Population projections, 112 (Exercise 10), 448 (Exercises 9–14)
Precalculus course, time and percentage of topics learned in, 1068 (Exercise 43)
President, probability of Republican, 1028 (Exercise 65)
Price reductions, 132 (Exercise 142), 233–34
  on digital camera, 105
  price before, 105, 112 (Exercises 11–12), 114 (Exercise 58), 134 (Exercise 58)
Prison inmates per 100,000 U.S. residents, number of sentenced, 276 (Exercise 27)
Problem solving time, 375
Profit function, 741, 744 (Exercises 71–72), 777 (Exercise 17)
Profits
  corporate, from 2002 through 2006, 272 (Exercise 61)
  department store branches, 231 (Exercise 98)
  maximizing, 301 (Exercise 103), 339 (Exercise 27), 385 (Exercise 8), 796 (Exercise 17), 802 (Exercise 61), 803 (Exercise 18)
  maximum daily, 794, 817 (Exercise 67)
  maximum monthly, 796 (Exercise 15)
  on newsprint/writing paper, 802 (Exercise 60)
  production and sales for gains in, 127 (Exercises 116–117)
  total daily, 791, 802
  total monthly, 796 (Exercise 15)
Projectile, path of, 384 (Exercise 92), 934 (Exercises 83–84), 948 (Exercise 59). See also Ball; Baseball; Football
Propeller
  of airplane, linear speed of, 580 (Exercise 20)
  on wind generator, angular speed of, 580 (Exercise 19)
Pyramid volume, 385 (Exercise 98)

**R**

Radiation intensity and distance of radiation machine, 377 (Exercise 29)
Radio sales, 231 (Exercise 97)
Radio show programming, 1012 (Exercise 43)
Radios produced and sold, 743–44 (Exercises 67–72)
Radio station, locating illegal, 653 (Exercise 48)
Radio station call letters, 1012 (Exercise 36)
Radio tower(s)
  on coast, distance of ship from, 899 (Exercise 62)
  height of, 109
  location of ship between, 947 (Exercise 26)
Radio waves, simple harmonic motion of, 576 (Exercise 62)
Raffle prizes, 1012 (Exercises 18, 20), 1013 (Exercises 60, 62)
Railway crossing sign, length of arcs formed by cross on, 474 (Exercise 91)
Rain gutter cross-sectional area, 263 (Exercise 17), 300 (Exercises 71–72)
Ramp
  computing work of pulling box along, 720 (Exercises 57–58)
  force and weight of box being pulled up, 710 (Exercises 75–76)
  magnitude of force required to keep object from sliding down, 710 (Exercises 77–78)
  vector components of force on boat on tilted, 716, 720 (Exercises 63–64)
  wheelchair, 108–9, 575 (Exercise 47)
Rate of change. See Average rate of change; Instantaneous rate of change
Rate of travel
  average rate and time traveled, 163 (Exercise 107)
  average rate on a round-trip commute, 81 (Exercise 92)
Razor blades sold, 755 (Exercise 36)
Real-estate sales and prices (U.S.), 987 (Exercise 19)
Records, linear speed of 45-rpm, 472
Rectangle
  area of, 45 (Exercises 119–120)
  golden, 44 (Exercise 117)
  perimeter of, 45 (Exercises 119–120), 81 (Exercises 95–96), 101 (Exercise 173), 384 (Exercise 84)

Rectangle dimensions, 113 (Exercises 35–36), 325 (Exercises 53–54), 367 (Exercises 79–80), 746 (Exercises 91–92), 774, 775 (Exercises 57–60), 801 (Exercise 36), 803 (Exercise 17), 804 (Exercise 34)
  bedroom, 132 (Exercise 146)
  carpet, 134 (Exercise 56)
  maximizing enclosed area, 297
Rectangular box
  dimensions, 325 (Exercise 52)
  surface area of, 276 (Exercise 38)
Rectangular field/lot
  area of, as function of one dimension, 276 (Exercise 37)
  cost of fencing, 1086 (Exercise 35)
  dimensions of, 132 (Exercise 144)
  fencing to enclose, 263 (Exercises 21–26), 274 (Exercise 125)
Rectangular garden
  area of, 257–59
  cost of enclosing, 263 (Exercise 30)
  doubling area with path around, 107–8
  maximizing area within fencing of, 1086 (Exercise 33)
  path/border around, dimensions of, 113 (Exercises 28–30)
Redwood trees, finding height of, 654 (Exercise 57)
Reflecting mirror, flashlight using parabolic, 908–9, 910 (Exercises 61–62)
Reflecting telescopes, 908
Relativity, Einstein's special theory of, 30, 42, 44 (Exercise 118), 1061 (Exercises 59–60)
Religious affiliation, college students claiming no, 148
Repair bill, cost of parts and labor on, 113 (Exercises 43–44)
Residential community costs, adult, 963, 968–69
Restaurant tables and maximum occupancy, 746 (Exercise 90)
Resultant forces, 707–8, 710 (Exercises 71–74), 711 (Exercises 79–80), 725 (Exercise 94), 726 (Exercise 21)
  of two tugboats pulling ship, 710 (Exercises 72–73), 712 (Exercise 114)
Retirement, savings needed for health-care expenses during, 450 (Exercise 52)
Revenue
  as function of ticket price, 255–56, 262 (Exercises 9–12)
  game attendance and, 262 (Exercises 9–10)
  hotel room cost and, 274 (Exercise 123)
  maximum daily, 300 (Exercise 74)
  maximum monthly, 300 (Exercise 73)
Revenue and cost functions, 739, 740, 743–44 (Exercises 67–72), 777 (Exercise 17)
  break-even points, 744 (Exercises 73–76), 799 (Exercise 6), 803 (Exercise 13)
Reversibility of thought, 56
Roads to expressway, length of, 265 (Exercise 46)
Robotic exoskeleton, cost of manufacturing, 340, 352–53
Roller coasters, instantaneous velocity of, 1079–80
Rolling motion, 932
Roof of A-frame cabin, finding length of, 724 (Exercise 17)
Rotating beam of light, distance from point, 547 (Exercise 59), 548 (Exercise 64)
Roulette wheel, independent events on, 1025
Royal flush (poker hand), probability of, 1011
Rug's length and width, 775 (Exercise 60)
Runner's pulse, 435 (Exercise 133)
Running shoes, manufacturing, break-even analysis of, 741
Running track, area enclosed by, 263 (Exercises 27–28)

**S**

Sabbatical to earn master's degree, investment in annuity for, 984 (Exercises 77–78)
Sailing angle to 10-knot wind, sailing speed and, 674 (Exercises 85–87, 96), 684 (Exercises 45–49)
Salaries
  anticipated earnings, 984 (Exercise 68)

average, for various jobs, 111 (Exercises 3–4)
average weekly, 274 (Exercise 121)
celebrity earnings, 102–3
choosing between pay arrangements, 1035 (Exercise 38)
comparing, 970 (Exercises 63–64), 972, 984 (Exercise 74)
earnings with overtime, 458 (Exercise 20)
gender gap, at private colleges, 103
gross amount per paycheck, 113 (Exercise 46)
length of time to earn $1000, 101
lifetime computation, 977–78, 984 (Exercise 73)
maximum weekly earnings, 796 (Exercise 16)
salesperson's earnings/commissions, 132 (Exercise 143), 1035 (Exercise 38)
in sixth year, 1032 (Exercise 53)
teachers' earnings, 965–66
total, 971 (Exercise 68), 984 (Exercise 74), 1031 (Exercise 29), 1032 (Exercise 53), 1034 (Exercise 15)
total weekly earnings, 796 (Exercise 16)
of U.S. senators, 963
weekly, 101 (Exercise 171)
Sales. See also Price reductions
  computer, 66 (Exercise 115)
  price and advertising budget and, 374–75
  radio, 231 (Exercise 97)
  real estate, 987 (Exercise 19)
  television, 66 (Exercise 116)
  theater ticket, 755 (Exercise 35)
Salesperson's earnings, 132 (Exercise 143), 1035 (Exercise 38)
Satellite dish, 910 (Exercises 63–64), 911 (Exercises 68, 74)
  placement of receiver for, 947 (Exercise 38)
Satellite radio manufacturing costs, 386 (Exercise 26)
Savings
  and compound interest, 434 (Exercises 105–112)
  geometric sequencing, 984 (Exercises 65–66)
  needed for health-care expenses during retirement, 450 (Exercise 52)
  total, 984 (Exercises 71–72)
Scattering experiments, 899 (Exercise 64)
Scheduling appearances, ways of, 1012 (Exercises 37–38), 1013 (Exercise 64)
Scholarship funds, investment in annuity for, 985 (Exercises 81–82)
Seasons, 501
Seconds in a year, 29 (Exercise 122)
Security cameras at school, percentage of students ages 12-18 seeing, 1031 (Exercise 27)
Semielliptical archway and truck clearance, 874, 882–83, 884 (Exercises 65–66), 912 (Exercise 28), 946 (Exercise 13)
Shaded region areas, 55 (Exercises 95–96), 66 (Exercises 117–120)
Shading process, 985 (Exercise 87)
Shadow
  hyperbolic, 886
  length of, 710 (Exercises 69–70)
Shark, weight of a great white, length and, 372
Ship
  bearing of. See Boat/ship, finding bearing of
  distance from lighthouse, 582 (Exercise 124)
  leaving harbor at same time, distance between after three hours, 662 (Exercise 39)
  location between two radio towers, 947 (Exercise 26)
Shipping cost, 271 (Exercise 44). See also Mailing costs
Ship tracking system, 775 (Exercise 56)
"Shortest time" problems, 932
Shot put
  parabolic paths of, 299 (Exercises 57–58)
  throwing distance, 585, 617 (Exercise 94), 654 (Exercise 53)
Sign dimensions, rectangular, 112 (Exercise 23)
Simple harmonic motion, 726 (Exercise 15), 1036 (Exercise 44)
  modeling, 570–73, 576 (Exercises 59–62), 583 (Exercises 24, 126–129)
  radio waves, 576 (Exercise 62)
  tuning fork, 576 (Exercise 61)

Simple interest, 260
Skydiver's fall, 372, 384 (Exercise 94), 987 (Exercise 18)
Sled, pulling
  computing work of, 719
  forces exerted, 710 (Exercise 66)
Sleep
  awakenings at night, by age and gender, 145 (Exercises 57–60)
  coffee consumption and, 458 (Exercise 17)
  death rate and hours of, 748, 752–53
  hours of, on typical night, 1015
  hours slept per day, by age, 241–42 (Exercises 65–66)
Smokers, probability of suffering from some ailments, 1001–2 (Exercises 57–58)
Smoking-related deaths and disease's incidence ratios, 356–57 (Exercises 93–96), 358 (Exercise 110). See also Cigarette consumption of U.S. adults
Snowfall, graphs describing, 146 (Exercises 75–78)
Soccer field dimension, 112 (Exercise 17)
Social class ladder, U.S., 869–70 (Exercise 7)
Social Security benefits/costs, 134 (Exercises 51–53), 745 (Exercise 82)
Soft-drink can
  minimizing aluminum in, 252
  surface area of, 259
Soft drink consumption, 252
Sonic boom, hyperbolic shape of, 896
Sound
  amplitude and frequency of, 622
  from touching buttons on touch-tone phone, 619, 624 (Exercises 45–46, 52), 625 (Exercises 58, 70)
Sound intensity, 378 (Exercise 35), 412 (Exercises 117–118), 421 (Exercise 103), 450 (Exercise 53), 457 (Exercise 19)
Sound quality, amusia and, 596, 598
Space exploration and relativity theory, 30, 42, 44 (Exercise 118), 1061 (Exercise 60)
Spaceguard Survey, 899 (Exercise 73)
Spam as percentage of e-mail, 44 (Exercise 115)
Spatial orientation, age and, 1048 (Exercise 69)
Speed. See also Linear speed
  angular, 471, 580 (Exercise 19)
  of blood, 27
  on expressway, recommended safe distance between cars and, 1048 (Exercise 68)
  ground, 711 (Exercises 83–84), 712 (Exercise 113)
  Mach speed of aircraft, 617 (Exercises 80–81)
Speed, linear, 474 (Exercises 97–100)
  of airplane propeller, 580 (Exercise 20)
  of animals on carousel, 471, 474 (Exercises 100, 110)
  of wind machine propeller, 472
Speed skating, winning time for women in, 276 (Exercise 35)
Sphere with changing radius, surface area of, 1081 (Exercise 41)
Spinner, probability of pointer landing in specific way, 1023, 1027 (Exercises 43–44), 1033 (Exercises 93–95), 1034 (Exercise 30)
Spring, ball attached to. See Ball attached to spring
Spring, simple harmonic motion of object attached to, 570–73
  ball attached to spring, 570–72, 638 (Exercises 133–134), 641 (Exercise 68)
  distance of object from rest position, 574 (Exercises 17–20), 583 (Exercises 128–129)
  frequency of, 574 (Exercises 21–28), 575 (Exercises 37–40)
  maximum displacement of, 574 (Exercises 21–28), 575 (Exercises 37–40)
  phase shift of motion, 575 (Exercises 37–40)
  time required for one cycle, 574 (Exercises 21–28), 575 (Exercises 37–40)
Square
  with changing side, area of, 1081 (Exercises 37–38)
  enlarged, length of side of original, 112 (Exercises 25–26)

Stadium seats, 971 (Exercise 71)

Standbys for airline seats, 1013 (Exercise 52)

Starship moving in space, length with respect to observer on Earth, 1061 (Exercise 59)

Statue of Liberty, distance of ship from base of, 575 (Exercise 43)

Stereo speaker loudness, 385 (Exercise 96)

Stolen plants, 114 (Exercise 62)

Stonehenge, raising stones of, 500 (Exercise 67)

Stopping distances
  for cars at selected speeds, 359, 367 (Exercises 77–78)
  for motorcycles, at selected speeds, 384 (Exercise 91)
  for trucks at various speeds, 368 (Exercises 92–93)

Strontium-90, decay of, 440

Student government elections, 1009

Students
  probability of selecting specific, 1034 (Exercise 28)
  saying school is not drug free, percentage of, 1087 (Exercise 40)

Sun, finding angle of elevation of, 497, 499 (Exercises 54–55), 501 (Exercise 73), 515 (Exercise 30), 575 (Exercise 48), 581 (Exercise 44)

Supply and demand, 744 (Exercises 77–78)

Supply-side economics, 325 (Exercises 55–56)

Surface area
  of box with square base and top, 274 (Exercise 126)
  of open box with square base, 1087 (Exercise 39)
  of rectangular box, 276 (Exercise 38)
  of soft-drink can, 259
  of sphere with changing radius, 1081 (Exercise 41)

Surveying
  bearings in, 569
  to find distance between two points on opposite banks of river, 653 (Exercise 50)

Suspension bridges, parabolas formed by, 907, 911 (Exercises 65–66)

Swimming pool dimensions, 112 (Exercises 18, 20)
  path around pool, 112 (Exercise 22)

Synthesizers, musical sounds modeled by, 566, 572

**T**

Takeout meals, average number of, 162–63 (Exercises 103–104)

Target, probability of hitting, 1028 (Exercise 68)

Task mastery, 422 (Exercise 104), 455 (Exercise 49)

Taxes
  bills, 127 (Exercise 114)
  Federal Tax Rate Schedule of taxes owed, 176–77 (Exercises 93–94)
  IRAs as tax-deferred savings plans, 979
  number of words, in millions, in federal tax code, 398 (Exercises 71–72)
  owed by single taxpayer in 2007, 1068 (Exercise 45)
  rebate and multiplier effect, 982, 985 (Exercise 86)
  tax rate percentage and revenue, 325 (Exercises 55–56)
  tax returns filed and audited, by taxable income (2006), 1023–24
  top marginal income tax rates in U.S., 270 (Exercises 9–14)
  U.S. population and total tax collections, 29 (Exercises 115–116)

Tax preparation costs, 130 (Exercises 38–39)

Teachers' earnings, 965–66

Telephone numbers in United States, 1005–6, 1034 (Exercise 21)

Telephone plans
  cellular plans, 127 (Exercise 109), 169–70, 176 (Exercises 79–82), 178 (Exercise 121)
  local, 134 (Exercise 60)
  long-distance, 101 (Exercise 172), 127 (Exercise 113), 253–55, 266 (Exercise 63), 274 (Exercise 122)

Telephone pole
  angle between guy wire and, 500 (Exercises 59–60)
  tilted, finding length of, 654 (Exercise 55)

Telescope, reflecting, 908

Television
  channels available in average U.S. household, 68 (Exercise 42)
  households with HDTV sets, 446
  nonprogram minutes in hour of prime-time cable, 100 (Exercises 143–144)

Television programming of movies, 1012 (Exercise 40)

Television sale, 66 (Exercise 116)

Television screen dimensions, 775 (Exercise 59)

Temperature
  atmospheric carbon dioxide concentration and global, 135, 187–88
  average monthly, 535 (Exercise 86), 536 (Exercises 109–110)
  body, variation in, 582 (Exercise 81)
  carbon dioxide concentration and global, 187–88
  of cooling cup of coffee, 454 (Exercise 12)
  cricket chirps per minute and, 243 (Exercises 89–90)
  degree-days, 971 (Exercise 83)
  and depth of water, 377 (Exercise 28)
  in enclosed vehicle, increase in, 409, 450 (Exercise 54)
  Fahrenheit-Celsius interconversions, 16 (Exercises 17–18), 127 (Exercise 110), 242 (Exercise 69)
  home, as a function of time, 218–19 (Exercises 137–140)
  Newton's Law of Cooling to model, 442–43, 449 (Exercises 47–50), 451 (Exercise 83), 456 (Exercise 89), 1086 (Exercise 34)
  time-temperature flu scenario, 164–65

Tennis court dimensions, 112 (Exercise 19)

Text messaging in the U.S., 456 (Exercise 91)

Theater attendance, maximizing revenue from, 797 (Exercise 21)

Theater seats, 971 (Exercise 70), 1032 (Exercise 30)

Theater ticket sales, 755 (Exercise 35)

Thefts in U.S., 382 (Exercise 28)

Throwing distance, 585, 607, 616 (Exercise 79)
  angle of elevation of, 638 (Exercises 135–136), 641 (Exercise 69)
  maximum height of thrown ball, 726 (Exercise 14)
  shot put, 299 (Exercises 57–58), 585, 617 (Exercise 94), 654 (Exercise 53)

Ticket price
  number of airline passengers and, 266 (Exercise 64)
  revenue as function of, 255–56, 262 (Exercises 9–12)
  U.S. film admissions and admission charges, 29 (Exercises 117–118)

Tides, behavior of, 375, 475, 488 (Exercise 84), 501
  modeling cycle of, 532
  modeling water depth and, 535 (Exercises 87–88)

Time
  decrease in motion of oscillating object over, 571
  distance of skydiver's fall and, 372, 384 (Exercise 94), 987 (Exercise 18)
  home temperature as a function of, 218–19 (Exercises 137–140)
  involved in uniform motion, 354

Time traveled
  average rate and, 163 (Exercise 107)
  driving rate and, 372–73
  as function of average velocity, 353–54, 357 (Exercises 98–99), 384 (Exercise 83)
  as function of distance, 266 (Exercise 67)

Total economic impact of factory on town, 985 (Exercise 85), 1032 (Exercise 55)

Touch-tone phone, sounds from touching buttons on, 619, 624 (Exercises 45–46, 52), 625 (Exercises 58, 70)

Tower
  angle of elevation between point on ground and top of, 584 (Exercise 20)
  height of, finding, 109, 567, 575 (Exercise 41)
  length of two guy wires anchoring, 663 (Exercises 47–48)

Track and field, maximizing area of, 301 (Exercise 104)

Track-and-field records, 261 (Exercise 3)

Traffic control, 818, 822–23, 825 (Exercises 29–33), 826 (Exercises 40, 46), 870 (Exercise 12)

Trains leaving station at same time, distance between, 685 (Exercise 9)

Transformations of an image, 837–38, 840 (Exercises 53–60), 870 (Exercises 31–32)

Transition to adulthood, percentage having completed, 840 (Exercise 61)

Travel. *See* Distance traveled; Rate of travel

Tree, finding height of, 654 (Exercises 52, 57), 685 (Exercise 11)

Tree yield, maximizing, 300 (Exercises 75–76), 382 (Exercise 23)

Triangle, area of, 660, 866–67 (Exercises 53–54)

Triangular piece of land
  cost of, 663 (Exercises 51–52), 724 (Exercise 21)
  dimensions of right, 114 (Exercise 57)
  length of sides of, 724 (Exercise 20)

Truck rental costs, 127 (Exercise 112), 950 (Exercise 19)

Trucks, stopping distances for, at selected speeds, 368 (Exercises 92–93)

Tugboats towing ship, resultant force of two, 710 (Exercises 72–73), 712 (Exercise 114)

Tuning fork
  eardrum vibrations from, 606 (Exercise 80)
  simple harmonic motion on, 576 (Exercise 61)

**U**

Unemployment and years of education, 383 (Exercise 81)

Uniform motion, 353–54, 738–39
  average velocity of airplane, 738–39, 743 (Exercises 61–62)
  average velocity of boat and current, 739, 743 (Exercises 63–66)
  time involved in, 354

U.S. Capitol Building, elliptical ceiling in Statuary Hall in, 884 (Exercise 67)

Universe imagery, 900

**V**

Vacation cabin, number of people sharing cost of, 134 (Exercise 59)

Vacation condominium, number of owners sharing, 113 (Exercise 38)

Vacation lodgings, 788 (Exercise 83)

Vacation plan packages, cost of, 800 (Exercise 19)

Vacation time, European vs. American, 111 (Exercise 2)

Vaccine, flu, mixture for, 163 (Exercise 108), 736–38

Value of an annuity, 984–85 (Exercises 77–84)

Velocity
  average, 113 (Exercises 39–42), 199–200, 353–54, 357 (Exercises 98–99), 384 (Exercise 83), 738–39, 743 (Exercises 61–62), 747 (Exercise 107), 800 (Exercise 11), 803 (Exercise 15), 1078 (Exercise 38)
  instantaneous, 1078–80, 1081 (Exercises 43–46), 1082 (Exercise 76), 1085 (Exercises 16, 60), 1087 (Exercise 38)

Velocity vector
  of boat, 708
  of plane, 708
  of wind, 707, 708, 711 (Exercises 85–86)

Verbal ability, age and, 1048 (Exercise 70)

Vertical pole supported by wire, 134 (Exercise 57)

Videos rented, number of one-day and three-day, 719 (Exercise 52)

Violin string length and frequency, 374

Vitamin content, 825 (Exercise 34)

Volume(s)
  average rate of change of, 1077–78, 1085 (Exercise 58)
  of carry-on luggage, 337 (Exercises 61–64)
  of cone, 266 (Exercise 70), 376
  of gas under pressure, 1087 (Exercise 37)
  of given figures, 55 (Exercises 108–109)
  for given regions, 66 (Exercises 121–122)
  instantaneous rate of change of, 1077–78, 1081 (Exercise 42), 1085 (Exercises 58–59)
  of open box, 55 (Exercises 93–94), 256–57, 262 (Exercises 15–16)

of package whose front is a square, 264 (Exercises 33–34)

of pyramid, 385 (Exercise 98)

Voters
  abortion polars as a percentage of, 744–45 (Exercise 79)
  by age and gender, 841 (Exercise 64)

Voting systems usage, 127 (Exercises 107–108)

**W**

Wagon, computing work of pulling, 718, 719, 720 (Exercises 55–56), 726 (Exercise 22)

Walking speed and city population, 444, 455 (Exercise 82)

Walnut tree yield, 276 (Exercise 36)
  maximum, 300 (Exercise 75)

Wardrobe selection, 1004

Warehouse, cost of building, 263 (Exercise 29)

Washington Monument, angle of elevation to top of, 499 (Exercise 56)

Water pipe, number of houses supplied by, 377 (Exercise 26)

Water pressure and depth, 369–70

Water supply produced by snowpack, 384 (Exercise 93)

Water temperature and depth, 377 (Exercise 28)

Water used in a shower, 371

Water wheel, linear speed of, 474 (Exercise 99)

Weight
  elephant's, age and, 435 (Exercise 134)
  of great white shark, length and, 372
  and height recommendations/calculations, 99–100 (Exercises 137–138), 113 (Exercise 45), 377 (Exercise 25), 778, 783, 788 (Exercises 77–80)
  moon weight of person given Earth weight, 377 (Exercise 22)
  volume of blood and body, 370–71

Weightlifting, 450 (Exercise 65)
  work done by weightlifter, 720 (Exercise 73)

Weight-loss surgeries in United States, number of, 444

Wheelchair manufacturing
  break-even analysis of, 740–41
  costs of, 353

Wheelchair ramp
  angle of elevation of, 575 (Exercise 47)
  vertical distance of, 108–9

Wheel rotation, centimeters moved with, 474 (Exercise 92)

Whispering gallery, 881, 884 (Exercises 67–68), 948 (Exercise 9)

White House, 816–17 (Exercise 50)

Will distribution, 114 (Exercise 61)

Wind
  average velocity of, 747 (Exercise 107), 800 (Exercise 11), 803 (Exercise 15)
  velocity vector of, 707, 708, 711 (Exercises 85–86)

Wind force, 378 (Exercise 38)

Wind generator
  angular speed of propeller on, 580 (Exercise 19)
  linear speed of propeller of, 472

Wind pressure, 378 (Exercise 53)

Wine consumption, 299 (Exercise 59)
  heart disease and moderate, 191 (Exercise 104)

Wing span of jet fighter, finding, 655 (Exercise 77)

Wire length, 113 (Exercises 33–34), 263 (Exercise 18)

Witch of Agnesi, 934 (Exercise 80)

Women, average level of happiness at different times of day, 242 (Exercise 68). *See also* Gender

Work, changing pattern of, in U.S. (1900–2005), 776 (Exercise 63)

Work, computing, 718–19, 720 (Exercises 53–62, 72–73)
  crane lifting boulder, 720 (Exercise 54)
  dragging crate, 725 (Exercise 104)
  pulling box up ramp, 720 (Exercises 57–58)
  pulling wagon, 718, 719, 720 (Exercises 55–56), 726 (Exercise 22)
  pushing car, 718, 720 (Exercise 53)
  of weightlifter, 720 (Exercise 73)

**Y**

Yacht, dividing cost of, 109–10

# Subject Index

## A

Absolute value, 9–11
  of complex number, 687–88
  definition of, 9
  evaluating, 9–10
  to find distance between two points, 11
  properties of, 11
Absolute value bars
  rewriting absolute value equation without, 89
  rewriting inequalities without, 123
Absolute value equations, solving, 88–89
Absolute value inequalities, solving, 122–24
Abstract algebra, 835
Acute angle, 461
  in right triangle, as complements, 494
  in right triangle, trigonometric functions of, 490–91
Adams, John Quincy, 881, 884
Addition
  associative property of, 12
  commutative property of, 11–12
  of complex numbers, 279–80
  distributive property of multiplication over, 12
  of functions, 222, 223, 224
  identity property of, 12
  inverse property of, 12
  of like radicals, 34
  matrix, 828–30
  of polynomial in two variables, 51
  of polynomials, 47–48
  of rational expressions with common denominators, 72
  of rational expressions with different denominators, 72–75
  of real numbers, 11–12
  of square roots, 34–35
  vector, 703–4, 705
Addition method
  nonlinear systems solved by, 770–73
  systems of linear equations in three variables solved by, 749–50
  systems of linear equations in two variables solved by, 731–34
  variables eliminated using, 731–34, 749–50, 770–73
Addition property of inequality, 119
Additive identity, 12
  for matrices, 829, 830
Additive inverses, 13
  for matrices, 829, 830
Aging rate of astronaut, 30, 42
Algebra, Fundamental Theorem of, 332
Algebraic expressions
  containing fractional and negative exponents, factoring, 64–65
  defined, 2
  evaluating, 3
  properties of, 11–13
  properties of negatives applied to, 14–15
  simplifying, 13–14, 15, 83
  terms of, 13
Algebra of functions, 222–24
  difference, 222
  product, 222
  quotient, 222
  sum, 222, 223, 224
  using, 222–24

Ambiguous case, triangle in, 647
  solving, using Law of Sines, 647–50
Amount of rotation formula, 917
Amplitude
  of cosine function, 526–29
  of simple harmonic motion, 571, 573
  of sine function, 517–23
  of sine wave, 622
Amusia, sound quality and, 598
Analytic geometry, 136
Analytic trigonometry, 585–642
  double-angle formulas, 607–10, 614
  half-angle formulas, 611–14
  power-reducing formulas, 610–11, 614
  product-to-sum formulas, 619–20
  sum and difference formulas, 596–607, 614
  sum-to-product formulas, 620–22
  trigonometric equations, 626–39
  verifying trigonometric identities, 586–96
*And* probabilities with independent events, 1024–25
Angle(s), 460–75
  acute, 461, 490–91, 494
  central, 462, 463
  conversion between degrees and radians, 463–64
  coterminal, 468–70, 507–8
  direction, 706, 707–8
  equations involving multiple, 628–29
  formed by revolutions of terminal sides, 465–67
  initial side of, 460
  lying in quadrant, 461
  measuring, using degrees, 461, 467, 512
  measuring, using radians, 462–63, 467, 512
  naming, 460
  negative, 461, 467
  notation, 461
  obtuse, 461
  positive, 460, 467
  quadrantal, 461, 502, 503–4, 512
  reference, 505–11, 512
  right, 461
  in standard position, 460, 461
  in standard position, drawing, 465–67
  straight, 461
  terminal side of, 460
  between two vectors, 714–15
  vertex of, 460
Angle of depression, 495
Angle of elevation, 495
  determining, 497
  problem solving using, 496–98
Angular speed, 471–72
  linear speed in terms of, 471–72
Annuities, 978–80
  value of, 978–80
Architecture
  angles in, 460
  hyperbolas in, 886, 896
Area
  formulas for, 106
  maximizing, 297
  of oblique triangle, 650
  of a rectangle with fixed perimeter, modeling, 257–59
  of triangle, Heron's formula for, 660, A2–A3
Argument of complex number, 688

Arithmetic sequences, 963–71
  applications with, 968–69
  common difference of, 963, 964–65
  defined, 963
  general term of, 964–66, 967
  sum of first *n* terms of, 966–69
  writing terms of, 964
Armstrong, Neil, 377
Arrow notation, 341–43
Arrows
  in graph, 155
  in limit notation, 1039
  showing orientation of curve, 926
*Ars Magna* (Cardano), 326
Associative property
  of addition, 12
  and English language, 12
  of matrix addition, 830
  of matrix multiplication, 836
  of multiplication, 12
  of scalar multiplication, 831, 836
Asteroids, 767
Asymptotes, 342
  horizontal, 345–46, 390, 391, 404–5, 440
  of hyperbola, 889–90, 891, 892, 894, 896, 916, A5–A6
  slant, of rational functions, 351–52
  vertical, 343–45, 390, 391, 404–5
Augmented matrix, 806–7, 808, 810–14, 818–22, 847, 848
Average cost, business problems involving, 352–53
Average cost function, 352–53
Average rate of change, 195–200, 1071, 1076–78
  of a function, 196–200
  slope as, 195–96
Average velocity, 199–200, 1078
  time involved in uniform motion and, 353–54
Axis
  imaginary, 686–87
  polar, 664–65
  real, 686–87
Axis of symmetry, 286–87, 939
  of parabola, 286–87, 901, 902–3, 905–8
  polar axis as, 937, 938, 941

## B

Babbage, Charles, 856
Base
  change-of-base property, 419–20
  natural (*e*), 393–96, 410, 446–47
Bearings
  defined, 569
  solving problems involving, 569–70
Berlin Airlift, 790–91
Binomial(s), 47
  cubing, 51
  dividing polynomial by, 316
  multiplying trinomial and, 48–49
  product of two, 49–50
  squaring, 51, 52
Binomial coefficients, 996–97
Binomial difference, square of, 51
Binomial expansions, 997–99
  finding particular term in, 999–1000
  patterns in, 997
Binomial sum, square of, 52
Binomial Theorem, 997–99
Biorhythms, 459
Blood alcohol concentration, 430–31
Body shape, ideal, 727

Boundary points, 359–60
  locating on number line, 360, 362, 364
Braces, 5
Brackets, 115
Branches, of hyperbola, 886
Break-even analysis, 739–41
Break-even point, 739–41
Breathing cycle, modeling air flow in, 531
Burrows, Christopher J., 908
Business
  average cost for, 352–53
  functions, 739–41

## C

Calculator. *See also* Graphing calculators/graphing utilities; Scientific calculators
  changing angle from degree, minute, second notation to decimal form, 462
  degree vs. radian mode, setting, 485
  evaluating inverse trigonometric functions with, 558
  evaluating trigonometric functions using, 485–86
  inverse trigonometric function keys on, 634
  radian mode on, 634
  solving trigonometric equation using, 634–35
Calculus, 1037–87. *See also* Limits
  change study in, 199
  derivatives, 1070–82
  fractional expressions in, 77–78
  instantaneous velocity in, 200, 1078–80
  in Japan, 1055
  motion and change analyzed in, 1038, 1070
  partial fraction decomposition in, 756
  transition from precalculus to, B1
Carbon dating
  and artistic development, 439
  and Dead Sea Scrolls, 439–40
Cardano, Girolamo, 284, 326
Cardioids, 679
Cartesian coordinate system, 136. *See also* Rectangular coordinate system
Cayley, Arthur, 835
Centaurus galaxy, 996
Center
  of circle, 246, 247–48
  of ellipse, 874
  of hyperbola, 886
Central angle, 462, 463
  length of circular arc intercepted by, 470–71
Centrifugal force, modeling, 376
Change-of-base property, 419–20
  proof of, A1–A2
Chaos, 686
Chaos theory, 643
China, "Pascal's" triangle discovered in, 1000
Circles, 243, 246–49, 874
  area and perimeter formulas for, 106
  defined, 246
  general form of equation of, 248–49
  identifying, without completing the square, 914
  identifying, without rotation of axes, 922–23

Circles, (*cont.*)
  in polar coordinates, 676–77
  standard form of equation of,
    246–48, 249
  unit, 475–76
Circular arc, length of, 470–71
Circular cylinder
  surface area formula for, 259
  volume formula for, 106
Circular functions, 477. *See also*
  Trigonometric functions
Circular path, linear and angular
    speed describing motion on,
    471–72
"Clearing equation of fractions," 85
Closed dots, 155
Closed interval, 115
Coded matrix, 851, 852–53
Coding, matrix inverses for, 851–53
Coding matrix, 851, 852–53
Coefficient matrix, 850
Coefficients, 13, 51
  binomial, 996–97
  correlation, 444–45, 446
  leading, 47, 303
  Leading Coefficient Test, 304–6
Cofactor, 865
Cofunction identities, 495
Cofunctions, 494
  of complements, 599
Column matrices, 850
Combinations, 1008–11
  defined, 1008
  formula for, 1009–11
  permutations compared to,
    1009, 1010
  probability and, 1020
Combined variation, 374–75
Combining like terms, 13, 48
Comets
  hyperbolic orbit of, 896
  parabolic paths, 908
Common difference, of arithmetic
    sequence, 963, 964–65
Common logarithms, 406–8
  changing base to, 419–20
  introducing, 419–20
  properties of, 407
Common ratio, of geometric sequence,
    972, 976
Commutative property, 12
  of addition, 11–12
  of matrix addition, 830
  of multiplication, 12
  noncommutativity of matrix
    multiplication, 834
Complements, cofunctions of599
  equal cofunctions, using, 494–95
Completing the square, 92–93
  converting general form of circle's
    equation to standard form by,
    248–49
  to derive quadratic formula, 93
Complex conjugates
  dividing complex numbers using,
    280–81
  as solution to quadratic
    equations, 283
Complex fractions. *See* Complex
  rational expressions
Complex *n*th root, 693
Complex numbers, 278–85, 686–98
  absolute value of, 687–88
  adding and subtracting, 279–80
  dividing, 280–81
  equality of, 279
  Mandelbrot set, 686, 695
  multiplying, 280, 689–90
  plotting, in complex plane, 687
  in polar form, 688–95, A3
  powers of, in polar form, 691–93
  product of two, in polar form, 689–90

quotient of two, in polar form,
    690–91
  in rectangular form, 688, 689
  roots of, in polar form, 693–95
  simplified, 279
  in standard form, 279
Complex plane, 686
  plotting the complex number on,
    687
Complex rational expressions, 75–77
  simplifying by multiplying by
    one, 76
Complex sixth root, 693
Composite functions, 224–28
  decomposing functions, 229
  forming, 224–27
  writing function as composition,
    229
Compound inequalities, 121–22
  solving those involving "and, "121
Compound interest, 395–96, 980
  formulas for, 396, 431, 437, 978
Computer, history behind, 856
Computer graphics, matrices and,
    837–38
Condensing logarithmic expressions,
    418–19
  properties for, 418
Cone, volume formula for, 106
Conic sections, 873–925
  circles, 106, 243, 246–49, 676–77, 874,
    914, 923
  defined, 874
  degenerate, 908
  ellipses, 874–85, 914, 919–20, 923,
    931, 935–36, 938, A5
  focus-directrix definitions of,
    935–36
  hyperbolas, 874, 886–900, 914, 916,
    923, 935–36, 940–41
  identifying, without completing the
    square, 913–14
  identifying, without rotation of
    axes, 922–23
  parabolas, 286–92, 874, 900–912,
    914, 922, 930, 935–36, 939–40
  parametric equations and, 925–35
  in polar coordinates, 935–44
  rotated, graphing equation of,
    921–22
  rotation of axes, 913–25
  standard forms of, transforming
    rotated conics to, 917–22
Conjugates, 36–37
  of complex number, 280–81
  to divide complex numbers, using,
    280–81
  multiplying, 36–37
  as solution to quadratic equations,
    283
Consistent systems, 735
Constant, coefficient of, 13
Constant function, 165, 166, 184, 303
  limits of, 1050–51
Constant matrix, 850
Constant numerators, partial fraction
    decomposition with, 759–60,
    764–65
Constant of variation, 370, 373
Constant term, 47
Constraints, in linear programming,
    791–92
Continuity, limits and, 1062–69
Continuous compounding of interest,
    395–96, 431, 437
Continuous function
  graph of, 1062
  at a number, determining,
    1063–64
Continuous graphs, 303
Converse of the Pythagorean
  Theorem, 109

Coordinates. *See* Polar coordinates;
  Rectangular coordinates
Copernicus, Nicolaus, 136, 942
Correlation coefficient, 444–45, 446
Cosecant (csc)
  as cofunction of secant, 495
  defined, 490
  evaluating, 491–92
  of 45°, evaluating, 493
Cosecant curve
  characteristics of, 542
  sine curve to obtain, 543–44
Cosecant function
  graph of, 542–44, 545
  as odd function, 481
Cosine (cos)
  as cofunction of sine, 494, 495
  defined, 490
  difference formula for, 597–99, 614
  of difference of two angles, 597–99
  double-angle formula for,
    607–9, 614
  evaluating, 491–92
  of 45°, evaluating, 493, 494
  half-angle formula for, 611, 614
  Law of Cosines, 656–64, 714
  product-to-sum formulas for,
    619–20
  rotation of axes and, 915
  sum formula for, 599–602, 614
  sum-to-product formulas for,
    620–21
  of 30° and 60°, evaluating, 493–94
  verifying an identity by changing to,
    587–88, 589, 591–92
Cosine curves, 525
  to obtain a secant curve, 544
  vertical shifts of, 529–30
Cosine function
  domain of, 479, 526
  in equation for simple harmonic
    motion, 571–72
  as even function, 480–81, 526
  of form $y = A \cos Bx$, 526–28
  of form $y = A \cos (Bx - C)$,
    528–29
  graph of $y = \cos x$, 525–26, 545
  inverse, 553–55, 557
  inverse properties, 559
  key points in, 527, 528–29, 530
  period, 525, 526
  periodic properties of, 484
  range, 479, 526
  reference angle to evaluate,
    509–10
  repetitive behavior of, 485
  solving right triangles using, 566
  variations of, graphing, 526–29
  vertical shifts of cosine curve,
    529–30
Cost, 739
Cost function, 352–53, 739, 741
Cotangent (cot)
  as cofunction of tangent, 495
  defined, 490
  evaluating, 491–92
  of 45°, evaluating, 493
Cotangent curve, characteristics
    of, 541
Cotangent function
  graph of, 540–42, 545
  as odd function, 481
  periodic properties of, 484
  reference angle to evaluate,
    509–10
Coterminal angles, 468–70
  finding, 468–70
  finding reference angles for angles
    greater than 360° or less than
    −3° using, 507
Counting principles, 1004–6
Cramer, Gabriel, 856

Cramer's rule, 856, 858–59
  with inconsistent and dependent
    systems, 864
  system of linear equations in three
    variables solved using, 862–64
  system of linear equations in two
    variables solved using, 858–59
  for systems with four or more
    equations, 865
Crick, Francis, 931
Cryptogram, encoding and decoding,
    851
Crystal, David, 1012
Cube(s)
  factoring sum and difference of,
    62–63
  surface area formula for, 259
  volume formula for, 106
Cube roots, 38
  combining, 39
Cubing a binomial, 51
Cycles, 475, 501
Cycloid, 932, 934
Cylinder. *See* Circular cylinder

**D**

*Dark Knight, The* (film), 550
Data, modeling, 187–88, 752–53
  with slope-intercept form, 188
Dead Sea Scrolls, and carbon-14
    dating, 439–40
Dean, James, 1008
Decaying entity, 437
Decimal notation
  converting from scientific notation
    to, 23
  converting to scientific notation
    from, 24
Decomposing functions, 229
Decomposition of vector into two
    orthogonal vectors, 717–18
Decreasing function, 164–66
  relative maximum/minimum,
    166–67
Degenerate conic sections, 909
Degree(s)
  of $ax^n$, 46
  converting between radians and,
    463–64
  fractional parts of (minutes and
    seconds), 462
  measuring angles using, 461–62,
    467, 512
  of nonzero constant, 46
  of polynomial, 46, 47, 51
  of polynomial in two variables, 51
  of term $ax^ny^m$, 51
  turning points of polynomial
    function and, 309–10
Degree-day, 971
DeMoivre, Abraham, 691
DeMoivre's Theorem, 691–95
  for finding complex roots, 693–95
Denominator(s), 13. *See also* Least
    common denominator (LCD)
  adding rational expressions with the
    same, 72
  factors of, partial fraction
    decomposition and, 757–65
  negative exponents in, 19
  rationalizing, 35–37
  rationalizing those containing two
    terms, 36–37
  subtracting rational expressions
    with the same, 72
  zero as limit of, 1058–60
Dependent equations, 735, 752, 820–21
Dependent systems, geometric
    possibilities for, 821
Dependent systems, identifying
  determinants used for, 864
  matrices used for, 820–21

Dependent variables, 150
Derek, Jeter, 925, 933
Derivatives, 1070–82
    applications of, 1076–80
    of a function, 1075–80
    instantaneous rate of change, finding, 1076–78
    instantaneous velocity, finding, 1078–80
    roller coasters and, 1079
Descartes, René, 136, 334
Descartes's Rule of Signs, 333–35
Determinants, 856–68
    higher-order, 865
    inconsistent and dependent systems identified with, 864
    second-order, 856–57
    solving systems of linear equations in two variables using, 857–59
    systems of linear equations in three variables solved using, 862–64
    third-order, 859–62
Difference
    binomial, square of, 51
    of cubes, factoring, 62–63
    of functions, 222
    limit of, 1052, 1057
    of two terms, product of, 51, 52
    of two vectors, 701
Difference engine, 856
Difference formulas
    for cosines, 597–99, 614
    for sines, 599–602
    for tangents, 602–3
Difference of two squares, 60–61
    factoring, 60–61, 63
Difference quotient, 171
Digital photography, matrices and, 836–37
Dinosaurs, extinction theory, 767
Directed distance, 902
Directed line segments, 699
Direction
    equal vectors with same magnitude and, 699–700
    of vector, reversing, 700
    writing a vector in terms of its magnitude and, 706–7
Direction angle, 706, 707–8
Directrix
    focus-directrix definitions of conic sections, 935–36
    of parabola, 901, 902–5
Direct variation, 369–72
    in combined variation, 374–75
    with powers, 371
    and problem solving, 370–72
Discontinuous function, at a number, 1063, 1064
    determining for what numbers, 1065–66
Discriminant, 95
    for determining number/type of solutions, 95
    negative, 283
    using, 95
Distance
    directed, 902
    from origin to point on graph, modeling, 261
    between two points on real number line, 11
Distance formula, 244–45, 246, 261, 875
    in derivation of Law of Cosines, 657
    equal vectors and, 699
    finding magnitude of vector using, 702
    in proof of identity for cosine of difference of two angles, 597

Distributive property(ies), 13–14
    adding and subtracting square roots, 34
    of matrix multiplication, 836
    of multiplication over addition, 12
    for multiplying complex numbers, 280
    for multiplying monomial and polynomial that is not monomial, 48
    properties of negatives and, 14–15
    of scalar multiplication, 831
Division. See also Quotient rule
    of complex numbers, 280–81
    of complex numbers in polar form, 690–91
    definition of, 13
    long, 316–19
    with numbers in scientific notation, 25
    of polynomial by binomial, 316
    of polynomials, 316–26
    of radical expressions, 38–39
    of rational expressions, 71–72
    of real numbers, 13
    simplifying complex rational expressions by, 76
    synthetic, 319–21, 322, 323
Division Algorithm, 318–19, 322
DNA, parametrization of, 931
Domain, 147, 149
    of any quadratic function, 292
    of arithmetic sequence, 964
    of composite function, 225, 226, 228
    of cosecant function, 542
    of cosine function, 479, 526
    of cotangent function, 541
    determining, 223, 224
    of function, 157–59, 220–22
    graphing the rectangular equation of curve defined parametrically and, 927–28
    identifying, from function's graph, 157–59
    of inverse sine function, 550–51, 553, 554
    of logarithmic function, 406
    of natural logarithmic function, 408
    of rational expression, 69
    of rational function, 340–41
    of relation, 147
    of secant function, 543
    of sequence, 952
    of sine function, 478, 479, 517
    of tangent function, 538
Domain-restricted function, finding the inverse of, 240
Dot product, 713–21
    alternative formula for, 714, 716
    angle between two vectors and, 714–15
    application of, 718–19
    definition, 713
    orthogonal vectors and, 715–16
    projection of vector onto another vector and of two orthogonal vectors, 716–17
    properties of, 714, A4
    of two vectors, 713–14
    vector as sum of two orthogonal vectors, 717–18
Double-angle formulas, 607–10, 614
    deriving power-reducing formulas using, 610–11
Double-angle identity, solving trigonometric equation using, 632
Doubling time, savings and, 431

**E**

Earthquake magnitude, 400, 408
Eccentricity, 935–36
    of planetary orbits, 942

Einstein's theory of relativity, 30, 42
Elements
    of matrix, 806, 832, 833
    of set, 5
Elevation, angle of, 495–98
Eliminating the parameter, 927–29
Eliminating variables. See Variables, eliminating
Ellipse(s), 874–85, A5
    applications with, 881–83
    definition of, 874
    eccentricity for, 936
    elliptical planetary orbits, 942
    focus-directrix definition of, 935–36
    graphing, 876–81
    graphing those centered at origin, 876–78
    graphing those not centered at origin, 879–81
    horizontal and vertical elongations of, 875
    identifying, without completing the square, 914
    identifying, without rotation of axes, 923
    parametric vs. rectangular representation of, 930–31
    polar equation of, graphing, 938
    rotated, transforming to standard form, 919–20
    standard form of equation of, 875–78, A5
Ellipsis, 5
Empirical probability, 1015–17
    formula, 1015
    with real-world data, 1015–17
Empty set, 6, 87, 786, 819
e (natural base), 410
    in continuous compounding formula, 396
    evaluating functions with, 393–94
    expressing exponential model in, 446–47
End behavior, 303–6
    determining, 310
Endeavor space shuttle, 908
English language, associative property and, 12
English sentences, and inequalities, 118
Equal and unequal one-sided limits, 1044–45
Equality of complex numbers, 279
Equal matrices, 828
Equals sign, 3, 779
Equal vectors, 699–700
Equation(s), 3. See also Linear equations; Polynomial equations
    absolute value, 88–89
    dependent, 735, 752, 820–21
    equivalent, 83
    exponential, 423–27, 430–32
    functions as, 150–51
    graphing, 137–43
    graphing, using point-plotting method, 137–38
    inverse variation, 373
    logarithmic, 427–32
    matrix, solving, 831–32, 850–51
    polar, 670–72, 675
    rational, 86–87
    trigonometric, 626–39
    in two variables, 137
    of variation, 370
    word problems solved using, 102–11
Equation of line
    general form, 185–86, 187, 195
    horizontal lines, 184, 187
    parallel to given line, 193–94
    point-slope form of, 180–82, 187, 193–94, 195, 1073, 1074

    slope-intercept form of, 182–83, 185, 187, 188, 193–94, 1073–74
    tangent lines, 1073–74
    various forms of, summarizing, 187
    vertical lines, 184–85, 187
Equation of the inverse, finding, 235–37
Equilibrium, 711
Equilibrium position, 571
Equivalent equations, 83
Equivalent inequalities, 118, 119
Ethiopia, 436
Euler, Leonhard, 410
Evaluating an algebraic expression, 3
Evaluating the function, 152
    piecewise function, 169–71
Even function, 167–69
    cosine function as, 526
    definition of, 167
    secant function as, 543
    $y$-axis symmetry and, 168–69
Even multiplicity, zero of, 308
Even-odd identities, 586
Event(s)
    defined, 1017
    empirical probabilities assigned to, 1015
    independent, 1024–25
    mutually exclusive, 1021–22
    non-mutually exclusive, 1022–24
    theoretical probability of, 1017
Even trigonometric function, 480–81
    to find exact values, 481
Exact value
    cosine of sum to find, using, 601
    half-angle formula to find, 612
    sine of sum to find, using, 600–602
Exact values
    of composite functions with inverse trigonometric functions, 558–62
    of $\cos^{-1}x$, 554–55
    difference formula for cosines to find, 598–99
    double-angle formulas to find, 608–9
    of $\sin^{-1}x$, 552–53
    of $\tan^{-1}x$, 556–57
    of trigonometric functions at $t = \pi/4$, 479–80
    using even and odd functions to find, 481
Expanding a logarithmic expression, 414–17
    and power rule, 415–16, 418
    and product rule, 414
    properties for, 416
    and quotient rule, 414–15
Expanding binomials, 997–99
Expanding the summation notation, 957–58
Expansion by minors, 860, 862
Experiment, 1017
Exponential equations
    applications of, 430–32
    defined, 423
    natural logarithms used in solving, 424–27
    solving, 423–27
Exponential expression, 2–3
    dividing, quotient rule for, 20
    multiplying, product rule for, 20
    simplifying, 21–22, 41–42
Exponential form, 401
    changing from, to logarithmic form, 401–2
    changing from logarithmic form to, 401
    location of base and exponent in, 401
Exponential functions, 387–400
    characteristics of, 391
    defined, 388
    evaluating, 389
    examples of, 388

Exponential functions, (cont.)
  expressing model in base e, 446–47
  graphing, 389–91, 403–4
  modeling data with, 442–47
  natural, 393
  transformations involving, 392–93
Exponential growth, 974
Exponential growth and decay
  models, 436–41
Exponential notation, 2
Exponential REGression option,
  graphing utility, 445
Exponents, 2, 19–22
  fractional, factoring involving,
    64–65
  and large numbers, 23
  negative, 19, 64–65
  negative integers as, 19
  power rule for, 20
  products-raised-to-powers rule
    for, 20
  properties of, 19–20
  quotient-raised-to-power rule for,
    20
  rational, 39–42
  zero, 20
Extraneous solutions, 97

**F**

Face cards, 1019
Factorial notation, 955–56
Factorials, from 0 through 20, 955
Factoring
  algebraic expressions containing
    fractional and negative
    exponents, 64–65
  difference of two squares, 60–61, 63
  to find limits, 1058–59
  by grouping, 57, 63, 64
  perfect square trinomials, 61–62, 63
  polynomials, 56–67
  quadratic equations solved by,
    89–91, 96
  separating different functions in
    trigonometric equation using,
    630–31
  over the set of integers, 56
  sum and difference of two cubes,
    62–63
  trinomials in two variables, 60
  trinomials whose leading coefficient
    is not 1, 59
  trinomial with leading coefficient of
    1, 58–59
  verifying an identity using, 588–89
Factoring completely, 56, 61
Factoring out Greatest Common
  Factor, 57, 63, 64
Factors
  in denominator, partial fraction
    decomposition and, 757–65
  of polynomials, 319
  of term, 13
Factor Theorem, 322–23, 332
Fermat, Pierre de, 136, 987, 995
Fermat's Last Theorem, 987, 995
Ferrari, 326–27
Fibonacci (Leonardo of Pisa), 952
Fibonacci numbers, on piano
  keyboard, 952
Fibonacci sequence, 952
Finite sequences, 952
First terms, in binomial, 50
Fixed cost, 739–40
Focus-directrix definitions of conic
  sections, 935–36
Focus (foci)
  of ellipse, 874
  of parabola, 901, 902–5
FOIL method
  and factoring by grouping, 57
  and factoring trinomials, 59, 60

for multiplying complex numbers,
  280, 690
for multiplying polynomials, 49–50
for multiplying polynomials in two
  variables, 52
for multiplying sum and difference
  of two terms, 51
Force(s)
  computing work done by, 718–19
Force vector, 707–8
Formula(s), 3–5
  amount of rotation, 917
  for area, perimeter, and volume, 106
  Binomial Theorem, 998
  for combinations, 1009–11
  compound interest, 396, 431,
    437, 978
  distance, 244–45, 246, 261, 597, 657,
    699, 702, 875
  double-angle, 607–10, 614
  empirical probability, 1015
  exponential growth and decay, 437
  for finding limits, 1051, 1057
  functions from, 256–61
  for general term of arithmetic
    sequence, 965, 966, 967
  for general term of geometric
    sequence, 973–75
  half-angle, 611–14
  linear speed, 471–72
  and mathematical models, 3–5
  midpoint, 245
  permutations, 1007
  power-reducing, 610–11, 614
  product-to-sum, 619–20
  quadratic, 94
  radian measure, 463
  recursion, 954–55
  rotation of axes, 914–16
  Schwarzschild, 27
  simple interest, 260
  slope of the tangent line, 1072
  solving for variable in, 87–88
  special-product, 51, 52
  sum and difference, 596–607, 614
  sum of first n terms of an arithmetic
    sequence, 967
  sum of first n terms of geometric
    sequence, 975
  sum-to-product, 620–22
  for surface area, 259
  Tartaglia's secret, 326
  uniform motion, 353–54, 738
  value of an annuity, 978–79, 980
  variation, 369
Fourier, John, 572
Fraction(s)
  complex. See Complex rational
    expressions
  with factorials, evaluating, 956
  linear equations with, 85
  partial, 756
  partial fraction decomposition,
    756–67
  writing repeating decimal as,
    981–82
Fractional equation. See Rational
  equations
Fractional exponents, factoring
  algebraic expressions containing,
    64–65
Fractional expressions
  in calculus, 77–78
  verifying an identity by combining,
    590
Free-falling object, modeling position
  of, 365–66
Frequency, 572
  of object in simple harmonic
    motion, 572, 573
  of sine wave, 622

Function(s), 147–276. See also
    Exponential functions;
    Logarithmic functions;
    Polynomial functions; Quadratic
    functions; Rational functions
  algebra of, 222–24
  analyzing graphs of, 155–57
  average cost, 352–53
  average rate of change, 196–200
  business, 739–41
  combinations of, 220–28
  composite, 224–28
  constant, 165, 166, 184, 303, 1050–51
  continuous, 1062, 1063–64
  cost, 352–53, 739, 741
  defined, 149
  derivative of, 1075–80
  determining domain, 223, 224
  difference quotients of, 171
  discontinuous, at a number, 1063,
    1064, 1065–66
  domain of, 157–59, 220–22
  as equations, 150–51
  evaluating, 152
  even, 167–69
  even trigonometric, 480–81
  finding a limit by graphing, 1042
  from formulas, 256–61
  graphing, 153–54, 164–78, 204–5
  graphs of common, recognizing,
    204–5
  greatest integer, 171
  identifying intercepts from graph
    of, 159
  identity, 1050–51
  increasing and decreasing, 164–66
  inverse, 232–43, 401
  linear, 153, 178–92
  modeling with, 252–66
  objective, 791, 794–95
  odd, 167–69
  odd trigonometric, 480–81
  one-to-one, 239–40
  parametric equations for,
    finding, 930
  periodic, 483–85
  piecewise, 169–71, 1042, 1058,
    1065–66
  profit, 741
  quadratic, 256, 286–301, 303, 752–53
  range of, 157–59
  reciprocal, 341–42
  relations as, 149
  relative maximum or relative
    minimum of, 166–67
  revenue, 739, 741
  step, 171
  sum of (addition of), 222, 223, 224
  transformation of, 204–19
  from verbal descriptions, 252–56
  vertical line test for, 154–55
  zeros of, 159
Function machine, 151, 152
Function notation, 151–53
Fundamental Counting Principle,
  1004–6, 1007
  applications of, 1004–6
  defined, 1004
Fundamental Theorem of Algebra,
  332
Fundamental trigonometric identities,
  586–96
  defined, 586
  to verify other identities, using,
    586–96

**G**

Galileo, 136
Galois, Evariste, 327
Games of chance, theoretical
  probability in, 1018–20
Gauss, Carl Friedrich, 332, 808, 813

Gaussian elimination, 808–13, 818–23
  applied to dependent systems,
    820–21
  applied to inconsistent systems,
    818–19
  applied to systems with more
    variables than equations, 821–22
  applied to systems without unique
    solutions, 818–21, 822–23
  solving problems using, 822–23
Gauss-Jordan elimination, 813–14,
  847, 848
General form
  of equation of circle, 248–49
  of quadratic equation, 89, 93, 94, 283
General form of equation of a line,
  185–86, 187
  perpendicular lines, 195
  using intercepts to graph, 186–87
General second-degree equation,
  914–15
  graphing, 920
  transformed to standard equations
    of conic sections, 917–22
General term
  of arithmetic sequence, 964–66,
    967
  of geometric sequence, 973–75
  of sequence, 952–53
Geometric figures, formulas for area,
  perimeter, and volume, 106
Geometric formula, obtaining a
  function from, 256–57
Geometric population growth, 974–75
Geometric sequences, 972–80
  applications with, 977–80
  common ratio of, 972, 976
  defined, 972
  general term of, 973–75
  sum of first n terms of, 975–78
  writing terms of, 973
Geometric series, 980–82
  infinite, 980–82
Gleick, James, 643
Glenn, John, 935, 943
Graphing calculators/graphing
  utilities, 139
  adding and subtracting matrices,
    829
  angle of elevation problems on, 497
  binomial coefficients computed
    with, 998
  change-of-base property to graph
    logarithmic functions on, 420
  checking partial fraction
    decomposition on, 763
  checking solutions to trigonometric
    equation on, 633
  checking tables and graphs on, 154
  circles graphed on, 246, 249
  combinations on, 1011
  common logarithms evaluated
    on, 407
  computations with scientific
    notation on, 25
  converting from decimal to
    scientific notation on, 24
  derivative of function, 1078
  determinant of matrix evaluated
    on, 861
  DRAW TANGENT feature, 1073
  ellipse graphed on, 877
  equations graphed on, 139–41
  e to various powers evaluated
    on, 393
  evaluating trigonometric functions
    using, 485–86
  exponential expressions evaluated
    on, 389
  Exponential REGression
    option, 445
  factorials found on, 955

functions evaluated on, 152
graphing polar equation using, 676
greatest integer function on, 171
inverse sine key, 497
inverse trigonometric functions on, 557
keystroke sequences for rational exponents, 41
linear system with unique solution on, 851
Logarithmic REGression option, 444
logistic growth function on, 441
matrix multiplication on, 834
maximum function feature, 257, 297
minimum function feature, 259, 261, 753
modeling data with, 444–45
modeling from formulas on, 256–57, 259, 261
models for scatter plots obtained on, 188
multiplicative inverse of matrix on, 845, 849
parabola on, 903, 904, 906, 907
parametric mode and radian mode of, 931
permutations on, 1007
plane curve represented by parametric equations on, 927
polar mode, 938
polar-to-rectangular point conversion on, 668
providing evidence of identity on, 587
quadratic regression program, 359
rational functions graphed with, 344–45
rectangular-to-polar point conversion on, 670
reduced row-echelon form on, 814
row-echelon form on, 810, 812–13
SHADE feature, 780
SINe REGression feature, 530
solving systems on, 731
statistical menu, 359
sum of first *n* terms of arithmetic sequence on, 968
sum of first *n* terms of geometric sequence on, 977
sum of sequence on, 957–58
TABLE feature on, 296, 430, 445, 587, 630, 763, 1039
TABLE SETUP function, 140
terms of sequences, 952
verifying model of periodic behavior with, 532
verifying observations on, 602
verifying solution set for logarithmic equation, 428
verifying solution set for polynomial inequality, 361, 362
verifying solution set for rational inequality, 364
verifying solutions of trigonometric equation quadratic in form on, 630
verifying solution to scalar multiplication, 830
verifying verbal models with, 254
ZERO feature, 307, 309
zeros of polynomial function on, 306–7
ZOOM SQUARE setting, 247, 249, 877
Graphing quadratic functions in form $f(x) = ax^2 + bx + c$, 289–92
identifying a conic section without, 913–14
quadratic equations solved by, 92–93

Graphs/graphing
asymptotes of, horizontal and vertical, 390, 391, 404–5
circles, 247
of complex numbers, 687
continuous, 303
of continuous function, 1062
of cosecant function, 542–44, 545
of cosine function, 525–29, 545
of cotangent function, 540–42, 545
ellipse, 876–81
equations, 137–43
even functions, 167–69
exponential functions, 389–91, 403–4
finding limits using, 1041–42, 1044–45
functions, 153–54, 164–78, 204–5
general second-degree equation, 920
and horizontal line test, 237–39
horizontal shifts, 207–9, 213, 214, 215, 392, 405
horizontal stretching and shrinking, 212–13, 214, 392, 405
hyperbolas, 890–96
information obtained from, 155–57
interpreting information given by, 141–43
inverse functions, 239
inverse trigonometric functions, 557
lemniscates, 682
limaçons, 679
line, 141
linear inequalities in two variables, 778–82
logarithmic functions, 403–6
modeling periodic behavior, 530–32
nonlinear inequalities in two variables, 781–82
odd functions, 167–69
one-to-one function, 239
parabolas, 902–7
plane curves defined by parametric equations, 926–27
polar equation of conic, 937–41
polar equations, 675–76
polynomial functions, 303–6, 309–11
quadratic functions, 286–92
rational functions, 346–51
real numbers, 8
reciprocal function, 342
rectangular equation of curve defined parametrically, 927–29
reflection about the *x*-axis, 209–10
reflection about the *y*-axis, 210
reflections of, 209–10, 213, 239, 392, 405, 406
relative maximum or relative minimum on, 166–67
rose curves, 680–81
secant function, 542–44
sequences, 953–54
sequences of transformations, 213–15
sine function, 515–25, 545
smooth, 303
step functions, 171
systems of linear equations in two variables solved by, 729, 734–35
systems of linear inequalities, 784–86
tangent function, 537–40, 545
of transformations of functions, 204–19
using intercepts, 140–41, 186–87
vertical lines, 184
vertical shifts, 205–6, 213, 214, 215
vertical shifts of sinusoidal, 529–30
vertical stretching and shrinking, 211–12, 213, 214, 215, 392, 405
Gravitation, Newton's formula for, 375
Greater than or equal to symbol, 9, 115

Greater than symbol, 115
absolute value inequalities using, 122
Greatest common binomial factor, factoring out, 57
Greatest Common Factor (GCF), 56–57
factoring out, 57, 63, 64
Greatest integer function, 171
Ground speed, 711
Grouping/grouping method, factoring by, 57, 63, 64
Growing entity, 437
Growth models, logistic, 440–41
Growth rate, for world population, 436

**H**

Half-angle formulas, 611–14
Half-life, 439
Half-planes, 778–80
Halley's Comet, 882, 896, 908
Harding, Warren G., 619
Harmonic motion, simple, 570–73
Harvey, William, 136
Hendrix, Jimi, 1008
Heron's formula, 660, A2–A3
Higher-order determinants, 865
Horizontal asymptote(s)
definition of, 345
of exponential function, 404–5
locating, 345–46
in logistic growth model, 440
of rational functions, 345–46, 348, 349, 350, 353
*x*-axis as, 390, 391
Horizontal component of vector, 702
Horizontal lines, 187
equations of, 184, 187
Horizontal line test
applying, 237–39
for inverse functions, 237–39
Horizontal shifts, 207–9, 213, 214, 215
combining vertical shifts and, 208–9
of exponential function, 392
to left, 208, 209
of logarithmic function, 405
to right, 207
Horizontal stretching or shrinking, 212–13, 214
of exponential function, 392
of logarithmic function, 405
Hubble Space Telescope, 900, 908
Hyperbolas, 874, 886–900
applications with, 896–97
asymptotes of, 889–90, 891, 892, 894, 896, 916, A5–A6
definition of, 886
eccentricity for, 936
focus-directrix definition of, 935–36
graphing, 890–96
identifying, without completing the square, 914
identifying, without rotation of axes, 923
polar equation of, graphing, 940–41
standard form of equation of, 886–89, 893, 916
Hyperbolic cosine function, 400
Hyperbolic sine function, 400
Hypocycloid, 934
Hypotenuse, of right triangle, 108, 490
Pythagorean Theorem to find length of, 491, 492

**I**

IBM, 856
Identities, 626
for cosine of difference of two angles, 597–99
double-angle formulas, 607–10, 614
fundamental trigonometric, 586–96

half-angle formulas, 611–14
principal trigonometric, 607–18
product-to-sum formulas, 619–20
quotient, 482, 586
solving trigonometric equations using, 631–34
sum-to-product formulas, 620–22
trigonometric. *See* Trigonometric identities
verifying. *See* Verifying an identity
Identity function, limits of, 1050–51
Identity property
of addition, 12
of multiplication, 12
scalar, 831
*i* (imaginary unit), 278–79
square roots of negative numbers in terms of, 281–82
Imaginary axis, 686–87
Imaginary numbers, 278
Imaginary part, of complex number, 278
Incidence ratio, 356
Inconsistent systems, 734–35, 752
determinants used for identifying, 865
geometric possibilities for, 819
matrices used for identifying, 818–19
Increasing function, 164–66
relative maximum/minimum, 166–67
Independent events, 1024–25
Independent variable, 150
Index, 37
reducing, 42
Index of summation, 957, 958
Individual Retirement Account, 978, 979–80
Induction. *See* Mathematical induction
Inequalities
absolute value, 122–24
compound, 121–22
and English sentences, 118
equivalent, 118, 119
isolating *x* in middle of, 121
polynomial, 359–62, 364–66
rational, 362–64
solution set of, 115
solving, 118–21
triangle, 11
Inequality symbols, 9, 115, 779, 781
reversal of direction of, 119
Infinite geometric series, 980–82
sum of, 980–82
Infinite interval, 115
Infinite sequence, 952
Infinity symbol, 115
Initial point
of directed line segment, 699
of vector at origin (position vector), 702
Initial side of angle, 460
Inside terms, in binomial, 50
Instantaneous rate of change, 1071, 1072, 1075
finding, 1076–78
Instantaneous velocity, 200, 1078–80
Integers, 7
Intercepts
for graphing linear equations, 186–87
graphing using, 140–41, 186–87
identifying, 141
identifying, from function's graph, 159
Interest
compound, 395–96, 431, 437, 978, 980
simple, 260
Interest rates, doubling time and, 431

Intermediate Value Theorem, 309
Intersection of sets, 5–6, 220
Intersections of intervals, 116–17
Interval notation, 115–16, 121, 220
    to represent function's domain and
      range, 157
Intervals
    closed, 115
    infinite, 115
    intersections and unions of, 116–17
    open, 115, 165, 166
    on real number line, 115
    satisfying polynomial inequality,
      361, 362
    satisfying rational inequality, 364
    on which function increases,
      decreases, or is constant, 164–66
Inverse
    additive, 13, 829, 830
    equation of the, finding, 235–37
    multiplicative (reciprocal), 13, 71
Inverse cosine function, 553–55
    defined, 554
    exact values of, 554–55
    inverse properties, 559
Inverse function(s), 232–43, 550
    defined, 234
    of exponential function. *See*
      Logarithmic functions
    finding, 235–37
    graphing, 239
    horizontal line test for, 237–39
    inverse of domain-restricted
      function, finding, 240
    notation, 234
    verifying, 235
Inverse property(ies)
    of addition, 12
    of logarithms, 403
    of multiplication, 12
    using, 409
Inverse sine function, 497, 550–53
    defined, 551
    exact values of, finding, 552–53
    inverse properties, 559
    notation, 551
    simplifying expression
      involving, 562
Inverse tangent function, 555–57
    defined, 555
    exact values of, 556–57
    inverse properties, 559
Inverse trigonometric functions,
    550–65
    exact values of composite functions
      with, 558–62
    inverse properties, 559
    using calculator to evaluate, 558
Inverse variation, 372–74
    in combined variation, 374–75
    equations, 373
    problem solving, 373–74
Inverted cycloid, 932
Invertible square matrix, 845, 849
Investments
    choosing between, 396
    and compound interest, 395–96,
      431, 980
Irrational number, 7
    as exponent in exponential
      function, 389
    natural base $e$, 393–94, 410, 446–47
    as solutions to quadratic
      equations, 95
Isolating $x$ in the middle of
    inequality, 121
Isosceles right triangle, 492–93

**J**

Japan, calculus in, 1055
Job offers, 972
Joint variation, 375–76

Joplin, Janis, 1008
Jordan, Wilhelm, 813

**K**

Kepler, Johannes, 881, 942
Kidney stone disintegration,
    873, 882

**L**

Laffer, Arthur, 325
Large numbers
    and exponents, 23
    names of, 23
Last terms, in binomial, 50
Latus rectum of parabola, 903–4,
    906, 907
Law of Cosines, 656–64, A2–A3
    applications of, 659–60
    defined, 657
    derivation, 656–57
    deriving formula for dot product
      using, 714
    solving oblique triangles using,
      657–59
Law of Sines, 644–55, 658, 659
    ambiguous case, solving triangle in,
      647–50
    applications of, 650–51
    area of oblique triangle, finding, 650
    defined, 644
    derivation of, 644–45
    solving oblique triangle using,
      645–46
Leading coefficient, 47, 303
Leading Coefficient Test, 304–6
Leaning Tower of Pisa, 365–66
Least common denominator (LCD)
    finding, 73–74
    in solving linear equation involving
      fractions, 85
    in solving rational equations, 86, 87
Ledger, Heath, 1008
Left-hand limit, 1043, 1044
Legs, of right triangle, 108
Leibniz, Gottfried, 1050, 1052
Lemniscates, 682
Length of circular arc, 470–71
Less than or equal to symbol, 9, 115
Light, theory of, 932
Like radicals, 34
    adding and subtracting, 34
Like terms, 13
    combining, 13, 48
Limaçon, 679
Limitations, inequalities to describe,
    791–92
Limit notation, 1039
    for one-sided limits, 1043
Limits, 199, 343, 1038–69, B1
    of constant functions, 1050–51
    continuity and, 1062–69
    derivative of a function and,
      1075–76
    of difference, 1052, 1057
    factoring to find, 1058–59
    finding, using graphs, 1041–42,
      1044–45
    finding, using properties of limits,
      1050–62
    finding, using tables, 1039–41
    of fractional expressions when limit
      of denominator is zero, 1058–60
    of identity function, 1050–51
    instantaneous rate of change, 1072,
      1076–78
    of monomial, 1054
    one-sided, 1043–45, 1058
    of polynomial, 1055
    of power, 1055–56, 1057
    of product, 1053, 1057
    properties of, 1051–60
    of quotient, 1056–57

rationalizing a numerator to find,
    1059–60
    of root, 1056, 1057
    slope of tangent line, 1072, 1073–74
    of sum, 1052, 1057
Line(s)
    directed line segment, 699
    equations of, 187. *See also* Equation
      of line
    parallel, 193–95, 734
    perpendicular, 193–95
    regression, 179
    secant, 196–97, 1071, 1072
    slope of, 179–80
Linear combination of vectors, 702
Linear equations, 82–85
    defined, 82
    with fractions, 85
    intercepts used for graphing, 186–87
    in one variable, 82
    solving, 83
    in three variables, 748
Linear Factorization Theorem, 332–33
Linear factors
    partial fraction decomposition with,
      759–61
    partial fraction decomposition with
      distinct, 757–59
Linear functions, 153, 178–92, 303
    constant function, 165, 166, 184, 303
    data modeled with, 187–88
    graphing in slope-intercept form,
      182–83
    limit of, 1055
Linear inequalities
    problem solving with, 125
    properties of, 119
    solving, 118–21
    systems of, 784–86, 790–95
Linear inequalities in one
    variable, 115
    solving, 118–21
Linear inequalities in two variables,
    778–82
    graphing, 778–82
Linear numerators, partial fraction
    decomposition with, 761, 763–65
Linear programming, 790–98
    constraints in, 791–92
    objective functions in, 791, 794–95
    problem solving with, 793–95
Linear speed, 471–72
    in terms of angular speed, 471–72
Linear systems. *See* Systems of linear
    equations
Line graphs, 141
    interpreting, 141–43
Line segments, midpoint of, 245
Lissajous Curve, 934
Logarithmic equations, 427–32
    applications of, 430–32
    defined, 427
    one-to-one property of logarithms
      to solve, 429–30
    product rule used for solving, 428
    quotient rule used for solving, 429
    solving, 427–30
Logarithmic expressions
    condensing, 418–19
    expanding, 414–17
Logarithmic form, 401
    changing from exponential form to,
      401–2
    changing to exponential form
      from, 401
    equations in, 401
    location of base and exponent
      in, 401
Logarithmic functions, 400–413
    with base $b$, 401
    change-of-base property to
      graph, 420

common, 406–8
    definition of, 400
    domain of, 406
    graphs of, 403–6
    modeling data with, 442–47
    natural, 408–9
    transformations involving, 405–6
Logarithmic properties, 413–22
    change-of-base property, 419–20
    involving one, 402
    power rule, 415–16, 418, 419
    product rule, 414, 416, 418, 428
    quotient rule, 414–15, 416, 418,
      419, 429
    using, 402–3
Logarithmic REGression option,
    graphing utility, 444
Logarithms
    common, 406–8, 419–20
    evaluating, 402
    inverse properties of, 403
    natural, 408–9, 419, 420, 425–27
    one-to-one property of, solving
      logarithmic equations using,
      429–30
    properties of, A1–A2
Logistic growth model, 440–41
Long division, polynomial, 316–19
Lower limit of summation, 957, 958

**M**

Mach, Ernst, 617
Magnitude
    of directed line segment, 699
    and direction. *See* Vector(s)
    equal vectors with same direction
      and, 699–700
    scalars involving, 699
    of single point, 701
    of vector in rectangular coordinates,
      finding, 702–3
    writing vector in terms of its
      direction and, 707
Main diagonal, 807
Major axis, of ellipse, 875, 876,
    877, 880
Malthus, Thomas, 974
Mandelbrot set, 686, 695
Mansfield, Jayne, 727
Mathematical induction, 987–95
    domino analogy illustrating, 989
    principle of, 987–91
    proving statements about positive
      integers using, 991–94
    steps in proof by, 989
Mathematical modeling, 3. *See also*
    Modeling
    and formulas, 3–5
Mathematics, universality of, 1000
Matrix equations, solving, 831–32
    using inverse of matrix, 850–51
Matrix (matrices), 805–72
    augmented, 806–7, 808, 810–14,
      818–22, 847, 848
    coded, 851, 852–53
    coding, 851, 852–53
    coefficient, 850
    column, 850
    constant, 850
    determinant of $2 \times 2$, 856–57
    determinant of $3 \times 3$, 859–62
    equal, 828
    inconsistent and dependent systems
      identified with, 818–21
    linear systems solved using,
      806–17
    multiplicative inverse of, 843–56
    nonsquare, 845
    notation for, 827–28
    of order $m \times n$, 827
    square, 827, 843–50
    zero, 829

Matrix operations, 827–42
  addition, 828–30
  applications, 836–38
  multiplication, 832–36
  scalar multiplication, 830–31
  solving matrix equations involving, 831–32
  subtraction, 828–30
Matrix row operations, 807–13
Maximized quantity, objective function describing, 791, 794–95
Maximum, relative, 166–67
Maximum point
  on cosine curve, 544
  in graph of cosine function, 527, 529
  in graph of sine function, 517, 518–19, 520, 521, 522, 524, 525
  on sine curve, 543
Maximum value of quadratic functions, 292–97
Midpoint formula, 245
Minimized quantity, objective function describing, 791
Minimum, relative, 166–67
Minimum function feature, on graphing utility, 753
Minimum point
  on cosine curve, 544
  in graph of cosine function, 527, 529
  in graph of sine function, 517, 518–19, 520, 521, 522, 524, 525
  on sine curve, 543
Minimum value of quadratic functions, 292–97
Minor, 860, 865
  expansion by, 860, 862
Minor axis, of ellipse, 875, 880
Mixture problem, solving, 736–38
Model breakdown, 5
Modeling
  of data with exponential and logarithmic functions, 440–47
  with functions, 252–66
  music, 572
  periodic behavior, 530–32
  simple harmonic motion, 570–73
  with systems of linear inequalities, 783
  with variation, 369–79
  verbal models, 252–56
Modulus of complex number, 688
Monomials, 47
  limit of, 1054
  multiplying, 48
  multiplying polynomial and, 48
  multiplying polynomial that is not monomial and, 49
Monroe, Marilyn, 1008
Monteverdi, 136
Morphing, 204
Morrison, Jim, 1008
Motion
  and change analyzed in calculus, 1038, 1070
  simple harmonic, 570–73
  uniform, 353–54, 738–39
Moving object, parametric representation of, 930–31
Multiple angles, trigonometric equations involving, 628–29
Multiple representation of points, 666
Multiplication
  associative property of, 12
  of binomial and trinomial, 48–49
  commutative property of, 12
  of complex numbers, 280
  of complex numbers in polar form, 689–90
  of conjugates, 36–37
  distributive property of, over addition, 12
  identity property of, 12

inverse property of, 12
  matrix, 832–36
  of monomial and polynomial, 48
  of monomials, 48
  with numbers in scientific notation, 25
  of numerator and denominator by same factor, verifying an identity by, 590–91
  of polynomials, 48–50
  of polynomials in two variables, 52
  product rule. *See* Product rule
  of rational expressions, 70–71
  of real numbers, 12
  scalar, 700, 704, 705, 830–31
  of sum and difference of two terms, 51, 52
Multiplication property of inequality, 119
Multiplicative identity matrix, 843
Multiplicative inverse of matrix, 843–56
  applications to coding, 851–53
  of $n \times n$ matrices with $n$ greater than 2, 847–49
  quick method for finding, 846
  solving systems of equations using, 850–51
  of a square matrix, 843–51
Multiplicative inverse (or reciprocal), 13, 71
Multiplicities of zeros, $x$-intercepts and, 308–9, 311
Multiplier effect, and tax rebates, 982
Music
  modeling572
  sinusoidal sound, 622
  sound quality and amusia, 598
Mutually exclusive events, 1021–22

**N**

National Education Association, 965
Natural base ($e$), 393–95, 410, 446–47
Natural exponential function, 393
Natural logarithms, 408–9
  changing base to, 420
  exponential equations solved using, 425–27
  introducing, 419–20
  properties of, 409
Natural numbers, 7
$n$ compounding periods per year, 395
Negative angles, 461
  degree and radian measures of selected, 467
Negative discriminants, 283
Negative-exponent rule, 19
Negative exponents, 19, 64–65
Negative integers, as exponents, 19
Negative multiplication property of inequality, 119
Negative numbers
  multiplying a vector by, 700
  principal square root of, 281–82
  square root of, 31, 32
  square root of, as multiples of $i$, 278
  square root of, operations with, 281–82
Negative real zeros, 334
Negative reciprocal, 194, 195
Negative slope, 180
Negative square root, 31
Negative units, 8
Newton, Isaac, 410, 442
  calculus developed by, 1050, 1052
  gravitation formula of, 375
Newton's Law of Cooling, 442–43
$n$ factorial ($n!$), 410
Nolan, Christopher, 550
Nonlinear inequality in two variables, graphing, 782

Nonlinear systems, 767–77
  applications with, 773–74
  recognizing, 767
  solving by addition method, 770–73
  solving by substitution, 768–70
Nonsingular square matrix, 845
Nonsquare matrix, 845
Nonsquare systems, 821–22
North Korea, 436
$n$th-order determinant, 865
$n$th partial sum, 966, 975
$n$th roots
  even and odd, 38
  of real numbers, 37
  solving radical equations containing, 97
Null set, 6
Numbers, sets of, 5
  irrational numbers, 7
  rational numbers, 7
  real numbers, 7–8
Numerator(s), 13
  partial fraction decomposition with constant, 759–60, 764
  partial fraction decomposition with linear, 761, 763–65
  rationalizing, 78–79
  rationalizing, to find limits, 1059–60
Numerical coefficient, 13

**O**

Objective functions, in linear programming, 791, 794–95
Oblique triangle, 644
  abbreviating known measurements in, 645
  area of, finding, 650
  solving, using Law of Cosines, 657–59
  solving, using Law of Sines, 645–46
Obtuse angle, 461
Odd function, 167–69
  cosecant function as, 542
  cotangent function as, 541
  definition of, 167
  and origin symmetry, 169
  sine function as, 517
  tangent function as, 537, 538
Odd multiplicity, zero of, 308
Odd trigonometric function, 480–81
  to find exact values, 481
One radian, 462
One-sided limits, 1043–45, 1058
  equal and unequal, 1044–45
  finding, by using graph, 1044–45
  left-hand and right-hand, 1043, 1044
  using limit properties to find, 1058
One-to-one correspondence, 8
One-to-one functions, 239
Open dots, 155
Open intervals, 115, 165, 166
Opposites (additive inverses), 13
Orbits, planetary, 942
Order, distinguishing between combination and permutation and, 1009
Ordered pairs, 136–37
  as solutions of systems, 728–29
Ordered triples, as solution of system of linear equation in three variables, 748–49, 819
Order of operations, 3
Orientation, 926
Origin, 8, 136
  graphing ellipse centered at, 876–78
  graphing ellipse not centered at, 879–81
  graphing hyperbolas centered at, 890–93
  graphing hyperbolas not centered at, 893–96
  graphing parabolas with vertices at, 902–4

graphing parabolas with vertices not at, 905–7
  modeling distance to point on graph from, 261
Origin symmetry, 169, 538
*Or* probabilities
  with events that are not mutually exclusive, 1022–24
  with mutually exclusive events, 1021–22
  with real-world data, 1023–24
Orthogonal vectors, 715–16
  dot product and, 715–16
  vector as sum of two, 716–18
Oscillatory motion, modeling, 570
  diminishing motion with increasing time, 571
  simple harmonic motion, 570–73
Outside terms, in binomial, 50

**P**

Parabolas, 286–92, 874, 900–912
  applications with, 907–9
  and axis of symmetry, 286–87, 901, 902, 905–8
  definition of, 900–901
  downward opening, 286, 287, 288, 291, 292, 902, 904, 905
  eccentricity for, 936
  finding parametric equations for, 930
  focus-directrix definition of, 935–36
  in form $f(x) = ax^2 + bx + c$, 289–92
  in form $f(x) = a(x - h)^2 + k$, 287–89
  graphing, 902–7
  identifying, without completing the square, 914
  identifying, without rotation of axes, 923
  latus rectum of, 903–4, 906, 907
  leftward opening, 902, 905
  polar equation of, graphing, 939–40
  rightward opening, 903, 905
  standard form of equation of, 901–5, 906, 907
  translations of, 905–7
  upward opening, 286, 287, 288, 289, 292, 902, 905
Parallel lines, 193–95
  inconsistent system and, 734
  and slope, 193–94
Parallel vectors, 715–16
Parameter, 926
  eliminating the, 927–29
Parametric equations, 925–35
  advantages over rectangular equations, 930–31
  defined, 926
  for function $y = f(x)$, finding, 930
  plane curves and, 925–29
Parentheses, 5
  and distributive property, 14
  in interval notation, 115
  and simplifying algebraic expressions, 13–14, 15
Partial fraction, 756
Partial fraction decomposition, 756–67
  with distinct linear factors, 757–59
  idea behind, 756–57
  with prime, nonrepeated quadratic factors, 761–63
  with prime, repeated quadratic factor, 763–65
  with repeated linear factors, 759–61
  steps in, 759
Pascal, Blaise, 136, 1000
Pascal's triangle, 1000
Perfect $n$th power, 38
Perfect square, 32
  greatest perfect square factor, 33, 35

Perfect square trinomials, 61–62, 63, 92
  factoring, 61–62, 63
Perimeter, formulas for, 106
Period, 483
  of cosecant function, 542
  of cosine function, 525, 526–29
  of cotangent function, 541
  of secant function, 543
  of simple harmonic motion, 571, 573
  of sine function, 517–23, 629
  of tangent function, 537, 538, 628
Periodic functions, 483–85
  definition of, 483
  modeling periodic behavior, 530–32
Permutations, 1006–8
  combinations compared to, 1009, 1010
  defined, 1007
  notation, 1006
  of $n$ things taken $r$ at a time, 1007
Perpendicular lines, 193–95
  and slope, 194
Phase shift, 522–23, 528
Phi $(\phi)$, 6
Photography, digital, 836–37
Picture cards, 1019
Piecewise function, 169–71
  discontinuous, determining for what numbers, 1065–66
  finding a limit by graphing, 1042
  properties of limits and, 1058
Pixels, 836, 837
Plane curves, 925–29
  defined, 926
  defined by parametric equations, graphing, 926–27
  finding parametric equations, 930
Planetary motion, modeling, 942
Plotting points in rectangular system, 136–37
Point conversion
  polar-to-rectangular, 667–68
  rectangular-to-polar, 668–69
Point-plotting method, 676
  graphing equation using, 137–38
  graphing plane curves described by parametric equations, 926–27
  graphing polar equation by, 676–77
Points, plotting
  in polar coordinate system, 664–65
  in rectangular coordinate system, 136–37
Point-slope form of equation of line, 180–82, 187
  parallel lines, 193–94
  perpendicular lines, 195
  tangent line, 1073, 1074
  writing, 181–82
Polar axis, 664–65
  as axis of symmetry, 937, 938, 941
  symmetry with respect to, 677, 937, 938, 941
Polar coordinates, 664–75
  circles in, 676–77
  conic sections in, 935–44
  equation conversion from rectangular coordinates to, 670
  equation conversion to rectangular coordinates from, 671–72
  multiple sets of, for given point, 666
  plotting points with, 665–66
  point conversion from rectangular coordinates to, 668–69
  point conversion to rectangular coordinates from, 667–68
  relations between rectangular coordinates and, 667–68
  sign of $r$ and point's location in, 665
  tests for symmetry in, 677

Polar coordinate system, 664–65
  multiple representation of points in, 666
  plotting points in, 664–65
Polar equation, 670–72, 675
  conversion to rectangular equation, 671–72
  converting rectangular equation to, 670
  graphs of, 675–76
  for planetary orbits, 942
Polar equations of conics, 936–41
  graphing, 937–41
  standard forms of, 936–37
Polar form of complex number, 688–95
  defined, 688
  powers of complex numbers, 691–93
  product of two complex numbers, 689–90
  quotient of two complex numbers, 690–91, A3
  roots of complex numbers, 693–95
Polar grids, 675
  graphing polar equations on, 675
Pole, 664
  symmetry with respect to, 677, 678
Polk, James K., 619
Polynomial(s), 46–67
  adding, 47–48
  defined, 46, 47
  degree of, 46, 47, 51
  dividing, 316–26
  dividing by those containing more than one term, 316–19
  dividing using synthetic division, 319–21
  factoring, 56–67
  factoring completely, 56
  limit of, 1055
  long division of, 316–19
  prime (irreducible over the integers), 56, 61
  strategy for factoring, 58, 63–64
  subtracting, 47–48
  in two variables, 51
  vocabulary of, 46–47
Polynomial equations
  Factor Theorem to solve, 322–23
  Fundamental Theorem of Algebra and roots of, 332
  properties of, 332
  solving for roots of, 330–32
  Tartaglia's formula giving root for third degree, 326–27
Polynomial functions, 302–15
  continuous at every number, 1065
  definition of, 303
  of degree $n$, 303
  end behavior of, 303–6, 310
  even-degree, 304, 305, 306
  example of, 277
  with given zeros, finding, 332–33
  graphs of, 303–6, 309–11
  Intermediate Value Theorem for polynomials, 309
  multiplicities of zeros of, 308–9, 311
  odd-degree, 304, 305
  quadratic functions, 286–301, 303, 752–53
  rational zeros of, 327–28
  Remainder Theorem used for evaluating, 322
  turning points of, 309–10, 311
  zeros of, 306–7, 311, 326–39
Polynomial inequality, 359–62
  definition of, 359
  solving, 359–62
  solving problems modeled by, 364–66
Polynomial multiplication, 48–49
  FOIL method used in, 49–50

multiplying monomial and polynomial that is not monomial, 49
  polynomials in two variables, 52
  when neither is monomial, 49
Population growth
  geometric, 974–75
  U.S., modeling, 437–39
  world, 436
Position function for a free-falling object near Earth's surface, 365–66
Position vector, 702
Positive angles, 460
  degree and radian measures of selected, 467
  in terms of revolutions of angle's terminal side around origin, 467
Positive multiplication property of inequality, 119
Positive (or principal) square root, 31, 32, 281–82
  definition of, 31
Positive real zeros, 334
Positive slope, 180
Positive units, 8
Power, limit of a, 1055–56, 1057
Power-reducing formulas, 610–11, 614
Power rule, 415–16, 418, 419
  for exponents (powers to powers), 20
Powers of complex numbers in polar form, 691–93
Precalculus, transition to calculus from, B1
Prime polynomials, 56, 61
Prince, Richard E., 913
Principal, 395
Principal $n$th root, 37
Principal square root, 281
  of $a^2$, 32
  definition of, 31
  of negative number, 281–82
Probability, 1015–28
  combinations and, 1020
  empirical, 1015–17
  of event not occurring, 1020–21
  *or* probabilities with events that are not mutually exclusive, 1022–24
  *or* probabilities with mutually exclusive events, 1021–22
  *and* probabilities with independent events, 1024–25
  theoretical, 1017–20
Problem solving
  involving maximizing/minimizing quadratic functions, 293–97
  With linear inequalities, 125
  with linear programming, 793–95
  with scientific notation, 26–27
  with systems of linear equations, 736–41
  uniform motion problem, 738–39
  word problems, 102–11
Product(s)
  of functions, 222
  limit of, 1053, 1057
  minimizing, 296
  of rational expressions, 70–71
  special, 52
  special-product formula, 51, 52
  of sum and difference of two terms, 51, 52
  of two binomials, 49–50
  of two complex numbers in polar form, 689–90
  of two matrices, defined, 833
Product rule, 20, 414, 416, 418
  proof of, A1
  for radicals, 38–39

for solving logarithmic equations, 428
  for square roots, 32–33
  using, 414
Products-raised-to-powers rule, 20
Product-to-sum formulas, 619–20
Profit function, 741
  gain or loss, 741
Projectiles, 286
Pythagorean identities, 483, 586
  eliminating the parameter and, 928–29
  solving trigonometric equation using, 633
Pythagorean Theorem, 108–9
  converse of, 109
  and distance between two points, 244

**Q**

Quadrantal angle, 461, 502
  degree and radian measures of, 512
  trigonometric functions of, 503–4, 512
Quadrants, 136
  signs of trigonometric functions and, 504–5, 512
  in which angle lies, finding, 505
Quadratic equations
  with complex imaginary solutions, 283
  defined, 89
  determining most efficient method for solving, 95–96
  discriminant of, 95
  in general form, 89, 93, 94, 283
  irrational solutions to, 95
  rational solutions to, 95
  solving by completing the square, 92–93
  solving by factoring, 89–91, 96
  solving by square root property, 91–92, 95, 96
  solving using quadratic formula, 93–94, 96
Quadratic factors in denominator of rational expression
  prime, nonrepeated, 761–63
  prime, repeated, 763–65
Quadratic formula, 93–94, 283
  deriving, 93
  graph of circle and, 249
  quadratic equations solved with, 93–94, 96
  trigonometric equation solved using calculator and, 635
Quadratic functions, 256, 277, 286–301, 303, 752–53
  applications of, 293–97
  defined, 286
  graphs of, 286–92
  minimum and maximum values of, 292–93
  in standard form, 287–92
Quadratic in form, solving trigonometric equations, 629–30
Quantities
  scalar, 699
  vector. *See* Vector(s)
Quarterly compounding of interest, 395
Quotient(s), 13
  of complex numbers in polar form, 690–91, A3
  difference, 171
  of functions, 222
  limit of a, 1056–57
  of two rational expressions, 71–72
Quotient identities, 482, 586

Quotient rule, 20, 414–15, 416, 418, 419
  for radicals, 38–39
  for solving logarithmic equations,
    414–15, 416, 418, 419, 429
  for square roots, 33–34
  using, 415
Quotients-raised-to-powers rule, 20

**R**

Radian(s)
  converting between degrees and,
    463–64
  definition of, 462
Radian measure, 462–63, 467, 512
  computing, 463
Radical(s), 37
  like, 34
  simplifying fractional expression
    containing, 77–78
Radical equations, 96–98
  solving, 97–98
  solving those containing $n$th roots, 97
Radical expressions, 31
  adding and subtracting, 34–35
  dividing, 38–39
  product rule for, 38–39
  quotient rule for, 38–39
  simplifying, 32, 34
  simplifying using rational
    exponents, 41
Radical sign, 31
Radical symbols, 31
Radicand, 31, 37
Radius, of circle, 246, 247–48
  linear speed as product of angular
    speed and, 471
Ramirez, Manny, 951
Range, 149
  of any quadratic function, 292
  of cosecant function, 542
  of cosine function, 479, 526
  of cotangent function, 541
  identifying, from function's graph,
    157–59
  of relation, 147
  of secant function, 543
  of sine function, 478, 479, 517
  of tangent function, 538
Rate of change
  average, 195–200, 1071, 1076–78
  instantaneous, 1071, 1072, 1075,
    1076–78
  slope as, 195–96
Rational equations, 86–87
  solving, 86–87
Rational exponents, 39–42
  defining, 39
  with numerators other than one,
    40–41
  properties of, 41
  radical expressions simplified
    using, 41
  reducing the index of, 42
  simplifying expressions with, 41–42
Rational expressions, 68–79
  addition of those with common
    denominators, 72
  addition of those with different
    denominators, 72–75
  complex, 75–77
  defined, 69
  dividing, 71–72
  domain of, excluding numbers
    from, 69
  multiplying, 70–71
  partial fraction decompositions for,
    756–67
  simplifying, 70
  subtraction of those with common
    denominators, 72
  subtraction of those with different
    denominators, 72–75

Rational functions, 340–58
  applications, 352–54
  domain of, 340–41
  graphs of, 346–51
  horizontal asymptote of, 345–46,
    348, 349, 350, 353
  inverse variation equation as, 373
  reciprocal function and, 341–42
  slant asymptotes of, 351–52
  vertical asymptotes of, 343–45, 348,
    349, 350
Rational inequalities, 362–64
  solving, 362–64
Rationalizing denominators, 35–37
  containing two terms, 36–37
Rationalizing the numerator, 78–79
  to find limits, 1059–60
Rational numbers, 7
Rational Zero Theorem, 327–28, 329
Ray, 460
Real axis, 686–87
Real number line, 8
  distance between two points on, 11
  intervals on, 115
Real numbers, 8
  adding, 11–12
  dividing, 13
  multiplying, 12
  ordering, 9
  properties of, 11–13
  set of, 6–8
  subsets of, 6–7
  subtracting, 13
  trigonometric functions of, 476–78
Real part, of complex number, 278
Reciprocal function, 341–42
  defined, 341
  graph of, 342
Reciprocal identities, 481–82, 586
Reciprocal (or multiplicative inverse),
    13, 71
  negative, 194, 195
Rectangle
  area and perimeter formulas for,
    106, 107
  with fixed perimeter, modeling area
    of, 257–59
Rectangular coordinates
  equation conversion from polar to,
    671–72
  equation conversion to polar
    coordinates from, 670
  point conversion from polar to,
    667–68
  point conversion to polar
    coordinates from, 668–69
  relations between polar coordinates
    and, 667
Rectangular coordinate system, 136
  circle in, 243
  distance between two points on,
    244
  ellipse on, 875–76
  graphing equations in, 137–38
  points plotted in, 136–37
  vectors in, 701–3
Rectangular equation of curve
  defined parametrically, finding
    and graphing, 927–29
Rectangular form, complex number
  in, 688
  converting from polar form to, 689
Rectangular solid
  surface area formula for, 259
  volume formula for, 106
  volume of, 256–57
Recursion formulas, 954–55
Reduced row-echelon form, 813
Reference angles, 505–11
  for angles greater than 360° ($-2\pi$),
    or less than $-3°(-2\pi)$,
    finding, 507

definition of, 506
  evaluating trigonometric functions
    using, 508–11, 512
  finding, 506–8
Reflecting light, and parabolas, 908–9
Reflections of graphs, 209–10, 213
  of exponential function, 392
  of logarithmic function, 405, 406
  one-to-one functions, 239
  about $x$-axis, 209–10
  about $y$-axis, 210
Regression line, 179
Relations, 147–48
  defined, 147
  as functions, 149
Relative maximum, 166–67
Relative minimum, 166–67
Relativity, Einstein's theory of, 30, 42
Remainder Theorem to evaluate
  polynomial function, 322
Repeated factorization, 61
Repeating decimals, 7
  written as fractions, 981–82
Repetitive behavior of sine, cosine,
  and tangent functions, 485
Representative numbers
  test value, solving polynomial
    inequalities at, 360, 361, 362
  test value, solving rational
    inequality at, 364
Resultant force vector, 707–8
Resultant vector, 700–701
Revenue, 739
Revenue function, 739, 741
Richter scale, 400, 408
Right angle, 461
Right-hand limit, 1043, 1044
Right triangle, 108
  isosceles, 492–93
  names of sides of, 490
  solving a, 566–68
  solving problem using two, 568
  special, 512
Right triangle trigonometry, 489–501.
  *See also* Trigonometric functions
  applications of, 495–97
Rise, 179
Rodriguez, Alex, 951
Roller coasters, derivatives and, 1079
Rolling motion, 932
Root(s)
  of complex numbers in polar form,
    693–95
  limit of a, 1056, 1057
Roots of equations, 83
  polynomial equation, 306, 330–32
Rose curves, 680–81
  with eight petals, 681
  with five petals, 681
  with four petals, 680–81
  with three petals, 681
Roster method, 5
Rotational motion, 932
Rotation of axes, 913–25
  equations of rotated conics in
    standard form, writing, 917–22
  formulas, using, 914–16
  identifying conic sections without,
    922–23
  identifying conic sections without
    completing the square, 913–14
Row-echelon form, 808, 810, 812–13
Row equivalent, 807
Row operations, 807–8
  on augmented matrix, 807–13
Run, 179
Rutherford, Ernest, 899

**S**

St. Mary's Cathedral (San Francisco),
  886
Saint-Vincent, Grégoire de, 410

Salaries
  comparing, 972
  lifetime computation, 977–78
Sample space, 1017, 1019–20
Satisfying the equation, 83, 137
Satisfying the inequality, 115, 778
Savings, and doubling time, 431
Savings plans, tax-deferred, 979
Scalar, 699
  dot product of two vectors as, 713
Scalar components of vector, 702
Scalar identity property, 831
Scalar multiple, 700, 830
Scalar multiplication, 700, 705, 830–31
  with vector in terms of i and j, 704
Scatter plots, 179, 187, 188, 443–44,
  445, 446
Schwarzchild formula, 27
Scientific calculators
  angle of elevation problems on, 497
  combinations on, 1011
  common logarithms evaluated
    on, 407
  computations with scientific
    notation on, 25
  converting from decimal to
    scientific notation on, 24
  evaluating $e$ to various powers, 393
  evaluating trigonometric functions
    using, 485–86
  exponential expressions evaluated
    on, 389
  factorials found with, 955
  inverse sine key, 497
  inverse trigonometric functions
    on, 558
  keystroke sequences for rational
    exponents, 41
Scientific notation, 23–27
  computations with, 25
  converting from decimal notation
    to, 24–25
  converting to decimal notation
    from, 23
  defined, 23
  problem solving with, 26–27
Secant curve
  characteristics of, 543
  cosine curve to obtain, 544
Secant function
  as even function, 481
  graph of, 542–44
  reference angle to evaluate, 511
Secant line, 196–97, 1071
  slope of, 1072
Secant (sec)
  as cofunction of cosecant, 495
  defined, 490
  evaluating, 491–92
  of 45°, evaluating, 493
Second-degree equation, general,
  914–15
Second-degree polynomial
  equation, 89
Second-order determinants,
  evaluating, 856–57
Seki Kowa, 1055
Semiannual compounding of
  interest, 395
Sense of the inequality, changing, 119
Sequences, 952–62
  arithmetic, 963–71
  defined, 952
  defined using recursion formulas,
    954–55
  factorial notation, 955–56
  Fibonacci, 952
  finding particular terms of, from
    general term, 953
  finite, 952
  geometric, 972–80
  graph of, 953–54

Sequences, (cont.)
  infinite, 952
  summation notation, 956–59
  of transformations, 213–15
Series, geometric, 980–82
  infinite, 980–82
Set(s), 5–8
  empty, 6, 87, 786, 819
  intersection of, 5–6, 220
  of irrational numbers, 7
  of numbers, 5
  of rational numbers, 7
  of real numbers, 6–8
  union of, 6, 220
Set-builder notation, 5, 115, 116,
    121, 122
  to represent function's domain and
    range, 157
Set notation for *or* probabilities with
  mutually exclusive events, 1021
Sherpa, Ang Rita, 489
Shrinking graphs
  horizontal, 212–13, 214, 392, 405
  vertical, 211–12, 214
$\Sigma$, 957
Signs
  Descartes's Rule of Signs, 333–35
  of trigonometric functions, 504–5, 512
Simple harmonic motion, 570–73
  analyzing, 572–73
  diminishing motion with increasing
    time, 571
  finding equation for object in,
    571–72
  frequency of object in, 572, 573
Simple interest formula, 260
Simplifying algebraic expressions,
    13–14, 15
Simplifying complex numbers, 279
Simplifying complex rational
    expressions
  by dividing, 76
  by multiplying by one, 76
Simplifying exponential expressions,
    21–22
  common errors in, 22
  with rational exponents, 41–42
Simplifying fractional expression
  containing radicals, 77–78
Simplifying radical expressions, 32,
    34, 41
Simplifying rational expressions, 70
Simplifying square roots, 32
Sine curve, 516
  to obtain cosecant curve, 543–44
  stretching and shrinking, 517–18
  vertical shifts of, 529–30
Sine function
  amplitude of, 517–23
  domain, 517
  domain and range of, 478, 479
  in form $y = A \sin Bx$, 520–22
  in form $y = A \sin (Bx - C)$,
    522–25
  graph of, 515–25, 545
  inverse, 550–53, 557, 562
  inverse properties, 559
  key points in graphing, 517–19, 520,
    522, 524, 525
  modeling periodic behavior, 530–32
  as odd function, 480–81, 517
  period, 517–23, 629
  periodic properties of, 484
  properties of, 517
  of quadrantal angles, 503–4
  range, 517
  reference angle to evaluate, 509
  repetitive behavior of, 485
  solving right triangles using, 568
  variations of $y = \sin x$, graphing,
    517–25
  vertical shifts of sine curve, 529–30

Sine (sin)
  as cofunction of cosine, 494, 495
  defined, 490
  double-angle formula for,
    607–9, 614
  evaluating, 491–92
  of 45°, evaluating, 493, 494
  half-angle formula for, 611, 614
  inverse, 497
  Law of Sines, 644–55, 658, 659
  product-to-sum formulas for, 619
  rotation of axes and, 915
  sum and difference formulas for,
    599–602, 614
  sum-to-product formulas for,
    620–21
  of 30° and 60°, evaluating, 493–94
  verifying an identity by changing to,
    587–88, 589, 591–92
Sine waves, 622
Singular square matrix, 845
Sinusoidal functions, modeling
  musical sounds with, 572
Sinusoidal graphs, 526
  vertical shifts of, 529–30
Sinusoidal sounds, 622
Slant asymptotes, 351–52
Slope
  as average rate of change, 195–96
  defined, 179, 195
  interpreting, 195–96
  of line, 179–80
  negative, 180
  notation for, 179
  and parallel lines, 193–94
  and perpendicular lines, 194
  point-slope form of the equation of
    a line, 180–82, 187, 193–94, 195
  positive, 180
  as rate of change, 195–96
  of secant line, 1072
  undefined, 180
  zero, 180
Slope-intercept form of equation of
    line, 182–83, 185, 187
  linear functions graphed in, 182–83
  modeling data with, 188
  parallel lines, 193–94
  perpendicular lines, 194
  tangent line, 1073–74
Smooth graphs, 303
Solution(s), 626
  of equation in two variables, 137
  extraneous, 97
  of inequality, 115
  of inequality in two variables, 778
  of linear equation in one
    variable, 83
  of nonlinear system in two
    variables, 767
  of polynomial equation, 306, 330–32
  of system of linear equations,
    728–29
  of system of linear equations in
    three variables, 748–49, 819
  of system of linear inequalities,
    783, 784
  of trigonometric equation, finding,
    626–28
Solution set
  of inequality, 115
  of linear equation in one
    variable, 83
  of nonlinear system in two
    variables, 767
  of system of linear equations in
    three variables, 748
  of system of linear inequalities, 784
Solving a formula for a variable, 87–88
Solving an inequality, 115
Solving an oblique triangle, 645–46
  using Law of Sines, 645–46

Solving a right triangle, 566–68
Solving linear equations, 83
Sonic boom, hyperbolic shape of, 896
Sound quality and amusia, 598
Sounds, sinusoidal, 622
Space, photographs sent back
  from, 837
Spaceguard Survey (NASA), 899
Space Telescope Science Institute, 908
Special products, using, 50–51, 52
Speed
  angular, 471–72
  ground, 711
  linear, 471–72
Speed of light, 27, 42
Sphere
  surface area formula for, 259
  volume formula for, 106
Square
  area and perimeter formulas
    for, 106
  perfect, 32
Square brackets, 5
Square matrix, 827
  invertible or nonsingular, 845, 849
  multiplicative identity matrix of
    order $n$, 843
  multiplicative inverse of, 843–51
  singular, 845
Square of binomial difference, 51
Square of binomial sum, 51
Square root property, quadratic
  equations solved by, 91–92, 95, 96
Square roots, 7, 31–37
  adding and subtracting, 34–35
  evaluating, 31–32
  product rule for, 32–33
  quotient rule for, 33–34
  simplified, 32
Square roots of negative numbers, 32
  as multiples of $i$, 278
  multiplying, 281–82
Standard form
  complex numbers in, 279
  of equation of circle, 246–48, 249
  of equation of ellipse, 875–78, A5
  of equation of hyperbola, 886–89,
    893, 916
  of equation of parabola, 901–5,
    906, 907
  of polynomial, 46
  of quadratic function, graphing,
    287–92
  transforming rotated conics to,
    917–22
Standard position, angle in, 460, 461
  drawing, 465–67
Standard viewing rectangle, 139
Statuary Hall (U.S. Capitol Building),
    881, 884
Step functions, 171
Straight angle, 461
Stretching graphs
  horizontal, 212–13, 214, 392, 405
  vertical, 211–12, 214, 215
Subscripts, 47
Subsets of real numbers, 6–7
Substitution
  for eliminating variables, 729–31,
    749, 768–70
  nonlinear systems solved by,
    768–70
  systems of linear equations in two
    variables solved by, 729–31
Subtraction
  of complex numbers, 279–80
  definition of, 13
  of like radicals, 34
  matrix, 828–30
  of polynomials, 47–48
  of polynomials in two variables, 51
  of radical expressions, 34–35

  of rational expressions with
    common denominators, 72
  of rational expressions with
    different denominators, 72–75
  of real numbers, 13
  of square roots, 34–35
  vector, 703–4
Sum
  binomial, square of, 51
  of cubes, factoring, 62–63
  of first $n$ terms of arithmetic
    sequence, 966–69
  of first $n$ terms of geometric
    sequence, 975–78
  of functions, 222, 223, 224
  of infinite geometric series, 980–82
  limit of, 1052, 1057
  of two terms, product of, 51, 52
Sum and difference formulas,
    596–607, 614
  for cosines, 597–602, 614
  for sines, 599–602, 614
  for tangents, 602–3, 614
Summation notation, 956–59
  properties of sums, 959
  using, 957–58
  writing sums in, 959
Sum-to-product formulas, 620–21
Supercomputers, 810
Surface area
  common formulas for, 259
  of cylinder with fixed volume,
    modeling, 259
Switch-and-solve strategy, 235
Symbols
  approximation, 6
  for binomial coefficients, 996
  for elements in sets, 5
  greater than, 115, 122
  greater than or equal to, 9, 115
  inequality, 9, 115, 119, 779, 781
  infinity, 115
  less than or equal to, 9, 115
  negative square root, 31
  radical, 31
  sigma, in adding terms of
    sequence, 957
  square root, 31
  for subsets of real numbers, 7
Symmetry
  axis of, 286–87, 901, 902, 905–8, 937,
    938, 939, 941
  even and odd functions and, 167–69
  graphing a polar equation using,
    677–82
  with respect to origin, 169, 538
  with respect to polar axis, 677, 937,
    938, 941
  with respect to $y$-axis, 168, 311, 677,
    937, 939
  tests for, in polar coordinates, 677
Synthesizers, 566
Synthetic division, 319–21, 322, 323
  polynomials divided using, 319–21
Systems of equations. *See* Systems of
    linear equations
Systems of inequalities. *See* Systems of
    linear inequalities
Systems of linear equations, 728
  business applications using, 739–41
  matrix solutions to, 806–17
  multiplicative inverses of matrices
    to solve, 850–51
  problem solving using, 736–41
Systems of linear equations in three
    variables, 748–56
  Gaussian elimination applied to,
    818–23
  inconsistent and dependent
    systems, 752
  problem solving with, 752–53
  solution of, 748–49

solving by eliminating variables, 749–52

solving by using matrices, 808–10

solving those with missing terms, 751–52

solving using determinants and Cramer's rule, 862–64

Systems of linear equations in two variables, 728–47

determining if ordered pair is solution of, 728–29

with infinitely many solutions, 734, 735–36

with no solutions, 734–36

number of solutions to, 734–36

solving, using determinants and Cramer's rule, 857–59

solving by addition method, 731–34

solving by graphing, 729, 734–35

solving by substitution method, 729–31

Systems of linear inequalities

applications of, 790–95

graphing, 784–86

modeling with, 783

solution of, 783

Systems of nonlinear equations in two variables, 767–77

applications with, 773–74

recognizing, 767

solving by addition method, 770–73

solving by substitution method, 768–70

**T**

Tables, creating

with graphing utility, 140, 296, 430, 445, 587, 630, 763, 1039

of solutions of equations in two variables, 140

Tables, finding limits using, 1039–41

Tangent curve, characteristics of, 538

Tangent function

domain, 538

finding bearing using, 570

graph of, 537–40, 545

inverse, 555–57

inverse properties, 559

as odd function, 481, 537, 538

period, 537, 538, 628

periodic properties of, 484

of quadrantal angles, 503–4

range, 538

reference angle to evaluate, 509

repetitive behavior of, 485

solving right triangles using, 566, 567, 568

vertical asymptote of, 537–38, 539–40

Tangent lines, 1071–74

point-slope equation of, 1073, 1074

slope-intercept equation of, 1073–74

slope of, derivative and, 1075–76

slope of, to curve at point, 1072–73

Tangent (tan)

as cofunction of cotangent, 495

defined, 490

double-angle formula for, 607–8, 609, 614

evaluating, 491–92

of 45°, evaluating, 493, 494

half-angle formula for, 611, 614

sum and difference formulas for, 602–3, 614

of 30° and 60°, evaluating, 494

Tartaglia's formula giving root for third-degree polynomial equation, 326–27

Tax-deferred savings plans, 979

Tax rebates, and multiplier effect, 982

Telephone numbers, running out of, 1005

Terminal point of directed line segment, 699

Terminal side of angle, 460

angle lies in quadrant of, 461

angles formed by revolutions of, 465–67

Terminating decimals, 7

Terms

of algebraic expressions, 13

constant, 47

finding, in binomial expansion, 999–1000

of geometric sequence, 973–74

like, 13

multiplying sum and difference of, 51, 52

outside/last/inside/first, in binomial, 50

of sequence, written from general term, 952

of sequences involving factorials, finding, 955–56

Test point

graphing linear inequalities without using, 781–82

graphing linear inequality in two variables, 779–80

graphing nonlinear inequalities in two variables, 782

Test value, 360, 361, 362, 364

Theoretical probability, 1017–20

computing, 1017–19

computing without listing event and sample space, 1019–20

Third-order determinants

defined, 860

evaluating, 860–62

Tidal cycle, modeling, 532

Time involved in uniform motion, 353–54

Total economic impact, 985

Transformations of functions, 204–19

exponential functions, 392–93

horizontal shifts, 207–9, 213, 214, 215, 392, 393, 405

horizontal stretching and shrinking, 212–13, 214, 392, 405

logarithmic functions, 405–6, 408–9

rational functions, 346–47

recognizing graphs of common functions and, 204–5

reflections of graphs, 209–10, 213, 239, 392, 405, 406

sequences of, 213–15

vertical shifts, 205–6, 213, 214, 215, 392, 405

vertical stretching and shrinking, 211–12, 213, 214, 215, 392, 405

Translations. *See also* Vertical shifts (translations)

of ellipses, 879–81

of hyperbolas, 893–96

of parabolas, 905–7

Transverse axis, of hyperbola, 886, 887

Trapezoid, area and perimeter formulas for, 106

Tree diagram, 1004

Triangle

area and perimeter formulas for, 106

Heron's formula for area of, 660, A2–A3

oblique, 644, 645–46, 650, 657–59

Pascal's, 1000

right, 108

solving a right, 566–68

Triangle inequality, 11

Triangular numbers, 1000

Trigonometric equations, 626–39

calculator to solve, using, 634–35

defined, 626

factoring to separate two different functions in, 630–31

finding all solutions of, 626–28

identities to solve, using, 631–34

involving single trigonometric function, 627–28

with multiple angles, 628–29

quadratic in form, 629–30

Trigonometric functions

of any angle, 501–14

cofunction identities, 495

and complements, 494–95

definitions of, in terms of unit circle, 477–78

equations involving single, 627–28

evaluating, 503, 505

even and odd, 480–81

finding values of, 477–78

of 45°, evaluating, 493, 494, 512

function values for some special angles, 492–94

fundamental identities, recognizing and using, 481–83

graphs of, 545. *See also* Graphs/graphing; *specific trigonometric functions*

inverse, 550–65

modeling periodic phenomena with, 483–84

of quadrantal angles, 503–4, 512

of real numbers, 476–78

reducing power of, 610–11

reference angles to evaluate, 508–11, 512

right triangle definitions of, 490

signs of, 504–5, 512

at $t = \pi/4$, 479–80

of 30° and 60°, evaluating, 493–94, 512

using calculator to evaluate, 485–86

using right triangles to evaluate, 491–92

Trigonometric functions, applications of, 566–73

bearings, solving problems involving, 569–70

simple harmonic motion, 570–73

solving right triangles, 566–68

Trigonometric identities, 481–83

eliminating the parameter and, 928

fundamental, 586–96

principal, 607–18

Pythagorean identities, 483, 586, 633

quotient identities, 482, 586

reciprocal identities, 481–82, 586

Trigonometry. *See also* Right triangle trigonometry

defined, 489

uses of, 489

Trinomials, 47

factoring those whose leading coefficient is not 1, 59

factoring those with leading coefficient of 1, 58–59

multiplying binomial and, 48–49

perfect square, 61–62, 63, 92

in two variables, factoring, 60

Turning points, 309–10

maximum number of, 311

**U**

Undefined slope, 180

Uniform motion, 353–54, 738–39

formula, 353, 738–39

solving problem of, 738–39

Union of sets, 6, 220

defined, 6

solution sets, 788

Unions of intervals, 116–17

Unit circle, 475–76

definitions of trigonometric functions in terms of, 477–78

factoring to separate two different functions in, 630–31

Unit distance, 8

U.S. Census Bureau, 974

United States population, modeling growth of, 437–39

Unit vectors, 701–6

finding, in same direction as given nonzero vector, 705–6

**i** and **j**, 701–5

Upper limit of summation, 957, 958

**V**

Value, of second-order determinant, 857

Value of an annuity, 978–80

Variable cost, 740

Variables, 2

dependent, 150

independent, 150

solving for, in formulas, 87–88

Variables, eliminating

addition method of, 731–34, 749–50, 770–73

solving linear system in three variables by, 749–50

solving linear systems in two variables by, 729–34, 749–51

solving nonlinear systems by, 768–73

substitution method of, 729–31, 749–52, 768–70

Variation

combined, 374–75

constant of, 370, 373

direct, 369–72

equations of, 370

formulas, 369

inverse, 372–74

joint, 375–76

modeling using, 369–79

Variation problems, solving, 370–72

Vector(s), 698–712

adding and subtracting, in terms of **i** and **j**, 703–4

angle between two, 714–15

applications of, 707–8

difference of two, 701

directed line segments and geometric, 699–701

dot product of, 713–14

equal, using magnitude and direction to show, 699–700

force, 707–8

orthogonal, 715–16

parallel, 715–16

position, 702

projection of vector onto another vector, 716–17

properties of vector addition and scalar multiplication, 705

in rectangular coordinate system, 701–3

relationships between, 699

resultant, 700–701, 707–8

scalar multiplication with, 700, 705

scalar multiplication with, in terms of **i** and **j**, 704

as sum of two orthogonal vectors, 716–18

unit, 701–6

velocity, 707, 708

writing, in terms of magnitude and direction, 707

zero, 705

Vector components of force, 716

Vector components of **v**, 717

Vector projection of **v** onto **w**, 716–17

Velocity

average, 199–200, 353–54, 1078

instantaneous, 200, 1078–80

Velocity vector, 707, 708

Verbal models, 252–56

Verifying an identity, 586–87
   changing to sines and cosines for, 587–88, 589, 591–92
   combining fractional expressions for, 590
   difference formula for cosines for, 599
   guidelines for verifying trigonometric identities, 593
   half-angle formula for, 613
   multiplying numerator and denominator by same factor for, 590–91
   sum and difference formulas for tangents for, 603
   sum-to-product formulas to, 621–22
   using factoring, 588–89
   using fundamental identities to, 586–96
   using two techniques, 589
   working with both sides separately in, 592
Vertex of angle, 460
Vertex (vertices), 793, 794
   of ellipse, 875
   of hyperbola, 886, 887, 888–89, 891, 892, 894, 895
   of parabola, 286, 287, 288, 289–90, 292, 901, 905, 906–7
Vertical asymptotes
   of cosecant function, 542
   of cotangent function, 541
   defined, 343
   locating, 343
   of logarithmic function, 405–6
   of rational function, 343–45, 348, 349, 350
   of secant function, 543
   of tangent function, 537–38, 539–40
   y-axis as, 405–6

Vertical component of vector, 702
Vertical lines, 187
   equations of, 184–85
   graphs of, 184
Vertical line test, for functions, 154–55
Vertical shifts (translations), 205–6, 213, 214, 215
   combining horizontal shifts and, 208–9
   downward, 206
   of exponential function, 392
   of logarithmic function, 405
   of sinusoidal graphs, 529–30
   upward, 206
Vertical stretching and shrinking, 211–12, 213, 214, 215
   of exponential function, 392
   of logarithmic function, 405
Viewing rectangle
   on graphing utility, 139
   understanding, 139–40
Volume
   formulas for, 106
   of rectangular solid, 106, 256–57

**W**

Wadlow, Robert, 377
Walters, Barbara, 995
Washburn, Brad, 498
Watson, James, 931
Weierstrass, Karl, 1050
Whispering gallery, 881
Whole numbers, 7
Wiles, Andrew, 987, 995
Witch of Agnesi, 934
Wolf population, 394
Word problems, solving, 102–11
   strategy for, 102

Work, 713
   definition of, 718
   dot product to compute, 718–19
World population
   future of, 446–47
   growth in, 436
   modeling data about, 445–47
   rewriting model in base e, 446–47

**X**

x-axis, 136
   as horizontal asymptote, 390, 391
   reflection about, 209–10
x-coordinate, 136, 140
   horizontal stretching and shrinking and, 212–13
x-intercept, 140, 141, 186
   on cosine curve, 544
   of cotangent function, 541, 542
   of function, 159
   graphing quadratic function in standard form, 288, 291–92
   in graph of cosine function, 527, 529
   in graph of sine function, 517, 518–19, 520, 522, 525
   multiplicity and, 308, 311
   on sine curve, 543
   solving polynomial inequalities and, 360
   of tangent function, 538, 539, 540

**Y**

y-axis, 136
   as axis of symmetry, 937, 939
   even function symmetric with respect to, 168–69, 311
   reflection about, 210

symmetry with respect to, 677, 937, 939
   as vertical asymptote, 405–6
y-coordinate, 136, 140
   vertical shifts and, 205
   vertical stretching and shrinking and, 211–12
y-intercept, 140, 141, 182–83, 186
   of function, 159
   graphing polynomial function and, 311
   graphing quadratic function in standard form, 288, 291–92
   graphing using slope and, 182–83

**Z**

Zero, as limit of denominator, 1058–60
Zero-exponent rule, 20
Zero factorial (0!), 955
Zero matrix, 829
Zero-Product Principle, 89–90, 96
Zero slope, 180
Zeros of a function, 159
Zeros of polynomial functions, 306–7, 311, 326–39
   Descartes's Rule of Signs and, 333–35
   finding, 328–30
   Intermediate Value Theorem and, 309
   kinds of, 327
   Linear Factorization Theorem, 332–33
   multiplicities of, 308–9, 311
   rational, 327–28
Zero vector, 705
Zero with multiplicity k, 308
Zoom in/zoom out, on graphing utilities, 139–40

**Chapter Test Prep Video CD**

**System Requirements**
**Windows® Users:**
• Pentium II 300 MHz processor
• Windows XP Service Pack 2 or Vista
• In addition to the minimum RAM required by the operating system, this CD-ROM requires 64 MB RAM
• 71 MB available hard drive space (optional - for minimum QuickTime installation if necessary)
• 800 x 600 resolution
• 8x or faster CD-ROM drive
• QuickTime 7.x (for best performance we recommend version 7.4 or higher)
• Sound card

**Macintosh® Users:**
• Mac OS 10.x
   • In addition to the minimum RAM required by the operating system, this CD-ROM requires 64 MB RAM
• 25 MB available hard drive space (optional - for minimum QuickTime installation if necessary)
• 800 x 600 resolution
• 8x or faster CD-ROM drive
• QuickTime 7.x (for best performance we recommend version 7.4 or higher)

The QuickTime player may already be installed on your computer, but if it is not, you can download it from Apple's website:
* Go to http://www.apple.com/quicktime/download/
* Select your operating system and follow the on-screen instructions to download the free player.

**How to get started with the Chapter Test Prep Video CD:**
Insert the CD into your CD-ROM drive. For Windows users, the program should launch automatically. If it does not, or if you have auto-launch turned off, you will need to open the program manually.

**To open the Chapter Test Prep Video CD manually:**
**Windows Users:** (1) Double-click on "My Computer" and locate your CD-ROM drive. It is usually the D: drive. (2) Right-click on the CD-ROM drive and select "Open" to view the contents of the CD. (3) Double-click on the "START" file to open the Home page of the Chapter Test Prep program. (4) From the Home page you can select any of the available resources by clicking on the buttons in the top menu bar.

**Macintosh Users:** (1) Locate the CD-ROM Icon on your desktop and double-click it to view the contents of the CD. (2) Double-click on the "START" file to open the Home page of the Pass the Test program. (3) From the Home page you can select any of the available resources by clicking on the buttons in the top menu bar.

**For Pearson's technical support:**
• Visit us online anytime at http://247pearsoned.custhelp.com/, where you can search our knowledgebase for common solutions, view product alerts, and review all options for additional assistance. NOTE: Pearson does not support and/or assist with third-party software. For technical assistance with the QuickTime player, please visit Apple's website at http://www.info.apple.com/usen/quicktime

Apple, Macintosh, and QuickTime are trademarks of Apple, Inc., registered in the U.S. and other countries.

# Photo Credits

**TABLE OF CONTENTS** **p. iii** John-Francis Bourke/zefa/Corbis; BIOS Klein & Hubert/Peter Arnold, Inc.; Rubberball/Jupiter Images-Rubberball Royalty Free; Getty Images **p. iv** Frank Siteman/Stock Boston; Phil McCarten/PhotoEdit Inc.; CinemaPhoto/Corbis/Bettmann; CORBIS-NY **p. v** Christoph Weihs/Shutterstock; Comstock/Jupiter Images Royalty Free; Masterfile Royalty Free Division; Dave King/Graham High at Centaur Studios-modelmaker © Dorling Kindersley **p. vi** John Hicks/Getty Images, Inc.-Taxi; Petr Fajkos/Shutterstock; ESA/A. Schaller (STSci)/NASA Headquarters; National Institute for Biological Standards and Control (U.K.)/Science Photo Library/Photo Researchers, Inc.

**CHAPTER P** **CO** John-Francis Bourke/zefa/Corbis **p. 2** Brian Snyder/Getty Images, Inc.-Allsport Photography **p. 3 (left)** Moodboard/ Corbis Royalty Free; **(right)** Comstock/MaXx Images **p. 8** Burke/Triolo/ Jupiter Images-Picture Arts Corporation/Brand X Pictures Royalty Free **p. 18** FOXTROT © 2000 Bill Amend. Reprinted with permission of UNIVERSAL PRESS SYNDICATE. All rights reserved. **p. 19** National Geographic/Superstock Royalty Free **p. 30** Albert Einstein and related rights ™/© of The Hebrew University of Jerusalem, used under license. Represented exclusively by Corbis Corporation. **p. 42** Salvador Dali "The Persistence of Memory" 1931, oil on canvas, $9\frac{1}{2} \times 13$ in. (24.1 × 33 cm). The Museum of Modern Art/Licensed by Scala-Art Resource, NY. © 1999 Demart Pro Arte, Geneva/Artists Rights Society (ARS), New York. **p. 44** John G. Ross/Photo Researchers, Inc. **p. 45** PEANUTS © United Feature Syndicate, Inc. **p. 46 (top)** Courtesy of Robert Blitzer; **(bottom)** Jupiter Images/Brand X/Alamy Images Royalty Free **p. 53** Steve Lyne/Getty Images, Inc.-Dex Images **p. 56** Steve Shott © Dorling Kindersley **p. 68** Jupiter Images/Thinkstock **p. 82** Image Source/Corbis/Image Source/Royalty Free **p. 101 (Howard Stern)** Stuart Ramson/AP Wide World Photos; **(Dr. Phil McGraw)** Frederick M. Brown/Getty Images; **(Brad Pitt)** Piyal Hosain/Fotos International/Getty Images; **(Kobe Bryant)** Lucy Nicholson/Corbis/ Reuters America LLC; **(Chief executive)** PictureIndia/Getty Images, Inc. Asia Images Group-Royalty free; **(Doctor)** © Red Chopstocks/Getty Images; **(High school teacher)** Moodboard/Corbis Royalty Free; **(Janitor)** Creatas Images/Jupiter Images Royalty Free **p. 102 (Oprah Winfrey)** AP Wide World Photos; **(Jerry Seinfeld)** Brian Zak/Sipa Press/UNICEF/AP Wide World Photos; **(Simon Cowell)** Dan Steinberg/AP Wide World Photos; **(David Letterman)** Hirsch Michael/Corbis/Sygma; **(Donald Trump)** AP Wide World Photos **p. 113** Everett Collection **p. 114** Aaron McCoy/Jupiter Images

**CHAPTER 1** **CO** BIOS Klein & Hubert/Peter Arnold, Inc. **p. 136** Getty Images **p. 142** Nick Dolding/Getty Images, Inc.-Stone Allstock **p. 147** National Institute for Biological Standards and Control (U.K.)/ Science Photo Library/Photo Researchers, Inc. **p. 164** Stock Connection Blue/Alamy Images **p. 178 (top)** Copyright © Scott Kim, scottkim.com. All rights reserved. **(bottom)** Gautam Narang/IFA Bilderteam/Jupiter Images **p. 192 (left)** Jupiter Images/FoodPix/ Creatas/Brand X/Banana Stock/PictureQuest; **(right)** Sharon L. Jonz/Workbook Stock/Jupiter Images-Picture Arts Corporation **p. 202** John Serafin **p. 204** Everett Collection **p. 209** SuperStock, Inc. **p. 220 (left)** Elisa Cicinelli/Jupiter Images-Picture Arts Corporation/Brand X Pictures Royalty Free; **(right)** Hemera Technologies/PhotoObjects.net/Jupiter Images Royalty Free **p. 232** © Lauren Victoria Burke/CORBIS All rights reserved. **p. 243 (top)** B.C. by permission of Johnny Hart and Creators Syndicate, Inc. **(bottom)** Scott Berner/Index Stock Imagery/ www.photos.com/Jupiter Images **p. 252** Todd A. Gipstein/Corbis/ Bettmann

**CHAPTER 2** **CO** Christoph Weihs/Shutterstock **p. 278** © 2005 Roz Chast from Cartoonbank.com. All rights reserved. **p. 285** © 2007 GJ Caulkins **p. 286 (top)** Jim W. Grace/Photo Researchers, Inc.; **(bottom left)** Simon Bruty; **(bottom right)** Copyright © 1981 Scott Kim, scottkim.com. All rights reserved. **p. 302** N. Hashimoto/Corbis/Sygma **p. 316** Treat Davidson/Photo Researchers, Inc. **p. 326** From Hieraymi Candi, "Ni Mediolanensis Medio (Basel, 1554)," Cardano portrait, frontispiece. Smithsonian Institution Libraries. © 2003 Smithsonian Institution. **p. 334** Courtesy of the Library of Congress **pp. 340, 353** Yuriko Nakao/Corbis/ Reuters America LLC **p. 342** Courtesy of knuckletattoos.com **p. 359** © The New Yorker Collection 1995 Warren Miller from cartoonbank.com. All Rights Reserved. **p. 369 (left)** Alex Segre/Alamy Images; **(right)** Moodboard/Alamy Images **p. 370** © Stan Fellerman/Corbis **p. 372** Superstock Royalty Free **p. 376 (top and bottom)** David Madison/PCN Photography **p. 377** UPI/Corbis/ Bettmann

**CHAPTER 3** **CO** Plush Studios/Alamy Images **p. 388** Michael Newman/PhotoEdit Inc. **p. 394** Tim Davis/Corbis Royalty Free **p. 400** Roger Ressmeyer/CORBIS_NY **p. 413** Mark Thomas/Photo Researchers, Inc. **p. 423** Purestock/Superstock Royalty Free **p. 436** Franck Boston/ Shutterstock **p. 439** CORBIS-NY

**CHAPTER 4** **CO** Rubberball/Jupiter Images-Rubberball Royalty Free **p. 460** San Francisco MOMA/Olivier Laude Photography **p. 471** Pictor/ImageState Media Partners Limited **p. 475 (top and bottom)** Laszlo Podor/Alamy **p. 488** Dale O'Dell Photography **p. 489** Petr Fajkos/Shutterstock **p. 498** Janet Foster/Masterfile Corporation **p. 500** Hugh Sitton/Getty Images Inc.-Stone Allstock **p. 501 (top)** Wesley Hitt/Photographer's Choice/ Getty Images Inc.-Photographer's Choice; **(bottom)** nagelestock.com/ Alamy Images **p. 515** Rubberball/Getty Creative/Getty Images Inc.-Rubberball Royalty Free **p. 537** Roger Harris/Photo Researchers, Inc. **p. 550** Warner Bros./Courtesy Everett Collection **p. 566** Scott Kleinman/Stone/Getty Images **p. 573** Paul Sakuma/AP Wide World Photos

**CHAPTER 5** **CO** John Hicks/Getty Images, Inc.-Taxi **p. 586** Jay Brousseau/Getty Images, Inc.-Image Bank **p. 596** Idamini/Alamy Images **p. 607** Masterfile Royalty Free Division **p. 619 (left)** MPI/ Stringer/Getty Images, Inc.-Hulton Archive Photos; **(right)** Tropical Press Agency/Getty Images, Inc.-Hulton Archive Photos **p. 626** Dia Max/ Getty Images

**CHAPTER 6** **CO** Science Photo Library/Steve Allen/Photo Researchers, Inc. **p. 644** Frank Clarkson **p. 656** CarverMostardi /Alamy **p. 675** SeaSee/Kos Picture Source/Getty Images **p. 686** R. F. Voss "29-Fold M-set Seahorse" computer-generated image. © 1990 R. F. Voss/IBM Research **p. 697** Stamp from the private collection of Professor C. M. Lang, photography by Gary J. Shulfer, University of Wisconsin, Stevens Point. "Germany: #5"; Scott Standard Postage Stamp Catalogue, Scott Pub. Co., Sidney, Ohio **pp. 698, 701** Stephen T. Thornton/Tom Cogill **p. 699** Jeff Greenberg/Photo Researchers, Inc. **p. 713** Andrea Comas/Corbis/Reuters America LLC **p. 718** Gregory K. Scott/Photo Researchers, Inc. **p. 720 (top and bottom left)** Robert E. Daemmrich/Bob Daemmrich Photography, Inc.; **(right)** © Mimmo Jodice/CORBIS

**CHAPTER 7** **CO Bob Grieser/AP Images** **p. 728** Inspirestock/ Jupiter Images-Picture Arts Corporation/Brand X Pictures Royalty Free **p. 740** Raveendran/Agence France Presse/Getty Images **p. 743** PEANUTS © United Feature Syndicate, Inc. **p. 748** David W. Hamilton/Getty Images Inc.-Stone Allstock **p. 756** Comstock/Jupiter Images Royalty Free **p. 767** Dave King/Graham High at Centaur Studios-modelmaker © Dorling Kindersley **p. 778 (left and right)** Karl Prouse/ Catwalking/Getty Images **p. 790** AP Wide World Photos **p. 792** Pascal Parrot/ Corbis/Sygma **p. 800 (left)** Gustav Klimt (1862–1918) "Mrs. Adele Bloch-Bauer, I", 1907. Oil on canvas, 138 × 138 cm. Private Collection. Photo: Erich Lessing/Art Resource, NY; **(right)** Pablo Picasso (1881–1973) "Boy with a Pipe", 1905 (oil on canvas). Collection of Mr. and Mrs. John Hay Whitney, New York, USA. © DACS/The Bridgeman Art Library. © 2008 Estate of Pablo Picasso/Artists Rights Society (ARS), New York.

**CHAPTER 8** **CO** Tim Ridley © Dorling Kindersley **p. 806** © Mike Watson/CORBIS All Rights Reserved. **p. 818** Yellow Dog Productions/Getty Images Inc.-Image Bank **p. 827** Colin Anderson/ Jupiter Images/Brand X/Alamy Images **p. 835** The Granger Collection **p. 837** NASA/Tim Furniss/Genesis Space Photo Library **p. 842** RCA Communications, Inc. **p. 856** David Parker/Science Museum/Science Photo Library/Photo Researchers, Inc.

**CHAPTER 9** **CO** ESA/A. Schaller (STSci)/NASA Headquarters **p. 874** © Kevin Fleming/CORBIS **p. 882** David R. Austen Photography Group **p. 886** Andrea Pistolesi **p. 900** Jeff Hester and Paul Scowen (Arizona State University), and NASA **p. 908** Space Telescope Science Institute **p. 913** Richard E. Prince "The Cone of Apollonius" (detail), fiberglass, steel, paint, graphite, 51 × 18 × 14 in. Collection: Vancouver Art Gallery, Vancouver, Canada. Photo courtesy of Equinox Gallery, Vancouver, Canada. **p. 925** Jeff Gross/Getty Images **p. 932** Richard Megna/Fundamental Photographs, NYC **p. 935** NASA/Getty Images, Inc.-Liaison

**CHAPTER 10** **CO** G. Paul Burnett/The New York Times/Redux Pictures **p. 952** Brian Hagiwara/Jupiter Images-Botanica **p. 962** Harry Blair **p. 963** Image Source/Getty Images Inc.-Image Source Royalty Free **p. 972** Tim Ridley © Dorling Kindersley **p. 974** Richard Lord/The Image Works **p. 977** U.S. Bureau of Engraving and Printing **p. 987** Charles Rex Arbogast/AP Wide World Photos **p. 996** Dr. Rudolph Schild/Science Photo Library/Photo Researchers, Inc. **p. 1000** From Science and Civilization in China, Vol. 3, pg. 135, Fig. "Pascal's triangle as depicted by Chu Shih Chieh," by Joseph Needham, 1959. Reprinted with the permission of Cambridge University Press. **p. 1003** Jupiter/Corbis Royalty Free **p. 1005 (top)** SuperStock, Inc.; **(bottom)** Apple/Splash News/Newscom **p. 1008 (Marilyn Monroe)** 20th Century Fox Film Corp. All rights reserved. Courtesy Everett Collection; **(James Dean)** Imapress/Globe Photos, Inc.; **(Jim Morrison)** Michael Ochs Archives Ltd./Getty Images Inc.-Los Angeles; **(Janis Joplin)** AP Wide World Photos; **(Jimi Hendrix)** Pictorial Press Ltd./Alamy Images **p. 1015** © Rolf Bruderer/CORBIS All Rights Reserved. **p. 1020** © Damon Higgins/The Palm Beach Post **p. 1025** UPI/Corbis/Bettmann

**CHAPTER 11** **CO** Cary Wolinsky/Getty Images **p. 1038** Mark Cooper/Corbis/Bettmann **p. 1050 (left and right)** The Granger Collection **p. 1062** Getty Images, Inc.-PhotoDisc **p. 1070** Masterfile Royalty Free Division **p. 1079** Alan Thornton/Getty Images Inc.-Stone Allstock

# Definitions, Rules, and Formulas

## THE REAL NUMBERS

Natural Numbers: $\{1, 2, 3, \ldots\}$

Whole Numbers: $\{0, 1, 2, 3, \ldots\}$

Integers: $\{\ldots, -3, -2, -1, 0, 1, 2, 3, \ldots\}$

Rational Numbers: $\{\frac{a}{b} \mid a$ and $b$ are integers, $b \neq 0\}$

Irrational Numbers: $\{x \mid x$ is real and not rational$\}$

## PROPERTIES OF ADDITION AND MULTIPLICATION

Commutative: $a + b = b + a; ab = ba$

Associative: $(a + b) + c = a + (b + c);$
$$(ab)c = a(bc)$$

Distributive: $a(b + c) = ab + ac; a(b - c) = ab - ac$

Identity: $a + 0 = a; a \cdot 1 = a$

Inverse: $a + (-a) = 0; a \cdot \frac{1}{a} = 1 \ (a \neq 0)$

Multiplication Properties: $(-1)a = -a;$
$(-1)(-a) = a; a \cdot 0 = 0; (-a)(b) = (a)(-b) = -ab;$
$(-a)(-b) = ab$

## EXPONENTS

### Definitions of Rational Exponents

**1.** $a^{\frac{1}{n}} = \sqrt[n]{a}$

**2.** $a^{\frac{m}{n}} = \left(\sqrt[n]{a}\right)^m$ or $\sqrt[n]{a^m}$

**3.** $a^{-\frac{m}{n}} = \dfrac{1}{a^{\frac{m}{n}}}$

### Properties of Rational Exponents

If $m$ and $n$ are rational exponents, and $a$ and $b$ are real numbers for which the following expressions are defined, then

**1.** $b^m \cdot b^n = b^{m+n}$

**2.** $\dfrac{b^m}{b^n} = b^{m-n}$

**3.** $\left(b^m\right)^n = b^{mn}$

**4.** $(ab)^n = a^n b^n$

**5.** $\left(\dfrac{a}{b}\right)^n = \dfrac{a^n}{b^n}$

## RADICALS

If $\sqrt[n]{a}$ and $\sqrt[n]{b}$ are real numbers, then

**1.** If $n$ is even, then $\sqrt[n]{a^n} = |a|$.

**2.** If $n$ is odd, then $\sqrt[n]{a^n} = a$.

**3.** The product rule: $\sqrt[n]{a} \cdot \sqrt[n]{b} = \sqrt[n]{ab}$

**4.** The quotient rule: $\dfrac{\sqrt[n]{a}}{\sqrt[n]{b}} = \sqrt[n]{\dfrac{a}{b}}$

## INTERVAL NOTATION, SET-BUILDER NOTATION, AND GRAPHS

$(a, b) = \{x \mid a < x < b\}$

$[a, b) = \{x \mid a \leq x < b\}$

$(a, b] = \{x \mid a < x \leq b\}$

$[a, b] = \{x \mid a \leq x \leq b\}$

$(-\infty, b) = \{x \mid x < b\}$

$(-\infty, b] = \{x \mid x \leq b\}$

$(a, \infty) = \{x \mid x > a\}$

$[a, \infty) = \{x \mid x \geq a\}$

$(-\infty, \infty) = \{x \mid x$ is a real number$\} = \{x \mid x \in R\}$

## SLOPE FORMULA

$$\text{slope } (m) = \frac{\text{change in } y}{\text{change in } x} = \frac{y_2 - y_1}{x_2 - x_1} \quad (x_1 \neq x_2)$$

## EQUATIONS OF LINES

**1.** *Slope-intercept form:* $y = mx + b$
$m$ is the line's slope and $b$ is its $y$-intercept.

**2.** *General form:* $Ax + By + C = 0$

**3.** *Point-slope form:* $y - y_1 = m(x - x_1)$
$m$ is the line's slope and $(x_1, y_1)$ is a fixed point on the line.

**4.** *Horizontal line parallel to the $x$-axis:* $y = b$

**5.** *Vertical line parallel to the $y$-axis:* $x = a$

## ABSOLUTE VALUE

**1.** $|x| = \begin{cases} x & \text{if } x \geq 0 \\ -x & \text{if } x < 0 \end{cases}$

**2.** If $|x| = c$, then $x = c$ or $x = -c. \ (c > 0)$

**3.** If $|x| < c$, then $-c < x < c. \ (c > 0)$

**4.** If $|x| > c$, then $x < -c$ or $x > c. \ (c > 0)$

# SPECIAL FACTORIZATIONS

**1.** *Difference of two squares:*
$$A^2 - B^2 = (A + B)(A - B)$$

**2.** *Perfect square trinomials:*
$$A^2 + 2AB + B^2 = (A + B)^2$$
$$A^2 - 2AB + B^2 = (A - B)^2$$

**3.** *Sum of two cubes:*
$$A^3 + B^3 = (A + B)(A^2 - AB + B^2)$$

**4.** *Difference of two cubes:*
$$A^3 - B^3 = (A - B)(A^2 + AB + B^2)$$

# ALGEBRA'S COMMON GRAPHS

**Identity Function**

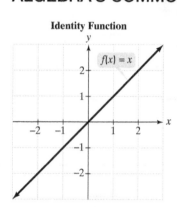

**Absolute Value Function**

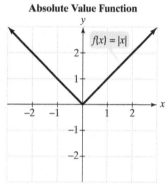

**Standard Quadratic Function**

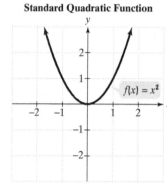

**Square Root Function**

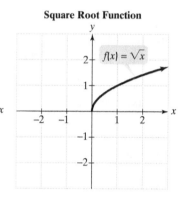

**Standard Cubic Function**

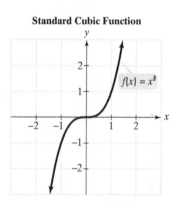

**Cube Root Function**

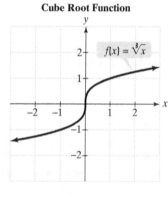

**Greatest Integer Function**

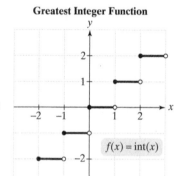

**Reciprocal Function**

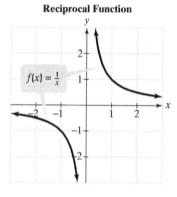

# TRANSFORMATIONS

In each case, $c$ represents a positive real number.

| Function | Draw the graph of $f$ and: |
|---|---|
| **Vertical translations** $\begin{cases} y = f(x) + c \\ y = f(x) - c \end{cases}$ | Shift $f$ upward $c$ units. <br> Shift $f$ downward $c$ units. |
| **Horizontal translations** $\begin{cases} y = f(x - c) \\ y = f(x + c) \end{cases}$ | Shift $f$ to the right $c$ units. <br> Shift $f$ to the left $c$ units. |
| **Reflections** $\begin{cases} y = -f(x) \\ y = f(-x) \end{cases}$ | Reflect $f$ about the $x$-axis. <br> Reflect $f$ about the $y$-axis. |
| **Vertical Stretching or Shrinking** $\begin{cases} y = cf(x); c > 1 \\ y = cf(x); 0 < c < 1 \end{cases}$ | Vertically stretch $f$, multiplying each of its $y$-coordinates by $c$. <br> Vertically shrink $f$, multiplying each of its $y$-coordinates by $c$. |
| **Horizontal Stretching or Shrinking** $\begin{cases} y = f(cx); c > 1 \\ y = f(cx); 0 < c < 1 \end{cases}$ | Horizontally shrink $f$, dividing each of its $x$-coordinates by $c$. <br> Horizontally stretch $f$, dividing each of its $x$-coordinates by $c$. |

# DISTANCE AND MIDPOINT FORMULAS

**1.** The distance from $(x_1, y_1)$ to $(x_2, y_2)$ is

$$\sqrt{(x_2 - x_1)^2 + (y_2 - y_1)^2}.$$

**2.** The midpoint of the line segment with endpoints $(x_1, y_1)$ and $(x_2, y_2)$ is

$$\left(\frac{x_1 + x_2}{2}, \frac{y_1 + y_2}{2}\right).$$

# QUADRATIC FORMULA

The solutions of $ax^2 + bx + c = 0$ with $a \neq 0$ are

$$x = \frac{-b \pm \sqrt{b^2 - 4ac}}{2a}.$$

# FUNCTIONS

**1.** Linear Function: $f(x) = mx + b$
Graph is a line with slope $m$ and $y$-intercept $b$.

**2.** Quadratic Function: $f(x) = ax^2 + bx + c, a \neq 0$

Graph is a parabola with vertex at $x = -\dfrac{b}{2a}$.

Quadratic Function: $f(x) = a(x - h)^2 + k$
In this form, the parabola's vertex is $(h, k)$.

**3.** nth-Degree Polynomial Function:
$f(x) = a_n x^n + a_{n-1}x^{n-1} + a_{n-2}x^{n-2} + \cdots + a_1 x + a_0, a_n \neq 0$
For $n$ odd and $a_n > 0$, graph falls to the left and rises to the right.
For $n$ odd and $a_n < 0$, graph rises to the left and falls to the right.
For $n$ even and $a_n > 0$, graph rises to the left and rises to the right.
For $n$ even and $a_n < 0$, graph falls to the left and falls to the right.

**4.** Rational Function: $f(x) = \dfrac{p(x)}{q(x)}$, $p(x)$ and $q(x)$ are
polynomials, $q(x) \neq 0$

**5.** Exponential Function: $f(x) = b^x, b > 0, b \neq 1$
Graphs:

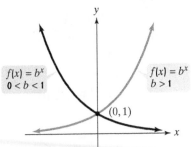

**6.** Logarithmic Function: $f(x) = \log_b x, b > 0, b \neq 1$
$y = \log_b x$ is equivalent to $x = b^y$.

Graph:

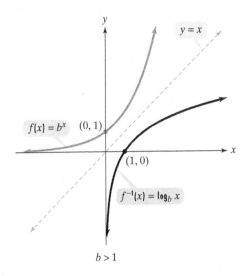

# PROPERTIES OF LOGARITHMS

**1.** $\log_b(MN) = \log_b M + \log_b N$

**2.** $\log_b\left(\dfrac{M}{N}\right) = \log_b M - \log_b N$

**3.** $\log_b M^p = p \log_b M$

**4.** $\log_b M = \dfrac{\log_a M}{\log_a b} = \dfrac{\ln M}{\ln b} = \dfrac{\log M}{\log b}$

**5.** $\log_b b^x = x; \quad \ln e^x = x$

**6.** $b^{\log_b x} = x; \quad e^{\ln x} = x$

# INVERSE OF A 2 × 2 MATRIX

If $A = \begin{bmatrix} a & b \\ c & d \end{bmatrix}$, then $A^{-1} = \dfrac{1}{ad - bc}\begin{bmatrix} d & -b \\ -c & a \end{bmatrix}$, where
$ad - bc \neq 0$.

# CRAMER'S RULE

If

$$a_{11}x_1 + a_{12}x_2 + a_{13}x_3 + \cdots + a_{1n}x_n = b_1$$
$$a_{21}x_1 + a_{22}x_2 + a_{23}x_3 + \cdots + a_{2n}x_n = b_2$$
$$a_{31}x_1 + a_{32}x_2 + a_{33}x_3 + \cdots + a_{3n}x_n = b_3$$
$$\vdots$$
$$a_{n1}x_1 + a_{n2}x_2 + a_{n3}x_3 + \cdots + a_{nn}x_n = b_n$$

then $x_i = \dfrac{D_i}{D}, D \neq 0$.

$D$: determinant of the system's coefficients
$D_i$: determinant in which coefficients of $x_i$ are replaced by $b_1$, $b_2, b_3, \ldots, b_n$.

# CONIC SECTIONS

### Circle

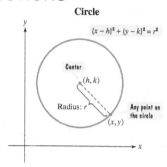

### Ellipse

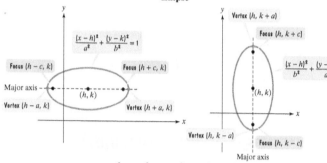

$$a^2 > b^2 \text{ and } c^2 = a^2 - b^2$$

### Hyperbola

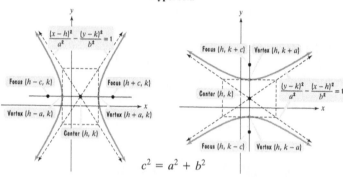

$$c^2 = a^2 + b^2$$

### Parabola

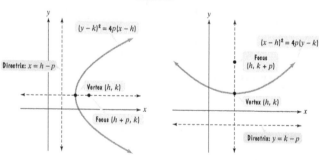

# SEQUENCES

1. Infinite Sequence:

$$\{a_n\} = a_1, a_2, a_3, \ldots, a_n, \ldots$$

2. Summation Notation:

$$\sum_{i=1}^{n} a_i = a_1 + a_2 + a_3 + \cdots + a_n$$

3. $n$th Term of an Arithmetic Sequence:

$$a_n = a_1 + (n-1)d$$

4. Sum of First $n$ Terms of an Arithmetic Sequence:

$$S_n = \frac{n}{2}(a_1 + a_n)$$

5. $n$th Term of a Geometric Sequence: $a_n = a_1 r^{n-1}$

6. Sum of First $n$ Terms of a Geometric Sequence:

$$S_n = \frac{a_1(1 - r^n)}{1 - r} \quad (r \neq 1)$$

7. Sum of an Infinite Geometric Series with $|r| < 1$:

$$S = \frac{a_1}{1 - r}$$

# THE BINOMIAL THEOREM

1. $n! = n(n-1)(n-2)\cdots 3 \cdot 2 \cdot 1; 0! = 1$

2. $\displaystyle \binom{n}{r} = \frac{n!}{r!\,(n-r)!}$

3. Binomial Theorem:

$$(a+b)^n = \binom{n}{0}a^n + \binom{n}{1}a^{n-1}b$$
$$+ \binom{n}{2}a^{n-2}b^2 + \cdots + \binom{n}{n}b^n$$

# PERMUTATIONS, COMBINATIONS, AND PROBABILITY

1. $_nP_r$, the number of permutations of $n$ elements taken $r$ at a time, is given by

$$_nP_r = \frac{n!}{(n-r)!}.$$

2. $_nC_r$, the number of combinations of $n$ elements taken $r$ at a time, is given by

$$_nC_r = \frac{n!}{(n-r)!\,r!}.$$

3. *Probability of an Event:* $P(E) = \dfrac{n(E)}{n(S)}$, where

$n(E) = $ the number of outcomes in event $E$ and $n(S) = $ the number of outcomes in the sample space.

# UNIT CIRCLE DEFINITIONS OF TRIGONOMETRIC FUNCTIONS

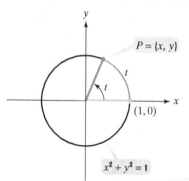

$\sin t = y$ $\qquad \csc t = \dfrac{1}{y}, \quad y \neq 0$

$\cos t = x$ $\qquad \sec t = \dfrac{1}{x}, \quad x \neq 0$

$\tan t = \dfrac{y}{x}, \quad x \neq 0$ $\qquad \cot t = \dfrac{x}{y}, \quad y \neq 0$

# RIGHT TRIANGLE DEFINITIONS OF TRIGONOMETRIC FUNCTIONS

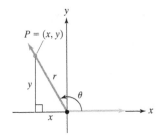

Length of the hypotenuse

Length of the side opposite $\theta$

Length of the side adjacent to $\theta$

$$\sin \theta = \frac{\text{opp.}}{\text{hyp.}} = \frac{a}{c} \qquad \csc \theta = \frac{\text{hyp.}}{\text{opp.}} = \frac{c}{a}$$

$$\cos \theta = \frac{\text{adj.}}{\text{hyp.}} = \frac{b}{c} \qquad \sec \theta = \frac{\text{hyp.}}{\text{adj.}} = \frac{c}{b}$$

$$\tan \theta = \frac{\text{opp.}}{\text{adj.}} = \frac{a}{b} \qquad \cot \theta = \frac{\text{adj.}}{\text{opp.}} = \frac{b}{a}$$

# TRIGONOMETRIC FUNCTIONS OF ANY ANGLE

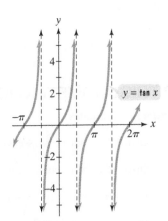

$$\sin \theta = \frac{y}{r} \qquad \csc \theta = \frac{r}{y}, \quad y \neq 0$$

$$\cos \theta = \frac{x}{r} \qquad \sec \theta = \frac{r}{x}, \quad x \neq 0$$

$$\tan \theta = \frac{y}{x}, \quad x \neq 0 \qquad \cot \theta = \frac{x}{y}, \quad y \neq 0$$

# GRAPHS OF TRIGONOMETRIC FUNCTIONS

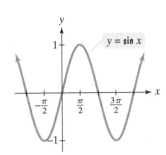

$y = \sin x$

**Domain**: all real numbers: $(-\infty, \infty)$
**Range**: $[-1, 1]$
**Period**: $2\pi$

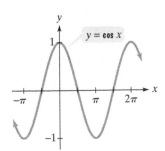

$y = \cos x$

**Domain**: all real numbers: $(-\infty, \infty)$
**Range**: $[-1, 1]$
**Period**: $2\pi$

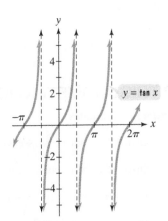

$y = \tan x$

**Domain**: all real numbers except odd multiples of $\frac{\pi}{2}$
**Range**: all real numbers
**Period**: $\pi$

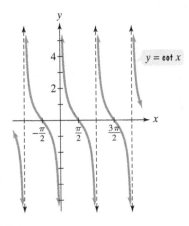

$y = \cot x$

**Domain**: all real numbers except integral multiples of $\pi$
**Range**: all real numbers
**Period**: $\pi$

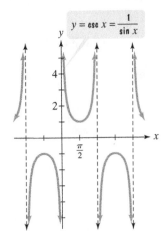

$y = \csc x = \dfrac{1}{\sin x}$

**Domain**: all real numbers except integral multiples of $\pi$
**Range**: $(-\infty, -1] \cup [1, \infty)$
**Period**: $2\pi$

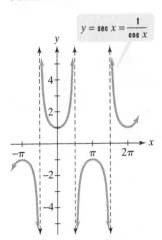

$y = \sec x = \dfrac{1}{\cos x}$

**Domain**: all real numbers except odd multiples of $\frac{\pi}{2}$
**Range**: $(-\infty, -1] \cup [1, \infty)$
**Period**: $2\pi$

# FUNDAMENTAL TRIGONOMETRIC IDENTITIES

## Reciprocal Identities

$$\sin x = \frac{1}{\csc x} \qquad \csc x = \frac{1}{\sin x}$$

$$\cos x = \frac{1}{\sec x} \qquad \sec x = \frac{1}{\cos x}$$

$$\tan x = \frac{1}{\cot x} \qquad \cot x = \frac{1}{\tan x}$$

## Quotient Identities

$$\tan x = \frac{\sin x}{\cos x} \qquad \cot x = \frac{\cos x}{\sin x}$$

## Pythagorean Identities

$$\sin^2 x + \cos^2 x = 1$$
$$1 + \tan^2 x = \sec^2 x$$
$$1 + \cot^2 x = \csc^2 x$$

## Even-Odd Identities

$$\sin(-x) = -\sin x \qquad \cos(-x) = \cos x \qquad \tan(-x) = -\tan x$$
$$\csc(-x) = -\csc x \qquad \sec(-x) = \sec x \qquad \cot(-x) = -\cot x$$

# OTHER TRIGONOMETRIC IDENTITIES

## Sum and Difference Formulas

$$\sin(\alpha + \beta) = \sin\alpha\cos\beta + \cos\alpha\sin\beta$$

$$\sin(\alpha - \beta) = \sin\alpha\cos\beta - \cos\alpha\sin\beta$$

$$\cos(\alpha + \beta) = \cos\alpha\cos\beta - \sin\alpha\sin\beta$$

$$\cos(\alpha - \beta) = \cos\alpha\cos\beta + \sin\alpha\sin\beta$$

$$\tan(\alpha + \beta) = \frac{\tan\alpha + \tan\beta}{1 - \tan\alpha\tan\beta}$$

$$\tan(\alpha - \beta) = \frac{\tan\alpha - \tan\beta}{1 + \tan\alpha\tan\beta}$$

## Double-Angle Formulas

$$\sin 2\theta = 2\sin\theta\cos\theta$$

$$\cos 2\theta = \cos^2\theta - \sin^2\theta = 2\cos^2\theta - 1 = 1 - 2\sin^2\theta$$

$$\tan 2\theta = \frac{2\tan\theta}{1 - \tan^2\theta}$$

## Power-Reducing Formulas

$$\sin^2\theta = \frac{1 - \cos 2\theta}{2}$$

$$\cos^2\theta = \frac{1 + \cos 2\theta}{2}$$

$$\tan^2\theta = \frac{1 - \cos 2\theta}{1 + \cos 2\theta}$$

## Half-Angle Formulas

$$\sin\frac{\alpha}{2} = \pm\sqrt{\frac{1 - \cos\alpha}{2}}$$

$$\cos\frac{\alpha}{2} = \pm\sqrt{\frac{1 + \cos\alpha}{2}}$$

$$\tan\frac{\alpha}{2} = \pm\sqrt{\frac{1 - \cos\alpha}{1 + \cos\alpha}} = \frac{1 - \cos\alpha}{\sin\alpha} = \frac{\sin\alpha}{1 + \cos\alpha}$$

# OBLIQUE TRIANGLES

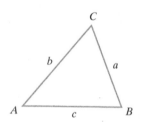

## Law of Sines

$$\frac{a}{\sin A} = \frac{b}{\sin B} = \frac{c}{\sin C}$$

## Law of Cosines

$$a^2 = b^2 + c^2 - 2bc\cos A$$

$$b^2 = a^2 + c^2 - 2ac\cos B$$

$$c^2 = a^2 + b^2 - 2ab\cos C$$